HANDBOOK OF
Psychological Assessment, Case Conceptualization, and Treatment

Michel Hersen, Editor-in-Chief

HANDBOOK OF
Psychological Assessment, Case Conceptualization, and Treatment

Volume 1   **Adults**

Volume Editors
Michel Hersen and Johan Rosqvist

John Wiley & Sons, Inc.

Published by John Wiley & Sons, Inc., Hoboken, New Jersey.
Published simultaneously in Canada.

Wiley Bicentennial Logo: Richard J. Pacifico

Library of Congress Cataloging-in-Publication Data:

Handbook of psychological assessment, case conceptualization, and
    treatment / editor-in-chief, Michel Hersen.
        p. ; cm.
    Includes bibliographical references and index.
    ISBN-13: 978-0-471-77999-5 (cloth) Volume 1: Adults
    ISBN-13: 978-0-471-78000-7 (cloth) Volume 2: Children and Adolescents
    ISBN-13: 978-0-471-77998-8 (cloth) Set 1. Psychology,
Pathological—Handbooks, manuals, etc.   I. Hersen, Michel.   II. Rosqvist, Johan.
    III. Reitman, David
    [DNLM: 1. Mental Disorders—diagnosis.   2. Mental Disorders—therapy.
    WM 141 H2374 2008]
    RC454.H352 2008
    616.89—dc22   2007026314

Printed in the United States of America.

10 9 8 7 6 5 4 3 2 1

Contents

v

Preface to Volume 1

Many books have been written on assessment, conceptualization, and treatment over the past few decades. However, for the most part, these three issues critical to developing the most effective treatment regimens for clients have not been linked in systematic fashion across the age spectrum. In this two-volume set, we believe that we have filled a gap in the literature. Volume I does so for adults, while Volume II considers the issues in children and adolescents.

In Volume 1 on adults the chapters are divided into three parts. Part I (General Issues) has six chapters dealing with an Overview of Behavioral Assessment with Adults, Diagnostic Issues, Behavioral Conceptualization, Overview of Behavioral Treatment with Adults, Medical and Pharmacological Issues, and Ethical Issues.

Part II deals with Assessment, Conceptualization, and Treatment of Specific Disorders, while Part III considers Special Issues, such as Marital Distress, Sexual Deviation, Adults with Developmental Disabilities, Older Adults, Insomnia, Health Anxiety, and Compulsive Hoarding.

In Parts II and III, authors were encouraged to include the following topics in their chapters: Description of the Disorder, Diagnosis and Assessment, Conceptualization, Behavioral Treatment, Medical Treatment (if relevant), and a detailed Case Description. Authors were also encouraged to consider the following issues in the section on Conceptualization: learning and modeling, life events, genetic influences, physical affecting behavior, drugs affecting behavior, and cultural and diversity issues.

We believe that the way this volume is structured provides a valuable teaching tool so that students have a more holistic view of psychopathology, its etiology, and its ultimate remediation. The Case Description was included to help concretize the thinking of our experts and to help students understand the more subtle transitions and connections of assessment, conceptualization, and treatment.

Acknowledgments

Many individuals have contributed to the fruition of this work. First, we thank our contributors who agreed to share their thinking and expertise with us. Second, we thank Carole Londerée for her technical help throughout the process of putting together this volume. Third, we thank Cynthia Polance and Christopher Brown for their work on the indexes. And finally, but hardly least of all, we thank our editorial friends at John Wiley who understood the importance of this project and who helped us keep on track to completion.

MICHEL HERSEN
JOHAN ROSQVIST

Portland, Oregon

Contributors

Gordon J.G. Asmundson, Ph.D
Anxiety and Illness Behaviours
    Laboratory
University of Regina
Regina, Saskatchewan, Canada

Krissan Alvarez, MA
Department of Psychology
University of Nevada—Las Vegas
Las Vegas, Nevada

Michael R. Basso, PhD
Department of Psychology
University of Tulsa
Tulsa, Oklahoma

F. Michler Bishop, PhD, CAS
Alcohol and Substance Abuse
    Services
Dr. Albert Ellis Institute
New York, New York

Thröstur Björgvinsson, PhD
The Menninger Clinic
Houston, Texas

Dennis R. Combs, PhD
Department of Psychology
University of Texas at Tyler
Tyler, Texas

Jean Cottraux, MD, PhD
Hopital Neurologique
Unite de Traitement de L'Anxiete,
Bron Cedex, France

Michelle G. Craske, PhD
Department of Psychology
University of California—
    Los Angeles
Los Angeles, California

Natalie Dautovich
Counseling Department
University of Florida
Gainesville, Florida

Felicia De la Garza-Mercer
Graduate Psychology Program
University of California—Los Angeles
Los Angeles, California

Brad C. Donohue, PhD
Department of Psychology
University of Nevada—Las Vegas
Las Vegas, Nevada

Brian D. Doss, PhD
Department of Psychology
Texas A&M University
College Station, Texas

Michel J. Dugas, PhD
Department of Psychology
Concordia University
Montréal, Québec, Canada

Barry A. Edelstein, PhD
Department of Psychology
West Virginia University
Morgantown, West Virginia

Kylie Francis
Department of Psychology
Concordia University
Montréal, Québec, Canada

Philip Gehrman, PhD
Department of Social Sciences
University of the Sciences—Philadelphia
Philadelphia, Pennsylvania

Gerald Goldstein, PhD
Psychology Service
Veterans Affairs Medical Center
Pittsburgh, Pennsylvania

Michelle Haring, PhD
British Columbia Women's
   Hospital and Health Centre, North
   Shore Stress and Anxiety Clinic
Vancouver, British Columbia,
Canada

John Hart
The Menninger Clinic
Houston, Texas

Richard G. Heimberg, PhD
Adult Anxiety Clinic
Temple University
Philadelphia, Pennsylvania

Derek R. Hopko, PhD
Department of Psychology
University of Tennessee—
   Knoxville
Knoxville, Tennessee

William G. Iacono, PhD
Psychology Department
University of Minnesota
Minneapolis, Minnesota

Maureen C. Kenny, PhD
Department of Educational
   and Psychological Studies
Florida International
   University
Miami, Florida

William J. Koch, PhD
Department of Psychiatry
University of British Columbia
Vancouver, British Columbia

Mark A. Lau, PhD
BC Mental Health and Addiction
   Services 201-601 West Broadway
Vancouver, British Columbia,
   Canada

Sumer N. Ledet, MA
Department of Psychology
University of Tulsa
Tulsa, Oklahoma

C. W. Lejuez, PhD
Department of Psychology
University of Maryland
College Park, Maryland

Kenneth L. Lichstein, PhD
Department of Psychology
The University of Alabama
Tuscaloosa, Alabama

Nicholas A. Maltby, PhD
Institute of Living
University of Connecticut School
   of Medicine
Hartford, Connecticut

Naomi R. Marmorstein, PhD
Department of Psychology
Rutgers University—Camden
Camden, New Jersey

L. E. Marshall
Rockwood Psychological Services
Kingston, Ontario, Canada

W. L. Marshall, PhD
Rockwood Psychological Services
Kingston, Ontario, Canada

Christina M. McCrae, PhD
Center for Gerontological
   Studies and Department
   of Psychology
University of Florida
Gainesville, Florida

Suzanne A. Meunier, PhD
Institute of Living
University of Connecticut School
   of Medicine
Hartford, Connecticut

Catherine Miller, PhD
School of Professional Psychology
Pacific University
Hillsboro, Oregon

Alexandra Mitchell
Department of Psychology
Texas A&M University
College Station, Texas

Maria Nazarian, PhD
Department of Psychology
University of California—Los
    Angeles
Los Angeles, California

M. D. O'Brien, PhD
Rockwood Psychological Services
Kingston, Ontario, Canada

William H. O'Brien, MA
Department of Psychology
Bowling Green State University
Bowling Green, Ohio

Brian P. O'Connor, PhD
Department of Psychiatry
Lakehead University
Thunder Bay, Ontario

Sarah M. C. Robertson
Department of Psychology
University of Tennessee—Knoxville
Knoxville, Tennessee

Thomas L. Rodebaugh, PhD
Washington University—St. Louis
St. Louis, Missouri

Luke T. Schultz
Adult Anxiety Clinic
Temple University
Philadelphia, Pennsylvania

Heather Schwetschenau
Department of Psychology
Bowling Green State
    University
Bowling Green, Ohio

G. A. Serran
Rockwood Psychological
    Services
Kingston, Ontario, Canada

Kathryn A. Sexton, PhD
Department of Psychology
Concordia University
Montréal, Québec, Canada

Alissa Sherry, PhD
Department of Educational
    Psychology
University of Texas—Austin
Austin, Texas

Tiffany M. Stewart, PhD
Pennington Biomedical Research
    Center
Baton Rouge, Louisiana

Sarah A. Stoner
Department of Psychology
West Virginia University
Morgantown, West Virginia

Peter Sturmey, PhD
Department of Psychology
Queens College, CUNY
New York, New York

Marlene Taube-Schiff, PhD
Psychosocial Oncology
    and Palliative Care Department
Princess Margaret Hospital
Toronto, Ontario, Canada

Daniel J. Taylor, PhD
Department of Psychology
University of Texas
Denton, Texas

Steven Taylor, PhD
Department of Psychiatry
University of British Columbia
Vancouver, British Columbia, Canada

David F. Tolin, PhD
Anxiety Disorders Center/Institute
    of Living
University of Connecticut
Hartford, Connecticut

Paula Truax, PhD
Clinical Psychologist
Kaiser Permanente
Portland, Oregon

Jill L. Wanner, MA
Department of Psychology,
University of Tulsa
Tulsa, Oklahoma

Margaret R. Whilde
Department of Educational
    Psychology
The University of Texas—
    Austin
Austin, Texas

Laura Widman
Department of Psychology
University of Tennessee—
    Knoxville
Knoxville, Tennessee

Donald A. Williamson, PhD
Pennington Biomedical
    Research Center
Baton Rouge, Louisiana

Charles B. Winick, PsyD
Psych Team
Cooper City, Florida

Erin Woodhead
Department of Psychology
West Virginia University
Morgantown, West Virginia

Sara Wright, MS
School of Professional Psychology
Pacific University
Hillsboro, Oregon

PART I

GENERAL ISSUES

CHAPTER 1

Overview of Behavioral Assessment with Adults

MAUREEN C. KENNY, KRISANN ALVAREZ,
BRAD C. DONOHUE, AND CHARLES B. WINICK

HISTORICAL DEVELOPMENT

Behavioral assessment stems from early research in classical and operant conditioning that demonstrated how behavioral and emotional responses could be conditioned, or in effect learned (Watson & Rayner, 1920). Treatments based on behavioral principles were then initiated to ameliorate various problem behaviors (Jones, 1924). Despite the increase in the use of behavioral therapy in the late 1950s, behavioral assessment measures were not commonly utilized in a clinical context until the mid-1960s. Early behavioral assessment focused on the observation of behavior patterns. Specifically, assessment focused on quantifying the frequency, rate, and duration of behaviors that were very specifically described to enhance reliability (Ullmann & Krasner, 1965). The publication of *Complex Human Behavior* (Staats, 1963) and *Behavior Analysis* (Kanfer & Saslow, 1965) increased interest in the field.

In the 1970s, behavioral assessment expanded in application and focus. The concept that situational variables influenced behavior led researchers to investigate individuals' behaviors within larger social contexts such as family, school, and business. In addition, assessment expanded to include feelings, sensations, internal imagery, cognitions, interpersonal relations, and psychophysiological functioning (Lazarus, 1973). To adequately assess these content areas, indirect measures, such as self-reports and ratings by significant others were included in behavioral assessments (Cone, 1977, 1978).

Diversification of behavioral assessment continued throughout the 1980s and 1990s with incorporation of other disciplines and traditions. Indeed, in a review of articles published in behavioral assessment journals in the early to mid-1980s, only 15% indicated observation as a mode of assessment (Fernandez-Ballesteros, 1988). Such diversity garnered interest in the topic and resulted in an increase in journal articles related to behavioral assessment. As a result, in the span of 3 years, articles containing the term "behavioral assessment" increased from 50 articles in 1980 to 200 articles in 1983

3

(Fernandez-Ballesteros, 1993). Inclusion of other disciplines was evident in a review of *Behavior Therapy* and *Behavior Research and Therapy* from 1988 through 1991 in which 53% of articles detailed the utilization of standardized trait questionnaires (Haynes & Uchigakiuchi, 1993). Moreover, 82% of the articles that included trait measures did so in conjunction with traditional behavioral assessment methodologies. Along a slightly different vein, objective measures of behavior (e.g., urine drug screens to detect drug use) have become customarily administered with subjective measures of behavior (e.g., ratings of satisfaction with drug use) in controlled treatment outcome studies (e.g., Azrin et al., 2001). Thus, behavioral assessment has developed over multiple decades and continues to expand through the incorporation of traditional forms of assessment and application to various fields.

CONCEPTUAL FOUNDATIONS

CONTRASTS WITH TRADITIONAL ASSESSMENT

Despite recent incorporation of traditional assessment strategies in behavioral assessment, differences between behavioral and traditional assessment models lie within contrasting conceptual foundations. Traditional assessment including psychodynamic and personality approaches assume that behavior is the result of stable, internal, psychological processes. The assumption of this methodology is that behavior is the expression of enduring, underlying personality traits. Therefore, emphasis of traditional assessment is on the measurement of internal experiences and underlying traits (O'Brien & Haynes, 2005). The stable nature of these traits does not lend itself to modification through therapy. In addition, traditional assessment requires the acceptance of abstract constructs used to conceptualize underlying traits that are not amenable to empirical investigation. These limitations, among others, led to development of behavioral assessment strategies.

Perhaps the most distinctive trait of behavioral assessment is the emphasis on situational determinants of behavior and exclusion of trait assumptions. Behavioral assessment highlights the importance of environmental contributions and assumes that behavior is situation specific. Assessment in this tradition emphasizes the measurement of environmental factors, situation specific behavior, and recently has incorporated the examination of cognitive processes (O'Brien & Haynes, 2005). Behavior is considered to be initiated and maintained through a dynamic process and thus is assessed across time and environments. This dynamic process is assessed through the investigation of the antecedents and consequences of behavior. These variables include stimuli that precede, co-occur, and follow behaviors of interest.

The emphasis on situational determinants in behavioral assessment lends itself to sensitivity to individual differences. Behavioral assessment accepts that individuals differ in past experiences and present environmental variables and allows for individualized application of assessment strategies (O'Brien & Haynes, 2005). Individualized application can be utilized to better understand the factors initiating and maintaining behavior as similar behavior may be a function of differing contextual variables across individuals. Unlike traditional assessment, such specificity provides for direct therapeutic application. Identification of contributing variables allows for behavior modification through the manipulation of the environment (Nelson & Hayes, 1979).

Behavioral assessment is also distinct from traditional assessment in its emphasis on empirical evaluation. The focus of behavioral assessment on specific actions and contextual variables is better suited for empirical testing than conceptual trait characteristics utilized in traditional assessment (Goldfried & Kent, 1972). Application of empirical evaluation in behavioral assessment involves specific definitions of behavior, monitoring of contextual variables, systematic observation, and the use of validated instruments. Several studies evaluating the reliability and validity of diagnoses, behavioral observation, and self-report inventories highlight the importance of empirical validation in behavioral assessment (Follette & Hayes, 1992).

BASIC ISSUES IN BEHAVIORAL ASSESSMENT

Assessment is a necessary first step in behavioral therapy. In many ways, it is the complementary partner of behavioral treatment. Behavioral assessment ideally occurs prior to commencing treatment to assess requisite goals for treatment, during treatment to assist in measuring therapeutic progress and adequacy of selected treatments, and after treatment to determine final outcomes and appropriateness of treatment termination.

Behavioral assessment is typically organized in three distinct, and increasingly molecular stages. The first stage, or level, of behavioral assessment is focused on the identification of global behaviors (e.g., noncompliance, sleep disturbance) that are most contributory to the presenting problem. These behaviors are particularly distressing, disruptive to daily functioning, socially unacceptable, or dangerous or detrimental to health and well being. The focus of assessment then shifts to determining the syndrome or cluster of symptoms that influence the onset of problem behaviors. Assessment concludes with an assessment of the system. This view holds that the individual is a system, whereby one symptom disturbance affects functioning in another area.

Although behavioral assessment and the *Diagnostic and Statistical Manual of Mental Disorders,* fourth edition, text revision (*DSM-IV-TR;* American Psychiatric Association, 2000) began on much different tracks (the former growing out of behavior therapy and the latter linked to the medical model), they have developed a working relationship and can be used in conjunction with one another. For instance, behavioral assessment is often relied on to assist in diagnosing *DSM-IV* diagnoses, as these syndromes are often based on quantifiable actions that are quite amenable to behavioral assessment practices. The nosologic scheme of the *DSM* sets forth a descriptive set of behaviors that are necessary for diagnosis in a particular area. This is analogous to the syndrome level of assessment discussed previously; where by a cluster of symptoms (which delineate a diagnosis) are identified as targets of treatment. Additionally, the *DSM* list of psychosocial stressors is consistent with behaviorism's emphasis on environmental factors (Tyron, 1998). The atheoretical nature of the *DSM* does not preclude explanations of disorders based on behavioral theory. However, the *DSM* is based on a nomotheic system (classifying groups of similar individuals), while behavioral assessment is idiographic (unique to the individual) (Nelson-Gray & Paulson, 2004). A synthesis of behavioral assessment and *DSM,* where behavioral assessment is used to create a treatment that may be best for a specific individual, is possible.

Behavioral assessment may include many different instruments and types of assessment strategies. The domains that often need to be attended to when working with a client may best be assessed in different ways including self-report, self-monitoring and recording, surveys, direct behavioral recordings, and physiological assessment (Barlow, 2005). Generally, the start of an assessment identifies what behaviors are of interest. This usually involves some behavioral excess (e.g., crying all the time) or deficit (e.g., unable to speak in social situations) (Tyron, 1998). Sometimes direct observation of the client is essential, as this method is generally the most validated method of specified behaviors, particularly when motivation is lacking. However, this method is relatively costly as compared with subjective self-report measures (i.e., questionnaires and other retrospective rating by others). Moreover, as compared with direct observation, subjective measures are easier to implement (i.e., direct observation often requires the assessor to travel to naturalistic environments). Assessment in the natural environment is preferred, but not always feasible and so artificial laboratory testing circumstances may be used (Tyron, 1998). Physiological responses (which can impact target behavior) can also be measured directly, requiring relevant equipment and expertise. The various methods of behavioral assessment will be reviewed later in the chapter.

FUNCTIONAL ASSESSMENT

Functional assessment is often confused with *functional analysis* (O'Neill, 2005). However, these terms are distinct from one another (Gresham, Quinn, & Restori, 1999; Herner, 1994). Functional assessment refers to the utilization of methods and techniques to identify target behaviors, including stimuli that precede (i.e., antecedents) and follow (i.e., consequences, target behaviors); conducting a functional analysis; and developing treatment interventions. Functional analysis is limited to the process by which environmental events are manipulated to estimate their impact on target behaviors, and is, therefore, a component of functional assessment.

IDENTIFICATION OF TARGET BEHAVIORS

The first step in the functional assessment process is the identification of target behaviors. Generally, the clinician and client work together to identify target problem behaviors. This process begins by broadly identifying behavioral patterns, and later specifying these behavioral patterns into well-defined behaviors (Donohue, Ammerman, & Zelis, 1998), including the manner by which these behaviors are performed, as well as their frequency, duration, and severity (O'Neill, 2005).

FUNCTIONAL ANALYSIS

Functional analysis involves formulating hypotheses regarding the function, or purpose, of target behaviors (Gresham et al., 1999). Relationships between the variables that proceed, co-occur, and follow target behaviors are examined through the ABC model of functional analysis (i.e., antecedents, behaviors, consequences). An extension of this model, the SORC model includes antecedent stimuli (S), factors inherent to organism (O), target response (R), and consequences (C) (Goldfried & Sprafkin, 1976). This model includes current environmental stimuli and consequences, as well as individual physiology and learning history. The way in which this information is obtained and utilized is dependent on the method of functional analysis.

Indirect functional analysis involves utilization of interviewing procedures that are specifically designed to identify the function of relationships existing between target behaviors and relevant antecedents and consequences (Iwata & Worsdell, 2005). In this process, clinicians formulate hypotheses about the maintenance of target behaviors through inquiry about antecedents and consequences. Behavior analysts may assess interviewee beliefs about how the behavior is maintained, how the problem may be solved, and successful and unsuccessful strategies that may have been used to cope with target behaviors. This method is easily implemented. However, verbal reports have been reported to be unreliable (Sturmey, 1994).

Descriptive functional analysis involves systematic observation of target behavior to aid in hypothesis formulation (Sulzer-Azaroff & Mayer, 1977). Data obtained in this method is utilized in the formulation of hypotheses regarding the function of target behaviors. These hypotheses are confirmed or disconfirmed by examining the correlations between occurrence of target behaviors and antecedents and consequences. Descriptive functional analysis is a more reliable method than indirect functional analysis, as it does not rely upon self-report. However, this method relies on correlations and fails to provide a means of experimentally testing hypotheses (Iwata & Worsdell, 2005).

Experimental functional analysis is the method of experimentally manipulating the environment to develop and test hypotheses that are pertinent to the maintenance of target behaviors. Environmental events may be presented or withdrawn for short time periods to assess the affect on target behaviors (O'Neill, 2005). Behavior occurrence during these trials is compared to identify the function of the target behaviors and the maintaining variables (Iwata & Worsdell, 2005). Although this method is relatively time consuming, experimental manipulation offers great promise when accurate assessment is wanting.

TREATMENT INTERVENTIONS

Once target behaviors and their functional relationships have been identified, treatment intervention may be developed and implemented. When multiple target behaviors are identified, the clinician may choose to initially focus on a single behavior or address multiple behaviors concurrently. It is customary to initially target the behavior causing greatest distress to the client, thus assisting the client in being able to attend to other behaviors. Another approach is to first target the behavior most amenable to change so that the client is encouraged by the effect of treatment (O'Leary & Wilson, 1975). When the client lacks motivation, the clinician may choose to first address the behavior that is most disruptive to the client's significant others (Tharp & Wetzel, 1969). In addressing multiple behaviors concurrently, clinicians must examine whether behaviors are influenced by one another. Related behaviors are referred to as *response classes*. Response classes include behaviors that have seemingly different characteristics, but have similar effects on the environment or contextual variables (O'Neill, 2005).

SELF-REPORT ASSESSMENT

Information from self-report assessment strategies (e.g., questionnaires, self-monitoring) is obtained directly from the client. Self-report methods are cost-effective, easily administered, and amenable to the assessment of motoric, physiological, and cognitive processes (Cone, 1978). Self-report assessment generally requires less time and resources than other forms of assessment, such as behavioral observation. The primary criticism of self-reports is that client's may provide inaccurate information due to various factors, including intentional false reporting and memory deficits. However,

Barlow, Hayes, and Nelson (1984) argued the client's perception of their problem is an important component of the therapeutic process, and Evans (1986) noted that the theoretical assumptions of behavioral assessment do not include unconscious processes that would lead to distortion of self-reports of behavior.

SELF-REPORT MEASURES/INSTRUMENTS

Self-report measures present clients with statements regarding the presence, frequency, or severity of their thoughts and behaviors. Measures differ in the their number of items, but frequently utilize a Likert-type response scale (e.g., 7 = Extremely happy, 1 = Extremely unhappy). Standardized rating scales and problem behavior checklists are generally paper-and-pencil measures. However, some measures may be administered via computer. Computer-administered assessments often have the advantage of automated scoring, which can reduce the time of assessment interpretation. Although most measures are completed by the client, some measures may be completed by significant others or family members to gain a greater understanding of the problem.

Self-report measures vary in their degree of specificity. Some instruments assess multiple domains (e.g., depression, anxiety, conduct problems) broadly, while others assess specific behavioral categories more comprehensively. Determination of the type of measure to employ is dependent upon the objective of assessment. General measures are beneficial in the initial stages of assessment to identify the areas in which the client is experiencing greatest relative difficulty. Specific measures are useful when the clinician is interested in assessing detailed information about a client's identified problem and usually are administered once the initial target behaviors have been identified during broad-based assessment. Determination of which measure to use should include an examination of the reliability and validity of potential instruments because self-report inventories vary in degree of psychometric validation.

The Symptom Checklist-90-Revised (SCL-90-R; Derogatis, 1994) is a broad-based self-report checklist that assesses nine dimensions (i.e., Somatization, Obsessive-Compulsive, Interpersonal Sensitivity, Depression, Anxiety, Hostility, Phobic Anxiety, Paranoid Ideation, and Psychoticism) and three global indices of distress (i.e., Global Severity Index, Positive Symptom Distress Index, and Positive Symptom Total). Clients respond to 90 items measuring symptom presence and severity on a 5-point rating scale ranging from "not at all" to "extremely." The SCL-90-R may be utilized to initially identify problems and measure treatment progress and outcomes. The SCL-90-R includes computer-based administration requiring approximately 12 to 15 minutes. The SCL-90-R has been reported to have above satisfactory ratings of internal consistency (Derogatis, Rickels, & Rock, 1976; Horowitz, Rosenberg, Baer, Ureno, & Villasenor, 1988), and high levels of convergent-discriminant validity (see Derogatis, 1983). Most SCL-90-R item stems are behaviorally specified, (e.g., shouting or throwing things) although some are not amenable to functional analysis (e.g., never feeling close to another person).

Beck Depression Inventory II   The Beck Depression Inventory Second Edition (BDI-II; Beck, Brown, & Steer, 1996a) is a specific self-report inventory used to assess the presence and severity of various symptoms of depression. The measure consists of 21 items; each item has four alternative responses from which the individual can choose, which are then scored, 0 to 3. The BDI-II is available in a paper-and-pencil version. Total administration requires approximately 5 minutes and may be conducted by the clinician or self-administered by the client. The BDI-II has been reported to have good reliability, and high content and convergent validity (Beck, Brown, & Steer, 1996b). Although frequently utilized to measure depression, many of the items are designed to measure cognitive processes (e.g., I feel that I am a total failure as a person) limiting its application to traditional functional assessment.

SELF-MONITORING

Self-monitoring is the process of "systematically observing and recording aspects of one's own behavior" (Bornstein, Hamilton, & Bornstein, 1986, p. 176). Functionally related internal and external environmental events may be recorded to gain better understanding of the client's behavior (Cone, 1999). This form of self-report assessment is frequently used in clinical psychology. Indeed, in a survey of behavioral practitioners, 83% reported using self-monitoring with their clients (Elliott, Miltenberger, Kaster-Bundgaard, & Lumley, 1996).

Clients may use self-monitoring to track thoughts, feelings, and behaviors. Client recordings may include the frequency and duration of target behavior, as well as relevant antecedents and consequences to assist in understanding the function of behavior. Because clients are responsible for monitoring their behavior, the client and clinician should agree on operational definitions of the target behavior and relevant contextual variables to be monitored (Korotitsch & Nelson-Gray, 1999). Some authors reported finding increased accuracy when clients were trained in how to monitor behavior (Hamilton & Bornstein, 1977; Nelson, Lapinski, & Boykin, 1978). Thus, clients should have a thorough understanding of the recording process.

The way in which self-monitoring is structured may vary. Clients may record behavior at every occurrence, during a specific time period, or during specific situations. Barton, Blanchard, and Veazy (1999) recommend that the time period monitored by clients be specific to the monitored behavior and purpose of the data. Cone (1999) suggested that clinicians consider: (a) when and how frequent behavior should be monitored, (b) the time period for monitoring, (c) what is to be recorded, (d) the format of the record, (e) whether and how to use cues, (f) the number of different variables to be recorded, and (g) any techniques for assuring compliance.

Clients most often record their behavior on paper-and-pencil forms, although counters, tape recorders, and journals are also useful in the monitoring process. Paper-and-pencil forms and counters can quickly capture the frequency of behavior. Unlike counters, paper-and-pencil forms allow detailed information including severity ratings and contextual variables to be recorded. Tape recorders and journals offer the additional advantage of comprehensive verbatim responses, although much of the information recorded may be irrelevant to the treatment plan.

Self-monitoring may assist in the initial assessment process through identification of target behaviors and relevant contextual variables. Monitoring can also be used to establish baseline rates of behavior (Ciminero, Nelson, & Lipinski, 1977; Korotisch & Nelson-Gray, 1999). This gathering of information further contributes to the development of a functional analysis through the formulation of hypotheses regarding target behavior and maintaining variables. When diagnostic classification is unclear, self-monitoring can aid in appropriate diagnosis. Treatment plans can then be developed accordingly (Korotisch & Nelson-Gray, 1999).

Utilization of self-monitoring during treatment assists clients in gaining increased awareness of behavior occurrence and behavior management (Korotitsch & Nelson-Gray, 1999; Wilson & Vitousek, 1999). Indeed, merely attending to the occurrence of behavior may alter behavior in the direction of the therapeutic goal (Baird & Nelson-Gray, 1999). Monitoring can also be used in treatment to monitor treatment gains and outcomes. Recordings throughout treatment can be compared to base rate information to assess behavior changes. If behavior change is not reflected in recordings, intervention strategies may be altered.

Self-monitoring is an inexpensive, convenient technique that requires less of the clinician's time and resources than other methods (e.g., behavioral observation). In addition to convenience, self-monitoring is less intrusive. Since clients record behaviors themselves, there is no need for the presence of observers, and recordings are less likely to be biased by observer perception. Clients are also benefited by being provided with a method of attending to their behavior and responses. Bornstein and colleagues (1986) noted the immediate self-derived feedback outside of therapy through self-reporting methods empowers clients. Self-monitoring also has a wide range of application.

Despite benefits of self-monitoring, the technique is not without criticism. Reactivity to monitoring may occur. Response reactivity occurs when clients purposely alter their report of behavior as a result of attention (Ciminero et al., 1977). Frequency or severity of problem behavior may be inflated to signal need for treatment (Craske & Tsao, 1999), or underreported if the client fears negative consequences for failing to reflect treatment gains. Contrarily, clients may underreport problem behavior to impress the therapist or "get out" of therapy commitments. Accuracy may also be affected by the limitations of memory. If the client records retrospectively, aspects of the monitored variables may not be remembered. Further, easily remembered events might be recorded as occurring more frequently (Craske & Tsao, 1999). To increase accuracy of data, observer load is an important consideration (Hayes & Cavior, 1977, 1980). Baird and Nelson-Gray (1999) suggest it is best to initiate the monitoring process with a few behaviors, and gradually increase the number of monitored behaviors with the passage of time.

BEHAVIORAL INTERVIEWS

Behavioral interviewing uses the framework of learning principles (i.e., operant and classical conditioning) to elicit information from the client, and initiate functional analysis of the problem (Sarwer & Sayers, 1998). The interview is often the first step in identifying the problem behavior(s), generating hypotheses, and gathering information (Glass & Arnkoff, 1989). Most clients are cooperative and provide detailed information regarding their problems and the antecedents and consequences. However, there are times when clients are not able to fully describe what is wrong. In instances such as these, it may be helpful for the clinician to ascertain motivations for the referral.

Interviews used in behavioral assessment vary in structure. The content and organization of unstructured interviews is dependent upon the clinician and the goal of the interview. Semi-structured and structured interviews are less flexible. Semi-structured interviews include standardized questions and formats, but do permit the clinician leeway to ask follow-up questions, select questions to ask from an available list, and permit idiosyncratic queries. Structured interviews are fully structured interviews that clearly delineate the format of the interview and the questions to be read verbatim by the clinician. They do not allow rephrasing or additional questions to be posed to the client.

Unstructured Interviews   Clinicians frequently use unstructured interviews at the outset of the assessment and therapeutic process to identify client's problem. The clinician works with the client to identify, and operationally define the problem. Lazarus (1973) proposed the BASIC ID approach to assessing content areas in interviews [i.e., behavior (B), affect (A), sensation (S), imagery (I), cognitions (C), interpersonal relationships (I), and possible drug utilization (D)]. Assessment of medical history is customary, as medical conditions may contribute to problem behavior. In keeping with behavioral assumptions, interviews are chiefly focused on current problem behavior, contextual variables, and treatment utility. The history of the problem may be assessed, but the emphasis is on recent events.

Kratochwill (1985) provides a four-stage format relevant to discussing topics during an unstructured interview:

1. Problem identification is the specification of problem to establish base rates and treatment goals.
2. Problem analysis is the assessment of contextual variables and client resources.
3. Plan implementation is the proposed data collection for evaluation of treatment progress.
4. Treatment evaluation concerns how pre- and postlevels of behavior will be compared.

Witt and Elliott (1983) suggested a more detailed organization for unstructured interviews:

1. The clinician begins by providing an overview of the interview agenda and a rationale for problem specification.
2. Clinician and client work together to identify and clearly define problem behaviors.
3. The problem behavior is further defined by assessing frequency, duration, and intensity.
4. Relevant antecedents and consequences are identified.
5. Realistic treatment goals and deadlines are discussed and agreed upon by the clinician and client.
6. The client's strengths are identified.
7. Any behavior to be recorded and the method of the recording are identified.
8. The way in which treatment efficacy will be assessed is discussed.
9. The clinician summarizes the information discussed and obtains agreement from the client.

These suggestions provide the clinician with a format for organizing unstructured interviews. However, clinicians have the freedom to vary the content of the interview, the specific questions posed, and the amount of time spent on each area. Unstructured interviews should be tailored to the client's needs and responses during the interview process. Through individualization of the interview, the clinician may obtain information from the client that would not have otherwise been disclosed.

A major advantage of unstructured interviews is the flexibility to assess multiple areas and spontaneously alter the interview format based on information obtained. In addition to identifying problem behavior and contextual variables, unstructured interviews provide an opportunity for clinicians to formulate and inquire about hypotheses regarding the function of behavior. Depending on the information obtained, the clinician may determine whether further assessment measures are necessitated. Flexibility of the unstructured interview allows the clinician to explore client initiated content, and provide empathy, which may assist in establishing rapport. The interaction also provides an opportunity for the clinician to gain an impression of the client, and may serve as an observation measure if the client displays problem behavior during the interview.

Semi-Structured and Structured Interviews   Semi-structured and structured interviews provide an organized approach to interviewing. Both forms of interview provide clinicians with a standardized set of questions, sequence for asking questions, and behavior ratings. The difference lies in the degree of structure. Semi-structured interviews allow clinicians to rephrase questions and ask additional questions for clarification. Structured interviews require clinicians to ask questions verbatim without deviation. This may be beneficial for interviewers with less experience and clinical skill, provided they receive training on the specific interview.

As compared with unstructured interviews, clinicians may achieve more accurate diagnoses through the use of semi-structured and structured interviews as they assure coverage of diagnostic criteria. Diagnostic accuracy is particularly important in research, and clinical settings for which accurate classification is crucial (i.e., forensic settings). Structured interviews are also used to verify diagnostic impressions gained during unstructured interviews. If clinicians are unsure of a client's diagnosis, they may use a semi-structured or structured interview to assist in differential diagnosis. The emphasis on diagnostic criteria, however, does not provide a thorough examination of contextual variables.

Although structured interviews have been criticized for failing to provide an opportunity to build rapport (Segal & Coolidge, 2003), they have demonstrated greater reliability and validity than unstructured interviews (Rogers, 2001; Segal & Coolidge, 2003). Reliability across interviewers is an important aspect of assessment when working with managed care systems that require diagnostic certainty and base reimbursement on diagnosis. Reliable measures also provide a more accurate measure of treatment outcome. However, it is important to note that psychometric properties vary across specific interviews, as indicated below.

STRUCTURED CLINICAL INTERVIEW FOR *DSM-IV* AXIS I DISORDERS   The Structured Clinical Interview for *DSM-IV* Axis I Disorders (SCID-I) is a semi-structured interview for assessing *Diagnostic and Statistical Manual* disorders *(DSM-IV)* (American Psychiatric Association, 1994) Axis I disorders. Multiple versions of the interview are available depending on the type of client to be interviewed and the setting in which the interview is to be conducted (e.g., patient/nonpatient client, research/clinical setting). The clinical version (SCID-CV; First, Spitzer, Gibbon, & Williams, 1997) provides open-ended prompts with close-ended follow-up questions to assess both current (i.e., within the past month) and lifetime symptomology. The interview is comprised of 6 major modules: Mood Episodes, Psychotic Symptoms, Psychotic Disorders, Mood Disorders, Substance Use Disorders, and Anxiety and other Disorders, and requires 30 to 90 minutes for administration. However, the clinician has the discretion to utilize all modules, or chose the modules that are most relevant to the client's presenting problem. The SCID-I has been used as the "gold standard" for validity (e.g., Shear, Greeno, & Kang, 2000; Steiner, Tebes, & Sledge, 1995). Reliability is generally good, and varies across modules (Zanarini, et al., 2000).

DIAGNOSTIC INTERVIEW SCHEDULE FOR *DSM-IV*   The Diagnostic Interview Schedule (DIS-IV) for *DSM-IV* (Robins et al., 2000) is a fully structured interview for assessing *DSM-IV* (American Psychiatric Association, 1994) disorders. All questions and probes are provided, and presented verbatim. Questions are close-ended as a means of limiting variability. The DIS-IV requires 90 to 120 minutes to administer. Clinicians may choose which modules to administer, or utilize the optional termination points within each disorder section if the client does not endorse sufficient symptoms. Given the complexity of the interview, training is recommended.

DIRECT BEHAVIORAL OBSERVATION

Behavioral observation of specified behaviors is the hallmark of behavioral assessment (Algozzine, Konrad, & Test, 2005) and is the preferred method of obtaining information about problem behaviors (Groth-Marnat, 2003). Jordan and Franklin (2003) report behavioral observation is one of the most effective measures of frequency and duration of behavior. Although other methods are more commonly utilized, these methods are more likely to be influenced by reporting biases. The more removed from the time and place of the occurrence of the behavior, the more indirect the assessment and the greater chance of error. Behavioral observation should ideally occur in naturalistic environments (e.g., home, school, work), and should involve a range of appropriate and inappropriate social behavior (Algozzine et al., 2005). In conducting in vivo assessment the observer has little control over the behaviors that are observed. In vivo observations are most effective when assessing high frequency, global behaviors and are valuable for measuring change following clinical intervention (Groth-Marnat, 2003).

Defining the target behavior, in measurable, observable terms is a necessary first step to behavioral observation (Groth-Marnat, 2003). Any definition of a behavior should include specific examples of behavioral performance to assist in achieving sufficient reliability between raters. For some behaviors, such as measuring how many alcoholic beverages the client consumes (e.g., 12 ounces of beer, 5 ounces of wine), this is an easy process. Other behaviors, such as assertiveness, are more difficult and must be clearly defined (e.g., refusing an offer to ingest an alcoholic beverage). The target behaviors for observation will be derived from information obtained from the interview, anecdotal observations (e.g., observation of argument with spouse in waiting room), self-report inventories, and other assessment strategies (Groth-Marnat, 2003).

An observational assessment generally focuses on the here and now. Thus, the clinician's attention is focused on the immediate behavior, its antecedents (what happened just before the behavior) and its consequences (what happens right afterward). In conducting informal observations, an observer may observe behavior for a specific period of time and provide a narrative summary of relevant actions, often called a *narrative recording*. For example, a clinician working with an individual who self-reports social skill deficits may observe this person at a party. The clinician would then return to the office and make notes of observed actions. This type of observation is very helpful in defining more specific areas for future assessment to be measured quantitatively (Groth-Marnat, 2003). Formal observations identify previously defined behaviors. In a formal observation, the observer decides ahead of time who will be observed, what they will be doing, when and where the observation will take place, and how the behavior will be counted. The behavior must be operationalized prior to the observation so that the observer is able to measure it and keep a record. An example of a well-defined behavior would be, "asking a coworker how she is feeling during a work break," whereas a poorly defined behavior would be, "being friendly." Once the target behavior occurs, the clinician records its occurrence, along with relevant antecedents (e.g., presence of one person who smiles, solving a work-related problem successfully) and consequences (e.g., person returns salutation).

It is necessary to fully understand the various dimensions of behavior prior to conducting formal observations (Algozzine et al., 2005). For instance, *frequency* is the number of times an individual engages in the target behavior within a given time frame; the clinician must be clear about when the behavior begins and ends (e.g., Sam swore at his supervisee three times during the 8-hour work day). Rates per minute, hour or day can be derived from frequency data, thereby allowing comparisons across observations. Duration is how long the individual engages in the target behavior during the specified time period (e.g., Sam engaged in a conversation with his coworker for 2 minutes during the 1-hour lunch). Latency refers to the length of time that elapses between the antecedent stimulus and the onset of the behavior (e.g., Thirty minutes after Sam arrived home, he began crying). The *magnitude* of the behavior is the force, intensity, or severity of the behavior, but relies on a qualitative judgment (1 = Extremely angry, 5 = Extremely happy). What the behavior looks like motorically is the *topography* of behavior, while *locus* is where the behavior occurs.

PARTICIPANT AND NONPARTICIPANT OBSERVERS

O'Brien, Kaplar, and Haynes (2005) describe both nonparticipant and participant observers. Nonparticipant observers are generally individuals who are trained to record the occurrence of behaviors and contributing variables. These individuals are not, however, part of the client's environment. They receive formal training and are hired to conduct the observations and collect data on the problem behavior and causal variables. One downfall of this type of assessment is the cost associated with the training and hiring of such individuals. Participant observers are involved in the client's natural environment. They may include family members, coworkers, teachers, hospital staff, or other caregivers. Due to their regular involvement in the client's life, they are able to conduct observations in many different settings across substantial periods of time. There are drawbacks to utilizing these individuals. Given their multiple roles and responsibilities, they are generally able to record a limited number of events. In addition, their reports may be biased due to their relationship with the client, thus affecting objectivity of their recordings (O'Brien et al., 2005).

Direct behavioral observation can also be conducted with more than one observer at a time, making it a very effective measurement strategy (Jordan & Franklin, 2003). Two observers might be used in a residential or hospital setting. For instance, both a nurse and a mental health technician might be trained to observe a client's behavior, and would record their observations. Then, interobserver agreement could be obtained as a measure of reliability. The use of two observers is time consuming, expensive, and not always practical, usually demanding an assessment of interrater/interobserver reliability.

By-Products   By-products occur when an observer codes stimuli that are indicators of the behavior of interest (e.g., urinalysis to assess cocaine use, bruises to assess perpetration of child maltreatment, movie ticket stubs to assess attendance at a movie; Jordan & Franklin, 2003). Advantages of this method include precise quantification, relative noninvasiveness, and ease of implementation. However, Bloom, Fischer and Orme (2003) note some problems with behavior byproducts including that the information is generally limited to quantity, many behaviors do not have by-products, and the clinician must be certain that the by-product is reflective of the target behavior. The validity of information gained from the collection of by-products is also questionable (e.g., tampered urinalysis, bruises reflect accidents rather than perpetration of abusive behavior, movie tickets are collected prior to movie) because it is sometimes difficult to verify.

Methods of Data Recording   There are distinct methods of recording behavior (Algozzine et al., 2005). *Event recording,* the simplest and most efficient system, measures the occurrence of behavior. The observer must wait for the behavior to occur, and then record relevant information. This method is useful for aggressive actions, greetings, or verbal expressions (Groth-Marnat, 2003). It is especially effective when recording behaviors that have low frequencies, different types of behaviors, and when measuring change over long periods of time. However, it may be difficult to use this method for situations in which target behaviors have poorly defined beginnings and endings, and attention is difficult to sustain. *Interval recording* measures whether the behavior occurs within a predetermined time interval. This can be done in whole or part, meaning the interval can be separated into a specific number of time intervals (blocks of time) or the entire time period is used. For example, a period of 30 minutes can be divided into three equal, 10-minute intervals. Then the observer monitors the client to see if the target behavior occurs during that time interval (Jordan & Franklin, 2003).

Audio or video recording is also used as a method of observation that is less intrusive than an observer presenting in the room, and reduces the chances of reactivity from the client. Given the complexity of behavior, and the rapidness with which it may occur, video taping of behavior can allow for subsequent analysis without fear the observer "missing" important data. Sometimes, observers are not able to record behavior in the units of measurement that are needed (e.g., seconds) as accurately as an instrument can (Tyron, 1998), and instruments may be less invasive than observers. Technological advances have assisted observers by providing computers for recording purposes or digital-data storage devices which can provide counts of behavior and numerous calculations about rates, intervals, and reliability (Baer, Harrison, Fradenburg, Peterson, & Milla, 2005). However, the user of such equipment must be prepared for the rather lengthy dubbing process after the recording takes place and the possibility of equipment failure.

Analog Observation   When direct observation is not possible, analog observations may occur. In these situations, a controlled clinical situation analogous to the natural environment is created so the target behavior may be observed (e.g., simulated bar to observe alcohol use behaviors). Indeed, there are many instances in which behaviors of interest may not occur in the presence of an observer (e.g., binge eating, fire setting, antisocial acts). Thus, analog assessment is one acceptable alternative. Importantly, the results of analog assessments may not be generalizable to the natural environment (Gresham et al., 1999).

Limitations There are some significant limitations associated with behavioral observation. The accuracy of observational data can be compromised if the target behavior is not clearly defined, the observer is not trained or objective, and the time intervals are not equal or numbers of response opportunities are not equal (Algozzinee al., 2005). Direct behavioral observation is expensive (O'Brien et al., 2005) and labor intensive (observers must be recruited, trained, supported, and the data entered and analyzed). Additionally, observer reactivity occurs when the presence of the observer can influence the behavior being observed (e.g., a conspicuous observer) or the client increases socially desirable behaviors while decreasing undesirable ones (Tyron, 1998). The observer may also have a lapse in attention and discuss the data with others (Groth-Marnat, 2003). Nevertheless, one of the chief advantages of behavioral observation is that the observer is permitted to examine behaviors that clients or significant others may be unable to report with sufficient detail or accuracy.

PSYCHOPHYSIOLOGICAL ASSESSMENT

Given the tradition of the "mind-body" connection, the use of instruments to assess physiological processes underlying psychological disorders is important. Physiological responses are activities of the body's muscles that can be measured with precision through technical and mechanical indicators of client behavior (Jordan & Franklin, 2003). For example, assessment of cardiovascular measures such as heart rate and blood pressure are important in the assessment and treatment of anxiety disorders (Sturgis & Gramling, 1998). Utilization of psychophysiological recordings permits direct, observable, and measurable data. Many psychological disorders are accompanied by physiological changes (sleep disturbances, gastrointestinal changes, heart rate, body temperature) that can be measured through instrumentation (Iverson, Stampfer, & Gaetz, 2002). The validity and reliability of such measurements is generally high. Much like behavioral assessment in general, psychophysiological measures can be used to initially assess the target problem, and later, to monitor outcome (Turpin, 1991).

The choice of which psychophysiological responses to measure depends on whether the target behavior is considered a primary defining characteristic or only part of the symptoms associated with the behavior (Sturgis & Gramling, 1998). For example, heart rate increase in anxious clients is only part of the symptom picture, while increased blood pressure in hypertensive clients is a defining feature of the disorder. Selection of the responses for measurement should also be guided by whether they involve the autonomic nervous system or the hypothamalus-pitutary-adrenal cortex system. The former relates to stimuli eliciting a startle response or requiring a physical or cognitive effort, while the later is stimulated from more chronic stressors which are uncontrollable. The clinician must also consider the invasiveness, convenience, and acceptability of the measuring device (Sturgis & Gramling, 1998). Some commonly measured responses are heart rate and blood pressure, galvanic skin response (skin conductance), brain activity (electroencephalography; EEG); muscle response (electromyography; EMG), respiration, eye movement, and hand temperature. These measurements allow psychological problems to be translated into specific physiological indices (Groth-Marnat, 2003).

Anxiety disorders are one domain in which assessment of psychophysiological indices seems extremely important. Alpers, Wilhelm and Roth (2005) report that a comprehensive assessment of a client with anxiety requires both self-report and physiological assessment. Turpin (1991) states that adding psychophysiological techniques to "clinical assessment, particularly within the context of anxiety disorders, may yield unique information that might help to determine both the direction and effectiveness of therapeutic interventions" (p. 366). One such example is circadian heart patterns that have been found to be associated with a number of anxiety disorders (Iverson et al., 2002). These authors report that this method is a "noninvasive, inexpensive, minute-by-minute index of autonomic nervous system dysfunction" (p. 202). Mussgay and Ruddel (2004) suggest a thorough cardiovascular examination of all clients with anxiety disorders that may assist in devising a more complex treatment regime, including exercise. They performed a continuous assessment of EEG, blood pressure, breathing patterns and other cardiovascular indices that allowed the calculation of heart rate variances. Further, Alper et al. (2005) found that respiratory and autonomic system measures are valid diagnostic and treatment outcome criteria for phobic disorders.

Another area in which psychophysiological measurements are made is sexual disorders. For men, a penile strain gauge is used to obtain a direct measure of penile circumference. As the penis expands in the aroused state, the strain gauge records the changes on a polygraph (Barlow & Durand, 2005). This could be used to diagnose primary or secondary erectile dysfunction. Additionally, biofeedback measures are used with clients experiencing headaches.

Given that there are an increasing number of disorders that may require psychophysiological assessment, the laboratory is no longer the main setting for such research (Turpin, 1991). There are now ambulatory methods for psychophysiological recordings that allow clients to move about freely and can be used in the client's home or work setting, thus moving assessment to the real world and increasing its generalizability. Strides have been made to produce user-friendly software and hardware as well as compact computers that are available to most any clinician at a modest cost. As advances are made in ambulatory measuring devices, these would be of greater interest to clinicians who work outside of laboratory settings.

Despite its advantages, there are some limitations to physiological assessment. Skill, expertise, and training are essential for those who are conducting these assessments. At times, the measures produce inconsistent results due to procedural or technical difficulties or the nature of the behavior (Barlow & Durand, 2005). Given this, clinicians must be highly trained in the area in which they are obtaining these measurements. There is also often an adaptation that takes place when the client arrives at the clinic for psychophysiological assessment. Most measurements require that the client remain still (e.g., blood pressure measurement), which may be difficult, especially if the situation itself is anxiety provoking. The use of the instrumentation may also impact the physiological responses of the client. If the assessment requires multiple transducers, video cameras, and other devices, the greater the physiological response of the client (Sturgis & Gramling, 1998). Some clients may also demonstrate habituation responses (reduction in behavior following presentation of stimuli) over time. Finally, the instrumentation is generally recording physiological responses that are very minor and the equipment must be sensitive to recording only those responses that are meaningful and not extraneous.

Reliability and validity are a concern with psychophysiological measurements also. To ensure not only the safety of the client, but to obtain reliable and valid measurements, proper preparation of the skin, electrode placement and proper care of the instruments is necessary. In a naturalistic setting where physiological assessment is taking place, it may be extremely difficult to filter out "noise" or sources of artifact. For example, temperature, and food and beverage intake may all affect psychophysiological measures and are not easily controlled. However, heart rate is one psychophysiological measurement that is highly reliable and easy to measure, even when a client is ambulatory (Sturgis & Gramling, 1998).

RELIABILITY AND VALIDITY

As mentioned previously in this chapter, behavioral assessment differs from traditional assessment; although it shares some of the same issues with respect to reliability and validity, it also possesses unique concerns in these areas. Reliability and validity are both fundamental to ensure accuracy of assessments. Potential sources of error, which affect reliability and validity, in turn could lead to biased case conceptualizations and interventions (Haynes, 2006).

The relationship between reliability and validity is complex. Reliability is necessary, but not a sufficient condition for validity. Best practice within behavioral assessment should aim at a balance between validity and reliability, with a priority given to validity while cognizant of the importance of reliability (Baer et al., 2005). If a measurement is reliable, but is not valid (not what the assessor intended to measure) then it has little value. Demonstrating reliability and validity of assessment data is important to ensure confidence that the results of the assessment have some degree of consistency (ability to be reproduced) while accurately represent the construct measured (behavior; Shriver, Anderson, & Proctor, 2001).

RELIABILITY

Reliability refers to the consistency or reproducibility of the results obtained from an assessment method. The ways in which reliability are established relate to determining how much measurement error is present in different conditions. Some of the standard methods of determining reliability used in traditional assessments are internal consistency, equivalent forms, test-retest, interrater, and standard error of measurement (Shriver et al., 2001). Reliability is related to the degree of confidence that similar results would be found over different occasions, raters or samples of the same behavior (Linn & Gronlund, 2000).

Behavioral assessment strives to take into consideration psychometric considerations, however, many concepts require different interpretations. For instance, normative comparisons are not as important in behavioral assessment as they are in traditional settings due to the emphasis of the former on a client's own level of functioning (Groth-Marnat, 2003). Additionally, inconsistency and instability in scores, which traditionally would be viewed as affecting reliability, are interpreted differently by behavioral assessors (Silva, 1993). While many may report this as error in the observation system, it may be interpreted as instability of the behavior or true changes in the behavior (Haynes, 2006). However, having two raters (whose interrater reliability would be examined) would determine potential errors in the observation system. With regard to test-retest reliability, low test-retest reliability is likely to be interpreted as due to environmental conditions rather than error during data collection (Groth-Marnat, 2003).

VALIDITY

Validity is defined as an evaluation of the adequacy and "the appropriateness of the interpretations of the results of an assessment procedure" (Linn & Gronlund, 2000, p. 75). Essentially this means the information gained from the test or assessment and inferences derived from there are appropriate, useful, and meaningful (Osterlind, 2006); the test or instrument measures what it is intended to measure. The validity of an assessment is not simply described as existing or not, rather it is based on a particular use and or purpose. Validity is best thought of in terms of degree, rather than all or none. The most common descriptions of validity use the terms, high, moderate, and low validity.

In traditional assessment, there has been a tripartite focus of validity: content, construct, and criterion related. However, these constructs may not be as applicable in behavioral assessment. Content validity refers to how well this assessment procedure or task represents the domain of behavior to be measured. Initially in behavioral assessment, content validity was approached informally by including in questionnaires and observational strategies what was rationally considered to be studied. For instance, a measure of depression would include statements that were believed to represent what symptoms most depressed people are experiencing (Groth-Marnat, 2003). Construct validity refers to "empirical evidence that supports the posited existence of a hypothetical construct and indicates that an assessment device, does in fact, measure that construct" (Popham, 2002, p. 363). This can be done in several ways including intervention studies, differential-population studies and related-measures studies (see Popham, 2002, for a complete review). Finally, criterion related validity refers to the relationship between the current measure and some future measure. Difficulties in this area have been similar to those raised in traditional assessment, namely, generalizability to different populations, settings and methods of administration (Groth-Marnat, 2003). Generalizability becomes an issue when behaviors that are observed in an office setting are representative of behaviors that would be displayed at home (Tyron, 1998). Behaviorists should obtain enough information across different settings in order to be considered valid and generalizable.

High face validity, sometimes thought to affect responding, can be an advantage in behavioral assessments. Face validity refers to the fact that "the appearance of a test seems to coincide with the use to which the test is being put" (Popham, 2002, p. 65). Knight and Godfrey (1995) report that behaviorally based memory tests that are high in face validity increase the likelihood that the client will be motivated to perform well and receive appropriate encouragement from others (caregivers, staff, clinicians) to perform their best. Face-valid measures are likely to be perceived as relevant to the client's problem, as they use behaviorally referenced items related to the clients' concerns.

Self-Report   Historically, self-report measures, initially used to gain a direct report from the client, relied on content and face validity (Groth-Marnat, 2003). This method received much criticism for response bias, questionable reliability and validity, lack of norms, and client honesty in responding. Clients may under or over report behavior, be inaccurate in their own self recording of behavior, and fall prey to distortion when engaging in retrospective reporting (O'Donohue, Beitz, & Byrd, 2006). However, it may be better to think of self-report questionnaires as assessment tools, rather than psychometrically sound tests. To assist in conducting a thorough assessment, self-report measures should be administered with other measures from other sources, and processed through a lens of reliability and validity by the assessor. In fact, when multiple measures are applied reliability is increased regardless of the measurement device.

Behavioral Observation   In direct observation, reliability is often reported as the percentage agreement between observers. Observer agreement tells us the degree to which two similarly trained observers record behavior. This can be achieved by having different observers independently observe and record the behavior and then compute the interobserver reliability (e.g., percentage agreement or nonagreement). Sometimes two observers may not agree on the presence or absence of the target behavior (Tyron, 1998). Baer et al. (2005) discuss one way to ensure that high reliabilities are not achieved by chance (high interrater reliability). They recommend checking to see how often the observers agree the target behavior occurred and how often it did not occur, respectively, occurrence reliability and nonoccurence reliability.

Assuming reliability, validity across observers is a concern because not all observers possess the same threshold for observing the target behavior (Baer, et al., 2005). Ways to handle this are to more specifically define the topography of the behavior or create subcategories of behavior that are all recorded. Validity may also be comprised by observer distraction, so efforts should be made to create an environment that is minimally distracting for observers, while maintaining a typical environment for the behavior to occur. Additionally, a type of validity that may be unique to behavioral assessment is observer validity that is how accurately the observer records the behavior in a direct behavioral observation (Tyron, 1998). Finally, reactivity of the client can become a significant source of concern (O'Donohue et al., 2006). By virtue of being observed, clients may behave differently than if they were not. Indeed, it may result in genuine changes in behavior. Here the distinction between reliability and validity becomes clearer. The reliability of the information obtained by the observation is high, but the validity is questionable. The observer would be wise to not record the subject's responses and behaviors that appeared to be due to reactivity.

Reliability across different behavioral observational strategies varies based on a number of factors including observer expectancies, interference from nontarget persons, as well as a number of observer errors (i.e., halo effects, primacy effects, leniency in scoring). When there are highly structured procedures, reliability is increased. Understandably, observation conducted in a laboratory or controlled setting will have higher reliability then one conducted in a natural environment. There are ways for bias to be reduced and reliability to be increased, such as through highly structured procedures as systematic sampling (a procedure that allows each person in the population to have a known and equal probability of being selected).

To measure behaviors reliably, the definition of a behavior to record must be made clear to observers. For observable behaviors, staff who are conducting observations should be trained adequately to minimize the effects of reactivity of subjects, accurately record behavior and avoid interpretations, and leave the interpretations to the clinician. Measurement becomes much less reliable when dealing with internal cognitions where direct observation is not possible and the clinician relies on self-report by the client.

SUMMARY

Behavioral assessment is a psychological assessment paradigm that is based on theory, research, and practice. Founded in behavioral theory, over the past 20 years, there has been considerable research to support behavioral assessment methods. Behavioral assessment is concerned with the preceding events and resulting consequences of behavior, as well as ways to change these behaviors. Given the wide variety of treatment options available to clinicians, a thorough, broad-based assessment is a critical first step to ensure treatment success. There are several options available to the clinician desiring to conduct a behavioral assessment including functional assessment of behavior, self-report measures and instruments, interview techniques, direct behavioral observation, and psychophysiological recordings. Functional assessment includes identifying target behaviors, conducting a functional analysis, and developing treatment strategies. Self-report assessment obtains information directly from the client and includes interviews, self-report measures, self-monitoring and recording. Although there are multiple benefits to these methods, clients may not always provide accurate information on their behavior. Behavioral observation can be one of the most useful methods of assessment, due to its high validity and reliability. As with all forms of assessment, it has a number of limitations, including cost, observer bias, and necessary training. Some behavioral problems can be assessed through psychophysiological assessment that focuses on direct, observable data of physiological changes. Advanced methods of assessment including ambulatory recording devices make this type of assessment accessible to most clinicians. Psychometric concepts of traditional assessments, such as validity and reliability, have a distinctive role in and their relevance to behavioral assessment were discussed, with an emphasis on a balance between the two and a consideration of the unique issues inherent in behavioral assessment. Behavioral assessment is important before, during, and after intervention.

REFERENCES

Algozzine, R., Konrad, M., & Test, W. (2005). Direct observation. In M. Hersen, G. Sugai, & R. Horner (Eds.), *Encyclopedia of behavior modification and cognitive behavior therapy: Vol. 3. Educational applications* (pp. 1266–1269). Thousand Oaks, CA: Sage.

Alpers, G. W., Wilhelm, F. H., & Roth, W. T. (2005). Psychophysiological assessment during exposure in driving phobic patients. *Journal of Abnormal Psychology, 114*, 126–139.

American Psychiatric Association. (1994). *Diagnostic and statistical manual of mental disorders* (4th ed.). Washington, DC: Author.

American Psychiatric Association. (2000). *Diagnostic and statistical manual of mental disorders* (4th ed., text rev.). Washington, DC: Author.

Azrin, N. H., Donohue, B., Teichner, G., Crum, T., Howell, J., & DeCato, L. (2001). A controlled evaluation and description of individual-cognitive problem solving and family-behavioral therapies in conduct-disordered and substance dependent youth. *Journal of Child and Adolescent Substance Abuse, 11*, 1–43.

Baer, D., Harrison, R., Fradenburg, L., Peterson, D., & Milla, S. (2005). Some pragmatics in the valid and reliable recording of directly observed behavior. *Research on Social Work, 15*(6), 440–451.

Baird, S., & Nelson-Gray, R. O. (1999). Direct observation and selfmonitoring. In S. C. Hayes, D. H. Barlow, & R. O. Nelson-Gray (Eds.), *The scientist practitioner: Research and accountability in the age of managed care* (2nd ed., pp. 353–386). Boston: Allyn & Bacon.

Barlow, D. H. (2005). What's new about evidence-based assessment? *Psychological Assessment, 17,* 308–311.

Barlow, D. H., & Durand, M. (2005). *Abnormal psychology: An integrative approach.* Belmont, CA: Wadsworth/Thompson Learning.

Barlow, D. H., Hayes, S. C., & Nelson, R. O. (1984). *The scientist-practitioner: Research and accountability in clinical and educational settings.* New York: Pergamon Press.

Barton, K. A., Blanchard, E. B., & Veazy, C. (1999). Self-monitoring as an assessment strategy in behavioral medicine. *Psychological Assessment, 11,* 490–497.

Beck, A. T., Brown, G., & Steer, R. A. (1996a). *Beck Depression Inventory II Manual.* San Antonio, TX: Psychological Corporation.

Beck, A. T., Brown, G., & Steer, R. A. (1996b). *Beck Depression Inventory II (BDI-II).* San Antonio, TX: Psychological Corporation.

Bloom, M., Fischer, J., & Orme, J. (2003). *Evaluating practice: Guidelines for the accountable professional.* Boston: Allyn & Bacon.

Bornstein, P. H., Hamilton, S. B., & Bornstein, M. T. (1986). Self-monitoring procedures. In A. R. Ciminero, C. S. Calhoun, & H. E. Adams (Eds.), *Handbook of behavioral assessment* (pp. 176–222). New York: Wiley.

Ciminero, A. R., Nelson, R. O., & Lipinski, D. P. (1977). Self-monitoring procedures. In A. R. Ciminero, K. S. Calhoun, & H. E. Adams (Eds.), *Handbook of behavioral assessment* (pp. 195–232). New York: Wiley.

Cone, J. D. (1977). The relevance of reliability and validity for behavioral assessment. *Behavior Therapy, 8,* 411–426.

Cone, J. D. (1978). The behavioral assessment grid (BAG): A conceptual framework and taxonomy. *Behavior Therapy, 9,* 882–888.

Cone, J. D. (1999). Introduction to the special section on self-monitoring: A major assessment method in clinical psychology. *Psychological Assessment, 11,* 411–414.

Craske, M. G., & Tsao, J. C. I. (1999). Self-monitoring with panic and anxiety disorders. *Psychological Assessment, 11,* 466–479.

Derogatis, L. R. (1983). *The SCL-90-R Manual II: Administration, scoring, and procedures.* Towson, MD: Clinical Psychometric Research.

Derogatis, L. R. (1994). *SCL-90-R: Symptom Checklist-90-R.* Minneapolis, MN: National Computer Systems.

Derogatis, L. R., Rickels, K., & Rock, A. (1976). The SCL-90 and the MMPI: A step in the validation of a new self-report scale. *British Journal of Psychiatry, 128,* 280–289.

Donohue, B., Ammerman, R., & Zelis, K. (1998). Child abuse and neglect. In T. S. Watson & F. M. Gresham (Eds.), *Handbook of child behavior therapy* (pp. 183–202). New York: Plenum Press.

Elliott, A. J., Miltenberger, R. G., Kaster-Bundgaard, J., & Lumley, V. (1996). A national survey of assessment and therapy used by behavior therapists. *Cognitive and Behavioral Practice, 3,* 107–125.

Evans, I. M. (1986). Response structure and the triple-response-mode concept. In R. O. Nelson & S. C. Hayes (Eds.), *Conceptual foundations of behavioral assessment* (pp. 131–155). New York: Guilford Press.

Fernandez-Ballesteros, R. (1988). *Que escriben los evaluadores conductuales?* [english translation] Unpublished manuscript, Universidad Autonoma de Madrid.

Fernandez-Ballesteros, R. (1993). Behavioral assessment: Dying, vanishing or still running. *European Journal of Psychological Assessment, 9,* 159–174.

First, M. B., Spitzer, R. L., Gibbon, M., & Williams, J. B. W. (1997). *Structured Clinical Interview for DSM-IV Axis I Disorders-Clinician Version (SCID-CV).* Washington, DC: American Psychiatric Press.

Follette, W. C., & Hayes, S. C. (1992). Behavioral assessment in the DSM era. *Behavioral Assessment, 14*(3/4), 293–295.

Glass, C. R., & Arnkoff, B. D. (1989). Behavioral assessment of social anxiety and social phobia. *Clinical Psychology Review, 9,* 75–90.

Goldfried, M. R., & Kent, R. N. (1972). Traditional versus behavioral assessment: A comparison of methodological and theoretical assumptions. *Psychological Bulletin, 77,* 409–420.

Goldfried, M. R., & Sprafkin, J. N. (1976). Behavioral personality assessment. In J. T. Spence, R. C. Carson, & J. Thibaut (Eds.), *Behavioral approaches to therapy* (pp. 295–321). Morristown, NJ: General Learning Press.

Gresham, F. M., Quinn, M. M., & Restori, A. (1999). Methodological issues in functional analysis: Generalizability to other disability groups. *Behavioral Disorders, 24,* 180–182.

Groth-Marnat, G. (2003). Behavioral assessment. In G. Groth-Marnat (Ed.), *Handbook of psychological assessment* (pp. 103–128). New York: Wiley.

Hamilton, S. B., & Bornstein, P. H. (1977). Increasing the accuracy of self-recording in speech anxious undergraduates through the use of self-monitoring training and reliability enhancement procedures. *Journal of Consulting and Clinical Psychology, 45,* 1076–1085.

Hayes, S. C., & Cavior, N. (1977). Multiple tracking and the reactivity of self-monitoring: Pt. I. Negative behaviors. *Behavior Therapy, 8,* 819–831.

Hayes, S. C., & Cavior, N. (1980). Multiple tracking and the reactivity of self-monitoring: Pt. II. Positive behaviors. *Behavioral Assessment, 2,* 283–296.

Haynes, S. N. (2006). Psychometric considerations. In M. Hersen (Ed.), *Clinician's handbook of adult behavioral assessment* (pp. 17–41). Burlington, MA: Elsevier Academic Press.

Haynes, S. N., & Uchigakiuchi, P. (1993). Incorporating personality measures in behavioral assessment: Nuts in a fruitcake or raisins in a Mai Tai? *Behavior Modification, 17,* 72–91.

Herner, R. B. (1994). Functional assessment: Contributions and future directions. *Journal of Applied Behavior Analysis, 27,* 401–404.

Horowitz, L. M., Rosenberg, S. E., Baer, B. A., Ureno, G., & Villasenor, V. S. (1988). Inventory of interpersonal problems: Psychometric properties. *Journal of Consulting and Clinical Psychology, 56,* 885–892.

Iverson, G. I., Stampfer, H., & Gaetz, M. (2002, Fall). Reliability of circadian heart pattern analysis in psychiatry. *Psychiatric Quarterly, 73,* 195–203.

Iwata, B. A., & Worsdell, A. S. (2005). Implications of functional analysis methodology for the design of intervention programs. *Exceptionality, 13,* 25–34.

Jones, M. C. (1924). The elimination of children's fears. *Journal of Experimental Psychology, 7,* 382–390.

Jordan, C., & Franklin, C. (2003). *Clinical assessment for social workers: Quantitative and qualitative methods* (2nd ed.). Chicago: Lyceum Books.

Kanfer, F. H., & Saslow, G. (1965). Behavioral analysis: An alternative to diagnostic classification. *Archives of General Psychiatry, 12,* 529–538.

Knight, R., & Godfrey, H. (1995). Behavioral and self report methods. In A. Baddeley, B. Wilson, & F. Watts (Eds.), *Handbook of memory disorders* (pp. 393–410). Oxford, England: Wiley.

Korotitsch, W. J., & Nelson-Gray, R. O. (1999). An overview of self-monitoring research in assessment and treatment. *Psychological Assessment, 11,* 415–425.

Kratochwill, T. R. (1985). Selection of target behaviors in behavioral consultation. *Behavior Assessment, 7,* 49–61.

Lazarus, A. A. (1973). Multimodel behavior therapy: Treating the "BASIC ID." *Journal of Nervous and Mental Diseases, 156,* 404–411.

Linn, R., & Gronlund, N. (2000). *Measurement and assessment in teaching* (8th ed.). Upper Saddle River, NJ: Prentice-Hall.

Mussgay, L., & Ruddel, H. (2004). Autonomic dysfunctions in patients with anxiety throughout therapy. *Journal of Psychophysiology, 18*, 27–37.

Nelson, R. O., & Hayes, S. C. (1979). Some current dimensions of behavioral assessment. *Behavioral Assessment, 1*, 1–16.

Nelson, R. O., Lipinski, D. P., & Boykin, R. A. (1978). The effects of self-recorders' training and the obtrusiveness of the self-recording device on the accuracy and reactivity of self-monitoring. *Behavior Therapy, 9*, 200–208.

Nelson-Gray, R., & Paulson, J. (2004). Behavioral assessment and the DSM system. In S. Haynes, E. Heiby, & M. Hersen (Eds.), *Comprehensive handbook of psychological assessment: Vol. 3. Behavioral assessment* (pp. 470–488). Hoboken, NJ: Wiley.

O'Brien, W. H., & Haynes, S. N. (2005). Behavioral assessment. In M. Hersen & J. Rosqvist (Eds.), *Encyclopedia of behavior modification and cognitive behavior therapy* (Vol. 2, pp. 704–711). Thousand Oaks, CA: Sage.

O'Brien, W. H., Kaplar, M., & Haynes, S. (2005). Behavioral assessment. In M. Hersen & J. Rosqvist (Eds.), *Encyclopedia of behavior modification and cognitive behavior therapy: Vol. 1. Adult clinical applications* (pp. 82–90). Thousand Oaks, CA: Sage.

O'Donohue, W., Beitz, K., & Byrd, M. (2006). Overview of behavioral assessment with adults. In M. Hersen (Ed.), *Clinician's handbook of adult behavioral assessment* (pp. 3–16). Burlington, MA: Elsevier Academic Press.

O'Neill, R. (2005). Functional behavioral assessment of problem behavior. In M. Hersen & J. Rosqvist (Eds.), *Encyclopedia of behavior modification and cognitive behavior therapy* (Vol. 3, pp. 1322–1328). Thousand Oaks, CA: Sage.

Osterlind, S. (2006). *Modern measurement: Theory, principles, and applications of mental appraisal.* Upper Saddle River, NJ: Pearson Education.

Popham, W. J. (2002). *Classroom assessment: What teachers need to know* (3rd ed.). Boston: Allyn & Bacon.

Robins, L. N., Cottler, L. B., Bucholz, K. K., Compton, W. N., North, C. S., & Rourke, K. (2000). *The Diagnostic Interview Schedule for DSM-IV* (DIS-IV). St. Louis, MO: Washington University School of Medicine.

Rogers, R. (2001). *Handbook of diagnostic and structured interviewing.* New York: Guilford Press.

Sarwer, D., & Sayers, S. (1998). Behavioral interviewing. In A. Bellack & M. Hersen (Eds.), *Behavioral assessment: A practical handbook* (pp. 763–778). Boston: Allyn & Bacon.

Segal, D. L., & Coolidge, F. L. (2003). Structured interviewing and DSM classification. In M. Hersen & S. Turner (Eds.), *Adult psychopathology and diagnosis* (4th ed., pp. 72–103). Hoboken, NJ: Wiley.

Shear, M. K., Greeno, C., & Kang, J. (2000). Diagnosis of nonpsychotic patients in community clinics. *American Journal of Psychiatry, 157*, 581–587.

Shriver, M., Anderson, C., & Proctor, B. (2001). Evaluating the validity of functional behavior assessment. *School Psychology Review, 30*(2), 180–192.

Silva, F. (1993). *Psychometric foundations and behavioral assessment.* Newbury Park, CA: Sage.

Staats, A. W. (1963). *Complex human behavior.* New York: Holt, Rinehart and Winston.

Steiner, J. L., Tebes, J. K., & Sledge, W. H. (1995). A comparison of the structured clinical interview for DSM-III-R and clinical diagnoses. *Journal of Nervous and Mental Disorders, 183*, 365–369.

Sturgis, E., & Gramling, S. (1998). Psychophysiological assessment. In A. Bellack & M. Hersen (Eds.), *Behavioral assessment: A practical handbook* (pp. 126–157). Boston: Allyn & Bacon.

Sturmey, P. (1994). Assessing the functions of aberrant behaviors: A review of psychometric instruments. *Journal of Autism and Developmental Disorders, 24*, 293–304.

Sulzer-Azaroff, B., & Mayer, G. R. (1977). *Applying behavior-analysis procedures with children and youth.* New York: Holt, Rinehart and Winston.

Tharp, R. G., & Wetzel, R. J. (1969). *Behavior modification in the natural environment.* New York: Academic Press.

Turpin, G. (1991). The psychophysiological assessment of anxiety disorders three-systems measurement and beyond. *Psychological Assessment: A Journal of Consulting and Clinical Psychology, 3*(3), 366–375.

Tyron, W. (1998). Behavioral observation. In A. Bellack & M. Hersen (Eds.), *Behavioral assessment: A practical handbook* (pp. 79–103). Boston: Allyn & Bacon.

Ullmann, L. P., & Krasner, L. A. (1965). *Case studies in behavior modification: A systematic extension of learning principles.* New York: Holt, Rinehart and Winston.

Watson, J. B., & Rayner, R. (1920). Conditioned emotional reactions. *Journal of Experimental Psychology, 3,* 1–14.

Wilson, G. T., & Vitousek, K. M. (1999). Self-monitoring in the assessment of eating disorders. *Psychological Assessment, 11,* 480–489.

Witt, J. N., & Elliott, S. N. (1983). Assessment in behavioral consultation: The initial interview. *School Psychology Review, 12,* 42–49.

Zanarini, M. C., Skodol, A. E., Bender, D., Dolan, R., Sanislow, C., & Schaefer, E., et al. (2000). The Collaborative Longitudinal Personality Disorders Study: Reliability of Axis I and II diagnoses. *Journal of Personality Disorders, 14,* 291–299.

CHAPTER 2

Diagnostic Issues

NAOMI R. MARMORSTEIN AND WILLIAM G. IACONO

Classification may be defined as the process of assigning objects to groups based on common characteristics. A classification system used in a scientific context, such as that of species in biology or mental disorders in psychology, is often called a *taxonomy*. In this chapter, we review the purposes of classification, characteristics of a good classification system, definition of a mental disorder, the history of the classification of mental disorders, the current psychiatric classification system, and several current issues in classification (the use of a categorical versus dimensional approaches, the meaning and implications of comorbidity, developmental considerations, and cultural issues). We then briefly discuss issues facing future revisions of the psychiatric classification system. By the end of the chapter, you will have an understanding of the currently accepted classification system for psychopathology, how it was developed, the strengths and limitations of this approach, and potential future directions in the classification of psychopathology.

PURPOSES OF CLASSIFICATION

Why classify? Although some argue for an approach in which each person's symptoms are evaluated and treated on a completely individualized basis, there are several compelling reasons to seek similarities in people's symptoms and to classify symptoms based on these similarities. First, classification facilitates research. Scientists need to use the same definitions of disorders; otherwise, each researcher would be forced to rely on idiosyncratic criteria to arrive at a given diagnosis, thereby sacrificing the comparability of findings across studies. When scientists use the same disorder definitions, research findings from one setting can be better generalized to another, and knowledge about particular psychopathological syndromes can advance more smoothly and rapidly.

Second, classification facilitates clinical work. If a treatment has been shown to be effective with a particular disorder, then a clinician presented with a client with that disorder will know how to treat it. In addition, diagnoses have prognostic implications, and thus convey important information to both the treatment provider and the client about the typical course of the disorder as well as what to expect from the treatment. Classification also helps to organize clinical information about a particular patient in a coherent way. For example, it is easier to conceptualize and remember that a particular patient has major depression than that she has a constellation of symptoms that might include sad mood, difficulty sleeping, reduced appetite, hopeless feelings, and suicidal ideation.

Third, classification provides for a common nomenclature that facilitates professional communication. This language allows researchers to communicate with other scientists (e.g., people designing studies meant to further investigate the findings from another lab), clinicians to communicate with each other (e.g., a psychologist describing the problems of someone that he or she is referring for inpatient hospitalization), and for the sharing of information between researchers and clinicians (e.g., a clinician looking to the research literature for guidance on how to treat a patient with a particular disorder).

Fourth, classification increases our understanding of psychopathology in ways that can influence both our understanding of human nature and our efforts to facilitate mental health and prevent psychopathology. Through research and clinical efforts, we can gain information about the types of mental health problems that people tend to exhibit as well as their etiology. This can inform our understanding of how healthy development occurs and thereby improve our ability to enhance psychological adjustment and prevent psychopathology.

However, objections to classification of psychopathology have been raised. Although some of these objections are based on incorrect ideas about classification, some of the concerns merit consideration. Despite recent attempts to develop classification systems that are atheoretical (see later discussion), current classification systems are rooted in a *medical model.* That is, they assume that psychiatric problems can be categorized and classified in similar ways to nonpsychiatric disease states, and that these problems exist within an individual. Some professionals—including behaviorists, who prefer to focus on modifying reinforcers to change discrete problem behaviors, and culturally focused psychologists, who place more emphasis on broader contextual factors than on pathology existing within individuals—object to this fundamental assumption. In addition, the process of assigning diagnoses based on psychological symptoms raises concerns about *labeling,* including the social stigma frequently attached to having a psychological disorder. Being told one has a particular disorder may lead to a self-fulfilling prophesy that increases dysfunction (e.g., "I have major depression, therefore I cannot perform my job"). In addition, naming a phenomenon is not the same as understanding it. Although mental health professionals are aware of this, it is all too easy to slip into thinking that because one has performed a thorough assessment and found that a patient has a particular disorder, one truly understands the person's problems. Although the diagnostic process can certainly provide clues as to etiology and/or treatment strategies, an accurate diagnosis should not be confused with a thorough understanding of an individual presenting for mental health treatment.

It is important to remember that psychopathology classification systems also serve practical purposes; although they are not developed for these purposes, we need to acknowledge them. As an example, youth with some forms of diagnosed psychopathology may be eligible for special services from their school districts; thus, the decision to diagnose a child may have significant implications for his or her receipt (or nonreceipt) of services and for the cost to society of providing these services. In addition, billing systems for mental health professionals typically rely on codes that correspond to different diagnostic categories; a particular type of diagnosis may be necessary in order for clinicians to be reimbursed for treating clients. On the other hand, a diagnosis may inadvertently limit access to a variety of forms of health care, such as when health insurance companies decline to insure (or charge extremely high rates to insure) people who have been diagnosed with particular mental health problems. Although a thorough examination of these topics is beyond the scope of this chapter, it is important to remember that classification systems in general as well as their application to particular cases may have wide-ranging implications for the individual, his or her future, and the cost incurred by society.

CHARACTERISTICS OF A GOOD CLASSIFICATION SYSTEM

Given the need for a classification system of some sort, what are characteristics of a good taxonomy of mental health problems? That is, on what dimensions should we evaluate possible classification systems, so that we may have a clear rationale for deciding whether a system is adequate and/or for choosing one method of classification over another?

First, any useful classification system must be reliable. Reliability is a broad term that refers to the concept of consistency. The type of reliability that is most relevant for classification systems is interrater reliability, which refers to the degree to which two raters (in this instance, typically mental health professionals) reach the same conclusion regarding the appropriate diagnosis. If a particular patient is assessed by two clinicians and they reach different decisions about which diagnosis is appropriate, this should cause one to question the interrater reliability of the diagnostic system (of course, differing assessment techniques may also yield differing degrees of interrater reliability, but an in-depth discussion of that is beyond the scope of this chapter). Another type of reliability that can also relate to classification systems is test-retest reliability. This refers to the tendency of a diagnostic system to yield the same diagnosis regardless of when it is used. If a patient is assessed on one day, and then returns for another assessment the next day, it would be concerning if he or she received a different diagnosis on the two visits. That said, some degree of fluctuation in psychological symptoms over time is to be expected; therefore, perfect test-retest reliability is not realistic, nor is it necessarily desirable.

Second, classification systems must be valid. Validity refers to the concept of accuracy: is this diagnostic system measuring what it is supposed to be measuring? Validity is predicated on reliability: if a diagnostic system is unreliable—it yields a different diagnosis depending on which clinician uses it or the particular time at which a client is assessed—then it cannot be accurate. However, a diagnostic system can be reliable but not valid—it can measure something consistently, but the entity that it measures may not be what it is supposed to be. Robins and Guze (1970) outlined a "gold standard" for the validation of psychiatric syndromes that involved five phases: clinical description, laboratory studies, distinguishing this from other disorders, follow-up studies, and family studies. Since that time, others have suggested additional validators (e.g., Andreason, 1995; Kendler, 1990), but these steps constitute the core of the validation process for psychiatric disorders. However, as pointed out by Rounsaville and colleagues (Rounsaville et al., 2002), these criteria for diagnostic validity may not always point to the same answer. For example, to maximize the consistency of outcome of schizophrenia in follow-up studies (Robins and

Guze's fourth criterion), a narrow diagnostic category (requiring especially severe symptoms and a relatively long duration of symptoms prior to diagnosis) would be appropriate. However, to maximize findings that schizophrenia tends to aggregate in families from family studies (Robins and Guze's fifth criterion), a much broader diagnosis—including other psychotic disorders and schizophrenia-related personality disorders—would be appropriate. Therefore, even determining how the validity of diagnostic categories should be studied is difficult.

Further complicating the study of the validity of psychiatric diagnoses is the fact that there is no gold standard—that is, there is no objectively verifiable pathology, such as a blood test or a brain scan, to which we can compare our diagnostic system. Therefore, criterion validity—the degree of agreement between an assessment method and an objective, external criterion—cannot be rigorously assessed. We must rely, then, on attempting to establish construct validity—the notion that what we call a psychiatric syndrome actually corresponds to a real-world entity that behaves as it should according to our theory of that disorder. Clearly, then, establishing validity of a diagnosis or a diagnostic system is a matter of degree, based on accumulating evidence that either supports or refutes the notion that our definitions of mental disorders correspond with constellations of symptoms in the real world and with theoretically predicted etiologies, correlates, and outcomes.

Reliability and validity are not characteristics that a diagnostic system "has" or "does not have." No system is perfectly reliable or valid, and most have some degree of reliability and validity. What is important is that a particular system have at least a reasonable degree of both, and that the development of new diagnostic systems be guided by efforts to maximize reliability and validity. It is also important to remember that different elements of a given diagnostic system may vary in their reliability and validity—or even in the extent to which their reliability and validity have been examined. Thus, even within a particular diagnostic system, some elements may have excellent reliability and validity, some may have moderate to poor reliability and validity, and others may simply be lacking in data on these characteristics. This has prompted some to discuss the possibility that our diagnostic system should add a rating system indicating which diagnoses have relatively more and less support for their validity. Although this would certainly make the use of these diagnoses more straightforward, it would also introduce a new set of problems, including on what basis the ratings would be assigned and how these ratings would affect practical considerations such as the willingness of insurance companies to reimburse providers for the treatment of relatively less-valid disorders (see Rounsaville et al., 2002, for a more thorough discussion of this idea).

Practically speaking, a classification system must also be clinically useful: clinicians must find it helpful in assessing and treating their patients. This involves a diagnostic system being standard enough that it facilitates communication with other professionals, straightforward enough that it helps clinicians organize the information they have collected about each patient, and meaningful enough that it aids in the development of hypotheses about the etiology and treatment of each client's disorder.

DEFINITION OF A MENTAL DISORDER

Because classification efforts in psychiatry and psychology focus on mental disorders, a clear definition of a mental disorder is necessary. Unfortunately, a straightforward definition agreed on by professionals in the field has been elusive. Several difficult questions arise when such a definition is attempted: (a) what should be called a "disorder"? For example, if a person seems to be more dependent on other people than most people are, should that be considered a disorder ("dependent personality disorder")? (b) which disorders fall under the category of "mental disorders"? For example, are learning disabilities mental disorders or should they be characterized as neurological disorders? Given the growing body of evidence indicating that psychiatric disorders frequently have physical correlates and physical disorders frequently have emotional symptoms, it may be inappropriate even to attempt to differentiate between physical and mental disorders.

One frequently discussed definition of mental disorder was proposed by Wakefield (1992) and is referred to as the "harmful dysfunction" definition, which has as its basis the functions that humans have been evolutionarily selected to perform:

> I proposed that disorder means harmful dysfunction, where dysfunctions are failures of internal mechanisms to perform naturally selected [i.e., evolutionarily adaptive] functions. . . . the HD [harmful dysfunction] analysis proposes that a disorder attribution requires both a scientific judgment that there exists a failure of designed function and a value judgment that the design failure harms the individual. (Wakefield, 1999, p. 374)

Although many researchers have praised this definition of mental disorder (e.g., Richters & Hinshaw, 1997; Spitzer, 1997), others have criticized it, primarily because it requires value judgments by the clinician or researcher regarding what functions humans have evolved to perform and also what harms a particular individual. In addition, some have pointed out that natural selection may produce extreme variability in behavior among different people (Lilienfeld & Marino, 1995) and some disorders may reflect naturally selected traits (Jensen et al., 1997).

Other professionals have suggested other definitions of psychopathology. For example, Ossorio (1985) proposed that psychopathology can be described this way: "When a person is in a pathological state there is a significant restriction on his ability (a) to engage in deliberate action and, equivalently, (b) to participate in the social practices of the community." However, this definition has been critiqued for not sufficiently distinguishing normality from abnormality and physical from mental disorders (e.g., Widiger, 1997). Clearly, despite the efforts of many mental health professionals, an agreed-on definition of psychopathology has not been achieved.

The current version of the diagnostic manual includes a relatively explicit definition of the term *mental disorder,* with inclusion and exclusion criteria, in its introduction. However, it acknowledges that "no definition adequately specifies precise boundaries for the concept of 'mental disorder'" (American Psychiatric Association, 2000). The multipart definition is as follows:

> In DSM-IV, each of the mental disorders is conceptualized as a clinically significant behavioral or psychological syndrome or pattern that occurs in an individual and that is associated with present distress (e.g., a painful symptom) or disability (i.e., impairment in one or more important areas of functioning) or with a significantly increased risk of suffering death, pain, disability, or an important loss of freedom. In addition, this syndrome or pattern must not be merely an expectable and culturally sanctioned response to a particular event, for example, the death of a loved one. Whatever its original cause, it must currently be considered a manifestation of a behavior, psychological, or

biological dysfunction in the individual. Neither deviant behavior (e.g., political, religious, or sexual) nor conflicts that are primarily between the individual and society are mental disorders unless the deviance or conflict is a symptom of dysfunction in the individual, as described above. (American Psychiatric Association, 2000, p. xxxi)

HISTORY OF THE CLASSIFICATION OF MENTAL DISORDERS

Modern classification efforts can be traced back to the nineteenth-century work of Emil Kraepelin, a German psychiatrist. Often called the "father of psychiatric diagnosis," the structure of Kraepelin's classification system—the categories that were chapter titles in his textbooks—is still used today. Kraepelin believed that mental disorders were manifestations of disease states (the medical model) and he based his classifications primarily on grouping disorders with similar courses together (Blashfield, 1984). He distinguished between dementia praecox (similar to what we now call schizophrenia) and manic-depressive insanity (similar to what we now call bipolar disorder) and delineated 11 other main classes of psychiatric disorders.

Classification efforts in the United States lagged behind those in Europe. In 1917, the United States adopted a classification system that was based on Kraepelin's categories, but from then until World War II, interest in classification was low. Because troops in World War II were sometimes discharged due to psychiatric reasons, interest in classification then grew—however, because of a lack of standardization, by the end of the war there were four different classification systems in active use in the United States (Blashfield, 1984). Because of this, the American Psychiatric Association decided to develop a standard system for use in the United States, and the first edition of the *Diagnostic and Statistical Manual of Mental Disorders* (*DSM*) was published in 1952. It was based on the psychiatric section of the International Classification of Diseases (*ICD*), a general disease diagnostic manual published by the World Health Organization. A revision of the *DSM* was published in 1968 (*DSM-II*; American Psychiatric Association, 1968), but both the first and second editions were characterized by limited reliability and critiqued for their heavily psychoanalytic bent. Many researchers were frustrated by the presumption that psychoanalytic theoretical concepts underlie all psychological symptoms and the lack of interrater reliability (due, at least in part, to the need to infer various unconscious conflicts in order to assign diagnoses) limited the utility of the systems. Likewise, clinicians who did not take a psychoanalytic approach in their work were frustrated by what they saw as a lack of validity in these diagnostic manuals.

Therefore, a movement to standardize and remove theory from diagnostic systems began. In 1972, a group of researchers at Washington University in St. Louis delineated specific criteria for 15 diagnoses, often called the Feighner criteria (Feighner et al., 1972). Several years later, a group of researchers at the New York State Psychiatric Institute published criteria for 25 diagnoses, again with the goal of developing atheoretical, specific, reliable criteria (Spitzer, Endicott, & Robins, 1979).

These two sets of criteria, and the research efforts they were based on, led to a dramatic change in the third edition of the *DSM* (*DSM-III*; American Psychiatric Association, 1980). The *DSM-III* differed from the editions before it in three major ways. First, the authors attempted to be atheoretical. Psychoanalytic language and concepts were removed from the manual, and there was an attempt to be strictly descriptive in the criteria sets. Related to this, the revision committees attempted to improve the reliability and validity of the criteria, primarily by increasing the emphasis on observable and quantifiable features and decreasing the emphasis on putative causal factors. Third, the third edition of the *DSM* included, for the first time, a multiaxial diagnostic system. In addition to a focus on major clinical disorders (then placed on Axis I), the multiaxial system represented an attempt to encourage clinicians to obtain and record information about the patient's functioning and environment in a variety of different domains. In particular, personality disorders were put on a separate axis (Axis II) from the major clinical disorders (Axis I) in order to encourage clinicians to assess people for these diagnoses even when they also had a major clinical syndrome (Frances, 1980). The revised current version of these axes is described when the *DSM-IV* is discussed in depth in a later section.

As an example of the dramatic shift from *DSM-II* to *DSM-III*, it is instructive to examine the diagnoses of depressive disorders. Depression in *DSM-II* consisted of a "depressive neurosis" diagnosis that was defined partially by a nonspecific depressed mood ("depression") and more by an etiology ("an excessive reaction . . . due to an internal conflict or to an identifiable event such as the loss of a love object or cherished possession"). In the *DSM-III* criteria, references to etiology are avoided and the symptoms descriptions are far more specific. In addition, there are now three potential diagnoses that a person with a diagnosis of *DSM-II* "depressive neurosis" may evidence: major depressive disorder (one or more major depressive episodes, which represent severe depressive symptoms), dysthymia (a longer-term but somewhat less severe syndrome), and adjustment disorder with depressed mood (depressive symptoms in reaction to a stressor).

Since the *DSM-III*, adjustments have been made to the *DSM*, but no major shifts in the conceptualization of mental disorders or the value system behind the *DSM* have occurred. In 1987, a revised third edition—intended to be a fine-tuning of the *DSM-III*—was published (*DSM-III-R*; American Psychiatric Association, 1987); it eliminated many hierarchy requirements (i.e., requiring that a particular diagnosis *not* be assigned if another diagnosis was assigned) and increased the polythetic nature of many disorders (in which a number of possible symptoms are listed, of which only a subset are required to qualify for the diagnosis). In 1994, a fourth edition (*DSM-IV*; American Psychiatric Association, 1994) was published. In the fourth edition, there was an attempt to revise criteria fairly conservatively, based as much as possible on research evidence, including literature reviews, field trials, and re-analyses of existing data sets. The *DSM-IV* revision also included more acknowledgment of the role of culture in psychopathology; this is discussed in more depth later (under "Cultural Considerations"). Some clinicians and researchers objected to the frequent revision of the diagnostic manual; for clinicians, it raised questions regarding potentially changing clients' diagnoses, and for researchers, especially those conducting longitudinal studies, it raised questions about which diagnostic criteria to use (i.e., whether to always use the most up-to-date criteria and sacrifice the comparability of diagnoses across time, or whether to use the criteria that were in use when the study was started and risk appearing outdated). Therefore, the psychiatric community appeared to become more conservative in the revision of the manuals and especially the diagnostic criteria themselves. In 2000, the American Psychiatric Association published a text revision of *DSM-IV* (*DSM-IV-TR*), which involved no changes to the diagnostic criteria but instead only changes to the text accompanying the criteria, to reflect advances in knowledge about the disorders that had occurred after the publication of the *DSM-IV*. As discussed below, the next revision of the *DSM* has begun and is expected to be published in approximately 2011.

The number of disorders delineated in each edition of the *DSM* has increased dramatically, from 108 in the first edition of the *DSM* to nearly 300 in the current *DSM-IV*. This has prompted critics to assert that normal behavior is being pathologized (e.g., McHugh, 1999) and that this growth in *DSM* diagnoses reflects the "invention" of psychiatric diagnoses, not the discovery of actual new syndromes (e.g., Follette & Houts, 1996).

The other diagnostic system in widespread use is the International Statistical Classification of Diseases and Related Health Problems, commonly called the *International Classification of Diseases* or *ICD*, which is published by the World Health Organization and is the world standard for reporting health statistics (World Health Organization, 1992). It has a chapter entitled "Mental and Behavioral Disorders" that contains psychiatric syndromes, similar to the *DSM*. The *ICD* has a longer history that the *DSM*, having grown out of the Bertillon Classification of Causes of Death in the late 1800s. A revised version of this classification system, called the International List of Causes of Death, was published in 1900; it has been revised every 7 to 14 years since; the most recent (10th) edition was published in 1992. The revision process for the *ICD-11* began in 2004 and is scheduled for approval in 2011 and implementation in 2013.

Although similar to the *DSM-IV* in most ways, the *ICD-10* does differ from the *DSM* system. Broadly speaking, the *ICD-10* does not tend to require impairment for syndromes to be diagnosed, while the *DSM-IV* does. A comparison between the two systems indicated that *ICD-10* diagnoses were assigned more frequently than *DSM-IV* diagnoses. When substance-related diagnoses, affective disorders, and anxiety disorders were examined, 32% of those who met diagnostic criteria for a disorder in one system did not qualify for a diagnosis in the other system (Andrews, Slade, & Peters, 1999). Given the widespread use of both systems around the world, it would seem important for future revisions of both systems to make an attempt to make them as similar as possible, so that psychiatric research evidence and world health statistics could be as comparable as possible.

CURRENT DIAGNOSTIC SYSTEM (*DSM-IV-TR*)

The *DSM-IV* uses a prototypical approach to diagnosis, which is a variant on a categorical approach. In a prototypical diagnostic system, certain characteristics are viewed as essential to the concept of each disorder, while other features may vary across individuals. For example, to be diagnosed with major depression, a person must experience either depressed mood or loss of interest in things previously enjoyed (anhedonia) for most of the day, nearly every day for at least 2 weeks. Without at least one of these symptoms, by definition, a person does not have major depression. In addition, to qualify for this diagnosis, a person must experience at least five out of nine total symptoms of depression. One person may experience a persistent depressed mood and four of the remaining "nonessential" symptoms, while a second person may experience anhedonia and four of the remaining "nonessential" symptoms, three out of the four of which are different from the first person. Thus, two people may both be experiencing major depressive episodes but only have one symptom in common, as long as they both are displaying an "essential feature" of depression and some combination of at least four other symptoms.

As mentioned above, the *DSM-IV* continues the 5-axis approach to diagnosis begun in the *DSM-III*; indeed, even more emphasis is placed on the multiaxial approach in the *DSM-IV*. Axis I contains the clinical syndromes—the major mental disorders that most frequently bring people to treatment. Nearly all psychiatric disorders are included on Axis I, from schizophrenia to sexual disorders to phobias. Typically, these are characterized by impairment in functioning, subjective feelings of distress, or both, and are frequently characterized by having a time-limited or episodic course. They are also generally perceived as unwanted and uncomfortable (e.g., ego-dystonic) by the patient. Axis II contains the remaining disorders discussed in the *DSM,* those that are conceived of as beginning in childhood or adolescence and persisting through adulthood: specifically, the personality disorders and cognitive impairment (mental retardation). These are pervasive, affecting patients in many or all domains of life; they also tend to be chronic and are frequently perceived by the patient as "just how they are" and not as though something is wrong with them (e.g., ego-syntonic).

Axes III, IV, and V include supplemental information; these axes codify information that may be important to an understanding of the case but does not affect the actual psychiatric diagnosis. Axis III contains any medical conditions that the person has. This includes conditions that may be directly relevant to the person's Axis I disorder (e.g., a thyroid condition that may be related to major depression) as well as those not directly related to the Axis I disorder (e.g., an illness that may act as a stressor, or an illness that may be treated with a medication that could interact with a prescribed psychiatric medication). Axis IV contains current and recent stressors; these may affect the etiology, presentation, prognosis, or course of the disorder. Again, these may be directly related to the Axis I disorder (e.g., a traumatic event as a stressor on Axis IV, with posttraumatic stress disorder as the Axis I disorder) or more distally related (e.g., the loss of a job, which may have exacerbated a preexisting generalized anxiety disorder). The *DSM-IV* provides a listing of potential categories that stressors may fall under; the clinician then indicates which stressor(s) the client is experiencing or has recently experienced. Axis V is the Global Assessment of Functioning (GAF) scale, which provides an indication of the clinician's judgment of the person's overall level of functioning. Functioning is rated on a scale ranging from 1 ("Persistent danger of severely hurting self or others . . . OR persistent inability to maintain minimal personal hygiene OR serious suicidal act . . . ") to 100 ("superior functioning in a wide range of activities . . . "); guidelines for each 10-point range are provided. Ratings on this scale can provide a record of a client's decline or improvement over time, and can also indicate how impaired someone with a particular diagnosis is. For example, although the diagnostic criteria for a major depressive episode specify that the person must be experiencing some degree of impairment, a person in the midst of a major depressive episode may rate a 1 if he or she has recently made a serious suicide attempt or as high as approximately 70 if he or she is only experiencing "some difficulty in social, occupational, or school functioning."

In order to illustrate use of this multiaxial diagnostic system, we will briefly examine the case of a hypothetical client named Susan. Susan is a 43-year-old woman who presents with a depressed mood, frequent crying, and feelings of despair. She has been having these feelings to some degree for approximately 4 months, and they became worse after her boyfriend broke up with her 3 weeks ago. Upon interview, she reports having six of the nine symptoms of a major depressive episode (enough for a diagnosis). She reports having had one other similar episode in the past, shortly after she graduated from college when she was laid off from a job. She denies any history of manic symptoms. Based on interview and observational data, she appears to be of average intellectual ability and does not have any significant personality disorder symptoms. She denies having any serious medical problems, though she does report intermittent migraine headaches. For the past 3 months, she has been continuing to go to work and perform adequately at her job, though she reports that this has been more difficult than usual, especially in the past 3 weeks. She has withdrawn from family and friends, however, and now spends all of her time outside of work watching television. Susan's *DSM-IV* multiaxial diagnosis would be as follows:

Axis I: Major depressive disorder, recurrent

Axis II: No diagnosis

Axis III: Migraine headaches

Axis IV: Problems with primary support group (recent breakup with boyfriend)

Axis V: GAF = 55 (highest in past 3 months)

DIAGNOSTIC ISSUES

COMORBIDITY

The term *comorbidity* has been the subject of substantial debate and confusion within the psychopathology literature. When originally used in the medical literature, it referred to "any distinct additional entity that has existed or that may occur during the clinical course of a patient who has the index disease under study" (Feinstein, 1970, p. 467). Since that time, it has been used in many ways, including to refer simply to the existence of two psychological disorders occurring within the same individual, at either the same or different points in time. Although some argue cogently for the use of the term comorbidity only to refer to true disease states—those for which the underlying pathologies and etiologies are clearly defined (Lilienfeld, Waldman, & Israel, 1994)—the psychopathology literature has increasingly used this term to refer broadly to any co-occurrence of more than one disorder in a single person. Following this definition, it has become clear that comorbidity among mental disorders is the rule, rather than the exception. This is the case among population-based samples (e.g., Kessler, Chiu, Demler, & Walters, 2005) and even more so among clinical samples (e.g., Galbaud du Fort, Newman, & Bland, 1993).

The observation that mental health disorders tend to co-occur at rates greater than chance may be due to both methodological and substantive factors. One substantive explanation for comorbidity is that risk factors for different forms of psychopathology may be the same or highly intercorrelated. For example, growing up in poverty and being raised by an abusive, drug-abusing parent could be related to a wide variety of problems in adulthood. Similarly, having a (perhaps genetically mediated) impulsive personality style could predispose a person to a variety of *DSM* disorders. In addition, risk factors are often correlated with one another; for example, having a parent who is highly impulsive and aggressive could lead to a child having a genetic predisposition toward those traits, growing up in a dangerous neighborhood because the parent is unable to hold a steady enough job to facilitate a move to a safer neighborhood, and experiencing the modeling and perhaps reinforcement of antisocial behavior. Another substantive explanation for observed comorbidity is that having one disorder may actually put a person at risk for another distinct disorder. For example, having conduct disorder could put a youth at risk for getting in trouble at school, with parents, or with the law; the stress created by these problems could result in the development of major depression. Alternatively, a person with major depression may discover that using alcohol alleviates their depressive feelings; they may then use increasing quantities of alcohol on a more and more frequent basis, leading to the development of alcohol dependence (the "self-medication hypothesis" or "negative affect alcoholism"; e.g., Zucker, 1986).

Several methodological factors may result in the appearance of comorbidity, even when there is no actual co-occurrence of two (or more) distinct disorders. First, it is possible that the two co-occurring disorders actually represent a third distinct syndrome. For example, the possibility of including a "mixed anxiety-depression" diagnostic category has frequently been discussed, because anxiety and depressive disorders so often co-occur (e.g., Tyrer, 2001). In fact, this diagnosis is included in the *ICD-10* and in the appendix for criteria sets provided for further study in the *DSM-IV.* There could also be problems with use of the diagnostic system. For example, clinicians may simply have difficult distinguishing between closely related disorders and may therefore end up diagnosing two disorders when only one is actually present. Two other methodological explanations for the high rates of observed comorbidity have implications for our overall approach to diagnosis. First is the problem of "fuzzy boundaries" (e.g., Lilienfeld & Marino, 1995), which refers to the fact that certain disorders appear to blend into other disorders at their edges. For example, someone with severe schizotypal personality disorder may not be very different from someone with relatively mild schizophrenia. Thus, in some cases, a diagnostic assessment may involve a judgment call regarding whether certain behaviors or experiences are severe enough to call symptoms and whether or not those symptoms "add up to" one disorder or two. Second, there is increasing evidence of the hierarchical nature of many forms of psychopathology. For example, a "distressed affectivity" or negative affectivity trait appears to be common to both anxiety and depressive disorders (Watson, 2005) and an "externalizing spectrum" consisting of antisocial behavior and substance use-related problems and related to an underlying disinhibition trait has been proposed and received some empirical support (Krueger, Markon, Patrick, & Iacono, 2005). If multiple forms of psychopathology are part of the same spectrum of disorders, with related etiologies and correlates, then comorbidity among disorders on the same spectrum would be expected. These last two explanations of comorbidity relate closely to the next diagnostic issue that we consider: the use of dimensional versus categorical approaches.

DIMENSIONAL VERSUS CATEGORICAL APPROACHES TO CLASSIFICATION

Dimensional approaches to the classification of mental disorders presuppose that abnormal functioning represents one extreme end of a dimension of functioning, while categorical approaches implicitly presuppose that mental disorders represent a distinct entity that is qualitatively distinct from normal functioning. The debate over which type of approach more accurately represents the nature of mental illness is long-standing (e.g., Kendell, 1975) and has intensified with the recognition that disorders frequently co-occur within an individual (see previous discussion on comorbidity) and treatments—both pharmacologic and psychotherapeutic—are typically not disorder-specific. These observations argue against the notion that each mental disorder is a discrete entity with a unique etiology and treatment.

Recent methodological advances have enabled more sophisticated examinations of these questions. Specifically, taxometric analyses (e.g., Meehl, 2004) allow for the examination of whether a set of symptoms covary in ways consistent with a continuous distribution (which would argue for a dimensional view of the symptoms) or a categorical distribution (which would argue for a categorical view of the disorder). Although taxometric studies of psychopathology can be critiqued (see Widiger & Samuel, 2005 for a review of potential problems with taxometric studies), the results of sound taxometric analyses of major types of psychopathology indicate that many, if not most, types of psychopathology fall on a continuum: *DSM* categories do not tend to correspond to discrete taxons. Although the evidence is most clear for personality disorders (e.g., Trull & Durrett, 2005), converging evidence points to the accuracy of dimensional views of schizophrenia (e.g., Tsuang, Stone, & Faraone, 2000), depression (Hankin, Fraley, Lahey, & Waldman, 2005), anxiety disorders (Ruscio, Borkovec, & Ruscio, 2001), alcoholism (Krueger et al., 2004), and potentially other classes of disorders as well.

In addition, some evidence challenges the broad categories of disorders that the *DSM* uses (e.g., mood disorders, anxiety disorders). For example, posttraumatic stress disorder may be better conceptualized as a dissociative disorder (due to its symptoms of depersonalization and detachment) than an anxiety disorder (Davidson & Foa, 1991; see Clark, Watson, & Reynolds, 1995 for a more complete discussion of this issue). Even the distinction between Axis I and Axis II disorders is not clear-cut: for example, schizotypal personality disorder and schizophrenia may fall on a continuum, and borderline personality disorder is closely related to mood disorders and may represent a variant of them (see Widiger & Shea, 1991). There is also mounting evidence that broad dimensions (e.g., an externalizing dimension, encompassing antisocial behavior, substance use, and disinhibited personality traits) of behavior may accurately represent the distribution of symptoms and perhaps share a common etiology (e.g., Krueger et al., 2005; Mineka, Watson, & Clark, 1998). Therefore, a hierarchical system of dimensional categories, in which broad factors (such as internalizing and externalizing syndromes) are at the top of the hierarchy and more specific problems (e.g., generalized anxiety, social anxiety) are at lower levels of the hierarchy, may more accurately represent the pattern of occurrence of psychological symptoms in the population.

Accumulation of evidence that most mental disorders truly exist in the population on a continuum has naturally led to discussion of whether a dimensional model of classification should be used as our standard diagnostic system. Clinical utility is a key prerequisite for the use of such an approach (e.g., First, 2005; Widiger, 2005). That is, if a dimensional model is simply too difficult to use, then attempting to implement such a model will at best be frustrating and at worst result in the misdiagnosis and subsequent poor treatment of many clients. Categorical models appear more straightforward: a particular patient is conceptualized as either having or not having a particular disorder, and the name of that disorder appears to capture most of the key information regarding the person's presenting problem and necessary for the treatment of the problem. Therefore, these more familiar systems appear easier to use by busy mental health professionals. In addition, nonmental health professionals who are involved in the care of mental health patients (such as primary care physicians, health insurance representatives, etc.) are used to working with categorical diagnoses (i.e., when medical—nonmental health—syndromes and diseases are involved), and the adoption of a dimensional system would require corresponding changes in record keeping and administration. However, as Widiger (2005) points out, diagnostic categories may be frustrating to use because they frequently do not adequately capture the nature, complexity, or severity of a particular client's problems and frequently clients exhibit several related but nonidentical disorders (as discussed previously). Clinicians may appreciate the additional validity gained through the use of a dimensional system. However, communication among professionals would likely become more complex; it is easier to simply name the diagnosis that a particular client has than it is to describe where he or she falls on several dimensions.

Widiger (2005) raised another potential objection to the adoption of a dimensional approach to the classification of mental disorders: credibility. Currently, many mental health professionals view themselves as treating psychiatric pathologies, much as nonpsychiatrist physicians treat diseases. If psychopathology is reconceptualized as a set of dimensions onto which both "normal" and "abnormal" people fall, it may either decrease the credibility of mental health professions or cause mental disorders to seem unimportant. However, the apparent distinction between mental and medical health problems—with the dimensional mental health problems seeming less important— is not an accurate distinction; for example, no one would argue that extremely high blood pressure or a dangerously high fever should not be treated simply because both are measured using continuous scales. Thus, although it would require an adjustment in thinking, there is no apparent reason that a change to a dimensional system should decrease the importance of mental health professionals' work or trivialize mental disorders.

DEVELOPMENTAL CONSIDERATIONS

The *DSM*'s primary acknowledgment of development within individuals occurs in its placement of some disorders in a chapter entitled "Disorders Usually First Diagnosed in Infancy, Childhood, or Adolescence." However, there is evidence that some disorders placed in that chapter may occur across the life span (e.g., ADHD; Barkley, Fischer, Smallish, & Fletcher, 2006; Biederman et al., 2006) and other disorders not placed in that chapter tend to begin in childhood and adolescence (e.g., 75% of adults with major depressive disorder had their first major depressive episode prior to age 18; Kim-Cohen et al., 2003). Thus, although existence of this chapter is reflective of the traditional distinction between adult and child psychiatry, and between adult clinical psychology and child clinical psychology, it may not be reflective of any true distinction between disorders that tend to begin in childhood or adolescence and those that tend to begin later.

There are two primary ways that development is considered in relation to the *DSM*. First, there are issues of how psychiatric disorders develop within a person over time, and second, there are questions of the applicability of *DSM* criteria to children and adolescents and how the expression of certain disorders may change as people develop. We consider each of these in turn.

The *DSM* criteria capture a static snapshot of psychiatric symptoms. With a few exceptions (e.g., the requirement that symptoms of personality disorders be present prior to age 18, duration requirements for the diagnosis of certain disorders), criteria sets do not specify factors that may have led to the emergence of disorders. This practice is consistent with the goal of achieving increased diagnostic reliability, but it also gives the impression that psychiatric disorders are static, discrete entities existing within individuals, and therefore ignores the extensive research on the role of attachment processes, gene-environment interactions, contextual factors and life events, and culture. Developmental psychopathologists, who study abnormal (i.e., psychopathological) developmental processes as a variant of normal developmental processes, emphasize the complex interplay of risk and protective factors that lead up to the emergence of a diagnosable disorder and predict the re-emergence of healthy functioning even after a disorder is present. From this perspective, the *DSM* system is simplistic and does not readily lend itself to optimal clinical or research efforts that view the transactions between the entire person and his or her environment in a comprehensive way.

Related to this, the *DSM* rarely acknowledges the differing expressions of psychiatric symptoms that may occur at different ages. However, there is a reasonably extensive literature documenting change with development of the symptoms characteristic of many disorders. For example, young children with separation anxiety disorder frequently have nightmares and excessively fear separation from their attachment figures, while older children with the same disorder may display a reluctance to go to school and physical symptoms relating to separation.

Implications of potential developmental differences in the presentations of two other disorders—one traditionally thought of as a childhood disorder, and the other traditionally thought of as a disorder that only occurs during late adolescence and adulthood—have been the subject of substantial debate in recent years. First, we know that among people with attention-deficit hyperactivity disorder (ADHD), hyperactive-impulsive symptoms tend to decrease over time (e.g., Hart, Lahey, Loeber, Applegate, & Frick, 1995). This has led some authors to note that using the symptom list in the *DSM* could result in a larger percentage of young children, compared to adolescents and adults, being diagnosed with ADHD imply due to these developmental trends (Barkley, Fischer, Smallish, & Fletcher, 2002), therefore, the list of diagnostic criteria is unlikely to apply equally well to people across all ages (Barkley, 2003). The potential existence of ADHD in adulthood has been the subject of much study and debate in recent years. It is clear that ADHD in childhood is related to negative developmental outcomes in adulthood (e.g., Cantwell, 1996), though the actual persistence of ADHD symptomatology into adulthood (and resulting questions regarding the need for more developmentally sensitive ADHD criteria for adults) remains under debate (as reviewed by Willoughby, 2003). Conversely, potential existence of bipolar disorder among prepubertal children has been the subject of much controversy in recent years. Although discrete manic episodes, as defined by the *DSM*, rarely occur in young children, some children do exhibit extremely overactive, aggressive behavior along with severe deficits in emotion regulation and grandiosity. The core controversy is whether or not it is appropriate to classify these children as having bipolar disorder even though they do not fit the traditional criteria. In part because it remains unclear whether these children will grow up to have traditionally defined bipolar disorder and in part because of the difficulty in interpreting grandiose and euphoric symptoms among young children (e.g., if a 5-year-old says that he can fly, is that a grandiose delusion? Or normal wishful thinking? Or a delayed understanding of gravity? Or normal fantasy play?), it is unclear whether children with these symptoms should be classified as having bipolar disorder (see Carlson, 2005 for a comprehensive discussion of these issues). The situation is complicated by the fact that children with this constellation of symptoms do not fit neatly into any other diagnostic category yet are clearly troubled, at risk for a variety of negative outcomes, and in need of treatment. Both adult ADHD and childhood bipolar disorder present challenges to the *DSM* classification system that can be resolved by a combination of more research and more developmentally sensitive sets of diagnostic criteria.

In some cases, the *DSM* specifies age requirements even though empirical evidence does not support these cutoffs. For example, attention-deficit hyperactivity disorder must start prior to age 7, but evidence does not support the notion that that requirement is psychometrically sound or clinically meaningful (Applegate et al., 1997; Barkley & Beiderman, 1997). In addition, the diagnosis of antisocial personality disorder requires that conduct disorder be present prior to age 15; however, evidence indicates that people who exhibit antisocial behavior in adulthood in the absence of conduct disorder prior to age 15 are quite similar to those who exhibit both antisocial behavior in adulthood and conduct disorder prior to age 15 (Marmorstein, 2006; Marmorstein & Iacono, 2005). Therefore, it seems that empirical evidence needs to be taken into account in a more comprehensive way when age cutoffs are being determined.

In addition to these specific variants in how different disorders may (or may not) be expressed at different ages, prominent developmental theorists have been calling for a more developmental framework for classifying children's psychological problems that acknowledges the developmental tasks that children face (e.g., children must cope adaptively with changing demands over time, such as starting school in early childhood and forming romantic attachments in adolescence) and the transactions that occur between children and their environment (e.g., Garber, 1984; Jensen & Hoagwood, 1997). Although the *DSM* framework may provide a valid way to assess psychopathology among preschoolers (Keenan & Wakschlag, 2002), there have been attempts to develop supplementary diagnostic tools that can easily be applied to preschool children (e.g., the Preschool Age Psychiatric Assessment; Egger, Ascher, & Angold, 1999) since even the criteria for "Disorders Usually First Diagnosed in Infancy, Childhood, or Adolescence" sometimes are difficult to apply to these very young children. Intervention with these preschool-aged children may be important in the prevention of more severe problems later.

Cultural Considerations

The fact that culture affects psychopathology is clear, but incorporating cultural considerations in a comprehensive way into a diagnostic system for mental disorders is quite challenging. As noted by Alarcon et al. (2002, pp. 221–222), cultural factors can influence mental health and illness and the diagnostic process in a number of ways: "1) define and create specific sources of stress and distress; 2) shape the form and quality of illness experience; 3) influence the symptomatology of generalized distress and of specific syndromes; 4) determine the interpretation of symptoms and hence their subsequent cognitive and social impact; 5) provide specific modes of coping with distress; 6) guide help-seeking and the response to treatment; and 7) govern social responses to distress and disability (Alarcon, Westermeyer, Foulks, & Ruiz, 1999; Kirmayer & Young, 1999)."

The *DSM-IV* incorporates culture in four primary ways. First, at the end of the introduction, a short section encourages the clinician to be aware of cultural factors that may impact psychopathology. Second, when specific disorders are discussed, frequently cross-cultural variations in prevalence and symptomatology are included (under sections typically labeled "Culture, Age, and Gender Features"). Third, guidelines for a cultural formulation are presented in an appendix. The five elements of the formulation, meant to supplement the five diagnostic axes, are: (1) "The cultural identity of the individual" (his or her cultural reference group(s)), (2) "cultural explanations of the individual's illness" (including idioms of distress and explanatory models), (3) "cultural factors related to the . . . environment and . . . functioning" (e.g., stressors and support networks), (4) "cultural elements of the relationship between the individual and the clinician" (such as differences in culture and/or social status), and (5) "overall cultural assessment" (a formulation of how these cultural factors will influence diagnosis and treatment; APA, 1994, pp. 843–844). Fourth, a glossary of "culture-bound syndromes" is included in an appendix. This includes definitions of terms used to refer to syndromes that occur in nonnative United States residents; these syndromes have varying degrees of similarity to traditionally defined forms of psychopathology (Mezzich et al., 1999).

Although these elements represent significantly more inclusion of cultural factors than in previous editions of the *DSM,* they have come under significant attack. For example, members of the National Institutes of Mental Health's Group on Culture and Diagnosis critiqued the *DSM-IV* for marginalizing cultural considerations. For example, they assert that the placement of "culture-bound syndromes" in an appendix and the deletion of their proposed "Western Culture-bound syndrome" reduce these disorders to being a "museum of exotica" (Mezzich et al., 1999). These authors also discuss the core tension inherent in trying to incorporate culture into a diagnostic manual that takes a primarily biomedical approach.

Cultural psychologists interpret the entire process of developing a diagnostic system as a culturally mediated enterprise that reflects the values and beliefs of the dominant culture. In contrast, the dominant biomedical diagnostic paradigm seeks to find core patterns of psychological problems that theoretically should not be dependent on particular cultural or social characteristics. Therefore, the two approaches cannot be integrated in a way that is likely to be satisfactory to professionals from both perspectives. A traditional biomedical diagnostician is likely to be offended by the notion that what he or she is doing simply represents a statement of his or her cultural values, while a culturally focused mental health professional is likely to be frustrated by the perception that the dominant diagnostic model fails to fully incorporate his or her clients' cultural perspectives and experiences. For this reason, incorporating a comprehensive understanding of culture as the basis for all human experiences and interactions would require a complete paradigm shift—something that seems unlikely, at least in the near future.

SUMMARY

Preliminary work for the *DSM-V* began in 1999 with the formation of groups of researchers who identified research priorities for the next edition. These groups were assembled by a joint project of the American Psychiatric Association and the National Institutes of Mental Health, National Institute on Drug Abuse, and National Institute on Alcohol Abuse and Alcoholism in an attempt to identify lines of research that would enhance the evidence base informing future revisions of the *DSM* so that researchers would be more likely to pursue these issues. Their discussions and research recommendations were published in book form in 2002 (Kupfer, First, & Regier, 2002). The revision process began soon after; a conference series on particular diagnostic subgroupings, jointly sponsored by the American Psychiatric Association and the National Institutes of Health, is underway (with conferences taking place between 2004 and 2007) and a target publication date of 2011 has been set.

The committee preparing the 5th edition of the *DSM* will face a number of significant challenges, including broad issues that have implications for both professionals' and the public's conceptualization of mental health and illness. The most pressing broad issue relates to categorical versus dimensional approaches to psychopathology. As discussed earlier, accumulating research has been pointing for some time now toward dimensional approaches being more accurately representative of how psychopathological symptoms are distributed in the population, at least for many disorders. However, the revision committee will have to decide whether the other, more practical considerations discussed above and/or the weight of tradition outweigh this fact to the degree that a categorical approach should be maintained. Widiger and Samuel (2005) have suggested that the diagnosis of mental retardation be used as a model for future revisions of the diagnostic system. Currently, mental retardation is assessed using a normally distributed, dimensional scale (an intelligence quotient, or IQ, as defined by intelligence tests that assess a number of different functions), and it is diagnosed using a cut-point (an IQ of 70 or below) combined with the requirement that clinically significant impairment also be present. This cut-point is meaningful in the sense that people whose intelligence falls below it typically experience difficulty in functioning, but no one argues that an IQ score of 69 is qualitatively different from one of 71. As Widiger and Samuel point out, this sort of approach could maintain many of the advantages of a strictly categorical approach while acknowledging the empirical reality that psychopathological symptoms tend to be distributed dimensionally; thus, it could move both professionals and the public toward a more nuanced understanding of the nature of psychopathology.

Prevalence of comorbidity, which likely relates in part to the hierarchical nature of psychopathology, is also likely to become a more pressing issue as clinicians and researchers grow increasingly frustrated by the practice of attempting to distinguish between similar syndromes and sometimes diagnosing numerous closely related disorders in a single person. Although evidence for the broad structure of psychopathology may be too new to affect the structure of the 5th edition of the *DSM*, it seems likely that in the future it could result in broad change in diagnostic practices. In the meantime, this evidence should at least be incorporated into the text of the *DSM-V*, with some recommendations about how clinicians and researchers can thoughtfully use it in their assessments and resulting diagnoses.

Developmental questions are also becoming increasingly important as more and more youth are being diagnosed with formerly "adult" disorders such as bipolar disorder (prompting cover-page stories in popular magazines such as *Time* magazine; Kluger et al., 2002) and many are being treated with psychotropic medications, including antipsychotics and other medications historically used primarily for the treatment of adults (Olfson, Blanco, Liu, Moreno, & Laje, 2006). Increased discussion of alternative expressions of disorders among children (especially for disorders such as bipolar disorder) and adults (for disorders such as ADHD) will be necessary to guide both clinicians and researchers. In addition, work on developmentally modified criteria for major depression in preschool children has begun (e.g., Luby et al., 2003), and more attention to the mental health needs of these very young children could be helpful in preventing later, more severe conditions. On the other end of the developmental spectrum, following the initial research agenda "white papers" for *DSM-V*, an additional paper was developed to focus on geriatric mental health issues; as the baby-boom generation ages, issues relating to the diagnosis and treatment of psychopathology among older Americans will become more pressing.

As the American society becomes more multicultural and also as technology enables Americans to become more aware of and integrated with other cultures around the world, questions about culture are also likely to increase in importance and become increasingly relevant to clinicians and researchers, including those who do not specializing in working with minority or immigrant populations. Thus, a continually growing emphasis on the influence of culture on the expression and treatment of mental health problems is both warranted and likely.

The potential inclusion of relational disorders—problems occurring in the relationship or bond between people—is also an issue in need of examination by the editors of the *DSM-V.* Like an integrative consideration of cultural factors, this would require a conceptual shift for the *DSM,* which traditionally has conceptualized psychopathology as something that occurs within an individual. However, many similarities between relational disorders and more traditionally defined psychopathology can be delineated (see First et al., 2002), and it is clear that relationship problems such as expressed emotion adversely affect both psychiatric and medical conditions (e.g., Butzlaff & Hooley, 1998). Although research in this area is less well developed than in some of the areas discussed in this chapter, consideration of these factors is likely to increase in importance as research into the definition of these disorders—and their reliability and validity—increases.

Systems for the diagnosis of psychiatric syndromes have evolved substantially in the past century, and these developments have both facilitated and been informed by research on the origins, nature, and treatment of psychopathology. We can look forward to future diagnostic systems being increasingly reflective of emerging research findings and spurring the field to a deeper understanding of psychopathology; these developments will facilitate the more accurate assessment and treatment of people suffering from mental illness.

REFERENCES

Alarcon, R. D., Bell, C. C., Kirmayer, L. J., Lin, K.-M., Ustun, B., & Wisner, K. L. (2002). Beyond the funhouse mirrors: Research agenda on culture and psychiatric diagnosis. In D. J. Kupfer, M. B. First, & D. A. Regier (Eds.), *A research agenda for DSM-V* (pp. 219–281). Washington, DC: American Psychiatric Association.

Alarcon, R. D., Westermeyer, J., Foulks, E. F., & Ruiz, P. (1999). Clinical relevance of contemporary cultural psychiatry. *Journal of Nervous and Mental Diseases, 187,* 465–471.

American Psychiatric Association. (1952). *Diagnostic and statistical manual of mental disorders.* Washington, DC: Author.

American Psychiatric Association. (1968). *Diagnostic and statistical manual of mental disorders* (2nd ed.). Washington, DC: Author.

American Psychiatric Association. (1980). *Diagnostic and statistical manual of mental disorders* (3rd ed.). Washington, DC: Author.

American Psychiatric Association. (1987). *Diagnostic and statistical manual of mental disorders* (3rd ed., rev.). Washington, DC: Author.

American Psychiatric Association. (1994). *Diagnostic and statistical manual of mental disorders* (4th ed.). Washington, DC: Author.

American Psychiatric Association. (2000). *Diagnostic and statistical manual of mental disorders* (4th ed., text rev.). Washington, DC: Author.

Andreasen, N. C. (1995). The validation of psychiatric diagnosis: New models and approaches. *American Journal of Psychiatry, 152,* 161–162.

Andrews, G., Slade, T., & Peters, L. (1999). Classification in psychiatry: ICD-10 versus DSM-IV. *British Journal of Psychiatry, 174,* 3–5.

Applegate, B., Lahey, B. B., Hart, E. L., Biederman, J., Hynd, G. W., Barkely, R. A., et al. (1997). Validity of the age-of-onset criterion for ADHD: A report from the DSM-IV field trials. *Journal of the American Academy of Child and Adolescent Psychiatry, 36,* 1211–1221.

Barkley, R. A. (2003). Issues in the diagnosis of attention-deficit/hyperactivity disorder in children. *Brain and Development, 25,* 77–83.

Barkley, R. A., & Biederman, J. (1997). Toward a broader definition of the age-of-onset criterion for attention-deficit hyperactivity disorder. *Journal of the American Academy of Child and Adolescent Psychiatry, 36,* 1204–1210.

Barkley, R. A., Fischer, M., Smallish, L., & Fletcher, K. (2002). The persistence of attention-deficit/hyperactivity disorder into young adulthood as a function of reporting source and definition of disorder. *Journal of Abnormal Psychology, 111,* 279–289.

Barkley, R. A., Fischer, M., Smallish, L., & Fletcher, K. (2006). Young adult outcome of hyperactive children: Adaptive functioning in major life activities. *Journal of the American Academy of Child and Adolescent Psychiatry, 45,* 192–202.

Biederman, J., Monuteaux, M. C., Mick, E., Spencer, T., Wilens, T. E., Silva, J. M., et al. (2006). Young adult outcome of attention deficit hyperactivity disorder: A controlled 10-year follow-up study. *Psychological Medicine, 36,* 167–179.

Blashfield, R. K. (1984). *The classification of psychopathology: Neo-Kraepelian and quantitative approaches.* New York: Plenum Press.

Butzlaff, R. L., & Hooley, J. M. (1998). Expressed emotion and psychiatric relapse: A meta-analysis. *Archives of General Psychiatry, 55,* 549–562.

Cantwell, D. P. (1996). Attention deficit disorder: A review of the past 10 years. *Journal of the American Academy of Child and Adolescent Psychiatry, 35,* 978–987.

Carlson, G. A. (2005). Early onset bipolar disorder: Clinical and research considerations. *Journal of Clinical Child and Adolescent Psychology, 34,* 333–343.

Clark, L. A., Watson, D., & Reynolds, S. (1995). Diagnosis and classification of psychopathology: Challenges to the current system and future directions. *Annual Review of Psychology, 46,* 121–153.

Davidson, J. R. T., & Foa, E. B. (1991). Diagnostic issues in posttraumatic stress disorder: Considerations for the DSM-IV. *Journal of Abnormal Psychology, 100,* 346–355.

Egger, H. L., Ascher, B. H., & Angold, A. (1999). *The preschool age psychiatric assessment: Version 1.1.* Unpublished interview schedule, Center for Developmental Epidemiology, Department of Psychiatry and Behavioral Sciences, Duke University Medical Center.

Feighner, J. P., Robins, E., Guze, S. B., Woodruff, R. A., Winokur, G., & Munoz, R. (1972). Diagnostic criteria for use in psychiatric research. *Archives of General Psychiatry, 26,* 57–63.

Feinstein, A. R. (1970). The pre-therapeutic classification of co-morbidity in chronic disease. *Journal of Chronic Diseases, 23,* 455–468.

First, M. B. (2005). Clinical utility: A prerequisite for the adoption of a dimensional approach in DSM. *Journal of Abnormal Psychology, 114,* 560–564.

First, M. B., Bell, C. C., Cuthbert, B., Krystal, J. H., Malison, R., Offord, D. R., et al. (2002). Personality disorders and relational disorders. In D. J. Kupfer, M. B. First, & D. A. Regier (Eds.), *A research agenda for DSM-V* (pp. 123–200). Washington, DC: American Psychiatric Association.

Follett, W. C., & Houts, A. C. (1996). Models of scientific progress and the role of theory in taxonomy development: A case study of the DSM. *Journal of Consulting and Clinical Psychology, 64,* 1120–1132.

Frances, A. J. (1980). The DSM-III personality disorders section: A commentary. *American Journal of Psychiatry, 137,* 1050–1054.

Galbaud du Fort, G., Newman, S. C., & Bland, R. C. (1993). Psychiatric comorbidity and treatment seeking: Sources of selection bias in the study of clinical populations. *Journal of Nervous and Mental Diseases, 181,* 467–474.

Garber, J. (1984). Classification of childhood psychopathology: A developmental perspective. *Child Development, 55*, 30–48.

Hankin, B. L., Fraley, R. C., Lahey, B. B., & Waldman, I. D. (2005). Is depression best viewed as a continuum or discrete category? A taxometric analysis of childhood and adolescent depression in a population-based sample. *Journal of Abnormal Psychology, 114*, 96–110.

Hart, E. L., Lahey, B. B., Loeber, R., Applegate, B., & Frick, P. J. (1995). Developmental change in attention-deficit hyperactivity disorder in boys: A four-year longitudinal study. *Journal of Abnormal Child Psychology, 23*, 729–749.

Jensen, P. S., & Hoagwood, K. (1997). The book of names: DSM-IV in context. *Development and Psychopathology, 9*, 231–249.

Jensen, P. S., Mrazek, D., Knapp, P. K., Steinberg, L., Pfeffer, C., Schowalter, J., et al. (1997). Evolution and revolution in child psychiatry: ADHD as a disorder of adaptation. *Journal of the American Academy of Child and Adolescent Psychiatry, 36*, 1672–1681.

Keenan, K., & Wakschlag, L. S. (2002). Can a valid diagnosis of disruptive behavior disorder be made in preschool children? *American Journal of Psychiatry, 159*, 351–358.

Kendell, R. E. (1975). *The role of diagnosis in psychiatry.* Oxford, England: Blackwell Scientific.

Kendler, K. S. (1990). Toward a scientific psychiatric nosology: Strengths and limitations. *Archives of General Psychiatry, 47*, 969–973.

Kessler, R. C., Chiu, W. T., Demler, O., & Walters, E. E. (2005). Prevalence, severity, and co-morbidity of 12-month DSM-IV disorders in the National Comorbidity Survey Replication. *Archives of General Psychiatry, 62*, 617–627.

Kim-Cohen, J., Caspi, A., Moffitt, T. E., Harrington, H., Milne, B. J., & Poulton, R. (2003). Prior juvenile diagnoses in adults with mental disorder. *Archives of General Psychiatry, 60*, 709–717.

Kirmayer, L. F., & Young, A. (1999). Culture and context in the evolutionary concept of mental disorder. *Journal of Abnormal Psychology, 108*, 446–452.

Kluger, J., Song, S., Cray, D., Ressner, J., DeQuine, J., Sattley, M., et al. (2002). Young and bipolar. *Time, 160*(8), 38–48.

Krueger, R. F., Markon, K. E., Patrick, C. J., & Iacono, W. G. (2005). Externalizing psychopathology in adulthood: A dimensional-spectrum conceptualization and its implications for DSM-V. *Journal of Abnormal Psychology, 114*, 537–550.

Krueger, R. F., Nichol, P. E., Hicks, B. M., Markon, K. E., Patrick, C. J., Iacono, W. G., et al. (2004). Using latent trait modeling to conceptualize an alcohol problems continuum. *Psychological Assessment, 16*, 107–119.

Kupfer, D. J., First, M. B., & Regier, D. A. (Eds.). (2002). *A research agenda for DSM-V.* Washington, DC: American Psychiatric Association.

Lilienfeld, S. O., & Marino, L. (1995). Mental disorder as a Roschian concept: A critique of Wakefield's "harmful dysfunction" analysis. *Journal of Abnormal Psychology, 104*, 411–420.

Lilienfeld, S. O., Waldman, I. D., & Israel, A. C. (1994). A critical examination of the use of the term and concept of *comorbidity* in psychopathology research. *Clinical Psychology: Science and Practice, 1*, 71–83.

Luby, J. L., Mrakotsky, C., Heffelfinger, A., Brown, K., Hessler, M., & Spitznagel, E. (2003). Modification of DSM-IV criteria for depressed preschool children. *American Journal of Psychiatry, 160*, 1169–1172.

Marmorstein, N. R. (2006). Adult antisocial behavior without conduct disorder: Demographic characteristics and risk for co-occurring psychopathology. *Canadian Journal of Psychiatry, 51*, 226–233.

Marmorstein, N. R., & Iacono, W. G. (2005). Longitudinal follow-up of adolescents with late-onset antisocial behavior: A pathological yet overlooked group. *Journal of the American Academy of Child and Adolescent Psychiatry, 44,* 1284–1291.

McHugh, P. R. (1999). How psychiatry lost its way. *Commentary, 108,* 32–38.

Meehl, P. E. (2004). What's in a taxon? *Journal of Abnormal Psychology, 113,* 39–43.

Mezzich, J. E., Kirmayer, L. J., Kleinman, A., Fabrega, H., Parron, D. L., Good, B. J., et al. (1999). The place of culture in DSM-IV. *Journal of Nervous and Mental Diseases, 187,* 457–464.

Mineka, S., Watson, D., & Clark, L. A. (1998). Comorbidity of anxiety and unipolar mood disorders. *Annual Review of Psychology, 49,* 377–412.

Olfson, M., Blanco, C., Liu, L., Moreno, C., & Laje, G. (2006). National trends in the outpatient treatment of children and adolescents with antipsychotic drugs. *Archives of General Psychiatry, 63,* 679–685.

Ossorio, P. G. (1985). Pathology. *Advances in Descriptive Psychology, 4,* 151–201.

Richters, J. E., & Hinshaw, S. (1997). Psychiatry's turbid solution. *Clinical Psychology: Science and Practice, 4,* 276–280.

Robins, E., & Guze, S. B. (1970). Establishment of diagnostic validity in psychiatric illness: Its application to schizophrenia. *American Journal of Psychiatry, 126,* 983–987.

Rounsaville, B. J., Alarcon, R. D., Andrews, G., Jackson, J. S., Kendell, R. E., & Kendler, K. (2002). Basic nomenclature issues for DSM-V. In D. J. Kupfer, M. B. First, & D. A. Regier (Eds.), *A research agenda for DSM-V* (pp. 1–30). Washington, DC: American Psychiatric Association.

Ruscio, A. M., Borkovec, T. D., & Ruscio, J. (2001). A taxometric investigation of the latent structure of worry. *Journal of Abnormal Psychology, 110,* 413–422.

Spitzer, R. L. (1997). Brief comments from a psychiatric nosologist weary from his own attempts to define mental disorder: Why Ossorio's definition muddles and Wakefield's "harmful dysfunction" illuminates the issues. *Clinical Psychology: Science and Practice, 4,* 259–266.

Spitzer, R. L., Endicott, J., & Robins, E. (1979). Research diagnostic criteria: Rationale and reliability. *Archives of General Psychiatry, 36,* 773–782.

Trull, T. J., & Durrett, C. A. (2005). Categorical and dimensional models of personality disorder. *Annual Review of Clinical Psychology, 1,* 355–380.

Tsuang, M. T., Stone, W. S., & Faraone, S. V. (2000). Toward reformulating the diagnosis of schizophrenia. *American Journal of Psychiatry, 157*(7), 1041–1050.

Tyrer, P. (2001). The case for cothymia: Mixed anxiety and depression as a single diagnosis. *British Journal of Psychiatry, 179,* 191–193.

Wakefield, J. C. (1992). The concept of mental disorder: On the boundary between biological facts and social values. *American Psychologist, 47,* 373–388.

Wakefield, J. C. (1999). Evolutionary versus prototype analyses of the concept of disorder. *Journal of Abnormal Psychology, 108,* 374–399.

Watson, D. (2005). Rethinking the mood and anxiety disorders: A quantitative hierarchical model for DSM-V. *Journal of Abnormal Psychology, 114,* 522–536.

Widiger, T. A. (1997). The construct of mental disorder. *Clinical Psychology: Science and Practice, 4,* 262–266.

Widiger, T. A. (2005). A dimensional model of psychopathology. *Psychopathology, 38,* 211–214.

Widiger, T. A., & Samuel, D. B. (2005). Diagnostic categories or dimensions? A question for the diagnostic and statistical manual of mental disorders (5th ed.). *Journal of Abnormal Psychology, 114,* 494–504.

Widiger, T. A., & Shea, T. (1991). Differentiation of Axis I and Axis II disorders. *Journal of Abnormal Psychology, 100,* 399–406.

Willoughby, M. T. (2003). Developmental course of ADHD symptomatology during the transition from childhood to adolescence: A review with recommendations. *Journal of Child Psychology and Psychiatry, 44,* 88–106.

World Health Organization. (1992). *International statistical classification of diseases and related health problems* (10th rev.). Geneva, Switzerland: Author.

Zucker, R. A. (1986). The four alcoholisms: A developmental account of the etiological process. *Nebraska Symposium on Motivation, 34,* 27–83.

CHAPTER 3

Behavioral Conceptualization

SARA WRIGHT AND PAULA TRUAX

This chapter provides a framework for understanding and applying behavioral theory to clinical practice in the form of case conceptualization. Case conceptualization "effectively links a client's presenting problem to a treatment plan as well as provides the basis for tailoring treatment to clients needs and expectations" (Sperry, 2005). In other words, a case conceptualization answers the following questions: What happened? Why did it happen? and What can be done about it and how? Behavioral case conceptualization draws on behavioral theory to understand clients, including the emphasis on observable behaviors and learning principles. In contrast to other theoretical orientations, the conceptualization of the presenting problem focuses on observable client behaviors to answer the question of "What happened?" Additionally, hypotheses about the cause and maintenance of behavior are developed using learning theory that describes all behavior as acquired, maintained, and changed through the internal and external events that precede and follow them. The causal and maintenance hypotheses answer the question "Why did it happen?" Finally, treatment interventions are developed to answer the question "What can be done about it and how?" These interventions are based on theory of change that states that change occurs through manipulation of antecedents and consequences of behavior.

Case conceptualization using a behavioral perspective has several strengths, including the treatment effectiveness research and the compatibility with the current managed care environment. The current state of clinical psychology emphasizes the importance of using treatment interventions shown to be effective in targeting and reducing mental health disorders. This shift in focus was clearly seen when the American Psychological Association (APA) developed a task force to determine and define empirically validated or empirically supported treatments (Division 12 Task Force, 1995). Most of these empirically supported treatments were behavioral or cognitive-behavioral treatment interventions. The large amount of research that supports behavioral therapy as an effective intervention points to the advantage in using a behavioral case conceptualization framework.

Behavioral treatment is also compatible with the current managed care environment. The current managed care companies heavily favor treatment that is efficient, empirically supported, and includes specific goals and interventions. Efficiency refers to number of sessions that a health care company will provide; often, the company will grant a specified number of sessions. Research suggests that behavioral interventions may be the most efficient and cost-effective interventions available (Antonuccio, Thomas, & Dutton, 1997). Although the exact number of sessions depends on the complexity of the presenting problems, often behavioral treatments last between 10 and 20 sessions. Further, citing the large body of effectiveness research on behavioral interventions in the treatment plan may facilitate managed care approval of additional sessions. Additionally, managed care companies may better comprehend specific, behavioral descriptions of problems and interventions than descriptions from other theoretical orientations (Hoyt, 1995). Current proliferation of treatment manuals and protocols has made it even easier to describe and implement these interventions. Behavioral case conceptualization provides a cohesive framework to develop specific treatment goals and interventions, all of which is beneficial when clinicians are working within the current managed care environment.

APPLYING THE SCIENTIFIC METHOD TO THE CLINICAL SETTING

Beyond the logistical advantages just mentioned, a behavioral framework is desirable because the structure is similar to the scientific method. Behavioral therapy is closely linked to the methodology of science and closely follows the principles of a scientific experiment both in research and application. Stricker and Trierweiler (1995) encourage clinicians to be "local clinical scientists" in which the scientific method is applied in working with each client. The traditional scientific method consists of the following steps: (1) observing a phenomenon; (2) developing hypotheses that may explain the phenomenon; (3) testing the hypotheses through experiments; and (4) observing the outcome to analyze the validity of the original hypotheses. If needed, steps 2 through 5 are repeated. In Table 3.1, the parallels between the scientific method and clinical settings are described. Each of these steps is explained in more detail later in the chapter.

OBSERVATION: ASSESSMENT

The assessment phase is crucial in the development of a behavioral case conceptualization. Similar to the first step in the scientific method, the focus is on observing the clients' behaviors in several different ways. Although it is difficult to directly observe clients in their own natural environment, clinicians can utilize several different methods to obtain this critical information. Semi-structured interviews, self-report measures, mental status examination, reports from others, and self-monitoring are all possible methods. The assessment phase also includes identifying and defining treatment targets, as well as assessing the context in which behaviors occur.

CLINICAL INTERVIEW

This is by far the most common method of gathering information about clients. However, there is great variability in the type of interview used and the degree

Table 3.1

Parallels in Scientific Method and Local Clinical Scientist Model in Clinical Setting

Scientific Method	Local Clinical Scientist Model
Observe	1. The *observation* phase is similar to the initial assessment phase in therapy. Gathering information about the problem that will be used in later steps is the focus. Information concerning the presenting problem, including remote and recent context is gathered.
Develop hypotheses	2. The *developing hypotheses* phase occurs during the treatment planning process. Clinicians develop hypotheses about the cause and maintenance of the presenting problems, as well as hypotheses about treatment. Hypotheses about treatment are used to develop specific goals, interventions, and outcome measures.
Test hypotheses	3. *Testing hypotheses* occurs when the treatment plan is implemented with clients. Treatment closely follows the hypotheses developed in the treatment plan.
Observe outcome	4. *Observing the outcome* is similar to reviewing the progress made in therapy. Progress is measured through standardized and ideographic measures completed by the client.
Revise hypotheses	5. *Revising the hypotheses* occurs if treatment goals have not been successfully met. Changes in hypotheses about cause, maintenance, and treatment may be needed.
Test new hypotheses	6. *Test new hypotheses* according to revised treatment plan. Repeat steps 4 through 6.

of structure followed. Research supports the utility of semi-structured interviews, such as the Structured Clinical Interview Disorder-Clinician Version (SCID-CV; First, Spitzer, Gibbon, & Williams, 1996) because it has been found to be a more reliable and valid assessment tool than the clinician developed interview. For example, Miller, Dasher, Collins, Griffiths, and Brown (2001) compared structured versus unstructured interviews for making diagnoses with 56 inpatients. When consensus diagnoses using the LEAD criteria (L = Longitudinal evaluation of symptomatology, E = Evaluation by expert consensus, AD = All Data from multiple sources) were used as the gold standard, structured approaches such as the SCID-CV were most accurate. The SCID-CV is used primarily for diagnostic purposes and closely follows the *Diagnostic and Statistical Manual-IV-TR (DSM-IV-TR;* American Psychiatric Association, 2000) diagnostic criteria for most Axis I disorders. More information about the SCID can be found in the *Users Guide for SCID Manual* (First, Spitzer, Gibbon, & Williams, 1997). Another commonly used semi-structured interview is the Anxiety Disorder Inventory Schedule (ADIS; DiNardo, Brown, & Barlow, 1994). This assessment tool focuses primarily on anxiety disorders and contains specific questions regarding symptom intensity, duration, and frequency.

Finally, it is important to obtain information about the clients' psychosocial history, including childhood, education, employment, marital, social, substance use, and medical issues. Clinicians' methods of gathering this information are varied; however, from a behavioral perspective, the focus is on how history is impacting current behaviors and assessing the context in which the presenting problem occurs. By using the Functional Analytic Interview (Cormier & Cormier, 1998), clinicians can also gather information concerning the antecedents, consequences, and secondary gain of target behaviors. This information regarding behavioral context is central to behavioral case conceptualization.

STANDARDIZED SELF-REPORT MEASURES

Self-report measures provide clinicians with more objective, reliable, and quantifiable information concerning client's overall distress as well as specific symptoms. Standardized measures have also been normed on a clinical population, which allow comparison of client's scores to others who suffer from similar disorders. Clinicians often have clients complete these measures before conducting the interview, as well as throughout therapy to assess change. Broadband measures of distress, such as the Outcome-Questionnaire-45 (OQ-45, Lambert, Okiishi, Finch, & Johnson, 1998) or the Brief Symptom Inventory (BSI; Dertogatis, 1993), provide overall assessment of clients' daily functioning and can be helpful in tracking distress in multiple life roles. Specific measures, such as the Beck Depression Inventory-II (BDI-II; Beck, Steer, & Brown, 1996) and the Beck Anxiety Inventory (BAI; Beck & Steer, 1993), obtain information concerning the presence and intensity of key diagnostic and clinical symptoms of depression and anxiety disorders. Disorder specific measures, such as the Social Interaction Anxiety Scale (SIAS; Mattick & Clarke, 1998) for social phobia or the Impact of Events Scale (IES; Horowitz, Wilner, & Alvarez, 1979) for posttraumatic stress disorder, are helpful to assess problem severity once a diagnosis has been determined. Although self-report measures can provide more objective assessment of client's symptoms, administration and scoring can be time consuming. Therefore, it is important to reinforce the importance of the measure completion by regularly reviewing the results with clients in session.

MENTAL STATUS EXAMINATION

A mental status examination should be conducted during the intake in an effort to assess behavioral and cognitive aspects of mental functioning. Behavioral aspects are assessed through clinician observation and include general appearance, mood, and flow of thought. Cognitive aspects are assessed through questioning and include thought content, perception, cognition, insight, and judgment. The examination consists of indirect observation (e.g., client appearance, ability to answer questions, affect, and physical movement) and directed questions (e.g., "Do you ever see or hear things that other people may not?"). The Folstein Mini-Mental Status Exam (MMSE; Folstein, Folstein, & McHugh, 1975) is a brief, more structured assessment of these aspects of functioning. Clinicians should always assess mental status, although the formality and length of the exam may be tailored to the apparent client impairment (Morrison, 1995b).

REPORTS FROM OTHERS

In some cases, it is appropriate to interview significant others in the client's life, such as physician, past mental health treatment provider, parents, spouse, or coworkers. Before contacting others, clinicians have a legal and ethical responsibility to obtain release of information from the client. Physicians and past mental health providers may provide important additional information concerning diagnoses, past mental health distress, and/or current medical conditions. Parents, spouse, or coworkers may provide a more objective observation or assessment of client functioning in important areas of life, such as work and interpersonal relationships.

SELF-MONITORING

Clients may gather data concerning their own functioning through self-monitoring of mood and behaviors. For example, clients who suffer from depression may regularly record the intensity, frequency, and/or duration of mood and activities on a tracking sheet. Clinicians may also have clients do in-session self-monitoring using methods such as the Subjective Unit of Distress Scale (SUDS; Wolpe, 1958), with anchors such as 1 = Almost no anxiety and 10 = Maximum anxiety. This method of assessment also has the benefit of educating the client more about their current symptoms. However, self-monitoring at times can be time consuming and/or inaccurate due to the client concerns about social desirability or lack of insight.

OTHER ASSESSMENT MEASURES

As mentioned previously, it is most desirable to directly observe client behaviors. Logistically, this is very difficult to due, considering the time requirements and inevitable impact of clinicians' presence on the client in natural setting. However, some naturalistic observation can occur through videotaping sessions, videotaping at home, or home visits. Videotaping sessions for later review can be beneficial for clients who have little insight into their own behaviors. For instance, clients with social phobia often are not aware of the interpersonal cues they are sending; thus, watching the videotape of a role-play practice of social skills can be very beneficial. Additionally, clinicians can request for clients to make a videotape at home so that clinicians can review tapes with clients in session and can gain insight into the contexts in which behavior occurs. For example, clinicians working with families may request a recording of a family meal to observe typical interactions between family members. Finally, clinicians may conduct home visits to observe the client's typical environment, if feasible for both the client and clinician.

The following case is discussed in the context of behavioral conceptualization.

Case Description

Ms. X is a 35-year-old employed, single, Indian female with two children. She sought treatment for a primary problem of anxiety in social situations, both at work and with friends. A secondary concern was a recent development of depressed mood and loss of interest in previously enjoyed activities. She expressed more concern about getting help for her anxiety at work because she has recently been offered a new position that includes more presentations and public speaking. She appeared more ambivalent about treatment for her shift in mood.

(continued)

Ms. X reported that she has "always been shy," but that in the past year she has experienced intense anxiety while giving presentations at work or socially with coworkers. She also stated that she feels anxious at her children's school functions, particularly when talking with other parents. She said that she is worried what other people think of her presentations and often assumes the worst. She reported that her most effective coping strategy is to avoid all unnecessary social situations. When in social situations, she arrives late and leaves early, does not speak unless asked direct questions, and does not make eye contact with others.

Ms. X reported that she noticed a change in mood about a month ago when a long-term romantic relationship ended. She stated that she has been crying "all the time," has difficulty sleeping, and eats "to numb the pain." She also reported feeling guilty for the break up and does not have as much energy to play with her children. She denied any thoughts of suicide now or in the past.

On the basis of the Social Interaction Anxiety Scale (SIAS; Mattick & Clark, 1998) and the Social Phobia Scale (SPS; Mattick & Clark, 1998), Ms. X is experiencing clinically elevated anxiety concerning social interactions (SIAS = 45) and performance in social situations (SPS = 50). Additionally, her score on the Beck Depression Inventory-II (BDI-II; Beck et al., 1996) indicated moderate depression (BDI-II = 23). Similarly, baseline self-monitoring by Ms. X suggested that her average anxiety in a social situations was an 8 and her average daily depression was a 6 (on a 0–10 point scale with large numbers signifying greater severity).

TARGET BEHAVIORS FOR TREATMENT

The process of identifying and selecting target behavior is a crucial first step for treatment. Within this step, clinicians take time to operationally define the target behaviors, create a time line of those behaviors, and formalize diagnoses to best describe the problematic behaviors.

OPERATIONAL DEFINITIONS

Behavioral theorists emphasize value of observable behaviors now and in the past, have deemphasized nonobservable behaviors. Traditional behavior theorists focused only on overt behaviors—those that could clearly be observed by others. Overt behaviors include both verbal (such as rate or content of speech) and nonverbal (such as frowning, crying, or) communication. Overt behaviors also include motor behaviors, such as avoidance of feared situations, social isolation, or excessive eating. More recently, behavioral therapy includes covert, or nonobservable behaviors; most notably, internal cognitions. Aaron Beck and David Barlow have led the movement to include automatic thoughts, dysfunctional schemas, and core beliefs (Barlow, 1998; Beck, Rush, Shaw, & Emery, 1979). Covert behaviors include thoughts, feelings, images, and physical sensations. An anxious client may be thinking, "I must leave if I feel anxious," feeling restless or fidgety, imagining rejection in social situations, and experiencing rapid heart beat and dizziness. Both overt and covert behaviors can be behavioral target behaviors.

Target behaviors should be operationally defined early in treatment to clearly identify problems, measure progress, and ultimately determine treatment success. Although the tendency in psychology is to often describe a person by traits and labels, behaviorists focus on observable behavior. By focusing on what can be observed, ambiguity and subjectivity of both the client and clinician are minimized. Therefore, an operational definition of behavior should include observable, specific, and measurable aspects. A dialogue follows in which the clinician is gathering information about the behavioral manifestation of internal states to formulate operational definitions of Ms. X's problems. Although the conversation is focused on her social anxiety, these questions could also be asked about her depressive symptoms.

THERAPIST: How would I know by looking at you that you were feeling anxious? (behavioral manifestations of overt and covert behaviors)

Ms. X: I would become quiet, my face would flush, I would fidget, and I would avoid eye contact.

THERAPIST: What have others told you they have observed about your behavior while feeling you were feeling anxious? (behavioral manifestations of overt and covert behaviors)

Ms. X: Other people usually don't see me anxious; I usually avoid people when I feel this way.

THERAPIST: So other people may notice that you are not present in social gathering. What have others told you about your presentations when you have been forced to do them? (behavioral manifestations of overt and covert behaviors)

Ms. X: Well, everyone is very reassuring after I tell them I didn't think I did well. Most people say they didn't notice my shaky voice or fidgeting. My boss once told me that I was avoiding eye contact during my initial interview.

THERAPIST: So most people are not aware of your nervousness, even though you are very aware of it. How has feeling anxious affected the way you communicate with others? (behavioral manifestations of overt and covert behaviors)

Ms. X: I try to avoid conversation with strangers. With my coworkers that I feel more comfortable with, I usually agree with them and smile a lot so that the focus is not on me. At school functions for my children, I usually talk quietly to others and laugh at all their jokes. If there is silence, then I excuse myself and leave.

THERAPIST: It sounds like social situations are very difficult for you. And how has feeling anxious affected your work? (behavioral manifestations of overt and covert behaviors)

Ms. X: Well, I may not take this promotion if it means having to do more presentations. I dread the days when I have to talk at meetings and often feel distracted for the whole day before if I know I will be doing a presentation soon.

THERAPIST: Well, I hope that we can work together to make sure that your anxiety doesn't negatively affect your career decisions. Now I want to get some more specific information about what your anxiety feels like inside of your body. To get this information, I want to use a number scale in which 0 means the least possible anxiety you can imagine feeling and 10 means the most possible anxiety you can imagine feeling. How anxious do you feel right now? (intensity of internal anxiety)

Ms. X: About a 4.

THERAPIST: And how anxious have you felt on average over the last week? (intensity of internal anxiety)

Ms. X: About a 5.

THERAPIST: So it sounds like you are at a constant mid-range anxiety level, which can be very tiring. How anxious did you feel during the most recent presentation you gave? How long did that last? (intensity and duration of internal anxiety)

Ms. X: About an 8. Probably for the hour before the presentation, during the presentation, and for 10 minutes afterwards.

THERAPIST: Wow, I can see how being that anxious could really make presentations unpleasant. How frequently during an average day to you notice feeling more anxious than a 5? (frequency of internal anxiety)

Ms. X: Probably about three times a day. Especially when I first arrive at work and when I leave, as I have to say hello to people and engage in polite small talk.

THERAPIST: How anxious are you during the best times of the week? How long did that last? (intensity and duration of internal anxiety)

Ms. X: When I am at home, I am not anxious at all—probably a 1 or 2 because there is a possibility someone would call or stop by the house. Usually every night for about 2 hours, as long as it just myself and the kids.

THERAPIST: I'm glad that you have some time during your day that you can relax; that time is very important.

These questions by the therapist helped gather important information, including how Ms. X's anxiety manifests in her behavior. Also, the therapist gathered information on the intensity and frequency of social anxiety. At times, it is difficult for clients to answer these questions due to lack of awareness about their symptoms. When this occurs, it can be helpful to have clients monitor their anxiety over the following week or even interview others who may have information.

TIME LINE

After defining the target intensity, frequency, and behavioral manifestations of the target behavior, the next step is creating a time line to recreate the history of the target behavior. The process of developing a time line often helps the client increase understanding of the problem. The complexity of the time line is up to the clinician, who may want to consider both the desired information and the historical knowledge of the client. Ideally, the time line would begin at the first onset of the problem and end with the present date. Depending on the length of that time period, the clinician can generate time markers for the middle. Clinicians should encourage clients to remember significant events that occurred along the time line, as well as the severity and intensity of the target behavior. If possible, it is also helpful to include culturally relevant events in an effort to assess the impact of sociocultural events on symptoms. For Ms. X, it would be helpful to collaboratively create a time line for both her social anxiety and depression. Utilizing the time line in Figure 3.1, the clinician and Ms. X could add in significant events that occurred in the past 6 months. For example, Ms. X's separation from her partner occurred in April, which may have contributed to the increase in her depression. Her job

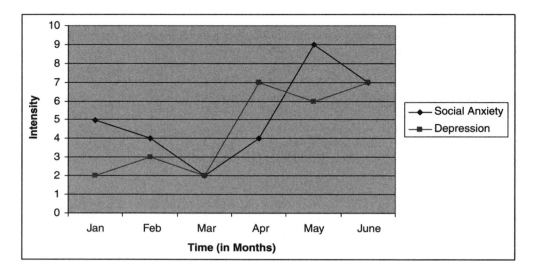

Figure 3.1 Ms. X's self-report of the time line for Social Anxiety and Depression severity on 0–10 rating scale with 0 = None and 10 = Severe.

promotion offer occurred in May, which may have contributed to the increase in her anxiety.

DIAGNOSIS

After determining treatment targets and developing a time line of symptomology, the clinician often has a sufficient understanding of the client's symptoms to determine a diagnosis. The current diagnostic classification system is in the *DSM-IV-TR* (American Psychiatric Association, 2000) and closely follows the medical model of diagnosis. Usefulness of diagnosis is debated within most theoretical orientations because there are numerous advantages and disadvantages. The advantages of using a diagnostic system include the idea that diagnosis gives psychologists a way of discussing clients in a more efficient way. In other words, clinicians have a simpler way of talking about clusters of symptoms that usually exist together. However, this more efficient way of talking often makes the inaccurate assumption that disorders look exactly the same in different people. Another reason that diagnoses are used is that managed care often requires a diagnosis for reimbursement, so most clinicians use them on a regular basis. Additionally, an accurate diagnosis can help to inform the treatment interventions used. The disadvantages of the *DSM-IV-TR* diagnostic system include the negative stigma attached to certain mental disorders, minimization of the uniqueness of each client, and the arbitrary nature of numeric criteria needed to qualify for a diagnosis. Behavioral theorists also criticize the diagnostic criteria because it focuses more on the topography of the symptoms (i.e., what do these symptoms look like) and less on the function of the behavior (i.e., what purpose is this behavior serving; Follette & Houts, 1996). Regardless of the advantages and disadvantages of the current system, diagnosis remains a routine practice for clinicians.

For Ms. X, the following diagnoses and justifications were assigned based on the assessment information gathered:

Axis I: 300.23 Social Phobia
          Major Depressive Disorder, Single Episode, Moderate
Axis II: V71.09 No diagnosis
Axis III: None, per client's self-report
Axis IV: Distress in workplace, End of significant relationship
Axis V: 60–70

Ms. X is suffering from Social Phobia, as evidenced by a persistent fear of social performance situations. She reports fear of scrutiny by others, particularly in performance situations. When in social situations, she experiences anxiety, although she realizes that her fear is excessive. She avoids social situations, particularly giving public speeches and going to social gathering at her children's school. The avoidance and anxiety when she does not avoid causes interference in her job performance. The fear and avoidance is not better accounted for by substance use, a known medical disorder, or other mental disorders. Ms. X is also suffering from Major Depressive Disorder, Single Episode, Moderate, as evidenced by her depressed mood and decreased interest in previously enjoyed activities in the preceding month. She also endorses insomnia, overeating, feelings of worthlessness, and loss of energy. She denies previous depressive episodes and the modifier of moderate was given due to the severity of her symptoms.

Ms. X does not appear to meet criteria for a personality disorder, as there is no current evidence of long-term, characterological, or maladaptive patterns. On Axis III, she denies any medical problems, although she has not received a physical in over a year. On Axis IV, the distress caused by the social phobia is preventing her from accepting a job promotion. Additionally, she recently ended a long-term romantic relationship, which may be contributing to her depressed mood. Finally, she receives a current GAF score range of 60–70, due to the moderate level of her symptoms and impairment in occupational functioning.

IMPORTANCE OF CONTEXT/ENVIRONMENT

The final step in assessment of the client's presenting problem is evaluation of the context, or environment, in which the behavior occurs. The context includes both the remote environment, which includes the client's history, and the recent context, which includes the client's current environment. The remote context is best understood using the biopsychosocial model. The recent context focuses on the antecedents and consequences that are maintaining the behavior.

REMOTE CONTEXT

The remote context refers to client history that is relevant to the presenting problem. While it is impossible to know what directly caused the presenting problem, it is possible to develop hypotheses about contributing factors based on history. Behavioral therapists often use the biopsychosocial model when assessing for important contributing factors. The biopsychosocial model includes the following factors:

biological, physical, substance use, learning and modeling, life events, sociocultural, and life events.

Biological Many studies support the idea that people can be genetically predisposed to develop certain psychological disorders. The genetic predisposition is often thought to be hereditary; that is, if parents suffer from a mental health disorder, then their children are more likely to suffer from one as well. For example, people who have first-degree family members who suffer from social phobia are three times more likely to develop the disorder themselves (Fyer, Mannuzza, Chapman, Liebowitz, & Klein, 1993; Reich & Yates, 1988). This family trend has been found to be true even after factoring out the environmental influences parents have on children. For example, there was a 24.4% concordance rate for monozygotic twins compared to 15.3% concordance rate for dizygotic twins, which indicates genetic factors contribute to approximately 30% of the occurrence of social anxiety (Kendler, Neale, Kesslar, Heath, & Eaves, 1992). Therefore, it is important for clinicians to obtain a thorough family psychiatric history, including parents and grandparents. Often, clinicians will hear from clients that a parent, aunt or uncle, or grandparent had a similar psychological disorder. This information can also be helpful in determining the course of treatment. Some research suggests that when certain disorders, such as depression, have a genetic component, they may respond more effectively to psychotropic medication (Jarrett, 1995).

Ms. X described her mother as a shy person, as well, who did not enjoy going to family gatherings or holiday parties. However, she reported that her mother was never diagnosed with a mental health disorder. She also reported that her father was often "depressed and withdrawn from the family." She also mentioned that despite these difficulties, her parents believed it was "unnecessary" to seek out a mental health treatment provider.

Physical Assessment A thorough medical history is necessary for case conceptualization because there are several medical conditions that can cause or contribute to psychological distress. For instance, changes in thyroid functioning can directly lead to changes in mood, including depressive episodes. For a list of medical conditions that have been found to be related to psychological disorder, see Morrison's book (1995a) *DSM-IV Made Easy: The Clinician's Guide to Diagnosis.* Additionally, research has shown that some people are more sensitive to physiological symptoms of anxiety. Therefore, being more sensitive and reactive to the physiological symptoms of anxiety may contribute to development, as well as the severity and distress, associated with panic symptoms (Schmidt, Joiner, Staab, & Williams, 2003).

Ms. X reported no significant medical conditions. She reported that her last physical examination was less than one year ago and stated that the physician declared she was in good health.

Substance Use Given the high prevalence of substance use in American culture, it is important to assess all types of substance use, including alcohol, tobacco, illegal drugs, prescription drugs, alternative medications, and over-the-counter medications. Research suggests that the comorbidity rate of substance use and psychological disorders is significant. For example, over 30% of individuals with an anxiety disorder also have a substance use disorder (Brady, 2002). Substances can cause, maintain, and/or exacerbate psychological disorders. Substance use can also impede treatment progress for a variety of reasons. Therefore, it is important to assess on a continual basis in treatment for any changes in substance use.

Ms. X did report that she recently stopped taking birth control pills (Ortho-TriCyclen) due to the end of her romantic relationship. She also reported that she drinks alcohol (typically two to three glasses of wine) approximately one time per month in social situations such as parties to help "loosen me up."

Learning and Modeling   The importance of learning and modeling cannot be overstated. As very young children, the world is navigated by learning certain behaviors. Much of this type of learning and modeling occurs from observing parents and family members. Therefore, it is important to learn what family members did when feeling anxious, sad, or angry because this was likely a modeling experience for the child. Additionally, how the client was treated (in terms of reinforcement or punishment) as a child when experiencing or expressing feelings is most likely how the client learned to cope with feelings. For example, Linehan's (1993) theory on the etiology or development of Borderline Personality Disorder (BPD) emphasizes the idea of an invalidating environment, in which the child was not reinforced (through attention) for expressing emotions until the child was explosive—which is a common symptom of BPD.

As mentioned earlier, Ms. X's mother was often quiet in social situations and did not enjoy these experiences. Therefore, Ms. X may be currently modeling her mother's quiet behavior, and such withdrawn behavior may lead to punishing responses or a lack of reinforcing responses. Additionally, she may be modeling how her father withdrew from the family when depressed; through observing his behavior, she had learned that when experiencing sadness, it is important to retreat from people and activities.

Life Events   Through the intake process, clients are likely to report significant current or past life events. Although it is difficult to determine whether a life event directly caused a psychological disorder, it is important to recognize possible antecedents and consequences the client has experienced in relation to major life events. Additionally, some research suggests that a significant life stressor often corresponds with the onset or worsening of depression. Specifically, Rounsaville, Weissman, Prusoff, and Herceg-Baron (1979) found that 50% of individuals seeking treatment for depression reported having marital or romantic relationship conflict. Thus, assessment of past and current difficult life events as well as coping methods may clarify the effectiveness of existing coping strategies.

Ms. X's recent end of a significant romantic relationship is likely to be a significant life event to consider, especially since it corresponds with her depressed mood. Additionally, the recent job promotion offer prompted her to seek treatment, which suggests the significance of this event. Ms. X did not report any significant events in her childhood, such as abuse or trauma, but did state that her parents' marriage was not "happy." She also reported that she moved often because her father was in computer sales and often had to relocate the family. Therefore, she changed schools frequently and never had long-time friendships.

Sociocultural Factors   The importance of sociocultural issues in the development and treatment of psychological disorder is emphasized in the contemporary literature. Specifically, Hays (2001) ADRESSING model recommends examining the following areas of diversity: **A**ge, **D**evelopmental or acquired disabilities, **R**eligion, **E**thnicity,

Socioeconomic status, Sexual orientation, Indigenous heritage, National origin, and Gender. All of these areas of diversity may have influenced the values that have been learned or modeled to the client. These diversity areas should be considered to develop a culturally responsive diagnosis and treatment plan.

For Ms. X, the relevant diversity issues in which she is not a member of the privileged class are ethnicity (she identifies herself as first-generation Indian American) and gender (female). She was raised in the United States and reported that both of her parents were born in India and moved to the United States when they were children. Ms. X learned many traditional Indian values, which may have influenced her presenting problems of anxiety and depression. Given her parents' reluctance to seek psychological treatment for their own difficulties, Ms. X may have learned that "Therapy is not helpful. If I go to therapy, then I am showing my weaknesses to others." Such diversity issues are important to consider when determining diagnosis and treatment planning.

RECENT CONTEXT

In addition to the remote context, the recent context of the target behavior is integral to treatment. Recent context refers to both the antecedents, which occur directly before the behavior, and consequences, which occur directly after the behavior. Antecedents and consequences can be either internal (i.e., thoughts and emotions) or external (i.e., environment) events. At the most basic level, recent context refers to all pieces that come together for learning to occur. People engage in behavior because of past learning experiences. Both antecedents and consequences serve to maintain, or reinforce, the behavior and will likely be targeted in treatment.

Gathering information about the recent context can be difficult for several reasons. First, clients may not be aware of the antecedents and consequences maintaining their problematic behaviors. Frequently, people are not monitoring their thoughts, emotions, and surrounding environment when engaging in behavior (for example, clients who have panic attacks often are so focused on physiological symptoms that they fail to identify other events). Second, clients may be hesitant to acknowledge the reinforcing nature of behaviors they are trying to reduce. For example, clients who suffer from anxiety may be hesitant to admit to avoidance tactics because of the possibility of having to stop avoidance behavior. Finally, clients may agree with the clinicians' hypotheses about what is reinforcing the behavior due to social desirability factors. Linehan's DBT treatment emphasizes the importance of having clients identify the contingencies of a certain behavior or event (Linehan, 2003). It may be helpful to have clients generate a specific, recent example of the behavior. Then, the client and clinician can work together to identify the antecedents and consequences. The questions that follow illustrate example clinician questions used to illicit relevant information. These questions are specific to the case example of Ms. X.

Antecedents   As mentioned, antecedents are any factors that occur directly before the behavior and act to increase the likelihood of that behavior occurring. Antecedents do not directly cause the behavior to occur, but increase the likelihood due to past situations in which the antecedent was present, the target behavior occurred and was reinforced.

Antecedents to psychological issues can be either internal (i.e., thoughts, feelings, physical sensations, and images) or external (i.e., situation, people, location). For example, antecedents to alcohol use often include internal events such as the thought

"I can't stand not drinking," feelings such as loneliness or anger, sensations such as dry throat, the smell of alcohol, or images such as having fun with friends at a bar. External events may include being at a bar, having a friend offer a drink, or being in a grocery store that sells alcohol. None of these antecedents directly cause someone to drink, but they likely increase the probability of drinking. This information may be pivotal to intervention. Questions to illicit information about antecedents for most recent target behavior include the following:

> When was the most recent time you were socially anxious (i.e., greater than an 8 on a scale of 0–10)?
>
> What was happening around you right before you became anxious? (environmental)
> - Where were you? (location)
> - Who was with you? What were they doing? (people)
> - What was going on? (situation)
>
> What were you doing right before the attack? (behavioral)
>
> What was happening inside of you right before the attack? (internal)
>
> What were you feeling? (physical)
>
> What emotions or feelings were you having? (emotional)
>
> What thoughts were going through your head? (cognitive)

Consequences As mentioned, consequences are any factors that occur directly after the behavior and act to increase or decrease the probability of that behavior occurring again in the future. Because consequences include events that increase and decrease the probability, there are more different types of consequences. If a consequence increases the probability of a behavior re-occurring, it is considered a reinforcer. If a consequence decreases the probability of a behavior re-occurring, it is considered a punisher. Both reinforcers and punishers can be further divided according to whether an increase or decrease in the consequence leads to change in target behavior. These consequences are listed next with possible examples for Ms. X:

- *Positive reinforcement:* Increase of this type of pleasurable consequence increases the likelihood of target behavior occurring in future. For example, Ms. X may have received positive attention from her mother when she stayed home from school due to anxiety.
- *Negative reinforcement:* Decrease of this type of aversive consequence increases the likelihood of target behavior occurring in the future. For example, Ms. X arrives late and leaves early to social gatherings, thus avoiding perceived awkward introductions and goodbyes. This relief is probably experienced as reinforcing and thus it is more likely she will continue to arrive late and leave early.
- *Positive punishment:* Increase of this type of aversive consequence decreases the likelihood of target behavior occurring in the future. For example, Ms. X experiences increased anxiety when giving presentations at work and thus is less likely to give presentations.
- *Negative punishment:* Decrease in this type of positive consequence decreases the likelihood of target behavior occurring in the future. For example, Ms. X experiences less enjoyment and pleasure when playing with her children and thus is less likely to engage in play with them in the future.

Because the target behaviors are most often considered undesirable behavior, the focus is usually on reducing the availability of consequences that increase the likelihood of the behavior occurring. Possible clinician questions to illicit information about the client's experience of consequences include:

Exacerbating Factors

What happens outside of you that makes the situation worse? What do you do and say? What do others do and say? What about the situation makes it worse?

What happens inside of you after the social situation ends or presentation ends?

What do you feel emotional and physically? What do you say to yourself?

Mitigating Factors

What happens outside of you that makes the situation better?

What happens inside of you after the situation that makes the situation better?

Secondary Gain

Is there any relief from any other external activities as a result of this problem?

Have your work or home responsibilities changed? Have others changed their demands on you? Have you changed your demands on yourself? Are you getting any compensation as a result of this problem?

Is there any part of any time in this problem that you experience some relief from something uncomfortable inside of you? Do you experience any physical or emotional relief during this problem?

Assessment of both recent and remote context is key to behavioral case conceptualization because of the emphasis on learning. The context, or environment, that is unique to each client needs to be assessed so that clinicians can understand why target behaviors are occurring. The information about remote context will be used to develop hypotheses about cause, while the information about recent context will be used to develop hypotheses about maintenance. Ultimately, the information will also be used to manipulate the context and change the target behaviors.

DEVELOPING HYPOTHESES: TREATMENT PLANNING PHASE

After collecting information in the observation phase, in next phase hypotheses are developed about cause, maintenance, and treatment of the client's presenting problems. These hypotheses should be developed directly from the assessment of the client and knowledge about behavioral theory. This section is divided into hypotheses about causal factors, maintenance factors, and treatment planning.

HYPOTHESES ABOUT CAUSAL FACTORS

Much of the information used to develop hypotheses about cause has already been gathered during the biopsychosocial assessment. Therefore, hypotheses are usually separated into the following factors: biological, physical, substance use, learning and modeling, life events, and sociocultural influences. However, the next step is to use the biopsychosocial information collected and determine which aspects of the client's remote context are likely to have contributed to the development of the presenting problem. The focus may also be on internal and external factors in the recent context immediately before the problem developed.

Given the information provided in the biopsychosocial assessment, it is likely that biological, learning and modeling, life events, and sociocultural factors influenced the development of Ms. X's presenting problems. For Ms. X, the likely hypotheses about cause are:

- Given Ms. X's description of her mother as "shy" and her father as "withdrawn," it is likely there is a genetic and/or learning component to her Social Phobia and Depression. Because her parents did not seek mental health treatment, it is unknown for certain whether either met diagnostic criteria for a mental health disorder. However, both depression and anxiety disorder are known to have biological predispositions. Additionally, Ms. X may have learned and modeled from her mother that social events are not enjoyable and from her father that the best way to deal with sadness is to withdrawal.
- Ms. X's sociocultural background may have influenced the development of her presenting problems. She reported a value of her parents not to seek mental health treatment; therefore, her family culture de-emphasized the importance of mental health. Also, research has shown that women are more likely to develop anxiety and depressive disorders (e.g., Parker, & Hadzi-Pavlovic, 2004). Further information about her level of ethnic minority identity development is needed to determine the level of identification to Indian and American cultures.
- Three significant life events likely contributed to the development of her anxiety and depression. First, the end of a serious romantic relationship likely influenced her mood, thoughts, and behaviors. Second, the promotion to a job that requires more public speaking is likely contributing to her social anxiety. Last, the consistent change in schooling at an early age likely caused difficulties making friendships, which may have generalized to anxiety in social situations.

HYPOTHESES ABOUT MAINTENANCE

Through assessment of the recent context described previously, clinicians gather information that can be used in the development of hypotheses about maintenance. The focus is on how the presenting problem is being maintained or reinforced; in other words, how is this behavior being maintained despite the client's desire for change? Often, clients are not aware that what they consider problematic behavior is being reinforced in some way. Behavior theorists state that a behavior does not occur unless it is reinforced. Clinicians need to use information gathered through functional assessment to determine likely antecedents and consequences that are maintaining the client's behaviors.

Research has found common maintenance factors for different disorders. For depression, the research suggests that lack of engagement in behaviors or activities that are enjoyable or provide a sense of mastery maintains depression. Once clients become depressed, they are less active and that pattern is maintained by low energy and lack of positive reinforcement. Therefore, the focus of treatment is often re-engaging depressed clients in these activities. In terms of cognitions, depressed clients often report several distortions, such as "I'm never going to be successful," "I am a bad person because I am depressed," or "Things will never get better. I will always be alone." Therefore, the focus of treatment is also on challenging these cognitions and encouraging more realistic thinking. For anxiety, research suggests that avoidance of feared activities maintains the anxiety through negative reinforcement. As clients who are anxious about certain situations continue to avoid those situations, their behavior is reinforced because they avoid feeling anxious (which provides relief) and their behavior further confirms the fear of that situation. Therefore, beliefs such as "This situation is awful," "I won't be able to stand my anxiety if I have to feel it again," and "It's so much easier to avoid my fears than to face them" are often commonly reported by clients who have an anxiety disorder. Given these common maintenance factors, clinicians can assess for whether these behaviors or cognitions exist for their clients.

Likely maintenance factors for Ms. X are:

Maintenance Factors for Depression

- Reduction in pleasurable activities due to avoidance of anxiety provoking situations (i.e., social gatherings) and low motivation (i.e., no energy to play with her children).
- Belief that important to withdraw when feeling sadness.

Maintenance Factors for Anxiety

- Negative reinforcement (relief) experienced when she escapes an anxiety provoking situation such as presentations or social gatherings.
- Excessive focus on her internal experience distracts from involvement (and thus enjoyment) of other people.
- Distortions about her appearance in social situations (i.e., "Everyone is noticing I am nervous," "I must look awful").
- Reassurance from others after her presentations when she expresses doubts (positive reinforcement).

After developing hypotheses about maintenance of the presenting problems, the clinician can generate treatment hypotheses.

HYPOTHESES ABOUT TREATMENT

Several factors should be considered when developing hypotheses about treatment, including relevant research literature, client priorities of presenting concerns, and feasibility concerns. Feasibility of treatment includes factors such as time limitations, session limitations, and competence or expertise of clinician. Additionally, the hypotheses about cause and maintenance are crucial to determine treatment interventions.

Functional Relationships   The behavioral theory for change states that change in the antecedents or consequences of a target behavior will result in change of the behavior itself. Therefore, importance of an accurate understanding of the relationship between antecedents, behavior, and consequences cannot be overstated. If changes occurs in the antecedents or consequences and the target behavior remains unchanged, the relationship between these factors is most likely misunderstood. The contingency should be re-examined and the treatment intervention will likely need to be changed. If, for example, a client is depressed and the functional assessment suggests that the antecedent is negative social interactions while the primary exacerbating consequence is verbally abusive interchanges, then social skills training would probably be a more appropriate focused intervention.

Empirical Literature   Given the fast pace at which research is produced on the most effective interventions, it is important for clinicians to consult the literature when beginning treatment with a client. With proliferation of treatment protocols and manuals, it is not difficult to find specific, effective interventions. Despite criticisms of manualized treatments, the research suggests that these efficacious treatments are also effective in nonresearch settings (e.g., Addis et al., 2004, 2006). Additionally, research has shown that clinicians can be flexible and adapt the protocols to their personal style or the client's unique problems and not lose the effectiveness of the interventions (Kendall, Chu, Gifford, Hayes, & Nauta, 1998; Otto, 2000). For beginning clinicians, the specificity provided in protocols creates easy-to-implement interventions.

For Ms. X's presenting problems, there is a substantial amount of research literature on effective interventions for both social phobia and depression. Research on social phobia suggests that a combination of cognitive and behavioral interventions is the most effective treatment (Heimberg & Juster, 1995; Taylor, 1996). Behavioral treatment models include exposure (both in vivo and imaginal) and social skills training (Rapee, 1995; Turner, Beidel, Cooley, Woody, & Messer, 1994). Cognitive treatment models emphasize the role of cognitions in this disorder, as the *DSM-IV-TR* diagnostic criteria include the presence of cognitions concerning feared, negative evaluation by others. Therefore, Clark's (2001) model of treatment focuses on cognitive restructuring, as people with social phobia often report excessively high standards for social performance and unconditional negative beliefs about the self. Finally, research on depression suggests a combination of behavioral interventions (including behavioral activation) and cognitive interventions (including cognitive restructuring) is an effective treatment (Butler, Chapman, Forman, & Beck, 2006).

Prioritization of Presenting Concerns   When determining prioritization of treatment targets, clinicians should consider the nature and severity of the concerns, client preference, and client stage of change. Linehan (1993) provides clear guidelines for prioritization of treatment goals based on the nature of the problems. She suggests that treatment goals should first focus on life-threatening behaviors (including suicidal and parasuicidal behaviors), then therapy interfering behaviors (including not participating in therapy sessions and not completing homework), and subsequently severe quality of life concerns (substance use, domestic violence, and housing concerns). After these concerns are addressed, focus of therapy shifts to other presenting problems, such as depression or anxiety. Severity of presenting problems should be evaluated in terms of interference in daily functioning and higher priority should be given to more severe problems. Clients' preferences are extremely important, both because clients are often clear about what they would like to work on first and because listening to their preferences cements the therapeutic relationship. Similar to preference is current stage of change, which refers to the client's amount of motivation to work on current concerns. The client's stage of change frequently varies for different problems and thus therapy is likely more successful if the focus is on the problem that the client has the most motivation to change. Booth, Dale, and Ansari (1984), for example, found that clients seeking treatment for substance abuse were more successful in reducing drinking when they chose their goals as compared to when the therapists chose the goals. Therefore, treatment is more likely to be successful if the focus is on what the client would like to change. All of these factors should be considered when the clinician and client are determining the prioritization of concerns.

For Ms. X's presenting problems, prioritization of concerns should be developed. In terms of the nature of her concerns, there are currently no life-threatening behaviors, therapy interfering behaviors, or severe quality of life concerns; therefore, the presenting concerns of anxiety and depression can be immediately focused on. In relation to severity of her anxiety and depression, it appears that the anxiety is most directly interfering with her daily functioning at work. Additionally, Ms. X reported that she is more interested in reducing her anxiety and is less concerned about her depressed mood. Therefore, she appears to be in the preparation stage of change for addressing the anxiety, and contemplative stage of change for addressing her depression. Her stage of change could be also assessed more formally with a questionnaire such as the Change Assessment Scale (Dozois, Westra, Collins, Fung, & Garry, 2004). The presenting concerns would be prioritized so that anxiety is addressed before the depression.

Feasibility Concerns   As mentioned, feasibility of treatment includes time and session limitations, as well as the competence of the clinician. The current state of the health insurance environment places limitations on the number of reimbursable sessions. Therefore, clinicians will often have only 8 to 12 sessions to treat the presenting problems. Treatment should not exceed these limits unless there is an agreement in place for how the cost of sessions will be covered. Additionally, clinicians should assess the treatment duration the client is willing to commit to because some clients may have limitations in their schedules. Finally, the clinician should assess their own competence to treat the presenting concerns. According to the APA Code of Ethics, a clinician should always practice within the realm of his or her expertise. If the presenting concern is outside the competence of the clinician, then an appropriate referral should be made.

HYPOTHESES ABOUT MS. X'S TREATMENT

After reviewing the empirical literature, functional relationships, prioritization of concerns, and feasibility, hypotheses about treatment can be developed. The hypotheses for Ms. X are:

- Ms. X's Social Phobia exacerbates and maintains her Depression through confirming beliefs of inadequacy and avoidance of potentially pleasurable activities.
- Treatment will be most effective if the social phobia is addressed first, as it fits with the prioritization of concerns and the research literature.
- Social phobia treatment will be effective if the focus is on her cognitions in social situations, as they are exacerbating her anxiety and preventing her from public speaking. Additionally, interventions (such as exposure) will be needed to extinguish the escape response that is currently negatively reinforced by relief from anxiety.

- Social phobia treatment will also decrease anxiety in social situations by providing social skills training and public speaking practice.
- A reduction in social phobia will result in a reduction in depression, as well. As she increases her social contact, she will become more behaviorally activated (i.e., behavioral activation is a CBT treatment component for depression) and challenge her depressogenic beliefs (i.e., cognitive challenging is the second CBT depression treatment component).

Treatment Plan Collaboration

After the therapist has generated hypotheses about treatment, the next step is to collaborate with the client about their goals for treatment. Treatment planning should be a collaborative process, as the therapeutic relationship is key to successful treatment. In fact, Lambert (1992) found that the therapeutic relationship accounts for 30% of treatment progress, while technique accounts for only 15% of progress. Additionally, Tryon and Winograd (2001) found that clients who reported that they had been collaboratively involved in goal-setting generally had better outcomes. Therefore, clinicians should present the treatment planning process with confidence, competence, and interest in hearing clients' goals for treatment.

Goals

Treatment goals should be consistent with hypotheses concerning treatment and specific so that the therapist and client can evaluate treatment progress. Setting specific goals increases the effectiveness of treatment (James, Thorn, & Williams, 1993), enhances collaboration between therapist and client (Tracey & Kokotovic, 1989), and sufficiently meets the needs of the current managed care environment (Antonuccio et al., 1997). Treatment goals should meet the following SMART criteria developed by Locke and Latham (1990).

- *Specific:* Goals should target specific variables with observable referents that are relevant to the client's presenting concerns (e.g., intensity of depressed mood; frequency of night awakenings). Specificity helps to determine the most accurate treatment intervention.
- *Measurable:* Goals should include an observable, objective scale of measurement that is meaningful to the client (e.g., on a scale of 0–10; daily frequency).
- *Anchored:* To assess whether sufficient progress was made, goals should include both the current level and the desired level at the end of treatment (e.g., intensity of depressed mood will be reduced from a daily average of 9 to a daily average of 5).
- *Realistic:* Goals should be realistic given the client's current and past functioning as well as available treatment time. It is important to distinguish between ideal and realistic, as they are not always the same.
- *Time line:* Goals should include a target date for the goals to be accomplished. On the target date, the goals should be reviewed with the client to determine whether the goals have been resolved or need to be renewed.

INTERVENTIONS

In addition to specific goals, the treatment plan should include specific interventions to achieve those goals. Interventions should be developed based on treatment literature, including empirically supported protocols.

MEASUREMENTS

After determining specific goals, regular measurement of progress is needed to assess whether the treatment goals have been met. Measuring progress provides an objective view of client change. A combination of standardized (e.g., Beck Anxiety Inventory) and ideographic measures (e.g., intensity of anxiety on self-defined 0–10 scale) are recommended to assess progress.

Figure 3.2 is a treatment plan for Ms. X. The treatment plan includes goals that met the SMART criteria, specific interventions, and both standardized and ideographic measurements.

Primary Presenting Problem: Ms. X is a 35-year-old woman with two children who is presenting with a primary problem of social phobia. Her problem appears to be interfering with her work and her social support system, which is contributing to her feelings of loneliness and isolation. She is also presenting with depression, as evidenced by depressed mood, loss of interest in activities, insomnia, and weight loss. She prioritized her concerns as follows:

Top Priority Concerns:
1. Increased anxiety in performance or public speaking situations.
2. Increased time worrying about others' perceptions of her.
3. Increased overall daily anxiety.

Secondary Priority Concerns:
1. Depressed mood and loss of energy, particularly playing with her children.
2. Decreased appetite and sleep loss.

Specific Goals:
1. Reducing anxiety in public speaking from an average of 8 (ratings based on subjective units of distress scale, or SUDS, 1 = Minimal anxiety, 10 = Maximum anxiety) to an average of a 3.
2. Reducing time spent worrying about others' perceptions from 80% of the time to 30% of the time.
3. Increase time spent at social activities, from staying for 50% of the time to 100% of the time.
4. Increase time spent playing with children, from 20 minutes a day to 1 hour a day.

Interventions to Address Each Goal:
1. Client will learn to identify cognitive distortions and challenge these thoughts with more realistic, moderate alternative thoughts to aid in goals 1, 2, and 3.
2. Client will learn social skills, including public speaking skills to aid in goal 1.
3. Client will develop a hierarchy of anxiety provoking social situations and engage in in vivo exposure to these situations to aid in goals 1, 2, and 3.
4. Client will engage in activity scheduling and reward planning to aid in goal 4.

Figure 3.2 Ms. X treatment plan.

Referrals (Medication, Physical, Assessment, Other Counseling Provider, etc.):

No referrals are needed at this time.

Measurement of Each Goal:
1. Anxiety tracking sheet for public speaking (rate on SUDS scale 1–10) (goal 1).
2. Percentage of time spent worrying daily (goal 2).
3. Percentage of time spent at social activities (goal 3).
4. Tracking sheet for time spent with children (goal 4).
5. SIAS and SPS administered weekly (measure of social anxiety) (goals 1, 2, & 3).
6. BDI-II administered weekly (measure of depression) (goal 4).

Client Strengths and Obstacles:

Ms. X is bright, motivated, and performing well in many areas of her life. She appears committed to treatment for her social anxiety because she is aware of the negative impact on her career. Her primary obstacle will likely be the significant duration and early onset of her social anxiety. However, she states that she is willing to try and change.

Prioritized Summary and Time Frame:

The social anxiety will be the initial focus of treatment. The depression may be somewhat alleviated with the social anxiety treatment, but if not, will be addressed later. It is anticipated that this treatment plan will be completed in 12–14 weekly sessions.

———————————   ———————————————   ———————————————   ———————————————
Client Signature   Date   Therapist Signature   Date

Figure 3.2   *(Continued)*

TESTING HYPOTHESES: IMPLEMENTING TREATMENT PLAN

After conducting observations through assessment and developing hypotheses about treatment, the next phase in behavioral case conceptualization is testing the hypotheses by implementing the treatment plan. Ideally, the treatment plan is implemented as originally developed and the client makes progress in treatment. However, given that clients and their surrounding context are changing throughout the treatment, it is likely that therapists will need to be flexible in their implementation based on changing client needs. One criticism of cognitive-behavioral and behavior interventions is the level of rigidity in which they are implemented (Feeny, Hembree, & Zoellner, 2003; Strupp & Anderson, 1997); the protocols that have been developed allow for creativity and an individualistic application based on each client (Kendall et al., 1998; Otto, 2000). Additionally, if treatment progress is not being made, it is imperative that therapists return to the observation phase to develop new hypotheses and revise the original treatment plan. A brief description of the implementation phase of treatment for Ms. X follows:

Sessions 1–5

- *Education:* Throughout the course of treatment, Ms. X was educated about physiology of anxiety, role of escape and avoidance in maintaining anxiety, and components of social anxiety. Additionally, he learned about the rationale behind cognitive restructuring and exposure as primary treatment interventions.

- *Cognitive restructuring:* Ms. X learned to identify and challenge beliefs that occurred preceding, during, and after social situations. Beliefs about others ("They think I'm stupid") and herself ("I should never be nervous") were challenged and more realistic beliefs were developed. Ms. X completed automatic thought records in and out of session.
- *Identification of safety behaviors:* Ms. X identified which behaviors she does in social situations in an effort to reduce the likelihood of embarrassment. These behaviors include smiling, laughing excessively, and not initiating conversation. Once identified, Ms. X was instructed to decrease the use of these behaviors, especially during exposure.

Session 6–12

- *Constructed and implemented in vivo exposure hierarchy:* Ms. X developed a hierarchy of anxiety-provoking social situations. The hierarchy ranged from little anxiety (i.e., walking into work in the morning and greeting people) to severe anxiety (i.e., giving a presentation to strangers and her boss). After developing the hierarchy, Ms. X gradually and deliberately exposed herself to these situations. Ms. X repeatedly exposed herself to the situation until she did not experience anxiety greater than a 3 on SUDS scale before moving onto the next level in the hierarchy.
- *Social skills training:* The therapist and Ms. X conducted role-plays to identify skills deficit areas. The role-plays included public speaking, engaging in small talk, and asking questions. The therapist modeled the skills and then had Ms. X practice them in role with the therapist. These skills were then applied during in vivo exposures.

Session 12–14

- *Behavioral activation and reward planning:* The focus of therapy shifted to reducing depressive symptoms. The intervention included scheduling pleasurable activities, such as spending time with her children, and mastery activities, such as organizing her desk. To ensure the activities were reinforced, the therapist and Ms. X developed rewards to enjoy after completing activities. The therapist also had Ms. X schedule social activities, as they would serve as an anxiety exposure and behavioral activation.
- Reviewed progress based on measure collected throughout treatment to determine if all treatment goals had been met.

OBSERVING TREATMENT OUTCOME

After implementing the treatment plan, the next step is to determine whether significant progress was made and whether the hypotheses about treatment were supported. Assessment measures are crucial at this step because they provide objective criteria for treatment progress. Although the measures should be discussed regularly, a more complete discussion should occur when the original treatment plan has been completed. If possible, the therapist can present a visual representation of symptoms to the client to facilitate discussion about progress. Although standardized measures are

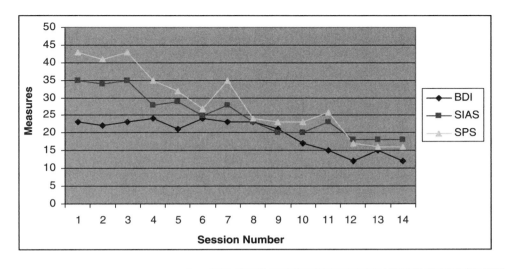

Figure 3.3 Ms. X's treatment progress on the BDI-II, SIAS, and SPS.

important progress indicators, clients need to also feel that significant improvement has been made. See Figure 3.3 for an example of Ms. X's treatment progress.

As can be seen, Ms. X's assessment measures appear to signify reduction in both anxiety and depression. The social anxiety measures at intake were clinically elevated concerning social interactions (SIAS = 45) and (SPS = 50). At Session 14, her SIAS score was 18 and her SPS score was 16, which are both within the nonclinical range of functioning. Her BDI-II score at intake was 23; her BDI-II score at Session 14 was 12, which is within the minimal range of depression.

In addition to standardized measures of change, ideographic measures should be addressed. At intake, Ms. X stated that her average anxiety in social situations was an 8 and her average daily depression was a 6. At session 14, Ms. X stated that her average anxiety reduced to a 3 and her depression was a 2. She also reported that she worries about others' perceptions of her about 20% of the time and stated that she gets nervous about 10 minutes before presenting (instead of hours before). She also reported that she is able to engage in social activities for the full time, as she arrives on time and does not leave early. She also reported that she is spending more time playing with her children and is enjoying their time together.

Despite positive changes in both the standardized and ideographic measures, Ms. X reported that she often still feels depressed when thinking about the end of her long-term relationship. She also continued to endorse feelings of worthlessness and loss of interest in pursuing any future romantic relationships. Given her concerns, despite BDI-II scores in the nonclinical range, it was concluded that further examination of the original hypotheses and possible revisions may be needed.

REVISING THE HYPOTHESES

After reviewing the treatment outcomes, it may be necessary to develop more hypotheses to address any treatment goals have not been met. To develop more treatment hypotheses, clinicians may need to return to the observation phase and reassess the original presenting concerns. Hypotheses concerning cause and maintenance factors may be incorrect due to missing information. Alternatively, the treatment plan may need to be revised if goals are too vague or unrealistic. Clients may also express new goals for treatment after completing the original treatment plan. Once new hypotheses are developed, a revised treatment plan is completed according to the previous guidelines. The treatment plan is then implemented and outcomes are reassessed.

For Ms. X, further examination was needed of the original hypotheses regarding cause, maintenance, and treatment. Ms. X reported several cognitive distortions when discussing the relationship, such as "It was all my fault the relationship ended," "I am worthless without a relationship," and "I will never be able to find someone else." This suggests that an important antecedent to her depressed mood was self-depreciating thoughts. Given this additional information, new hypotheses regarding her depression were developed:

- Ms. X depression is exacerbated and maintained by thoughts of worthlessness and guilt concerning the end of her relationship.
- Depression treatment will be more effective if interventions include cognitive restructuring, including challenging her standards, labels, and predictions concerning future relationships.
- Cognitive restructuring is consistent with hypothesized functional relationship, has data to support its effectiveness (Hollon, 2003) and is feasible for the client.

These hypotheses would then be included into a revised treatment plan and implemented.

The results would be reviewed and if Ms. X's depression continued, the plan would be revised.

SUMMARY

Behavioral case conceptualization uses a scientific framework to understand the presenting problem and develop effective treatment interventions. Similar to a scientist, the clinician assesses the client (Observation Phase), develops a treatment plan (Developing Hypotheses Phase), implements the treatment plans (Testing Hypotheses Phase), assesses outcomes (Observing the Outcome Phase), and revises the hypotheses about treatment if needed (Revising Hypotheses Phase). The observation phase includes several different types of assessment, as well as processing of identifying treatment targets and assessing the context in which the behavior occurs. The developing hypotheses phase includes creating hypotheses about cause, maintenance, and treatment, which are used to develop a cohesive treatment plan. The implementation of treatment plans includes appropriately following the treatment plan goals. The assessment phase includes summarizing the treatment progress with both standardized and ideographic measures. The final phase includes revisiting the hypotheses developed in the second phase in an effort to increase the treatment effectiveness. By utilizing this behavioral framework, clinicians can help their clients achieve better mental health in an effective and efficient manner.

REFERENCES

Addis, M. E., Hatgis, C., Cardemil, E., Jacob, K., Krasnow, A. D., & Mansfield, A. (2006). Effectiveness of cognitive-behavioral treatment for panic disorder versus treatment as usual in a managed care setting: Two-year follow-up. *Journal of Consulting and Clinical Psychology, 74,* 377–385.

Addis, M. E., Hatgis, C., Krasnow, A. D., Jacob, K., Bourne, L., & Mansfield, A. (2004). Effectiveness of cognitive-behavioral treatment for panic disorder versus treatment as usual in a managed care setting. *Journal of Consulting and Clinical Psychology, 72,* 625–635.

American Psychiatric Association. (2000). *Diagnostic and statistical manual of mental disorders* (4th ed., text rev.). Washington, DC: Author.

Antonuccio, D. L., Thomas, M., & Dutton, W. G. (1997). A cost-effectiveness analysis of cognitive behavior therapy and fluoxetine (prozac) in the treatment of depression. *Behavior Therapy, 28*(2), 187–210.

Barlow, D. H. (1998). *Anxiety and its disorders: The nature and treatment of anxiety and panic.* New York: Guilford Press.

Beck, A. T., Rush, A. J., Shaw, B. F., & Emery, G. (1979). *Cognitive therapy of depression.* New York: Guilford Press.

Beck, A. T., & Steer, R. A. (1993). *Beck Anxiety Inventory Manual.* San Antonio, TX: Psychological Corporation.

Beck, A. T., Steer, R. A., & Brown, G. K. (1996). *Beck-Depression Inventory* (2nd ed.). San Antonio, TX: Psychological Corporation.

Booth, P. G., Dale, B., & Ansari, J. (1984) Problem drinkers' goal choice and treatment outcome: A preliminary study. *Addictive Behaviors, 9,* 357–364.

Brady, K. (2002). Comorbidity of substance use disorders and Axis I psychiatric disorders. *Medscape Psychiatry, 7*(1), 10–16.

Butler, A. C., Chapman, J. E., Forman, E. M., & Beck, A. T. (2006). The empirical status of cognitive-behavioral therapy: A review of meta-analyses. *Clinical Psychology Review, 26,* 17–31.

Clark, D. M. (2001). A cognitive perspective on social phobia. In R. Crozier & L. E. Alden (Eds.), *International handbook of social anxiety* (pp. 405–430). Chichester, England: Wiley.

Cormier, S., & Cormier, B. (1998). *Interviewing strategies for helpers: Fundamental skills and cognitive behavioral interventions.* Pacific Grove, CA: Brooks/Cole.

Derogatis, L. R. (1993). *Brief symptom inventory: Administration, scoring, and procedures manual.* Minneapolis, MN: National Computer Systems.

DiNardo, P. A., Brown, T. A., & Barlow, D. H. (1994). *Anxiety disorders interview schedule for DSM-IV: Clinicians manual.* Albany, NY: Graywind Publications.

Division 12 Task Force. (1995). Training in and dissemination of empirically validated psychological treatments: Report and recommendations. *Clinical Psychologist, 48,* 3–23.

Dozois, D. J. A., Westra, H. A., Collins, K. A., Fung, T. S., & Garry, J. K. F. (2004). Stages of change in anxiety: Psychometric properties of the University of Rhode Island Change Assessment (URICA) scale. *Behavior Research and Therapy, 42,* 711–729.

Feeny, N. C., Hembree, E. A., & Zoellner, L. A. (2003). Myths regarding exposure therapy for PTSD. *Cognitive and Behavioral Practice, 10,* 85–90.

First, M. B., Spitzer, R. L., Gibbon, M., & Williams, J. B. W. (1996). *Structured Clinical Interview for DSM-IV Axis I Disorders, Clinician Version* (SCID-CV). Washington, DC: American Psychiatric Press.

First, M. B., Spitzer, R. L., Gibbon, M., & Williams, J. B. W. (1997). *Users guide for Structured Clinical Interview for DSM-IV Axis I Disorders, Clinical Version.* Washington, DC: American Psychiatric Press.

Follette, W. C., & Houts, A. C. (1996). Models of scientific progress and the role of theory in taxonomy development: A case study of the DSM. *Journal of Consulting and Clinical Psychology, 64*(6), 1120–1132.

Folstein, M. F., Folstein, S. E., & McHugh, P. R. (1975). "Mini-mental-state": A practical method for grading the cognitive state of patients for the clinician. *Journal of Psychiatric Research, 12,* 189–198.

Fyer, A. J., Mannuzza, S., Chapman, T. F., Liebowitz, M. R., & Klein, D. F. (1993). A direct interview family study of social phobia. *Archives of General Psychiatry, 50,* 286–293.

Hays, P. A. (2001). *Addressing cultural complexities in practice: A framework for clinicians and counselors.* Washington, DC: American Psychological Association Books.

Heimberg, R. G., & Juster, H. R. (1995). Cognitive-behavioral treatments: Literature review. In R. G. Heimberg, M. R. Liebowitz, D. A. Hope, & F. R. Schneier (Eds.), *Social phobia: Diagnosis, assessment, and treatment* (pp. 261–309). New York: Guilford Press.

Hollon, S. D. (2003). Does cognitive therapy have an enduring effect? *Cognitive Therapy and Research, 27*(1), 71–75.

Horowitz, M., Wilner, N. J., & Alvarez, W. (1979). Impact of events scale: A measure of subjective stress. *Psychosomatic Medicine, 41,* 209–218.

Hoyt, M. F. (1995). *Brief therapy and managed care: Readings for contemporary practice.* San Francisco: Jossey-Bass.

James, L. D., Thorn, B. E., & Williams, D. A. (1993). Goal specification in cognitive-behavioral therapy for chronic headache pain. *Behavior Therapy, 24,* 305–320.

Jarrett, R. B. (1995). Comparing and combining short-term psychotherapy and pharmacotherapy for depression. In E. E. Beckham & W. R. Leber (Eds.), *Handbook of depression* (2nd ed.). New York: Guilford Press.

Kendall, P. C., Chu, B., Gifford, A., Hayes, C., & Nauta, M. (1998). Breathing life into a manual: Flexibility and creativity with manual-based treatment. *Cognitive and Behavioral Practice, 5,* 177–198.

Kendler, K. S., Neale, M. C., Kesslar, R. C., Heath, A. C., & Eaves, L. J. (1992). The genetic epidemiology of phobias in women: The interrelations of agoraphobia, social phobia, situational phobia, and simple phobia. *Archives of General Psychiatry, 49,* 273–281.

Lambert, M. J. (1992). Implications of outcome research for psychotherapy integration. In J. C. Norcross & M. R. Goldfield (Eds.), *Handbooks of psychotherapy integration* (pp. 94–129). New York: Basic Books.

Lambert, M. J., Okiishi, J. C., Finch, A. E., & Johnson, L. D. (1998). Outcome assessment: From conceptualization to implementation. *Professional Psychology: Research and Practice, 29,* 63–70.

Linehan, M. (1993). *Cognitive-behavioral treatment of borderline personality disorder.* New York: Guilford Press.

Locke, E. A., & Latham, G. P. (1990). *A theory of goal setting and task performance.* Englewood Cliffs, NJ: Prentice Hall.

Mattick, R. P., & Clarke, J. C. (1998). Development and validation of measures of social phobia scrutiny fear and social interaction anxiety. *Behavior Research and Therapy, 36,* 455–470.

Miller, P. R., Dasher, R., Collins, R., Griffiths, P., & Brown, F. (2001). Inpatient diagnostic assessments: Pt. 1. Accuracy of structured versus unstructured interviews. *Psychiatric Research, 105*(3), 255–264.

Morrison, J. (1995a). *DSM-IV made easy: The clinician's guide to diagnosis.* New York: Guilford Press.

Morrison, J. (1995b). *The first interview: Revised for DSM-IV.* New York: Guilford Press.

Otto, M. W. (2000). Stories and metaphors in cognitive-behavior therapy. *Cognitive and Behavioral Practice, 7,* 166–172.

Parker, G., & Hadzi-Pavlovic, D. (2004). Is the female preponderance in major depression secondary to a gender difference in specific anxiety disorders? *Psychological Medicine, 34,* 461–470.

Rapee, R. M. (1995). Descriptive psychopathology of social phobia. In R. G. Heimberg, M. R. Liebowitz, D. A. Hope, & F. R. Schneier (Eds.), *Social phobia: Diagnosis, assessment, and treatment* (pp. 41–66). New York: Guilford Press.

Reich, J., & Yates, W. (1988). Family history of psychiatric disorders in social phobia. *Comprehensive Psychiatry, 29,* 72–75.

Rounsaville, B. J., Weissman, M. M., Prusoff, B. A., & Herceg-Baron, R. L. (1979). Marital disputes and treatment outcome in depressed women. *Comprehensive Psychiatry, 20,* 483–490.

Schmidt, N. B., Joiner, T. E., Jr., Staab, J. P., & Williams, F. M. (2003). Health perceptions and anxiety sensitivity in patients with panic disorder. *Journal of Psychopathology and Behavioral Assessment, 25,* 139–145.

Sperry, L. (2005). Case conceptualizations: The missing link between theory and practice. *Family Journal: Counseling and Therapy for Couples and Families, 13*(1), 71–76.

Stricker, G., & Trierweiler, S. J. (1995). The local clinical scientist: A bridge between science and practice. *American Psychologist, 50*(12), 995–1002.

Strupp, H. H., & Anderson, T. (1997). On the limitations of therapy manuals. *Clinical Psychology: Science and Practice, 4,* 76–82.

Taylor, S. (1996). Meta-analysis of cognitive-behavioral treatments for social phobia. *Journal of Behavior Therapy and Experimental Psychiatry, 27*(1), 1–9.

Tracey, T. J., & Kokotovic, A. M. (1989). Working alliance in the early phase of counseling. *Journal of Counseling Psychology, 37,* 16–21.

Tryon, G. S., & Winograd, G. (2001). Goal consensus and collaboration. *Psychotherapy, 38,* 385–389.

Turner, S. M., Beidel, D. C., Cooley, M. R., Woody, S. R., & Messer, S. C. (1994). A multicomponent behavioral treatment for social phobia: Social effectiveness training. *Behavior Research and Therapy, 32*(4), 381–390.

Wolpe, J. (1958). *Psychotherapy by reciprocal inhibition.* Stanford, CA: Stanford University Press.

CHAPTER 4

Overview of Behavioral Treatment with Adults

WILLIAM H. O'BRIEN AND HEATHER SCHWETSCHENAU

Behavior therapy is a field of research and clinical practice that emerged in the 1950s and grew into a well-supported approach to the treatment of human psychopathology (cf. Dobson, 2000; Leichsenring, Hiller, Weissberg, & Leibing, 2006; Nathan & Gorman, 1998, 2002). The unique characteristics of behavioral therapy with adults are made more distinct when they are contrasted with alternative psychotherapy approaches. The sharpest contrasts tend to be yielded when psychoanalytic and/or psychodynamic approaches are compared to behavioral approaches. A brief case example provides insight into some of the more fundamental differences. It also serves as an example of why many behavior therapists are so firmly committed to this most important field of inquiry and intervention.

CASE DESCRIPTION

The case we examine involves a young woman who was admitted to a psychiatric unit of a major university-affiliated medical center for chronic diabetes noncompliance. The magnitude and chronicity of her noncompliance had led to a number of medical complications and her health was becoming increasingly fragile. After admission, the patient Sarah was referred for psychological evaluation and treatment. Because the hospital staff was comprised of two groups of psychologists (the behavior therapy clinic psychologists and the psychiatry service psychologists) who had very different clinical approaches (the former were behaviorally oriented and the latter endorsed a traditional psychoanalytic orientation), it was possible to compare and contrast these two models of case conceptualization and treatment.

The psychoanalytic psychologists were the primary care providers in this instance because of staffing patterns at the hospital (i.e., the behavior therapy psychologists tended to provide services on the medical units of the hospital, whereas the psychoanalytic staff provided service in the psychiatric unit). After conducting a diagnostic assessment (unstructured interview, Rorschach test, Draw-a-Person Test,

Thematic Apperception Test), a psychoanalytic case conceptualization was developed. In essence, it was postulated that Sarah's noncompliance arose from unconscious conflicts that were triggered by insulin injections. Drawing from psychoanalytic theory, it was argued that the unconscious conflicts were sexual in nature and that the injection of insulin was symbolically experienced as penile insertion and ejaculation from Sarah's father. This hypothesis was supported by Sarah's report of significant conflict with her father over her noncompliance and her extreme anxiety about "allowing herself to be penetrated" by the syringe. It was further argued that association between these sexual fantasies and insulin injection were formed because Sarah's diabetes had developed during a critical stage of psychosexual development (her early childhood) where issues related to sexualized father-daughter fantasies were prominent.

Nondirective, transference-focused therapy was recommended for Sarah. The principal goal of therapy was to provide a supportive environment where Sarah could examine the underlying reasons for her noncompliance and gain better control of it through enhanced insight. Sarah was provided with psychoanalytically oriented therapy on a daily basis throughout her inpatient stay (approximately 2 weeks). At discharge, she reported feeling more in control of her anxiety and that she had gained a greater willingness to endure insulin injections. No quantitative measures of outcome were obtained.

CASE CONCEPTUALIZATION

The behavior therapy psychologists discussed the case conceptualization and offered an alternative viewpoint during staff meetings. They agreed that anxiety was a prominent aspect of Sarah's difficulties. They further agreed that insulin injections appeared to trigger these feelings of intense anxiety. From a behavioral perspective, however, the cause of anxiety and subsequent treatment recommendations diverged substantially from psychoanalytic conceptions. The behavioral position was that Sarah was experiencing anxiety with insulin injections because of classically conditioned fear responses and negatively reinforced avoidance behaviors. During the assessment interview, Sarah had reported that when she attempted to inject herself with insulin, she would experience very vivid images of the insulin circulating in her veins and an image of her pancreas "rotting" inside of her abdomen. She could not remember when the images first appeared, but that they were disgusting and very frightening. Thus, the syringe was functioning as a conditioned stimulus for a conditioned fear response. By avoiding the injection and distracting herself with other activities and/or thoughts, she was able temporarily to reduce her anxiety. These avoidance behaviors were negatively reinforced through anxiety reduction.

BEHAVIORAL TREATMENT

Treatment recommendations from a behavioral position were clear: (a) provide Sarah with a learning-based explanation for how and why her anxiety was triggered by injections from a behavioral perspective, (b) develop with Sarah strategies designed to identify and challenge disturbing cognitions, (c) provide Sarah with graded exposure to insulin injections using a collaboratively developed hierarchy in the context of a supportive therapeutic relationship, and (d) collect measures of fear and avoidance throughout the intervention to gauge progress.

Discussions between the psychoanalytic and behavioral psychologists were typical of the historical, and continuing, divergence between the two approaches. The behavioral psychologists tended to be very skeptical of the fanciful and seemingly absurd narrative linking injections to sexualized striving for the father. They also questioned efficacy of the various assessment and treatment procedures for a person with this type of presenting problem. Alternatively, the psychoanalytic psychologists suggested that the behavioral conceptualization and treatment recommendations were superficial, simplistic, mechanistic, and likely to cause symptom substitution (i.e., the injection fear might subside, but another symptom representing the unaltered unconscious conflict would emerge).

At the end of the day, a truce was drawn because the behavioral psychologists were able to reinterpret the process and outcome of the psychoanalytic psychotherapy. Specifically, they speculated that the nondirective and supportive therapy may be construed as a form of imaginal exposure therapy. That is, Sarah was systematically prompted by the nondirective therapist to explore the disturbing images and feelings in a supportive environment. Over time, her fear responses subsided as a function of experimental extinction and possible reciprocal inhibition (i.e., pairing the exploration of disturbing thoughts with supportive and reassuring therapist behavior). *Pragmatic, logical, scientific, creative,* and *enthusiastic* are the terms that come to mind when we think of this case example and behavior therapy in general. Although it may be interesting and even fun to ponder the deep and hidden meanings of behavior, our pragmatic focus constrains fanciful analyses in favor of practical and logical exploration of processes and treatments that are based on reasonable science. Creativity and enthusiasm are two additional terms that many may not immediately associate with behavior therapy, yet they are clearly a hallmark of the field. Developing even straightforward interventions, such as a graded exposure hierarchy, requires significant creativity and careful exploration of myriad factors that comprise a client's construction of fear. In addition, conducting behavior therapy also requires constant and creative modification of interventions and interpersonal interactions with the client to remain focused on central concerns. Finally, behavior therapists are a spirited and enthusiastic collection of researchers and clinicians who are willing to leave the artificial and constraining influence of a 50-minute psychotherapy session in an outpatient office and accompany clients to settings where their lives actually occur.

The primary goal of this chapter is to provide a sense of the essential characteristics of behavior therapy and an idea of how it has expanded across the past 50 years. To achieve this, we review the theoretical and epistemological characteristics of behavior therapy. We then present a review of how assessment data is collected and integrated for the purposes of treatment design. Following this, we examine how the field has expanded and evolved to reach its current status as a worldwide approach that has garnered widespread research support. Finally, we present thoughts about the current status and future directions of behavior therapy.

THEORETICAL AND EPISTEMOLOGICAL CHARACTERISTICS OF BEHAVIOR THERAPY

Behavior therapy has several fundamental assumptions that differentiate it from other approaches. The first and most important characteristic is *functional contextualism* (Hayes, 2004; Haynes & O'Brien, 2000). This assumption posits that target behaviors (i.e., cognitive, affective, physiological, and overt-motor responses that are the focus of treatment) are not randomly emitted, but occur as a function of complex causal influences that arise from intrapersonal events (e.g., internal causal factors such as physiological states, cognitive experiences, learning history), interpersonal events (e.g., social relationships), and nonsocial environmental events (e.g., settings, time of day).

Functional contextualism also supports the belief that the fundamental unit of analysis in behavior therapy is the *relationship* between target behaviors and the contexts in which they occur (Fletcher & Hayes, 2005). As a result, target behaviors cannot be meaningfully isolated and evaluated for form and content. Instead, the behavior therapist focuses on the function of target behaviors—how and why they occur within specific and well-defined environmental, social, and intraindividual contexts.

Empiricism is a second characteristic associated with behavior therapy and the many techniques subsumed within it. The empirical assumption guides the therapist to develop careful operational definitions of target behaviors and contextual factors in assessment and treatment design. Further, the preferred type of operational definition requires minimal inference and permits the therapist to obtain quantitative measurement of target behaviors, contextual variables, and the relationships among them. The empirical assumption also supports the strong allegiance to using objective data and quantitative methods (as opposed to intuition) to evaluate treatment process and outcome. Finally, the empirical assumption supports use of hypothetico-deductive methods in both research and clinical applications—in essence, the scientist-practitioner approach to clinical work (O'Brien, Kaplar, & McGrath, 2004; G. S. Watson & Gross, 1999).

A third characteristic of behavioral approaches is the use of *learning theories* as a basis for understanding how and why target behaviors are acquired, maintained, and changed (Guevremont & Spiegler, 2002; G. S. Watson & Gross, 1999). Here, the therapist draws from the very well-established corpora of theory and research in classical conditioning, operant conditioning, social learning theory, and/or relational frame theory to generate plausible hypotheses about the function of target behaviors. In addition, the therapist develops intervention strategies and understands the mechanism through which the strategies operate, using learning theories as a guide.

An *idiographic emphasis* is a fourth characteristic of behavior therapy. Because it is believed that behavior arises as a function of unique interactions among target behaviors and contextual events, it is also believed that optimal understanding results when assessment, case conceptualization, and treatments are designed at the individual level (Haynes & O'Brien, 2000). In addition, because empirical methods are the preferred mode for evaluating process and outcomes, case conceptualizations and treatment evaluations will tend to rely on methodological and statistical procedures that permit plausible causal inference using data collected from an individual client (O'Brien et al., 2004).

The fifth characteristic of behavior therapy is what we term *behavioral plasticity* (cf. O'Brien & Haynes, 1993). This assumption supports the belief that virtually any target behavior can be changed through the careful analysis of its function and the application of learning principles in an intervention. Therefore, for every target behavior encountered, there may be a unique combination of contextual variables that can be used to produce a significant and positive change.

Finally, behavioral therapies endorse a *multivariate* assumption that proposes that target behaviors are comprised of many components. Each target behavior is related to many other behaviors. These correlated behaviors may be either adaptive or problematic. It is further assumed that most behaviors are controlled by more than one contextual factor (Hayes, 2004).

In summary, behavior therapy carries with it several characteristics about why target behaviors occur, the favored manner for evaluating data, the preferred level of analysis, the possibility for change, and an assumption of multideterminism. At the operational level, these assumptions are evidenced in the use of specific assessment and therapy procedures that are designed to yield data from carefully defined and well-validated measures of target behaviors and causal events for an individual client.

FUNCTIONAL ANALYSIS: A TEMPLATE FOR TREATMENT DESIGN

The aforementioned assumptions are embedded in strategies used to gather information about the form and function of behavior. In turn, this information is used to conceptualize client difficulties, design interventions, and evaluate outcomes. This process of gathering and integrating information within the behavioral paradigm is often referred to as a *functional analysis* (Haynes & O'Brien, 1990, 2000) that integrates two behavioral assessment outcomes: (1) target behavior description and (2) a model of relationships between target behaviors and controlling contextual factors. The strategies used to construct a functional analysis are described in the following sections.

PROBLEM BEHAVIOR DESCRIPTION

In line with the empirical assumption, an important aspect of behavioral assessment and consequent functional analysis is to generate precise and quantifiable definitions of target behaviors. This is a challenging task because target behaviors can be described in an infinite number of ways. For most clinical applications, however, modes and parameters of problem behaviors are of primary interest. The term *mode* refers to four interrelated sets of target behaviors: (1) cognitive responses, (2) affective responses, (3) physiological responses, and (4) overt-motor responses. The term *parameter* refers to the dimensions of a target behavior that are emphasized in assessment, such as intensity, frequency, latency, and duration.

To clarify how target behavior descriptions are generated, consider how an experience such as evaluation anxiety can be detailed. In terms of mode, anxiety can be defined in terms of cognitions (e.g., a belief in the possibility that catastrophic outcomes may occur with evaluation, worry, concentration difficulties), affective responses (e.g., a perception of anxious arousal), physiological responses (e.g., increased heart rate, increased blood pressure, sympathetic nervous system activation), and overt-motor responses (e.g., avoidance, escape). Individual differences in target behavior modes are commonly encountered in behavior therapy. Some clients with evaluation anxiety report severe physical symptoms of anxiety but limited cognitive experiences and behavioral expression of the anxiety. Other clients with evaluation anxiety may experience intense thoughts about catastrophic outcomes and severe escape and avoidance behavior.

Each of the aforementioned modes of problem behavior can also be evaluated in terms of intensity (e.g., how strongly a client believes in the possibility of catastrophic outcomes), frequency (e.g., how often anxious arousal occurs), and duration (e.g., how long anxious arousal lasts). Again, individual differences are frequently observed.

Some clients experience infrequent but intense and debilitating bouts of evaluation anxiety of short duration, whereas others experience frequent bouts of evaluation anxiety that are less intense and longer in duration.

IDENTIFYING AND EVALUATING RELATIONSHIPS BETWEEN TARGET BEHAVIORS AND CONTROLLING CONTEXTUAL FACTORS

After generating operational definitions of target behaviors, the behavior therapist focuses on identification of controlling contextual factors. Two major types of causes are often explored: (1) historical events that exert an impact on the problem behavior (e.g., learning history) and (2) contemporary events that are operating in the client's current environment. These controlling contextual factors often fall into three main categories of variables: (1) social/interpersonal factors (e.g., interactions with others), (2) nonsocial environmental factors (e.g., settings, time of day), and (3) intrapersonal factors (e.g., cognitive processes and structures, physiological capacities; O'Brien & Haynes, 1993).

After controlling contextual factors have been identified, the behavior therapist will attempt to characterize the relationships that exist among: (a) target behaviors, (b) contextual factors, and (c) contextual factors and target behaviors. Several behavioral assessment methods (e.g., interviewing, self-monitoring, systematic observation, experimentation) and data analytic techniques (e.g., contingency table construction, Bayesian analyses, graphing, single subject designs) can be used to help behavior therapists identify and evaluate potential relationships among problem behaviors and causes. Each of these methods differs with respect to cost efficiency, behavior mode for which they are best suited, and sources of error (for a more complete discussion of these factors in assessment, see Haynes & O'Brien, 2000).

We recommend that behavior therapists generate informal causal models, labeled functional analytic causal models (FACM), to depict functional analyses. An FACM is a diagram that graphically illustrates the important, controllable, and contemporary relationships among target behaviors and controlling contextual factors for an individual client. We find them to be useful in several ways. First, FACMs systematize the clinical decision-making process and thereby encourage the therapist to consider the complexity of the case and the nature of relationships that exist among problem behaviors and causes. Second, they encourage greater integration of assessment data with treatment design. Third, FACMs provide an easily interpretable and parsimonious summarization of a functional analysis. Finally, they provide assistance with the design of idiographic and behaviorally based interventions that can be designed.

An example of an FACM for a client presenting with "white coat hypertension" is presented in Figure 4.1. This client, a young man in excellent physical condition and with no known medical illnesses, presented to our behavioral medicine clinic after he repeatedly failed a physical for entry into a pilot training program for a branch of the armed services. Although his blood pressure was within normal limits when he tested it at home and in our laboratory, it would rise to hypertensive levels when he was examined by armed forces physicians.

We conducted a behavioral assessment of this young man using interviewing, self-report inventory administration (e.g., stress inventories, anxiety inventories, anger inventories), self-monitoring of blood pressure, and observation of cardiovascular responses under varied conditions (e.g., resting baseline, cognitive stressor, a simulated physical with a confederate acting as an armed forces physician).

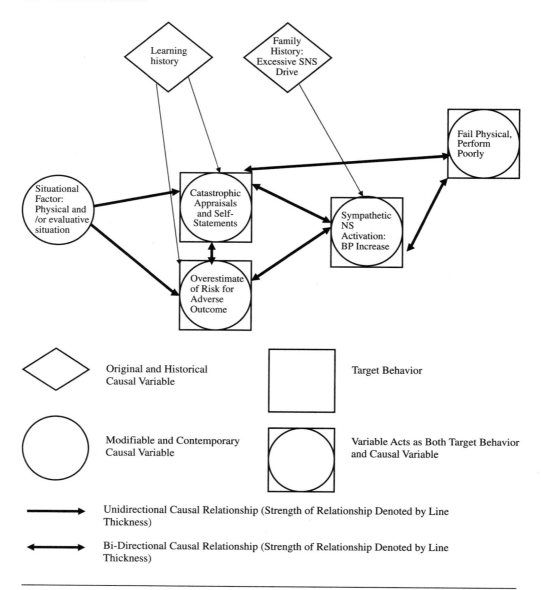

Figure 4.1   Functional analytic causal model of a client with white coat hypertension.

The FACM, which synthesized our assessment data, hypothesizes that on exposure to evaluative situations (e.g., taking a physical) the client was apt to generate catastrophic appraisals about the possible consequences of failure (e.g., loss of meaning and purpose as a human being, being a failure). These cognitive appraisals triggered psychophysiological responses associated with sympathetic nervous system activation (increased cardiovascular activation, peripheral vasoconstriction) that were principally manifested in elevated blood pressure. In addition, he had a positive family history for essential hypertension that likely contributed to increased cardiovascular reactivity to stress. In an effort to control these appraisals and physiological responses, the client would tend to escape or avoid evaluative situations whenever possible. In turn, he had limited opportunities to acquire, practice, and apply self-regulation skills in high-stakes evaluative situations. In addition, when escape was not possible (e.g., a medical exam), he experienced ever-increasing levels of anxious apprehension. When failure or less-than-hoped-for performance in evaluative situations occurred, the strength of his belief in the threatening aspects of evaluative situations was reinforced.

The treatment for this client was based on the FACM and familiarity with the behavioral literature regarding techniques that can be used to modify problematic cognitive experiences, excessive cardiovascular reactivity, and anxiety-based avoidance behaviors. Daily monitoring of blood pressure and perceived stress were recommended to help the client gain increased awareness of contextual factors leading to elevated blood pressure in the natural environment. Biofeedback and relaxation training were provided to help the client gain increased control of his physiological reactivity. Self-instructional training was recommended to help the client learn to stop catastrophic thinking and reappraise evaluative situations as more benign. Finally, graded exposure was used to help the client learn to successfully manage blood pressure examination procedures (i.e., experience without excessive blood pressure reactivity) that were contrived to simulate real-world blood pressure measurements in an armed services physical.

The multicomponent treatment developed and provided for this client used treatment procedures that were described in behavioral journals and books. They were also disseminated in courses, workshops, and seminars (many of which were presented at the annual convention of the Association for the Advancement of Behavior Therapy, now known as the Association for the Advancement of Cognitive Behavioral Therapy). These varied techniques were developed and tested over 50 years of behavior therapy. An examination of the growth and development of behavior therapy and associated intervention techniques follows.

THREE WAVES OF BEHAVIOR THERAPY

It is currently a very exciting time in the evolution of behavior therapy. As the field has expanded and embraced new models of understanding and associated intervention techniques, there has been a growing debate about the nature of change and mechanisms underlying change in some of the oldest and most well-established interventions. To characterize these changes, it can be instructive to organize the field of behavior therapy into three *waves* of evolution (Hayes, 2004). The first wave is represented by development and application of interventions based on classical conditioning and operant conditioning principles. This wave also corresponds to the beginning years of behavior therapy. The second wave can be thought of as a phase where cognitive variables and interventions targeting cognitive variables were incorporated into behavior therapy. The third wave of behavior therapy can be thought of as the recent expansion into areas of human experience that have not been traditionally associated with behavior therapy (e.g., conceptualization of self, life meaning and purpose, spirituality), use of interventions that take a significantly different approach to behavior change (e.g., acceptance, "transference" interpretations, mindfulness), and curiously a theoretical and philosophical stance that represents a recommitment to the most fundamental principles of radical behaviorism.

In the following sections, we present the basic principles contained in each wave of behavior therapy. Following this, we describe how these principles are used to account for the development of problematic behavior. We then summarize some of the most commonly used interventions that arise from these principles.

WAVE 1: APPLICATIONS OF CONDITIONING TO THE ANALYSIS AND TREATMENT OF TARGET BEHAVIORS

The first wave of behavior therapy emerged out of theoretical developments and research findings in classical and operant conditioning. The first wave of behavior therapy also represented a rejection of psychoanalytic approaches that were thought of as overly elaborate (if not absurd), excessively pessimistic, untestable, and ineffective (e.g., Hayes, 2004; Wolpe, 1963, 1971). It was not easy for the pioneers of behavior therapy to lay the foundations of our field. As noted by Guevremont and Spiegler (1998), "... facing skepticism from traditional professionals, having to work under adverse conditions, and nonetheless demonstrating effectiveness was a common experience for early behavior therapist through at least the mid-1970s" (p. 19). At the time, psychoanalytic writers cautioned that approaches based on learning theory were simplistic, mechanistic, cold-hearted, and potentially damaging to client well-being. Additionally, it was argued that the use of learning-based approaches would lead to temporary change in behavior but not to structural and lasting changes that were needed for true client improvement (Weitzman, 1969). Despite the presence of such objections, early behavior therapy pioneers pressed forward with research investigating how classical conditioning and operant conditioning principles could be used to account for development and treatment of behavioral disorders.

One of the primary Wave 1 learning approaches was classical conditioning and its associated principles. Drawing from the research conducted by experimental works of classical conditioning researchers (e.g., Pavlov, 1941; Skinner, 1938; J. B. Watson & Rayner, 1920), the first wave of behavior therapists conducted basic research focused on how classical conditioning principles could account for the acquisition, maintenance, and change in target behaviors (e.g., Mowrer, 1960). An excellent example of this line of research is represented in the work of Joseph Wolpe. Through careful experimentation on animals and humans, Wolpe (1952a, 1952b) demonstrated that neuroses and anxiety related disorders could plausibly arise from classical conditioning processes. After demonstrating that anxiety states and phobic reactions could be induced using classical conditioning, Wolpe then demonstrated that these same responses could be deconditioned using principles of experimental extinction and reciprocal inhibition (Wolpe, 1958; Wolpe & Lazarus, 1966; Wolpe, Salter, & Reyna, 1964). Later called *systematic desensitization*, these procedures were demonstrated to lead to rapid and substantial reductions in anxiety and avoidance behaviors among persons presenting with a wide assortment of fears and phobias (Wolpe, 1997).

Following Wolpe's lead, other researchers demonstrated that classical conditioning can account for the acquisition and/or maintenance of a wide array of problem behaviors and behavioral disorders in adults and children (e.g., Antoni & Roemer, 2003; Craighead & Craighead, 2003; Craske & Hermans, 2006). They also represented a departure from the psychoanalytic perspectives that, at that time, had accumulated scant research support using reasonable standards of scientific scrutiny (cf. Wolpe, 1963, 1971, 1997).

Having established the link between classical conditioning processes and various forms of psychopathology, researchers focused their attention on the use of conditioning principles to modify problem behavior. As noted earlier, one of the most familiar procedures developed from this framework is systematic desensitization. Wolpe's systematic desensitization procedures received widespread support in clinical and research settings. Further research examined the key components of this therapeutic technique. Modifications and enhancements to the technique were subsequently developed and tested with many target behaviors (see Table 4.1). The general findings from these varied research lines indicates that: (a) exposure to the conditioned stimulus without the presence of the unconditioned stimulus is a critical component of virtually all behavioral treatments for classically conditioned disorders; (b) imaginal exposure yields less powerful effects than in vivo exposure; (c) in some instances, better results are obtained with a graded exposure approach while in other instances massed exposure (sometimes referred to as flooding) promotes more optimal outcomes; and (d) providing relaxation training to promote reciprocal inhibition does not appear to reliably enhance outcomes (Barlow, Pincus, Heinrichs, & Choate, 2003).

The other major learning theory explored during Wave 1 was operant conditioning. Here behavior therapists drew on the works of J. B. Watson (1919), Skinner (1938, 1974), Hull (1952), and many others in an effort to understand the ways that operant conditioning principles (e.g., contingencies of reinforcement and punishment, stimulus generalization, stimulus discrimination, stimulus control, extinction) could account for the acquisition, maintenance, and change in a wide range of target behaviors and disorders that are commonly seen in outpatient and inpatient settings (cf. Antoni, Ledley, & Heimburg, 2006; Tarrier, 2006).

Table 4.1
Therapeutic Techniques Emerging from Wave 1

Intervention Goal	*Intervention Technique*	*Illustrative Articles*
Classical Conditioning		
Reduce symptoms and associated avoidant behavior in presence of distressing stimuli	Systematic desensitization Graded exposure therapy Flooding Implosion therapy	Wolpe (1990); Trull, Nietzel, & Main (1988); Marshall (1985); Keane et al. (1989)
Decrease physiological activation associated with distressing stimuli	Relaxation training	Ost, Jerremalm, & Johansson (1981)
Operant Conditioning		
Increase adaptive behavior/Decrease maladaptive behavior through use of reinforcement and punishment	Token economy Contingency management Shaping Chaining	Ayllon & Azrin (1968); Petry (2000)
Learn to recognize and control physiological responses	Biofeedback	Blanchard, Theobald, Williamson, Silver, & Brown (1978)

Many types of behavioral interventions were developed using operant conditioning principles as the framework (see Table 4.1). These varied interventions and techniques have been shown to produce significant and lasting change in many randomized control outcome trials and single-subject investigations. In essence, the Wave 1 interventions laid the foundations for the entire behavior therapy movement and these procedures continue to form the cornerstone of all behavioral interventions.

WAVE 2: COGNITIVE EXPANSION

As noted by Hayes (2004), the second wave of behavior therapy emerged out of a growing recognition that there were important aspects of human experience such as thoughts and felt emotions that seemed to be underemphasized in Wave 1 interventions. It was not the case that these interventions could not accommodate these experiences, rather Wave 1 behavior therapists tended to eschew using unobservable intrapsychic responses as causal variables or mediational variables. Rejection of intrapsychic variables as causes or mediators arose from the Watsonian position that it was critically important for a science of behavior to conform to strict empiricism—the use of direct observation to confirm or disconfirm the plausibility of a hypothesis or a theory. Because thoughts and felt emotions could not be directly observed, they were not be used as explanatory variables. Instead, attention was directed to the observable context in which behavior occurs. Additionally, in line with Skinner's arguments (1974, 1986, 1990), it was argued that thoughts and felt emotions did not account for meaningful or unique amounts of variance in target behavior onset, maintenance, or change. That is, these intrapsychic experiences were thought of as outcome variables that were noncausally correlated with other observable outcome variables such as target behaviors.

Introduction of cognitive variables (i.e., cognitive content such as the specific form of a thought; cognitive process such as mechanisms of perception, storage, and retrieval as well as biases, heuristics, and errors) into behavior therapy was spearheaded by behavior therapy researchers who drew on the works of social learning theorists (e.g., Bandura, 1969, 1977) as well as cognitive psychologists (e.g., Estes, 1975, 1978) and took the position that cognitive variables functioned as important mediators between contextual stimuli and observable responses (e.g., Meichenbaum, 1977). As such, they could account for unique variance in target behavior occurrence and also function as causal variables. A prototypical model of this mediated relationship can be found in Beck's cognitive model of depression (cf. Beck, Rush, Shaw, & Emery, 1979). According to Beck and colleagues, depression arises from negative automatic thoughts about the self (e.g., incapable, helpless), the person's life circumstances (e.g., unfair, uncontrollable), and the person's future (e.g., hopeless). This *cognitive triad* is acquired through adverse life experiences and is maintained by dysfunctional cognitive processes (e.g., overgeneralization, selective abstraction, dichotomous thinking) and structures labeled "schemas." The automatic thoughts, cognitive processes, and schemas are activated by specific contextual events (e.g., daily stressors) and lead to problematic behavioral and emotional responses (e.g., withdrawal, guilt, sadness). Similar mediational models of behavior were offered by Meichenbaum (1977), Mahoney (cf. Mahoney & Kazdin, 1979), Lazarus (1976), and Barlow (1988).

Because cognitive variables are presumed to act as important causal agents in behavioral disorders, treatment techniques were (and continue to be) designed to

Table 4.2
Therapeutic Techniques Emerging from Wave 2

Intervention Goal	Intervention Technique	Illustrative Articles
Identify problematic thoughts	Thought records Labeling cognitive distortions	Beck, Rush, Shaw, & Emery (1979); Barlow & Cerny (1988); Meichenbaum (1985); Fairburn (1985); Salkovskis & Clark (1991); Brown, O'Leary & Barlow (1994); Zinbarg, Craske, & Barlow (1993)
Challenge and eliminate problematic thoughts	Examining past evidence Challenging absolutes Challenging dichotomous thinking Direct disputation Reattribution Decatastrophizing Cognitive restructuring Positive self-statements	
Control recurrent thoughts	Thought stopping Distraction Scheduling time for problematic thoughts	

modify their form and content (see Table 4.2). Generally, the many types of cognitive-behavioral interventions contain four interrelated elements:

1. The therapist focuses on identification of the form, frequency, and intensity of problematic cognitions. For example, in panic disorder, it is thought that several cognitive problems were occurring such as risk overestimation, catastrophic thinking, and attentional narrowing (Barlow, 1988; Barlow, Raffa, & Cohen, 2002). Similarly, as noted earlier, depression was thought to be associated with myriad problematic cognitive processes and structures (Beck et al., 1979).
2. The client is provided with psychoeducation about how cognitive variables were an important aspect of his or her behavioral disorder.
3. The therapist and client develop strategies designed to identify, stop, confront, and/or nullify the problematic cognitive experience. These confrontational strategies typically involve using logic, corrective experiences (e.g., collecting data on your thoughts and affective experiences), and the recitation of alternative adaptive thoughts as a means for changing cognitive content.
4. In line with Wave 1 interventions, the Wave 2 interventions typically contain interventions directed toward inducing behavior change using principles of classical and operant conditioning (e.g., graded exposure, contingency management, skills building).

In summary, Wave 2 behavior therapies added cognitive variables into behavioral conceptualizations of disordered behavior. In addition, techniques were developed that were aimed at helping the client reduce the frequency, intensity, and/or duration of problematic cognitions. Effectiveness of these many cognitive-behavioral interventions is quite well established. For example, nearly all of the empirically supported treatments identified by the American Psychological Association's (APA) Task Force on Treatments That Work are cognitive-behavioral in nature and technique (Nathan & Gorman, 1998, 2002). Further, meta-analyses of the treatment outcome literature indicate that cognitive-behavioral interventions yield large and robust improvements in client functioning across a number of psychiatric conditions and behavioral disorders (e.g., Butler, Chapman, Forman, & Beck, 2006; Lipsey & Wilson, 1990). Finally, the effects of these interventions tend to be larger than those found for alternative therapies (Giles, 1993).

WAVE 3: RECOMMITMENT TO RADICAL BEHAVIORISM AND FORAYS INTO NEW DOMAINS OF HUMAN EXPERIENCE

Waves 1 and 2 of behavior therapy yielded unprecedented gains in the conceptualization and treatment of a vast number of problems encountered by clients in clinical settings. As noted earlier, the success of these interventions is evident in their widespread empirical support and capacity to promote significant and lasting changes in client behavior. However, a growing number of behavioral interventions have been developed that are quite different from their predecessors. Examples of these third-wave interventions include acceptance and commitment therapy (ACT; Hayes, Strosahl, & Wilson, 1999), dialectical behavior therapy (Linehan, 1993, Linehan et al., 2006), functional analytic behavior therapy (Kohlenberg et al., 2004), and mindfulness cognitive therapy (Hayes, Follette, & Linehan, 2004; Segal, Williams, & Teasdale, 2002).

These new therapies diverge from Waves 1 and 2 therapies in terms of targets of treatment, techniques, and theoretical/philosophical stance. In terms of treatment targets, the Wave 3 approaches have expanded into areas of human experience and behavior therapy that were underemphasized in the Wave 2 approaches. Examples of such treatment targets include suffering, acceptance, defusion, values identification, valued living, spirituality, existential meaning, dialectical reasoning, and the client-therapist relationship. Similar to the expansion into cognitive domains that marked the transition from Wave 1 to Wave 2 therapies, the current expansion partially arises from recognition among many researchers and clinicians that these human experiences are critically important in both adaptive and nonadaptive behavioral functioning (Hayes, Luoma, Bond, Masuda, & Lillis, 2006). It should be noted, however, that the Wave 3 approaches are also designed to treat most, if not all, of the target behaviors subsumed within Waves 1 and 2 of behavior therapy.

The techniques deployed in the Wave 3 therapies are unique in many respects (see Table 4.3). This is most evident in techniques targeting cognitive variables. Whereas Wave 2 therapies emphasize *control* of problematic cognitive experiences using various confrontational tactics (e.g., challenging, applying logic, collecting evidence for and against a belief), the Wave 3 therapies (especially ACT) encourage the client to *accept* the presence of problematic cognitive experiences because it is believed that they cannot be eliminated or controlled due to the architecture of consciousness and language (Hayes, 2004). In addition to accepting these problematic cognitive experiences, the client is encouraged to simply *note their occurrence* and work toward *defusing* or

Table 4.3
Therapeutic Techniques Emerging from Wave 3

Intervention Goal	Intervention Technique	Illustrative Articles
Increased acceptance of distressing thoughts	Creative hopelessness Letting go of the struggle as an alternative to control Distress tolerance skills Willingness diary Defusing language through deliteralization Teaching nonjudgmental awareness of self	Eifert & Forsyth (2005); Hayes & Pankey (2002); Hayes, Strosahl, & Wilson (1999); Teasdale et al. (2000); Segal, Williams, & Teasdale (2002); Linehan (1993)
Increased emotional tolerance	Identify and label emotions Identify obstacles to changing emotions Increase mindfulness to current emotions Reduce vulnerability to perceived literal meaning of emotions Distress tolerance skills	
Increased contact with present moment and transcendent self	Meditation Mindfulness training Experiential exercises	
Commitment and action toward a valued life	Defining valued directions Goal setting Using values and goals to guide actions Skills training	

deliteralizing them. Taken together, the goal of this particular aspect of therapy, sometimes referred to as *mindfulness training* (Segal et al., 2002), is to help the client learn to dissociate problematic thoughts and behavioral action—in essence, alter the function of problematic thoughts rather than their content or form (Hayes et al., 1999). The behavior change techniques in Wave 3 therapies also differ. Whereas Wave 2 therapies tend to employ an eliminative approach and focus on *symptom reduction* (e.g., reduce escape and avoidance behavior), Wave 3 therapies employ a constructive approach and focus on assisting the client to actively move toward *valued living*. In essence, the client is encouraged to organize his or her behavior around appetitive goals rather than avoidance of pain and suffering.

Last, the philosophical and theoretical foundations for the Wave 3 therapies diverge from Waves 1 and 2. As noted by Hayes (2004), the Wave 3 therapies are rooted in functional contextualism and constructivism, whereas the Wave 2 approaches tend to be rooted in a mechanistic and positivistic conception of functionalism. The differences between these two philosophical stances are substantial: From a traditional Wave 1or Wave 2 point of view, disordered behavior can be broken down into its constituent parts (e.g., thoughts, feelings, actions) and the relationships among these parts can be analyzed separately. From this perspective, it is logical to take the position, for example, that a dysfunctional thought can *lead to* or *cause* a specific behavioral response. It is also logical to assume that it is critically important to learn to control thoughts in order to control behavior.

A functional-contextual philosophy, however, takes the position that psychological experiences must be thought of as a whole event—target behaviors occur in *relation to*, and *derive meaning from,* ongoing external and internal contexts. Consider the example of walking. In one context, walking functions as a means for a person to solve a problem that has arisen in the external world (e.g., moving from one location to another to obtain food). In another context, walking may function as a means for avoiding or reducing emotional activation (e.g., walking to relieve stress or anger). It is important to note that the form of the behavior is identical in both instances, but the function differs. Further, walking when taken alone and out of context is neither adaptive nor maladaptive. These evaluative labels can only be applied when walking is considered along with the context. The same basic example can be used for cognition. Like walking, any particular cognition is neither adaptive nor maladaptive, right nor wrong, good nor bad. These evaluative labels can only be applied within a particular context.

In Wave 3 behavior therapy, the context of literality or believability (i.e., the context wherein the person believes in the accuracy or truthfulness of the thought) creates the possibility for cognitions to exert harmful effects and guide the person toward potentially problematic behaviors (e.g., avoidance). Thus, if a depressed person were to experience the thought "I am no good" and *believe it to be literally true,* then he or she will experience adverse emotional activation and tend to engage in actions designed to escape from the thoughts and associated feelings (e.g., withdraw). Alternatively, if the same depressed person experienced the same thought within a context of defusion (e.g., where the thought is recognized as a thought and nothing more), then adverse emotional activation and avoidance behaviors are unnecessary. So, in Wave 3 treatments, the thought "I am no good," in and of itself, need not be targeted for intervention. Instead, the function of the thought and the context in which it occurs are the proper targets for treatment using the techniques described earlier and summarized in Table 4.3.

Applying an ACT approach to the client presented earlier in this chapter illustrates the differences between Wave 2 and Wave 3 approaches. As noted earlier, the intervention provided to this client consisted of Wave 2 intervention components. The cognitive therapy component was designed to help him detect and then replace problematic appraisals (e.g., "I am a loser if I fail the physical") with more adaptive appraisals (e.g., "It is important to pass the physical, but failing does not mean that I am a loser"). In addition, relaxation and biofeedback training were provided to assist with the control of excessive physiological reactivity. Finally, exposure therapy was provided to promote extinction of the fear and avoidance responses and also help him learn to use his newly developed coping skills within the context of a simulated evaluative environment. As is clear with each set of techniques, the principal theme of the intervention was to help the client learn to *control* his cognitions for the purposes of *reducing* and/or *eliminating* problematic *symptoms.*

An ACT approach would take a diametrically opposed stance to the management of cognitions, physiological reactivity, and avoidance behaviors. Specifically, the goal of an ACT intervention would be for the client to recognize that catastrophic thoughts are nothing more than thoughts. They are words and/or ideas that stream through consciousness just like any other thought. Thus, they need not be controlled nor taken as the literal truth of his situation (i.e., that failure will lead to a meaningless life). The intervention would emphasize *not controlling* thoughts and instead encourage the client to *defuse* the thoughts by experiencing them from the perspective of an observer or transcendent self. Further, rather than focus on symptom reduction, the goal would be to help the client articulate important values (e.g., a wish to have a meaningful life in which he provides and receives love from family and where his work is important and makes a contribution to society) and then organize therapy (and his daily actions) around the pursuit of those values. Thus, it would be noted that becoming a pilot is only one means to an end and that there are many other aspects of valued living that he can, and should, pursue.

SUMMARY

Several fundamental assumptions (functional contextualism, empiricism, learning theories as guideposts, idiographic emphasis, behavioral plasticity, multivariate determinism) are unique to behavior therapy and guide the assessment and treatment process. Behavioral interventions are often designed using assessment methods that permit the therapist to obtain empirical measures of well-defined target behaviors, contextual factors, and the relationships among them. This detailed, and often complex, assessment information is typically summarized in a functional analysis that, in turn, can be used as a guide for idiographic treatment design.

The behavior therapy techniques that are currently used to modify target behaviors were developed and tested over the past 50 years. In addition, the growth and development of the field can be characterized as three waves, each representing distinct types of advances in theory and technique. Presently, behavior therapy is a vital and constantly evolving approach to the assessment and treatment of virtually all forms of disordered human behavior. The new Wave 3 therapies are creating excitement and debate in the field as we continue to press forward with our attempts to further advance and refine the use of scientifically supported psychotherapy.

REFERENCES

Antoni, M. M., Ledley, D. R., & Heimburg, R. G. (2006). *Improving outcomes and preventing relapse in cognitive-behavioral therapy.* New York: Guilford Press.

Antoni, M. M., & Roemer, L. (2003). Behavior therapy. In A. S. Gurman & S. B. Messer (Eds.), *Essential psychotherapies: Theory and practice* (2nd ed., pp. 182–223). New York: Guilford Press.

Ayllon, T., & Azrin, N. (1968). *The token economy: A motivational system for therapy and rehabilitation.* New York: Appleton-Century-Crofts.

Bandura, A. (1969). *Principles of behavior modification.* New York: Holt, Rinehart and Winston.

Bandura, A. (1977). *Social learning theory.* Oxford, England: Prentice-Hall.

Barlow, D. H. (1988). *Anxiety and its disorders: The nature and treatment of anxiety and panic.* New York: Guilford Press.

Barlow, D. H., & Cerny, J. A. (1988). *Psychological treatment of panic.* New York: Guilford Press.

Barlow, D. H., Pincus, D. B., Heinrichs, N., & Choate, M. L. (2003). Anxiety disorders. In G. Strickler & T. A. Widiger (Eds.), *Handbook of psychology: Vol. 8. Clinical psychology* (pp. 119–148). Hoboken, NJ: Wiley.

Barlow, D. H., Raffa, S. D., & Cohen, E. M. (2002). Psychosocial treatments for panic disorders, phobias, and generalized anxiety disorder. In P. E. Nathan & J. M. Gorman (Eds.), *A guide to treatments that work* (2nd ed., pp. 301–335). New York: Oxford University Press.

Beck, A. T., Rush, A. J., Shaw, B. F., & Emery, G. (1979). *Cognitive therapy of depression.* New York: Guilford Press.

Blanchard, E. B., Theobald, D. E., Williamson, D. A., Silver, B. V., & Brown, D. A. (1978). Temperature biofeedback in the treatment of migraine headaches. *Archives of General Psychiatry, 35,* 581–588.

Brown, T., O'Leary, T., & Barlow, D. H. (1994). Generalized anxiety disorder. In D. H. Barlow (Ed.), *Clinical handbook of psychological disorders* (pp. 154–209). New York: Guilford Press.

Butler, A. C., Chapman, J. E., Forman, E. M., & Beck, A. T. (2006). The empirical status of cognitive-behavioral therapy: A review of meta-analyses. *Clinical Psychology Review, 26,* 17–31.

Craighead, W. E., & Craighead, L. W. (2003). Behavioral and cognitive-behavioral psychotherapy. In G. Strickler & T. A. Widiger (Eds.), *Handbook of psychology: Vol. 8. Clinical psychology* (pp. 279–300). Hoboken, NJ: Wiley.

Craske, M. G., & Hermans, D. (2006). *Fear and learning: From basic process to clinical implications.* Washington, DC: American Psychological Association.

Dobson, K. S. (2000). *Handbook of cognitive-behavioral therapies* (2nd ed.). New York: Guilford Press.

Eifert, G. H., & Forsyth, J. P. (2005). *Acceptance and commitment therapy for anxiety disorders: A practitioner's treatment guide to using mindfulness, acceptance, and values-based behavior change strategies.* Oakland, CA: New Harbinger.

Estes, W. K. (1975). *Handbook of learning and cognitive processes: Pt. I. Introduction to concepts and issues.* Hillsdale, NJ: Erlbaum.

Estes, W. K. (1978). *Handbook of learning and cognitive processes: Pt. VI. Language functioning in cognitive theory.* Hillsdale, NJ: Erlbaum.

Fairburn, C. G. (1985). Cognitive-behavioral treatment for bulimia. In D. M. Garner & P. E. Garfinkel (Eds.), *Handbook of psychotherapy for anorexia nervosa and bulimia* (pp. 160–192). New York: Plenum Press.

Fletcher, L., & Hayes, S. C. (2005). Relational frame theory, acceptance and commitment therapy, and a functional analytic definition of mindfulness. *Journal of Rational-Emotive and Cognitive Behavior Therapy, 23,* 315–336.

Giles, T. R. (1993). *Handbook of effective psychotherapy.* New York: Plenum Press.

Guevremont, D. C., & Spiegler, M. D. (1998). *Contemporary behavior therapy* (3rd ed.). Pacific Grove, CA: Brooks/Cole.

Guevremont, D. C., & Spiegler, M. D. (2002). *Contemporary behavior therapy* (4th ed.). New York: Wadsworth.

Hayes, S. C. (2004). Acceptance and commitment therapy, relational frame theory, and the third wave of behavioral and cognitive therapies. *Behavior Therapy, 35,* 639–665.

Hayes, S. C., Follette, V. M., & Linehan, M. M. (2004). *Mindfulness and acceptance: Expanding the cognitive-behavioral tradition.* New York: Guilford Press.

Hayes, S. C., Luoma, J. B., Bond, F. W., Masuda, A., & Lillis, J. (2006). Acceptance and commitment therapy: Model, processes and outcomes. *Behavior Research and Therapy, 44,* 1–25.

Hayes, S. C., & Pankey, J. (2002). Experiential avoidance, cognitive fusion, and an ACT approach to anorexia nervosa. *Cognitive and Behavioral Practice, 9,* 243–247.

Hayes, S. C., Strosahl, K., & Wilson, K. G. (1999). *Acceptance and commitment therapy: An experiential approach to behavior change.* New York: Guilford Press.

Haynes, S. N., & O'Brien, W. H. (1990). The functional analysis in behavior therapy. *Clinical Psychology Review, 10,* 649–668.

Haynes, S. N., & O'Brien, W. H. (2000). *Principles and practice of behavioral assessment.* New York: Plenum Press.

Hull, C. L. (1952). *A behavior system: An introduction to behavior theory concerning the individual organism*. New Haven, CT: Yale University Press.

Keane, T. M., Fairbank, J. A., Caddell, J. M., & Zimering, R. T. (1989). Implosive (flooding) therapy reduced symptoms of PTSD in Vietnam combat veterans. *Behavior Therapy, 20,* 245–260.

Kohlenberg, R. J., Kanter, J. W., Bolling, M., Wexner, R., Parker, C., & Tsai, M. (2004). Functional analytic psychotherapy, cognitive therapy, and acceptance. In S. C. Hayes, V. M. Follette, & M. M. Linehan (Eds.), *Mindfulness and acceptance: Expanding the cognitive-behavioral tradition* (pp. 96–119). New York: Guilford Press.

Lazarus, A. A. (1976). *Multimodal behavior therapy*. New York: Springer.

Leichsenring, F., Hiller, W., Weissberg, M., & Leibing, E. (2006). Cognitive-behavioral therapy and psychodynamic psychotherapy: Techniques, efficacy, and indications. *American Journal of Psychotherapy, 60,* 233–259.

Linehan, M. M. (1993). *Skills training manual for treating borderline personality disorder*. New York: Guilford Press.

Linehan, M. M., Comtois, K. A., Murray, A. M., Brown, M. Z., Gallop, R. J., Heard, H. L., et al. (2006). Two-year randomized controlled trial and follow-up of dialectical behavior therapy versus therapy by experts for suicidal behaviors and borderline personality disorder. *Archives of General Psychiatry, 63,* 757–766.

Lipsey, M. W., & Wilson, D. B. (1990). The efficacy of psychological, educational, and behavioral treatment. *American Psychologist, 48,* 1181–1209.

Mahoney, M. J., & Kazdin, A. E. (1979). Cognitive behavior modification: Misconceptions and premature evacuation. *Psychological Bulletin, 86,* 1044–1049.

Marshall, W. L. (1985). The effects of variable exposure in flooding therapy. *Behavior Therapy, 16,* 117–135.

Meichenbaum, D. (1977). *Cognitive-behavior modification: An integrative approach*. New York: Plenum Press.

Meichenbaum, D. (1985). *Stress inoculation training*. New York: Pergamon Press.

Mowrer, O. H. (1960). *Learning theory and behavior*. New York: Wiley.

Nathan, P. E., & Gorman, J. M. (1998). *A guide to treatments that work*. New York: Oxford University Press.

Nathan, P. E., & Gorman, J. M. (2002). *A guide to treatments that work* (2nd ed.). New York: Oxford University Press.

O'Brien, W. H., & Haynes, S. N. (1993). Behavioral assessment in the psychiatric setting. In A. S. Bellack & M. Hersen (Eds.), *Handbook of behavior therapy in the psychiatric setting* (pp. 39–73). New York: Plenum Press.

O'Brien, W. H., Kaplar, M., & McGrath, J. J. (2004). Broadly-based causal models of behavior disorders. In M. Hersen, S. N. Haynes, & E. M. Heiby (Eds.), *Handbook of psychological assessment: Vol. 3: Behavioral assessment* (pp. 69–93). Hoboken, NJ: Wiley.

Ost, L.-G., Jerremalm, A., & Johansson, J. (1981). Individual response patterns and the effects of different behavioral methods in the treatment of social phobia. *Behavior Research and Therapy, 19,* 1–16.

Pavlov, I. P. (1941). *Conditioned reflexes and psychiatry* (W. Horsley Gantt, Trans.). New York: International.

Petry, N. M. (2000). A comprehensive guide to the application of contingency management procedures in clinical settings. *Drug and Alcohol Dependence, 58,* 9–25.

Salkovskis, P. M., & Clark, D. M. (1991). Cognitive treatment of panic disorder. *Journal of Cognitive Psychotherapy, 3,* 215–226.

Segal, Z. V., Williams, J. M., & Teasdale, J. D. (2002). *Mindfulness-based cognitive therapy for depression: A new approach to preventing relapse*. New York: Guilford Press.

Skinner, B. F. (1938). *The behavior of organisms: An experimental analysis.* Oxford, England: Appleton-Century.

Skinner, B. F. (1974). *About behaviorism.* Oxford, England: Knopf.

Skinner, B. F. (1986). Why I am not a cognitive psychologist. In L. Terry & L. Robertson (Eds.), *Approaches to cognition: Contrasts and controversies* (pp. 79–90). Hillsdale, NJ: Earlbaum.

Skinner, B. F. (1990). Can psychology be a science of the mind? *American Psychologist, 45,* 1206–1210.

Tarrier, N. (2006). *Case formulation in cognitive-behavioral therapy: The treatment of challenging and complex cases.* New York: Routledge/Taylor.

Teasdale, J. D., Segal, Z. V., Williams, J. G., Ridgeway, V. A., Soulsby, J. M., & Lau, M. A. (2000). Prevention of relapse/recurrence in major depression by mindfulness-based cognitive therapy. *Journal of Consulting and Clinical Psychology, 68,* 615–623.

Trull T. J, Nietzel, M. T., & Main A. (1988). The use of meta-analysis to assess the clinical significance of behaviour therapy for agoraphobia. *Behavior Therapy, 19,* 527–538.

Watson, G. S., & Gross, A. M. (1999). Behavior therapy. In M. Hersen & A. S. Bellack (Eds.), *Comparative interventions for adult disorders* (2nd ed., pp. 25–47). New York: Wiley.

Watson, J. B. (1919). *Psychology from the standpoint of a behaviorist.* Philadelphia: Lippincott.

Watson, J. B., & Raynor, R. (1920). Conditioned emotional reactions. *Journal of Experimental Psychology, 3,* 1–14.

Weitzman, B. (1969). Behavior therapy and psychotherapy. *Psychological Review, 74,* 300–317.

Wolpe, J. (1952a). Experimental neurosis as learned behavior. *British Journal of Psychology, 43,* 243–268.

Wolpe, J. (1952b). The formation of negative habits: A neurophysiological view. *Psychological Review, 59,* 290–299.

Wolpe, J. (1958). *Psychotherapy by reciprocal inhibition.* Oxford, England: Stanford University Press.

Wolpe, J. (1963). Psychotherapy: The nonscientific heritage and the new science. *Behavior Research and Therapy, 1,* 23–28.

Wolpe, J. (1971). The behavioristic conception of neurosis: A reply to two critics. *Psychological Review, 78,* 341–343.

Wolpe, J. (1990). *Practice of behavior therapy* (4th ed.). New York: Pergamon Press.

Wolpe, J. (1997). From psychoanalytic to behavioral methods in anxiety disorders: A continuing evolution. In J. K. Zeig (Ed.), *The evolution of psychotherapy: The third conference* (pp. 107–116). Philadelphia: Brunner/Mazel.

Wolpe, J., & Lazarus, A. A. (1966). *Behavior therapy techniques: A guide to the treatment of neuroses.* Elmsford, NY: Pergamon Press.

Wolpe, J., Salter, A., & Reyna, L. J. (1964). *The conditioning therapies.* Oxford, England: Holt, Rinehart and Winston.

Zinbarg, R. E., Craske, M. G., & Barlow, D. H. (1993). *Therapist's guide for the mastery of your anxiety and worry program.* San Antonio, TX: Psychological Corporation.

CHAPTER 5

Medical and Pharmacological Issues in Assessment, Conceptualization, and Treatment

JEAN COTTRAUX

This chapter would have the length of a voluminous treatise to fully embrace the scope and answer the questions suggested by its title. For the sake of clarity, we deal only with five selected topics:

1. Bridging the mind-body gap: Conceptual challenges of the biopsychosocial model, behavioral medicine, and psychosomatics
2. Relation between stress and illness: Assessment and treatment of coronary heart disease and its complications
3. Assessment of factors affecting individual vulnerability
4. Drug and psychological interventions: Obsessive-compulsive disorder psychobiological models and management
5. Cognitive neuroscience approaches: New assessment tools for psychotherapies and drugs

BRIDGING THE MIND-BODY GAP: CONCEPTUAL CHALLENGES OF THE BIOPSYCHOSOCIAL MODEL, BEHAVIORAL MEDICINE, AND PSYCHOSOMATICS

The statement about the relations between soul and body in ancient Greek *Soma Sema* translates as, "The body is a tomb." The Greek root *sem* refers also to semiology, the science of signs. Medicine was based on semiology because, before the advent of biological measurement and imagery techniques, diagnoses were built on the interpretations of physical signs and self-reports by patients. At the other end of the philosophical specter, Napoleon Bonaparte said, "Anatomy is destiny," representing a strong case for the influence of genetics on individual behavior.

95

In Western civilization, the chasm between mind and body is still present. Descartes described the dichotomy between *res cogitans* (thinking thing), the soul with no spatiotemporal reality, and *res extensa* (spatially extended thing), the material of which body machinery is made. The current distinction between biological and psychological models reflects the persistence of such an ancient conception.

This dichotomized belief system is still operating both in the popular wisdom and more surprisingly in the scientific enterprise despite repeated warnings and attempts to bridge the conceptual gap. Two attempts have been made: (1) Engel (1977) proposed a biopsychosocial model, and (2) the behavioral medicine movement established more scientific bases to explore and expand the old concept of *psychosomatics*, coined by Heinroth in 1818.

ARE WE BEYOND DUALISM? THE BIOPSYCHOSOCIAL MODEL TODAY

George Engel (1977) suggested that the physician as scientist must operate concurrently in two modes: (1) observational and (2) relational. The observational mode consists of collecting empirical data and emphasizes accurate measurement and description. The relational mode, on the contrary, is concerned with language, symbols, thoughts, and feelings. Empathy is the hallmark of the approach by which private experience is organized and communicated through dialogue with the physician who learns the nature and history of the patients' experiences and clarifies their meaning. These two modes should not constitute separate alternatives but be integrated in everyday practice. Engel's biopsychosocial model envisioned the study and treatment of interacting systems at cellular, tissue, organic, interpersonal, and environmental levels (Borrell-Carrió, Suchman, & Epstein, 2004). Table 5.1 presents this argument.

Engel's perspective was influential on *DSM-III* (American Psychiatric Association, 1980) formulation of the four Axes: Axis I, diagnoses; Axis II, personality; Axis III, physical disorders or condition; and Axis IV, severity of psychosocial stressors. Axis V, global assessment of functioning, was added in *DSM-IV* (American Psychiatric Association, 1987).

Table 5.1
Engel's Critique of Biomedicine

A biochemical alteration does not translate directly into an illness. Conversely, psychological alterations may, under certain circumstances, manifest as illnesses or forms of suffering that constitute health problems, including, at times, biologically measurable correlates.

The presence of a biological alteration does not shed light on the meaning of the symptoms for the patient and the physician.

Psychosocial variables are important antecedents of susceptibility, severity, and course of any illness.

Adopting a sick role is not necessarily associated with the presence of a biological alteration.

The success of the biological treatments is influenced by psychosocial factors. For example, the placebo has powerful effects.

The patient-clinician relationship influences medical outcomes, especially, because of its influence on adherence to a chosen treatment.

Patients are deeply influenced by the way in which they are studied. Conversely, their subjects influence the scientists engaged in any study.

Where are we almost 30 years after the formulation of the biopsychosocial model by Engel and 25 years after *DSM-III*? Mind-Brain dualism is still here and it has been empirically studied. Miresco and Kirmayer (2006) observed that, despite attempts in psychiatry to adopt an integrative biopsychosocial model, social scientists have observed that psychiatrists continue to operate according to a mind-brain dichotomy in ways that are often covert. Moreover, they suggested that the same cognitive schemas that people use to make judgments of responsibility led to dualistic reasoning among clinicians. The study consisted of self-report questionnaires sent to psychiatrists and psychologists in the department of psychiatry at McGill University. A total of 127 faculty members were included in the analysis. In response to clinical vignettes, participants rated level of intentionality, controllability, responsibility, and blame attributable to the patients, as well as the importance of neurobiological, psychological, and social factors in explaining the patients' symptoms. Factor analysis revealed a single dimension of responsibility regarding the patients' illnesses that correlated positively with ratings of psychological etiology and negatively with ratings of neurobiological etiology. Psychological and neurobiological ratings were inversely correlated. Multivariate analyses supported these results. The conclusion was that mental health professionals continue to employ a mind-brain dichotomy when reasoning about clinical cases. The more a behavioral problem was seen as originating in psychological processes, the more a patient tended to be viewed as responsible and blameworthy for his or her symptoms. Conversely, the more behaviors were attributed to neurobiological causes, the less likely patients were considered to be responsible and blameworthy.

Cognitive modeling by the prestigious spiritualist Western tradition and social differential reinforcement may anchor such beliefs and professional behaviors. The biopsychosocial model is not really applied because the specialists practicing psychotherapy and those practicing psychopharmacology are not always the same and have different goals and incentives. Another explanation can also be found in the vested interests of researchers and drug companies that sponsor research for mental or physical disorders.

BEHAVIORAL MEDICINE AND PSYCHOSOMATIC APPROACHES

The evidence produced by clinical studies that psychological factors influence the body and vice versa has long been recognized from Hippocratic teaching to psychoanalytically oriented psychosomatic medicine. Learning and cognitive theories have been applied to medical illnesses to overcome the mind-body dualism. Proposed are new short-term therapies for modifying behaviors, emotions, and cognitions that represent antecedents or maintaining factors of health or illness.

Hence, classical holistic medicine has been progressively prolonged by a new branch of psychology called *behavioral medicine*—or *health psychology, consultation-liaison, psychosomatics,* or *medical psychology,* depending on the country of origin or theoretical orientation. The evidence demonstrated by epidemiological studies of the association of social and behavioral risk factors in physical diseases like cancer, alcoholism, heart diseases, obesity, and so on gave rise to numerous interventions and controlled studies.

G. E. Schwartz and Weiss (1978) defined *behavioral medicine* as the interdisciplinary field concerned with development and integration of behavioral and biomedical science knowledge and techniques relevant to health and illness and the application of this knowledge and these techniques to prevention, diagnosis, treatment, and rehabilitation. This widely accepted definition emphasized the integration of biomedical and behavioral knowledge and techniques. It was further proposed to integrate relevant parts of epidemiology, anthropology, sociology, psychology, physiology, pharmacology, nutrition, neuroanatomy, endocrinology, immunology, and the various branches of medicine and public health, as well as related professions such as dentistry, social work, and health education. This integration was presented as the ultimate goal in the field. The scope of behavioral medicine extends from research efforts to understand basic brain-body mechanism interactions, to clinical diagnosis and intervention, to public health disease prevention, and health promotion strategies. This definition underlines both the importance of studying psychosocial factors and the need for basic etiological research. Behavioral medicine represents also the application of cognitive-behavioral therapy (CBT) to the field of so-called medical illnesses.

COGNITIVE-BEHAVIORAL THERAPY: PRACTICAL MANAGEMENT OF MEDICAL ILLNESSES

For psychiatric disorders or psychological problems, 12 criteria define CBT's clinical application to medical problems:

1. *Therapy is based on empirical collaboration.* An agenda is set for each session, and patients and therapists interact based on an empirical collaboration or therapeutic alliance to solve psychological problems related to health and illness. Motivation of the patient to change has to be tested before starting. Because the patient is the main agent of change, the therapist should help him to clarify his goals and the means that therapy will use to help him.
2. *Therapy is centered on current problems.* Therapist and patient agree on the selection of target behaviors with the patient and contract on the goals of the treatment.
3. *Functional analysis targets problems.* Functional analysis is carried out with the patient to single out target problems to analyze their current antecedents and consequences. Cognitive variables, images, thoughts, emotions, and beliefs system are related to ongoing emotions and behaviors. Although the main focus is on those factors maintaining current behavior, the past history of the patient is also noted if it has some relevance to problems in the here and now. Historical aspects are not neglected if they represent possible antecedents of the current problems. Functional analysis has to make the history of early development and critical life events in relation with the patient's current complaints.
4. *Continuous measurement is used.* Target problem behaviors, cognitions, and emotions before, during, and after (posttest and follow-up points) therapy usually last up to 1 year after the end of the treatment. Other measures, especially personality measures, should be used to complement a too-restricted measurement of target behaviors.
5. *Treatment program is defined with patient.* A treatment program usually takes 10 to 25 sessions and is defined with the patient. Its rationale and techniques are explained to the patient. The term of the therapy is fixed in advance. Sessions are given once or twice a week in individual sessions or group format. In general, patients and therapists have manuals.

6. *Therapy presents a structured format.* Each session starts with an agenda of the topics and problems that are to be dealt with in the session. At the end of each session, real-life homework is agreed on with the patient and its completion evaluated at the next session.

7. *Ongoing functional analysis is implemented.* This is carried out to understand new or unexpected problems. At the last session, patient and therapist agree on a maintenance program.

8. *Follow-up and booster sessions are implemented.* The patient is generally followed for up to 1 year after the end of the treatment to insure the quality of the outcomes and assess the durable effectiveness of the treatment. Booster sessions are scheduled if needed.

9. *Techniques are clearly defined.* Techniques have to be empirically tested in single-case experimental designs and at a later stage in controlled trials. They are based on learning principles (e.g., classical and operant conditioning, social learning theory) but also on cognitive principles related to information-processing models. The techniques are designed to teach the patient new coping skills or to improve old ones that are failing. Some basic techniques are used.

10. *Emotional responses are modified.* Relaxation, exposure in imagination to fearful situations, biofeedback, or stress management techniques may be used to reduce anxiety, fear, or anger confronted by a medically ill patient.

11. *Behavioral Methods Are Implemented.* For instance, a person may use assertion training to cope with anger and learn how to decrease aggressive speech and behaviors in relating to others. For example, problem solving in seven points (D'Zurilla & Nezu, 1999) represents both a way to assess the patients and a way to help him or her to find a solution for a problem. It could be a medical illness with the urge to be adaptive to the loss it represents; hence, depression is common in the medically ill (Fava & Sonino, 2000). Problem solving aims to reduce feelings of helplessness and anxiety when the patient is confronted with a medical illness. Problem solving is a better stress reduction tool than relaxation because it develops coping strategies in the patients. Relaxation alone, drugs, alcohol, or street drugs represent a way to avoid a painful situation instead of coping with it. Such avoidance may increase depressive interpretations and emotions and lead to helplessness, after a stage of prolonged anxiety. Drug and alcohol effects increase depression. Relaxation is only able to alleviate anxiety and prepare the patient for active coping and problem solving.

12. *Cognitive methods are implemented.* The therapist could question and challenge irrational anger and hostile thoughts in a patient suffering from a coronary prone pattern. The therapist may also implement problem-solving techniques and relaxation induced by physical or psychological cues to cope with a difficult social encounter. At a deeper level, basic schemas about overachievement, irrational beliefs about perfectionism (unrelenting standards), and fear of rejection should be discussed. The discussion is led in a Socratic manner with the patients. However, at some point, empathic confrontation to the schema is recommended. This modification of the way the patient sees him- or herself, the outer world, and the future purports to change his or her lifestyle. For instance, a man with a type A behavior pattern may change his philosophy of life and hence stop confronting others with anger or hostility because he always sees them as potential competitors.

Self-Management Development

Cognitive-behavioral therapy aims at developing the patient's control over his or her own problem behaviors. Self-control is an important issue in most of the cases of medically ill patients. Patients have first to monitor their risk behaviors, then to self-record them, and finally to implement a self-management program designed with the therapist. The patient reinforces the positive effects of this program (self-reinforcement). The effects of the behavior change on the environment may foster in return a better quality of life, better interpersonal relationships, and more satisfying personal achievements. Both insight and outsight should be enhanced. Mahoney and Thoresen (1974) coined the concept of outsight. They meant that being aware of the environmental contingencies regulating behaviors in a detrimental way is necessary to implement behavioral and cognitive change. Environmental control has to be made conscious; they referred to this process as *outsight*, as opposed to *insight*, a word coined by early Gestalt psychology and designing the internal rearrangement of meaning. The word *insight* was then used by psychoanalysis to describe a new awareness of inner psychological problems or conflicts.

Developing outsight is especially useful for smoking, alcoholism, eating disorders, sexual dysfunctions, aggressive driving, overwork, burnout, chronic fatigue, and so on. Many of these types of patients are first referred to a department of medicine and too often have repeated and costly examinations before psychological intervention. Avoidance of both external and internal problems may delay the appropriate psychological intervention.

Limitations of the medical model and responses to the patients' untold questions are to be pointed out. Assessment instruments to reveal hidden problems do exist, but they are not routine practice in all medical department. An improvement of the training of medical students in health psychology could fill the gap between a pure physical approach of the syndromes and a more humanist understanding to uncover the emotional needs of the patient.

Goals of Intervention: Quality of Life and Psychological Well-Being

Quality of life, especially in chronic diseases, has become the focus of an increasing number of publications. Ryff and Singer (1996) suggested that psychological well-being plays a buffering role in coping with stress and has a favorable impact on disease course, especially breast cancer, showing important immunological and endocrine connotations. Other examples are concerned with the role of optimism and coping style in transplantation outcome, anxiety, hope in the course of medical disorders, and the relationship between life satisfaction and cardiologic variables.

RELATION BETWEEN STRESS AND ILLNESS: ASSESSMENT AND TREATMENT OF CORONARY HEART DISEASE AND ITS COMPLICATIONS

A high proportion of coronary heart disease can be predicted from classic risk factors including cigarette smoking, lack of physical exercise, obesity, raised blood cholesterol, and high blood pressure. Various psychological risk factors such as type A behavior and hostility/anger have been identified. Behavior therapy has been used as a method to modifying the risk behavior in individuals.

Type A Behavior and Coronary Heart Disease

Type A behavior pattern has been characterized, after Osler at the turn of the century, by Friedman and Rosenman (1974) as a complex of behavioral traits, including excessive competitive drive, aggression, impatience, and time urgency, that suggest the presence of a chronic struggle against time and other people. This is a dimensional concept with the other end of the spectrum being represented by the relaxed and easy-going type B. Accordingly, the type A is a statistical construct depending on an accurate evaluation based on paper-and-pencil tests or a more sophisticated videotaped structured interview that was validated by Friedman and Rosenman.

The modification of type A behavioral pattern has been proposed to prevent relapses and death after coronary heart disease. Following many years of research all over the world, the type A behavior pattern is more than a dubious concept. Today, researchers consider anger/hostility and aggression as the core risk factors for type A behavior pattern (Roskies, 1987; Roskies et al., 1986).

There is controlled evidence of the effectiveness of modifying type A pattern and some controlled evidence of the positive effects of such modifications on the recurrence of coronary events. In general, the programs are presented in groups of 5 to 10 participants and are completed in 12 sessions that cover five modules: (1) relaxation, (2) cognitive restructuring, (3) social skills training, (4) problem solving, and (5) stress-anger management training.

A study by Friedman et al. (1984) compared 270 patients who received simple medical counseling to 592 patients who received the same treatment plus type A behavior management (relaxation, cognitive therapy, lifestyle modification) in a CBT program. At a 3-year follow-up, both coronary heart disease relapses and type A behavior were found to be significantly decreased in the group receiving the CBT program. The effects of the behavior modification were superior to the effects of the simple medical counseling. Nunes, Frank, and Kornfeld (1987) in a meta-analytic literature review of 18 controlled studies concluded that psychological interventions may have a positive effect on coronary heart disease prognosis and justify more research on their clinical applications. Combined reduction of coronary events was 50% after 3 years.

Psychological and Physical Treatment for the Complications of Coronary Heart Disease

Epidemiological and experimental evidence supports a causal association between psychological factors and risk of sudden cardiac death. An implantable cardioverter defibrillator (ICD) that delivers shock in case of ventricular arrhythmias is used widely to prevent fatal arrhythmias. The negative effects of stress on shock delivery has been demonstrated in ICD patients. Lampert, Baron, McPherson, and Lee (2002) reported that the World Trade Center 9/11 terrorist attacks more than doubled the frequency of life-threatening ventricular arrhythmias in patients with ICDs. Hence, an ICD represents a good model to study cardiac and psychological stress responses and the patient's coping mechanisms. Any time the patient feels a shock, it means he or she was close to dying and was rescued by the ICD. Such an experience may lead to posttraumatic stress disorder (PTSD) or anticipatory anxiety with insomnia. In turn, anxiety may increase arrhythmic events.

A study (Chevalier et al., 2006) was designed to ascertain whether CBT resulted in a decrease of arrhythmic events requiring ICD intervention through an improvement of the sympatho-vagal balance. Seventy of 250 consecutive ICD patients were randomly assigned to CBT plus conventional medical care ($n = 35$) or conventional medical care alone ($n = 35$).

Cognitive-behavioral therapy was administered to small groups (4 to 6 participants) by a team of one psychologist and one psychiatrist who were qualified to practice CBT and who were experienced in applying CBT for the treatment of anxiety disorders. They used a manual written specifically for this study and received special training in stress management for physical disorders. The patients also received a manual written in lay language that provided information on stress and stress management and that explained the steps of CBT. Six 2-hour sessions were given, one every 2 weeks over a period of 3 months: The first session was about stress and relaxation. A relaxation tape was given to the participants, who were encouraged to practice daily. The second session included a cognitive restructuring method used for confronting stressors. The third session was on the techniques of positive interindividual communication and role-playing was used to modify conflicting issues. The fourth and fifth sessions addressed problem-solving methods. The sixth session proposed a plan for dealing with everyday stressors. Practical homework was given after each session and recorded.

Quality of life was assessed at baseline, at 3 months, and at 1 year. Heart rate variability was analyzed on serial 24-hours Holter recordings. The primary outcome measure was the shock delivery frequency. Secondary outcomes were heart rate variability indexes, quality of life, and psychological status. Although not statistically different, the number of patients with shocks was less in the CBT group than in the conventional treatment group (3 versus 6 at a 12-month follow-up, respectively). At 3 months, in patients without anti-arrhythmic drugs, none of the CBT group had experienced arrhythmic events requiring ICD intervention, as compared to 4 in the control arm ($p < 0.05$). Also at the 3-month follow-up, anxiety, measured on the Hamilton Anxiety Rating Scale, was significantly less in the CBT group as compared to the control group. At a 12-month follow-up, although anxiety was still significantly lower in the CBT group, there was no difference in the number of arrhythmic events requiring therapy between groups. Some of the heart rate variability measures improved significantly in the CBT group as compared to the control group.

By decreasing anxiety and possibly improving sympatho-vagal balance, CBT may decrease the propensity to ventricular arrhythmias in ICD patients without anti-arrhythmic drugs. These effects appear however to be limited in time and suggest that a maintenance program would be required for these patients.

ASSESSMENT OF FACTORS AFFECTING INDIVIDUAL VULNERABILITY

Psychosocial and biological factors continuously interact in the course of medical and psychiatric disorder. Their balance fosters the individual and unique qualities of experience and also shapes the attitude toward a given episode of physical illness. The same is true for so-called psychological problems and disorders. Several factors, both physical and psychosocial (Fava & Sonino, 2000), have been implied to modulate individual vulnerability to disease. They should be part of assessment of both psychological and physical disturbances.

GENETICS

A study by Uhl and Grow (2004) showed that brain and nervous system disorders may cost the United States as much as $1.2 trillion annually and affect millions of Americans each year. The twin data reported suggested that more than 40% of the societal burden of brain disorders was likely to be genetically mediated. Most of the disease burden arises from complex genetic factors as well as from environmental influences. The authors concluded that the large sizes of these burdens should encourage careful molecular and clinical work to link disease-vulnerability allelic variants with the pathogenesis, clinical characteristics, prevention, diagnostics, and therapeutics of brain disorders. It should also be acknowledged that environmental factors are of paramount importance and are to be assessed because they explain 60% of the social burden of neuropsychiatric disorders.

One study of identical twins reared together (hence, sharing the same genetic endowment and education among other environmental influences) has demonstrated some singular and specific life events are more important than education to explain the psychopathological processes. The twins, in this study, had suffered from child abuse; but the intensity of the violence was discordant in cotwins on a rating scale with three degrees: (1) nongenital, (2) genital, and (3) intercourse. The more violent the child abuse had been, the more severe the later psychiatric problems and/or addiction to drugs. Familial factors and genetics appeared unrelated to the intensity of these psychiatric problems. This suggested a direct causal link between child abuse intensity and psychopathology (Kendler et al., 2000).

RECENT LIFE EVENTS AND PSYCHOIMMUNOLOGY

The notion that life events with an adverse meaning and detrimental effect may be followed by ill health is a common observation. Within a multifactorial frame of reference, stressful life events have been consistently associated with several medical disorders, especially immunology-related disorders. For example, Kiecolt-Glaser et al. (1988) showed immune function reduction after divorce in cases of marital distress.

AIDS represents an example, with one study showing that HIV-positive patients are more prone to develop the full picture of AIDS when they are facing adverse life events. Sixty-two HIV-infected gay men, who were asymptomatic at baseline, were assessed systematically at 6-month intervals. Severe stress and depressive symptoms were independently related to decreases on immune measures from entry to up to 7.5-year follow-up, with some men showing declines in CD8+ T cells, CD56+, and CD16+ NK cell subsets. Subjects most likely to have decreases on these immune measures were those who scored above the median on both stress and depressive symptoms. These data suggest that stress and depressive symptoms may have clinical implications for the course of AIDS (Leserman et al., 1997). The same group in a subsequent study with a 7.5 year followup (Leserman et al., 2000) found, in 82 gay men with HIV infection, that faster progression to AIDS was related to average stressful events, higher serum cortisol, and lower satisfaction with social support.

CHRONIC STRESS

Dramatic life changes are not the only source of psychological stress. Subtle and long-standing life situations are not negligible; a good example is represented by a constant and apparently justified overwork with marital, professional conflicts, overachievement, and loss of interest for emotional life. By middle age, patients with unrelenting standards become "victims of duty" and are prone to depression and/or physical problems. Psychometric and biological measures of chronic stress are currently developed in laboratories involved with psychoneuroendocrinology of human diseases. This represents an emerging trend in psychosomatic problems assessment (Fava & Sonino, 2000).

EARLY LIFE EVENTS

Disturbance of attachment process have been subjected to scientific inquiry (Bowlby, 1988). Insecure attachment may be an antecedent of emotional disturbances. Early adverse life events, for instance mother-infant separation without a good maternal substitute, may render the human individual more vulnerable to the effects of stress later in life by long-lived alteration in corticotropin-releasing-hormone-containing neural circuits. The same is true for traumatic events in childhood, especially sexual abuse. The association of childhood physical and sexual abuse with medical disorders has been in the past decade a subject for psychobiological inquiry. This is true for the whole field of PTSD. Some studies reported biological marker change (e.g., dexamethasone test alteration or neuropeptides chronic increase; Yehuda, 1998; Yehuda, Brand, & Yang, 2006). In the same way, brain imagery state markers reflect abnormalities (e.g., hippocampic volume diminution or disconnection between temporal and prefrontal regions have been reported in person suffering from PTSD; Bremner et al., 2003; Lanius et al., 2004).

PERSONALITY

Personality disorders such as borderline personality disorder (BPD) may be the consequence of early adverse events imprinting on the brain and psychological functioning as shown in the preceding section of this chapter. Basic research on nonassociative learning (e.g., long-term potentiation and sensitization related to memory neurochemistry; Kandel, 2006) may ultimately explain the underlying processes. Neural systems related to the suppression of unwanted memories are beginning to be investigated by neuroimagery (Anderson et al., 2004). This research will help bridge the gap between environmental and genetic influences.

TEMPERAMENT AND CHARACTER

A medical illness may represent a consequence of personality disorder or trait. Study of twins has shown the heritability of personality traits such as continuity from normal to pathologic subjects, as well as emotional dysregulation, dissocial behavior, inhibition, and compulsivity. But personality is made both of *temperament,* whose traits are related to genetics, and *character,* which is the result of conditioning life events in each patient's history. Cloninger (1998) proposed a comprehensive model showing the subtle interactions of these different levels of causality. Research has confirmed four dimensions of temperament: (1) novelty seeking, (2) harm avoidance, (3) reward dependence, and (4) persistence. These dimensions are independently heritable, manifest early in life, and involve preconceptual biases in perceptual memory and habit formation. Cloninger (1998, 1999) added three dimensions of character evaluating the extent to which a person identifies him- or herself as an autonomous individual, an integral part of humanity, and an integral part of the universe as a whole. These aspects of the self-concept correspond to three character dimensions: (1) self-directedness, (2) cooperativeness, and (3) self-transcendence. This psychobiological model may be related to the current status and the physical or psychological complaints of the patient. The questionnaire deriving from Cloninger's model may be used to assess the personality of the patient.

ASSESSMENT OF PERSONALITY TRAITS RELATED TO ILLNESSES

Two personality constructs can potentially affect general vulnerability to disease: (1) the relationship between coronary heart disease and the so-called type A behavior pattern and (2) the psychological construct of *alexithymia* and related models, that was introduced by Sifneos (1973) to describe an impoverished fantasy life with a material way of thinking and an inability to use appropriate words to describe emotions. The inhibition of emotional expression and particularly a lifelong tendency to suppress anger have been found to involve an increased risk for a variety of health problems, both using the alexithymia or similar concepts.

A neighboring conceptualization was proposed in the 1960s by the French psychoanalyst Pierre Marty (Jasmin, Lê, Marty, Herzberg, & Psycho-Oncologic Group, 1990) who attempted to relate breast cancer and some other psychosomatic illnesses to a cognitive construct *La pensée opératoire* (utilitarian thought) that would be the clinical surface expression of a specific deep mental structure.

However, despite advances in our understanding of the relationship between the brain and the immune system, it is premature to conclude that a relationship between suppressed emotion and cancer is demonstrated. A review of scientific evidence reached the conclusion that, to date, alexithymia remains a controversial concept, particularly in its assessment (Fava & Sonino, 2000).

ASSESSMENT OF COGNITIVE SCHEMAS AND PERSONALITY

Schemas serve to interpret the environment and its relation to the person by the assignment of meaning. The function of the schemas is to control various psychological systems, including behavioral, motivational emotional, attention, and memory. When cognitive distortions take place, errors in cognitive contents and processing do occur. Specific cognitive vulnerabilities predisposing to specific disorders can be found in any psychopathological condition. From at theoretical standpoint, Beck, Freeman, Davis, and associates (2004) proposed to distinguish three levels of cognition:

1. The preconscious or automatic level that is represented by automatic thoughts.
2. The conscious level.
3. The meta-cognitive level that produces realistic, adaptive, or rational responses.

Cottraux and Blackburn (2001) distinguish, from a clinical perspective, four levels of information processing:

1. *Cognitive schemas store postulates and basic assumptions about incoming information.* Postulates can be unconditional (e.g., "I am worthless") or conditional

(e.g., "If the others knew me better they would understand I am worthless"). Only information that fits the maladaptive schemas is allowed to be processed until reaching full awareness; this is termed *tunnelization*.

2. *The cognitive process (or operations) are active.* At this level, cognitive distortions are also active. Assimilation to the content of the schema is preponderant over accommodation to facts of life. Arbitrary inference, selective abstraction, personalization, overgeneralization, use of cognitive heuristics instead of hypothetico-deductive thought reflect the preponderance of *top-down* cognitive processes over *bottom-up* ones.

3. *Cognitive process translates the deep structure (i.e., schema) into surface structure (i.e., preconscious automatic thoughts).* Automatic thoughts are cognitive products or events, operationally defined as inner monologues, dialogues, or images that are not conscious unless the person's attention is focused on them.

4. *Maintenance of the schema is similar to a self-fulfilling prophecy.* The consequence of behavior confirms cognitive distortion.

Personality Schemas versus Axis I Schemas

Schemas are stored in long-term memory, remaining nonconscious and latent, but they can be triggered by events that recall the past interactions that shaped them. Because most of the events that made up the personality are interpersonal and reflect the prolonged influence of significant others during childhood and adolescence, schemas can be activated by trivial everyday events or more dramatic life events related to developmental phases (e.g., professional achievement, loving relationship, dependence/independence problems, separation, social dominance and submission, grief, aging, illness, adaptation to social and economical circumstances). Personality schemas are more pervasive, enduring, stable, and rigid than schemas underlying Axis I disorders. They take over more functional schemas and block them. That prepotency of the personality schemas may result in their generalization to many situations that are less and less related to the original situations that once shaped them. Schemas may also spread from Axis II to Axis I syndromes when personality disorders are associated with Axis I syndromes. This generalization process has been referred to as the *cognitive shift*.

Young, Klosko, and Weishaar (2003) place greater emphasis on early maladaptive schemas. Young et al. also attach more emphasis to affects associated with core schemas and hence advocate the use of interventions to bring emotional change. They delineate three processes that maintain the rigidity of the schemas: (1) schema surrender, (2) schema avoidance, and (3) schema compensation.

Schema Surrender

The cognitive processes are selective attention to confirmatory evidence and the neglect or minimization of contradictory evidence ensures the stability of dysfunctional schema. The persistence of self-defeating behaviors that may have been adaptive in the past also contributes to schema maintenance though the repetition of the same negative experiences. For example, the actions of a woman who divorces her violent, alcoholic husband and remarries the same type of individual help to maintain her schema: "I am worthless; I cannot do anything right."

Schema Avoidance

Schemas that are associated with intense negative affects tend to be avoided. A variety of cognitive, affective, and behavioral strategies may be used for this purpose. Cognitive avoidance may involve automatic or volitional attempts to block thoughts and images that trigger schema. Affective avoidance strategies include not having any feelings; feeling empty; engaging in self-harm, drug addiction, or alcoholism; or experiencing psychosomatic symptoms. Behavioral avoidance strategies are more evident when they involve avoidance of social situations.

Schema Compensation

Compensation involves the occurrence of cognitive and behavioral patterns that are the opposite from those predicted by the early maladaptive schema. For example, an excessively dependent individual may develop excessive autonomy and a refusal to accept help and advice. Compensation strategies are partially successful attempts to challenge the schema, but overcompensation creates new problems. It also masks core beliefs, making it difficult to identify and modify them.

Assessment of Personality Schemas

Young et al. (2003) developed the Schema Questionnaire (YSQ) to assess 16 schemas organized into five problem areas: (1) disconnection and rejection, (2) impaired autonomy and performance, (3) impaired limits, (4) other directedness, and (5) overvigilance and inhibition. The second version of this questionnaire the YSQ-II has been validated by Schmidt, Joiner, Young, and Telch (1995) as well as Lee, Taylor, and Dunn (1999). This second, shortened version (75 items) is easier to administrate and has been validated in English (Welburn, Coristine, Dagg, Pontrefact, & Jordan, 2002) and French versions (Lachenal-Chevallet, Mauchand, Cottraux, Bouvard, & Martin, 2006).

Empirical Testing of Young's Model for Borderline Personality Disorder

Personality modes, according to Young's model are fluctuating emotional states, whereas schemas represent a stable trait. Young has proposed a schema mode model of BPD that allows us to relate cognition with emotion in those patients. He hypothesized that BPD patients tend to flip from 1 of 4 maladaptive schema modes to another: (1) Detached Protector, (2) Punitive Parent, (3) Abused/Abandoned Child, and (4) Angry/Impulsive Child. Patients can also be seen under the effects of one adaptive mode: the Healthy Adult mode.

A study by Arntz, Klokman, and Sieswerda (2005) represents the first empirical test of this model. Eighteen BPD patients, 18 cluster-C personality disorder (PD) patients, and 18 nonpatient female controls filled out trait and state versions of a newly developed schema mode questionnaire, assessing cognitions, feelings, and behaviors characteristic of seven schema modes. Using a crossover design, subjects watched a "neutral" and an "emotional" movie sequence designed to activate borderline emotions. The order of the film presentations was balanced. After watching each movie, subjects again filled out the schema mode questionnaire, state version. Trait as well as state versions indicated that borderline patients indeed characterized high scores on four maladaptive modes. Borderline personality disorder patients were lowest on the Healthy Adult mode. The stress induction method induced negative emotions in all groups. In borderline patients, the Detached Protector mode increased significantly more than in both control groups.

THERAPEUTIC TESTING OF THE EARLY SCHEMA MODEL BY SCHEMA-FOCUSED THERAPY

Upstream biological factors may in part explain BPD (Gunderson, 2001). Moreover, BPD's evolution is often complicated by medical problems and patients are often referred to medical or surgery department for eating disorders, alcoholism, self-mutilation, car accidents, suicidal attempts with physical injuries, somatization disorder, physical consequences of drug addiction, AIDS, hepatitis resulting from alcoholism, and impulsive use of street drugs associated with medications prescribed by several physicians. The discovery in consultation-liaison of the underlying personality that is responsible for these medical complications, some being possibly fatal, may lead to psychological treatment and/or medication such as antidepressants, neuroleptics, or mood stabilizers.

Linehan's (1993) pioneering work showed the possibility to improve impulsivity in BPD women with or without drug addiction. A breakthrough study (Giesen-Bloo et al., 2006) compared the effectiveness of schema-focused therapy (SFT) and psychodynamically based transference-focused psychotherapy (TFP) in patients with BPD. A multicenter randomized, two-group design in four general community mental health centers was conducted. Eighty-eight patients who were evaluated with a Borderline Personality Disorder Severity Index, fourth version scored greater than a predetermined cutoff score. The patients took medications in the two groups without statistical differences. The drugs were prescribed according to good clinical practice. The Borderline Personality Disorder Severity Index, quality of life, general psychopathologic dysfunctions, and measures of personality concepts (including the YSQ) were assessed. Patient assessments were made before randomization and then every 3 months for 3 years. Data on 44 SFT patients and 42 TFP patients were available for intent-to-treat analysis. The sociodemographic and clinical characteristics of the groups were similar at baseline. Survival analyses revealed a higher dropout risk for TFP patients than for SFT patients. After 3 years of treatment, survival analyses demonstrated that significantly more SFT patients recovered or showed reliable clinical improvement on the Borderline Personality Disorder Severity Index. Analysis of covariance showed that they also improved more in general psychopathologic dysfunction, measures of SFT/TFP personality concepts, and quality of life measures. This important study and the studies by Linehan's group give some hope for these patients requiring both biological and psychological care. Moreover, the Giesen-Bloo et al. (2006) study represents the first controlled test of the SFT model.

DRUG AND PSYCHOLOGICAL INTERVENTIONS: OBSESSIVE-COMPULSIVE DISORDER PSYCHOBIOLOGICAL MODELS AND MANAGEMENT

Evidence-based medicine (EBM) began in Canada at the Mac Master University in 1981 and expanded to the United States, the United Kingdom, and some countries in

Europe (Gray, 2004). Evidence-based medicine uses a five-step approach:

1. Formulate the question.
2. Search for answers.
3. Appraise the evidence.
4. Apply the results.
5. Assess the outcomes.

Evidence-based medicine puts the emphasis on the quality of the proof and uses randomized controlled trials as the gold standard to construct an argumentation for or against a given treatment. The experimental orientation of EBM was designed to replace the prevalent *opinion-based* or *eminence-based* medicine by a continuous and objective assessment and to eliminate ineffective or dangerous treatment. Evidence-based medicine attempts to answer the methodological issues raised by a scientific assessment of the efficacy of psychotherapies and medications based on two assumptions: (1) the characteristics of the patients are included (what diseases are the studies based on; what is the level of severity of the disease and possibly its comorbidities) and (2) the level of improvement of the patients at the end of treatment is known.

GENERAL PROBLEMS IN EVIDENCE-BASED MEDICINE

The description of the target diseases and definition of treatment goals may differ depending on the studies and according to the underlying theoretical frameworks. This renders comparisons between treatments difficult. Nevertheless, insofar as a treatment is proposed for a given syndrome, improvement in the syndrome represents a common standard to assess the different psychotherapies and medications. A number of factors may influence the course of a treatment and therefore its assessment, including the nature and severity of the disorder, life events, family and social environment, the placebo effect, the treatment method or technique used, the therapeutic relationship (with positive or negative consequences), the combination effects of treatments, and covert biological change.

The scientific assessment of medication and psychotherapy raises three main methodological questions:

1. What is the definition of the population of patients to be treated?
2. How do we measure the efficacy of a therapy or a medication?
3. How do we prove this efficacy?

DEFINING A STUDY POPULATION

Classifications from *ICD-10* (World Health Organization, 1992) or *DSM-IV-TR* (American Psychiatric Association, 2000) are widely used with patients, but their potential misuses and abuses have been constantly discussed in the past 10 years.

DSM-IV categories are not mutually exclusive; comorbidity represents the rule rather than the exception; comorbid personality disorders are found in 30% to 50% of the outpatients seen in the psychiatry department (Zimmermann, Rothschild, & Chehminski, 2005). But, too often, the drug companies are making randomized controlled trials with drugs for one single isolated Axis I disorder without taking into account the four other Axes, and exclude cases with comorbidity. Such a limitation allows marketing of drugs, without taking into account the biological and psychoso-cial factors that may render the medication effective or not in everyday practice. A clear-cut message is all that is needed: "A new and effective drug for disease X." In this instance, marketing imperatives controls both research content and scientific publication. In this regard, *DSM* is criticized, especially in Europe, for what it did not intend to be and should not be—a mere collection of syndromes and symp-toms for biologically oriented psychiatry, drug companies, and prescribing physi-cians.

Increasing attention has been paid in the literature to the potential conflicts of in-terest in clinical medicine and biomedical sciences, particularly in scientific journals and advisory panels. The degree and type of financial ties to the pharmaceutical in-dustry of panel members responsible for revisions of the *DSM* have been investigated (Cosgrove et al., 2006). By using multimodal screening techniques, the authors in-vestigated the financial ties to the pharmaceutical industry of 170 panel members who contributed to the diagnostic criteria produced for the *DSM-IV* and the *DSM-IV-TR*. The outcomes showed that 95 (56%) had one or more financial associations with companies in the pharmaceutical industry. All of the members of the panels on mood disorders, schizophrenia, and other psychotic disorders had financial ties to drug companies. The authors concluded that connections were especially strong in those diagnostic areas where drugs are the first-line treatments for mental disor-ders. Full disclosure by *DSM* panel members of their financial relationships with drug companies used in the treatment of mental illness was recommended.

Prior to the publication of *DSM-V* in 2012, there is time to correct this biological drift and come back to an integrative and more scientific model.

MEASURING EFFICACY OF THERAPY AND MEDICINE

In terms of the measurement of the effects of psychotherapies and medication, the studies use many evaluation scales of symptoms, behavior, and methods of psycho-logical and interpersonal functioning. These scales have been validated for various psychopathological problems. They may be completed either by the clinician or the patient. Personality questionnaires or ad-hoc measurements are also found in some studies depending on the hypotheses tested. In vivo behavioral tests provide a di-rect measurement of a person's performances and may be very different from the evaluation scales.

Correctly conducted evaluation studies report many criteria and measurements, allowing the range of conclusions to be extended. Some of these studies also analyze features of the therapeutic process in detail. Alongside changes in scores from con-tinuous scales, the studies refer occasionally to general discontinuous criteria, criteria for good results, or end point criteria. A single positive/negative end point criterion (success/failure) may be used or, alternatively, a principle end point and secondary end points.

Statistically significant changes measured in a group using a scale may occasionally only reflect mediocre clinical results, the mean value of which is sufficient to make statistical tests significant if the statistical power is high because of a large number of patients included. Conversely, lack of change in the mean value of a scale score may more rarely be accompanied by clinically beneficial changes in some patients or in a subgroup of patients. Expressing the magnitude of the effect obtained in the *average* subject in the study for people receiving the treatment or its comparator (placebo or other treatment) is close to the effect size and is necessary information in addition to the classical statistical tests.

Meta-analysis is a quantitative approach to a literature review that estimates the magnitude of the effect obtained in the *treated subject* compared to the *control subject* from the effect size. This analysis is based on the concept that all of the studies represent a quantum of information connected to the aim of the research subject and that each study provides its own contribution. The assumption made is that all of the studies included represent a sample of all possible studies on the subject in question.

Proving Efficacy

Quality of Life Measurement   Research on quality of life measurement seeks essentially two kinds of information, the functional status of the individual and the patient's appraisal of health. Measures of disease alone are insufficient to describe the subjective burden and real-life consequences such as loss of well-being, demoralization, and difficulties in fulfilling personal and family responsibilities. But quality of life measurements are often poorly designed (Fava & Sonino, 2000). Positive health is often regarded as the absence of illness, despite the fact that, 50 years ago, the World Health Organization defined *health* as a "state of complete physical, mental, and social well-being and not merely the absence of disease or infirmity."

The Question of Scientific Proof and Its Limits   Several guidelines have been used by various agencies around the world to establish the level of proof for a given treatment and to suggest guidelines for patient care. In general, the treatments are classified on three grades with some variations according to country (INSERM, Canceil et al., 2004):

> *Grade A:* Proven efficacy—Positive meta-analyses or several well-conducted randomized controlled trials with sufficient sample size
>
> *Grade B:* Presumption of efficacy—A few controlled trials with limited sample size, cohort studies
>
> *Grade C:* No proven efficacy—Case studies, experts' opinions

One of the critiques faced by EBM lies in the difference between efficacy found in randomized trials and effectiveness found in the practical application of the treatments in clinical everyday practice. A meta-analysis (Shadish et al., 1997) gave an answer to this question for the psychological treatments, especially CBT. It showed that psychotherapies worked not only in randomized controlled trials but also in clinically representative conditions. This work has to be replicated for medications.

Example: Obsessive-Compulsive Disorder

Examination of obsessive-compulsive disorder's (OCD) etiological and therapeutic issues exemplifies the intricacy of biological and psychological factors both in conceptualization and treatment of this enduring condition. It also analyzes some of the problems faced by EBM.

Both genetic and environmental influences have been considered as factors in OCD and OCD spectrum disorders. Pauls, Asobrock, Goodman, Rasmussen, and Leckman (1995) demonstrated that OCD was five times as frequent in families of OCD probands compared to controls. Moreover, they suggested a genetic heterogeneity with three forms of OCD: (1) familial cases with tics or Tourette syndrome, (2) familial cases with only obsessions and compulsions, and (3) nonfamilial sporadic cases. Although still speculative, a correlation between Syndenham chorea and obsessive-compulsive symptoms in children has been suggested by Swedo et al. (1997).

Since the seminal study of Baxter et al. (1987) with positron emission tomography (PET), neuroimaging techniques have been extensively used, accumulating a wealth of data over the past 20 years and suggesting specific dysfunction of neural pathways in OCD (Cottraux & Gérard, 1998). Positron emission tomography activation studies with O^{15} suggested the existence of three OCD subtypes with different patterns of activation in fronto-striatal regions (Cottraux et al., 1996; Mataix-Cols et al., 2004): (1) washing, (2) checking and (3) hoarding.

Both serotonin reuptake inhibitors (SSRIs) and CBT have been found to be effective in OCD. Cognitive-behavioral therapy is presented under the form of exposure and response prevention (ERP), cognitive therapy (CT), or a mixture of the two methods. There is no clear-cut and long-lasting advantage of CT over ERP in controlled trials (Cottraux et al., 2001).

Studies on Medication

In a meta-analysis (Greist, Jefferson, Kobak, Katzelnick, & Serlin, 1995) of placebo-controlled trials, it was found that clomipramine, fluoxetine, fluvoxamine, and sertraline were all superior to placebo. Greist et al. (1995) also found that the three SSRIs were comparable to each other in efficacy and that clomipramine was more effective than the SSRIs. Stein, Spadaccini, and Hollander (1995) conducted a meta-analysis of pharmacotherapy trials for OCD. In placebo-controlled trials, SSRIs (clomipramine, fluoxetine, fluvoxamine, and sertraline) had a significant effect size, with clomipramine being more effective than fluoxetine.

Another meta-analytic review of the efficacy of drug treatments (Piccinelli et al., 1995) found that SSRIs (clomipramine, fluoxetine, fluvoxamine, and sertraline) were effective in the short term. Although the improvement rate over placebo was greater for clomipramine than for SSRIs, a direct comparison between these drugs showed that they had similar therapeutic efficacy on obsessive-compulsive symptoms. Concomitant high levels of depression at the outset did not seem necessary for clomipramine or SSRIs to improve obsessive-compulsive symptoms.

In a meta-analysis comparing pharmacological treatments of OCD (clomipramine, fluoxetine, fluvoxamine, paroxetine, and sertraline; Kobak, Greist, Jefferson, Katzelnick, & Henk, 1998), clomipramine was better than SSRIs as a class, with the exception of fluoxetine. But when the year of publication was controlled, no significant difference was found between clomipramine and the other SSRIs, either as a group or in head-to-head trials. Moreover, no difference in dropout rates was found. The authors concluded that this statistical difference is probably not clinically significant enough to warrant first-choice treatment, given the greater lethality of clomipramine in overdose, which is linked to its cardiac effects (ventricular fibrillation).

Medication versus Cognitive-Behavioral Therapy

Three main meta-analyses have examined the effects of drugs and/or CBT in OCD. The first study combined 86 trials (from 1970 to 1993) and found no difference between antidepressants alone, CBT, and their combination (Van Balkom et al., 1994). Another meta-analysis (combining 77 trials between 1973 and 1997, yielding 106 comparisons) found that CBT was equivalent or better than treatment with SSRIs (Kobak et al., 1998). A third meta-analysis found SSRIs, CT, and ERP to be similarly effective (Abramowitz, 1997).

COMBINING MEDICATION AND COGNITIVE-BEHAVIORAL THERAPY

Some controlled trials studied the effectiveness of drugs and CBT combined or alone. Cottraux, Mollard, Bouvard, and Marks (1993) found that ERP combined with flu-voxamine or placebo had better outcomes than fluvoxamine alone, on the relapse rate, and 1 year after discontinuation of treatment. More recently, a controlled study by Nakatani et al. (2005) found a superiority of CBT over fluvoxamine but had no combined condition.

A trial by Foa et al. (2005) tested the relative and combined efficacy of clomipramine and ERP in the treatment of OCD in adults. The trial compared ERP, clomipramine, their combination, and pill placebo. It was conducted at a center known for expertise in pharmacotherapy, a second center known for its expertise in ERP, and a third center with expertise in both treatments. Participants were adult outpatients ($n = 122$) with OCD. Interventions included ERP for 4 weeks, followed by eight weekly maintenance sessions, and/or clomipramine administered for 12 weeks, to a maximum dose of 250 mg/day. The main outcome measures were the Yale-Brown Obsessive Compulsive Scale (Y-BOCS; Goodman et al., 1989) total score and response rates determined by the Clinical Global Impressions Improvement Scale. At week 12, the effects of all active treatments were superior to placebo. The effect of ERP did not differ from that of ERP plus clomipramine, and both were superior to clomipramine only. Intent-to-treat and completer response rates were, respectively, 62% and 86% for ERP, 42% and 48% for clomipramine, 70% and 79% for ERP plus clomipramine, and 8% and 10% for placebo.

Clomipramine, ERP, and their combination were all efficacious treatments for OCD. Foa et al. (2005) suggested that intensive ERP might be superior to clomipramine and, by implication, to other SSRIs. The findings were obtained by an intensive ERP program of 15 two-hour sessions (1 each weekday) over 3 weeks and a daily exposure and response prevention time of up to 2 hours a day. This may be impossible to implement in most therapeutic settings and requires very compliant patients. As suggested by the authors, this may represent the gold standard for patients who fail to benefit from a less intensive form of treatment.

A paper by Tenneij, Van Megen, Denys, and Westenberg (2005) brings new interesting conclusions on the combined approach. The novel approach used in this RCT was to initiate CBT in people who were responders to an adequate trial of venlafaxine or paroxetine. At 6-month follow-up, medication plus CBT was better than medication alone with a higher rate of people in remission.

ASSESSING THE REFRACTORY PATIENT

To date, there is no clear consensus on the definition of *refractory patients* or on what to do with them. An international group of experts made some recommendations to define the refractory or resistant patient (Pallanti et al., 2002), proposing a definition of the therapeutic response to drugs or CBT (see Tables 5.2 and 5.3).

Table 5.2
Criteria for Therapeutic Response for OCD

   I. Cure: No illness: Y-BOCS < 8
  II. Remission: Y-BOCS < 16
 III. Full response: Y-BOCS decrease: 35%, CGI = 1 or 2
 IV. Partial response: Y-BOCS decrease between 25% and 35%
  V. No response: Less than 25% Y-BOCS decrease, CGI = 4
 VI. Relapse: Symptoms return: CGI = 6, or increase of 25% on the Y-BOCS after three months of an adequate treatment
VII. No change or worsening with all the available treatments

---

CGI = Clinical Global Impressions Scale; Y-BOCS = Yale-Brown Obsessive-Compulsive Scale (Goodman et al., 1989).

Source: "Treatment Non-Response in OCD: Methodological Issues and Operational Definitions," by Pallanti et al., 2002, *International Journal of Clinical Neuropsychopharmacology, 5,* pp. 181–191.

The response rate is still too low in many patients; the 25% decrease on the Y-BOCS required as proof of efficacy in drug studies is rather overoptimistic. This magnitude of change will not affect dramatically the life of most of the patients. Pallanti's et al. (2002) requirement of a 35% decrease on the Y-BOCS seems more realistic.

In sum, the current *DSM* diagnosis of OCD covers probably heterogeneous conditions. At this very moment, genetics, neuroimagery, and clinical descriptions are not in line. Current research suggests that OCD is not an anxiety disorder, but a disorder in its own right, with subtypes. This is the only anxiety disorder with a sex ratio that equals 1, whereas other anxiety disorders (panic, agoraphobia, specific

Table 5.3
Levels of Nonresponse for OCD

    I. SSRI or CBT
   II. SSRI + CBT
  III. Two successive SSRIs + CBT
  IV. Three successive SSRIs + CBT
   V. Three successive SSRIs (including clomipramine) + CBT
  VI. Three successive SSRIs (including augmented clomipramine) + CBT
 VII. Three successive SSRIs (including augmented clomipramine) + CBT + psychoeducation and other psychotropic drugs (benzodiazepines, neuroleptics, mood stabilizers, psychostimulants)
VIII. Three successive SSRIs including intravenous clomipramine + CBT + psychoeducation
  IX. Three successive SSRIs including intravenous clomipramine + CBT + psychoeducation and other psychotropic drugs: Venlafaxine, MAOIs
   X. Failure of all the treatments: Psychosurgery could be considered

---

CBT = Cognitive-behavioral therapy; MAOIs = Monoamine oxidase inhibitors; SSRIs = Selective serotonin reuptake inhibitors.

Source: "Treatment Non-Response in OCD: Methodological Issues and Operational Definitions," by Pallanti et al., 2002, *International Journal of Clinical Neuropsychopharmacology, 5,* pp. 181–191. *Source:* Pallanti et al., 2002.

phobias, PTSD, GAD) demonstrate a predominance of women (Rasmussen & Eisen, 1998).

To conclude, we should be reminded that some patients would remain refractory to any kind of treatment. Hence, further psychobiological research is needed to help the chronic and treatment-refractory patients.

COGNITIVE NEUROSCIENCE APPROACHES: NEW ASSESSMENT TOOLS FOR PSYCHOTHERAPIES AND DRUGS

Cognitive neurosciences are slowly but surely solving the mind-body separation problem. Virtually all psychiatric conditions and most of the cognitive psychology issues have been explored in the past 20 years. Only studies dealing with psychotherapies or comparing drugs to psychotherapies are reviewed in this chapter.

Studies that used cerebral neuroimagery before and after therapy are scarce compared to studies dealing with basic brain research or drugs. Hard data exist only for CBT and interpersonal therapy (IPT). Only four troubles have been explored: (1) OCD, (2) social anxiety disorder, (3) specific phobias, and (4) depression.

NEUROBIOLOGICAL CHANGE PROCESSES IN DRUG AND PSYCHOLOGICAL TREATMENTS FOR OBSESSIVE-COMPULSIVE DISORDER

Neuroimagery studies found similar brain sites of action for both medication and CBT. Baxter et al. (1992) used an 18-fluoro-deoxy-glucose (FDG) PET in patients with OCD before and after treatment with either fluoxetine or ERP. After treatment, the glucose metabolic rate ratio for the right caudate/ipsilateral hemisphere was decreased significantly compared with pretreatment values in responders to both drug and ERP. Percentage change in OCD symptom ratings correlated significantly with the percentage of the ratio right caudate/ipislateral hemisphere change with drug therapy, and there was a trend toward significance for this same correlation with ERP. By grouping together all responders to either treatment, right orbital cortex/hemisphere was significantly correlated with ipsilateral caudate/hemisphere and thalamus/hemisphere before treatment but not after. Differences, before and after treatment, were significant. J. M. Schwartz, Stoessel, Baxter, Martin, and Phelps (1996) studied 9 OCD patients with an 18-FDG PET before and after 10 weeks of structured ERP and CT. Results were analyzed both alone and combined with those from 9 similar subjects from the Baxter et al. (1992) earlier-mentioned study. Exposure and response prevention responders had significant bilateral decreases in caudate glucose metabolic rates that were greater than those seen in nonresponders to treatment. Before treatment, there were significant correlations of brain activity between the orbital gyri and the head of the caudate nucleus and the orbital gyri and thalamus on the right. Correlations decreased significantly in responders. This study replicated Baxter et al.'s (1992) findings. Nakatani et al. (2003) (13) studied the effects of BT on the cerebral blood flow of OCD patients with the Single Positron Emission Computerized Tomography (SPECT) Xenon method. Therapist-aided ERP was applied to 31 patients who were refractory to treatment. Some patients received medication (clomipramine). The 22 responders to CT showed a decrease of cerebral blood flow in the right caudate nucleus, regardless of the presence or absence of clomipramine treatment.

Neurobiological Change Processes in Drug and Psychological Treatments for Social Phobia (Anxiety Disorder)

The seminal work by LeDoux (1996) demonstrated the central role of amygdala in the neuromodulation of emotional processes and cognitions that mediate behavioral responses to fear stimuli. Since then, several works with neuroimagery techniques have shown the role of amygdala in the fear responses to new faces or others' gaze, or they have tried to measure gaze aversion in anxiety disorders and normal controls (Armony, Corbo, Clement, & Brunet, 2005; Birbaumer et al., 1998; Garrett, Menon, Mackenzie, & Reiss, 2004; Tillfors et al., 2001). An increase of amygdala functioning may represent a temperamental trait marker (or endo phenotype) in infants that is revealed by functional magnetic resonance imaging (fMRI) measuring the response to new faces (C. E. Schwartz & Rauch, 2004; C. E. Schwartz, Wright, Shin, Kagan, & Rauch, 2003). Hariri et al. (2005) correlated a susceptibility gene for affective disorder and the response of human amygdala to angry faces in an fMRI standardized stimulation paradigm.

Furmark et al. (2002) used O^{15} PET in 18 social *DSM-IV* phobic patients who were randomized in three groups: (1) the antidepressant citalopram, (2) CBT, or (3) waiting list. A behavioral task—presenting a speech in front of 6 to 8 persons—provoked anxiety just before the PET examination that was made before and after 9 weeks of treatment. There was no difference in efficacy in the two groups. The main PET finding was that responders to both treatments demonstrated a decrease of the amygdala complex hyperactivity.

Neurobiological Change Processes in Drug and Psychological Treatments for Depression

The outcomes of IT versus antidepressants in depression remain contradictory in two studies. Brody et al. (2001) made an 18-FDG PET study that compared paroxetine and an untreated normal control group. Before treatment, the patients had increased activity in the prefrontal cortex, the caudate nucleus, and the thalamus and decreased metabolism in the temporal lobe. After 12 weeks of treatment, the abnormalities were corrected in the two groups. However, the study was not fully controlled as the patients chose their treatment, either paroxetine or CBT. An attempt to replicate the Brody et al. (2001), with venlafaxine compared to IPT, did not find the same pattern of activation and therapeutic response, but this study used the SPECT technetium method, which is different.

Goldapple et al. (2004) studied depression with 18-FDG PET. They compared a group of 17 unipolar depressed patient treated with CBT with 13 unipolar depressed patients treated with the antidepressant paroxetine. Fourteen patients responded to CBT and were entered into the statistical analysis. The study was not randomized. Two patterns of effectiveness were delineated. Responders to paroxetine modulated certain sites: Prefrontal regions showed increased activity, while hippocampal and cingulated subgenual regions showed decreased activity. Some changes were specific to the CBT responders: Increased activity in hippocampal regions and, in the dorsal cingulate gyrus, there was decreased activity in the frontal cortex.

It could also be interesting to compare the placebo to active psychotherapies or drugs. To date, there is only a preliminary work. An 18-FDG PET study (Mayberg et al., 2002) compared placebo versus antidepressant in a small sample of male depressed patients. Placebo response was associated with regional metabolic increases in the prefrontal, anterior cingulate, premotor, parietal, posterior insula, and posterior cingulated regions. They also showed metabolic decreases involving the subgenual cingulate, parahippocampus, and thalamus. These regions of change overlapped those seen in responders-administered active fluoxetine. Fluoxetine response was associated with additional subcortical and limbic changes in the brainstem, striatum, anterior insula, and hippocampus.

NEUROBIOLOGICAL CHANGE PROCESSES PSYCHOLOGICAL TREATMENTS FOR SPECIFIC PHOBIAS

To date, there is only in one study (Paquette et al., 2003) on specific phobia. It has a provocative title: "Change the Mind and You Change the Brain: Effects of Cognitive-Behavioral Therapy on the Neural Correlates of Spider Phobia." The well-designed study was included 12 subjects who presented with spider phobia and who were treated with CBT. They were measured by MRI, when watching films that showed spiders or butterflies (control condition). At pretest, a comparison was made with a normal control group. Controls demonstrated activation in the middle left occipital and inferior temporal. In the phobics, there was a dorsolateral prefrontal activation that may correspond, according to the authors, to an "adaptive meta cognition." There was also a para-hippocampal increase corresponding to the activation of the contextual memory related to fear. Cognitive-behavioral therapy was effective in reducing prefrontal and hippocampal regions hyperactivity in these spider phobic patients.

Future research with the new imagery tool, magneto encephalography (MEG; Amo et al., 2004; Cage et al., 2003), will be easier than using PET or fMRI and will certainly bring new ideas for the conceptualization and measurement of emotional disorders.

SUMMARY

At the end of this chapter, are we in a better position to bridge the mind-body gap? The fascinating research programs we reviewed definitely anchor psychology and psychotherapy effects studies in cognitive neurosciences and bridge the mind-body gap. They can be combined with psychoneuroimmunology, genetic, and environmental factors studies to develop new paradigms.

Because it is more than a hard science, a business, or a pill-engineering practice, medicine remains an art that applies technical knowledge to the uniqueness of the individual. Forgetting that point may lead the patients to alternative medicine, religion, or any enterprise that seems to take into account his or her emotional burden. This is the challenge of this century.

REFERENCES

Abramowitz, J. S. (1997). Effectiveness of psychological and pharmacological treatments for obsessive-compulsive disorder: A quantitative review. *Journal of Consulting and Clinical Psychology, 65,* 44–52.

American Psychiatric Association. (1980). *Diagnostic and statistical manual of mental disorders* (3rd ed.). Washington, DC: Author.

American Psychiatric Association. (1987). *Diagnostic and statistical manual of mental disorders* (3rd ed., rev.). Washington, DC: Author.

American Psychiatric Association. (2000). *Diagnostic and statistical manual of mental disorders* (4th ed., text rev.). Washington, DC: Author.

Amo, C., Quesney, L. F., Ortiz T., Maestu, F., Fernandez, A., Lopez-Ibor, M. I., et al. (2004, February). Limbic paroxysmal magnetoencephalographic activity in 12 obsessive-compulsive disorder patients: A new diagnostic finding. *Journal of Clinical Psychiatry, 65*(2), 156–162.

Anderson, M. C., Ochsner, K., Kuhl, B., Cooper, J., Robertson, E., Gabrieli, S. W., et al. (2004, January). Neural system underlying suppression of unwanted memories. *Science, 303,* 234–235.

Armony, J. L., Corbo, V., Clement, M. H., & Brunet, A. (2005). Amygdala response in patients with acute PTSD to masked and unmasked emotional facial expressions. *American Journal of Psychiatry, 162*(10), 1961–1963.

Arntz, A., Klokman, J., & Sieswerda, S. (2005). An experimental test of the schema mode model of borderline personality disorder. *Journal of Behavior Therapy and Experimental Psychiatry, 36*(3), 226–239.

Baxter, L., Phelps, M., Mazziota, J., Guze, B., Schwartz, J., & Selin, C. (1987). Local cerebral glucose metabolic rates in obsessive-compulsive disorders. *Archives of General Psychiatry, 44,* 211–221.

Baxter, L., Schwartz, J., Bergman, K., Szuba, M., Guze, B., Mazziota, J., et al. (1992). Caudate glucose metabolic rate changes with both drug and behavior therapy for obsessive-compulsive disorder. *Archives of General Psychiatry, 49,* 681–689.

Beck, A. T., Freeman, A., Davis, D. D., & Associates (2004). *Cognitive therapy of personality disorders* (2nd ed.). New York: Guilford Press.

Birbaumer, N., Grodd, W., Diedrich, O., Klose, M., Schneider, F., Weiss, U., et al. (1998). FMRI reveals amygdala activation to human faces in social phobics. *NeuroReport, 9,* 1223–1226.

Borrell-Carrió, F., Suchman, A. L., & Epstein, R. M. (2004). The bio psychosocial model 25 years later: Principles, practice and scientific inquiry. *Annals of Family Medicine, 2*(6), 576–582.

Bowlby, J. (1988). *A secure base: Clinical application of attachment theory.* London: Routledge.

Bremner, J. D., Narayan, M., Staib, L. H., Southwick, S. M., Mcglashan, T., & Charney, D. S. (2003). Neural correlates of memories of childhood sexual abuse in women with and without posttraumatic stress disorder. *Journal of Psychiatry Research, 37*(2), 109–115.

Brody, A. L., Saxena, S., Stoessel, P., Gillies, L. A., Fairbanks, L. A., Alborzian, S., et al. (2001). Regional brain metabolic changes in patients with major depression treated with either paroxetine or interpersonal therapy. *Archives of General Psychiatry, 58,* 631–640.

Canceil, O., Cottraux, J., Falissard, B., Flament, M., Miermont, J., Swendsen, J., et al. (2004). *INSERM: Psychothérapie: Trois approches évaluées* [Expertise Collective]. Synthesis available in English at http://www.inserm.fr/fr/inserm/programmes/expertise_collective.

Chevalier, P., Cottraux, J., Mollard, E., Yao, S., Burri, H., Restier, L., et al. (2006). Prevention of implantable-defibrillator shocks by cognitive behavioral therapy: A pilot trial. *American Heart Journal, 151*(1), 191e1–191e6.

Cloninger, C. R. (1998). The genetics and psychobiology of the seven-factor model of personality. *Annual Review of Psychiatry, 17,* 63–92.

Cloninger, C. R. (1999). *Personality and psychopathology.* Washington, DC: American Psychiatric Press.

Cosgrove, L., Krimsky, S., Vijayaraghavana, M., & Schneider, L. (2006). Financial Ties between DSM-IV Panel Members and the Pharmaceutical Industry. *Psychotherapy and Psychosomatics, 75,* 154–160.

Cottraux, J., & Blackburn, I. M. (2001). Cognitive therapy for personality disorders. In J. Livesley (Ed.), *Handbook of personality disorders* (pp. 377–399). New York: Guilford Press.

Cottraux, J., & Gérard, D. (1998). Neuroimaging and neuroanatomical issues in obsessive compulsive disorder towards an integrative model: Perceived impulsivity. In R. Swinson, M. Anthony, S. Rachman, & M. Richter (Eds.), *Obsessive compulsive disorder: Theory research and treatment* (pp. 154–180). New York: Guilford Press.

Cottraux, J., Gérard, D., Cinotti, L., Froment, J. C., Deiber, M. P., Le Bars, D., et al. (1996). A controlled PET-scan study of neutral and obsessive auditory stimulations in obsessive-compulsive disorder. *Psychiatry Research, 60,* 101–112.

Cottraux, J., Mollard, E., Bouvard, M., & Marks, I. (1993). Fluvoxamine or combination treatment in obsessive-compulsive disorder: One-year follow-up. *Psychiatry Research, 49,* 63–75.

Cottraux, J., Note, I., Yao, S. N., Lafont, S., Note, B., Mollard, E., et al. (2001). A randomized controlled trial of cognitive therapy versus intensive behavior therapy in obsessive-compulsive disorder. *Psychotherapy and Psychosomatics, 70,* 288–297.

D'Zurilla, T. J., & Nezu, A. M. (1999). *Problem solving therapy*. New York: Springer.

Engel, G. L. (1977). The need for a new medical model: A challenge for biomedicine. *Science, 196,* 129–136.

Fava, G. A., & Sonino, N. (2000). Psychosomatic medicine: Emerging trends and perspectives. *Psychotherapy and Psychosomatics, 69,* 184–197.

Foa, E. B., Liebowitz, M. R., Kozak, M. J., Davies, S., Campeas, R., Franklin, M. E., et al. (2005). Randomized, placebo-controlled trial of exposure and ritual prevention, clomipramine, and their combination in the treatment of obsessive-compulsive disorder. *American Journal of Psychiatry, 162,* 151–161.

Friedman, M., & Rosenman, R. H. (1974). *Type A behavior and your heart*. New York: Knopf.

Friedman, M., Thoresen, G., Gill, J., Powell, L., Ulmer, D., Thomson, L., et al. (1984). Alteration of type A behavior and reduction in cardiac recurrences in post-myocardial infarction patients. *American Heart Journal, 108*(2), 237–248.

Furmark, T., Tillfors, M., Marteinsdottir, I., Fisher, H., Pissiota, A., Langström, B., et al. (2002). Common changes in cerebral blood flow in patients with social phobia treated with citalopram or cognitive-behavioral therapy. *Archives of General Psychiatry, 59,* 425–433.

Garrett, A. S., Menon, V., Mackenzie, K., & Reiss, A. L. (2004). Here's looking at you, kid: Neural systems underlying face and gaze processing in fragile X syndrome. *Archives of General Psychiatry, 61,* 281–288.

Giesen-Bloo, J., Van Dyck, R., Spinhoven, P., Van Tilburg, W., Dirksen, C., Van Asselt, T., et al. (2006). Outpatient psychotherapy for borderline personality disorder randomized trial of schema-focused therapy versus transference-focused psychotherapy. *Archives of General Psychiatry, 63,* 649–658.

Goldapple, K., Segal, Z., Garson, C., Lau, M., Bieling, P., Kennedy, S., et al. (2004). Modulation of corticolimbic pathways in major depression: Treatment specific effects of cognitive behavior therapy. *Archives of General Psychiatry, 61,* 34–40.

Goodman, W. K., Price, H., Rasmussen, S., Mazure, R., Fleischman, R., Hill, C., et al. (1989). The Yale Brown Obsessive Compulsive Scale: Pt. 1. Development use and reliability. *Archives of General Psychiatry, 46,* 1006–1011.

Gray, G. E. (2004). *Evidence based psychiatry*. Washington, DC: American Psychiatric Publishing.

Greist, J. H., Jefferson, J. W., Kobak, K. A., Katzelnick, D. J., & Serlin, R. C. (1995). Efficacy and tolerability of serotonin transport inhibitors in obsessive-compulsive disorder: A meta-analysis. *Archives of General Psychiatry, 52,* 53–60.

Gunderson, J. G. (2001). *Borderline personality disorder: A clinical guide*. Washington, DC: American Psychiatric Publishing.

Hariri, A. R., Drabant, E. M., Munoz, K. E., Kolachana, B. S., Mattay, V. S., Egan, M. F., et al. (2005). A susceptibility gene for affective disorders and the response of the human amygdala. *Archives of General Psychiatry, 62,* 146–152.

Jasmin, C., Lê, M. G., Marty, P., Herzberg, R., & Psycho-Oncologic Group. (1990). Evidence for a link between certain psychosocial factors and the risk of breast cancer in a case-control study. *Annals of Oncology, 1,* 22–29.

Kandel, E. (2006). *In search of memory: The emergence of a new science of mind.* New York: Norton.

Kendler, K. S., Bulik, C. M., Silberg, J., Hettema, J. M., Myers, J., & Prescott, C. A. (2000). Childhood sexual abuse and adult psychiatric and substance use disorders in women: An epidemiological and cotwin control analysis. *Archives of General Psychiatry, 57,* 953–959.

Kiecolt-Glaser, J. K., Kennedy, S., Malkoff, S., Fisher, L., Speicher, C. E., & Glaser, R. (1988). Marital discord and immunity in males. *Psychosomatic Medicine, 50,* 213–229.

Kobak, K. A., Greist, J. H., Jefferson, J. W., Katzelnick, D. J., & Henk, H. J. (1998). Behavioral versus pharmacological treatments of obsessive compulsive disorder: A meta-analysis. *Psychopharmacology, 136,* 205–216.

Lachenal-Chevallet, K., Mauchand, P., Cottraux, J., Bouvard, M., & Martin, R. (2006). Factor Analysis of the Schema Questionnaire-Short Form in a Nonclinical Sample. *Journal of Cognitive Psychotherapy: An International Quarterly, 20*(3), 217–224.

Lampert, R., Baron, S. J., McPherson, C. A., & Lee, F. A. (2002). Heart rate variability during the week of September 11, 2001. *Journal of the American Medical Association, 288–*575.

Lanius, R. A., Williamson, P. C., Densmore, M., Boksman, K., Neufeld, R. W., Gati, J. S., et al. (2004). The nature of traumatic memories: A 4-T functional connectivity analysis. *American Journal of Psychiatry, 161,* 36–44.

LeDoux, J. (1996). *The emotional brain.* New York: Simon & Schuster.

Lee, C. W., Taylor, G., & Dunn, J. (1999). Factor structure of the schema questionnaire in a large clinical sample. *Cognitive Therapy and Research, 23,* 441–451.

Leserman, J., Petitto, J. M., Golden, R. N., Gaynes, B. N., Gu, H., Perkins, D. O., et al. (2000). Impact of stressful life events, depression, social support, coping, and cortisol on progression to AIDS. *American Journal of Psychiatry, 157*(8), 1221.

Leserman, J., Petitto, J. M., Perkins, D. O., Folds, J. D., Golden, R. N., & Evans, D. L. (1997). Severe stress, depressive symptoms, and changes in lymphocyte subsets in human immunodeficiency virus-infected men: A 2-year follow-up study. *Archives of General Psychiatry, 54,* 279–285.

Linehan, M. (1993). *Cognitive–behavioral treatment of borderline personality disorder.* New York: Guilford Press.

Mahoney, M., & Thoresen, C. (1974). *Self-control: Power to the person.* Monterey, CA: Brooks/Cole.

Mataix-Cols, D., Wooderson, S., Lawrence, N., Brammer, M. J., Speckens, A., & Phillips, M. L. (2004). Distinct neural correlates of washing, checking, and hoarding symptoms dimensions in obsessive compulsive disorder. *Archives of General Psychiatry, 61,* 564–576.

Mayberg, H. S., Silva, J. A., Brannan, S. K., Tekell, J. L., Mahurin, R. K., McGinnis, S., et al. (2002). The functional neuroanatomy of the placebo effect. *American Journal of Psychiatry, 159,* 728–737.

Miresco, M. J., & Kirmayer, L. J. (2006). The persistence of mind-brain dualism in psychiatric reasoning about clinical scenarios. *American Journal of Psychiatry, 163,* 913–918.

Nakatani, E., Nakagawa, A., Ohara, Y., Goto, S., Uozumi, N., Iwakiri, M., et al. (2003). Effects of behavior therapy on regional cerebral blood flow in obsessive compulsive disorder. *Psychiatry Research: Neuroimaging, 124,* 113–120.

Nakatani, E., Nakagawa, A., Nakao, T., Yoshizato, C., Nabeyama, M., Kudo, A., et al. (2005). A randomized controlled trial of Japanese patients with obsessive-compulsive disorder: Effectiveness of behavior therapy and fluvoxamine. *Psychotherapy and Psychosomatics, 74,* 269–276.

Nunes, E., Frank, K., & Kornfeld, D. (1987). Psychologic treatment for the type A behavior pattern and for coronary heart disease: A meta-analysis of the literature. *Psychosomatic Medicine, 48*(2), 159–173.

Pallanti, S., Hollander, E., Bienstock, C., Koran L., Leckman, J., Marazatti, D., et al. (2002). Treatment non-response in OCD: Methodological issues and operational definitions. *International Journal of Clinical Neuropsychopharmacology, 5*, 181–191.

Paquette, V., Levesque, J., Mensour, B., Leroux, J. M., Beaudoin, G., Bourgoin, P., et al. (2003). Change the mind and you change the brain: Effects of cognitive-behavioral therapy on the neural correlates of spider phobia. *NeuroImage, 18*, 401–409.

Pauls, D. L., Asobrock, J. P., Goodman, W., Rasmussen, S., & Leckman, J. F. (1995). A family study of obsessive-compulsive disorder. *American Journal of Psychiatry, 152*, 76–84.

Piccinnelli, M., Pini, S., Bellantuono, C., & Wilkinson, G. (1995). Efficacy of drug treatment in obsessive-compulsive disorder: A meta-analytic review. *British Journal of Psychiatry, 166*, 424–443.

Rasmussen, S. A., & Eisen, J. L. (1998). The epidemiology and clinical features of obsessive compulsive disorder. In M. A. Jenike, L. Baer, & W. E. Minichiello (Eds.), *Obsessive compulsive disorder, practical management* (3rd ed., pp. 12–43). Saint Louis, MO: Mosby.

Roskies, E. (1987). *Stress management for the healthy type A.* New York: Guilford Press.

Roskies, E., Seraganian, P., Oseasohn, R., Hanley, J. A., Collu, R., Martin, N., et al. (1986). The Montreal Type A intervention project: Major findings. *Health Psychology, 5*, 45–69.

Ryff, C. D., & Singer, B. (1996). Psychological well-being. *Psychotherapy and Psychosomatics, 65*, 14–23.

Schmidt, N. B., Joiner, T. E., Young, J. E., & Telch, M. J. (1995). The schema questionnaire: Investigation of psychometric properties and the hierarchical structure and measure of maladaptive schemas. *Cognitive Therapy and Research, 19*(5), 295–321.

Schwartz, C. E., & Rauch, S. L. (2004). Temperament and its implications for neuroimaging of anxiety disorders. *CNS spectrums, 9*(4), 284–291.

Schwartz, C. E., Wright, C., Shin, L., Kagan, J., & Rauch, S. (2003). Inhibited and uninhibited infants "grown up": Adult amygdala response to novelty. *Science, 300*, 1952–1953.

Schwartz, G. E., & Weiss, S. M. (1978). Behavioral medicine revisited: An amended definition. *Journal of Behavioral Medicine, 1*, 249.

Schwartz, J. M., Stoessel, P. W., Baxter, L. R., Martin, K. M., & Phelps, M. (1996). Systematic changes in cerebral glucose metabolic rate after successful behavior modification treatment of obsessive compulsive disorder. *Archives of General Psychiatry, 53*, 109–113.

Shadish, R. W., Matt, G. E., Navarro, A. M., Siegle, G., Crits-Cristoph, P., Hazelrigg, M. D., et al. (1997). Evidence that therapy works in clinically representative conditions. *Journal of Consulting and Clinical Psychology, 65*(3), 355–365.

Sifneos, P. E. (1973). The prevalence of alexithymic characteristics in psychosomatic patients. *Psychotherapy and Psychosomatics, 22*, 255–262.

Stein, D. J., Spadaccini, E., & Hollander, E. (1995). Meta-analysis of pharmacotherapy trials for obsessive-compulsive disorder. *International Clinical Psychopharmacology, 10*, 11–18.

Swedo, S. E., Leonard, H. L., Mittleman, B. B., Allen, A. J., Rapoport, J., Dow, S. P., et al. (1997). Identification of children with pediatric autoimmune neuropsychiatric disorder associated with streptococcal infections by a marker associated with rheumatic fever. *American Journal of Psychiatry, 154*, 110–112.

Tenneij, N. H., Van Megen, H. J. G. M., Denys, D. A. J. P., & Westenberg, H. G. M. (2005). Behavior therapy augments response of patients with obsessive-compulsive disorder responding to drug treatment. *Journal of Clinical Psychiatry, 66*(9), 1169–1175.

Tillfors, M. T., Furmak, T., Marsteinsdottir, I., Fischer, H., Pissiota, A., Langström, B., et al. (2001). Cerebral blood flow in subjects with social phobia during stressful speaking tasks: A PET study. *American Journal of Psychiatry, 158*(8), 1220–1226.

Uhl, G. R., & Grow, R. W. (2004). The burden of complex genetics in brain disorders. *Archives of General Psychiatry, 61,* 223–229.

Van Balkom, A. J. L. M., Van Oppen, P., Vermeulen, A. W. A., Van Dyck, R., Nauta, M. C. E., & Vorst, H. C. M. (1994). A meta-analysis on the treatment of obsessive compulsive disorder: A comparison of anti-depressants, behavior and cognitive therapy. *Clinical Psychology Review, 14,* 359–381.

Welburn, K., Coristine, M., Dagg, P., Pontrefact, A., & Jordan, S. (2002). The schema questionnaire-short form: Factor analysis and relationship between schemas and symptoms. *Cognitive Therapy and Research, 26,* 519–530.

World Health Organization. (1992). *ICD-10: International classification of diseases.* Geneva, Switzerland: Author.

Yehuda, R. (1998). *Psychological trauma.* Washington, DC: American Psychiatric Press.

Yehuda, R., Brand, S., & Yang, R. K. (2006). Plasma neuropeptide y concentrations in combat exposed veterans: Relationship to trauma exposure, recovery from PTSD, and coping. *Biological Psychiatry, 59,* 660–663.

Young, J., Klosko, J., & Weishaar, M. (2003). *Schema therapy: A practitioner guide.* New York: Guilford Press.

Zimmermann, M., Rothschild, L., & Chehminski, I. (2005). The prevalence of DSM-IV personality disorders in psychiatric outpatients. *American Journal of Psychiatry, 162*(10), 1911–1918.

CHAPTER 6

Ethical Issues

CATHERINE MILLER

Assessment, case conceptualization, and treatment comprise the three main ingredients of an effective helping relationship. Assessment may be defined as "a process for evaluating behavior, psychological constructs, and/or characteristics of individuals or groups for the purpose of making decisions regarding classification, selection, placement, diagnosis, or intervention" (American Psychological Association, 2000, p. 7). Case conceptualization may be defined as a working hypothesis about the causes, precipitants, and maintaining influences of the client's problems based on the psychologist's theoretical orientation (Eells, 1997; Freeman & Miller, 2002). In addition, a good case conceptualization should include possible treatment ideas (Bruch, 1998; Persons & Tompkins, 1997). Treatment or intervention may be defined as utilizing evidence-based techniques to ameliorate psychological symptoms such as depression or anxiety. Assessment, conceptualization, and treatment should be considered as "both sequential and part of a feedback loop" in the therapy process (Meier, 1999, p. 847).

A plethora of ethical concerns arises throughout the assessment, case conceptualization, and treatment phases of therapy. Although overwhelming at first glance, these varied ethical concerns actually can be boiled down to four broad ethical issues: competence, informed consent, confidentiality, and multiple relationships. The first and most basic ethical issue is that of *competence*. Weiner (1989) declared that "competence is prerequisite for ethicality," stating that although it is possible "to be competent without being ethical, it is not possible to be ethical without being competent" (p. 829). The most recent American Psychological Association (APA) Ethical Principles of Psychologists and Code of Conduct (hereafter referred to as the APA Ethics Code) emphasizes importance of competence in Standard 2.01, stating that psychologists provide services only within the boundaries of their competence. Before considering themselves competent to provide services to clients, psychologists must obtain education, training, supervised experience, consultation, study, or professional experiences (APA, 2002).

A second important ethical issue is that of *informed consent*. Before initiating any services with a client, informed consent from that client must be obtained. To be truly informed, consent must be given (a) voluntarily, (b) by a legally competent person, and (c) after that person is fully informed about the nature and purpose of the clinical services (Bersoff, 1995; Everstine et al., 1980). First, a client's consent must be obtained voluntarily, without "coercion, . . . duress, pressure, or undue excitement or influence" (Koocher & Keith-Spiegel, 1998, p. 417). Second, a client must be legally competent or capable of granting consent. Unless deemed incompetent by the legal system, all adults are presumed capable of giving consent. When working with children or adults deemed legally incompetent, substitute consent should be obtained from parents, legal guardians, or from the court (Everstine et al., 1980; Miller & Evans, 2004). In addition, information should be given to the legally incompetent client in developmentally appropriate language, and assent, or agreement, should be obtained from the client (Keith-Spiegel, 1983). Finally, a client must be given sufficient information to make an informed decision regarding consent. Although it is not necessary to review all possible outcome scenarios, it is necessary to provide facts a reasonable person would need in arriving at an informed decision (Welfel, 1998).

Closely related to informed consent is the issue of *confidentiality*. Koocher and Keith-Spiegel (1998) define confidentiality as "a general standard of professional conduct that obliges a professional not to discuss information about a client with anyone" (p. 116). Confidentiality is a necessary ingredient for effective psychological services because without candid client participation assessment results can be invalid, diagnoses inaccurate, and therapy ineffective (DeKraai & Sales, 1982). Standard 4.01 of the Ethics Code states that a psychologist should take precautions to protect and maintain confidential information (APA, 2002), and most states have passed laws that establish confidentiality rules and exceptions (U.S. Department of Health and Human Services, 1999). In addition, the federal government recently passed the Health Insurance Portability and Accountability Act (HIPAA, 1996) that sets a federal floor on confidentiality, requiring explicit client authorization for release of information to third parties.

The final important ethical issue is that of *multiple relationships*. Standard 3.05 of the Ethics Code defines two types of multiple relationships. In the first type, the psychologist engages in more than one professional relationship with the client (e.g., therapist and business partner). In the second type, the psychologist engages in both a professional (i.e., therapist) and a social relationship (i.e., dating partner) with the client. These relationships may be concurrent or consecutive. The Ethics Code does not prohibit all multiple relationships; instead, Standard 3.05 proscribes only those that "could reasonably be expected to impair the psychologist's objectivity, competence, or effectiveness in performing his or her functions as a psychologist, or otherwise risks exploitation or harm to the person with whom the professional relationship exists" (APA, 2002, p. 1065).

In this chapter, the three clinical activities of assessment, case conceptualization, and treatment are examined in relation to the four ethical issues of competence, informed consent, confidentiality, and multiple relationships to produce a list of 12 ethical proficiencies (see Table 6.1). Each proficiency is discussed in detail and suggestions for psychologists are given to ensure proficiency in each area.

Table 6.1

Proficiencies and Ethical Issues within Assessment, Case Conceptualization, and Treatment

Proficiencies	Main Ethical Issues
ASSESSMENT	
1. Ability to obtain consent from clients for assessment	Informed consent/Multiple relationships
2. Ability to select relevant assessment devices	Competence
3. Ability to appropriately administer and interpret assessment devices	Competence
4. Ability to thoroughly and accurately integrate assessment results	Competence
5. Ability to determine if/when to release test data/test materials	Informed consent/ Confidentiality
Case Conceptualization	
6. Ability to integrate assessment results and theoretical orientation	Competence
7. Ability to develop testable treatment hypotheses	Competence
TREATMENT	
8. Ability to obtain consent from clients for treatment	Informed consent/Multiple relationships
9. Ability to utilize evidence-based techniques	Competence
10. Ability to monitor treatment outcomes	Competence
11. Ability to determine if/when to release treatment information	Informed consent/ Confidentiality
12. Ability to set appropriate boundaries	Multiple relationships

ASSESSMENT

PROFICIENCY 1: ABILITY TO OBTAIN CONSENT FROM CLIENTS FOR ASSESSMENT

There are two main ethical issues involved in obtaining consent for assessment. Clearly, there is the issue of informed consent. In addition, the issue of multiple relationships must be considered. Information about informed consent for assessment is contained in Standard 9.03 of the Ethics Code. This standard requires psychologists to "obtain informed consent for assessments, evaluations, or diagnostic services" by providing potential test takers with "an explanation of the nature and purpose of the assessment, fees, involvement of third parties, and limits of confidentiality and sufficient opportunity for the client/patient to ask questions and receive answers" (APA, 2002, p. 1071). It is imperative that such information be provided to and consent obtained from the test taker prior to the initiation of the assessment process. Informed consent may be desirable to obtain even when not required (e.g., court-ordered assessment). Further, even when informed consent is not required, it is advisable to inform test takers of the testing process unless such information will threaten the psychometric properties of the instrument or test (APA, 1996).

The issue of multiple relationships should be addressed by establishing during the informed consent process the parameters of the assessment role (i.e., assessment as part of therapy or separate from therapy). Although the terms *assessment* and *evaluation* are frequently used interchangeably in the literature, a distinction between the two terms helps to clarify appropriate boundaries. As previously stated, assessment may be defined as an ongoing part of therapy to help with diagnosis as well as with the monitoring of treatment outcome. An evaluation, however, may be defined as a time-limited examination of a person's functioning, referred by a third party (e.g., courts, school district, physician), and used to diagnose a condition or answer another specific referral question. Psychologists *should* routinely engage in regular assessment of their clients; however, psychologists should *not* conduct evaluations, such as custody evaluations, of clients being seen for therapy (APA, 1991). Once a psychologist has taken on the therapist role with a client, conducting an objective, unbiased evaluation is not possible. It is also not recommended that psychologists move in the reverse direction (from evaluator to therapist). Although this situation is not as ethically questionable, it is potentially rife with clinical difficulties, and the situation should be clearly discussed with the potential client prior to initiating therapy services.

PROFICIENCY 2: ABILITY TO SELECT RELEVANT ASSESSMENT DEVICES

The main ethical issue involved in selection of relevant assessment devices is competence. Psychologists must understand the concept of relevance and must have a sufficient knowledge base of psychometric properties to appropriately select assessment devices for each client. First, psychologists should employ only tests that meet a standard of relevance to the needs of a particular client (Anastasi, 1988). A client's right to privacy must be respected, as the "process of arriving at the diagnosis, of prodding the client for details of his or her experience, is in many ways an invasion of privacy no less severe than a physical examination by a medical doctor or an audit by the IRS" (Welfel, 1998, p. 218). In other words, assessment should be conducted for a good reason, as "testing for its own sake, or because of an institutional mandate, is inappropriate" (Welfel, 1998, p. 226).

Second, psychologists must understand general psychometric properties. Standard 9.02 requires psychologists to utilize "assessment instruments whose validity and reliability have been established for use with members of the population tested" (APA, 2002, p. 1071). If these psychometric properties have not yet been established, Standard 9.02 requires psychologists to describe any limitations of the results and interpretations. Therefore, psychologists should be trained in and have a thorough understanding of general psychometric properties prior to assessing clients (APA, 1998,

2000; Turner, DeMers, Fox, & Reed, 2001). Such general properties include descriptive statistics (e.g., measures of central tendency, measures of variation, correlation coefficients), types of scales and scores, types of reliability and sources of variability, types of validity, and normative interpretation of test scores (see APA, 2000, for a complete list of properties).

In addition to knowledge of general psychometric properties, psychologists must know how to flexibly apply this knowledge to particular testing situations. For example, in most testing situations, psychologists should employ only current measures rather than obsolete devices to ensure that the normative sample is appropriate (APA, 2002; Fremouw, Johansson-Love, Tyner, & Strunk, 2006). However, when attempting to compare scores across time, it may be more helpful to utilize the version of the device on which the client was originally tested rather than the new version, in an effort to reduce variability. As a second example, in most testing situations, psychologists should only use tests that are reliable and that have been validated for the purpose at hand, as "a test that is reliable, valid, and quite useful for one purpose may be useless or inappropriate for another" (Koocher & Keith-Spiegel, 1998, p. 149). However, psychologists must be flexible in test selection when considering client ethnic, racial, cultural, gender, age, and linguistic variables (APA, 1990, 2000; Sandoval, Frisby, Geisinger, Scheuneman, & Grenier, 1998; Turner et al., 2001) because there may not be reliable and valid instruments with similar normative samples.

PROFICIENCY 3: ABILITY TO APPROPRIATELY ADMINISTER AND INTERPRET ASSESSMENT DEVICES

The main ethical issue involved in administration and interpretation of assessment devices is competence. The exact amount of training and supervised experience needed before one is competent in assessment has never been clearly articulated. The APA did attempt to develop a three-tiered qualification system in 1950 to clarify the experience necessary prior to administering different tests (as cited in APA, 2000). In this qualification system, psychological tests were labeled as Level A, B, or C. Level A included vocational proficiency tests that were appropriate for administration and interpretation by nonpsychologists. Level B included general intelligence tests and interest inventories that required some technical knowledge of test construction, statistics, and individual differences. Level C included individually administered tests of intelligence, personality tests, and projective methods that required at least a master's degree in psychology and 1 year of supervised experience. Although test publishers still refer to such categorization in test catalogs (Moreland, Eyde, Robertson, Primoff, & Most, 1995), this qualification system has not been endorsed by APA since 1974 (APA, 2000).

Currently, psychologists are given very general advice to employ only those tests they have been trained to administer and to avoid using instruments with which they have no training or experience (Adams & Luscher, 2003). APA has resisted quantifying the amount of supervision needed for each test because some tests, such as the third edition revision of the revised Wechsler Adult Intelligence Scales (WAIS-III; Wechsler, 1997) or the Rorschach Inkblot test (Rorschach, 1921/1942) are more difficult to learn (APA, 2000). In addition, each test user arrives at the testing situation with different experience and knowledge; therefore, "a specific prescribed format or mechanism for supervision cannot be described for each test user" (Turner et al., 2001, p. 1104).

With few guidelines available on requisite qualifications of testers, psychologists have been "left to address this matter on the basis of their own awareness of their competencies and limitations" (Koocher & Keith-Spiegel, 1998, p. 156). Psychologists are advised to obtain supervision on the administration and scoring of *each* test, as "competence in the use of one test or one group of tests [does not] imply competence in any other test" (Welfel, 1998, p. 226). In addition, psychologists should continue to obtain supervision "of sufficient intensity and duration" until the supervisor judges that mastery of each test is acquired (APA, 2000, p. 32). Finally, psychologists ideally should obtain supervision in the specific settings in which assessment will occur (APA, 2000).

In addition to training and supervision, a second issue in the administration and interpretation of assessment devices is that of responsibility for appropriate test usage. Standard 9.09 of the Ethics Code states that "psychologists retain responsibility for the appropriate application, interpretation, and use of assessment instruments, whether they score and interpret such tests themselves or use automated or other services" (APA, 2002, p. 1072). In other words, students or assistants may administer tests, and automated services may score tests; however, the trained professional is still responsible for appropriate administration and interpretation of scores.

A third issue in the administration and interpretation of assessment devices is that of outdated test data. Standard 9.08 of the Ethics Code states, "psychologists do not base their assessment or intervention decisions or recommendations on data or test results that are outdated for the current purpose" (APA, 2002, p. 1072). How long test results may be relied on depends primarily on the construct being measured (Welfel, 1998). Tests that measure rapidly changing constructs, such as depressed (e.g., Beck Depression Inventory—Second Edition [BDI-II]; A. T. Beck, Steer, & Brown, 1996) or anxious moods (e.g., Beck Anxiety Inventory [BAI]; A. T. Beck & Steer, 1990), may be valid only for several days or weeks. Other tests that measure more stable personality constructs, such as the Minnesota Multiphasic Personality Inventory—Second Edition (MMPI-II; Butcher, Dahlstrom, Graham, Tellegen, & Kaemmer, 1989) may be valid for several months.

Additional issues may need to be considered when administering tests to individuals with disabilities or when interpreting scores of individuals from differing cultural or ethnic backgrounds. When testing clients with disabilities, psychologists must recognize that many available assessment devices were not developed and normed for individuals with disabilities. Although strongly encouraged to follow *all* standardized procedures when administering tests, psychologists may consider changing the standardized administration procedures to accommodate clients with disabilities. If administration is changed, psychologists must understand the impact of such changes on reliability and validity estimates (APA, 2000). Psychologists may find guidance on these issues in various publications, including the *Standards for Educational and Psychological Testing* (SEPT; Joint Committee of the American Educational Research Association, the American Psychological Association, and the National Council on Measurement in Education, 1999) and *Guidelines for Adapting Educational and Psychological Tests: A Progress Report* (Hambleton, 1994).

When interpreting scores from clients from diverse backgrounds, it is the duty of the psychologist to seek information and consultation if necessary (Knapp & VandeCreek, 2006). At a minimum, psychologists should be familiar with research on test bias for different racial, ethnic, cultural, gender, and linguistic groups. In addition, they should be familiar with research on the influence of psychological characteristics, such as stereotype threat, on test performance (APA, 2000). Psychologists may seek guidance on these issues in various articles, including Steele and Aronson's seminal study in 1995 on stereotype threat and Reschly's 1981 discussion of bias and IQ testing.

PROFICIENCY 4: ABILITY TO THOROUGHLY AND ACCURATELY INTEGRATE ASSESSMENT RESULTS

The main ethical issue involved in the integration of assessment results is competence. Competent psychologists resist any temptation to base clinical or other decisions on one test result or assessment finding (Miller, 2006). Standard 9.01 of the Ethics Code (APA, 2002) requires psychologists to "base the opinions contained in their recommendations, reports, and diagnostic or evaluative statements . . . on information and techniques sufficient to substantiate their findings" (p. 1071). To obtain sufficient information, psychologists should utilize multiple methods of assessment (APA, 2000). There are five main methods of assessment from which to choose, and psychologists should utilize two or more methods in assessing a client (Cone, 1978). First, there are interview schedules, such as the Structured Clinical Interview for DSM-IV Axis I Disorders—Clinician Version (SCID-CV; First, Spitzer, Gibbon, & Williams, 1996). Second, there are self-report forms, such as the BDI-II (A. T. Beck et al., 1996) or the MMPI-II (Butcher et al., 1989). Third, there are self-monitoring forms, such as thought logs (J. S. Beck, 1995). Fourth, there are ratings-by-others, such as the Child Behavior Checklist (CBCL; Achenbach, 1991) or the Conners Rating Scales—Revised (CRS-R; Conners, 1997). Finally, there are direct observation systems, such as the Dyadic Parent-Child Interaction Coding System—Second Edition (DPICS-II; Eyberg, Bessmer, Newcomb, Edwards, & Robinson, 1994). If it is not possible to reasonably obtain a sufficient amount of information using these multiple methods of assessment, Standard 9.01 goes on to state that psychologists should "clarify the probable impact of their limited information on the reliability and validity of their opinions, and appropriately limit the nature and extent of their conclusions or recommendations" (APA, 2002, p. 1071).

PROFICIENCY 5: ABILITY TO DETERMINE IF/WHEN TO RELEASE TEST DATA/TEST MATERIALS

Two main ethical issues are involved in the release of assessment materials or results: (1) informed consent and (2) confidentiality. Regarding informed consent, clients must be given information on who will have access to assessment results prior to beginning the assessment process.

Maintaining confidentiality of assessment results is a more complex issue. Standard 9.04 of the Ethics Code states, "pursuant to a client/patient release, psychologists provide test data to the client/patient or other persons identified in the release" (APA, 2002, p. 1071). There are two important components of this standard: First is the definition of test data that includes the following: (a) raw and scaled scores, (b) specific answers provided by the client, (c) portions of test materials that include client responses, and (d) any notes taken by the psychologist regarding the verbal and nonverbal behavior of the client during the assessment. It is important to note that this definition does not include test materials, defined as the actual instrument, stimuli, manuals, test questions, or protocols. Standard 9.11 of the Ethics Code (APA, 2002) requires psychologists to protect the integrity and security of the test materials and prohibits them from releasing test materials. Second, Standard 9.04 suggests that assessment results may be released to the test taker and/or third parties.

In regards to releasing assessment results to the test taker, Standard 9.10 of the Ethics Code requires psychologists to "take reasonable steps to ensure that explanations of results are given to the individual or designated representative unless the nature of the relationship precludes provision of an explanation of results (such as in some organizational consulting, preemployment or security screenings, and forensic evaluations)" (APA, 2002, p. 1072). If at all possible, assessment results should be communicated to the test taker via a copy of the written report and/or an oral feedback session (APA, 1996, 2000; Welfel, 1998). To avoid misinterpretation and misunderstanding, all communication should be direct and free from technical language (Koocher & Keith-Spiegel, 1998). If it is not possible to communicate assessment results to the test taker, that information must be provided to the test taker during the initial informed consent process.

In regards to releasing assessment results to third parties, psychologists may only reveal test data if the client consents or if ordered to do so by the law (Smith, 2003). Standard 9.04 of the Ethics Code (APA, 2002) does allow psychologists to withhold assessment results if this action protects the client or others from considerable harm (Erard, 2004) or if inappropriate or inaccurate use of the data is anticipated.

CASE CONCEPTUALIZATION

PROFICIENCY 6: ABILITY TO INTEGRATE ASSESSMENT RESULTS AND THEORETICAL ORIENTATION

The main ethical issue involved in integrating assessment results and theoretical orientation is competence. Because a good case conceptualization is based on an identified theory (Clark, 1999; Eells, 1997; Meier, 1999), psychologists must strive to clearly articulate their own theoretical orientation and be familiar with the assumptions underlying that particular model (Freeman & Miller, 2002). Specifically, a good case conceptualization should clearly specify the following, based on an identifiable theory: (a) hypotheses about the causes of the presenting problems, (b) hypotheses about the maintaining variables, and (c) theories of change.

PROFICIENCY 7: ABILITY TO DEVELOP TESTABLE TREATMENT HYPOTHESES

The main ethical issue involved in development of testable treatment hypotheses is competence. Regardless of which theoretical orientation is employed, a case conceptualization should be considered a set of hypotheses about a particular client that can be tested throughout treatment (Clark, 1999; Eells, 1997; Haynes, 1998; Persons, 2000). There must be an ongoing process of testing the hypotheses by implementing treatment techniques and then monitoring treatment outcome (Tompkins, 1999). In other words, a case conceptualization should be used in every session to guide ongoing treatment decisions (Persons, 2000). If treatment outcomes are negative or show no change, many therapists assume that such treatment techniques should be modified (Meier, 1999). However, it is also possible that the original hypotheses are incorrect and that the case conceptualization must be revised based on the new data obtained from repeated assessment and treatment outcome (Tompkins, 1999). By repeating this process throughout treatment, fewer treatment failures and improved client compliance with therapeutic tasks may result (Clark, 1999).

TREATMENT

PROFICIENCY 8: ABILITY TO OBTAIN CONSENT FROM CLIENTS FOR TREATMENT

There are two main ethical issues involved in obtaining consent for treatment. As with consent for assessment, the two issues are informed consent and multiple relationships. Informed consent is addressed in Standard 10.01 of the Ethics Code. This standard states that psychologists have an affirmative duty to "inform clients/patients as early as is feasible in the therapeutic relationship about the nature and anticipated course of therapy" (APA, 2002, p. 1072). Because the Ethics Code offers few specifics regarding the amount and type of information to provide to clients when obtaining informed consent to treatment, two other sources may be considered by psychologists. First, a DC Circuit court of Appeals case in 1972 (*Canterbury v. Spence*) introduced the "reasonable patient" concept. Following surgery to repair a ruptured disc that resulted in paralysis, a patient sued the surgeon, stating that the risk of paralysis was never discussed. The resulting court opinion stated that physicians have an affirmative duty to impart as much information as a reasonable patient would require, regardless of whether the patient asks for such information. Second, the Department of Health, Education, and Welfare (DHEW; as cited in Keith-Spiegel, 1983) issued guidelines in 1971 instructing researchers to provide the following information to all potential research subjects: (a) a fair and understandable explanation of the nature of the activity, its purpose, and the procedures to be followed, including an identification of those that are experimental; (b) an understandable description of the attendant discomforts and risks that may reasonably be expected to occur; (c) an understandable description of any benefits that may reasonably be expected to ensue; (d) an understandable disclosure of any appropriate alternative procedures that may be advantageous for the participant; (e) an offer to answer any inquiries concerning the procedures to be used; and (f) an understanding that the person is free to withdraw his or her consent and discontinue participation in the project or activity at any time without prejudice. Although neither the court opinion nor the DHEW guidelines speak directly to consent for treatment, these sources of information suggest that psychologists provide, at a minimum, the following information to all clients prior to implementing treatment: (a) potential benefits and risks of the contemplated treatment, (b) expected prognosis with and without treatment, and (c) any possible alternative treatments.

When providing services to couples and/or families, additional information must be provided. Standard 10.02 of the Ethics Code requires psychologists providing services to several related persons (e.g., spouses, significant others, or parents and children) to "take reasonable steps to clarify at the outset (1) which of the individuals are clients/patients and (2) the relationship the psychologist will have with each person. This clarification includes the psychologist's role and the probable uses of the services provided or the information obtained" (APA, 2002, pp. 1072–1073). If conflicts arise, psychologists should "take reasonable steps to clarify and modify, or withdraw from, roles appropriately" (APA, 2002, p. 1073).

Regardless of therapy modality (individual or family/couples), written consent documents that specify such things as client rights and responsibilities, limitations of confidentiality, and fees for services should be utilized in every case to ensure that consent is truly informed. These written consent documents should be read and signed by each client. They should also be reviewed orally with each client in language that is appropriate to the client's level of understanding and free from technical jargon or colloquial terminology (Mann, 1994; Welfel, 1998). In general, consent forms should be written at no higher than a seventh grade reading level (Miller, 2002). In addition to ensuring informed consent to treatment, written forms have been shown to have positive treatment effects. For example, Handelsman (1990) found that the use of written consent forms increased clients' positive judgments of therapists' experience, likeability, and trustworthiness.

PROFICIENCY 9: ABILITY TO UTILIZE EVIDENCE-BASED TECHNIQUES

The main ethical issue involved in the utilization of evidence-based techniques is competence. Evidence-based techniques are those treatments that have been supported in efficacy and effectiveness research studies (Kazdin & Weisz, 2003). Nowhere in the Ethics Code does it state that only evidence-based techniques must be used. However, Standard 10.01 of the Ethics Code does state that psychologists should inform their clients of "the developing nature of treatment" that may be interpreted to include the level of available research support (APA, 2002, p. 1072). Good practice suggests that psychologists should utilize treatments that have established research support for each client's presenting problems.

PROFICIENCY 10: ABILITY TO MONITOR TREATMENT OUTCOMES

The main ethical issue involved in monitoring treatment outcomes is competence. Standard 10.10 of the Ethics Code states that "psychologists terminate therapy when it becomes reasonably clear that the client/patient no longer needs the service, is not likely to benefit, or is being harmed by continued services" (APA, 2002, p. 1073). Clients and psychologists must work together to continually monitor symptoms and progress in treatment because Standard 10.10 suggests that it is unethical to continue seeing clients when they are not benefiting from the services. Utilizing multiple methods of assessment of client-presenting problems and/or symptoms on an ongoing basis will allow psychologists to quickly alter treatment techniques or to recommend termination of services if necessary.

PROFICIENCY 11: ABILITY TO DETERMINE IF/WHEN TO RELEASE TREATMENT INFORMATION

There are two main ethical issues involved in the decision to release treatment information: (1) confidentiality and (2) informed consent. The most common scenario requiring this decision to be made is one involving disclosure of potential harm to self or others. In these types of situations, legal statutes and/or case law (e.g., *Tarasoff v. Regents of the University of California*, 1976) allows psychologists to disclose confidential information without the consent of the client. All 50 states have legal statutes that mandate disclosure of various information, including child abuse, elder abuse, suicide, and/or imminent harm to self or others (Knapp & VandeCreek, 2006). Due to varying statutory requirements and case laws, psychologists must be aware of the requirements within the state in which they practice.

Proficiency 12: Ability to Set Appropriate Treatment Boundaries

The main ethical issue involved in setting appropriate boundaries is multiple relationships. As previously stated, only multiple relationships that could reasonably be expected to harm clients are prohibited. Specifically, the Ethics Code (APA, 2002) explicitly prohibits sexual relationships between psychologists and their clients. Such relationships have been shown to cause harm to clients, even to the point of suicide (Bouhoutsos, Holroyd, Lerman, Forer, & Greenberg, 1983). Primarily, Standard 10.05 prohibits psychologists from engaging in sexual intimacies with current therapy clients/patients. In addition, Standard 10.06 prohibits psychologists from engaging in sexual intimacies with "individuals they know to be close relatives, guardians, or significant others of current clients/patients" (APA, 2002, p. 1073). Standard 10.07 prohibits psychologists from accepting as therapy clients "persons with whom they have engaged in sexual intimacies" in the past (APA, 2002, p. 1073). Finally, Standard 10.08 prohibits psychologists from engaging in sexual intimacies "with former clients/patients for at least 2 years after cessation or termination of therapy" (APA, 2002, p. 1073). Even after the 2-year interval, Standard 10.08 discourages psychologists from engaging in such intimacies "except in the most unusual circumstances" by requiring psychologists to "bear the burden of demonstrating that there has been no exploitation" in any sexual situation (APA, 2002, p. 1073).

SUMMARY

In summary, an ethical psychologist is one who strives to work toward the best interests of the client. This means that the psychologist must work only within the bounds of his or her competence, must fully inform the client of the nature and potential outcomes of their work together, must respect and protect the client's confidentiality, and must strive to maintain professional boundaries. Each part of therapy (assessment, case conceptualization, and treatment) brings up its own unique ethical situations. However, by focusing at the outset of each case on the 12 proficiencies presented in this chapter, psychologists may prevent many ethical issues from occurring. At a minimum, by routinely focusing on the 12 proficiencies, psychologists may be better prepared to address any ethical dilemmas that do arise.

REFERENCES

Achenbach, T. M. (1991). *Manual for the Child Behavior Checklist/4-81 and 1991 profile*. Burlington: University of Vermont, Department of Psychiatry.

Adams, H. E., & Luscher, K. A. (2003). Ethical considerations in psychological assessment. In W. O'Donohue & K. Ferguson (Eds.), *Handbook of professional ethics for psychologists: Issues, questions, and controversies* (pp. 275–283). Thousand Oaks, CA: Sage.

American Psychological Association. (1990). *Guidelines for providers of psychological services to ethnic, linguistic, and culturally diverse populations*. Washington, DC: Author.

American Psychological Association (Committee on Ethical Guidelines for Forensic Psychologists). (1991). Specialty guidelines for forensic psychologists. *Law and Human Behavior, 15*(6), 655–665.

American Psychological Association (Committee on Psychological Tests and Assessment). (1996). Statement on the disclosure of test data. *American Psychologist, 51*(6), 644–648.

American Psychological Association (Test Taker Rights and Responsibilities Working Group of the Joint Committee on Test Taking Practices). (1998). *Rights and responsibilities of test takers: Guidelines and expectations.* Retrieved August 15, 2006, from http://www.apa.org/science/ttrr.html.

American Psychological Association. (2000). *Report of the task force on test user qualifications.* Retrieved August 15, 2006, from http://www.apa.org/science/tuq.pdf.

American Psychological Association. (2002). Ethical principles of psychologists and code of conduct. *American Psychologist, 57*(12), 1060–1073.

Anastasi, A. (1988). *Psychological testing* (6th ed.). New York: Macmillan.

Beck, A. T., & Steer, R. A. (1990). *Beck Anxiety Inventory (BAI).* San Antonio, TX: Psychological Corporation.

Beck, A. T., Steer, R. A., & Brown, G. K. (1996). *Beck Depression Inventory-II (BDI-II) manual.* San Antonio, TX: Psychological Corporation.

Beck, J. S. (1995). *Cognitive therapy: Basics and beyond.* New York: Guilford Press.

Bersoff, D. N. (Ed.). (1995). *Ethical conflicts in psychology.* Washington, DC: American Psychological Association.

Bouhoutsos, J., Holroyd, J., Lerman, H., Forer, B. R., & Greenberg, M. (1983). Sexual intimacy between psychotherapists and patients. *Professional Psychology: Research and Practice, 14,* 185–196.

Bruch, M. H. (1998). Cognitive-behavioral case formulation. In E. Sanavio (Ed.), *Behavior and cognitive therapy today: Essays in honor of Hans J. Eysenk* (pp. 31–48). Kidlington, Oxford, England: Pergamon Press.

Butcher, J. N., Dahlstrom, W. G., Graham, J. R., Tellegen, A., & Kaemmer, B. (1989). *Minnesota Multiphasic Personality Inventory-2 (MMPI-2): Manual for administration and scoring.* Minneapolis: University of Minnesota Press.

Canterbury v. Spence, 150 U.S. App. DC. 263 (1972).

Clark, D. A. (1999). Case conceptualization and treatment failure: A commentary. *Journal of Cognitive Psychotherapy: An International Quarterly, 13,* 331–337.

Cone, J. D. (1978). The behavioral assessment grid (BAG): A conceptual framework and a taxonomy. *Behavior Therapy, 9*(5), 882–888.

Conners, C. K. (1997). *Conners Rating Scales—Revised (CRS-R).* North Tonawanda, NY: Multi-Health Systems.

DeKraai, M. B., & Sales, B. D. (1982). Privileged communications of psychologists. *Professional Psychology, 32,* 372–388.

Eells, T. D. (1997). *Handbook of psychotherapy case formulation.* New York: Guilford Press.

Erard, R. E. (2004). Release of test data under the 2002 ethics code and the HIPAA privacy rule: A raw deal or just a half-baked idea? *Journal of Personality Assessment, 82*(1), 23–30.

Everstine, L., Everstine, D. S., Heymann, G. M., True, R. H., Frey, D. H., Johnson, H. G., et al. (1980). Privacy and confidentiality in psychotherapy. *American Psychologist, 35,* 828–840.

Eyberg, S., Bessmer, J., Newcomb, K., Edwards, D., & Robinson, R. (1994). *Dyadic parent-child interaction coding system-II: A manual.* Gainesville: University of Florida.

First, M. B., Spitzer, R. L., Gibbon, M., & Williams, J. B. W. (1996). *Structured Clinical Interview for DSM-IV Axis I Disorders, Clinician Version (SCID-CV).* Washington, DC: American Psychiatric Press.

Freeman, K. A., & Miller, C. A. (2002). Behavioral case conceptualization for children and adolescents. In M. Hersen (Ed.), *Clinical behavior therapy: Adults and children* (pp. 239–255). Hoboken, NJ: Wiley.

Fremouw, W., Johansson-Love, J., Tyner, E., & Strunk, J. (2006). Ethical/legal issues. In M. Hersen (Ed.), *Clinician's handbook of adult behavioral assessment* (pp. 547–565). San Diego, CA: Elsevier Academic Press.

Hambleton, R. K. (1994). Guidelines for adapting educational and psychological tests: A progress report. *European Journal of Psychological Assessment, 10*, 229–244.

Handelsman, M. M. (1990). Do written consent forms influence clients' first impressions of therapists? *Professional Psychology: Research and Practice, 21*(6), 451–454.

Haynes, S. N. (1998). On the changing nature of behavioral assessment. In A. S. Bellack & M. Hersen (Eds.), *Behavioral assessment: A practical handbook* (4th ed., pp. 1–21). Boston: Allyn & Bacon.

Health Insurance Portability and Accountability Act (HIPAA), Pub. L. No. 104-191 (1996).

Joint Committee of the American Educational Research Association, the American Psychological Association, and the National Council on Measurement in Education. (1999). *Standards for educational and psychological testing*. Washington, DC: AERA.

Kazdin, A. E., & Weisz, J. R. (Eds.). (2003). *Evidence-based psychotherapies for children and adolescents*. New York: Guilford Press.

Keith-Spiegel, P. (1983). Children and consent to participate in research. In G. B. Melton, G. P. Koocher, & M. J. Saks (Eds.), *Childrens' competence to consent* (pp. 179–211). New York: Plenum Press.

Knapp, S. J., & VandeCreek, L. D. (2006). *Practical ethics for psychologists: A positive approach*. Washington, DC: American Psychological Association.

Koocher, G. P., & Keith-Spiegel, P. (1998). *Ethics in psychology: Professional standards and cases* (2nd ed.). New York: Oxford University Press.

Mann, T. (1994). Informed consent for psychological research: Do subjects comprehend consent forms and understand their legal rights? *Psychological Science, 5*, 140–143.

Meier, S. T. (1999). Training the practitioner-scientist: Bridging case conceptualization, assessment, and intervention. *Counseling Psychologist, 27*, 846–869.

Miller, C. A. (2002, November). *Update on ethical and legal issues*. Workshop presented at Pacific University.

Miller, C. A. (2006). Ethical and legal issues. In M. Hersen (Ed.), *Clinician's handbook of child behavioral assessment* (pp. 631–644). San Diego, CA: Elsevier Academic Press.

Miller, C. A., & Evans, B. B. (2004). Ethical issues in assessment. In M. Hersen (Ed.), *Psychological assessment in clinical practice: A pragmatic guide* (pp. 21–32). New York: Brunner-Routledge.

Moreland, K. L., Eyde, L. D., Robertson, G. J., Primoff, E. S., & Most, R. B. (1995). Assessment of test user qualifications: A research-based measurement procedure. *American Psychologist, 50*, 14–23.

Persons, J. B. (2000, November). *Cognitive-behavioral case formulation and treatment planning*. Paper presented at the annual meeting of the Association for the Advancement of Behavior Therapy, New Orleans, LA.

Persons, J. B., & Tompkins, M. A. (1997). Cognitive-behavioral case formulation. In T. D. Eells (Ed.), *Handbook of psychotherapy case formulation* (pp. 314–339). New York: Guilford Press.

Reschly, D. J. (1981). Psychological testing in educational classification and placement. *American Psychologist, 36*(10), 1094–1102.

Rorschach, H. (1942). *Psychodiagnostics: A diagnostic test based on perception* (P. Lemkau & B. Kronenberg, Trans.). New York: Grune & Stratton. (Original work published 1921)

Sandoval, J., Frisby, C. L., Geisinger, K. F., Scheuneman, J. D., & Grenier, J. R. (Eds.). (1998). *Test interpretation and diversity: Achieving equity in assessment*. Washington, DC: American Psychological Association.

Smith, D. (2003). What you need to know about the new code. *Monitor on Psychology, 34*(1), 62.

Steele, C. M., & Aronson, J. (1995). Stereotype threat and the intellectual test performance of African Americans. *Journal of Personality and Social Psychology, 69*, 797–811.

Tarasoff v. Regents of the University of California, 17 Cal.3d 425 (1976).

Tompkins, M. A. (1999). Using case formulation to manage treatment nonresponse. *Journal of Cognitive Psychotherapy: An International Quarterly, 13*, 317–331.

Turner, S. M., DeMers, S. T., Fox, H. R., & Reed, G. M. (2001). APA's guidelines for test user qualifications. *American Psychologist, 56*(12), 1099–1113.

U.S. Department of Health and Human Services. (1999). *Mental health: A report of the surgeon general—Executive summary.* Rockville, MD: U.S. Department of Health and Human Services, Substance Abuse and Mental Health Services Administration, Center for Mental Health Services, National Institutes of Health, National Institute of Mental Health.

Wechsler, D. (1997). *Wechsler Adult Intelligence Scale-III.* San Antonio, TX: Psychological Corporation.

Weiner, I. B. (1989). On competence and ethicality in psychodiagnostic assessment. *Journal of Personality Assessment, 53*(4), 827–831.

Welfel, E. R. (1998). *Ethics in counseling and psychotherapy.* Pacific Grove, CA: Brooks/Cole.

PART II

ASSESSMENT, CONCEPTUALIZATION, AND TREATMENT OF SPECIFIC DISORDERS

CHAPTER 7

Specific Phobias

DEREK R. HOPKO, SARAH M. C. ROBERTSON,
LAURA WIDMAN, AND C. W. LEJUEZ

T he predominant feature of specific phobias is a strong and persistent fear of an object or situation that deviates markedly from societal norms and creates significant distress or impairment in functioning. Specific phobias are included under the broader diagnostic category of anxiety disorders (*DSM-IV-TR*; American Psychiatric Association, 2000) and represent a highly prevalent and potentially debilitating class of disorders. Accordingly, researchers and clinicians must make continued strides toward a better understanding of the etiological factors associated with the onset and persistence of specific phobias, as well as to continue to develop effective assessment and intervention strategies that will assist in the recognition of specific phobias and help to attenuate associated symptoms. As a move in this direction, this chapter highlights characteristic symptoms and epidemiological data on specific phobias, elucidates a range of diagnostic and assessment strategies, focuses on conceptual factors associated with the development and sustenance of specific phobias, addresses the most current cognitive-behavioral and pharmacological interventions for these conditions, and concludes with a case depicting the psychological assessment, case conceptualization, and treatment of a patient presenting with a specific phobia.

DESCRIPTION OF THE DISORDERS

Anxiety, fear, panic, and *stress* are normative existential phenomena that affect all human beings to some capacity, with marked variability in terms of environmental stimuli that elicit these reactions as well as the frequency and severity of responses that follow. Although such descriptive terminology often is used interchangeably, important phenomenological differences have been identified that assist in differentiating among these emotional states, with fear- and panic-related responding generally considered more similar than anxiety- or stress-related responding (Barlow, 2002). Although a specific phobia is considered an anxiety disorder, more intense panic and fear-related responding is quite common in those diagnosed with a specific phobia and is reflected in current diagnostic nomenclature. According to the *DSM-IV-TR* (American Psychiatric Association, 2000), a specific phobia involves a "marked and persistent fear that is excessive or unreasonable, cued by the presence (or anticipation) of a specific object or situation." In addition, individuals must: (a) experience the fear nearly every time the feared object or situation is encountered, (b) recognize the fear is excessive or unreasonable, (c) avoid the feared object or situation or endure exposure with intense anxiety, (d) experience significant distress and/or functional impairment from the fear or avoidance behavior, and (e) have had the problem for a minimum of 6 months. Although the scientific and clinical utility of creating a typology of specific phobias has been questioned on various grounds (Antony, Brown, & Barlow, 1997; Antony & Swinson, 2000; Muris, Schmidt, & Merckelbach, 1999), five primary subtypes of specific phobias have been identified including (1) *animal type* (e.g., spiders, dogs, insects), (2) *natural environment type* (e.g., heights, storms, water), (3) *blood-injection-injury type* (e.g., seeing blood, getting an injection), (4) *situational type* (e.g., flying, elevators, enclosed places), and (5) *other type* (e.g., situations that may lead to vomiting or choking; in children, avoidance of loud sounds or costumed characters).

The prevalence and functional impact of specific phobias is quite remarkable. Based on large-scale epidemiological studies that have incorporated structured diagnostic interviewing strategies, both the Epidemiological Catchment Area (ECA) study (Eaton, Dryman, & Weissman, 1991) and National Comorbidity Survey (NCS; Magee, Eaton, Wittchen, McGonagle, & Kessler, 1996) estimate the lifetime prevalence of specific phobias at approximately 11%. In examining differential lifetime prevalence rates of various phobias, the literature is fairly consistent in that approximately 5% to 7% of adult Americans will experience an animal phobia or height phobia during their lifetime, with slightly fewer developing phobias associated with enclosed spaces, flying, and storms (i.e., 3% to 4% for each; Bourdon et al., 1988; Curtis, Magee, Eaton, Wittchen, & Kessler, 1998; Fredrikson, Annas, Fischer, & Wik, 1996). As reported in a number of investigations incorporating epidemiological, clinical, and student samples (Bourdon et al., 1988; Cornelius & Averill, 1983; Curtis et al., 1998; Goisman et al., 1998) and for several plausible reasons (cf. Barlow, 2002), gender differences also are apparent, with females more likely to be diagnosed with specific phobias related to animals, lightning, enclosed places, and darkness (Fredrikson et al., 1996). Gender differences appear less likely in phobias related to heights, flying, injections, and dental experiences (Fredrikson et al., 1996). In relation to age of onset, although research largely is cross-sectional and retrospective in design, it appears that animal phobias and blood injection phobias may emerge earlier in childhood, whereas driving phobias and claustrophobia may develop more frequently in young adulthood (Antony et al., 1997; Bourdon et al., 1988; Marks & Gelder, 1966; Ost, 1987). Progressing through adulthood, data suggest equivalent prevalence rates between younger and older adults across most specific phobias, with the exception of storm and height phobias that may be more prevalent among older cohorts (Fredrikson et al., 1996).

Functional impairment associated with specific phobias also is quite extensive, including maladaptive cognitive processes and distorted beliefs (Jones & Menzies, 2000; Menzies & Clarke, 1995a; Rachman & Cuk, 1992; Woody & Teachman, 2000), substantial avoidance behaviors (Barlow, Allen, & Choate, 2004; Huijding & de Jong, 2006; Tolin, Lohr, Lee, & Sawchuk, 1999; Woody & Tolin, 2002) that may be associated with decreased engagement in pleasurable or rewarding behaviors and depressive affect (Lewinsohn, 1974), and poorer adherence to medical regimens in the case of individuals with blood-injection phobias (Mollema, Snoek, Ader, Heine, & van der Ploeg, 2001). Moreover, individuals with a specific phobia tend to be more vulnerable toward developing other specific phobias and there is a positive relationship between the number of phobias experienced and the likelihood of being diagnosed with other anxiety disorders such as panic disorder, generalized anxiety disorder (GAD), and social phobia (Curtis et al., 1998). Interestingly, relative to other anxiety disorders, individuals with specific phobias seem less likely to be diagnosed with depression and substance use disorders (Lehman, Patterson, Brown, & Barlow, 1998; Schatzberg, Samson, Rothschild, Bond, & Regier, 1998).

DIAGNOSIS AND ASSESSMENT

Several assessment strategies have been developed to assess for specific phobias and may generally be characterized in the domains of unstructured or structured interviews, self-report measures, observational methods, and functional analysis.

UNSTRUCTURED AND STRUCTURED INTERVIEWS

The structure of clinical interviews has tremendous variability, ranging from primarily unstructured and completely flexible approaches to more restrictive and goal-directed structured clinical interviews. Regardless of which interviewing strategy is chosen, several central issues should be considered when assessing for specific phobias. The degree to which certain objects and situations elicit fear should be assessed, including the breadth and severity of fears, and whether fear and anxiety results in a substantial degree of behavioral avoidance. The extent of distress and functional impairment associated with the phobic reaction also should be determined. Other pertinent information to be obtained would involve an understanding of the etiology of the specific phobia; physiological, cognitive, and behavioral manifestations of fear; prior psychosocial and pharmacological treatment; and various familial factors (Antony & Swinson, 2000). With the purpose of exploring such issues, and acknowledging limited practicality in certain clinical settings, various structured (clinician-rated) interviews may facilitate this process. These interviews would include the Structured Clinical Interview for DSM-IV—Patient Version (SCID-I/P; First, Spitzer, Gibbon, & Williams, 1996), Anxiety Disorders Interview Schedule (ADIS-IV; T. A. Brown, DiNardo, & Barlow, 1994), Schedule for Affective Disorders and Schizophrenia—Lifetime Anxiety Version (SADS-LA; Fyer et al., 1989; Mannuzza et al., 1989), Diagnostic Interview Schedule (DIS-IV; Robins, Cottler, Bucholz, & Compton, 1995), and the Primary Care Evaluation of Mental Disorders (PRIME-MD; Spitzer et al., 1994). Indeed, these structured interviews differ on a multitude of dimensions (Blanchard & Brown, 1998), and the decision of which (if any) to incorporate should be based on practical issues as well as clinicians' skill and competence toward comprehensively assessing relevant issues and content areas in the absence of these methods (Antony & Swinson, 2000).

SELF-REPORT MEASURES

Self-report measures of specific phobias are useful as screening instruments, auxiliaries in the diagnostic process, tools for monitoring progress across treatment sessions, and outcome measures for assessing the efficacy and effectiveness of various psychosocial and pharmacological interventions. Scales are available to assess a range of content areas, including affective, verbal-cognitive, somatic, behavioral, and social symptoms of specific phobias. At present, there are at least 40 measures designed to assess for symptoms associated with specific phobias. The majority of these instruments have adequate to excellent psychometric properties (see Antony, Orsillo, & Roemer, 2001, for a comprehensive review). A few of the most commonly utilized measures include the Blood-Injection Symptom Scale (BISS; Page, Bennett, Carter, Smith, & Woodmore, 1997), the Fear Survey Schedule (FSS; Wolpe & Lang, 1964), the Fear Questionnaire (FQ; Marks & Mathews, 1979), the Medical Fear Survey (MFS; Kleinknecht, Thorndike, & Walls, 1996), and the Spider Phobia Beliefs Questionnaire (SPBQ; Arntz, Lavy, van den Berg, & van Rijsoort, 1993).

OBSERVATIONAL METHODS

Observational methods of assessing symptoms of specific phobias are used to measure the frequency and duration of observable (overt-motor) behaviors as well as physiological indices of fear. The most common tool for assessing overt fear responses is the behavioral avoidance test (BAT). Perhaps a more valid index of behavioral responding than retrospective recall and self-report, BATs allow for direct observation of patient behavior when exposed to feared stimuli. As indicated in previous works (Antony et al., 2001; Antony & Swinson, 2000), BAT assessment may be either *progressive* or *selective* in nature. With *progressive BATs*, patients are required to approach feared stimuli in a gradual manner, with fearful responding measured at each hierarchical level. For example, a patient with a flying phobia may engage in a BAT that includes reserving a plane flight, thinking about a flight 1 week before departure, thinking about a flight the evening before departure, packing luggage in the morning, taking a taxi cab to the airport, checking in luggage, maneuvering through security, waiting for boarding, actually boarding an aircraft, taxiing down the runway, preparing for takeoff, speeding down the runway, cruising at 30,000 feet, and landing in an aircraft. Variables to be assessed might include subjective units of discomfort (SUDS; Wolpe, 1958) ratings at each step, or anxious cognitions experienced in each instance. Alternatively, when feasible, physiological indices such as heart rate, respiratory rate, and skin conductance also could be measured. By contrast, *selective BATs* involve more of a nonsystematic approach in which patients might be required to enter one or more situations (from a hierarchy) in a nonprogressive and somewhat divergent manner. For example, the patient with a flying phobia might be asked to fly on an airplane (directly related to the phobia), climb a sizeable ladder (to assess a more general fear of height), and engage in interoceptive exposure exercises such as hyperventilation or intense exercise (to assess symptoms of panic). Although both progressive and selective BATs are commonly used, the choice to use one or the other largely depends on clinician and patient preferences, time constraints, and the presenting symptoms of the patient and corresponding case conceptualization. Regardless of which method is chosen, it is recommended that BATs be repeated intermittently throughout and following treatment to assess patient progress.

As a complement to interviewing strategies, self-report measures, and BATs, behavioral monitoring logs or diaries may be used to provide information about anxiety-related responding as well as patients' sources of environmental reinforcement. These methods are used extensively in the context of treating various anxiety and mood disorders and are incorporated in a number of different treatment manuals (Andrews et al., 2003; Craske, Antony, & Barlow, 1997; Lejuez, Hopko, & Hopko, 2002; Lewinsohn, Munoz, Youngren, & Zeiss, 1986). Although the specific data being recorded varies somewhat across anxiety disorders and with respect to unique patient variables and symptoms, commonly recorded information would include day and time of exposure to feared stimulus, a description of the situation and antecedent variables, highlighting of specific symptoms and their intensity, specific anxious thoughts and any coping statements used in the situation, physiological experiences, a description of anxiety or fear-related behaviors that would include an indication of avoidance or escape tendencies, and monitoring of the consequences that follow from engaging in particular behaviors. Recording behaviors in this way simultaneously allows for a more comprehensive psychological assessment and conveniently provides a baseline by which patient progress can be evaluated throughout treatment. Given that anxiety disorders frequently coexist with mood disorders, diaries and monitoring logs that assess the frequency and duration of depressive behaviors as well as healthy nondepressive activities may assist in assessment, treatment planning, and measurement of treatment outcome (Lejuez et al., 2002; Martell, Addis, & Jacobson, 2001). Research has indicated that daily diaries can be useful in assessing both immediate and future reward value of current behaviors, that reward value ratings correlate highly with self-report measures of negative affect, and that mildly depressed and nondepressed students can be distinguished via response style on these measures (Hopko, Armento, Chambers, Cantu, & Lejuez, 2003).

Functional Analysis

Functional analysis generally refers to the process of identifying important, controllable, and causal environmental factors that may be related to the etiology and maintenance of pathological symptoms (Haynes & O'Brien, 1990). Applied to specific phobias, functional analysis involves the operational definition of undesirable (nonhealthy) fear-related behaviors such as escape, avoidance, and freezing or immobility (Marks, 1987). Strategies for conducting functional analysis include interviews with the patient and significant others, naturalistic observation, and/or the manipulation of specific situations that result in an increase or decrease of target behaviors (O'Neill, Horner, Albin, Storey, & Sprague, 1990). Often incorporating daily monitoring procedures, phobic patients may be asked to record phobic (target) behaviors, the context (e.g., time, place, surroundings) in which they occur, and the consequences that follow. With all functional analytic strategies, the therapist is concerned with identifying the function (or maintaining reinforcers) of the particular phobic behaviors exhibited by the patient. These behaviors may develop and persist because of response-contingent positive reinforcement and may be maintained via the experience of pleasant consequences (e.g., other people completing responsibilities; attention and sympathy) and/or as a result of removing aversive experiences (i.e., contact with the phobic object).

In addition to using functional analytic techniques to understand overt behavior, these strategies also may be useful for understanding maladaptive thought processes associated with fear-related responding. Indeed, through strategies that include the use of thought-monitoring logs or various thought-sampling methods (Csikszentmihalyi & Larson, 1987; Hurlburt, 1997), functional analysis can be used to identify specific thought patterns elicited by certain environmental events and how these cognitions may correspond with fearful affect and behavior. These same methods also may be utilized to assess change during and following psychotherapy that focuses on restructuring maladaptive or irrational cognitions.

Functional analysis methods may be useful in integrating assessment data or developing hypotheses about factors maintaining phobic behaviors and may greatly assist in the formulation of a treatment plan. From a pragmatic standpoint, the practice of conducting functional analysis requires extensive training and skill and is largely based on complex causal models of behavior disorders. Accordingly, it is not surprising that the literature suggests that pretreatment functional analyses are infrequently conducted (Haynes & O'Brien, 1990) and only rarely implemented in the assessment and treatment of specific phobias. Functional analytic strategies may be quite useful in generating specific treatment goals, as a method of intervention, and as a complement to other strategies to assess phobic disorders (Haynes, 1998).

CONCEPTUALIZATION

LEARNING AND MODELING

A substantial body of research has examined etiological models of phobia acquisition (Antony & Swinson, 2000; Craske, 2003; Mineka & Zinbarg, 1996; Mowrer, 1939; Ost & Hugdahl, 1981; Rachman, 1976, 1977, 1978; Rimm & Lefebvre, 1987) including conditioning, cognitive, and evolutionary paradigms. In the earliest of conditioning models, Mowrer (1939) highlighted a two-stage process in which phobias were developed through a classical conditioning process and were maintained through operant conditioning principles or the avoidance associated with negative reinforcement. However, more than 6 decades of research on the etiology of specific phobias has indicated that the development of specific phobias may be much more multifaceted, with many phobias originating without direct conditioning. These research efforts resulted in a subsequent expansion of the fear acquisition model with three distinct pathways proposed as relevant toward understanding the etiology of phobias (Rachman, 1976, 1977). In addition to the first pathway, *direct conditioning*, Rachman (1976) suggested that phobias may also develop via observing another individual behave fearfully in the presence of a feared object or situation (the second pathway, *vicarious conditioning*) or through receiving *information and instruction*, the third pathway, such as when an individual develops an animal phobia by reading or watching television programs about malicious dog attacks.

A large body of research has supported Rachman's extended model (Antony & Barlow, 1997) although the contention continues to be that direct conditioning experiences tend to be more frequently reported than either vicarious acquisition or informational onsets (Barlow, 2002). Using a sample of animal phobics, social phobics, and claustrophobics, Ost and Hugdahl (1981) demonstrated that 58% of individuals asserted that direct conditioning experiences were directly linked to the onset of their phobia, whereas 17% attributed the phobia to vicarious experiences, 10% to information, and 15% being unable to recall the specific circumstances associated with the development of the anxiety disorder. More comprehensive estimates of the impact of direct traumatic experiences indicate that between 27% to 67% of individuals with animal fears, 69% of those with claustrophobia, 50% to 100% of individuals with blood-injection-injury phobias, and 70% of people with driving phobias may have had direct conditioning experiences (cf. Craske, 2003). In contrast, retrospective estimates for vicarious acquisition of phobias range from 9% for claustrophobia (Ost & Hugdahl, 1981) to 28% to 71% for animal fears (Fredrikson, Fischer, & Wik, 1997; King, Clowes-Hollins, & Ollendick, 1997; Merckelbach, Arntz, Arrindell, & de Jong, 1992). Comparatively, retrospective estimates for informational transmission as the primary etiological factor in phobias range from 11% for claustrophobia (Ost & Hugdahl, 1981) to 6% to 15% for animal fears (Fredrikson, Fischer, et al., 1997; King et al., 1997; Merckelbach et al., 1992). A good body of comparative research also supports the generalization of direct and vicarious conditioning models toward understanding fear experienced by various animal species (Barlow, 2002; Mineka, Davidson, Cook, & Keir, 1984; Mineka & Zinbarg, 1996).

A revised three-pathway model (Rachman, 1976) has provided a more comprehensive theoretical basis by which to examine the etiology of phobias. It also is true that tremendous variability has been documented across studies with respect to the relative significance of etiological pathways. Among the many reasons for these discrepancies are different approaches to deriving specific diagnoses, periodic use of poorly diagnosed samples (i.e., uncontrolled coexistent psychiatric disorders), divergent methods of determining which events should be allocated as causal toward phobia development, examination of single versus multiple events, and so forth. Despite these limitations, a number of recent methodological advances have resulted in better quality research that allow for a firmer understanding of fear acquisition (Barlow, 2002), including (a) researchers are beginning to more carefully diagnose and document patient samples; (b) research designs are increasingly incorporating comparison groups of individuals without phobias; and perhaps most important (c) researchers are beginning to focus more heavily on recruiting child samples (Poulton, Menzies, Craske, Langley, & Silva, 1999). This longitudinal method allows for stronger assertions regarding issues of causality and avoids the many problems associated with retrospective accounts of behaviors and experiences.

As programs of research continue to be refined, two additional pressing issues will need to be addressed and better accommodated into existing theoretical models. First, there is good evidence that the three primary pathways do not exclusively account for the development of phobic responding. Whether they actually occurred, many individuals cannot recall precipitating events. Second, many individuals experience what would generally be considered a traumatic conditioning experience (direct or vicarious) or have substantial exposure to information and yet do not develop a specific phobia. Factors that seem to protect (or buffer) against the potential impact of environmental stressors as well as those associated with increased vulnerability and diathesis toward developing this disorder must therefore be further explored. Finally, because evolutionary models may account for variance in understanding fear acquisition (Harris & Menzies, 1996; Menzies & Clarke, 1995b), further pursuing innate predispositions and biological preparedness factors that may pertain to phobia development will be an important area of research.

LIFE EVENTS

As addressed in the previous section, data suggest life events that involve direct (traumatic) conditioning, vicarious conditioning, or information and instruction may contribute to the onset and persistence of specific phobias. In a recent model of the etiology of specific phobias (Barlow, 2002), these direct and vicarious experiences represent life events that elicit *true alarms*. These true alarms are physiological, cognitive, and behavioral responses that are elicited by an object or situation in a particular context. However, whether a specific phobia evolves out of this life experience is dependent on many contextual factors (Barlow, 2002; Mineka & Zinbarg, 1996). For example, stress-in-dynamic-context anxiety models (SIDCA; Mineka & Zinbarg, 1996) highlight the importance of constitutional factors such as temperament, past experiential history (e.g., previous exposure to uncontrollable life events; prior traumatic conditioning), current contextual factors at the time of the stressor (e.g., whether there are reliable predictors of the stressor; whether it can be controlled), and future impact of the stressor (e.g., degree of forgetting that transpires following the stressful event; breadth and intensity of later exposures to stressful events). In addition to these variables, generalized biological vulnerabilities also may mediate the relationship between stressful life events and the development of specific phobias. These vulnerabilities may take the form of selective associations or heritable tendencies that provide for a biological preparedness to develop fears to certain objects that represent a threat to human beings (e.g., heights, snakes). They also might involve low thresholds for specific defense reactions such as decreased alarm resistance and heightened vasovagal responses (Barlow, 2002). It is precisely these contextual factors and biological vulnerabilities that may allow us to answer relevant questions such as why (a) many people who have traumatic conditioning histories do not develop phobias, (b) human beings are more apt to develop fears and phobias to specific objects and situations, and (c) responses conditioned to fear-relevant objects are more resistant to extinction than responses conditioned to fear-irrelevant objects (McNally, 1987; Mineka & Zinbarg, 1996). Another issue that can be addressed in these contextual models is the answer to why a large number of individuals may develop a specific phobia despite never having a direct conditioning experience. In this view, biological and psychological vulnerabilities (e.g., "physiological sensations are dangerous"; "bad thoughts are dangerous") may interact with several life experiences. Stress that is experienced due to negative life events may result in *false alarms* (i.e., anxiety-related responding) that become associated with predisposed or prepared situations (Barlow, 2002). It has been demonstrated that the life experiences that precipitate phobia onset often do not resemble the situations feared (Magee, 1999; Reiss, 1991). So in essence, life events and experiences may directly elicit a phobic reaction through direct conditioning and associated vulnerabilities or, more indirectly, by eliciting stress that weakens psychological immunity and setting the occasion for an inappropriate response in the presence of given environmental objects or situations.

Given the relation between life events and the direct or indirect development of specific phobias and other psychiatric disorders (Coddington, 1972a, 1972b; Goodyer & Altham, 1991; Magee, 1999), to what degree can these events be qualified or quantified? A single stressful event or a multiplicity of stressful events may elicit anxiety disorders though it appears that the more chronic and intense the exposure to environmental stress, the greater the likelihood of developing psychopathology (Kessler, Davis, & Kendler, 1997). A number of specific life events have been associated with the onset of anxiety disorders, including natural and manmade disasters, parental death, parental divorce (prior to the child becoming 16 years of age), parental psychopathology, physical assaults, threats with weapons or kidnapping, witnessing the serious injury or death of another, shock on hearing of a terrible event that occurred to another, rape or molestation of a relative or nonrelative, and combat in war (Burnam et al., 1988; Galea et al., 2002; Kessler et al., 1997; Magee, 1999; McFarlane,

Clayer, & Bookless, 1997; Otto, Boos, Dalbert, Schops, & Hoyer, 2006). Of these variables, loss of a mother before age 10, violence at the hands of an adult, verbal aggression between parents, and parental divorce may be more strongly related to phobia acquisition (Magee, 1999; Tweed, Schoenbach, George, & Blazer, 1989) with the effects of other life events being largely nonspecific to particular disorders (Kessler et al., 1997).

Research exploring the impact of life events in the etiology of specific phobias and other anxiety disorders is in large part limited by its cross-sectional and retrospective nature, greatly restricting the ability to draw conclusions on causal relationships. Focused programs of longitudinal research will be necessary to better disentangle how negative life events influence the development of specific phobias, with attention to the complex interrelations among biological processes, psychological vulnerabilities, general (i.e., life stress) and specific environmental influences (i.e., direct conditioning), and the many other contextual factors outlined earlier in the SIDCA model (Mineka & Zinbarg, 1996). Among the many lines of research that are worthwhile to pursue, the role of perceived predictability and control over life experiences may be uniquely associated with certain anxiety disorders, including panic disorder and specific phobias (Magee, 1999; Zvolensky, Lejuez, & Eifert, 2000).

GENETIC INFLUENCES

Over the past 3 decades, several twin and family studies have attempted to identify the genetic basis of specific phobias. In general, these studies suggest a strong genetic influence for specific phobias, with some heritability estimates up to 50% (e.g., Kendler, Karkowski, & Prescott, 1999; Lichtenstein & Annas, 2000). Across twin studies, monozygotic twins show higher specific phobia concordance than dizygotic twins (Kendler, Myers, Prescott, & Neale, 2001; Lichtenstein & Annas, 2000; Torgersen, 1979), providing evidence for a genetic basis of this disorder. Further supporting this contention, through utilization of multivariate genetic analyses, a recent study of over 5,000 individuals from a large twin study found specific phobias may have a unique genetic factor not associated with other anxiety disorders (Hettema, Prescott, Myers, Neale, & Kendler, 2005). Family studies also support a genetic basis of phobia development. Research by Fyer and colleagues (Fyer, Mannuzza, Chapman, Martin, & Klein, 1995; Fyer et al., 1990) demonstrated that rates of specific phobia were three to four times more common in relatives of phobic patients than relatives of nonphobic individuals. Similarly, a familial study of women with snake or spider phobias found that parental prevalence rates of these phobias were elevated beyond what would be expected in a normal population (Fredrikson, Annas, & Wik, 1997). Together, these findings suggest there may be a distinct genetic pathway(s) in the etiology of specific phobias.

Although strong evidence suggests a genetic basis for specific phobias, it should be noted that research also indicates environmental factors are very consequential. Specifically, one study of anxiety disorders among twin pairs found the prevalence rate of simple phobias was similar between twins of anxiety probands and comparison probands, and did not differ between monozygotic and dizygotic twins (Skre, Onstad, Torgersen, Lygren, & Kringlen, 1993). When considering these results in the context of other genetic evidence, it seems likely that both genetic and environmental factors contribute to the development of specific phobias. However, it is also possible genetic influences vary within specific phobias. Studies suggest animal phobias may have the strongest genetic influence with heritability estimates ranging from 35% to 66% across studies (for review, see Skre, Onstad, Torgersen, Lygren, & Kringlen, 2000). In contrast, situational phobias may have the weakest genetic basis (Skre et al., 2000). Future studies that clearly specify the specific phobia under investigation and directly compare heritability indices among phobia subtypes may help us better understand the genetic basis of these disorders.

NEUROIMAGING

In addition to twin and family studies, advances in neuroimaging technology over the past decade have made it possible to examine the neural substrates associated with specific phobias. At present, approximately a dozen studies have been published using positron emission tomography (PET), magnetic resonance imaging (MRI), functional magnetic resonance imaging (fMRI), and single photon emission computed tomography (SPECT) scans to detect neuroanatomical differences between individuals with specific phobias and healthy controls. At least seven studies have utilized PET scans to compare regional cerebral blood flow in individuals with animal phobia under exposure and neutral conditions (Fredrikson, et al., 1993; Fredrikson, Wik, Annas, Ericson, & Stone-Elander, 1995; Mountz et al., 1989; Rauch et al., 1995; Reiman, 1997; Veltman, Tuinebreijer, Winkelman, Lammertsma, & Emmelkamp, 2004; Wik et al., 1993). Of the seven, one study found no change in cerebral blood flow between conditions (Mountz et al., 1989), and six found significant change in blood flow during exposure to the phobic stimulus (Fredrikson et al., 1993, 1995; Rauch et al., 1995; Reiman, 1997; Wik et al., 1993) although these changes were in different cortical areas and occasionally in different directions. Whereas some studies found decreased blood flow in the orbitofrontal and temporal lobes (e.g., Fredrikson et al., 1995; Wik et al., 1993), one study found increased blood flow in these regions (Rauch et al., 1995). In an attempt to reconcile these differing results, a seventh study by Veltman and colleagues (2004) compared 11 individuals with spider phobias to 6 healthy controls and examined habituation to phobic stimuli. For the phobic group, prolonged exposure to the phobic stimuli resulted in significant decreases in cerebral blood flow in the bilaterial anterior medial temporal lobe, including the amygdala. The authors suggested that amygdala habituation observed in this study may have been missed in earlier studies, highlighting the potential role of the amygdala in both phobic fear acquisition and habituation.

At least four studies have used MRI to investigate the neuroanatomy of specific phobias. In the most recent study, Schienle and colleagues (Schienle, Schafer, Walter, Stark, & Vaitl, 2005) examined fear and disgust reactivity in 10 individuals with spider phobias and 13 controls. Relative to individuals in the control group, the phobia sample exhibited increased activation in the visual association cortex, right dorsolateral prefrontal cortex, right hippocampus, and amygdala. Similar to these findings, Dilger et al. (2003) found increased amygdala activation in individuals with spider phobias relative to controls, further demonstrating the important role of the amygdala in phobic disorders. In a related fMRI study, Wright and colleagues (Wright, Martis, McMullin, Shin, & Rauch, 2003) examined whether increased amygdala activity would be present for phobic individuals under neutral conditions. To test this, 10 individuals with small animal phobias and 10 controls were exposed to visually presented human faces expressing emotional reactions. No differences in amygdala activation were found between phobic and control participants. However, there was increased right posterior insular activation among individuals with phobias, even under neutral conditions (for discussion, see Wright et al., 2003). Finally, MRI scans were used to investigate the cortical thickness of 10 individuals with specific phobia and 10 matched healthy controls. Results revealed that individuals with specific phobias had greater cortical thickness in the paralimbic and sensory cortex regions than healthy controls (Rauch et al., 2004). Although these researchers acknowledge the significance of this increased cortical thickness is unclear, they suggest it could signal a vulnerability factor toward developing phobic reactions.

Although the field of neuroimaging is growing rapidly and has the potential to greatly enhance our understanding of the neuroanatomical basis of specific phobias, at present the limited number of studies, small sample sizes, varied results, and cross-sectional data make it difficult to draw firm conclusions. For example, it is presently impossible to determine if the differences in neural structure (Rauch et al., 2004) and cerebral blood flow (e.g., Veltman et al., 2004) between phobics and healthy controls precede or follow phobia development. Longitudinal work and replication of the neuroimaging studies that currently exist will contribute greatly to our understanding of specific phobia development.

CULTURAL AND DIVERSITY ISSUES

African Americans   In general, research suggests African Americans are at an increased risk for developing specific phobias. Findings from over 18,000 individuals in the National Institutes of Mental Health Epidemiological Catchment Area (ECA) study of five U.S. cities found that compared to Hispanic and non-Black individuals, Black females were significantly more likely to have at least one simple phobia (Bourdon et al., 1988). There was also a nonsignificant trend in this study for Black males to be diagnosed with simple phobias more often than Hispanic and non-Black individuals. Using a subsample of the ECA survey, a separate study found the 1-month prevalence rate of phobic disorders was one-and-a-half times greater for Blacks than Whites, even controlling for significant demographic and socioeconomic factors (D. R. Brown, Eaton, & Sussman, 1990). From the U.S. National Comorbidity Study (NCS) that incorporated a nationwide stratified sample of over 8,000 individuals, Curtis and colleagues (1998) found that African Americans were at risk for an increased number of phobias. Although these findings suggest African Americans are at greater risk for specific phobia than Caucasians and Hispanics, at least one recent study found no significant differences between these groups. Breslau et al. (2006) compared rates of several anxiety disorders, including specific phobias across 5,000 participants from the National Comorbidity Study Replication (NCS-R), a nationally representative follow-up study to the NCS. Lifetime rates of specific phobia did not differ between African Americans, non-Hispanic Whites, and Hispanics, even when age, education, and onset of the disorder were controlled. In fact, African Americans actually showed decreased rates of anxiety disorders in general.

Hispanics   Using ECA survey data, Karno et al. (1989) conducted one of the first studies to examine racial differences in phobia prevalence among Hispanics. Higher prevalence rates were found among U.S.-born Mexican Americans (12.7%) relative to immigrant Mexican Americans (7.8%) or native non-Hispanic Whites (6.8%). Phobia rates did not statistically differ across the latter two groups. These researchers suggested the differences between immigrant and U.S.-born Hispanics may be due to the tendency for less distressed individuals to migrate from Mexico to the United States. It is also possible these differences are attributable to acculturation issues, as evidenced by one study that found Hispanic Americans who reported higher levels of U.S. acculturation also reported more phobic symptoms (Escobar, Karno, Burnam, Hough, & Golding, 1988). In further support of these findings, NCS data revealed that relative to non-Hispanics, Hispanics were at greater risk for developing specific phobias (Curtis et al., 1998). Taken together, findings suggest that Hispanic Americans, particularly those born in the United States, are at greater vulnerability for specific phobias than Caucasians. However, these data also should be interpreted in the context of a more recent study where no differences in the rates of specific phobias were evident across Hispanics, non-Hispanic Whites, and African Americans (Breslau et al., 2006).

Other Minority Groups   To the authors' knowledge, Asian Americans, Native Americans, and many other racial minority groups have largely been excluded in prevalence rate comparisons of specific phobias. However, Asian Americans were included in one study that combined specific phobias with agoraphobia and social phobia using a subsample of participants from the ECA study (Zhang & Snowden, 1999). Significant group differences were discovered in lifetime rates of phobias among Whites (11.5%), Blacks (19.9%), Hispanics (12.7%), and Asian Americans (6.6%), with the latter group having the lowest prevalence of phobias. Although it is impossible to determine the direct effects of race on the development of specific phobias from this single finding, it certainly suggests the need to further explore whether specific phobia vulnerability is lower among Asian Americans relative to other racial groups.

Geographic Differences (Region/Urbanicity/Country)

Differences within the United States   Two published studies have examined residential location in association to specific phobias in the United States. First, in the NCS study, Curtis et al. (1998) found no differences in specific phobia rates by region or urban residential status. Similarly, a study of urban-rural differences by George, Hughes, and Blazer (1986) compared rates of anxiety disorders across residents of one urban county (Durham County, North Carolina) to four rural North Carolina counties. Although urban residents appeared more vulnerable toward developing panic disorder and agoraphobia, no urban-rural differences were detected for specific phobias, and no between-group differences were found when participants were compared across demographic variables.

Differences across Countries   Comparing specific phobias across countries is a difficult task. Standard diagnostic criteria, such as those found in the *DSM-IV TR* (American Psychiatric Association, 2000), may not apply cross-culturally as some manifestations of anxiety are culturally specific (for discussion, see Guarnaccia, 1997). Also, a paucity of data exists on this topic, and results of the few international studies that have been done must therefore be interpreted cautiously. A literature review revealed only three studies that examined rates of specific phobias across countries. Chambers, Yeragani, and Keshavan (1986) compared 39 phobic individuals from India with 39 diagnosed individuals from the United Kingdom and found specific phobias of animals, darkness, bad weather, sudden death, and illness were all more common in India than the United Kingdom. Similar work was done comparing rates of phobias between Puerto Rican and U.S. citizens (Rubio-Stipec, Shrout, Bird, Canino, & Bravo,

1989; Shrout et al., 1992), but agoraphobia and social phobia were highlighted in the data analyses with no specific focus on the relative rates of specific phobias across countries. Likewise, exploration into cross-cultural differences in fear has found that children from African countries report higher levels of fear than children from the United States, Australia, and China (Ingman, Ollendick, & Akande, 1999). However, it is unclear if the fears reported in these studies are phenomenologically indicative of symptoms associated with specific phobias.

Education, Class, and Socioeconomic Status   An empirical link between specific phobias and education or social class has yet to be identified. In a study of phobias among 449 adult women, Costello (1982) found that social class, employment, and education were unrelated to phobic disorders. Likewise, using the ECA sample of over 18,000 men and women, Bourdon et al. (1988) found that education, socioeconomic status, and marital status were unrelated to simple phobias. Finally, the Breslau et al. (2006) study that incorporated the NCS-R sample found no significant difference in lifetime prevalence of specific phobias among racial groups when examining parental education and participant education status.

Religion   At present, examinations of religions affiliation or beliefs and specific phobias are sparse. One study examined religion and anxiety disorders in a sample of 1,025 young, 645 middle, and 1,299 elderly adults from a single cite of the ECA survey (Koenig, Ford, George, Blazer, & Medor, 1993). In this study, religious affiliation, actions, and beliefs were largely unrelated to specific phobias with one exception. Young adults who reported religion was very important to them had higher rates of simple phobia than those who said religion was somewhat or not at all important. Replication of this finding and more research in this area is needed.

Sexual Orientation   There are currently no data examining the relationship between sexual orientation and specific phobias although limited research exploring sexual orientation and social phobia does exist (e.g., Eckleberry, Jodie, & Dohrenwend, 2005; Golwyn & Sevlie, 1993). Examining this diversity issue in relationship to specific phobia may be a fruitful avenue for future research.

BEHAVIORAL TREATMENT

Cognitive-behavioral therapy and associated treatment manuals (Antony, Craske, & Barlow, 1995; Craske et al., 1997) are considered empirically supported interventions for specific phobias (Chambless & Ollendick, 2001; DeRubeis & Crits-Christoph, 1998). Although relatively less studied, there also are data to suggest similar interventions may be useful when implemented with children and adolescents (King, Heyne, & Ollendick, 2005). Cognitive-behavioral interventions generally are considered the treatment of choice for specific phobias and include four primary intervention methods: (1) exposure-based interventions, (2) eye movement desensitization and reprocessing (EMDR), (3) cognitive therapy, and (4) applied tension for blood phobias.

EXPOSURE-BASED INTERVENTIONS

Exposure-based psychotherapy for anxiety disorders is considered one of the hallmarks of behavior therapy and can be traced back to the early works of Joseph Wolpe when he highlighted the process of systematic desensitization (Wolpe, 1973). Systematic desensitization involves three primary stages: First, patients are trained in the use of progressive muscle relaxation. Second, the therapist and patient collaboratively construct an anxiety hierarchy where feared stimuli are documented according to the perceived level of patient stress. Third, imaginal exposure procedures are then used to systematically move through the hierarchy, with patients encouraged to utilize previously learned relaxation strategies to combat intrusive cognitions and physiological arousal that may be elicited by engaging in imaginal exercises. As the efficiency and usefulness of incorporating relaxation-based components has come to be questioned, and the notion has been solidified that exposure may be the active mechanism of change (Al-Kubaisy, Marks, Logsdail, & Marks, 1992; Barlow, 2002; Gilroy, Kirkby, Daniels, Menzies, & Montgomery, 2000; Ost, Lindahl, Sterner, & Jerremalm, 1984), *pure* exposure interventions have come to be the preferred behavioral intervention for specific phobias. There is also some contention that in vivo exposure interventions may be somewhat more effective than imaginal procedures (Barlow, 2002; Emmelkamp & Wessels, 1975). To date, an ever growing body of research is supporting the efficacy of in vivo exposure for many specific phobias (cf. Barlow, 2002), including fear of flying (Ost, Brandberg, & Alm, 1997), water (Menzies & Clarke, 1993), spiders (Gotestam, 2002; Hellstrom & Ost, 1995; Ost, 1996), snakes (Gauthier & Marshall, 1997), heights (Bourque & Ladouceur, 1980), enclosed places (Craske, Mohlman, Yi, Glover, & Valeri, 1995), and blood (Cox, Mohr, & Epstein, 2004; Ost, Fellenius, & Sterner, 1991).

The frequency and duration of exposure-based interventions is considerably variable and, quite interestingly, even single (2- to 3-hour) sessions have demonstrated success in treating specific phobias (Gotestam, 2002; Ost, 1989). Although research generally suggests that therapist-assisted exposure may be more beneficial than independently conducted exposure (Barlow, 2002; O'Brien & Kelley, 1980), there are some data to suggest manualized exposure therapy that is administered in a clinic setting may produce clinically meaningful prepost treatment gains in a substantial proportion of patients (Hellstrom & Ost, 1995). In one study that compared six 60-minute sessions of clinician-accompanied exposure plus self-exposure, self-exposure only, and self-relaxation with no exposure (Al-Kubaisy et al., 1992), both exposure groups were found to be superior to the self-relaxation group at posttreatment as well as at 6-month follow-up. Furthermore, clinician-accompanied exposure did not significantly enhance the earlier treatment outcome that achieved by patients in the self-exposure condition.

One of the other questions that has been raised is the degree to which exposure therapy is useful in the form of vicarious or modeled exposure. In at least two studies, patients treated with either direct (observing another individual being treated in person) or indirect (observing treatment via a videotape) observation were less responsive to psychotherapy relative to a group of individuals treated through direct exposure (Menzies & Clarke, 1993; Ost, Ferebee, & Furmark, 1997). Somewhat more supportive of the potential efficacy of modeled exposure, Gotestam (2002) examined the relative impact of direct, model, and video exposure in treating individuals with spider phobia. Evidenced by self-report questionnaires of cognitions, physiological sensations, and self-efficacy, all three groups had a similar outcome following a single session of group therapy, with individuals in the direct exposure condition faring mildly better at 12-month follow-up. Given the etiological role that vicarious conditioning may play insofar as the development of specific phobias and the paucity of data exploring vicarious reconditioning, more programmatic work is necessary to definitively indicate the efficacy of this form of exposure.

In addition to the use of videotape procedures, other technological advances have been used to treat specific phobias. For example, there are a number of studies that have used virtual reality to expose patients to flying (Kahan, Tanzer, Darvin, & Borer, 2000; Rothbaum, Hodges, Smith, Lee, & Price, 2000), heights (Rothbaum et al., 1995), and spiders (Carlin, Hoffman, & Weghorst, 1997). Although methodological limitations are inherent, in two randomized controlled trials that have been conducted, virtual reality therapy outperformed a waitlist control condition in the treatment of individuals with height phobias (Rothbaum et al., 1995) and was equivalent to direct exposure in the treatment of individuals with a flying phobia (Rothbaum et al., 2000). Computer-administered interventions, radio contact, and mobile phone strategies also have shown some promise in treating individuals with spider and driving phobias (Flynn, Taylor, & Pollard, 1992; Smith, Kirkby, Montgomery, & Daniels, 1997). In a randomized controlled trial, computer-aided vicarious exposure was comparable to live exposure therapy in the treatment of spider phobias and that both were superior to a relaxation placebo (Gilroy et al., 2000). Given that these programs are only about a decade old, considerably more systematic research is necessary to validate technological methods of exposure in treating specific phobias.

Considering the fairly sizeable literature on the efficacy of exposure therapy for specific phobias, it is remarkable how little progress has been made toward identifying patient variables that are associated with treatment outcome. In one study that assessed 14 possible self-report, demographic, physiological, and behavioral variables across four outcome studies, only diastolic blood pressure at preassessment and treatment credibility (in another sample) were determined to predict posttreatment response (Hellstrom & Ost, 1996). In another study, trait anxiety was deemed predictive of exposure treatment response in patients with spider phobias (Muris, Mayer, & Merckelbach, 1998). In the final analysis, Hellstrom and Ost (1996) concluded, "despite the many years of research in this area, there are no common opinions of prognostic variables in the outcome of anxiety disorders" (p. 410). Beyond patient characteristics, there are some variables associated with treatment administration that appear to affect treatment outcome. Among these variables, it is conceivable that predictable exposures to feared stimuli, massed versus spaced exposure, conducting exposure sessions in multiple contexts, incorporating varied stimuli that resemble the target stimulus, and reduced distraction may have a positive impact on treatment response (Barlow, 2002).

Eye Movement Desensitization and Reprocessing

Based on the pioneering work of Francine Shapiro (1989), EMDR incorporates psychodynamic, cognitive behavioral, interpersonal, experiential, and body-centered therapies. In the context of specific phobias, patients are asked to identify the most vivid visual image related to their phobia, along with associated negative cognitions, emotions, and physiological sensations. Patients also identify a preferred positive belief. The patient is then instructed to focus on the image, negative cognitions, and physiological sensations while simultaneously moving his or her eyes back and forth, following the therapist's fingers as they move across his or her field of vision for 20 to 30 seconds or more. The clinician then instructs the patient to let his mind go blank and experience whatever thought, feeling, image, memory, or sensation is noticed.

This process is repeated numerous times throughout the therapy session until the patient reports no distress related to the targeted (phobic) memory. The patient is then instructed to refocus on the preferred positive belief identified at the beginning of the session while simultaneously engaging in the eye movements. This process continues until the patient reports increased confidence in the positive belief and limited distress related to the phobic memory.

Case studies of the efficacy of EMDR with specific phobias initially yielded some positive findings in relation to the treatment of injection-blood phobias, claustrophobia, and spider phobias (Kleinknecht, 1993; Lohr, Tolin, & Kleinknecht, 1995, 1996; Muris & Merckelbach, 1995). However, larger group designs suggest EMDR may be inferior to the more traditional exposure-based therapies (Muris, Merckelbach, Holdrinet, & Sijsenaar, 1998; Muris, Merckelbach, van Haaften, & Mayer, 1997) and that EMDR may represent nothing more than an elaborated form of imaginal exposure (Barlow, 2002; Lohr, Tolin, & Lilienfeld, 1998). Shapiro (1999) has argued that findings are limited by substantial methodological flaws, the most important of which is a failure to incorporate the complete EMDR treatment protocol. When the comprehensive EMDR package is utilized (De Jongh, Ten Broeke, & Renssen, 1999; De Jongh, van den Oord, & Ten Broeke, 2002), Shapiro (2001) has argued that EMDR may be quite effective in treating specific phobias. Nonetheless, researchers have stated, "EMDR has little to offer for the treatment of specific phobias" (Barlow, 2002, p. 415) and generally includes elements (i.e., eye movements) that are not empirically supported and are nonessential for attenuation of clinical symptoms.

Cognitive Therapy

Although cognitive therapy is considered an efficacious treatment for a variety of anxiety disorders and clinical depression (DeRubeis & Crits-Christoph, 1998), literature examining cognitive therapy for specific phobias is actually quite sparse, probably related to more programmatic research efforts directed toward investigating exposure-based interventions. Through use of self-instructional training and cognitive restructuring methods, a majority of the research into cognitive therapy has involved an application toward dental phobias. Across nine 90-minute group sessions, Jerremalm, Jansson, and Ost (1986) demonstrated that self-instructional training was as useful as a gradual exposure intervention, and others have demonstrated that even a single-session of cognitive therapy may increase coping in patients with dental phobia prior to dental procedures (De Jongh et al., 1995). Cognitive therapy has also shown some utility in the treatment of driving phobias (Townend, 2003), claustrophobia (Booth & Rachman, 1992), and animal phobias (Craske et al., 1995). Although cognitive therapy may be somewhat effective in the treatment of specific phobias, a more concentrated research effort is necessary across a greater breadth of phobias to determine whether it approximates the treatment gains established via exposure therapy.

Applied Tension

Although a myriad of physiological, cognitive, and behavioral symptoms are associated with specific phobias, fainting is a response that appears relatively specific to blood phobias as a result of vasovagal syncope and associated decreases in blood pressure heart rate and muscle tension (Antony et al., 1997; Antony & Swinson, 2000). Applied muscle tension appears to be a useful strategy to counteract this response, and it involves muscle tensing of the arms and legs (while maintaining steady breathing) that is followed by increased blood pressure and inhibition of the fainting response. A number of studies have supported this intervention as effective in treating blood phobias (Kozak & Montgomery, 1981; Ost & Sterner, 1987), with one study finding applied tension to be more effective than exposure alone (Ost et al., 1991).

MEDICAL TREATMENT

Primary care physicians, psychiatrists, and nurse practitioners have been utilizing pharmacotherapy for the treatment of anxiety disorders for about half a century. Within this time frame, a variety of medication classes have been approved by the Food and Drug Administration for the treatment of pathological anxiety, including barbiturates, benzodiazepines, tricyclic antidepressants (TCA), monoamine oxidase inhibitors (MAOIs), selective serotonin reuptake inhibitors (SSRIs), and serotonin-norepinephrine reuptake inhibitors (SNRIs; Spiegel, Wiegel, Baker, & Greene, 2000). For example, imipramine, clomipramine (TCAs), alprazolam and other benzodiazepines, as well as paroxetine, citalopram, fluoxetine, fluvoxamine, and sertraline (types of SSRIs) are all effective in the treatment of panic disorder (Barlow, 2002; Roy-Byrne & Cowley, 1998; Spiegel et al., 2000). For GAD, there is good evidence supporting the efficacy of benzodiazepines, azapirones (e.g., buspirone), and antidepressants (e.g., imipramine and paroxetine; Roemer, Orsillo, & Barlow, 2002; Roy-Byrne & Cowley, 1998; Spiegel et al., 2000). For social anxiety disorder, there are substantial data supporting the use of MAOIs, SSRIs, benzodiazepines, antidepressants, and beta-blockers (Hofmann & Barlow, 2002; Roy-Byrne & Cowley, 1998; Spiegel et al., 2000). In contrast, very few studies have examined the effectiveness of pharmacological treatments in the treatment of specific phobias. One reason this occurs is the common misconception that specific phobias are more normative and less interfering anxiety responses and therefore don't require pharmacological treatment. In addition, methodological limitations on some level prohibit research into pharmacological interventions, such as difficulties inherent in recruiting patients with specific phobias who are free of coexistent mental illnesses. Finally, because many view specific phobias as normative, patients with specific phobias are often reluctant to take medication for their condition. These factors result in relatively little research on the pharmacological treatment of specific phobias compared to other anxiety disorders.

Despite these obstacles, a few studies have documented the importance of pharmacotherapy in the treatment of specific phobias. For example, a European study aimed to assess which pharmacological treatments psychiatrists prescribed for their patients as a function of their diagnosis (Uhlenhuth, Blater, Ban, & Yang, 1999). The results of this study demonstrated that in 1997, 45% of surveyed psychiatrists felt it was necessary to treat specific phobias with pharmacotherapy. Of those psychiatrists who prescribed medications to patients with specific phobias, 44% prescribed a benzodiazepine, 30% prescribed an SSRI, 11% prescribed a TCA, 7% prescribed a MAOI, 4% prescribed buspirone, and 4% prescribed a beta-blocker. Indeed, psychiatrists and primary care physicians have utilized several different pharmacological treatments in the treatment of specific phobia and there is no predominant pharmacotherapy algorithm, in large part due to inadequate programmatic research assessing the relative efficacy of different medications in the treatment of specific phobias.

Several case studies have demonstrated the potential efficacy of pharmacotherapy in the treatment of specific phobias. For example, Abene and Hamilton (1998) found that when treating two patients with a specific phobia and comorbid depression with fluoxetine, both fear of flying and depressive symptoms attenuated over time. An additional case study reported the use of fluvoxamine in treating a preadolescent with a specific phobia (Balon, 1999). This particular patient was 11 years old, and his mother refused behavioral psychotherapy. A low dose of fluvoxamine was initiated, and the patient noted significant improvement over a 3-week treatment period. An invited comment to this case study (Allgulander, 1999) also noted the potential benefit of paroxetine in the treatment of specific phobias, and others have identified fluoxetine as a potentially effective medical regimen (Viswanathan & Paradis, 1991). Although these case studies are not randomized controlled trials and have other methodological limitations, they have served to highlight the potential positive effects of pharmacotherapy in the treatment of specific phobias.

A few randomized trials have been completed to assess the efficacy of pharmacological interventions in the treatment of specific phobias. A study by Thom, Sartory, and Johren (2000) compared the relative efficacy of two treatments for dental phobia, pharmacological treatment (midazolam) versus psychosocial treatment (one session of cognitive-behavioral therapy). Results of this study indicated that both the pharmacological group and the psychological treatment group demonstrated an equivalent improvement in anxiety ratings. However, those in the pharmacological group relapsed sooner than those in the psychosocial treatment condition. Another randomized trial assessed the efficacy of timolol relative to placebo control in the treatment of flying phobias (Campos, Solyom, & Koelink, 1984). Results of this study demonstrated no significant differences in the subjective assessment of fear and anxiety between the timolol group and the placebo group. However, participants in the timolol group were observed to have inhibited tachycardia during exposure when compared to participants in the placebo group. A more recent randomized trial examined the effects of a cognitive enhancer (D-cycloserine) on symptoms of acrophobia (Ressler et al., 2004). All participants in the study received two sessions of exposure therapy that involved a simulation of rising in a glass elevator. Participants were randomly assigned to receive either the active medication or placebo in addition to the virtual reality exposure therapy. Results demonstrated that participants in the active medication group had significantly more improvement than the placebo group as measured by their real-world symptoms of acrophobia, number of times exposed to heights, and acrophobia-related anxiety. Another study assessed the effectiveness of diazepam in the treatment of patients with animal phobias (Whitehead, Robinson, Blackwell, & Stutz, 1978). Participants were randomly assigned to receive either placebo or diazepam while flooding procedures were administered over a 3-week treatment period. Participants in the diazepam group did not demonstrate greater treatment effects over those identified in the placebo group. Similarly, it was demonstrated that exposure therapy for spider phobia was not enhanced with the addition of alprazolam (Zoellner, Craske, Hussain, Lewis, & Echeveri, 1996).

Randomized medication trials for the treatment of specific phobias have produced mixed results. Whereas some trials have demonstrated the superiority of medication to placebo, others have shown no difference between treatment and control conditions. More systematic research that incorporates larger, more representative samples is clearly needed to advance our knowledge about the specific role of pharmacotherapy in the treatment of specific phobias.

Case Description

Client Description

Janey was a 34-year-old married Caucasian female with one young child at home. She previously was employed as an aesthetician for several years, although she was staying at home with her child when she presented for treatment. Her husband was gainfully employed as a computer programmer, and Janey reported that they had a strong marriage with adequate communication and minimal conflict.

Presenting Complaints

Janey presented to therapy with symptoms of a specific phobia of storms. She reported being extremely anxious in the presence of storms and noted that she could not stand the thought of being alone during a storm. Janey reported that she didn't regularly feel these symptoms of anxiety, and that anxiety-related responses occurred only in the presence of storms. Janey was a frequent viewer of the weather channel and avid surfer of Internet weather sites. She made an effort to avoid storms whenever possible; when a severe storm was predicted to strike her hometown, she would travel with her child to a location where she believed the storm would miss. She would stay in these locations, sometimes overnight, and generally was able to avoid encountering storms. Cognitive symptoms of the storm phobia included thoughts of being swept away by the storm and thoughts that she and her family would die in the storm. Physiological symptoms included hyperventilation, increased heart rate, respiratory rate, perspiration, and trembling. Behavioral symptoms include geographical displacement, canceling plans with friends and family if a storm was coming, and spending excessive amounts of time watching the local weather channel and surfing the Internet.

Janey also presented to therapy with symptoms of depression (depressed mood, loss of interest, decreased sleep, decreased appetite, feelings of hopelessness). She felt dissatisfied with her life because she enjoyed being an esthetician, and now felt increasing pressure to stay at home with her child. Although she enjoyed spending time with her daughter, she felt as though she was "stuck." She was in a life transition and was having difficulty adjusting to her increasing mothering responsibilities. She also reported that her life as a stay-at-home mom was isolating and lonely. Cognitive symptoms of depression include thoughts of worthlessness and low self-esteem, including "I am a terrible mother" and "I don't deserve to be a mother." Physiological symptoms of depression include feeling lethargic, slowed motorically, and without energy. Behavioral symptoms of depression include decreased time with members of her social system, avoidance of church, and diminished time in recreational activities.

History of the Disorder

Janey had a family history of anxiety and depression, including a biological mother who sought treatment for symptoms shortly after the birth of her first

(continued)

child. Janey also recalled several aversive experiences with storms that seemed directly related to her current phobia. Perhaps most significantly, Janey recalled an experience when she was 13 years of age. She had been outside playing with her dog when she noticed that dark clouds were approaching. She continued to play, until a fairly steady rain began to fall. As the rain quickened, she ran toward the house and began knocking on the door because it was locked. Janey's mother was inside housecleaning, and mistakenly thought that Janey had already come into the house. Janey began to panic as the storm worsened, pounding the door more intensely and screaming out to her mother. As the thunder and lightning increased in intensity, Janey began to cry uncontrollably. When she saw lightning strike in the distance, her fear escalated even further and she broke a pane of glass on the door. Finally, her mother came to the door, let her in, and comforted her as much as possible. In addition to this event, Janey experienced what would be more of a vicarious conditioning of her storm phobia when she watched the movie *Twister,* a film highlighting the devastation and destruction associated with tornado disasters. Janey also reported feelings of dysthymia for as long as she could remember, but indicated that symptoms seemed to have gotten increasingly worse over the past year as her avoidance of storms increased and her identity became more unstable with changing roles.

Psychological Assessment

The Anxiety Disorders Interview Schedule (ADIS-IV; T. A. Brown et al., 1994) was administered to Janey at the beginning of treatment. Janey met criteria for specific phobia (storms) as well as major depressive disorder (MDD; American Psychiatric Association, 2000). Consistent with the results of the ADIS-IV, Janey completed the Beck Depression Inventory (BDI-II) and scored a 24, indicative of a moderate level of depression. Because Janey met criteria for MDD, she completed daily diaries in which she reported her primary activities during 1 week. These diaries suggested that Janey spent the majority of her time care-givng, sleeping, doing household chores, and watching television, much of which did not bring her great pleasure or satisfaction. In addition to the daily diaries, an assessment of her life goals and values was completed to determine more precisely the types of activities she might find rewarding. These strategies are integral components of the Behavioral Activation Treatment for Depression (BATD; Lejuez et al., 2002). Janey reported that she valued spending time with family and friends, developing her spirituality, becoming more physically active, and developing her creative side by painting and writing.

Case Conceptualization

The case formulation was based on the stimulus-organism-response-consequence (SORC) model (Goldfried & Sprafkin, 1976). Applied to this case, the behavior targeted for change was extensive avoidance of several environmental situations. Among the *stimuli* that elicited this avoidance were storm clouds, thunder, lightning, and rain, as well as Internet, television, or radio-transmitted reports of threatening weather. *Organismic* variables included a family history of anxiety and depressive problems. Largely as a consequence of her learning history, avoidance of anxiety-inducing stimuli was negatively reinforced in that Janey avoided aversive *responses* associated with these stimuli. As mentioned earlier, these included maladaptive responses in all three response systems: (1) motoric, (2) physiological, and (3) cognitive. In addition to escape and avoidance associated with anxiety-eliciting situations, Janey had ceased to expose herself to previously rewarding behaviors that included spending quality time with her husband, going to church, exercising, and being engaged in arts and crafts. Withdrawal from these reinforcement contingencies was conceptualized as a critical factor toward maintaining her depressive affect. The *consequences* of Janey's responses included inadequate exposure to anxiety-eliciting situations that inhibited the extinction process and lack of response-contingent positive reinforcement that contributed to negative affect.

Course of Treatment

Behavioral treatment was implemented for the treatment of Janey's storm phobia. First, a behavioral hierarchy was created to identify activities that would serve as the basis to expose Janey to her phobia. This hierarchy was created in a collaborative manner and involved identification of eight different activities. For each activity listed, Janey reported how much she feared and avoided each activity. These ratings were completed on a 0 to 10 Likert-type scale (least fear or avoidance [1] to most fear or avoidance [10]). The behavioral hierarchy are shown in Table 7.1.

Table 7.1
Fear and Avoidance Hierarchy

Activity	Associated Fear (0–10)	Avoidance
1. Talking about storms	1	3
2. Reading a book about storms	2	4
3. Watching a movie about storms	4	5
4. Listening to audio tapes of storms	6	5
5. Imagining the presence of a storm	7	6
6. Imagining conditioning experience of childhood	8	8
7. Staying at home during storm on main floor with family	9	8
8. Staying at home during storm on main floor alone	10	10

The first exposure exercise, talking about storms, was completed in session. For all exposure exercises, subjective units of discomfort (SUDS) ratings were used, with exposure being terminated following a minimum of a 50% reduction in SUDS. Janey described her fears about storms in great deal with substantial focus on discussing the nature of storms, different kinds of storms, and potential damage caused by storms. As a second stage, Janey checked out a book at the local library that described storms. Next, she was able to rent a documentary about thunderstorms, which she watched with her husband. She was then given the task to watch the film alone, which she completed successfully. Although

(continued)

not specifically assigned to Janey, she and her husband rented and watched the movie *Twister,* a significant event given her history. Janey then purchased audio-tapes of storm recordings and listened to them at home. She started off listening to them at a low volume, and gradually increased the volume over a period of several days. We then completed imaginal exercises in session where the therapist described a detailed picture of a storm, and Janey imagined herself in the presence of a storm. During this stage of therapy, which lasted a few weeks, heavy emphasis was placed on recounting and reliving the early direct conditioning experience of her childhood. She was then given the task of remaining at home during a storm. At first, Janey remained with her family during the storm. Once this task was completed successfully on three occasions, she stayed at home during a storm by herself. Janey was able to proceed through this behavioral hierarchy over the course of 12 weeks. Cognitive restructuring strategies and relaxation techniques were also implemented to help Janey progress through the hierarchy. By the end of treatment, Janey was able to remain in her home on the main level throughout the presence of a storm. Janey also reported significant reductions in her anxiety level.

After Janey had completed this behavioral hierarchy and felt more com-fortable with storms, we transitioned the focus of treatment to her depression. Proceeding through the specific phobia hierarchy created behavioral momentum, and Janey reported that working on her storm phobia had somewhat improved her mood. However, she still reported experiencing the majority of depressive symptoms she reported on intake. Thus, it was decided that work in this area would be beneficial for long-term gains. A BATD was implemented to help Janey understand the relationship between her activities and mood. It was first important to consider Janey's values and goals to determine what behaviors would be appropriate for a behavioral checklist. As previously mentioned, Janey reported that she valued spending time with family and friends, developing her spirituality, becoming more physically active, and developing her creative side by painting and writing. Specific activities were then created that targeted each overarching value. For example, Janey stated that going out to dinner with her husband and having a play date with her daughter and her best friend were target goals associated with her value of becoming closer to family and friends. Once each target activity was selected, Janey determined an ideal amount of time that she would like to spend completing each activity, as well as the number of times per week spent completing each activity. Treatment involved spending progressively more time on each activity until ideal goals were accomplished. Progressing through this behavior checklist decreased Janey's level of depression on the BDI-II. Over the course of 12 weeks, her BDI score decreased from 24 to 6.

In summary, Janey's specific phobia of storms was treated effectively through implementation of behavioral exposure aimed at extinguishing Janey's fears of storms. Next, her depression was treated through utilization of BATD, which involved the selection and implementation of specific activities related to each of her life values. The combination of behavioral exposure and behavioral activation resulted in a decreased level of anxiety related to her storm phobia as well as decreased levels of depression.

SUMMARY

Specific phobias represent a highly prevalent and potentially debilitating class of disorders. Based on large-scale epidemiological studies that have incorporated structured diagnostic interviewing strategies, both the Epidemiological Catchment Area (ECA) study (Eaton et al., 1991) and the National Comorbidity Survey (NCS; Magee et al., 1996) estimate the lifetime prevalence of specific phobias at approximately 11%. Functional impairment associated with specific phobias also is quite extensive, including maladaptive cognitive processes and distorted beliefs (Jones & Menzies, 2000; Menzies & Clarke, 1995a; Rachman & Cuk, 1992; Woody & Teachman, 2000), substantial avoidance behaviors (Barlow et al., 2004; Huijding & de Jong, 2006; Tolin et al., 1999; Woody & Tolin, 2002) that may be associated with decreased engagement in pleasurable or rewarding behaviors and depressive affect (Lewinsohn, 1974), and poorer adherence to medical regimens in the case of individuals with blood-injection phobias (Mollema et al., 2001). Moreover, individuals with a specific phobia tend to be more vulnerable toward developing other specific phobias and there is a positive relationship between the number of phobias experienced and the likelihood of being diagnosed with other anxiety disorders such as panic disorder, GAD, and social phobia (Curtis et al., 1998).

Given the prevalence and functional impact of specific phobias, researchers and clinicians must make continued strides toward better understanding etiological factors associated with the onset and persistence of specific phobias, as well as continue to develop effective assessment and intervention strategies that will assist in the recognition of specific phobias and help to attenuate associated symptoms. As a move in this direction, this chapter highlights characteristic symptoms and epidemiological data on specific phobias, elucidates a range of diagnostic and assessment strategies, focuses on conceptual factors associated with the development and sustenance of specific phobias, addresses the most current cognitive-behavioral and pharmacological interventions for these conditions, and concludes with a case illustration depicting the psychological assessment, case conceptualization, and treatment of a patient presenting with a specific phobia.

REFERENCES

Abene, M. V., & Hamilton, J. D. (1998). Resolution of fear of flying with fluoxetine treatment. *Journal of Anxiety Disorders, 12,* 599–603.

Al-Kubaisy, T., Marks, I. M., Logsdail, S., & Marks, M. P. (1992). Role of exposure homework in phobia reduction: A controlled study. *Behavior Therapy, 23,* 599–621.

Allgulander, C. (1999). "Fluvoxamine for phobia of storms:" Comment. *Acta Psychiatrica Scandinavica, 100,* 245–246.

American Psychiatric Association. (2000). *Diagnostic and statistical manual of mental disorders* (4th ed., text rev.). Washington, DC: Author.

Andrews, G., Creamer, M., Crino, R., Hunt, C., Lampe, L., & Page, A. (2003). *The treatment of anxiety disorders: Clinician guides and patient manuals* (2nd ed.). Cambridge: Cambridge University Press.

Antony, M. M., & Barlow, D. H. (1997). Social and specific phobias. In A. Tasman, J. Kay, & J. A. Lieberman (Eds.), *Psychiatry* (pp. 1037–1059). Philadelphia: Saunders.

Antony, M. M., Brown, T. A., & Barlow, D. H. (1997). Heterogeneity among specific phobia types in DSM-IV. *Behavior Research and Therapy, 35,* 1089–1100.

Antony, M. M., Craske, M. G., & Barlow, D. H. (1995). *Mastery of your specific phobia: Client manual*. San Antonio, TX: Psychological Corporation/Graywind Publications.

Antony, M. M., Orsillo, S. M., & Roemer, L. (2001). *Practitioner's guide to empirically based measures of anxiety*. New York: Kluwer Academic/Plenum Press.

Antony, M. M., & Swinson, R. P. (2000). *Phobic disorders and panic in adults: A guide to assessment and treatment*. Washington, DC: American Psychological Association.

Arntz, A., Lavy, E., van den Berg, G., & van Rijsoort, S. (1993). Negative beliefs of spider phobics: A psychometric evaluation of the Spider Phobia Beliefs Questionnaire. *Advances in Behavior Research and Therapy, 15,* 257–277.

Balon, R. (1999). Fluvoxamine for phobia of storms. *Acta Psychiatrica Scandinavica, 100,* 244–246.

Barlow, D. H. (2002). *Anxiety and its disorders: The nature and treatment of anxiety and panic* (2nd ed.). New York: Guilford Press.

Barlow, D. H., Allen, L. B., & Choate, M. L. (2004). Toward a unified treatment of emotional disorders. *Behavior Therapy, 35,* 205–230.

Blanchard, J. J., & Brown, S. B. (1998). Structured diagnostic interview schedules. In C. R. Reynolds (Ed.), *Comprehensive clinical psychology: Vol. 3. Assessment* (pp. 97–130). New York: Elsevier Science.

Booth, R., & Rachman, S. (1992). The reduction of claustrophobia: Pt. I. *Behavior Research and Therapy, 30,* 207–221.

Bourdon, K. H., Boyd, J. H., Rae, D. S., Burns, B. J., Thompson, J. W., & Locke, B. Z. (1988). Gender differences in phobias: Results of the ECA community study. *Journal of Anxiety Disorders, 2,* 227–241.

Bourque, P., & Ladouceur, R. (1980). An investigation of various performance-based treatments with acrophobics. *Behavior Research and Therapy, 18,* 161–170.

Breslau, J., Aguilar-Gaxiola, S., Kendler, K. S., Su, M., Williams, D., & Kessler, R. C. (2006). Specifying race-ethnic differences in risk for psychiatric disorder in a USA national sample. *Psychological Medicine, 36,* 57–68.

Brown, D. R., Eaton, W. W., & Sussman, L. (1990). Racial differences in prevalence of phobic disorders. *Journal of Nervous and Mental Diseases, 178,* 434–441.

Brown, T. A., DiNardo, P. A., & Barlow, D. H. (1994). *The Anxiety Disorder Interview Schedule for DSM-IV*. Albany: State University of New York, Center for Stress and Anxiety Disorders.

Burnam, M. A., Stein, J. A., Golding, J. M., Siegel, J. M., Sorenson, S. B., Forsythe, A. B., et al. (1988). Sexual assault and mental disorders in a community population. *Journal of Consulting and Clinical Psychology, 56,* 843–850.

Campos, P. E., Solyom, L., & Koelink, A. (1984). The effects of timolol mealeate on subjective and physiological components of air travel phobia. *Canadian Journal of Psychiatry, 29,* 570–574.

Carlin, A. S., Hoffman, H. G., & Weghorst, S. (1997). Virtual reality and tactile augmentation in the treatment of spider phobia: A case report. *Behavior Research and Therapy, 35,* 153–158.

Chambers, J., Yeragani, V. K., & Keshavan, M. S. (1986). Phobias in India and the United Kingdom: A trans-cultural study. *Acta Psychiatrica Scandinavica, 74,* 388–391.

Chambless, D. L., & Ollendick, T. H. (2001). Empirically supported psychological interventions: Controversies and evidence. *Annual Review of Psychology, 52,* 685–716.

Coddington, R. D. (1972a). The significance of life events as etiologic factors in the disease of children: Pt. I. A survey of professional workers. *Journal of Psychosomatic Research, 16,* 7–18.

Coddington, R. D. (1972b). The significance of life events as etiologic factors in the disease of children: Pt. II. A study of a normal population. *Journal of Psychosomatic Research, 16,* 205–213.

Cornelius, R. R., & Averill, J. R. (1983). Sex differences in fear of spiders. *Journal of Personality and Social Psychology, 45,* 377–383.

Costello, C. G. (1982). Fears and phobias in women: A community study. *Journal of Abnormal Psychology, 91*, 280–286.

Cox, D., Mohr, D. C., & Epstein, L. (2004). Treating self-injection phobia in patients prescribed injectable medications: A case example illustrating a six-session treatment model. *Cognitive and Behavioral Practice, 11*, 278–283.

Craske, M. G. (2003). *Origins of phobias and anxiety disorders: Why more women than men?* Amsterdam: Elsevier.

Craske, M. G., Antony, M. M., & Barlow, D. H. (1997). *Mastery of your specific phobia: Therapist guide.* San Antonio, TX: Psychological Corporation.

Craske, M. G., Mohlman, J., Yi, J., Glover, D., & Valeri, S. (1995). Treatment of claustrophobia and snake/spider phobias: Fear of arousal and fear of context. *Behavior Research and Therapy, 33*, 197–203.

Csikszentmihalyi, M., & Larson, R. (1987). Validity and reliability of the experience sampling method. *Journal of Nervous and Mental Diseases, 175*, 526–536.

Curtis, G. C., Magee, W. J., Eaton, W. W., Wittchen, H. U., & Kessler, R. C. (1998). Specific fears and phobias: Epidemiology and classification. *British Journal of Psychiatry, 173*, 212–217.

De Jongh, A., Muris, P., Horst, G. T., van Zuuren, F., Schoenmaker, N., & Makkes, P. (1995). One-session cognitive treatment of dental phobia: Preparing dental phobics for treatment by restructuring negative cognitions. *Behavior Research and Therapy, 33*, 947–954.

De Jongh, A., Ten Broeke, E., & Renssen, M. R. (1999). Treatment of specific phobias with eye movement desensitization and reprocessing (EMDR): Research, protocol, and application. *Journal of Anxiety Disorders, 13*, 69–85.

De Jongh, A., van den Oord, H. J. M., & Ten Broeke, E. (2002). Efficacy of eye movement desensitization and reprocessing (EMDR) in the treatment of specific phobias: Four single-case studies on dental phobia. *Journal of Clinical Psychology, 58*, 1489–1503.

DeRubeis, R. J., & Crits-Christoph, P. (1998). Empirically supported individual and group treatments for adult mental disorders. *Journal of Consulting and Clinical Psychology, 66*, 37–52.

Dilger, S., Straube, T., Mentzel, H. J., Fitzek, C., Reichenbach, J., Hecht, S., et al. (2003). Brain activation to phobia-related pictures in spider phobic humans: An event-related functional magnetic resonance imaging study. *Neuroscience Letters, 248*, 29–32.

Eaton, W. W., Dryman, A., & Weissman, M. M. (1991). Panic and phobia. In L. N. Robins & D. A. Regier (Eds.), *Psychiatric disorders in America: The epidemiological Catchment Area Study* (pp. 155–179). New York: Free Press.

Eckleberry, H., Jodie, G., & Dohrenwend, A. (2005). Sociocultural interpretations of social phobia in a non-heterosexual female. *Journal of Homosexuality, 49*, 103–117.

Emmelkamp, P. M. G., & Wessels, H. (1975). Flooding in imagination versus flooding in vivo: A comparison with agoraphobics. *Behavior Research and Therapy, 13*, 7–15.

Escobar, J. I., Karno, M., Burnam, A., Hough, R. L., & Golding, J. (1988). Distribution of major mental disorders in an U.S. metropolis. *Acta Psychiatric Scandinavica, 78*, 45–53.

First, M. B., Spitzer, R. L., Gibbon, M., & Williams, J. (1996). *Structured Clinical Interview for DSM-IV Axis I Disorders—Patient Edition (SCID-I/P, Version 2.0)* New York: New York Psychiatric Institute, Biometrics Research Department.

Flynn, T. M., Taylor, P., & Pollard, C. A. (1992). Use of mobile phones in the behavioral treatment of driving phobias. *Journal of Behavior Therapy and Experimental Psychiatry, 23*, 299–302.

Fredrikson, M., Annas, P., Fischer, H., & Wik, G. (1996). Gender and age differences in the prevalence of specific fears and phobias. *Behavior Research and Therapy, 26*, 241–244.

Fredrikson, M., Annas, P., & Wik, G. (1997). Parental history, aversive exposure and the development of snake and spider phobia in women. *Behavior Research and Therapy, 35*, 23–28.

Fredrikson, M., Fischer, H., & Wik, G. (1997). Cerebral blood flow during anxiety provocation. *Journal of Clinical Psychiatry, 58,* 16–21.

Fredrikson, M., Wik, G., Annas, P., Ericson, K., & Stone-Elander, S. (1995). Functional neuroanatomy of visually elicited simple phobic fear: Additional data and theoretical analysis. *Psychophysiology, 32,* 43–48.

Fredrikson, M., Wik, G., Greitz, T., Eriksson, L., Stone-Elander, S., Ericson, K., et al. (1993). Regional cerebral blood flow during experimental phobic fear. *Psychophysiology, 30,* 126–130.

Fyer, A. J., Mannuzza, S., Chapman, T. F., Martin, L. Y., & Klein, D. F. (1995). Specificity in familial aggregation of phobic disorders. *Archives of General Psychiatry, 52,* 564–573.

Fyer, A. J., Mannuzza, S., Gallops, M. S., Martin, L. Y., Aaronson, C., Gorman, J. M., et al. (1990). Familial transmission of simple phobias and fears: A preliminary report. *Archives of General Psychiatry, 47,* 252–256.

Fyer, A. J., Mannuzza, S., Martin, L. Y., Gallops, M. S., Endicott, J., Schleyer, B., et al. (1989). Reliability of anxiety assessment: Pt. II. Symptom assessment. *Archives of General Psychiatry, 46,* 1102–1110.

Galea, S., Ahern, J., Resnick, H., Kilpatrick, D., Bucuvalas, M., Gold, J., et al. (2002). Psychological sequelae of the September 11 terrorist attacks in New York City. *New England Journal of Medicine, 346,* 982–987.

Gauthier, J., & Marshall, W. L. (1977). The determination of optimal exposure to phobic stimuli in flooding therapy. *Behavior Research and Therapy, 15,* 403–410.

George, L. K., Hughes, D. C., & Blazer, D. G. (1986). Urban/rural differences in the prevalence of anxiety disorders. *American Journal of Social Psychiatry, 6,* 249–258.

Gilroy, L. J., Kirkby, K. C., Daniels, B. A., Menzies, B. A., & Montgomery, I. M. (2000). Controlled comparison of computer-aided vicarious exposure versus live exposure in the treatment of spider phobia. *Behavior Therapy, 31,* 733–744.

Goisman, R. M., Allsworth, J., Rogers, M. P., Warshaw, M. G., Goldenberg, I., Vasile, R. G., et al. (1998). Simple phobia as a comorbid anxiety disorder. *Depression and Anxiety, 7,* 105–112.

Goldfried, M. R., & Sprafkin, J. N. (1976). Behavioral personality assessment. In J. T. Spence, R. C. Carson, & J. W. Thibaut (Eds.), *Behavioral approaches to therapy* (pp. 295–321). Morristown, NJ: General Learning Press.

Golwyn, D. H., & Sevlie, C. P. (1993). Adventitious change in homosexual behavior during treatment of social phobia with phenelzine. *Journal of Clinical Psychiatry, 54,* 39–40.

Goodyer, I. M., & Altham, P. M. (1991). Lifetime exit events and recent social and family adversities in anxious and depressed school-age children and adolescents. *Journal of Affective Disorders, 21,* 219–228.

Gotestam, K. G. (2002). One session group treatment of spider phobia by direct or modeled exposure. *Cognitive Behavior Therapy, 31,* 18–24.

Guarnaccia, P. J. (1997). A cross-cultural perspective on anxiety disorders. In S. Freidman (Ed.), *Cultural issues in the treatment of anxiety* (pp. 3–20). New York: Guilford Press.

Harris, L. M., & Menzies, R. G. (1996). Origins of specific fears: A comparison of associative and non-associative accounts. *Anxiety, 2,* 248–250.

Haynes, S. N. (1998). The assessment-treatment relationship and functional analysis in behavior therapy. *European Journal of Psychological Assessment, 14,* 26–35.

Haynes, S. N., & O'Brien, W. H. (1990). Functional analysis in behavior therapy. *Clinical Psychology Review, 10,* 649–668.

Hellstrom, K., & Ost, L. G. (1995). One-session therapist directed exposure versus two forms of manual directed self-exposure in the treatment of spider phobia. *Behavior Research and Therapy, 33,* 959–965.

Hellstrom, K., & Ost, L. G. (1996). Prediction of outcome in the treatment of specific phobia: A cross validation study. *Behavior Research and Therapy, 34,* 403–411.

Hettema, J. M., Prescott, C. A., Myers, J. M., Neale, M. C., & Kendler, K. S. (2005). The structure of genetic and environmental risk factors for anxiety disorders in men and women. *Archives of General Psychiatry, 62,* 182–189.

Hofmann, S. G., & Barlow, D. H. (2002). Social phobia (social anxiety disorder). In D. H. Barlow (Ed.), *Anxiety and its disorders: The nature and treatment of anxiety and panic* (2nd ed., pp. 454–476). New York: Guilford Press.

Hopko, D. R., Armento, M., Chambers, L., Cantu, M., & Lejuez, C. W. (2003). The use of daily diaries to assess the relations among mood state, overt behavior, and reward value of activities. *Behavior Research and Therapy, 41,* 1137–1148.

Huijding, J., & de Jong, P. J. (2006). Specific predictive power of automatic spider-related affective associations for controllable and uncontrollable fear responses toward spiders. *Behavior Research and Therapy, 44,* 161–176.

Hurlburt, R. T. (1997). Randomly sampling thinking in the natural environment. *Journal of Consulting and Clinical Psychology, 65,* 941–949.

Ingman, K. A., Ollendick, T. H., & Akande, A. (1999). Cross-cultural aspects of fears in African children and adolescents. *Behavior Research and Therapy, 37,* 337–345.

Jerremalm, A., Jansson, L., & Ost, L. G. (1986). Individual response patterns and the effects of different behavioral methods in the treatment of dental phobia. *Behavior Research and Therapy, 24,* 171–180.

Jones, M. K., & Menzies, R. G. (2000). Danger expectancies, self-efficacy, and insight in spider phobia. *Behavior Research and Therapy, 38,* 585–600.

Kahan, M., Tanzer, J., Darvin, D., & Borer F. (2000). Virtual reality-assisted cognitive-behavioral treatment for fear of flying: Acute treatment and follow-up. *CyberPsychology and Behavior, 3,* 387–392.

Karno, M., Golding, J. M., Burnam, M. A., Hough, R. L., Escobar, J. I., Wells, K. M., et al. (1989). Anxiety disorders among Mexican Americans and non-Hispanic Whites in Los Angeles. *Journal of Nervous and Mental Diseases, 177,* 202–209.

Kendler, K. S., Karkowski, L. M., & Prescott, C. A. (1999). The assessment of dependence in the study of stressful life events: Validation using a twin design. *Psychological Medicine, 29,* 1455–1460.

Kendler, K. S., Myers, J., Prescott, C. A., & Neale, M. C. (2001). The genetic epidemiology of irrational fears and phobias in men. *Archives of General Psychiatry, 58,* 257–267.

Kessler, R. C., Davis, C. G., & Kendler, K. S. (1997). Childhood adversity and adult psychiatric disorder in the U.S. National Comorbidity Survey. *Psychological Medicine, 27,* 1101–1119.

King, N. J., Clowes-Hollins, V., & Ollendick, T. H. (1997). The etiology of childhood dog phobia. *Behavior Research and Therapy, 35,* 77.

King, N. J., Heyne, D., & Ollendick, T. H. (2005). Cognitive-behavioral treatments for anxiety and phobic disorders in children and adolescents: A review. *Behavioral Disorders, 30,* 241–257.

Kleinknecht, R. A. (1993). Rapid treatment of blood and injection phobias with eye movement desensitization. *Journal of Behavior Therapy and Experimental Psychopathology, 24,* 211–217.

Kleinknecht, R. A., Thorndike, R. M., & Walls, M. M. (1996). Factorial dimensions and correlates of blood, injury, injection, and related medical fears: Cross validation of the Medical Fear Survey. *Behavior Research and Therapy, 34,* 323–331.

Koenig, H., Ford, S. M., George, L. K., Blazer, D. G., & Meador, K. G. (1993). Religion and anxiety disorder: An examination and comparison of associations in young, middle-aged, and elderly adults. *Journal of Anxiety Disorders, 7,* 321–342.

Kozak, M. J., & Montgomery, G. K. (1981). Multimodal behavioral treatment of recurrent injury-scene elicited fainting (vasodepressor syncope). *Behavioral Psychotherapy, 9*, 316–321.

Lehman, C. L., Patterson, M. D., Brown, T. A., & Barlow, D. H. (1998, November). *Lifetime alcohol use disorders in patients with anxiety or mood disorders.* Paper presented at the 32nd Annual Convention of the Association for the Advancement of Behavior Therapy, Washington, DC.

Lejuez, C. W., Hopko, D. R., & Hopko, S. D. (2002). *The brief behavioral activation treatment for depression (BATD): A comprehensive patient guide.* Boston: Pearson Custom Publishing.

Lewinsohn, P. M. (1974). A behavioral approach to depression. In R. M. Friedman & M. M. Katz (Eds.), *The psychology of depression: Contemporary theory and research* (pp. 157–185). New York: Wiley.

Lewinsohn, P. M., Munoz, R. F., Youngren, M. A., & Zeiss, A. M. (1986). *Control your depression.* New York: Prentice-Hall.

Lichtenstein, P., & Annas, P. (2000). Heritability and prevalence of specific fears and phobias in childhood. *Journal of Child Psychology and Psychiatry, 41*, 927–937.

Lohr, J. M., Tolin, D. F., & Kleinknecht, R. A. (1995). Eye movement desensitization of medical phobias: Two case studies. *Journal of Behavior Therapy and Experimental Psychiatry, 26*, 141–151.

Lohr, J. M., Tolin, D. F., & Kleinknecht, R. A. (1996). An intensive design investigation of eye movement desensitization and reprocessing of claustrophobia. *Journal of Anxiety Disorders, 10*, 73–88.

Lohr, J. M., Tolin, D. F., & Lilienfeld, S. O. (1998). Efficacy of eye movement desensitization and reprocessing: Implications for behavior therapy. *Behavior Therapy, 29*, 123–156.

Magee, W. J. (1999). Effects of life experiences on phobia onset. *Social Psychiatry and Psychiatric Epidemiology, 34*, 343–351.

Magee, W. J., Eaton, W. W., Wittchen, H. U., McGonagle, K. A., & Kessler, R. C. (1996). Agoraphobia, simple phobia, and social phobia in the national comorbidity survey. *Archives of General Psychiatry, 53*, 159–168.

Mannuzza, S., Fyer, A. J., Martin, L. Y., Gallops, M. S., Endicott, J., Gorman, J., et al. (1989). Reliability of anxiety assessment: Pt. I. Diagnostic agreement. *Archives of General Psychiatry, 46*, 1093–1101.

Marks, I. M. (1987). *Fears, phobias, and rituals: Panic, anxiety, and their disorders.* New York: Oxford University Press.

Marks, I. M., & Gelder, M. G. (1966). Different ages of onset in varieties of phobia. *American Journal of Psychiatry, 123*, 247–254.

Marks, I. M., & Mathews, A. M. (1979). Brief standard self-rating for phobic patients. *Behavior Research and Therapy, 17*, 263–267.

Martell, C. R., Addis, M. E., & Jacobson, N. S. (2001). *Depression in context: Strategies for guided action.* New York: Norton.

McFarlane, A. C., Clayer, J. R., & Bookless, C. L. (1997). Psychiatric morbidity following a natural disaster: An Australian bushfire. *Social Psychiatry and Psychiatric Epidemiology, 32*, 261–268.

McNally, R. J. (1987). Preparedness and phobias: A review. *Psychological Bulletin, 101*, 283–303.

Menzies, R. G., & Clarke, J. C. (1993). A comparison of in vivo and vicarious exposure in the treatment of childhood water phobia. *Behavior Research and Therapy, 31*, 9–15.

Menzies, R. G., & Clarke, J. C. (1995a). Danger expectancies and insight in acrophobia. *Behavior Research and Therapy, 33*, 215–221.

Menzies, R. G., & Clarke, J. C. (1995b). The etiology of phobias: A non-associative account. *Clinical Psychology Review, 15*, 23–48.

Merckelbach, H., Arntz, A., Arrindell, W. A., & de Jong, P. J. (1992). Pathways to spider phobia. *Behavior Research and Therapy, 30*, 543–546.

Mineka, S., Davidson, M., Cook, M., & Keir, R. (1984). Observational conditioning of fear in rhesus monkeys. *Journal of Abnormal Psychology, 93,* 355–372.

Mineka, S., & Zinbarg, R. (1996). Conditioning and ethological models of anxiety disorders: Stress-in-dynamic context anxiety models. In D. Hope (Ed.), *Nebraska Symposium on Motivation* (pp. 135–210). Lincoln: University of Nebraska Press.

Mollema, E. D., Snoek, F. J., Ader, H. J., Heine, R. J., & Van Der Ploeg, H. M. (2001). Insulin-treated diabetes patients with fear of self-injecting or fear of self-testing: Psychological comorbidity and general well-being. *Journal of Psychosomatic Research, 51,* 665–672.

Mountz, J. M., Modell, J. G., Wilson, M. W., Curtis, G. G., Lee, M. A., Schmaltz, S., et al. (1989). Positron emission tomographic evaluation of cerebral blood flow during state anxiety in simple phobia. *Archives of General Psychiatry, 46,* 501–504.

Mowrer, O. H. (1939). Anxiety and learning. *Psychological Bulletin, 36,* 517–518.

Muris, P., Mayer, B., & Merkelbach, H. (1998). Trait anxiety as a predictor of behavior therapy outcome in spider phobia. *Behavioral and Cognitive Psychotherapy, 26,* 87–91.

Muris, P., & Merckelbach, H. (1995). Treating spider phobia with eye movement desensitization and reprocessing: Two case reports. *Journal of Anxiety Disorders, 9,* 439–449.

Muris, P., Merckelbach, H., Holdrinet, I., & Sijsenaar, M. (1998). Treating phobic children: Effects of EMDR versus exposure. *Journal of Consulting and Clinical Psychology, 66,* 193–198.

Muris, P., Merckelbach, H., van Haaften, H., & Mayer, B. (1997). Eye movement desensitization and reprocessing versus exposure in vivo: A single-session crossover study of spider phobic children. *British Journal of Psychiatry, 171,* 82–86.

Muris, P., Schmidt, H., & Merckelbach, H. (1999). The structure of specific phobia symptoms among children and adolescents. *Behavior Research and Therapy, 37,* 863–868.

O'Brien, T. P., & Kelley, J. E. (1980). A comparison of self-directed and therapist-directed practice for fear reduction. *Behavior Research and Therapy, 18,* 573–579.

O'Neill, R. E., Horner, R. H., Albin, R. W., Storey, K., & Sprague, J. R. (1990). *Functional analysis of problem behavior: A practical assessment guide.* Sycamore, IL: Sycamore Press.

Ost, L. G. (1987). Age of onset of different phobias. *Journal of Abnormal Psychology, 96,* 223–229.

Ost, L. G. (1989). One-session treatment for specific phobias. *Behavior Research and Therapy, 27,* 1–7.

Ost, L. G. (1996). One session group treatment for spider phobia. *Behavior Research and Therapy, 34,* 707–715.

Ost, L. G., Brandberg, M., & Alm, T. (1997). One versus five sessions of exposure in the treatment of flying phobia. *Behavior Research and Therapy, 35,* 987–996.

Ost, L. G., Fellenius, J., & Sterner, U. (1991). Applied tension, exposure in vivo, and tension-only in the treatment of blood phobia. *Behavior Research and Therapy, 29,* 561–574.

Ost, L. G., Ferebee, I., & Furmark, T. (1997). One-session group therapy of spider phobia: Direct versus indirect treatments. *Behavior Research and Therapy, 35,* 721–732.

Ost, L. G., & Hugdahl, K. (1981). Acquisition of phobias and anxiety response patterns in clinical patients. *Behavior Research and Therapy, 19,* 439–447.

Ost, L. G., Lindahl, I. L., Sterner, U., & Jerremalm, A. (1984). Exposure in vivo versus applied relaxation in the treatment of blood phobia. *Behavior Research and Therapy, 22,* 205–216.

Ost, L. G., & Sterner, U. (1987). Applied tension: A specific behavioral method for treatment of blood phobia. *Behavior Research and Therapy, 25,* 25–29.

Otto, K., Boos, A., Dalbert, C., Schops, D., & Hoyer, J. (2006). Posttraumatic symptoms, depression, and anxiety of flood victims: The impact of a belief in a just world. *Personality and Individual Differences, 40,* 1075–1084.

Page, A. C., Bennett, K. S., Carter, O., Smith, J., & Woodmore, K. (1997). The Blood-Injection Symptom Scale (BISS): Assessing a structure of phobic symptoms elicited by blood and injections. *Behavior Research and Therapy, 35,* 457–464.

Poulton, R., Menzies, R. G., Craske, M. G., Langley, J. D., & Silva, P. A. (1999). Water trauma and swimming experiences up to age 9 and fear of water at age 18: A longitudinal study. *Behavior Research and Therapy, 37,* 39–48.

Rachman, S. (1976). The passing of the two-stage theory of fear and avoidance: Fresh possibilities. *Behavior Research and Therapy, 14,* 125–134.

Rachman, S. (1977). The conditioning theory of fear acquisition: A critical examination. *Behavior Research and Therapy, 15,* 375–387.

Rachman, S. (1978). *Fear and courage.* Oxford, England: Freeman.

Rachman, S., & Cuk, M. (1992). Fearful distortions. *Behavior Research and Therapy, 30,* 583–589.

Rauch, S. L., Savage, C. R., Alpert, N. M., Miguel, E. C., Baer, L., Breiter, H. C., et al. (1995). A positron emission tomographic study of simple phobic symptom provocation. *Archives of General Psychiatry, 52,* 20–28.

Rauch, S. L., Wright, C. I., Martis, B., Busa, E., McMullin, K. G., Shin, L. M., et al. (2004). A Magnetic Resonance Imaging Study of Cortical Thickness in Animal Phobia. *Biological Psychiatry, 55,* 946–952.

Reiman, E. M. (1997). The application of positron emission tomography to the study of normal and pathologic emotions. *Journal of Clinical Psychiatry, 58,* 4–12.

Reiss, S. (1991). Expectancy model of fear, anxiety, and panic. *Clinical Psychology Review, 11,* 141–153.

Ressler, K. J., Rothbaum, B. O., Tannenbaum, L., Anderson, P., Graap, K., Zimand, E., et al. (2004). Cognitive enhancers as adjuncts to psychotherapy. *Archives of General Psychiatry, 61,* 1136–1144.

Rimm, D. C., & Lefebvre, R. C. (1987). Phobic disorders. In S. M. Turner, K. S. Calhoun, & H. E. Adams (Eds.), *Handbook of clinical behavior therapy* (pp. 19–37). New York: Wiley.

Robins, L. N., Cottler, L., Bucholz, K., & Compton, W. (1995). *The Diagnostic Interview Schedule, Version IV.* St. Louis, MO: Washington University School of Medicine.

Roemer, L., Orsillo, S. M., & Barlow, D. H. (2002). Generalized anxiety disorder. In D. H. Barlow (Ed.), *Anxiety and its disorders: The nature and treatment of anxiety and panic* (2nd ed., pp. 477–515). New York: Guilford Press.

Rothbaum, B. O., Hodges, L. F., Kooper, R., Opdyke, D., Williford, J. S., & North, M. (1995). Virtual reality graded exposure in the treatment of acrophobia: A case report. *Behavior Therapy, 26,* 547–554.

Rothbaum, B. O., Hodges, L. F., Smith, S., Lee, J. H., & Price L. (2000). A controlled study of virtual reality exposure for the fear of flying. *Journal of Consulting and Clinical Psychology, 68,* 1020–1026.

Roy-Byrne, P. P., & Cowley, D. S. (1998). Pharmacological treatment of panic, generalized anxiety, and phobic disorders. In P. E. Nathan & J. M. Gorman (Eds.), *A guide to treatments that work* (pp. 319–338). New York: Oxford University Press.

Rubio-Stipec, M., Shrout, P., Bird, H., Canino, G., & Bravo, M. (1989). Symptom scales of the Diagnostic Interview Schedule: Factor results in Hispanic and Anglo samples. *Psychological Assessment, 1,* 30–34.

Schatzberg, A. F., Samson, J. A., Rothschild, A. J., Bond, T. C., & Regier, D. A. (1998). McLean Hospital Depression Research Facility: Early-onset phobic disorders and adult-onset major depression. *British Journal of Psychiatry, 173,* 29–34.

Schienle, A., Schafer, A., Walter, B., Stark, R., & Vaitl, D. (2005). Brain activation of spider phobics towards disorder-relevant, generally disgust- and fear-inducing pictures. *Neuroscience Letters, 388,* 1–6.

Shapiro, F. (1989). Eye movement desensitization: A new treatment for post-traumatic stress disorder. *Journal of Behavior Therapy and Experimental Psychiatry, 20,* 211–217.

Shapiro, F. (1999). Eye movement desensitization and reprocessing (EMDR) and the anxiety disorders: Clinical and research implications of an integrated psychotherapy treatment. *Journal of Anxiety Disorders, 13,* 35–67.

Shapiro, F. (2001). *Eye movement desensitization and reprocessing: Basic principles, protocols and procedures* (2nd ed.). New York: Guilford Press.

Shrout, P. E., Canino, G. J., Bird, H. R., Rubio-Stipec, M., Bravo, M., & Burnam, M. A. (1992). Mental health status among Puerto Ricans, Mexican Americans, and non-Hispanic Whites. *American Journal of Community Psychology, 20,* 729–752.

Skre, I., Onstad, S., Torgersen, S., Lygren, S., & Kringlen, E. (1993). A twin study of DSM-III-R anxiety disorders. *Acta Psychiatrica Scandinavica, 88,* 85–92.

Skre, I., Onstad, S., Torgersen, S., Lygren, S., & Kringlen, E. (2000). The heritability of common phobic fear: A twin study of a clinical sample. *Journal of Anxiety Disorders, 14,* 549–562.

Smith, K. L., Kirkby, K. C., Montgomery, I. M., & Daniels, B. A. (1997). Computer-delivered modeling of exposure for spider phobia: Relevant versus irrelevant exposure. *Journal of Anxiety Disorders, 11,* 489–497.

Spiegel, D. A., Wiegel, M., Baker, S. L., & Greene, K. A. I. (2000). Pharmacotherapy of anxiety disorders. In D. I. Mostofsky & D. H. Barlow (Eds.), *The management of stress and anxiety in medical disorders* (pp. 36–65). Boston: Allyn & Bacon.

Spitzer, R. L., Williams, J. B., Kroenke, K., Linzer, M., deGruy, F. V. III, Hahn, S. R., et al. (1994). Utility of a new procedure for diagnosing mental disorders in primary care: The PRIME-MD 1000 study. *Journal of the American Medical Association, 272,* 1749–1756.

Thom, A., Sartory, G., & Johren, P. (2000). Comparison between one-session psychological treatment and benzodiazepine in dental phobia. *Journal of Consulting and Clinical Psychology, 68,* 378–387.

Tolin, D. F., Lohr, J. M., Lee, T. C., & Sawchuk, C. N. (1999). Visual avoidance in specific phobia. *Behavior Research and Therapy, 37,* 63–70.

Torgersen, S. (1979). The nature and origin of common phobic fears. *British Journal of Psychiatry, 134,* 343–351.

Townend, M. (2003). Cognitive therapy for driving phobias: Two single case studies. *Behavioral and Cognitive Psychotherapy, 31,* 369–375.

Tweed, J. L., Schoenbach, V. J., George, L. K., & Blazer, D. G. (1989). The effects of childhood parental death and divorce on six-month history of anxiety disorders. *British Journal of Psychiatry, 154,* 823–828.

Uhlenhuth, E. H., Blater, M. B., Ban, T. A., & Yang, K. (1999). Trends in recommendations for the pharmacotherapy of anxiety disorders by an international expert panel, 1992–1997. *European Neuropsychopharmacology, 9,* 393–398.

Veltman, D. J., Tuinebreijer, W. E., Winkelman, D., Lammertsma, A. A., & Emmelkamp, P. M. G. (2004). Neurophysiological correlates of habituation during exposure in spider phobia. *Psychiatry Research: Neuroimaging, 132,* 149–158.

Viswanathan, R., & Paradis, C. (1991). *Treatment of cancer phobia with fluoxetine* [Letter to the editor]. *American Journal of Psychiatry, 8,* 1090.

Whitehead, W. E., Robinson, A., Blackwell, B., & Stutz, R. M. (1978). Flooding treatment of phobias: Does chronic diazepam increase effectiveness? *Journal of Behavior Therapy and Experimental Psychiatry, 9,* 219–225.

Wik, G., Fredrikson, M., Ericson, K., Eriksson, L., Stone-Elander, S., & Greitz, T. (1993). A functional cerebral response to frightening visual stimulation. *Psychiatry Research: Neuroimaging, 50,* 15–24.

Wolpe, J. (1958). *Psychotherapy by reciprocal inhibition.* Stanford, CA: Standford University Press.

Wolpe, J. (1973). *The practice of behavior therapy* (2nd ed.). New York: Pergamon Press.

Wolpe, J., & Lang, P. J. (1964). A Fear Survey Schedule for use in behavior therapy. *Behavior Research and Therapy, 2,* 27–30.

Woody, S. R., & Teachman, B. (2000). Intersection of disgust and fear: Normative and pathological views. *Clinical Psychology: Science and Practice, 7,* 291–311.

Woody, S. R., & Tolin, D. F. (2002). The relationship between disgust sensitivity and avoidant behavior: Studies of clinical and nonclinical samples. *Journal of Anxiety Disorders, 16,* 543–559.

Wright, C. I., Martis, B., McMullin, K., Shin, L. M., & Rauch, S. L. (2003). Amygdala and insular responses to emotionally valenced human faces in small animal specific phobia. *Biological Psychiatry, 54,* 1067–1076.

Zhang, A. Y., & Snowden, L. R. (1999). Ethnic characteristics of mental disorders in five U.S. communities. *Cultural Diversity and Ethnic Minority Psychology, 5,* 134–146.

Zoellner, L. A., Craske, M. G., Hussain, A., Lewis, M., & Echeveri, A. (1996, November). *Contextual effects of alprazolam during exposure therapy.* Paper presented at the 30th annual Convention of the Association for the Advancement of Behavior Therapy, New York.

Zvolensky, M. J., Lejuez, C. W., & Eifert, G. H. (2000). The effects of prediction and control of aversive events on anxiety: An operational reformulation. *Behavior Research and Therapy, 38,* 653–663.

CHAPTER 8

Panic and Agoraphobia

MARIA NAZARIAN AND MICHELLE G. CRASKE

DESCRIPTION OF THE DISORDER

I wasn't sure what was happening to me that evening, but I was extremely scared! All of a sudden, my heart was pounding, it felt like it was going to jump out of my chest, and I couldn't breathe. I really thought I was dying! The room started spinning, I started sweating and shaking, and I got nauseous. I had [my wife] rush me to the hospital, but by the time the doctor could see me, I was feeling fine. I was convinced I had a heart attack, but the tests came out negative. I'm relieved that nothing is wrong with my heart, but I am really afraid it might happen again. What if it happens while I'm driving? Heart palpitations, nausea, dizziness, shortness of breath, chest pain, sweating, trembling, tingling, feeling of choking, chills or hot flushes, and derealization are examples of the physical symptoms present during a panic attack, in addition to the cognitive symptoms, such as fear of dying, going crazy, or losing control. According to the *DSM-IV* (American Psychiatric Association, 1994), a panic attack is a distinct episode of extreme apprehension during which individuals experience at least 4 of the 13 symptoms, with a sudden onset and with the intensity of symptoms reaching peak within 10 minutes. Panic attacks may occur as part of various anxiety disorders as *cued* attacks. However, a diagnosis of panic disorder is given in the case of recurrent *unexpected* panic attacks, followed by at least 1 month of persistent concern about their recurrence and their consequences or by a significant change in behavior consequent to the attacks (American Psychiatric Association, 1994).

Panic attacks may occur with a different combination of symptoms across individuals and may vary in intensity and symptom presentation in the same person (Rapee, Craske, & Barlow, 1990). Generally, individuals report more than four symptoms during a panic attack (Fyer & Rassnick, 1990), yet some experience *limited-symptom* attacks where they endorse less than four symptoms. Although some limited-symptom attacks can be quite debilitating, most are reported by patients as less intense and are associated with an observably smaller increase in heart rate compared to *full-blown* panic attacks (C. B. Taylor et al., 1986). Limited-symptom attacks rarely occur in the absence of full-blown attacks, but they can still lead to phobic avoidance.

Panic disorder can occur with or without agoraphobia or avoidance of, or endurance with dread of, situations and places from which escape might be difficult or where help might be unattainable in case of a panic attack or paniclike symptoms (American Psychiatric Association, 1994). Agoraphobia without a history of panic suggests the same situational anxiety and avoidance exclusive of full-blown panic attacks. Individuals display varying forms of agoraphobia and level of impairment or interference, and thus the degree of agoraphobia varies from mild to severe. The diagnosis of panic disorder with mild agoraphobia may be given to an individual who is uncomfortable using public transportation but who continues to take the subway to work on most days and occasionally turns down an offer to go to the movies or a concert. He or she may feel some discomfort in these situations and prefer to sit close to an exit to make sure escape is uncomplicated in case of a panic attack. A person with moderate agoraphobia might choose to drive or walk to work instead of using public transportation, or he or she might take the subway only when accompanied by a supportive friend and may avoid movie theatres and concert halls altogether. An individual with severe agoraphobia might have difficulty leaving the home unless absolutely necessary or when accompanied, and might not be able to accomplish much, including work, without the help of others.

In addition to agoraphobic avoidance, individuals with panic disorder often engage in other behaviors designed to protect themselves in the event of panic attacks (White & Barlow, 2002). These behaviors can include reassurance seeking and other safety behaviors (e.g., knowing the locale of medical facilities), reliance on safety signals (e.g., having a cell phone or a friend), and avoiding certain somatic sensations such as those caused by caffeine or exercise (i.e., "interoceptive avoidance").

Panic disorder with agoraphobia can be very incapacitating and costly, both personally and on a societal level (e.g., Greenberg et al., 1999). The somatic symptoms of a panic attack often lead people to think that they are experiencing a medical problem, and thus they seek medical as opposed to psychological care. Individuals with panic disorder utilize resources in the medical setting more frequently than the general public and people with other psychiatric disorders, therefore accruing considerable costs for themselves and imposing on the health care system. This is particularly true for panic disordered individuals who have other comorbid psychiatric disorders (Roy-Byrne et al., 1999). Appropriate assessment and treatment of panic disorder and agoraphobia may minimize these personal and community costs.

RELATIONSHIP BETWEEN PANIC AND AGORAPHOBIA

From an evolutionary standpoint, fear is a natural and adaptive response to threatening stimuli. However, such fear experienced during the first unexpected panic attack is often unjustified due to the lack of an identifiable trigger or antecedent. Barlow (1988, 2002) described this initial panic attack as a "false alarm," when the fear system is activated to produce a panic attack in biologically and psychologically susceptible persons. These individuals then develop hypervigilance for internal sensations (i.e., interoceptive awareness) and become exceptionally aware of any minor somatic changes, no matter how harmless or natural. Slight changes in their physiology that are similar to their panic attack symptoms become signs of danger and elicit anxiety about having another panic attack, which is often the motivation for agoraphobic avoidance. Therefore, agoraphobia is thought to be precipitated by the anticipation of panic (Cox, Endler, & Swinson, 1995; Craske & Barlow, 1988), by anxiety sensitivity, or by a set of beliefs that anxiety symptoms are detrimental (White, Brown, Somers, & Barlow, 2006).

There is evidence that initial panic attacks occurring in uncontrollable situations or where escape would be difficult (e.g., driving on the freeway) are followed by higher levels of anxiety when compared to those occurring in controllable situations (e.g., being at home; Craske, Miller, Rotunda, & Barlow, 1990). Recently, White and colleagues (2006) found that perception of control over threatening situations functioned as a moderator in the relationship between anxiety sensitivity and agoraphobia. Anxiety sensitivity and agoraphobia were more strongly positively correlated in individuals who scored low on perceived control.

However, not everyone with panic disorder develops agoraphobia, and the extent of agoraphobia that emerges is highly variable (Craske & Barlow, 1988). Various factors have been investigated as potential predictors of agoraphobia. Although agoraphobia tends to increase as history of panic lengthens, a significant proportion of individuals panic for many years without developing agoraphobic limitations. Nor is agoraphobia related to age of onset or frequency of panic (Cox et al., 1995; Craske & Barlow, 1988; Rapee & Murrell, 1988). Some studies report more intense physical symptoms during panic attacks when there is more agoraphobia (e.g., De Jong & Bouman, 1995; Goisman et al., 1994; Noyes, Clancy, Garvey, & Anderson, 1987; Telch, Brouillard, Telch, Agras, & Taylor, 1989). Others fail to find such differences (e.g., Cox et al., 1995; Craske et al., 1990). Nor do fears of dying, going crazy, or losing control relate to level of agoraphobia (Cox et al., 1995; Craske, Rapee, & Barlow, 1988). However, concerns about social consequences of panicking may be stronger when there is more agoraphobia (Amering et al., 1997; De Jong & Bouman, 1995; Rapee & Murrell, 1988; Telch et al., 1989). Occupational status also predicts agoraphobia, accounting for 18% of the variance in one study (De Jong & Bouman, 1995). Perhaps the strongest predictor of agoraphobia is gender. The ratio of males to females shifts dramatically in the direction of female predominance as the level of agoraphobia worsens (e.g., Thyer, Himle, Curtis, Cameron, & Nesse, 1985).

Nocturnal Panic

A subset of individuals with panic disorder experiences nocturnal panic attacks. Nocturnal panic refers to waking from sleep in a state of panic with symptoms that are very similar to panic attacks during wakeful states (Craske & Barlow, 1989; Uhde, 1994). Nocturnal panic does *not* refer to waking from sleep and panicking after a lapse of waking time or to nighttime arousals induced by nightmares or environmental stimuli (e.g., unexpected noises). Instead, nocturnal panic is an abrupt waking from sleep in a state of panic without an obvious trigger. Nocturnal panic attacks reportedly most often occur between one and three hours after sleep onset and only occasionally occur more than once per night (Craske & Barlow, 1989).

Although epidemiological studies have not been conducted, surveys of select clinical groups suggest that nocturnal panic is relatively common among individuals with panic disorder, with 44% to 71% reporting experiencing nocturnal panic at least once and 30% to 45% having repeated nocturnal panics (Craske & Barlow, 1989; Krystal, Woods, Hill, & Charney, 1991; Mellman & Uhde, 1989; Roy-Byrne, Mellman, & Uhde, 1988; Uhde, 1994). Individuals who suffer frequent nocturnal panics often become fearful of sleep and attempt to delay sleep onset. Avoidance of sleep may result in chronic sleep deprivation, in turn precipitating more nocturnal panics (Uhde, 1994).

DIAGNOSIS AND ASSESSMENT

As with any psychiatric disorder, a complete and reliable assessment is essential to making an accurate diagnosis of panic disorder with agoraphobia, as well as creating an effective treatment plan. In addition, regular assessment during treatment is important in monitoring progress and adapting treatment goals and procedures as necessary. A diagnosis of panic disorder is established best by using a clinical interview that reliably targets the *DSM-IV* diagnostic criteria and provides unequivocal results. The Anxiety Disorders Interview Schedule for DSM-IV (ADIS-IV; Brown, DiNardo, & Barlow, 1994) is a semi-structured interview that was designed for the diagnosis of anxiety disorders in particular. It facilitates a reliable method of gathering the necessary information to make differential diagnosis among anxiety disorders and offers the ability to distinguish between clinical and subclinical presentations of a disorder. In addition, ADIS-IV allows diagnosis of other comorbid *DSM-IV* Axis I disorders that may be present (e.g., mood disorders, hypochondriasis) that help generate a more complete clinical presentation of the individual. It is essential to obtain data on the frequency, intensity, and duration of panic attacks, as well as details on avoidance behavior to be able to tailor treatment accordingly. In addition to clinical intake interviews, other self-report instruments, including self-monitoring forms, can be utilized in the ongoing symptom monitoring of panic disorder and agoraphobia because they may provide a more objective measure on the present frequency and intensity of symptoms during treatment (Craske & Tsao, 1999).

Evaluation of the subjective experience, including cognitive and emotional, is only one component of the complete assessment of panic disorder and agoraphobia. Because it is widely agreed that emotions are expressed in the subjective, physiological, and behavioral systems, it is important to include the behavioral component and, if possible, the physiological component in the assessment of panic disorder. Behavioral assessment, often called behavioral avoidance, tests (BAT) are important in determining the extent of agoraphobic and interoceptive avoidance, as well as in case conceptualization, in executing a suitable treatment plan and in monitoring progress or redirecting treatment goals. Although behavioral tests were originally designed to be used in research settings, they are useful clinical tools because they provide an objective assessment of agoraphobic avoidance that might be different from what patients believe they can endure in specific situations.

Behavioral tests can be standardized or individualized. A standardized behavioral test designed to assess the severity of agoraphobia usually entails walking or driving an established route, whereas an individualized test usually involves a range of idiosyncratic tasks that are rated in the moderate to high difficulty range by the patient. In both tests, anxiety levels are rated at regular intervals using a subjective unit of distress scale (SUDS) and the degree of approach (i.e., refused, attempted but escaped, or completed) and the level of accomplishment (e.g., distance traveled) are recorded. Examples of standardized behavioral tests targeting interoceptive sensations include spinning in a circle, running in place, hyperventilating, and breathing through a straw (Antony, Ledley, Liss, & Swinson, 2006). Anxiety levels before, during, and after each task as well as task duration are recorded.

Psychophysiological measures (e.g., heart rate, respiration, and galvanic skin response) can be valuable assessment tools in the evaluation of response to treatment for panic disorder and agoraphobia (Craske, Lang, Aikins, & Mystkowski, 2005). In addition to providing an objective measure of progress, they can be useful therapeutic tools in challenging and correcting common misperceptions in individuals with panic disorder regarding their physiological function.

Such a functional analysis, incorporating information about the cognitive, behavioral, and physiological components of panic disorder with agoraphobia, facilitates a thorough assessment in an effort to determine the way in which the disorder presents itself in each person. This information combined with data regarding age, gender, socioeconomic status, degree of social support, and medical or other problems, (i.e., biopsychosocial assessment) is ideal in designing the best and most personalized treatment for each individual.

DIFFERENTIAL DIAGNOSIS

Panic attacks can occur in the context of other anxiety disorders, and in most cases they should be subsumed under that diagnosis rather than being diagnosed separately as panic disorder. However, it can be difficult to determine which diagnosis is more appropriate, especially if panic attacks are a significant concern. The experience of fear in cued versus unexpected panic attacks is similar; however, cognitive symptoms of fear of dying, going crazy, or losing control are not especially present in panic attacks experienced by persons with anxiety disorders other than panic disorder, such as specific phobias (Craske, Zarate, Burton, & Barlow, 1993). Therefore, whereas cognitive symptoms are not essential in defining a panic attack, they are significant in the definition of panic disorder (Barlow, Brown, & Craske, 1994). It is important to discuss these differences in the context of social phobia and specific phobia.

Social Phobia An individual with social phobia may experience panic attacks in social situations where he or she may become extremely nervous or afraid of being evaluated or humiliated. Socially phobic persons may be likely to avoid such situations due to their anticipatory anxiety of negative judgment or embarrassment. Similarly, it is common for individuals with panic disorder with agoraphobia to avoid public places to prevent embarrassment in the event of a panic attack. One important distinction is that persons with panic disorder tend to avoid social situations because of worries about having a panic attack or feeling embarrassed if they were to have a panic attack in public. Therefore, their primary fear is having a panic attack in front of others and feeling humiliated as a result. However, individuals with social phobia tend to avoid social situations because of concerns about doing or saying something that could cause embarrassment or negative evaluation. Therefore, their primary fear is of being humiliated in public and not necessarily of having a panic attack. Often, the panic attack might cause further embarrassment in socially anxious individuals, but it is neither a primary concern nor the main reason for avoiding social situations. In addition, individuals with panic disorder and agoraphobia may continue to feel anxious even when playing a passive role in a social setting, whereas a socially phobic patient is more likely to feel relaxed in that situation where he or she is not the center of attention and where he or she does not anticipate being evaluated or judged (Dattilio & Salas-Auvert, 2000). Another distinction between social phobia and panic disorder with agoraphobia is in the interpretation of physiological changes due to anxiety: Individuals with panic disorder interpret somatic changes as a sign of imminent threat, whereas socially anxious individuals are more likely to perceive physiological changes such as blushing or sweating as a cause of humiliation (Dattilio & Salas-Auvert, 2000).

Specific Phobia Persons experiencing specific phobia usually have a circumscribed focus of fear although exposure to the phobic stimulus might trigger a panic attack. Panic attacks in specific phobia are quite predictable and phobic avoidance is usually directly related to the phobic stimulus, though avoidance may generalize to objects or situations related to the phobic stimulus. However, panic attacks in panic disorder are less predictable and agoraphobia is directly related to the fear of having a panic attack. An individual suffering from panic disorder with agoraphobia might avoid flying specifically because he or she is afraid of having a panic attack on an airplane. In contrast, a person with a specific phobia of flying might avoid traveling by airplane strictly because he or she is afraid a plane could crash. The latter situational fear is not related to having a panic attack.

COMORBID MOOD DISORDERS

Individuals with panic disorder and agoraphobia are at high risk for comorbid mood disorders (e.g., Brown, Campbell, Lehman, Grisham, & Mancill, 2001). Thus, assessment and diagnosis of such disorders is emphasized in the implementation and delivery of treatment for primary panic disorder. Panic disorder with agoraphobia is more likely to predate the onset of a mood disorder in most individuals. However, the opposite is also possible, as well as the simultaneous development of both disorders (Breier, Charney, & Heninger, 1984; Kaufman & Charney, 2000). One theory regarding the overlap of panic and mood disorders suggests the presence of stressful life events as an etiologic association between the two types of disorders (e.g., Roy-Byrne, Geraci, & Uhde, 1986). Other theories include genetic predispositions (Levinson et al., 2003) and neurobiological vulnerabilities (Ninan & Dunlop, 2005). Regardless of the cause, comorbid depression in panic disordered individuals increases the severity and chronicity of panic, causes further impairment in functioning, and heightens the risk of alcohol and substance abuse (Kaufman & Charney, 2000). In addition, an increased risk of suicidality in panic disorder is related to comorbid depression although some researchers have found that comorbid disorders are not necessary for this elevation in risk of suicidality (e.g., Johnson, Weissman, & Klerman, 1990). Although some researchers have suggested that interventions for comorbid depression may be necessary in the treatment of principal panic disorder (Woody, McLean, Taylor, & Koch, 1999), others have found that cognitive-behavioral treatment of panic disorder yielded positive benefits for co-occurring disorders and that the degree of generalization to comorbid conditions was predicted by the degree of mastery in the targeted disorder (e.g., Tsao, Mystkowski, Zucker, & Craske, 2002).

In addition to unipolar depression, bipolar disorder sometimes is comorbid with panic disorder with or without agoraphobia. In particular, the higher comorbidity rates between panic and bipolar disorder seem to be most prominent in the bipolar I subtype (Simon et al., 2004). Theories of this connection focus on genetic and neurobiological predictors (discussed later). Panic and other anxiety disorders have been found to lower the age of bipolar disorder onset, exacerbate the course of bipolar disorder, reduce the quality of life and functioning, and increase rates of suicidality significantly (Simon et al., 2004). There is much focus on the effects of panic disorder on bipolar disorder; however, symptoms of bipolar disorder also may exacerbate the severity of panic disorder. More research is needed in determining the best ways to address bipolar disorder in treating primary panic disorder with and without agoraphobia, and vice versa.

Comorbid Medical Illness

In some cases, medical illness may precede onset of panic disorder and generate anxiety as a result of the physical symptoms associated with the medical condition, whereas in other cases a medical disorder may onset later and function as an exacerbating factor of preexisting panic disorder (Simon & Fischmann, 2005). Numerous studies have found that respiratory disease (e.g., asthma or chronic obstructive pulmonary disease; COPD) is a risk factor for panic and other anxiety disorders (e.g., Smoller & Otto, 1998). In addition, comorbid anxiety disorders are thought to intensify the subjective rating of symptoms related to respiratory difficulties (Dales, Spitzer, Schechter, & Suissa, 1989). Smoller and Otto (1998) found that treating COPD patients with an antidepressant medication improved both mood and anxiety symptoms, including shortness of breath and exercise tolerance, in the absence of changes in pulmonary function. Therefore, Simon and Fischmann (2005) deduce that, although COPD is a chronic medical condition, treating comorbid panic disorder may diminish symptoms for both medical and anxiety disorders.

The somatic symptoms of a panic attack (e.g., heart palpitations and chest pain) are not easily distinguishable from symptoms of cardiac problems and therefore lead individuals suffering from a panic attack into the emergency room for medical care. Studies have found that panic disorder is undiagnosed in 33% to 98% of individuals who are admitted into the emergency room with complaints of chest pain (Beitman et al., 1989; Lynch & Galbraith, 2003). Others have found that 21% of patients with panic disorder also have cardiac problems, including myocardial infarction (MI; Carter et al., 1992). The relationship between anxiety disorders, in particular panic disorder, and cardiac problems is thought to be due to reduced heart rate variability, a physiological abnormality. Decreased heart rate variability in anxious individuals is a risk factor for arrhythmias and sudden death from MI (Kawachi, Sparrow, Vokonas, & Weiss, 1994).

CONCEPTUALIZATION

Vulnerability Factors

Aside from the role of neuroticism as a nonspecific vulnerability factor for all emotional disorders (Mineka, Watson, & Clark, 1998), central to current theorizing about panic disorder is the notion of anxiety sensitivity (Reiss, 1980), or the belief that anxiety and its associated symptoms may cause deleterious physical, social, and psychological consequences that extend beyond any immediate physical discomfort during an episode of anxiety or panic. Anxiety sensitivity is elevated across most anxiety disorders, but it is particularly elevated in panic disorder (e.g., S. Taylor, Koch, & McNally, 1992; Zinbarg & Barlow, 1996), especially the physical concerns subscale (Zinbarg & Barlow, 1996; Zinbarg, Barlow, & Brown, 1997). Therefore, beliefs that physical symptoms of anxiety are harmful seem to be particularly relevant to panic disorder. Several longitudinal studies indicate that high scores on the Anxiety Sensitivity Index predict the onset of panic attacks over 1- to 4-year intervals in adolescents (Hayward, Killen, Kraemer, & Taylor, 2000), college students (Maller & Reiss, 1992), and community samples with specific phobias or no anxiety disorders (Ehlers, 1995). The predictive relationship remains after controlling for prior depression (Hayward et al., 2000). In addition, Anxiety Sensitivity Index scores predicted spontaneous panic attacks and worry about panic (and anxiety more generally) during an acute military stressor (i.e., 5 weeks of basic training), even after controlling for history of panic attacks and trait anxiety (Schmidt, Lerew, & Jackson, 1997). However, it is important to note that anxiety sensitivity accounted for only a relatively small portion of the variance and neuroticism was a better predictor of panic attacks.

Other studies highlight the role of medical illnesses in predicting later panic disorder. For example, using the Dunedin Multidisciplinary Study database, we found that experience with personal respiratory disturbance and parental ill health as a youth predicted panic disorder at the ages of 18 or 21 (Craske, Poulton, Tsao, & Plotkin, 2001). In addition, more respiratory disturbance is reported in the history of panic disorder patients compared to other anxiety disordered groups (Verburg, Griez, Meijer, & Pols, 1995). Medical adversity as a child has been related to increased risk for later anxiety disorders and there may be a particular affinity with panic disorder. Also, community-based studies have found a link between childhood sexual and physical abuse and increased rates of panic attacks and panic disorder among adults in the general population (Kendler et al., 2000; Stein et al. 1996). More recently, Goodwin, Fergusson, and Horwood (2005), using longitudinal data, found a significant relationship between development of panic disorder in young adulthood and experience of childhood sexual and physical abuse, but not interparental violence, even after adjusting for common confounding variables.

Panic disordered patients as well as nonclinical panickers appear to have heightened awareness of, or ability to detect, bodily sensations of arousal (e.g., Ehlers & Breuer, 1992, 1996; Ehlers, Breuer, Dohn, & Feigenbaum, 1995; Zoellner & Craske, 1999). Discrepant findings (e.g., Antony et al., 1995; Rapee, 1994) exist, but they have been attributed to methodological artifact (Ehlers & Breuer, 1996). Ability to perceive heart beat, in particular, appears to be a relatively stable individual difference variable, given that it does not differ between untreated and treated panic disorder patients (Ehlers & Breuer, 1992) or from before to after successful treatment (Antony, Meadows, Brown, & Barlow, 1994; Ehlers et al., 1995). Thus, interoceptive accuracy may be a predisposing trait for panic disorder. Ehlers and Breuer (1996) conclude, "although good interoception is considered neither a necessary or a sufficient condition for panic disorder, it may enhance the probability of panic by increasing the probability of perceiving sensations that may trigger an attack if perceived as dangerous" (p. 174).

Separate from interoception is the issue of physiological propensity to acute and intense autonomic activation. Some evidence points to a unique genetic influence on the reported experience of breathlessness, heart pounding, and a sense of terror (Kendler, Heath, Martin, & Eaves, 1987). Perhaps cardiovascular reactivity presents a unique physiological predisposition for panic disorder. Consistent with this notion is the evidence that panic disorder patients report having experienced paniclike and cardiac sensations, although less intense and frightening, prior to their first panic attack (Craske et al., 1990; Keyl & Eaton, 1990). However, these studies are based on symptom reporting rather than physiological measurement, and thus the findings may pertain more to interoception than to physiological propensity.

Maintaining Factors

The initial panic attack, or false alarm, often occurs during a stressful period or follows a significant life change. Acute "fear of fear" that develops after initial panic attacks in *vulnerable individuals* refers to fear of certain bodily sensations associated with panic attacks (e.g., racing heart, dizziness, paresthesias; Barlow, 1988; Goldstein & Chambless, 1978) and is attributed to two factors: The first is *interoceptive conditioning*, or conditioned fear of internal cues (e.g., elevated heart rate) because of their association with intense fear, pain, or distress (Razran, 1961). Specifically, interoceptive conditioning refers to low-level somatic sensations of arousal or anxiety becoming conditioned stimuli so that early somatic components of the anxiety response come to elicit significant bursts of anxiety or panic (Bouton, Mineka, & Barlow, 2001). An extensive body of experimental literature attests to the robustness of interceptive conditioning (e.g., Dworkin & Dworkin, 1999). In addition, interoceptive conditioned responses are not dependent on conscious awareness of triggering cues (Block, Ghoneim, Fowles, Kumar, & Pathak, 1987; Lennartz & Weinberger, 1992; Razran, 1961). Within this model, slight changes in relevant bodily functions that are not consciously recognized may elicit conditioned fear and panic due to previous pairings with the terror of panic (Barlow, 1988; Bouton et al., 2001).

The second factor offered by Clark (1986) to explain acute fear of panic-related body sensations involves catastrophic misappraisals of bodily sensations (i.e., misinterpretation of sensations as signs of imminent death, loss of control). Debate continues as to the significance of catastrophic misappraisals of bodily sensations versus conditioned (i.e., emotional, noncognitively mediated) fear responding (Bouton et al., 2001). Bouton et al. (2001) propose that catastrophic misappraisals may accompany panic attacks because they are a natural part of the constellation of responses that go with panic or because they have been encouraged and reinforced much like sick role behaviors during childhood. In addition, such thoughts may become conditioned stimuli that trigger anxiety and panic, as demonstrated via panic induction through presentation of pairs of words involving sensations and catastrophic outcomes (Clark et al., 1988). In this case, catastrophic cognitions may well be sufficient to elicit conditioned panic attacks but not necessary.

An acute fear of bodily sensations is likely to generate ongoing distress for a number of reasons: In the immediate sense, autonomic arousal generated by fear in turn intensifies the sensations that are feared, thus creating a reciprocating cycle of fear and sensations that sustains until autonomic arousal exhausts or safety is perceived. In addition, because bodily sensations that trigger panic attacks are not always immediately obvious, they may generate the perception of unexpected or "out of the blue" panic attacks (Barlow, 1988). Furthermore, even when interoceptive cues are identifiable, they tend to be less predictable than external stimuli. For example, an accelerated heart rate may be produced by excitement, anger, fear, sexual arousal, stimulants, stress, inefficient breathing, or natural variations in heart rate, to name a few, and may shift rapidly and independently of veridical contextual variables, thus creating unpredictability—and unpredictable aversive events are more anxiety provoking than predictable ones (Mineka, Cook, & Miller, 1984).

Not only are bodily sensations less predictable, but like other internally generated stimuli such as threat-related images, they are also less controllable than clearly discernible external stimuli. That is, the ability to terminate a bodily sensation is likely to be substantially weaker than the ability to terminate a clearly defined external situation if by only physically escaping the situation; uncontrollability of aversive stimuli also elevates distress (e.g., Maier, Laudenslager, & Ryan, 1985; Mineka et al., 1984). Unpredictability and uncontrollability are seen as enhancing general levels of anxiety about "When is it going to happen again?" and "What do I do when it happens?"

For these reasons, fears of bodily sensations are likely to generate pervasive distress, thereby contributing to high levels of chronic anxious apprehension (Barlow, 1988). In turn, anxious apprehension increases the likelihood of panic by directly increasing the availability of sensations that have become conditioned cues for panic and/or by increasing attentional vigilance for these bodily cues. Thus, a maintaining cycle of panic and anxious apprehension develops. Subtle avoidance behaviors are believed to maintain negative beliefs about feared bodily sensations (Barlow & Craske, 1994; Clark & Ehlers, 1993). Examples include holding onto objects or persons for fears of fainting, sitting and remaining still for fears of heart attack, and moving slowly or searching for an escape for fears of acting foolish (Salkovskis, Clark, & Gelder, 1996). Finally, anxiety may develop over specific contexts in which occurrence of panic would be particularly troubling (i.e., situations associated with impairment, entrapment, negative social evaluation, and distance from safety). These anxieties could contribute to agoraphobia, which in turn maintains distress by preventing disconfirmation of catastrophic misappraisals and extinction of conditioned responding.

GENETIC INFLUENCES

Evidence from family studies suggests an increased prevalence of panic disorder or agoraphobia among family members of patients with the disorder, compared to control families (e.g., Crowe, Noyes, Pauls, & Slymen, 1983; Moran & Andrews, 1985). Crowe et al. (1983) did not find any differences in frequency of generalized anxiety disorder (GAD) among family members of patients with panic disorder versus controls. To examine more closely the evidence for genetic transmission, Torgersen (1983) studied panic disorder and agoraphobia among twins in Norway. He found a significantly higher rate of "anxiety disorder with panic attack" in monozygotic than dizygotic twins. However, other researchers have failed to find this difference (Andrews, Stewart, Allen, & Henderson, 1990). Torgersen did not find a significant relationship between presence of panic in one twin and GAD in the cotwin, suggesting that panic is more likely to be inherited and may have a separate heritability. Moran and Andrews (1985) concluded that there may be an inherited nonspecific diathesis for agoraphobia, rather than a specific gene, and that the development of this cluster of symptoms is still dependent on environmental factors such as stress.

It is possible that a deficiency in serotonin (5-HT) neurotransmission may be linked to vulnerability to panic attacks and panic disorder (Maron et al., 2005). A study comparing individuals diagnosed with panic disorder with and without agoraphobia to a group of matched controls found evidence supporting the hypothesis that genetic variations associated with lower serotonin neurotransmission are related to panic disorder in a sample consisting mostly of women (Maron et al., 2005). However, analyses of specific genetic markers remain preliminary and inconsistent. For example, panic disorder has been linked to a locus on chromosome 13 (Hamilton et al., 2003; Schumacher et al., 2005) and chromosome 9 (Thorgeirsson et al., 2003), but the exact genes remain unknown. Findings regarding markers for the cholecystokinin-BE receptor gene have been inconsistent (Hamilton et al., 2001; van Megen, Westenberg, Den Boer, & Kahn, 1996). Association and linkage studies implicate the adenosine receptor gene in panic disorder (Deckert et al., 1998; Hamilton et al. 2004), but studies of genes involved in neurotransmitter systems associated with fear and anxiety have produced inconsistent results (Roy-Byrne, Stein, & Craske, in press).

Physical Affecting Behavior

Behavioral tests discussed earlier provide some evidence that a person's emotions and behaviors can be affected by physical changes that often trigger maladaptive ways of thinking. Behavioral tests are used to assess the degree to which individuals with panic disorder are sensitive to interoceptive cues. These include hyperventilating and spinning in place, which induce sensations associated with panic attacks (e.g., shortness of breath and dizziness). In addition to using such information in a clinical setting, some researchers have examined panic-inducing tasks in a laboratory setting, including carbon dioxide inhalation and central nervous system stimulants that elicit sensations of shortness of breath or choking and of increased heart rate, respectively (e.g., Charney, Heninger, & Jatlow, 1985; Woods, Charney, Goodman, & Heninger, 1987). Again, it seems that even slight changes in somatic sensations can lead to fear and panic in individuals vulnerable to panic disorder. Because the individual interprets the initial sensations as threatening or harmful, the fight-flight response is activated as if to protect the body from danger. The fight-flight response is hardwired and unconditioned and it includes, among other things, autonomic arousal. It involves the sympathetic nervous system, which is an all-or-none system, immediately activating all of it parts. This may explain why most panic attacks involve many different symptoms that occur almost instantaneously. As the sympathetic nervous system becomes active, it releases adrenalin and noradrenalin that continue sympathetic nervous system activity and increase it for some time. Eventually, the parasympathetic nervous system is activated to restore relaxation. Panic cannot continue forever, nor spiral to ever increasing and possibly damaging levels. However, adrenalin and noradrenalin may remain in the bloodstream for a while after the relaxing system has taken over, suggesting that the individual cannot feel fully relaxed until those chemicals have been eradicated from the bloodstream.

During unexpected panic attacks, the amygdala, which is the central command for emotions and emotional memory, is presumed to be activated. As the fear subsides, it is assumed that an emotional memory of the event is formed that is characterized by the strengthening of connections among neurons in the amygdala (Ninan & Dunlop, 2005). As a result, fear becomes conditioned and future events, whether definite or anticipated, that correspond to elements of this emotional memory are presumed to trigger the fear and panic response (Ninan & Dunlop, 2005). In addition to emotional memory, an autobiographical memory of the events is hypothesized to develop in the hippocampus, which is the center for such explicit memories (Ninan & Dunlop, 2005). The important role of the hippocampus is the registering of the context in which the panic attack occurred, and this contextual learning contributes to the association of external cues with the fear response. This may lead to situational avoidance, which is believed to involve the prefrontal cortex and its links with the amygdala (Ninan & Dunlop, 2005). This connection is hypothesized to prohibit the extinction of avoidant behavior and lead to the lasting learned avoidance of objects and situations (Ninan & Dunlop, 2005).

Drugs Affecting Behavior

Though it is true that individuals with emotional disorders, including panic disorder, may use substances to self-medicate, there is some evidence pointing to drugs as precipitating factors for panic attack and perhaps panic disorder. Last, Barlow, and

O'Brien (1984) found that 12% of their sample reported experiencing a "false alarm" due to a drug reaction. It is often difficult to distinguish whether alcohol use or anxiety came first, and perhaps they each play a role in initiating the other, but Kushner, Sher, and Beitman (1990) reported that panic disorder and GAD are more likely than other anxiety disorders to result from excessive alcohol consumption. Kushner, Abrams, and Borchardt (2000) confirmed that anxiety disorders and alcohol use disorders play a role in each other's onset and that anxiety influences the maintenance and recurrence of alcohol use disorders. Therefore, when anxiety and panic are self-medicated with alcohol, the consequence can be a consistently worsening self-destructive pattern, due both to the effects of drug addition and the intensifying of anxiety and panic related to alcohol use (Kushner et al., 2000).

In addition to alcohol, other drugs such as cocaine have been associated with panic attacks. One study found many of their participants reported that heavy use of cocaine triggered panic attacks and subsequent panic disorder, despite discontinuation of cocaine use (Louie et al., 1996). Caffeine also has been found to be associated with increased anxiety and panic symptoms. In a survey of caffeine use, individuals diagnosed with panic disorder, but not those diagnosed with major depressive disorder, reported higher levels of anxiety with increasing amounts of caffeine consumption and strong reactivity to just one cup of coffee (Boulenger, Uhde, Wolff, & Post, 1984). In a laboratory panic induction experiment using caffeine, individuals with panic disorder reported increased subjective and somatic anxiety that correlated significantly with caffeine levels in their bloodstream, and 71% of them believed this cluster of symptoms to be similar to their typical panic attacks (Charney et al., 1985). Notably, the panicogenic effects of caffeine and other drugs may represent fear of bodily sensations.

Cultural and Diversity Issues

Similar to other anxiety disorders, women are more likely to be diagnosed with panic disorder than men (see Craske, 2003). Lifetime prevalence of panic disorder and agoraphobia without history of panic disorder is twice as high in women as it is in men (Kessler et al., 1994). Also, a higher rate of women than men report more severe agoraphobia (White & Barlow, 2002). Some have hypothesized that increased degree of avoidance in women may be due to the cultural acceptance of avoidance in women but not in men (White & Barlow, 2002). Others have found that gender (i.e., masculinity versus femininity) rather than sex is more closely associated with situational avoidance (Chambless & Mason, 1986). That is, they found that, irrespective of sex, those who reported less "masculine" traits on a sex role scale endorsed more agoraphobic avoidance. In a more recent study, Arrindell and colleagues (2003) used data from 11 countries to examine the relationship between national levels of agoraphobia and the femininity or masculinity of the nation. That is, they were interested in comparing cultures that promoted equality between men and women (i.e., a high feminine society, such as Sweden) with cultures that emphasized different and more traditional sex roles for men and women, such as Japan. After correcting for sex and age, they found that scores of national agoraphobic fear were significantly higher in more masculine societies compared to more feminine societies. Thus, it is not only important to consider individual differences in masculinity-femininity or sex roles, but also to take into account the overall national/cultural values and demands affecting agoraphobia and emotional disorders in general.

Though facial expression of some emotions is known to be universal, expression of emotion overall is established as being dependent upon cultural factors. Therefore, as expected, cultural differences exist in the manifestation or presentation of psychiatric disorders and they are important in assessment and treatment of these disorders, including panic disorder and agoraphobia. Guarnaccia and colleagues have studied "ataque de nervios" in Puerto Rico (Guarnaccia, Canino, Rubio-Stipec, & Bravo, 1993) as it is endorsed in Hispanic populations in Latin American and Caribbean areas (Barlow, 2002). The symptoms of ataque de nervios include somatic sensations similar to those reported in panic attacks as well as shouting, cursing, crying, falling to the ground, and/or memory loss following the attack (Barlow, 2002). Ataque de nervios often occurs during stressful periods and they are recognized as an appropriate stress reaction (Guarnaccia, Rubio-Stipec, & Canino, 1989).

A phenomenon known as "heart distress" is reported mostly by Iranian women from lower socioeconomic classes (Good, 1977), and its symptoms are often somatic in nature and focus on the heart (i.e., heart palpitations or faintness). Some have thought that this syndrome resembles the Western category of depression, whereas others classify it as anxiety, especially panic (Barlow, 2002). However, a recent study assessing panic attacks in university students in Iran found a presentation of panic in their sample that is similar to the Western notion of panic disorder (Nazemi et al., 2003).

Another interesting phenomenon is found in Cambodian refugees, also named Khmers, who come from a culture with several cultural syndromes related to fears about physiological arousal (Hinton, Um, & Ba, 2001). *Kyol goeu*, translated as wind overload, is the belief that when a person is unhealthy (i.e., worry, sleep disturbance, poorer nutrition), he or she has too much wind in the diaphragm or belly caused by poor circulation and blockage of blood and wind vessels (Hinton et al., 2001). The excess wind is believed to constrict on the abdomen causing nausea, to compress the heart resulting in less efficient pumping, and to cause soreness in the neck (Hinton et al., 2001). In addition, when the wind reaches the head, dizziness, blurred vision, and faintness are felt (Hinton et al., 2001). Khmers believe that these circulatory blockages can have severe consequences that may result in death. Panic attacks are triggered by the interoceptive symptoms reported as a result of blockage, in particular dizziness, thus orthostatic panic and "sore neck" are the main ways in which panic attacks are presented in this culture. During times of stress or increased anxiety, the individual believes his or her body is weakened and begins to pay particular attention to physiological changes and signs of wind blockage. Thus, sensations resulting from normal activities such as standing up quickly may signal imminent danger and may trigger a panic attack (i.e., orthostatic panic).

BEHAVIORAL TREATMENT

Based on treatment outcome studies, cognitive-behavioral therapy (CBT) and pharmacological treatment are found to be effective and the treatments of choice for panic disorder with and without agoraphobia. Although research indicates a short-term benefit to a combined approach of CBT with psychotropic medications, the evidence does not point to any advantage over the long term and sometimes point to a disadvantage in terms of higher relapse rates when medications are combined with CBT (Smits, O'Cleirigh, & Otto, 2006). A cognitive-behavioral approach applies several ingredients that target the physiological, cognitive, and behavioral aspects of panic disorder and agoraphobic avoidance. Each element is designed to work on key characteristics and symptoms of the disorder, based on many laboratory and clinical findings that support their use. Usually, the treatment is brief, is completed within three to 4 months, can be administered in an individual or group format, and is highly effective, with approximately 76% of clients panic-free following treatment and 78% at follow-up (see Craske, 1999, for more detail). The structured sessions focus mainly on current symptoms.

Central to CBT is learning that fear and anxiety as well as the stimuli with which they are associated are not harmful. This is most effectively learned through direct experience (i.e., exposure) and is facilitated by discussion and verbal processing (i.e., cognitive restructuring). Reducing fear and anxiety is not an immediate goal of treatment. Through processes of exposure and cognitive restructuring, fear and the associated stimuli become less threatening, and consequently fear and anxiety eventually subsides.

Cognitive-behavioral treatment is based on the cognitive-behavioral model of emotional responding, such that thoughts and behaviors influence emotional responding, and, in turn, emotions influence cognitive and behavioral responding. These pathways can become maladaptive when thoughts and behaviors reinforce the threat value of emotions and associated stimuli (i.e., perception of threat and avoidant behavioral responses). Stress exacerbates maladaptive cycles among thoughts, behaviors and emotions, and it can be generated by these cycles themselves. However, eliminating life stress alone is rarely effective and is not the focus of treatment due to the need to transform self-perpetuating cycles that exist among threat appraisals, behaviors, and emotions. Also, early life events may be important to current functioning and insight about their contributory role may aid in development of control, but insight alone is rarely effective because of the self-perpetuating cycles described. Therefore, treatment does not emphasize insight unless critical learning incidents currently contribute to ongoing maintenance of distress. For example, insight about the effects of early life events may be beneficial if current panic attacks are linked with the unexpected loss of a client's father due to cardiac arrest when a client was very young, which the individual now views as evidence for his or her own early demise.

To decrease the perceived threat of emotions and associated stimuli, the individual observes and monitors his or her responses, develops an objective perspective of the relationships among thoughts, behaviors, and emotions, and gains a framework for understanding fear and anxiety as well as an understanding of how to learn different ways of responding. Next, the individual identifies thoughts and behaviors that contribute to emotional distress and carries out exercises to learn how to think and act differently. Conceptually, this involves building a new associative network of thoughts, feelings, and behaviors that compete with existing learned associations surrounding specific objects and situations. Rehearsal through repetitive exposure is required for the new competing associative network to become the preferred response option in the natural setting and over the long term.

Cognitive-behavioral therapy involves several different components, including psychoeducation, self-monitoring, breathing retraining (although the value of this particular component is questionable), cognitive restructuring, and exposure to internal and external feared cues as well as relapse prevention. Homework assignments are given regularly throughout treatment and each session usually begins with the review of the previous week's homework. The client is offered feedback on all homework material, focusing specifically on addressing difficulties and problems as well as re-inforcing accomplishments.

Cognitive-behavioral therapy begins with educational concepts as a way of correcting misconceptions and developing a model that explains and corresponds with the treatment. The educational information can be revisited at any time throughout subsequent sessions, especially as a way of correcting cognitive distortions. Psychoeducation for panic disorder focuses on the physiology of fear, given that physical symptoms of fear are often misinterpreted; emphasis is given to the protective and adaptive (as opposed to harmful) purpose of fear. The individual is informed of the causes of fear, including biological, psychological, and environmental stressors. Although knowing the causes of fear and panic is not necessary for treating the disorder, this type of information is included in the psychoeducation because misconceptions about causes can contribute unnecessarily to anxiety. Once the purpose and causes of fear are discussed, the components of fear and panic are introduced: physical, cognitive, and behavioral. Then the interactions among these three components are discussed in terms of negative cycles and ways to interrupt them. This also warrants an explanation of the ways in which the CBT will target these components and their interactions.

Along with the psychoeducation, objective self-monitoring is introduced as a skill for becoming a personal scientist of one's own reactions. The goal of self-monitoring is to play the role of an outside observer rather than to judge emotional responding; to be able to describe the physical, cognitive, and behavioral components of one's own responses objectively. Monitoring facilitates detection of specific triggers and conditions under which panic attacks occur. This contributes to a greater objective understanding and begins the process of identifying relevant cues for exposure therapy. Self-monitoring is emphasized in the initial stages of therapy but is continuously reinforced throughout treatment. This task can be demonstrated during session and given as homework assignment for practice.

Prior to exposure therapy, the client is taught the basic coping skill of slowed diaphragmatic breathing to interrupt the state of physiological overreactivity and facilitate corrective thinking and active confronting of fear-provoking stimuli. Each inhalation is accompanied by the count of breaths and each exhalation is accompanied by "relax," which reminds clients to focus on relaxing sensations. Breathing retraining is demonstrated during the session and the individual is assigned as homework assignment the practicing of the task twice daily for 5 to 10 minutes. The technique is reviewed at the beginning of each subsequent session as needed and practice of breathing retraining outside of the session is reinforced. Notably, there is some evidence to suggest that breathing retraining is not essential to treatment outcome and, in some cases, may become a maladaptive safety-seeking behavior.

Typically, cognitive therapy begins with discussion of the role of thoughts in generating emotions, to provide a treatment rationale. Next, thoughts are recognized as hypotheses rather than fact and therefore are open to questioning and challenge. Detailed self-monitoring of emotions and associated cognitions is instituted to identify specific beliefs, appraisals, and assumptions. Once relevant cognitions are identified, they are categorized into types of typical errors that occur during heightened emotion, such as overestimations of risk of negative events or catastrophizing of event meaning. The process of categorization, or labeling of thoughts, is consistent with a personal scientist model and facilitates an objective perspective by which the validity of the thoughts can be evaluated. Thus, in labeling the type of cognitive distortion, the client is encouraged to use an empirical approach to examine the validity of his or her thoughts by considering all of the available evidence. Therapists use Socratic questioning to help clients make guided discoveries and question their anxious thoughts. Next, alternative hypotheses are generated that are more evidence based. In addition to surface level appraisals (e.g., "That person is frowning at me because I look foolish"), core level beliefs or schemata (e.g., "I am not strong enough to withstand further distress" or "I am unlikeable") are questioned in the same way. Cognitive restructuring is not intended as a direct means of minimizing fear, anxiety, or unpleasant symptoms. Instead, cognitive restructuring is intended to correct distorted thinking; eventually fear and anxiety will subside, but their diminution is not the first goal of cognitive therapy.

Exposure is a critical phase of treatment and once begun should become the major focus of treatment sessions as well as between-treatment session homework. Limited exposure practice is of small benefit and may even be detrimental; thus concentrated exposure practice is essential. For the treatment of panic disorder with agoraphobia, the exposure is designed to gather data that disconfirm misappraisals and extinguish conditioned emotional responses to bodily sensations through interoceptive exposure, as well as to external situations and contexts through in vivo exposure.

In interoceptive exposure, the goal is to deliberately induce feared physical sensations to permit corrective learning that facilitates easy dismissal of such sensations in the future. Following the standard list of exercises mentioned earlier when describing the behavioral assessment, such as hyperventilating and spinning, the therapist models each exercise and encourages the client to attempt each one and to provide ratings after each induction of sensations, level of distress, and similarity to regular panic sensations. Using a graduated approach, exposure begins with the less distressing physical exercises and continues with the more distressing exercises. It is essential that the client endure sensations beyond the point at which they are first noticed, for at least 30 seconds to 1 minute, because early termination of the task may eliminate the opportunity to learn that the sensations are not harmful and that the anxiety can be tolerated. The coping skills of cognitive restructuring and slowing diaphragmatic breathing are used after each exercise, followed by a discussion of what was learned during the exercise about bodily sensations, fear, and avoidance. These interoceptive exercises are practiced daily outside of the therapy session to consolidate the process of learning. As clients learn that they can tolerate a certain level of distress by being exposed to internal cues of fear and panic, prolonged exposure to such stimuli is introduced. The client learns that bodily sensations and fear itself are not harmful, and that fear diminishes over days of repeated practice. Naturalistic interoceptive activities inherently induce somatic sensations (e.g., caffeine consumption, exercise). A list of common activities is provided to the client and a hierarchy is constructed based on the level of fear that each activity would elicit. Repeated exposure to these activities follows the same procedures as other exposure exercises.

In vivo exposure is introduced simultaneously with interoceptive exposure. As with interoceptive exposure, exposure to feared situations (e.g., driving) involves removal of safety signals and maladaptive coping. Graduated in vivo exposure proceeds from the least to the most distressing items on a hierarchy of feared and avoided situations. Given the recent advances in research, showing that neither physiological habituation nor the amount of fear reduction *in an exposure trial* is predictive of overall outcome (see Craske & Mystkowski, 2006), and given that self-efficacy through performance accomplishment is predictive of overall phobia reductions (e.g., Williams,

1992), and that toleration of fear and anxiety may be a more critical learning experience than the elimination of fear and anxiety (see Eifert & Forsyth, 2005), the focus now is on staying in the phobic situation until the specified time at which clients learn that what they are most worried about never or rarely happens or that they can cope with the phobic stimulus and tolerate the anxiety. Thus, length of a given exposure trial is not based on fear reduction but based on the conditions necessary for new learning that eventually leads fear and anxiety to subside across trials of exposure. Essentially, level of fear or fear reduction within a given trial of exposure is no longer considered an index of learning, but rather a reflection of performance; learning is best measured by the level of anxiety that is experienced the next time the phobic situation is encountered or at some later time. As with interoceptive exposure, exposure to feared and avoided situations involves removal of safety signals and safety behaviors. Safety signals provide patients a sense of safety from panic, loss of control, physical injury, or embarrassment. Examples include other people, water, money (to call for help), empty or full medication bottles, exit signs, and familiar landmarks when traveling. Safety behaviors similarly provide a sense of safety, and include seeking reassurance, or checking for exits. Reliance on safety signals and safety behaviors maintain excessive anxiety in the long term, even though they attenuate distress in the short term. The client identifies his or her own safety signals with the therapist's guidance who works with the client in finding ways in which the safety signals and safety behaviors can be eliminated gradually.

Cognitive-behavioral treatment for panic disorder and agoraphobia is designed as a short-term intervention with a key objective of teaching clients the skills necessary to become their own therapist. Therefore, a good therapist is like a coach who helps the client develop skills that can be used following the end of therapy. This is the purpose of relying on homework assignment and the active participation of the client. The therapist gradually diminishes involvement and guides the client to answer questions on his or her own, leading to a natural and expected end of treatment. In the effort to prevent relapse, the therapist reminds the client of the general principles of maintaining progress. Clients are encouraged to set up deliberate practices to deal with situations that elicit anxiety and to manage their anxiety by slowed abdominal breathing and generating alternative thoughts in those situations. They are reminded to be more aware of their ways of thinking and behaving when life stress increases because this is when panic and anxiety are likely to resurge. In addition, clients are reminded that setbacks may occur on their road to recovery or self-management of fear and anxiety. These lapses may be experienced as flare-ups of anxious symptoms or reinstatement of avoidance behavior. It is essential that clients do not confuse a lapse or a setback as a complete relapse or complete failure. The most important thing to do under conditions of lapse or flare-up of symptoms is to repeat the skills learned during cognitive-behavioral therapy: breathing retraining, cognitive restructuring, and exposure.

Efficacy of Behavioral Treatment

Cognitive-behavioral therapy for panic disorder typically yields panic-free rates in the range of 70% to 80% and high end-state rates (i.e., within normative ranges of functioning) in the range of 50% to 70% (e.g., Barlow, Craske, Cerny, & Klosko, 1989; Clark et al., 1994). Two meta-analyses reported very large effect sizes of 1.55 and 0.90 for CBT for panic disorder (Mitte, 2005). Also, results generally maintain over follow-up intervals for as long as 2 years (Craske, Brown, & Barlow, 1991). One analysis of individual profiles over time suggested a less optimistic picture in that one third of clients who were panic-free 24 months after CBT had experienced a panic attack in the preceding year, and 27% had received additional treatment for panic over that same interval of time (Brown & Barlow, 1995). Nevertheless, this approach to analysis did not take into account the general trend toward continuing improvement over time. Thus, rates of eventual therapeutic success may be underestimated when success is defined by continuous panic-free status since the end of active treatment.

The effectiveness extends to patients who experience nocturnal panic attacks (Craske, et al., 2005). Also, CBT is effective even when there is comorbidity, and some studies indicate that comorbidity does not reduce the effectiveness of CBT for panic disorder (e.g., Brown, Antony, & Barlow, 1995; McLean, Woody, Taylor, & Koch, 1998). Furthermore, CBT results in improvements in comorbid conditions (Brown et al., 1995; Tsao, Lewin, & Craske, 1998; Tsao, Mystkowski, Zucker, & Craske, 2002, 2005). In other words, co-occurring symptoms of depression and other anxiety disorders tend to improve after CBT for panic disorder. However, one study suggested that the benefits for comorbid conditions may lessen over time, when assessed 2 years later (Brown et al., 1995). Nonetheless, the general finding of improvement in comorbidity is significant because it suggests the value of remaining focused on the treatment for panic disorder even when comorbidity is present because the comorbidity will be benefited as well, at least up to 1 year. Applications of panic control treatment (PCT) have proven very helpful in lowering relapse rates on discontinuation of high potency benzodiazepines (e.g., Otto et al., 1993; Spiegel, Bruce, Gregg, & Nuzzarello, 1994).

Results from CBT for agoraphobia are slightly less effective than CBT for panic disorder with minimal agoraphobia, although outcomes tend to improve from post to follow-up assessment. Furthermore, Fava, Zielezny, Savron, and Grandi (1995) found that only 18.5% of their panic-free clients relapsed over a period of 5 to 7 years after exposure-based treatment for agoraphobia. Some research suggests that the trend for improvement after acute treatment is facilitated by involvement of significant others in every aspect of treatment (e.g., Cerny, Barlow, Craske, & Himadi, 1987). Recently, an intensive, 8-day treatment, using a sensation-focused PCT approach was developed for individuals with moderate to severe agoraphobia, and initial results are promising (Morissette, Spiegel, & Heinrichs, 2005).

Attempts have been made to dismantle the different components of CBT for panic and agoraphobia. The results are somewhat confusing, and dependent on the samples used (e.g., mild versus severe levels of agoraphobia) and the exact comparisons made. It appears that the cognitive therapy component may be effective (e.g., Williams & Falbo, 1996) even when conducted in full isolation from exposure and behavioral procedures (e.g., Salkovskis, Clark, & Hackman, 1991), and is more effective than applied relaxation (e.g., Arntz & van den Hout, 1996; Beck, Stanley, Baldwin, Deagle, & Averill, 1994; Clark et al., 1994). However, some studies find that cognitive therapy does not improve outcome when added to in vivo exposure treatment for agoraphobia (e.g., Rijken, Kraaimaat, de Ruiter, & Garssen, 1992; van den Hout, Arntz, & Hoekstra, 1994). Similarly, one study found that breathing skills training and repeated interoceptive exposure to hyperventilation did not improve outcome beyond in vivo exposure alone for agoraphobia (de Beurs, van Balkom, Lange, Koele, & van Dyke, 1995) and we found that breathing skills training was slightly less effective than interoceptive exposure when each was added to cognitive restructuring (Craske, Rowe, Lewin, & Noriega-Dimitri, 1997). Clearly, more dismantling research is needed.

Most of the studies described in the previous sections averaged around 11 to 12 treatment sessions. Four to 6 sessions of PCT (Craske, Maidenberg, & Bystritsky, 1995; Roy-Byrne et al., 2005) seem effective also, although the results were not as effective as those typically seen with 11 or 12 treatment sessions. However, another study demonstrated equally effective results when delivering CBT for panic disorder across the standard 12 sessions versus approximately 6 sessions (Clark et al., 1999), and a pilot study indicated good effectiveness with intensive CBT over 2 days (Deacon & Abramowitz, 2006).

Self-directed treatments, with minimal direct therapist contact, are very beneficial for highly motivated and educated clients (e.g., Ghosh & Marks, 1987; Gould & Clum, 1995; Gould, Clum, & Shapiro, 1993). Computerized versions of CBT for panic disorder now exist. Computer-assisted and Internet versions of CBT are effective for panic disorder (e.g., Richards, Klein, & Carlbring, 2003). In one study, a 4-session computer-assisted CBT for panic disorder was less effective than a 12-session PCT at posttreatment although they were equally effective at follow-up (Newman, Kenardy, Herman, & Taylor, 1997). However, findings from computerized programs for emotional disorders in general indicate that such treatments are more acceptable and successful when they are combined with therapist involvement (e.g., Carlbring, Ekselius, & Andersson, 2003).

MEDICAL TREATMENT

A variety of pharmacological treatment options is available for panic disorder with agoraphobia. There are several medications commonly used to treat the disorder as well as combinations of medical agents, some often combined with behavioral treatment, and all of which can be beneficial with some negative side effects for patients. Medical treatment of panic disorder has evolved over the past several decades and improved in efficacy (Spiegel, Wiegel, Baker, & Greene, 2000). Traditionally, pharmacotherapy for panic disorder involved tricyclic antidepressants (TCAs), such as imipramine, as well as monoamine oxidase inhibitors (MAOIs) and barbiturates (White & Barlow, 2002). Monoamine oxidase inhibitors, though effective in treating panic disorder, are now typically only prescribed after other better-tolerated options have proven ineffective; this is due mainly to their side effects, such as weight gain and hypotension (Pollack, 2005). Since the 1980s, benzodiazepine medications have been used to treat panic disorder more safely and to offer an alternative to medications with harmful side effects. More recently, selective serotonin reuptake inhibitors (SSRIs) and serotonin-norepinephrine reuptake inhibitors (SNRIs) became first-line prescribed medications for various mood and anxiety disorders, including panic disorder. Studies comparing TCAs, SSRIs, and benzodiazepines have concluded generally that the three types of medications produced similar effects; however, it is important to consider advantages and disadvantages of each as well as their effectiveness in treating panic disorder.

TRICYCLIC ANTIDEPRESSANTS

Several studies have found TCAs to demonstrate short-term and long-term effectiveness (e.g., Mavissakalian & Perel, 1999), and they continue to be touted by many as the gold standard for pharmacological treatment in panic disorder (Spiegel et al., 2000). However, TCA users often complain of unpleasant side effects, such as dry mouth, nausea, weight gain, and fatigue, resulting in high attrition rates. There is also significant toxicity in overdose of TCAs, and they do not seem to be effective in treating comorbid disorders. In addition, research shows that imipramine does not act directly on panic attacks, but rather on generalized anxiety and anticipatory anxiety symptoms. Nevertheless, imipramine is thought to facilitate exposure treatment by reducing anxiety and somatic sensations, which function as cues for panic attacks (White & Barlow, 2002).

Benzodiazepines

These medications are generally found to be safe and become effective quickly; those who take them do not report as many side effects as with other antianxiety medication (Spiegel et al., 2000). Unfortunately, they lead to tolerance, physiological dependence, and abuse. It seems most tolerance related to benzodiazepines develops to the tranquilizing effects and perhaps only some to the anxiolytic effects. With regular use, most individuals taking these agents over a long period of time endorse physiological dependence on discontinuation of the medication, endorsing withdrawal symptoms such as "confusion" and "heightened sensory perception" (Pecknold, Swinson, Kuch, & Lewis, 1988). Therefore, it is necessary that the dosage be tapered by the prescribing clinician to prevent such harsh withdrawal symptoms. Although individuals prone to substance abuse may abuse benzodiazepines, they are very rarely misused in individuals without such a predisposition.

Serotonin Reuptake Inhibitors

Despite limited evidence of the SSRIs' superiority in effectiveness over other anxiolytics, currently many believe them to be the top-of-the-line medications for treating panic disorder and agoraphobia. Patients and clinicians favor them because they are thought to be safer. Selective serotonin reuptake inhibitors users are not at risk for abuse or dependence of the medication, and SSRIs are less likely to interact negatively with alcohol than benzodiazepines. Randomized, placebo-controlled studies have found SSRIs to be efficacious in treating panic disorder, where most patients (i.e., up 75%) were panic-free by posttreatment. Moreover, SNRIs have demonstrated efficacy in such treatments, though not yet approved by the Food and Drug Administration for the treatment of panic disorder. Selective serotonin reuptake inhibitors and SNRIs are effective in treating comorbid disorders often associated with panic disorder, such as depression, generalized anxiety disorder, and social phobia. However, SSRI users are not immune to negative side effects. These patients often complain of gastrointestinal problems, sexual impairment, and jittering or agitation. Another disadvantage is the length of time SSRIs require for becoming effective (usually longer than 2 to 3 weeks). Therefore, SSRIs require a more gradual increase in dosage and may be prescribed in combination with a sleep medication, for short-term use, to circumvent the central nervous system-activating effects of the SSRI (White & Barlow, 2002).

Case Description

Joanne was a 24-year-old teacher who had been experiencing panic attacks for the past 2 years. She was married, had a 3-year-old daughter, and worked full-time. Her husband, John, was an engineer and they lived in Los Angeles, California. Joanne had her first panic attack while she was driving on the freeway on a warm and muggy morning. She reported that her level of stress was unusually elevated as she was adjusting to simultaneously fulfilling her role as a mother, wife, and teacher. She had been drinking more coffee (three cups a day) than usual to give her the energy she needed to take care of her responsibilities. Road construction was causing delays in her commute and she had been late to work a couple of times that week. She was worried that she might not be able to accomplish her morning tasks that day and that she might have to work late to complete them, which meant that she would be late in picking up her daughter from daycare. As these thoughts rushed through her mind, she noticed her heart pounding and had difficulty breathing, which were followed by a flood of other physical symptoms, such as trembling and dizziness, and the thought that she might die. She pulled over immediately and called an ambulance that drove her to the emergency room. The tests did not reveal any medical cause for her symptoms and she was discharged home.

The first panic attack had an immediate and significant impact on Joanne's life. After her return home from the hospital, she asked for 3 days of sick leave from her job and stayed home for the majority of that time to avoid driving. She became very concerned about having more panic attacks, especially while driving. Since that time, she avoided highway and long distance driving, even as a passenger, which was quite limiting for her. This increased her commute to work by a half an hour in each direction and it took her considerably longer to run errands or visit her friends. Also, she saw her sister, Sarah who lived in San Diego, only twice per year despite their close relationship. She and John used to drive to visit Sarah and Albert about once a month.

Since her first panic attack, most of Joanne's panic attacks started with slightly increased heart rate, which often happened when she became impatient with students or in other situations where she had to wait. The first attack in her car left her with a hypersensitivity to her heart rate, breathing, tingling sensations, and dizziness. She remembered that during her first panic attack, her immediate concern was losing control of her car and facing the consequences of a possible crash or even death. Those sensations were very frightening because they seemed to come unexpectedly without an identifiable reason or origin. Frequency of her panic attacks increased gradually after her first one and depended on the level of stress she was experiencing at the time. For example, she had fewer panic attacks during the summer when she was not working. Joanne reported having an average of five full-blown and several limited-symptom panic attacks per week. They were often triggered by situations in which she felt trapped and places where help would not be available in case of a panic attack. For example, she experienced panic attacks in the classroom while she was teaching, at the salon while she was getting a haircut, and while she was waiting in line at the bank or supermarket. She often escaped those situations as soon as she felt panicky and returned once she had calmed down, which caused some problems at work. She asked the teacher in the classroom next door to keep an eye on her students so she could "get some air." Eventually, she began to anticipate panic attacks in these situations as well as others. The thought that she might have a panic attack usually was followed by hypervigilance of somatic sensations, which increased

(continued)

the likelihood that she would experience more symptoms that would quickly escalate to a full-blown panic attack. Joanne's fear generalized to unfamiliar places and crowds that she endured with intense anxiety; she preferred to be accompanied by John or a good friend.

During the initial diagnostic interview, Joanne reported that her chief complaint was worrying about the panic attacks, the fear that something was very wrong, and the limitations imposed on her life due to these attacks. Since her first panic attack, she read information on the Internet regarding her symptoms and understood that her symptoms fell under the category of panic disorder. However, she was convinced that there must be something wrong with her heart and that she might fall seriously ill or even die. Therefore, she continued to seek medical treatment and did not accept the benzodiazepines or SSRIs offered by her general practitioner. Joanne did not suffer from any known medical illness and did not endorse any personal history of psychopathology, except for a brief depressive episode when she started college and rare occurrence of paniclike symptoms during periods of very high stress. She reported feeling depressed over the past several months, which, in combination with her limitations due to panic and agoraphobia, was causing some arguments with John. She reported that her father became depressed after a heart attack a few years ago, and she described her mother as a very anxious person who constantly worried about the health and welfare of her family members. Her brother died in a motorcycle accident when he was 20 and her sister Sarah had bouts of anxiety and depression.

Following her diagnostic interview using the ADIS-IV, Joanne was provided with a number of self-report measures to provide information for treatment planning, such as to rate specific aspects of her mood, anxiety, panic, and agoraphobia that were used again following treatment to assess therapeutic change. Information from these measures, the self-monitoring forms, and the ADIS-IV was used to help construct exposure hierarchies for both interoceptive and in vivo exercises. Individualized behavioral tests were used to assess degree of agoraphobic avoidance and standardized tasks were used to determine the level of interoceptive sensitivity. Joanne was asked to attempt two tasks prior to her first therapy session that she rated as moderately difficult: shopping at the supermarket on a weeknight when it was relatively crowded with long lines, and to drive through an unfamiliar neighborhood with a passenger (her husband or friend). She was able to attempt both tasks, but did not complete the driving task. She immediately asked her husband to switch seats with her and to drive them back to the familiar part of the neighborhood. To assess fear of bodily sensations and level of impairment, Joanne participated in exercises to induce interoceptive sensations associated with panic attacks. These behavioral tests included running in place for a minute, breathing through a straw for two minutes, and hyperventilating for 30 seconds. Joanne endorsed moderate to high levels of anxiety during each task and was not able to complete the hyperventilation after 10 seconds. During these exercises, Joanne wore a heart rate monitor used to provide her with feedback on her physiological changes during the tasks. Although Joanne believed her heart rate must have been dangerously elevated while she was running in place and hyperventilating, her actual heart rate was only slightly increased.

Joanne experienced her first panic attack in her early 20s. This is a period common for the increase in life stressors due to the many changes that often occur at this age. This was particularly true for Joanne who got married as soon as she completed college and gave birth to her daughter a year later. She was starting her career as a teacher when she was faced with taking care of her daughter and her responsibilities in the traditional role of a wife. John worked long hours and often traveled for work, leaving Joanne almost completely responsible for the household and their daughter. In addition to these chronic stressors, Joanne was experiencing acute stress on the day of her first panic attack. Traffic due to road construction led her to worry about being late to work and the consequences of her tardiness. These thoughts were combined with increased caffeine intake and the warm stuffy weather to produce increased heart rate, difficulty breathing, and trembling sensations, which probably contributed to the onset of her symptoms on that day. Since that first episode, Joanne observed that she often felt panicky when she was rushing to work or an appointment and had consumed coffee. Therefore, she gradually stopped drinking coffee, which seemed to act as a conditioned stimulus triggering a panic response. She also started to avoid other conditioned stimuli, such as physical exertion that increased her heart rate, hot and stuffy rooms where she sensed difficulty breathing, and skipping meals that often resulted in trembling. Joanne reported severe apprehension about experiencing another attack. The possibility of having an attack was on her mind frequently and she was forced to plan activities based on how she would escape from situations in case of an attack. She completely avoided places where escape would be difficult or impossible or where a panic attack could lead to serious injury or death (i.e., driving on the freeway). It was clear that Joanne's fear of somatic sensations associated with panic and anxiety were key components in her maladaptive behavior and increased emotional distress. The belief that she might be prone to serious physical illness, possibly having inherited her father's cardiovascular disease, motivated her hypervigilance of her body. Even though her mother was always worried about health, Joanne was able to dismiss her mother's warnings of possible illness. However, she continued to notice any new sensation and wonder if it was an indication of a health problem, which she was able also to dismiss eventually. Her tendency to question bodily changes exacerbated her symptoms of panic disorder and helped develop her agoraphobic behavior.

Joanne completed 12 sessions of CBT for panic disorder and agoraphobia. She was very eager to learn about the disorder and appreciated the explanation of the physiology of fear, which emphasized the protective aspects of the fear response. Given that she was very articulate and aware of her thoughts, she quickly grasped the notion of self-monitoring and demonstrated an understanding of the benefits of such observations after she was introduced to the cognitive-behavioral model. Because her breathing was quite shallow, Joanne required multiple demonstrations of the slow diaphragmatic breathing technique and reported difficulties in practicing it at home. Her reluctance to relax her body was addressed in session in terms of noticing changes in her body that seemed unusual. She was eager to monitor her thoughts, behaviors, and physical

(continued)

responses, and she eventually practiced her breathing exercises regularly after having a better understanding of the conditioning of the fear response. With guidance, Joanne learned to generate alternative ways of thinking in situations where she responded with anxiety and fear and eagerly practiced these exercises outside of session. Joanne's maladaptive cognitions were challenged in the effort to help generate new responses. For example, when asked why she is afraid of increases in her heart rate, Joanne responded, "Because I might have a panic attack." When questioned further with "What would happen if you had a panic attack?" Joanne answered, "I might have a heart attack or even die." Then, there was a discussion involving the numerous panic attacks she has endured without ever having a heart attack or dying. This type of cognitive restructuring required regular practice to ensure it became an automatic way of thinking and replaced prior cognitive distortions. Once she had her coping skills in place (i.e., breathing retraining and cognitive restructuring), exposure began with panic symptoms induced in session followed by prolonged repeated exposure. She reported difficulty practicing the interoceptive exposure exercises at home. This was addressed during the next session, and the educational material was revisited accordingly. After creating an agoraphobia hierarchy, Joanne practiced facing difficult situations, such as going to the grocery store and driving in unfamiliar places several times. Although she was reluctant to complete the driving task on her own initially, she gradually felt more comfortable and did not need John or her friend to accompany her.

After completion of treatment, Joanne was administered the ADIS-IV and the other self-report instruments completed at the initial assessment. Although much improved, she continued to endorse some symptoms of panic disorder and agoraphobia, mainly because she continued to experience limited-symptom attacks two or three times monthly and to avoid driving on freeways and long distance. Though her depression was not directly addressed in therapy, her mood improved significantly and she reported a much better quality of life. She was encouraged to practice her coping skills when she felt anxious, especially when she was undergoing increased levels of stress. She was also encouraged to practice imagining driving on the freeway to prepare herself to complete the task in person when she felt ready.

As part of the gradual fading of treatment, a follow-up session was scheduled 3 months posttreatment. Follow-ups are important both to assess the maintenance of treatment gains and to intervene if needed. Joanne underwent another series of assessments, including the ADIS-IV and the standardized behavioral tests. She had not experienced a full-blown panic attack and the frequency of her limited-symptom attacks were the same as they were at the end of treatment. She still was not driving on freeways regularly, but she was practicing driving gradually increasing distances. The farthest distance driven on the freeway was 6 miles at the follow-up, and her goal was to be able to drive to work the fastest way, which required a 10-mile drive on the freeway. Her report of symptoms was confirmed by the behavioral tests. In addition, she did not endorse any signs or symptoms of depressed mood that was present at intake and present at low levels at posttreatment. It was agreed that future follow-ups would take place over the phone periodically as needed.

SUMMARY

The diagnosis of panic disorder with agoraphobia is given when an individual is having recurrent unexpected panic attacks accompanied by worry about future attacks and anxiety in and avoidance of situations where escape might be difficult in case of panic. In addition to assessment of the subjective experience, behavioral tests are important in determining severity of symptoms and in planning individualized treatment. A thorough biopsychosocial assessment is important to differentiate panic disorder from other disorders and to be aware of comorbid psychiatric and medical illness, as well as other social factors that can play a role in maintaining and/or exacerbating symptoms of panic disorder. Panic disorder is thought to develop in individuals with vulnerability factors, such as anxiety sensitivity, medical illness, and physiological propensity to autonomic activation. Such individuals learn to become afraid of bodily sensations after having the first panic attack and apply catastrophic misappraisals to the sensations related to panic. Such fear and cognitive misappraisals work together to maintain the disorder and contribute to agoraphobia. Because the individual interprets initial sensations as threatening or harmful, the fight-flight response is activated, heightening the anxiety response. Activation of the amygdala during unexpected panic attacks strengthens the emotional memory and facilitates conditioning of the fear response.

Based on outcome studies, CBT and pharmacological treatment are found to be effective and treatments of choice for panic disorder with and without agoraphobia. Central to CBT is learning that fear and anxiety as well as the stimuli with which they are associated are not harmful. This is most effectively learned through direct experience (i.e., exposure) and is facilitated by discussion and verbal processing (i.e., cognitive restructuring).

REFERENCES

American Psychiatric Association. (1994). *Diagnostic and statistical manual of mental disorders* (4th ed.). Washington, DC: Author.

Amering, M., Katschnig, H., Berger, P., Windhaber, J., Baischer, W., & Dantendorfer, K. (1997). Embarrassment about the first panic attack predicts agoraphobia in panic disorder patients. *Behavior Research and Therapy, 35,* 517–521.

Andrews, G., Stewart, G., Allen, R., & Henderson, A. S. (1990). The genetics of six neurotic disorders: A twin study. *Journal of Affective Disorders, 19,* 23–29.

Antony, M. M., Brown, T. A., Craske, M. G., Barlow, D. H., Mitchell, W. B., & Meadows, E. A. (1995). Accuracy of heartbeat perception in panic disorder, social phobia, and nonanxious subjects. *Journal of Anxiety Disorders, 9,* 355–371.

Antony, M. M., Ledley, D. B., Liss, A., & Swinson, R. P. (2006). Responses to symptom induction exercises in panic disorder. *Behavior Research and Therapy, 44,* 85–98.

Antony, M. M., Meadows, E. A., Brown, T. A., & Barlow, D. H. (1994). Cardiac awareness before and after cognitive-behavioral treatment for panic disorder. *Journal of Anxiety Disorders, 8,* 341–350.

Arntz, A., & van den Hout, M. (1996). Psychological treatments of panic disorder without agoraphobia: Cognitive therapy versus applied relaxation. *Behavior Research and Therapy, 34,* 113–121.

Arrindell, W. A., Eisemann, M., Richter, J., Oei, T. P. S., Caballo, V. E., van der Ende, J., et al. (2003). Masculinity-femininity as a national characteristic and its relationship with national agoraphobic fear levels: Fodor's sex role hypothesis revitalized. *Behavior Research and Therapy, 41*, 795–807.

Barlow, D. H. (1988). *Anxiety and its disorders: The nature and treatment of anxiety and panic.* New York: Guilford Press.

Barlow, D. H. (2002). *Anxiety and its disorders: The nature and treatment of anxiety and panic* (2nd ed.). New York: Guilford Press.

Barlow, D. H., Brown, T. A., & Craske, M. G. (1994). Definitions of panic attacks and panic disorder in the DSM-IV: Implications for research. *Journal of Abnormal Psychology, 103*(3), 553–564.

Barlow, D. H., & Craske, M. G. (1994). *Mastery of your anxiety and panic-II.* San Antonio, TX: Harcourt Brace.

Barlow, D. H., Craske, M. G., Cerny, J. A., & Klosko, J. S. (1989). Behavioral treatment of panic disorder. *Behavior Therapy, 20*, 261–282.

Beck, J. G., Stanley, M. A., Baldwin, L. E., Deagle, E. A., & Averill, P. M. (1995). Comparison of cognitive therapy and relaxation training for panic disorder. *Journal of Consulting and Clinical Psychology, 62*, 818–826.

Beitman, B. D., Mukerji, V., Lamberti, J. W., Schmid, L., DeRosear, L., Kushner, M., et al. (1989). Panic disorder in patients with chest pain and angiographically normal coronary arteries. *American Journal of Cardiology, 63*, 1399–1403.

Block, R. I., Ghoneim, M. M., Fowles, D. C., Kumar, V., & Pathak, D. (1987). Effects of a sub-anesthetic concentration of nitrous oxide on establishment, elicitation, and semantic and phonemic generalization of classically conditioned skin conductance responses. *Pharmacology, Biochemistry and Behavior, 28*, 7–14.

Boulenger, J. P., Uhde, T. W., Wolff, E. A., & Post, R. M. (1984). Increased sensitivity to caffeine in patients with panic disorder. *Archives of General Psychiatry, 41*, 1067–1071.

Bouton, M. E., Mineka, S., & Barlow, D. H. (2001). A modern learning-theory perspective on the etiology of panic disorder. *Psychological Review, 108*(1), 4–32.

Breier, A., Charney, D. S., & Heninger, G. B. (1984). Major depression in patients with agoraphobia and panic disorder. *Archives of General Psychiatry, 41*, 1129–1135.

Brown, T. A., Antony, M. M., & Barlow, D. H. (1995). Diagnostic comorbidity in panic disorder: Effect on treatment outcome and course of comorbid diagnoses following treatment. *Journal of Consulting and Clinical Psychology, 63*, 408–418.

Brown, T. A., & Barlow, D. H. (1995). Long-term outcome in cognitive-behavioral treatment of panic disorder: Clinical predictors and alternative strategies for assessment. *Journal of Consulting and Clinical Psychology, 63*, 754–765.

Brown, T., A., Campbell, L. A., Lehman, C. L., Grisham, J. R., & Mancill, R. B. (2001). Current and lifetime comorbidity of the DSM-IV anxiety and mood disorders in a large clinical sample. *Journal of Abnormal Psychology, 110*, 49–58.

Brown, T. A., DiNardo, P. A., & Barlow, D. H. (1994). *Anxiety Disorders Interview Schedule for DSM-IV (ADIS-IV).* Albany, NY: Graywind.

Carlbring, P., Ekselius, L., & Andersson, G. (2003). Treatment of panic disorder via the Internet: A randomized trial of CBT versus applied relaxation. *Journal of Behavior Therapy and Experimental Psychiatry, 34*, 129–140.

Carter, C., Maddock, R., Amsterdam, E., McCormick, S., Waters, C., & Billett, J. (1992). Panic disorder and chest pain in the coronary care unit. *Psychosomatics, 33*, 302–309.

Cerny, J. A., Barlow, D. H., Craske, M. G., & Himadi, W. G. (1987). Couples treatment of agoraphobia: A 2-year follow-up. *Behavior Therapy, 18*, 401–415.

Chambless, D. L., & Mason, J. (1986). Sex, sex-role stereotyping and agoraphobia. *Behavior Research and Therapy, 24*, 231–235.

Charney, D. S., Heninger, G. R., & Jatlow, P. I. (1985). Increased anxiogenic effects of caffeine in panic disorders. *Archives of General Psychiatry, 42*, 223–243.

Clark, D. M. (1986). A cognitive approach to panic. *Behavior Research and Therapy, 24*, 461–470.

Clark, D. M., & Ehlers, A. (1993). An overview of the cognitive theory and treatment of panic disorder. *Applied and Preventive Psychology, 2*, 131–139.

Clark, D. M., Salkovskis, P. M., Gelder, M., Koehler, C., Martin, M., Anastasiades, P., et al. (1988). Test of a cognitive theory of panic. In I. Hand & H. U. Wittchen (Eds.), *Panic and phobias: Pt. II. Treatments and variables affecting course and outcome* (pp. 71–90). Berlin, Germany: Springer-Verlag.

Clark, D. M., Salkovskis, P. M., Hackmann, A., Middleton, H., Anastasiades, P., & Gelder, M. (1994). A comparison of cognitive therapy, applied relaxation, and imipramine in the treatment of panic disorder: A randomized controlled trial. *British Journal of Psychiatry, 164*, 759–769.

Clark, D. M., Salkovskis, P. M., Hackmann, A., Wells, A., Ludgate, J., & Gelder, M. (1999). Brief cognitive therapy for panic disorder: A randomized controlled trial. *Journal of Consulting and Clinical Psychology, 67*, 583–589.

Cox, B. J., Endler, N. S., & Swinson, R. P. (1995). An examination of levels of agoraphobic severity in panic disorder. *Behavior Research and Therapy, 33*, 57–62.

Craske, M. G. (1999). *Anxiety disorders: Psychological approaches to theory and treatment.* Boulder, CO: Westview Press.

Craske, M. G. (2003). *Origins of phobias and anxiety disorders: Why more women than men?* Oxford, England: Elsevier.

Craske, M. G., & Barlow, D. H. (1988). A review of the relationship between panic and avoidance. *Clinical Psychology Review, 8*, 667–685.

Craske, M. G., & Barlow, D. H. (1989). Nocturnal panic. *Journal of Nervous and Mental Diseases, 177*(3), 160–167.

Craske, M. G., Brown, T. A., & Barlow, D. H. (1991). Behavioral treatment of panic disorder: A 2-year follow-up. *Behavior Therapy, 22*, 289–304.

Craske, M. G., Lang, A. J., Aikins, D., & Mystkowski, J. L. (2005). Cognitive behavioral therapy for nocturnal panic. *Behavior Therapy, 36*, 43–54.

Craske, M. G., Maidenberg, E., & Bystritsky, A. (1995). Brief cognitive-behavioral versus non directive therapy for panic disorder. *Journal of Behavior Therapy and Experimental Psychiatry, 26*, 113–120.

Craske, M. G., Miller, P. P., Rotunda, R., & Barlow, D. H. (1990). A descriptive report of features of initial unexpected panic attacks in minimal and extensive avoiders. *Behavior Research and Therapy, 28*, 395–400.

Craske, M. G., & Mystkowski, J. L. (2006). Exposure therapy and extinction: Clinical studies. In M. G. Craske, D. Hermans, & D. Vansteenwegen (Eds.), *Fear and learning: From basic processes to clinical implications* (pp. 217–233). Washington, DC: American Psychological Association.

Craske, M. G., Poulton, R., Tsao, J. C. I., & Plotkin, D. (2001). Paths to panic-agoraphobia: An exploratory analysis from age 3 to 21 in an unselected birth cohort. *American Journal of Child and Adolescent Psychiatry, 40*, 556–563.

Craske, M. G., Rapee, R. M., & Barlow, D. H. (1988). The significance of panic-expectancy for individual patterns of avoidance. *Behavior Therapy, 19*, 577–592.

Craske, M. G., Rowe, M., Lewin, M., & Noriego-Dimitri, R. (1997). Interoceptive exposure versus breathing retraining within cognitive-behavioral therapy for panic disorder with agoraphobia. *British Journal of Clinical Psychology, 36*, 85–99.

Craske, M. G., & Tsao, J. C. (1999). Self-monitoring with panic and anxiety disorders. *Psychological Assessment, 11*, 466–479.

Craske, M. G., Zarate, R., Burton, T., & Barlow, D. H. (1993). Specific fears and panic attacks: A survey of clinical and nonclinical samples. *Journal of Anxiety Disorders, 7*, 1–19.

Crowe, R. R., Noyes, R., Pauls, D. L., & Slymen, D. J. (1983). A family study of panic disorder. *Archives of General Psychiatry, 40*, 1065–1069.

Dales, R. E., Spitzer, W. O., Schechter, M. T., & Suissa, S. (1989). The influence of psychological status on respiratory symptom reporting. *American Review of Respiratory Disease, 139*, 1459–1463.

Dattilio, F. M., & Salas-Auvert, J. A. (2000). *Panic disorder: Assessment and treatment through a wide-angle lens.* Phoenex, AZ: Zeig, Tucker.

Deacon, B., & Abramowitz, J. (2006). A pilot study of 2-day cognitive-behavioral therapy for panic disorder. *Behavior Research and Therapy, 44*, 807–817.

de Beurs, E., van Balkom, A. J., Lange, A., Koele, P., & van Dyke, R. (1995). Treatment of panic disorder with agoraphobia: Comparison of fluvoxamine, placebo, and psychological panic management combined with exposure and of exposure in vivo alone. *American Journal of Psychiatry, 152*, 683–691.

Deckert, J., Nothen, M. M., Franke, P., Delmo, C., Fritze, J., Knapp, M., et al. (1998). Systematic mutation screening and association study of the A1 and A2a adenosine receptor genes in panic disorder suggest a contribution of the A2a gene to the development of disease. *Molecular Psychiatry, 3*, 81–85.

De Jong, G. M., & Bouman, T. K. (1995). Panic disorder: A baseline period. Predictability of agoraphobic avoidance behavior. *Journal of Anxiety Disorder, 9*, 185–199.

Dworkin, B. R., & Dworkin, S. (1999). Heterotopic and homotopic classical conditioning of the baroreflex. *Integrative Physiological and Behavioral Science, 34*, 158–176.

Ehlers, A. (1995). A 1-year prospective study of panic attacks: Clinical course and factors associated with maintenance. *Journal of Abnormal Psychology, 104*, 164–172.

Ehlers, A., & Breuer, P. (1992). Increased cardiac awareness in panic disorder. *Journal of Abnormal Psychology, 101*, 371–382.

Ehlers, A., & Breuer, P. (1996). How good are patients with panic disorder at perceiving their heartbeats? *Biological Psychology, 42*, 165–182.

Ehlers, A., Breuer, P., Dohn, D., & Fiegenbaum, W. (1995). Heartbeat perception and panic disorder: Possible explanations for discrepant findings. *Behavior Research and Therapy, 33*, 69–76.

Eifert, G. H., & Forsyth, J. P. (2005). *Acceptance and commitment therapy for anxiety disorders: A practitioner's treatment guide to using mindfulness, acceptance, and value-based behavior change strategies.* Oakland, CA: New Harbinger.

Fava, G. A., Zielezny, M., Savron, G., & Grandi, S. (1995). Long-term effects of behavioral treatment for panic disorder and agoraphobia. *British Journal of Psychiatry, 166*, 87–92.

Fyer, A. J., & Rassnick, H. (1990). *Frequency of symptom thresholds for panic disorder: Report to the DSM-IV Anxiety Disorders Work Group.* New York: New York State Psychiatric Institute.

Ghosh, A., & Marks, I. M. (1987). Self-treatment of agoraphobia by exposure. *Behavior Therapy, 18*, 3–16.

Goisman, R. M., Warshaw, M. G., Peterson, L. G., Rogers, M. P., Cuneo, P., Hunt, M. F., et al. (1994). Panic, agoraphobia, and panic disorder with agoraphobia: Data from a multicenter anxiety disorders study. *Journal of Nervous and Mental Diseases, 182*, 72–79.

Goldstein, A. J., & Chambless, D. L. (1978). A reanalysis of agoraphobia. *Behavior Therapy, 9*, 47–59.

Good, B. J. (1977). The heart of what's the matter: The semantics of illness in Iran. *Culture, Medicine, and Psychiatry, 1*, 25–58.

Goodwin, R. D., Fergusson, D. M., & Horwood, L. J. (2005). Childhood abuse and familial violence and the risk of panic attacks and panic disorder in young adulthood. *Psychological Medicine, 35,* 881–890.

Gould, R. A., & Clum, G. A. (1995). Self-help plus minimal therapist contact in the treatment of panic disorder: A replication and extension. *Behavior Therapy, 26,* 533–546.

Gould, R. A., Clum, G. A., & Shapiro, D. (1993). The use of bibliotherapy in the treatment of panic: A preliminary investigation. *Behavior Therapy, 24,* 241–252.

Greenberg, P. E., Sisitsky, T., Kessler, R. C., Finkelstein, S. N., Berndt, E. R., Davidson, J. R. T., et al. (1999). The economic burden of anxiety disorders in the 1990s. *Journal of Clinical Psychiatry, 60*(7), 427–435.

Guarnaccia, P. J., Canino, G., Rubio-Stipec, M., & Bravo, M. (1993). The prevalence of *ataques de nervios* in Puerto Rico Disaster Study. *Journal of Nervous and Mental Diseases, 181,* 157–165.

Guarnaccia, P. J., Rubio-Stipec, M., & Canino, G. (1989). *Ataques de nervios* in the Puerto Rican Diagnostic Interview Schedule: The impact of cultural categories on psychiatric epidemiology. *Culture, Medicine, and Psychiatry, 13,* 275–295.

Hamilton, S. P., Fyer, A. J., Durner, M., Heiman, G. A., Baisre de Leon, A., Hodge, S. E., et al. (2003). Further genetic evidence for a panic disorder syndrome mapping to chromosome 13q. *Proceedings of the National Academy of Sciences, USA, 100,* 2550–2555.

Hamilton, S. P., Slager, S. L., De Leon, A. B., Heiman, G. A., Klein, D. F., Hodge, S. E., et al. (2004). Evidence for genetic linkage between a polymorphism in the adenosine 2A receptor and panic disorder. *Neuropsychopharmacology, 29,* 558–565.

Hamilton, S. P., Slager, S. L., Helleby, L., Heiman, G. A., Klein, D. F., Hodge, S. E., et al. (2001). No association or linkage between polymorphisms in the genes encoding cholecystokinin and the cholecystokinin B receptor and panic disorder. *Molecular Psychiatry, 6,* 59–65.

Hayward, C., Killen, J. D., Kraemer, H. C., & Taylor, C. B. (2000). Predictors of panic attacks in adolescents. *Journal of the American Academy of Child and Adolescent Psychiatry, 39*(2), 1–8.

Hinton, D., Um, K., & Ba, P. (2001). *Kyol Goeu* [wind overload]: Pt. I. A cultural syndrome of orthostatic panic among Khmer refugees. *Transcultural Psychiatry, 38*(4), 403–432.

Johnson, J., Weissman, M. M., & Klerman, G. L. (1990). Panic disorder, comorbidity, and suicide attempts. *Archives of General Psychiatry, 47,* 805–808.

Kaufman, J., & Charney, D. (2000). Comorbidity of mood and anxiety disorders. *Depression and Anxiety, 12,* 69–76.

Kawachi, I., Sparrow, D., Vokonas, P. S., & Weiss, S. T. (1994). Symptoms of anxiety and risk of coronary heart disease: The Normative Aging Study. *Circulation, 90,* 2225–2229.

Kendler, K. S., Bulik, C. M., Silberg, J., Hettema, J. M., Myers, J., & Prescott, C. A. (2000). Childhood sexual abuse and adult psychiatric and substance use disorders in women: An epidemiological and Cotwin Control Analysis. *Archives of General Psychiatry, 57,* 953–959.

Kendler, K. S., Heath, A. C., Martin, N. G., & Eaves, L. J. (1987). Symptoms of anxiety and symptoms of depression: Same genes, different environments? *Archives of General Psychiatry, 44,* 451–457.

Kessler, R. C., McGonagle, K. A., Zhao, S., Nelson, C. B., Hughes, M., Eshelman, S., et al. (1994). Lifetime and 12-month prevalence of DSM-III-R psychiatric disorders in the United States: Results from the National Comorbidity Survey. *Archives of General Psychiatry, 51,* 8–19.

Keyl, P. M., & Eaton, W. W. (1990). Risk factors for the onset of panic disorder and other panic attacks in a prospective, population-based study. *American Journal of Epidemiology, 131,* 301–311.

Krystal, J. H., Woods, S. W., Hill, C. L., & Charney, D. S. (1991). Characteristics of panic attack subtypes: Assessment of spontaneous panic, situational panic, sleep panic, and limited symptom attacks. *Comprehensive Psychiatry, 32,* 474–480.

Kushner, M. G., Abrams, K., & Borchardt, C. (2000). The relationship between anxiety disorders and alcohol use disorders: A review of major perspectives and findings. *Clinical Psychology Review, 20*(2), 149–171.

Kushner, M. G., Sher, K. J., & Beitman, B. D. (1990). The relation between alcohol problems and the anxiety disorders. *American Journal of Psychiatry, 147,* 685–695.

Last, C. G., Barlow, D. H., & O'Brien, G. T. (1984). Precipitants of agoraphobia: Role of stressful life events. *Psychological Reports, 54,* 567–570.

Lennartz, R. C., & Weinberger, N. M. (1992). Analysis of response systems in Pavlovian conditioning reveals rapidly versus slowly acquired conditioned responses: Support for two factors, implications for behavior and neurobiology. *Psychobiology, 20,* 93–119.

Levinson, D. F., Zubenko, G. S., Crowe, R. R., DePaulo, R. J., Scheftner, W. S., Weissman, M. M., et al. (2003). Genetics of recurrent early-onset depression (GenRED): Design and preliminary clinical characteristics of a repository sample for genetic linkage studies. *American Journal of Medical Genetics, 119B,* 118–130.

Louie, A. K., Lannon, R. A., Rutzick, E. A., Browne, D., Lewis, T. B., & Jones, R. (1996). Clinical features of cocaine-induced panic. *Society of Biological Psychiatry, 40,* 938–940.

Lynch, P., & Galbraith, K. M. (2003). Panic in the emergency room. *Canadian Journal of Psychiatry, 48,* 361–366.

Maier, S. F., Laudenslager, M. L., & Ryan, S. M. (1985). Stressor controllability, immune function and endogenous opiates. In F. R. Brush, & J. B. Overmeier (Eds.), *Affect, conditioning and cognition: Essays on the determinants of behavior* (pp. 183–201). Hillsdale, NJ: Erlbaum.

Maller, R. G., & Reiss, S. (1992). Anxiety sensitivity in 1984 and panic attacks in 1987. *Journal of Anxiety Disorders, 6,* 241–247.

Maron, E., Lang, A., Gunnar, T., Liivlaid, L., Tõru, I., Must, A., et al. (2005). Associations between serotonin-related gene polymorphisms and panic disorder. *International Journal of Neuropsychopharmacology, 8,* 261–266.

Mavissakalian, M. R., & Perel, J. M. (1999). Long-term maintenance and discontinuation of imipramine therapy in panic disorder with agoraphobia. *Archives of General Psychiatry, 56,* 821–827.

McLean, P. D., Woody, S., Taylor, S., & Koch, W. J. (1998). Comorbid panic disorder and major depression: Implications for cognitive-behavioral therapy. *Journal of Consulting and Clinical Psychology, 66,* 240–247.

Mellman, T. A., & Uhde, T. W. (1989). Sleep panic attacks: New clinical findings and theoretical implications. *American Journal of Psychiatry, 146,* 1204–1207.

Mineka, S., Cook, M., & Miller, S. (1984). Fear conditioned with escapable and inescapable shock: The effects of a feedback stimulus. *Journal of Experimental Psychology: Animal Behavior Processes, 10,* 307–323.

Mineka, S., Watson, D., & Clark, L. A. (1998). Comorbidity of anxiety and unipolar mood disorders. *Annual Review of Psychology, 49,* 377–412.

Mitte, K. A. (2005). Meta-analysis of the efficacy of psycho- and pharmacotherapy in panic disorder with and without agoraphobia. *Journal of Affective Disorders, 88,* 27–45.

Moran, C., & Andrews, G. (1985). The familial occurrence of agoraphobia. *British Journal of Psychiatry, 146,* 262–267.

Morissette, S. B., Spiegel, D. A., & Heinrichs, N. (2005). Sensation-focused intensive treatment for panic disorder with moderate to severe agoraphobia. *Cognitive and Behavioral Practice, 12,* 17–29.

Nazemi, H., Kleinknecht, R. A., Dinnel, D. L., Lonner, W. J., Nazemi, S., Shamlo, S., et al. (2003). A study of panic attacks in university students of Iran. *Journal of Psychopathology and Behavioral Assessment, 25*(3), 191–201.

Newman, M. G., Kenardy, J., Herman, S., & Taylor, C. B. (1997). Comparison of palmtop-computer-assisted brief cognitive-behavioral treatment to cognitive-behavioral treatment for panic disorder. *Journal of Consulting and Clinical Psychology, 65,* 178–183.

Ninan, P. T., & Dunlop, B. W. (2005). Neurobiology and etiology of panic disorder. *Journal of Clinical Psychiatry, 66*(4), 3–7.

Noyes, R., Clancy, J., Garvey, M. J., & Anderson, D. J. (1987). Is agoraphobia a variant of panic disorder or a separate illness? *Journal of Anxiety Disorders, 1,* 3–13.

Otto, M. W., Pollack, M. H., Sachs, G. S., Teiter, S. R., Meltzer-Brody, S., & Rosenbaum, J. F. (1993). Discontinuation of benzodiazepine treatment: Efficacy of cognitive-behavioral therapy for patients with panic disorder. *American Journal of Psychiatry, 150,* 1485–1490.

Pecknold, J. C., Swinson, R. P., Kuch, K., & Lewis, C. P. (1988). Alprazolam in panic disorder and agoraphobia: Results from a multicenter trial—Discontinuation effects. *Archives of General Psychiatry, 45,* 429–436.

Pollack, M. H. (2005). The pharmacotherapy of panic disorder. *Journal of Clinical Psychiatry, 66,* 23–27.

Rapee, R. M. (1994). Detection of somatic sensations in panic disorder. *Behavior Research and Therapy, 32,* 825–831.

Rapee, R. M., Craske, M. G., & Barlow, D. H. (1990). Subject described features of panic attacks using a new self-monitoring form. *Journal of Anxiety Disorders, 4,* 171–181.

Rapee, R. M., & Murrell, E. (1988). Predictors of agoraphobic avoidance. *Journal of Anxiety Disorder, 2,* 203–217.

Razran, G. (1961). The observable unconscious and the inferable conscious in current Soviet psychophysiology: Interoceptive conditioning, semantic conditioning, and the orienting reflex. *Psychological Review, 68,* 81–150.

Reiss, S. (1980). Pavlovian conditioning and human fear: An expectancy model. *Behavior Therapy, 11,* 380–396.

Richards, J., Klein, B., & Carlbring, P. (2003). Internet-based treatment for panic disorder. *Cognitive Behavior Therapy, 32,* 125–135.

Rijken, H., Kraaimaat, F., de Ruiter, C., & Garssen, B. (1992). A follow-up study on short-term treatment of agoraphobia. *Behavior Research and Therapy, 30,* 63–66.

Roy-Byrne, P. P., Craske, M. G., Stein, M. B., Sullivan, G., Bystritsky, A., Katon, W., et al. (2005). A randomized effectiveness trial of cognitive-behavioral therapy and medication for primary care panic disorder. *Archives of General Psychiatry, 62,* 290–298.

Roy-Byrne, P. P., Geraci, M., & Uhde, T. W. (1986). Life events and the onset of panic disorder. *American Journal of Psychiatry, 143,* 1424–1427.

Roy-Byrne, P. P., Mellman, T. A., & Uhde, T. W. (1988). Biologic findings in panic disorder: Neuroendocrine and sleep-related abnormalities [Special issue]. *Journal of Anxiety Disorders: Perspectives on Panic-Related Disorders, 2,* 17–29.

Roy-Byrne, P. P., Stein, M. B., & Craske, M. G. (in press). Panic disorder. *Lancet.*

Roy-Byrne, P. P., Stein, M. B., Russo, J., Mercier, E., Thomas, R., McQuaid, J., et al. (1999). Panic disorder in the primary care setting. *Journal of Clinical Psychiatry, 60,* 492–499.

Salkovskis, P. M., Clark, D. M., & Gelder, M. G. (1996). Cognition-behavior links in the persistence of panic. *Behavior and Research Therapy, 34,* 453–458.

Salkovskis, P. M., Clark, D. M., & Hackmann, A. (1991). Treatment of panic attacks using cognitive therapy without exposure or breathing retraining. *Behavior Research and Therapy, 29,* 161–166.

Schmidt, N. B., Lerew, D. R., & Jackson, R. J. (1997). The role of anxiety sensitivity in the pathogenesis of panic: Prospective evaluation of spontaneous panic attacks during acute stress. *Journal of Abnormal Psychology, 106*(3), 355–364.

Schumacher, J., Jamra, R. A., Becker, T., Klopp, N., Franke, P., Jacob, C., et al. (2005). Investigation of the DAOA/G30 locus in panic disorder. *Molecular Psychiatry, 10,* 428–429.

Simon, N. M., & Fischmann, D. (2005). The implications of medical and psychiatric comorbidity with panic disorder. *Journal of Clinical Psychiatry, 66,* 8–15.

Simon, N. M., Otto, M., Wisniewski, S., Fossey, M., Sagduyu, K., Frank, E., et al. (2004). Anxiety disorder comorbidity in bipolar disorder patients: Data from the first 500 participants in the Systematic Treatment Enhancement Program for Bipolar Disorder (STEP-BD). *American Journal of Psychiatry, 161,* 2222–2229.

Smits, J. A. J., O'Cleirigh, C. M., & Otto, M. W. (2006). Combining cognitive-behavioral therapy and pharmacotherapy for the treatment of panic disorder. *Journal of Cognitive Psychotherapy: An International Quarterly, 20*(1), 75–84.

Smoller, J. W., & Otto, M. W. (1998). Panic, dyspnea, and asthma. *Current Opinion in Pulmonary Medicine, 4,* 40–45.

Spiegel, D. A., Bruce, T. J., Gregg, S., F., & Nuzzarello, A. (1994). Does cognitive behavior therapy assist slow taper alprazolam discontinuation in panic disorder? *American Journal of Psychiatry, 151,* 876–881.

Spiegel, D. A., Wiegel, M., Baker, S. L., & Greene, K. A. I. (2000). Pharmacotherapy of anxiety disorders. In D. I. Mostofsky & D. H. Barlow (Eds.), *The management of stress and anxiety in medical disorders.* Boston: Allyn & Bacon.

Stein, M. B., Walker, J. R., Anderson, G., Hazen, A. L., Ross, C. A., Eldridge, G., et al. (1996). Childhood physical and sexual abuse in patients with anxiety disorders and a community sample. *American Journal of Psychiatry, 153,* 275–277.

Taylor, C. B., Sheikh, J., Agras, W. S., Roth, W. T., Margraf, J., Ehlers, A., et al. (1986). Self-report of panic attacks: Agreement with heart rate changes. *American Journal of Psychiatry, 143,* 478–482.

Taylor, S., Koch, W. J., & McNally, R. J. (1992). How does anxiety sensitivity vary across the anxiety disorders? *Journal of Anxiety Disorders, 6,* 249–259.

Telch, M. J., Brouillard, M., Telch, C. F., Agras, W. S., & Taylor, C. B. (1989). Role of cognitive appraisal in panic-related avoidance. *Behavior Research and Therapy, 27,* 373–383.

Thorgeirsson, T. E., Oskarsson, H., Desnica, N., Kostic, J. P., Stefansson, J. G., Kolbeinsson, H., et al. (2003). Anxiety with panic disorder linked to chromosome 9q in Iceland. *American Journal of Human Genetics, 72,* 1221–1230.

Thyer, B. A., Himle, L., Curtis, G. C., Cameron, O. G., & Nesse, R. M. (1985). A comparison of panic disorder and agoraphobia with panic attacks. *Comprehensive Psychiatry, 26,* 208–214.

Torgersen, S. (1983). Genetic factors in anxiety disorders. *Archives of General Psychiatry, 40,* 1085–1089.

Tsao, J. C. I., Lewin, M. R., & Craske, M. G. (1998). The effects of cognitive-behavioral therapy for panic disorder on comorbid conditions. *Journal of Anxiety Disorders, 12,* 357–371.

Tsao, J. C. I., Mystkowski, J. L., Zucker, B. G., & Craske, M. G. (2002). Effects of cognitive-behavioral therapy for panic disorder on comorbid conditions: Replication and extension. *Behavior Therapy, 33,* 493–509.

Tsao, J. C. I., Mystkowski, J. L., Zucker, B. G., & Craske, M. G. (2005). Impact of cognitive-behavioral therapy for panic disorder on comorbidity: A controlled investigation. *Behavior Research and Therapy, 43,* 959–970.

Uhde, T. W. (1994). The anxiety disorders: Phenomenology and treatment of core symptoms and associated sleep disturbance. In M. Kryger, T. Roth, & W. Dement (Eds.), *Principles and practice of sleep medicine* (pp. 871–898). Philadelphia: Saunders.

van den Hout, M., Arntz, A., & Hoekstra, R. (1994). Exposure reduced agoraphobia but not panic, and cognitive therapy reduced panic but not agoraphobia. *Behavior Research and Therapy, 32,* 447–451.

van Megen, H. J., Westenberg, H. G., Den Boer, J. A., & Kahn, R. S. (1996). The panic-inducing properties of the cholecystokinin tetrapeptide CCK4 in patients with panic disorder. *European Neuropsychopharmacology, 6,* 187–194.

Verburg, K., Griez, E., Meijer, J., & Pols, H. (1995). Respiratory disorders as a possible predisposing factor for panic disorder. *Journal of Affective Disorder, 33,* 129–134.

White, K. S., & Barlow, D. H. (2002). Panic disorder and agoraphobia. In D. H. Barlow (Ed.), *Anxiety and its disorders* (2nd ed., pp. 328–379). New York: Guilford Press.

White, K. S., Brown, T. A., Somers, T. J., & Barlow, D. H. (2006). Avoidance behavior in panic disorder: The moderating influence of perceived control. *Behavior Research and Therapy, 44,* 147–157.

Williams, S. L. (1992). Perceived self-efficacy and phobic disability. In R. Schwarzer (Ed.), *Self-efficacy: Thought control of action* (pp. 149–176). Washington, DC: Hemisphere.

Williams, S. L., & Falbo, J. (1996). Cognitive and performance-based treatments for panic attacks in people with varying degrees of agoraphobic disability. *Behavior Research and Therapy, 34,* 253–264.

Woods, S. W., Charney, D. S., Goodman, W. K., & Heninger, G. R. (1987). Carbon dioxide-induced anxiety: Behavioral, physiologic, and biochemical effects of 5% CO_2 in panic disorder patients and 5% and 7.5% CO_2 in healthy subjects. *Archives of General Psychiatry, 44,* 365–375.

Woody, S., McLean, P., Taylor, S., & Koch, W. J. (1999). Treatment of major depression in the context of panic disorder. *Journal of Affective Disorders, 53,* 163–174.

Zinbarg, R. E., & Barlow, D. H. (1996). Structure of anxiety and that anxiety disorders: A hierarchical model. *Journal of Abnormal Psychology, 105*(2), 181–193.

Zinbarg, R. E., Barlow, D. H., & Brown, T. A. (1997). Hierarchical structure and general factor saturation of the Anxiety Sensitivity Index: Evidence and implication. *Psychological Assessment, 9,* 277–284.

Zoellner, L. A., & Craske, M. G. (1999). Interoceptive accuracy and panic. *Behavior Research and Therapy, 37,* 1141–1158.

CHAPTER 9

Social Anxiety Disorder

LUKE T. SCHULTZ, RICHARD G. HEIMBERG,
AND THOMAS L. RODEBAUGH

DESCRIPTION OF THE DISORDER

An individual with social anxiety disorder often defines his or her life with two powerful experiences: crippling fear and social isolation. Indeed, as an anxiety disorder, social anxiety disorder is best understood by "marked and persistent fear" of social situations, which are typically "avoided ... or ... endured with dread" (American Psychiatric Association, 1994, p. 450). In social anxiety disorder, the feared stimuli are situations in which the individual may be evaluated by other people, because socially anxious individuals fear that they will be embarrassed or humiliated. In particular, socially anxious individuals commonly fear that they will behave in a way that will result in other people thinking they are weak, unintelligent, or awkward, or that others will notice their anxiety. Research suggests that persons with social anxiety disorder also fear positive evaluation, such as receiving complimentary feedback from others, possibly because they believe that others will come to expect more from them in the future and they will not be able to maintain the elevated status that is implied (Gilbert, 2001; Weeks, Heimberg, & Rodebaugh, 2006). Clearly, these feared outcomes are more likely when the person with social anxiety disorder is in the presence of other people (i.e., when he is engaged in a social situation).

Social situations naturally assume many forms, and in the social anxiety disorder literature, they generally fall into two major domains: social interaction situations and performance situations. In social interaction situations, the person is engaged in conversation in dyads or small groups, such as initiating and/or maintaining conversations, asking for a date, or speaking with authority figures. Performance situations can be as formal and demanding as public speaking or as informal and spontaneous as signing forms in front of others or eating in a crowded cafeteria. Although interaction and performance situations are often quite different in terms of the expectations involved, socially anxious individuals typically see themselves as the object of an audience's evaluation in each, resulting in significant anxiety.

Anxiety in social situations may be experienced physiologically and often involves symptoms such as heart palpitations, sweating, trembling, and abdominal distress.

Some individuals with social anxiety experience severe and intense physical symptoms that meet diagnostic criteria for a panic attack (see Jack, Heimberg, & Mennin, 1999; Scott, Heimberg, & Jack, 2000). Panic attacks in social anxiety disorder are differentiated from those in panic disorder, in that they are triggered and exacerbated by situations that are specifically associated with the feared outcome of evaluation by others. Furthermore, Jack et al. (1999) found that individuals with social anxiety disorder who experience such situationally bound panic attacks experience significantly greater anxiety in and avoidance of social situations as well as greater anxiety sensitivity and feelings of hopelessness than do their nonpanicking counterparts.

Whether interacting with other people or performing in front of them, the person with social anxiety disorder perceives that she may do or say something to make a fool of herself. Thus, the most efficient behavior to prevent this outcome is to avoid social situations whenever possible. Such behavior not only appears to be a reasonable short-term strategy, but it would also be evolutionarily adaptive if embarrassing oneself in public leads to the risk of social estrangement or even expulsion (Trower & Gilbert, 1989). Socially anxious individuals may engage in complete situational avoidance, such as declining an invitation to a party, or they may avoid in more subtle ways. For instance, an individual with social anxiety disorder may attend the party but stay close to the side of someone she knows very well, not venturing into conversations with strangers. In addition to avoidance behaviors, socially anxious individuals often engage in behavior to compensate for what they believe to be visible signs of anxiety or its consequences. Wells et al. (1995) and D. M. Clark (2001) have labeled these efforts *safety behaviors* (also see D. M. Clark & Wells, 1995). For example, a woman with social anxiety disorder believes that she blushes when giving reports to her colleagues; in meetings, she holds her hands to her face in an attempt to prevent others from noticing her skin coloration. This behavior may be similar in function to overt avoidance because it is an attempt to reduce the likelihood of evaluation by others. However, it may work against the anxious individual's goal of deflecting attention away from herself and strengthen her maladaptive belief that she could not have "survived" the situation without it.

Social anxiety disorder was not officially recognized as a diagnostic category until the publication of *DSM-III* (American Psychiatric Association, 1980). However, after its nosological birth, it was described as an acute fear of and desire to avoid a *specific* social situation. For example, someone could be diagnosed with social anxiety disorder (also known as social phobia) if she feared public speaking or eating in public. If an individual demonstrated significant fear and avoidance of social interaction situations, she would be assigned a diagnosis of avoidant personality disorder rather than social anxiety disorder. Nevertheless, social anxiety disorder has come to be recognized as a disorder associated with significant anxiety and impairment in a number of domains (see Schneier et al, 1994; Schneier, Johnson, Hornig, Liebowitz, & Weissman, 1992). Beginning with *DSM-III-R* (American Psychiatric Association, 1987), and continuing in *DSM-IV* (American Psychiatric Association, 1994), the generalized subtype of social anxiety disorder was introduced, marking the official recognition of the potential breadth of fears in this disorder.

Assignment of the generalized subtype confers the understanding that the anxious individual fears "most" social situations (American Psychiatric Association, 1994, p. 451). Individuals who do not meet criteria for the generalized subtype are said to have nongeneralized social anxiety disorder, which is considered a "heterogeneous group" (American Psychiatric Association, 1994; p. 452) because this diagnosis is assigned if only one performance situation is feared (e.g., public speaking) or if several, but not most, situations are feared. In addition to the introduction of subtypes of social anxiety disorder in *DSM-III-R*, the criteria were changed so that broad interpersonal fears were no longer assigned only to avoidant personality disorder and excluded from social anxiety disorder. There has been ongoing debate about the similarity of generalized social anxiety disorder and avoidant personality disorder, and some have suggested that the criteria for these two disorders are simply too similar (Holt, Heimberg, & Hope, 1992; Turner, Beidel, & Townsley, 1992). Although controversy remains, social anxiety may best be understood as existing on a continuum (Kollman, Brown, Liverant, & Hofmann, 2006), with the combination of generalized social anxiety disorder and avoidant personality disorder at the most severe pole (Heimberg, 1996).

Social anxiety disorder is clearly associated with much distress and discomfort, which has been linked to significant interpersonal, intimate, and occupational impairment. For instance, individuals with social anxiety disorder have reported significant impairment in general and romantic relationships (Turner, Beidel, Dancu, & Keys, 1986), are more likely than nonanxious individuals to be divorced or never to have married (Wittchen, Stein, & Kessler, 1999), and have reported significant difficulty in making and sustaining friendships (Whisman, Sheldon, & Goering, 2000). People with social anxiety disorder also demonstrate substantial impairment at work. In their review of the literature, Ballenger et al. (1998) reported that at least one-third of individuals with social anxiety disorder believed that this disorder reduced their productivity at work.

In the United States, a great number of people experience the distress and impairment of social anxiety disorder. In Kessler, Chiu, Demler, Merikangas, and Walters's (2005) National Comorbidity Study Replication, social anxiety disorder had a 12-month prevalence of 6.8%, second highest among the Axis I psychiatric disorders, comparable to specific phobias (8.7%) and major depression (6.7%). Kessler, Berglund, et al. (2005) also reported that social anxiety disorder ranks fourth in lifetime prevalence at 12.1%, following only major depression (16.6%), alcohol abuse (13.2%), and specific phobia (12.5%). In the original National Comorbidity Survey, rates of *DSM-III-R* social anxiety disorder were especially high in particular groups such as women and in individuals who lived with their parents, did not have a college education, were never married, or who were in the lowest income brackets (W. J. Magee, Eaton, Wittchen, McGonagle, & Kessler, 1996).

Social anxiety disorder is most commonly diagnosed in the presence of another disorder. W. J. Magee et al. (1996) found that 81% of individuals with social anxiety disorder met criteria for some other disorder. Most commonly, individuals with social anxiety disorder met criteria for an additional anxiety disorder (57%) with high rates of comorbid specific phobia (38%), agoraphobia (23%) posttraumatic stress disorder (16%) and generalized anxiety disorder (13%). Comorbid mood disorders were also quite common (41%), and many of these cases met criteria for major depressive disorder (37%). Not surprisingly, individuals with social anxiety disorder often met criteria for a substance use disorder (40%), particularly alcohol dependence (24%).

Its associated impairment and remarkable prevalence indicate that social anxiety disorder is a significant problem for a great number of people. Furthermore, rates of comorbidity suggest that the intense fear in social anxiety disorder rarely occurs in isolation from depression, substance misuse, and other severe forms of anxiety. Certainly importance of accurate assessment, thorough conceptualization, and effective treatment are paramount. Since its introduction into the psychiatric nosology, social anxiety disorder has gained attention and respect, and there has been a great increase in our understanding of the disorder. Next we review and evaluate recent advances in identifying, conceptualizing, and treating social anxiety disorder.

DIAGNOSIS AND ASSESSMENT

STRUCTURED CLINICAL INTERVIEWS

A common tool in the diagnosis of Axis I disorders is the semi-structured diagnostic interview. In the diagnosis of social anxiety disorder, the Structured Clinical Interview for *DSM-IV* Axis I Disorders-Patient Edition (SCID; First, Spitzer, Gibbon, & Williams, 2002) is one of the most common. Although it probes all Axis I disorders, the SCID includes a series of screening questions meant to inform the interviewer of the likelihood of a diagnosis being met, and thus, the necessity of further probing. Diagnosticians can terminate a particular diagnostic module if screening does not yield positive endorsement. Therefore, the SCID may be efficiently administered while allowing for accurate differential diagnosis. Ventura, Liberman, Green, Shaner, and Mintz (1998) found strong agreement on symptoms ($\kappa = .76$) and good accuracy of diagnosis (83%) in a general clinical sample when less-experienced SCID-IV evaluators' ratings were compared to the ratings of more experienced interviewers over a period of 5 years. Although the SCID may be lauded for its efficiency, the speed at which it can be administered, and its psychometric strength, it may also be criticized for a lack of depth in assessing symptom presentation. For this reason, it may not be ideal in the planning of cognitive behavioral therapy for social anxiety disorder.

The Anxiety Disorders Interview Schedule for *DSM-IV: Lifetime Version* (ADIS; DiNardo, Brown, & Barlow, 1994) is also a frequently used semi-structured diagnostic interview in social anxiety research and treatment. In addition to detailed modules assessing the several anxiety disorders, it also includes modules for disorders that are commonly comorbid with anxiety, such as mood disorders, somatoform disorders, and the substance use disorders. Within all of its modules, the ADIS requires the assessment of a number of symptoms that may make it less time-efficient than the SCID, yet potentially more informative. Also, the ADIS probes a number of the cognitive and situational cues for the experience of anxiety among the disorders assessed. Specificity of this information, lacking in the SCID, can be particularly useful in the planning of cognitive behavioral treatment for social anxiety disorder. Like the SCID, the ADIS has demonstrated considerable psychometric strength. For instance, T. A. Brown, DiNardo, Lehman, and Campbell (2001) found the ADIS to have good interrater reliability in the diagnosis of social anxiety disorder ($\kappa = .77$).

CLINICIAN-ADMINISTERED MEASURES

Although structured interviews are helpful in the initial identification of social anxiety disorder, more focused clinician-administered measures of the disorder are also available for the further exploration of severity and morbidity. The Liebowitz (1987) Social Anxiety Scale (LSAS) is a widely used measure in research and treatment. The LSAS assesses fear and avoidance in 11 social and 13 performance situations. Respondents indicate the severity of their fear and extent of their avoidance for each item/situation based on prescribed Likert-type scales. Responses on each scale range from 0 (None; Never, respectively) to 3 (Severe; Usually, respectively). The LSAS provides a total scale score to indicate overall social anxiety as well as subscale scores of total fear, total avoidance, and fear and avoidance in both social and performance situations. Other subscales have been derived on the basis of factor analysis and may provide more specifically focused information for treatment planning (e.g., Safren et al., 1999). The LSAS is psychometrically strong, with excellent internal consistency ($\alpha = .96$; Heimberg et al., 1999) and good convergent validity (Heimberg, Mueller, Holt, Hope, & Liebowitz, 1992). It also discriminates well between persons with social anxiety disorder and those with another anxiety disorder (Heimberg & Holaway, 2006). Using a receiver operating characteristics analysis, Mennin et al. (2002) determined that a total score of 30 on the LSAS was sufficient to confer an accurate diagnosis of social anxiety disorder, and a score of 60 accurately identified the generalized subtype. The LSAS is also a useful and sensitive measure of symptom change in both cognitive behavioral and pharmacological treatment of social anxiety disorder (Heimberg et al., 1998). With its relatively structured format, the LSAS has been shown to be an effective self-report measure as well (Fresco et al., 2001).

The Brief Social Phobia Scale (BSPS; Davidson et al., 1991) is a clinician-administered measure used most commonly in studies of pharmacotherapy. The BSPS assesses fear and avoidance of seven social situations as well as the severity of four physiological anxiety symptoms that may occur when the interviewee experiences or thinks about the feared situations. The items on each subscale are rated on 0–4 Likert-type scales. The BSPS has demonstrated relatively strong psychometric properties including good temporal consistency (Davidson et al., 1997) and interrater reliability (Davidson et al., 1991). Although the overall scale and the fear and avoidance subscales demonstrated good internal consistency, the physiological subscale did not. Additionally, the three subscales of the BSPS have not been confirmed by factor analysis. Rather an exploratory factor analysis demonstrated that the BSPS may possess a more complex six-factor solution (Davidson et al., 1997). However, the BSPS has been shown to have good convergent validity (Davidson et al., 1991) and sensitivity to the effects of pharmacotherapy (Davidson et al., 1997) and cognitive behavioral therapy (Davidson et al., 2004).

SELF-REPORT MEASURES

Self-report measures are extremely useful and universally employed in the evaluation of social anxiety disorder. Such response inventories allow clients to rate their experiences efficiently, without the need to meet with a trained diagnostician or clinical evaluator. Included next is brief review of such measures (see Hart, Jack, Turk, & Heimberg, 1999, for a more in-depth review of social anxiety assessment devices).

The Social Interaction Anxiety Scale (SIAS) and the Social Phobia Scale (SPS; Mattick & Clarke, 1998) are two commonly administered self-report scales. They were designed to assess the two major domains of social anxiety defined above: social interaction situations and situations in which a person may be scrutinized by others (often performance situations), respectively. Although both types of situations are likely to be feared by individuals with social anxiety disorder, it is not uncommon for socially anxious clients to endorse greater fear in one particular domain. Both scales are composed of 20 items and rated on five-point Likert-type scales (the published version of the SIAS has just 19 items; however, the version most commonly used was distributed prior to the published version and contains 20 items; see Cox & Swinson, 1995). The SIAS and the SPS have demonstrated excellent psychometric properties, such as strong internal consistency (αs = .88 to .94), high temporal stability (rs = .91 and .93), and accurate discrimination between patients with social anxiety disorder and those with other disorders (E. J. Brown et al., 1997; Heimberg et al., 1992). Also, both measures have been found to have good convergent and discriminant validity (Heimberg et al., 1992; Mattick & Clarke, 1998) and treatment sensitivity (Ries et al., 1998). However, recent data suggest that the three reverse scored items of the SIAS do not contribute usefully to the total score (Rodebaugh, Woods, Heimberg, Liebowitz, & Schneier, 2006).

The Social Phobia and Anxiety Inventory (SPAI; Turner, Beidel, Dancu, & Stanley, 1989) is a comprehensive scale that measures cognitive, behavioral, and somatic aspects of social anxiety in both interaction and performance situations. The SPAI consists of 45 items, however 21 items require multiple responses, for 109 individual responses altogether. Although such length may preclude the administration of the SPAI in certain treatment/research settings, the large information yield and the psychometric strengths of the measure (and the benefits of its usage in treatment planning) should not be ignored. For instance, the SPAI has demonstrated good internal consistency (Turner et al., 1989) and convergent (Herbert, Bellack, & Hope, 1991; Ries et al., 1998) and discriminant (Herbert et al., 1991) validity.

The Social Phobia Inventory (SPIN; Connor et al., 2000) is a relatively new self-report measure that has not yet received as much as attention as the measures listed above, but is used frequently in trials of pharmacological treatment of social anxiety disorder. Based on the BSPS (Davidson et al., 1991), the SPIN consists of three subscales (17 items in total), which assess socially anxious respondents' fear, avoidance, and physiological arousal. The SPIN has demonstrated good psychometric properties such as internal consistency, temporal stability, and sensitivity to the effects of pharmacotherapy (Antony, Coons, McCabe, Ashbaugh, & Swinson, 2006; Connor et al., 2000). Antony et al. (2006) also have found the SPIN to differentiate well between socially anxiety disorder, panic disorder, and obsessive-compulsive disorder. An abbreviated 3-item version of the SPIN, the Mini-SPIN, has shown good sensitivity and specificity in the identification of social anxiety disorder, both in general patient samples (Connor, Kobak, Churchill, Katzelnick, & Davidson, 2001) and in patients seeking treatment for anxiety (Weeks, Spokas, & Heimberg, in press).

Interviews and questionnaires in this section have been valuable in the study of social anxiety disorder, and most of those presented have earned good marks in psychometric studies. However, the measurement of social anxiety does not end with anxiety because many other areas of assessment have received much attention. For example, information processing in the anxiety disorders has received a great deal of attention in recent years, and research in social anxiety has demonstrated attentional bias to threat (see Bögels & Mansell, 2004), biased interpretation of ambiguous social cues (see Hirsch & Clark, 2004) and memory biases (see Coles & Heimberg, 2002). In addition to cognitive assessment of social anxiety, behavioral assessment tests have been employed (e.g., Fydrich, Chambless, Perry, Buergner, & Beazley, 1998; Harb, Eng, Zaider, & Heimberg, 2003). In a controlled environment, such role-play (typically social interaction or public speaking) tasks can provide researchers and clinicians with much information regarding a client's behavior (e.g., safety behaviors, avoidance tendencies, etc) at times of high anxiety, especially given repeated demonstrations that patients with social anxiety disorder underestimate the quality of their social performance (e.g., Rapee & Lim, 1992; Stopa & Clark, 1993). Last, it is also important to measure the impact of the disorder or its treatment on disability, impairment, and life satisfaction. Several measures such as the Liebowitz Self-Rated Disability Scale (Schneier et al., 1994), the Sheehan Disability Scale (Sheehan, 1983), the Disability Profile (Schneier et al., 1994), and the Quality of Life Inventory (Frisch, Cornell, Villanueva, & Retzlaff, 1992) have demonstrated strong psychometric properties in samples of patients with social anxiety disorder (Hambrick, Turk, Heimberg, Schneier, & Liebowitz, 2004) and may be usefully employed for these purposes.

CONCEPTUALIZATION

Cognitive Behavioral Conceptualization

Cognitive behavioral conceptualizations have provided fertile ground for empirical exploration of social anxiety disorder (e.g., D. M. Clark & Wells, 1995; Rapee & Heimberg, 1997). Rapee and Heimberg (1997) outlined a model of social anxiety disorder with emphasis on the interplay of cognitive, behavioral, and affective components of anxiety. This dynamic process has been implicated in the situational experience of anxiety in both normal and pathological social fears and grows from a biopsychosocial foundation.

As described earlier, the initial stage of the social anxiety response inevitably begins with the detection/perception of a potential audience. According to A. T. Beck and Emery (1985), the experience of anxiety is expected when danger or threat is perceived. Accordingly, the socially anxious individual appraises social evaluation (negative or positive) as inherently dangerous, and the *potential* presence of other people makes more likely the possibility of evaluative threat. Thus, in social anxiety disorder, anxiety is experienced when the individual simply suspects that he may be scrutinized by others, meaning that he need not stand at a podium in a crowded room or attend a job interview to feel threatened. Rather, simply walking ahead of someone on the street or approaching the checkout line at a grocery store may trigger anxiety. Such an understanding defines social situations rather liberally; nevertheless, socially anxious individuals commonly describe such situations as particularly anxiety provoking.

In the presence of threat (i.e., after the detection of an audience), socially anxious individuals may become increasingly vigilant for cues that would signal the realization of their feared outcomes (A. T. Beck & Emery, 1985). Typically in social situations, this information is seldom provided unambiguously; however, individuals with social anxiety disorder consistently attend to three sources for possible information on the proximity of feared outcomes: environmental cues, a mental representation of how they believe they appear to others, and cognitive, behavioral, and affective cues related to the severity of their anxiety in the moment (Rapee & Heimberg, 1997).

Over the past 15 years, much research has been published demonstrating the possible bias of cognitive processes in social anxiety, with attentional bias garnering the most support (see Bögels & Mansell, 2004). Studies in this area have demonstrated that socially anxious individuals allocate attention more quickly to words associated with negative evaluation (e.g., *failure*; Asmundson & Stein, 1994; Hope, Rapee, Heimberg, & Dombeck, 1990) and pictures of disapproving faces (e.g., Mogg, Philippot, & Bradley, 2004) than do nonanxious controls, and these effects have also been extended to more ecologically valid settings, such as perception of audience behaviors during public speaking tasks (e.g., Veljaca & Rapee, 1998). Interpretations of these results suggest that social anxiety is maintained by rapid and consistent detection of danger in social situations, resulting in apparent confirmation of social concerns followed by ongoing fear and avoidance of similar future occasions.

Indeed, individuals with social anxiety disorder tend to detect negative cues despite the presence of more positive alternatives (e.g., noticing one audience member yawning while three others nod and smile). However, social situations are replete with ambiguous cues and feedback that could be interpreted as innocuous and neutral, positive and complimentary, or negative and threatening. For example, an interaction partner's furrowed brow could mean that she has a headache, that she finds the conversation topic intellectually stimulating, or that she is annoyed. Evidence suggests that individuals with social anxiety disorder tend to interpret socially ambiguous feedback as negative, whereas individuals low in social anxiety tend to make neutral or even positive interpretations (Amir, Foa, & Coles, 1998; Stopa & Clark, 2000). Similarly, individuals with social anxiety disorder have demonstrated biases in their predictions of negative social outcomes, such as "Someone you know will not say hello to you" (Foa, Franklin, Perry, & Herbert, 1996). Foa et al. found that, compared to nonanxious controls, individuals with generalized social anxiety disorder judged a negative outcome of such events to be more likely and more costly. Also, there may be interactions between attentional and interpretive biases in social anxiety. If individuals with social anxiety disorder are more liberal in their determination of what constitutes negative feedback (e.g., Veljaca & Rapee, 1998) and tend to interpret ambiguous situations as negative (Stopa & Clark, 2000), then there is more potential threat to be detected, and they are highly likely to find it.

Cognitive behavioral conceptualizations suggest that the socially anxious individual also focuses on an internal, mental representation of the self as seen by the audience. According to Rapee and Heimberg (1997), this representation may be an image or a vague sense of how one appears to others, which likely involves seeing oneself as if through the eyes of the audience (also see D. M. Clark & Wells, 1995). Evidence indeed suggests that socially anxious individuals may be more likely to see themselves from an observer perspective during anxiety-provoking social situations and from a field perspective (i.e., as if through their own eyes) during nonsocial situations (Wells, Clark, & Ahmad, 1998; Wells & Papageorgiou, 1999). Also, individuals with social anxiety disorder are most likely to see themselves from the observer perspective when they are engaged in high anxiety situations, as opposed to situations that provoke low or moderate levels of anxiety (Coles, Turk, Heimberg, & Fresco, 2001). Research has suggested that this internal representation/image may be based, in part, on autobiographical memories of past socially stressful situations that may have been influential in the development or exacerbation of an individual's social anxiety disorder (Hackmann, Clark, & McManus, 2000; Hackmann, Surawy, & Clark, 1998).

Cognitive, physiological, and behavioral symptoms are also integral components to the social anxiety model. Socially anxious individuals have been shown to experience negative thoughts about their performance during social situations, are likely to judge their performance more harshly than others do, but may assume that others endorse similarly evaluations of their performance (Stopa & Clark, 1993). Physiological symptoms (e.g., blushing, trembling, sweating) are also potentially problematic in social situations. Socially anxious persons overestimate visibility of these symptoms (Alden & Wallace, 1995; McEwan & Devins, 1983) and conclude that when others do, in fact, notice them, they will attribute these symptoms to severe anxiety or mental illness (Roth, Antony, & Swinson, 2001). Negative cognition and fear of appearing anxious have a significant impact on the socially anxious individual's behavior during social situations. For instance, socially anxious individuals may employ a number of safety behaviors to address the "information" they receive from their negatively biased cognitions and predictions about the visibility of their anxiety, which may actually interfere with their performance (D. M. Clark & Wells, 1995). In some studies, observers rated socially anxious individuals as performing slightly worse in social situations than they rated nonanxious controls; however, these performance ratings were still significantly better than the ratings made by the socially anxious individuals themselves (Rapee & Lim, 1992; Stopa & Clark, 1993).

Considered in isolation, there is much evidence to indicate that socially anxious individuals attend to external threat in a biased manner, interpret ambiguous social cues as negative, focus on themselves from an observer perspective, and experience negative cognitions, severe physiological anxiety symptoms, and compromised performance. However, theorists have suggested that these processes do not operate in isolation (Hirsch, Mathews, & Clark, 2006; Rapee & Heimberg, 1997). Recent research has demonstrated that manipulation of one source of bias may have causal implications for other sources of bias. For example, manipulation of the mental representation of the self (particularly through imagery manipulation) appears to have a direct influence on cognitive and affective processes during social situations (e.g., Hirsch, Mathews, Clark, Williams, & Morrison, 2003; Vassilopoulos, 2005). In addition, Rapee and Heimberg have suggested that this relationship may operate as a positive feedback loop, such that biased attention to threat may influence the mental representation of the self. The implications for the interrelationships of the components of this model are significant. The mental representation of the self is based on the inputs outlined previously; however, these inputs are biased because socially anxious persons are more likely to notice negative audience behaviors than positive, experience negative thoughts, make inaccurate assumptions about the visibility of their anxiety, and underestimate their own performance. Therefore because an individual with social anxiety disorder looks to his mental representation for information about how he comes across, he necessarily sees a negatively biased caricature informed by anxious feelings and assumptions about others' evaluations when, realistically, the data needed to support such self-assessment cannot be obtained in ambiguous social situations.

During social situations, the complex interaction of external and internal information typically provides the socially anxious person with evidence for the conclusion that his performance has fallen short in a number of ways. Having gathered much negative information from a number of sources, the socially anxious individual then weighs the likelihood that his feared consequences will be realized (Rapee & Heimberg, 1997). To do this, he compares his evaluation of his performance to what he believes the audience expects of him. Therefore, if the individual believes that he is likely to meet the expectations of the audience despite his shortcomings, he will be less likely to experience anxiety (Carver & Scheier, 1981; Rapee & Heimberg, 1997). For people with social anxiety disorder, however, this conclusion is unlikely because they rate their feared outcomes as *more* likely and the consequences as more severe than nonanxious individuals do, perpetuating their cycle of fear (Foa et al., 1996).

Etiology

A complete conceptualization of social anxiety disorder must also consider potential causes, such as biological and environmental contributors. Familial contributions to social anxiety disorder have been identified. In one study, 16% of relatives of individuals with social anxiety disorder were also diagnosed with the disorder, whereas just 5% of nonanxious controls' relatives were so diagnosed (Fyer, Mannuzza, Chapman, Liebowitz, & Klein, 1993). Interestingly, relatives of patients with social anxiety disordered were *no* more likely to have been diagnosed with any other anxiety disorder than the relatives of controls. Therefore, there appears to be shared morbidity in families that is specific to social anxiety. Evidence also suggests that the frequency of social anxiety disorder within one's relatives varies by subtype (Mannuzza et al., 1995). When first-degree relatives were administered diagnostic interviews, relatives of patients with generalized social anxiety disorder were more likely to meet criteria of any subtype of social anxiety disorder (16%) than relatives of patients with nongeneralized social anxiety disorder (6%) or nonanxious controls (6%). In a similar study, Stein et al. (1998) showed that 26% of the relatives of patients with generalized social anxiety disorder met criteria for the generalized subtype and nearly 20% met criteria for avoidant personality disorder. By comparison, 2.7% and 0% of the relatives of nonanxious controls met criteria for these diagnoses. Although studies such as these clearly provide evidence that social anxiety symptoms may be shared among family members, genetic contributions cannot be assumed without more specific comparisons (e.g., twin studies).

Though few, twin studies have allowed for the measurement of genetic factors. Kendler, Neale, Kessler, Heath, and Eaves (1992) found that 24% of the monozygotic twins of individuals with social anxiety disorder also met criteria, compared to 15% of dizygotic twins. Further analysis has shown that nearly 21% of the variance in social anxiety disorder's development was accounted for by specific genetic factors, with 10% of the variance accounted for by a genetic predisposition that may be shared by specific phobias. This research group reassessed the same cohort of twins 8 years later (Kendler, Karkowski, & Prescott, 1999). With data from two assessments several years apart, Kendler and colleagues effectively accounted for measurement error in their analyses, finding social anxiety disorder's heritability to be closer to 50%. However, although rates of heritability may be higher than initially suggested, Kendler et al. (1999) emphasize that they are lower than those found in depression, suggesting a relatively higher significance of environmental factors in the etiology of social anxiety disorder.

Environmental factors that may contribute to the development of social anxiety disorder include parental influences and significant life experiences. Bruch, Heimberg, Berger, and Collins (1989) compared socially anxious subjects' and agoraphobic subjects' ratings of their mothers. Socially anxious participants recalled their mothers as being more fearful and avoidant of social interactions, as well as more likely to shelter them from social situations during childhood. Further evidence indicates that individuals with social anxiety disorder have parents who are more likely to discipline their children with shame and to place a greater emphasis on the opinions of others than are parents of nonanxious individuals (Bruch & Heimberg, 1994). A study of adolescents still living with their parents also points to the importance of parental influence, finding that participants with social anxiety disorder were more likely to rate their parents as rejecting and overprotective than participants without social anxiety disorder (Lieb et al., 2000).

In addition to parental factors, particular life events have been implicated in the development of social anxiety disorder. As mentioned, research has explored autobiographical events, the memories and images of which may trigger or exacerbate anxiety as individuals enter social situations (Hackmann et al., 1998, 2000). In addition, Erwin, Heimberg, Marx, and Franklin (in press) interviewed a number of individuals with social anxiety disorder who endorsed extremely stressful past social events (e.g., being publicly ridiculed by a parent or teacher). Although these social events did not qualify as criterion A traumas experienced by those with posttraumatic stress disorder (PTSD), more than one-third of those who experienced these events would otherwise have met criteria for PTSD. In general, these individuals also experienced more symptoms of hyperarousal and cognitive and emotional avoidance than nonanxious controls who had experienced similar events. Although socially anxious participants did not significantly differ from nonanxious controls in number of re-experiencing symptoms, they did endorse several such experiences, lending further support to the findings of Hackmann et al. (1998, 2000). Importantly, ongoing negative events such as bullying in childhood may also be important in the etiology of social anxiety, and evidence suggests that one form of bullying, teasing, is associated with a number of interpersonal problems later in life (Ledley et al., 2006) including trait anxiety, social anxiety, anxiety sensitivity, and depression (Roth, Coles, & Heimberg, 2002).

In addition to direct genetic contributions, child-rearing effects, and the influence of significant, negative life events, theorists have also suggested that a diathesis-stress model may explain social anxiety. The temperamental state known as "behavioral inhibition" has been tapped as a likely diathesis (Kagan, Reznick, & Snidman, 1988; Rosenbaum, Biederman, Pollock, & Hirshfeld, 1994). Behavioral inhibition has generally been defined as a temperament evident in young children marked by a tendency to withdraw from unfamiliar stimuli such as new people, environments, or objects. Behavioral inhibition is an appealing candidate diathesis, given its apparent links to social anxiety disorder in later life. In a longitudinal study, 61% of children who were classified as behaviorally inhibited as children met criteria for social anxiety disorder 11 years later, whereas only 27% of noninhibited children went on to meet similar criteria (Schwartz, Snidman, & Kagan, 1999).

DRUGS AFFECTING BEHAVIOR

Several studies have demonstrated significant overlap between social anxiety disorder and substance misuse; in particular, alcohol abuse and dependence are often comorbid with social anxiety disorder. Nearly half of individuals with a lifetime diagnosis of social anxiety disorder meet criteria also for a lifetime diagnosis of alcohol abuse or dependence (Grant et al., 2005). The 12-month prevalence of alcohol use disorders among individuals with social anxiety disorder is 13.1% (Grant et al., 2005), compared to only 8.5% among the general population (Grant et al., 2004). Also, social anxiety disorder is associated with higher rates of alcohol use disorders than most other anxiety disorders (Kessler et al., 1997; Kessler, Berglund, et al., 2005).

By definition, social anxiety disorder is associated with impairment in a number of life domains as well as ongoing fear and distress. It is therefore unsurprising that a large number of socially anxious individuals abuse a depressant such as alcohol. Despite the logical connection between alcohol misuse and intense social fears, little research substantiates the potential causal relationship. Some evidence suggests that many people with social anxiety disorder use alcohol to dampen fear in social situations (Turner et al., 1986). Turner et al. found that roughly half of their social anxiety disordered sample drank alcohol to lessen anxiety before and during parties. Similarly, large percentages of individuals with social anxiety disorder report that they drink alcohol intentionally to relieve anxiety before speaking to an authority figure (57%), while eating with other people (42%), or when forced to be the center of attention (43%; Smail, Stockwell, Canter, & Hodgson, 1984). Individuals with social anxiety disorder have also endorsed greater intention (than nonanxious controls) to use alcohol during social situations in which there would be strangers present (Holle, Heimberg, Sweet, & Holt, 1995). Given its effect in reducing social anxiety (see Tran, Haaga, & Chambless, 1997), intentional alcohol consumption for the purpose of easing social interaction/performance may be regarded as a safety behavior. If one is not apt to feel anxious, physiological symptoms become less likely, which may change the content of the mental representation of the self and thereby free up attentional resources. Importantly, sufficient alcohol consumption may, in fact, make negative evaluation (or at least being the center of attention) *more* likely. Excessive alcohol consumption may actually mimic feared anxiety symptoms such as blushing, dry mouth, and impaired speech and attention. Last, the negatively and positively reinforcing nature of alcohol consumption coupled with constant threat of social interaction in normal life makes alcohol dependence a dangerous possibility for individuals with social anxiety disorder.

Cultural and Diversity Issues

As in most areas of psychopathology research, cultural and diversity issues in social anxiety disorder may be extremely important, yet are regrettably understudied. Social anxiety research has demonstrated the importance for continued study of cultural issues. For instance, studies using self-report questionnaires have found that African Americans score slightly higher on some measures of social anxiety. Schultz et al. (2006) found that African Americans scored significantly higher on the Appraisal of Social Concerns Scale (Telch et al., 2004) than Caucasians. Similarly, Fresco et al. (2001) found that African Americans scored higher than Caucasians on the self-report version of the Liebowitz (1987) Social Anxiety Scale; however, this difference was not evident when the same respondents were assessed with the clinician-administered version. Importantly, none of the clinical interviewers in this study were African American. In line with these results were those of Okazaki, Liu, Longworth, and Minn (2002), who found that Asian Americans scored higher than Caucasians on measures of trait social anxiety; however, these differences were not evident in anxiety ratings made by third-party assessors. Ultimately, it is difficult to determine from such studies what these apparent differences mean. For example, the scales in question could be biased, leading to higher scores; alternatively, they could be accurate in detecting a difference between groups that may be missed by clinicians. Techniques such as item response theory (see Embertson & Reise, 2000) may be useful in elucidating such questions in the future.

Taijin kyofusho has recently gained greater attention in Western research. Identified by *DSM-IV* as a disorder primarily diagnosed in Asian countries such as Japan and Korea, *taijin kyofusho* is defined as a pervasive fear of causing discomfort to other people. There are several subtypes of this disorder, differing with the setting in which offense to others might occur. Despite its traditional definition (and that found in *DSM-IV*), researchers have recently claimed that *taijin kyofusho* may be more closely related to social anxiety disorder in core symptoms than initially expected. Specifically, L. Magee, Rodebaugh, and Heimberg (in press) and Suzuki, Takei, Kawai, Minabe, and Mori (2003) have claimed that the fear of offending/causing discomfort in others may actually be better defined as a fear of being evaluated negatively by that person, after the offense. Altogether, social anxiety disorder research has demonstrated differences between ethnic groups that may point toward important areas for future research.

MEDICAL TREATMENT

Much research has also demonstrated particular efficacy for pharmacological treatments for social anxiety disorder. Meta-analyses (Blanco, Antia, & Liebowitz, 2002; Hidalgo, Barnett, & Davidson, 2001; Van der Linden, Stein, & van Balkom, 2000) and more recent studies (e.g., Davidson et al., 2004) have shown a number of medications to be efficacious, including monoamine-oxidase inhibitors (MAOIs), selective serotonin reuptake inhibitors (SSRIs), and norepinephrine-serotonin reuptake inhibitors. Phenelzine sulfate, a MAOI, has been shown to be efficacious for over two-thirds of patients with social anxiety disorder and has demonstrated an overall between-groups effect size of 1.02, which is the largest among the medications studied (Blanco et al., 2002). However, other drugs, such as clonazepam (a benzodiazepine), gabapentin (an anticonvulsant), brofaromine (a reversible MAOI), and several SSRIs have demonstrated similar effect sizes. Although quite effective, phenelzine poses serious health risks that require patients to adhere strictly to prescribed diets. Therefore, SSRIs are considered first-line pharmacological treatment given their tolerability, safety, and efficacy in treating social anxiety disorder and many commonly comorbid conditions, whereas phenelzine is typically prescribed to those who do not respond to safer medications (Blanco et al., 2002).

COGNITIVE BEHAVIORAL TREATMENT

Cognitive behavioral therapy (CBT) has been the most widely studied and consistently empirically supported treatment for social anxiety disorder. Cognitive behavioral treatments have been delivered in both group (e.g., Davidson et al., 2004; Heimberg et al., 1998) and individual (e.g., D. M. Clark et al., 2003; Zaider, Heimberg, Roth, Hope, & Turk, 2003) formats, without much difference in efficacy (Lucas & Telch, 1993; Scholing & Emmelkamp, 1993; but see Stangier et al., 2003). Cognitive behavioral therapy typically includes the assembly of a few key components described below (also see the Case Description for applied examples).

First, as suggested, an individual's beliefs during situations, not the situations themselves, generate anxiety (A. T. Beck & Emery, 1985); individuals with social anxiety disorder engage in excessively negative thinking about themselves, which is associated with increased anxiety and compromised social performance (Stopa & Clark, 1993). The types of thinking errors generated by socially anxious individuals are numerous, but typically include negatively biased interpretation of ambiguous cues and assumed factual knowledge regarding the thoughts and intentions of others (for greater detail regarding social anxiety-relevant thinking errors, see Heimberg and Becker, 2002; Hope, Heimberg, Juster, & Turk, 2000; and the Case Description). A. T. Beck and Emery (1985) described such negative thoughts as "automatic" given their apparent consistency and spontaneity. Cognitive restructuring, then, is a CBT component that specifically targets such negative automatic thinking before, during, and after social situations. As a therapeutic technique, cognitive restructuring typically involves the client's identifying and labeling automatic thoughts, then challenging them with adaptive statements based on fact and observation, as opposed to inference and conjecture. Ultimately, the goal of cognitive restructuring is to assist the client in altering the cognitive filter that distorts incoming social information.

Second, CBT for social anxiety disorder typically involves exposure to feared stimuli, which has long been recognized as integral to fear reduction (e.g., Foa & Kozak, 1986; Lang, 1977, 1979; Wolpe, 1958). Foa and Kozak (1986) suggest that anxiety disorders are maintained by a "fear structure," an escape/avoidance program activated by the perception of feared stimuli (e.g., an audience in social anxiety disorder). The socially anxious individual defines the audience as dangerous and escape or avoidance as the effective antidote. Anxiety is reduced, the escape behavior is negatively reinforced, and stimuli (threat cues) and responses (escape behaviors) continue to hold inaccurate and maladaptive meaning. In the treatment of social anxiety disorder, the goal of exposure is essentially to eliminate avoidant/escapist response elements and challenge the meaning of the stimulus elements. Habituation of anxiety is paired with the absence of feared consequences, and therapeutic learning may occur (Lang, 1979). Because exposure to feared situations presents socially anxious individuals with information that may weaken their fear structure, it is a very useful when coupled with cognitive restructuring because therapist and client can compare inaccurate predictions with actual outcomes generated during exposures (Heimberg & Becker, 2002; Hope et al., 2000).

In CBT for social anxiety disorder, applied relaxation and social skills training have also been employed, although less extensively than cognitive restructuring and exposure techniques. Applied relaxation involves the practice of progressive muscle relaxation (Bernstein, Borkovec, & Hazlett-Stevens, 2000) and their application during times of high anxiety, such as anxiety-provoking social situations (e.g., Ost, 1987). Therefore, applied relaxation may derive at least some of its efficacy from the mechanisms underlying exposure treatment. Social skills training has also been used in combination with CBT techniques (e.g., Davidson et al., 2004) based on the rationale that individuals with social anxiety disorder are deficient in social skill. Research has shown that individuals with social anxiety disorder may perform more poorly during social interactions than those without the disorder (Stopa & Clark, 1993). However, this effect has not been consistently demonstrated (e.g., Rapee & Lim, 1992), and one may argue that hypervigilance for threat cues (e.g., Veljaca & Rapee, 1998) and the focus of attention on self-images during times of high anxiety (e.g., Coles et al., 2001) are responsible for compromised cognitive resources and thus poorer social performance (also see Bögels, Sijbers, & Voncken, 2006). Nevertheless, one study has demonstrated that social skills training may augment the efficacy of group CBT consisting of exposure and cognitive restructuring (Herbert et al., 2005).

Treatment of social anxiety disorder with cognitive behavioral techniques has been evaluated in a number of studies. Meta-analyses have examined these studies and are reported here (Chambless & Hope, 1996; Fedoroff & Taylor, 2001; Feske & Chambless, 1995; Gould, Buckminster, Pollack, Otto, & Yap, 1997; Taylor, 1996). The major findings of these meta-analytic studies are addressed in terms of their effects sizes, indicating symptom reduction. Cohen's *d* is utilized as a measure of an intervention's effectiveness given its independence from sample size and the standardization of results offered. Cohen (1988) categorizes effect sizes by magnitude, including small (0.2), medium (0.5), and large (0.8) effects.

Of the cognitive behavioral techniques included in the meta-analyses (cognitive restructuring, exposure, cognitive restructuring plus exposure, applied relaxation, and social skills training), all demonstrated moderate to large effect sizes from pretreatment to posttreatment (within-group) as well as compared to control conditions (between-groups). Comparisons between CBT components and control conditions also offered some evidence for the added benefit of cognitive restructuring plus exposure. For instance, Taylor's (1996) meta-analysis included studies with exposure alone, cognitive restructuring alone, cognitive restructuring plus exposure, and social skills training as active CBT conditions. Cognitive restructuring plus exposure outperformed its isolated components and social skills training when compared to control conditions. In a more recent meta-analysis, these results were again demonstrated, however, only on observer ratings of social anxiety (Fedoroff & Taylor, 2001). Also, group and individual CBT formats appeared to be similarly efficacious (see Fedoroff & Taylor, 2001; Gould et al., 1997; Taylor, 1996). The meta-analyses described included studies with follow-up assessments 2 to 12 months posttreatment, and CBT conditions were associated with maintenance of (or continued improvement in) therapeutic gains at these later assessments.

Comparisons between components themselves (without regard to control conditions) did not demonstrate significant effects. Several of the meta-analyses found that cognitive restructuring plus exposure was nonsignificantly more effective in symptom reduction than were cognitive restructuring alone, social skills training alone and applied relaxation (Fedoroff & Taylor, 2001; Gould et al; 1997; Taylor, 1996). Comparisons between exposure alone and cognitive restructuring plus exposure yielded no evidence (significant or otherwise) of differences between these two conditions.

As they were defined earlier, cognitive restructuring and exposure techniques appear to be natural therapeutic complements. Put simply, cognitive restructuring involves the challenging of automatic thoughts, and exposure to feared situations allows for optimal testing of thoughts. Therefore, the meta-analytic results suggesting that the addition of exposure to cognitive restructuring provides no significant benefit above and beyond the isolated components may be surprising. However, theorists have argued that presumed separation of the two techniques may be unrealistic (e.g., Rodebaugh, Holaway, & Heimberg, 2004). Indeed, cognitive and behavioral techniques may be inseparable because clients receiving exposure are likely engaged in informal self- or therapist-guided cognitive restructuring of their beliefs.

Additional studies have been reported since the publication of the above meta-analyses. D. M. Clark et al. (2003) conducted a study comparing cognitive therapy with fluoxetine and placebo treatments. The protocol for cognitive therapy was predicated on D. M. Clark and Wells's (1995) cognitive model of social anxiety and emphasizes redirecting the socially anxious individual's focus away from internal imagery and toward external events while also abandoning safety behaviors. These goals are often accomplished with the use of video feedback (e.g., Rapee & Hayman, 1996). In addition, Clark et al. reported implementing cognitive strategies during exposure exercises, similar to those outlined earlier. Clark et al.'s treatment was significantly more efficacious than both fluoxetine and placebo conditions, and gains were maintained at 1-year follow-up. The within-group effect size for the CBT condition was greater than 2.0, which is large. D. M. Clark et al. (2006) also compared cognitive therapy to exposure plus applied relaxation and a waitlist control condition, again finding cognitive therapy to be a superior treatment. Compared to exposure plus applied relaxation, cognitive therapy evidenced a large between-groups effect size of 1.17. Compared to the control group, both active treatments were shown to be efficacious; however, cognitive therapy demonstrated a larger between-groups effect size than exposure plus applied relaxation ($ds = 2.63, 1.46$, respectively). Zaider, Heimberg,

Roth, et al. (2003) offered an individualized CBT format manualized and adapted from Heimberg and Becker (2002) and Hope et al. (2000), which they compared with a waitlist control group. Self-report measures and clinician-administered measures of social anxiety disorder symptoms suggest significant symptom reduction, evidencing large between-groups effect sizes, averaging 1.19.

Davidson et al. (2004) compared cognitive behavioral group therapy (based on Heimberg's group CBT, with added social skills training) with fluoxetine, pill placebo, and combination conditions. The CBT alone condition evidenced a large within-group effect size from pre- to posttreatment and a moderate between-groups effect size compared to the placebo condition. Hofmann (2004) compared cognitive behavioral group therapy (based on Heimberg, 1991) to an exposure alone group and a waitlist control group. Group CBT and exposure alone demonstrated similar, significant change from pre- to posttreatment (within-group $ds = 0.72$ & 0.52, respectively), whereas the control condition did not; however, clients who received CBT demonstrated continued improvement at 6-month follow-up (within-group $d = 1.55$), whereas those who received exposure alone did not (within-group $d = 0.68$). Furthermore, change in estimations of social consequences mediated symptom reduction in *both* active conditions at posttreatment (see Rodebaugh et al., 2004). However, Hofmann concludes that *direct* cognitive interventions have a more durable effect on social anxiety disorder. Mörtberg, Karlsson, Fyring, and Sundin (2006) showed that cognitive behavioral group therapy (based on Heimberg and Becker's treatment) may also be efficacious when offered in an intensive format. Clients in the active CBT condition who met with therapists every day for 2 weeks evidenced significant reductions on a number of clinician-administered and self-report measures, whereas those in the wait-list control condition generally did not. However the pre- to posttreatment within-group effect size ($d = 0.56$) for the CBT condition appears to be more modest than the large effect sizes reported earlier.

Stangier, Heidenreich, Peitz, Lauterbach, and Clark (2003) compared individual CBT (similar to that offered by D. M. Clark et al., 2003) with group CBT and waitlist conditions. The individual treatment was more effective, demonstrating a large effect size ($d = 1.17$) compared to the waitlist condition, whereas the group treatment evidenced a medium effect size compared to the waitlist condition ($d = 0.55$). However, this is the only study indicating the superiority of individual over group treatment for social anxiety disorder.

Considered altogether, meta-analyses and more recently published studies have demonstrated with great consistency that cognitive behavioral treatments are particularly efficacious, with a majority of studies reporting large effect sizes. Comparisons of CBT treatment components have generally found that cognitive restructuring plus exposure is associated with nonsignificantly better outcome; however, comparing these two components separately provides less clear, and arguably less useful, information. Individual and group formats have both been shown to be highly efficacious; however, direct comparison of these treatment formats does not suggest a clear favorite.

Therefore, given the promise of CBT, researchers have also investigated and identified a number of predictors of positive CBT outcome. First, expectancy for improvement is significantly associated with actual improvement in treatment. For instance, the expectancy ratings of individuals with social anxiety disorder beginning CBT contributed to the prediction of posttreatment outcome above and beyond the contribution of pretreatment symptom severity. Furthermore, pretreatment expectancy was a significant predictor of self-reported social anxiety and depression at treatment's end (Safren, Heimberg, & Juster, 1997).

A major treatment component of CBT involves between-session exercises intended to facilitate the generalization of treatment gains, and these assignments typically include cognitive restructuring and exposure exercises (see Hope et al., 2000). Adherence to such prescribed homework assignments has been associated with positive treatment outcome, and evidence has suggested that adherence to particular components of CBT homework assignments may be differentially predictive of outcome. For instance, adherence to between-session cognitive restructuring and exposure assignments predicts posttreatment outcome better than adherence to assignments early in treatment related more to psychoeducation (Leung & Heimberg, 1996). However, other studies have not replicated these effects (Edelmann & Chambless, 1995; Woody & Adessky, 2002).

Severity of social anxiety disorder has also been associated with improvement during CBT. Although the magnitude of change on outcome measures across subtypes has been relatively uniform, persons with generalized social anxiety disorder are nevertheless more impaired both before and after treatment (e.g., E. J. Brown, Heimberg, & Juster, 1995). Brown et al. reported that an additional diagnosis of avoidant personality disorder had little impact on the outcome for CBT for clients with generalized social anxiety disorder; however, in another study, an additional diagnosis of avoidant personality disorder predicted poorer treatment response (Feske et al., 1995).

Comorbid Axis I conditions are also important factors in treatment response. Erwin, Heimberg, Juster, and Mindlin (2002) found that clients with social anxiety disorder and a comorbid anxiety disorder responded to CBT similarly to clients with social anxiety disorder alone. However, Chambless, Tran, and Glass (1997) found that depression was a significant predictor of outcome in CBT for social anxiety disorder because depressed clients were less likely to improve than nondepressed clients. Erwin et al. (2002) found that depressed social anxiety disorder clients improved in a fashion similar to those without depression, although they were more severely impaired than nondepressed individuals both before and after treatment.

Finally, anger is a significant predictor of CBT outcome as well. In a study by Erwin, Heimberg, Schneier, and Liebowitz (2003), individuals with high levels of trait anger were more likely to terminate treatment prematurely. Also, levels of state and trait anger and anger suppression before treatment were significantly correlated with posttreatment severity of social anxiety.

COGNITIVE BEHAVIORAL THERAPY VERSUS PHARMACOTHERAPY

Clearly, CBT and pharmacotherapy are efficacious treatments for social anxiety disorder; however, data comparing these treatments are mixed. Gould et al.'s (1997) meta-analysis demonstrated that both approaches were significantly more efficacious than control conditions, although not different from one another. However, the more recent meta-analysis by Fedoroff and Taylor (2001) suggested that benzodiazepines are more efficacious than CBT (although SSRIs and MAOIs are not).

Studies directly comparing CBT and pharmacotherapy are few. Heimberg et al. (1998) compared cognitive behavioral group therapy (see Heimberg & Becker, 2002) with phenelzine sulfate, pill placebo, and a credible psychological control condition (Educational Supportive Group Psychotherapy). At posttreatment (week 12), CBT and phenelzine demonstrated comparable rates of response (75% and 77% of treatment completers, respectively), which was significantly greater than both placebo conditions. Despite similar response rates at the end of treatment, participants receiving phenelzine met criteria for treatment response earlier than those receiving CBT. After 6 weeks of treatment, over half of those receiving phenelzine met response criteria, compared to just 28% of CBT participants. However after a 6-month maintenance phase and a 6-month follow-up period, half of those who had received phenelzine had relapsed, whereas this was the case for only 17% of CBT participants (Liebowitz et al., 1999). Thus phenelzine worked faster to reduce social anxiety symptoms, but those who received CBT were more likely to enjoy lasting benefits.

Davidson et al. (2004) utilized a five-arm design to compare group CBT (see earlier discussion), fluoxetine, pill placebo, CBT plus fluoxetine, and CBT plus placebo. All active treatment conditions outperformed pill placebo, but none of the active treatments performed differently. As also reported by Heimberg et al. (1998), participants receiving fluoxetine improved more quickly than those receiving CBT. Follow-up data were collected but are not yet available. A number of other studies have also reported direct comparisons of CBT and pharmacotherapy; however, they are complicated by self-exposure instructions in the medication condition or lack of control groups, and thus are not reviewed here (e.g., D. M. Clark et al., 2003; Gerlernter et al., 1991; Otto et al., 2000).

COGNITIVE BEHAVIORAL THERAPY PLUS PHARMACOTHERAPY

Independently, CBT and pharmacotherapy have received much support; however, there are fewer data to support the combination of these two approaches. Although it is apparent that some medication treatments may work more quickly than CBT (e.g., Davidson et al., 2004; Heimberg et al., 1998), the existing evidence for the utility of their combination is mixed. Studies have drawn various conclusions suggesting that the addition of pharmacotherapy to CBT performs no better than a placebo (e.g., D. B. Clark & Agras, 1991), is better than a placebo but no better than the individual treatments alone (Davidson et al., 2004), or is modestly beneficial (Heimberg, 2003). In addressing these findings, Rodebaugh and Heimberg (2005) have suggested that the simple combination of treatments is not likely to be as efficacious as a combination that capitalizes on the each treatment's strengths. For example, initial pharmacological treatment might allow for faster symptom reduction, and the addition of CBT might confer increased protection against relapse, especially if medication could be tapered before the termination of CBT.

Case Description

Presenting Problem and Initial Assessment

Melissa was a 27-year-old Caucasian woman who worked as a bank teller. She reported that she experienced much anxiety in the presence of other people and expressed interest in a course of CBT for social anxiety. Melissa had been taking

(continued)

paroxetine for social anxiety disorder for the previous 3 months. However, her social anxiety was severe enough to require additional therapeutic attention.

Before Melissa began taking paroxetine, she had met with a diagnostician who administered the ADIS-IV-L and determined that she met criteria for generalized social anxiety disorder. During the ADIS interview, Melissa had endorsed fears of a number of social interaction and performance situations, such as attending parties, speaking up at meetings and classes, public speaking, dating situations, initiating and maintaining conversations, and being assertive. Melissa did not meet criteria for any other current Axis I disorders; however, she had experienced two previous episodes of major depression.

Melissa explained that, although paroxetine was generally successful in decreasing some of her anxiety in social situations (e.g., she described herself as slightly "more talkative" with coworkers), she continued to feel significantly nervous about the "major stuff" such as dating and occasions when others might directly observe her performance, such in as public speaking situations. Although Melissa endorsed a modest degree of overt avoidance in these situations, she admitted that she often engaged in a number of safety behaviors such as rehearsing formal speeches excessively in anticipation of their presentation. Melissa expressed hope that CBT would help her make additional progress.

Before CBT, Melissa's symptoms of social anxiety and depression were assessed. An independent evaluator administered the social phobia module of the ADIS-IV (current version; T. A. Brown, DiNardo, & Barlow, 1994) and determined that Melissa still met diagnostic criteria for social anxiety disorder. Melissa endorsed ongoing fear and avoidance of participating at meetings and classes, formal speaking, dating, and initiating and maintaining conversations. Melissa feared that she would give others a negative impression of herself. She received a score of 34 on the LSAS, surpassing the clinical cutoff recommended by Mennin et al. (2002), and a rating of 4 on the Clinical Global Impressions Scale (CGI, severity version; Guy, 1976; Zaider, Heimberg, Fresco, Schneier, & Liebowitz, 2003), indicating moderate severity of symptoms and life impairment. Melissa also completed several questionnaires, including the Social Interaction Anxiety Scale, the Social Phobia Scale, and the Brief Fear of Negative Evaluation Scale (Leary, 1983) on which she endorsed moderate to high levels of fear of interacting with, performing in front of, and being judged negatively by others. Based on this evaluation, individual CBT for was recommended.

Course of Treatment

Melissa's treatment was based on the cognitive behavioral model of social anxiety disorder proposed by Rapee and Heimberg (1997; see earlier discussion) and utilized the individual CBT protocol developed by Hope et al. (2000). Melissa and her therapist addressed the major domains of her anxiety experience, particularly the physiological, cognitive, and behavioral components. Melissa explained that despite her improvements with paroxetine, her feared social situations continued to cause heart pounding, blushing, shaking, and dizziness. She found these symptoms distressing in themselves, but she was additionally concerned that they would be noticeable to others in social situations (i.e., interaction partners or audience members), which would inevitably lead them to think less of her. Melissa also reported that her physiological symptoms were very distressing and impaired her performance in social situations.

Melissa and her therapist also identified the cognitive components of her anxiety. Melissa saw her lack of confidence in social domains as "a major problem" in her life, leading to her feeling anxious and invariably coming across to others as ineffectual. Unlike many clients with social anxiety disorder, Melissa recognized that many of her thoughts during social situations were negative, some which may have been exaggerations. However, she also reported that as her arousal increased in social situations, such negative thoughts seemed inevitable and unstoppable, and they interfered with her ability to concentrate on the social demands of the situation.

Behaviorally, Melissa engaged in a modest degree of overt avoidance; however, she reported that she could deliver a public speech (her greatest social fear) in order to avoid significant professional consequences. Similarly, she spoke with strangers and attended parties despite great anxiety. Melissa and her therapist identified several forms of subtle avoidance (e.g., avoiding eye contact; speaking only to close friends at parties) as well as safety behaviors (e.g., speaking to unfamiliar people but only about clearly innocuous, "small talk" topics instead of personally relevant, inherently more sensitive issues). Importantly, as Melissa and her therapist took inventory of behaviors meant to preclude evaluation by others, Melissa remarked that she realized that such behaviors actually worked *against* her goal of engaging in enjoyable social interactions.

With Melissa's understanding of the cognitive behavioral model of social anxiety disorder in place, she and her therapist began mapping particular areas of intervention. They generated a list of specific social situations that were difficult for her. Subsequently, the level of anxiety aroused by each situation was rated (scored on a scale ranging from 0, "no anxiety" to 100 "highest anxiety imaginable") as was Melissa's tendency to avoid each situation (ranging from 0, "never" to 100 "always"). Incorporating such affective and behavioral information, Melissa ranked these situations on a hierarchy. Unsurprisingly, Melissa described "giving a public speech" to be her "worst" situation, which she assigned an anxiety rating of 96 and an avoidance rating of 98. Also ranked high on Melissa's hierarchy were other social performance tasks such as "speaking in an informal group," as well as social interaction situations such as "small talk with authority figures" and "small talk with coworkers." Thus with the establishment of her hierarchy, Melissa was prepared for the next major step in the treatment program: identifying and challenging her negative automatic thoughts in these situations.

Melissa realized early in treatment that her socially relevant catastrophic thinking and overgeneralizations were not rooted in logic. These illogical thoughts increased her anxiety, decreased her confidence, and, ultimately, interfered with her performance. Indeed, many of Melissa's thoughts in anticipation of and during social situations were negative, seemingly spontaneous, and based on errors of assumption, interpretation, and biased attention. One of the first goals of the cognitive component to treatment was to practice identifying these thoughts and the lapses in logic associated with them. Therefore, Melissa was

(continued)

instructed about the types of thinking errors (J. S. Beck, 1995) most common to social anxiety disorder. Melissa identified several errors common in her thinking about social situations, which included making predictions about what she "knows" will happen in social situations (i.e., fortune telling), placing social demands on herself with the understanding that failure to meet those demands will result in certain negative evaluation (i.e., should/must statements), assuming anxiety in circumscribed situations (e.g., speaking to her supervisor) was equivalent to complete social ineptitude (i.e., overgeneralizing/catastrophizing) and labeling herself or her actions with a negative, descriptive shorthand (e.g., awkward and boring). As one of their first exercises, Melissa and her therapist reflected on a recent experience in which she approached a superior at work to speak with her casually. Melissa listed several thoughts that she had in anticipation of that encounter, including "She does not like me," "I'm nobody," and "I should be friendlier." Melissa successfully identified several thinking errors in these automatic thoughts such that she predicted negative outcomes of events that had yet to occur, assumed she knew what her boss was thinking, labeled herself with emotionally loaded negative terms, and placed ambiguous demands on herself. Importantly, Melissa recognized that as the terrifying conversation unfolded, she did not question the accuracy of her negative automatic thoughts but believed them to be true. Accepting that she was unimportant and disliked by the person with whom she was speaking precipitated a significant spike in her anxiety before and during the interaction, also driving her strong desire to escape the conversation and to avoid similar interactions in the future. With this realization, Melissa and her therapist began to consider more adaptive (and accurate) methods for appraising social situations.

As therapy progressed, Melissa and her therapist considered that there may have been more lingering anxiety related to social interaction than was initially apparent. Therefore, they directed many of their cognitive restructuring efforts toward this domain. As discussed earlier, an ongoing concern for Melissa was that she would bore others or that they would find her uninteresting. Given the causal link between negative thinking and the exacerbation of her anxiety, Melissa felt quite anxious every day at work because she was unavoidably confronted with social interaction with coworkers. Therefore, the importance of cognitive change in this area was clear, and Melissa made much progress with skills she acquired in cognitive restructuring. Specifically, Melissa's therapist provided her with a number of questions for the purpose of challenging her negative cognitions. These questions were aimed at underscoring the illogic of thinking errors and thus provided Melissa with ammunition to reappraise inherently anxiety-provoking thoughts from the outset. For example, in instances in which Melissa told herself that she was "boring" and that her coworkers would find her "uninteresting," she became adept at identifying thinking errors and, with the help of her therapist, applying disputing questions. Particularly helpful to Melissa were coping challenges such as "What evidence do I have that I will not be interesting?" and "Is it possible that the quality of the interaction could fall on a continuum between good and bad?" Melissa recognized that there were a number of alternative perspectives that she might take in any single social encounter and that the perspectives facilitated by empirical social appraisal less consistently resulted in the assessment of a social situation as dangerous, reducing her anxiety. Finally, she and her therapist consolidated the empirical conclusions made during the challenging of her automatic thoughts and generated a short "rational response." Melissa's therapist instructed her in using this response as an adaptive and positive counter to her habitual, negative automatic thoughts; thus, it was intended as a short reminder of the evidence generated during cognitive restructuring.

With continued cognitive restructuring, Melissa and her therapist recognized themes that seemed to arise in her listing of automatic thoughts, specifically involving labeling herself as boring and inadequate, as well as placing demands on herself that typically required her to perform perfectly. In an exercise described as "peeling the onion" (Hope et al., 2000), Melissa and her therapist came to agree that Melissa's automatic thoughts may be closely related to a core belief of "I am inadequate and unacceptable. Therefore, I must always work exceptionally hard to ensure that others will not recognize this fundamental flaw." Melissa and her therapist discussed the notion that her core belief itself was contingent on thinking errors, as well as the impact it had on her anxiety and her efforts to compensate for her perceived deficits.

Melissa made further improvements in the cognitive domain with the addition of the behavioral component of treatment, which may be most clearly illustrated with regard to her exposure to social performance situations, which she continued to endorse as her most feared and avoided social domain. Exposure began with the role-playing of situations that evoked a moderate amount of anxiety and progressed to more anxiety-evoking situations.

Melissa and her therapist concluded each session with an agreement on in vivo exposures intended to transfer her in-session gains (acquired through role play and subsequent cognitive restructuring) to similar situations in her life, with their potentially greater social consequences and rewards. A particularly important experience in this capacity involved attending a job-related training and orientation seminar. With the employment of her increasingly sophisticated cognitive skills, Melissa was able to refute several automatic thoughts such as "I don't belong here" and "they are all smarter than I" with rational responses such as "I am capable of professional achievement." She was able to reappraise the situation quickly, and as a result, she was able to enjoy the opportunity to network and learn new skills without the added pressure she typically put on herself.

By her fourteenth session, Melissa continued to demonstrate successful identification and refutation of her automatic thoughts (and by this late point in treatment, her core belief) through behavioral exposure exercises. In addition, she had made substantial stepwise progress toward the top of her fear and avoidance hierarchy and was ready and willing to attempt a social activity that she ranked at the top early in treatment. Melissa and her therapist agreed on an exposure that involved the delivery of a formal speech to a small audience. In their discussion of the logistics of the exercise, she established several factors that would be challenging for her but that would allow for maximal empirical testing of cognitions she had not yet abandoned. For example, Melissa was to stand at

(continued)

a podium and address an audience comprised of a number of highly educated individuals (which ultimately included a PhD psychologist, several doctoral students, and a smaller number of undergraduates). In addition, Melissa chose to speak about a topic concerning a professional plan that she hoped to institute at work. The nature of the topic posed a significant challenge because it was related not just to her competence at work, but to her own personal creativity. The sensitivity of the topic and the potentially critical audience proved ideal for challenging Melissa's core belief and more intractable automatic thoughts.

As usual, Melissa and her therapist targeted negative thoughts and thinking errors. In anticipation of the speech, Melissa experienced such thoughts as "I will forget something" and "If I make mistakes, I am a failure as a person." With identification of thinking errors and the application of disputing questions, she was successful in generating an empirical rational response, which in this case was "I don't need to be perfect." Also, as prescribed in the treatment protocol, she and her therapist agreed on a behavioral goal, something Melissa could plan to achieve in her speech that would test her assumptions about perfectionism. She decided to "take a risk" during the exposure by stating something that she knew to be incorrect and later calling attention to her "error."

Exposure itself began with Melissa taking the podium in front of the audience and immediately beginning her speech. At the end of each minute, her therapist prompted Melissa to write down her current level of anxiety (rated on a 0–100 scale) as well as to utter aloud her rational response (audience members simultaneously recorded their ratings of her apparent anxiety). During the speech, Melissa referred to a term in her plan that she did not fully understand, meeting her behavioral goal.

After the speech, Melissa took several questions from the audience and subsequently shared her anxiety ratings with her therapist and the audience. In turn, members of the audience shared their ratings as well. As can be seen in Figure 9.1, Melissa's anxiety ratings were considerably higher than the average

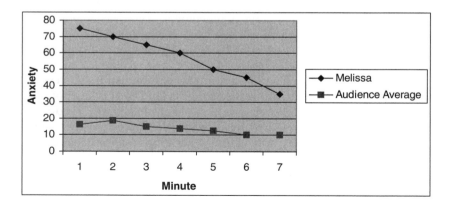

Figure 9.1 Comparing Melissa's ratings of her anxiety and those of her audience during exposure to her most feared social situation.

ratings made by the audience. Although her arousal demonstrated relatively linear habituation, her lowest rating was nearly 15 points higher than the highest average rating from the audience. Immediately after the exposure and again in her later sessions, she expressed great surprise that, despite the subjectively intense and almost intolerable level of anxiety that she experienced during her speech, audience members were not able to detect more than minor arousal that might otherwise be attributable to excitement (rather than paralyzing fear). Although she experienced several automatic negative thoughts during the speech, Melissa reported that she felt substantially less anxious as she recited her rational response. Importantly, the exposure allowed her to challenge her assumptions about perfectionism and her more global sense of competence in an experimental manner.

In her final (sixteenth) session, Melissa and her therapist re-rated the social situations from her fear and avoidance hierarchy. Her ratings dropped 70 to 80 points in her previously most feared situations. Particularly encouraging to Melissa was the recognition that she only rated two situations above 50 anxiety points ("dealing with unreasonable people" and "giving a speech"). Although she still found these situations to be somewhat difficult, she was quite confident that she would not feel the need to avoid them and that she was likely to excel in each if given the opportunity.

Termination and Posttreatment Assessment

When treatment had ended, Melissa was again evaluated by an independent assessor on a number of social anxiety measures. On the social phobia module of the ADIS (current version), she no longer met the *DSM-IV* criteria for social anxiety disorder. Additionally, she evidenced reductions in LSAS, CGI, and SPS scores. Furthermore, Melissa was evaluated 6 months after the termination of her treatment. At that time, she had maintained the gains she made in treatment and even continued to improve on a number of measures (e.g., LSAS and CGI). The case presented in this chapter was unique in some of the idiosyncratic concerns presented by Melissa. However, the goal of the case presentation is to bring to life the improvements made by clients in the growing number of studies that support the efficacy of CBT for social anxiety disorder. In Melissa's case, cognitive restructuring of problematic patterns of thinking coupled with empirical testing of beliefs through exposure to anxiety-evoking stimuli was particularly effective. Importantly, such gains can be made in just several months—Melissa demonstrated significant improvement in her anxiety and her life in only 16 sessions. Although these gains were achieved in a relatively short period of time, she continued to improve in the several months that followed.

REFERENCES

Alden, L. E., & Wallace, S. T. (1995). Social phobia and social appraisal in successful and unsuccessful social interactions. *Behavior Research and Therapy, 33,* 497–505.

American Psychiatric Association. (1980). *Diagnostic and statistical manual of mental disorders* (3rd ed.). Washington, DC: Author.

American Psychiatric Association. (1987). *Diagnostic and statistical manual of mental disorders* (3rd ed., rev.). Washington, DC: Author.

American Psychiatric Association. (1994). *Diagnostic and statistical manual of mental disorders* (4th ed.). Washington, DC: Author.

Amir, N., Foa, E. B., & Coles, M. E. (1998). Negative interpretation bias in social phobia. *Behavior Research and Therapy, 36,* 959–970.

Antony, M. M., Coons, M. J., McCabe, R. E., Ashbaugh, A., & Swinson, R. P. (2006). Psychometric properties of the Social Phobia Inventory: Further evaluation. *Behavior Research and Therapy, 44,* 1177–1185.

Asmundson, G. J. G., & Stein, M. B. (1994). Selective processing of social threat in patients with generalized social phobia: Evaluation using a dot-probe paradigm. *Journal of Anxiety Disorders, 8,* 107–117.

Ballenger, J., Davidson, J., Lecrubier, Y., Nutt, D., Bobes, J., Beidel, D., et al. (1998). Consensus statement on social anxiety disorder from the International Consensus Group on Depression and Anxiety. *Journal of Clinical Psychiatry, 59,* 54–60.

Beck, A. T., & Emery, G. (1985). *Anxiety disorders and phobias: A cognitive perspective.* New York: Basic Books.

Beck, J. S. (1995). *Cognitive therapy: Basics and beyond.* New York: Guilford Press.

Bernstein, D. A., Borkovec, T. D., & Hazlett-Stevens, H. (2000). *New directions in progressive relaxation training: A guidebook for helping professionals.* Westport, CT: Praeger.

Blanco, C., Antia, S. X., & Liebowitz, M. R. (2002). Pharmacological treatment of social anxiety disorder. *Biological Psychiatry, 51,* 109–120.

Bögels, S. M., & Mansell, W. (2004). Attention processes in the maintenance and treatment of social phobia: Hypervigilance, avoidance and self-focused attention. *Clinical Psychology Review, 24,* 827–856.

Bögels, S. M., Sijbers, G. F. V., & Voncken, M. (2006). Mindfulness and task concentration training for social phobia: A pilot study. *Journal of Cognitive Psychotherapy, 20,* 33–44.

Brown, E. J., Heimberg, R. G., & Juster, H. R. (1995). Social phobia subtype and avoidant personality disorder: Effect on severity of social phobia, impairment, and outcome of cognitive-behavioral treatment. *Behavior Therapy, 26,* 467–486.

Brown, E. J., Turovsky, J., Heimberg, R. G., Juster, H. R., Brown, T. A., & Barlow, D. H. (1997). Validation of the Social Interaction Anxiety Scale and the Social Phobia Scale across the anxiety disorders. *Psychological Assessment, 9,* 21–27.

Brown, T. A., DiNardo, P., & Barlow, D. H. (1994). *Anxiety Disorders Interview Schedule for DSM-IV (ADIS-IV).* New York: Oxford University Press.

Brown, T. A., DiNardo, P. A., Lehman, C. L., & Campbell, L. A. (2001). Reliability of DSM-IV anxiety and mood disorders: Implications for the classification of emotional disorders. *Journal of Abnormal Psychology, 110,* 49–58.

Bruch, M. A., & Heimberg, R. G. (1994). Differences in perceptions of parental and personal characteristics between generalized and nongeneralized social phobics. *Journal of Anxiety Disorders, 8,* 155–168.

Bruch, M. A., Heimberg, R. G., Berger, P., & Collins, T. M. (1989). Social phobia and perceptions of early prenatal and personal characteristics. *Anxiety Research, 2,* 57–65.

Carver, C. S., & Scheier, M. F. (1981). *Attention and self-regulation: A control-theory approach to human behavior.* New York: Springer-Verlag.

Chambless, D. L., & Hope, D. A. (1996). Cognitive approaches to the psychopathology and treatment of social phobia. In P. M. Salkovskis (Ed.), *Frontiers of cognitive therapy* (pp. 345–382). New York: Guilford Press.

Chambless, D. L., Tran, G. Q., & Glass, C. R. (1997). Predictors of response to cognitive-behavioral group therapy for social phobia. *Journal of Anxiety Disorders, 11*, 221–240.

Clark, D. B., & Agras, W. S. (1991). The assessment and treatment of performance anxiety in musicians. *American Journal of Psychiatry, 148*, 598–605.

Clark, D. M. (2001). A cognitive perspective on social phobia. In W. R. Crozier & L. E. Alden (Eds.), *International handbook of social anxiety: Concepts, research and interventions relating to the self and shyness* (pp. 405–430). New York: Wiley.

Clark, D. M., Ehlers, A., Hackmann, A., McManus, F., Fennell, M., Grey, N., et al. (2006). Cognitive therapy versus exposure and applied relaxation in social phobia: A randomized controlled trial. *Journal of Consulting and Clinical Psychology, 74*, 568–578.

Clark, D. M., Ehlers, A., McManus, F., Hackmann, A., Fennell, M., Campbell, H., et al. (2003). Cognitive therapy versus fluoxetine in generalized social phobia: A randomized placebo controlled trial. *Journal of Consulting and Clinical Psychology, 71*, 1058–1067.

Clark, D. M., & Wells, A. (1995). A cognitive model of social phobia. In R. G. Heimberg, M. Liebowitz, D. A. Hope, & F. R. Schneier (Eds.), *Social phobia: Diagnosis, assessment and treatment* (pp. 69–93). New York: Guilford Press.

Cohen, J. (1988). *Statistical power analysis for the behavioral sciences* (2nd ed.). Hillsdale, NJ: Erlbaum.

Coles, M. E., & Heimberg, R. G. (2002). Memory biases in the anxiety disorders: Current status. *Clinical Psychology Review, 22*, 587–627.

Coles, M. E., Turk, C. L., Heimberg, R. G., & Fresco, D. M. (2001). Effects of varying levels of anxiety within social situations: Relationships to memory perspective and attributions in social phobia. *Behavior Research and Therapy, 39*, 651–665.

Connor, K. M., Davidson, J. R. T., Churchill, L. E., Sherwood, A., Foa, E. B., & Weisler, R. H. (2000). Psychometric properties of the Social Phobia Inventory (SPIN): A new self-rating scale. *British Journal of Psychiatry, 176*, 379–386.

Connor, K. M., Kobak, K. A., Churchill, L. E., Katzelnick, D., & Davidson, J. R. T. (2001). Mini-SPIN: A brief screening assessment for generalized social anxiety disorder. *Depression and Anxiety, 14*, 137–140.

Cox, B. J., & Swinson, R. P. (1995). Assessment and measurement. In M. B. Stein (Ed.), *Social phobia: Clinical and research perspectives* (pp. 261–291). Washington, DC: American Psychiatric Press.

Davidson, J. R. T., Foa, E. B., Huppert, J. D., Keefe, F. J., Franklin, M. E., Compton, J. S., et al. (2004). Fluoxetine, comprehensive cognitive behavioral therapy, and placebo in generalized social phobia. *Archives of General Psychiatry, 61*, 1005–1013.

Davidson, J. R. T., Miner, C. M., DeVeaughGeiss, J., Tupler, L. A., Colket, J. T., & Potts, N. L. S. (1997). The Brief Social Phobia Scale: A psychometric evaluation. *Psychological Medicine, 27*, 161–166.

Davidson, J. R. T., Potts, N. L. S., Richichi, E. A., Krishnan, R. R., Ford, S. M., Smith, R. D., et al. (1991). The Brief Social Phobia Scale. *Journal of Clinical Psychiatry, 52*, 48–51.

DiNardo, P. A., Brown, T. A., & Barlow, D. H. (1994). *Anxiety Disorders Interview Schedule for DSM-IV: Lifetime version* (ADIS-IV-L). New York: Oxford University Press.

Edelmann, R. E., & Chambless, D. L. (1995). Adherence during session and homework in cognitive-behavioral group treatment of social phobia. *Behavior Research and Therapy, 33*, 573–577.

Embretson, S. E., & Reise, S. P. (2000). *Item response theory for psychologists.* Mahwah, NJ: Erlbaum.

Erwin, B. A., Heimberg, R. G., Juster, H., & Mindlin, M. (2002). Comorbid anxiety and mood disorders among persons with social anxiety disorder. *Behavior Research and Therapy, 40*, 19–35.

Erwin, B. A., Heimberg, R. G., Marx, B. P., & Franklin, M. E. (in press). Traumatic and so-cially stressful life events among persons with social anxiety disorder. *Journal of Anxiety Disorders.*

Erwin, B. A., Heimberg, R. G., Schneier, F. R., & Liebowitz, M. R. (2003). Anger experience and expression in social anxiety disorder: Pretreatment profile and predictors of attrition and response to cognitive-behavioral treatment. *Behavior Therapy, 34,* 331–350.

Fedoroff, I. C., & Taylor, S. T. (2001). Psychological and pharmacological treatments of social phobia: A meta-analysis. *Journal of Clinical Psychopharmacology, 21,* 311–324.

Feske, U., & Chambless, D. L. (1995). Cognitive behavioral versus exposure only treatment for social phobia: A meta-analysis. *Behavior Therapy, 26,* 695–720.

First, M. B., Spitzer, R. L., Gibbon, M., & Williams, J. (2002). *Structured Clinical Interview for DSM-IV Axis I Disorders—Patient Edition (SCID-I/P).* New York: Biometrics Research Department, New York State Psychiatric Institute.

Foa, E. B., Franklin, M. E., Perry, K. J., & Herbert, J. D. (1996). Cognitive biases in generalized social phobia. *Journal of Abnormal Psychology, 105,* 433–439.

Foa, E. B., & Kozak, M. J. (1986). Emotional processing of fear: Exposure to corrective informa-tion. *Psychological Bulletin, 99,* 20–35.

Fresco, D. M., Coles, M. E., Heimberg, R. G., Liebowitz, M. R., Hami, S., Stein, M. B., et al. (2001). The Liebowitz Social Anxiety Scale: A comparison of the psychometric properties of the self-report and clinician-administered formats. *Psychological Medicine, 31,* 1025–1035.

Frisch, M., Cornell, J., Villanueva, M., & Retzlaff, P. (1992). Clinical validation of the Quality of Life Inventory: A measure of life satisfaction for use in treatment planning and outcome assessment. *Psychological Assessment, 4,* 92–101.

Fydrich, T., Chambless, D. L., Perry, K. J., Buergner, F., & Beazley, M. B. (1998). Behavioral assessment of social performance: A rating system for social phobia. *Behavior Research and Therapy, 36,* 995–1010.

Fyer, A. J., Mannuzza, S., Chapman, T. F., Liebowitz, M. R., & Klein, D. F. (1993). A direct family interview study of social phobia. *Archives of General Psychiatry, 50,* 286–293.

Gerlernter, C. S., Uhde, T. W., Cimbolic, P., Arnkoff, D. B., Vittone, B. J., Tancer, M. E., et al. (1991). Cognitive-behavioral and pharmacological treatments of social phobia: A controlled study. *Archives of General Psychiatry, 48,* 938–945.

Gilbert, P. (2001). Evolution and social anxiety: The role of attraction, social competition, and social hierarchies. *Psychiatric Clinics of North America, 24,* 723–751.

Gould, R. A., Buckminster, S., Pollack, M. H., Otto, M., & Yap, L. (1997). Cognitive-behavioral and pharmacological treatment for social phobia: A meta-analysis. *Clinical Psychology: Science and Practice, 4,* 291–306.

Grant, B. F., Hasin, D. S., Blanco, C., Stinson, F. S., Chou, S. P., Goldstein, R. B., et al. (2005). The epidemiology of social anxiety disorder in the United States: Results from the National Epidemiologic Survey on Alcohol and Related Conditions. *Journal of Clinical Psychiatry, 66,* 1351–1361.

Grant, B. F., Stinson, F. S., Dawson, D. A., Chou, S. P., Ruan, J., & Pickering, R. P. (2004). Co-occurrence of 12-month alcohol and drug use disorders and personality disorders in the United States: Results from the National Epidemiologic Survey on Alcohol and Related Conditions. *Archives of General Psychiatry, 61,* 361–368.

Guy, W. (Ed.). (1976). *ECDEU assessment for psychopharmacology* (Rev. ed.). Rockville, MD: NIMH Publication.

Hackmann, A., Clark, D. M., & McManus, F. (2000). Recurrent images and early memories in social phobia. *Behavior Research and Therapy, 38,* 601–610.

Hackmann, A., Surawy, C., & Clark, D. M. (1998). Seeing yourself through others' eyes: A study of spontaneously occurring images in social phobia. *Behavioral and Cognitive Psychotherapy, 26,* 3–12.

Hambrick, J. P., Turk, C. L., Heimberg, R. G., Schneier, F. R., & Liebowitz, M. R. (2004). Psychometric properties of disability measures among patients with social anxiety disorder. *Journal of Anxiety Disorders, 18,* 825–839.

Harb, G. C., Eng, W., Zaider, T., & Heimberg, R. G. (2003). Behavioral assessment of public speaking anxiety using a modified version of the Social Performance Rating Scale. *Behavior Research and Therapy, 41,* 1373–1380.

Hart, T. A., Jack, M. S., Turk, C. L., & Heimberg, R. G. (1999). Issues for the measurement of social anxiety disorder. In H. G. M. Westenberg & J. A. Den Boer (Eds.), *Social anxiety disorder* (pp. 133–155). Amsterdam: Syn-Thesis.

Heimberg, R. G. (1991). *Cognitive behavioral treatment of social phobia in a group setting: A treatment manual.* Unpublished treatment manual, Center for Stress and Anxiety Disorders, Albany, State University of New York.

Heimberg, R. G. (1996). Social phobia, avoidant personality disorder and the multiaxial conceptualization of interpersonal anxiety. In P. M. Salkovskis (Ed.), *Trends in cognitive and behavioral therapies* (pp. 43–61). Chichester, England: Wiley.

Heimberg, R. G. (2003, March). *Cognitive-behavioral and psychotherapeutic strategies for social anxiety disorder.* Paper presented at the annual meeting of the Anxiety Disorders Association of America, Toronto, Ontario, Canada.

Heimberg, R. G., & Becker, R. E. (2002). *Cognitive behavioral group therapy for social phobia: Basic mechanisms and clinical applications.* New York: Guilford Press.

Heimberg, R. G., & Holaway, R. M. (2006). *An examination of the known-groups validity of the Liebowitz Social Anxiety Scale.* Manuscript submitted for publication.

Heimberg, R. G., Horner, K. J., Juster, H. R., Safren, S. A., Brown, E. J., Schneier, F. R., et al. (1999). Psychometric properties of the Liebowitz Social Anxiety Scale. *Psychological Medicine, 29,* 199–212.

Heimberg, R. G., Liebowitz, M. R., Hope, D. A., Schneier, F. R., Holt, C. S., Welkowitz, L., et al. (1998). Cognitive behavioral group therapy versus phenelzine in social phobia: 12-week outcome. *Archives of General Psychiatry, 55,* 1133–1141.

Heimberg, R. G., Mueller, G. P., Holt, C. S., Hope, D. A., & Liebowitz, M. R. (1992). Assessment of anxiety in social interaction and being observed by others: The Social Interaction Anxiety Scale and the Social Phobia Scale. *Behavior Therapy, 23,* 53–73.

Herbert, J. D., Bellack, A. S., & Hope, D. A. (1991). Concurrent validity of the Social Phobia and Anxiety Inventory. *Journal of Psychopathology and Behavioral Assessment, 13,* 357–368.

Herbert, J. D., Gaudiano, B. A., Rheingold, A. A., Myers, V. H., Dalrymple, K., & Nolan, E. M. (2005). Social skills training augments the effectiveness of cognitive behavioral group therapy for social anxiety disorder. *Behavior Therapy, 36,* 125–138.

Hidalgo, R. B., Barnett, S. D., & Davidson, J. R. T. (2001). Social anxiety disorder in review: Two decades of progress. *International Journal of Neuropsychopharmacology, 4,* 279–298.

Hirsch, C. R., & Clark, D. M. (2004). Information-processing bias in social phobia. *Clinical Psychology Review, 24,* 799–825.

Hirsch, C. R., Mathews, A., & Clark, D. M. (2006). Imagery and interpretations in social phobia: Support for the combined cognitive biases hypothesis. *Behavior Therapy, 37.*

Hirsch, C. R., Mathews, A., Clark, D. M., Williams, R., & Morrison, J. (2003). Negative self-imagery blocks inferences. *Behavior Research and Therapy, 41,* 1383–1396.

Hofmann, S. G. (2004). Cognitive mediation of treatment change in social phobia. *Journal of Consulting and Clinical Psychology, 72,* 392–399.

Holle, C., Heimberg, R. G., Sweet, R. A., & Holt, C. S. (1995). Alcohol and caffeine use by social phobics: An initial inquiry into drinking patterns and behavior. *Behavior Research and Therapy, 33*, 561–566.

Holt, C. S., Heimberg, R. G., & Hope, D. A. (1992). Avoidant personality disorder and the generalized subtype of in social phobia. *Journal of Abnormal Psychology, 101*, 318–325.

Hope, D. A., Heimberg, R. G., Juster, H. R., & Turk, C. L. (2000). *Managing social anxiety: A cognitive-behavioral therapy approach.* New York: Oxford University Press.

Hope, D. A., Rapee, R. M., Heimberg, R. G., & Dombeck, M. J. (1990). Representation of the self in social phobia: Vulnerability to social threat. *Cognitive Therapy and Research, 14*, 177–189.

Jack, M. S., Heimberg, R. G., & Mennin, D. S. (1999). Situational panic attacks: Impact on distress and impairment among patients with social phobia. *Depression and Anxiety, 10*, 112–118.

Kagan, J., Reznick, J. S., & Snidman, N. (1988). Biological bases of childhood shyness. *Science, 240*, 167–171.

Kendler, K. S., Karkowski, L. M., & Prescott, C. A. (1999). Fears and phobias: Reliability and heritability. *Psychological Medicine, 29*, 539–553.

Kendler, K. S., Neale, M. C., Kessler, R. C., Heath, A. C., & Eaves, L. J. (1992). The genetic epidemiology of phobias in women: The interrelations of agoraphobia, social phobia, situational phobia, and simple phobia. *Archives of General Psychiatry, 49*, 273–281.

Kessler, R. C., Berglund, P. D., Demler, O., Olga, J. R., Merikangas, K. R., & Walters, E. E. (2005). Lifetime prevalence and age-of-onset distributions of DSM-IV disorders in the National Comorbidity Survey Replication. *Archives of General Psychiatry, 62*, 593–602.

Kessler, R. C., Chiu, W. T., Demler, O., Merikangas, K., & Walters, E. E. (2005). Prevalence, severity, and comorbidity of 12-month DSM-IV disorders in the National Comorbidity Survey Replication. *Archives of General Psychiatry, 62*, 617–627.

Kessler, R. C., Crum, R. M., Warner, L. A., Nelson, C. B., Schulenberg, J., & Anthony, J. C. (1997). Lifetime co-occurrence of DSM-III-R alcohol abuse and dependence with other psychiatric disorders in the National Comorbidity Survey. *Archives of General Psychiatry, 54*, 313–321.

Kollman, D. M., Brown, T. A., Liverant, G. I., & Hofmann, S. G. (2006). A taxometric investigation of the latent structure of social anxiety disorder in outpatients with anxiety and mood disorders. *Depression and Anxiety, 23*, 190–199.

Lang, P. J. (1977). Imagery in therapy: An information processing analysis of fear. *Behavior Therapy, 8*, 862–886.

Lang, P. J. (1979). A bio-informational theory of emotional imagery. *Psychophysiology, 16*, 495–512.

Leary, M. R. (1983). A brief version of the Fear of Negative Evaluation Scale. *Personality and Social Psychology Bulletin, 9*, 371–375.

Ledley, D. R., Storch, E. A., Coles, M. E., Heimberg, R. G., Moser, J., & Bravata, E. A. (2006). The relationship between childhood teasing and later interpersonal functioning. *Journal of Psychopathology and Behavioral Assessment, 28*, 33–40.

Leung, A. W., & Heimberg, R. G. (1996). Homework compliance, perceptions of control, and outcome of cognitive-behavioral treatment for social phobia. *Behavior Research and Therapy, 34*, 423–432.

Lieb, R., Wittchen, H. U., Hofler, M., Fuetsch, M., Stein, M. B., & Merikangas, K. R. (2000). Parental psychopathology, parenting styles, and the risk of social phobia in offspring. *Archives of General Psychiatry, 57*, 859–866.

Liebowitz, M. R. (1987). Social phobia. *Modern Problems in Pharmacopsychiatry, 22*, 141–173.

Liebowitz, M. R., Heimberg, R. G., Schneier, F. R., Hope, D. A., Davies, S., Holt, C. S., et al. (1999). Cognitive-behavioral group therapy versus phenelzine in social phobia: Long-term outcome. *Depression and Anxiety, 10*, 89–98.

Lucas, R. A., & Telch, M. J. (1993, November). *Group versus individual treatment of social phobia.* Paper presented at the annual meeting for the Association for the Advancement of Behavior Therapy, Atlanta, GA.

Magee, L., Rodebaugh, T. L., & Heimberg, R. G., (in press). Negative evaluation is the feared consequence of making others uncomfortable: A response to Rector, Kocovski, and Ryder. *Journal of Social and Clinical Psychology.*

Magee, W. J., Eaton, W. W., Wittchen, H. U., McGonagle, K. A., & Kessler, R. C. (1996). Agoraphobia, simple phobia, and social phobia in the National Comorbidity Survey. *Archives of General Psychiatry, 53,* 159–168.

Mannuzza, S., Schneier, F. R., Chapman, T. F., Liebowitz, M. R., Klein, D. F., & Fyer, A. J. (1995). Generalized social phobia: Reliability and validity. *Archives of General Psychiatry, 52,* 230–237.

Mattick, R. P., & Clarke, J. C. (1998). Development and validation of measures of social phobia scrutiny fear and social interaction anxiety. *Behavior Research and Therapy, 36,* 455–470.

McEwan, K. L., & Devins, G. M. (1983). Is increased arousal in social anxiety noticed by others? *Journal of Abnormal Psychology, 92,* 417–421.

Mennin, D. S., Fresco, D. M., Heimberg, R. G., Schneier, F. R., Davies, S. O., & Liebowitz, M. R. (2002). Screening for social anxiety disorder in the clinical setting: Using the Liebowitz Social Anxiety Scale. *Journal of Anxiety Disorders, 16,* 661–673.

Mogg, K., Philippot, P., & Bradley, B. P. (2004). Selective attention to angry faces in clinical social phobia. *Journal of Abnormal Psychology, 113,* 160–165.

Mörtberg, E., Karlsson, A., Fyring, C., & Sundin, O. (2006). Intensive cognitive-behavioral group treatment (CBGT) of social phobia: A randomized controlled study. *Journal of Anxiety Disorders, 20,* 646–660.

Okazaki, S., Liu, J. F., Longworth, S. L., & Minn, J. Y. (2002). Asian American-White American differences in expressions of social anxiety: A replication and extension. *Cultural Diversity and Ethnic Minority Psychology, 8,* 234–247.

Ost, L. G. (1987). Applied relaxation: Description of a coping technique and review of controlled studies. *Behavior Research and Therapy, 25,* 397–409.

Otto, M. W., Pollack, M. H., Gould, R. A., Worthington, J. J., McArdle, E. T., Rosenbaum, J. F., et al. (2000). A comparison of the efficacy of clonazepam and cognitive-behavioral group therapy for the treatment of social phobia. *Journal of Anxiety Disorders, 14,* 345–358.

Rapee, R. M., & Hayman, K. (1996). The effects of video feedback on the self-evaluation of performance in socially anxious subjects. *Behavior Research and Therapy, 34,* 315–322.

Rapee, R. M., & Heimberg, R. G. (1997). A cognitive-behavioral model of anxiety in social phobia. *Behavior Research and Therapy, 35,* 741–756.

Rapee, R. M., & Lim, L. (1992). Discrepancy between self- and observer ratings of performance in social phobics. *Journal of Abnormal Psychology, 101,* 728–731.

Ries, B. J., McNeil, D. W., Boone, M. L., Turk, C. L., Carter, L. E., & Heimberg, R. G. (1998). Assessment of contemporary social phobia verbal report instruments. *Behavior Research and Therapy, 36,* 983–994.

Rodebaugh, T. L., & Heimberg, R. G. (2005). Combined treatment for social anxiety disorder. *Journal of Cognitive Psychotherapy: An International Quarterly, 19,* 331–345.

Rodebaugh, T. L., Holaway, R. M., & Heimberg, R. G. (2004). The treatment of social anxiety disorder. *Clinical Psychology Review, 24,* 883–908.

Rodebaugh, T. L., Woods, C. M., Heimberg, R. G., Liebowitz, M. R., & Schneier, F. R. (2006). The factor structure and screening utility of the Social Interaction Anxiety Scale. *Psychological Assessment, 18,* 231–237.

Rosenbaum, J. F., Biederman, J., Pollock, R. A., & Hirshfeld, D. R. (1994). The etiology of social phobia. *Journal of Clinical Psychiatry, 55*(Suppl. 6), 10–16.

Roth, D. A., Antony, M. M., & Swinson, R. P. (2001). Interpretations for anxiety symptoms in social phobia. *Behavior Research and Therapy, 39,* 129–138.

Roth, D. A., Coles, M. E., & Heimberg, R. G. (2002). The relationship between memories for childhood teasing and anxiety and depression in adulthood. *Journal of Anxiety Disorders, 16,* 149–164.

Safren, S. A., Heimberg, R. G., Horner, K. J., Juster, H. R., Schneier, F. R., & Liebowitz, M. R. (1999). Factor structure of social fears: The Liebowitz Social Anxiety Scale. *Journal of Anxiety Disorders, 13,* 253–270.

Safren, S. A., Heimberg, R. G., & Juster, H. R. (1997). Client expectancies and their relationship to pretreatment symtomatology and outcome of cognitive-behavioral group treatment for social phobia. *Journal of Consulting and Clinical Psychology, 65,* 694–698.

Schneier, F. R., Heckelman, L. R., Garfinkel, R., Campeas, R., Fallon, B. A., Gitow, A., et al. (1994). Functional impairment in social phobia. *Journal of Clinical Psychiatry, 55,* 322–331.

Schneier, F. R., Johnson, J., Hornig, C. D., Liebowitz, M. R., & Weissman, M. M. (1992). Social phobia: Comorbidity and morbidity in an epidemiologic sample. *Archives of General Psychiatry, 49,* 282–288.

Scholing, A., & Emmelkamp, P. M. G. (1993). Exposure with and without cognitive therapy for generalized social phobia: Effects of individual and group treatment. *Behavior Research and Therapy, 31,* 667–681.

Schultz, L. T., Heimberg, R. G., Rodebaugh, T. L., Schneier, F. R., Liebowitz, M. R., & Telch, M. J. (2006). The Appraisal of Social Concerns Scale: Psychometric validation with a clinical sample of patients with social anxiety disorder. *Behavior Therapy, 37.*

Schwartz, C. E., Snidman, N., & Kagan, J. (1999). Adolescent social anxiety as an outcome of inhibited temperament in childhood. *Journal of the American Academy of Child and Adolescent Psychiatry, 38,* 1008–1015.

Scott, E. L., Heimberg, R. G., & Jack, M. S. (2000). Anxiety sensitivity in social phobia: A comparison between social phobics with and without panic attacks. *Depression and Anxiety, 12,* 189–192.

Sheehan, D. (1983). *The anxiety disease.* New York: Scribner.

Smail, P., Stockwell, T., Canter, S., & Hodgson, R. (1984). Alcohol dependence and phobic anxiety states: Pt. I. A prevalence study. *British Journal of Psychiatry, 144,* 53–57.

Stangier, U., Heidenreich, T., Peitz, M., Lauterbach, W., & Clark, D. M. (2003). Cognitive therapy for social phobia: Individual versus group treatment. *Behavior Research and Therapy, 41,* 991–1007.

Stein, M. B., Chartier, M. J., Hazen, A. L., Kozak, M. V., Tancer, M. E., Lander, S., et al. (1998). A direct interview family study of generalized social phobia. *American Journal of Psychiatry, 155,* 90–97.

Stopa, L., & Clark, D. M. (1993). Cognitive processes in social phobia. *Behavior Research and Therapy, 31,* 255–267.

Stopa, L., & Clark, D. M. (2000). Social phobia and interpretation of social events. *Behavior Research and Therapy, 38,* 273–283.

Suzuki, K., Takei, N., Kawai, M., Minabe, Y., & Mori, N. (2003). Is taijin kyofusho a culture-bound syndrome? *American Journal of Psychiatry, 160,* 1358.

Taylor, S. (1996). Meta-analysis of cognitive-behavioral treatments for social phobia. *Journal of Behavior Therapy and Experimental Psychiatry, 27,* 1–9.

Telch, M. J., Lucas, R. A., Smits, J. A. J., Powers, M. B., Heimberg, R. G., & Hart, T. (2004). Appraisal of social concerns: A cognitive assessment instrument for social phobia. *Depression and Anxiety, 19*, 217–224.

Tran, G. Q., Haaga, D. A. F., & Chambless, D. L. (1997). Expecting that alcohol use will reduce social anxiety moderates the relation between social anxiety and alcohol consumption. *Cognitive Therapy and Research, 21*, 535–553.

Trower, P., & Gilbert, P. (1989). New theoretical conceptions of social anxiety and social phobia. *Clinical Psychology Review, 9*, 19–35.

Turner, S. M., Beidel, D., Dancu, C., & Keys, D. (1986). Psychopathology of social phobia and comparison to avoidant personality disorder. *Journal of Abnormal Psychology, 95*, 389–394.

Turner, S. M., Beidel, D. C., Dancu, C. V., & Stanley, M. A. (1989). An empirically derived inventory to measure social fears and anxiety: The Social Phobia and Anxiety Inventory. *Psychological Assessment, 1*, 35–40.

Turner, S. M., Beidel, D. C., & Townsley, R. M. (1992). Social phobia: A comparison of specific and generalized subtype and avoidant personality disorder. *Journal of Abnormal Psychology, 101*, 326–331.

Van der Linden, G. J., Stein, D. J., & van Balkom, A. J. (2000). The efficacy of the selective serotonin reuptake inhibitors for social anxiety disorder (social phobia): A meta-analysis of randomized controlled trials. *International Clinical Psychopharmacology, 15*(Suppl. 2), S15–S23.

Vassilopoulos, S. (2005). Social anxiety and the effects of engaging in mental imagery. *Cognitive Therapy and Research, 29*, 261–277.

Veljaca, K., & Rapee, R. M. (1998). Detection of negative and positive audience behaviors by socially anxious subjects. *Behavior Research and Therapy, 36*, 311–321.

Ventura, J., Liberman, R. P., Green, M. F., Shaner, A., & Mintz, J. (1998). Training and quality assurance with Structured Clinical Interview for DSM-IV (SCID-I/P). *Psychiatry Research, 79*, 163–173.

Weeks, J. W., Heimberg, R. G., & Rodebaugh, T. L. (2006). *The Fear of Positive Evaluation Scale: Assessing a proposed cognitive component of social anxiety disorder.* Manuscript submitted for publication.

Weeks, J. W., Spokas, M. E., & Heimberg, R. G. (in press). Psychometric evaluation of the Mini-Social Phobia Inventory (Mini-SPIN) in a treatment-seeking sample. *Depression and Anxiety.*

Wells, A., Clark, D. M., & Ahmad, S. (1998). How do I look with my mind's eye: Perspective taking in social phobic imagery. *Behavior Research and Therapy, 36*, 631–634.

Wells, A., Clark, D. M., Salkovskis, P., Ludgate, J., Hackmann, A., & Gelder, M. (1995). Social phobia: The role of in-situation safety behaviors in maintaining anxiety and negative beliefs. *Behavior Therapy, 26*, 153–161.

Wells, A., & Papageorgiou, C. (1999). The observer perspective: Biased imagery in social phobia, agoraphobia, and blood/injury phobia. *Behavior Research and Therapy, 37*, 653–658.

Whisman, M., Sheldon, C., & Goering, P. (2000). Psychiatric disorders and dissatisfaction with social relationships: Does type of relationship matter? *Journal of Abnormal Psychology, 109*, 803–808.

Wittchen, H.-U., Stein, M. B., & Kessler, R. C. (1999). Social fears and social phobia in a community sample of adolescents and young adults: Prevalence, risk factors, and comorbidity. *Psychological Medicine, 29*, 309–323.

Wolpe, J. (1958). *Psychotherapy by reciprocal inhibition.* Palo Alto, CA: Stanford University Press.

Woody, S. R., & Adessky, R. S. (2002). Therapeutic alliance, group cohesion, and homework compliance during cognitive-behavioral group treatment of social phobia. *Behavior Therapy, 33,* 5–27.

Zaider, T. I., Heimberg, R. G., Fresco, D. M., Schneier, F. R., & Liebowitz, M. R. (2003). Evaluation of the Clinical Global Impression Scale among individuals with social anxiety disorder. *Psychological Medicine, 33,* 611–622.

Zaider, T. I., Heimberg, R. G., Roth, D. A., Hope, D. A., & Turk, C. L. (2003, November). *Individual CBT for social anxiety disorder: Preliminary findings.* Paper presented at the meeting of the Association for Advancement of Behavior Therapy, Boston.

CHAPTER 10

Obsessive-Compulsive Disorder

THRÖSTUR BJÖRGVINSSON AND JOHN HART

DESCRIPTION OF THE DISORDER

Obsessive-Compulsive Disorder (OCD) is often a severe, frequently debilitating anxiety disorder that affects approximately 2% of the population. The disorder affects males and females equally, with a modal onset of 6 to 15 years of age for males and 20 to 29 for females. The disorder appears cross-culturally around the world with similar prevalence rates. Although the etiology of OCD is not established, neurobiological, genetic, cognitive, and behavioral factors have been implicated (Abramowitz & Houts, 2006; Jenike, 1998). Obsessive-Compulsive Disorder is characterized by (a) obsessions, defined as unwanted, disturbing, and intrusive thoughts, images, or impulses that are generally seen by the individual as excessive, irrational, and ego-alien; and (b) compulsions, defined as repetitive behaviors and mental acts that neutralize obsessions and reduce emotional distress (American Psychiatric Association, 2000). Although in a limited number of cases a patient may have only obsessions or compulsions, the vast majority of patients experience both.

Obsessive-Compulsive Disorder has a substantial effect on sufferers' quality of life (Eisen, Mancebo, Pinto, Coles, & Rasmussen, 2006), in a recent 5-year prospective naturalistic study ($N = 197$), found that a third of the sample was unable to work due to psychopathology. This study found impairments compared to community norms in all domains of sufferers' life, including performance of household duties, subjective sense of well-being, social relationships, and the ability to enjoy leisure activities. Interestingly, this study found that the strongest correlation between impaired quality of life and severity of obsessions. Only the ability to work was associated with severity of compulsions. In fact, the World Health Organization (2001) has ranked OCD as one of the most debilitating disorders and estimated that in 2000 OCD was among the top 20 causes of illness-related disability for people ages 15 to 44.

The disorder is much more common than previously considered. Studies in the 1950s and 1960s indicated that OCD made up a small proportion of psychiatric patients, ranging from 1% to 4%. Currently it is estimated that 1% to 2% of the *general population* meets the diagnostic criteria for OCD at any given time, with a lifetime prevalence of 2% to 3% (Karno, Golding, Sorenson, & Burnam, 1988). Some epidemiological studies have suggested that OCD is the fourth most common mental disorder, following phobias, substance abuse, and Major Depression (Karno et al., 1988). Ranking disorders according to frequency is controversial due to various factors, such as accuracy of diagnosis and sample size, but the fact remains that OCD is a prevalent mental disorder. In addition, many patients struggle with comorbid conditions such as depression or substance abuse. While there is discrepancy in comorbidity rates reported by various studies, the most consistent finding is that 50% to 65% of patients with OCD have at least one additional mental disorder (e.g., Antony, Downie, & Swinson, 1998).

Intrusive obsessive thoughts and repetitive compulsive behaviors have intrigued people for centuries. A classic example is Shakespeare's powerful depiction of Lady Macbeth's guilt-driven hand-washing compulsion. One of the earliest descriptions of "obsessions" was provided by Westphal, a German neurologist who wrote a paper titled "Über Zwangsvorstellungen" in the year 1887. In that paper he defined obsessions as the following: "Thoughts which come to the foreground of consciousness in spite of and contrary to the will of the patient and which he is unable to suppress although he recognizes them as not characteristic of himself" (quoted in Reed, 1985, p. 1). Westphal considered obsessions likely either a prodromal or integral part of Schizophrenia. Although his ideas are now widely accepted as incorrect, his definition of obsessions was very much on target and still have utility well over a century later. As early as 1903, Janet described a successful treatment of compulsions, and Freud (1909/1955) presented an intriguing account of obsessional neurosis in his description of the Rat Man. Meyer (1966) was the first to describe the use of exposure and response techniques in two patients with OCD.

Although intrusive thoughts and compulsive ritual-like behaviors are observed in the general population, such phenomena are seen as pathological in OCD patients because they can be extremely time-consuming, cause enormous distress, and are often in direct contradiction to a person's sense of self, personal values, or life goals. Mataix-Cols, Rosario-Campos, and Leckman (2005) argue that OCD can be understood as a spectrum of overlapping syndromes that may coexist in any patient, be continuous with normal obsessive-compulsive phenomena, and extend beyond the traditional boundaries of OCD.

Typically, OCD is viewed as a heterogeneous phenomenon that is categorized into subtypes based on symptom presentation concerning obsessional theme and ritual type. The disorder presents with diverse symptoms, such as struggles with aggressive, sexual, contamination, and religious obsessions, and various checking, cleaning, and "just so" rituals, whereby the person feels compelled to perform an action repeatedly until it "feels right." Close examination and comparison among OCD patients clearly suggests that there are consistent OCD symptom themes, with several subclassifications being suggested. One classification system, proposing four clusters of obsessive and compulsive symptoms, has received increased support through factor analysis utilizing major OCD assessment questionnaires (Leckman et al., 1997; Summerfeldt, Richter, Antony, & Swinson, 1999). What has emerged from these analyses are four obsession clusters: (1) contamination; (2) aggressive, sexual, religious, somatic; (3) symmetry; and (4) hoarding. In addition, four clusters of compulsions have emerged: (1) cleaning; (2) checking; (3) ordering, arranging, counting, and repeating rituals; and (4) hoarding and collecting. A fifth cluster, unacceptable thoughts, has been identified by Abramowitz, Franklin, Schwartz, and Furr (2003). Other subtypes have been proposed based on clinical characteristics such as age of onset and comorbid diagnoses, particularly tic disorders (Mataix-Cols, 2006; Mataix-Cols et al., 2005).

Other attempts to define OCD have included the concept of a spectrum of disorders that share overlapping symptoms. Hollander and colleagues (Hollander, Friedberg, Wasserman, Yeh, & Iyengar, 2005) have identified three categories of obsessive-compulsive spectrum disorders (OCSDs): (1) neurological disorders with repetitive behaviors (e.g., tic disorders); (2) impulse control disorders (e.g., trichotillomania); and (3) body image, body sensitization, and body weight concern disorders (e.g., Body Dysmorphic Disorder). Shared characteristics of OCSD and OCD include age of onset, clinical course, family history, neurobiology, and treatment response. Moreover, Hollander and his associates conceptualize OCSDs along a continuum of compulsivity and impulsivity. In this conceptualization, Hollander and colleagues describe compulsive behaviors as risk aversive and as driven by the need to decrease distress. They also describe impulsive behaviors as risk taking and driven by the desire to increase gratification or stimulation. The common factor in this continuum is the inability to inhibit repetitive behaviors regardless of the underlying drives. If the OCSDs are added to OCD prevalence rates, the total prevalence may be as high as 10% of the general population of the United States (Hollander & Wong, 1995).

Mataix-Cols (2006) has proposed a multidimensional conceptualization of OCD as a spectrum of potentially overlapping syndromes that are continuous with so-called normal obsessive-compulsive phenomena and can be observed in other psychiatric disorders. This view is an attempt to bridge the gap between the belief that OCD is a unitary disorder and that each subtype of OCD is a different disorder with a separate phenomenology, cause, and treatment. The multidimensional view would account for both common and unique casual factors within a set of overlapping symptom presentations. In addition, according to the multidimensional model, general anxiety common to OCD and many other psychiatric disorders may have evolved to contend with nonspecific threat through increased vigilance and physiological arousal, whereas OCD symptom dimensions may have evolved to cope with specific threats, as in washing to keep clean, hoarding to have plenty of food, and checking to keep safe. Furthermore, an inflated sense of responsibility could be observed in many conditions but would be most pronounced in individuals with aggressive or checking symptoms. An important feature of this multidimensional model is that symptoms can coexist in any individual, be continuous with normal phenomena, and extend beyond traditional boundaries of OCD.

DIAGNOSIS AND ASSESSMENT

The *Diagnostic and Statistical Manual of Mental Disorders* (*DSM-IV-TR*; American Psychiatric Association, 2000) classifies OCD as an anxiety disorder characterized by obsessive thoughts and compulsive actions. Table 10.1 provides a summary of the *DSM-IV-TR* diagnostic criteria. A patient meets the diagnostic criteria of *DSM-IV* if these symptoms are a significant source of distress or significantly interfere with social or occupational functioning. These obsessive symptoms are usually recurrent, persistent, and unwanted thoughts, impulses, or images that are resisted by the patient. Compulsive actions appear as purposeful and ritualistic behavior, often aimed at reducing anxiety triggered by obsessions, or they are completed according to rigid rules. Compulsions can include either physical or mental rituals.

Table 10.1

Diagnostic Criteria for OCD According to *DSM-IV-TR*

Either obsessions or compulsions:

CRITERION A

Obsessions are repetitive and persistent thoughts, images, or impulses that are at some point experienced as intrusive and inappropriate and cause marked distress; they are not about real-life problems; the person attempts to ignore or suppress the thoughts, images, or impulses, or neutralize them with some other thought or action; and they are recognized as a product of the person's own mind.

Compulsions are repetitive behaviors or mental acts that the person feels compelled to perform in response to an obsession or in accordance with rigid rules; the behaviors or mental acts are aimed at preventing or reducing distress or preventing some dreaded event or situation; and they are either clearly perceived as excessive or are not connected in a realistic way with what they are intended to neutralize.

CRITERION B

The patient recognizes at some point that his or her obsessions and compulsions are excessive or unreasonable.

CRITERION C

The obsessions and compulsions cause marked distress for the patient, are time consuming (at least one hour per day), or significantly interfere with day-to-day activities or with social or occupational functioning.

CRITERION D

The content of obsessions or compulsions is not better explained by another Axis I disorder.

CRITERION E

Obsessions or compulsions are not due to direct physiological effects of substance abuse or general medical condition.

Note: It is possible to specify if the patient has OCD *with poor insight*, if for most of the time the patient does not consider his or her obsessions and compulsions excessive or unreasonable.

Adapted from the *Diagnostic and Statistical Manual of Mental Disorders*, fourth edition, text revision (pp. 462–463), by American Psychiatric Association, 2000, Washington, DC, Author.

ASSESSMENT

It is very important to recognize that assessment is a fluid and flexible process and the basis for effective treatment. A thorough assessment provides the opportunity to build a therapeutic relationship through psychoeducation and careful assessment of the nature and maintenance of symptoms. When a therapist appears to understand the bizarreness of the patient's obsessions, the patient often feels validated, which typically strengthens the therapeutic alliance. In the initial interview, the therapist formulates a diagnostic impression, including a primary diagnosis and diagnosis of any existing comorbid conditions, based on the patient's chief complaint and symptom presentation. It is important to gauge the history of the illness, the level of insight the patient exhibits, and what (if anything) has worked in the past and why.

STRUCTURED INTERVIEWS

There are two empirically validated structured interviews with good reliability and validity that can be used to assess for an OCD diagnosis based on *DSM-IV-TR* criteria. The two structured interviews are the Anxiety Disorder Interview Schedule for *DSM-IV* (DiNardo, Moras, Barlow, Rapee, & Brown, 1993) and the Structured Clinical

Interview for *DSM-IV* (First, Spitzer, Gibbon, & Williams, 2002; First, Spitzer, Williams, & Gibbon, 1996).

SEMI-STRUCTURED INTERVIEWS

Semi-structured interviews are very effective in evaluating the form or theme of obsessions and compulsions. The most widely used measure is the Yale-Brown Obsessive Compulsive Scale (Y-BOCS; Goodman, Price, Rasmussen, Mazure, Delgado, et al., 1989; Goodman, Price, Rasmussen, Mazure, Fleischmann, et al., 1989). The Y-BOCS has both a symptom checklist and a severity rating scale. The Y-BOCS checklist consists of over 50 symptoms, and patients are asked if they have ever experienced these symptoms, now or in the past. Not only is the Y-BOCS symptom checklist important for collecting information about a patient's symptom history, but it also provides the therapist with information about the problem areas that need further focus in treatment. The measure provides a useful framework for the therapist and patient to identify and understand the functional relationship between specific obsessions and compulsions. The Y-BOCS Severity scale consists of 10 questions, five about obsessions and five about compulsions. The questions are about how much time the obsessions and compulsions occupy during any given day, how much they interfere in functioning, how distressing they are, how much they are resisted, and how much control the patient has over them. Score for each question range from 0 to 4. Hence, patients can get a score of 20 for obsessions and 20 for compulsions, resulting in a total score of 40. A common way of breaking down the severity ratings of the Y-BOCS is demonstrated in Table 10.2.

The Y-BOCS has become the gold standard in assessing a patient's progress in treatment (Steketee, 1993), but it has several limitations. In the assessment of symptoms, it is very important to assess OCD symptoms only, not symptoms of other anxiety disorders. Also, there is a problematic issue with one item on the scale, item 4. This asks patients to rate how much they resist their obsessions, but the answer usually does not give an accurate picture of where they stand in treatment. The more they resist, the lower their score is on this scale (i.e., less severe, more motivated). However, at the end of treatment most patients have learned that it is futile to resist obsessions and actually have learned not to resist them. If the question is asked as directed, then patients score higher on Y-BOCS as they improve. To get around this, clinicians usually ask patients how much they use the therapeutic techniques that they have learned in dealing with OCD—although it truly affects the reliability and validity of the total Y-BOCS score.

Another semi-structured interview that is frequently used and possesses good reliability and validity is the Brown Assessment of Beliefs Scale (BABS; Eisen et al.,

Table 10.2
Yale-Brown Obsessive Compulsive Scale—Severity Ratings

Y-BOCS Score	Severity of Symptoms
0–7	Subclinical (asymptomatic)
8–15	Mild
16–23	Moderate
24–31	Severe
32–40	Extreme

1998). The BABS is a measure of insight into obsessions and compulsions. Patients first identify one or two obsessional fears and then answer seven items that reflect patients' insight into their particular fear. Given the fact that depression is highly concurrent with OCD, the Hamilton Rating Scale for Depression (HRSD; Hamilton, 1960) also has utility in the assessment of patients with OCD. This is a semi-structured interview that the clinician administers and has acceptable psychometric properties.

SELF-REPORT MEASURES

There are several available self-report instruments that can be utilized as supplements to the structured and semi-structured interviews. In fact, the Y-BOCS has been studied as a self-report instrument and has demonstrated reasonable validity (e.g., Steketee, Frost, & Bogart, 1996). Still, using the Y-BOCS as a self-report measure with children and adolescents, as well as with patients with poor insight, is a questionable practice.

One new and promising 18-item measure of a wide range of OCD symptoms is the Obsessive Compulsive Inventory—Revised (Foa, Huppert et al., 2002). It has promising psychometric properties and is reliable and valid. In addition, Beck and his colleagues have designed two frequently used self-report measures for depression and anxiety called the Beck Depression Inventory (Beck, Ward, Mendelson, Mock, & Erbaugh, 1961) and the Beck Anxiety Inventory (Beck, Epstein, Brown, & Steer, 1988), respectively. The Beck Depression Inventory is also available in a second edition (Beck, Steer, & Brown, 1996). Other noteworthy measures, all with reasonable psychometric properties, are the Obsessive Beliefs Questionnaire (OBQ) and the Responsibility Interpretations Questionnaire (Obsessive Compulsive Cognitions Working Group [OCCWG], 2003, 2005), the Overvalued Ideation Scale (Neziroglu, McKay, Yaryura-Tobias, Stevens, & Todaro, 1999), the Symmetry, Ordering, and Arranging Questionnaire (Radomsky & Rachman, 2004), the Thought Action Fusion Scale (Rassin, Merckelbach, Muris, & Schmidt, 2001; Shafran, Thordarson, & Rachman, 1996), and the Vancouver Obsessional Compulsive Inventory (Thordarson et al., 2004).

CONCEPTUALIZATION

LEARNING AND MODELING

Although intrusive thoughts and compulsive, ritual-like behaviors are observed in the general population, such phenomena are seen as pathological in OCD patients because they can be extremely time-consuming, cause enormous distress, and often are in direct contradiction to a person's sense of self or life goals. As previously stated, the etiology of OCD is not established, but neurobiological, evolutionary, genetic, cognitive, and behavioral factors have been implicated (e.g., Abramowitz & Houts, 2006; Jenike, 1998). It is broadly accepted that OCD symptoms are maintained through the initiation of compulsions or rituals that serve to neutralize obsessions. The subsequent reduction in anxiety serves as a negative reinforcer that maintains the compulsive behaviors. Mowrer's (1960) two-factor learning model has been used as an explanation for the maintenance of OCD symptoms. In Mowrer's theory, fears are acquired through classical conditioning and maintained through operant conditioning when an individual learns to escape aversive stimuli and subsequently avoid such stimuli. Learned avoidance responses are extremely resistant to extinction, which potentially explains the durability and persistence of compulsive rituals. The most effective way to extinguish avoidance responses is to block them during prolonged exposure to the conditioned stimulus, as in exposure and response prevention (ERP), the most widely accepted treatment for OCD. Meyer (1966) was the first to describe the use of exposure and response techniques in two patients with OCD. Although some patients can identify a traumatic experience at the onset of their obsessive-compulsive symptoms, research has failed to find good evidence of traumatic conditioning history in the origin of many cases of OCD (Mineka & Zinbarg, 2006).

According to Salkovskis and colleagues (Salkovskis, Forrester, Richards, & Morrison, 1998), the two-factor process theory provided a useful framework for conceptualizing ERP. However, they argue that the model falls short for several reasons: (a) the limitations of ERP, (b) the need to take into account phenomenological and experiential observations not encompassed by behavioral theories, and (c) the inability to discriminate between anxiety disorders. The nature of obsessions is more endogenous than phobic experiences and supports a more cognitive explanation (Clark, 2004). Additionally, some individuals do not experience a reduction in anxiety (and may even experience an increase) after the completion of their rituals or avoidant responses (Rachman, 2004). Moreover, the behavioral account does not explain why many cases of OCD occur without any apparent pairing and conditioning from aversive or traumatic events (Clark, 2004).

Rachman (1997, 1998a, 1998b) proposed that obsessions are caused by catastrophic misinterpretations of an individual's thoughts, images, and impulses. Moreover, he suggested that obsessions will stay as long as the misinterpretations persist and will diminish or disappear if the misinterpretation is weakened or eliminated. People with OCD often attach salience and personal significance to their intrusive thoughts. These misinterpretations and faulty appraisals will result in an attempt to control the appearance and frequency of the intrusive thought. It is important to note that about 85% of people who do not have a psychiatric diagnosis endorse having intrusive thoughts that are similar in content to the obsessional themes common in OCD sufferers (Rachman & de Silva, 1978). Rachman (1997) defined the misinterpretation of significance as having the following qualities: (a) The thought is important; (b) the thought is very personal; (c) the thought is ego-alien; (d) the thought is believed to have potential consequences; and (e) the potential consequences are serious. According to Clark (2004), two main processes by which unwanted intrusions are escalated into obsessions are faulty appraisals and strategies to control the intrusive thoughts through neutralization, compulsions, or avoidances. Continued faulty appraisals and attempts to control intrusive thoughts will lead to a subsequent increase in the frequency and intensity of a person's obsessions.

An inflated responsibility model has been presented by Salkovskis (1985; Salkovskis, Forrester, & Richards, 1998; Salkovskis, Shafran, Rachman, & Freeston, 1999). Salkovskis argues that ideas that are of importance and that reflect the current concerns of a person will be given processing priority. Intrusive thoughts are experienced as neutral at their initial occurrence but may take on positive or negative significance given the individual's prior experience or current context. In addition to having a high personal significance, an intrusive thought will be paired with a person's belief in his or her level of responsibility to cope with the potentialities and outcomes raised by the intrusive thought. An individual's inflated assessment of his or her personal level of responsibility to prevent harm to self or others is determined by his or her general assumptions, beliefs, and current "online" appraisals (Cougle, Salkovskis, & Wahl, 2007). If the level of responsibility for preventing harm is inflated, then a person is driven to carry out strategies to prevent the catastrophic harm from occurring, even if the probability of such an occurrence is minimal. In addition, people with inflated responsibility beliefs presume that not preventing harm or not attempting to prevent harm is morally equivalent to causing harm. Thus, people with this level of responsibility are concerned with acts of commission and omission. An overestimated sense of responsibility has been associated primarily with checking compulsions (Arntz, Voncken, & Goosen, 2007; Foa, Sacks, Tolin, Prezworski, & Amir, 2002; Rachman, 2002; Shafran, 1997). Recent evidence has emerged to support this theory across other OCD subtypes (Cougle et al., 2007).

In addition to inflated responsibility beliefs, people with obsessions misinterpret the significance of their intrusive thoughts. Whether or not an individual experiences thoughts as ego-alien is an important factor in the development of an obsession (Rachman, 1997). Consider the example of people who value being compassionate and nonviolent but have intrusions that are physically aggressive; if these individuals misinterpret the significance of their thoughts, this may raise doubts in their mind about their character. They may erroneously assume that they are not as nonviolent as believed since they are capable of having such horrific thoughts. Rachman has identified four types that are frequently found in misinterpretation of significance: immoral, antisocial, dangerous, and insane.

Wells (2002; Fisher & Wells, 2005a) has developed a metacognitive model of OCD that emphasizes beliefs about the importance, meaning, and power of thoughts, as well as the need to control thoughts and perform rituals. In doing so, he and his associates developed a measure, the Metacognitions Questionnaire, that identifies five domains: (1) positive beliefs about worries; (2) beliefs about uncontrollability; (3) beliefs about cognitive confidence; (4) general negative beliefs, including beliefs about responsibility, superstition, and punishment; and (5) cognitive self-consciousness. In addition, the model includes *fusion beliefs* based on Rachman's and colleagues (e.g., Rachman, Thordarson, Shagran, & Woddy, 1995) concept of thought action fusion, in which the obsessional activity and a forbidden action are morally equivalent. The metacognitive model identifies three elements of fusion beliefs: (1) thought-event fusion, which indicates that having the thought means the thought is happening, will happen, or has happened; (2) thought-action fusion, which is the belief that having particular thoughts will lead to the uncontrollable commission of unwanted acts; and (3) thought-object fusion, which concerns the belief that thoughts, feelings, and memories can be transferred into objects and/or caught from objects.

Myers and Wells (2005) found that fusion beliefs and two other metacognitive domains (i.e., the need to control one's thoughts and beliefs about uncontrollability and the danger of thoughts and feelings) were significantly correlated with obsessive-compulsive symptoms. In this model, inflated responsibility was considered a consequence of metacognitive beliefs rather than a primary construct. To test the model's clinical utility, Fisher and Wells (2005a) compared ERP to a treatment that consisted of a brief, 5-minute exposure to obsessional fears followed by challenges to metacognitive beliefs. Preliminary evidence suggests that the brief exposure and metacognitive work were more effective in providing reductions in anxiety, thought fusion beliefs, and urges to neutralize compared to ERP.

Other domains of the metacognitive model have been shown to relate to OCD. Hermans, Martens, De Cort, Pieters, and Eelen (2003) found that OCD patients showed less confidence in their memory for actions, less confidence in their ability to discriminate actions from imaginations, and less ability maintaining focused attention. These findings support the notion that OCD sufferers lack confidence in their cognitive processes compared to the notion that OCD sufferers experience deficits in memory and attention. Cognitive self-consciousness (CSC) has been shown to discriminate OCD from other anxiety disorders (Janeck, Calamari, Riemann, & Heffelfinger, 2003). Cognitive self-consciousness is defined as the focusing of attention on thought processes (e.g., "I pay close attention to how my mind works"). Janeck et al. argued that excessively reflecting upon one's thoughts may increase the opportunities for negative appraisals of intrusive thoughts and elevate the risk for developing OCD. Marker, Calamari, Woodard, and Riemann (2006) found that high scores in CSC were related to symptom severity and poor performance on an implicit learning task. In contrast to typical individuals who experience their stream of consciousness as fluid thoughts that infrequently prompt attention allocation, individuals high in CSC are highly aware of their thoughts (Marker et al., 2006). Increased attention to thoughts has been significantly linked to negative appraisals of intrusive thoughts (Cohen & Calamari, 2004). Rauch and Savage (2000) hypothesize that OCD is associated with cognitive gating processes that result in impaired implicit learning ability and a compensatory reliance on explicit learning. They propose that varied clinical presentations of OCD and OCSDs may reflect a fundamental impairment in neural mechanisms that underlie procedural learning.

More recent work, such as the work of the Obsessive Compulsive Cognitions Work Group (1997), has endeavored to look at differences and similarities in beliefs specific to OCD. This group has identified six belief domains (overestimation of threat, intolerance of uncertainty, importance of thoughts, control of thoughts, responsibility, and perfectionism) likely to be important in the study of the phenomenology of and treatment-related change in OCD. Further investigations by the OCCWG (2001, 2003, 2005) have led to the development of the Obsessive Beliefs Questionnaire 87. Subsequent factor analyses of the OBQ-87 yielded an inventory (OBQ-44) with a 44-item total scale with three subscales (Responsibility/Threat Estimation, Perfectionism/Certainty, and Importance/Control of Thoughts). Several attempts have been made to identify subtypes based on obsessional beliefs. For example, Calamari et al. (2006) found that the symmetry/ordering subtype was positively correlated with Perfectionism/Certainty beliefs. They also reported that membership in the unacceptable thoughts, identified by Abramowitz, Franklin, et al. (2003), was associated with Importance/Control of Thoughts beliefs. Taylor et al. (2006) made a similar finding in identifying these subgroups. These studies are important inasmuch as they present the possibility in which there is a subgroup of OCD sufferers for whom dysfunctional beliefs potentially do not play a role in the etiology or maintenance of their OCD. Further study needs to be pursued as there could be other, more salient cognitive factors involved that are not currently identified by the OCD measures now available.

A recent attempt to classify obsessions has been undertaken by Lee and colleagues (Lee & Kwon, 2003; Lee & Telch, 2005). These researchers have found evidence of different types of obsessions: autogenous obsessions that are consistent with the traditional understanding of obsessional thinking, and reactive obsessions that share a phenomenological overlap with rumination and worry. Autogenous obsessions are experienced as ego-dystonic and irrational. Individuals with these obsessions attempt to suppress or expel them from consciousness and frequently utilize avoidant control strategies to neutralize unwanted thoughts through covert or overt ritualized behaviors that are often of a magical or superstitious nature. Such thoughts typically involve blasphemous or immoral and sexual or aggressive themes. Individuals with autogenous obsessions are vulnerable to misinterpretations of the significance of their thoughts; often the thoughts are misinterpreted as representations of one's self or character (Clark, 2004). Conversely, those with reactive obsessions tend to view their thoughts as more realistic and rational, although the thoughts are generally considered excessive by the individual. The themes of thoughts that are categorized as reactive include contamination, making mistakes, and asymmetry. Rather than attempting to expel their obsessional thoughts, these individuals commit themselves to developing coping strategies to prevent the unwanted catastrophic occurrences that their fears represent. Individuals with reactive obsessions may employ cognitive strategies similar to worry to keep themselves and others safe through increased environmental vigilance. Without these cognitive strategies, individuals may feel excessively vulnerable to environmental threat.

LIFE EVENTS

A numbers of elements may be responsible for the existence of obsessions, including the presence of dysphoria, personality variables, periods of stress, heightened arousal, and perceived loss of control. There is a great deal of evidence that stress increases the likelihood of intrusive thoughts and that intrusive thoughts are the raw material for developing obsessions. The risk of OCD has been reported to be 10 times greater in patients with Posttraumatic Stress Disorder (de Silva & Marks, 1999).

One life event that has been associated with precipitation or exacerbation of OCD is pregnancy and childbirth. Neziroglu, Anemone, and Yaryura-Tobias (1992) found that of the 59 women in their sample who had at least one child, 39% reported onset of OCD during pregnancy. In a longitudinal study of first-time mothers and fathers, Abramowitz, Nelson, Rygwall, and Khandker (2007) found that the tendency for first-time mothers and fathers to negatively interpret the presence and meaning of unwanted intrusive infant-related thoughts early in the postpartum period mediated the relationship between prechildhood beliefs and late postpartum obsessive-compulsive beliefs. The association between pregnancy and the onset of obsessive-compulsive symptoms clearly warrants further research on psychological and biological factors associated with pregnancy and OCD (Neziroglu et al.,1992).

There have been some attempts to identify family environment variables in the etiology and maintenance of OCD. Yoshida, Taga, Matsumoto, and Fukui (2005) found evidence in a Japanese sample that paternal controlling and interfering attitudes were linked to the development of OCD and depression with obsessive traits. In another study, Alonso et al. (2004) found that perceived negative parental characteristics were associated with the hoarding subtype. However, Alonso et al. did find that across all subtypes, OCD patients showed a significant tendency to see their fathers as more rejecting as compared to controls. Steketee, Lam, Chambless, Rodebaugh, and McCullough (2007) found that perceived criticism from a family member may interfere with patients' positive response to behavior therapy. In another study, Renshaw, Chambless, and Steketee (2006) found that high expressed emotion in the form of hostility was associated with family members' attributional beliefs about the amount of responsibility and control that the sufferer has over his or her symptoms. Although the findings on the role of the family environment are not well understood, there is enough relevant research that indicates that family therapy or involvement of the family should always be considered in clinical assessment and treatment of OCD.

GENETIC INFLUENCES

Although there has been great interest in the family transmission of OCD, the genetic factors are not yet well understood. Issues of heterogeneity, assertive mating, and gene-gene and gene-environment interactions complicate our understanding of genetic factors (Hanna, 2000). Monozygotic twins show significantly higher rates of obsessive-compulsive symptoms than do dizygotic twins, and first-degree relatives of OCD sufferers have been found to have the disorder at a rate 3 to 12 times greater than the population at large (Grados, Walkup, & Walford, 2003). The rate of OCD in first-degree probands with OCD was found to be 10.3% to 11.7% and was significantly higher then nonpsychiatric controls (Nestadt et al., 2000).

Many candidate genes related to the serotonin, dopamine, and glutaminergic systems are thought to be implicated in the pathophysiology of OCD. Several ambitious and ongoing studies have as their primary aim to clarify the genetic influences on the development of OCD, including a six-site collaboration called The OCD Collaborative Genetic Study (Samuels et al., 2006) and the OC Foundations Genetic Collaborative among nine universities (David L. Pauls, personal communication, 2006).

PHYSICAL FACTORS AFFECTING BEHAVIOR

Neuropsychology Cognitions associated with OCD might best be described as an inability to inhibit and direct attention from distressing thoughts and images toward more pleasant or less distressing mental experiences. A variety of studies have been conducted in recent years to determine whether there are underlying neuropsychological dysfunctions common to patients with OCD. Overall, neuropsychological studies have yielded divergent results concerning executive functioning and nonverbal memory functions in patients with OCD compared to controls. The interest in neuropsychological dysfunction has been sparked by clinical observations. Most OCD patients express the belief that their obsessions are irrational and their compulsions are senseless, yet they are unable to banish obsessions from their minds and feel compelled to ritualize, thus suggesting a deficit in cognitive control associated with problems of executive function. Similarly, OCD patients report excessive doubting, which presumably is linked to difficulties in memory function. These difficulties might be related to encoding problems or to an insufficient level of confidence in memory function for facilitating neutralization of the obsessions (Greisberg & McKay, 2003).

Several memory deficits have been reported in OCD patients. Purcell and colleagues (Purcell, Maruff, Kyrios, & Pantelis, 1998) found that OCD patients had deficits in spatial working memory and motor speed. These patients were impaired on a measure of visual recall, suggesting that memory impairments were secondary to deficits in their ability to use organizational strategies (Savage et al., 1999, 2000). Additionally, Savage found that verbal memory, not generally known to be affected in OCD patients, is impaired when an organizational strategy is required. Deficits in nonverbal fluency, controlled attention, abstract reasoning, and cognitive flexibility have also been reported (Schmidtke, Schorb, Winkelmann, & Hohagen, 1998). Cavedini and his colleagues (Cavedini, Gorini, & Bellodi, 2006) found decision-making deficits in OCD patients, and these deficits have been correlated with treatment resistance. Set-shifting difficulties have been implicated in a number of studies (Abbruzzese, Ferri, & Scarone, 1997; Aycicegi, Dinn, Harris, & Erkmen, 2003; Watkins et al., 2005).

Despite these findings, other studies have found contradictory findings. Simpson and colleagues (2006) found no difference between current OCD patients and healthy controls on a number of frequently researched neuropsychological functions (e.g., visual memory, motor speed, cognitive flexibility), including those specifically given by Purcell et al. (1998) and Savage et al. (2000). One exception was the poor performance of the OCD patients on the Benton Visual Retention Test scores, consistent with visual memory dysfunction (Simpson et al., 2006). However, similar scores have been found with social phobia patients (L. J. Cohen et al., 1996) and therefore may not be exclusive to OCD. In the same study, OCD patients did not differ from healthy controls in the Rey-Osterrieth Complex Figure Test (RCFT). Moreover, Simpson et al. found no differences in set-shifting deficits between current OCD patients and healthy controls, consistent with the findings of several other studies (Basso, Bornstein, Carona, & Morton, 2001; Moritz, Fricke, Wagner, & Hand, 2001; Purcell et al., 1998). Contrary to the Cavedini et al. (2006) study, at least two studies (Nielen, Veltman, de Jong, Mulder, & den Boer, 2002) found intact decision-making abilities in OCD patients.

These mixed findings can be interpreted in different ways. The contradictory results across studies may be due, at least partially, to different matching criteria, divergent methodological procedures, and not controlling for comorbidities. The Simpson et al. (2006) study, like most studies, did not take into account different subtypes of OCD, medication versus no medication, and treatment history. Although there has been no substantial evidence of a relationship between obsessive-compulsive subtypes and performance on neuropsychological tests (e.g., Kuelz, Hohagen, & Voderholzer, 2004), Hartl and colleagues (2004) found that individuals with hoarding behavior showed deficits in delayed recall and poor organizational strategies on the RCFT. Continued research into the neuropsychological underpinnings is warranted. There is enough evidence to conclude that there are substantial numbers of OCD sufferers who have neuropsychological deficits. Patients with neuropsychological deficits may represent a subtype that may have prognostic and treatment implications.

Neurobiology   Obsessive-Compulsive Disorder is widely considered a neurobiological disorder that implicates the loops that connect the orbitofrontal cortex and anterior cingulate, the basal ganglia, and the medial thalamus. Baxter et al. (1996) conceptualize OCD as an antagonism between the direct and indirect striatopallidal pathways of the basal ganglia. The direct pathway has numerous connections to the orbitofrontal cortex and anterior cingulate that are speculated to facilitate routines. The indirect pathway is well connected to the dorsal lateral prefrontal cortex and is thought to act as an on/off switching mechanism that is involved in the starting and stopping of routines set in motion by the direct pathways. Thus, OCD is conceptualized as the interaction between (a) the overfunctioning of the loop between the orbitofrontal and anterior cingulate and (b) the indirect striatopallidal pathway within the basal ganglia in which the orbitofrontal and anterior cingulated circuit remains on continuous activation, producing obsessive thoughts and uncontrollable doubt. The ineffective functioning of the indirect pathway is unable to curtail the repetition of routines and habitual behavior that are expressed as rituals.

Schwartz and colleagues (Saxena, Brody, Schwartz, & Baxter, 1998; Schwartz, 1998, 1999) have developed a model of OCD that involves the head of the caudate nucleus, whose functioning is modified by information salient to the individual. A dysfunction in this area may lead to inadequate learning to promote and generate novel and relevant patterns of behavior in response to changing information. Thus, the error detection mechanism remains in hyperalert, reducing the patient's inability to perceive the reinforcing nature of important changes in environmental conditions. Responses to this information processing will result in ineffective and repetitive strategies in the form of overt and covert rituals.

DRUGS AFFECTING BEHAVIOR

Serotonin appears to play an important role in the pathophysiology of OCD, although the evidence for this is indirect. Serotonin reuptake inhibitor (SRI) antidepressants are undoubtedly effective in the treatment of OCD. The leading neurochemical theory—the serotonin (or serotonergic) hypothesis—postulates that OCD symptoms stem from abnormalities in the serotonin systems. Antidepressants that exert their main influence on other neurotransmitter systems—not serotonin systems—are largely ineffective in the treatment of OCD. It would therefore be tempting to point to a primary serotonergic problem underlying OCD, but this does not necessarily follow. Instead, it may be that alteration of serotonergic systems may allow the brain to compensate for some other problem underlying OCD (Rauch, Corá-Locatelli, & Greenberg, 2002).

Another theory postulates that glutamate dysfunction may be intrinsic to OCD (Carlsson, 2001). This theory suggests that enhanced prefrontal glutamatergic activity leads to overactivity in both the direct (behaviorally stimulating) and indirect (behaviorally inhibitory) orbitofrontal-subcortical circuits. This interesting theory accounts for both the behaviorally activated symptoms of OCD (repetition, cleaning, etc.) and the behaviorally inhibited symptoms (slowness, difficulty initiating behaviors, overly cautious attitude). To date, the glutamate-modulating drug lamotrigine has not been found to be useful in reducing OCD symptoms (Kumar & Khanna, 2000).

Despite these findings, modification of serotonin (5-HT) systems remains the primary medication approach to the treatment of OCD (Davidson & Björgvinsson, 2003). How serotonin systems exert their therapeutic effects has been the topic of considerable research, and focus has increasingly been on specific 5-HT receptors. Response to SRIs in OCD patients generally requires 8 to 10 weeks of chronic treatment, far longer than the time for response in depression. This timing correlates closely with the time it takes SRIs to down-regulate 5-HT_{1D} autoreceptors in the orbitofrontal cortex, providing a clue to the possible therapeutic mechanism of SRIs in OCD patients (Hollander, Kaplan, Allen, & Cartwright, 2000).

CULTURAL AND DIVERSITY ISSUES

Symptom presentation of OCD is consistent across cultures (Weissman et al., 1994). Weissman and his colleagues, using the *DSM-III* criteria for OCD, compared community surveys in seven countries: the United States, Canada, Puerto Rico, Germany, Taiwan, Korea, and New Zealand. They reported that the OCD annual prevalence rates are remarkably consistent among these countries, ranging from 1.1% in Korea and New Zealand to 1.8% in Puerto Rico. The exception was Taiwan, with a 0.4% prevalence rate; consistent with other studies, when standard practices are used, Taiwan tends to have the lowest prevalence rates for all psychiatric disorders. These findings suggest the robustness of OCD as a disorder in diverse parts of the world and are often cited as further evidence of the neurobiological basis of OCD. However, the content of obsessions and compulsions tend to be culture-specific (Akhtar, Wig, Varma, Pershad, & Verma, 1975). Using a sample of 82 OCD patients from India, Akhtar et al.

reported that dirt and contamination obsessions were more prevalent compared to similar samples in the United States; religious and sexual obsessions were rare. Some studies indicate that religious obsessions may be more prevalent in countries or cultures with moral codes that are based on strict religiosity (e.g., Rasmussen & Eisen, 1992).

BEHAVIORAL TREATMENT

Efficacy of behavior therapy, specifically exposure and response prevention, for patients struggling with OCD has been clearly established. Several meta-analyses and clinical significance analyses indicate that 60% to 80% of patients who complete the treatment, particularly those who engage in treatment with compliance and motivation, get significantly better (e.g., Abramowitz, 1997; Fisher & Wells, 2005b). The definition of significant improvement usually refers to a 35% or higher reduction in Y-BOCS scores (see Pallanti & Quercioli, 2006), the measure most frequently used to gauge patients' response to treatment. The Y-BOCS is referred to as the gold standard for assessing treatment response (Steketee, 1993), but it is not without problems, as previously discussed. The behavior treatment of OCD is focused and usually time-limited; the most standard time frame for treatment is 12 to 20 sessions (e.g., Abramowitz, 1997).

Exposure and response prevention are performed by first creating a fear hierarchy of situations that trigger OCD anxiety. The items on such a hierarchy include both external cues (e.g., seeing or touching something dirty or leaving without checking if the stove is off) and internal cues (e.g., thoughts, images, or impulses that trigger anxiety). Effective ERP treatment includes assessment of the patient's avoidances, safety behaviors, and covert neutralizations (mental rituals), which are then incorporated into the exposure hierarchy. The feared situations and triggers are ranked from least to greatest distress-provoking OCD trigger to create the exposure hierarchy. The patient usually starts with mildly to moderately challenging OCD triggers, not the lowest. This is because lower level exposures often provide minimal gains that many patients dismiss in the face of dealing with more difficult OCD triggers. The patient then gradually moves up the fear hierarchy (after successful habituation to the OCD trigger being challenged) by confronting increasingly challenging distress-provoking situations (e.g., touching a perceived contaminated item). There are two types of exposures used: *in vivo* (repeated confrontation with the actual OCD triggering stimulus) and *imaginal* exposures (planned thinking or imaginal confrontation of the OCD trigger without the ritual). For example, imaginal exposures are used either to prepare the patient to complete the in vivo exposure (e.g., imagining touching a dirty doorknob without washing his or her hands) or in situations where it is not feasible (e.g., confronting harming or aggressive obsessions). Usually, clinicians use these concurrently. That is, they have the patient directly confront the OCD trigger and then use imaginal exposures to confront the thoughts and images that result from completing these exposures. Having the patient write out the actual OCD scenario is a common practice. This is also where modern technology has helped the clinicians. In the past, many clinicians have used answering machine tapes to create an endless loop of the recorded feared consequence that would repeat itself every 30 to 60 seconds. Now clinicians can use technology such as burning CDs or recording audio clips that are used with MP3 players to create imaginal exposure scripts that the patient can use in treatment. There are also promising developments in treating anxiety disorders using virtual reality techniques (see Rothbaum, 2006). Virtual exposure therapy may have its use in treating OCD, especially enhancing the delivery of imaginal exposures with response prevention.

Every exposure is followed by response prevention, in which the patient does not complete the compulsive act and learns that the anxiety generated will gradually decrease on its own without performing the assumed necessary compulsion or avoidance behavior. This process is referred to as habituation, and when it occurs, OCD-related situations trigger less anxiety and less of an urge to ritualize. This is usually completed in a systematic and incremental manner, but sometimes in very rapid fashion, when it is referred to as flooding. Habituation occurs as the patient learns that the anxiety generated will gradually decrease on its own without performing the assumed necessary compulsion or avoidance behavior. Both exposure *and* response prevention are necessary to reduce OCD symptoms. Frequent and repetitive ERP practice produces better outcomes than less practice with large gaps of time between practice. Gains are typically maintained for longer periods and generalize to a greater degree when treatment is intensive, for example having 90-minute ERP sessions 3 to 5 times per week for many weeks (Abramowitz, Foa, & Franklin, 2003; Neziroglu, Henricksen, & Yaryura-Tobias, 2006).

Although ERP is a very potent treatment for OCD, it has some limitations. One is that many patients decline recommendation to engage in ERP and therefore do not appear in intent-to-treat evaluations of treatment efficacy, nor are they among the completers. If these patients and those who drop out of ERP prior to completing the treatment are included in responder rate estimates, the response rate decreases to about 55% (Stanley & Turner, 1995).

More recently, cognitive therapy (CT) specific to core beliefs typically held by persons with OCD has been shown to be effective in significant OCD symptom reduction (Clark, 2004; Frost & Steketee, 2002; van Oppen et al., 1995). Cognitive therapy is first and foremost educational and collaborative. It aims at identifying and correcting dysfunctional beliefs or faulty appraisals of obsessional stimuli. According to the cognitive-behavioral model of OCD, these beliefs lead to obsessional fears and responses that are maladaptive, reinforce specific core beliefs, and maintain dysfunctional neutralization responses. Although the data clearly demonstrate that the most effective treatment for OCD is ERP, promising data are emerging about the efficacy of CT (Clark, 2004). Specifically, CT demonstrated efficacy in reducing dropout rates among patients in treatment and in enhancing motivation (e.g., Kozak & Coles, 2005).

In an attempt to shed some light on how effective CBT truly is in treating OCD, Fisher and Wells (2005b) conducted clinical significance analyses using two criteria: the Jacobson methodology for defining clinical significance (Jacobson, Roberts, Berns, & McGlinchey, 1999) and an "asymptomatic" criterion based on the Y-BOCS Severity scores. Using data from five recent studies (since 2002) when treatment response is defined by Jacobson's methodology, ERP appears to be the most effective treatment available, with success rates of 50% to 60%. It was more effective than CT and medication management. When an "asymptomatic" criterion is used and a Y-BOCS score of equal to or lower than 7, both ERP and CT have equally low rates of recovery, approximately 25%. A review of findings from OCD treatment studies completed by Franklin and Foa (2002) also concludes that ERP is the most effective treatment available today for OCD, more effective than pharmacotherapy and CT. Furthermore, they concluded that the efficacy of ERP is highly dependent on being delivered in an optimal manner utilizing prolonged exposures—at least 90 minutes—with strict response prevention. As it stands, ERP is the most effective treatment for OCD. However, many patients do not respond to ERP, and those that do are not "asymptomatic." As a result, promising new CBT approaches are being developed and tested.

Lack of well-trained therapists experienced in ERP makes the utilization of this treatment less practical and less accessible than medication treatment provided by qualified psychiatrists. There continue to be tremendous misconceptions about implementing ERP, and it continues to be vastly underutilized (see Rosqvist, 2005). For example, some clinicians still hold the belief that they will ultimately damage the therapeutic relationship and patients' coping by having them revisit what they fear through exposure. Additionally, the belief lingers that ERP does not go after the real root of the problem and therefore symptoms will emerge in other forms. These beliefs have clearly been proven wrong by extensive research on the efficacy of ERP (e.g., Rosqvist, 2005).

Although many psychodynamically trained clinicians do in fact treat individuals with OCD, there is little evidence that such treatment is effective in ameliorating the OCD symptoms. As there is a clear need for more clinicians trained in cognitive-behavioral therapy for OCD, it may be possible for practitioners trained in psychodynamic or other modalities to learn how to effectively implement ERP. Bram and Björgvinsson (2004) identify the many challenges that such cross-theoretical training evokes, including the therapist's own anxiety about ERP, understanding the mechanism for change, and reconsidering therapeutic boundaries within behavioral therapy (Bram & Björgvinsson, 2004).

Recently, several third-wave behavioral and cognitive interventions have been developed that target the function of cognitions and emotions rather than their form, frequency, or situational sensitivity. Acceptance and commitment therapy (ACT) is one such development (Hayes, Strosahl, & Wilson, 1999). One of the major processes underlying ACT is *cognitive defusion*, which involves the arranging of verbal contexts to help decrease the believability of patients' thoughts. It also aims at reducing the tendency to respond in the presence of these thoughts while not necessarily decreasing their frequency or altering their form. Another construct in ACT is the decrease in *experiential avoidance*, which is defined as the escape from or avoidance of unwanted private events, even when doing so causes psychological harm. Thus ACT purports to help patients develop a new relationship with obsessive thoughts and anxious feelings, for instance, helping a patient discover that a thought is just a thought and anxiety is an emotion to be felt. It has been suggested that ACT is a viable way to treat OCD, as demonstrated by a recent study by Twohig, Hayes, and Masuda (2006). The ACT protocol used in this study did not use exposure and habituation in a traditional fashion. Instead, patients were encouraged to practice acceptance and defusion while engaging in valued activities. This small but promising multiple baseline study showed good results in decreasing compulsions as well as self-reported depression and anxiety.

MEDICAL TREATMENT

Although clearly influenced by learning principles, OCD is a biologically based disorder, and as such, medication is an important component of treatment. The disorder's symptomatology has been linked to a difficulty in adequately regulating the brain neurotransmitter serotonin. The exact mechanisms for this still remain unclear; however,

SRIs can help to reduce OCD symptoms. This occurs by slowing the reuptake of serotonin, thus making more serotonin available for the receiving brain cells to use. About 40% to 60% of patients with OCD show significant improvement during treatment with SRIs (Davidson & Björgvinsson, 2003; Dougherty, Rauch, & Jenike, 2004). The SRIs clomipramine (Anafranil), sertraline (Zoloft), fluoxetine (Prozac), fluvoxamine (Luvox), citalopram (Celexa), and paroxetine (Paxil) have all demonstrated efficacy as pharmacotherapy in reducing OCD symptoms in several double-blind, randomized, and placebo-controlled research studies (Dougherty et al., 2004). Of those, clomipramine was the first to receive U.S. Food and Drug Administration approval for OCD (Clomipramine Collaborative Study Group, 1991).

Augmentation therapy with serotonergic agents, dopaminergic agents, and GABA agents suggests that response rates can increase to 70% to 80% (Greist et al., 2003). Because neither ERP nor serotonergic medications by themselves have been effective for all OCD sufferers, a combination is typically recommended as the treatment of choice (Jenike, 2004).

Case Description

Sarah, a 15-year-old, was the youngest of three. She came to the specialized inpatient OCD treatment program with her parents and older sister. The parents had sought out several therapists in a major metropolitan area for months, but were turned down by several psychiatrists and other outpatient therapists. All stated that her symptoms were too severe for outpatient practice and that they could not help her. Therefore, the parents decided to seek out specialty inpatient treatment, but Sarah was not a willing participant. She was very upset at the prospect of being left alone at a "mental" hospital and clearly stated that she did not want to engage in treatment. The initial agreement that we were able to work out was that if she worked hard in her treatment for 2 weeks and was able to meet specific target goals, she could go home and attempt intensive outpatient treatment.

At the onset of treatment, her OCD symptoms were all-consuming. Her entire life was more or less consumed by obsessions and compulsions. Her main symptoms were harming obsessions (triggered mostly by numbers and colors), sexual obsessions, contamination fears, checking, and contamination. Due to her OCD symptoms, she had dropped out of school several months before, was unable to sleep in her own bed, and could not enter her own room, or sometimes her own house. It was very difficult for her to take showers that lasted less than 2 hours, to put certain clothes on, to wear certain colors, and to look at carpet or big squares with four corners. She felt intense urges to complete rituals to prevent harm to herself and her family.

When she was 13, she was doing well at school, had many friends, and participated in various school activities, gymnastics being her favorite. Then her showers began to take a very long time and her parents noticed that she

(continued)

was struggling with leaving the house without excessive reassurance from her mother and elaborate checking rituals.

At onset of treatment her main obsessions and compulsions included the following:

Obsessions

- Harm obsessions—primarily about harm coming to her family, concerns about sexually molesting a child (these obsessions were clearly ego-dystonic).
- Contamination obsessions—feeling "contaminated" after a bad harming thought.
- Colors—especially around "gangs" at her previous schools and bad associations with those particular colors.
- Scrupulosity/morality—especially around cheating. She "cheated" if she talked to students about the issue before taking a test and therefore had to answer incorrectly on the test.
- Different bad numbers—but "666" was always bad; 6, $6 + 6 + 6 = 18$, 2, 3 were bad, but this would change by the hour, sometimes by the minute.
- Letters—would become bad, for example a, b, c, d would become 1, 2, 3, 4 on a multiple-choice test, and she would be unable to answer any question because it was tied to bad number.

Compulsions

- Excessive washing—often after a bad harming thought (usually washed at least 4 or more times, but it depended on what the bad number was at that time).
- Mental rituals focused on the number 7—which was always a good number. She explained that the number seven was good because God created the world in 7 days according to her Christian beliefs.
- Avoiding "bad" numbers, letters, and colors—she was unable to wear clothes with "bad" colors.

At the onset of treatment Sarah's Children Yale-Brown Obsessive Compulsive Scale (CY-BOCS) was in the extreme range (36 out of 40). She scored equally on both obsessions (total = 18) and compulsions (total = 18). She was very anxious about being in the program, but was not depressed and had good insight into her OCD. Her obsessions were clearly ego-dystonic. Initially, we attempted to build a treatment alliance through education to the cognitive-behavioral therapy model and to create a shared framework for addressing the OCD symptoms with the construction of an exposure hierarchy.

The treatment alliance allowed us to utilize the following:

- Imaginal exposures—around bad numbers, colors, and other harming themes.
- In vivo exposures—for example, she put on a yellow T-shirt for the first time in over a year.

- Cognitive restructuring—practice challenging the faulty appraisals and dysfunctional neutralizations about her family and her exaggerated sense of responsibility.
- Relapse prevention—practiced skills with family, at home, and confronted her fears in home environment.

Sarah rapidly took ownership of her treatment. After the first successful ERP she saw the merit of the treatment. Her peers in the treatment program were also a great influence on her and were able to create a frame of reference for her about what it means to have OCD. Prior to entering treatment she felt very isolated, misunderstood, and ashamed of her obsessions. Realizing that other patients struggled with similar issues and that they were actively engaged in treatment created a tremendous motivational boost for Sarah and helped her significantly in completing her ERPs effectively. She systematically continued to complete a minimum of 2 hours of ERP daily, with emphasis on very strict and complete response prevention. After 6 weeks of treatment, she returned home to her parents to engage in outpatient practice. At discharge, her CY-BOCS was 4 (in the subclinical or asymptomatic range), dropping from 36 to 4, indicating an 89% reduction. She did not take any medication at any time throughout the treatment and was very proud of her achievement that was due to her ERP work. She was anxious about returning home and resuming sleeping in her own bed, which had been a trigger for so many obsessions and compulsions. She was able to practice imaginal exposures and various other techniques and did in fact do well on her return home. One year postdischarge, her OCD remained in the subclinical range while taking no medication and attending school full time.

SUMMARY

Obsessive-compulsive disorder is often a severe, frequently debilitating anxiety disorder that affects approximately 2% of the population, affecting males and females equally. The disorder appears cross-culturally around the world with similar prevalence rates. It is characterized by (a) obsessions, defined as unwanted, disturbing, and intrusive thoughts, images, or impulses that are generally seen by the individual as excessive, irrational, and ego-alien; and (b) compulsions, defined as repetitive behaviors and mental acts that neutralize obsessions and reduce emotional distress. In a limited number of cases a patient may have only obsessions or compulsions, but the vast majority of patients experience both.

Although the etiology of OCD is not established, neurobiological, genetic, cognitive, and behavioral factors have all been implicated. Development of OCD is clearly influenced by learning principles. It is broadly accepted that OCD symptoms are maintained through the initiation of compulsions or rituals that serve to neutralize obsessions. Subsequent reduction in anxiety serves as a negative reinforcer that maintains the compulsive behaviors. Several cognitive models have also been proposed. Rachman (1997, 1998a, 1998b) proposed that obsessions are caused by catastrophic misinterpretations of an individual's thoughts, images, and impulses. Salkovskis (1985; Salkovskis et al., 1998, 1999) has presented an inflated responsibility model, and Wells (2002; Fisher & Wells, 2005a) has developed a metacognitive model of OCD that emphasizes beliefs about the importance, meaning, and power of thoughts, as well as the need to control thoughts and perform rituals.

Cognitive-behavioral therapy is an effective treatment for OCD that utilizes ERP along with pharmacotherapy. Despite the availability of these effective evidence-based treatments, up to 25% of patients fail to benefit from them. More recently, other modes of treatment have been developed to further increase the effectiveness of cognitive-behavioral interventions. Interventions based on traditional cognitive approaches that challenge core beliefs have been shown to be effective. Acceptance-based therapies such as ACT and treatments based on metacognitive principles also show promise and need to be researched further. These new treatment approaches are currently being developed and researched with the hope that treatments for OCD will continue to improve the quality of life for OCD sufferers.

REFERENCES

Abbruzzese, M., Ferri, S., & Scarone, S. (1997). The selective breakdown of frontal functions in patients with obsessive-compulsive disorder and in patients with schizophrenia: A double dissociation experimental finding. *Neuropsychologia, 35,* 907–912.

Abramowitz, J. S. (1997). Effectiveness of psychological and pharmacological treatments for obsessive-compulsive disorder: A quantitative review. *Journal of Consulting and Clinical Psychology, 65,* 44–52.

Abramowitz, J. S., Foa, E. B., & Franklin, M. E. (2003). Exposure and ritual prevention for obsessive-compulsive disorder: Effects of intensive versus twice-weekly sessions. *Journal of Consulting and Clinical Psychology, 71,* 394–398.

Abramowitz, J. S., Franklin, M., Schwartz, S., & Furr, J. (2003). Symptom presentation and outcome of cognitive-behavior therapy for obsessive-compulsive disorder. *Journal of Consulting and Clinical Psychology, 71,* 1049–1057.

Abramowitz, J. S., & Houts, A. C. (2006). *Concept and controversies in obsessive-compulsive disorder.* New York: Springer.

Abramowitz, J. S., Nelson, C. A., Rygwall, R., & Khandker, M. (2007). The cognitive mediation of obsessive-compulsive symptoms: A longitudinal study. *Journal of Anxiety Disorders, 21,* 91–104.

Akhtar, S., Wig, N. N., Varma, V. K., Pershad, D., & Verma, S. K. (1975). A phenomenological analysis of symptoms in obsessive-compulsive neurosis. *British Journal of Psychiatry, 127,* 342–348.

Alonso, P., Menchón, J., Mataix-Cols, D., Pifarré, J., Urretavizcaya, M., Crespo, J. M., et al. (2004). Perceived parental rearing style in obsessive-compulsive disorder: Relation to symptom dimensions. *Psychiatry Research, 127*(3), 267–278.

American Psychiatric Association. (2000). *Diagnostic and statistical manual of mental disorders* (4th ed., text rev.). Washington, DC: Author.

Antony, M. M., Downie, F., & Swinson, R. P. (1998). Diagnostic issues and epidemiology in obsessive-compulsive disorder. In R. P Swinson, M. M. Antony, S. Rachman, & M. A. Richter (Eds.), *Obsessive-compulsive disorder: Theory, research, and treatment* (pp. 3–32). New York: Guilford Press.

Arntz, A., Voncken, M., & Goosen, A. C. (2007). Responsibility and obsessive-compulsive disorder: An experimental test. *Behavior Research and Therapy, 45,* 425–435.

Aycicegi, A., Dinn, W. M., Harris, C. L., & Erkmen, H. (2003). Neuropsychological function in obsessive-compulsive disorder: Effects of comorbid conditions on task performance. *European Psychiatry, 18,* 241–248.

Basso, M. R., Bornstein, R. A., Carona, F., & Morton, R. (2001). Depression accounts for executive function deficits in obsessive-compulsive disorder. *Neuropsychiatry, Neuropsychology, and Behavioral Neurology, 14,* 241–245.

Baxter, L. R., Jr., Saxena, S., Brody, A. L., Ackermann, R. F., Colgan, M., Schwartz, J. M., et al. (1996). Brain mediation of obsessive-compulsive disorder symptoms: Evidence from functional brain imaging studies in the human and nonhuman primate. *Seminars in Clinical Neuropsychiatry, 1,* 32–47.

Beck, A. T., Epstein, N., Brown, G., & Steer, R. A. (1988). An inventory for measuring clinical anxiety: Psychometric properties. *Journal of Consulting and Clinical Psychology, 56,* 893–897.

Beck, A. T., Steer, R. A., & Brown, G. K. (1996). *Beck Depression Inventory manual* (2nd ed.). San Antonio TX: Psychological Corporation.

Beck, A. T., Ward, C. H., Mendelson, M., Mock, J., & Erbaugh, J. (1961). An inventory for measuring depression. *Archives of General Psychiatry, 4,* 561–571.

Bram, T., & Björgvinsson, T. (2004). A psychodynamic clinician's foray into cognitive-behavioral therapy utilizing exposure and ritual prevention for OCD. *American Journal of Psychotherapy, 58,* 304–320.

Calamari, J. E., Cohen, R. J., Rector, N. A., Szacun-Shimizu, K., Riemann, B. C., & Norberg, M. M. (2006). Dysfunctional belief-based obsessive-compulsive disorder subgroups. *Behavior Research and Therapy, 44,* 1347–1360.

Carlsson, M. L. (2001). On the role of prefrontal cortex glutamate for the antithetical phenomenology of obsessive compulsive disorder and attention deficit hyperactivity disorder. *Progress in Neuro-Psychopharmacology and Biological Psychiatry, 25,* 5–26.

Cavedini, P., Gorini, A., & Bellodi, L. (2006). Understanding obsessive-compulsive disorder: Focus on decision making. *Neuropsychology Review, 16,* 3–15.

Clark, D. A. (2004). *Cognitive-behavioral therapy for OCD.* New York: Guilford Press.

Clomipramine Collaborative Study Group. (1991). Clomipramine in the treatment of patient with obsessive-compulsive disorder. *Archives of General Psychiatry, 48,* 730–738.

Cohen, L. J., Hollander, E., DeCaria, C. M., Stein, D. J., Simeon, D., Liebowitz, M. R., et al. (1996). Specificity of neuropsychological impairment in obsessive-compulsive disorder: A comparison with social phobic and normal control subjects. *Journal of Psychiatry and Clinical Neurosciences, 8,* 82–85.

Cohen, R. J., & Calamari, J. E. (2004). Thought-focused attention and obsessive-compulsive symptoms: An evaluation of cognitive self-consciousness in a nonclinical sample. *Cognitive Therapy and Research, 28,* 457–471.

Cougle, J. R., Salkovskis, P. M., & Wahl, K. (2007). Perception of memory ability and confidence in recollections in obsessive-compulsive checking. *Journal of Anxiety Disorders, 21,* 118–130.

Davidson, J., & Björgvinsson, T. (2003). Current and future treatments of obsessive-compulsive-disorder. *Expert Opinion on Investigational Drugs, 12,* 993–1001.

de Silva, P., & Marks, M. (1999). The role of traumatic experiences in the genesis of obsessive-compulsive disorder. *Behavior Research and Therapy, 37,* 941–951.

DiNardo, P., Moras, K., Barlow, D. H., Rapee, R. M., & Brown, T. A. (1993). Reliability of DSM-III-R anxiety disorder categories: Using the Anxiety Disorders Interview Schedule—Revised (ADIS-R). *Archives of General Psychiatry, 50,* 251–256.

Dougherty, D. D., Rauch, S. L., & Jenike, M. A. (2004). Pharmacotherapy for obsessive-compulsive disorder. *Journal of Clinical Psychology, 60,* 1195–1202.

Eisen, J. L., Mancebo, M. A., Pinto, A., Coles, M. E., & Rasmussen, S. A. (2006). Impact of obsessive-compulsive disorder on quality of life. *Comprehensive Psychiatry, 47,* 270–275.

Eisen, J. L., Phillips, K. A., Baer, L., Beer, D. A., Atala, K. D., & Rasmussen, S. A. (1998). The Brown Assessment of Beliefs Scale: Reliability and validity. *American Journal of Psychiatry, 155,* 102–108.

First, M. B., Spitzer, R. L., Gibbon, M., & Williams, J. B. W. (2002). *Structured Clinical Interview for DSM-IV-TR Axis I Disorders, research version, non-patient edition* (SCID-I/NP). New York: Biometrics Research, New York State Psychiatric Institute.

First, M. B., Spitzer, R. L., Williams, J. B. W., & Gibbon, M. (1996). *Structured Clinical Interview for DSM-IV* (SCID). Washington, DC: American Psychiatric Association.

Fisher, P. L., & Wells, A. (2005a). Experimental modification of beliefs in obsessive-compulsive disorder: A test of the metacognitive model. *Behavior Research and Therapy, 43,* 821–829.

Fisher, P. L., & Wells, A. (2005b). How effective are cognitive and behavioral treatments for obsessive-compulsive disorder? A clinical significance analysis. *Behavior Research and Therapy, 43,* 1543–1558.

Foa, E. B., Huppert, J. D., Leiberg, S., Langner, R., Kichic, R., Hajcak, G., et al. (2002). The Obsessive-Compulsive Inventory: Development and validation of a short version. *Psychological Assessment, 14,* 485–496.

Foa, E. B., Sacks, M. B., Tolin, D. F., Prezworski, A., & Amir, N. (2002). Inflated perception of responsibility for harm in OCD patients with and without checking compulsions: A replication and extension. *Journal of Anxiety Disorders, 16,* 443–453.

Franklin, M. E., & Foa, E. (2002). Cognitive behavioral treatments for obsessive compulsive disorder. In P. E. Nathan & J. M. Gorman (Eds.), *Guides to treatments that work* (pp. 367–386). New York: Oxford University Press.

Freud, S. (1955). Notes upon a case of obsessional neurosis. In J. Strachey (Ed.), *The complete psychological works of Sigmund Freud* (Vol. 10, pp. 153–249). London: Hogarth Press. (Original work published 1909)

Frost, R. O., & Steketee, G. (2002). *Cognitive approaches to obsessions and compulsions: Theory, assessment, and treatment.* Oxford: Elsevier.

Goodman, W. K., Price, L. H., Rasmussen, S. A., Mazure, C., Delgado, P., Heninger, G. R., et al. (1989). The Yale-Brown Obsessive Compulsive Scale: Pt. II. Validity. *Archives of General Psychiatry, 46,* 1012–1016.

Goodman, W. K., Price, L. H., Rasmussen, S. A., Mazure, C., Fleischmann, R. L., Hill, C. L., et al. (1989). The Yale-Brown Obsessive Compulsive Scale: Pt. I. Development, use, and reliability. *Archives of General Psychiatry, 46,* 1006–1011.

Grados, M. A., Walkup, J., & Walford, S. (2003). Genetics of obsessive compulsive disorders: New findings and challenges. *Brain and Development, 25,* 55–61.

Greisberg, S., & McKay, D. (2003). Neuropsychology of obsessive-compulsive disorder: A review and treatment implications. *Clinical Psychology Review, 23,* 95–117.

Greist, J. H., Bandelow, B., Hollander, E., Marazziti, D., Montgomery, S. A., Nutt, D. J., et al. (2003). WCA recommendations for the long-term treatment of obsessive-compulsive disorder in adults. *CNS Spectrums, 8,* 7–16.

Hamilton, M. (1960). A rating scale for depression. *Journal of Neurology, Neurosurgery, and Psychiatry, 23,* 56–62.

Hanna, G. L. (2000). Clinical and family-genetic studies of childhood obsessive-compulsive disorder. In W. K. Goodman, M. V. Rudorfer, & J. D. Maser (Eds.), *Obsessive-compulsive disorder: Contemporary issues in treatment* (pp. 133–154). Mahwah, NJ: Erlbaum.

Hartl, T. L., Frost, R. O., Allen, G. J., Deckersbach, T., Steketee, G., Duffany, S. R., et al. (2004). Actual and perceived memory deficits in individuals with compulsive hoarding. *Depression and Anxiety, 20*(2), 59–69.

Hayes, S., Strosahl, K. D., & Wilson, K. G. (1999). *Acceptance and commitment therapy: An experiential approach to behavioral change.* New York: Guilford Press.

Hermans, D., Martens, K., De Cort, K., Pieters, G., & Eelen, P. (2003). Reality monitoring and metacognitive beliefs related to cognitive confidence in obsessive-compulsive disorder. *Behavior Research and Therapy, 41,* 383–401.

Hollander, E., Friedberg, J. P., Wasserman, S., Yeh, C., & Iyengar, R. (2005). The case for the OCD spectrum. In J. S. Abramowitz & A. C. Houts (Eds.), *Concepts and controversies in obsessive-compulsive disorder* (pp. 95–113). New York: Springer.

Hollander, E., Kaplan, A., Allen, A., & Cartwright, C. (2000). Pharmacotherapy for obsessive-compulsive disorder. *Psychiatric Clinics of North America, 23,* 643–656.

Hollander, E., & Wong, C. M. (1995). Obsessive-compulsive spectrum disorders. *Journal of Clinical Psychiatry, 56,* 53–55.

Jacobson, N. S., Roberts, L. J., Berns, S. B., & McGlinchey, J. B. (1999). Methods for defining and determining the clinical significance of treatment effects: Description, application, and alternatives. *Journal of Consulting and Clinical Psychology, 67,* 300–307.

Janeck, A. S., Calamari, J. E., Riemann, B. R., & Heffelfinger, S. K. (2003). Too much thinking about thinking? Meta-cognitive differences in obsessive-compulsive disorder. *Journal of Anxiety Disorders, 17,* 181–195.

Janet, P. (1903). *Les obsessions et la psychasthénie.* Paris: Félix Alcan.

Jenike, M. A. (1998). Theories of etiology. In M. A. Jenike, L. Baer, & W. E. Minichiello (Eds.), *Obsessive-compulsive disorder: Practical management* (3rd ed., pp. 203–221). St. Louis, MO: Mosby.

Jenike, M. A. (2004). Clinical practice: Obsessive-compulsive disorder. *New England Journal of Medicine, 350,* 259–265.

Karno, M., Golding, J. M., Sorenson, S. B., & Burnam, M. A. (1988). The epidemiology of obsessive-compulsive disorder in five U.S. communities. *Archives of General Psychiatry, 45,* 1094–1099.

Kozak, M. J., & Coles, M. E. (2005). Treatment for OCD: Unleashing the power of exposure. In J. S. Abramowitz & A. C. Houts (Eds.), *Concepts and controversies in obsessive-compulsive disorder* (pp. 283–304). New York: Springer.

Kuelz, A. K., Hohagen, F., & Voderholzer, U. (2004). Neuropsychological performance in obsessive-compulsive disorder: A critical review. *Biological Psychology, 65,* 185–236.

Kumar, T. C., & Khanna, S. (2000). Lamotrigine augmentation of serotonin re-uptake inhibitors in obsessive-compulsive disorder. *Australian and New Zealand Journal of Psychiatry, 34,* 527–528.

Leckman, J. F., Grice, D. E., Boardman, J., Zhang, H., Vitale, A., Bondi, C., et al. (1997). Symptoms of obsessive-compulsive disorder. *American Journal of Psychiatry, 154,* 911–917.

Lee, H. J., & Kwon, S. M. (2003). Two different types of obsession: Autogenous obsessions and reactive obsessions. *Behavior Research and Therapy, 41,* 11–29.

Lee, H. J., & Telch, M. J. (2005). Autogenous/reactive obsessions and their relationship with OCD symptoms and schizotypal personality features. *Journal of Anxiety Disorders, 19,* 793–805.

Marker, C. D., Calamari, J. E., Woodard, J. L., & Riemann, B. C. (2006). Cognitive self-consciousness, implicit learning, and obsessive-compulsive disorder. *Journal of Anxiety Disorders, 20,* 389–407.

Mataix-Cols, D. (2006). Deconstructing obsessive-compulsive disorder: A multidimensional perspective. *Current Opinions in Psychiatry, 19,* 1984–1989.

Mataix-Cols, D., Rosario-Campos, M. C., & Leckman, J. F. (2005). A multidimensional model of obsessive-compulsive disorder. *American Journal of Psychiatry, 162,* 228–238.

Meyer, V. (1966). Modification of expectations in cases with obsessional rituals. *Behavior Research and Therapy, 4,* 273–280.

Mineka, S., & Zinbarg, R. (2006). A contemporary learning theory perspective on the etiology of anxiety disorders: It's not what you thought it was. *American Psychologist, 61,* 10–26.

Moritz, S., Fricke, S., Wagner, M., & Hand, I. (2001). Further evidence for delayed alternation deficits in obsessive-compulsive disorder. *Journal of Nervous and Mental Diseases, 189,* 562–564.

Mowrer, O. H. (1960). *Learning theory and behavior.* New York: Wiley.

Myers, S. G., & Wells, A. (2005). Obsessive-compulsive symptoms: The contribution of metacognitions and responsibility. *Journal of Anxiety Disorders, 19,* 806–817.

Nestadt, G., Samuels, J., Riddle, M., Bienvenu, O. J., Liang, K. Y., LaBuda, M., et al. (2000). A family study of obsessive–compulsive disorder. *Archives of General Psychiatry, 57,* 358–363.

Neziroglu, F., Anemone, R., & Yaryura-Tobias, J. (1992). Onset of obsessive-compulsive disorder in pregnancy. *American Journal of Psychiatry, 149,* 947–950.

Neziroglu, F., Henricksen, J., & Yaryura-Tobias, J. A. (2006). Psychotherapy of obsessive-compulsive disorder and spectrum: Established facts and advances, 1995–2005. *Psychiatric Clinics of North America, 29,* 585–604.

Neziroglu, F., McKay, D., Yaryura-Tobias, J. A., Stevens, K. P., & Todaro, J. (1999). The Overvalued Ideas Scale: Development, reliability and validity in obsessive-compulsive disorder. *Behavior Research and Therapy, 37,* 881–902.

Nielen, M. M., Veltman, D. J., de Jong, R., Mulder, G., & den Boer, J. A. (2002). Decision making performance in obsessive compulsive disorder. *Journal of Affective Disorders, 69,* 257–260.

Obsessive Compulsive Cognitions Working Group. (1997). Cognitive assessment of obsessive-compulsive disorder. *Behavior Research and Therapy, 35,* 667–681.

Obsessive Compulsive Cognitions Working Group. (2001). Development and initial validation of the Obsessive Beliefs Questionnaire and the Interpretation of Intrusions Inventory. *Behavior Research and Therapy, 39,* 987–1006.

Obsessive Compulsive Cognitions Working Group. (2003). Psychometric validation of the Obsessive Beliefs Questionnaire and the Interpretation of Intrusions Inventory: Part I. *Behavior Research and Therapy, 41,* 1245–1264.

Obsessive Compulsive Cognitions Working Group. (2005). Psychometric validation of the Obsessive Beliefs Questionnaire and the Interpretation of Intrusions Inventory: Part II. Factor analyses and testing of a brief version. *Behavior Research and Therapy, 43,* 1527–1542.

Pallanti, S., & Quercioli, L. (2006). Treatment-refractory obsessive-compulsive disorder: Methodological issues, operational definitions and therapeutic lines. *Progress in Neuro-Psychopharmacology and Biological Psychiatry, 30,* 400–412.

Purcell, R., Maruff, P., Kyrios, M., & Pantelis, C. (1998). Cognitive deficits in obsessive-compulsive disorder on tests of frontal-striatal function. *Biological Psychiatry, 43,* 348–357.

Rachman, S. (1997). A cognitive theory of obsessions. *Behavior Research and Therapy, 35,* 793–802.

Rachman, S. (1998a). A cognitive theory of obsessions: Elaborations. *Behavior Research and Therapy, 36,* 385–401.

Rachman, S. (1998b). Progress toward a cognitive clinical psychology. *Journal of Psychosomatic Research, 45,* 387–389.

Rachman, S. (2002). A cognitive theory of compulsive checking. *Behavior Research and Therapy, 40,* 625–639.

Rachman, S. (2004). Fear of contamination. *Behavior Research and Therapy, 42,* 1227–1255.

Rachman, S., & de Silva, P. (1978). Abnormal and normal obsessions. *Behavior Research and Therapy, 16,* 233–248.

Rachman, S., Thordarson, D. S., Shafran, R., & Woddy, S. R. (1995). Perceived responsibility: Structure and significance. *Behavior Research and Therapy, 33,* 779–784.

Radomsky, A. S., & Rachman, S. (2004). Symmetry, ordering and arranging compulsive behavior. *Behavior Research and Therapy, 42,* 893–913.

Rasmussen, S. A., & Eisen, J. L. (1992). The epidemiology and clinical features of obsessive compulsive disorder. *Psychiatric Clinics of North America, 15,* 743–758.

Rassin, E., Merckelbach, H., Muris, P., & Schmidt, H. (2001). The Thought-Action Fusion Scale: Further evidence for its reliability and validity. *Behavior Research and Therapy, 39,* 537–544.

Rauch, S. L., Corá-Locatelli, G., & Greenberg, B. D. (2002). Pathogenesis of obsessive-compulsive disorder. In D. J. Stein & E. Hollander (Eds.), *Textbook of anxiety disorders* (pp. 191–205). Washington, DC: American Psychiatric Publishing.

Rauch, S. L., & Savage, C. R. (2000). Investigating cortico-striatal pathophysiology in obsessive compulsive disorders: Procedural learning and imaging probes. In W. K. Goodman, M. V. Rudorfer, & J. D. Maser (Eds.), *Obsessive-compulsive disorder: Contemporary issues in treatment* (pp. 133–154). Mahwah, NJ: Erlbaum.

Reed, G. F. (1985). *Obsessional experience and compulsive behavior: A cognitive-structural approach.* New York: Academic Press.

Renshaw, K. D., Chambless, D. L., & Steketee, G. (2006). The relationship of relatives' attributions to their expressed emotion and to patients' improvement in treatment for anxiety disorders. *Behavior Research and Therapy, 37,* 159–169.

Rosqvist, J. (2005). *Exposure treatments for anxiety disorders: A practitioner's guide to concepts, methods and evidence-based practice.* New York: Routledge.

Rothbaum, B. O. (2006). Virtual reality exposure therapy. In B. O. Rothbaum (Ed.), *Pathological anxiety: Emotional processing in etiology and treatment* (pp. 227–244). New York: Guilford Press.

Salkovskis, P. M. (1985). Obsessional-compulsive problems: A cognitive-behavioral analysis. *Behavior Research and Therapy, 23,* 571–583.

Salkovskis, P. M., Forrester, E., & Richards, C. (1998). Cognitive-behavioral approach to understanding obsessional thinking. *British Journal of Psychiatry, (35),* 53–63.

Salkovskis, P. M., Forrester, E., Richards, H. C., & Morrison, M. (1998). The devil is in the detail: Conceptualizing and treating obsessional problems. In N. Tarrier, A. Wells, & G. Haddock (Eds.), *Treating complex cases: The cognitive behavioral therapy approach* (pp. 47–80). New York: Wiley.

Salkovskis, P. M., Shafran, R., Rachman, S., & Freeston, M. H. (1999). Multiple pathways to inflated responsibility beliefs in obsessional problems: Possible origins and implications for therapy and research. *Behavior Research and Therapy, 37,* 1055–1072.

Samuels, J. F., Riddle, M. A., Greenberg, B. D., Fyer, A. J., McCracken, J. T., Rauch, S. L., et al. (2006). The OCD Collaborative Genetics Study: Methods and sample description. *American Journal of Medical Genetics: Pt. B. Neuropsychiatric Genetics, 141,* 201–207.

Savage, C. R., Baer, L., Keuthen, N. J., Brown, H. D., Rauch, S. L., & Jenike, M. A. (1999). Organizational strategies mediate nonverbal memory impairment in obsessive-compulsive disorder. *Biological Psychiatry, 45,* 905–916.

Savage, C. R., Deckersbach, T., Wilhelm, S., Rauch, S. L., Baer, L., Reid, T., et al. (2000). Strategic processing and episodic memory impairment in obsessive compulsive disorder. *Neuropsychology, 14,* 141–151.

Saxena, S., Brody, A. L., Schwartz, J. M., & Baxter, L. R. (1998). Neuroimaging and frontal-subcortical circuitry in obsessive-compulsive disorder. *British Journal of Psychiatry, (35),* 26–37.

Schmidtke, K., Schorb, A., Winkelmann, G., & Hohagen, F. (1998). Cognitive frontal lobe dysfunction in obsessive-compulsive disorder. *Biological Psychiatry, 43,* 666–673.

Schwartz, J. M. (1998). Neuroanatomical aspects of cognitive-behavioral therapy response in obsessive-compulsive disorder: An evolving perspective on brain and behavior. *British Journal of Psychiatry, (35)*, 38–44.

Schwartz, J. M. (1999). A role for volition and attention in the generation of new brain circuitry: Toward a neurobiology of mental force. *Journal of Consciousness Studies, 6*, 115–142.

Shafran, R. (1997). The manipulation of responsibility in obsessive-compulsive disorder. *British Journal of Clinical Psychology, 36*, 397–407.

Shafran, R., Thordarson, D. S., & Rachman, S. (1996). Thought-action fusion in obsessive compulsive disorder. *Journal of Anxiety Disorders, 10*, 379–391.

Simpson, H. B., Rosen, W., Huppert, J. D., Lin, S. H., Foa, E. B., & Liebowitz, M. R. (2006). Are there reliable neuropsychological deficits in obsessive-compulsive disorder? *Journal of Psychiatric Research, 40*, 247–257.

Stanley, M. A., & Turner, S. M. (1995). Current status of pharmacological and behavioral treatment of obsessive compulsive disorder. *Behavior Therapy, 26*, 163–186.

Steketee, G. S. (1993). *Treatment of obsessive-compulsive disorder.* New York: Guilford Press.

Steketee, G. S., Frost, R., & Bogart, K. (1996). The Yale-Brown Obsessive Compulsive Scale: Interview versus self-report. *Behavior Research and Therapy, 34*, 675–684.

Steketee, G. S., Lam, J. N., Chambless, D. L., Rodebaugh, T. L., & McCullough, C. E. (2007). Effects of perceived criticism on anxiety and depression during behavioral treatment of anxiety disorders. *Behavior Research and Therapy, 45*, 11–19.

Summerfeldt, L. J., Richter, M. A., Antony, M. M., & Swinson, R. P. (1999). Symptom structure in obsessive-compulsive disorder: A confirmatory factor-analytic study. *Behavior Research and Therapy, 37*, 297–311.

Taylor, S., Abramowitz, J. S., McKay, D., Calamari, J. E., Sookman, D., Kyrios, M., et al. (2006). Do dysfunctional beliefs play a role in all types of obsessive-compulsive disorder? *Journal of Anxiety Disorders, 20*, 85–97.

Thordarson, D. S., Radomsky, A. S., Rachman, S., Shafran, R., Sawchuk, C. N., & Hakstian, A. (2004). The Vancouver Obsessional Compulsive Inventory (VOCI). *Behavior Research and Therapy, 42*, 1289–1314.

Twohig, M. P., Hayes, S. C., & Masuda, A. (2006). Increasing willingness to experience obsessions: Acceptance and commitment therapy as a treatment for obsessive-compulsive disorder. *Behavior Therapy, 37*, 3–13.

van Oppen, P., de Haan, E., van Balkom, A. J., Spinhoven, P., Hoogduin, K., & van Dyck, R. (1995). Cognitive therapy and exposure in vivo in the treatment of obsessive compulsive disorder. *Behavior Research and Therapy, 33*, 379–390.

Watkins, L. H., Sahakian, B. J., Robertson, M. M., Veale, D. M., Rogers, R. D., Pickard, K. M., et al. (2005). Executive function in Tourette's syndrome and obsessive-compulsive disorder. *Psychological Medicine, 35*, 571–582.

Weissman, M. M., Bland, R. C., Canino, G. J., Greenwald, S., Hwu, H. G., Lee, C. K., et al. (1994). The cross national epidemiology of obsessive compulsive disorder (The Cross National Collaborative Group). *Journal of Clinical Psychiatry, 55*, 5–10.

Wells, A. (2002). *Emotional disorders and metacognitions: Innovative cognitive therapy.* Hoboken, NJ: Wiley.

World Health Organization. (2001). *The world health report 2001—Mental health: New understanding, new hope.* Geneva, Switzerland: Author.

Yoshida, T., Taga, C., Matsumoto, Y., & Fukui, K. (2005). Paternal overprotection in obsessive-compulsive disorder and depression with obsessive traits. *Psychiatry and Clinical Neurosciences, 59*, 533–538.

CHAPTER 11

Posttraumatic Stress Disorder

WILLIAM J. KOCH AND MICHELLE HARING

DESCRIPTION OF THE DISORDER

Posttraumatic Stress Disorder (PTSD; American Psychiatric Association, 2000) is a condition consisting of a variety of anxiety, depressive, and other emotional symptoms of distress that are thought to be precipitated by a person's direct exposure to extremely threatening events. Intrusive (i.e., involuntary) and distressing memories of specific threatening events are considered unique to PTSD. Other symptoms of PTSD overlap with other mental disorders. For example, reduced interest in social and recreational activities that appears as one of the Cluster C symptoms of PTSD is also a symptom of depression; the hypervigilance symptoms found in Cluster D of PTSD are part of the symptoms of Generalized Anxiety Disorder; and the behavioral avoidance of trauma reminders symptom found in Cluster C of PTSD overlaps with behavioral avoidance found in specific phobias.

Occurrence of such involuntary distressing memories of traumatic events has been recognized for centuries. For example, Samuel Pepys described residual symptoms of what we now call PTSD in his diary note of February 28, 1667, in which he described his continued distress about the great London fire of September 1666:

> It is strange to think how to this very day I cannot sleep a-night without great terrors of fire; and this very night I could not sleep till almost 2 in the morning through thoughts of fire. (Samuel Pepys Diary 1666—Great Fire)

During the nineteenth century, growing interest by medical professionals in adverse emotional responses to extremely threatening events led to a plethora of contextually related terms to describe such responses, for example, railway mind (Harrington, 1996) and soldier's heart (Tomb, 1994), reflecting the observations of cases of emotional distress following railway trauma and civil war trauma, respectively. However, it was not until the involvement of U.S. troops in the Vietnam War, with the subsequent increase in claims of disability related to combat experience, that the term PTSD became codified by the American Psychiatric Association in their *Diagnostic and Statistical Manual of Mental Disorders* (*DSM-III*; American Psychiatric Association, 1980).

Since inclusion of this diagnosis in *DSM-III*, research concerning PTSD, trauma, and related topics has increased exponentially, and use of this concept has influenced popular culture, the media, and law. Burgeoning research and public interest in PTSD in the past quarter-century has led to significant refinement in our conceptualization and understanding of this important disorder.

First, research has demonstrated that the presumed causal raw material of PTSD, traumatic events, is in fact much more common than was originally thought. In fact, most studies examining exposure to potentially traumatic events (PTEs) have shown that more than 60% of respondents have experienced at least one PTE in their life (Norris, 1992). For this reason, the initial diagnostic criteria for PTSD, which described it as a response that is confined to exposure to an "event outside the range of usual human experiences" (American Psychiatric Association, 1987), have been amended to focus more specifically on the experience of a PTE in combination with a particular emotional response to this event. This change was made in large part to account for this notable discrepancy between exposure to traumatic events and the development of PTSD.

Second, only a minority of exposed persons develop PTSD, with lifetime prevalence estimates hovering around 8% (Breslau, Davis, Andreski, & Peterson, 1991). This finding, in combination with the high base rate of PTEs, leads to an obvious conclusion that the development of PTSD must not be randomly distributed. In fact, there is a substantial research literature showing that development of PTSD is made more likely by a variety of pretrauma personal factors, such as previous anxiety proneness, depression, and other adverse life experiences (Bowman, 1999).

Third, despite early formulations that the unusually threatening nature of the trauma was critical for development of adverse emotional responses, more recent research demonstrates that the best predictors of the development of PTSD are various facets of the person's initial emotional, cognitive, and behavioral response to the traumatic event (e.g., Ehlers, Mayou, & Bryant, 1998). Early research showing this phenomenon led to what was at the time a controversial change in the *DSM* diagnostic criteria that gave greater credence to the person's response to the traumatic event in *DSM-IV* (American Psychiatric Association, 1994; e.g., that the person respond with intense fear, helplessness, or horror). Such controversy stems from the history of disability and compensation claims arising from trauma exposure since the nineteenth century (see review by Koch, Douglas, Nicholls, & O'Neill, 2006).

Fourth, the impact of trauma exposure and of PTSD in particular has been increasingly implicated in economic functioning (e.g., Fairbank, Ebert, & Zarkin, 1999) and physical illness (e.g., Schnurr & Green, 2004). This has led to forensic mental health professionals being called on to assess the impact of trauma on individuals' emotional and physical well-being and their ability to function in important domains, as insurance claims are increasingly initiated by traumatized individuals seeking restitution for psychological injuries.

In short, research concerning people's responses to traumatic events has evolved rapidly in the past quarter-century to the point that we now have a more nuanced appreciation of the ubiquity of trauma in daily life, individual differences in trauma response, the influences of individuals' initial emotional response on later coping with trauma exposure, and the impact of trauma and subsequent distress on economic functioning and physical health.

DIAGNOSIS AND ASSESSMENT

Diagnostic criteria for PTSD cover four domains, as well as duration (1 month) and disability/distress requirements. This disorder is unique because it is the only condition in the *DSM* that requires assessment of an environmental or social event as part of the diagnosis. Thus, the person-event combination being assessed must satisfy both of the following: (Criterion A1) "The person experienced, witnessed, or was confronted with an event or events that involved actual or threatened death or serious injury, or a threat to the physical integrity of self or others," and (Criterion A2) "The person's response involved intense fear, helplessness, or horror" (American Psychiatric Association, 2000, p. 467).

Assessment of Criterion A

This unique requirement demands that clinicians investigate two phenomena that they are seldom trained to assess: (1) occurrence and objective characteristics of a traumatic event (e.g., motor vehicle collision and resulting physical injuries), and (2) the person's mental and emotional state at some date that could be any time from days to years in the past. This assessment task is made more complicated by three conundrums. First, most clinicians tend to underinvestigate the occurrence of PTEs in their daily practice. Second, objective characteristics of PTEs (e.g., dollar value of damage to a car in a motor vehicle collision, extent of physical injuries) have little or no utility with respect to predicting the onset of PTSD. Third, retrospective estimations of people's subjective emotional states are exceedingly unreliable. We discuss a conservative method for assessing Criterion A in this section.

If part of the diagnosis of PTSD is dependent on the individual's experience with traumatic events, it behooves clinicians to screen for PTEs. Several self-report and interview screening tools are available (e.g., Stressful Life Events Screening Questionnaire: Goodman, Corcoran, Turner, Yuan, & Green, 1998; Traumatic Life Events Questionnaire: Kubany et al., 2000). Following such screening, however, the clinician must evaluate a number of domains of the event itself and the individual's response to the event. First, although scientific research has offered up equivocal data supporting a dose-response relationship between objective trauma severity and subsequent PTSD status, thoughtful assessors will ask themselves, "Would a reasonable person feel that his or her physical or emotional well-being was threatened by this event?" Not all motor vehicle accident experiences or coercive sexual experiences are the same, and clinicians should spend some time on evaluating the objectively threatening aspects of individual PTEs experienced by their clients. Interwoven with such investigation, the individual's initial emotional and physiological reaction to the event should be investigated. This will involve determining the extent to which he or she experienced severe fear at the time of the event, whether he or she responded with a panic attack (e.g., Bryant & Panasetis, 2001) or with dissociative symptoms (e.g., Ursano et al., 1999), whether objective evidence for excessive physiological arousal at the time exists (Shalev et al., 1998), and what the trauma survivor thought the worst-case scenario might have been at the time.

Symptomatic Assessment of PTSD

Once one has established that the individual being assessed has suffered a PTE with an initially adverse emotional response, one can move on to assessing whether he or she suffers from PTSD symptoms. To meet formal diagnostic criteria, a person must suffer one or more of the five reexperiencing symptoms (Criterion B, e.g., upsetting nightmares), three or more of the seven avoidance/numbing symptoms (Criterion C, e.g., avoidance of physical or social reminders of the event, emotional numbing), and two or more of the five hyperarousal symptoms (Criterion D, e.g., sleep disturbance). Assessment of such symptoms requires a detailed inquiry about frequency and severity of such symptoms, as opposed to a mere checklist accounting of, for example, nightmares. The Clinician's Assessment of PTSD Scale (CAPS; Blake et al., 1990) is one of the best validated semi-structured interviews for assessing in detail PTSD symptoms (see, e.g., review in Chapter 3 of Koch et al., 2006). The CAPS formulates questions in the following manner:

> Have you ever had unwanted memories of (event)? What were they like? . . . How often have you had these memories in the past month? . . . How much distress or discomfort did these memories cause you? Were you able to put them out of your mind and think about something else? How hard did you have to try? How much did they interfere with your life? (CAPS-DX; Blake et al., 1998, p. 3)

A set of questions like this results in the assessor then scoring the relative frequency of the symptom on a scale of 0 (never) to 4 (daily or almost every day), and severity on a scale of 0 (none) to 4 (extreme, incapacitating distress, cannot dismiss memories, unable to continue activities). As the reader can imagine, many respondents will achieve frequency and severity scores somewhere between 0 and 4, but few will achieve scores of 4. Thus, the assessment of PTSD requires relatively detailed inquiry about each of the potential 17 symptoms. The developers of this interview (Blake et al., 1990) recommended using a combined frequency plus severity score of 3 (e.g., rating of 2 on frequency and 1 on severity) as the cutoff for determining a symptom to be of clinical significance, and then diagnosing PTSD based on the individual's having sufficient clinically significant symptoms according to *DSM* rules. Subsequent studies (Blanchard et al., 1995; Weathers, Ruscio, & Keane, 1999) evaluated different strategies for using CAPS-obtained data in identifying cases of PTSD. In brief, these two different research groups found that rates of PTSD varied from 27% to 82%, dependent on the stringency of symptom severity scores and total CAPS scores set as the PTSD threshold. For example, in the Weathers et al. study, the original rule of 3 originally adopted by Blake et al. resulted in the highest rates of PTSD (48% to 82%), and a combination rule of 3 plus total symptom severity score of 65 resulted in relatively equal false negatives and false positives and a PTSD rate of 34% to 59%. This research suggests that the rules clinicians use to define a symptom as present or absent and the cutoff they use for total symptom frequency and severity have a significant impact on PTSD prevalence.

For a number of reasons, PTSD is a mental health condition that requires a multitrait, multimethod model of assessment (Campbell & Fiske, 1959). The latter term reflects the scientific consensus that most psychological phenomena are multidimensional and that different sources or methods of assessing such phenomena will provide richer and more diverse perspectives on the particular phenomenon (e.g., PTSD) being assessed (G. J. Meyer, 2002). For this reason, a diversity of self-report tests of PTSD symptoms and related constructs have been developed and are commonly used in research and clinical assessments of individuals presenting with distress associated with traumatic experiences. Similarly, use of information taken from sources other than the client himself or herself (known as collateral sources), such as family members, is often obtained to broaden the perspective of the individual client's psychological distress and daily functioning. Such collateral information is particularly important with respect to PTSD because it is an increasingly common claim made in personal injury lawsuits and worker's compensation disability cases and because forensic experts recommend the use of assessment data beyond that supplied by the client (Melton, Petrila, Poythress, & Slobogin, 1997).

Symptomatic status can be assessed via either semi-structured interview or via a plethora of self-report screening measures, such as the PTSD Checklist (Weathers & Ford, 1996), of which there are both civilian and combat veteran versions. The reader should appreciate that, although such self-report screening tools correlate highly with interview-based diagnoses, they may overestimate symptomatic status because of their transparent nature and the absence of the opportunity for clarification of positive responses. For a more detailed review of such instruments, the reader is referred to Koch et al. (2006).

Beyond the assessment of PTSD diagnostic status and symptom severity, a comprehensive clinical assessment will evaluate the following areas that have implications for prognosis and treatment: (a) comorbid diagnoses, and (b) negative prognostic indicators. We next selectively describe these factors along with selected research literature.

COMMON COMORBID CONDITIONS

A number of other stress-related anxiety, mood, substance, and somatic disorders occurs concurrently with PTSD at higher than expected rates. In particular, depression occurs concurrently in between 33% and 50% of PTSD cases (e.g., Blanchard et al., 2003; Brown, Campbell, Lehman, Grisham, & Mancill, 2001) and can negatively influence treatment outcome (e.g., Taylor et al., 2001). Thus, it is important to screen for depressed mood in PTSD cases.

Panic Disorder is also highly comorbid with PTSD (Brown et al., 2001) and may have commonalities with PTSD, in particular because panic attacks are common in PTSD sufferers during their initial reaction to PTEs (Bryant & Panasetis, 2001). Also, PTSD sufferers, like Panic Disorder clients, have high levels of anxiety sensitivity (Taylor, Koch, & McNally, 1992). A high frequency of panic attacks or fear of such attacks and the bodily sensations associated with them can complicate treatment of PTSD.

Generalized Anxiety Disorder, a condition characterized by excessive worry proneness, also appears to occur at a high rate in PTSD sufferers (e.g., Blanchard et al., 2003). It may complicate the presentation of PTSD cases, as illustrated in the case we present later in the chapter, and has been shown in some research to be a negative prognostic indicator for the treatment of PTSD.

Substance abuse (Stewart, 1996) is a relatively common clinical problem associated with exposure to PTEs and is also commonly comorbid with PTSD. It appears that PTSD sufferers often use alcohol and other substances to sedate themselves (e.g., Stewart, Conrod, Pihl, & Dongier, 1999). Given that substance abuse is a potentially disabling health problem in its own right and that ongoing substance abuse may interfere with successful treatment of PTSD, astute clinicians must screen for such problems. Chronic pain and somatization disorders commonly occur in PTSD cases and may complicate both the prognosis and the treatment of PTSD.

NEGATIVE PROGNOSTIC INDICATORS

When assessing a PTSD sufferer, it is critical to consider those factors known to predict a negative outcome. Several research groups using varied trauma populations have investigated predictors of treatment outcome, most commonly for variants of cognitive-behavioral and exposure therapy. A variety of pretrauma historical variables, comorbid medical and psychological conditions or states, and posttrauma environmental variables have been found to predict negative outcomes. However, the reader should be aware that this research area has a number of conflicting findings.

As might be predicted from a learning theory perspective, previous exposure to trauma as a child and the number of previous traumas both predict a worse outcome for PTSD sufferers following an adult trauma, even if subjects receive evidence-based treatment (e.g., Hembree, Street, Riggs, & Foa, 2004). Such findings are most parsimoniously explained as suggesting that these multiply traumatized individuals have stronger learning histories concerning danger and the need for self-protection and thus may require additional or more varied treatment to achieve good outcomes.

A number of comorbid conditions appear to interfere with successful treatment of PTSD and thus merit evaluation during initial assessment of possible PTSD cases. Chronic pain conditions (as is common in motor vehicle collision survivors) both predict the development of PTSD and negative responses to PTSD treatment. Whether pain serves as an ongoing reminder of the incident trauma, or whether it merely diverts the individual's coping resources from dealing with his or her PTSD, chronic pain should be treated either before or concurrently with PTSD for best effects.

Many PTSD sufferers also present with problematic anger, some of which may be focused on the perpetrator of their trauma (e.g., the other driver), at professionals involved in their care, or at family members or friends. Anger, whether measured as a trait or as the person's expressed anger at another person, is a negative indicator. There is some evidence that anger experienced during prolonged imaginal exposure interferes with the habituation of anxiety (Foa, Riggs, Massie, & Yarczower, 1995).

Alcohol and prescription sedative use have also been implicated in negative outcome following cognitive-behavioral treatment of PTSD (van Minnen, Arntz, & Keijsers, 2002). It seems likely that active substance abuse of any kind will interfere with treatment of PTSD. More significantly, however, may be the interfering effects of sedative prescriptions because of (a) their ubiquitous use in the general population and (b) their apparent interference with the process of habituation during exposure therapy.

Depression (e.g., Taylor et al., 2001) and Generalized Anxiety Disorder (Tarrier, Sommerfield, Pilgrim, & Faragher, 2000), when occurring concurrently with PTSD, have also been found to predict worse outcome.

The impact of several of these variables is predicted in the outcome of Taylor et al.'s (2001) study. These authors conducted a large ($N = 50$) open trial of cognitive-behavioral therapy for PTSD following motor vehicle accidents. Following treatment, the authors performed a statistical cluster analysis to separate those patients who showed significant improvement in their PTSD symptoms (termed "responders," $n = 30$) and those patients who showed relatively little improvement ("partial responders," $n = 20$). Before treatment, partial responders experienced more severe numbing symptoms, greater depression, more severe pain, and greater trait anger.

CONCEPTUALIZATION

In this section, we discuss psychological models of Posttraumatic Stress Disorder and the evolution of such models over the past 25 years.

LEARNING THEORY MODELS

Initial learning theory models of PTSD drew on Mowrer's (1960) two-factor learning theory. Essentially, two-factor learning theory proposes that through classical conditioning, a neutral stimulus (e.g., travel in a motor vehicle) is paired with an aversive unconditioned stimulus (e.g., serious physical injury, the perception that one might die violently). Through temporal contiguity, the previously neutral stimulus comes to elicit anxiety and takes on the function of a conditioned stimulus (CS; e.g., the individual is now anxious when driving in similar traffic situations). Subsequently, the new CS is paired temporally with other neutral stimuli (e.g., other traffic situations), leading to anxiety over a broader array of situations. To cope with exposure to anxiety-provoking CSs, the individual then learns to avoid such CSs (e.g., reducing the amount he or she drives) or to quickly escape from such situations (e.g., terminates driving episodes prematurely). This theory is useful for explaining generalized fear and avoidance in PTSD sufferers, but has been criticized for inadequately accounting for other commonly observed symptoms of PTSD, such as excessive startle responses and reexperiencing symptoms such as nightmares.

More recent work (see Mineka & Zinbarg, 2006, for a brief review) suggests that contemporary learning theory that incorporates concepts such as learned helplessness, and the opioid-mediated effects of stress-induced passivity, may explain more of the observed symptoms than earlier appreciated. For example, there is evidence from both animal and human research that exposure to uncontrollable and/or unpredictable stress results in high levels of generalized arousal and passive avoidance behavior. There is also some anecdotal evidence at the human level that trauma survivors who were less surprised by the traumatic event or who engaged in active resistance to being victimized are less likely to develop PTSD. In this enhanced learning theory perspective, symptoms of emotional numbing are thought to be a form of analgesia that functions to terminate or dampen aversive arousal (e.g., Pitman, Van der Kolk, Orr, & Greenberg, 1990). There is a growing research base suggesting that active—versus passive—responses during the traumatic event will inoculate individuals from developing PTSD (e.g., Dunsmore, Clark, & Ehlers, 2001). In short, learning theory models of PTSD appear able to explain much of the fear, behavioral avoidance, reminder distress, emotional numbing, and hypervigilance symptoms of PTSD. However, learning theory models have been criticized for being unable to explain reexperiencing symptoms (e.g., intrusive memories, nightmares, flashbacks).

COGNITIVE MODELS

This explanatory failure of traditional learning theory led Foa, Steketee, and Rothbaum (1989) to develop an associative network cognitive model of PTSD. The reader should note that there have been several other associative network models proposed for

PTSD, although Foa et al.'s article is most often cited.* In brief, associative network theories of PTSD suggest that maladaptive fear networks comprise long-term memory elements concerning stimulus information about feared objects, information about the person's cognitive, physiological, and behavioral responses to the feared objects, and information linking stimuli and responses together. Thus, a PTSD sufferer may encounter an activity or event (e.g., driving a car) that bears some similarity to memories of a feared activity or event (his or her motor vehicle accident), which reminder will activate the fear network, including maladaptive responses of physiological arousal and physical escape behaviors. Network theory explains the success of exposure therapy (see later discussion) as occurring through modification of the maladaptive fear network through extinction of the fear reaction via repeated exposure to the upsetting memory and (differentiating it from classical learning theory) through alterations of the maladaptive expectancies of the PTSD sufferer (e.g., that the anxiety will be unbearable, that he or she will lose control of his or her emotions). Reexperiencing symptoms are explained by network theory as occurring because the overlapping networks of stimulus-response memories (e.g., watching a television show with an ambulance scene triggers memories of ambulances, including the ambulance attending one's own accident) lead to frequent triggering of maladaptive fear responses despite being physically removed from the original scene of the trauma. Thus, even interoceptive sensations (e.g., chest pain during physical exertion) may trigger the fear network that includes chest pain (secondary to broken ribs) associated with a motor vehicle accident and fear for one's life. Network theory accounts for emotional numbing symptoms as representing the effortful avoidance of emotions that may trigger the fear network, and hyperarousal symptoms as a function of ongoing low-level activation of the fear network (i.e., the individual's inability to entirely avoid reminders of the trauma). Network theories are most helpful in explaining reexperiencing symptoms of PTSD and potentially add to our understanding of the workings of exposure therapy.

Schema theories have also been applied to PTSD, most prominently by Horowitz (e.g., Horowitz, Wilner, Kaltreider, & Alvarez, 1980) and Janoff-Bulman (e.g., Janoff-Bulman, 1985). Horowitz's schema theory of PTSD derives from psychodynamic theory, by which he argued that individuals exposed to trauma must match new (trauma-related) information to old information about the world in order to complete a coherent schema. Thus, emotional numbing is thought to be a psychological defense against experiencing the distress associated with the disparity between the traumatized person's previous schemas (e.g., of safety) and his or her new traumatic experience. According to Horowitz's model, the completion tendency (i.e., attempt to assimilate new traumatic information into preexisting schemas of safety) conflicts with the defense mechanisms of numbing.

Janoff-Bulman's (1985) model is a social cognition model that proposes that individuals experiencing trauma suffer more when the trauma violates some assumption of safety they had about the world or themselves. Thus, reexperiencing symptoms are the result of the individual's need to assimilate threatening information into previously more benign schemas. Both schema models suggest that reexperiencing memories of the trauma are ultimately adaptive and support the utility of exposure therapy.

Brewin (2001) proposed a dual representation theory of PTSD that suggests that individuals have both verbally accessible memories and situationally accessible memories of traumatic events. Situationally accessible memories theoretically are accessible

---

*A detailed review of the varied cognitive models of PTSD can be found in Dalgleish (2004).

only when cued by stimuli associated with the frightening trauma, whereas verbally accessible memories are accessible during conversation. This theory proposes that exposure therapy will fail if it does not access situationally accessible memories during trauma recall.

Ehlers and Clark (2000) proposed a cognitive theory of PTSD that suggests that individuals' appraisal of the trauma or of their own responses (e.g., intrusive memories, loss of control) are critical in maintaining PTSD. Thus, PTSD sufferers are thought to remain in their maladaptive fearful and vigilant state because of some combination of their changed appraisals of the world as a dangerous place (e.g., automobile travel is inherently dangerous, all men are rapists) or of their own vulnerability (e.g., having these intrusive thoughts means I'm a poor coper). As the reader can tell, this theory suggests that overcoming such appraisals should be central to therapy.

These various cognitive theories of PTSD appear to add to, but do not supplant, learning theory explanations of PTSD. All these theories make similar predictions with respect to the utility of exposure therapy, although Brewin's (2001) dual representation theory and Ehlers and Clark's (2000) theory may help to explain why exposure therapy is not always effective.

LIFE EVENTS

By definition, PTSD is associated with traumatic and threatening life events. The breadth of types of such threatening events has been stretched in recent years to include such events as life-threatening illness (e.g., cancer), loss of family members via violent death, physical injuries induced by motor vehicle accidents, sexual assault and sexual harassment, schoolyard and workplace bullying, exposure to natural or man-made disasters, combat exposure, torture, and refugee status.

There is some evidence that traumatic events are summative in their effects (e.g., the finding that victims of childhood sexual abuse or other adverse childhood experiences are at higher risk to develop PTSD as adults following other trauma exposure). There is also evidence that further stressors exacerbate individuals' PTSD status or interfere with recovery.

GENETIC INFLUENCES

Research on the genetics of PTSD has explored two pathways through which genetics may influence the development of PTSD. First, genes may influence exposure to certain types of traumatic events. For example, individuals with certain types of personality traits (e.g., antisocial personality) may be more prone to finding or putting themselves in situations that are at high risk for trauma. Second, genetics may influence the likelihood of developing PTSD symptoms following exposure to a traumatic event. Research in this area is complicated by a number of factors, including a broadly defined phenotype (i.e., the considerable variability in symptomatology among individuals with the diagnosis), the specific requirement for environmental exposure, and the high frequency of comorbid psychiatric illness (Radant, Tsuang, Peskind, McFall, & Raskind, 2001). Genetic contributions to PTSD have been explored through family studies, twin studies, and, more recently, through gene association studies that attempt to isolate the location and specific allele that influences genetic vulnerability to PTSD.

Family studies have examined the relatives of individuals with PTSD to determine whether rates of PTSD or other psychiatric illnesses are higher in these groups relative to the families of traumatized individuals without PTSD (e.g., Davidson, Swartz, Storck, Krishnan, & Hammett, 1985; Reich, Lyons, & Kai, 1996; Sack, Clarke, & Seeley, 1995). To date, the major finding to emerge from this research is that a family history of PTSD or anxiety or depressive disorders may increase risk for PTSD, which may suggest a genetic link. Of course, it is also possible that a negative shared family environment, such as a violent household, could explain this relationship.

Twin studies offer a better understanding of the relative contributions of genetic and environmental factors to the development of PTSD. The majority of the twin studies in this area have used the Vietnam Era Twin Registry, a database of records from male-male twin pairs who served in the Vietnam War. In a landmark study, True and colleagues (1993) found that monozygotic (i.e., genetically identical) twins were more concordant for a variety of PTSD symptoms than were dizygotic twins, suggesting a strong role for genetics. Moreover, even after controlling for differences in exposure to trauma, up to 30% of the variance in PTSD symptoms could be explained by genetic factors. In a twin study published the same year using a different sample, Skre and colleagues (Skre, Onstad, Torgeson, Lygren, & Kringlen, 1993) found that diagnoses of PTSD in one twin were found only if the other twin also had some form of anxiety disorder.

Interestingly, more recent studies have suggested that genetic factors may play an important role in both trauma exposure and the experience of PTSD symptoms following trauma. For example, in a study using data from the Vietnam Era Twin Registry, Koenen and colleagues (2002, 2005) found that preexisting Conduct Disorder was a risk factor for both trauma exposure and PTSD symptoms in a dose-response way. Similarly, a study using a community sample of both male and female twin pairs (Stein, Jang, Taylor, Vernon, & Livesley, 2002) suggested that shared genetic influences were important for both exposure to assaultive trauma and the experience of PTSD symptoms following trauma.

Despite the accumulating evidence that genetic influences are important in PTSD, later twin studies using the Vietnam Era Twin Registry have suggested that genetic vulnerabilities to PTSD overlap with vulnerabilities to other types of psychopathology. Chantarujikapong and colleagues (2001) found that genetic influences common to symptoms of Generalized Anxiety Disorder and Panic Disorder account for 21.3% of the genetic variance in PTSD, and genetic influences specific to PTSD account for 13.6% of the genetic variance in PTSD. Similar findings using the same dataset have been reported for drug and alcohol dependence (Xian et al., 2000) and Major Depressive Disorder (Koenen et al., 2003). Additional research using datasets other than the Vietnam Era Twin Registry would help to clarify the generalizability of these findings.

The final line of research bearing on the role of genetics in PTSD has attempted to identify specific genes that may confer additional risk for PTSD. Most of the research in this area has examined genes related to dopamine type 2 receptors, as this neurotransmitter is related to fear conditioning. However, the findings of these studies have been mixed, and to date no clear conclusions are possible from this line of research (Koenen, 2005).

Overall, research on the genetics of PTSD has suggested that genetic factors play a role in PTSD, both in terms of exposure to traumatic events and in terms of the later development of symptoms of PTSD. Moreover, the same genetic factors may be responsible for both of these vulnerabilities (Stein et al., 2002). However, the extent to which these genetic factors convey specific vulnerability to PTSD versus more general vulnerability to psychopathology is not clear.

DRUGS AFFECTING BEHAVIOR

There is limited but growing evidence that trauma survivors and PTSD sufferers in particular use alcohol and other psychoactive substances to self-medicate distress (Stewart et al., 1999). This may account for the relatively high rates of comorbidity between PTSD and substance abuse. Furthermore, it is likely that substance abuse, whether recreational or prescription, serves to maintain psychological distress in PTSD sufferers.

CULTURE AFFECTS ON BEHAVIOR

Minority groups are more likely to be the victim of many forms of trauma (e.g., torture, refugee status), and there is some evidence for higher rates of PTSD in some ethnic minorities (e.g., North American Indians, Hispanics). However, there are substantial differences between heterogeneous minority groups and within trauma categories (e.g., sexual harassment). There are also substantial differences between physical and economic environments that may mediate higher rates of trauma exposure or higher rates of PTSD. There is little strong evidence that ethnocultural status is a risk factor for PTSD once risk factors such as exposure to trauma and socioeconomic status are adequately controlled. For more detail, the interested reader should see the review by Koch et al. (2006).

GENDER AND TRAUMA

It is well-established (see review in Koch et al., 2006) that women face twice the risk of developing PTSD as do men. However, this increased risk of developing PTSD may have less to do with gender than it does with a number of other factors. For example, many PTEs will have different subjective meanings to women than to men (e.g., sexual harassment; DeSouza & Fansler, 2003), and the same event may have objectively more injurious consequences to women than to men (e.g., physical assault). Women may be more likely to suffer other nontraumatic stressors that can make them less likely to recover from PTEs (e.g., Byrne, Resnick, Kilpatrick, Best, & Saunders, 1999). In short, although it is clear that women suffer a higher prevalence of PTSD than do men, the reasons for this may reside in sociocultural, physical, and economic factors rather than in gender per se.

BEHAVIORAL TREATMENT

Behavioral treatment strategies for PTSD have focused on three separate models of intervention. The most extensively studied area is the treatment of chronic PTSD (defined as longer than 3 months) via either open trials or randomized controlled trials, the latter utilizing either wait-list controls or alternative psychological treatments (e.g., supportive counseling, relaxation training). Early intervention strategies targeted either nonselected survivors of large-scale or individual traumas via a single session of debriefing, or survivors who initially exhibit a high level of distress and provided them with a limited number of treatment sessions.

EARLY INTERVENTION TO PREVENT PTSD

Rachman (1980) argued that maladaptive behavioral patterns may be more amenable to change shortly after exposure to traumatic events, and thus prior to the effects of excessive avoidance and escape behavior. Such theorizing, as well as societal influences (e.g., labor-management negotiations for emergency workers such as firefighters and police), encouraged the development of early intervention strategies such as critical incident stress debriefing (CISD), first described by Mitchell (1983). This intervention presumes that normalizing discussion following traumatic stressors will inhibit subsequent psychological distress. Critical incident stress debriefing has typically been evaluated with nonselected survivors of traumatic events and is presented as a group-administered, single-session intervention. Although these debriefing protocols are now quite commonly prescribed for emergency workers and for victims of mass disasters, empirical evaluations of such treatment have shown disappointing results (e.g., see review by Bisson, 2003). Despite several well-controlled evaluations, it does not appear that CISD or similar early interventions applied to nonselected trauma survivors provide any protection from developing PTSD, although there may be other, nonclinical benefits to providing such programs.

There is reason for more optimism about early interventions that target highly distressed survivors and use several sessions of individually administered cognitive-behavioral therapy. Since Acute Stress Disorder (ASD; American Psychiatric Association, 2000) was introduced as a diagnostic category in *DSM-IV*, some researchers have selected ASD sufferers for early intervention trials. The disorder is defined as a reaction to traumatic stress that occurs up to 4 weeks after the index trauma. Preliminary prospective studies suggest that between 60% and 80% of individuals meeting criteria for ASD following a traumatic event will meet criteria for PTSD up to 2 years later (e.g., Harvey & Bryant, 2000).

Researchers from three different sites have found that individuals suffering acute distress in the first month posttrauma who received 4 to 6 sessions of cognitive-behavioral therapy were less symptomatic at 6- or 12-month follow-ups than were subjects in various control groups such as supportive counseling or assessment-only (e.g., Bryant, Moulds, & Nixon, 2003; Echeburua, de Corral, Sarasua, & Zubizarreta, 1996; Foa, Hearst-Ikeda, & Perry, 1995). Acute PTSD and ASD cases may benefit from early intervention of a specific cognitive-behavioral nature. The success of such interventions begs the question of the practicality of screening large numbers of trauma survivors to detect those distressed and vulnerable individuals who may respond positively to early intervention.

BEHAVIORAL TREATMENT OF CHRONIC PTSD

Numerous controlled and open trials of treatment for PTSD lead to the conclusion that cognitive-behavioral therapy (CBT) appears to be the main efficacious psychological treatment for chronic PTSD. Cognitive-behavioral therapy is a label that encompasses a number of similar, yet distinct therapy protocols. Four variations of CBT developed specifically for PTSD have been evaluated and found to be efficacious: stress inoculation training (Veronen & Kilpatrick, 1983), prolonged exposure (Foa et al., 1999), cognitive processing therapy (Resick & Schnicke, 1992), and CBT based on Ehlers and Clark's (2000) cognitive model of PTSD. The efficacy of cognitive-behavioral interventions for chronic PTSD has been demonstrated with different trauma populations, including sexual assault victims, adult survivors of childhood abuse, motor vehicle accident survivors, and veterans.

Prolonged exposure treatment typically includes education about PTSD; breathing retraining; in vivo hierarchy construction and graded repeated exposure (e.g., to different driving situations for PTSD motor vehicle accident victims); prolonged imaginal exposure to trauma memories (e.g., to the assault or subject motor vehicle accident); and imaginal exposure debriefing. Imaginal exposure requires clients to relive the trauma in imagination for a prolonged period of time (typically 45 to 60 minutes). Therapists use various techniques to help clients achieve maximal habituation of anxiety and fear to distressing trauma memories.

Stress inoculation training interventions focus on skills to cope with trauma-related anxiety and other stress-related difficulties. This includes education about PTSD, breathing retraining, applied relaxation, thought stopping, cognitive restructuring, and guided self-dialogue.

Cognitive processing therapy focuses mainly on cognitive therapy and exposure for victims of sexual assault. Exposure is implemented through detailed written accounts of the index trauma that sexual assault survivors read to both themselves and the therapist (similar to that used in prolonged exposure). Consistent with traditional cognitive therapy, the therapist employing cognitive processing therapy identifies distorted beliefs that clients may have about the assault or themselves (e.g., other people's evaluation of the rape victim, subjects' appraisal of reexperiencing symptoms as indications that they are "losing their mind"); challenges these beliefs; and works to create more balanced, realistic beliefs.

The different variants of CBT are all efficacious and appear generally equivalent in outcome.

SPECIAL ISSUES IN BEHAVIORAL TREATMENT OF PTSD

Panic   There is increasing evidence that panic attacks, whether spontaneous or triggered by exposure to reminders of the index trauma, occur frequently in PTSD patients. For example, Falsetti and Resnick (1997) found that 69% of treatment-seeking trauma survivors reported at least one panic attack in the 2 weeks prior to assessment. Falsetti, Resnick, Davis, and Gallagher (2001) developed a specific PTSD treatment protocol (multiple-channel exposure therapy) for comorbid PTSD and Panic Disorder. This implies that PTSD patients who also suffer significantly from panic attacks may require specific treatment for panic and thus may require more treatment in total. Some researchers are beginning to investigate the utility of interoceptive exposure (a behavioral treatment procedure used for Panic Disorder) in the treatment of PTSD (Walde & Taylor, 2005). This is based on the findings of frequent panic attacks in PTSD patients, as well as data suggesting that PTSD patients have excessive sensitivity to body sensations similar to that of Panic Disorder patients (e.g., Taylor et al., 1992).

Guilt and Shame   Perhaps unique within the general PTSD population, many combat-related PTSD survivors experience feelings of both victimization and perpetration of trauma (Foa & Meadows, 1997). Similarly, shame is a common emotion among victims of sexual assault, often associated with either unsupportive reactions from family members or friends following disclosure of the assault or their own negative evaluations of their initially passive response to the assault. Victims of domestic violence may also be more prone to guilt and shame related to their perceived "choice" of the abusive relationship (Kubany, Hill, & Owens, 2003). These same authors developed a variant of CBT for PTSD, referred to as cognitive trauma therapy for formerly battered women. This treatment targets (a) perceived self-responsibility for negative events in the relationship, (b) avoidance of self-protective actions, (c) constraints based on other values such as the sanctity of marriage, and (d) self-blame. Cognitive trauma therapy for formerly battered women also focuses on assertiveness, reducing and managing unwanted contacts with the ex-spouse, and avoidance of future abuse.

PTSD Sufferers Who May Still Be in Danger   With victims of sexual assault, the possibility of revictimization, particularly for women living in troubled neighborhoods or relationships, is a reality to be addressed throughout the course of treatment (Foa & Meadows, 1997). Treatment should focus on differentiating safe from unsafe situations, particularly when conducting the in vivo exposure aspect of the therapy.

Similar to this caveat about treating sexual assault victims, domestic violence victims often experience continuing risk of repeated assault. Such risk may actually increase when an abused person has left the abusive relationship, when he or she may be stalked by the perpetrator. Unique to domestic violence, well-intentioned family members may interfere with victims' attempts to leave the relationship.

Concurrent Pain Conditions   Individuals who suffer both emotional and physical trauma, primarily via either motor vehicle accidents or industrial accidents, will frequently suffer from concurrent pain conditions secondary to orthopedic or soft-tissue injuries. Severity of continuing pain complaints often interferes with CBT for PTSD (e.g., Taylor et al., 2001), and thus CBT of PTSD concurrent with chronic pain conditions is best coordinated with the patient's pain management program.

Concurrent Depression   Because depressive affect compromises individuals' tolerance of emotional distress and impairs motivation, many patients whose PTSD developed after a motor vehicle accident will require help with their depressive condition. This may be most parsimoniously dealt with through behavioral activation such as pleasant event scheduling (e.g., Blanchard et al., 2003).

Treatment of Anger in PTSD Clients   A limited amount of work has been conducted with respect to treating problematic anger in PTSD sufferers. Chemtob, Novaco, Hamada, and Gross (1997) evaluated a 12-session stress inoculation intervention for anger for Vietnam veterans with PTSD and high levels of anger. Although the treatment appeared to successfully reduce anger, it was notable that almost half the subjects in the entire study dropped out of treatment. A great deal of work remains to be done in this particular area.

Treatment of Substance Abuse with PTSD Clients   Recently some research has emerged with respect to treating individuals with comorbid PTSD and substance abuse (e.g., Najavits, Weiss, Shaw, & Muenz, 1998). Najavits et al. conducted an open trial of a 24-session CBT treatment for these comorbid conditions. Completers improved from pretreatment to 3-month posttreatment follow-up on measures of substance use, PTSD symptoms, and somatic complaints. However, as in the study by Chemtob et al. (1997) for excessively angry PTSD subjects, this sample had a high (37%) dropout rate.

Special Issues in In Vivo Exposure   In vivo exposure therapy is a critical part of
PTSD treatment for those clients who have substantial avoidance habits (e.g., avoidance of social situations, of automobile travel). Although it would be unethical to pur-
posefully place the client in an overtly dangerous situation during therapy, therapists
must collaborate with the client to determine what a "reasonable person" would consider excessive avoidance and set goals for in vivo exposure assignments that will
provide the client greater mobility, freedom of movement, and social involvement.
Travel avoidance following a motor vehicle accident provides a cogent example of
this process.

Those PTSD clients whose disorder developed after a motor vehicle accident are
infrequently entirely avoidant of automobile travel. They typically have some limited
mobility that allows them to commute to work or attend other necessary engagements.
However, they are very likely to give up recreational driving (e.g., spur-of-the-moment
errands, driving for pleasure) and are likely to constrain their commuting routes (e.g.,
limited time in car, limited variety of routes). The fact that they can commute to work
sometimes leads clients and their therapists to believe that driving avoidance is not a
significant problem. As well, individual differences with respect to passenger versus
driver fear and avoidance are common; that is, some individuals are more fearful of
passenger travel, and others more fearful of actual driving.

Basic principles of in vivo exposure treatment for individuals fearful and avoidant
of motor vehicle travel include (a) remaining in the feared situation until their anxiety
declines in intensity, (b) altering danger and safety appraisals through repeated and
prolonged benign exposure to motor vehicle travel, and (c) suppressing maladaptive
safety behaviors that increase patients' sense of safety but become "crutches."

Because the auto traffic environment is neither easily controlled nor constant, in
vivo exposure treatment requires that patients repeat their exposure to specific situations that elicit fear (e.g., intersections, freeway on-ramps), rather than just spending
a certain amount of time in a vehicle. The therapist must keep in mind that the feared
situation is not just being in a car, but it is those frequently short-lived traffic situations
that elicit rushes of fear in the individual patient. Thus, in vivo exposure therapy for
these patients often includes "looping" exposures (Koch & Taylor, 1995) to ensure that
clients' emotional distress to specific traffic triggers can successfully habituate.

In vivo exposure is, of course, a potential learning experience in which PTSD sufferers' negative appraisals of the danger in driving or traveling as a passenger can
be empirically tested. Thus, such exposure assignments should be presented as opportunities to learn new safety information, and every travel episode without actual
collisions should be used as a learning experience (e.g., "What did you learn in yester-
day's drive on the highway about the safety of travel?"). Sometimes one can address
safety and danger appraisals without the client actually traveling in a vehicle. For
example, one can turn the client into a traffic observer and ask him or her to monitor
the number of vehicles passing through a busy intersection and the number of actual
collisions so that he or she can compute a probability of collision to use in challenging
his or her danger appraisals.

Finally, most of these patients will exhibit "safety compulsions" (e.g., use of imagi-
nary brakes on the passenger side, backseat driving) that serve to maintain high levels
of vigilance and fearfulness. As with other anxiety disorders, it is helpful to suppress
such safety compulsions during in vivo exposure assignments to achieve maximum
therapeutic impact.

Ethnicity and Treatment Outcome   To our knowledge, only three studies have examined ethnic minorities' differential response to treatment of PTSD. Rosenheck, Fontana, and Cottrol (1995) found that African American veterans participated less in therapy, showed poorer attendance, and had less improvement on outcome measures compared to Caucasian veterans. However, the same research group (Rosenheck & Fontana, 1996) could not replicate this finding. Another study examined the response of Caucasian and African American women to treatment of PTSD following sexual and nonsexual assault (Zoellner, Feeny, Fitzgibbons, & Foa, 1999). These authors found no differences between Caucasian and African American women on several measures, including pretreatment functioning, dropout rates, and overall treatment efficacy. Little is known about the response of other ethnic minorities to PTSD treatment.

MEDICAL TREATMENT

Early Intervention

There have been only limited research trials evaluating pharmaceutical prevention of PTSD. Pitman et al. (2002) found that 40 mg of propranolol administered four times daily for 10 days beginning within 6 hours of accident trauma resulted in decreased heart rate and skin conductance reactivity to mental imagery of the trauma, as compared to a placebo group. There were, however, no differences in PTSD symptoms between the two groups. Saxe et al. (2001) found that the amount of morphine administered during initial hospitalization due to burn injury predicted lower PTSD symptoms at 6-month follow-up. There is some evidence that short-term use of sedative benzodiazepines may be helpful with PTSD cases in their early stages. Mellman, Byers, and Augenstein (1998) found that use of benzodiazepines for sleep disturbance in PTSD patients between 1 and 3 months posttrauma resulted in reduced PTSD symptoms. It is clear that much more research is necessary before pharmaceutical treatments can be confidently prescribed as preventive interventions for trauma victims.

Pharmacological Treatment of Chronic PTSD

Increasing evidence supports the effectiveness of selective serotonin reuptake inhibitors (SSRIs) and monoamine oxidase inhibitors (MAOIs) in reducing PTSD symptomatology. Davidson and his colleagues (e.g., Davidson, Rothbaum, van der Kolk, Sikes, & Farfel, 2001) in a series of three controlled trials have found sertraline to outperform placebo on the vast majority of PTSD symptoms, particularly with the numbing and arousal clusters of symptoms.

There also are several open-trial studies for the treatment of PTSD with various SSRIs. Fluvoxamine has demonstrated some effectiveness for PTSD symptoms, particularly with combat-related trauma (e.g., Escalona, Canive, Calais, & Davidson, 2002). Citalopram has demonstrated symptom reduction in a preliminary study with 14 adults (Seedat et al., 2002). There is also evidence that nefazodone decreases PTSD symptoms in combat veterans (Garfield, Fichtner, Leveroni, & Mahableshwarkar, 2001). However, Lubin, Weizman, Shmushkevitz, and Valevski (2002) completed an open-label preliminary study of naltrexone and found that the minor clinical improvements found did not warrant use due to the severity of side effects. Overall, it appears that the family of SSRIs demonstrates moderate but clinically significant improvement in PTSD symptomatology and overall functioning across a wide variety of trauma populations. Thus, there is evidence of efficacy for some SSRIs in the treatment of PTSD

Case Description

The following case of PTSD was chosen because (a) it was triggered by the most common type of precipitating trauma, a motor vehicle accident; (b) it illustrates the influence of predisposing factors on the development of PTSD; (c) it provides an example of a common pattern of comorbidity in PTSD patients; and (d) it illustrates common issues in the treatment of PTSD.

Presenting Complaints

Ms. N. was a 33-year-old married female who lived with her husband and two small children in a small city. She worked as a unit clerk in an emergency ward. Upon initial assessment, she complained of fear and avoidance of automobile travel, excessive worry about her children's and husband's safety, particularly during motor vehicle travel, and frequent headaches. These symptoms had arisen following a motor vehicle accident.

Trauma Description

Ms. N. was involved in a motor vehicle collision 16 months before the assessment. She and her husband were passengers in a van driving to a dinner outing with two other couples. She saw the oncoming impact with another car in an intersection and reacted fearfully in anticipation. The air bags deployed on contact, and she became frightened that the vehicle was on fire because of the air bag gas. After the vehicle stopped, Ms. N. quickly verified that none of the people riding in the rear seats of the vehicle had been seriously injured. However, her female friend in the right front seat was moaning, and this frightened Ms. N. The driver was bloodied but attending to her friend. She could hear that emergency vehicles were on the way. She then realized that children were crying in the other vehicle, so she went to investigate and learned that there were two children in car seats in the other vehicle. The children were not seriously injured but were distraught and had some visible bruising. She subsequently learned that the other driver was impaired, which further upset her. As she and her husband were not seriously injured, they took a taxi to the emergency room. On the way, she began to mentally review the consequences if she had herself been killed (e.g., "[I] thought of my kids. Who would take care of them?"). She became very upset in the hospital emergency room at that time and received tranquilizing medication.

Assessment

Ms. N. was assessed via a combination of the CAPS (Blake et al., 1998), the Anxiety Disorders Interview Schedule for *DSM-IV* (ADIS-IV; DiNardo, Brown, & Barlow, 1994), and a number of psychological tests.

Ms. N. reported experiencing once- or twice-weekly intrusive and distressing images of the collision, intermittent nightmares involving cars running off

(continued)

the road, and at least weekly emotional upset when reminded of the accident, accompanied by shortness of breath, heart palpitations, and trembling. Triggers of emotional distress included driving or riding in a car, knowing that her children had to ride in a car, and hearing (over the hospital PA system) of children being admitted to the emergency room. Notably, she frequently had headaches following attempts to drive a vehicle. Thus, she met Criterion B (reexperiencing symptoms) of PTSD.

Ms. N. avoided thinking or talking about the accident by changing the topic of conversations and distraction (e.g., reading, watching TV). She made significant efforts to avoid television programming depicting accidents or injury. She was markedly driving-avoidant, which led to interference with her work life as she would refuse shifts offered to her if they required a longer commute. She also reported decreased interest in exercise and socializing and lowered libido. Thus, she met Criterion C (avoidance/numbing symptoms) of PTSD.

Ms. N. also reported having nightly disrupted sleep, excessive irritability, frequent problems with concentration (e.g., "always in a daydream") both at home and at work, and was excessively vigilant to various threats (e.g., overly concerned about children's safety at home; when at work and hears of a child being admitted with injuries has to check to ensure it is not one of her children). Thus, she met Criterion D (hyperarousal symptoms). Her CAPS PTS Symptom Severity total score was 52. This is below the score of 65, which Weathers, Ruscio, & Keane (1999) noted as the most stringent standard for diagnosing PTSD on the CAPS. Nonetheless, it demonstrates relatively severe psychological distress.

Ms. N. also met criteria for a number of other diagnoses. For many years prior to the accident, she had been experiencing excessive worry about minor matters such as punctuality ("never late"), work and school performance, her family's safety and well-being (especially the safety of her children), finances, interpersonal issues (e.g., what her friends think of her), her own health (checks herself for different problems excessively), and her family members' health (e.g., husband, mother, children, including excessive concern about potential illnesses in her children and for which she repeatedly sought reassurance from her family physician). She also experienced a wide variety of symptoms of tension, including restlessness, excessive fatigue, concentration problems, irritability, muscle tension, and sleep disturbance. Although she had been like this for several years, she indicated that most of these worries, particularly those revolving around her children's safety, had increased in frequency and intensity since the car accident. Based on this information, she met diagnostic criteria for Generalized Anxiety Disorder (GAD; American Psychiatric Association, 2000).

Ms. N. also described a moderate fear of driving and of riding as a car passenger. Her fear of car travel began shortly after the car accident, and may be best considered part of her PTSD. When fearful in a car, she experienced heart palpitations, shortness of breath, and tingling sensations. Thus she had some limited symptoms of panic attacks while in the car. Her core fears at these times were that she would die in an accident, that her children would die or be injured, and—if she dies—her children would be left without her.

Ms. N. also complained of specific somatic difficulties, including frequent headaches, often brought on by car travel but more generally stress-related; a long-standing problem with abdominal pain and diarrhea (previous diagnosis of irritable bowel syndrome); and a past history of anorexia. Her anorexic behavior ceased at around the time she became pregnant with her first child.

Ms. N.'s symptoms caused only minor impairment in her social functioning (primarily limiting her activities with her husband and reducing somewhat her recreational and social interests), but had a substantial impact on her work functioning, as her fears of car travel made her less willing to commute to work, especially if it required travel outside of her usual schedule and route.

Psychological test results were consistent with diagnoses of GAD, PTSD, and a specific phobia of driving. Further, test results showed Ms. N. to be highly vigilant to body sensations, with a very elevated score on the Anxiety Sensitivity Index (Peterson & Reiss, 1987). Anxiety sensitivity is known to be elevated in trauma victims (Taylor et al., 1992).

Collateral information from a friend and from Ms. N.'s husband suggested that she was very anxious in a car or when anticipating a long drive and responded with strong emotional upset to reminders of the accident. Her husband noted that since the accident, she engaged in significant "backseat driving": calling his attention to traffic lights, the movements of other motorists, and potentially hazardous road conditions. He also noted her tendency to hold on to the armrests and make braking motions on the passenger side of the vehicle.

More generally, they described her as excessively responsible, excessively worried, and stressed. They noted sleep disturbance, complaints about nightmares, and irritability. Finally, these respondents noted that Ms. N. was often bothered by physical symptoms, including muscle tension, headaches, and fatigue. Her husband noted that her worst area of functioning was commuting to work.

Relevant Psychosocial History

Ms. N. grew up as the youngest child in a blended family, consisting of her mother, stepfather, two significantly older stepsisters, and two twin sisters who were 14 months older than she. She described her childhood in positive terms and noted that she was very active in a variety of recreational activities. She described the family environment as "supportive." She denied exposure to child abuse, neglect, or domestic violence as a child. She reported that she became very independent early in life, at least partially because of the health problems of her two older twin sisters. She often found herself assuming a caretaker role with her sisters, and upon completion of high school pursued postsecondary training that prepared her for her current position as a unit clerk in a busy emergency ward. This job provided her with exposure to many multiply severely injured patients, some of whom succumbed to their injuries. It is of note that hospital emergency room workers have a high rate of PTSD symptoms (e.g., Laposa & Alden, 2003).

Ms. N. described an extensive social support system but appeared to take on excessive responsibility for the well-being of both friends and extended family members. Until the motor vehicle collision, she had a very active recreational and social life. At intake, Ms. N. also reported varied health and other psychosocial

(continued)

stressors in her extended family (e.g., the recent death of one of her stepsisters due to cancer).

Case Conceptualization

Ms. N. presented with symptoms of moderately severe PTSD following a motor vehicle accident as well as a lengthy history of excessive worry and anxiety meeting criteria for GAD. Her preexisting tendency to worry about the well-being of family members and her possibly heightened awareness of bodily harm and mortality issues (i.e., exposure to ongoing illness through her childhood and to significant bodily injury and death related to her job) likely predisposed her to the development of PTSD following the accident. Occurrence of the accident, and in particular, involvement of an impaired driver with children in the vehicle, appears to have exacerbated these preexisting worries and activated schemas related to risk and danger, not only related to motor vehicle travel, but also to other potential sources of harm (e.g., illness). Maintaining factors included her avoidance of thinking or speaking about the accident and reminders of the accident (e.g., television programs), extensive safety behaviors while riding as a passenger (and possibly while driving, such as overcautiousness), a tendency to selectively attend to risky driving behaviors while disregarding information and evidence consistent with safe driving and travel, and her continuing exposure to vehicular accident danger during her hospital employment. Positive prognostic indicators included her strong social support system and the lack of comorbid mood or substance abuse disorders. Negative prognostic indicators included the duration and intensity of her PTSD symptoms, her tendency to experience limited symptom panic attacks during vehicle travel, and her long-standing anxiety. Given these indicators, her prognosis was judged to be guardedly optimistic.

Course of Treatment and Assessment of Progress

Ms. N. was treated in 15 sessions of individual CBT for PTSD. Treatment progress was measured using the Post-Traumatic Symptoms Scale—Self Report version every third session and by obtaining repeated ratings of distress associated with specific treatment targets (e.g., level of distress while completing righthand turns). A more complete battery, including the Penn State Worry Questionnaire (T. J. Meyer, Miller, Metzger, & Borkovec, 1990) and the Anxiety Sensitivity Index (Peterson & Reiss, 1987), was completed pretreatment, following the eighth session, and again at posttreatment and follow-up. Initial sessions involved providing psychoeducation about the nature of PTSD and effective treatment approaches, as well as a detailed explanation of the recommended treatment interventions as they related to her case conceptualization. The role of avoidance (both overt and covert), safety behaviors and selective attention in maintaining her symptoms was emphasized. Ms. N.'s husband was included in an early session, which allowed him a better understanding of what to expect in terms of symptom change (e.g., an initial increase in symptom severity following the initiation of imaginal exposure) and to secure his cooperation in encouraging his wife to participate fully in homework assignments (e.g., facilitating the creation of opportunities for driving practice, encouraging her to drop safety behaviors while traveling as a passenger).

Following this psychoeducational phase of treatment, Ms. N. was asked to write a detailed account of her memories of the accident, including as much detail as possible. She was also asked to include her fears and concerns about what could have happened. This script was revised a couple of times in session until it was judged to be sufficiently detailed to allow for elicitation of a strong fear response and effective processing of thoughts and feelings related to the trauma. Following a review of the concepts of exposure and habituation, Ms. N. was instructed spend at least 1 hour per day engaged in review of this script and to track her distress over the course of these exposure sessions to permit evaluation of her habituation process. As expected, she experienced an initial increase in PTSD symptoms following the initiation of imaginal exposure, followed by a steep and steady decline in her reactivity to the script, as well as in her overall PTSD symptoms over 2 weeks of exposure.

In preparation for the next phase of treatment, a hierarchy of feared driving situations (including both riding as a passenger and driving herself) was created and a list of safety behaviors was compiled. Ms. N. was provided with instructions for completing "looping" driving exposures in which she would repeat the same driving maneuver (e.g., right hand turns) over and over again while dropping safety behaviors. Following the initiation of driving exposures, Ms. N. experienced an increase in her physical symptoms, including headaches, and often culminating in limited symptom panic episodes during planned exposures. Due to her distress over these symptoms, her compliance with driving assignments became spotty, and this was addressed in treatment. Ms. N. was provided with training in diaphragmatic breathing and progressive muscle relaxation. She was also reminded that these symptoms were uncomfortable but nondangerous manifestations of the body's fight-or-flight response and would decrease over time as her perception of the dangerousness of the situation normalized. Some interoceptive exposure to increased heart rate and shortness of breath using hyperventilation and stair running was conducted to decrease her fear of these physical symptoms.

Later on in treatment, Ms. N.'s beliefs and automatic thoughts related to the dangerousness of motor vehicle travel were elicited and challenged using standard cognitive restructuring techniques. To further decrease her perceptions of the risk associated with driving, she was given a series of assignments involving counting the number of vehicles passing through a busy intersection and observing (a) frequency of actual accidents and (b) the frequency of safe driving behaviors (e.g., use of turn signals, shoulder checks, braking before turns). This enabled her to compute a risk estimate for the likelihood of collision and drew her attention to safe driving behaviors instead of "near misses" and unsafe driving behaviors. She reported that this exercise was particularly useful in decreasing the perceived risk associated with motor vehicle travel.

Following the 10th session, Ms. N.'s treatment sessions were spaced out to once every 2 to 4 weeks. She gradually assumed primary responsibility for identifying situations that required further practice and designing appropriate practice exercises. The importance of continued practice of the skills and techniques learned in treatment following the end of formal treatment was emphasized.

(continued)

At the end of treatment, her scores on the Post-Traumatic Symptoms Scale—Self Report had dropped to within half a standard deviation of the nontraumatized norms. Her scores on the Anxiety Sensitivity Index (ASI) and, to a lesser extent, the Penn State Worry Questionnaire had also decreased significantly. An independent rater using an abbreviated version of the ADIS-IV rated her as being in partial remission.

Follow-Up

Ms. N. was reassessed at 6 months posttreatment by a brief telephone interview and through the completion of a questionnaire battery. Overall, she had maintained her treatment gains. Her PTSD symptoms remained low. She reported that she had experienced a temporary resurgence in symptoms and associated avoidance behaviors a couple of months earlier, related to a friend's motor vehicle accident, which she felt had "reactivated" her fears and general sense of the dangerousness of motor vehicle travel. At that time, she had recontacted her primary therapist, who provided her with encouragement and some guidance in planning a series of in vivo exposures (e.g., looping exposure assignments involving making lefthand turns, as her friend had been hit while making a lefthand turn into a parking lot) as well as assistance with cognitive restructuring (i.e., "Just because my friend was involved in an accident does not mean that the overall risk of car travel has increased"). With such minimal assistance, she was able to minimize the seriousness of this relapse in symptoms and prevent a full relapse. She indicated that she continued to experience some problems with excessive worry and excessive feelings of responsibility for ensuring the well-being of others (e.g., vigilance to possible health problems in her family members), but overall felt that her symptoms had not worsened since the last treatment contact.

Treatment Implications of the Case

Ms. N.'s case illustrates the importance of providing a clear case conceptualization and treatment rationale to clients as well as to support persons who may be involved in or affected by important treatment assignments (e.g., imaginal exposure, driving exposure). It also illustrates the importance of addressing comorbid problems (e.g., panic attacks) when they impact the client's ability to comply with treatment recommendations for the primary problem of PTSD. Finally, as in this case, it is often useful to arrange for booster sessions a few months after the end of treatment to ensure that the client is continuing to practice skills learned in treatment and is maintaining treatment gains.

SUMMARY

Posttraumatic Stress Disorder is a mental health condition comprising reexperiencing, avoidance, emotional numbing, and hypervigilance symptoms. Such PTSD symptoms as nightmares have been observed for centuries. The diagnosis of PTSD represents the current consensus conceptualization of maladaptive coping subsequent to threatening traumatic experiences such as assault, combat exposure, and transportation accidents.

This mental health condition has significant economic implications because of (a) the ubiquity of potentially traumatic events in modern society, (b) the association of PTSD with reduced economic and physical well-being, and (c) the potential for legal action in personal injury lawsuits or worker's compensation claims. It is also unique among mental health disorders because of its high rate of comorbidity with other anxiety disorders and depression, as well as with somatic disorders. The latter relationship is complex but suggests that PTSD may account for excessive health care utilization. There are many pitfalls in the assessment of PTSD, thus reliable and valid diagnosis requires a multitrait-multimethod assessment via semi-structured interview, self-report screening tests for PTSD symptoms, measures of correlated constructs, and collateral information. Over the past 2 decades, research suggests that the most efficacious treatments for PTSD are variants of CBT involving prolonged imaginal exposure and forms of cognitive therapy targeting maladaptive safety beliefs. Some progress has been made with respect to early intervention with trauma survivors, but single-session debriefing treatments appear to be of little benefit. It is still too early to conclude whether pharmaceutical treatments have major benefit, although antidepressant medications are commonly prescribed to PTSD sufferers.

REFERENCES

American Psychiatric Association. (1980). *Diagnostic and statistical manual of mental disorders* (3rd ed.). Washington, DC: Author.

American Psychiatric Association. (1987). *Diagnostic and statistical manual of mental disorders* (3rd ed., rev.). Washington, DC: Author.

American Psychiatric Association. (1994). *Diagnostic and statistical manual of mental disorders* (4th ed.). Washington, DC: Author.

American Psychiatric Association. (2000). *Diagnostic and statistical manual of mental disorders* (4th ed., text rev.). Washington, DC: Author.

Bisson, J. I. (2003). Single-session early psychological interventions following traumatic events. *Clinical Psychology Review, 23,* 481–499.

Blake, D. D., Weathers, F., Nagy, L. M., Kaloupek, D. G., Chamey, D. S., & Keane, T. M. (1998). *Clinician-Administered PTSD Scale for DSM–IV.* Boston: National Center for Posttraumatic Stress Disorder.

Blake, D. D., Weathers, F., Nagy, L. M., Kaloupek, D. G., Klauminzer, G., Chamey, D. S., et al. (1990). A clinician ratings scale for assessing clinical and lifetime PTSD: The CAPS-1. *Behavior Therapist, 13,* 187–188.

Blanchard, E. B., Hickling, E. J., Devineni, T., Veazey, C., Galovski, T., Mundy, E., et al. (2003). A controlled evaluation of cognitive behavioral therapy for posttraumatic stress in motor vehicle accident survivors. *Behavior Research and Therapy, 41,* 79–96.

Blanchard, E. B., Hickling, E. J., Taylor, A. E., Fomeris, C. A., Loos, W., & Jaccard, J. (1995). Effects of varying scoring rules of the Clinician Administered PTSD (CAPS) for the diagnosis of posttraumatic stress disorder in motor vehicle accident victims. *Behavior Research and Therapy, 33,* 471–475.

Bowman, M. L. (1999). Individual differences in posttraumatic distress: Problems with the DSM-IV model. *Canadian Journal of Psychiatry, 44,* 21–33.

Breslau, N., Davis, G. C., Andreski, P., & Peterson, E. L. (1991). Traumatic events and posttraumatic stress disorder in an urban population of young adults. *Archives of General Psychiatry, 48,* 216–222.

Brewin, C. R. (2001). A cognitive neuroscience account of posttraumatic stress disorder and its treatment. *Behavior Research and Therapy, 39,* 373–393.

Brown, T. A., Campbell, L. A., Lehman, C. L., Grisham, J. R., & Mancill, R. B. (2001). Current and lifetime comorbidity of the DSM-IV anxiety and mood disorders in a large clinical sample. *Journal of Abnormal Psychology, 110,* 585–599.

Bryant, R. A., Moulds, M. L., & Nixon, R. V. (2003). Cognitive behavior therapy of acute stress disorder: A 4-year follow-up. *Behavior Research and Therapy, 41,* 489–494.

Bryant, R. A., & Panasetis, P. (2001). Panic symptoms during trauma and acute stress disorder. *Behavior Research and Therapy, 39,* 961–966.

Byrne, C. A., Resnick, H. S., Kilpatrick, D. G., Best, C. L., & Saunders, B. E. (1999). The socioeconomic impact of interpersonal violence on women. *Journal of Consulting and Clinical Psychology, 67,* 362–366.

Campbell, D. T., & Fiske, D. W. (1959). Convergent and discriminant validation by the multitrait-multimethod matrix. *Psychological Bulletin, 56,* 81–105.

Chantarujikapong, S. I., Scherrer, J. F., Xian, H., Eisen, S. A., Lyons, M. J., Goldberg, J., et al. (2001). A twin study of generalized anxiety disorder symptoms, panic disorder symptoms and posttraumatic stress disorder in men. *Psychiatry Research, 103,* 133–145.

Chemtob, C. M., Novaco, R. W., Hamada, R. S., & Gross, D. M. (1997). Cognitive behavioral treatment for severe anger in posttraumatic stress disorder. *Journal of Consulting and Clinical Psychology, 65,* 184–189.

Dalgleish, T. (2004). Cognitive approaches to posttraumatic stress disorder: The evolution of multirepresentational theorizing. *Psychological Bulletin, 130,* 228–260.

Davidson, J. R. T., Rothbaum, B. O., van der Kolk, B. A., Sikes, C. R., & Farfel, G. M. (2001). Multicenter, double-blind comparison of sertraline and placebo in the treatment of posttraumatic stress disorder. *Archives of General Psychiatry, 58,* 485–492.

Davidson, J. R. T., Swartz, M., Storck, M., Krishnan, K. R. R., & Hammett, E. (1985). A diagnostic and family study of posttraumatic stress disorder. *American Journal of Psychiatry, 142,* 90–93.

DeSouza, E., & Fansler, A. G. (2003). Contrapower sexual harassment: A survey of students and faculty members. *Sex Roles, 48,* 529–542.

DiNardo, P. A., Brown, T. A., & Barlow, D. H. (1994). *Anxiety Disorders Interview Schedule for DSM-IV: Lifetime version* (ADIS-IV-L). Albany, NY: Graywind.

Dunsmore, E., Clark, D. M., & Ehlers, A. (2001). A prospective investigation of the role of cognitive factors in persistent posttraumatic stress disorder (PTSD) after physical or sexual assault. *Behavior Research and Therapy, 39,* 1063–1084.

Echeburua, E., de Corral, P., Sarasua, B., & Zubizarreta, I. (1996). Treatment of acute posttraumatic stress disorder in rape victims: An experimental study. *Journal of Anxiety Disorders, 10,* 185–199.

Ehlers, A., & Clark, D. M. (2000). A cognitive model of posttraumatic stress disorder. *Behavior Research and Therapy, 38,* 319–345.

Ehlers, A., Mayou, R. A., & Bryant, B. (1998). Psychological predictors of chronic posttraumatic stress disorder after motor vehicle accidents. *Journal of Abnormal Psychology, 107,* 508–519.

Escalona, R., Canive, J., Calais, L. A., & Davidson, J. T. (2002). Fluvoxamine treatment in veterans with combat-related post-traumatic stress disorder. *Depression and Anxiety, 15,* 29–33.

Fairbank, J. A., Ebert, L., & Zarkin, G. A. (1999). Socioeconomic consequences of traumatic stress. In P. A. Saigh & J. D. Bremner (Eds.), *Posttraumatic stress disorder: A comprehensive text* (pp. 180–198). Boston: Allyn & Bacon.

Falsetti, S. A., & Resnick, H. S. (1997). Frequency and severity of panic attack symptoms in a treatment seeking sample of trauma victims. *Journal of Traumatic Stress, 10,* 683–689.

Falsetti, S. A., Resnick, H. S., Davis, J., & Gallagher, N. G. (2001). Treatment of posttraumatic stress disorder with comorbid panic attacks: Combining cognitive processing therapy with panic control treatment techniques. *Group Dynamics, 5,* 252–260.

Foa, E. B., Dancu, C. V., Hembree, E. A., Jaycox, L. H., Meadows, E. A., & Street, G. P. (1999). A comparison of exposure therapy, stress inoculation training, and their combination for reducing posttraumatic stress disorder in female assault victims. *Journal of Consulting and Clinical Psychology, 67,* 194–200.

Foa, E. B., Hearst-Ikeda, D., & Perry, K. J. (1995). Evaluation of a brief cognitive-behavioral program for the prevention of chronic PTSD in recent assault victims. *Journal of Consulting and Clinical Psychology, 63,* 948–955.

Foa, E. B., & Meadows, E. A. (1997). Psychosocial treatments for posttraumatic stress disorder: A critical review. *Annual Review of Psychology, 48,* 449–480.

Foa, E. B., Riggs, D. S., Massie, E. D., & Yarczower, M. (1995). The impact of fear activation and anger on the efficacy of exposure treatment for posttraumatic stress disorder. *Behavior Therapy, 26,* 487–499.

Foa, E. B., Steketee, G., & Rothbaum, B. O. (1989). Behavioral/cognitive conceptualization of post-traumatic stress disorder. *Behavior Therapy, 20,* 155–176.

Garfield, D. A. S., Fichtner, C. G., Leveroni, C., & Mahableshwarkar, A. (2001). Open trial of nefazodone for combat veterans with posttraumatic stress disorder. *Journal of Traumatic Stress, 13,* 453–460.

Goodman, L. A., Corcoran, C., Turner, K., Yuan, N., & Green, B. L. (1998). Assessing traumatic event exposure: General issues and preliminary findings for the Stressful Life Events Screening Questionnaire. *Journal of Traumatic Stress, 11,* 521–542.

Harrington, R. (1996). The "railway spine" diagnosis and Victorian responses to PTSD. *Journal of Psychosomatic Research, 40,* 11–14.

Harvey, A. G., & Bryant, R. A. (2000). A 2-year prospective evaluation of the relationship between acute stress disorder and posttraumatic stress disorder following mild traumatic brain injury. *American Journal of Psychiatry, 157,* 626–628.

Hembree, E. A., Street, G. P., Riggs, D. S., & Foa, E. B. (2004). Do assault-related variables predict response to cognitive behavioral treatment for PTSD? *Journal of Consulting and Clinical Psychology, 72,* 531–534.

Horowitz, M. J., Wilner, N., Kaltreider, N., & Alvarez, W. (1980). Signs and symptoms of post-traumatic stress disorder. *Archives of General Psychiatry, 37,* 85–92.

Janoff-Bulman, R. (Ed.). (1985). *The aftermath of victimization: Rebuilding shattered assumptions.* New York: Brunner/Mazel.

Koch, W. J., Douglas, K. S., Nicholls, T. L., & O'Neill, M. L. (2006). *Psychological injuries: Forensic assessment, treatment, and law.* New York: Oxford University Press.

Koch, W. J., & Taylor, S. (1995). Assessment and treatment of motor vehicle accident victims. *Cognitive and Behavioral Practice, 2,* 327–342.

Koenen, K. C. (2005). Genetics of PTSD: A neglected area? *Psychiatric Times, 22*(9). http://psychiatrictimes.com/showArticle.jhtml?articleId=170100940

Koenen, K. C., Fu, Q. J., Lyons, M. J., Toomey, R., Goldberg, J., Eisen, S. A., et al. (2005). Juvenile conduct disorder as a risk factor for trauma exposure and post-traumatic stress disorder. *Journal of Traumatic Stress, 18,* 23–32.

Koenen, K. C., Harley, R., Lyons, M. J., Wolfe, J., Simpson, J. C., Goldberg, J., et al. (2002). A twin registry study of familial and individual risk factors for trauma exposure and posttraumatic stress disorder. *Journal of Nervous and Mental Diseases, 190,* 209–218.

Koenen, K. C., Lyons, M. J., Goldberg, J., Simpson, J., Williams, W. M., Cloitre, M., et al. (2003). A high risk twin study of combat-related PTSD comorbidity. *Twin Research, 6,* 218–226.

Kubany, E. S., Haynes, S. N., Leisen, M. B., Owens, J. A., Kaplan, A. S., Watson, S. B., et al. (2000). Development and preliminary validation of a brief broad-spectrum measure of trauma exposure: The Traumatic Life Events Questionnaire. *Psychological Assessment, 12,* 210–224.

Kubany, E. S., Hill, E. E., & Owens, J. A. (2003). Cognitive trauma therapy for battered women with PTSD: Preliminary findings. *Journal of Traumatic Stress, 16,* 81–91.

Laposa, J. M., & Alden, L. E. (2003). Posttraumatic stress disorder in the emergency room: Exploration of a cognitive model. *Behavior Research and Therapy, 41,* 49–65.

Lubin, G., Weizman, A., Shmushkevitz, M., & Valevski, A. (2002). Short-term treatment of post-traumatic stress disorder with naltrexone: An open-label preliminary study. *Human Psychopharmacology, 17,* 181–185.

Mellman, T. A., Byers, P. M., & Augenstein, J. S. (1998). Pilot evaluation of hypnotic medication during acute traumatic stress response. *Journal of Traumatic Stress, 11,* 563–569.

Melton, G. B., Petrila, J., Poythress, N. G., & Slobogin, C. (1997). *Psychological evaluations for the courts: A handbook for mental health professionals and lawyers* (2nd ed.). New York: Guilford Press.

Meyer, G. J. (2002). Implications of information-gathering methods for a refined taxonomy of psychopathology. In L. E. Beutler & M. L. Malik (Eds.), *Rethinking the DSM: A psychological perspective* (pp. 69–106). Washington, DC: American Psychological Association.

Meyer, T. J., Miller, M. L., Metzger, R. L., & Borkovec, T. D. (1990). Development and validation of the Penn State Worry Questionnaire. *Behavior Research and Therapy, 28,* 487–495.

Mineka, S., & Zinbarg, R. (2006). A contemporary learning theory perspective on the etiology of anxiety disorders: It's not what you thought it was. *American Psychologist, 61,* 10–26.

Mitchell, J. T. (1983, January). When disaster strikes: The critical incident stress debriefing process. *Journal of the American Medical Society,* 336–339.

Mowrer, O. H. (1960). *Learning theory and behavior.* New York: Wiley.

Najavits, L. M., Weiss, R. D., Shaw, S. R., & Muenz, L. R. (1998). "Seeking safety": Outcome of a new cognitive-behavioral psychotherapy for women with posttraumatic stress disorder and substance dependence. *Journal of Traumatic Stress, 11,* 437–456.

Norris, F. H. (1992). Epidemiology of trauma: Frequency and impact of different potentially traumatic events on different demographic groups. *Journal of Consulting and Clinical Psychology, 60,* 409–418.

Peterson, R. A., & Reiss, S. (1987). *Anxiety sensitivity index manual.* Palos Heights, IL: International Diagnostic Systems.

Pitman, R. K., Sanders, K. M., Zusman, R. M., Healy, A. R., Cheema, F., Lasko, N. B., et al. (2002). Pilot study of secondary prevention of posttraumatic stress disorder with propranolol. *Biological Psychiatry, 51,* 189–192.

Pitman, R. K., Van der Kolk, B., Orr, S., & Greenberg, M. (1990). Naloxone-reversible analgesic response to combat-related stimuli in posttraumatic stress disorder: A pilot study. *Archives of General Psychiatry, 47,* 541–544.

Rachman, S. (1980). Emotional processing. *Behavior Research and Therapy, 18,* 51–59.

Radant, A., Tsuang, D., Peskind, E. R., McFall, M., & Raskind, W. (2001). Biological markers and diagnostic accuracy in the genetics of post-traumatic stress disorder. *Psychiatry Research, 102,* 203–214.

Reich, J., Lyons, M. J., & Kai, B. (1996). Familial vulnerability factors to posttraumatic stress disorder in male military veterans. *Acta Psychiatrica Scandinavica, 93,* 105–112.

Resick, P. A., & Schnicke, M. K. (1992). Cognitive processing therapy for sexual assault victims. *Journal of Consulting and Clinical Psychology, 60,* 748–756.

Rosenheck, R., & Fontana, A. (1996). Race and outcome of treatment for veterans suffering from PTSD. *Journal of Traumatic Stress, 9,* 343–351.

Rosenheck, R., Fontana, A., & Cottrol, C. (1995). Effects of clinician-veteran racial pairing in the treatment of posttraumatic stress disorder. *American Journal of Psychiatry, 152,* 555–563.

Sack, W. H., Clarke, G. N., & Seeley, J. (1995). Posttraumatic stress disorder across two generations of Cambodian refugees. *Journal of the American Academy of Child and Adolescent Psychiatry, 34,* 1160–1166.

Samuel Pepys Diary 1666—Great Fire. Retrieved June 9, 2006, from http://www.pepys.info/fire.html#anchor600522.

Saxe, G., Stoddar, F., Courtney, D., Cunningham, K., Chawla, N., Sheridan, R., et al. (2001). Relationship between acute morphine and the course of PTSD in children with burns. *Journal of the American Academy of Child and Adolescent Psychiatry, 40,* 915–921.

Schnurr, P. P., & Green, B. L. (2004). *Trauma and health: Physical health consequences of exposure to extreme stress.* Washington, DC: American Psychological Association.

Seedat, S., Stein, D. J., Ziervogel, C., Middleton, T., Kaminer, D., Emsley, R. A., et al. (2002). Comparison of response to a selective serotonin reuptake inhibitor in children, adolescents, and adults with posttraumatic stress disorder. *Journal of Child and Adolescent Psychopharmacology, 12,* 37–46.

Shalev, A. Y., Sahar, T., Freedman, S., Peri, T., Glick, N., Brandes, D., et al. (1998). A prospective study of heart rate response following trauma and the subsequent development of posttraumatic stress disorder. *Archives of General Psychiatry, 55,* 553–559.

Skre, I., Onstad, S., Torgeson, S., Lygren, S., & Kringlen, E. A. (1993). A twin study of DSM-III-R anxiety disorders. *Acta Psychiatrica Scandinavica, 88,* 85–92.

Stein, M. B., Jang, K. L., Taylor, S., Vernon, P. A., & Livesley, W. J. (2002). Genetic and environmental influences on trauma exposure and posttraumatic stress disorder symptoms: A twin study. *American Journal of Psychiatry, 159,* 1675–1681.

Stewart, S. H. (1996). Alcohol abuse in individuals exposed to trauma: A critical review. *Psychological Bulletin, 120,* 83–112.

Stewart, S. H., Conrod, P. J., Pihl, R. O., & Dongier, M. (1999). Relations between posttraumatic stress symptom dimensions and substance dependence in a community-recruited sample of substance-abusing women. *Psychology of Addictive Behaviors, 13,* 78–88.

Tarrier, N., Sommerfield, C., Pilgrim, H., & Faragher, B. (2000). Factors associated with outcome of cognitive-behavioral treatment of chronic post-traumatic stress disorder. *Behavior Research and Therapy, 38,* 191–202.

Taylor, S., Fedoroff, I. C., Koch, W. J., Thordarson, D. S., Fecteau, G., & Nicki, R. M. (2001). Posttraumatic stress disorder arising after road traffic collisions: Patterns of response to cognitive-behavior therapy. *Journal of Consulting and Clinical Psychology, 69,* 541–551.

Taylor, S., Koch, W. J., & McNally, R. J. (1992). How does anxiety sensitivity vary across the anxiety disorders? *Journal of Anxiety Disorders, 6,* 249–259.

Tomb, D. A. (1994). The phenomenology of post-traumatic stress disorder. *Psychiatric Clinics of North America, 17,* 237–250.

True, W. R., Rice, J., Eisen, S. A., Heath, A. C., Goldberg, J., Lyons, M. J., et al. (1993). A twin study of genetic and environmental contributions to liability for posttraumatic stress symptoms. *Archives of General Psychiatry, 50,* 257–264.

Ursano, R. J., Fullerton, C. S., Epstein, R. S., Crowley, B., Vance, K., Kao, T. C., et al. (1999). Peritraumatic dissociation and posttraumatic stress disorder following motor vehicle accidents. *American Journal of Psychiatry, 156,* 1808–1810.

van Minnen, A., Arntz, A., & Keijsers, G. P. J. (2002). Prolonged exposure in patients with chronic PTSD: Predictors of treatment outcome and dropout. *Behavior Research and Therapy, 40,* 439–457.

Veronen, L. J., & Kilpatrick, D. G. (1983). Stress management for rape victims. In D. Meichenbaum & M. E. Jaremko (Eds.), *Stress reduction and prevention* (pp. 341–374). New York: Plenum Press.

Walde, J., & Taylor, S. (2005). Interoceptive exposure therapy combined with trauma-related exposure therapy for post-traumatic stress disorder: A case report. *Cognitive Behavior Therapy, 34*, 34–40.

Weathers, F. W., & Ford, J. (1996). Psychometric review of PTSD Checklist. In B. H. Stamm (Ed.), *Measurement of stress, trauma, and adaptation* (pp. 250–251). Lutherville, MD: Sidran Press.

Weathers, F. W., Ruscio, A. M., & Keane, T. M. (1999). Psychometric properties of nine scoring rules for the Clinician-Administered Posttraumatic Stress Disorder Scale. *Psychological Assessment, 11*, 124–133.

Xian, H., Chantarujikapong, S. I., Scherrer, J. F., Eisen, S. A., Lyons, M. J., Goldberg, J., et al. (2001). Genetic and environmental influences on posttraumatic stress disorder, alcohol and drug dependence in twin pairs. *Drug and Alcohol Dependence, 61*, 95–102.

Zoellner, L. A., Feeny, N. C., Fitzgibbons, L. A., & Foa, E. B. (1999). Response of African American and Caucasian women to cognitive behavioral therapy for PTSD. *Behavior Therapy, 30*, 581–595.

CHAPTER 12

Generalized Anxiety Disorder

KATHRYN A. SEXTON, KYLIE FRANCIS, AND MICHEL J. DUGAS

DESCRIPTION OF THE DISORDER

SYMPTOMS

According to the fourth edition of the *Diagnostic and Statistical Manual of Mental Disorders* (*DSM-IV-TR*; American Psychiatric Association, 2000), Generalized Anxiety Disorder (GAD) is characterized by high levels of excessive worry and anxiety about a number of topics, experienced more days than not for at least 6 months. The excessive worry is accompanied by three or more somatic symptoms: restlessness, fatigue, difficulty concentrating, irritability, muscle tension, and sleep disturbance. The worry is experienced as uncontrollable, and the cognitive and somatic symptoms cause significant distress or impairment in social, occupational, or other areas of functioning. Several researchers have noted that GAD is one of the most disabling anxiety disorders, with levels of impairment comparable to depression and chronic physical illness (see Wittchen, 2002, for a review). The disorder has also been associated with a substantial increase in the use of health care services and greater employment-related disability costs compared to nonclinical populations (Koerner et al., 2004; Wittchen, 2002).

Although there has been some debate concerning which somatic symptoms are specific to GAD (see Brown, Marten, & Barlow, 1995), the *DSM-IV-TR* currently includes the six somatic symptoms found to be most commonly endorsed by individuals with GAD compared to other anxiety disorders (Marten et al., 1993). Though symptoms of autonomic hyperarousal are no longer part of the criteria for GAD in the *DSM-IV-TR*, these symptoms in particular may help to distinguish GAD from mood disorders (Brown et al., 1995) given that these two diagnostic categories are not always reliably distinguished by *DSM-IV-TR* criteria (Brown, DiNardo, Lehman, & Campbell, 2001). Brown and colleagues (1995) have also suggested that a diagnostic cutoff of four as opposed to three somatic symptoms may be more useful for distinguishing GAD from other anxiety disorders, while preserving a similar level of diagnostic sensitivity.

Since the *DSM-III-R*, and now in the *DSM-IV-TR* (American Psychiatric Association, 1987, 2000), GAD is defined by the presence of its cardinal feature, excessive and uncontrollable worry, rather than being a residual category for anxiety as it was in earlier editions of the *DSM*. Worry has been defined as "a cognitive phenomenon . . . concerned with future events where there is uncertainty about the outcome, the future being thought about is a negative one, and this is accompanied by feelings of anxiety" (MacLeod, Williams, & Bekerian, 1991, p. 478). Worry is also present in other anxiety disorders and in nonclinical populations, but individuals with GAD appear to worry more often and for longer periods (Dupuy, Beaudoin, Rhéaume, Ladouceur, & Dugas, 2001). In addition, individuals with GAD tend to perceive their worry as harmful and dangerous (Ruscio & Borkovec, 2004), uncontrollable, less realistic, and less likely to be mitigated by attempts to cope (Craske, Rapee, Jackel, & Barlow, 1989).

Research examining the typical worries experienced by individuals with GAD (Shadick, Roemer, Hopkins, & Borkovec, 1991) and by the general population (e.g., Dugas, Freeston, Doucet, Lachance, & Ladouceur, 1995) has found some consistency in reported worry themes. In both clinical and nonclinical populations, worries tend to focus on intimate relationships, family, finances, work, and issues such as punctuality and daily hassles (Craske et al., 1989; Dugas, Freeston, et al., 1995; Shadick et al., 1991). Although the presence of worry about these topics does not therefore differentiate GAD from other anxiety disorders or from nonclinical groups (Dugas, Freeston, et al., 1998), some studies suggest that individuals with GAD worry more about their health and minor issues, and less about finances, than do controls (Craske et al., 1989; Roemer, Molina, & Borkovec, 1997). Furthermore, compared to those with other anxiety disorders, patients with primary GAD seem to worry significantly more about the future (Dugas, Freeston, et al., 1998).

Some variation in worry themes has also been noted in elderly as compared to young and middle-aged adults. Elderly worriers, for instance, tend to worry more about family concerns, world issues (Hunt, Wisocki, & Yanko, 2003), and their health (Doucet, Ladouceur, Freeston, & Dugas, 1998; Hunt et al., 2003), and less about their future, work, and finances (Doucet et al., 1998). It should be noted, however, that elderly populations tend to worry less overall (Doucet et al., 1998; Hunt et al., 2003). In contrast, adolescent worriers are concerned with school, relationships with friends and family, love relationships, their own future, and finances (Gosselin et al., 1998). Thus, specific worry themes may vary more with developmental context (Gosselin et al., 1998; Ladouceur, Freeston, Fournier, Dugas, & Doucet, 2002) or with individuals' immediate life events (Dugas, Freeston, et al., 1995) than with clinical status.

EPIDEMIOLOGY

Generalized Anxiety Disorder has a current 1.5% to 3% prevalence rate in the general population, a 1-year prevalence rate between 3% and 5%, and a lifetime prevalence rate between 4% and 7% (Kessler & Wittchen, 2002), with women being twice as likely to develop GAD as men (Carter, Wittchen, Pfister, & Kessler, 2001). Prevalence rates of GAD in clinical settings tend to be higher; approximately 8% of individuals seeking help in a primary care setting have been found to have GAD, which is higher than for any other anxiety disorder (Kessler & Wittchen, 2002).

Whereas other anxiety disorders often emerge in adolescence or young adulthood, the onset of GAD is usually in early middle age; as such, GAD prevalence rates tend to increase with age (Carter et al., 2001; Wittchen & Hoyer, 2001). For women, the likelihood of GAD onset increases substantially after the age of 35, whereas for men such increase most often occurs after the age of 45 (Wittchen & Hoyer, 2001). The course of GAD has been shown to be highly chronic: One prospective, naturalistic study found that only 38% of individuals with GAD had a period of full remission lasting longer than 2 months within a 5-year period (Kessler & Wittchen, 2002).

The majority of individuals with GAD also presents with comorbid anxiety or mood disorders (Kessler & Wittchen, 2002). Social Phobia, Major Depressive Disorder, Panic Disorder with or without agoraphobia, and specific phobia are among the most common co-occurring diagnoses; one study found that the prevalence of these comorbid disorders in a GAD population was 36%, 26%, 15%, and 12%, respectively (Brown, Campbell, Lehman, Grisham, & Mancill, 2001). Comorbidity rates also tend to be higher among individuals seeking treatment, although comorbidity with mood disorders is high even in community populations (Kessler & Wittchen, 2002). Although these comorbidity rates are higher than for other anxiety disorders, Kessler (2000) found that the effect of comorbid conditions on the onset, course, and severity of GAD was similar to the effect of comorbidity in other anxiety and mood disorders. In addition, noncomorbid GAD has been associated with similar (Kessler et al., 2002; Kessler, DuPont, Berglund, & Wittchen, 1999) and sometimes higher (Kessler et al., 2002) levels of impairment as GAD with comorbidity, suggesting that even uncomplicated GAD produces substantial impairment.

CONCEPTUALIZATION

Current conceptualizations of GAD are outlined using a model of worry developed by Dugas, Gagnon, Ladouceur, and Freeston (1998). This model postulates that a higher order dispositional characteristic, intolerance of uncertainty, contributes directly to worry while also influencing other worry-related processes. Three lower order factors—positive beliefs about worry, negative problem orientation, and cognitive avoidance—are also included as processes that contribute directly to worry. This model is only one of several current models of GAD, but it has received considerable empirical support, and moreover includes some of the principal components of other models. Where applicable, research related to other prominent models of GAD is presented. Specifically, aspects of Borkovec and colleagues' (Borkovec, Ray, & Stöber, 1998) cognitive avoidance model, Wells's (1995, 1999, 2002) metacognitive model, and Mennin and colleagues' (Mennin, Heimberg, Turk, & Fresco, 2002, 2005) emotion dysregulation model are discussed.

INTOLERANCE OF UNCERTAINTY

Intolerance of uncertainty is the central component of the model of GAD proposed by Dugas, Gagnon, and colleagues (1998). Defined as *a dispositional characteristic that results from a set of negative beliefs about uncertainty and its implications* (Dugas & Robichaud, 2007), intolerance of uncertainty includes beliefs that uncertainty is unfair and stressful, interferes with functioning, and should be avoided (Buhr & Dugas, 2002). Intolerance of uncertainty has been shown to be specifically related to worry even when controlling for anxiety (Buhr & Dugas, 2002), processes associated with obsessions/compulsions or panic (such as beliefs about responsibility and anxiety sensitivity; Dugas, Gosselin, & Ladouceur, 2001), depressive symptoms (Buhr & Dugas, 2002; Dugas, Schwartz, & Francis, 2004), dysfunctional attitudes (Dugas, Schwartz, et al., 2004), perfectionism, and perceived sense of control (Buhr & Dugas, 2006). Intolerance of uncertainty has also demonstrated specificity to GAD as compared to nonclinical and other anxiety disorder populations (Dugas, Marchand, & Ladouceur, 2005; Ladouceur et al., 1999). Further, in GAD populations, intolerance of uncertainty is associated with greater worry and somatic symptom severity, and distinguishes mild from moderate and severe GAD (Dugas et al., 2007).

Although a direct causal link between intolerance of uncertainty and worry has yet to be established, there is evidence to suggest such a relationship. For example, Tallis, Eysenck, and Mathews (1991) demonstrated that high worriers have elevated evidence requirements in decision making. Similarly, Ladouceur, Talbot, and Dugas (1997) found that intolerance of uncertainty was associated with elevated evidence requirements on a task of moderate ambiguity. Ladouceur, Gosselin, and Dugas (2000) found that experimentally increasing levels of intolerance of uncertainty led to higher levels of worry, and decreasing intolerance of uncertainty lowered worry in a nonclinical sample.

Intolerance of Uncertainty and Information Processing   It has been proposed that intolerance of uncertainty contributes to worry by affecting the way individuals attend to, appraise, and retain information—particularly ambiguous information—in their environment. Intolerance of uncertainty is thought to directly affect information processing through biased attention, interpretation, and recall of ambiguous stimuli, resulting in greater worry about the outcome of uncertain events (Koerner & Dugas, 2006). For instance, Dugas, Hedayati, and colleagues (2005) found that individuals high in intolerance of uncertainty recalled significantly more uncertainty-related words and fewer neutral words and made more threatening interpretations of ambiguous situations than individuals low in intolerance of uncertainty. Intolerance of uncertainty was also found to account for a significant proportion of the variance in threatening interpretations of ambiguous situations after accounting for levels of anxiety, depression, and worry (Dugas, Hedayati, et al., 2005). Further, Koerner and Dugas (2007) found that individuals high in intolerance of uncertainty made significantly more negative appraisals of both negative and ambiguous pictorial stimuli. At high levels of intolerance of uncertainty, a specific cognitive avoidance strategy, thought suppression, was related to more negative appraisals of ambiguous and negative stimuli. The researchers proposed that intolerance of uncertainty, while it may increase the perceived need to engage in cognitive avoidance, may at high levels interfere with those strategies, such as thought suppression, that are used to reduce the emotional discomfort aroused by ambiguity (Koerner & Dugas, 2007).

Beliefs about Worry

Intolerance of uncertainty may lead to worry through biased processing of information; it may also influence worry through the component processes described in Dugas and colleagues' (Dugas, Gagnon, et al., 1998) model. One of these components, beliefs about worry, is based on the finding that individuals with GAD appear to hold specific beliefs about the act of worrying itself, which distinguishes them from nonclinical samples.

Positive Beliefs about Worry   Individuals with GAD often report that they believe their worry has a useful or positive function, such as providing distraction from more emotionally distressing topics (Borkovec & Roemer, 1995). Research has identified as many as five domains of positive beliefs about worry (Francis & Dugas, 2004): that worry is motivating, facilitates problem solving, protects against negative emotions such as guilt, is a positive personality trait, and can, as a mental act, directly alter events (thought-action fusion). These positive beliefs have been found among individuals with GAD regardless of the particular worry theme (Gosselin et al., 2006).

More recent investigations have suggested that positive beliefs about worry may be most relevant at earlier stages in the development of excessive worry. Specifically, positive beliefs have been found to be significantly correlated with levels of worry among low rather than high worriers (Bakerman, Buhr, Koerner, & Dugas, 2004; Holowka, Dugas, Francis, & Laugesen, 2000). Bakerman and colleagues' study also found that one positive belief in particular, the belief that worry is a positive personality trait, was specifically related to worry among nonclinical worriers; this belief in particular may therefore be more relevant to the development than the maintenance of worry. Nonetheless, Ladouceur, Blais, Freeston, and Dugas (1998) found that positive beliefs about worry differentiated individuals meeting diagnostic criteria for GAD from nonclinical moderate worriers.

Negative Beliefs about Worry   Despite the prevalence of positive beliefs about worry in GAD populations, negative appraisals of worry are also commonly reported. Specifically, negative beliefs such as the belief that worry disrupts performance, exaggerates the problem, and causes emotional discomfort have been shown to correlate with both excessive and nonclinical worry (Davey, Tallis, & Capuzzo, 1996). According to Wells's (1999, 2002) metacognitive theory of GAD, a distinguishing feature of pathological worry is the presence of type 2 or metaworry, that is, worry about the negative consequences of the act of worrying itself. In a validation of Wells's (1995, 1999, 2002) metacognitive model of GAD, Wells and Carter (1999) found that metaworry significantly predicted excessive worry after controlling for other types of worry (e.g., social and health worries) and trait anxiety. Further, Wells and Carter found that negative as opposed to positive beliefs about worry, including the belief that worry is uncontrollable and therefore dangerous, distinguished GAD patients from nonclinical controls and from those with other anxiety disorders or depression. Similarly, Davis and Valentiner (2000) found that a discriminant function composed of negative beliefs about the danger and uncontrollability of worry correctly classified 79.8% of GAD worriers, anxious nonworriers, and nonanxious controls.

Mineka (2004) has proposed that beliefs about worry may be acquired as a result of learning experiences in which there is a perceived association between worry and the avoidance of negative outcomes. For example, avoidance of negative outcomes (often low-probability events) may be attributed to worrying that is seen as preventive or preparatory (Borkovec, Hazlett-Stevens, & Diaz, 1999). Similarly, positive beliefs about worry may be reinforced when worry precedes successful problem solving (Koerner & Dugas, 2006). Negative beliefs about worry as being uncontrollable or dangerous may also be reinforced when worry is followed by negative consequences such as increased anxiety (Borkovec, Lyonfields, Wiser, & Deihl, 1993), enhanced perception of threat (Dugas, Hedayati, et al., 2005; Koerner & Dugas, 2007), and intrusive thoughts about the source of worry (Butler, Wells, & Dewick, 1995; Wells & Papageorgiou, 1995).

Negative Problem Orientation

Early research suggested that high levels of worry were associated with impairments in problem solving (Borkovec, 1985). Later investigations, however, showed that deficits in problem solving were more specifically related to negative attitudes toward problem solving than to a lack of skill per se (Dugas, Freeston, & Ladouceur, 1997; Dugas, Letarte, Freeston, & Ladouceur, 1995). In other words, individuals with GAD tend to have a negative problem orientation: They perceive problems as highly challenging and perceive themselves as unable to cope with their problems. Robichaud and Dugas (2005b) found that a negative problem orientation significantly predicted levels of worry after accounting for neuroticism, pessimism, and sense of control; further, a negative problem orientation was more specifically related to worry than to depression.

In a further exploration of problem orientation, Dugas and colleagues (1997) found that intolerance of uncertainty and negative problem orientation made both unique and shared contributions to high levels of worry. These researchers proposed that intolerance of uncertainty is a higher order construct that leads directly to worry and to negative problem orientation, which may also be worsened by an additional construct, intolerance of emotional arousal. More specifically, intolerance of uncertainty and intolerance of emotional arousal may lead to a negative problem orientation by (a) directing attention to the ambiguous or uncertain aspects of a problem, thereby enhancing the perceived threat; and (b) creating greater emotional arousal in problem situations, or leading individuals to overestimate the extent of their emotional arousal and therefore underestimate their ability to problem-solve effectively.

Cognitive Avoidant Function of Worry

According to Borkovec and colleagues' (1998) cognitive avoidance model, worry, which is predominantly verbal-linguistic, functions to avoid the heightened physiological arousal associated with images of feared negative outcomes. For instance, Borkovec and colleagues (1993) have noted that instructing individuals to worry just prior to visualizing a fear-provoking scenario suppresses the increased heart rate observed among individuals in a high-imagery condition (Borkovec & Inz, 1990). Further, worry was associated with decreased vividness of mental imagery and increased subjective ratings of fear in response to phobic stimuli. Thus, worry may serve an avoidant function which reduces anxiety in the short term (e.g., Butler et al., 1995) but impedes successful emotional processing in the long term (Borkovec et al., 1998). Stöber (1998) has demonstrated that worry is less concrete than mental images, and suggests that worry may thereby impede emotional processing; this reduced concreteness could also explain the difficulties in problem elaboration associated with worry.

Recent investigations have found that several cognitive avoidance strategies are associated with excessive worry and may serve a similar function. Thought suppression in particular has been associated with excessive worry (e.g., Dugas, Gagnon, et al., 1998; Ladouceur et al., 1999), as have thought substitution, the transformation of images into verbal thoughts, distraction, and the avoidance of threatening stimuli that trigger intrusive thoughts (Sexton & Dugas, 2007). Sexton and Dugas found that, as suggested by Borkovec and colleagues (Borkovec & Inz, 1990; Borkovec et al., 1998), the tendency to employ these cognitive avoidance strategies was associated with high levels of fear of somatic anxiety symptoms and, furthermore, that employing these strategies was associated with negative beliefs about worry as proposed by Wells (1995, 1999).

EMOTION DYSREGULATION: WORRY AS AVOIDANCE OF EMOTIONAL EXPERIENCING

Mennin and colleagues (2002, 2005) propose that GAD worry may be explained by an emotion dysregulation model. They found that nonclinical high worriers and GAD patients alike show heightened emotional intensity, greater difficulty identifying and describing emotions, greater fear of emotional responses, and less ability to self-soothe. These authors have suggested that these deficits in emotion regulation may account for the tendency to use worry as a cognitive avoidance strategy. Turk and colleagues (Turk, Heimberg, Luterek, Mennin, & Fresco, 2005) further demonstrated that certain emotion regulation deficits, including a tendency to experience emotions more intensely and to pay more attention to one's own emotional reactions, were specific to GAD as compared to Social Anxiety Disorder.

DEVELOPMENTAL FACTORS

Life Events   Newman and Bland (1994) noted that in the year before diagnosis, individuals with GAD often reported the occurrence of significant, negative, or stressful life events, particularly negative marital events or the forming of new social connections. There was no direct association, however, between GAD and a given type of life event, as these events also preceded Major Depression. Kendler and colleagues (Kendler, Hettema, Butera, Gardner, & Prescott, 2003), however, found that stressful life events characterized by loss or danger predicted the onset of GAD as opposed to depression. In contrast, other researchers have found no association between the number of recent negative life events and diagnostic status (Mancuso, Townsend, & Mercante, 1993), or between the number of childhood or past-year negative events and the likelihood of a current diagnosis of Major Depression or GAD (Dean & White, 1996). Garnefski, Kraaij, and Spinhoven (2001) have suggested that an individual's cognitive and emotional reactions to a negative event, rather than the occurrence of a negative event per se, may constitute a risk factor for anxiety and mood disorders. Consistent with this view, Brantley and colleagues (Brantley, Mehan, Ames, & Jones, 1999) found that GAD patients reported more minor negative life events and rated these events as significantly more stressful than did controls. For the most part, however, these investigations have not specifically examined life events leading to the development of GAD as opposed to other anxiety and mood disorders.

Genetic Influences   Research on the potential genetic basis of GAD suggests that approximately 32% of the variance in GAD symptomatology may be due to genetic factors (Hettema, Neale, & Kendler, 2001). Research also indicates that GAD and other anxiety disorders share a common genetic vulnerability to anxiety (Chantarujikapong et al., 2001; Scherrer et al., 2000). However, GAD appears to have a stronger genetic relationship to Major Depressive Disorder than to other anxiety disorders (Kendler, 1996; Kendler, Neale, Kessler, Heath, & Eaves, 1992; Kendler et al., 1995). Moreover, the genetic relationship between GAD and depression does not seem to be explained by the relationship between GAD and other anxiety disorders (Kendler et al., 1995). It may be most accurate, therefore, to conceptualize GAD as having a shared underlying vulnerability to anxiety, while still possessing a specific genetic relationship to depression. However, GAD does not appear to be associated with substantial disorder-specific genetic influences (Chantarujikapong et al., 2001; Kendler et al., 1995).

Peer Influences   Researchers have found that for adolescents and young adults, worry content is primarily social, relating to self-confidence, assertiveness, and relationships. For older adults, in contrast, worries may primarily focus on issues related to aging, though these concerns might also entail worries about the social consequences of aging (Ladouceur et al., 2002). Worry often has a prominent social component, yet few studies have investigated the social basis for this type of worry. Recently, however, Eng and Heimberg (2006) examined interpersonal correlates of GAD among undergraduate students who met diagnostic criteria for GAD. These researchers found no differences in attachment with peers, in perceived social support, or in other-rated friendship quality; however, GAD participants did report less secure parental attachment.

Parental Issues   Anxiety has known associations with childhood family experiences (Rapee, 1997), but the association between parenting and the development of GAD in mid adulthood has not been closely examined. Nevertheless, there is some evidence that certain perceived parental rearing behaviors, including rejection, anxious rearing (Muris, Meesters, Merckelbach, & Hülsenbeck, 2000), and parental control (Muris & Merckelbach, 1998), are associated with worry and GAD symptoms in children. Similarly, adults diagnosed with GAD have been found to retrospectively report an "affectionless control" or "affectionate constraint" style of parenting, both of which are characterized by high parental overprotection (Silove, Parker, Hadzi-Pavlovic, Manicavasagar, & Blaszczynski, 1991). However, prospective investigation of the enduring consequences of these styles of parenting on the incidence of GAD in adulthood is needed.

Cultural and Diversity Issues

Although GAD is prevalent in many cultures worldwide, there has been little investigation of cross-cultural differences in the disorder (Carter et al., 2001). In one study, Scott and colleagues (Scott, Eng, & Heimberg, 2002) found that Caucasian, African American, and Asian American samples of undergraduate students did not significantly differ in levels of worry, prevalence of worry, GAD diagnoses, or worry themes. Caucasians and Asian Americans, however, did self-report higher levels of worry on a nonclinical measure when compared to African Americans. On the same measure, Caucasians and Asian Americans reported significantly more worry about relationships, about a lack of confidence, about work incompetence, and about having an aimless future than did African Americans. Caucasian participants in turn reported more concern about having an aimless future than did Asian Americans. There was also a nonsignificant trend for Caucasians to be more likely to meet GAD diagnostic criteria by a self-report screening questionnaire.

Given the markedly higher prevalence of worry among women, greater attention has been devoted to examining sex differences in worry and GAD. Robichaud, Dugas, and Conway (2003) found that women reported significantly more worry about a broad range of topics than men; this difference was greatest at high levels of worry. With respect to cognitive processes underlying worry, women and men were not found to differ on levels of intolerance of uncertainty or positive beliefs about worry. However, women were found to have a significantly more negative problem orientation and to engage in more thought suppression. Conversely, among men, positive beliefs about worry were more highly related to worry about a range of topics. Despite these differences, correlations between cognitive processes and measures of worry were highly similar across gender. It may be, therefore, that women are more likely to engage in cognitive processes such as cognitive avoidance, or may possess a more negative problem orientation, which puts them at greater risk of developing high levels of worry. The reason for the gender differences in these cognitive processes, however, is not yet well understood.

DIAGNOSIS AND ASSESSMENT

Screening Instruments

The Worry and Anxiety Questionnaire   The Worry and Anxiety Questionnaire (WAQ; Dugas, Freeston, et al., 2001) is an 11-item brief screening instrument for the assessment of *DSM-IV-TR* (American Psychiatric Association, 2000) GAD. As a diagnostic screener, the WAQ is particularly useful as it employs continuous as opposed to dichotomous ratings of symptoms and can therefore be employed as a measure of symptom severity. Individuals are asked to list up to six of their primary worry themes and are then asked to rate the extent to which their worry is excessive (rated on a 9-point Likert scale ranging from 0 = Not at all excessive to 8 = Totally excessive), is difficult to control (ranging from 0 = No difficulty to 8 = Extreme difficulty), and is interfering with their life (ranging from 0 = Not at all to 8 = Very severely). Individuals also rate the frequency of their worry during the course of the preceding 6 months (ranging from 0 = Never to 8 = Every day). The WAQ also includes a list of the six somatic symptoms included in the *DSM-IV-TR* diagnostic criteria for GAD, each of which is rated in terms of severity on a 9-point Likert scale, ranging from 0 = Not at all to 8 = Very severely. The WAQ is thus a particularly useful measure of GAD somatic symptoms that are not assessed by the other self-report measures included here.

Screening tools such as the WAQ are designed to have a high level of sensitivity to detect most, if not all, probable cases of GAD; specificity and a formal diagnosis of GAD can then be established with a structured or semi-structured clinical interview. The WAQ has nonetheless demonstrated both sensitivity and specificity as a screening instrument for GAD. For example, 78% of a nonclinical sample with worry scores in the highest quartile met diagnostic criteria on the WAQ, whereas none in the lowest quartile met diagnostic criteria (Dugas, Freeston, et al., 2001). In a clinical sample, the WAQ also correctly identified 89.5% of a sample of patients diagnosed with GAD using the Anxiety Disorders Interview Schedule for *DSM-III-R*, and misclassified only 5.3% of a nonclinical comparison group (Dugas, Freeston, et al., 2001). The WAQ has shown good test-retest reliability after 9 weeks (Dugas, Freeston, et al., 2001) and moreover is sensitive to gains made over the course of cognitive-behavioral treatment for GAD (Ladouceur, Dugas, et al., 2000), making it a useful tool for monitoring treatment progress and outcome.

CLINICIAN-ADMINISTERED SEMI-STRUCTURED CLINICAL INTERVIEWS

The Anxiety Disorders Interview Schedule for DSM-IV The Anxiety Disorders Interview Schedule for *DSM-IV* (ADIS-IV; Brown, DiNardo, & Barlow, 1994) is one of the most commonly used semi-structured interviews for the diagnosis of *DSM-IV-TR* (American Psychiatric Association, 2000) anxiety disorders. The ADIS-IV also assesses for the presence of possible comorbid mood, somatoform, and substance use disorders. The greatest advantage to the ADIS-IV is its dimensional nature: Rather than relying solely on dichotomous diagnoses, the ADIS-IV provides a severity rating for symptoms, ranging on a scale from 0 to 8. The ADIS-IV can therefore provide information about nonclinical symptomatology, yet consistency with the *DSM-IV-TR* can be maintained (a score of 4 or greater indicates a disorder that meets diagnostic criteria, scores of 1 to 3 indicate subthreshold presentations, and 0 denotes the absence of symptoms). This dimensional assessment is more in line with current conceptualizations of psychopathology as existing on a continuum (Brown, DiNardo, et al., 2001). The ADIS-IV also includes questions about the etiology of the disorder, such as questions about recent life stresses (Summerfeldt & Antony, 2002), as well as more detailed questions about diagnostic subtypes. The ADIS-IV is available in both current and lifetime versions; the current version takes approximately 45 to 60 minutes to administer, whereas the lifetime version can take from 2 to 4 hours (Summerfeldt & Antony, 2002). The ADIS-IV has shown good interrater agreement for current ($\kappa = .67$ for primary GAD, $\kappa = .65$ for primary or comorbid GAD) and lifetime ($\kappa = .65$; Brown, DiNardo, et al., 2001) diagnoses of GAD. The ADIS-IV dimensional ratings of GAD symptoms have also shown good interrater reliability ($r = .73$ for excessive worry, $r = .78$ for the uncontrollability of worry, $r = .83$ for somatic symptoms, and $r = .72$ for ratings of clinical severity; Brown, DiNardo, et al., 2001, reprinted in Grisham, Brown, & Campbell, 2004).

SELF-REPORT MEASURES OF GAD SYMPTOMS

The Penn State Worry Questionnaire The Penn State Worry Questionnaire (PSWQ; Meyer, Miller, Metzger, & Borkovec, 1990) is one of the most commonly used measures of excessive generalized worry. The PSWQ is composed of 16 items measuring worry frequency and intensity and includes items such as "I know I shouldn't worry about things but I just can't help it" and "I am always worrying about something." Items are rated on a 5-point Likert scale ranging from 1 = Not at all typical to 5 = Very typical. The PSWQ has been shown to have excellent internal consistency ($\alpha = .86$ to .95) and good temporal stability, ranging from $r = .74$ to .93 over a 4-week period (Meyer et al., 1990; Molina & Borkovec, 1994). The PSWQ has also shown good to excellent sensitivity and specificity when used as a GAD screen in clinical and nonclinical samples (Behar, Alcaine, Zuellig, & Borkovec, 2003). Furthermore, the PSWQ successfully discriminates individuals with GAD from those with other anxiety disorders (Brown, Antony, & Barlow, 1992). The PSWQ has demonstrated convergent validity, being more highly correlated with other worry-related process measures than with measures of anxiety or depression (Brown et al., 1992; Molina & Borkovec, 1994).

SELF-REPORT MEASURES OF WORRY-RELATED PROCESSES

The Intolerance of Uncertainty Scale The central component of the model of GAD proposed by Dugas, Gagnon, and colleagues (1998) is assessed by the 27-item

Intolerance of Uncertainty Scale (IUS; French version: Freeston, Rhéaume, Letarte, Dugas, & Ladouceur, 1994; English translation: Buhr & Dugas, 2002), which assesses different negative beliefs about uncertainty and its implications. Examples of items on the IUS include "Uncertainty keeps me from living a full life" and "When I am uncertain, I can't go forward." These items are rated on a 5-point Likert scale ranging from 1 = Not at all characteristic of me to 5 = Entirely characteristic of me. The English translation of the original French measure has shown excellent internal consistency and temporal stability as well as convergent, criterion, and discriminant validity (Buhr & Dugas, 2002). Although the IUS was initially found to have five factors, a four-factorial structure was deemed to be more interpretable (Buhr & Dugas, 2002). Cross-cultural examination of the IUS, however, has demonstrated that item loadings across the four- and five-factor structures varies considerably among Caucasian, African American, Hispanic/Latino, and Southeast Asian populations (Norton, 2005). Despite this finding, the IUS demonstrated similarly strong reliability and validity across these ethnic groups (Norton, 2005).

The Why Worry-II   The Why Worry-II (WW-II; French version: Gosselin et al., 2003; English translation: Holowka et al., 2000), which is a revision of the earlier Why Worry scale, comprises 25 items assessing five categories of positive beliefs about the usefulness of worry, specifically, that worry (1) aids in problem solving, (2) motivates, (3) protects against negative emotions, (4) can alter actual events (thought-action fusion), and (5) is a positive personality trait. The English translation of the WW-II has demonstrated excellent internal consistency for the total score ($\alpha = .93$), and for its five subscales: subscale 1 ($\alpha = .81$); subscale 2 ($\alpha = .84$); subscale 3 ($\alpha = .81$); subscale 4 ($\alpha = .75$); subscale 5 ($\alpha = .71$). In addition, the WW-II has demonstrated good stability ($r = .80$) over 6 weeks (Holowka et al., 2000).

The Negative Problem Orientation Questionnaire   The Negative Problem Orientation Questionnaire (NPOQ; French version: Gosselin, Ladouceur, & Pelletier, 2001; English translation: Robichaud & Dugas, 2005a) is a 12-item measure of negative attitudes toward problems and one's ability to solve them. These items are rated on a 5-point Likert scale ranging from 1 = Not at all true of me to 5 = Extremely true of me. Examples of items on the NPOQ include "I often doubt my capacity to solve problems" and "I often see my problems as bigger than they really are." The English version of the NPOQ has shown excellent internal consistency ($\alpha = .92$) and good test-retest reliability ($r = .80$ over 5 weeks) and has been found to have a unifactorial structure (Robichaud & Dugas, 2005a). The NPOQ has demonstrated convergent and divergent validity with other measures of negative and positive problem orientation, respectively (Robichaud & Dugas, 2005a). The NPOQ has also shown strong correlations with measures of worry, anxiety, and depression (Robichaud & Dugas, 2005a; Robichaud & Dugas, 2005b).

The Cognitive Avoidance Questionnaire   The Cognitive Avoidance Questionnaire (CAQ; French version: Gosselin et al., 2002; English translation: Sexton & Dugas, in press) is a self-report measure of five cognitive avoidance strategies: thought substitution, transformation of images into thoughts, distraction, avoidance of threatening stimuli, and thought suppression. The CAQ consists of 25 items that are divided into five 5-item subscales, rated on a 5-point Likert scale ranging from 1 = Not at all typical to 5 = Completely typical. The English translation of the CAQ has shown excellent internal consistency ($\alpha = .95$) and good temporal stability over a

4- to 6-week period ($r = 85$). The five-subscale structure of the CAQ has been supported in confirmatory factor analysis, although the overall goodness of fit was lower than conventional standards (Sexton & Dugas, in press). In addition, the five subscales have shown good to excellent internal consistency ($\alpha = .86$ for Thought Suppression; $\alpha = .73$ for Thought Substitution; $\alpha = .89$ for Distraction; $\alpha = .87$ for Avoidance of Threatening Stimuli; and $\alpha = .87$ for Transformation of Images into Thoughts). The CAQ has shown evidence of convergent and criterion-related validity with measures of worry and worry-related processes, convergent validity with measures of thought suppression and information-avoidant coping, and divergent validity with adaptive forms of information seeking (Sexton & Dugas, in press).

COGNITIVE-BEHAVIORAL TREATMENT

The treatment described in this section was formulated by Dugas and colleagues (Dugas & Ladouceur, 2000; Ladouceur, Dugas, et al., 2000) based on the Dugas, Gagnon, et al. (1998) model of GAD described earlier. However, it should be emphasized that other efficacious treatments for GAD are available. For example, Borkovec and colleagues (Borkovec & Costello, 1993; Borkovec, Newman, Pincus, & Lytle, 2002) have demonstrated that a cognitive-behavioral treatment that includes cognitive therapy, self-control desensitization, and applied relaxation effectively produces long-term reductions in worry and GAD somatic symptoms. Wells and King (2006) evaluated a metacognitive treatment for GAD that targets negative beliefs about the uncontrollability and dangers of worry, as well as the usefulness of worrying and other thought control strategies. Mennin (2004) recently proposed a treatment targeting emotion dysregulation in GAD. Borkovec and Ruscio (2001) provide a more detailed review of these treatment approaches and outcomes.

COMPONENTS OF A COGNITIVE-BEHAVIORAL TREATMENT

The treatment proposed by Dugas, Ladouceur, and colleagues (Dugas & Ladouceur, 2000; Ladouceur, Dugas, et al., 2000) targets the four components of their model of GAD: positive beliefs about worry, negative problem orientation and problem-solving skills, cognitive avoidance, and intolerance of uncertainty. Treatment typically consists of 12 to 16 sessions, which include many standard cognitive-behavioral treatment strategies, such as psychoeducation, cognitive reevaluation, and exposure. Typically, beliefs about worry and negative problem orientation are addressed in the first stages of therapy, and cognitive avoidance is addressed later. As intolerance of uncertainty has been found to play a key role in worry, beliefs about uncertainty are challenged throughout therapy.

Presentation of the Treatment Rationale   Treatment begins with psychoeducation about the nature of worry, GAD, and contributing processes. Diagnostic criteria for GAD are reviewed, and the uncontrollable and excessive nature of the worry is denoted as the defining characteristic of GAD. In addition, clients are given an accessible definition of worry, specifically, that worry is a series of thoughts about potential future negative events that is accompanied by anxiety. During the initial sessions, the rationale for the treatment strategies is also presented. Clients are told that because research has shown that reductions in worry lead to reductions in somatic anxiety symptoms, worry will be the main focus of treatment. In addition, the role of intolerance of uncertainty in maintaining high levels of worry is discussed. It is emphasized that the purpose of therapy is not to reduce uncertainty (which is a normal part of life), but rather to help clients recognize their intolerance of uncertainty and subsequently accept and cope with uncertainty. Finally, the collaborative and structured nature of cognitive-behavioral therapy, its focus on the here and now, the emphasis on between-session exercises, and the goal of helping the client to become his or her own therapist are discussed.

Worry Awareness Training   At the beginning of treatment, daily monitoring of worry is introduced as a means to increase awareness of worry and to help clients discern different types of worry. In particular, two types of worry are distinguished: worry about actual, current problems and worry about hypothetical future events. The idea that different strategies are needed to cope with different types of worry is then presented, thereby introducing the rationale for addressing problem orientation and problem solving (for worries about actual problems) and for engaging in cognitive exposure (for worries about hypothetical events). Clients are given a standard form on which to record their worries at predetermined times each day.

Coping with Uncertainty   During the initial sessions of therapy, the central role of intolerance of uncertainty in excessive worry is presented. First, the therapist explains that people who worry excessively are intolerant of uncertainty, meaning that they find uncertainty stressful, unacceptable, and disruptive. The therapist goes on to explain that intolerance of uncertainty is therefore the "motor" that drives worry, as it leads people to focus on uncertainties and consequently to worry about potential negative outcomes. Patients with GAD often respond to the presentation of intolerance of uncertainty with relief: "That's *exactly* how I feel—I can't stand uncertainty!" The therapist can also present the idea that high worriers have an "allergy" to uncertainty. For example, someone who is allergic to peanuts will have an extreme allergic reaction to even a microscopic amount of peanut; likewise, an individual who is intolerant of uncertainty will have an extreme "allergic" reaction (excessive worry) to even a small amount of uncertainty. The therapist can then help clients to identify the manifestations of intolerance of uncertainty in their own lives, for example, that uncertain situations lead to worry, over planning, excessive information seeking, or even complete avoidance of uncertain situations. Subsequently, the therapist and client discuss what can be done to help the client cope, given his or her "allergy" to uncertainty. The client may respond that eliminating uncertainty would solve his or her problems. After some discussion, however, it will be apparent to the client that attempts to eliminate uncertainty are not only time- and energy-consuming but futile, because uncertainty is an inevitable part of life. Moreover, the therapist can remind the client that attempts to eliminate uncertainty lead to increased anxiety, worry, and eventual exhaustion. The client is therefore left with the only logical option: to learn to become more tolerant of uncertainty. The therapist explains that this is the underlying goal of therapy and that each component of treatment will help the client to become more tolerant of uncertainty. The therapist begins by assigning simple between-session exercises that will help clients to gradually increase their tolerance for uncertainty. For example, clients can learn to tolerate uncertainty by not double-checking a minor memorandum before it is mailed. Similarly, clients can expose themselves to low-risk events with an uncertain outcome, such as going to a well-known restaurant but ordering an unfamiliar dish from the menu.

Reevaluating Positive Beliefs about Worry   As previously noted, there is some debate about the relevance of positive beliefs at clinical levels of worry. However, a discussion of beliefs about the usefulness of worry has proven useful in the early stages of treatment, as it provides a motivational component that helps to engage clients in the therapeutic process. Furthermore, successful cognitive-behavioral treatment of GAD has been shown to reduce positive beliefs about worry (Borkovec et al., 1999; Dugas, Savard, et al., 2004; Laberge, Dugas, & Ladouceur, 2000), and therefore addressing these beliefs during treatment seems warranted. A role-play exercise is used to reevaluate the usefulness of worrying. First, the therapist and client identify the positive beliefs about worry held by the client, and the client is instructed to list the advantages and disadvantages of these beliefs. Subsequently, the client is asked first to defend these positive beliefs about worry (for example, by playing the role of a defense lawyer), and then is encouraged to take a more "prosecutorial" role and challenge those beliefs. The goal of this exercise is not to change clients' beliefs outright, but to encourage them to begin questioning the validity of their beliefs. Further, reexamining positive beliefs about worry helps to increase a client's tolerance for uncertainty by introducing the idea that trying to control future events through worry may not be an effective way to cope with potential future threats.

Problem-Solving and Problem Orientation Training   As previously mentioned, worry has been associated with a negative problem orientation rather than a lack of actual problem-solving skills. Problem-solving training has nevertheless been shown to be beneficial in the treatment of GAD (Ladouceur, Dugas, et al., 2000; Provencher, Dugas, & Ladouceur, 2004). This may be because worry impairs some steps of the problem-solving process, such as problem elaboration (e.g., Stöber, 1998) and decision making (e.g., Tallis et al., 1991). Problem-solving training may also help individuals to differentiate between worry about hypothetical and actual problems, while providing coping strategies for the latter. In addition, successful problem-solving experiences are likely to boost confidence and increase readiness for later stages of treatment.

Problem-solving training (D'Zurilla, 1986) begins with a description of the five basic problem-solving steps: (1) identification of the client's problem orientation, (2) problem definition and goal formulation, (3) generation of alternative solutions, (4) decision making, and (5) solution implementation and verification. These steps are then practiced and applied to specific problems that the client is currently experiencing. Intolerance of uncertainty is addressed throughout this process by encouraging clients to proceed through the problem-solving steps, even though they may feel uncertain about their choices and the eventual outcome. Throughout the problem-solving process, problem orientation is targeted by encouraging clients to see problems as a normal part of life and to view problems as challenges or opportunities rather than threats. The therapist points out that recognizing and dealing with problems quickly prevents them from becoming bigger and less manageable. Clients are therefore encouraged to make a list of "recurring problems" to help them sooner identify problems. Clients are also encouraged to use their emotional reactions as cues that a problem has arisen.

Counteracting Cognitive Avoidance with Exposure   To help clients overcome their tendency to avoid upsetting mental content, cognitive (or imaginal) exposure techniques are introduced. Cognitive exposure is specifically applied to worries concerning future hypothetical events, that is, feared situations that have not, and may never, occur and are therefore not available for interventions such as problem solving.

The rationale for cognitive exposure is presented and discussed with the client. Using graphs depicting anxiety levels over time, the therapist explains how different forms of avoidance can reduce anxiety in the short term but maintain and even intensify anxiety in the long term. The therapist explains that by engaging in worry, clients will reduce their somatic anxiety, but because they are avoiding specific and vivid mental imagery, they will be unable to emotionally process or digest their core fears.

To provide an exposure to these core fears, a cognitive exposure scenario is developed. The exposure scenario is a joint effort, typically written during the session, so that the therapist can identify and remove any neutralization or avoidance in the scenario. The downward arrow technique is used to help clients identify their core fears. Clients are then instructed to write about their fears using first-person language and vivid, concrete details. Clients are also encouraged to incorporate ambiguous elements into their scenarios, thereby providing an exposure to uncertainty. Once an appropriate exposure scenario has been written and read during the session, the scenario is recorded onto a looped tape or compact disc. Clients are instructed to listen to the exposure scenario every day for a period of 30 to 60 minutes, or until their anxiety levels decrease; clients are also asked to monitor and record their levels of anxiety and worry before, during, and after each exposure. This enables the client and therapist to monitor progress and determine when the feared scenario has been adequately processed (i.e., when anxiety levels decrease), which typically takes 1 to 3 weeks. Through exposure to these scenarios, the meaning of the feared event will gradually change, and clients will be able to view the possibility of feared events as less threatening.

Our research team has recently begun to investigate the usefulness of written exposure, following a procedure developed by Pennebaker and Beall (1986). Written exposure has the advantage of being a more engaging and active task than standard cognitive exposure and may therefore lead to increased activation of the fear network (Goldman, Dugas, Sexton, & Gervais, in press). In addition, because the client rewrites the scenario during each exposure, written exposure is more flexible and can be adapted to changes in the client's fears, including changes in context. Clients should be instructed to describe in vivid detail their worst fear being realized, including their cognitive, behavioral, and emotional reactions. In addition, clients should be encouraged to elaborate and expand on their scenario with each successive exposure (Goldman et al., in press).

Relapse Prevention   To consolidate gains made during treatment, the final session is devoted to relapse prevention. The client's progress is reviewed, and treatment is framed as an ongoing process in which the client has now become his or her own therapist. Clients are therefore encouraged to continue applying the strategies they have learned during therapy and to self-monitor their ability to cope with uncertainty and worry. Expectations about future relapse are also addressed, and it is emphasized that fluctuations in levels of worry and anxiety are normal. Specifically, clients are told that a lapse (a temporary increase in symptoms) does not necessarily denote a relapse (i.e., a full return of GAD worry and somatic symptoms); what is important is that clients recognize these fluctuations and continue to apply treatment strategies that enable them to cope with worry and uncertainty.

EFFICACY OF COGNITIVE-BEHAVIORAL APPROACHES

The treatment just described has been evaluated in two randomized controlled clinical trials. Ladouceur, Dugas, and colleagues (2000) found that compared to a wait-list control group, the treatment group showed significant decreases in worry, anxiety, depression, and ADIS-IV-rated GAD clinical severity. When the wait-list group had received treatment, the combined sample of 26 participants also demonstrated these significant decreases, with pre- to posttreatment effect sizes ranging from $d' = .87$ to $d' = 3.19$. These decreases were maintained at 6- and 12-month follow-up. Furthermore, this cognitive-behavioral intervention led to significant and lasting decreases in intolerance of uncertainty. At posttest, 77% of participants no longer met GAD diagnostic criteria; at 12 months, 62% had achieved high responder status, and 58% had maintained a high end state of functioning. In addition, although somatic symptoms were not directly targeted in treatment (i.e., no relaxation training component was included), participants nonetheless showed significant decreases in GAD somatic symptoms, which were maintained at 12 months.

In a further evaluation, Dugas, Savard, and colleagues (2004) compared the cognitive-behavioral treatment with a relaxation-based intervention for GAD. At posttest, both treatment groups demonstrated the expected reductions in GAD symptomatology, including reductions in levels of worry and GAD somatic symptoms. Intolerance of uncertainty decreased in both groups, but only the cognitive-behavioral group showed reductions in the other targeted processes, namely, positive beliefs about worry, negative problem orientation, and cognitive avoidance. As such, this study provided further empirical support for the cognitive-behavioral treatment based on the four-component model of GAD.

Effects of Cognitive-Behavioral Treatment on Worry-Related Processes   Two further studies of this treatment have examined the effect of targeting specific processes on levels of worry among GAD participants. Dugas and Ladouceur (2000) examined the relationship between change in intolerance and uncertainty and change in worry. They applied time-series analysis to daily ratings of symptoms during treatment and found that for three of four participants with GAD, changes in intolerance of uncertainty preceded changes in worry; in no case, however, did change in worry precede change in intolerance of uncertainty. Provencher et al. (2004) targeted two other components of the model by applying problem-solving training and cognitive exposure in a case replication series. Participants received either problem-solving training (for actual situations) or cognitive exposure (for hypothetical situations), and all participants reevaluated positive beliefs about worry and received relapse prevention. Both treatments produced significant and enduring change in excessive worry, GAD somatic symptoms, anxiety, and depression, which was maintained at 6-month follow-up. At posttest, 66.7% of treatment completers had achieved high end state functioning, and this number rose to 83.3% at 6 months. Thus, problem orientation and problem-solving training as well as cognitive exposure appear to be active components in the cognitive-behavioral treatment of GAD.

Effectiveness of Individual and Group Treatment Formats   Dugas and colleagues (2003) applied this individual cognitive-behavioral treatment to groups of four to six GAD participants. Treatment consisted of 14 weekly 2-hour sessions conducted by two clinical psychologists. At posttreatment, participants showed significant decreases in worry, GAD somatic symptoms, anxiety, depression, and intolerance of uncertainty, and increases in social adjustment. Not only were treatment gains maintained at 6-, 12-, and 24-month follow-ups, but worry and intolerance of uncertainty significantly *decreased* over this period. At posttest, 60% of participants no longer met GAD diagnostic criteria; this percentage increased over time (88% at 6 months, 83% at 12 months, and 95% at 24 months). Although this study did not directly compare group and individual treatments, these results are somewhat similar to those found for individual therapy (i.e., Ladouceur, Dugas, et al., 2000), suggesting that a group format is a viable option.

Case Description

Case Introduction

Ellen is a 41-year old woman who works as an administrator in a large office supplies company. She has been married for 20 years and has two sons, ages 15 and 18. Ellen said that she has a good relationship with her husband but worries about the strain her anxiety is placing on her marriage. She mentioned that her younger son is having problems at school, which is a major source of worry for her; although her older son is doing well, she said she worries about his future. Ellen agreed that she has "always been a worrier," but said that her worry and anxiety increased significantly about 3 years ago, when she was offered a management position at her company. She said that she was initially happy about her promotion, but found it extremely stressful because it involved more responsibilities and fewer guidelines than her previous position. She said she quickly became overwhelmed with worry about whether she was doing a good job and spent increasing amounts of time checking her work and worrying about her decisions, which made it increasingly difficult for her to meet her deadlines. In addition, she was asked to supervise several other employees, which she said was very stressful because she has always been afraid of confronting or upsetting others.

Presenting Complaints

Ellen said that 3 months ago her worries and physical symptoms of anxiety became so severe that she had to obtain sick leave from work. While her job continues to be a major source of worry, she said that she currently also worries about her children, her health, social interactions, and everyday tasks around the house. She said that she probably spends about 5 hours a day worrying and is unable to stop worrying once she begins. She describes herself as constantly tense and "wound up," with muscle tension particularly in her neck and shoulders. She said she often has trouble getting to sleep because she lies awake at night with her thoughts racing. All of these symptoms have left Ellen feeling physically exhausted, drained, and very irritable with her husband and children. When she first obtained sick leave, she was prescribed lorazepam, 0.5 mg per day, by her family doctor. She said that although this "took the edge off" her

(continued)

anxiety, most of her symptoms remained, and they returned in full force when she recently attempted to return to work.

History

Ellen described herself as a shy and anxious child, with few friends her own age, but very close to her younger brother. She said that she had worried about her school performance beginning in grade school; however, she said this was "probably a good thing," because she felt it led to her academic success. She said that although she had a good relationship with her father, he had a demanding career and was not very involved in the family. She said that she was closer to her mother, whom she described as a "mother hen," who worried about everything, especially her children. In retrospect, Ellen said her mother probably also experienced episodes of depression during her childhood. She recalled feeling very protective of her mother and brother, with whom she often assumed a caretaking role.

Assessment

Ellen was first asked to fill out the WAQ (Dugas, Freeston, et al., 2001) as a screen for GAD symptoms. Her scores showed that her worry was excessive, difficult to control, and interfered significantly with her life. In addition, she endorsed these symptoms at severe to very severe levels (scores ranging from 6 to 8 on the Likert scale).

The ADIS-IV (Brown et al., 1994) was then used to establish a formal diagnosis of GAD. Because Ellen reported considerable worry about social interactions, particular focus was also placed on the Social Phobia section of the ADIS-IV. Ellen stated that she not only worried about social interactions, but would also avoid social interactions when she could (i.e., giving feedback to employees, speaking to her boss), due to her intense fear of offending or being rejected by others. Nevertheless, she said that her worry about different aspects of her life, combined with her symptoms of physical tension, were currently most disturbing to her. Therefore, she was assigned a primary diagnosis of GAD (diagnostic severity of 6 on the 8-point scale) and a secondary diagnosis of Social Phobia (diagnostic severity of 4).

Finally, Ellen was asked to fill out self-report measures of GAD symptoms and processes. Her scores on the PSWQ (Meyer et al., 1990) confirmed excessive levels of worry; her ratings on the IUS (Buhr & Dugas, 2002) were correspondingly high. On the WW-II (Holowka et al., 2000), Ellen endorsed several items relating to worry as motivating and a positive personality trait. Her scores on the NPOQ (Robichaud & Dugas, 2005a) showed that Ellen had a tendency to view problems as dangerous and difficult to solve. Her ratings on the CAQ (Sexton & Dugas, in press) showed that she tended to replace upsetting mental images with verbal-linguistic thought (i.e., worry).

Case Conceptualization

Given the description of her mother's personality, it is likely that Ellen inherited a genetic predisposition for anxiety which contributed to the development of both GAD and Social Phobia. In addition, she had early modeling experiences of her mother's anxious care-giving style, which are likely to have contributed to her later tendency to worry. In Ellen's current situation, it was apparent that her inability to deal with the uncertainty inherent in several aspects of her life, particularly in her job, was leading to excessive and debilitating worry. Because GAD was clearly the primary disorder in this case, and because her secondary diagnosis was also likely to benefit from treatment for her primary disorder, worry and intolerance of uncertainty were the central targets of therapy.

Initially, Ellen maintained that her problems stemmed from a lack of information about her responsibilities at work. After a discussion about intolerance of uncertainty, however, she acknowledged that trying to eliminate the uncertainty in her job had only created further problems. With the therapist, Ellen discussed how intolerance of uncertainty had led to worry in other areas of her life. As treatment progressed, Ellen conceded that because it is impossible to eliminate uncertainty, she might try to learn to tolerate it. Tolerating uncertainty was the underlying goal in all aspects of the treatment. For example, during a discussion of Ellen's belief that worry is a positive personality trait, the therapist suggested that this belief may be rooted in the idea that worrying shows that one is a "good parent." When problem orientation was being addressed, Ellen said that she feels problems are dangerous because "anything could go wrong" and that she finds proceeding through subsequent problem-solving steps difficult because she can never be certain she is making the right decision. The therapist therefore worked with Ellen to help her tolerate the uncertainty inherent in making decisions and carrying out problem-solving steps. Finally, Ellen's cognitive exposure scenario involved the loss of her job due to her inability to meet deadlines, with catastrophic consequences for her family. In creating her scenario, Ellen was encouraged to include uncertain aspects, for example, "Because I lost my job we won't be able to make payments on the house, and then we could lose the house, or we might keep the house but get deeper and deeper into debt."

COURSE OF TREATMENT AND ASSESSMENT OF PROGRESS

During treatment, Ellen was asked to keep track of her levels of anxiety and worry in a portable booklet, which allowed her and the therapist to monitor her progress easily. Measures such as the WAQ (Dugas, Freeston, et al., 2001) are also useful, as they have been shown to be sensitive to changes in treatment (Ladouceur, Dugas, et al., 2000). Furthermore, an alternative version of the PSWQ (Stöber & Bittencourt, 1998) can be used to assess worry over the past week alone. In addition to her self-monitoring, Ellen filled out the WAQ (Dugas, Freeston, et al., 2001), the IUS (Buhr & Dugas, 2002), the WW-II (Holowka et al., 2000), the NPOQ (Robichaud & Dugas, 2005a), and the CAQ (Sexton & Dugas, in press) at mid- and posttreatment to monitor change in GAD-related processes. Finally, the ADIS-IV (Brown et al., 1994) was readministered at the end of treatment to provide an index of pre- to posttreatment change. At the end of treatment, Ellen no longer met ADIS-IV criteria for GAD or Social Phobia, although she did have some residual symptoms (GAD: residual symptom severity of 2; social phobia: residual symptom severity of 1).

COMPLICATING FACTORS: COMORBIDITY

As in Ellen's case, co-occurring diagnoses are common among GAD clients. However, research suggests that a comorbid diagnosis such as Social Phobia is unlikely to interfere with treatment gains; in fact, one study found that most comorbid diagnoses decreased following treatment, even though they were not addressed during therapy (Provencher, Ladouceur, & Dugas, 2006). If a client has a comorbid diagnosis of Panic Disorder, however, this may present a more serious complication. Provencher and colleagues found that at 6 months following treatment for GAD, patients with a secondary diagnosis of Panic Disorder were less likely to have reached a high end state of functioning. The researchers speculated that this may be due to remaining panic-specific processes, such as fear of emotional arousal (anxiety sensitivity), which are not targeted or attenuated during the treatment of GAD. Treatments for clients with comorbid GAD and Panic Disorder should therefore include some intervention to address the fear of anxiety. In fact, Labrecque, Dugas, Marchand, and Letarte (2006) have recently found preliminary support for a cognitive-behavioral treatment that targets intolerance of emotional arousal in addition to the four components of the treatment outlined in this chapter.

FOLLOW-UP

When possible, clients should be reassessed at 6, 12, and 24 months with the ADIS-IV (Brown et al., 1994), as well as with self-report measures of GAD symptoms and processes. This will provide the clinician information not only about the diagnostic status of the client via the ADIS-IV, but also about any increases in processes such as intolerance of uncertainty, which may indicate impending relapse. Any changes in the client's symptoms can be addressed during booster therapy sessions at 3, 6, 12, and 24 months.

TREATMENT IMPLICATIONS OF THE CASE

Even though Ellen's somatic symptoms of anxiety were not addressed during the treatment, they had nevertheless decreased at posttest. Ellen noted that she not only felt less anxious, but was much less fatigued and in a more positive mood. As previous studies have shown, GAD symptoms can be significantly reduced by targeting intolerance of uncertainty (Dugas & Ladouceur, 2000; Dugas, Savard, et al., 2004). This finding underscores the importance of applying treatments that are research-driven and that target the specific processes thought to underlie the disorder—in this case, intolerance of uncertainty, beliefs about worry, problem orientation and problem solving, and cognitive avoidance. At 6-month follow-up, Ellen's residual symptoms had further diminished, and she observed that although she still tends to worry, she now knows how to deal with it effectively. Specifically, she said she has begun to tolerate inevitable uncertainties and to use anxiety as a cue that a problem has arisen, rather than worrying fruitlessly as she would have in the past. She also said that she has reduced her medications and has been able to resume work on a part-time basis. Ellen said she still finds her supervisory duties at work anxiety-provoking, but she is better able to face these situations because she now feels she has the tools to help her cope with worry and anxiety.

SUMMARY

Generalized Anxiety Disorder is characterized by excessive and uncontrollable worry and anxiety about a number of topics. To conform to the diagnostic criteria for GAD, the worry must be experienced more days than not for at least 6 months and must be accompanied by somatic symptoms such as restlessness, fatigue, difficulty concentrating, irritability, muscle tension, and sleep disturbance. The disorder affects 1.5% to 3% of the general population, is more common in women than in men, most often onsets in early middle age, and frequently presents with comorbid anxiety and mood disorders (Carter, Wittchen, Pfister, & Kessler, 2001; Kessler & Wittchen, 2002; Wittchen & Hoyer, 2001). It is also associated with substantial impairment and is highly chronic (Kessler & Wittchen, 2002). A model of GAD proposed by Dugas, Gagnon, and colleagues (1998) identified intolerance of uncertainty as a key component involved in excessive and uncontrollable worry. Research suggests that intolerance of uncertainty is specifically associated with worry in GAD populations (Dugas, Marchand, & Ladouceur, 2005) and that it may lead to worry through biased processing of ambiguous information (e.g., Dugas, Hedayati, et al., 2005; Koerner & Dugas, 2007). In addition, intolerance of uncertainty has been conceptualized as a higher order variable that interacts with other component processes described in Dugas and colleagues' model. Three other component processes that have been associated with excessive worry are included in this model: positive beliefs about worry, negative problem orientation, and cognitive avoidance. More specifically, individuals with GAD appear to hold positive beliefs about worry (they believe that worry is useful); tend to have a negative problem orientation (they perceive problems as highly challenging and themselves as unable to cope with problems); and engage in cognitive avoidance (they use worry and other cognitive strategies to avoid the experience of anxiety).

Tools commonly used for the assessment of GAD symptoms and associated processes were described. A cognitive-behavioral treatment targeting the components of the model was proposed (see Dugas & Ladouceur, 2000; Ladouceur, Dugas, et al., 2000). This treatment begins with presentation of the treatment rationale, followed by worry awareness training, strategies for increasing tolerance of uncertainty, reevaluation of positive beliefs about worry, problem solving and problem orientation training, imaginal exposure to counteract cognitive avoidance, and relapse prevention. Three randomized control trials have shown this treatment to be efficacious in both individual and group formats (Dugas et al., 2003; Dugas, Savard, et al., 2004; Ladouceur, Dugas, et al., 2000). Specifically, this treatment has been found to produce lasting decreases in worry and GAD somatic symptoms, which are maintained over 1- and 2-year periods. Further, this treatment has been shown to produce change in worry-related processes, including decreases in intolerance of uncertainty (Dugas & Ladouceur, 2000; Dugas, Savard, et al., 2004) and decreases in positive beliefs about worry, negative problem orientation, and cognitive avoidance (Dugas, Savard, et al., 2004).

REFERENCES

American Psychiatric Association. (1987). *Diagnostic and statistical manual of mental disorders* (3rd ed., rev.). Washington, DC: Author.

American Psychiatric Association. (2000). *Diagnostic and statistical manual of mental disorders* (4th ed., text rev.). Washington, DC: Author.

Bakerman, D., Buhr, K., Koerner, N., & Dugas, M. J. (2004, November). *Exploring the link between positive beliefs about worry and worry.* Poster session presented at the annual convention of the Association for the Advancement of Behavior Therapy, New Orleans, LA.

Behar, E., Alcaine, O., Zuellig, A. R., & Borkovec, T. D. (2003). Screening for generalized anxiety disorder using the Penn State Worry Questionnaire: A receiver operating characteristic analysis. *Journal of Behavior Therapy and Experimental Psychiatry, 34,* 25–43.

Borkovec, T. D. (1985). Worry: A potentially valuable concept. *Behavior Research and Therapy, 23,* 481–482.

Borkovec, T. D., & Costello, E. (1993). Efficacy of applied relaxation and cognitive-behavioral therapy in the treatment of GAD. *Journal of Consulting and Clinical Psychology, 61,* 611–619.

Borkovec, T. D., Hazlett-Stevens, H., & Diaz, M. L. (1999). The role of positive beliefs about worry in generalized anxiety disorder and its treatment. *Clinical Psychology and Psychotherapy, 6,* 126–138.

Borkovec, T. D., & Inz, J. (1990). The nature of worry in generalized anxiety disorder: A predominance of thought activity. *Behavior Research and Therapy, 28,* 153–158.

Borkovec, T. D., Lyonfields, J. D., Wiser, S. L., & Deihl, L. (1993). The role of worrisome thinking in the suppression of cardiovascular response to phobic imagery. *Behavior Research and Therapy, 31,* 321–324.

Borkovec, T. D., Newman, M. G., Pincus, A. L., & Lytle, R. (2002). A component analysis of cognitive-behavioral therapy for generalized anxiety disorder and the role of interpersonal problems. *Journal of Consulting and Clinical Psychology, 70,* 288–298.

Borkovec, T. D., Ray, W. J., & Stöber, J. (1998). Worry: A cognitive phenomenon intimately linked to affective, physiological, and interpersonal behavioral processes. *Cognitive Therapy and Research, 22,* 561–576.

Borkovec, T. D., & Roemer, L. (1995). Perceived functions of worry among generalized anxiety disorders subjects: Distraction from more emotionally distressing topics? *Journal of Behavior Therapy and Experimental Psychiatry, 26,* 25–30.

Borkovec, T. D., & Ruscio, A. M. (2001). Psychotherapy for generalized anxiety disorder. *Journal of Clinical Psychiatry, 62,* 37–42.

Brantley, P. J., Mehan, D. J., Ames, S. C., & Jones, G. N. (1999). Minor stressors and generalized anxiety disorder among low-income patients attending primary care clinics. *Journal of Nervous and Mental Diseases, 187,* 435–440.

Brown, T. A., Antony, M. M., & Barlow, D. H. (1992). Psychometric properties of the Penn State Worry Questionnaire in a clinical anxiety disorders sample. *Behavior Research and Therapy, 30,* 33–37.

Brown, T. A., Campbell, L. A., Lehman, C. L., Grisham, J. R., & Mancill, R. B. (2001). Current and lifetime comorbidity of the DSM-IV anxiety and mood disorders in a large clinical sample. *Journal of Abnormal Psychology, 110,* 585–599.

Brown, T. A., DiNardo, P. A., & Barlow, D. H. (1994). *Anxiety Disorders Interview Schedule for DSM-IV (ADIS-IV).* Albany, NY: Graywind.

Brown, T. A., DiNardo, P. A., Lehman, C. L., & Campbell, L. A. (2001). Reliability of DSM-IV anxiety and mood disorders: Implications for the classification of emotional disorders. *Journal of Abnormal Psychology, 110,* 49–58.

Brown, T. A., Marten, P. A., & Barlow, D. H. (1995). Discriminant validity of the symptoms constituting the DSM-III-R and DSM-IV associated symptom criterion of generalized anxiety disorder. *Journal of Anxiety Disorders, 9,* 317–328.

Buhr, K., & Dugas, M. J. (2002). The Intolerance of Uncertainty Scale: Psychometric properties of the English version. *Behavior Research and Therapy, 40,* 931–345.

Buhr, K., & Dugas, M. J. (2006). Investigating the construct validity of intolerance of uncertainty and its unique relationship with worry. *Journal of Anxiety Disorders, 20*, 222–236.

Butler, G., Wells, A., & Dewick, H. (1995). Differential effects of worry and imagery after exposure to a stressful stimulus: A pilot study. *Behavioral and Cognitive Psychotherapy, 23*, 45–56.

Carter, R. M., Wittchen, H.-U., Pfister, H., & Kessler R. (2001). One-year prevalence of subthreshold and threshold DSM-IV generalized anxiety disorder in a nationally representative sample. *Depression and Anxiety, 13*, 78–88.

Chantarujikapong, S. I., Scherrer, J. F., Xian, H., Eisen, S. A., Lyons, M. J., Goldberg, J., et al. (2001). A twin study of generalized anxiety disorder symptoms, panic disorder symptoms, and post-traumatic stress disorder in men. *Psychiatry Research, 103*, 133–145.

Craske, M. G., Rapee, R. M., Jackel, L., & Barlow, D. H. (1989). Qualitative dimensions of worry in DSM-III-R generalized anxiety disorder subjects and nonanxious participants. *Behavior Research and Therapy, 27*, 397–402.

Davey, G. C. L., Tallis, F., & Capuzzo, N. (1996). Beliefs about the consequences of worrying. *Cognitive Therapy and Research, 20*, 499–520.

Davis, R. N., & Valentiner, D. P. (2000). Does meta-cognitive theory enhance our understanding of pathological worry and anxiety? *Personality and Individual Differences, 29*, 513–526.

Dean, C., & White, A. P. (1996). A twin study examining the effect of parity on the prevalence of psychiatric disorder. *Journal of Affective Disorders, 38*, 145–152.

Doucet, C., Ladouceur, R., Freeston, M. H., & Dugas, M. J. (1998). Thèmes d'inquiétudes et tendance à s'inquiéter chez les aînés [Worry themes and the tendency to worry in older adults]. *Canadian Journal on Aging/La Revue canadienne du vieillissement, 17*, 361–371.

Dugas, M. J., Freeston, M. H., Doucet, C. D., Lachance, S., & Ladouceur, R. (1995). Structured versus free-recall measures: Effect on report of worry themes. *Personality and Individual Differences, 18*, 355–361.

Dugas, M. J., Freeston, M. H., & Ladouceur, R. (1997). Intolerance of uncertainty and problem orientation in worry. *Cognitive Therapy and Research, 21*, 593–606.

Dugas, M. J., Freeston, M. H., Ladouceur, R., Rhéaume, J., Provencher, M., & Boisvert, J.-M. (1998). Worry themes in primary GAD, secondary GAD, and other anxiety disorders. *Journal of Anxiety Disorders, 12*, 253–261.

Dugas, M. J., Freeston, M. H., Provencher, M. D., Lachance, S., Ladouceur, R., & Gosselin, P. (2001). Le questionnaire sur l'inquiétude et l'anxiété : Validation dans des échantillons non cliniques et cliniques [The Worry and Anxiety Questionnaire: Validation in non-clinical and clinical samples]. *Journal de Thérapie Comportemental et Cognitive, 11*, 31–36.

Dugas, M. J., Gagnon, F., Ladouceur, R., & Freeston, H. (1998). Generalized anxiety disorder: A preliminary test of a conceptual model. *Behavior Research and Therapy, 36*, 215–226.

Dugas, M. J., Gosselin, P., & Ladouceur, R. (2001). Intolerance of uncertainty and worry: Investigating specificity in a nonclinical sample. *Cognitive Therapy and Research, 25*, 551–558.

Dugas, M. J., Hedayati, M., Karavidas, A., Buhr, K., Francis, K., & Phillips, N. A. (2005). Intolerance of uncertainty and information processing: Evidence of biased recall and interpretations. *Cognitive Therapy and Research, 29*, 57–70.

Dugas, M. J., & Ladouceur, R. (2000). Treatment of GAD: Targeting intolerance of uncertainty in two types of worry. *Behavior Modification, 24*, 635–657.

Dugas, M. J., Ladouceur, R., Léger, E., Freeston, M. H., Langlois, F., Provencher, M., et al. (2003). Group cognitive-behavioral therapy for generalized anxiety disorder: Treatment outcome and long-term follow-up. *Journal of Consulting and Clinical Psychology, 71*, 821–825.

Dugas, M. J., Letarte, H., Freeston, M. H., & Ladouceur, R. (1995). Worry and problem solving: Evidence of a specific relationship. *Cognitive Therapy and Research, 19*, 109–120.

Dugas, M. J., Marchand, A., & Ladouceur, R. (2005). Further validation of a cognitive-behavioral model of generalized anxiety disorder: Diagnostic and symptom specificity. *Journal of Anxiety Disorders, 19,* 329–343.

Dugas, M. J., & Robichaud, M. (2007). *Cognitive-behavioral treatment for generalized anxiety disorder: From science to practice.* New York: Routledge.

Dugas, M. J., Savard, P., Gaudet, A., Turcotte, J., Brillon, P., Leblanc, R., et al. (2004, November). Cognitive-behavioral therapy versus applied relaxation for generalized anxiety disorder: Differential outcomes and processes. In H. Hazlett-Stevens (chair), *New advances in the treatment of chronic worry and generalized anxiety disorder.* Symposium conducted at the 38th annual convention for the Association for Advancement of Behavior Therapy, New Orleans, LA.

Dugas, M. J., Savard, P., Gaudet, A., Turcotte, J., Laugesen, N., Robichaud, M., et al. (2007). Can the components of a cognitive model predict the severity of generalized anxiety disorder? *Behavior Therapy, 38,* 169–178.

Dugas, M. J., Schwartz, A., & Francis, K. (2004). Intolerance of uncertainty, worry, and depression. *Cognitive Therapy and Research, 28,* 835–842.

Dupuy, J.-B., Beaudoin, S., Rhéaume, J., Ladouceur, R., & Dugas, M. J. (2001). Worry: Daily self-report in clinical and non-clinical populations. *Behavior Research and Therapy, 39,* 1249–1255.

D'Zurilla, T. J. (1986). *Problem-solving therapy: A social competence approach to clinical intervention.* New York: Springer.

Eng, W., & Heimberg, R. G. (2006). Interpersonal correlates of generalized anxiety disorder: Self versus other perception. *Journal of Anxiety Disorders, 20,* 380–387.

Francis, K., & Dugas, M. J. (2004). Assessing positive beliefs about worry: Validation of a structured interview. *Personality and Individual Differences, 37,* 405–415.

Freeston, M. H., Rhéaume, J., Letarte, H., Dugas, M. J., & Ladouceur, R. (1994). Why do people worry? *Personality and Individual Differences, 17,* 791–802.

Garnefski, N., Kraaij, V., & Spinhoven, P. (2001). Negative life events, cognitive emotion regulation and emotional problems. *Personality and Individual Differences, 30,* 1311–1327.

Goldman, N., Dugas, M. J., Sexton, K. A., & Gervais, N. J. (in press). The impact of written exposure on worry: Efficacy and mechanisms. *Behavior Modification.*

Gosselin, P., Cloutier, M., Vaillancourt, L., Lemay, M., Perron, G., & Ladouceur, R. (2006). Différences individuelles au niveau des croyances erronées à l'égard des inquiétudes [Individual differences in erroneous beliefs about worry]. *Revue Canadienne des Sciences du Comportement, 38,* 41–49.

Gosselin, P., Laberge, M., Lemay, D., Freeston, M. H., Langlois, F., & Ladouceur, R. (1998, June). *Worry themes among high school students.* Poster session presented at the annual convention of the Canadian Psychological Association, Edmonton, Alberta, Canada.

Gosselin, P., Ladouceur, R., Langlois, F., Freeston, M. H., Dugas, M. J., & Bertrand, J. (2003). Développement et validation d'un nouvel instrument évaluant les croyances erronées à l'égard des inquiétudes [Development and validation of a new instrument to evaluate erroneous beliefs about worries]. *Revue Européenne de Psychologie Appliquée, 53,* 119–211.

Gosselin, P., Ladouceur, R., & Pelletier, O. (2001). Évaluation de l'attitude d'un individu face aux différents problèmes de vie: Le Questionnaire d'Attitude face aux Problèmes (QAP) [Evaluation of an individual's attitude toward daily life problems: The Negative Problem Orientation Questionnaire]. *Journal de Thérapie Comportementale et Cognitive, 15*(4), 141–153.

Gosselin, P., Langlois, F., Freeston, M. H., Ladouceur, R., Dugas, M. J., & Pelletier, O. (2002). Le Questionnaire d'Évitement Cognitif (QEC): Développement et validation auprès d'adultes et d'adolescents [The Cognitive Avoidance Questionnaire (CAQ): Development and validation among adult and adolescent samples]. *Journal de Thérapie Comportementale et Cognitive, 12,* 24–37.

Grisham, J. R., Brown, T. A., & Campbell, L. A. (2004). The Anxiety Disorders Interview Schedule for DSM-IV (ADIS-IV). In M. J. Hilsenroth & D. L. Segal (Eds.), *Comprehensive handbook of psychological assessment: Vol. 2. Personality assessment* (pp. 163–177). Hoboken, NJ: Wiley.

Hettema, J. M., Neale, M. C., & Kendler, K. S. (2001). A review and meta-analysis of the genetic epidemiology of anxiety disorders. *American Journal of Psychiatry, 158,* 1568–1578.

Holowka, D. W., Dugas, M. J., Francis, K., & Laugesen, N. (2000, November). *Measuring beliefs about worry: A psychometric evaluation of the Why Worry II Questionnaire.* Poster presented at the annual meeting of the Association for the Advancement of Behavior Therapy, New Orleans, LA.

Hunt, S., Wisocki, P., & Yanko, J. (2003). Worry and use of coping strategies among older and younger adults. *Anxiety Disorders, 17,* 547–560.

Kendler, K. S. (1996). Major depression and generalized anxiety disorder: Same genes, (partly) different environments: Revisited. *British Journal of Psychiatry, 168,* 68–75.

Kendler, K. S., Hettema, J. M., Butera, F., Gardner, C. O., & Prescott, C. A. (2003). Life event dimensions of loss, humiliation, entrapment, and danger in the prediction of onsets of major depression and generalized anxiety. *Archives of General Psychiatry, 60,* 789–795.

Kendler, K. S., Neale, M. C., Kessler, R. C., Heath, A. C., & Eaves, L. J. (1992). Major depression and generalized anxiety disorder. *Archives of General Psychiatry, 49,* 716–722.

Kendler, K. S., Walters, E. E., Neale, M. C., Kessler, R. C., Heath, A., & Eaves, L. J. (1995). The structure of the genetic and environmental risk factors for six major psychiatric disorders in women: Phobia, generalized anxiety disorder, panic disorder, bulimia, major depression, and alcoholism. *Archives of General Psychiatry, 52,* 374–382.

Kessler, R. C. (2000). The epidemiology of pure and comorbid generalized anxiety disorder: A review and evaluation of recent research. *Acta Psychiatrica Scandinavica, 102*(Suppl. 406), 7–13.

Kessler, R. C., Berglund, P. A., Dewit, D. J. Üstün, T. B., Wang, P. S., & Wittchen, H.-U. (2002). Distinguishing generalized anxiety disorder from major depression: Prevalence and impairment from current pure and comorbid disorders in the United States and Ontario. *International Journal of Methods in Psychiatric Research, 11,* 99–111.

Kessler, R. C., DuPont, R. L., Berglund, P., & Wittchen, H.-U. (1999). Impairment in pure and comorbid generalized anxiety disorder and major depression at 12 months in two national surveys. *American Journal of Psychiatry, 156,* 1915–1923.

Kessler, R. C., & Wittchen, H.-U. (2002). Patterns and correlates of generalized anxiety disorder in community samples [Special issue: Generalized anxiety disorder: New trends in diagnosis, management, and treatment]. *Journal of Clinical Psychiatry, 63*(Suppl. 8), 4–10.

Koerner, N., & Dugas, M. J. (2006). A cognitive model of generalized anxiety disorder: The role of intolerance of uncertainty. In G. C. L. Davey & A. Wells (Eds.), *Worry and its psychological disorders: Theory, assessment and treatment* (pp. 201–216). Chichester, West Sussex, England: Wiley.

Koerner, N., & Dugas, M. J. (2007). *Intolerance of uncertainty, cognitive avoidance, and their relation to interpretive processing.* Manuscript in preparation.

Koerner, N., Dugas, M. H., Savard, P., Gaudet, A., Turcotte, J., & Marchand, A. (2004). The economic burden of anxiety disorders in Canada. *Canadian Psychology, 45,* 191–201.

Laberge, M., Dugas, M. J., & Ladouceur, R. (2000). Modification des croyances relatives aux inquiétudes après traitement du trouble d'anxiété généralisée [Changes in dysfunctional beliefs about worry before and after a cognitive-behavioral treatment for people with generalized anxiety disorder]. *Revue Canadienne des Sciences du Comportement, 32,* 91–96.

Labrecque, J., Dugas, M. J., Marchand, A., & Letarte, A. (2006). Cognitive-behavioral therapy for comorbid generalized anxiety disorder and panic disorder with agoraphobia. *Behavior Modification, 30*, 383–410.

Ladouceur, R., Blais, F., Freeston, M. H., & Dugas, M. J. (1998). Problem solving and problem orientation in generalized anxiety disorder. *Journal of Anxiety Disorders, 12*, 139–152.

Ladouceur, R., Dugas, M. J., Freeston, M. H., Léger, E., Gagnon, F., & Thibodeau, N. (2000). Efficacy of a cognitive-behavioral treatment for generalized anxiety disorder: Evaluation in a controlled clinical trial. *Journal of Consulting and Clinical Psychology, 68*, 957–964.

Ladouceur, R., Dugas, M. J., Freeston, M. H., Rhéaume, J., Blais, J.-M., Boisvert, J.-M., et al. (1999). Specificity of generalized anxiety disorders symptoms and processes. *Behavior Therapy, 30*, 191–207.

Ladouceur, R., Freeston, M. H., Fournier, S., Dugas, M. J., & Doucet, C. (2002). The social basis of worry in three samples: High school students, university students, and older adults. *Behavioral and Cognitive Psychotherapy, 30*, 427–438.

Ladouceur, R., Gosselin, P., & Dugas, M. J. (2000). Experimental manipulation of intolerance of uncertainty: A study of a theoretical model of worry. *Behavior Research and Therapy, 38*, 933–941.

Ladouceur, R., Talbot, F., & Dugas, M. J. (1997). Behavioral expressions of intolerance of uncertainty in worry. *Behavior Modification, 21*, 355–371.

MacLeod, A. K., Williams, J. M. G., & Bekerian, D. A. (1991). Worry is reasonable: The role of explanations in pessimism about future personal events. *Journal of Abnormal Psychology, 100*, 478–486.

Mancuso, D. M., Townsend, M. H., & Mercante, D. E. (1993). Long-term follow-up of generalized anxiety disorder. *Comprehensive Psychiatry, 34*, 441–446.

Marten, P. A., Brown, T. A., Barlow, D. H., Borkovec, T. D., Shear, M. K., & Lydiard, R. B. (1993). Evaluation of the ratings comprising the associated symptom criterion of DSM-III-R generalized anxiety disorder. *Journal of Nervous and Mental Diseases, 181*, 676–682.

Mennin, D. S. (2004). An emotion regulation treatment for generalized anxiety disorder. *Clinical Psychology and Psychotherapy, 11*, 17–29.

Mennin, D. S., Heimberg, R. G., Turk, C. L., & Fresco, D. M. (2002). Applying an emotion regulation framework to integrative approaches to generalized anxiety disorder. *Clinical Psychology: Science and Practice, 9*, 85–90.

Mennin, D. S., Heimberg, R. G., Turk, C. L., & Fresco, D. M. (2005). Preliminary evidence for an emotion regulation deficit model of generalized anxiety disorder. *Behavior Research and Therapy, 43*, 1281–1310.

Meyer, T. J., Miller, M. L., Metzger, R. L., & Borkovec, T. D. (1990). Development and validation of the Penn State Worry Questionnaire. *Behavior Research and Therapy, 28*, 487–495.

Mineka, S. (2004). The positive and negative consequences of worry in the aetiology of generalized anxiety disorder: A learning theory perspective. In J. Yiend (Ed.), *Cognition, emotion and psychopathology: Theoretical, empirical and clinical directions* (pp. 29–48). New York: Cambridge University Press.

Molina, S., & Borkovec, T. D. (1994). The Penn State Worry Questionnaire: Psychometric properties and associated characteristics. In G. C. L. Davey & F. Tallis (Eds.), *Worrying: Perspectives on theory, assessment and treatment* (pp. 265–283). New York: Wiley.

Muris, P., Meesters, C., Merckelbach, H., & Hülsenbeck, P. (2000). Worry in children is related to perceived parental rearing and attachment. *Behavior Research and Therapy, 38*, 487–497.

Muris, P., & Merckelbach, H. (1998). Perceived parental rearing behavior and anxiety disorders symptoms in normal children. *Personality and Individual Differences, 25*, 1199–1206.

Newman, S. C., & Bland, R. C. (1994). Life events and the 1-year prevalence of major depressive episode, generalized anxiety disorder, and panic disorder in a community sample. *Comprehensive Psychiatry, 35,* 76–82.

Norton, P. J. (2005). A psychometric analysis of the Intolerance of Uncertainty Scale among four racial groups. *Journal of Anxiety Disorders, 19,* 699–707.

Pennebaker, J. W., & Beall, S. K. (1986). Confronting a traumatic event: Toward an understanding of inhibition and disease. *Journal of Abnormal Psychology, 95,* 274–281.

Provencher, M. D., Dugas, M. J., & Ladouceur, R. (2004). Efficacy of problem-solving training and cognitive exposure in the treatment of generalized anxiety disorder: A case replication series. *Cognitive and Behavioral Practice, 11,* 404–414.

Provencher, M. D., Ladouceur, R., & Dugas, M. J. (2006). La comorbidité dans le trouble d'anxiété généralisée: Prévalence et évolution suite à une thérapie cognitive-comportemental [Comorbidity in generalized anxiety disorder: Prevalence and course after cognitive-behavioural therapy]. *La Revue Canadienne de Psychiatrie, 51,* 91–99.

Rapee, R. M. (1997). Potential role of childrearing practices in the development of anxiety and depression. *Clinical Psychology Review, 17,* 47–67.

Robichaud, M., & Dugas, M. J. (2005a). Negative problem orientation: Pt. 1. Psychometric properties of a new measure. *Behavior Research and Therapy, 43,* 391–401.

Robichaud, M., & Dugas, M. J. (2005b). Negative problem orientation: Pt. 2. Construct validity and specificity to worry. *Behavior Research and Therapy, 43,* 403–412.

Robichaud, M., Dugas, M. J., & Conway, M. (2003). Gender differences in worry and associated cognitive-behavioral variables. *Anxiety Disorders, 17,* 501–516.

Roemer, L., Molina, S., & Borkovec, T. D. (1997). An investigation of worry content among generally anxious individuals. *Journal of Nervous and Mental Diseases, 185,* 314–319.

Ruscio, A. M., & Borkovec, T. D. (2004). Experience and appraisal of worry among high worriers with and without generalized anxiety disorder. *Behavior Research and Therapy, 42,* 1469–1482.

Scherrer, J. F., True, W. R., Xian, H., Lyons, M. J., Eisen, S. A., Goldberg, J., et al. (2000). Evidence for genetic influences common and specific to symptoms of generalized anxiety and panic. *Journal of Affective Disorders, 57,* 25–35.

Scott, E. L., Eng, W., & Heimberg, R. G. (2002). Ethnic differences in worry in a nonclinical population. *Depression and Anxiety, 15,* 79–82.

Sexton, K. A., & Dugas, M. J. (in press). The Cognitive Avoidance Questionnaire: Validation of the English translation. *Journal of Anxiety Disorders.*

Sexton, K. A., & Dugas, M. J. (2007). *An investigation of the factors leading to cognitive avoidance in worry.* Manuscript submitted for publication.

Shadick, R. N., Roemer, L., Hopkins, M. B., & Borkovec, T. D. (1991). A description of patients diagnosed with DSM-III-R generalized anxiety disorder. *Journal of Nervous and Mental Diseases, 178,* 588–591.

Silove, D., Parker, G., Hadzi-Pavlovic, D., Manicavasagar, V., & Blaszczynski, A. (1991). Parental representations of patients with panic disorder and generalized anxiety disorder. *British Journal of Psychiatry, 159,* 835–841.

Stöber, J. (1998). Worry, problem elaboration and suppression of imagery: The role of concreteness. *Behavior Research and Therapy, 36,* 751–756.

Stöber, J., & Bittencourt, J. (1998). Weekly assessment of worry: An adaptation of the Penn State Worry Questionnaire for monitoring changes during treatment. *Behavior Research and Therapy, 36,* 645–656.

Summerfeldt, L. J., & Antony, M. M. (2002). Structured and semistructured diagnostic interviews. In M. M. Antony & D. H. Barlow (Eds.), *Handbook of assessment and treatment planning for psychological disorders* (pp. 3–37). New York: Guilford Press.

Tallis, R., Eysenck, M., & Mathews, A. (1991). Elevated evidence requirements and worry. *Personality and Individual Differences, 12,* 21–27.

Turk, C. L., Heimberg, R. G., Luterek, J. A., Mennin, D. S., & Fresco, D. M. (2005). Emotion dysregulation in generalized anxiety disorder: A comparison with social anxiety disorder. *Cognitive Therapy and Research, 29,* 89–106.

Wells, A. (1995). Meta-cognition and worry: A cognitive model of generalized anxiety disorder. *Behavioral and Cognitive Psychotherapy, 23,* 301–320.

Wells, A. (1999). A cognitive model of generalized anxiety disorder. *Behavior Modification, 23,* 526–555.

Wells, A. (2002). Worry, metacognition, and GAD: Nature, consequences, and treatment. *Journal of Cognitive Psychotherapy: An International Quarterly, 16,* 179–191.

Wells, A., & Carter, K. (1999). Preliminary tests of a cognitive model of generalized anxiety disorder. *Behavior Research and Therapy, 37,* 585–594.

Wells, A., & King, P. (2006). Metacognitive therapy for generalized anxiety disorder: An open trial. *Journal of Behavior Therapy and Experimental Psychiatry, 37,* 206–212.

Wells, A., & Papageorgiou, C. (1995). Worry and the incubation of intrusive images following stress. *Behavior Research and Therapy, 33,* 579–583.

Wittchen, H. U. (2002). Generalized anxiety disorder: Prevalence, burden, and cost to society. *Depression and anxiety, 16,* 162–171.

Wittchen, H.-U., & Hoyer, J. (2001). Generalized anxiety disorder: Nature and course. *Journal of Clinical Psychiatry, 62*(Suppl. 11), 15–19.

CHAPTER 13

Major Depressive Disorder

MARLENE TAUBE-SCHIFF AND MARK A. LAU

DESCRIPTION OF THE DISORDER

PREVALENCE

Depressive disorders have been referred to as the common colds of mental illness due to the staggering number of individuals affected by it. Lifetime prevalence estimates for Major Depressive Disorder (MDD) ranges from 15% to 17% (American Psychiatric Association APA, 2000a). The 12-month prevalence rate ranges from 6% to 7% (Kessler, Chiu, Demler, Merikangas, Walters, 2005), with prevalence rates approximately twice as high for women as for men. These numbers include only individuals meeting diagnostic criteria for MDD. However, Dysthymic Disorder, sometimes conceptualized as chronic sadness, shows many of the same symptoms as MDD, except that they are less severe. At any given time, approximately 3% of the population suffers from dysthymia (M. M. Weissman, Leaf, Bruce, & Florio, 1988). In addition, recent epidemiological studies have begun to investigate subsyndromal symptoms of depression, using the diagnostic criteria for minor depression and recurrent brief depression as described in the fourth edition of the *Diagnostic and Statistical Manual of Mental Disorders* (*DSM-IV-TR*; American Psychiatric Association, 2000a). These studies have revealed that rates of subsyndromal depression are as high as or higher than the rates of Major Depression in adults (e.g., Judd, Akiskal, & Paulus, 1997; Kessler, Zhao, Blazer, & Swartz, 1997).

COURSE AND RECURRENCE

Depression used to be regarded as a self-limiting and discrete disorder (Keller, 1994). An individual who recovered from an episode of depression was thought to be unlikely to become depressed again. As further evidence has accumulated, however, the understanding of the course of this disorder has changed dramatically. It is now estimated that at least 50% of those who recover from an initial episode of depression will have at least one subsequent depressive episode (Paykel et al., 1995), and that people with a history of two or more past episodes have a 70% to 80% likelihood of recurrence in their lifetimes (National Institute of Mental Health Consensus Development Conference Statement, 1985). The period of remission between episodes may be a few months or several years. Studies of the natural course of the disorder in treated individuals reveal that even after individuals "recover" from an episode of Major Depression, they often continue to exhibit both symptoms and psychosocial impairment (e.g., Judd et al., 1998, 2000).

SUICIDE

Suicidal thoughts and motivations are a symptom of depressive illness—not always an inevitable outcome of this illness (Gotlib & Hammen, 2002). The lifetime risk of suicide among the mood-disordered is estimated to be approximately 15% (Mann, 1998), which is 15 times higher than the risk in the general population. It is not entirely clear why some depressed individuals attempt suicide and others do not. However, a 10-year follow-up study of a large number of people with major depressive illness found that six factors were predictive of suicide within the first year: panic attacks, severe anxiety, reduced ability to concentrate, insomnia, moderate alcohol abuse, and reduced capacity for enjoyment (Fawcett et al., 1990). Also, suicide following 1 year of depressive symptoms was associated with severe hopelessness or suicidal thinking at the time of the initial illness, as well as previous suicide attempts. Recent research suggests that suicidality may have a familial component and be linked to a genetic predisposition, possibly serotonergic processes (also found to be associated with impulsivity and violence; Mann, Brent, & Arango, 2001).

DIAGNOSIS AND ASSESSMENT

DIAGNOSTIC CRITERIA

It has been debated in the literature whether depression exists in an all-or-none fashion or along a distributed graded continuum (see Joiner, Walker, Pettit, Perez, & Cukrowicz, 2005, for a review of this discussion). It should be noted that the former conceptualization is the most accepted, as illustrated by the commonly used diagnostic manuals described in the proceeding paragraphs.

Depression is most often diagnosed as a distinct *syndrome* and has well-characterized parameters, including disease course, comorbidity patterns, and treatment response (Joiner et al., 2005). The two most widely used systems of classification are the *DSM-IV-TR* (American Psychiatric Association, 2000a, primarily used in North America) and the *International Classification of Diseases*, version 10 (*ICD-10*; World Health Organization, 1992, primarily used in Europe). In order for a diagnosis of a Major Depressive Episode (MDE) to be made according to the *DSM-IV-TR*, a certain subset of criteria must be met. The two cardinal symptoms of an MDE, one of which must be experienced by the individual, are (1) at least 2 weeks of continuous depressed mood, or (2) at least 2 weeks of a loss of interest or pleasure in activities. In addition to either of these symptoms, the individual must experience at least four additional symptoms, including any of the following: significant weight loss (when not dieting) or weight gain (e.g., a change of more than 5% of body weight in a month) or a decrease in appetite; insomnia or hypersomnia; psychomotor agitation or retardation (must be observable by others and not simply subjective feelings of restlessness or retardation); fatigue or loss of energy; feelings of worthlessness or excessive or inappropriate guilt (which may present as delusional in severe depression); diminished ability to think or concentrate or indecisiveness; or recurrent thoughts of death (not just fear of dying), recurrent suicidal ideation without a specific plan, or a specific plan for committing suicide or a suicide attempt. Although the diagnostic criteria require that an MDE lasts at least 2 weeks, episodes usually last much longer; a duration of 6 to 9 months is more typical.

DYSTHYMIC DISORDER

According to the *DSM-IV-TR*, dysthymia is a chronic mood disorder with a duration of at least 2 years in adults and 1 year in adolescents. It is characterized by depressed mood for most of the day, more days than not, and is accompanied by at least two of following symptoms: poor appetite or overeating; insomnia or hypersomnia; low energy or fatigue; low self-esteem; poor concentration; difficulty making decisions; and feelings of hopelessness. For this diagnosis to be made individuals must have not experienced any manic or depressive episodes during the first 2 years of the illness. However, the individual may have experienced transient euthymic episodes of up to 2 months during the course of the illness. It should also be noted that, according to the *DSM-IV-TR,* Dysthymic Disorder is diagnosed only when an individual is currently experiencing these symptoms (i.e., a past diagnosis of dysthymia is not assigned).

Much of the criteria for MDD and dysthymia in the *ICD-10* are quite similar to that in the *DSM-IV-TR*, although the *ICD-10* breaks down the category of MDD into subcategories (mild depression, moderate depression, severe depression, dysthymia, very long-standing depression) according to very specific criteria. Although the *DSM-IV-TR* does use specifiers that enable the clinician or researcher to designate subtypes of depression (see later discussion), these are determined by the clinician or researcher in a somewhat more subjective manner. See Table 13.1 for an overview of the *ICD-10* criteria for depression.

SPECIFIERS

One category of specifiers used by the *DMS-IV-TR* is to aid the clinician in the description of severity. Severity is to be judged as mild, moderate, or severe (with or without psychotic features) based on the number and severity of criteria symptoms and the degree of functional disability and distress. Mild episodes are characterized by the presence of five or six depressive symptoms and either mild disability or the capacity to function normally but with much greater effort (American Psychiatric Association, 2000a). The "severe without psychotic features" specifier indicates the presence of most of the criteria symptoms along with observable disabilities in functioning. Moderate episodes fall in between these two categories. An episode is characterized as "severe with psychotic features" when the patient has reported experiencing delusions or hallucinations (typically auditory). These are most often consistent with the depressive themes (e.g., delusions of guilt, deserved punishment). Finally, there are remission specifiers for current and past episodes. Full remission requires a period of at least 2 months in which there are no significant symptoms of depression. Criteria for partial remission may be met in two ways: (1) Some symptoms of an MDE are still present, but full criteria are not met; or (2) there are no longer any significant symptoms of an MDE, but the period of remission has been less than 2 months.

Table 13.1
ICD-10 Criteria for Depression

DEPRESSIVE EPISODE
At least 2 weeks of depressed mood, reduction of energy, a decrease in activity, a loss of interest and decreased concentration, marked tiredness, disturbed sleep and appetite, lowered self-esteem and self-confidence, feelings of worthlessness or guilt.
The lowered mood varies little from day to day and is unresponsive. This low mood may also be accompanied by "somatic" symptoms, such as loss of pleasurable feelings, marked psychomotor retardation/agitation, weight loss/gain, and a loss of libido.

MILD DEPRESSION
Two or three of the above symptoms present; patient is distressed but probably able to continue with most daily activities.

MODERATE DEPRESSION
Four or more of the above symptoms present, and the patient is likely to have great difficulty in continuing with ordinary activities.

SEVERE DEPRESSION
Several of the above symptoms are marked and distressing; loss of self-esteem and ideas of worthlessness and guilt are most typical. Also common are suicidal thoughts and acts, along with a number of somatic symptoms. Sometimes psychotic symptoms such as hallucinations or delusions are present.

DYSTHYMIA
Chronic depressed mood lasting several years, not sufficiently severe enough to fulfill criteria for recurrent depressive disorder.

Source: The ICD-10 Classification of Mental Health and Behavior Disorders: Diagnostic Criteria for Research, by the World Health Organization, 1992, Geneva, Switzerland: Author.

COMORBIDITY

Occurrence of depression with another illness, be it psychiatric or medical, has been found to have a negative effect on treatment outcome often due to increased symptom severity or complexity (Boland & Keller, 2002). The following paragraphs briefly review some of the most common comorbid illnesses.

Double Depression   This course modifier occurs when an individual experiences both dysthymia and MDD. This is often diagnosed when a patient presents with a long-standing history of dysthymia as well as periods of time when symptoms meet diagnostic criteria for an MDE. Patients with this disorder most often experience illness chronically (Boland & Keller, 2002), and recovery from an episode is often limited to a lower level of depression or dysthymia (Keller, Lavori, Endicott, Coryell, & Klerman, 1983). Although recovery has been found to be more rapid with double depression, the level to which these individuals recover is not as beneficial, and relapses occur more often (Boland & Keller, 2002).

Anxiety Disorders   The most frequent condition comorbid with depression is anxiety, which occurs in as many as 50% of individuals diagnosed with depression (M. M. Weissman, Leckman, Merikangas, Gammon, & Prusoff, 1984). Considerable symptom overlap exists between depression and anxiety, including poor concentration, irritability, hypervigilance, fatigue, guilt, memory loss, sleep difficulties, and worry.

One approach to differentiating the close relationship between anxiety and depression is to conceptualize these disorders on three broad dimensions of emotion: negative affect (e.g., distress, anger, fear, guilt, worry); positive affect (e.g., excitement, delight, interest, pride); and anxious hyperarousal (physical signs of autonomic arousal such as racing heart and dizziness; Clark, Steer, & Beck, 1994). Whereas anxious and depressed individuals score high on measures of negative affect, anxious individuals score higher on measures of positive affect and anxious hyperarousal than do depressed people (Clark et al., 1994). Individuals presenting with high levels of negative affect and autonomic arousal but low levels of positive affect have formed a new diagnostic category, mixed anxiety-depression, that has been included in *DSM-IV-TR* as a diagnosis in need of further study.

Medical Illness   The diagnosis of depression within a medical population can often be complicated for a variety of reasons. For example, patients experiencing significant medical illnesses (e.g., cancer, renal disease) may experience some of the somatic symptoms of depression due to the medical illness as opposed to the presence of depression (e.g., fatigue, weight or appetite changes). This has led to the well-documented difficulty of underdetection or overdiagnosis of depressive disorders in chronic somatic illnesses (e.g., Chochinov, Wilson, Enns, & Lander, 1994; McDaniel, Musselmann, Porter, Reed, & Nemeroff, 1995). In addition, individuals with medical illnesses may experience depressive symptoms as the result of their illness and the adjustments that must occur in their lives. In these latter cases, the clinician must be cautious when assigning a primary diagnosis of MDD. It may be that a diagnosis of Adjustment Disorder with Depressed Mood is more appropriate when symptoms do not meet full diagnostic criteria for MDD and are best conceptualized in the context of the illness. Recently, Reuter, Raugust, Bengel, and Härter (2004) suggested that cognitive symptoms should receive special attention in discriminating primary affective disorders from adjustment disorders. Further, the medical treatment that individuals receive for their illness may cause symptoms similar to depression. For example, a patient undergoing chemotherapy will commonly report experiencing feelings of fatigue, appetite loss, and sleep disturbances. Due to this symptom overlap, alternative diagnostic approaches have been proposed. For example, some suggest excluding all somatic symptoms of depression (referred to as the "exclusive approach") or excluding symptoms most likely due to the somatic disease (referred to as the "etiologic approach"; for a discussion of these approaches with respect to cancer and depressive disorders, see Cohen-Cole, Brown, & McDaniel, 1993; Creed, 1997).

Assessment

Assessment of depressive symptoms may be done for a variety of clinical and research purposes. Because the full range of assessment tools cannot be covered in the following overview, the interested reader is directed to Nezu, Nezu, McClure, and Zwick (2002) and Joiner et al. (2005). This discussion focuses on various purposes for which an assessment may be conducted, including screening, diagnostic clarification, and symptom severity.

Screening   This type of assessment is often conducted to determine the presence of depressive symptoms as well as to identify individuals at risk of developing a depressive disorder (e.g., Alloy, 2001). These instruments are administered quickly and scored fairly easily, as the goal is to provide the user with a snapshot of the individual's symptoms. This provides information for further diagnostic evaluation and interventions (Nezu et al., 2002). Measures that have been used for screening that are characterized by a strong criterion-related validity include the Reynolds Depression Screening Inventory (W. M. Reynolds & Kobak, 1998) and the Harvard Department of Psychiatry/National Depression Screening Day questionnaire (Baer et al., 2000).

Diagnostic Assessment   One of the most widely used tools for the diagnosis of MDD is the Structured Clinical Interview for *DSM-IV* Axis I Disorders (SCID-I; First, Spitzer, Gibbon, & Williams, 1997). This is a standardized clinical interview used in both research and clinical settings. It comprises an open-ended interview, a semi-structured interview, and questions pertaining to specific symptoms that enable differential diagnosis. This instrument was structured to match the specific diagnostic criteria that have been defined in the *DSM-IV-TR* for Axis I disorders. This tool in its entirety often requires 90 to 120 minutes to administer. However, each disorder exists as a stand-alone module, which is very beneficial for symptom follow-up and targeted research populations. The general reliability and validity of the SCID have been found to vary greatly depending on the raters administering the SCID, the population tested, and the symptom severity of the patients (Joiner et al., 2005). It should be noted that given the labor intensity of SCID administration, clinicians might opt to perform a semi-structured interview. These can be conducted in various ways. Most important, the essentials to be covered include current and past psychiatric symptomatology, medical history, interpersonal and social functioning, and an overview of background history, often including developmental issues.

Symptom Severity   This type of assessment provides clinicians with a picture of symptom intensity prior to initiating treatment or a research study. It may also enable both the clinician and the patient to monitor changes in symptomatology throughout the course of treatment. Although structured clinical interviews provide valid and reliable assessments of symptoms, they are not practical for acquiring information about rapid symptom fluctuations (Joiner et al., 2005). Self-report measures such as the Beck Depression Inventory-Second Edition (BDI-II; Beck, Steer, & Brown, 1996) as well as brief clinician rating scales such as the Hamilton Rating Scale for Depression (HRSD; Hamilton, 1960) are preferable. Clinician ratings have been found to be more sensitive to symptom changes than self-report measures, although the accuracy of this heightened sensitivity is questionable (Lambert & Lambert, 1999). Interestingly, Vittengl, Clark, Kraft, and Jarrett (2005) recently found that the 17-item HRSD, the BDI (Beck, Ward, Mendelson, Mock, & Erbaugh, 1961), and the 30-item self-report and clinician-rated forms of the Inventory for Depressive Symptomatology (Rush, Gullion, Basco, Jarrett, & Trivedi, 1996) reflect similar symptom severity and change constructs during acute-phase cognitive therapy when administered to adult outpatients with recurrent MDD. They suggested that this may enable clinicians to decrease the number of tools used and time needed for assessment of recurrent MDD as well as allowing for comparisons with outcomes in other clinical trials.

Cultural Issues   As global awareness of mental health issues increases, cultural issues related to psychopathology assessment are becoming more relevant. Currently, there is no culture-specific assessment tool for depression. In fact, some argue that the assessment of depression itself is a Westernized construct, thereby making it difficult to diagnose in other cultural contexts (see Falicov, 2003, for an overview of this discussion). The culturally distinctive elements of the clinical presentation of patients with depression might reflect culture-specific symptoms or syndromes, which speaks to a potential need for a different diagnostic strategy and clinical intervention (Kirmayer, 2001). Thus, when assessing culturally diverse clients, it is imperative to ensure that a comprehensive picture of the client's functioning and other relevant medical history is obtained, as some somatic symptoms may present as bizarre when encountered outside of their cultural context and may lead clinicians to mistakenly diagnose psychosis (Kirmayer, 2001) when, in fact, the symptom may be very common within the client's cultural context. For example, sensations of "heat" or a "peppery feeling" in the head are common in equatorial regions of Africa (Ifabumuyi, 1981).

To aid with some of this complexity, the *DSM-IV-TR* has included an appendix listing descriptions of some *culture-bound syndromes.* These are locality-specific patterns of aberrant behavior or troubling experiences that have been described by various cultural groups. For example, *nervios* is described as a common idiom of distress among Latinos in the United States and Latin America. This "syndrome" refers to a wide range of symptoms, including emotional distress, somatic disturbance ("brain aches," tingling sensations, sleep difficulties, dizziness), and inability to function, often brought on by stressful life experiences.

CONCEPTUALIZATION

Risk factors for depression onset and recurrence involve a complex and dynamic interaction of biological, social, and psychological factors (Segal & Dobson, 1992; Teasdale, 1988). Our discussion, however, describes each of these factors in isolation.

BIOLOGICAL BASES OF DEPRESSION

Biological theories propose that depressive disorders are the result of an organic dysfunction which can be detected through studies of genetic, biochemical, or neurophysiological indices.

Genetic Influences Depression has been found to have a strong familial link (Hammen, 1991), and numerous family studies over the past 35 years estimate that first-degree relatives of people with depression are 2 to 5 times more likely to develop depression than individuals from the general population. Berrettini (2006) describes five well-designed studies in the literature on familial linkage of depression (Gershon et al., 1982; Maier & Lichtermann, 1993; Tsuang, Winokur, & Crowe, 1980; M. M. Weissman et al., 1984, 1993). These studies all illustrated that first-degree relatives of individuals with recurrent depression were at increased risk for recurrent depression, as compared with first-degree relatives of control probands.

Twin studies have also been utilized to support the idea of a genetic predisposition in the development of depression. However, given that these studies demonstrate a higher rate of concordance for depression among monozygotic twins than dizygotic twins, some have argued that results can be explained due to identical twins sharing a more similar environment compared to fraternal pairs. However, McGuffin and his colleagues (McGuffin, Katz, Watkins, & Rutherford, 1996) showed that the concordance rates for twins reared apart did not differ from those reared together, thereby strengthening the genetic hypothesis. More recently, Sullivan, Eaves, Kendler, and Neale (2001) provided evidence from twin studies demonstrating 37% heritability in recurrent depression with a significant component of unique individual environmental risk but little shared environmental risk. Adoption studies have also been employed as a means of better understanding the potential genetic contribution to the development of mood disorders. For example, Wender et al. (1986) found that depression was 7 times more likely in biological relatives of depressed people than in biological relatives of control cases. Overall, the literature on family, twin, and adoption studies has demonstrated significant heritable risk components for recurrent depression (for review, see Berrettini, 2006).

Neurochemical Findings   The neurochemical conceptualization of depression has benefited from a great deal of research over the past 20 years. A complete overview of all potential neurotransmitters and neuromodulators in the pathophysiology of MDD would be too broad to cover in the current discussion. The interested reader, therefore, is directed to Delgado and Moreno (2006) for an in-depth review of these topics. The present discussion focuses primarily on the monoamine hypothesis of depression, as that has received the majority of attention by researchers. It should be noted that neuropeptides, such as opioids, somatostatin, and neuropeptide Y, have also been studied (Delgado & Moreno, 2006).

Research on the study of brain function began in the 1950s, and evidence soon implicated the likelihood of central nervous system dysfunction being subserved by two key neurotransmitters: the catecholamine norepinephrine (NE) and the indoleamine serotonin (5-hydroxytryptamine or 5-HT). These two monoamines were both found to regulate bodily functions such as energy levels, sleep, appetite, libido, and psychomotor behavior (Thase, Jindal, & Howland, 2002), which become disrupted during depressive states. Over the years, research has consistently found relationships between drug effects on monoamines (e.g., serotonin, norepinephrine, dopamine, and acetylcholine) and affective or behavior states (e.g., Pryor & Sulser, 1991). Some specific examples of these include the following: Drugs that deplete or inactivate centrally acting norepinephrine (reserpine-like drugs) produce sedation or depression, whereas drugs that increase or potentiate brain norepinephrine (monoamine oxidase inhibitors and tricyclic antidepressants) are associated with behavior stimulation/excitement and are generally associated with an antidepressant effect (Pryor & Sulser, 1991). Although these types of chemical changes actually take place within minutes, clinical practice has shown that antidepressants do not produce mood-altering effects for approximately 10 to 14 days. This suggests that antidepressants act via a delayed postsynaptor receptor-mediated event (Kalia, 2005).

Involvement of the serotonin neurotransmitter system has also been well researched. Although serotonin alone does not account for the entire pathophysiology of mood disorders, the interaction of serotonin with other neurotransmitters in the central nervous system has been considered to play an important role in the etiology of depression (Kalia, 2005; Meltzer & Lowy, 1987). For example, a variety of findings has implicated the serotonin system in the involvement of depression: Drugs increasing serotonergic activity exert antidepressant effects on patients; metabolites and/or 5-HT of serotonin are reduced in urinary or cerebrospinal fluid of patients with depression; and the 5-HT content in brains of suicide victims have been found to be low compared with controls (Murphy, Campbell, & Costa, 1978). In addition, preclinical studies in laboratory animals have found that altering the function of the serotonin system alters many of the behaviors and somatic functions that form the key features in clinical depression, including appetite, sleep, and sexual function, as well as changes in body temperature, pain sensitivity, and circadian rhythms (Maes & Meltzer, 1995).

Overall, these findings speak to the important role that neurochemicals play in the onset and maintenance of depression. It follows from this that medications that target these symptoms often play an important role in treating individuals with moderate to severe depressive symptoms. This is further discussed in the treatment section of this chapter.

Electrophysiological Findings Data from numerous studies have shown that individuals with depression display an asymmetrical resting electroencephalograph (EEG) pattern. They have been found to have higher alpha readings in the left frontal region of the brain than in the right frontal region (suggesting lower levels of cortical activity in the left frontal cortex; Henriques & Davidson, 1990). This asymmetry reliably distinguishes depressed from nondepressed individuals and remitted-depressed patients from never-depressed controls, and is stable across phases of depression (Henriques & Davidson, 1990). Therefore, frontal cortex EEG asymmetry has been suggested to be a risk marker for Major Depression and an indicator of the underlying disorder as opposed to just a reflection of mood.

Sleep Research As described, depressed patients often experience sleep difficulties such that they may find it difficult to fall asleep or to sleep continuously during the night or experience early morning awakening (Ford & Kamerow, 1990). Recordings of brain-related electrical activity taken from the scalp have shown that depressed patients have different sleep patterns than nondepressed controls. Electroencephalograph studies indicate that depressed patients show a decrease in slow-wave sleep and an earlier onset of *rapid eye movement (REM)* sleep, which is often associated with dreaming and more restful sleep. For example, the first period of REM sleep in nondepressed adults starts about 70 to 90 minutes after the person has fallen asleep. Depressed patients, however, tend to start having REM sleep at 60 minutes or less (C. F. Reynolds & Kupfer, 1987). One study demonstrated that some sleep disturbances are present in individuals who are at high genetic risk for depression (Lauer, Schreiber, Holsboer, & Krieg, 1995). In addition, the decrease in slow-wave sleep has been found to be consistent with reduced activity of the neurotransmitter serotonin, supporting hypotheses that would be predicted from the monoamine hypothesis (Thase & Kupfer, 1987).

Neuroimaging Studies The research on anatomical differences in patients with primary mood disorders has revealed less consistent findings compared to those for depressed patients with neurological disorders (Mayberg, 2006). However, hippocampal changes have been well-researched, and it is often found that volumes are consistently reduced (Campbell, Marriott, Nahmias, & MacQueen, 2004; Frodl et al., 2004; Sheline, Sanghavi, Mintun, & Gado, 1999; Videbech & Ravnkilde, 2004). It is possible that clinical correlates of depression (duration of illness, repeated episodes and treatment resistance) contribute to and are associated with these hippocampal changes (Campbell et al., 2004; Shah, Ebmeier, Glabus, & Goodwin, 1998; Shah, Glabus, Goodwin, & Ebmeier, 2002; Videbech & Ravnkilde, 2004). Therefore, until there are longitudinal studies conducted with depressed patients (as opposed to the current cross-sectional ones) that examine whether changes in the hippocampus are due to depression as opposed to the clinical characteristics of the illness, this issue will not completely be resolved (Ebmeier, Donaghey, & Steele, 2006).

Positron emission studies have found that patients with unipolar depression consistently demonstrate decreased brain activity in the left lateral prefrontal cortex (Baxter et al., 1989). Although abnormalities in the amygdala have occasionally been illustrated, reliable abnormalities in this region have not been reported (Mayberg, 2006). In geriatric subgroups of depressed patients, volume loss has been found in various subdivisions of the orbital frontal cortex (Ballmaier et al., 2004; Drevets et al., 1997; Lee et al., 2003) as well as increased ventricle size (Musselman et al., 1998) in studies using magnetic resonance imaging. It is not entirely clear what mechanisms may be responsible for these changes observed in depressed individuals. It has been thought that, consistent with animal models and studies of patients with Posttraumatic Stress Disorder, changes may be due to glucocorticoid neurotoxicity and stress-induced changes in structural plasticity (Mirescu, Peters, & Gould, 2004; Sapolsky, 2000).

INTERPERSONAL EFFECTS OF MOOD DISORDERS

Interpersonal models of depression focus on interactions between the individual and possible triggers in his or her social environment. These models propose that depressed individuals may interact with others in ways that elicit depressing or negative feedback, which then may lead to a loss of social support. Joiner (2002) reviewed literature on interpersonal areas of functioning found to be difficult for individuals experiencing depressive symptoms. For example, social and communication skills have been found to be problematic in depressed individuals. Specifically, depressed individuals (adults and children) have been found to negatively evaluate their own social skills as compared to nondepressed individuals (e.g., Lewinsohn, Mischel, Chaplin, & Barton, 1980; Segrin, 2001; Segrin & Dillard, 1992; Youngren & Lewinsohn, 1980). Interestingly, although depressed individuals do judge their own social skills more harshly than others do, their skills still have been rated objectively by others as lower than nondepressed individuals (Lewinsohn et al., 1980; Segrin, 1990, 2001). In a related area of research, depressed individuals have been found to speak more slowly, with less volume and voice modulation and longer pauses in their speech patterns, and they take longer to respond when someone addresses them as compared to nondepressed individuals (e.g., Talavera, Saiz-Ruiz, & Garcia-Toro, 1994; Teasdale, Fogarty, & Williams, 1980; Youngren & Lewinsohn, 1980). Given these findings, one may postulate that these interpersonal qualities would negatively impact individuals interacting with depressed people, possibly causing them to withdraw, which may invariably perpetuate the negative skills of the depressed individuals.

Another area of research has focused on how depressed individuals often have strained or problematic relationships, which may contribute to maintaining and exacerbating depressive symptoms (Coyne, 1976; Gotlib & Hammen, 1995). For example, Coyne and Calarco (1995) interviewed people who had a history of depression but were not currently depressed. Those who had had multiple experiences of depression interacted differently than those who had experienced only one episode. More specifically, those with multiple episodes usually lowered their expectations of what they could get from relationships with others and scaled back their ambitions.

Researchers have also examined the role of marital and family functioning with respect to the onset, maintenance, and relapse of depression. For example, in a recent review of retrospective studies, Anderson and her colleagues (Anderson, Beach, & Kaslow, 1999) concluded that marital discord might precipitate a depressive episode, particularly in women. In another study (Whisman & Bruce, 1999), it was found that dissatisfied spouses were nearly 3 times more likely than satisfied spouses to experience a depressive episode over a 12-month period following the initial assessment. It is important to note that these results do not rule out instances where the converse is true, that is, depression leading to marital discord. Depression may contribute to marital dissatisfaction (Coyne, 1976) through behaviors, such as constant reassurance-seeking behaviors from others, which can then interfere with the marital relationship (Joiner & Metalsky, 1995). Evidence supporting this notion comes from a study in which depressive symptoms were shown to predict level of marital satisfaction (Ulrich-Jakubowski, Russell, & O'Hara, 1988).

It is interesting to note, as pointed out by Joiner (2002), that interpersonal therapy (IPT, discussed later in detail) does not focus on these interpersonal domains (i.e., verbal and nonverbal behavior, excessive reassurance seeking). Instead, IPT focuses on the interpersonal realms of grief, role transitions, and role disputes. Although already shown to be effective, it may be possible that extending the scope of IPT to include these contexts may further improve its efficacy (Joiner, 2002).

PSYCHOLOGICAL FACTORS

In the past 30 years there has been a growing interest in the role of psychological factors in depressive disorders (Lau, Segal, & Williams, 2004). Although there are many psychological theories of depression, this section focuses on some of the more well-researched theories.

Cognitive Models of Depression   Cognitive models of depression emphasize the role of dysfunctional thinking patterns in the development and maintenance of MDD (e.g., Beck, 1967, 1987; Beck, Rush, Shaw, & Emery, 1979; Nolen-Hoeksema, 1991; Teasdale & Barnard, 1993). Beck (1967, 1987) has proposed that this type of dysfunctional thinking is evident at three levels. At the most manifest, symptomatic level are automatic thoughts; these are thoughts, or visual images, that seemingly occur involuntarily as part of one's ongoing stream of consciousness. They are characterized by (a) their instantaneous arousal in response to a stimulus; (b) their unquestioned plausibility; and (c) the fact that, while not always in the patient's focal awareness, they can be detected by shifting attention to how one is interpreting a given situation. For depressed individuals, the content of these automatic thoughts is predominantly negative regarding the self, the world, and the future (Beck, 1967; Beck et al., 1979). Beck has proposed that automatic thoughts arise from irrational beliefs or assumptions that are, in turn, products of dysfunctional self-schemas. A *schema* is a set of interconnected beliefs, information, and examples used to organize and simplify subsequent information on a topic. A person with a negative schema of the world or a negative self-schema often expects events to not work out, looks for evidence that they have not worked out, and misses important information that paints a different picture. Although negative schemata are not directly detectable, they lead to certain types of thinking errors or cognitive distortions, such as *overgeneralization* (drawing a broad conclusion on the basis of a single incident) or *all-or-nothing thinking* (seeing a situation only in extreme terms). A large body of research supports the major constituents of the cognitive model (for a review, see Clark, Beck, & Alford, 1999).

Another cognitive conceptualization of depression is that of the learned helplessness/hopelessness model (Abramson, Metalsky, & Alloy, 1989). This model of depression suggests that a basic cause of depression is one's expectation that bad events will occur and nothing can be done to prevent this from happening. Thus, depression arises from an individual's perceived lack of control over negative events. More specifically, a depressive reaction is most likely associated with explanations of negative events in terms of causes that are internal (to the individual), stable, and global. Therefore, the critical factor is not presence of the event itself, nor even the lack of control, but the actual *interpretation* of the situation.

In an extension of this work, Abramson et al. (1989) proposed that hopelessness is an immediately preceding and sufficient cause of depression and that there is a chain of events that builds toward the development of hopelessness in individuals and then results in depression. Therefore, the specific cognitive risk factor in this model is a general tendency to explain events in terms of stable and global causes, to view adverse events as having extremely unpleasant consequences, and to see bad events as lowering self-esteem. Overall, researchers have demonstrated that the cognitive tendency to attribute negative events to internal, stable, and global causes is associated with the severity of concurrent and future depression (for reviews, see Barnett & Gotlib, 1988; Brewin, 1985; Peterson & Seligman, 1984; Sweeney, Anderson, & Bailey, 1986). However, as pointed out by Henkel, Bussfeld, Möller, and Hegerl (2002), these studies have demonstrated only correlations between depression and hopelessness-type attributions, therefore not providing evidence for a causative model.

MEDICAL TREATMENT

PHARMACOTHERAPY

At present there are three major classes of antidepressants: monoamine oxidase inhibitors (MAOIs), tricyclics, and selective serotonin reuptake inhibitors (SSRIs). Common MAOIs include isocarboxazid (Marplan), phenelzine sulfate (Nardil), and tranylcypromine sulfate (Parnate). Tricyclics include amoxapine (Asendin), amitriptyline (Elavil), imipramine (Tofranil), and doxepin (Sinequan). The SSRIs include fluoxetine (Prozac), sertraline (Zoloft), and paroxetine (Paxil). Each class of antidepressant has a different mechanism of action as well as various side effects that must be monitored when taken by an individual. According to the practice guidelines published by the American Psychiatric Association (2000b), antidepressants should be provided for individuals experiencing moderate to severe depressive symptoms, unless electroconvulsive therapy has been planned (explained in more detail later in the chapter). In individuals with mild depressive symptoms, psychotherapy may be adequate without medication treatment, although medication may be used if preferred by the patient (American Psychiatric Association, 2000b).

Selective Serotonin Reuptake Inhibitors   The first antidepressant drugs of choice are often the SSRIs (American Psychiatric Association, 2000b; Gitlin, Suri, Altshuler, Zuckerbrow-Miller, & Fairbanks, 2002). As their name suggests, SSRIs delay the process of neurotransmitter reuptake so that they remain available longer to maintain optimal neuronal firing rates. They have been cited as particularly effective for individuals experiencing melancholic depression, in which the individual is unable to be cheered up by positive events, even momentarily. Although a great deal of interest has been devoted to the idea of SSRI use and increased violence and/or suicidality, there has been no confirmed increased risk of suicidal behavior with SSRIs as compared to other drugs (see Ebmeier et al., 2006, for a review of this controversy). An appealing use of the SSRIs for treating MDD is their relative lack of adverse side effects as compared to the other antidepressants. For example, the SSRIs are less cardiotoxic, safer in overdose, less likely to produce cognitive impairment, and have a more rapid onset than other antidepressants (Gelder, Dennis, Mayou, & Cowen, 1996). However, the administration of an SSRI in combination with an MAOI or other serotonergic agent may result in serotonin syndrome; symptoms include neurological effects, changes in mental state, cardiac arrhythmia, and possible progression to coma and death. In addition, one of the most commonly cited side effects of the SSRIs is orgasmic problems and decreased interest in sexual activity (Enserink, 1999).

Tricyclics   Tricyclics are the oldest class of antidepressants but are rarely used as first-line agents (Gitlin et al., 2002) due to their side effects. Gitlin et al. (2002) discusses several advantages of prescribing the tricyclics: their long history of efficacy, once-daily dosing, fairly low expense due to their generic availability, and the ability to measure their blood concentration, which often correlates with both their efficacy and toxicity (Perry, Zeilmann, & Arndt, 1994). The disadvantages of the tricyclics are unfortunately plentiful and include a long and gradual process of needing to slowly increase the dose until full effect occurs; a substantial side effect profile, including dry mouth, blurry vision, constipation, urinary hesitation, dizziness, sedation, and weight gain; possible exacerbation of other existing medical illnesses, particularly cardiac conditions; and high lethality in overdose (Roose & Spatz, 1999).

Monoamine Oxidase Inhibitors   The MAOIs inhibit the enzyme monoamine oxidase, which is involved in deactivating dopamine, norepinephrine, and serotonin, allowing these neurotransmitters to remain in the synaptic cleft for longer periods and stimulate increased rates of neuronal firing. The MAOIs are most effective for treating atypical depression, which includes symptoms of anxiety, reversed vegetative symptoms (e.g., hypersomnia, hyperphagia), and interpersonal sensitivity. People taking MAOIs must avoid foods containing tyramine, such as certain cheeses, chocolate, and red wine; in combination, such foods and MAOIs may increase risk of hypotension, stroke, or circulatory problems. Due to these potentially dangerous side effects and dietary restrictions, MAOIs are typically considered to be third- or fourth-choice antidepressants (Gitlin et al., 2002).

Newer Antidepressants   Since the late 1980s and early 1990s quite a few newer antidepressants have come on the market. These include bupropion (Wellbutrin), venlafaxine (Effexor), nefazodone (Serzone), and mirtazapine (Remeron). Each of these acts slightly differently and carries with it different types of side effects, making them more or less useful for certain individuals. For example, bupropion affects norepinephrine and dopamine and has no serotonergic effects (Ascher et al., 1995). The most common side effects associated with this drug are insomnia, anxiety, tremor, and headache. However, it has no sedating properties, causes no weight gain, and has very few sexual side effects—an important difference from the SSRIs.

Electroconvulsive Therapy   Recent research has improved our knowledge of the conditions under which electroconvulsive therapy (ECT) works and the types of disorder for which it is most effective (Enns & Reiss, 1992; Pankratz, 1980; Weiner & Coffey, 1991). Electroconvulsive therapy is now used mainly for major depression and Bipolar Disorder; it is also used, less commonly, in acute Schizophrenia with prominent affective or catatonic symptoms. It is important to note that ECT is most commonly used for the most severe cases in which individuals have not responded to other treatments. It is typically administered 2 to 3 times per week, with between 6 and 12 treatments. The treatments are modified by the use of anesthesia, muscle relaxants, and oxygen. With the development of the current treatment guidelines, the rate of complications and adverse effects has been markedly reduced to around 0.4% (Wijeratne, Halliday, & Lyndon, 1999). Nausea, headache, and muscle soreness are common, but these can be treated. The mortality rate is estimated to be 0.2 deaths per 100,000 treatments (Kramer, 1999), which is comparable to that reported for brief general anesthesia. The main adverse effect from ECT is memory impairment. Immediately after the seizure, there is usually a period of confusion. After the confusion clears, there is usually both retrograde amnesia (forgetting events prior to the seizure) and anterograde amnesia (forgetting events after the seizure). These usually subside in the weeks following the therapy but can be distressing to patients during therapy. A small proportion of patients complain of continuing memory impairment following ECT; however, this complaint is controversial, and it has yet to be clearly documented with empirical tests that longer term memory impairment actually occurs (Enns & Reiss, 1992). Overall, it is clear that ECT is a safe and effective treatment and should continue to be available as a therapeutic option.

PSYCHOTHERAPY TREATMENTS

Over the past 20 years, a number of new treatments, both psychological and somatic, has been developed that enable clinicians to treat depressed patients both quickly and comprehensively. Although relapse or the return of symptoms following recovery remains a problem, the acute features of a depressive episode can now be managed with greater confidence. Furthermore, as the stigma associated with having a clinical depression has decreased and public education has increased awareness of the signs and costs of this disorder, more people receive effective help (Olfson et al., 2002).

Although different psychotherapies may be employed by therapists when treating depressed individuals, Hollon et al. (2005; see also DeRubeis & Crits-Christoph, 1998) recently completed an extensive literature review and recommended the following treatments for depression based on their efficacy: cognitive (Beck et al., 1979); behavior (Bellack, Hersen, & Himmelhoch, 1983; Lewinsohn & Clarke, 1984; Lewinsohn, Steinmetz, Antonuccio, & Teri, 1984; Nezu, 1986; Rehm, Fuchs, Roth, Kornblith, & Romano, 1979); interpersonal (M. M. Weissman & Markowitz, 2002; M. M. Weissman, Markowitz, & Klerman, 2000); and cognitive behavior analysis system of psychotherapy (McCullough, 1984, 2000, 2001, 2003). The following discussion focuses on a review of these types of psychotherapies.

COGNITIVE-BEHAVIORAL THERAPY

Cognitive-behavioral therapy (CBT) has been the most influential and most widely researched psychotherapy for depression (Thase, 2001). This broad class of therapies has evolved over the past 50 years in what Hayes (2002) describes as three phases. In the first phase, learning theory and principles were systematically applied to develop specific behavior treatments for emotional disorders, including depression. The second phase was heralded by the arrival of cognitive therapy, which eclipsed purely behavioral models of psychopathology in favor of accounts featuring the role of attention, memory, and mental representation. The third phase, which is in its infancy, features treatments that combine the fundamental properties associated with the two earlier phases with elements derived from mindfulness meditation practices, including, for example, acceptance and commitment therapy. This discussion now turns to a more in-depth overview of CBT—an integration of both cognitive and behavioral therapeutic approaches.

Cognitive-behavioral therapy is a structured form of treatment, stemming from Beck's cognitive model of psychopathology, as described earlier. It is often short term, lasting 15 to 20 sessions, and is focused on the here and now. Its foundation (as with most psychotherapies) comes from a productive therapeutic alliance established between therapist and patient. The most important elements and interventions used to help depressed patients are summarized in this section, but the interested reader will find more detailed accounts elsewhere (e.g., Beck, 1995; Beck et al., 1979; Friedman & Thase, 2006; Greenberger & Padesky, 1995; Hollon, Haman, & Brown, 2002; Persons, 1989).

Session Structure   Therapists employing CBT often follow a structured format for the therapy session (Friedman & Thase, 2006). For example, the initial segment typically lasts 5 to 10 minutes and consists of a check-in regarding mood status as well as collaborative agenda setting. The second segment comprises the bulk of the session, during which homework (i.e., between-session work) from the previous week is reviewed and a new intervention may be introduced, often building on the strategy learned during the previous session. The final 5 to 10 minutes are spent discussing homework for the week as well as eliciting feedback from the patient.

Collaborative Empiricism   A key and defining feature of the therapeutic relationship in CBT is the idea of collaborative empiricism. Friedman and Thase (2006, p. 359) define this as "the stylistic fulcrum that permits the helping alliance to thrive within the artificial constraints of the structured sessions." This involves both therapist and patient adopting a scientific approach to discuss the dysfunctional thoughts and behaviors that the patient brings to the therapy sessions. This allows them to be observed, challenged, and potentially modified.

Psychoeducation   Psychoeducation plays an important role in CBT. Therapists adopting this approach convey information to the patient regarding the illness of depression, the rationale for employing the cognitive model, the types of strategies that will be used during the therapy, and the rationale for homework.

Behavioral Treatment   Behavioral interventions are especially helpful for dealing with a depressed person's lack of energy or motivation. Behavioral strategies include behavioral activation, graded task assignments, and mastery-pleasure exercises. When using these strategies, therapists and patients identify small behavior tasks that patients feel confident they can perform prior to the next session, possibly something as simple as deciding to get out of bed or keeping track of daily activities. Having done a specific activity, the depressed person may note changes in negative thoughts or may find evidence that can be used against self-defeating thoughts (Beck et al., 1979).

Modifying Automatic Negative Thoughts Training in self-monitoring is fundamental to most cognitive interventions. People are encouraged to bring ongoing records of thoughts (i.e., a daily record of dysfunctional thoughts), images, and feelings surrounding problematic situations to the therapy session. These records are preferable to retrospective accounts of events, as they are a more direct data source and are less likely to be influenced by the types of memory biases often present. The information collected in the records is then reviewed in session with the therapist.

Evidence Gathering and Generating Balanced Thoughts Automatic thoughts often have an absolute, black-and-white quality. Examples of such thoughts are "I'm a bad parent" and "I'm a stupid person." These constructs are often not an accurate reflection of reality. Patients are asked to then generate concrete evidence to both support and refute their cognitive distortions. In doing so they often are able to generate more balanced or realistic views of the situation. This will enable them to gain new perspectives on their automatic negative thoughts and catch themselves when engaging in these types of cognitive distortions.

Testing Beliefs through Behavioral Experiments In another approach for challenging negative beliefs, therapists encourage clients to regard their thoughts as scientific hypotheses that can then be tested. Designing effective experiments can require a good deal of creativity and ingenuity on the part of both the therapist and the client. One means of generating ideas for experiments involves considering the kind of evidence that could either support or refute the hypothesis in question. A series of such experiments could help weaken the acceptability of people's negative automatic thoughts and may provide evidence for more reasonable alternatives.

Relapse Prevention During the final stages of therapy, it is important to develop a wellness plan with the patient. This often involves identifying triggers for depressive symptoms and early warning signs that a depressive episode may be reoccurring. This allows patients to reflect on what form of action they would take should another episode occur in the future.

INTERPERSONAL THERAPY

Gerald Klerman and his colleagues in the 1970s devised interpersonal psychotherapy (IPT) by incorporating aspects of interpersonal theory and empirical research on interpersonal aspects of depression to treat outpatients with MDD. Since that time a manual has been developed to train therapists to deliver this approach (Klerman, 1984), and IPT has repeatedly been shown to be efficacious in the treatment of MDD in several randomized control trials (M. M. Weissman et al., 2000). Similar to CBT, IPT is a short-term approach emphasizing the here and now. Many clinical trials that have tested the efficacy of IPT have used structured treatment interventions involving approximately 16 sessions (Markowitz, 2006).

Interpersonal therapy (Klerman, Chevron, & Weissman, 1984) emphasizes that depression often arises due to disruptions in an individual's social adjustment.

Therapists employing IPT define depression as a treatable *medical illness* that is not the patient's fault (Markowitz, 2006). This allows patients to relieve themselves of any guilt they may feel due to the depression and enables them to become hopeful about treating their *illness* rather than changing *themselves.* The therapist, in essence, provides the patient with the "sick role" (Parsons, 1951), which explains what the illness is preventing the patient from doing while still encouraging the patient to work to recover his or her former "healthy" self. This model places great emphasis on understanding the roles played by family and friends and the patient's reactions to significant life stressors. Troubled or unresolved relationships are seen as contributing to depressed moods and locking the person into a cycle of ineffective coping. One common cause of depression, according to this model, is an abnormal grief reaction, in which mourning has been prolonged or avoided. Until that grieving is emotionally processed, the person will not be able to establish new relationships. Interpersonal role disputes, such as marital arguments or friction with workmates or friends, are also commonly experienced in depression. Role transitions such as leaving home for university, becoming a parent, changing careers, or retiring may also trigger depression if the person does not adapt well. People may be prone to depression if a deficit in interpersonal skills prevents them from building and maintaining relationships.

There are three phases to treatment (M. M. Weissman et al., 2000). In the early phase the goal is to enable the person to cope better with the depressive illness. Symptoms are reviewed, the diagnosis is confirmed, the need for medication is evaluated, and the person is offered education about depression. Individuals are reassured that they have a genuine illness, which they need not hide or feel stigmatized by, and are entitled to the lowered expectations that come with the sick role, as they would be for a broken leg. Once this has been explained, the interpersonal problems that may be related to depression are discussed. A specific problem area, or goal, is then identified and a plan for the therapy is outlined. The therapist's formulation of the depression will link the depressive symptoms to the patient's interpersonal situation (Markowitz & Swartz, 1997), centered on one of the following areas: (a) grief, (b) interpersonal role disputes, (c) role transitions, or (d) interpersonal deficits. Once the patient explicitly accepts the formulation for treatment, the work progresses to the second phase.

The second phase of treatment involves incorporating strategies that are focal to the specific interpersonal problem area (M. M. Weissman et al., 2000) related to the therapy goal. For example, to address grief (often complicated bereavement), IPT therapists will help patients to reconstruct their relationship with the departed, paying special attention to the expression of guilt, self-blame, and unfulfilled expectations (Klerman et al., 1984). They will also encourage patients to find new activities and relationships to compensate for the loss. When a role dispute is involved, therapists help patients to first identify the dispute, then explore options that may help to resolve the dispute, and then alter communication patterns or modify expectations to enable satisfactory resolution. When a role transition preceded depression, the therapist will help the person let go of the old role, mourning it if necessary, and explore the benefits and opportunities of the new role and the social skills and relationships that accompany it. If the patient believes that he or she lacks social relationships, the therapist will review past relationships and behaviors that may serve as a model for initiating new social contacts. Social skills training may also be used to give the person practice with social behaviors. In the final and termination phase of IPT, the patient's newly regained sense of competence is supported by recognizing and consolidating therapeutic gains that were made (Markowitz, 2006). As in other therapies, the patient is helped to anticipate triggers for and responses to depressive symptoms that might arise in the future.

COGNITIVE-BEHAVIORAL ANALYSIS SYSTEM OF PSYCHOTHERAPY

McCullough (2000) developed this therapeutic approach to address problems encountered in the treatment of chronic depression and dysthymia. Briefly, McCullough conceptualized chronic depression as the product of dysfunctional cognitions of helplessness, hopelessness, and failure. These cognitions are linked to a detached and maladaptive interpersonal style, which then becomes reinforced by poor problem solving. McCullough describes chronically depressed individuals as functioning at a "preoperational" stage of thinking. This implies that they engage in prelogical and precausal thinking, do not appreciate cause-and-effect reasoning, and draw conclusions that are static, global, and unchanging.

The goal of the cognitive-behavioral analysis system of psychotherapy is to teach depressed individuals how to think causally and logically. This is done by teaching them to engage in social problem solving at a higher development level, which may lead to the experience of more positive outcomes and improvement in interpersonal relationships. The intervention for gaining this awareness is to target the antecedent behaviors that produce relief or decrease the misery experienced by patients and then reinforce these new and more adaptive behaviors. Several techniques have been devised by McCullough (2000) for doing this: the situational analysis, the interpersonal discrimination exercise, the interpersonal transference hypothesis, and the significant other list. An overview of these techniques can be found in Friedman and Thase (2006). Overall, this therapeutic approach represents an amalgamation of cognitive, behavioral, and interpersonal strategies that are designed to motivate chronically depressed individuals and to help them develop much needed problem-solving and relationship skills.

COMBINATIONS OF PSYCHOLOGICAL AND PHARMACOLOGICAL TREATMENTS FOR DEPRESSION

Although a number of efficacious treatments exist for depression, they are not always effective for all patients. In particular, patients with moderate to severe symptoms of depression may be in need of combined pharmacotherapy and psychotherapy. Since the 1980s researchers have conducted clinical trials to determine differences in treatment outcome for depression by comparing the administration of medication alone, psychotherapy alone, and a combination of the two. Recently, Segal, Vincent, and Levitt (2002) reviewed this literature and provided some general conclusions on this topic.

Concurrent therapy is as effective as monotherapy for the treatment of a mild to moderate depressive disorder and shows evidence of a potential treatment advantage in cases where depression may be more severe (i.e., often implementing medication and then following this with short-term psychotherapy). Consecutive sequencing of pharmacotherapy and psychotherapy has demonstrated some benefit for both the conversion of partial to full response and the prevention of relapse and recurrence, especially in more severely depressed patients (Segal et al., 2002). Similarly, a Depression Guideline Panel (1993) suggested that psychotherapy should be added to medication in the treatment of depression if (a) the patient demonstrates a partial response to pharmacotherapy; (b) there is a partial or complete response to pharmacotherapy, but significant psychosocial stressors remain; or (c) there are problems with adherence to the medication regimen prescribed. When a nonresponse to psychotherapy alone is witnessed, the recommendation is that adding an antidepressant may be implemented following 6 weeks of no response or 12 weeks of a partial response. At this time it would be up to the clinician to determine whether to continue with psychotherapy or discontinue and continue on medication management alone (Depression Guideline Panel, 1993).

PREVENTIVE INTERVENTIONS

The majority of mental health resources are currently dedicated to the treatment of acute depressive episodes. However, as discussed earlier, MDD is now viewed as a chronic, lifelong illness with a high risk for relapse and/or recurrence (Berti Ceroni, Neri, & Pezzoli, 1984; Keller et al., 1983; for review, see Judd, 1997). Therefore, interventions directed at preventing relapse and recurrence of depression are critical to the overall management of this disorder. The Institutes of Medicine (IOM) report on preventing mental disorders (Mrazek & Haggerty, 1994) proposed two intervention categories in addition to treatment. First, preventive interventions include those that occur before the onset of the disorder and are designed to prevent its occurrence. Second are maintenance interventions that occur after the acute episode has remitted to prevent relapse or recurrence in those who have received treatment.

Within this category, the IOM further defined three sublevels. The first are universal preventive interventions, which are applied to entire communities without regard to risk. The second are selective preventive interventions, which target high-risk groups. Third are indicated preventive interventions, which target individuals who show early signs or symptoms of depression but do not yet meet criteria for an MDE. There is preliminary evidence supporting the potential benefits of all three approaches (e.g., Clarke et al., 1995; Munoz, Glish, Soo-hoo, & Robertson, 1982; Munoz et al., 1995), however, further research is required.

MAINTENANCE INTERVENTIONS

Current approaches for achieving prophylaxis of depression can be grouped into three broad categories. The first approach is to continue treatment beyond remission. Currently, maintenance pharmacotherapy is the best validated and most widely used approach to prophylaxis in depression. Continuation of psychotherapy in maintenance form can also be useful. Both IPT (Frank et al., 1990) and CBT (Jarrett et al., 2001) have been shown to significantly extend survival time following recovery. Finally, continuation of a combination of pharmacotherapy and psychotherapy (i.e., nefazodone cognitive-behavioral analysis system of psychotherapy; Klein et al., 2004) has also been shown to reduce the risk of recurrence.

A second approach is to use an acute treatment that provides long-term protection. The best evidence of this is when CBT has been used in the acute phase but is also effective in reducing subsequent relapse rates when compared to discontinuation of pharmacotherapy (e.g., Blackburn, Eunson, & Bishop, 1986; Evans et al., 1992; Shea, Widiger, & Klein, 1992; Simons, Murphy, Levine, & Wetzel, 1986).

A third approach is to use a different treatment for prophylaxis than was used to treat the acute episode. One example is using lithium augmentation of antidepressant treatment (Souza & Goodwin, 1991). Alternatively, pharmacotherapy for the acute episode has been combined with psychological prophylactic interventions following recovery. For example, Fava and colleagues (Fava, Rafanelli, Grandi, Conti, & Belluardo, 1998) combined pharmacotherapy of the acute episode with CBT upon recovery as the antidepressant medication was withdrawn. Finally, both cognitive therapy (Bockting et al., 2005) and mindfulness-based cognitive therapy (Ma & Teasdale, 2004; Teasdale et al., 2000) have been shown to significantly reduce the risk of depressive relapse in remitted depressed individuals with 5 or more, or 3 or more, previous episodes, respectively.

Case Description

Case Introduction

This is the case of a young man who was self-referred to an ambulatory tertiary care center. This outpatient clinic specializes in both group and individual therapy employing a CBT orientation for the treatment of depressive disorders.

Presenting Complaints

Mr. Smith, a 35-year-old single man, was on disability leave from his job at the time of his assessment. His chief presenting complaints included continuous periods of depressed mood over the past year as well as symptoms of anxiety.

History—Psychiatric

Mr. Smith reported that he had been struggling with his most recent bout of depression for the past 9 months. He noted that prior to the beginning of his most recent episode, he experienced job-related stressors. Although he was reluctant to attribute the onset of his depressive symptoms to these stressors, he was unable to describe any other stressors that occurred within the past year or prior to the onset of his depressive symptoms. He reported that during the past month he had experienced periods of depressed mood at least 50% of the time as well as a diminished interest and pleasure in almost all activities. In addition to these symptoms, he also reported decreased appetite, weight gain, sleep disturbances (insomnia), fatigue, diminished ability to concentrate, indecisiveness, and feelings of worthlessness. He also reported thoughts of death but denied any suicidal intent or plan. He reported experiencing five previous episodes of depression since 1988. Mr. Smith described his depressive episodes as being discrete, often lasting for several months, and then experiencing at least 2 months during which his mood remitted to what felt like his usual self. He reported never having been hospitalized in the past for any psychiatric difficulties and that he had never made any suicide attempts, nor was there any familial history of suicide.

At the time of the assessment, he had been receiving medication for his depressive symptoms for approximately 18 years. He reported that he was taking Effexor (112.5 mg) and Paxil (12.5 mg) for his mood- and anxiety-related symptoms.

History—General

Mr. Smith reported an unproblematic childhood. However, he did discuss how he always felt somewhat different from his parents and that they never quite "understood" him. He also indicated that he was occasionally able to confide in his mother while growing up, but not as often his father. He also discussed a traumatic event involving his father when he was 18 years old. He described being out with his mother and both of them returning home to find his father had died of a heart attack. He reported that this bothered him very much at the time, although he felt much better about it all these years later. He reported that he had a good relationship with his father when he was growing up and that his father was quiet—although he had a bad temper. His mother was still alive, and he described having a good relationship with her. At the time of the assessment, Mr. Smith was in a 2-year long-term relationship. He described being very similar to his partner and that this relationship brought him a great deal of joy. He reported that he did not have many close friends other than his girlfriend.

Generally, Mr. Smith stated that he expresses his feelings, opinions, and wishes in an appropriate manner—having the tendency to hold back and not express himself in an assertive manner to others. He noted that he has trouble asserting himself with people in positions of authority (e.g., bosses) and people with "strong" personalities and individuals that he considers to be more knowledgeable than he.

Assessment

The assessment consisted of both clinician-rated and self-report measures. To determine a diagnosis, the clinician-administered SCID was conducted. Symptoms were consistent with a diagnosis of recurrent Major Depressive Disorder, moderate severity. Mr. Smith also described symptoms consistent with a diagnosis of Social Phobia, Generalized Type (moderate), Generalized Anxiety Disorder (onset age 6), Alcohol Abuse, In Sustained Full Remission, Anxiolytic Substance Dependence, In Sustained Full Remission, and a past diagnosis of Panic Disorder. In accordance with these diagnoses, Mr. Smith scored in the clinically severe range on a self-report measure of depressive symptoms (BDI-II) and on a self-report measure of anxiety-related symptoms (Beck Anxiety Inventory; Beck, Epstein, Brown, & Steer, 1988).

Mr. Smith's responses on a questionnaire examining typical behaviors clients engage in when they are depressed (Response Style Questionnaire; Nolen-Hoeksema, 1991) revealed that he would often think, "Why can't I get going?" and "Why do I always react this way?" and that he focused on how hard it is to concentrate and how passive and unmotivated he feels. His score on a cognitive measure of dysfunctional attitudes (Dysfunctional Attitudes Scale; A. N. Weisman & Beck, 1978) was in the depressed range and revealed a tendency to heavily base his self-worth on the approval of others (within the context of his depression). In terms of his performance on a measure of depressogenic automatic thoughts (Automatic Thoughts Questionnaire; Hollon & Kendall, 1980), his frequency and belief of such thoughts was elevated and within the depressed range. His endorsement of the following thoughts captured his feelings of

(continued)

hopelessness and low self-worth: "My life's not going the way I want it to" and "I hate myself." Mr. Smith's overall score on a measure of psychological symptoms (Symptom Checklist-90—Revised; Derogatis, 1984) was elevated into the clinical range, indicating that he was experiencing significant levels of distress. Furthermore, his scores were elevated on seven of the nine clinical subscales: Depression (which measures feelings of sadness and hopelessness and physical symptoms associated with depression such as low energy and loss of interest), Interpersonal Sensitivity (which measures feelings of personal inadequacy and inferiority and being self-conscious), Anxiety (which measures feelings of nervousness, fear, and physical sensations associated with anxiety such as trembling and shaking), Psychoticism (which measures feelings of isolation, inappropriate guilt, and paranoia and delusional thinking), Hostility (which measures the presence of irritability, resentment, and anger), Somatization (which measures the presence of a variety of physical symptoms such as headaches, body pains, and gastrointestinal symptoms), and Obsessive-Compulsive (which measures recurring thoughts and impulses that are experienced as unwanted). The elevated level for psychoticism was most likely related to his isolation ("Feeling lonely even when you are with people") and his feeling that depression had compromised his functioning ("Never feeling close to another person"). He did not endorse items suggesting impaired reality testing, such as "Feeling that you are watched or talked about by others," "The idea that someone else can control your thoughts," or "Hearing voices that other people do not hear." It should also be noted that on the depression dimension, Mr. Smith endorsed moderate distress concerning thoughts of ending his life, which was consistent with his overall presentation of depressive symptomatology.

Case Conceptualization

It appeared that a central belief that Mr. Smith held was that his needs and demands were not as important as everyone else's. In addition, he seemed to believe that others would not like him for who he is and that his emotions must be hidden from everyone, even those closest to him. This led to feelings of inadequacy and a hesitation to be assertive with individuals in his life. This belief may have arisen as a result of living with a very assertive sibling who seemed to not only be able to speak her mind frequently but also have the family succumb to her demands on a regular basis. Conditional beliefs that had helped him to cope with this core belief might have included "If I am nice and go along with others' demands, regardless of my own, then others will like me and respect me" and "In order for others to like me I cannot reveal my opinions or negative emotions." The negative counterpart to such a conditional belief is "If I assert myself and voice my opinion, then others will not like me" and "If I reveal my negative emotions to others then they will not want to be in a relationship with me or associate with me." As a result of holding these assumptions, Mr. Smith tended to be passive and had difficulty asserting himself. In addition, he was not able to share his negative emotional experiences with those closest to him and so withdrew from social contact and felt very isolated when experiencing increases in depressive or anxious symptoms. Holding these assumptions likely also left him feeling alone even when he was with friends or family members because he was unable to be his "true" or whole self.

Course of Treatment and Assessment of Progress

Mr. Smith attended 15 of the 15 group sessions that were offered to him. He completed and discussed his homework assignments throughout the course of the group. He was an active participant during all group sessions. He would often share his homework and help others to understand their difficulties when they would become stuck in certain thoughts or trigger situations. He often served as a role model for the group in that he completed the homework, even when he found it difficult, and would comment on how he was going to try to work through specific problems.

Treatment comprised activity and mood monitoring and scheduling, monitoring automatic thoughts, evidence gathering, behavioral experiments, testing underlying assumptions, and some limited work on core beliefs. Treatment began by focusing on activity and mood monitoring and noting a pattern of decreased physical activity and engagement of pleasurable and rewarding activities resulting in decreased moods. Mr. Smith was not working when the group began and began to schedule time to work on his resume and look for work in a part-time employment situation. He also began to attend an interest class and would report to the group his progress in that domain. Through the course of the group he progressed to resuming work on a part-time basis and would discuss his anxieties about returning to work and how he was trying to tackle them. Treatment continued with learning how to identify automatic thoughts and label various emotions. Mr. Smith often found that his automatic thoughts focused on other people judging him or his not being as bright or as capable as others. Following work with thought records, the concept of underlying assumptions was introduced. Clients were taught how to set up behavioral experiments to test their underlying assumptions across a variety of situations. Mr. Smith engaged in a variety of behavioral experiments, some about himself and his abilities and some about the world and the way social justice is organized. He reported that he found these experiments useful and that they allowed him to begin to have a different perspective on himself and on the world. Two of the last sessions were spent identifying maladaptive core beliefs and promoting flexibility in terms of the extent that the client endorsed each core belief. The last session reviewed what each client had learned from therapy and their individual coping plans (including triggers, warning signs, and action plans).

Follow-Up

A routine 1-month follow-up session was conducted as part of the group therapy intervention. Mr. Smith noted during the follow-up that he had been doing well since the end of the group. The result of the SCID during follow-up indicated that he no longer met criteria for MDD. However, the result of another interview-administered measure (the HRSD) did indicate that he was experiencing partial symptoms of depression. These symptoms were important to note, and it was

(continued)

recommended that he continue to challenge his thoughts. He did, in fact, report that he was actively working on thought records and challenged his thoughts in situations where he notices his mood shifts. He stated that he finds this tool to be very useful and helpful on these occasions. Most of his scores on a variety of other measures decreased into an asymptomatic (i.e., "normal") range or subclinical range compared to his pretherapy measures. However, one or two measures evaluating the presence of depressive symptoms suggested that he was still experiencing some symptoms at a problematic level. Each measure was explained to him in terms of what the measure was investigating and how his scores had changed. In addition, the types of elevations and thoughts he did experience when he was depressed were discussed so that he could be more aware of that in the future.

Treatment Implications of the Case

This case nicely illustrates the use of CBT with an individual that displayed a great deal of psychological awareness during the initial assessment and was then able to engage in the therapeutic process. It also illustrates that at the time of follow-up, this individual, despite being engaged in therapy, receiving pharmacotherapy, and modifying his dysfunctional cognitions, still endorsed some depressive symptoms. Thus, although this case would be considered a treatment success, it still highlights that many individuals need to be acutely aware of their triggers and cognitions and continue to work on them well past treatment. It may be the case that this patient is able to continue to use these skills and thus keep his symptoms at bay. That, ultimately, is the hope of CBT. However, it may also be the case that an individual like this would benefit from some type of relapse prevention treatment, as described earlier. As effective as current therapies are, it appears that an ongoing challenge for clinicians and researchers will be to understand the mechanisms underlying depression, improve on existing treatments, and enable individuals to stay healthy for longer periods of time.

SUMMARY

Epidemiological data indicate that mood disorders are among the most common mental disorders. Diagnosis of a mood disorder requires interference with social and occupational function, bodily and behavioral symptoms, and a change in affect. Duration and severity will vary with individual presentations and are both considered during the assessment process. Dysthymic Disorder manifests many of the same symptoms as Major Depressive Disorder in a less severe form. To assess the presence of a mood disorder, clinicians may consider using structured or semi-structured interviews along with clinician-rated and self-report questionnaires.

Most researchers conceptualize MDD as multifactorial, involving the interaction of social, biological, and psychological variables. Biological theories have proposed that depressive disorders are the result of an organic dysfunction, which can be detected through studies of genetic, biochemical, and neurophysiological indices. Interpersonal models of depression focus on interactions between the individual and possible triggers in his or her social environment. These models propose that depressed individuals may interact with others in ways that elicit depressing or negative feedback, which then may lead to a loss of social support.

Cognitive models of depression emphasize the role of dysfunctional thinking patterns in the development and maintenance of MDD. These theories stress the mood-lowering effects of specific beliefs and expectations held by depressed individuals. These models hold that problems in affective regulation stem from the way in which rigid and self-punitive beliefs avoid being disconfirmed by the individual's experiences so that dysphoric moods are increasingly supported by the interpretation of events in the person's life.

Treatments for depression have improved greatly over the past 2 decades. Medical treatments for depression involve antidepressants (MAOIs, tricyclics, and SSRIs) that increase the availability of neurotransmitters. Newer drugs have fewer side effects. Electroconvulsive therapy, despite its poor public image, is another effective and safe technique. Psychological treatments, such as CBT, emphasize integrative strategies of behavior and cognitive techniques at different points in treatment. Early interventions may stress the need for activating and motivating depressed people to perform routine tasks; later in treatment, more focused work helps them dispel mistaken beliefs. Interpersonal therapy emphasizes the person's need to come to terms with recent losses or role changes. As effective as these treatments are, relapse of depression is still too common an occurrence. Therefore, researchers are also turning to the development of maintenance and preventive treatments to enable individuals to stay healthier for longer periods of time.

REFERENCES

Abramson, L. Y., Metalsky, G. I., & Alloy, L. B. (1989). Hopelessness depression: A theory-based subtype of depression. *Psychological Review, 96*(2), 358–372.

Alloy, L. B. (2001). The developmental origins of cognitive vulnerability to depression: Negative interpersonal context leads to personal vulnerability. *Cognitive Therapy and Research, 25*(4), 349–351.

American Psychiatric Association. (2000a). *Diagnostic and statistical manual of mental disorders* (4th ed., text rev.). Washington, DC: Author.

American Psychiatric Association. (2000b). *Practice guideline for the treatment of patients with major depressive disorder* (2nd ed.). Washington, DC: Author.

Anderson, P., Beach, S. R. H., & Kaslow, N. J. (1999). Marital discord and depression: The potential of attachment theory to guide integrative clinical intervention. In T. Joiner & J. C. Coyne (Eds.), *The interactional nature of depression: Advances in interpersonal approaches* (pp. 271–297). Washington, DC: American Psychological Association.

Ascher, J. A., Cole, J. O., Colin, J. N., Feighner, J. P., Ferris, R. M., Fibiger, H. C., et al. (1995). Bupropion: A review of its mechanism of antidepressant activity. *Journal of Clinical Psychiatry, 56*(9), 395–401.

Baer, L., Jacobs, D. G., Meszler-Reizes, J., Blais, M., Fava, M., Kessler, R., et al. (2000). Development of a brief screening instrument: The HANDS. *Psychotherapy and Psychosomatics, 69*(1), 35–41.

Ballmaier, M., Toga, A. W., Blanton, R. E., Sowell, E. R., Lavretsky, H., Peterson, J., et al. (2004). Anterior cingulate, gyrus rectus, and orbitofrontal abnormalities in elderly depressed patients: An MRI-based parcellation of the prefrontal cortex. *American Journal of Psychiatry, 161*, 99–108.

Barnett, P. A., & Gotlib, I. H. (1988). Dysfunctional attitudes and psychosocial stress: The differential prediction of future psychological symptomatology. *Motivation and Emotion, 12*(3), 251–270.

Baxter, L. R., Schwartz, J. M., Phelps, M. E., Mazziotta, J. C., Guze, B. H., Selin, C. E., et al. (1989). Reduction of prefrontal cortex glucose metabolism common to three types of depression. *Archives of General Psychiatry, 46*, 243–250.

Beck, A. T. (1967). *Depression.* New York: Harper & Row.

Beck, A. T. (1987). Cognitive models of depression. *Journal of Cognitive Psychotherapy, 1*(1), 5–37.

Beck, A. T. (1995). Cognitive therapy: Present and future. In M. J. Mahoney (Ed.), *Cognitive and constructive psychotherapies: Theory, research and practice* (pp. 29–40). New York: Springer.

Beck, A. T., Epstein, N., Brown, G., & Steer, R. A. (1988). An inventory for measuring clinical anxiety: Psychometric properties. *Journal of Consulting and Clinical Psychology, 56*(6), 893–897.

Beck, A. T., Rush, J. A., Shaw, B. S., & Emery, G. (1979). *Cognitive therapy of depression.* New York: Guilford Press.

Beck, A. T., Steer, R. A., & Brown, G. K. (1996). *Manual for the Beck Depression Inventory-II.* San Antonio, TX: Psychological Corporation.

Beck, A. T., Ward, C. H., Mendelson, M., Mock, J., & Erbaugh, J. (1961). An inventory for measuring depression. *Archives of General Psychiatry, 4*, 561–571.

Bellack, A. S., Hersen, M., & Himmelhoch, J. M. (1983). A comparison of social-skills training, pharmacotherapy and psychotherapy for depression. *Behavior Research and Therapy, 21*(2), 101–107.

Berrettini, W. (2006). Genetics of bipolar and unipolar disorders. In D. J. Stein, D. J. Kupfer, & A. F. Schatzberg (Eds.), *The American Psychiatric Publishing textbook of mood disorders* (pp. 235–247). Washington, DC: American Psychiatric Publishing.

Berti Ceroni, G., Neri, C., & Pezzoli, A. (1984). Chronicity in major depression: A naturalistic prospective study. *Journal of Affective Disorders, 7*(2), 123–132.

Blackburn, I. M., Eunson, K. M., & Bishop, S. (1986). A 2-year naturalistic follow-up of depressed patients treated with cognitive therapy, pharmacotherapy and a combination of both. *Journal of Affective Disorders, 10*(1), 67–75.

Bockting, C. L., Schene, A. H., Spinhoven, P., Koeter, M. W., Wouters, L. F., Huyser, J., et al. (2005). Preventing relapse/recurrence in recurrent depression with cognitive therapy: A randomized controlled trial. *Journal of Consulting and Clinical Psychology, 73*(4), 647–657.

Boland, R. J., & Keller, M. B. (2002). Course and outcome of depression. In I. H. Gotlib & C. L. Constance (Eds.), *Handbook of depression* (pp. 43–60). New York: Guilford Press.

Brewin, C. R. (1985). Depression and causal attributions: What is their relation? *Psychological Bulletin, 98*(2), 297–309.

Campbell, S., Marriott, M., Nahmias, C., & MacQueen, G. M. (2004). Lower hippocampal volume in patients suffering from depression: A meta-analysis. *American Journal of Psychiatry, 161*, 598–607.

Chochinov, H. M., Wilson, K. G., Enns, M., & Lander, S. (1994). Prevalence of depression in the terminally ill: Effects of diagnostic criteria and symptom threshold judgments. *American Journal of Psychiatry, 151*(4), 537–540.

Clark, D. A., Beck, A. T., & Alford, B. A. (1999). *Scientific foundations of cognitive therapy and therapy of depression.* New York: Wiley.

Clark, D. A., Steer, R. A., & Beck, A. T. (1994). Common and specific dimensions of self-reported anxiety and depression: Implications for the cognitive and tripartite models. *Journal of Abnormal Psychology, 103*(4), 645–654.

Clarke, G. N., Hawkins, W., Murphy, M., Sheeber, L. B., Lewinsohn, P. M., & Seeley, J.R. (1995). Targeted prevention of unipolar depressive disorder in an at-risk sample of high school adolescents: A randomized trial of a group cognitive intervention. *Journal of the American Academy of Child and Adolescent Psychiatry, 34,* 312–321.

Cohen-Cole, S. A., Brown, F. W., & McDaniel, J. S. (1993). Assessment of depression and grief reactions in the medically ill. In A. Stoudemire & B. S. Fogel (Eds.), *Psychiatric care of the medical patient* (pp. 53–69). New York: Oxford University Press.

Coyne, J. C. (1976). Depression and the response of others. *Journal of Abnormal Psychology, 85*(2), 186–193.

Coyne, J. C., & Calarco, M. M. (1995). Effects of the experience of depression: Application of focus group and survey methodologies. *Psychiatry: Interpersonal and Biological Processes, 58*(2), 149–163.

Creed, F. (1997). Assessing depression in the context of physical illness. In M. M. Robertson & C. L. E. Katona (Eds.), *Depression and physical illness* (pp. 3–20). New York: Wiley.

Delgado, P. L., & Moreno, F. A. (2006). Neurochemistry of mood disorders. In D. J. Stein, D. J. Kupfer, & A. F. Schatzberg (Eds.), *The American Psychiatric Publishing textbook of mood disorders* (pp. 101–116). Washington, DC: American Psychiatric Publishing.

Depression Guideline Panel. (1993). *Depression in primary care: Vol. 2. Treatment of major depression.* Hyattsville, MD: U.S. Department of Health and Human Services.

Derogatis, L. R. (1984). *SCL-90-R: Symptom Checklist-90—Revised.* Baltimore: Clinical Psychometrics Research.

DeRubeis, R. J., & Crits-Christoph, P. (1998). Empirically supported individual and group psychological treatments for adult mental disorders. *Journal of Consulting and Clinical Psychology, 66*(1), 37–52.

Drevets, W. C., Price, J. L., Simpson, J. R., Jr., Todd, R. D., Reich, T., Vannier, M., et. al. (1997). Subgenual prefrontal cortex abnormalities in mood disorders. *Nature, 386,* 824–827.

Ebmeier, K., Donaghey, C., & Steele, J. (2006). Recent developments and current controversies in depression. *Lancet, 367*(9505), 153–167.

Enns, M. W., & Reiss, J. P. (1992). Electroconvulsive therapy. *Canadian Journal of Psychiatry, 37*(10), 671–686.

Enserink, M. (1999). Can the placebo be the cure? *Science, 284*(5412), 238–240.

Evans, M. D., Hollon, S. D., DeRebeis, R. J., Piasecki, J. M., Grove, W. M., Garvey, M. J., et al. (1992). Differential relapse following cognitive therapy and pharmacotherapy for depression. *Archives of General Psychiatry, 49*(10), 802–808.

Falicov, C. J. (2003). Culture, society and gender in depression. *Journal of Family Therapy, 25*(4), 371–387.

Fava, G. A., Rafanelli, C., Grandi, S., Conti, S., & Belluardo, P. (1998). Prevention of recurrent depression with cognitive behavioral therapy. *Archives of General Psychiatry, 55,* 816–820.

Fawcett, J., Scheftner, W. A., Fogg, L., Clark, D. C., Young, M. A., Hedecker, D., et al. (1990). Time-related predictors of suicide in major affective disorder. *American Journal of Psychiatry, 147*(9), 1189–1194.

First, M. B., Spitzer, R. L., Gibbon, M., & Williams, J. B. (1997). *User's guide for the Structured Clinical Interview for DSM-IV Axis I Disorders: Clinical version.* Washington, DC: American Psychiatric Press.

Ford, D. E., & Kamerow, D. B. (1990). Screening for psychiatric and substance abuse disorders in clinical practice. *Journal of General Internal Medicine, 5*(Supp. 5), 37–41.

Frank, E., Kupfer, D. J., Perel, J. M., Cornes, C., Jarrett, D. B., Mallinger, A. G., et al. (1990). Three-year outcomes for maintenance therapies in recurrent depression. *Archives of General Psychiatry, 47*(12), 1093–1099.

Friedman, E. S., & Thase, M. E. (2006). Cognitive-behavior therapy for depression and dsythymia. In D. J. Stein, D. J. Kupfer, & A. F. Schatzberg (Eds.), *The American Psychiatric Publishing textbook for mood disorders* (pp. 353–371). Washington, DC: American Psychiatric Publishing.

Frodl, T., Meisenzahl, E. M., Zetzsche, T., Hohne, T., Banac, S., Schorr, C., et al. (2004). Hippocampal and amygdala changes in patients with major depressive disorder and healthy controls during a 1-year follow-up. *Journal of Clinical Psychiatry, 65*(4), 492–499.

Gelder, M., Dennis, G., Mayou, R., & Cowen, P. (1996). *Oxford textbook of psychiatry.* Oxford: Oxford University Press.

Gershon, E. S., Hamovit, J., Guroff, J. J., Dibble, E., Leckman, J. F., Sceery, W., et al. (1982). A family study of schizoaffective, bipolar I, bipolar II, unipolar, and normal control patients. *Archives of General Psychiatry, 39,* 1157–1167.

Gitlin, M. J., Suri, R., Altshuler, L., Zuckerbrow-Miller, J., & Fairbanks, L. (2002). Bupropion-sustained release as a treatment for SSRI-induced sexual side effects. *Journal of Sex and Marital Therapy, 28*(2), 131–138.

Gotlib, I. H., & Hammen, C. L. (1995). *Psychological aspects of depression: Toward an interpersonal cognitive-integration.* New York: Wiley.

Gotlib, I. H., & Hammen, C. L. (2002). *Handbook of depression.* New York: Guilford Press.

Greenberger, D., & Padesky, C. A. (1995). *Mind over mood.* New York: Guilford Press.

Hamilton, M. (1960). A rating scale for depression. *Journal of Neurology, Neurosurgery, and Psychiatry, 23,* 56–62.

Hammen, C. (1991). *Depression runs in families: The social context of risk and resilience in children of depressed mothers.* New York: Springer-Verlag.

Hayes, S. C. (2002). Getting to dissemination. *Clinical Psychology: Science and Practice, 9*(4), 410–415.

Henkel, V., Bussfeld, P., Möller, H.-J., & Hegerl, U. (2002). Cognitive-behavior theories of helplessness/hopelessness: Valid models of depression? *European Archives of Psychiatry and Clinical Neuroscience, 252*(5), 240–249.

Henriques, J. B., & Davidson, R. J. (1990). EEG activation asymmetries discriminate between depressed and control subjects. *Psychophysiology, 27,* 38.

Hollon, S. D., Haman, K. L., & Brown, L. L. (2002). Cognitive-behavior treatment of depression. In I. H. Gotlib & C. L. Hammen (Eds.), *Handbook of depression* (pp. 383–403). New York: Guilford Press.

Hollon, S. D., Jarrett, R. B., Nierenberg, A. A., Thase, M. E., Trivedi, M., & Rush, A. J. (2005). Psychotherapy and medication in the treatment of adult and geriatric depression: Which monotherapy or combined therapy? *Journal of Clinical Psychiatry, 66*(4), 455–468.

Hollon, S. D., & Kendall, P. C. (1980). Cognitive self-statements in depression: Development of an automatic thoughts questionnaire. *Cognitive Therapy and Research, 4*(4), 383–395.

Ifabumuyi, O. I. (1981). Depressive illness presenting as monosymptomatic hallucination: A case report. *African Journal of Psychiatry, 7*(1/2), 17–20.

Jarrett, R. B., Kraft, D., Doyle, J., Foster, B. M., Eaves, G. G., & Silver, P. C. (2001). Preventing recurrent depression using cognitive therapy with and without a continuation phase. *Archives of General Psychiatry, 58*(4), 381–388.

Joiner, T. E., Jr. (2002). Depression in its interpersonal context. In I. H. Gotlib & C. L. Hammen (Eds.), *Handbook of depression* (pp. 295–313). New York: Guilford Press.

Joiner, T. E., Jr. & Metalsky, G. I. (1995). A prospective test of an integrative interpersonal theory of depression: A naturalistic study of college roommates. *Journal of Personality and Social Psychology, 69,* 778–788.

Joiner, T. E., Walker, R. L., Pettit, J. W., Perez, M., & Cukrowicz, K. C. (2005). Evidence-based assessment of depression in adults. *Psychological Assessment, 17*(3), 267–277.

Judd, L. J. (1997). The clinical course of unipolar major depressive disorders. *Archives of General Psychiatry, 54,* 989–991.

Judd, L. L., Akiskal, H. S., Maser, J. D., Zeller, P. J., Endicott, J., Coryell, W., et al. (1998). Major depressive disorder: A prospective study of residual subthreshold depressive symptoms as predictor of rapid relapse. *Journal of Affective Disorders, 50*(2/3), 97–108.

Judd, L. L., Akiskal, H. S., & Paulus, M. P. (1997). The role and clinical significance of subsyndromal depressive symptoms (SSD) in unipolar major depressive disorder. *Journal of Affective Disorders, 45*(1/2), 5–17.

Judd, L. L., Paulus, M. J., Schettler, P. J., Akiskal, H. S., Endicott, J., Leon, A. C., et al. (2000). Does incomplete recovery from first lifetime major depressive episode herald a chronic course of illness? *American Journal of Psychiatry, 157*(9), 1501–1504.

Kalia, M. (2005). Neurological basis of depression: An update. *Metabolism, 54*(5), 24–27.

Keller, M. B. (1994). Depression: A long-term illness. *British Journal of Psychiatry, 165*(Suppl. 26), 9–15.

Keller, M. B., Lavori, P. W., Endicott, J., Coryell, W., & Klerman, G. L. (1983). Double depression: Two-year follow-up. *American Journal of Psychiatry, 140*(6), 689–694.

Kessler, R. C., Chiu, W. T., Demler, O., Merikangas, K. R., & Walters, E. E. (2005). Prevalence, severity, and comorbidity of twelve-month DSM-IV disorders in the National Comorbidity Survey Replication (NCS-R). *Archives of General Psychiatry, 62*(6), 617–627.

Kessler, R. C., Zhao, S., Blazer, D. G., & Swartz, M. (1997). Prevalence, correlates, and course of minor depression and major depression in the national comorbidity survey. *Journal of Affective Disorders, 45*(1), 19–30.

Kirmayer, L. J. (2001). Cultural variations in the clinical presentation of depression and anxiety: Implications for diagnosis and treatment. *Journal of Clinical Psychiatry, 62*(Suppl. 13), 22–28; discussion 29–30.

Klein, D. N., Santiago, N. J., Vivian, D., Blalock, J. A., Kocsis, J. H., Markowitz, J. C., et al. (2004). Cognitive-behavior analysis system of psychotherapy as a maintenance treatment for chronic depression. *Journal of Consulting and Clinical Psychology, 72*(4), 681–688.

Klerman, G. L. (1984). *Interpersonal psychotherapy of depression.* New York: Basic Books.

Klerman, G. L., Chevron, E., & Weissman, M. M. (1984). *Interpersonal psychotherapy for depression: A brief, focussed, specific strategy.* New York: Aronson.

Kramer, B. A. (1999). Use of ECT in California, revisited: 1984–1994. *Journal of ECT, 15,* 245–251.

Lambert, M. J., & Lambert, J. M. (1999). Use of psychological tests for assessing treatment outcome. In M. E. Maruish (Ed.), *The use of psychological testing for treatment planning and outcomes assessment* (2nd ed., pp. 115–151). Mahwah, NJ: Erlbaum.

Lau, M. A., Segal, Z. V., & Williams, J. M. G. (2004). Teasdale's differential activation hypothesis: Implications for mechanisms of depressive relapse and suicidal behavior. *Behavior Research and Therapy, 42*(9), 1001–1017.

Lauer, C. J., Schreiber, W., Holsboer, F., & Krieg, J. (1995). In quest of identifying vulnerability markers for psychiatric disorders by all-night polysomnography. *Archives of General Psychiatry, 52,* 145–153.

Lee, S., Payne, M. E., Steffens, D. C., McQuoid, D. R., Lai, T. L., Provenzale, J. M., et. al. (2003). Subcortical lesion severity and orbitofrontal cortex volume in geriatric depression. *Biological Psychiatry, 54,* 529–533.

Lewinsohn, P. M., & Clarke, G. (1984). Group treatment of depressed individuals: The Coping with Depression course. *Advances in Behavior Research and Therapy, 6,* 99–114.

Lewinsohn, P. M., Mischel, W., Chaplin, W., & Barton, R. (1980). Social competence and depression: The role of illusory self-perceptions. *Journal of Abnormal Psychology, 89*(2), 203–212.

Lewinsohn, P. M., Steinmetz, J. L., Antonuccio, D., & Teri, L. (1984). Group therapy for depression: The Coping with Depression course. *International Journal of Mental Health, 13*, 8–33.

Ma, S. H., & Teasdale, J. D. (2004). Mindfulness-based cognitive therapy for depression: Replication and exploration of differential relapse prevention effects. *Journal of Consulting and Clinical Psychology, 72*, 31–40.

Maes, M., & Meltzer, H. Y. (1995). The serotonin hypothesis of major depression. In F. E. Bloom & D. J. Kupfer (Eds.), *Psychopharmacology* (pp. 933–944). New York: Raven Press.

Maier, W., & Lichtermann, D. (1993). The genetic epidemiology of unipolar depression and panic disorder. *International Clinical Psychopharmacology, 8*(Supp. 1), 27–33.

Mann, J. J. (1998). The neurobiology of suicide. *Nature Medicine, 4*, 25–30.

Mann, J. J., Brent, D. A., & Arango, V. (2001). The neurobiology and genetics of suicide and attempted suicide: A focus on the serotonergic system. *Neuropsychopharmacology, 24*(5), 467–477.

Markowitz, J. C. (2006). The clinical conduct of interpersonal psychotherapy. *Focus, 4*, 179.

Markowitz, J. C., & Swartz, H. A. (1997). Case formulation in interpersonal psychotherapy of depression. In T. D. Eels (Ed.), *Handbook of psychotherapy case formulation* (pp. 192–222). New York: Guilford Press.

Mayberg, H. S. (2006). Defining neurocircuits in depression. *Psychiatric Annals, 36*, 259–266.

McCullough, J. P. (1984). Cognitive-behavior analysis system of psychotherapy: An interactional treatment approach for dysthymic disorder. *Psychiatry, 47*(3), 234–250.

McCullough, J. P. (2000). *Treatment for chronic depression: Cognitive behavior analysis of psychotherapy.* New York: Guilford Press.

McCullough, J. P. (2001). *Skills training manual for diagnosing and treating chronic depression: Cognitive behavior analysis system of psychotherapy.* New York: Guilford Press.

McCullough, J. P. (2003). *Treatment for chronic depression: Cognitive behavior analysis system of psychotherapy (CBASP).* New York: Guilford Press.

McDaniel, J. S., Musselmann, D. L., Porter, M. R., Reed, D. A., & Nemeroff, C. B. (1995). Depression in patients with cancer. *Archives of General Psychiatry, 52*, 89–99.

McGuffin, P., Katz, R., Watkins, S., & Rutherford, J. (1996). A hospital-based twin registry study of the heritability of DSM-IV unipolar depression. *Archives of General Psychiatry, 53*(2), 129–136.

Meltzer, H. Y., & Lowy, M. T. (1987). The serotonin hypothesis of depression. In H. Y. Meltzer (Ed.), *Psychopharmacology: The third generation of progress* (pp. 513–526). New York: Raven Press.

Mirescu, C., Peters, J. D., & Gould, E. (2004). Early life experience alters response of adult neurogenesis to stress. *Nature Neuroscience, 7*(8), 841–846.

Mrazek, P. B., & Haggerty, R. J. (1994). *Reducing risks for mental disorders: Frontiers for preventive intervention research.* Washington, DC: National Academy Press.

Munoz, R. F., Glish, M., Soo-hoo, T., & Robertson, J. L. (1982). The San Francisco Mood Survey Project: Preliminary work toward the prevention of depression. *American Journal of Community Psychology, 10*(3), 317–329.

Munoz, R. F., Yu-Wen, Y., Bernal, G., Perez-Stable, E. J., Sorensen, J. L., Hargreaves, W. A., et al. (1995). Prevention of depression with primary care patients: A randomized controlled trial. *American Journal of Community Psychology, 23*(2), 199–222.

Murphy, D. L., Campbell, I. C., & Costa, J. L. (1978). The brain serotonergic system in the affective disorders. *Progress in Neuropsychopharmacology, 2*(1), 5–31.

Musselman, D. L., DeBattista, D. M. H., Nathan, K. I., Kilts, C. D., Schatzberg, A. F., & Nemeroff, C. B. (1998). Biology of mood disorders. In A. F. Schatzberg & N. B. Nemeroff (Eds.), *The American Psychiatric Press textbook of psychopharmacology* (2nd ed., pp. 549–588). Washington, DC: American Psychiatric Press.

National Institute of Mental Health Consensus Development Conference Statement. (1985). Mood disorders: Pharmacologic prevention of recurrences. *American Journal of Psychiatry, 142*, 469–476.

Nezu, A. M. (1986). Efficacy of a social problem-solving therapy approach for unipolar depression. *Journal of Consulting and Clinical Psychology, 54*(2), 196–202.

Nezu, A. M., Nezu, C. M., McClure, K. S., & Zwick, M. L. (2002). Assessment of depression. In I. H. Gotlib & C. L. Hammen (Eds.), *Handbook of depression* (pp. 61–85). New York: Guilford Press.

Nolen-Hoeksema, S. (1991). Responses to depression and their effects on the duration of depressive episodes. *Journal of Abnormal Psychology, 100*(4), 569–582.

Olfson, M., Marcus, S. C., Druss, B., Elinson, L., Tanielian, T., & Pincus, H. A. (2002). National trends in the outpatient treatment of depression. *Journal of the American Medical Association, 287*, 203–209.

Pankratz, W. J. (1980). Electroconvulsive therapy: The position of the Canadian Psychiatric Association. *Canadian Journal of Psychiatry, 25*(6), 509–514.

Parsons, T. (1951). Illness and the role of the physician: A sociological perspective. *American Journal of Orthopsychiatry, 21*(3), 452–460.

Paykel, E. S., Ramana, R., Cooper, Z., Hayhurst, H., Kerr, J., & Barocka, A. (1995). Residual symptoms after partial remission: An important outcome in depression. *Psychological Medicine, 25*(6), 1171–1180.

Perry, P. J., Zeilmann, C., & Arndt, S. (1994). Tricyclic antidepressant concentrations in plasma: An estimate of their sensitivity and specificity as a predictor of response. *Journal of Clinical Psychopharmacology, 14*(4), 230–240.

Persons, J. B. (1989). *Cognitive therapy in practice: A case formulation approach.* New York: Norton.

Peterson, C., & Seligman, M. E. (1984). Causal explanations as a risk factor for depression: Theory and evidence. *Psychological Review, 91*(3), 347–374.

Pryor, J. C., & Sulser, F. (1991). Evolution of the monoamine hypothesis of depression. In R. Horton & C. Katona (Eds.), *Biological aspects of affective disorders* (pp. 78–94). New York: Academic Press.

Rehm, L. P., Fuchs, C. Z., Roth, D. M., Kornblith, S. J., & Romano, J. M. (1979). A comparison of self-control and assertion skills treatments in depression. *Behavior Therapy, 10*, 429–442.

Reuter, K., Raugust, S., Bengel, J., & Härter, M. (2004). Depressive symptom patterns and their consequences for diagnosis of affective disorders in cancer patients. *Supportive Care in Cancer, 12*(12), 864–870.

Reynolds, C. F., III, & Kupfer, D. J. (1987). Sleep research in affective illness: State of the art circa 1987. *Sleep, 10*(3), 199–215.

Reynolds, W. M., & Kobak, K. A. (1998). *Reynolds Depression Screening Inventory: Professional manual.* Odessa, FL: Psychological Assessment Resources.

Roose, S. P., & Spatz, E. (1999). Treating depression in patients with ischaemic heart disease. *Drug Safety, 20*(5), 459–465.

Rush, A. J., Gullion, C. M., Basco, M. R., Jarrett, R. B., & Trivedi, M. H. (1996). The Inventory of Depressive Symptomatology (IDS): Psychometric properties. *Psychological Medicine, 26*(3), 477–486.

Sapolsky, R. M. (2000). Stress hormones: Good and bad. *Neurobiology of Disease, 7*(5), 540–542.

Segal, Z. V., & Dobson, K. S. (1992). Cognitive models of depression: Report from a consensus development conference. *Psychological Inquiry, 3*(3), 219–224.

Segal, Z. V., Vincent, P., & Levitt, A. (2002). Efficacy of combined, sequential and crossover psychotherapy and pharmacotherapy in improving outcomes in depression. *Journal of Psychiatry and Neuroscience, 27*(4), 281–290.

Segrin, C. (1990). A meta-analytic review of social skill deficits in depression. *Communication Monographs, 57,* 292–308.

Segrin, C. (2001). *Interpersonal processes in psychological problems.* New York: Guilford Press.

Segrin, C., & Dillard, J. P. (1992). The interactional theory of depression: A meta-analysis of the research literature. *Journal of Social and Clinical Psychology, 11*(1), 43–70.

Shah, P. J., Ebmeier, K. P., Glabus, M. F., & Goodwin, G. M. (1998). Cortical gray matter reductions associated with treatment-resistant chronic unipolar depression. *Archives of General Psychiatry, 527,* 532.

Shah, P. J., Glabus, M. F., Goodwin, G. M., & Ebmeier, K. P. (2002). Chronic, treatment-resistant depression and right fronto-striatal atrophy. *British Journal of Psychiatry, 180,* 434–440.

Shea, M. T., Widiger, T. A., & Klein, M. H. (1992). Comorbidity of personality disorders and depression: Implications for treatment. *Journal of Consulting and Clinical Psychology, 60*(6), 857–868.

Sheline, Y. I., Sanghavi, M., Mintun, M. A., & Gado, M. H. (1999). Depression duration but not age predicts hippocampal volume loss in medically healthy women with recurrent major depression. *Journal of Neuroscience, 19*(12), 5034–5043.

Simons, A. D., Murphy, G. E., Levine, J. L., & Wetzel, R. D. (1986). Cognitive therapy and pharmacotherapy for depression: Sustained improvement over one year. *Archives of General Psychiatry, 43*(1), 43–48.

Souza, F. G., & Goodwin, G. M. (1991). Lithium treatment and prophylaxis in unipolar depression: A meta-analysis. *British Journal of Psychiatry, 158,* 666–675.

Sullivan, P. F., Eaves, L. J., Kendler, K. S., & Neale, M. C. (2001). Genetic case-control association studies in neuropsychiatry. *Archives of General Psychiatry, 58,* 1015–1024.

Sweeney, P. D., Anderson, K., & Bailey, S. (1986). Attributional style in depression: A meta-analytic review. *Journal of Personality and Social Psychology, 50*(5), 974–991.

Talavera, J. A., Saiz-Ruiz, J., & Garcia-Toro, M. (1994). Quantitative measurement of depression through speech analysis. *European Psychiatry, 9*(4), 185–193.

Teasdale, J. D. (1988). Cognitive vulnerability to persistent depression. *Cognition and Emotion, 2*(3), 247–274.

Teasdale, J. D., & Barnard, P. J. (1993). *Affect, cognition, and change: Remodeling depressive thought.* Hove, England: Erlbaum.

Teasdale, J. D., Fogarty, S. J., & Williams, J. M. (1980). Speech rate as a measure of short-term variation in depression. *British Journal of Social and Clinical Psychology, 19*(3), 271–278.

Teasdale, J. D., Segal, Z. V., Williams, J. M. G., Ridgeway, V. A., Soulsby, J. M., & Lau, M. A. (2000). Prevention of relapse/recurrence in major depression by mindfulness-based cognitive therapy. *Journal of Consulting and Clinical Psychology, 68*(4), 615–623.

Thase, M. E. (2001). Neuroimaging profiles and the differential therapies of depression. *Archives of General Psychiatry, 58,* 651–653.

Thase, M. E., Jindal, R., & Howland, R. H. (2002). Biological aspects of depression. In I. H. Gotlib & C. L. Hammen (Eds.), *Handbook of depression* (pp. 192–218). New York: Guilford Press.

Thase, M. E., & Kupfer, D. J. (1987). Characteristics of treatment-resistant depression. In J. Zohar & R. H. Belmaker (Eds.), *Treating resistant depression* (pp. 23–45). Great Neck, NY: PMA Publishing.

Tsuang, M. T., Winokur, G., & Crowe, R. R. (1980). Morbidity risks of schizophrenia and affective disorders among first-degree relatives of patients with schizophrenia, mania, depression and surgical conditions. *British Journal of Psychiatry, 137,* 497–504.

Ulrich-Jakubowski, D., Russell, D. W., & O'Hara, M. W. (1988). Marital adjustment difficulties: Cause or consequence of depressive symptomatology? *Journal of Social and Clinical Psychology, 7*(4), 312–318.

Videbech, P., & Ravnkilde, B. (2004). Hippocampal volume and depression: A meta-analysis of MRI studies. *American Journal of Psychiatry, 161,* 1957–1966.

Vittengl, J. R., Clark, L. A., Kraft, D., & Jarrett, R. B. (2005). Multiple measures, methods, and moments: A factor-analytic investigation of change in depressive symptoms during acute-phase cognitive therapy for depression. *Psychological Medicine, 35*(5), 693–704.

Weiner, R. D., & Coffey, C. E. (1991). Practical issues in the use of electroconvulsive therapy (ECT). *Psychiatric Medicine, 9*(1), 133–141.

Weissman, A. N., & Beck, A. T. (1978, April). *Development and validation of the Dysfunctional Attitudes Scale: A preliminary investigation.* Paper presented at the meeting of the American Educational Research Association, Toronto, Canada.

Weissman, M. M., Leaf, P. J., Bruce, M. L., & Florio, L. (1988). The epidemiology of dysthymia in five communities: Rates, risks, comorbidity, and treatment. *American Journal of Psychiatry, 145,* 815–819.

Weissman, M. M., Leckman, J. F., Merikangas, K. R., Gammon, G. D., & Prusoff, B. A. (1984). Depression and anxiety disorders in parents and children. *Archives of General Psychiatry, 41,* 845–852.

Weissman, M. M., & Markowitz, J. C. (2002). Interpersonal psychotherapy for depression. In I. H. Gotlib & C. L. Hammen (Eds.), *Handbook of depression* (pp. 404–421). New York: Guilford Press.

Weissman, M. M., Markowitz, J. C., & Klerman, G. L. (2000). *Comprehensive guide to interpersonal psychotherapy.* New York: Basic Books.

Weissman, M. M., Wickramaratne, P., Adams, P. B., Lish, J. D., Horwath, E., Charney, D., et al. (1993). The relationship between panic disorder and major depression: A new family study. *Archives of General Psychiatry, 50*(10), 767–780.

Wender, P. H., Kety, S. S., Rosenthal, D., Schulsinger, F., Ortmann, J., & Lunde, I. (1986). Psychiatric disorders in the biological and adoptive families of adopted individuals with affective disorders. *Archives of General Psychiatry, 43,* 923–929.

Whisman, M. A., & Bruce, M. L. (1999). Marital dissatisfaction and incidence of major depressive episode in a community sample. *Journal of Abnormal Psychology, 108*(4), 674–678.

Wijeratne, C., Halliday, G. S., & Lyndon, R. W. (1999). The recent status of electroconvulsive therapy: A systematic review. *Medical Journal of Australia, 171,* 250–254.

World Health Organization. (1992). *The ICD-10 classification of mental health and behavior disorders: Diagnostic criteria for research.* Geneva, Switzerland: Author.

Youngren, M. A., & Lewinsohn, P. M. (1980). The functional relation between depression and problematic interpersonal behavior. *Journal of Abnormal Psychology, 89*(3), 333–341.

CHAPTER 14

Schizophrenia

DENNIS R. COMBS, MICHAEL R. BASSO,
JILL L. WANNER, AND SUMER N. LEDET

DESCRIPTION OF THE DISORDER

Schizophrenia has profound and debilitating effects on individuals with the disorder, families, and society at large. The disorder is considered the most costly of all adult psychiatric illnesses (Knapp, Mangalore, & Simon, 2004). Despite the rise of community-based treatment, recent data suggest that about 25% of all psychiatric hospital beds are occupied by persons with Schizophrenia, and 50% of all inpatient hospital admissions are for the treatment of Schizophrenia (Miller, 1996; Terkelsen & Menikoff, 1995). In terms of financial costs, it is estimated that the United States spent about $62.7 billion on the treatment of Schizophrenia in 2002, with one third of that total ($22 billion) related to direct health care costs and treatment (Wu et al., 2005). In Canada, fiscal costs were estimated at $6.85 billion in 2004 (Goeree et al., 2005). Schizophrenia has consistently been one of the top 10 most disabling conditions in terms of illness-adjusted life years, and it accounts for 2.3% of the total burden worldwide (as reviewed in Mueser & McGurk, 2004; Murray & Lopez, 1996; Ustun et al., 1999). Most of the disability costs associated with Schizophrenia stem from a shorter life expectancy and lost productivity over a lifetime (Rössler, Salize, van Os, & Riecher-Rössler, 2005). Costs associated with the disorder are more than just financial, as families are asked to bear the burden of caring for persons with Schizophrenia (Gutierrez-Maldonado, Caqueo-Urizar, & Kavanagh, 2005; Magliano, Fiorillo, Rosa, & Maj, 2006; Rosenfarb, Bellack, & Aziz, 2006). Estimates suggest that between 25% and 60% of persons with Schizophrenia live with relatives, and an even higher percentage rely on relatives for their care and support (Goldman, 1982; Torrey, 2001). Clearly, Schizophrenia comes with a heavy price that all members of society must pay.

Despite more than 100 years of research on Schizophrenia, the disorder remains largely misunderstood, and public misconceptions abound. In addition to coping with the symptoms of Schizophrenia, persons with the disorder must overcome the stigma and negative perceptions as they attempt to access housing, employment, and health care services. Schizophrenia is considered a lifelong disorder and is associated with impairments in social, occupational, and community functioning. In fact, the social dysfunction appears to be more pronounced in Schizophrenia than in any other psychiatric disorder (Mueser & Bellack, 1998). However, the past 10 years have seen a dramatic rise in new methods to treat Schizophrenia, and new medical and psychological treatments give promise to those affected by the condition. Also, for the first time, there is an emphasis on recovery, not just symptom maintenance (Bellack, 2006; N. Jacobson & Greenley, 2001). This chapter provides an updated description of the clinical features of Schizophrenia with a focus on diagnosis and assessment, conceptualization, and treatments for the condition.

Schizophrenia is characterized by a variety of bizarre, strange, and puzzling symptoms that usually reflect a loss of contact with reality. The disorder can be frightening to individuals with the condition, family, and friends. Most persons, when asked to describe Schizophrenia, tend to focus on the clinical symptoms of the disorder, as these are the most visible. However, Schizophrenia also affects social and community functioning, cognition, and social cognition. We now turn our attention to describing the condition known as Schizophrenia.

Schizophrenia can be characterized by three types of symptoms: positive, negative, and disorganized (Arango, Kirkpatrick, & Buchanan, 2000; Ho, Black, & Andreasen, 2003; Liddle, 1987; Mueser, Curran, & McHugo, 1997; Van Der Does, Dingemans, Linszen, Nugter, & Scholte, 1993). Positive symptoms include sensory experiences or beliefs that are found in persons with the disorder and usually do not occur frequently in the normal population. Hallucinations (hearing voices or seeing visions) and delusions (strongly held beliefs without supporting evidence) are the most common positive symptoms. Persecutory delusions (i.e., belief that some entity, group, or person has clear, ongoing, or future intentions to harm the person; Bentall, Corcoran, Howard, Blackwood, & Kinderman, 2001) are the most common type of delusion found in Schizophrenia, and these beliefs tend to be associated with high levels of distress, anxiety, and worry (Appelbaum, Robbins, & Roth, 1999; as reviewed in Bentall et al., 2001). Persons with persecutory delusions tend to avoid others and social situations, which prevents disconfirmation of their beliefs. Grandiose delusions are also common in Schizophrenia and include beliefs of unrealistic power, wealth, intelligence, and fame (e.g., a person who believes he or she has the power to control world events with his or her thoughts). Auditory hallucinations occur in about 50% to 75% of persons with Schizophrenia and are by far the most common type of hallucination (Lindenmayer & Kahn, 2006). Auditory hallucinations can range from repeated sounds (buzzing, humming, noises, muffled speech) to clearly perceived voices of either sex and can occur intermittently or continuously. Voices may come from inside the person's head or from the outside. Auditory hallucinations are frequently derogatory, negative, or abusive, although some can be benevolent, comforting, and kind. Recent studies have shown that the power of and relationship that people have with their voices is a significant factor in their distress levels (Chadwick & Birchwood, 1995; Copolov, Mackinnon, & Trauer, 2004; Cutting, 1995). Some auditory hallucinations involve voices that keep a running commentary on the person's actions or consist of two or more voices having a conversation. Historically, visual hallucinations are believed to be less frequent in Schizophrenia (prevalence of 10% to 15%; Cutting, 1995) and related more to medical conditions. However, recent evidence suggests that these symptoms may be more common than initially believed, especially in more severe forms of the disorder (Bracha, Wolkowitz, Lohr, Karson, & Bigelow, 1989; Mueser, Bellack, & Brady, 1990).

In contrast, negative symptoms are defined as the lack of cognitions, emotions, and behaviors. Primary negative symptoms include flat or blunted affect (lack of emotional expressiveness or limited range of emotions), avolition (poor motivation, goal-directedness, or social drive), and poverty of speech (poor verbal expressiveness, speech with limited content or meaning). Primary negative symptoms are distinct from secondary negative symptoms, which arise from medication side effects, depression, or positive symptoms (inactivity due to delusions; American Psychiatric Association, 2000; Blanchard & Cohen, 2006; Kelley, van Kammen, & Allen, 1999). Long-term, persistent negative symptoms (e.g., deficit syndrome) are considered a poor prognostic indicator and are linked to impaired social functioning, poorer clinical outcomes, and greater brain and cognitive impairments (Amador et al., 1999; Harvey, Koren, Reichenberg, & Bowie, 2006; Kirkpatrick, Fenton, Carpenter, & Marder, 2006).

Disorganization includes problems in language, emotion, and behavior that are perceived as strange and bizarre by others. Persons with the disorder may display emotional expressions that are either too intense or out of context for the situation (e.g., laughing at a funeral). Their speech may be incoherent, tangential, or circumstantial (e.g., speech that is difficult to follow or understand), and their behavior may be strange or bizarre (e.g., wearing multiple layers of clothing, yelling at others on the street, mumbling, or talking to oneself).

Positive symptoms, negative symptoms, and disorganization have been formally incorporated in the diagnostic criteria for Schizophrenia found in the fourth edition of the *Diagnostic and Statistical Manual for Mental Disorders* (*DSM-IV-TR*; American Psychiatric Association, 2000). Current diagnostic and assessment instruments for Schizophrenia are closely linked to the *DSM-IV-TR* criteria for the disorder (discussed further in the Diagnosis and Assessment section).

SOCIAL AND FUNCTIONAL OUTCOME

Deficits in social functioning are a central feature of Schizophrenia (American Psychiatric Association, 2000). Persons exhibit a variety of social functioning deficits, such as poor social skills, lower social competence, poor community functioning, and impaired social problem solving (Corrigan & Penn, 2001; Green, 1996; Mueser, Bellack, Morrison, & Wixted, 1990). Problems in social functioning are believed to be independent of positive and negative symptoms, and these deficits generally do not improve following medication treatment (Bellack, Schooler, & Marder, 2004; Lenzenweger & Dworkin, 1996; Mueser, 2000; Penn & Mueser, 1996). Problems in social functioning are believed to be stable over time and are present prior to the initial onset of psychotic symptoms (Davidson, Stayner, & Haglund, 1998), following remission (D. G. Robinson, Woerner, McMeniman, Mendelowitz, & Bilder, 2004) and in the first-degree relatives of persons with Schizophrenia (Hans, Auerbach, Asarnow, Styr, & Marcus, 2000). Sadly, onset of psychotic symptoms in early adulthood coincides with important developmental milestones. Thus, persons with Schizophrenia are less likely to be married (Eaton, 1975; Munk-Jørgensen, 1987), complete higher levels of education (Kessler, Foster, Saunders, & Stang, 1995), or be employed (Marwaha & Johnson, 2004). Unemployment rates consistently average between 70% and 85% (Blyler, 2003; Mueser, Salyers, & Mueser, 2001; Rosenheck et al., 2006), and a substantial number end up relying on the social security disability system for financial support. Due to the lack of community resources for treatment programs, many end up incarcerated

(Lamb & Weinberger, 2005) or homeless (Susser, Struening, & Conover, 1989; Torrey, 2001).

COGNITIVE AND NEUROPSYCHOLOGICAL FUNCTIONING

In addition to positive and negative symptoms, persons with Schizophrenia also exhibit a wide range of cognitive and neuropsychological impairments. In fact, between 75% and 90% of persons with Schizophrenia show at least one area of cognitive impairment (as reviewed in Green et al., 2004; B. W. Palmer et al., 1997). The most common cognitive deficits are in verbal and visual learning and memory, working memory, attention and vigilance, abstract reasoning and executive functioning, and speed of information processing (Green et al., 2004; Heinrichs & Zakzanis, 1998). Cognitive deficits are so pervasive that they are now considered a core feature of Schizophrenia (Green et al., 2004; Wilk et al., 2005). The deficits appear to be relatively stable across the illness (Caspi et al., 2003; Heaton et al., 2001) and can be found in unmedicated and medicated persons (Saykin et al., 1991, 1994), children who are at high-risk for developing Schizophrenia (Erlenmeyer-Kimling et al., 2000), and nonpsychotic, first-degree relatives of a person with the disorder (Asarnow et al., 2002). The average performance deficit on most cognitive tasks averages about 1 to 2 standard deviations below that of normal individuals (Heinrichs, 2005), but not all individuals with Schizophrenia show cognitive impairment (Kremen, Seidman, Faraone, Toomey, & Tsuang, 2000). Understanding cognitive impairments associated with Schizophrenia is important because they impact functional outcomes such as community functioning, social problem solving, and social skill acquisition, but this relationship is based on cross-sectional studies (Green, 1996).

If attention, memory, and reasoning are impaired, then meeting your needs in a complex, fast-paced world becomes difficult. In fact, Green, Kern, Braff, and Mintz (2000) reported that between 20% and 50% of variance in functional outcome was attributed to neuropsychological and cognitive factors. Attempts at cognitive remediation have shown that specific cognitive abilities (attention, memory, executive functioning) can be improved with intensive practice and training (Brenner, Hodel, Roder, & Corrigan, 1992; Hogarty et al., 2004; Spaulding. Reed, Sullivan, Richardson, & Weiler, 1999; van der Gaag, Kern, van den Bosh, & Liberman, 2002), but what has not been clearly demonstrated is whether these gains generalize to community functioning (Kurtz, Moberg, Gur, & Gur, 2001; Pilling et al., 2002; Twamley, Jeste, & Bellack, 2003; Velligan, Kern, & Gold, 2006).

SOCIAL COGNITION

Despite the relationship between cognition and functional outcome, there is substantial portion of variance in outcome that remains unaccounted for (about 40% to 80%). Researchers have focused on social cognition in an attempt to better understand social functioning in Schizophrenia (Penn, Addington, & Pinkham, 2006; Penn, Combs, & Mohamed, 2001). Social cognition is defined as the way we perceive, interpret, and understand social information (Penn, Corrigan, Bentall, Racenstein, & Newman, 1997). Deficits in facial affect perception, social cue perception, theory of mind (inferring the intentions and motivations of others), attributional style, and problems in social knowledge have all been found in Schizophrenia (Brune, 2005; Corrigan & Penn, 2001; Edwards, Jackson, & Pattison, 2002). Persons with Schizophrenia consistently perform worse than persons with other psychiatric conditions and normal controls on emotion perception tasks, and the deficit appears to be greater for negative than positive emotions. Persons with persecutory delusions exhibit an attributional style in which they tend to blame others rather than situations for negative events (e.g., personalizing attributional style; see Garety & Freeman, 1999). Social cognition may help bridge the gap between basic cognitive processes and functional outcome; recent studies attempting to improve social cognition have met with success (Green et al., 2000; Penn & Combs, 2000). Finally, there appear to be neural pathways (prefrontal, fusiform gyrus, superior temporal lobe, and amygdala) that specifically process social and emotional information (Pinkham, Penn, Perkins, & Lieberman, 2003). It is not surprising that these same brain regions are also implicated in the pathogenesis of Schizophrenia. The exact nature of the relationship between cognition, social cognition, and functioning is still unclear, but social cognition appears to be an important component in understanding and even improving the lives of persons with Schizophrenia (Green, Oliver, Crawley, Penn, & Silverstein, 2005).

PREVALENCE, ONSET, AND COURSE

It is estimated that approximately 2.2 million persons in the United States have Schizophrenia (Narrow, Rae, Robins, & Reiger, 2002; Torrey, 2001). The incidence rate of newly diagnosed cases ranges from 11 to 70 per 100,000 persons (as reviewed in Eaton & Chen, 2006; Jablensky, 2000). The lifetime risk of developing Schizophrenia is believed to be about 1% for the general population and is relatively equivalent between men and women (Goldner, Hsu, Waraich, & Somers, 2002; Ho et al., 2003; Keith, Regier, & Rae, 1991; Saha, Chant, Welham, & McGrath, 2005).

As a general rule, Schizophrenia usually appears between the ages of 15 and 24 for both men and women (Eaton & Chen, 2006). Although the number of men with new cases of the disorder gradually decreases after the age of 25, there is a second peak in the number of females with new cases around the age of 45 (Häfner et al., 1998; Munk-Jørgensen, 1987), which may be due to the loss of estrogen as a protective factor on dopaminergic neurons. Currently, it is considered rare for children under the age of 12 to be diagnosed with Schizophrenia, and in many cases, these are more likely a form of Pervasive Developmental Disorder (Nicolson & Rapoport, 1999).

The progression of illness across the life span has been examined in research on children who are at high risk for developing Schizophrenia due to having one or both parents with the disorder. There is evidence to suggest that these children display some of the social and cognitive deficits even before appearance of psychotic symptoms. Videos of preschool children who later developed Schizophrenia showed less emotional expressivity and greater motor dysfunction compared to normal children (Schiffman et al., 2004; Walker, Grimes, Davis, & Smith, 1993). Data from the New York High Risk Project found deficits in verbal memory, attention, and motor functioning in children ages 7 to 12 who later developed Schizophrenia (Erlenmeyer-Kimling et al., 2000). As high-risk children progress in school and enter adolescence, a variety of behavior problems may appear, such as impulsivity, aggression, poor academic performance, and poor interpersonal and peer relations (Amminger et al., 1999; Baum & Walker, 1995; Fuller et al., 2002; Hans, Marcus, Henson, Auerbach, & Mirsky, 1992).

Onset of symptoms can be gradual and occur over many years, or it can be relatively sudden or acute in onset. Schizophrenia typically develops from prepsychotic features, which can include subtle cognitive, behavioral, and social deficits to the prodromal phase of the illness. Prodromal signs typically precede the active symptoms of Schizophrenia from a few weeks to several years and represent an intensification of the disorder that is evident to others (Perkins, Lieberman, & Lewis, 2006). Attenuated positive symptoms (e.g., magical thinking, ideas of reference), sleep problems, mood disturbance (e.g., anxiety, irritability, depression), suspiciousness, social isolation, and cognitive difficulties are common in the prodromal phase (Häfner, Maurer, Trendler, an der Heiden, & Schmidt, 2005; Malla & Payne, 2005; McGlashan, 1996; Norman, Scholten, Malla, & Ballageer, 2005; Yung & McGorry, 1996). The prodrome is usually followed by what is called the "first break" or first episode of psychosis (Lincoln & McGorry, 1995). First episode psychosis has the same diagnostic criteria as Schizophrenia, and many professionals diagnose first episode psychosis as Schizophreniform Disorder if a clear history cannot be obtained (symptoms less than 6 months of duration). However, it is crucial that treatment be initiated as early as possible as this improves clinical outcome (Malla, Norman, & Joober, 2005; as reviewed in Penn, Waldheter, Perkins, Mueser, & Liberman, 2005). Even though positive symptoms may improve in these individuals, data suggest that social functioning remains impaired (Tohen et al., 2000).

Although most persons with Schizophrenia show symptoms in late adolescence and early adulthood (ages 15 to 24), there are some individuals (20%; Harris & Jeste, 1988) who do not show symptoms until after the age of 40 or even 65. This type of Schizophrenia is believed to be distinct from the early-onset type and has been labeled "late-onset" or "very-late-onset" Schizophrenia (C. I. Cohen, 1990). Late-onset Schizophrenia is more common in women, and there is evidence of better social, educational, and occupational functioning as compared to early-onset Schizophrenia (Howard, Rabins, Seeman, & Jeste, 2000). Late-onset Schizophrenia is more likely to involve positive symptoms (visual, tactile, and olfactory hallucinations, persecutory delusions) than negative symptoms or disorganization (Bartels, Mueser, & Miles, 1998). Thus, it is important to emphasize that the symptoms of Schizophrenia can arise at any point in life and are a developmental phenomenon.

Clinical Outcome and Prognosis

Although Schizophrenia is considered a long-term psychiatric condition, there is considerable interindividual variability in the course and outcome of the disorder (Marengo, 1994). Thus, not all persons are equally affected. The onset, course, and prognosis of the illness appear to be partially moderated by sex (Haas & Garratt, 1998). Women tend to have later age of onset of the illness, spend less time in hospitals, have fewer negative symptoms, demonstrate less cognitive impairment, and have better social competence than men with the disorder (Goldstein, 1988; Häfner et al., 1993; Leung & Chue, 2000; Mueser, Bellack, Morrison, & Wade, 1990; Salem & Kring, 1998). It is possible that estrogen serves as a protective mechanism on dopamine neurons or that women have better coping strategies or more effective social networks (Castle & Murray, 1991; Flor-Henry, 1985; Halari et al., 2004), but no single theory has received strong support.

Outcome for recovery is poor to fair, but considerable variability in recovery rates has been reported across studies (DeSisto, Harding, McCormick, Ashikaga, & Brooks, 1995; Harding, Brooks, Ashikaga, Strauss, & Breier, 1987a, 1987b; Jobe & Harrow, 2005). Most of the studies measure outcome in terms of a symptom remission (i.e., a reduction in symptoms to nonproblematic levels; Andreasen et al., 2005), but more recent studies have focused on recovery, which is broader and involves subjective perceptions of improvement in social, community, occupational, and adaptive functioning (N. Jacobson & Greenley, 2001). In general, positive symptoms are more responsive to medication and psychosocial treatment than the negative, cognitive, and social functioning deficits (Greden & Tandon, 1991; Green et. al., 2005; Kane & Marder, 1993). Despite emphasis on recovery, not all persons with Schizophrenia have a positive outcome. In addition, it is generally estimated that 10% of persons with Schizophrenia will commit suicide (Bromet, Naz, Fochtmann, Carlson, & Tanenberg-Karant, 2005; Drake, Gates, Whitaker, & Cotton, 1985; Jobe & Harrow, 2005; Roy, 1986), but recent research examining suicide prevalence rates found estimates of around 5% (Inskip, Harris, & Barraclough, 1998; B. A. Palmer, Pankratz, & Bostwick, 2005). The management and prevention of suicide should be in the forefront of clinical concern when treating persons with Schizophrenia.

A recent review of 10 longitudinal studies on outcome in Schizophrenia, some of which followed individuals for over 20 years, reported that between 21% and 57% of persons showed periodic episodes of recovery (improved symptoms, greater social, educational, and occupational functioning; see Jobe & Harrow, 2005). In fact, some of these individuals showed extended periods of recovery without contact with the mental health care system (Harrow, Grossman, Jobe, & Herbener, 2005; Jobe & Harrow, 2005).

DIAGNOSIS AND ASSESSMENT

DIAGNOSIS

Diagnostic criteria for Schizophrenia are fairly similar across a variety of different diagnostic systems. In general, the diagnostic criteria specify some degree of social impairment, combined with positive and negative symptoms, lasting a significant duration (e.g., 6 months or more). The diagnostic criteria for Schizophrenia according to *DSM-IV-TR* (American Psychiatric Association, 2000) are summarized in Table 14.1.

Diagnosis of Schizophrenia requires a clinical interview with the individual, a thorough review of all available records, and standard medical evaluations to rule out the possible role of organic factors (e.g., CAT scan to rule out a brain tumor). In addition, because many persons with Schizophrenia are poor historians, information from significant others, such as family members, is often critical to establish a diagnosis. Use of family and other informants is especially important in the assessment of prodromal and prepsychotic states. Because of the wide variety of symptoms characteristic of Schizophrenia and variations in interviewing style and format across different clinical interviewers, the use of structured clinical interviews, such as the Structured Clinical Interview for *DSM-IV* (SCID; First, Spitzer, Gibbon, & Williams, 1996), can greatly enhance the reliability and validity of psychiatric diagnosis.

Structured clinical interviews have two main advantages over more open clinical interviews. First, structured interviews provide definitions of the key symptoms agreed upon by experts, thus making explicit the diagnostic criteria for the disorder. Second, by conducting the interview in a standardized format, including a specific sequence of questions, variations in interviewing style are minimized, thus enhancing the comparability of diagnostic assessments across different clinicians. The second point is especially crucial considering that most research studies of Schizophrenia employ structured interviews to establish diagnoses. It is important that interviewers

Table 14.1
DSM-IV-TR Diagnostic Criteria for Schizophrenia

A. *Characteristic symptoms:* Two (or more) of the following, each present for a significant portion of time during 1-month period (or less, if successfully treated):
   (1) delusions
   (2) hallucinations
   (3) disorganized speech (e.g., frequent derailment or incoherence)
   (4) grossly disorganized or catatonic behavior
   (5) negative symptoms (i.e., affective flattening, alogia, or avolition)
   Note: Only one Criteria A symptom is required if delusions are bizarre or hallucinations consist of a voice keeping up a running commentary on the person's behavior or thoughts, or two or more voices conversing with each other.

B. *Social/occupational dysfunction:* For a significant portion of the time since the onset of the disturbance, one or more major areas of functioning such as work, interpersonal relations, or self-care are markedly below the level achieved prior to the onset (or when the onset is in childhood or adolescence, failure to achieve expected level of interpersonal, academic, or occupational achievement).

C. *Duration:* Continuous signs of the disturbance persist for at least 6 months. This 6-month period must include at least 1 month of symptoms (or less, if successfully treated) that meet Criteria A (i.e., active-phase symptoms) and may include periods of prodromal or residual symptoms. During these prodromal or residual periods, the signs of the disturbance may be manifested by only negative symptoms or two or more symptoms listed in Criteria A present in an attenuated form (e.g., odd beliefs, unusual perceptual experiences).

D. *Schizoaffective and Mood Disorder exclusion:* Schizoaffective Disorder and Mood Disorder With Psychotic Features have been ruled out because either (1) no major Depressive, Manic, or Mixed Episodes have occurred concurrently with the active-phase symptoms or (2) if mood episodes have occurred during active-phase symptoms, their total duration has been brief relative to the duration of the active and residual periods.

E. *Substance/general medical condition exclusion:* The disturbance is not due to the direct physiological effects of a substance (e.g., a drug of abuse, a medication) or a general medical condition.

F. *Relationship to a Pervasive Developmental Disorder:* If there is a history of Autistic Disorder or another Pervasive Development Disorder, the additional diagnosis of Schizophrenia is made only if prominent delusions or hallucinations are also present for at least a month (or less, if successfully treated).

Source: Diagnostic and Statistical Manual of Mental Disorders, fourth edition, text revision, by American Psychiatric Association, 2000, Washington, DC: Author. Reprinted with permission from American Psychiatric Publishing, Inc.

are properly trained and interrater reliability with an expert rater is established before structured interviews are used. If the findings of clinical research studies are to be generalized into clinical practice, efforts must be taken to ensure the comparability of the clinical populations and the assessment techniques employed.

Symptoms of Schizophrenia overlap with many other psychiatric disorders. Establishing a diagnosis of Schizophrenia requires particularly close consideration of four other overlapping disorders: substance use disorders, affective disorders, Schizoaffective Disorder, and Delusional Disorder. We next discuss issues related to each of these disorders and the diagnosis of Schizophrenia.

Substance Use Disorders   Substance use disorders, such as alcohol dependence or drug abuse, can either be a differential diagnosis to Schizophrenia or a comorbid disorder (i.e., the individual can have both Schizophrenia *and* a substance use disorder). With respect to differential diagnosis, substance use disorders can interfere with a clinician's ability to diagnosis Schizophrenia and can lead to misdiagnosis if the substance abuse is covert, denied, or not reported accurately (Corty, Lehman, & Myers, 1993; Kranzler et al., 1995). Psychoactive substances, such as alcohol, PCP, LSD, marijuana, cocaine, and amphetamine, can produce symptoms that mimic those found in Schizophrenia, such as hallucinations, delusions, paranoia, and social withdrawal (Schuckit, 1995). In those cases where the substance is involved in the etiology of psychosis (i.e., onset of symptoms close in time to the use of the substance and the symptoms remit when the substance is stopped), a diagnosis of Substance-Induced Psychotic Disorder would be appropriate. Further complicating matters, use of many substances can exacerbate psychotic symptoms and, in many cases, can lead to a return of acute psychosis. Because diagnosis of Schizophrenia requires the presence of specific symptoms in the absence of identifiable organic or substance factors, the disorder can be diagnosed in persons with a history of substance use disorder only by examining the individual's functioning during sustained periods of abstinence from drugs or alcohol. When such periods of abstinence can be identified, a reliable diagnosis of Schizophrenia can be made. However, persons with Schizophrenia who have a long history of substance abuse, with few or no periods of abstinence, are more difficult to assess. For example, in a sample of 461 individuals admitted to a psychiatric hospital, a psychiatric diagnosis could neither be confirmed nor ruled out due to history of substance abuse in 71 persons (Lehman, Myers, Dixon, & Johnson, 1994).

Individuals with Schizophrenia tend to use smaller quantities of drugs and alcohol (M. Cohen & Klein, 1970; Crowley, Chesluk, Dilts, & Hart, 1974; Lehman et al., 1994) and rarely develop the full physical dependence syndrome that is often present in persons with a primary substance use disorder (Corse, Hirschinger, & Zanis, 1995; Drake et al., 1990; Test, Wallisch, Allness, & Ripp, 1989) or show other physical consequences of alcohol use (Mueser et al., 1999). Even very low scores on instruments developed for the primary substance use disorder population, such as the Addiction Severity Inventory, may be indicative of substance use disorder in persons with Schizophrenia (Appleby, Dyson, Altman, & Luchins, 1997; Corse et al., 1995; Lehman, Myers, Dixon, & Johnson, 1996). Because of the difficulties in using existing measures of substance abuse for people with Schizophrenia and other severe mental illnesses, a screening tool was developed specifically for these populations: the Dartmouth Assessment of Lifestyle Instrument (DALI; Rosenberg et al., 1998). The DALI is an 18-item questionnaire that has high classification accuracy for current substance use disorders of alcohol, cannabis, and cocaine for people with severe mental illness.

Despite difficulties involved in assessing comorbid substance abuse in persons with Schizophrenia, recent developments in this area indicate that if appropriate steps are taken, reliable diagnoses can be made (Drake, Rosenberg, & Mueser, 1996; Maisto, Carey, Carey, Gordon, & Gleason, 2000). The most critical recommendations for diagnosing substance abuse in Schizophrenia include (a) maintaining a high index of suspicion of current substance abuse, especially if a person has a past history of substance abuse; (b) using multiple assessment techniques, including self-report instruments, interviews, clinician reports, reports of significant others, and biological assays for the presence of substances, which are routinely collected on admission to inpatient treatment; and (c) being alert to signs that may be subtle indicators of the presence of a substance use disorder, such as unexplained symptom relapses, familial conflict, money management problems, and sudden depression or suicidality. Once a substance use disorder has been diagnosed, integrated treatment that addresses both the Schizophrenia and the substance use disorder (co-occurring disorders) is necessary to achieve a favorable clinical outcome (Drake, Mercer-McFadden, Mueser, McHugo, & Bond, 1998).

Mood Disorders   Schizophrenia overlaps more prominently with the major mood disorders than any other psychiatric disorder. The differential diagnosis of Schizophrenia from mood disorders is critical because the disorders respond to different treatments, particularly pharmacological interventions. Two different mood disorders can be especially difficult to distinguish from Schizophrenia: Bipolar Disorder and Major Depressive Disorder. The differential diagnosis of these disorders from Schizophrenia is complicated by the fact that mood symptoms are frequently present in all phases of Schizophrenia (prodrome, acute, and remission), and psychotic symptoms (e.g., hallucinations, delusions) may be present in persons with severe mood disorders (American Psychiatric Association, 2000; Pope & Lipinski, 1978).

The crux of making a differential diagnosis between Schizophrenia and a major mood disorder is determining whether psychotic symptoms are present *in the absence of* mood symptoms. If there is strong evidence that psychotic symptoms persist even when the person is not experiencing symptoms of mania or depression, then the diagnosis is either Schizophrenia or the closely related Schizoaffective Disorder (discussed later). If, on the other hand, symptoms of psychosis are present only during a mood episode but disappear when the person's mood symptoms stabilize or improve, the appropriate diagnosis is either Major Depressive Disorder with psychotic features or Bipolar Disorder. For example, it is common for people with Bipolar Disorder to have hallucinations and delusions during the height of a manic episode, but these psychotic symptoms remit when the person's mood becomes stable again. If the person experiences chronic mood problems, meeting criteria for manic, depressive, or mixed episodes, it may be difficult or impossible to establish a diagnosis of Schizophrenia because there are no sustained periods of stable mood.

Schizoaffective Disorder   Schizoaffective Disorder is a diagnostic entity that overlaps with both the mood disorders and Schizophrenia (American Psychiatric Association, 2000). Three conditions must be met for a person to be diagnosed with Schizoaffective Disorder: (a) The person must meet criteria for a mood episode (i.e., a 2-week period in which manic, depressive, or mixed mood features are present to a significant degree); (b) the person must also meet criteria for the symptoms of Schizophrenia during a period when he or she is not experiencing a mood syndrome (e.g., hallucinations or delusions in the absence of manic or depressive symptoms); and (c) the mood episode must be present for a substantial period of the person's psychiatric illness (i.e., a person who experiences brief, transient mood states and chronic psychosis and has other long-standing impairments would be diagnosed with Schizophrenia rather than Schizoaffective Disorder).

Schizoaffective Disorder and major mood disorders are frequently mistaken for one another because it is incorrectly assumed that Schizoaffective Disorder simply requires the presence of both psychotic and mood symptoms at the same time. Rather, as described in the preceding section, if psychotic symptoms always coincide with mood symptoms, the person has a mood disorder, whereas if psychotic symptoms are present in the absence of a mood episode, the person meets criteria for either Schizoaffective Disorder or Schizophrenia. Thus, Schizoaffective Disorder requires longitudinal information about the relationship between mood and psychosis to make a diagnosis. Often, this information is obtained from the individual but is subject to memory and self-reporting biases (i.e., poor insight or lack of awareness of mood states). The distinction between Schizophrenia and Schizoaffective Disorder can be more difficult to make because one must judge whether the affective symptoms have been present for a substantial part of the person's illness. Rules for determining the extent to which mood symptoms must be present to diagnose Schizoaffective Disorder have not been clearly established.

Although the differential diagnosis between Schizophrenia and Schizoaffective Disorder is difficult to make, clinical implications of this distinction are less important than between the mood disorders and either Schizophrenia or Schizoaffective Disorder. Research on family history and treatment response suggests that Schizophrenia and Schizoaffective Disorder are similar disorders and that they respond to the same interventions (Kramer et al., 1989; Levinson & Levitt, 1987; Levinson & Mowry, 1991; Mattes & Nayak, 1984). In fact, many studies of Schizophrenia routinely include persons with Schizoaffective Disorder and find few differences. Therefore, information provided in this chapter on Schizophrenia also pertains to Schizoaffective Disorder, and the differential diagnosis between the two is not of major importance from a clinical perspective.

Delusional Disorder   Delusions can be found in Schizophrenia, Schizoaffective Disorder, severe mood disorders, organic conditions, and Delusional Disorder. Persons with Delusional Disorder develop fixed, nonbizarre delusions but no other symptoms of Schizophrenia (auditory hallucinations, disorganization, negative symptoms). The delusions may lead to isolated problems with others, but compared to Schizophrenia, the person has good social, educational, and occupational functioning. Tactile and olfactory hallucinations can be present and are often incorporated into the delusional belief, possibly as an attempt to explain these unusual experiences. Delusional Disorder is more common in females (3:1 female-to-male ratio) and has a later age of onset (mean age of 40; Evans, Paulsen, Harris, Heaton, & Jeste, 1996; Manschreck, 1996; N. Yamada, Nakajima, & Noguchi, 1998). Delusional Disorder accounts for between 1% and 4% of all inpatient admissions and is relatively rare in outpatient clinical practice (Kendler, 1982). The differential diagnosis between Delusional Disorder and Schizophrenia is based on the presence of nonbizarre delusions and the absence of other symptoms of Schizophrenia. Nonbizarre delusions are based on events or situations that could occur in real life but are highly improbable and lack supporting evidence (Sedler, 1995). Examples of nonbizarre delusions are being watched, followed, spied on, harassed, loved, or poisoned. In contrast, bizarre delusions involve mechanisms not believed to exist in an individual's culture, such as beliefs of thought insertion, control, and broadcasting. In reality, the distinction between nonbizarre and bizarre beliefs is highly subjective and often difficult to make (Junginger, Barker, & Coe, 1992; Sammons, 2005). Many persons with delusions will provide convincing arguments that their beliefs are true, and a decision on whether the belief is plausible must often be made with very little corroborating evidence (Flaum, Arndt, & Andreasen, 1991; Jones, 1999). An examination of the person's history, premorbid and current functioning, and symptom profile can be useful in distinguishing Delusional

Disorder from Schizophrenia. A structured interview, such as the SCID, can be useful in assessing delusional beliefs along with the other symptoms of Schizophrenia.

PSYCHOLOGICAL ASSESSMENT

Diagnostic assessment provides important information about the potential utility of interventions for Schizophrenia (e.g., antipsychotic medications). However, assessment does not end with a diagnosis. It must be supplemented with additional psychological and biological assessments.

Psychological, Neuropsychological, and Social Competence Assessment   A range of different psychological formulations has been proposed for understanding Schizophrenia. For example, there are extensive writings about psychodynamic and psychoanalytic interpretations of Schizophrenia. Although this work has made contributions to the further development of these theories, these formulations do not appear to have improved the ability of clinicians to understand persons with this disorder or led to more effective interventions (Mueser & Berenbaum, 1990). Therefore, use of projective assessment techniques based on psychodynamic concepts of personality, such as the Rorschach and Thematic Apperception Test, are not considered here.

One of the primary areas to assess is severity of psychotic symptoms, as treatment response is judged by a reduction of symptoms (Andreasen et al., 2005). This includes an assessment of positive and negative symptoms, insight, and general psychopathology due to the high comorbidity with mood disorders. Measures such as the Positive and Negative Syndrome Scale (Kay, Fiszbein, & Opler, 1987), the Brief Psychiatric Rating Scale (Overall & Gorham, 1962), and the Psychotic Rating Scale (Haddock, McCarron, Tarrier, & Faragher, 1999) have been frequently used in Schizophrenia research and have good psychometric properties. Scales specific to positive (Scale for the Assessment of Positive Symptoms; Andreasen & Olsen, 1982) and negative (Scale for the Assessment of Negative Symptoms; Andreasen, 1982; Schedule for Deficit Syndrome; Kirkpatrick, Buchanan, McKenney, Alphs, & Carpenter, 1989) symptoms can be used for a more in-depth and detailed assessment of these areas. The Scale for the Unawareness of Mental Disorder can be used to assess level of insight in the disorder (see Amador & David, 2004). Commonly, these symptom and insight measures are used in conjunction with a structured diagnostic interview in the assessment of Schizophrenia.

As noted earlier, Schizophrenia is often associated with a variety of neuropsychological impairments. Core areas to assess in terms of cognitive functioning are verbal and visual learning and memory, working memory, attention and vigilance, abstract reasoning and executive functioning, speed of information processing, and social cognition. These areas are part of the National Institute of Mental Health—Measurement and Treatment Research to Improve Cognition in Schizophrenia battery (Green et al., 2004). This battery requires between 60 and 90 minutes to complete, and alternative forms are available for retest purposes. Having information on cognitive functioning in these areas will aid in examining the beneficial effects of antipsychotic medication on cognition. It is also important to consider the generalization of these impairments to different situations (i.e., transfer of training problems). Thus, assessment needs to be conducted with measures that are tied to real-world skills and demands (Bond, 1998; Drake & Becker, 1996; Wallace, Liberman, Tauber, & Wallace, 2000).

A great deal of research has been done on the functional assessment of social skills in people with Schizophrenia. Social skills refer to the individual behavioral components, such as eye contact, voice volume, and the specific choice of words, which, in combination, are necessary for effective communication with others (Mueser & Bellack, 1998). As previously described, poor social competence is a hallmark of Schizophrenia. Although not all problems in social functioning are the consequence of poor social skills, many social impairments appear to be related to skill deficits (Bellack, Morrison, Wixted, & Mueser, 1990).

A number of different strategies can be used to assess social competence. Clinical interviews can be a good place to start in identifying broad areas of social dysfunction. These interviews can focus on answering questions such as whether the patient is lonely? whether the patient would like more or closer friends, whether the patient is able to stand up for his or her rights, and whether the patient is able to get others to respond positively to him or her. Patient interviews are most informative when used in combination with information from significant others, such as family members and clinicians, who are familiar with the nature and quality of the patient's social interactions and/or with naturalistic observations of the patient's social interactions. The combination of these sources of information is useful for identifying specific areas in need of social skills training. A strategy for assessing social skills that yields the most specific type of information is role-play assessments. Role-plays usually involve brief simulated social interactions between the person and a confederate taking the role of an interactive partner. During role-plays, individuals are instructed to act as though the situation were actually happening in real life. Role-plays can be as brief as 30 seconds, to assess skill areas such as initiating conversations, or as long as several minutes, to assess skills such as problem-solving ability. Role-plays can be audiotaped or videotaped and later rated on specific social skill dimensions. A reliable and valid measure for social skill assessment is the Maryland Assessment of Social Competence (MASC; Bellack & Thomas-Lorman, 2003). The MASC is a structured role-play assessment that consists of 4 brief (3-minute) interactions. Following each role-play, ratings on verbal and nonverbal skills and overall effectiveness are made, which allows the clinician to examine social skills across different situations and contexts.

The broadest area of psychological assessment is community functioning, and improvement in this area is linked to the concept of recovery. Persons with Schizophrenia show not only poor social skills but poor adaptive functioning in the community. Independent living skills, quality of life, and social functioning may need to be assessed as part of a comprehensive assessment battery, especially when placement decisions are being made. The Social Functioning Scale (Birchwood, Smith, Cochrane, Wetton, & Copstake, 1990), Social Behavioral Schedule (Wykes & Sturt, 1986), and Multnomah Community Ability Scale (Dickerson, Origoni, Pater, Friedman, & Kordonski, 2003) can provide self-report and informant ratings for a wide range of functional and social behaviors. Performance-based measures, such as the UCSD Performance-Based Skills Assessment (Patterson, Goldman, McKibbin, Hughs, & Jeste, 2001) and the Independent Living Scales (Loeb, 1996; Revheim & Medalia, 2004) are useful in that persons must demonstrate their competency in different skill areas.

Family Assessment Assessment of family functioning has high relevance in Schizophrenia for two reasons. First, expressed emotion (EE), which refers to the presence of hostile, critical, or emotionally over involved attitudes and behaviors on the part of close relatives of persons with Schizophrenia, is an important stressor that can increase the chance of relapse and rehospitalization (Butzlaff & Hooley, 1998). Second, caring for an individual with a psychiatric illness can lead to significant burden on relatives (Webb et al., 1998), which ultimately can threaten their ability to continue to provide emotional and material support to the individual. Thus, a thorough assessment of these family factors is important to identify targets for family intervention.

A number of specific methods can be used to assess a negative emotional climate in the family and burden of the illness. Interviews with individual family members, including the person with Schizophrenia, as well as with the entire family, coupled with observation of more naturalistic family interactions can provide valuable information about the quality of family functioning. The vast majority of research on family EE has employed a semi-structured interview with individual family members, the Camberwell Family Interview (J. Leff & Vaughn, 1985). This instrument is primarily a research instrument, and it is too time-consuming to be used in clinical practice. Alternatives to the Camberwell Family Interview have been proposed (e.g., Magaña et al., 1986), although none has gained widespread acceptance yet. Several studies have successfully employed the Family Environment Scale (Moos & Moos, 1981), a self-report instrument completed by family members, which has been found to be related to symptoms and outcome in patients with Schizophrenia (Halford, Schweitzer, & Varghese, 1991).

Many instruments have been developed for the assessment of family burden. The most comprehensive instrument, with well-established psychometric properties, is the Family Experiences Interview Schedule (Tessler & Gamache, 1995). This measure provides information regarding both dimensions of subjective burden (e.g., emotional strain) and objective burden (e.g., economic impact), as well as specific areas in which burden is most severe (e.g., household tasks).

CONCEPTUALIZATION

LEARNING AND MODELING

Learning and modeling are not generally viewed as major factors in the etiology of Schizophrenia; however, they are considered maintenance factors of the disorder and integral aspects in the expression of some of its symptoms (e.g., delusions, hallucinations). Thus, the factors involved in the etiology of symptoms may be different from those that maintain it (Freeman, Garety, Kuipers, Fowler, & Bebbington, 2002). The role of learning and modeling in Schizophrenia has received little emphasis due to the rise of biological models of the disorder (genetic, brain impairments). There are a few exceptions, and the most significant behavioral model involves the development and maintenance of paranoia (Haynes, 1986). According to this model, paranoid behaviors stems from specific factors such as parental modeling, prompting, and reinforcing of paranoid thoughts. In addition, nonspecific determinants, including a socially isolated family, aversive parent-child interactions, and verbal-nonverbal discrepancies, facilitate the development of paranoia.

The notion that the symptoms of Schizophrenia, especially hallucinations and delusions, can be modified or maintained by contingencies present in the environment has received support over the years. For example, hallucinations or delusional statements will increase if a person receives reinforcement in the form of attention, reward, or escape from adverse tasks. In contrast, psychotic behavior will decrease if punishment or extinction methods are applied. Learning and modeling are currently more important in the treatment of Schizophrenia than in its etiology. We discuss intervention methods that involve learning and modeling principles (operant methods, social skills training) in more detail in the Behavioral Treatment section.

Life Events

Life events have been found to play an important role in the development of Schizophrenia (Cannon & Clarke, 2005). In broad terms, the stress-vulnerability model of Schizophrenia proposes that stressful life events interact with genetic or biological vulnerability factors, which lead to the emergence of psychosis (Liberman et al., 1986). Protective factors, such as seeking social support, utilizing systematic problem-solving techniques, or engaging in structured, meaningful activities, can ameliorate the harmful effects of stress on the disorder.

Although families do not cause Schizophrenia, there are important events and interactions between the family and the individual with Schizophrenia that deserve consideration. First, as previously mentioned, studies have found that critical attitudes and high levels of emotional over involvement (EE) on the part of the relatives toward the individual with Schizophrenia are strong predictors of the likelihood that persons with Schizophrenia will relapse and be rehospitalized (Butzlaff & Hooley, 1998). The importance of family factors is underscored by the fact that the severity of psychiatric illness or social skill impairments is not related to family EE (Mueser et al., 1993). Rather, family EE seems to act as a stressor, increasing the vulnerability of persons with Schizophrenia to relapse. A second important family consideration is the amount of burden on relatives caring for a mentally ill person. Family members of persons with Schizophrenia typically experience a wide range of negative emotions related to coping with the illness, such as anxiety, depression, guilt, and anger (Hatfield & Lefley, 1987, 1993; Oldridge & Hughes, 1992). Family burden may be related to levels of EE, ability to cope with the illness, and ultimately the ability of the family to successfully monitor and manage the symptoms of Schizophrenia in a family member (Mueser & Glynn, 1999). Thus, improving the structural, functional, and instrumental support of family members is an important goal in the treatment of Schizophrenia.

Environmental events that occur in the prenatal, perinatal, and postnatal period can also affect Schizophrenia. Maternal influenza or other infections, placental or uterine abnormalities, low birth weight, diabetes during pregnancy, hypoxia, or other obstetric complications may lead to increased risk of developing Schizophrenia (see Gilmore & Murray, 2006, for a review). According to the two-hit model of Schizophrenia, the disorder arises from the combination of a genetic vulnerability, which results in the preprogrammed disruption of neurons, and either nonoptimal child-rearing practices or obstetrical complications (Mednick et al., 1998).

Due to the severity of the disorder, many persons with Schizophrenia live in poverty (Bruce, Takeuchi, & Leaf, 1991). Some believe that Schizophrenia can lead to a gradual downward drift into a lower socioeconomic status as symptom severity and functional impairment increase over time (Aro, Aro, & Keskimaki, 1995; Silverton & Mednick, 1984). Dohrenwend et al. (1992) found evidence for social drift among persons with Schizophrenia, but this finding has not been consistently supported (Fox, 1990; Samele et al., 2001). Thus, researchers are unsure if persons with Schizophrenia tend to be born into poorer environments or if they tend to drift there.

Being a member of a minority group may also increase the risk for developing Schizophrenia or being hospitalized (Rabkin, 1979). Minority individuals may experience high levels of racism and discrimination, which can lead to higher levels of stress and physiological arousal (Clark, Anderson, Clark, & Williams, 1999). In terms of psychosis, there has been a link between the amount of perceived racism and paranoia among African Americans (Combs et al., 2006; A. M. Yamada, Barrio, Morrison, Sewell, & Jeste, 2006). In addition, certain ethnic and migratory groups, such as second-generation Afro-Caribbeans living in the United Kingdom (Boydell et al., 2001; Cantor-Graae & Selten, 2005; Hutchinson & Haasen, 2004), Dutch Antillean and Surinamese immigrants in Holland (Selten, Slaets, & Kahn, 1997), Finnish and Eastern and Southern European first- and second-generation immigrants in Sweden (Hjern, Wicks, & Dalman, 2004), and African Americans (Kirkbride et al., 2006), have shown higher rates of Schizophrenia (see Cantor-Graae & Selten, 2005, for a review).

Schizophrenia has also been associated with greater exposure to traumatic (Goodman, Dutton, & Harris, 1997) and violent (Hiday, Swartz, Swanson, Borum, & Wagner, 1999) events. Approximately 34% to 53% of individuals with severe mental illness report childhood sexual or physical abuse (Greenfield, Strakowski, Tohen, Batson, & Kolbrener, 1994; A. Jacobsen & Herald, 1990; Rose, Peabody, & Stratigeas, 1991; Ross, Anderson, & Clark, 1994). Exposure to traumatic events may lead to the development of Posttraumatic Stress Disorder (PTSD) in persons with Schizophrenia. The presence of PTSD in persons with Schizophrenia has been found to worsen the course of the disorder and complicate treatment (Mueser, Rosenberg, Goodman, & Trumbetta, 2002). Prevalence of PTSD among people with Schizophrenia and other severe mental illnesses ranges from 29% to 43% (Cascardi, Mueser, DeGirolomo, & Murrin, 1996; Craine, Henson, Colliver, & MacLean, 1988; Mueser, Bond, Drake, & Resnick, 1998; Mueser et al., 2004; Switzer et al., 1999). These rates are far in excess of the general population, which range from 8% to 12% (Breslau, Davis, Andreski, & Peterson, 1991; Kessler, Sonnega, Bromet, Hughes, & Nelson, 1995; Resnick, Kilpatrick, Dansky, Saunders, & Best, 1993).

GENETIC INFLUENCES

The etiology of Schizophrenia has been a topic of much debate over the past 100 years. Kraepelin (1919) and Bleuler (1911/1950) clearly viewed the illness as having a biological origin. However, from the 1920s to the 1960s alternative theories gained prominence, speculating that the disease was the result of psychogenic or family interactions (Bateson, Jackson, Haley, & Weakland, 1956; Fromm-Reichmann, 1950; Searles, 1965). These theories have not been supported empirically (Jacob, 1975; Waxler & Mishler, 1971). Moreover, in many cases, psychogenic theories fostered poor relationships between mental health professionals and relatives (Terkelsen, 1983), which have only begun to mend in recent years (Mueser & Glynn, 1999).

For over a century, clinicians have often noted that Schizophrenia tends to run in families. However, the clustering of Schizophrenia in family members could reflect learned behavior that is passed on from one generation to the next, rather than predisposing biological factors. In the 1950s and 1960s, two paradigms were developed for evaluating the genetic contributions to the illness. The first approach, the *high-risk* paradigm, involves examining the rate of Schizophrenia in adopted-away or biological offspring of mothers with Schizophrenia. If the rate of Schizophrenia in children of biological parents with Schizophrenia is higher than in the general population, even in the absence of contact with those parents, a role for genetic factors in developing the illness is supported. The second approach, the *monozygotic/dizygotic twin* paradigm, involves comparing the concordance rate of Schizophrenia in identical twins (monozygotic) to fraternal twins (dizygotic). Because monozygotic twins share the exact same gene pool, whereas dizygotic twins share only approximately half the gene pool, a higher concordance rate of Schizophrenia among monozygotic than dizygotic twins, even reared in the same environment, would support a role for genetic factors in the etiology of Schizophrenia.

Over the past 30 years, numerous studies employing either the high-risk or twin paradigm have been conducted, further examining the role of genetic factors in Schizophrenia. There has been almost uniform agreement across studies indicating that the risk of developing Schizophrenia in biological relatives of persons with Schizophrenia is greater than in the general population, even in the absence of any contact between the relatives (Kendler & Diehl, 1993). Thus, support exists for the role of genetic factors in the etiology of at least some cases of the disorder. For example, risk of developing Schizophrenia if one parent has the disorder is about 13% and rises to 50% if both parents have the disorder, compared to only 1% risk for the general population (Gottesman, 1991, 2001; McGuffin, Owen, & Farmer, 1995). Similarly, the concordance rate of one identical twin developing Schizophrenia if his or her cotwin has Schizophrenia is between 25% and 50% compared to about 6% to 15% for fraternal twins (Cardno et al., 1999; Faraone & Tsuang, 1985; Torrey, 1992; Walker, Downey, & Caspi, 1991).

The fact that identical twins do not have a 100% concordance rate of Schizophrenia (heritability rates = .81), as might be expected if the disorder were purely genetic, has raised intriguing questions about the etiology of Schizophrenia (see Sullivan, Kendler, & Neale, 2003). In a review of 40 studies on genetic risk, it was found that 80% of persons with psychotic symptoms do not have a single parent with the disorder, and 60% have a negative family history for Schizophrenia (Gottesman, 2001). It is likely that development of Schizophrenia results from an interaction between genetic and environmental factors. Results of a series of longitudinal studies support this case. Tienari (1991; Tienari et al., 1987, 2004) compared likelihood of developing Schizophrenia in three groups of children raised by adoptive families. Two groups of children had biological mothers with Schizophrenia, and the third group had biological mothers with no psychiatric disorder. The researchers divided the adoptive families of the children into two broad groups based on the level of disturbance present in the family: healthy adoptive families and disturbed adoptive families. Follow-up assessments were conducted to determine the presence of Schizophrenia and other severe psychiatric disorders in the adopted children raised in all three groups. The researchers found that biological children of mothers with Schizophrenia who were raised by adoptive families with high levels of disturbance were significantly more likely to develop Schizophrenia or another psychotic disorder (46%) than either similarly vulnerable children raised in families with low levels of disturbance (5%) or children with no biological vulnerability raised in either disturbed (24%) or healthy (3%) adoptive families. This study raises the intriguing possibility that some cases of Schizophrenia develop as a result of the interaction between biological vulnerability and environmental stress.

Finally, researchers have been interested in discovering genes and chromosomal areas involved in Schizophrenia. Current research has focused on several promising chromosomes (i.e., 1q, 22q) and genes that may be important in Schizophrenia

(Harrison & Owen, 2003; Lewis et al., 2003 as reviewed in Sullivan, Owen, O'Donovan & Freedman, 2006). Researchers are particularly interested in identifying genes found across family members with the disorder (linkage studies) or that directly relate to the underlying pathophysiology of Schizophrenia (e.g., genes that affect functioning of neurotransmitters such as dopamine, serotonin, or glutamate). This area of research has been generally hampered by the lack of independent replication of these genetic markers. The exact mechanism for genetic transmission of the disorder is unknown, but it appears that Schizophrenia does not follow a Mendelian pattern of inheritance. It is more likely that Schizophrenia is a polygenetic condition, or arises from an interaction of multiple genes, which increases the susceptibility to the disorder (Craddock, O'Donovan, & Owen, 2006; Miyamoto et al., 2003).

PHYSICAL FACTORS AFFECTING BEHAVIOR

Among his many contributions, Kraepelin (1919) was one of the first to assert that Schizophrenia resulted from cerebral pathology. For much of the past century, this suggestion went largely unsupported. However, as methods of data collection became increasingly sophisticated, the resulting literature grew to support Kraeplin's hypothesis. Indeed, abundant data collected over the past 2 decades imply a significant neuropathological substrate of Schizophrenia. Generally, this literature is based on studies that have employed brain imaging, postmortem analyses, and neuropsychological assessment.

Research involving imaging technology examines either of two aspects of cerebral integrity. Structural imaging (e.g., magnetic resonance imaging) assesses the volume of brain tissue or the presence of structural abnormalities. Functional imaging (e.g., functional magnetic resonance imaging) measures relative cerebral activation. Inasmuch as such imaging data deviate from normal, pathology is presumed.

With respect to structural imaging studies, evidence of global cerebral abnormalities has been inconclusive. Although people with Schizophrenia are apt to have abnormally reduced cortical gray matter and larger ventricles, these findings seem due to regionally specific anomalies (Shenton, Dickey, Frumin, & McCarley, 2001). In particular, the frontal lobes seem to be implicated in Schizophrenia. For instance, reduced total gray matter volume is commonly reported, as are reductions in white matter tissue. Additionally, the size of specific frontal regions and cortical gyri have been observed to be lower in people with Schizophrenia than in nonpatient groups. For instance, the dorsal lateral prefrontal, orbital, and medial frontal lobe regions are commonly observed to be smaller in people with Schizophrenia (Buchanan, Vladar, Barta, & Pearlson, 1998; Goldstein et al., 1999). Notably, the frontal lobes are presumed to be the neural substrate of planning, motivation, goal-directed activities, and capacity to inhibit impulses. Coincidentally, Schizophrenia is characterized by poor problem solving, apathy, and disorganized behavior. Thus, these frontal lobe anomalies may underlie some aspects of schizophrenic symptomatology. Indeed, some research reveals a relationship between frontal lobe abnormalities and severity of negative symptoms (Gur et al., 2000).

In addition to the frontal lobes, temporal lobe abnormalities have been reported. In particular, temporal lobe cortical volumes tend to be smaller in people with Schizophrenia (Shenton et al., 2001). Similar to the frontal lobes, however, some regions express this diminishment more saliently than others. For instance, the superior temporal gyrus, planum temporale, Heschl's gyrus, amygdala, hippocampus, and parahippocampal gyrus appear reduced in cortical volume (Bryant, Buchanan, Vladar, Brier, & Rothman, 1999). Implications of these abnormalities are uncertain. Yet, functions attributed to the temporal lobes are varied and include auditory processing, language, and memory. Schizophrenia is characterized by auditory hallucinations, disorganized language, and impaired memory, which reflect temporal lobe function. This suggestion is supported, albeit weakly, with some research revealing an association between temporal lobe volumes and severity of positive symptoms (Crespo-Facorro et al., 2004).

Apart from abnormalities involving the frontal and temporal lobes, other regions have been implicated in Schizophrenia. Specifically, ventricles are abnormally large as soon as symptom onset, and there are indications that they continue to enlarge over time (see DeLisi, Sakuma, Maurizio, Relja, & Hoff, 20044). Additionally, abnormal cerebral volumes have been observed in the parietal lobes, thalamus, and basal ganglia (Shenton et al., 2001). However, these findings have been inconsistently demonstrated in the literature, and their reliability and significance are uncertain.

Although the etiology of structural brain impairments has not been clearly determined, they appear to be present at the time of initial symptom onset. Moreover, a few longitudinal studies reveal further reductions in cortical volumes over time (Cahn et al., 2002; Gur et al., 1998; Mathalon, Sullivan, Lim, & Pfefferbaum, 2001). This suggests that cerebral anomalies precede symptom onset, thereby implying a neurodevelopmental etiology. Yet, owing to changes in cerebral structure over time, some further deterioration in cerebral integrity may occur, implying a progressive etiology.

Regarding functional abnormalities, many of the same regions implicated in structural imaging studies appear to manifest abnormal activation. In particular, frontal lobe structures demonstrate hypoactivation in people with Schizophrenia, especially when they perform tasks requiring working memory, vigilance, or concentration (e.g., Callicott et al., 2003). Specific regions in which this occurs include the dorsal lateral prefrontal cortex and medial frontal area. Curiously, in normal individuals, an inverse relationship appears to exist between frontal and temporal lobe activation during working memory tasks. Specifically, as frontal lobe activation increases, temporal lobe arousal tends to decrease. People with Schizophrenia do not manifest this pattern of reciprocal activation (Frith et al., 1995). Apart from these anomalies, few other areas have been identified that consistently manifest abnormal activation in Schizophrenia.

These structural and functional anomalies seem to correspond with abnormalities at the cellular level. In particular, Schizophrenia is associated with disordered arrangements of neurons, and this ultimately is reflected by abnormal distribution of neurons within cortical layers (Arnold, Ruscheinsky, & Han, 1997). In addition, Schizophrenia corresponds with decreased thickness of cortex, especially in the dorsal lateral prefrontal region (Harrison & Lewis, 2001). This thinning of cortex does not appear to reflect a loss of neurons (Thune, Uylings, & Pakkenberg, 2001). Indeed, most studies reveal no loss of cell number, and there is no atypical gliosis in Schizophrenia, as is commonly seen after necrosis. Rather, most investigations imply abnormal neuropil development (Selemon & Goldman-Rakic, 1999). The neuropil includes the axons, dendrites, and synaptic terminals rather than the cell body. Diminished neuropil has been observed in the dorsal lateral prefrontal cortex and in the hippocampus. Although there is little evidence of cellular loss in the cortex, at least one subcortical structure appears to lose neurons. Specifically, the thalamus and, to a lesser extent, the cingulate appear to have decreased neuronal counts (Byne et al., 2002). Taken together, these findings imply that frontal and temporal lobe regions possess abnormal interconnectivity, as evidenced by anomalous neuronal branching and distribution. Etiology of such pathology largely implies a developmental process. Specifically, normal neuronal migration occurs as early as the second trimester of fetal development and through the first few years of life, and modification of the neuropil is largely an adolescent event.

Corresponding with these cytoarchitectural abnormalities, neurotransmitters appear to be anomalous in Schizophrenia. In particular, the dopamine hypothesis of Schizophrenia was initially promulgated several decades ago. According to this model, excess dopamine yielded positive symptoms. Subsequently, a modified dopamine hypothesis has been proposed. In this model, subcortical dopamine (mesolimbic and nigrostriatal) circuits interact synergistically with frontal cortical dopamine systems (mesocortical) to yield excess subcortical dopamine activity and insufficient dopamine activation in the frontal cortex (Weinberger, 1987). The nature of this abnormal activation seems broad, as presynaptic storage, release, and reuptake of dopamine appears abnormal. Notably, in several studies, excess subcortical dopamine corresponded with severity of positive symptoms (Abi-Dargham & Moore, 2003). Yet, there is little evidence that dopamine levels correspond directly with negative symptoms, thereby suggesting involvement of other neurotransmitter systems. Indeed, glutamate, a diffusely distributed neurotransmitter, generally acts to increase arousal. In Schizophrenia, however, glutamate tends to have a diminished presence, and this correlates with severity of negative symptoms and possibly excess dopamine activity (see Coyle, 1996). Moreover, as glutamate antagonists are given to persons with schizophrenia, their symptoms exacerbate.

Collectively, the presence of structural, functional, cellular, and neuropsychological abnormalities indicates that Schizophrenia is associated with compelling cerebral dysfunction. The nature of this pathology is diffuse, and it appears severe. The etiology, as is the disease itself, is uncertain. Nonetheless, accumulating evidence implies that neuropathology in Schizophrenia is at least partially a result of abnormal neural development. Other factors, such as stressful life circumstances, may interact with individuals at risk to yield overt onset of symptoms (Keshavan, Gilbert, & Diwadkar, 2006).

DRUGS AFFECTING BEHAVIOR

Many substances, such as cannabis, amphetamines, PCP, and LSD, can mimic or produce the symptoms of Schizophrenia (Potvin, Stip, & Roy, 2005). Complexities of diagnosing Schizophrenia in the presence of substance use were highlighted earlier in the Psychological Assessment section. Recent attention has been directed at the link between cannabis and Schizophrenia; it is estimated that between 30% and 40% of persons with Schizophrenia report cannabis use (Fowler, Carr, Carter, & Lewin, 1998). Normal persons who abuse cannabis at very high levels can experience a "cannabis-induced psychosis," defined by perceptual disturbances, paranoia, and confusion. Some studies show that having these types of experiences may actually lead to the development of Schizophrenia-like symptoms (Arendt, Rosenberg, Foldager, & Perto, 2005). Cannabis use appears to increase the risk for developing Schizophrenia in persons already at high risk for the disorder (Andreasson, Allebeck, Engstrom, & Rydberg, 1987; Semple, McIntosh, & Lawrie, 2005), and persons with Schizophrenia who use cannabis develop the disorder earlier in their life than nonusers (Barnes, Mutsatsa, Hutton, Watt, & Joyce, 2006; Veen et al., 2004). Cannabis use has a negative impact on the course of the illness, with users having more frequent relapses and hospitalizations (Cuffel & Chase, 1994; Linszen, Dingemans, & Lenior, 1994). It is believed that cannabis may partially ameliorate the positive and negative symptoms of the disorder or attenuate the side effects related to antipsychotic medications (Bersani, Orlandi, Kotzalidis, & Pancheri, 2002; Smit, Bolier, & Cuijpers, 2004).

The substances most frequently linked to Schizophrenia are amphetamines and psychostimulants, which increase dopamine levels at the pre- and postsynaptic levels. Some persons with Schizophrenia may have an exacerbation of positive symptoms (hallucinations, delusions, paranoia) if amphetamines are used (as reviewed in Duncan, Sheitman, & Lieberman, 1999; Lieberman, Kane, & Alvir, 1987). In addition, normal persons who abuse amphetamines repeatedly can also exhibit psychotic symptoms (Potvin et al., 2005), and in many cases, these persons are indistinguishable from persons with paranoid Schizophrenia. It is believed that repeated amphetamine use may lead to the sensitization of dopamine neurons, which can persist for months after amphetamine use has ceased (T. E. Robinson & Becker, 1986; Strakowski, Sax, Setters, & Keck, 1996). Thus, amphetamines can worsen symptoms of Schizophrenia in existing patients and can lead to the onset of psychotic symptoms in normal persons who show a pattern of consistent abuse.

The positive, negative, and cognitive symptoms of Schizophrenia can also be produced by PCP and ketamine in normal individuals (Adler, Goldberg, Malhotra, Pickar, & Breier, 1998) and tend to exacerbate psychotic symptoms of persons with Schizophrenia (Lahti, Koffel, LaPorte, & Tamminga, 1995; Malhotra et al., 1997). Ketamine and PCP are NMDA receptor antagonists (glutamate), which is believed to increase dopaminergic activity in the mesocorticolimbic pathways, thus producing psychosis (Duncan et al., 1999). However, the role of PCP and ketamine in the development of Schizophrenia is not well studied, and the psychotic-like symptoms appear transient. The role of LSD in producing Schizophrenia has not been firmly supported, but its abuse can lead to distorted perceptual and sensory experiences. Use of LSD by persons who have Schizophrenia may lead to increased positive symptoms. It is believed that the action of LSD on the serotonergic system (5HT2 receptor agonists) may be helpful in further understanding Schizophrenia (Aghajanian & Marek, 2000).

In summary, although all of these substances can produce Schizophrenia-like symptoms in normals, their role in the disorder appears to be in the exacerbation of existing symptoms or raising the risk of developing the disorder among high-risk persons.

Culture and Diversity

It is widely believed that the prevalence of Schizophrenia is relatively consistent across different populations and cultures. In 1992, the World Health Organization published findings that similar incidence rates and symptom patterns of Schizophrenia were found across 10 different countries (Jablensky et al., 1992). However, the cross-cultural nature of Schizophrenia has not remained unchallenged, as some studies find widely differing rates (Eaton & Chen, 2006; Goldner et al., 2002). Furthermore, there is evidence that Schizophrenia is more heavily concentrated in urban areas of industrialized countries and may reflect the impact of poverty, stress, and/or poor health care. The prognosis for persons in more industrialized and developed countries is worse than for those in developing countries (Hopper, Nathan, & Wanderling, 2000; Jablensky, 2000; Jablensky et al., 2000; S. Leff, Sartorious, Jablensky, Korten, & Emberg, 1992).

A variety of different interpretations has been offered to account for the better prognosis of Schizophrenia in developing countries (Lefley, 1990). It has been suggested that there may be less discrepancy among social classes in developing countries, and persons with Schizophrenia may experience less stigma and social rejection (Fink & Tasman, 1992). Therefore, cultural acceptance of the social deviations present in Schizophrenia may enable persons in developing countries to live less stressful and more productive lives. Additionally, family ties may be stronger in developing countries, thus increasing support resources (Liberman, 1994; Lin & Kleinman, 1988). In contrast, Western societies tend to be more individualistic and place less emphasis on family ties and support (Lefley, 1990; Mueser & Glynn, 1999). Estroff (1989) argued that Western countries place considerable importance on the self, which may have an especially disabling effect on persons with Schizophrenia, whose sense of self is often fragile or fragmented.

The importance of religion and spirituality is often unaccounted for in Schizophrenia. Spiritual beliefs may shape development, phenomenology, and prognosis of the disorder. In the Puerto Rican culture, the notion of *espiritismo* involves the belief that the invisible spirit world and the visible world interact, and individuals strive for spiritual perfection (Comas-Díaz, 1981; Morales-Dorta, 1976), which may lead to a more favorable, less stigmatizing view of persons with hallucinations. Unfortunately, some religious practices and beliefs may complicate diagnosis and treatment (Moss, Fleck, & Strakowski, 2006). High levels of religiosity have been found in people with Schizophrenia (Brewerton, 1994), complicating the differentiation of delusional beliefs from culturally sanctioned religious beliefs (Huguelet, Mohr, Borras, Gillieron, & Brandt, 2006). For example, Peters, Day, McKenna, and Orbach (1999) found considerable overlap in delusional dimensions (conviction, preoccupation, and distress) between persons from new religious movements (Hare Krishnas and Druids) and persons with psychosis. Unfortunately, without a clear understanding of religious and cultural background, patients may be misdiagnosed. Because some ethnic groups differ in their willingness to disclose psychiatric symptoms to professionals, the influence of cultural norms is highly relevant for Schizophrenia. Skilbeck, Acosta, Yamamoto, and Evans (1984) found that African American persons were less likely to report symptoms than Hispanics or non-Hispanic Whites. Differences in the interpretation of mistrust for African Americans by White clinicians may lead to higher rates of diagnosing paranoid Schizophrenia (Adams, Dworkin, & Rosenberg, 1984; Combs et al., 2006; Combs, Penn, & Fenigstein, 2002; Kirkbride et al., 2006; Whaley, 1997). Mistrust may very well be an adaptive behavior in the face of racism and discrimination (Whaley, 2001). Thus, knowledge of cultural and ethnic norms is critical to avoid the possible misinterpretation of culturally bound beliefs, experiences, and practices when arriving at a diagnosis.

Cultural differences have also been found in the utilization of health care services. For example, African Americans tend to use more emergency services, and Hispanics and Asian Americans report less use of treatment services (Cheung & Snowden, 1990; Hough et al., 1987; Hu, Snowden, Jerrell, & Nguyen, 1991; Padgett, Patrick, Burns, & Schlesinger, 1994; Sue, Fujino, Hu, Takeuchi, & Zane, 1991). It has been suggested that matching client and provider in terms of ethnicity may improve the retention of minorities in treatment (Sue et al., 1991). In contrast, a recent study of Hispanic, African American, and White patients with Schizophrenia showed similar treatment outcomes, with the exception of slower rates of improvement in social functioning for African Americans (Bae, Brekke, & Bola, 2004). Thus, it appears that when treatment services are utilized consistently, outcomes for different ethnic groups approximate that of Whites.

Besides ethnic background, gender is also important in Schizophrenia. Women tend to have a later onset of the disorder, maintain greater social competence, have fewer and shorter hospitalizations, and have a better prognosis over time (Goldstein, 1988; Grossman, Harrow, Rosen, & Faull, 2006; Häfner et al., 1993; Leung & Chue, 2000; Mueser, Bellack, Morrison, & Wade, 1990; Salem & Kring, 1998). There is limited research concerning women in this area; most of the studies aimed at assessment and treatment of Schizophrenia are conducted on males (Kirkbride et al., 2006). In fact, the composition of research samples has ranged from 60% to 100% male. Thus, studies that focus on females with Schizophrenia, especially treatment outcome studies, should be conducted to determine if psychosocial and pharmacological treatments are equally efficacious for both men and women (Mueser, Levine, Bellack, Douglas, & Brady, 1990; Schaub, Behrendt, Brenner, Mueser, & Liberman, 1998; Smith et al., 1997). In fact, very little is known about late-onset Schizophrenia for females and how hormones affect psychosis (Mueser & McGurk, 2004).

BEHAVIORAL TREATMENT

Behavioral treatments for Schizophrenia have existed since the 1960s and have become increasingly more complex over time (Allyon & Haughton, 1964). Currently, the focus is on providing treatments that have sound empirical support; these treatments are collectively called empirically supported treatments or evidence-based practices (Baucom, Shoham, Mueser, Daiuto, & Stickle, 1998; Chambless & Ollendick, 2001; DeRubeis & Crits-Christoph, 1998). Given that between 25% and 60% of persons taking antipsychotics continue to report psychotic symptoms, behavioral treatments are important in maximizing recovery. Behavioral treatments have fared well in research; many efficacious treatments involve behavioral components. In this section, we focus on four types of behavioral treatments for Schizophrenia: (1) operant conditioning methods, (2) social skills training, (3) behavioral family therapy, and (4) cognitive-behavioral therapy.

The earliest treatments involved use of operant conditioning methods to reduce expression of delusional beliefs, hallucinations, and disorganized speech. Common interventions involved differential reinforcement, punishment, and extinction, and most of the research in this area has come from case studies (see Jimenez, Todman, Perez, Godoy, & Landon-Jimenez, 1996, for an example). However, complexity and heterogeneity of psychotic symptoms along with staffing problems have reduced the use of these methods in today's mental health system (Gomes-Schwartz, 1979; Schock, Clay, & Cipani, 1998). A modern example of operant conditioning methods can be found in attention-shaping programs, which provide positive reinforcement for paying attention to different tasks (Silverstein, Menditto, & Stuve, 2001). This method is useful as many persons with Schizophrenia may not be able to participate in traditional treatment programs due to their cognitive and attentional deficits. One specialized application of operant conditioning is the use of token economy systems to improve the adaptive behaviors (self-care, work, social interaction, treatment participation) of persons with Schizophrenia (see Dickerson, Tenhula, & Green-Paden, 2004, for a review). Token economies provide tokens to participants based on the performance of certain adaptive behaviors important in their treatment programs. These tokens can be used to purchase items or privileges that the person values, thus increasing the likelihood that the behaviors will continue. Recently, the Schizophrenia

Patient Outcomes Research Team (Lehman et al., 2004) listed token economies as a recommended, effective treatment for inpatient treatment facilities.

Social skills training (SST) is aimed at improving the social functioning and competence of persons with Schizophrenia. Persons with Schizophrenia have consistently been found to have worse social skills than persons with other psychiatric disorders (Bellack et al., 1990; Bellack, Mueser, Wade, Sayers, & Morrison, 1992; Mueser, Bellack, Douglas, & Wade, 1991). Approximately half of the persons with Schizophrenia demonstrate stable deficits in basic social skills compared to the nonpsychiatric populations (Mueser, Bellack, Douglas, & Morrison, 1991). In the absence of skills training, social skills tend to be stable over periods of time, as long as 6 months to 1 year (Mueser, Bellack, Douglas, & Morrison, 1991). Social skills training provides instruction on conversational skills, such as how to begin, maintain, and end conversations, express emotions appropriately, and resolve interpersonal conflict (Bellack, Sayers, Mueser, & Bennett, 1994; Douglas & Mueser, 1990; see Mueser & McGurk, 2004). Each social skill is broken down into different units: verbal, paralinguistic, and nonverbal components. To facilitate learning, SST involves didactic teaching, rehearsal, role-playing, corrective feedback, and modeling of appropriate social and communication skills, usually in a group setting (Bellack, Mueser, Gingerich, & Agresta, 2004). To reinforce gains made in the group session, participants are asked to continue to develop and practice these skills outside of the group sessions, which may improve the generalization of new skills into the real world (Glynn et al., 2002). Social skills training is usually conducted over 12 to 16 sessions, and inpatients may require smaller, more focused units to learn the material. Several randomized controlled trials of SST showed improvement in specific social skills and social adjustment and leisure skills, and therefore SST is currently considered a possibly efficacious treatment for Schizophrenia (DeRubeis & Crits-Christoph, 1998; Heinssen, Liberman, & Kopelowicz, 2000). However, the impact of SST on improving symptoms and community functioning or preventing relapse is less consistent (Bustillo, Lauriello, Horan, & Keith, 2001; see Penn & Mueser, 1996, for a review).

Behavioral family therapy (BFT) is based on teaching adaptive coping skills to ameliorate the deleterious effects of stress on Schizophrenia (i.e., expressed emotion). In addition, the burden that many families report when caring for a family member with Schizophrenia can lead to negative, hostile, and critical communication patterns. Even when unintended, family stress can lead to relapse and hospitalization among persons with Schizophrenia by impinging on the vulnerability factors of the disorder. Goals of BFT include reducing negative, hostile interactions between the patient and family members, providing psychoeducation about the disorder and its etiology, encouraging medication adherence, and developing and practicing problem-solving skills (Mueser & Glynn, 1999). The patient and family are taught problem-solving and communication skills and are then allowed to practice these techniques in the session and at home. Often, BFT is conducted with a single family, but modifications of this method have included a larger number of families and have focused on sharing coping skills for dealing with Schizophrenia (e.g., supportive family therapy). Recent reviews of the efficacy of BFT have shown that it leads to significant decreases in relapse rates, from about 60% to 30% (Baucom et al., 1998; Penn & Mueser, 1996; Pitschel-Walz, Leucht, Bauml, Kissling, & Engel, 2001). Currently, BFT is considered an efficacious treatment for Schizophrenia. A drawback of this method is that most studies show gains only after extended treatment periods (over 18 months; Baucom et al., 1998).

A recent modification of behavioral approaches is cognitive-behavioral therapy (CBT) for psychosis. This method has demonstrated efficacy in the treatment of a variety of psychotic symptoms and is emerging as an evidence-based practice (Dickerson, 2000; Gaudiano, 2005). Cognitive-behavioral therapy can be implemented as a comprehensive treatment package (Kingdon & Turkington, 2005) or for specific symptoms (delusions, hallucinations, negative symptoms; Haddock et al., 1998). In the United Kingdom, CBT for psychosis is officially recognized as an empirically based treatment and is recommended for all persons with Schizophrenia. Cognitive-behavioral therapy assumes that psychotic symptoms develop from information-processing biases in attention, appraisal, attribution, and belief formation (Rector & Beck, 2001). For example, persecutory delusions may be based on the interpretation of ambiguous events as negative and hostile, which increases anxiety and threat (Freeman et al., 2002). Similar to CBT for depression and anxiety, biases are changed through cognitive restructuring, behavioral experimentation, teaching and practicing coping skills, generating alternative attributions for events, and behavioral activation. Cognitive-behavioral therapy has been specifically effective in reducing conviction levels of delusional beliefs (Chadwick & Lowe, 1990) and frequency and distress associated with hallucinations (Bentall, Haddock, & Slade, 1994). In addition, researchers are beginning to apply CBT to acute and first episode psychosis with some success (Gaudiano, 2005; Zimmerman, Favrod, Trieu, & Pomini, 2005). Despite the substantial research evidence on CBT for psychosis, there remains a lack of dissemination and implementation in the United States (Dickerson, 2000).

MEDICAL TREATMENT

Antipsychotic medications are considered the mainstay in the medical treatment of Schizophrenia (Mueser & McGurk, 2004). Antipsychotic medications are currently classified as either first-generation (typicals) or second-generation (atypicals) drugs. First-generation medications, such as Thorazine, Haldol, and Prolixin, have been shown to be efficacious in reducing the positive symptoms of the disorder. However, the effectiveness of these drugs is tempered by their side effect profiles, which is largely responsible for their waning use in treatment (roughly 10% of individuals are prescribed these medications in the United States; Nasrallah & Smeltzer, 2003). First-generation antipsychotics block D2 dopamine receptors in the mesolimbic and mesocortical dopamine pathways; this mechanism of action is believed to lead to their antipsychotic effect (Duncan et al., 1999). But because blockade of dopamine neurons is nonspecific, they also affect the nigrostriatal pathway, which leads to an array of unwanted motor side effects, called extra pyramidal symptoms (EPS). Dystonia (painful muscle contractions or spasms), akathesia (restlessness, pacing), and parkinsonism (fine tremors, rigidity) are linked to the medications' affinity for the D2 receptor (higher affinity = greater EPS). Long-term administration of first-generation medications can lead to the development of tardive dyskinesia, in which the person exhibits involuntary hyperkinetic movements of the face, tongue, limbs, fingers, and trunk. Tardive dyskinesia is considered irreversible and cannot be accurately predicted, but it can be reduced by switching to an atypical antipsychotic medication with less dopamine antagonism.

In the 1990s, atypical antipsychotics were developed with the promise of improved treatment for Schizophrenia with greater efficacy and fewer side effects. As a general rule, atypical medications are less potent antagonists of the D2 receptor system (less potential for EPS) and affect several neurotransmitter systems (e.g., serotonin

[5-HT$_{2a/2c}$], norepinephrine, acetylcholine, glutamate). It is now recommended that atypical medications be considered the first line of treatment for Schizophrenia due to a lower risk for EPS in these medications (American Psychiatric Association, 2004; Marder et al., 2002; McEvoy, Scheifler, & Frances, 1999). However, atypicals do have their share of potential side effects, such as sedation, weight gain, abnormal heart activity (QT interval slowing), and diabetes. The first atypical medication, Clozaril, is effective in reducing treatment-resistant positive symptoms, negative symptoms, hostility, and suicidality (Lehman et al., 2004). However, Clozaril can produce a rare blood disorder called agranulocytosis (lowering of white blood cell counts) in some individuals and must be closely monitored; thus, Clozaril is usually not considered a first-line medication. A second benefit of atypical medications is a possible improvement in cognition, but the exact mechanism of improvement is unknown (Meltzer & McGurk, 1999). It is likely that atypical antipsychotics alter the balance of different neurotransmitters, thus leading to improved cognition (Keefe, Silva, Perkins, & Lieberman, 1999). However, it should be emphasized that no drug has been found to restore cognitive functioning to normal levels for all persons (Harvey, Bowie, & Loebel, 2006) or to improve social functioning (Breier, 2005). Also, it must be demonstrated that changes in cognitive functioning produced by these drugs mediate better social and occupational functioning following treatment (Green, 1996).

Despite efficacy of medication therapy, noncompliance remains a critical issue in the treatment of Schizophrenia (A. Buchanan, 1992; Fenton, Blyler, & Heinssen, 1997). About 50% of persons with Schizophrenia will discontinue their medication regimen within a year following initiation of treatment (as reviewed in Gilmer et al., 2004; Perkins, Lieberman, & Lewis, 2006), and noncompliance greatly increases risk of relapse and hospitalization (Hogarty & Ulrich, 1998; Olfson et al., 2000; Weiden, Kozma, Grogg, & Locklear, 2004). Noncompliance is likely due to a number of factors: poor rapport with provider, mistrust of the provider, lack of understanding of the treatment process, lack of perceived efficacy in the medication, or the emergence of side effects. Two recent studies highlight the widespread problem of noncompliance in Schizophrenia. First, the Clinical Antipsychotic Trials of Intervention Effectiveness randomly assigned 1,493 persons with Schizophrenia to 1 of 5 antipsychotic medications. Over the 18-month study period, 74% of these persons discontinued their medication despite a reduction in psychotic symptoms, which reflects the limited effectiveness of these medications due to noncompliance (Lieberman et al., 2005). Second, a study of 63,000 individuals with Schizophrenia in the Veterans Affairs medical system found widespread noncompliance in terms of filling needed prescriptions for both conventional and atypical antipsychotics (Valenstein et al., 2004). Overall, it seems that the improved side effect profiles of the atypicals do not translate into significantly better adherence rates (Dolder, Lacro, Dunn, & Jeste, 2002; Velligan, Lam, Ereshefsky, & Miller, 2003). In terms of enhancing compliance, it appears that specific interventions that target the cognitive, motivational, and behavioral aspects of compliance are most effective (see Dolder, Lacro, Leckband, & Jeste, 2003, for a review). Methods of improving medication compliance include use of depot or injectable antipsychotic medications, reducing the number of pills or complexity of treatment, allowing the person to become more involved in his or her treatment decisions (e.g., use of a treatment advocate), teaching persons how to include medication in their daily lives, providing reminders or cues to take their medications, educating about the importance of medication, and delivering medication to the individual's residence (Azrin & Teichner, 1998; Corrigan, Liberman, & Engle, 1990; Kemp, Hayward, Applewhaite,

Everitt, & David, 1996; Kemp, Kirov, Everitt, Hayward, & David, 1998; Velligan, Lam, et al., 2006; Velligan, Mueller, et al., 2006).

Case Description

Case Introduction

Bill, a 19-year-old single African American male, was brought to the local psychiatric hospital by law enforcement after he became belligerent and hostile with his mother and threatened to harm his younger siblings. He was considered a danger to self and others and was held for observation and treatment.

Presenting Complaints and History

At the hospital, Bill was agitated and aggressive, often yelling at staff to leave him alone. His speech was tangential, loose, and at times incoherent. His affect was labile and his mood was reported as "angry." He appeared to be responding to internal stimuli and was observed talking to himself in the admissions area. When asked why he was brought to the hospital, he reported that he was the target of a governmental conspiracy based on information he has about future world events. He reported that he hears the voice of a male person who tells him things about the future, but he was not sure who this voice was or why he was chosen to receive this information. Furthermore, he stated that his home was being monitored 24 hours a day and agents watch him from parked cars on the street. He believed that if given an opportunity he would be captured to get his information. He felt that the only safe place was at home in the attic, which he had cleared of surveillance devices. He ventures outside only if he has to and reports distress and anxiety when walking alone, especially at night. He described a recent event in which a store clerk stated that he needed to go into the back room to get some change. However, Bill knew that the clerk was summoning agents to seize him, and he ran home to avoid potential harm. He felt that the agents had offered his mother a substantial amount of money to turn him in, and he blamed her for his being admitted to the hospital. His mother reported that he has been acting "odd" for the past 9 months, She felt that she cannot communicate with him anymore. He reported using alcohol several times a week and smoking marijuana on the weekends. This was his first contact with the mental health system.

In terms of his community and psychosocial functioning, he quit school and was unemployed. In the prior year, he was employed for 2 months on a part-time basis for a local apartment complex performing custodial duties. Other jobs included a 1-week stint in house construction, from which he was fired for not showing up for work. He became isolative and has few friends or hobbies. He spends most of his time in the attic listening to music and chanting.

Assessment

After admission to the inpatient unit, Bill was administered an injection of Haldol and Ativan to reduce his agitation and psychosis. He was interviewed 2 days later and was informed of the purpose of the assessment. Testing consisted of diagnostic, symptom, and neuropsychological measures.

On a structured diagnostic interview (SCID), he endorsed several psychotic symptoms, including auditory hallucinations, persecutory delusions, and disorganized speech (e.g., tangential, loose). The belief that he was the target of a conspiracy was held with 100% conviction, and he rejected alternative explanations provided by the examiner. He did not display any bizarre behaviors during the interview, but did become overly excitable when discussing governmental plots. At other times, he was uninterested and apathetic. His affect was constricted (e.g., showed mild expressions). He expressed no goals, either short term or long term, other than just to "hang out." He denied the presence of depression, mania, or hypomania. He reported being nervous around others, but he stated that he must be on the alert for governmental agents who are always present and watching. He reported drinking about 3 to 4 beers on the weekend, but has not suffered any negative consequences. His marijuana use is episodic and inconsistent. He denied the use of amphetamines, cocaine, crack, LSD, and PCP. On a measure of symptom severity (Brief Psychiatric Rating Scale; BPRS), he endorsed items reflecting suspiciousness, hostility, thought insertion, and hallucinations. His BRPS score indicated moderate to severe levels of psychopathology.

On the Wechsler Adult Intelligence Scales III (WAIS-III), Bill obtained a Full-Scale Intelligence Quotient in the extremely low to borderline range (95%, confidence interval 62–70). His verbal and performance scores were in the borderline to low average (70–80) and extremely low ranges (55–68), respectively. In general, verbal abilities were significantly higher than performance. On the WAIS-III factor scores, he showed his lowest scores on tasks of processing speed and perceptual organization, while tasks of verbal and working memory were higher. On a test of attentional span, he correctly repeated 5 digits forward and 4 backward, which was in the low average range (age corrected SS = 5). On the Wechsler Memory Scale—Third Edition (WMS-III) (memory functioning), his ability to learn and encode new information was impaired (immediate memory index 60–76), but his ability to recall this material after a delay was improved (general memory index 75–91). His memory was further enhanced with cuing (auditory recognition memory 82–104). On a measure of abstraction and problem solving (Wisconsin Card Sorting Test), his overall performance was suggestive of mild impairment ($t = 41$). He completed a total of 3 categories (less than 5% out of 6 total) and made a total of 84 correct responses with 44 errors; 28 were perseverative errors and 16 were nonperseverative. On a measure of psychomotor processing, sequencing, and mental flexibility (Trail Making Test) he was slow, made several errors, and compared to others performed in the severe range of impairment for part A ($t = 16$) and in the moderate-severe range on part B ($t = 29$). Verbal (CFL Test [Word Fluency] test) and figural (Ruff Figural Fluency Test) fluency were also impaired. On measures of face (Benton Test of Facial Recognition) and visual (Judgment of Line Orientation) perception he showed scores in the normal range.

Additional information about Bill and the course and onset of his illness was obtained from his mother. She noted that for the past 2 years he had become

(continued)

more isolative and secretive. She felt that this behavior was normal, and he just needed his privacy. His grades in school declined (from B's to D's), and he started becoming interested in religion and the spirit world. She became more concerned when he stayed in his attic for 2 days listening to music and talking to himself following the loss of his job at the apartment complex. There is a family history on his mother's side of Schizophrenia (grandmother) and Bipolar Disorder (uncle). His birth was normal, and she could not recall any specific problems related to his delivery.

Case Conceptualization

Because this is Bill's first contact with the mental health system, he was considered a first episode patient. Many families are unsure of what is happening during the prepsychotic and prodromal phase of Schizophrenia and often wait to see if things improve. His mother's reaction is not unusual in this case. For Bill, there appears to be a period of gradually increasing symptoms, which may have been exacerbated by his being fired from his part-time job. Using the SCID, he does meet the *DSM-IV* criteria for Schizophrenia based on observable and clear evidence of hallucinations, delusions, disorganized speech, and negative symptoms. Although he did not appear disorganized in the interview, there is evidence from his family and at admission to support this aspect of the diagnostic criteria. The most prominent features in Bill's case are the presence of delusions and hallucinations; although there is some disorganization, this is not the most prominent feature of his illness. Thus, a diagnosis of Schizophrenia, paranoid type would be appropriate in this case.

In diagnosing Schizophrenia, especially in first episode patients, it is important to obtain a good time line regarding the onset and progression of symptoms. Bill's mother provided important additional information about his illness that could not be obtained reliably from Bill. Because the combination of prodromal and active symptoms were present for at least 6 months, the diagnosis of Schizophrenia and not Schizophreniform Disorder was appropriate. In terms of differential diagnoses, it is important to rule out mood disorders such as depression and bipolar conditions. The agitation observed in Schizophrenia can be confused with mania. However, absence of mania and depressive episodes are key in ruling out these conditions. It is also not uncommon for these individuals to have co-occurring substance use problems. In this case, use of alcohol and marijuana are present, but nonproblematic. It is important to obtain information about the relationship between symptoms and substance use to determine if a substance-induced condition is present. Finally, a baseline cognitive assessment was important to monitor his cognitive functioning over time and assist in treatment decisions. Problems in processing speed, memory, and executive functioning are all commonly found in Schizophrenia and may reflect the underlying pathophysiology of the disease.

Course of Treatment and Assessment of Progress

After his condition was stabilized, Bill was treated with an atypical antipsychotic medication (Zyprexa) over the course of a 2-week period at the hospital. To measure progress, the BPRS was administered each week and showed a gradual decline in symptom severity over time. He attended several psychotherapy groups during his treatment, which included groups on symptom management and coping skills, medication management, and relapse prevention. Social skills training or behavioral family therapy was not used in this case, as his stay was too brief for this type of intervention. However, these interventions could be part of his outpatient treatment program. He was provided case management services at the hospital and referred to a local community-based mental health center for follow-up outpatient treatment. He was discharged back to his home and verbalized an intention to "get better."

Complicating Factors

There are several complicating factors involved in Bill's case. First, the nature of his cognitive deficits may lead to difficulties in complying with and understanding his treatment program. Second, because this is his first admission, noncompliance needs to be addressed to ensure an optimal treatment response. Third, he has no transportation and his mother works during the day, which may lead to difficulties attending therapy and treatment appointments. Fourth, Bill is mistrustful of others, which can make establishing rapport with him difficult.

Managed Care Considerations

There were no managed care considerations in Bill's case.

Follow-Up

Bill attended the first 2 outpatient therapy appointments following hospitalization and verbalized taking his medications as prescribed. Unfortunately, he was switched to a different medication shortly thereafter and stopped taking his medications altogether after about 2 months. He doubted the need for the medication treatment and reported that it made him "tired all of the time." Cognitive-behavioral therapy for psychosis was begun, but he was passive and did not engage with the therapist. He was also enrolled in a vocational rehabilitation and supportive employment program, but he failed to attend the training sessions regularly. Bill was followed over the course of 1 year; due to his noncompliance with treatment he had 2 subsequent inpatient hospitalizations. Follow-up neuropsychological assessment at 1 year showed no significant improvements or decreases in his cognitive functioning. Bill exhibited a pattern of acute symptom exacerbations brought on by noncompliance and increased stress, which was followed by hospitalization. Once stable, he was released back home, where he began the cycle again. At the time of this writing, he had been court-committed to outpatient treatment, but medication compliance has remained a challenge.

TREATMENT IMPLICATIONS OF THE CASE

According to current practice guidelines, the first line of treatment for Schizophrenia is use of atypical antipsychotic medications. Atypical antipsychotics offer a more tolerable side effect profile than traditional medications with similar efficacy in reducing psychotic symptoms. For first-episode patients, the earlier treatment is initiated, the better the clinical response and long-term outcome. Although his clinical symptoms improved in the hospital, Bill's psychosocial and community functioning remained poor. Addressing his noncompliance should be the first target of treatment as it has been linked to more frequent relapse and hospitalization. Once he is stabilized, a variety of psychotherapies could be offered that may lead to further improvement: CBT for psychosis, SST, and/or BFT could provide important coping and symptom management skills. He was initially offered these types of therapies, but may have been too symptomatic to benefit from them. Attention to building rapport and increasing motivation for treatment should be part of any therapeutic relationship. If his substance use increases to problematic levels, a referral to programs specializing in co-occurring disorders (integrated treatment for Schizophrenia and substance abuse/dependence) may be useful. Reducing his cannabis use may help to prevent symptom exacerbations as well. Depending on his level of need, it may be useful to consider placement in an assertive community treatment program if he shows a pattern of repeated hospitalizations and noncompliance.

SUMMARY

Schizophrenia is a chronic psychiatric condition characterized by positive symptoms (hallucinations, delusions), negative symptoms (social withdrawal, apathy), and impairments in cognitive (executive functioning, memory) social-cognitive (emotion perception, theory of mind, attributions), and social (social skills, competence) functioning. Schizophrenia affects about 1% of the general population; about 2.2 million persons have the disorder in the United States. There is no consensus on the etiology of Schizophrenia, but there appear to be biological and environmental factors involved in the development, course, and outcome of the disorder. In terms of biological factors, genetics, brain and neurochemical impairments, and prenatal infections have received the most attention. Environmental stressors, expressed emotion, and delivery complications can either precipitate the onset of the illness or lead to greater relapse rates. The diagnosis of Schizophrenia is facilitated by clear and observable diagnostic criteria and is often made in conjunction with a structured interview. However, the overlap with mood and substance abuse conditions poses particular challenges in the differential diagnosis of Schizophrenia. The assessment of Schizophrenia is not complete without an examination of social skills, cognitive functioning, and social and community functioning.

In terms of treatment, antipsychotic medications are considered the first line of treatment and show efficacy in reducing symptoms, especially positive symptoms. However, adherence rates to medications are low, even with the widespread use of newer atypical medications. Psychosocial treatments such as SST, BFT, and CBT may lead to further improvement in functioning or in residual symptoms that do not respond to medication therapy. As with most disorders, the combination of medication and psychosocial treatments leads to the best outcome. As part of the development and refinement of treatments, attention to how diversity and culture impact the diagnosis, treatment, and outcome for Schizophrenia is needed. The focus on developing new treatments and emphasis on collaboration between the patient, family, and treatment professionals has provided a renewed sense of recovery for those persons with the condition.

REFERENCES

Abi-Dargham, A., & Moore, H. (2003). Prefrontal DA transmission at D1 receptors and the pathology of schizophrenia. *Neuroscientist, 9,* 404–416.

Adams, G. L., Dworkin, R. J., & Rosenberg, S. D. (1984). Diagnosis and pharmacotherapy issues in the care of Hispanics in the public sector. *American Journal of Psychiatry, 141,* 970–974.

Adler, C. M., Goldberg, T. E., Malhotra, A. K., Pickar, D., & Breier, A. (1998). Effects of ketamine on thought disorder, working memory, and semantics in healthy volunteers. *Biological Psychiatry, 43,* 811–816.

Aghajanian, G. K., & Marek, G. J. (2000). Serotonin model of schizophrenia: Emerging role of glutamate mechanisms. *Brain Research: Brain Research Reviews, 31*(2/3), 302–312.

Allyon, T., & Haughton, E. (1964). Modification of symptomatic verbal behavior of mental patients. *Behavior Research and Therapy, 2,* 87–97.

Amador, X. F., & David, A. (2004). *Insight and psychosis: Awareness of illness in schizophrenia and related disorders.* New York: Oxford University Press.

Amador, X. F., Kirkpatrick, B., Buchanan, R. W., Carpenter, W. T., Marcinko, L., & Yale, S. A. (1999). Stability of the diagnosis of deficit syndrome in schizophrenia. *American Journal of Psychiatry, 156,* 637–639.

American Psychiatric Association. (2000). *Diagnostic and statistical manual of mental disorders* (4th ed., text rev.). Washington, DC: Author.

American Psychiatric Association. (2004). *Practice guideline for the treatment of patients with schizophrenia* (2nd ed.). Washington, DC: Author.

Amminger, G. P., Pape, S., Rock, D., Roberts, S. A., Ott, S. L., Squires-Wheeler, E., et al. (1999). Relationship between childhood behavioral disturbance and later schizophrenia in the New York High-Risk Project. *American Journal of Psychiatry, 156,* 525–530.

Andreasen, N. C. (1982). Negative symptoms in schizophrenia: Definition and reliability. *Archives of General Psychiatry, 39,* 784–788.

Andreasen, N. C., Carpenter, W. T., Kane, J. M., Lasser, R. A., Marder, S. R., & Weinberger, D. R. (2005). Remission in schizophrenia: Proposed criteria and rational for consensus. *American Journal of Psychiatry, 162,* 441–449.

Andreasen, N. C., & Olsen, S. (1982). Negative versus positive schizophrenia: Definition and validation. *Archives of General Psychiatry, 39,* 784–788.

Andreasson, S., Allebeck, P., Engstrom, A., & Rydberg, U. (1987). Cannabis and schizophrenia. *Lancet, 2,* 1483–1486.

Appelbaum, P. S., Robbins, P. C., & Roth, L. H. (1999). Dimensional approach to delusions: Comparison across types and diagnoses. *American Journal of Psychiatry, 156,* 1938–1943.

Appleby, L., Dyson, V., Altman, E., & Luchins, D. (1997). Assessing substance use in multiproblem patients: Reliability and validity of the Addiction Severity Index in a mental hospital population. *Journal of Nervous and Mental Diseases, 185,* 159–165.

Arango, C., Kirkpatrick, B., & Buchanan, R. W. (2000). Neurological signs and the heterogeneity of schizophrenia. *American Journal of Psychiatry, 157,* 560–565.

Arendt, M., Rosenberg, R., Foldager, L., & Perto, G. (2005). Cannabis-induced psychosis and subsequent schizophrenia-spectrum disorders: Follow-up study of 535 incident cases. *British Journal of Psychiatry, 187,* 510–515.

Arnold, S. E., Ruscheinsky, D. D., & Han, L. Y. (1997). Further evidence of abnormal cytoarchitecture of the entorhinal cortex in schizophrenia using spatial point pattern analyses. *Biological Psychiatry, 42,* 639–647.

Aro, S., Aro, H., & Keskimaki, I. (1995). Socio-economic mobility among patients with schizophrenia or major affective disorder: A 17-year retrospective follow-up. *British Journal of Psychiatry, 166,* 759–767.

Asarnow, R. F., Nuechterlein, K. H., Subotnik, K. L., Fogelson, D., Torquato, R., Payne, D., et al. (2002). Neurocognitive impairments in non-psychotic parents of children with schizophrenia and attention deficit hyperactivity disorder: The UCLA family study. *Archives of General Psychiatry, 59*, 1053–1060.

Azrin, N. H., & Teichner, G. (1998). Evaluation of an instructional program for improving medication compliance for chronically mentally ill outpatients. *Behavior Research and Therapy, 36*, 849–861.

Bae, S., Brekke, J. S., & Bola, J. R. (2004). Ethnicity and treatment outcome variation in schizophrenia: A longitudinal study of community-based psychosocial rehabilitation interventions. *Journal of Nervous and Mental Diseases, 192*(9), 623–628.

Barnes, T. R., Mutsatsa, S. H., Hutton, S. B., Watt, H. C., & Joyce, E. M. (2006). Comorbid substance use and age at onset of schizophrenia. *British Journal of Psychiatry, 188*, 237–242.

Bartels, S. J., Mueser, K. T., & Miles, K. M. (1998). Schizophrenia. In M. Hersen & V. B. Van Hasselt (Eds.), *Handbook of clinical geropsychology* (pp. 173–194). New York: Plenum Press.

Bateson, G., Jackson, D. D., Haley, J., & Weakland, J. (1956). Toward a theory of schizophrenia. *Behavioral Science, 1*, 251–264.

Baucom, D. H., Shoham, V., Mueser, K. T., Daiuto, A. D., & Stickle, T. R. (1998). Empirically supported couple and family interventions for marital distress and adult mental health problems. *Journal of Consulting and Clinical Psychology, 66*, 53–88.

Baum, K. M., & Walker, E. F. (1995). Childhood behavioral precursors of adult symptom dimensions in schizophrenia. *Schizophrenia Research, 16*, 111–120.

Bellack, A. S. (2006). Scientific and consumer models of recovery in schizophrenia: Concordance, contrasts, and implications. *Schizophrenia Bulletin, 32*, 432–442.

Bellack, A. S., Morrison, R. L., Wixted, J. T., & Mueser, K. T. (1990). An analysis of social competence in schizophrenia. *British Journal of Psychiatry, 156*, 809–818.

Bellack, A. S., Mueser, K. T., Gingerich, S., & Agresta, J. (2004). *Social skills training for schizophrenia: A step-by-step guide* (2nd ed.). New York: Guilford Press.

Bellack, A. S., Mueser, K. T., Wade, J. H., Sayers, S. L., & Morrison, R. L. (1992). The ability of schizophrenics to perceive and cope with negative affect. *British Journal of Psychiatry, 160*, 473–480.

Bellack, A. S., Sayers, M., Mueser, K. T., & Bennett, M. (1994). An evaluation of social problem solving in schizophrenia. *Journal of Abnormal Psychology, 103*, 371–378.

Bellack, A. S., Schooler, N., & Marder, S. R. (2004). Do Clozapine and risperidone affect social competence and problem solving? *American Journal of Psychiatry, 161*, 364–367.

Bellack, A. S., & Thomas-Lohrman, S. (2003). *Maryland Assessment of Social Competence.* Unpublished assessment manual, Baltimore.

Bentall, R. P., Corcoran, R., Howard, R., Blackwood, N., & Kinderman, P. (2001). Persecutory delusions: A review and theoretical integration. *Clinical Psychology Review, 21*, 1143–1192.

Bentall, R. P., Haddock, G., & Slade, P. D. (1994). Cognitive behavior therapy for persistent auditory hallucinations. *Behavior Therapy, 25*, 51–66.

Bersani, G., Orlandi, V., Kotzalidis, G. D., & Pancheri, P. (2002). Cannabis and schizophrenia: Impact on onset, course, psychopathology and outcomes. *European Archives of Psychiatry and Clinical Neuroscience, 252*(2), 86–92.

Birchwood, M., Smith, J., Cochrane, R., Wetton, S., & Copstake, S. (1990). The Social Functioning Scale: The development and validation of a new scale of social adjustment for the use in family intervention programmes with schizophrenic patients. *British Journal of Psychiatry, 157*, 853–859.

Blanchard, J. J., & Cohen, A. S. (2006). The structure of negative symptoms within schizophrenia: Implications for assessment. *Schizophrenia Bulletin, 32*, 238–245.

Bleuler, E. (1950). *Dementia praecox or the group of schizophrenias* (J. Zinkin, Trans.). New York: International Universities Press. (Original work published 1911).

Blyler, C. R. (2003). Understanding the employment rate of people with schizophrenia: Different approaches lead to different implications for policy. In M. F. Lenzenweger & J. M. Hooley (Eds.), *Principles of experimental psychopathology: Essays in honor of Brendan A. Maher* (pp. 107–115). Washington, DC: American Psychological Association.

Bond, G. R. (1998). Principles of the individual placement and support model: Empirical support. *Psychiatric Rehabilitation Journal, 22,* 11–23.

Boydell, J., van Os J., McKenzie, K., Allardyce, J., Goel, R., McCreadie, R. G., et al. (2001). Incidence of schizophrenia in ethnic minorities in London: Ecological study into interactions with environment. *British Medical Journal, 323,* 1336–1338.

Bracha, H. S., Wolkowitz, O. M., Lohr, J. B., Karson, C. N., & Bigelow, L. B. (1989). High prevalence of visual hallucinations in research subjects with chronic schizophrenia. *American Journal of Psychiatry, 146,* 526–528.

Breier, A. (2005). Developing drugs for cognitive impairment in schizophrenia. *Schizophrenia Bulletin, 31,* 816–822.

Brenner, H. D., Hodel, B., Roder, V., & Corrigan, P. W. (1992). Treatment of cognitive dysfunctions and behavioral deficits in schizophrenia. *Schizophrenia Bulletin,* 18, 21–26.

Breslau, N., Davis, G. C., Andreski, P., & Peterson, E. (1991). Traumatic events and posttraumatic stress disorder in an urban population of young adults. *Archives of General Psychiatry, 48,* 216–222.

Brewerton, T. D. (1994). Hyperreligiosity in psychotic disorders. *Journal of Nervous and Mental Diseases, 182,* 302–304.

Bromet, E. J., Naz, B., Fochtmann, L. J., Carlson, G. A., & Tanenberg-Karant, M. (2005). Long-term diagnostic stability and outcome in recent first-episode cohort studies of schizophrenia. *Schizophrenia Bulletin, 31,* 639–649.

Bruce, M. L., Takeuchi, D. T., & Leaf, P. J. (1991). Poverty and psychiatric status: Longitudinal evidence from the New Haven Epidemiologic Catchment Area study. *Archives of General Psychiatry, 48,* 470–474.

Brune, M. (2005). "Theory of mind" in schizophrenia: A review of the literature. *Schizophrenia Bulletin, 31,* 21–42.

Bryant, N. L., Buchanan, R. W., Vladar, K., Brier, A., & Rothman, M. (1999). Gender differences in temporal lobe structures of patients with schizophrenia: A volumetric study. *American Journal of Psychiatry, 156,* 603–609.

Buchanan, A. (1992). A 2-year prospective study of treatment compliance in patients with schizophrenia. *Psychological Medicine, 22,* 787–797.

Buchanan, R. W., Vladar, K., Barta, P. E., & Pearlson, G. D. (1998). Structural evaluation of the prefrontal cortex in schizophrenia. *American Journal of Psychiatry, 155,* 1049–1055.

Bustillo, J. R., Lauriello, J., Horan, W. P., & Keith, S. J. (2001). The psychosocial treatment of schizophrenia: An update. *American Journal of Psychiatry, 158,* 163–175.

Butzlaff, R. L., & Hooley, J. M. (1998). Expressed emotion and psychiatric relapse: A meta-analysis. *Archives of General Psychiatry, 55,* 547–552.

Byne, W., Buchsbaum, M. S., Mattiace, L. A., Hazlett, E. A., Kemether, E., Elhakem, S. L., et al. (2002). Postmortem assessment of thalamic nuclear volumes in subjects with schizophrenia. *American Journal of Psychiatry, 159,* 59–65.

Cahn, W., Pol, H. E., Lems, E. B., van Haren, N., Schnack, H. G., van der Linden, J. A., et al. (2002). Brain volume changes in first episode schizophrenia: A 1-year follow-up study. *Archives of General Psychiatry, 59,* 1002–1010.

Callicott, J. H., Mattay, V. S., Verchinski, B. A., Marenco, S., Egan, M. F., & Weinberger, D. R. (2003). Complexity of prefrontal cortical dysfunction in schizophrenia: More up or down? *American Journal of Psychiatry, 160,* 2209–2215.

Cannon, T. D., & Clarke, M. C. (2005). Risk for schizophrenia: Broadening the concepts, pushing back the boundaries. *Schizophrenia Research, 79,* 5–13.

Cantor-Graae, E., & Selten, J. P. (2005). Schizophrenia and migration: A meta-analysis and review. *American Journal of Psychiatry, 162,* 12–24.

Cardno, A., Marshall, E. J., Coid, B., Macdonald, A. M., Ribchester, T. R., Davies, N. J., et al. (1999). Heritability estimates for psychotic disorders: The Maudsley twin psychosis series. *Archives of General Psychiatry, 56,* 162–168.

Cascardi, M., Mueser, K. T., DeGirolomo, J., & Murrin, M. (1996). Physical aggression against psychiatric inpatients by family members and partners: A descriptive study. *Psychiatric Services, 47,* 531–533.

Caspi, A., Reichenberg, A., Weiser, M., Rabinowitz, J., Kaplan, Z., Knobler, H., et al. (2003). Cognitive performance in schizophrenia patients assessed before and following the first psychotic episode. *Schizophrenia Research, 65,* 87–94.

Castle, D. J., & Murray, R. M. (1991). Editorial: The neurodevelopmental basis of sex differences in schizophrenia. *Psychological Medicine, 21,* 565–575.

Chadwick, P., & Birchwood, M. (1995). The omnipotence of voices: Pt. II: The Beliefs about Voices Questionnaire. *British Journal of Psychiatry, 166,* 773–776.

Chadwick, P. D. J., & Lowe, C. F. (1990). Measurement and modification of delusional beliefs. *Journal of Consulting and Clinical Psychology, 58,* 225–232.

Chambless, D., & Ollendick, T. (2001). Empirically supported psychological interventions: Controversies and evidence. *Annual Review of Psychology, 52,* 685–671.

Cheung, F. K., & Snowden, L. R. (1990). Community mental health and ethnic minority populations. *Community Mental Health Journal, 26,* 277–289.

Clark, R., Anderson, N. B., Clark, V. R., & Williams, D. R. (1999). Racism as a stressor for African Americans. *American Psychologist, 54,* 805–816.

Cohen, C. I. (1990). Outcome of schizophrenia into later life: An overview. *Gerontologist, 30,* 790–797.

Cohen, M., & Klein, D. F. (1970). Drug abuse in a young psychiatric population. *American Journal of Orthopsychiatry, 40,* 448–455.

Comas-Diaz, L. (1981). Puerto Rican espiritismo and psychotherapy. *American Journal of Orthopsychiatry, 51,* 636–645.

Combs, D. R., Penn, D. L., Cassisi, J., Michael, C. O., Wood, T. D., Wanner, J., et al. (2006). Perceived racism as a predictor of paranoia among African Americans. *Journal of Black Psychology, 32*(1), 87–104.

Combs, D. R., Penn, D. L., & Fenigstein, A. (2002). Ethnic differences in sub-clinical paranoia: An expansion of norms of the paranoia scale. *Cultural Diversity and Ethnic Minority Psychology, 8,* 248–256.

Copolov, D. L., Mackinnon, A., & Trauer, T. (2004). Correlates of the affective impact of auditory hallucinations in psychotic disorders. *Schizophrenia Bulletin, 30,* 163–171.

Corrigan, P. W., Liberman, R. P., & Engle, J. D. (1990). From noncompliance to collaboration in the treatment of schizophrenia. *Hospital and Community Psychiatry, 41,* 1203–1211.

Corrigan, P. W., & Penn, D. L. (2001). *Social cognition and schizophrenia.* Washington, DC: APA Press.

Corse, S. J., Hirschinger, N. B., & Zanis, D. (1995). The use of the Addiction Severity Index with people with severe mental illness. *Psychiatric Rehabilitation Journal, 19,* 9–18.

Corty, E., Lehman, A. F., & Myers, C. P. (1993). Influence of psychoactive substance use on the reliability of psychiatric diagnosis. *Journal of Consulting and Clinical Psychology, 61,* 165–170.

Coyle, J. T. (1996). The glutamatergic dysfunction hypothesis for schizophrenia. *Harvard Review of Psychiatry, 3,* 241–253.

Craddock, N., O'Donovan, M. C., & Owen, M. J. (2006). Genes for schizophrenia and bipolar disorder? Implications for psychiatric nosology. *Schizophrenia Bulletin, 32,* 9–16.

Craine, L. S., Henson, C. E., Colliver, J. A., & MacLean, D. G. (1988). Prevalence of a history of sexual abuse among female psychiatric patients in a state hospital system. *Hospital and Community Psychiatry, 39,* 300–304.

Crespo-Facorro, B., Kim, J.-J., Chemerinski, E., Magnotta, V., Andreasen, N. C., & Nopoulos, P. (2004). Morphometry of the superior temporal plane in schizophrenia: Relationship to clinical correlates. *Journal of Neuropsychiatry and Clinical Neuroscience, 16,* 284–294.

Crowley, T. J., Chesluk, D., Dilts, S., & Hart, R. (1974). Drug and alcohol abuse among psychiatric admissions. *Archives of General Psychiatry, 30,* 13–20.

Cuffel, B. J., & Chase, P. (1994). Remission and relapse of substance use disorders in schizophrenia: Results from a 1-year prospective study. *Journal of Nervous and Mental Diseases, 182,* 342–348.

Cutting, J. (1995). Descriptive psychopathology. In S. R. Hirsch & D. R. Weinberger (Eds.), *Schizophrenia* (pp. 15–27). Cambridge: Cambridge University Press.

Davidson, L., Stayner, D., & Haglund, K. E. (1998). Phenomenological perspectives on the social functioning of people with schizophrenia. In K. T. Mueser & N. Tarrier (Eds.), *Handbook of social functioning in schizophrenia* (pp. 97–120). Boston: Allyn & Bacon.

DeLisi, E., Sakuma, M., Maurizio, A. M., Relja, M., & Hoff, A. L., (2004). Cerebral ventricular change over the first 10 years after the onset of schizophrenia. *Psychiatry Research: Neuroimaging, 130*(10), 57–70.

DeRubeis, R. J., & Crits-Christoph, P. (1998). Empirically supported individual and group psychological treatments for adult mental disorders. *Journal of Consulting and Clinical Psychology, 66,* 37–52.

DeSisto, M. J., Harding, C. M., McCormick, R. V., Ashikaga, T., & Brooks, G. W. (1995). The Maine and Vermont 3-decade studies of serious mental illness: Pt. I. Matched comparison of cross-sectional outcome. *British Journal of Psychiatry, 167,* 331–342.

Dickerson, F. B. (2000). Cognitive behavioral psychotherapy for schizophrenia: A review of recent empirical studies. *Schizophrenia Research, 16,* 71–90.

Dickerson, F. B., Origoni, A. E., Pater, A., Friedman, B. K., & Kordonski, W. M. (2003). An expanded version of the Multnomah Community Ability Scale: Anchors and interview probes for the assessment of adults with serious mental illness. *Community Mental Health, 39,* 131–137.

Dickerson, F. B., Tenhula, W. N., & Green-Paden, L. D. (2004). The token economy of schizophrenia: Review of the literature and recommendations for future research. *Schizophrenia Research, 75,* 405–416.

Dohrenwend, B. R., Levav, I., Shrout, P. E., Schwartz, S., Naveh, G., Link, B. G., et al. (1992). Socioeconomic status and psychiatric disorders: The causation-selection issue. *Science, 255,* 946–952.

Dolder, C. R., Lacro, J. P., Dunn, L. B., & Jeste, D. V. (2002). Antipsychotic medication adherence: Is there a difference between typical and atypical agents? *American Journal of Psychiatry, 159,* 103–108.

Dolder, C. R., Lacro, J. P., Leckband, S., Jeste, D. V. (2003). Interventions to improve antipsychotic medication adherence: Review of recent literature. *Journal of Clinical Psychopharmacology, 23*(4), 389–399.

Douglas, M. S., & Mueser, K. T. (1990). Teaching conflict resolution skills to the chronically mentally ill: Social skills training groups for briefly hospitalized patients. *Behavior Modification,*
14, 519–547.

Drake, R. E., & Becker, D. R. (1996). The individual placement and support model of supported
employment. *Psychiatric Services, 47,* 473–475.

Drake, R. E., Gates, C., Whitaker, A., & Cotton, P. G. (1985). Suicide among schizophrenics: A
review. *Comprehensive Psychiatry, 26,* 90–100.

Drake, R. E., Mercer-McFadden, C., Mueser, K. T., McHugo, G. J., & Bond, G. R. (1998). Review
of integrated mental health and substance abuse treatment for patients with dual disorders.
Schizophrenia Bulletin, 24, 589–608.

Drake, R. E., Osher, F. C., Noordsy, D. L., Hurlbut, S. C., Teague, G. B., & Beaudett, M.
S. (1990). Diagnosis of alcohol use disorders in schizophrenia. *Schizophrenia Bulletin, 16,*
57–67.

Drake, R. E., Rosenberg, S. D., & Mueser, K. T. (1996). Assessment of substance use disorder in
persons with severe mental illness. In R. E. Drake & K. T. Mueser (Eds.), *Dual diagnosis of*
major mental illness and substance abuse disorder: Pt. II. Recent research and clinical implications.
New Directions in Mental Health Services (Vol. 70, pp. 3–17). San Francisco: Jossey-Bass.

Duncan, G. E., Sheitman, B. B., & Lieberman, J. A. (1999). An integrated view of pathophysiological models of schizophrenia. *Brain Research Reviews, 29,* 250–264.

Eaton, W. W. (1975). Marital status and schizophrenia. *Acta Psychiatrica Scandinavica, 52,* 320–329.

Eaton, W. W., & Chen, C. (2006). Epidemiology. In J. A. Lieberman, T. S. Stroup, & D. O. Perkins
(Eds.), *Textbook of schizophrenia* (pp. 17–38). Arlington, VA: APA Press.

Edwards, J., Jackson, H. J., & Pattison, P. E. (2002). Emotion recognition via facial expression
and affective prosody in schizophrenia: A methodological review. *Clinical Psychology Review,*
22, 789–832.

Erlenmeyer-Kimling, L., Rock, D., Roberts, S. A., Janal, M., Kestenbaum, C., Cornblatt, B., et al.
(2000). Attention, memory, and motor skills as childhood predictors of schizophrenia-related
psychoses: The New York High-Risk Project. *American Journal of Psychiatry, 157,* 1416–1422.

Estroff, S. E. (1989). Self, identity, and subjective experiences of schizophrenia: In search of the
subject. *Schizophrenia Bulletin, 15,* 189–196.

Evans, J. D., Paulsen, J. S., Harris, M. J., Heaton, R. K., & Jeste, D. V. (1996). A clinical and
neuropsychological comparison of delusional disorder and schizophrenia. *Journal of Neu-*
ropsychiatry and Clinical Neurosciences, 8, 281–286.

Faraone, S. V., & Tsuang, M. T. (1985). Quantitative models of the genetic transmission of
schizophrenia. *Psychological Bulletin, 98,* 41–66.

Fenton, W. S., Blyler, C. R., & Heinssen, R. K. (1997). Determinants of medication compliance
in schizophrenia: Empirical and clinical findings. *Schizophrenia Bulletin, 23,* 637–651.

Fink, P. J., & Tasman, A. (Eds.). (1992). *Stigma and mental illness.* Washington, DC: American
Psychiatric Press.

First, M. B., Spitzer, R. L., Gibbon, M., & Williams, J. B. W. (1996). *Structured Clinical Interview for*
Axes I and II DSM-IV Disorders—Patient edition (SCID-I/P). New York: Biometrics Research
Department, New York State Psychiatric Institute.

Flaum, M., Arndt, S., & Andreasen, N. C. (1991). The reliability of "bizarre" delusions. *Compar-*
ative Psychiatry, 32, 59–65.

Flor-Henry, P. (1985). Schizophrenia: Sex differences. *Canadian Journal of Psychiatry, 30,* 319–322.

Fowler, H., Carr, V. J., Carter, N., & Lewin, T. J. (1998). Pattern of current and lifetime substance
use in schizophrenia. *Schizophrenia Bulletin, 24,* 443–455.

Fox, J. W. (1990). Social class, mental illness, and social mobility: The social selection-drift
hypothesis for serious mental illness. *Journal of Health and Social Behavior, 31,* 344–353.

Freeman, D., Garety, P. A., Kuipers, E., Fowler, D., & Bebbington, P. E. (2002). A cognitive model of persecutory delusions. *British Journal of Clinical Psychology, 41*, 331–347.

Frith, C. D., Friston, K. J., Herold, S., Fletcher, P., Cahil, C., Dolan, R. J., et al. (1995). Regional brain activity in chronic schizophrenic patients during the performance of a verbal fluency task. *British Journal of Psychiatry, 167*, 343–349.

Fromm-Reichmann F. (1950). *Principles of intensive psychotherapy.* Chicago: University of Chicago Press.

Fuller, R., Nopoulos, P., Arndt, S., O'Leary, D., Ho, B., & Andreasen, N. C. (2002). Longitudinal assessment of premorbid cognitive functioning in patients with schizophrenia through examination of standardized scholastic test performance. *American Journal of Psychiatry, 159*, 1183–1189.

Garety, P. A., & Freeman, D. (1999). Cognitive approaches to delusions: A critical review of theories and evidence. *British Journal of Clinical Psychology, 38*, 113–154.

Gaudiano, B. A. (2005). Cognitive behavior therapies for psychotic disorders: Current empirical status and future directions. *Clinical Psychology: Science and Practice, 12*(1), 33–50.

Gilmer, T. P., Dolder, C. R., Lacro, J. P., Folsom, D. P., Lindamer, L., Garcia, P., et al. (2004). Adherence to treatment with antipsychotic medication and health care costs among Medicaid beneficiaries with schizophrenia. *American Journal of Psychiatry, 161*(1), 692–699.

Gilmore, J. H., & Murray, R. M. (2006). Prenatal and perinatal factors. In J. A. Lieberman, T. S. Stroup, & D. O. Perkins (Eds.), *Textbook of schizophrenia* (pp. 55–68). Arlington, VA: APA Press.

Glynn, S. M., Marder, S. R., Liberman, R. P., Blair, K., Wirshing, W. C., Wirshing, D. A., et al. (2002). Supplementing clinic-based skills training with manual-based community support sessions: Effects on social adjustment of patients with schizophrenia. *American Journal of Psychiatry, 159*, 829–837.

Goeree, R., Farahati, F., Burke, N., Blackhouse, G., O'Reilly, D., Pyne, J., et al. (2005). The economic burden of schizophrenia in Canada in 2004. *Current Medical Research and Opinion, 21*, 2017–2028.

Goldman, H. H. (1982). Mental illness and family burden: A public health perspective. *Hospital and Community Psychiatry, 33*, 557–560.

Goldner, E. M., Hsu, L., Waraich, P., & Somers, J. M. (2002). Prevalence and incidence studies of schizophrenic disorders: A systematic review of the literature. *Canadian Journal of Psychiatry, 47*, 833–843.

Goldstein, J. M. (1988). Gender differences in the course of schizophrenia. *American Journal of Psychiatry, 146*, 684–689.

Goldstein, J. M., Goodman, J. M., Seidman, L. J., Kennedy, D. N., Makris, N., Lee, H., et al. (1999). Cortical abnormalities in schizophrenia identified by structural magnetic resonance imaging. *Archives of General Psychiatry, 56*, 1165–1173.

Gomes-Schwartz, B. (1979). The modification of schizophrenic behavior. *Behavior Modification, 3*(4), 439–468.

Goodman, L. A., Dutton, M. A., & Harris, M. (1997). The relationship between violence dimensions and symptom severity among homeless, mentally ill women. *Journal of Traumatic Stress, 10*, 51–70.

Gottesman, I. I. (1991). *Schizophrenia genesis: The origins of madness.* New York: Freeman.

Gottesman, I. I. (2001). Psychopathology through a life span–genetic prism. *American Psychologist, 56*, 867–878.

Greden, J. F., & Tandon, R. (Eds.). (1991). *Negative schizophrenic symptoms: Pathophysiology and clinical implications.* Washington, DC: American Psychiatric Press.

Green, M. F. (1996). What are the functional consequences of neurocognitive deficits in schizophrenia? *American Journal of Psychiatry, 15,* 321–330.

Green, M. F., Kern, R. S., Braff, D. L., & Mintz, J. (2000). Neurocognitive deficits and functional outcome in schizophrenia: Are we measuring the "right stuff?" *Schizophrenia Bulletin, 26,* 119–136.

Green, M. F., Nuechterlein, K. H., Gold, J. M., Barch, D. M., Cohen, J., Essock, S., et al. (2004). Approaching a consensus battery for clinical trials in schizophrenia: The NIMH-MATRICS conference to select cognitive domains and test criteria. *Biological Psychiatry, 56,* 301–307.

Green, M. F., Olivier, B., Crawley, J. N., Penn, D. L., & Silverstein, S. (2005). Social cognition in schizophrenia: Recommendations from the measurement and treatment research to improve cognition in schizophrenia New Approaches Conference. *Schizophrenia Bulletin, 31,* 882–887.

Greenfield, S. F., Strakowski, S. M., Tohen, M., Batson, S. C., & Kolbrener, M. L. (1994). Childhood abuse in first-episode psychosis. *British Journal of Psychiatry, 164,* 831–834.

Grossman, L. S., Harrow, M., Rosen, C., & Faull, R. (2006). Sex differences in outcome and recovery for schizophrenia and other psychotic and nonpsychotic disorders. *Psychiatric Services, 57*(6), 844–850.

Gur, R. E., Cowell, P. E., Latshaw, A., Turetsky, B. I., Grossman, R. I., Arnold, S. E., et al. (2000). Reduced dorsal and orbital prefrontal gray matter volumes in schizophrenia. *Archives of General Psychiatry, 57,* 761–768.

Gur, R. E., Cowell, P., Turetsky, B. I., Gallacher, F., Cannon, T., Bilker, W., et al. (1998). A follow-up magnetic resonance imaging study of schizophrenia: Relationship of neuroanatomical changes to clinical and neurobehavioral measures. *Archives of General Psychiatry, 55,* 145–152.

Gutierrez-Maldonado, J., Caqueo-Urizar, A., & Kavanagh, D. J. (2005). Burden of care and general health in families of patients with schizophrenia. *Social Psychiatry and Psychiatric Epidemiology, 40,* 899–904.

Haas, G. L., & Garratt, L. S. (1998). Gender differences in social functioning. In K. T. Mueser & N. Tarrier (Eds.), *Handbook of social functioning in schizophrenia* (pp. 149–180). Boston: Allyn & Bacon.

Haddock, G., McCarron, J., Tarrier, N., & Faragher, E. B. (1999). Scales to measure dimensions of hallucinations and delusions: The Psychotic Symptom Rating Scales (PSYRATS). *Psychological Medicine, 29*(4), 879–89.

Haddock G., Tarrier, N., Spaulding, W., Yusupoff, L, Kinney, & C., McCarthy, E. (1998). Individual cognitive behavior therapy in the treatment of hallucinations and delusions. *Clinical Psychology Review, 18,* 821–838.

Häfner, H., an der Heiden, W., Behrens, S., Gattaz, W. F., Hambrecht, M., Löffler W., et al. (1998). Causes and consequences of the gender difference in age at onset of schizophrenia. *Schizophrenia Bulletin, 24,* 99–113.

Häfner, H., Maurer, K., Trendler, G., an der Heiden, W., & Schmidt, M. (2005). The early course of schizophrenia and depression. *European Archives of Psychiatry and Clinical Neuroscience, 255,* 167–173.

Häfner, H., Riecher-Rössler, A., an der Heiden, W., Maurer, K., Fätkenheuer, B., & Löffler, W. (1993). Generating and testing a causal explanation of the gender difference in age at first onset of schizophrenia. *Psychological Medicine, 23,* 925–940.

Halari, R., Kumari, V., Mehorotra, R., Wheeler, M., Hines, M., & Sharma, T. (2004). The relationship of sex hormones and cortisol with cognitive functioning in schizophrenia. *Journal of Pharmacology, 18,* 366–374.

Halford, W. K., Schweitzer, R. D., & Varghese, F. N. (1991). Effects of family environment on negative symptoms and quality of life on psychotic patients. *Hospital and Community Psychiatry, 42,* 1241–1247.

Hans, S. L., Auerbach, J. G., Asarnow, J. R., Styr, B., & Marcus, J. (2000). Social adjustment of adolescents at risk for schizophrenia: The Jerusalem Infant Development Study. *Journal of the American Academy of Child and Adolescent Psychiatry, 39*(11), 1406–1414.

Hans, S. L., Marcus, J., Henson, L., Auerbach, J. G., & Mirsky, A. F. (1992). Interpersonal behavior of children at risk for schizophrenia. *Psychiatry, 55,* 314–335.

Harding, C. M., Brooks, G. W., Ashikaga, T., Strauss, J. S., & Breier, A. (1987a). The Vermont Longitudinal Study of persons with severe mental illness: Pt. I. Methodology, study sample, and overall status 32 years later. *American Journal of Psychiatry, 144,* 718–726.

Harding, C. M., Brooks, G. W., Ashikaga, T., Strauss, J. S., & Breier, A. (1987b). The Vermont Longitudinal Study of persons with severe mental illness: Pt. II. Long-term outcome of subjects who retrospectively met DSM-III criteria for schizophrenia. *American Journal of Psychiatry, 144,* 727–735.

Harris, M. J., & Jeste, D. V. (1988). Late-onset schizophrenia: An overview. *Schizophrenia Bulletin, 14,* 39–45.

Harrison, P., & Lewis, D. (2001). Neuropathology in schizophrenia. In S. Hirsch & D. R. Weinberger (Eds.), *Schizophrenia* (pp. 310–325). Oxford: Blackwell Science.

Harrison, P. J., & Owen, M. J. (2003). Genes for schizophrenia: Recent findings and their pathophysiological implications. *Lancet, 361,* 417–419.

Harrow, M., Grossman, L. S., Jobe, T. H., & Herbener, E. S. (2005). Do patients with schizophrenia ever show periods of recovery? A 15-year multi-site follow-up study. *Schizophrenia Bulletin, 31,* 723–734.

Harvey, P. D., Bowie, C. R., & Loebel, A. (2006). Neuropsychological normalization with long-term atypical antipsychotic treatment: Results of a 6-month randomized, double-blind comparison of ziprasidone versus olanzapine. *Journal of Neuropsychiatry and Clinical Neurosciences, 18,* 54–63.

Harvey, P. D., Koren, D., Reichenberg, A., & Bowie, C. R. (2006). Negative symptoms and cognitive deficits: What is the nature of their relationship. *Schizophrenia Bulletin, 32,* 250–258.

Hatfield, A. B., & Lefley, H. P. (Eds.). (1987). *Families of the mentally ill: Coping and adaptation.* New York: Guilford Press.

Hatfield, A. B., & Lefley, H. P. (Eds.). (1993). *Surviving mental illness: Stress, coping, and adaptation.* New York: Guilford Press.

Haynes, S. (1986). Behavioral model of paranoid behaviors. *Behavior Therapy, 17,* 266–287.

Heaton, R. K., Gladsjo, J. A., Palmer, B. W., Kuck, J., Marcotte, T. D., & Jeste, D. V. (2001). Stability and course of neuropsychological deficits in schizophrenia. *Archives of General Psychiatry, 58,* 24–32.

Heinrichs, R. W. (2005). The primacy of cognition in schizophrenia. *American Psychologist, 60,* 229–242.

Heinrichs, R. W., & Zakzanis, K. K. (1998). Neurocognitive deficit in schizophrenia: A quantitative review of the evidence. *Neuropsychology, 12,* 426–445.

Heinssen, R. K., Liberman, R. P., & Kopelowicz, A. (2000). Psychosocial skills training for schizophrenia: Lessons from the laboratory. *Schizophrenia Bulletin, 26,* 21–46.

Hiday, V. A., Swartz, M. S., Swanson, J. W., Borum, R., & Wagner, H. R. (1999). Criminal victimization of persons with severe mental illness. *Psychiatric Services, 50,* 62–68.

Hjern, A., Wicks, S., & Dalman, C., (2004). Social adversity contributes to high morbidity in psychoses in immigrants—a national cohort study in two generations of Swedish residents. *Psychological Medicine, 34,* 1025–1033.

Ho, B. C., Black, D. W., & Andreasen, N. C. (2003). Schizophrenia and other psychotic disorders. In R. E. Hales & S. C. Yudosfsky (Eds.), *Textbook of clinical psychiatry* (4th ed., pp. 379–438). Washington, DC: American Psychiatric Publishing.

Hogarty, G. E., Flesher, S., Urlich, R., Carter, M., Greenwald, D., Pogue-Geile, M., et al. (2004). Cognitive enhancement therapy in schizophrenia. *Archives of General Psychiatry, 61*, 866–876.

Hogarty, G. E., & Ulrich, R. F. (1998). The limitations of antipsychotic medications on schizophrenia relapse and adjustment and the contribution of psychosocial treatment. *Journal of Psychiatric Research, 32*(3/4), 243–250.

Hopper, K., Nathan, S., & Wanderling, J. (2000). Revisiting the developed versus developing country distinction in course and outcome in schizophrenia: Results from ISoS, the WHO collaborative follow-up project. *Schizophrenia Bulletin, 26*(4), 835–846.

Hough, R. L., Landsverk, J. A., Karno, M., Burnam, A., Timbers, D. M., Escobar, J. I., et al. (1987). Utilization of health and mental health services by Los Angeles Mexican Americans and non-Hispanic Whites. *Archives of General Psychiatry, 44*, 702–709.

Howard, R., Rabins, P. V., Seeman, M. V., & Jeste, D. V. (2000). Late-onset schizophrenia and very-late-onset schizophrenia-like psychosis: An international consensus. *American Journal of Psychiatry, 157*, 172–178.

Hu, T., Snowden, L. R., Jerrell, J. M., & Nguyen, T. D. (1991). Ethnic populations in public mental health: Services choices and level of use. *American Journal of Public Health, 81*, 1429–1434.

Huguelet, P., Mohr, S., Borras, L., Gillieron, C., & Brandt, P. (2006). Spirituality and religious practices among outpatients with schizophrenia and their clinicians. *Psychiatric Services, 57*(3), 366–372.

Hutchinson, G., & Haasen, C. (2004). Migration and schizophrenia. *Social Psychiatry and Psychiatric Epidemiology, 39*(5), 350–357.

Inskip, H. M., Harris, E. C., & Barraclough, B. (1998). Lifetime risk of suicide for affective disorder, alcoholism, and schizophrenia. *British Journal of Psychiatry, 172*, 35–37.

Jablensky, A. (2000). Epidemiology of schizophrenia: The global burden of disease and disability. *European Archives of Psychiatry and Clinical Neuroscience, 250*, 274–285.

Jablensky, A., McGrath, J., Herman, H., Castle, D., Gureje, O., Evans, M., et al. (2000). Psychotic disorders in urban areas: An overview of the study on low prevalence disorders. *Australian and New Zealand Journal of Psychiatry, 34*, 221–236.

Jablensky, A., Sartorius, N., Ernberg, G., Anker, M., Korten, A., & Cooper, J. E. (1992). Schizophrenia: Manifestations, incidence, and course in different cultures. A World Health Organization 10 country study. *Psychological Medical Monograph Supplement, 20*, 1–97.

Jacob, T. (1975). Family interaction in disturbed and normal families: A methodological and substantive review. *Psychological Bulletin, 82*, 33–65.

Jacobson, A., & Herald, C. (1990). The relevance of childhood sexual abuse to adult psychiatric inpatient care. *Hospital and Community Psychiatry, 41*, 154–158.

Jacobson, N., & Greenley, D. (2001). What is recovery? A conceptual model. *Psychiatric Services, 52*(4), 482–485.

Jimenez, J. M., Todman, M., Perez, M., Godoy, J. F., & Landon-Jimenez, D. V. (1996). The behavioral treatment of auditory hallucinatory responding of a schizophrenic patient. *Journal of Behavioral Therapy and Experimental Psychiatry, 27*, 299–310.

Jobe, T. H., & Harrow, M. (2005). Long-term outcome of patients with schizophrenia: A review. *Canadian Journal of Psychiatry, 50*, 892–900.

Jones, E. (1999). The phenomenology of abnormal belief. *Philosophy, Psychiatry, and Psychology, 6*, 1–16.

Junginger, J., Barker, S., & Coe, D. (1992). Mood theme and bizarreness of delusions in schizophrenia and mood psychosis. *Journal of Abnormal Psychology, 101*, 287–292.

Kane, J. M., & Marder, S. R. (1993). Psychopharmacologic treatment of schizophrenia. *Schizophrenia Bulletin, 19*, 287–302.

Kay, S. R., Fiszbein, A., & Opler, L. A. (1987). The Positive and Negative Syndrome Scale (PANSS) for schizophrenia. *Schizophrenia Bulletin, 13*, 261–276.

Keefe, R. S. E., Silva, S. G., Perkins, D. O., & Lieberman, J. A. (1999). The effects of atypical antipsychotic drugs on neurocognitive impairment in schizophrenia: A review and meta-analysis. *Schizophrenia Bulletin, 25*(2), 210–222.

Keith, S. J., Regier, D. A., & Rae, D. S. (1991). Schizophrenic disorders. In L. N. Robins & D. A. Regier (Eds.), *Psychiatric disorders in America: The Epidemiologic Catchment Area Study* (pp. 33–52). New York: Free Press.

Kelley, M. E., van Kammen, D. P., & Allen, D. N. (1999). Empirical validation of primary negative symptoms: Independence from effects of negative symptoms and psychosis. *American Journal of Psychiatry, 156*, 406–411.

Kemp, R., Hayward, P., Applewhaite, G., Everitt, B., & David, A. (1996). Compliance therapy in psychotic patients: Randomised controlled trial. *British Medical Journal, 312*, 345–349.

Kemp, R., Kirov, G., Everitt, B., Hayward, P., & David, A. (1998). Randomised controlled trial of compliance therapy: Eighteen-month follow-up. *British Journal of Psychiatry, 173*, 271–272.

Kendler, K. S. (1982). Demography of paranoid psychosis (delusional disorder): A review and comparison with schizophrenia and affective illness. *Archives of General Psychiatry, 39*, 890–902.

Kendler, K. S., & Diehl, S. R. (1993). The genetics of schizophrenia. *Schizophrenia Bulletin, 19*, 261–285.

Keshavan, M. S., Gilbert, A. R., & Diwadkar, V. A. (2006). Neurodevelopmental theories. In J. A. Lieberman, T. S. Stroup, & D. O. Perkins (Eds.), *Textbook of schizophrenia* (pp. 69–84). Washington, DC: American Psychiatric Publishing.

Kessler, R. C., Foster, C. L., Saunders, W. B., & Stang, P. E. (1995). Social consequences of psychiatric disorders: Pt. I. Educational attainment. *American Journal of Psychiatry, 152*, 1026–1032.

Kessler, R. C., Sonnega, A., Bromet, E., Hughes, M., & Nelson, C. B. (1995). Posttraumatic stress disorder in the national comorbidity survey. *Archives of General Psychiatry, 52*, 1048–1060.

Kingdon, D. G., & Turkington, D. (2005). *Cognitive therapy of schizophrenia.* New York: Guilford Press.

Kirkbride, J. B., Fearon, P., Morgan, C., Dazzan, P., Morgan, K., Tarrant, J., et al. (2006). Heterogeneity in incidence rates of schizophrenia and other psychotic syndromes: Findings from the 3-center/ESOP study. *Archives of General Psychiatry, 63*, 250–258.

Kirkpatrick, B., Buchanan, R. W., McKenney, P. D., Alphs, L. D., & Carpenter, W. T., Jr. (1989). The Schedule for the Deficit Syndrome: An instrument for research in schizophrenia. *Psychiatry Research, 30*, 119–123.

Kirkpatrick, B., Fenton, W. S., Carpenter, W. T., & Marder, S. R. (2006). The NIMH-MATRICS consensus statement on negative symptoms. *Schizophrenia Bulletin, 32*, 214–219.

Knapp, M., Mangalore, R., & Simon, J. (2004). The global costs of schizophrenia. *Schizophrenia Bulletin, 30*, 279–293.

Kraepelin, E. (1919). *Dementia praecox and paraphrenia* (R. M. Barclay, Trans.). New York: R. E. Krieger Publishing.

Kramer, M. S., Vogel, W. H., DiJohnson, C., Dewey, D. A., Sheves, P., Cavicchia, S., et al. (1989). Antidepressants in "depressed" schizophrenic inpatients. *Archives of General Psychiatry, 46*, 922–928.

Kranzler, H. R., Kadden, R. M., Burleson, J. A., Babor, T. F., Apter, A., & Rounsaville, B. J. (1995). Validity of psychiatric diagnoses in patients with substance use disorders: Is the interview more important than the interviewer? *Comprehensive Psychiatry, 36*, 278–288.

Kremen, W. S., Seidman, L. J., Faraone, S. V., Toomey, R., & Tsuang, M. T. (2000). The paradox of normal neuropsychological function in schizophrenia. *Journal of Abnormal Psychology, 109,* 743–752.

Kurtz, M. M., Moberg, P. J., Gur, R. C., & Gur, R. E. (2001). Approaches to cognitive remediation of neuropsychological deficits in schizophrenia: A review and meta-analysis. *Neuropsychology Review, 11*(4), 197–210.

Lahti, A. C., Koffel, B., LaPorte, D., & Tamminga, C. A. (1995). Subanesthetic doses of ketamine stimulate psychosis in schizophrenia. *Neuropsychopharmacology, 13,* 9–19.

Lamb, H. R., & Weinberger, L. E. (2005). The shift of psychiatric inpatient care from hospitals to jails and prisons. *Journal of the American Academy of Psychiatry and Law, 33,* 529–534.

Leff, J., & Vaughn, C. (1985). *Expressed emotion in families: Its significance for mental illness.* New York: Guilford Press.

Leff, S., Sartorious, N., Jablensky, A., Korten, A., & Emberg, G. (1992). The international pilot study of schizophrenia: Five-year follow-up findings. *Psychological Medicine, 22,* 131–145.

Lefley, H. P. (1990). Culture and chronic mental illness. *Hospital and Community Psychiatry, 41,* 277–286.

Lehman, A. F., Kreyenbuhl, J., Buchanan, R. W., Dickerson, F. B., Dixon, L. B., Goldberg, R., et al. (2004). The schizophrenia Patient Outcomes Research Team (PORT): Updated treatment recommendations 2003. *Schizophrenia Bulletin, 30*(2), 193–217.

Lehman, A. F., Myers, C. P., Dixon, L. B., & Johnson, J. L. (1994). Defining subgroups of dual diagnosis patients for service planning. *Hospital and Community Psychiatry, 45,* 556–561.

Lehman, A. F., Myers, C. P., Dixon, L. B., & Johnson, J. L. (1996). Detection of substance use disorders among psychiatric inpatients. *Journal of Nervous and Mental Diseases, 184,* 228–233.

Lenzenweger, M. F., & Dworkin, R. H. (1996). The dimensions of schizophrenia phenomenology: Not one or two, at least three, perhaps four. *British Journal of Psychiatry, 168,* 432–440.

Leung, A., & Chue, P. (2000). Sex differences in schizophrenia: A review of the literature. *Acta Psychiatrica Scandinavica, 401,* 3–38.

Levinson, D. F., & Levitt, M. M. (1987). Schizoaffective mania reconsidered. *American Journal of Psychiatry, 144,* 415–425.

Levinson, D. F., & Mowry, B. J. (1991). Defining the schizophrenia spectrum: Issues for genetic linkage studies. *Schizophrenia Bulletin, 17,* 491–514.

Lewis, C. M., Levinson, D. F., Wise, L. H., DeLisi, L. E., Straub, R. E., Hovatta, I., et al. (2003). Genome scan meta-analysis of schizophrenia and bipolar disorder: Pt. II. *American Journal of Human Genetics, 73,* 34–48.

Liberman, R. P. (1994). Treatment and rehabilitation of the seriously mentally ill in China: Impressions of a society in transition. *American Journal of Orthopsychiatry, 64,* 68–77.

Liberman, R. P., Mueser, K. T., Wallace, C. J., Jacobs, H. E., Eckman, T., & Massel, H. K. (1986). Training skills in the psychiatrically disabled: Learning coping and competence. *Schizophrenia Bulletin, 12,* 631–647.

Liddle, P. F. (1987). Schizophrenic syndromes, cognitive performance and neurological dysfunction. *Psychological Medicine, 17,* 49–57.

Lieberman, J. A., Kane, J. M., & Alvir, J. A. J. (1987). Provocative tests with psychostimulant drugs in schizophrenia. *Psychopharmacology, 91,* 415–433.

Lieberman, J. A., Stroup, T. S., McEvoy, J. P., Swartz, M. S., Rosenheck, R. A., Perkins, D. O., et al. (2005). Effectiveness of antipsychotic drugs in patients with chronic schizophrenia. *New England Journal of Medicine, 353*(12), 1209–1223.

Lin, K.-M., & Kleinman, A. M. (1988). Psychopathology and clinical course of schizophrenia: A cross-cultural perspective. *Schizophrenia Bulletin, 14,* 555–567.

Lincoln, C. V., & McGorry, P. (1995). Who cares? Pathways to psychiatric care for young people experiencing a first episode of psychosis. *Psychiatric Services, 46,* 1166–1171.

Lindenmayer, J. P., & Khan, A. (2006). Psychopathology. In J. A. Lieberman, T. S. Stroup, & D. O. Perkins (Eds.), *Textbook of schizophrenia* (pp. 187–222). Arlington, VA: APA Press.

Linszen, D. H., Dingemans, P. M., & Lenior, M. E. (1994). Cannabis use and the course of recent onset schizophrenic disorders. *Archives of General Psychiatry, 51,* 273–279.

Loeb, P. A. (1996). *ILS: Independent Living Scales manual.* San Antonio, TX: Psychological Corporation.

Magaña, A. B., Goldstein, M. J., Karno, M., Miklowitz, D. J., Jenkins, J., & Falloon, I. R. H. (1986). A brief method for assessing expressed emotion in relatives of psychiatric patients. *Psychiatry Research, 17,* 203–212.

Magliano, L., Fiorillo, A., Rosa, C., & Maj, M. (2006). Family burden and social network in schizophrenia versus physical diseases: Preliminary results from an Italian national study. *Acta Psychiatrica Scandinavica Supplementum, 426,* 60–63.

Maisto, S. A., Carey, M. P., Carey, K. B., Gordon, C. M., & Gleason, J. R. (2000). Use of the AUDIT and the DAST-10 to identify alcohol and drug use disorders among adults with a severe and persistent mental illness. *Psychological Assessment, 12,* 186–192.

Malhotra, A. K., Oinals, D. A., Adler, C. M., Elman, I., Clifton, A., Pickar, D., et al. (1997). Ketamine-induced exacerbation of psychotic symptoms and cognitive impairment in neuroleptic-free schizophrenics. *Neuropsychopharmacology, 17,* 141–150.

Malla, A. K., Norman, R. M. G., & Joober, R. (2005). First-episode psychosis, early intervention, and outcome: What haven't we learned? *Canadian Journal of Psychiatry, 50,* 881–891.

Malla, A. K., & Payne, J. (2005). First-episode psychosis: Psychopathology, quality of life, and functional outcome. *Schizophrenia Bulletin, 31,* 650–671.

Manschreck, T. C. (1996). Delusional disorder: The recognition and management of paranoia. *Journal of Clinical Psychiatry, 57,* 32–38.

Marder, S. R., Essock, S. M., Miller, A. L., Buchanan, R. W., Davis, J. M., Kane, J. M., et al. (2002). The Mount Sinai conference on the pharmacotherapy of schizophrenia. *Schizophrenia Bulletin, 28*(1), 5–16.

Marengo, J. (1994). Classifying the courses of schizophrenia. *Schizophrenia Bulletin, 20,* 519–536.

Marwaha, S., & Johnson, S. (2004). Schizophrenia and employment: A review. *Social Psychiatry and Psychiatric Epidemiology, 39,* 337–349.

Mathalon, D. H., Sullivan, E. V., Lim, K. O., & Pfefferbaum, A. (2001). Progressive brain volume changes and the clinical course of schizophrenia in men: A longitudinal magnetic resonance imaging study. *Archives of General Psychiatry, 58,* 148–157.

Mattes, J. A., & Nayak, D. (1984). Lithium versus fluphenazine for prophylaxis in mainly schizophrenic schizoaffectives. *Biological Psychiatry, 19,* 445–449.

McEvoy, J. P., Scheifler, P. L., & Francis, A. (1999). Expert consensus guideline series: Treatment of schizophrenia. *Journal of Clinical Psychiatry, 60*(Suppl. 11), 1–72.

McGlashan, T. H. (1996). Early detection and intervention in schizophrenia: Research. *Schizophrenia Bulletin, 22,* 327–345.

McGuffin, P., Owen, M. J., & Farmer, A. E. (1995). Genetic basis of schizophrenia. *Lancet, 346,* 678–682.

Mednick, S. A., Watson, J. B., Huttunen, M., Cannon, T. D., Katila, H., Machon, R., et al. (1998). A two-hit working model of the etiology of schizophrenia. In M. F. Lenzenweger & R. H. Dworkin (Eds.), *Origins and development of schizophrenia: Advances in experimental psychopathology* (pp. 27–66). Washington, DC: American Psychological Association.

Meltzer, H. Y., & McGurk, S. R. (1999). The effect of clozapine, risperidone, and olanzapine on cognitive function in schizophrenia. *Schizophrenia Bulletin, 25*(2), 233–255.

Miller, D. D. (1996). Schizophrenia: Its etiology and impact. *Pharmacotherapy, 16,* 2–5.

Miyamoto, S., LaMantia, A. S., Duncan, G. E., Sullivan, P., Gilmore, J. H., & Lieberman, A. (2003). Recent advances in the neurobiology of schizophrenia. *Molecular Interventions, 3,* 27–39.

Moos, R. H., & Moos, B. S. (1981). *Family Environment Scale manual.* Palo Alto, CA: Consulting Psychologists Press.

Morales-Dorta, J. (1976). *Puerto Rican espiritismo: Religion and psychotherapy.* New York: Vantage Press.

Moss, Q., Fleck, D. E., & Strakowski, S. M. (2006). The influence of religious affiliation on time to first treatment and hospitalization. *Schizophrenia Research, 84*(2/3), 421–426.

Mueser, K. T. (2000). Cognitive functioning, social adjustment and long-term outcome in schizophrenia. In T. Sharma & P. D. Harvey (Eds.), *Cognition in schizophrenia: Impairments, importance, and treatment strategies* (pp. 157–177). New York: Oxford University Press.

Mueser, K. T., & Bellack, A. S. (1998). Social skills and social functioning. In K. T. Mueser & N. Tarrier (Eds.), *Social functioning in schizophrenia* (pp. 79–96). Boston: Allyn & Bacon.

Mueser, K. T., Bellack, A. S., & Brady, E. U. (1990). Hallucinations in schizophrenia. *Acta Psychiatrica Scandinavica, 82,* 26–29.

Mueser, K. T., Bellack, A. S., Douglas, M. S., & Morrison, R. L. (1991). Prevalence and stability of social skill deficits in schizophrenia. *Schizophrenia Research, 5,* 167–176.

Mueser, K. T., Bellack, A. S., Douglas, M. S., & Wade, J. H. (1991). Prediction of social skill acquisition in schizophrenic and major affective disorder patients from memory and symptomatology. *Psychiatry Research, 37,* 281–296.

Mueser, K. T., Bellack, A. S., Morrison, R. L., & Wade, J. H. (1990). Gender, social competence, and symptomatology in schizophrenia: A longitudinal analysis. *Journal of Abnormal Psychology, 99,* 138–147.

Mueser, K. T., Bellack, A. S., Morrison, R. L., & Wixted, J. T. (1990). Social competence in schizophrenia: Premorbid adjustment, social skill, and domains of functioning. *Journal of Psychiatric Research, 24,* 51–63.

Mueser, K. T., Bellack, A. S., Wade, J. H., Sayers, S. L., Tierney, A., & Haas, G. (1993). Expressed emotion, social skill, and response to negative affect in schizophrenia. *Journal of Abnormal Psychology, 102,* 339–351.

Mueser, K. T., & Berenbaum, H. (1990). Psychodynamic treatment of schizophrenia: Is there a future? *Psychological Medicine, 20,* 253–262.

Mueser, K. T., Bond, G. R., Drake, R. E., & Resnick, S. G. (1998). Models of community care for severe mental illness: A review of research on case management. *Schizophrenia Bulletin, 24,* 37–74.

Mueser, K. T., Curran, P. J., & McHugo, G. J. (1997). Factor structure of the Brief Psychiatric Rating Scale in schizophrenia. *Psychological Assessment, 9,* 196–204.

Mueser, K. T., & Glynn, S. M. (1999). *Behavioral family therapy for psychiatric disorders* (2nd ed.). Oakland, CA: New Harbinger Publications.

Mueser, K. T., Levine, S., Bellack, A. S., Douglas, M. S., & Brady, E. U. (1990). Social skills training for acute psychiatric patients. *Hospital and Community Psychiatry, 41,* 1249–1251.

Mueser, K. T., & McGurk, S. R. (2004). Schizophrenia. *Lancet, 363,* 2063–2072.

Mueser, K. T., Rosenberg, S. D., Drake, R. E., Miles, K. M., Wolford, G., Vidaver, R., et al. (1999). Conduct disorder, antisocial personality disorder, and substance use disorders in schizophrenia and major affective disorders. *Journal of Studies on Alcohol, 60,* 278–284.

Mueser, K. T., Rosenberg, S. D., Goodman, L. A., & Trumbetta, S. L. (2002). Trauma, PTSD, and the course of schizophrenia: An interactive model. *Schizophrenia Research, 53,* 123–143.

Mueser, K. T., Salyers, M. P., & Mueser, P. R. (2001). A prospective analysis of work in schizophrenia. *Schizophrenia Bulletin, 27,* 281–296.

Mueser, K. T., Salyers, M. P., Rosenberg, S. D., Goodman, L. A., Essock, S. M., Osher, F. C., et al. (2004). Interpersonal trauma and posttraumatic stress disorder in patients with severe mental illness: Demographic, clinical, and health correlates. *Schizophrenia Bulletin, 30,* 45–57.

Munk-Jørgensen, P. (1987). First-admission rates and marital status of schizophrenics. *Acta Psychiatrica Scandinavica, 76,* 210–216.

Murray, C. J. L., & Lopez, A. D. (Eds.). (1996). *The global burden of disease and injury series: Vol. I. A comprehensive assessment of mortality and disability from diseases, injuries, and risk factors in 1990 and projected to 2020.* Cambridge, MA: Harvard University Press.

Narrow, W. E., Rae, D. S., Robins, L. N., & Regier, D. A. (2002). Revised prevalence estimates of mental disorders in the United States. *Archives of General Psychiatry, 59,* 115–123.

Nasrallah, H. A., & Smeltzer, D. J. (2003). *Contemporary diagnosis and management of the patient with schizophrenia.* Newtown, PA: Handbooks for Health Care.

Nicolson, R., & Rapoport, J. L. (1999). Childhood-onset schizophrenia: Rare but worth studying. *Biological Psychiatry, 46,* 1418–28.

Norman, R. M., Scholten, D. J., Malla, A. K., & Ballageer, T. (2005). Early signs in schizophrenia spectrum disorders. *Journal of Nervous and Mental Diseases, 193,* 17–23.

Oldridge, M. L., & Hughes, I. C. T. (1992). Psychological well-being in families with a member suffering from schizophrenia. *British Journal of Psychiatry, 161,* 249–251.

Olfson, M., Mechanic, D., Hansell, S., Boyer, C. A., Walkup, J., & Weiden, P. J. (2000). Predicting medication non-compliance after hospital discharge among patients with schizophrenia. *Psychiatric Services, 51*(2), 216–222.

Overall, J. E., & Gorham, D. R. (1962). The Brief Psychiatric Rating Scale. *Psychological Reports, 10,* 799–812.

Padgett, D. K., Patrick, C., Burns, B. J., & Schlesinger, H. J. (1994). Women and outpatient mental health services: Use by Black, Hispanic, and White women in a national insured population. *Journal of Mental Health Administration, 21,* 347–360.

Palmer, B. A., Pankratz, V. S., & Bostwick, J. M. (2005). The lifetime risk of suicide in schizophrenia: A reexamination. *Archives of General Psychiatry, 62,* 247–253.

Palmer, B. W., Heaton, R. K., Paulsen, J. S., Kuck, J., Braff, D., Harris, M. J., et al. (1997). Is it possible to be schizophrenic yet neuropsychologically normal? *Neuropsychology, 11,* 437–446.

Patterson, T. L., Goldman, S., McKibbin, C. L., Hughs, T., & Jeste, D. (2001). UCSD performance-based skills assessment: Development of a new measure of everyday functioning for severely mentally ill adults. *Schizophrenia Bulletin, 27,* 235–245.

Penn, D. L., Addington, J., & Pinkham A. (2006). Social cognitive impairments. In J. A. Lieberman, T. S. Stroup, & D. O. Perkins (Eds.), *Textbook of schizophrenia* (pp. 17–38). Arlington, VA: APA Press.

Penn, D. L., & Combs, D. R. (2000). Modification of affect perception deficits in schizophrenia. *Schizophrenia Research, 25,* 100–107.

Penn, D. L., Combs, D. R., & Mohamed, S. (2001). Social cognition and social functioning in schizophrenia. In P. W. Corrigan & D. L. Penn (Eds.), *Social cognition and schizophrenia* (pp. 97–122). Washington, DC: APA press.

Penn, D. L., Corrigan, P. W., Bentall, R. P., Racenstein, J. M., & Newman, L. (1997). Social cognition in schizophrenia. *Psychological Bulletin, 121,* 114–132.

Penn, D. L., & Mueser, K. T. (1996). Research update on the psychosocial treatment of schizophrenia. *American Journal of Psychiatry, 153,* 607–617.

Penn, D. L., Waldheter, E. J., Perkins, D. O., Mueser, K. T., & Lieberman, J. A. (2005). Psychosocial treatment for first-episode psychosis: A research update. *American Journal of Psychiatry, 162,* 2220–2232.

Perkins, D. O., Lieberman, J. A., & Lewis, S. (2006). First episode. In J. A. Lieberman, T. S. Stroup, & D. O. Perkins (Eds.), *Textbook of schizophrenia* (pp. 353–364). Arlington, VA: APA Press.

Peters, E., Day, S., McKenna, J., & Orbach, G. (1999). Delusional ideation in religious and psychotic populations. *British Journal of Clinical Psychology, 38*, 83–96.

Pilling, S., Bebbington, P., Kuipers, E., Garety, P., Geddes, J., Martindale, B., et al. (2002). Psychological treatments in schizophrenia: Pt. II. Meta-analyses of randomized controlled trials of social skills training and cognitive remediation. *Psychological Medicine, 32*(5), 782–791.

Pinkham, A., Penn, D., Perkins, D., & Lieberman, J. (2003). Implications for the neural basis of social cognition for the study of schizophrenia. *American Journal of Psychiatry, 160*, 815–824.

Pitschel-Walz, G., Leucht, S., Bauml, J., Kissling, W., & Engel, R. R. (2001). The effect of family interventions on relapse and rehospitalization in schizophrenia: A meta-analysis. *Schizophrenia Bulletin, 27*, 73–92.

Pope, H. G., & Lipinski, J. F. (1978). Diagnosis in schizophrenia and manic-depressive illness. *Archives of General Psychiatry, 35*, 811–828.

Potvin, S., Stip, E., & Roy, J. Y. (2005). Toxic psychoses as pharmacological models of schizophrenia. *Current Psychiatry Reviews, 1*(1), 23–32.

Rabkin, J. G. (1979). Ethnic density and psychiatric hospitalization: Hazards of minority status. *American Journal of Psychiatry, 136*(12), 1562–1566.

Rector, N. A., & Beck, A. T. (2001). Cognitive behavioral therapy for schizophrenia: An empirical review. *Journal of Nervous and Mental Diseases, 189*, 278–287.

Resnick, H. S., Kilpatrick, D. G., Dansky, B. S., Saunders, B. E., & Best, C. L. (1993). Prevalence of civilian trauma and post-traumatic stress disorder in a representative national sample of women. *Journal of Consulting and Clinical Psychology, 61*, 984–991.

Revheim, N., & Medalia, A. (2004). The Independent Living Scales as a measure of functional outcome for schizophrenia. *Psychiatric Services, 55*, 1052–1054.

Robinson, D. G., Woerner, M. G., McMeniman, M., Mendelowitz, A., & Bilder, R. M. (2004). Symptomatic and functional recovery from a first episode of schizophrenia or schizoaffective disorder. *American Journal of Psychiatry, 161*, 473–479.

Robinson, T. E., & Becker, J. B. (1986). Enduring changes of brain and behavior produced by chronic amphetamine administration: A review and evaluation of animal models of amphetamine psychosis. *Brain Behavior Review, 11*, 157–198.

Rose, S. M., Peabody, C. G., & Stratigeas, B. (1991). Undetected abuse among intensive case management clients. *Hospital and Community Psychiatry, 42*, 499–503.

Rosenberg, S. D., Drake, R. E., Wolford, G. L., Mueser, K. T., Oxman, T. E., Vidaver, R. M., et al. (1998). Dartmouth Assessment of Lifestyle Instrument (DALI): A substance use disorder screen for people with severe mental illness. *American Journal of Psychiatry, 155*, 232–238.

Rosenfarb, I. S., Bellack, A. S., & Aziz, N. (2006). A sociocultural stress, appraisal, and coping model of subjective burden and family attitudes toward patients with schizophrenia. *Journal of Abnormal Psychology, 115*, 157–165.

Rosenheck, R., Leslie, D., Keefe, R., McEvoy, J., Swartz, M., Perkins, D., et al. (2006). Barriers to employment for people with schizophrenia. *American Journal of Psychiatry, 163*, 411–417.

Ross, C. A., Anderson, G., & Clark, P. (1994). Childhood abuse and the positive symptoms of schizophrenia. *Hospital and Community Psychiatry, 45*, 489–491.

Rössler, W., Salize, H. J., van Os, J., & Riecher-Rössler, A. (2005). Size of burden of schizophrenia and psychotic disorders. *European Neuropsychopharmacology, 15*, 399–409.

Roy, A. (Ed.). (1986). *Suicide*. Baltimore: Williams & Wilkins.

Saha, S., Chant, D., Welham, J., & McGrath, J. (2005). A systematic review of the prevalence of schizophrenia. *Public Library of Science, 2*, e141.

Salem, J. E., & Kring, A. M. (1998). The role of gender in the reduction of etiologic heterogeneity in schizophrenia. *Clinical Psychology Review, 18,* 795–819.

Samele, C., van Os, J., McKenzie, K., Wright, A., Gilvarry, C., Manley, C., et al. (2001). Does socioeconomic status predict course and outcome in patients with psychosis? *Social Psychiatry and Psychiatric Epidemiology, 36,* 573–581.

Sammons, M. T. (2005). Pharmacotherapy for delusional disorder and associated conditions. *Professional Psychology: Research and Practice, 36,* 476–479.

Saykin, A. J., Gur, R. C., Gur, R. E., Mozley, P. D., Mozley, L., Resnick, S. M., et al. (1991). Neuropsychological function in schizophrenia: Selective impairment in memory and learning. *Archives of General Psychiatry, 48,* 618–624.

Saykin, A. J., Shtasel, D. L., Gur, R. E., Kester, D. B., Mozley, L. H., Stafiniak, P., et al. (1994). Neuropsychological deficits in neuroleptic naïve patients with first-episode schizophrenia. *Archives of General Psychiatry, 51,* 124–131.

Schaub, A., Behrendt, B., Brenner, H. D., Mueser, K. T., & Liberman, R. P. (1998). Training schizophrenic patients to manage their symptoms: Predictors of treatment response to the German version of the Symptom Management Module. *Schizophrenia Research, 31,* 121–130.

Schiffman, J., Walker, E., Ekstrom, M., Schulsinger, F., Sorensen, H., & Mednick, S. (2004). Childhood videotaped social and neuromotor precursors of schizophrenia: A prospective investigation. *American Journal of Psychiatry, 161,* 2021–2027.

Schock, K., Clay, C., & Cipani, E. (1998). Making sense of schizophrenic symptoms: Delusional statements and behavior may be functional in purpose. *Journal of Behavior Therapy and Experimental Psychiatry, 29,* 131–141.

Schuckit, M. A. (1995). *Drug and alcohol abuse: A clinical guide to diagnosis and treatment* (Critical issues in psychiatry; 4th ed.). New York: Plenum Press.

Searles H. (1965). *Collected papers on schizophrenia and related subjects.* New York: International Universities Press.

Sedler, M. J. (1995). Understanding delusions. *Psychiatric Clinics of North America, 18,* 251–262.

Selemon, L. D., & Goldman-Rakic, P. S. (1999). The reduced neuropil hypothesis: A circuit based model of schizophrenia. *Biological Psychiatry, 45,* 17–25.

Selten, J.-P., Slaets, J. P. J., & Kahn, R .S. (1997), Schizophrenia in Surinamese and Dutch Antillean immigrants to the Netherlands: Evidence of an increased incidence. *Psychological Medicine, 27,* 807–811.

Semple, D. M., McIntosh, A. M., & Lawrie, S. M. (2005). Cannabis as a risk factor for psychosis: Systematic review. *Journal of Psychopharmacology, 19*(2), 187–194.

Shenton, M. E., Dickey, C. C., Frumin, M. & McCarley, R.W. (2001). A review of MRI findings in schizophrenia. *Schizophrenia Research, 49,* 1–52.

Silverstein, S. M., Menditto, A. A., & Stuve, P. (2001). Shaping attention span: An operant conditioning procedure to improve neurocognition and functioning in schizophrenia. *Schizophrenia Bulletin, 27,* 247–257.

Silverton, L., & Mednick, S. (1984). Class drift and schizophrenia. *Acta Psychiatrica Scandinavica, 70,* 304–309.

Skilbeck, W. M., Acosta, F. X., Yamamoto, J., & Evans, L. A. (1984). Self-reported psychiatric symptoms among Black, Hispanic, and White outpatients. *Journal of Clinical Psychology, 40,* 1184–1189.

Smit, F., Bolier, L., & Cuijpers, P. (2004). Cannabis use and the risk of schizophrenia. *Addiction, 99,* 425–430.

Smith, T. E., Hull, J. W., Anthony, D. T., Goodman, M., Hedayat-Harris, A., Felger, T., et al. (1997). Post-hospitalization treatment adherence of schizophrenic patients: Gender differences in skill acquisition. *Psychiatry Research, 69,* 123–129.

Spaulding, W. D., Reed, D., Sullivan, M., Richardson, C., & Weiler, M. (1999). Effects of cognitive treatment in psychiatric rehabilitation. *Schizophrenia Bulletin, 25,* 657–676.

Strakowski, S. M., Sax, K. W., Setters, M. J., & Keck, P. E. (1996). Enhanced response to repeated d-amphetamine challenge: Evidence for behavioral sensitization in humans. *Biological Psychiatry, 40,* 872–880.

Sue, S., Fujino, D. C., Hu, L. T., Takeuchi, D. T., & Zane, N. W. S. (1991). Community mental health services for ethnic minority groups: A test of the cultural responsiveness hypothesis. *Journal of Consulting and Clinical Psychology, 59,* 533–540.

Sullivan, P. F., Kendler, K. S., & Neale, M. C. (2003). Schizophrenia as a complex trait: Evidence from a meta analysis of twin studies. *Archives of General Psychiatry, 60,* 1187–1192.

Sullivan, P. F., Owen, M. J., O'Donovan, M. C., & Freedman, R. (2006). Genetics. In J. A. Lieberman, T. S. Stroup, & D. O. Perkins (Eds.), *Textbook of schizophrenia* (pp. 39–54). Arlington, VA: APA Press.

Susser, E., Struening, E. L., & Conover, S. (1989). Psychiatric problems in homeless men: Lifetime psychosis, substance use, and current distress in new arrivals at New York City shelters. *Archives of General Psychiatry, 46,* 845–850.

Switzer, G. E., Dew, M. A., Thompson, K., Goycoolea, J. M., Derricott, T., & Mullins, S. D. (1999). Posttraumatic stress disorder and service utilization among urban mental health center clients. *Journal of Traumatic Stress, 12,* 25–39.

Terkelsen, K. G. (1983). Schizophrenia and the family: Pt. II. Adverse effects of family therapy. *Family Process, 22,* 191–200.

Terkelsen, K. G., & Menikoff, A. (1995). Measuring costs of schizophrenia: Implications for the post-institutional era in the United States. *Pharmacoeconomics, 8,* 199–222.

Tessler, R., & Gamache, G. (1995). *Evaluating family experiences with severe mental illness: To be used in conjunction with the Family Experiences Interview Schedule (FEIS): The Evaluation Center @ HSRI toolkit.* Cambridge, MA: The Evaluation Center @ HSRI.

Test, M. A., Wallisch, L. S., Allness, D. J., & Ripp, K. (1989). Substance use in young adults with schizophrenic disorders. *Schizophrenia Bulletin, 15,* 465–476.

Thune, J. J., Uylings, H. B., & Pakkenberg, B. (2001). No deficit in total number of neurons in the prefrontal cortex in schizophrenics. *Journal of Psychiatric Research, 35,* 15–21.

Tienari, P. (1991). Interaction between genetic vulnerability and family environment: The Finnish adoptive family study of schizophrenia. *Acta Psychiatrica Scandinavica, 84,* 460–465.

Tienari, P., Sorri, A., Lahti, I., Naarala, M., Wahlberg, K., Moring, J., et al. (1987). Genetic and psychosocial factors in schizophrenia: The Finnish adoptive family study. *Schizophrenia Bulletin, 13,* 477–484.

Tienari, P., Wynne, L. C., Sorri, A., Lahti, I., Lasky, K., Moring, J., et al. (2004). Genotype-environment interaction in schizophrenia spectrum disorder. *British Journal of Psychiatry, 184,* 216–222.

Tohen, M., Strakowski, S. M., Zarate, C., Hennen, J., Stoll, A. L., Suppes, T., et al. (2000). The McLean-Harvard first episode project: Six month symptomatic and functional outcome in affective and nonaffective psychosis. *Biological Psychiatry, 48,* 467–476.

Torrey, E. F. (1992). Are we overestimating the genetic contribution to schizophrenia? *Schizophrenia Bulletin, 18,* 159–170.

Torrey, E. F. (2001). *Surviving schizophrenia* (4th ed.). New York: HarperCollins.

Twamley, E. W., Jeste, D. V., & Bellack, A. S. (2003). A review of cognitive training in schizophrenia. *Schizophrenia Bulletin, 29,* 359–382.

Ustun, T. B., Rehm, J., Chatterji, S., Saxena, S., Trotter, R., Room, R., et al. (1999). Multiple-informant ranking of the disabling effects of different health conditions in 14 countries: WHO/NIH Joint Project CAR Study group. *Lancet, 354,* 111–115.

Valenstein, M., Blow, F. C., Copeland, L. A., McCarthy, J. F., Zeber, J. E., Gillon, L., et al. (2004). Poor antipsychotic adherence among patients with schizophrenia: Medication and patient factors. *Schizophrenia Bulletin, 30*(2), 255–264.

Van Der Does, A. J. W., Dingemans, P. M. A. J., Linszen, D. H., Nugter, M. A., & Scholte, W. F. (1993). Symptom dimensions and cognitive and social functioning in recent-onset schizophrenia. *Psychological Medicine, 23*, 745–753.

van der Gaag, M., Kern, R. S., van den Bosch, R. J., & Liberman, R. P. (2002). A controlled trial of cognitive remediation in schizophrenia. *Schizophrenia Bulletin, 28*, 167–176.

Veen, N. D., Selten, J., van der Tweel, I., Feller, W. G., Hock, H. W., & Kahn, R. S. (2004). Cannabis use and age of onset of schizophrenia. *American Journal of Psychiatry, 161*, 501–506.

Velligan, D. I., Kern, R. S., & Gold, J. M. (2006). Cognitive rehabilitation for schizophrenia and the putative role of motivation and expectancies. *Schizophrenia Bulletin, 32*, 474–485.

Velligan, D. I., Lam, F., Ereshefsky, L., & Miller, A. L. (2003). Perspectives on medication adherence and atypical antipsychotic medications. *Psychiatric Services, 54*(5), 665–667.

Velligan, D. I., Lam, F., Glahn, D. C., Barrett, J. A., Maples, N. J., Ereshefsky, L., et al. (2006). Defining and assessing adherence to oral antipsychotics: A review of the literature. *Schizophrenia Bulletin, 32*(4), 724–742.

Velligan, D. I., Mueller, J., Wang, M., Dicocco, M., Diamond, P. M., Maples, N. J., et al. (2006). Use of environmental supports among patients with schizophrenia. *Psychiatry Services, 57*, 219–224.

Walker, E., Downey, G., & Caspi, A. (1991). Twin studies of psychopathology: Why do the concordance rates vary? *Schizophrenia Research, 5*, 211–221.

Walker, E. F., Grimes, K. E., Davis, D. M., & Smith, A. J. (1993). Childhood precursors of schizophrenia: Facial expressions of emotion. *American Journal of Psychiatry, 150*, 1654–1660.

Wallace, C. J., Liberman, R. P., Tauber, R., & Wallace, J. (2000). The Independent Living Skills Survey: A comprehensive measure of the community functioning of severely and persistently mentally ill individuals. *Schizophrenia Bulletin, 26*, 631–658.

Waxler, N. E., & Mishler, E. G. (1971). Parental interactions with schizophrenic children and well siblings. *Archives of General Psychiatry, 25*, 223–231.

Webb, C., Pfeiffer, M., Mueser, K. T., Mensch, E., DeGirolamo, J., & Levenson, D. F. (1998). Burden and well-being of caregivers for the severely mentally ill: The role of coping style and social support. *Schizophrenia Research, 34*, 169–180.

Weiden, P. J., Kozma, C., Grogg, A., & Locklear, J. (2004). Partial compliance and risk of rehospitalization among California Medicaid patients with schizophrenia. *Psychiatric Services, 55*(8), 886–891.

Weinberger, D. R. (1987). Implications of normal brain development for the pathogenesis of schizophrenia. *Archives of General Psychiatry, 44*, 660–669.

Whaley, A. L. (1997). Ethnicity, race, paranoia, and psychiatric diagnoses: Clinician bias versus socio-cultural differences. *Journal of Psychopathology and Behavioral Assessment, 19*, 1–20.

Whaley, A. L. (2001). Cultural mistrust: An important psychological construct for diagnosis and treatment of African-Americans. *Professional Psychology: Research and Practice, 32*, 555–562.

Wilk, C. M., Gold, J. M., McMahon, R. P., Humber, K., Iannone, V. N., & Buchanan, R. W. (2005). No, it is not possible to be schizophrenic yet neuropsychologically normal. *Neuropsychology, 6*, 778–786.

Wykes, T., & Sturt, E. (1986). The measurement of social behavior in psychiatric patients: An assessment of reliability and validity of the SBS schedule. *British Journal of Psychiatry, 148*, 1–11.

Wu, E. Q., Birnbaum, H. G., Shi, L., Ball, D. E., Kessler, R. C., Moulis, M., et al. (2005). The economic burden of schizophrenia in the United States in 2002. *Journal of Clinical Psychiatry, 66*, 1122–1129.

Yamada, A. M., Barrio, C., Morrison, S. W., Sewell, D., & Jeste, D. V. (2006). Cross-ethnic evaluation of psychotic symptom content in hospitalized middle-aged and older adults. *General Hospital Psychiatry, 28*, 161–168.

Yamada, N., Nakajima, S., & Noguchi, T. (1998). Age at onset of delusional disorder is dependent on the delusional theme. *Acta Psychiatrica Scandinavica, 97*, 122–124.

Yung, A. R., & McGorry, P. D. (1996). The initial prodrome in psychosis: Descriptive and qualitative aspects. *Australian and New Zealand Journal of Psychiatry, 30*, 587–599.

Zimmerman, G., Favrod, J., Trieu, V. H., & Pomini, V. (2005). The effect of cognitive behavioral treatment on the positive symptoms of schizophrenia spectrum disorders: A meta-analysis. *Schizophrenia Research, 77*, 1–9.

CHAPTER 15

Borderline Personality Disorder

ALISSA SHERRY AND MARGARET R. WHILDE

DESCRIPTION OF THE DISORDER

Borderline Personality Disorder (BPD) is one of 10 personality disorders described in the *Diagnostic and Statistical Manual of Mental Disorders* (*DSM-IV TR*; American Psychiatric Association, 2000). It is the most common disorder found in inpatient and outpatient treatment settings (Widiger & Trull, 1993) and is also prevalent in nonclinical populations (Gunderson & Zanarini, 1987). Estimates indicate that BPD affects 1% to 2% of the general population, about 10% of outpatients, and 20% of inpatients (Torgersen, Kringlen, & Cramer, 2001).

Borderline Personality Disorder is characterized by a pervasive pattern of instability in affect regulation, impulse control, interpersonal relationships, and self-image. Individuals diagnosed with BPD exhibit extreme mood fluctuations; outbursts of intense anger; suicidal, parasuicidal, and self-injurious behaviors; difficulties maintaining interpersonal relationships; a tendency to oscillate between idealization and devaluation of others; fear of abandonment that often leads to frantic efforts to maintain closeness; and problems establishing a coherent identity. This disorder has been identified as one of the most difficult conditions to treat, due to the frequency with which self-destructive behaviors impede treatment progress (Linehan, 1993), high therapy dropout rates (Gunderson, Frank, & Ronningstam, 1989; Skodol, Buckley, & Charles, 1983; Stevenson & Meares, 1992), and frequent comorbidity with other Axis I disorders, such as Major Depression (Pilkonis & Frank, 1988; J. H. Reich & Noyes, 1987; Sullivan, Joyce, & Mulder, 1994; Zimmerman & Mattia, 1999), Panic Disorder (J. H. Reich & Noyes, 1987; Zimmerman & Mattia, 1999), Bipolar Disorder (Benazzi, 2000; Kay, Altshuler, Ventura, & Mintz, 1999), eating disorders (Gartner, Marcus, Halmi, & Loranger, 1989; Matsunaga et al., 2000), Posttraumatic Stress Disorder (PTSD; Zimmerman & Mattia, 1999), and substance abuse disorders (Driessen, Veltrup, Wetterling, John, & Dilling, 1998; Nace, Davis, & Gaspari, 1991; Nace, Saxon, & Shore, 1983; Verheul, van den Brink, & Hartgers, 1998; Zimmerman & Mattia, 1999). In addition, Antisocial, Avoidant, Passive-Aggressive, Obsessive-Compulsive, and Depressive Personality Disorders are also often comorbid with BPD (Grilo, Sanislow, & McGlashan, 2002).

Since its inception, BPD has been a controversial diagnosis, in part because women are overrepresented in prevalence rates (American Psychiatric Association, 2000; Shaw & Proctor, 2005). The diagnosis has also been criticized for its apparent elasticity and frequent overlap with other conditions, particularly mood disorders and Antisocial and Histrionic Personality Disorders (Akiskal, 1985; Becker, 1997; Francis & Widiger, 1987; Kroll, 1993; Mack, 1975; Stone, 1990). Nevertheless, researchers and clinicians have continued to identify BPD as a useful framework for conceptualizing and treating patient distress (see Paris, 2005), and extensive efforts have been made to define and describe BPD with greater clarity and accuracy (see Andrulonis, Glueck, & Stroebel, 1982; Millon, 1987; Stone, 1990; Tramantano, Javier, & Colon, 2003).

Despite the *DSM's* atheoretical approach to diagnosis (American Psychiatric Association, 2001), BPD has a rich history of theoretical conceptualizations. The term "borderline" was introduced in 1938 by the psychoanalyst Adolph Stern to describe patients who appeared more disturbed than "neurotic" patients but who were not psychotic (Wirth-Cauchon, 2001). In other words, they were thought to straddle the "border" between a neurosis and a psychosis (Stern, 1938). This definition was eventually supplanted by formulations that emphasize oscillations in ego states, but the concept of borderline has continued to be invoked to describe individuals who are able to function effectively in well-structured situations but who become unstable and even psychotic when confronted with ambiguity and emotional uncertainty (see Horwitz et al., 1996; Knight, 1954). The concept of a borderline disorder began gaining attention within the psychoanalytic community in the early 1950s, and theorists wrote extensively about the condition during this period (Horwitz et al., 1996). It was not until 1980, however, with publication of the third edition of the *DSM*, that it was introduced as a formal diagnosis in the United States.

Otto Kernberg's (1975) psychoanalytic formulation of BPD draws heavily on mid-twentieth-century American ego psychology and British object relations theory, particularly the contributions of Melanie Klein. Kernberg's theory asserts that BPD has its origins in developmental challenges occurring between 6 and 36 months of age. Prior to this, infants have learned to rely heavily on "splitting" as a defense against intolerable affect. They have become adept, in other words, at actively separating good from bad experiences of themselves and others; they do this to protect and defend their good self- and object images from the strong feelings aroused by bad images and experiences. During the critical negotiation period that follows, children learn to integrate good and bad representations of themselves and others. According to Kernberg's theory, BPD develops during this phase, and it represents a failure to integrate good and bad images of self and others into a realistic self-concept or a sense of others as complex and whole. Individuals with BPD, according to Kernberg, become overrun during this developmental period with an excess of aggression and threatening negative representations, and they are forced to continue to rely on splitting as a defense against the intolerable feelings aroused by this. Such excessive use of splitting constitutes a developmental arrest, and it impedes their ability to develop a stable self-concept and an integrated ego that can manage impulses effectively and respond to external challenges. Kernberg also noted that individuals with BPD manifest a tendency to regress in close relationships and fuse or merge self- and object images; this can lead to transient psychotic episodes for some people in certain circumstances.

A second theoretical approach, attachment theory, asserts that BPD emerges during childhood in response to early patterns of interaction with caregivers (Bender, Farber, & Geller, 2001; Fonagy, Target, Gergely, Allen, & Bateman, 2003; Nickell,

Waudby, & Trull, 2002). Attachment theory's principal tenet is that affectional bonds between child and caregiver shape personality (Bowlby, 1969; Lopez, 1995). Early affectional bonds are internalized in the form of cognitive working models of self and others that work to organize cognition, affect, and behavior in close relationships, as well as shape self-image (Bowlby, 1973). Working models of the self consist of expectations about one's ability to elicit need-meeting responses from caregivers. Working models of others consist of expectations about the accessibility and responsiveness of caregivers (Bowlby, 1973). Bowlby hypothesized that the quality and intensity of early infant-caregiver relationships determine expectations about close relationships, which are generalized to other relationships as the individual develops. Attachment backgrounds of individuals with BPD are generally of poor quality and significant intensity, and the expectations generated by these experiences have been generalized in such a way that BPD clients anticipate their adult worlds in the same way they did as children, often as hostile, unsafe, and unpredictable.

A growing body of evidence supports an attachment etiology of BPD, suggesting that borderline traits are associated with insecure attachment styles (Bender et al., 2001; Brennan & Shaver, 1998; Laporte & Guttman, 1996; Liotti & Pasquini, 2000; Lyddon & Sherry, 2001; Paris, 1997, 1998; Sabo, 1997; Sherry, Lyddon, & Henson, in press; Sinha & Watson, 1997; Zanarini & Frankenburg, 1997). Risk factor research has contributed additional evidence of this relationship by outlining some of the specific threats to attachment that take place during the childhoods of individuals later diagnosed with BPD (Brown & Anderson, 1991; Goodwin, Cheeves, & Connell, 1989; Gunderson & Sabo, 1993; Landecker, 1992; Laporte & Guttman, 1996; Paris, 1997, 1998; Sabo, 1997; Wagner & Linehan, 1994).

Theodore Millon's (2000) sociocultural model of BPD draws heavily on social learning theory, biosocial theory, and evolutionary psychology, emphasizing the role of social structures and historical trends in the production and maintenance of BPD. According to Millon, the contemporary prevalence of BPD is attributable to two broad trends: (1) social customs that aggravate rather than remediate early, disturbed parent-child relationships and (2) the decreased power of reparative social institutions to compensate for these problems. Millon has speculated that a number of sociocultural trends have given rise to the fragmented psychic structures found in BPD. These include increased social stratification, unstable family structures, contradictory role models in the popular media, and the prevalence of substance abuse in contemporary culture. He has also hypothesized that the decline of institutions that have typically organized communities, the decreased reliance on kinship networks in child rearing, and a resurgence in social anonymity are exacerbating the problem of BPD.

Marsha Linehan's (1993, p. 1) dialectical behavior approach to BPD also makes use of biosocial theory by describing BPD as "a joint outcome of biological disposition, environmental context, and the transaction between the two during development." Linehan's theory is largely biologically based. According to Linehan, individuals with BPD possess a high degree of "emotional vulnerability," or sensitivity and responsiveness to emotional stimuli, as well as a tendency to return slowly to emotional baseline after they have been emotionally aroused. In addition, they have difficulty modulating affect. As a result, they are likely to manifest problems inhibiting inappropriate behavior related to strong affects, engaging in activities in the service of a goal in a manner that is not mood-dependent, soothing themselves when they are experiencing strong emotions, and focusing their attention when emotionally aroused.

There is no consensus as to the etiology of BPD, nor is there one theory that accounts for every behavior, affective experience, and cognitive disruption associated with BPD. The etiology of BPD is as complex as its clinical presentation. The following sections provide the reader with an overview of historical and recent theories and empirical findings that might create a best practice guide for the assessment and treatment of BPD.

DIAGNOSIS AND ASSESSMENT

The essential feature of BPD is a disruption in interpersonal relatedness that extends into areas of self-image, affect, and impulsivity. Although BPD features have been noted in children (Bemporad, Smith, Hanson, & Cicchetti, 1982; Crick, Murray-Close, & Woods, 2005), the *DSM-IV TR* (American Psychiatric Association, 2000) criteria limits diagnosis to adulthood while also acknowledging that its trajectory is developmental in nature. The *DSM-IV* criteria are as follows:

A pervasive pattern of instability of interpersonal relationships, self-image, and affects, and marked impulsivity beginning by early adulthood and present in a variety of contexts, as indicated by five (or more) of the following:

(1) frantic efforts to avoid real or imagined abandonment. **Note:** Do not include suicidal or self-mutilating behavior covered in Criterion 5.
(2) a pattern of unstable and intense interpersonal relationships characterized by alternating between extremes of idealization and devaluation.
(3) identity disturbance: markedly and persistently unstable self-image or sense of self.
(4) impulsivity in at least two areas that are potentially self-damaging (e.g., spending, sex, substance abuse, reckless driving, binge eating). **Note:** Do not include suicidal or self-mutilating behavior covered in Criterion 5.
(5) recurrent suicidal behavior, gestures, or threats, or self-mutilating behavior
(6) affective instability due to a marked reactivity of mood (e.g., intense episodic dysphoria, irritability, or anxiety usually lasting a few hours and only rarely more than a few days).
(7) chronic feelings of emptiness
(8) inappropriate, intense anger or difficulty controlling anger (e.g., frequent displays of temper, constant anger, recurrent physical fights).
(9) transient, stress-related paranoid ideation or severe dissociative symptoms. (American Psychiatric Association, 2000, p. 710)

The diagnosis and assessment of BPD can be difficult due to frequent comorbidity with other mental disorders and V codes in the *DSM*. In addition, diagnostic accuracy is only as good as the method used to diagnose. Many have criticized the *DSM* medical model of diagnosis by indicating that mental disorders are not true prototypes and that the nature of human behavior necessitates a system whereby variations and intensities can be accounted for. Widiger (1992) illustrates the shortcomings of the *DSM-IV* diagnostic system for personality disorders by noting that there are 149,495,616 different combinations of criteria that would warrant a diagnosis of Antisocial Personality Disorder. Similarly, there are 162 different possible combinations of borderline personality criteria in individuals who do not reach the clinical threshold for BPD (Widiger, 1992). This speaks not only to the weaknesses of the *DSM*, but also to the enormous heterogeneity of the BPD diagnosis. Some research has attempted to correlate psychological assessment findings with BPD traits in an effort to increase diagnostic accuracy. Findings from these efforts are summarized next.

Minnesota Multiphasic Personality Inventory

The Minnesota Multiphasic Personality Inventory, second edition (MMPI-2; Butcher, Dahlstrom, Graham, Tellegen, & Kaemmer, 1989) is the most widely researched personality instrument currently available. Since its development, there have been several attempts to create personality disorder scales utilizing the items on the MMPI (first edition). Morey, Waugh, and Blashfield (1985) created 11 personality disorder scales based on the MMPI that were meant to conform to the 11 personality disorders outlined in the third edition of the *DSM*. While numerous preliminary studies were conducted suggesting that Morey and his colleagues had generated what appeared to be valid and reliable scales (Hicklin & Widiger, 2000), revisions of both the *DSM* and the MMPI precluded further study of their efforts. Their work, however, served as a catalyst for the development of two personality disorder scales using the MMPI-2, which currently show promise (Levitt & Gotts, 1995; Somwaru & Ben-Porath, 1995). Both of these scales remain in various stages of validation and are not yet available for clinical use.

Millon Clinical Multiaxial Inventory

The third edition of the Millon Clinical Multiaxial Inventory (MCMI-III; Millon, Davis, & Millon, 1997) was normed and validated on a clinical population, using a base rate standardization technique instead of T-score standardization. Using it with a nonclinical population is therefore inappropriate; doing so will produce elevations in scores that do not reflect true elevations in symptomatology. The MCMI-III contains a Borderline Scale (Scale C), however, and items on Scale C reflect endorsements of anger, guilt, unstable mood, dependency-seeking behaviors, unstable relationships, and erratic moods. The scale was designed to reflect Millon's (1996) theory of borderline personality development, and it therefore highlights attachment, cognitive views of the self and other, and experience of pleasure and pain in personality functioning. Research on Scale C has been conducted primarily on earlier versions of the MCMI. Findings from this research indicate that Scale C could reflect BPD, but it could also simply reveal erratic emotionality associated with other personality or psychiatric disorders (Divac-Jovanovic, Svrakic, & Lecic-Tosevski, 1993; Strack, 2002). Using the MCMI-II, Nielsen, Hewitt, and Habke (1997) found that BPD patients had significant elevations on the Self-Defeating, Avoidant, Antisocial, and Passive-Aggressive subscales in addition to the Borderline subscale. Another study found that, compared to non-personality disordered inpatients, inpatients with BPD scored significantly higher on the instrument's Disclosure, Debasement, Passive-Aggressive, Self-Defeating, Borderline, and Major Depression scales (McCann, Flynn, & Gersh, 1992). To date, no studies have been undertaken to address validity issues for borderline samples on the MCMI-III. Extrapolating from earlier versions, it appears that Scale C has some utility, although interpreters should be careful not to overestimate its validity with respect to BPD specifically.

Personality Assessment Inventory

The Personality Assessment Inventory (PAI; Morey, 1991) has a four-subscale (PAI-BOR) composite that is most reflective of Kernberg's (1967, 1975) theory of BPD. The four subscales are Affective Instability (BOR-A), Identity Problems (BOR-I), Negative Relationships (BOR-N), and Self-Harm (BOR-S; Morey, 1991). Utilization of four subscales to measure this personality structure represents an acknowledgment of the complex nature of BPD, as well as its heterogeneity and the difficulty of pinpointing it accurately. To date, a handful of peer-reviewed studies have been conducted on the validity of the PAI Borderline Features Scale (PAI-BOR) with different samples. Morey suggests a raw score cutoff of 38 (*t*-score of 70) to indicate the presence of prominent features of BPD, but not necessarily a formal diagnosis of BPD. Because the PAI has been validated for use with clinical and nonclinical samples and results can been interpreted on a continuum, using the 38 raw score cutoff as a guideline is probably the best approach to interpreting scores on this instrument. Studies have shown that this cutoff score was able to correctly classify 81.8% of female inpatients and 77.3% of nonclinical female college students (Bell-Pringle, Pate, & Brown, 1997). However, Trull (1995) indicated that the cutoff was not sensitive enough to predict BPD features, based on his research utilizing a sample of 1,500 college undergraduates. In a study of 5,000 nonclinical adults, Jackson and Trull (2001) found a different factor structure for the PAI-BOR in their sample than was found in the original normative sample reported by Morey.

The continuum scoring of the PAI-BOR is an advantage of the PAI. Low scores (*t*-score $\leq$ 60) on the PAI-BOR are indicative of more healthy personality styles, whereas high scores (*t*-score $\geq$ 70) tend to reflect not only BPD, but possible variants of other *DSM* personality disorders, with symptoms including impulsivity and emotional lability, feeling misunderstood by others, anger, suspiciousness, anxiety, neediness, and ambivalence toward others. Elevations on the PAI-BOR scale along with elevations on all four subscales are more indicative of BPD than elevations on any one of the subscales independently. Markedly elevated scores (*t*-score $\geq$ 90), particularly in conjunction with elevations on scales assessing alcohol and drug abuse, suicide, and aggression, increase the reliability of a BPD diagnosis (Morey, 2003).

Rorschach Ink Blot Test

Second only to the MMPI, the Rorschach has been the most studied personality assessment instrument. Both the Rorschach and BPD have backgrounds in psychodynamic theory, so the available research using the Rorschach to predict BPD is a rich one. However, as Mihura (2006) cites, few use the Exner Comprehensive System (Exner, 2003), which is the preferred scoring system, because of its extensive normative data and validation history. Of the Exner studies, few have found indices that clearly discriminate between BPD and other disorders. This may be because such studies are overly simplistic, failing to consider the complex structure of both the Rorschach and the BPD diagnosis (Murray, 1993). It is suggested that the Rorschach may best be used as an approach to the ongoing assessment of indices related to stress, coping, intra- and interpersonal relations, affect modulation, and ideation in the context of psychotherapy (Murray, 1993). Mihura highlights a number of studies investigating the utility of the Rorschach in diagnosing and assessing BPD. Most involve psychodynamic scales constructed by other researchers in an attempt to find new ways of exploring the utility of the Rorschach.

Scales like the Separation-Individuation Scale (Coonerty, 1986), the Symbiotic Phenomena Content Scale (Hirshberg, 1989), the Transitional Object Scale (Greenberg, Craig, Seidman, Cooper, & Teele, 1987), and the Oral Dependency Scale (Masling, Rabie, & Blondheim, 1967) have provided some predictive validity, largely because they were developed to predict BPD traits. While the sheer number of these studies makes review of them outside the scope of this chapter, overall findings are similar to those of other personality instruments. That is, given the heterogeneity of BPD, within-group differences can be more informative of prognosis and treatment trajectory than between-group differences. The variability in scores thus precludes a definitive diagnosis of BPD to the exclusion of other personality or clinical disorders.

Overall, although published psychometric instruments provide some utility in the assessment and diagnosis of BPD, they should be used only in conjunction with a thorough clinical interview and an appreciation for each client's individual history. A complete history and diagnostic assessment can serve to fill in the gaps that assessment tools miss. In general, no one psychometric test should be used to diagnose a disorder, nor should psychometric tests alone be the basis for a diagnosis. In addition, a BPD diagnosis should always be a working diagnosis, open to revision and change over the course of treatment. Ongoing assessment should be employed, and careful attention should be paid to the Axis I diagnoses that often have BPD features. The use of semi-structured interviews for both Axis I and Axis II disorders, validated psychological assessment tools, and a thorough history should provide the clinician with the needed information to make a reliable working diagnosis with most clients.

CONCEPTUALIZATION

LEARNING AND MODELING

An emphasis on the role of interpersonal and social factors in conceptualizing BPD is pervasive in the literature. The majority of this literature focuses on early childhood experiences and risk factors that have been found in the histories of BPD clients. However, the literature is also careful to highlight that inheriting a particular set of risk factors does not necessarily guarantee a diagnosis of BPD, and not all clients with BPD have risk factor histories. This gap leaves space for other explanations accounting for BPD etiology. As Meehl (1972, 1977) highlights in his essays on etiology, the process of identifying causal factors for any psychological disorder is complicated, requiring the acknowledgment of both empirical and conceptual elements. These elements can vary greatly from necessary and directly causal influences to marginally statistical contributions to merely coincidental ones.

Learning theory is not pervasive in the BPD literature. The most notable author to employ this form of conceptualization is Millon (1987, 1996). At its core, Millon's theory is not solely a learning theory, but a combination of learning and environmental theories. His biosocial theory suggests that the increased pace of social change has contributed to, if not caused, the social and interpersonal deprivation of children, and that this deprivation represents a risk factor for the development of BPD in adulthood. Urbanization, increased mobility, and technology have created a social environment that is constantly shifting and complex. Such complexities create inconsistent, uncertain, and divergent demands on children, who then find it difficult to make decisions and find stability in the relationships around them. Included in these unstable relationships are parents, who are often too preoccupied with work and financial demands to be stable role models for children. The stress and pressure of an industrialized society often lead to parental bickering, separation, divorce, and remarriage. The result of this can be exposure to destructive models of learning; children may be led by their parents into cruel competition for contingent love and affection. The childhood search for the self as an individual is interrupted by virtue of these impingements, and internal schisms that mimic borderline behaviors begin to develop.

Life Events

Research investigating the life events that people with BPD have experienced is extremely rich. In fact, risk factor research permeates the BPD literature. In general, the childhoods of BPD clients are marked with a high number of traumatic events (Liotti & Pasquini, 2000; Paris, 1994, 1996); some researchers have even referred to the condition as a chronic form of PTSD (Herman & van der Kolk, 1987). Being a victim of childhood sexual abuse and incest greatly increases one's chances of developing BPD and is considered an indicator of poor prognosis; this is particularly true when abuse experiences occur at a young age, are repeated, and involve intrafamilial sexual abuse (Brown & Anderson, 1991; Goodwin et al., 1989; Gunderson & Sabo, 1993; Landecker, 1992; Laporte & Guttman, 1996; Paris, 1993; Sabo, 1997; Stone, 1990; Wagner & Linehan, 1994). It appears that the existence of sexual trauma is not as predictive of BPD as the level of severity of the trauma and its combination with other types of abuse (Goldman, D'Angelo, DeMaso, & Mezzacappa, 1992). Clients with BPD remember their father as more neglectful (Frank & Paris, 1981); they also report more difficulties with separation, more mood reactivity, and lower frustration tolerance during childhood and adolescence (D. B. Reich & Zanarini, 2001).

Loss and abandonment are also often found in BPD histories. Individuals with BPD have a significantly higher percentage of parental loss through divorce or death than people with other disorders (Grinker, Werble, & Drye, 1968; Walsh, 1977). They also have a higher incidence of prolonged separations in the first 5 years of life (Bradley, 1979), are more likely to come from divorced families, have a higher incidence of father loss (Soloff & Millward, 1983), and have more often experienced a developmentally important loss (Akiskal, 1985). There is some evidence to suggest that losses suffered by attachment figures could also create pathways to the development of BPD (Liotti & Pasquini, 2000). In addition, BPD clients have experienced a higher incidence of parental neglect, early separation and loss, parental psychopathology, and social disintegration (Paris, 1997, 1998). Moreover, the parenting that occurred when these clients were children is often described as overprotective, inconsistent, or demanding and as providing the child with very little sense of stability or structure by which to regulate his or her emotions (Laporte & Guttman, 1996). Some researchers have noted that caregivers are often inconsistently available during traumatic childhood events, and they have speculated that the emotional neglect and absence of adult attachment figures may be as powerful as actual traumatic events in the development of BPD (Sabo, 1997).

Given the overarching themes of loss, separation, parenting deficits, and trauma in conceptualizations of the etiology of BPD, many theorists have begun to explore attachment as an etiological mechanism for the development of BPD (Bender et al., 2001; Fonagy, 1998; Fonagy, Target, & Gergely, 2000; Lyddon & Sherry, 2001; Meyer, Pilkonis, Proietti, Heape, & Egan, 2001; Nickell et al., 2002; Sable, 1997a, 1997b; Sherry et al., in press). While some research has found direct connections between poor attachment histories and development of BPD through empirical research (Brennan & Shaver, 1998; Sherry et al., in press), others have noted that attachment may serve only as an indirect risk factor. For example, in a test of several plausible etiological models, Fossati et al. (2005) found that adult attachment patterns predicted impulsive and aggressive traits, which in turn predicted BPD. Broader theoretical conceptualizations of BPD, such as Parker's (1997) tripartite model, encompass attachment, environment, temperament, and biological vulnerability in a complex model of BPD etiology. Parker's model and others like it are currently being explored by scholars (Cloninger, 1997; Fossati et al., 2001; Graybar & Boutilier, 2002; Zanarini & Frankenburg, 1997). This research utilizing attachment theory and Parker's tripartite model represents an overwhelming consensus among scholars that environmental risk factors alone cannot predict BPD reliably and that more complex models need to be investigated to produce a true understanding of the pathways that lead to the development of the disorder.

GENETIC INFLUENCES

It is important to distinguish between biological influences and genetic influences when writing about BPD. Biological influences typically involve neurobiological causes of behavior, including the size or functioning of brain structures, the efficiency of neurotransmitter function, and/or hormonal or endocrine functioning. Genetics can contribute to these indicators, but they do not necessarily do so. Biological influences on BPD are summarized in a later section of this chapter, titled Physical Factors Affecting Behavior.

Genetic influences on BPD are best studied using twin or adoption studies to control for the environmental effects generated by family upbringing. Because research on life events is largely, if not exclusively, correlational in nature and measured in hindsight, direct causal indicators are limited (Paris, 1998). Few pure twin studies have been conducted on BPD. The most extensive study to date investigated 221 twin pairs, of which 92 were monozygotic (MZ) and 129 were dizygotic (DZ). Researchers found a statistically significant effect, with 35% probandwise concordance in the MZ pairs and 7% in the DZ pairs. Two models appeared to account for the effect. The first had a .69 additive genetic effect with no shared-in-families environmental effect. The second had a .57 additive genetic effect with a .11 shared-in-families effect (Torgersen et al., 2000). Although such findings show a strong genetic component for BPD, replication is needed.

One factor influencing genetic studies is a lack of uniform symptomatology concerning personality disorders. With most medical diseases, there are defining symptoms that are diagnostic of the disease, which can be objectively and categorically identified because diseases often do not exist on a continuum. Asthma, for example, has clear symptoms, such as difficulty breathing, coughing that will not stop, or wheezing, the presence of which is essential for the diagnosis. However, such is not the case for mental disorders. For BPD, there are multiple combinations that could produce a diagnosis, no one symptom is necessarily more or less diagnostic than others, most symptoms lie on a continuum rather than present dichotomously, and there are no truly reliable tests that can test for them; the profession relies completely on the variability of clinical judgment for diagnosis. In recognition of this, some genetic researchers have investigated the genetic predictability of a variety of traits that are associated with BPD. For example, traits such as anxiousness, identity problems, affective lability, cognitive dysregulation, and insecure attachment have been investigated. Using 686 twin dyads, researchers found genetic effects for these traits (Livesley, Jang, & Vernon, 1998) that account for greater amounts of variance than previous studies investigating the genetic contributors to BPD diagnosis. In addition, studies that focus on genetic contributions at the trait level provide a broader explanation for BPD and support a dimensional view of personality traits in general that can extend into normal personality variation. Considering the variability of diagnostic labeling, such studies likely provide a more realistic and useful picture of how genetic influences shape personality.

A few recent studies show additional promise in identifying genetic markers of BPD. Ni and colleagues (2006), for example, found the serotonin transporter gene (5-HTT) to distinguish between 89 BPD patients and 269 healthy controls. The serotonin transporter gene plays an important role in suicide, impulsive behavior, and emotional liability.

Physical Factors Affecting Behavior

Studies on the neurobiology of BPD have indicated impairments in systems that regulate impulsivity, aggression, and affect. However, neurobiological researchers have generally been careful not to conclude that BPD is caused solely by these indicators. A number of researchers have concluded that genetic influences, as well as environmental contributions, such as neglect, abuse, chronic stress, trauma, and maternal care, have implications for physiological regulation in the brain. Consistent with a biopsychosocial model, genetic tendencies may only become expressed when environments are conducive to that expression (Jang, Dick, Wolf, Livesley, & Paris, 2005; Pally, 2002). In this context, evidence of neurobiological indicators associated with BPD symptoms varies. Impulsive aggression has been noted in individuals with low levels of serotonin (Coccaro, 1998; Gurvits, Koenigsberg, & Siever, 2000; Oquendo & Mann, 2000). However, neurobiological mechanisms for identity disturbance are sparse and inconclusive (Pally, 2002). Other researchers have found differences in hippocampal size between BPD patients with comorbid PTSD and controls; this research suggests that small hippocampal size might be related to the psychotic symptoms noted in the symptom dyad represented by BPD and PTSD (Irle, Lange, & Sachsse, 2005). Overall, reviews suggest that the neurobiological factors of BPD are poorly understood (Lieb, Zanarini, Schmahl, Linehan, & Bohus, 2004). This research appears to be in its early stages, as newer neuroimaging techniques, which are considered to offer a great deal of fertile ground for further work, continue to be explored.

In a nonclinical sample of 226 women, DeSoto, Geary, Hoard, Sheldon, and Cooper (2003) investigated the relation between BPD symptoms and estrogen. In a series of three studies, findings indicated that variability of estrogen in women was predictive of the endorsement of more BPD symptoms. It was determined that extreme fluctuations of estrogen in women without BPD tendencies or normal fluctuations in women with BPD tendencies could be problematic. Although the study failed to assess progesterone, which had been previously associated with mood and cognition, it did relate the estrogen findings to individual differences in serotonin system sensitivity.

Not only do physiological indicators affect BPD, but BPD can have a profound impact on physical health. In a comprehensive study of 200 patients with BPD in remission and 64 patients with BPD, recovering from BPD was associated with better health overall, less use of costly medical services, and better health-related decisions.

Patients in remission were less likely to have a history of a syndromal medical conditions, such as chronic fatigue or fibromyalgia, as well as obesity, hypertension, diabetes, or osteoarthritis. They also reported less smoking and alcohol consumption, more exercise, less frequent use of sleep or pain medications, and fewer trips to the emergency room (Frankenburg & Zanarini, 2004, 2006). While this study attributed findings to overall health-related decisions and increased self-care, other studies have found more biological explanations, such as immune and endocrine dysfunction associated with depressive disorders in the context of BPD (Kahl et al., 2005).

DRUGS AFFECTING BEHAVIOR

Comorbid substance abuse disorders are common in people with BPD (Morgenstern, Langenbucher, Labouvie, & Miller, 1997), with the relationship being stronger for men than women (Zlotnick, Rothschild, & Zimmerman, 2002). Some research has suggested that 76% of patients with BPD abuse one or more substances, with the number of substances being used having a negative relationship to reported levels of depression (Hatzitaskos, Soldatos, Kokkevi, & Stefanis, 1999). The assessment of comorbid substance abuse when treating clients with BPD is essential, because both BPD and substance abuse disorders increase the likelihood of suicide attempts (Tidemalm, Elofsson, Stefansson, Waern, & Runeson, 2005). Overall, BPD substance abusers are less hostile, suspicious, and angry but do exhibit more anxiety, feelings of insufficiency, and suicide attempts (van den Bosch, Verheul, & van den Brink, 2001). In general, differences between BPD substance abusers and BPD nonabusers are not strong enough to warrant exclusion of substance abusing BPD patients from treatment. In fact, several studies have found dialectical behavioral therapy (DBT) to be effective in the treatment of BPD substance abusers (Dimeff, Rizvi, Brown, & Linehan, 2000; Linehan et al., 1999; van den Bosch, Koeter, Stijnen, Verheul, & van den Brink, 2005).

It should be noted that many of the impulsive, acting-out, and interpersonal difficulties that are diagnosed as BPD may actually be related to substance abuse. When someone with BPD abuses substances, the threshold for impulsivity is lowered and an increase in assault, sexual promiscuity or self-mutilation might appear (American Psychiatric Association, 2001). A thorough history of substance abuse and use is often forgotten in diagnostic and intake assessment, but it is an essential piece of information gathering for the assessment of BPD.

CULTURAL AND DIVERSITY ISSUES

Women currently account for a substantial majority (75%) of BPD diagnoses (American Psychiatric Association, 2000). Moreover, research on the relationship between ethnicity and BPD has identified higher rates of the disorder in American Hispanic than in Caucasian and African American clinical groups (Chavira et al., 2003). This overrepresentation in female and ethnically diverse populations signals that there are important cultural dynamics at play in the conceptualization and application of the diagnosis. In addition, the majority of the research on BPD involves female samples, silently perpetuating the idea that it is predominantly, if not only, found in women. In an investigation of 75 studies that provided unbiased estimates of sex ratios for BPD, it was found that the average proportion of women was 76% when semi-structured interviews were utilized for diagnosis (Widiger & Trull, 1993). Widiger and Trull have argued that, if sex bias was driving these prevalence rates, researchers would find higher female prevalence rates in studies using unstructured interviews than in those using semi-structured interviews. In fact, studies have found that female prevalence rates actually increase with interviews that are more structured (Henry & Cohen, 1983).

Although these studies have attempted to debunk the argument that differing prevalence rates in BPD are reflective of bias among clinicians, it is plausible that the diagnostic criteria of the *DSM* is the source of the bias. Feminist and multicultural scholars have also argued that current definitions of BPD fail to address sufficiently the role of culture and politics in giving rise to the characteristics and behaviors associated with the disorder (Becker, 1997; Daley, Burge, & Hammen, 2000; Herman, 1992; Hodges, 2003; Shaw & Proctor, 2005; Wirth-Cauchon, 2001). They have proposed that BPD "symptoms" represent efforts on the part of women and culturally diverse people to contend with the impact of systemic oppression, and they have advocated for an alternative theoretical approach to BPD, in which efforts are made to diagnose the cultural context that surrounds the individual rather than the individual herself (Cornett, 1993; Hodges, 2003; Shaw & Proctor, 2005).

Feminists have drawn particular attention to the relationship between gender-based violence, namely early sexual trauma, and BPD in adolescence and adulthood (Brown & Anderson, 1991; Daley et al., 2000; Goodwin et al., 1989; Gunderson & Sabo, 1993; Landecker, 1992; Laporte & Gutman, 1996; Sabo, 1997; Wagner & Linehan, 1994). They have argued that individuals diagnosed with BPD are in fact contending with the effects of systemic violence against women (Brown, 1994; Daley et al., 2000; Herman, 1992; Hodges, 2003). Herman and others have proposed that the symptoms of BPD are actually signs of traumatic stress in relation to prolonged and repeated experiences of victimization. On the basis of this argument, they have advocated for the replacement of BPD with PTSD or "Complex Posttraumatic Stress Disorder," to account for the role contextual social factors play in the development of client distress (Alexander & Muenzenmaier, 1998; Brown, 1994; Curtois, 1999; Herman, 1992; Hodges, 2003; Landecker, 1992; Zimmerman & Mattia, 1999).

Multicultural theorists have argued that symptoms associated with BPD can arise in response to feelings of marginality and powerlessness and in contexts in which an individual perceives himself or herself as experiencing social failure (see Miller, 1994, 1999). From this perspective, BPD may be attributable to social inequalities, such as racism or homophobia, rather than to individual pathology. In addition, it has been proposed that the process of acculturation can result in symptoms of BPD, such as identity confusion, feelings of emptiness, alienation, abandonment, loss of control, and anxiety (Hovey & Magana, 2002; Williams & Berry, 1991). Immigration and acculturation processes also typically disrupt families and activate intergenerational conflict (Negy & Snyder, 2000). These conditions have been identified as a source of mood instability, feelings of anger, and difficult interpersonal relationships (Chavira et al., 2003).

An additional critique levied by multicultural theorists is that BPD pathologizes personality characteristics and behaviors that are acceptable, normative, and even compulsory in certain cultural contexts, even though *DSM-IV* diagnostic criteria warn against this. For example, in Puerto Rican culture, men are expected to manifest strong emotions, such as anger, aggressiveness, and sexual attraction; these personality characteristics, which are culture-based, may account for higher rates of BPD in Hispanic populations (Casimir & Morrison, 1993; Chavira et al., 2003).

BEHAVIORAL TREATMENT

Dialectical behavioral therapy (Linehan, 1993) represents a modification of traditional cognitive-behavioral therapies for use with individuals diagnosed with BPD. Dialectical behavioral therapy was the first treatment shown via controlled studies to be effective with borderline personality (Linehan, Armstrong, Suarez, Allmon, & Heard, 1991; Linehan & Heard, 1993). The treatment utilizes therapeutic techniques that are found in many standard cognitive and behavioral programs, such as homework assignments, psychoeducational interventions, clear goal setting, ongoing assessment of behavior and treatment progress, and a collaborative working relationship between therapist and client (Linehan, 1993). In addition, DBT makes use of four tenets that integrate Eastern psychological and spiritual practices, as well as psychoanalytic insights into the role of transference-countertransference dynamics in therapy with individuals with BPD. These tenets include an emphasis on (1) dialectic processes, (2) the therapeutic relationship as crucial to treatment, (3) intervening in therapy-interfering behaviors on the part of both client and therapist, and (4) acceptance and validation of client behavior.

Dialectical behavioral therapy is predicated on a "dialectical worldview" that stresses the "fundamental nature of reality and persuasive dialogue and relationship" (Linehan, 1993, p. 1). Linehan has written that three aspects of this worldview inform the treatment strategies utilized in DBT. The first of these is an emphasis on understanding how parts of a whole are related to one another. Dialectical behavioral therapy addresses itself to the immediate and larger contexts that drive individual behavior, as well as the way behaviors and skill deficits exist in relation to, and mutually inform, one another. The second aspect is the valuing, rather than the rejection, of contradictions or polarities. Dialectical behavioral therapy challenges the dichotomous thinking that is characteristic of BPD and instead encourages clients to recognize contradictions and attempt to synthesize them. The third aspect is the proposition that reality is continuously changing. Here, DBT emphasizes the idea that the individual and the environment are constantly in transition. Rather than providing clients with a stable, consistent environment, DBT practitioners seek to help them become more comfortable with change. In addition, the therapist-client relationship is regarded as crucial in resolving BPD. Linehan has argued that a strong connection between client and therapist can mitigate the risks of suicidal behavior and dropout rates that frequently accompany the treatment process for individuals with BPD. Moreover, DBT calls for a sustained analysis throughout therapy to the role of both therapist and client in interfering with treatment interventions and goals. Linehan has written that this element of DBT is similar to the psychoanalytic analysis of transference-countertransference dynamics. Finally, a hallmark of DBT is an emphasis on acceptance rather than cognitive, emotional, or behavioral change. According to Linehan, DBT attempts to teach "clients to fully accept themselves and their world as they are in the moment" without an expectation that this acceptance will necessarily lead to improvement or progress (p. 6). The utilization of acceptance as a treatment strategy constitutes an integration of Eastern spiritual practice, particularly Zen practice, and traditional Western cognitive-behavioral treatment. It is designed to enhance the capacity of individuals with BPD to tolerate the emotional arousal brought about by internal and external sources of challenge or stress (Linehan, 1993).

Dialectical behavioral therapy is one of the most researched approaches to the treatment of BPD, with over 100 peer-reviewed articles and numerous book chapters.

A complete review of the effectiveness and efficacy studies conducted on the technique is beyond the scope of this chapter, but in general, DBT is associated with a significant reduction in symptomatology with inpatient groups (Kröger et al., 2006); reduction of suicidality and deliberate self-harm, hospitalization stays, psychiatric emergency room visits, and treatment dropout in outpatient groups (Linehan et al., 2006); lower levels of parasuicide and alcohol use (van den Bosch et al., 2005); and even decreases in depression and hopelessness in an intensive, 3-week treatment (McQuillan et al., 2005). These findings appear to be consistent throughout the literature.

Transference-focused psychotherapy (TFP; Clarkin, Yeomans, & Kernberg, 1999; Clarkin et al., 2001) is based on Kernberg's (1996) object relations model of BPD and emphasizes the importance of the therapeutic alliance and of insight, gleaned through the act of interpreting moment-to-moment transference-countertransference dynamics, in the resolution of BPD. Typically highly structured and twice weekly (Levy et al., 2006), TFP is predicated on the notion that a strong working alliance allows for the reworking of internalized, pathological early object relations. As the working alliance is continually monitored and fostered, individuals with BPD gain the opportunity for a "corrective emotional experience," in which new, more integrated representations of self and other can be consolidated (Clarkin, Yeomans, & Kernberg, 2006). In accordance with Kernberg's (1996) hypothesis that excess aggression is a driving force in producing the unstable, fragile ego and vulnerability to fragmentation that characterize BPD, considerable attention is paid to anger and hatred in the TFP approach (Clarkin et al., 2006). A firm structure and clear and consistent boundaries are emphasized in therapy to titrate the intensity of the treatment and keep negative emotions, such as rage, from destroying the working alliance. In addition, TFP is characterized by sustained and persistent analysis of negative transferences, such as hatred and rage. The analysis of anger and aggression is, in fact, posited as fundamental to the task of resolving the tendency to split self and others into all-good and all-bad representations.

A recent review indicated that TFP has been critically researched over the past 5 years, with considerable attention paid to it in non-English-speaking countries, such as Mexico, the Netherlands, and Denmark. Empirical findings overall tend to be supportive of the approach. One study using 23 female patients found that at the conclusion of a 12-month treatment regimen, patients were less suicidal and less self-injurious and had fewer hospitalizations for fewer numbers of days (Clarkin et al., 2001). However, the same study noted a dropout rate of slightly more than 19%, which is consistent with other studies, indicating that TFP may have higher dropout rates than cognitive-based treatments (Geisen-Bloo et al., 2006). A later randomized trial of 90 BPD clients investigated the efficacy of TFP in comparison to DBT and supportive psychotherapy. Findings indicated a reduction of anger and suicidality in the TFP and DBT groups, but not in the supportive group. All three groups noted a reduction in depression, anxiety, global functioning, and social adjustment (Clarkin, Levy, Lenzenweger, & Kernberg, 2004). Of note in this study was the finding, consistent with the theoretical assumptions of Kernberg (1996) , that TFP is useful in the reduction of anger. Only one study found TFP to be less effective than a cognitive-based treatment with a schema-based approach (Geisen-Bloo et al., 2006).

Recent trends attempting to pair atheoretical diagnostic labels with theoretically consistent etiology have led to additional treatment approaches that focus on the etiology of BPD, rather than its symptomatology. Attachment theory is one of these approaches. An attachment approach to the treatment of BPD was first introduced by

Fonagy (1998), who noted that severe personality pathology could be understood as a maladaptive and distorted strategy of attachment. Such attachment styles are a result of disruptions in early infancy, usually of a traumatic nature, which are currently affecting normal, intimate, interpersonal relationships. The therapist serves as a "secure base" from which clients can engage in an exploration of their problems. Sherry (in press) outlines a case study of a BPD client using an expanded application of Fonagy's tenets. A central goal of this approach is to provide disconfirming evidence regarding insecure attachment schemas, ultimately shifting assimilative cognitive structures into accommodative cognitive structures capable of organizing new information in healthy, secure, more adaptive approaches to everyday challenges. A brief description of this case is presented later in this chapter. An attachment approach to the treatment of BPD is new and has not yet been explored in efficacy or effectiveness studies.

MEDICAL TREATMENT

In a longitudinal study of BPD patients spanning 6 years, it was found that 40% were taking three or more concurrent medications, 20% were taking four or more, and 10% were taking five or more medications at the same time over the course of the follow-up (Zanarini, Frankenburg, Hennen, & Silk, 2004). The extent to which BPD is treated with pharmacological agents depends on which symptoms are being addressed. For example, medications differ with respect to the extent to which they can ameliorate affective instability, suicidal depressive states, intense anger, or transient psychotic episodes. A second consideration is the acuteness of the diagnosis and the extent to which the potential for suicide is present. Suicide completion rates in BPD clients have been found to be 10% (Paris, 2002). Pharmacological treatments for mental disorders are in constant flux as we learn more about the brain's response to medications, as new drugs are created, and as efficacy trials are completed. A technical discussion advocating for specific pharmacological treatments is outside the authors' expertise. Therefore, the current summary is meant to represent avenues for further exploration on the part of those readers qualified to administer psychotropic medication.

ANTIDEPRESSANTS

Antidepressants are used to treat symptoms of affective dysregulation, depressed mood, anger, impulsive aggression, and irritability common to individuals with BPD (American Psychiatric Association, 2001). There are three general classes of antidepressants: tricyclics, selective serotonin reuptake inhibitors (SSRI), and monoamine oxidase inhibitors (MAOI). Of these, tricyclic antidepressants appear to be the least effective. In addition, risk of toxicity is high, which is a particular concern when treating individuals prone to suicide attempts (Jensen & Andersen, 1989; Parsons et al., 1989). Therefore, use of this class of antidepressants is highly questionable. Monoamine oxidase inhibitors have demonstrated good outcomes for the treatment of BPD, particularly for anger, hostility, rejection sensitivity, impulsivity, and atypical depressive symptoms (American Psychiatric Association, 2001). Drugs found to be most effective include phenelzine (*Nardil*) and tranylcypromine (*Parnate*; Cornelius, Soloff, Perel, & Ulrich, 1993; Cowdry & Gardner, 1988; Parsons et al., 1989; Soloff et al., 1993). However, like the tricyclic class of antidepressants, the risk of toxicity with MAOIs is high. In addition, the use of MAOIs requires an extremely strict diet that, if violated, could lead to hypertension so severe it could cause death. Given that many clients with

BPD have a difficult time with treatment compliance, the additional burden of diet compliance may be unrealistic.

Selective serotonin reuptake inhibitors appear to be the treatment of choice among the antidepressants for treating BPD. Specifically, studies on fluoxetine (*Prozac*), venlafaxine (*Effexor*), and sertraline (*Zoloft*) have demonstrated efficacy for alleviating BPD symptoms such as irritability, cognitive-perceptual distortions, affective dysregulation, impulsivity, aggression, depressed mood, and even self-mutilation (Coccaro & Kavoussi, 1997; Cornelius, Soloff, Perel, & Ulrich, 1990; Kavoussi, Liu, & Coccaro, 1994; Markovitz, 1995; Markovitz, Calabrese, Charles, & Meltzer, 1991; Norden, 1989; Salzman et al., 1995). Studies have also demonstrated that different SSRIs can be tried if a client is nonresponsive to one of them (Markovitz, 1995). In addition, SSRIs have limited side effects, which tend to remit after the body has adjusted to the medication. They are also nontoxic and cannot be used as an overdosing agent. Overall, efficacy findings vary by drug. One double-blind, placebo-controlled study of 38 BPD women found improvements in mood lability but not in impulsivity and aggression. The researchers suggested that the finding could be gender-specific because the correlation between serotonin hypofunction and impulsive aggression has thus far been noted only in White males (Rinne, van den Brink, Wouters, & van Dyck, 2002).

MOOD STABILIZERS AND ANTICONVULSANTS

Acting-out behaviors and affective lability can sometimes be effectively managed with lithium carbonate or anticonvulsant mood stabilizers like carbamazepine (*Tegretol*), oxcarbazepine (*Trileptal*), valproic acid (*Valproate*), or divalproex sodium (*Depakote*; American Psychiatric Association, 2001). Both controlled studies and case studies have cited a decrease in mood swings among BPD patients who took lithium (LaWall & Wesselius, 1982; Rifkin, Levitan, Galewski, & Klein, 1972a, 1972b; Shader, Jackson, & Dodes, 1974). However, other studies have indicated that some of the effects of lithium, particularly on decreases in impulsivity, are noticeable to therapists but not to clients themselves (Links, Steiner, Boiago, & Irwin, 1990). Carbamazepine has been associated with fewer suicide attempts and improvements in anger, anxiety, and euphoria (Gardner & Cowdry, 1985, 1986), but this is juxtaposed against the warning that carbamazepine can be fatal if used as an overdosing agent (American Psychiatric Association, 2001). Carbamazepine has been shown in one study to cause melancholic depression among some patients (Gardner & Cowdry, 1986). Divalproex sodium has been shown to be effective in the reduction of anxiety and tension among BPD inpatients to the extent that they manifested a 68% decrease in time spent in seclusion (Wilcox, 1994). Although these patients did not have co-occurring psychiatric disorders, this study was nonetheless somewhat confounded by the fact that some patients were taking other medications at the time. In addition, five patients had co-occurring electroencephalograph abnormalities that predicted response improvement; this suggests that divalproex might be more effective for BPD patients with co-occurring EEG abnormalities. In another double-blind, placebo-controlled study of 52 outpatients, divalproex was found to reduce impulsive aggression, particularly in those with higher baseline levels of trait impulsivity and state aggression. The same study did not find significant effects for baseline affective instability (Hollander, Swann, Coccaro, Jiang, & Smith, 2005).

Anticonvulsants have undesirable and sometimes serious side effects and can be used as suicide agents (American Psychiatric Association, 2001). For these reasons,

SSRIs might be the best first response to manage BPD symptoms, followed by mood stabilizers. Studies have shown that divalproex sodium has been effective with patients who did not respond to SSRI treatments (Kavoussi, Liu, & Coccaro, 1998). Oxcarbezepine, a drug structurally related to carbamazepine with fewer unwanted side effects, was shown to improve subjective patient ratings of overall mental health, affective stability, impulsivity, anger outbursts, and interpersonal relationships in an Italian sample of 17 with BPD and no concurrent or previous episodes of psychotic or mood disorders (Bellino, Paradiso, & Bogetto, 2005). Overall, carbamazepine and valproic acid have not been shown to be effective in treating pathological aggression in patients with (Frankenburg & Zanarini, 2002) and without (Azouvi et al., 1999; Fava, 1997; Tariot et al., 1998) BPD. Aggression has been shown to be successfully treated with lamotrigine (*Lamictal*) alone in a randomized, double-blind, placebo-controlled study of 24 BPD women with a decrease in outward displays of anger and an increase in anger control on psychological measures of anger (Tritt et al., 2005). Finally, topiramate (*Topamax*) was used in a German sample of 74 women. Compared to placebo, topiramate influenced the subjective state of anger, readiness to react with anger, the tendency to direct anger outward, and desire to control anger. Reduced appetite and weight loss, in addition to fatigue and dizziness (Nickel et al., 2004), were side effects. This replicated nonplacebo trials on aggression conducted previously with samples of clients with other disorders (Janowsky, Kraus, Barnhill, Elamir, & Davis, 2003; Teter, Early, & Gibbs, 2000).

ANTIPSYCHOTICS

Antipsychotics are sometimes used to treat the anger, hostility, and psychotic symptoms of BPD (American Psychiatric Association, 2001), particularly when these symptoms are primary (Grootens & Verkes, 2003). Low doses, however, have recently been shown to be efficacious in the treatment of affective symptoms as well (American Psychiatric Association, 2001). Studies investigating treatment of these symptoms in particular can be difficult due to the high dropout rates of samples with chronic, severe symptoms (American Psychiatric Association, 2001). This leads to limited follow-up and generalizability of findings in some cases (Grootens & Verkens, 2003). However, for the most part, antipsychotics are some of the best-studied psychotropic medications for BPD and appear to be efficacious for psychotic symptoms, anger, and hostility, as well as global symptom severity (American Psychiatric Association, 2001). Drugs often associated with this group of medications include haloperidol (*Haldol*), chlorpromazine (*Thorazine*), thiothixene (*Navane*), and trifluoperazine, as well as atypical antipsychotics, such as clozapine (*Clozaril*), risperidone (*Risperdal*), olanzapine (*Zyprexa*), and quetiapine (*Seroquel*). Studies using olanzapine have provided additional clinical utility because olanzapine lacks the serious side effects typically found intolerable by patients, thus increasing its compliance rate. The most uncomfortable side effect noted in studies is weight gain. Studies have found olanzapine to be superior to placebo in the alleviation of BPD symptoms, such as anxiety, paranoia, anger, hostility, and interpersonal sensitivity. No difference was found in reports of depressive symptoms between the researchers' 19 experimental subjects and 9 controls (Zanarini & Frankenburg, 2001). Other studies have supported these findings, but also found a decrease in depressive symptoms when olanzapine was combined with DBT (Soler et al., 2005). Studies using clozapine have produced similar findings, with low doses ameliorating affective, impulsive, and psychotic features in a small sample of BPD patients (Benedetti, Sforzini, Colombo, Maffei, & Smeraldi, 1998). Quetiapine was studied in a sample of 23 outpatient individuals with BPD, including men and women with and without psychotic symptoms. Findings indicated that quetiapine contributed to a decrease in depression, anxiety, hostility, social adaptation, and global functioning for both groups. An additional decrease in thought disorder symptoms was noted for the psychotic symptoms group (Villeneuve & Lemelin, 2005).

A handful of studies have attempted to compare classes of drugs to measure the efficacy or effectiveness in treating specific symptoms of BPD. For example, haloperidol has been found to be more efficacious overall than amitriptyline (a tricyclic antidepressant) and more than phenelzine (an MAOI) in targeting symptoms of hostility and impulsivity. However, phenelzine was superior to haloperidol at targeting symptoms of depression, psychoticism, anxiety, and overall functioning (Cornelius, Soloff, Perel, & Ulrich, 1993; Soloff et al., 1986). The MAOI tranylcypromine and the mood stabilizer carbamazepine were found to be related to symptom improvement, as evidenced by physician ratings of 16 female outpatients with BPD. A marked decrease in the severity of behavioral acting out was noted by clinicians among patients taking carbamazepine. However, the patients themselves indicated they experienced improvement only with tranylcypromine (Cowdry & Gardner, 1988). A recent study comparing the SSRI fluoxetine to the atypical antipsychotic olanzapine found olanzapine to be superior to fluoxetine and to an olanzapine-fluoxetine combination in decreasing chronic dysphoria and impulsive aggression in 42 women (Zanarini, Frankenburg, & Parachini, 2004).

Pharmacological treatment has also been shown to vary depending on the etiological nature of BPD. For example, in a sample of 30 female BPD patients, the SSRI fluvoxamine (Luvox) was effective in women with a history of sustained child abuse in decreasing physiological indicators of stress and anxiety. Women without a history of child abuse did not have pretreatment elevations of physiological indicators of stress, so no change was noted (Rinne et al., 2003). Other medical approaches have not been studied intensely enough to draw definitive conclusions or have not been found to be effective. Use of anxiolytics for the treatment of BPD has not been thoroughly researched. One study using a hypertensive medication, clonidine, found that BPD patients demonstrated a decrease in the urge to self-harm and a decrease in inner tension within an hour of treatment, which suggests that drugs with anxiolytic effects may be useful in short-term treatment of acute BPD symptoms (Philipsen et al., 2004). Similar preliminary findings have been found with opiate antagonists using case studies, but double-blind studies have not replicated this experimentally (American Psychiatric Association, 2001). Electroconvulsant therapy (ECT) has also been investigated as a possible treatment for BPD due to the prominent depressive traits often found in BPD. However, studies have indicated that the depressive symptoms associated with BPD are not treated effectively with ECT, and ECT is not an appropriate medical approach for the treatment of BPD (American Psychiatric Association, 2001).

An analysis of studies conducted on medication therapy for BPD indicates that SSRIs and antipsychotics have the most supportive evidence in the treatment of affective dysregulation in BPD. This is followed by MAOIs (although dietary restrictions may limit the viability of this treatment) and finally mood stabilizers (American Psychiatric Association, 2001). For impulsive behavior control, SSRIs, MAOIs, lithium, and low-dose typical antipsychotics have the most supportive evidence (American Psychiatric Association, 2001). For cognitive-perceptual symptoms, low-dose typical antipsychotics, SSRIs, and MAOIs have the most support (American Psychiatric Association, 2001).

Case Description

There are numerous efficacy, effectiveness, and case study approaches to the treatment of BPD. Most recent investigations of treating this diagnosis focus on cognitive approaches, such as DBT. The current case description uses a short-term attachment theory approach in the treatment of a 48-year-old, never-married woman of Hispanic and African American decent named Thelma (a pseudonym). A more detailed description of this case has been published elsewhere (Sherry, in press). Thelma's case represents a fairly typical BPD presentation, especially in inpatient and day treatment settings, because in addition to her BPD diagnosis, she also suffered from multiple comorbid Axis I diagnoses. The hypothesis in treating her BPD in light of her numerous other diagnoses was that these diagnoses were actually being driven by her BPD. If her BPD could be ameliorated, then her Axis I disordered symptoms would remit as well.

Thelma was an identical twin with two older brothers and one older sister. She was the child of an African American mother and a Hispanic father, whom she never met. She was raised by her mother and stepfather, an alcoholic, who was emotionally abusive. She suspected her stepfather sexually abused her as well, but she had no clear memories of this. She did, however, remember her brothers molesting her. Her sexual abuse history was confirmed by her twin sister. Although she told her mother about the abuse, she said her mother blamed her for it and never protected her from her brothers. This pattern of placing the sons' welfare above the daughters' welfare was a theme in Thelma's relationship with her mother. Two of her siblings, one older brother and one older sister, had broken ties with the family, and Thelma had not talked to them in years. She described a close relationship with her twin, but this relationship was also marked by manipulation on the part of the twin toward Thelma. Thelma's twin sister had a cocaine addiction and frequently withheld affection from Thelma and made Thelma feel guilty for not giving her sister money when she had spent her money on drugs. This was similar to how Thelma's mother manipulated her by withholding affection, love, and emotional support if Thelma did not meet her mother's physical, emotional, and financial needs.

Thelma seemed to be devoid of sexual or gender identity. She had never dated and had never participated in a consensual romantic or sexual relationship in her lifetime. She expressed no desire for these things, citing intrusive images of sexual abuse as her reason. She also dressed androgynously and once mentioned discomfort with her female sex; she did not want to pursue discussion of this. She also had no friends, and her social support system consisted of her mother and twin sister.

Thelma had a lengthy treatment history and had been on psychiatric disability for 18 years. The depth of her treatment, however, had been limited, with Medicaid typically covering only brief (30 minutes) monthly visits to her psychiatric caseworker and somewhat longer (45 minutes) visits to her psychiatrist on a quarterly basis. Such visits targeted medication effectiveness, side effects, and basic emotional skills training. Thelma had a long list of ineffective treatment attempts using SSRIs. Psychotherapy was available sporadically and usually on a time-limited basis when she was in acute crisis as a substitute

(continued)

for inpatient care. In some cases, she attended day treatment programs. She reported temporary success from these interactions but ultimately was unable to translate her success to day-to-day functioning in the long term. She presented to the psychiatric floor of the public hospital numerous times, to the point that staff knew her by name. Counterintuitively, because of this, she rarely received inpatient care. She was usually labeled "a borderline" and released within 24 hours.

Symptomatically, Thelma had a long-standing depression as well as a history of suicidal and self-mutilating behavior, the latter of which had left over 100 scars on her arms from cutting. She reported that her self-mutilating behaviors helped her cope when she thought no one would listen to her or when her feelings were too overwhelming to identify. She was notably hypervigilant to her surroundings, and she often manifested a pronounced startle response. She also reported intrusive traumatic thoughts. She had a long-standing eating disorder; for the previous 8 years she had binged and purged on a regular basis. This left her with tooth chipping and decay, as well as chronic sores in her mouth. In all, she met diagnoses for PTSD, Major Depressive Disorder, and Bulimia Nervosa on Axis I.

It is not uncommon for people with BPD to have multiple Axis I disorders. It appears that, in many cases, having a BPD diagnosis compromises otherwise sufficient ego strength and psychological resources. Initially, treatment with Thelma focused on her Axis I complaints, in large part because they were presented by her as the most pressing issues she was facing; in addition, her eating disorder was posing a health risk. After 2 months of cognitive interventions (homework assignments, food journals, etc.) showed no improvement, however, it was determined that Thelma's BPD diagnosis was the driving force behind her Axis I symptoms and that it was actually her BPD that needed to be treated. Thelma's BPD symptoms included engaging in frantic efforts to avoid abandonment through dysfunctional approach-avoidance behaviors like cutting. She had dysfunctional and limited interpersonal relationships that were intense, unstable, and a constant source of disappointment. Her sense of self was unstable, with confusion around core issues of self, such as sexuality, gender, and racial identity. She engaged in impulsive dysfunctional behaviors, including overspending, self-mutilating, binge eating, and attempting suicide. Within this myriad of behaviors and feelings was a chronic sense of emptiness, hopelessness, and futility. Treating her BPD represented a shift from previous interventions and from the managed care model of psychiatric treatment, but it was concluded that BPD symptoms clearly explained Thelma's Axis I symptoms and thus needed to be addressed.

Prior to this time, Thelma was frequently turned away from intensive inpatient psychiatric treatment precisely *because* of her BPD. This approach, though intended to be cost-effective, potentially increases treatment costs for individuals with BPD. Interestingly, it is also incongruent with approaches to other medical conditions. For example, it would seem ridiculous for medicine to advocate for the amputation of feet or limbs secondary to the lack of circulation caused by untreated diabetes. Instead, long-term management and treatment of diabetes, also an incurable disease, is considered best practice because it prevents the development of other, more detrimental medical problems. The decision to treat Thelma's BPD followed this rationale. It was determined at the time that the etiology of Thelma's BPD was a history of disappointment with attachment figures in her life, coupled with abuse and neglect by those attachment figures, resulting in a pervasive and intense insecure attachment style. Shifting this attachment style to one of security became the goal of treatment, and the method was simply providing a secure base from which Thelma could explore her own interpersonal and intrapsychic issues. This was particularly important for Thelma in that the attachment figures she had in her past and present were neglectful and abusive. She had no template for healthy interpersonal relatedness.

At the onset of psychotherapy, Thelma's primary need was different from that proposed by the clinician. Initially, the clinician wanted to reduce Thelma's Axis I symptoms, but Thelma's true need was to connect in a meaningful way with another person. Once such incongruence was recognized, the shift to an attachment approach began. Initially, this approach consisted of simply spending time with Thelma to get to know her; a humanistic stance of unconditional positive regard was adopted. Early topics included the weather, movies, and funny stories from the week apart. Slowly, Thelma was able to share more, and she explored her relationship with her sister, her mother, why she had so few friendships, her financial concerns, and in one session her concern about her gender identity. The one exception to this stance was monitoring and following Thelma's suicidal ideation and self-mutilation through ongoing, frank discussions about safety. Often these discussions can come across as legalistic, impersonal attempts at controlling behavior, but they were cast in this treatment in an interpersonal light focusing on the importance of the relationship between the clinician and the client.

Therapy unfolded at Thelma's pace, and she was never pushed to go further than she wanted. The supportive relationship communicated both trust in Thelma's ability to talk about what she needed to on her own terms, as well as a secure base to which she could return if she felt she had gone too far. Thelma had control over the sessions. She had been a long-time mental health consumer and knew that psychotherapy was the place to talk about troubling or concerning themes. The clinician allowed her to discuss these issues in her own time with no agenda to expose them, but no attempt to avoid them either. Therapy was a process of ongoing negotiation. Rather than suggesting she discuss a specific issue, such as her child abuse, she was asked if she felt comfortable doing so that particular day. If not, the discussion turned to the emotional blocks she was experiencing. Traditional boundaries were relaxed with Thelma as well. When she articulated a need to be seen more than once a week, it was generally granted. If it could not be granted, it was for practical reasons rather than "boundary setting" reasons, and she and the clinician negotiated other ways her needs could get met in the context of the therapeutic relationship. Phone calls were returned immediately, and during times the clinician knew were stressful for her, the clinician would initiate calls to touch base in between sessions to see how she was doing. All of these decisions were based on the assumption that the creation of a secure base was paramount to treatment. Similarly, no such interventions were begun without careful consideration on the part of the clinician because the clinician would have to be committed to maintaining this level of care for as long as was needed.

(continued)

In the first 6 months, Thelma's self-mutilating and suicidal behavior continued from time to time. She admitted herself to the hospital preemptively two times before she hurt herself and was praised by the clinician for taking care of herself. These events were processed from an interpersonal perspective. At one point, Thelma cut her wrists and called the clinician on the phone to report the incident. The clinician called the mobile crisis unit, and Thelma was taken to the emergency room for stitches. During her recovery time in the ER, she left against medical advice and had to be admitted to the hospital via transportation by the sheriff's department. While on the psychiatric unit for a month, Thelma remained suicidal, even attempting suicide again in between 15-minute suicide checks. However, the clinician visited Thelma daily and attempted to maintain the secure base that had been created in the preceding 6 months. The therapist also tried to instill in Thelma a sense of self-efficacy around her mental health issues by recounting for her the gains she had made in therapy so far. In addition to these efforts, she was placed on the mood stabilizer Depakote. Toward the end of her hospitalization, her impulsiveness and depression began to lift, and she was discharged with no suicidal ideation.

Once discharged and stable, Thelma was referred to group therapy in addition to individual therapy. Her group therapist was also her individual therapist, so her perceptions of events that happened in group therapy could be processed in individual treatment with someone who was also privy to the sessions. Due to Thelma's long-standing insecure attachments with others, it was felt this was a good opportunity to help her identify ways people support her and try to connect with her, whereas in the past she had been unable to recognize these efforts. It was during these times that her cognitive working models of others and of herself began to make the most dramatic shifts.

Because the therapist's position was time-limited and an attachment approach was utilized, termination and transfer to a new therapist were discussed from the first day of treatment. Transfer involved Thelma's having several meetings with both her new and old therapists together, as well as several sessions individually but prior to formal termination with her first therapist. This gave Thelma the opportunity to come back to her secure base to discuss her fears and apprehensions about her new therapist and receive the supportive assurance from that secure base that she would be able to handle the change effectively. In an idiosyncratic decision, it was also decided that Thelma would be able to contact her old therapist through letters sent by her new therapist. This is something a participating therapist must be willing to follow through with, including the agreement to answer such letters in a timely fashion. This extends the notion of the secure base and reduces feelings of abandonment. This time in therapy was also an opportunity for one of the only healthy goodbyes Thelma had had in her life. This particular goodbye was not synonymous with rejection or abandonment. This was highlighted through the exchange of meaningful but inexpensive gifts and weeks of processing and discussing the departure.

A brief list of the shift to an attachment approach can be found in Table 15.1. From this approach, Thelma experienced several core changes that came to light during the treatment year, through her letter communications and through conversations with her new therapist. In time, Thelma was able to juxtapose her relationship with the clinician to her relationship with others in her life that created insecurity for her. The secure relationship she developed with her clinician became a new standard for what she wanted her relationships to be like. Her challenge was to determine how to create security in other relationships in her life. Severing ties with her mother and sister was not an option for her. Instead, helping Thelma negotiate a sense of autonomy with her family became one of many focal points in therapy. Thelma also reported making new friends with neighbors in her building for the first time in her life. She began wearing dresses and makeup, styling her hair, and otherwise exploring her gender identity. For the year and a half her progress was followed, she reported no more feelings of suicide and presented to the hospital much less frequently and only in instances in which she needed added support. She never needed to be admitted. She also stopped binging and purging completely and no longer met the criteria for an eating disorder. She reported improved relationships with her mother and twin sister as a result of more appropriate boundaries she was able to set with them. She wrote that she enjoyed working with her new therapist and that this relationship was a strong one, although she had to stop going about 2 years later due to knee surgery that immobilized her for some time.

Table 15.1
Shifting to an Attachment Approach to the Treatment of Borderline Personality Disorder

Shift	*Purpose*
Treating the symptom → Addressing the etiology	Similar to physical disorders like diabetes, treating BPD from an etiological perspective is more likely to address the core driving forces that impair functioning.
Resistance should be eliminated → Resistance should be understood[1]	Resistance is fear within the attachment organization that needs are not going to get met. It is a protective reaction and should be respected.
"Boundary pushing" should be eliminated or punished → Boundary pushing is an indication to the clinician that the client's needs are not being met	Attachment disordered clients push boundaries because of their almost insatiable anxious attachment. Negotiate a way to meet these needs with the client, even if it is more than what is done for other clients (extra phone calls, longer sessions), reduces anxiety, and reduces the need for clients to engage in this behavior.
Quantity and content of sessions → Quality and intensity of the therapeutic relationship	What symptoms get eradicated in 10 sessions or less is not as important as creating a relationship that serves as a secure base for the client to feel safe.

(continued)

Table 15.1
(*Continued*)

Shift	Purpose
Solve or fix → To shift	The goal is not to solve or fix client problems, but to shift internal working models from insecure models to secure ones through a patient, affirming, supportive relationship. Axis I symptoms are addressed, but are secondary to building the relationship.
Investment in the outcome → Investment in the process	Often clinician frustration occurs when clients continue to engage in destructive behavior. Shifting to an investment in the process of the relationship provides a place to reflect care and concern to the client while minimizing anger and frustration. Such care and concern contributes to the establishment of a secure base.
First-order change → Second-order change[2]	First-order change refers to change without change, or change in a system without change in the core structure of the system. Second-order change refers to changes in the fundamental core structure of the system.
Reality as real → Reality as subjective	It is unproductive to challenge client perceptions of reality in situations where clients have felt abused, neglected, or rejected. It is more important to validate the client's perception of events because this validation contributes to the security of the relationship. There is plenty of time for testing perceptions once security in the relationship is firmly established.
Dictating treatment to the client → Negotiating treatment with the client	The clinician regularly asks the client what is and is not working for him or her and makes adjustments accordingly. Negotiation is a strong element to this. When the therapist has a concern about a potential adjustment being unhealthy for the client, it is discussed with the client's emotional needs paramount superseding traditional therapeutic boundaries and rules.

[1] See Lyddon, W. J. (1993). Contrast, contradiction, and change in psychotherapy. *Psychotherapy, 30,* 383–390.
[2] See Lyddon, W. J. (1990). First- and second-order change: Implications for rationalist and constructivist cognitive therapies. *Journal of Counseling and Development, 69,* 122–127.

This case highlights a shift from traditional thoughts about the treatment of BPD, particularly those that imply that the disorder is not treatable and therefore should not be covered under insurance plans. The reality is that such assumptions and policies likely do more to prolong treatment, ultimately increasing costs. Because of the case study design, it is unclear to what extent Thelma's improvement could be attributed to the attachment approach utilized or to her new therapist, her medication change, or simply time. At a minimum, the goal of the short-term attachment approach was to provide her with a foundation for exploration with future mental health professionals, which it seemed to achieve.

Lyddon (1990) refers to approaches like the one utilized here as treatments that focus on second-order change. Approaches that emphasize first-order change tend to focus on the reduction of Axis I symptomatology. First-order change refers to "any change in a system that does not produce a change in the structure of the system" (p. 122). Because the core structure of the system remains relatively untouched, change is not expected to last, and the client eventually returns to pretreatment levels of functioning over the long term. This explains the revolving door often seen in BPD patients, including Thelma. However, second-order change alters the fundamental core structure of the system. As Lyddon notes, second-order change requires a developmental change in cognitive structures. In addition, it also requires the recognition of and attention to etiological structures that have become dysfunctional over time. An attachment approach to the treatment of BPD appears to meet both of these requirements, ultimately lessening the impact of Axis I symptoms which develop in the context of the BPD diagnosis. The goal is to establish new cognitive beliefs about others as trustworthy, attentive, and predictable through a secure, predictable relationship with a therapist. The theory and hope is that this template will generalize to others, including new treating professionals (provided the humanistic stance is present), and that long-term learning can thus be achieved.

This approach may not work with all BPD clients. An evaluation regarding goodness of fit between this approach and a particular client should focus on the etiological nature of the disorder. As demonstrated throughout this chapter, there are a number of pathways to the development of BPD. Millon (1996) conceptualizes BPD clients as having personal histories that reinforce the notion that they will never be able to trust others enough to gain all of the affection and support they need. At the same time, he explains a number of different subtypes of the disorder that are useful in creating working hypotheses around treatment and prognosis. Thelma most likely typified Millon's "discouraged borderline" prototype. However, the extent to which an attachment approach might be effective with other borderline subtypes remains unexplored.

SUMMARY

Borderline Personality Disorder is the most common disorder found in inpatient and outpatient treatment settings. It is characterized by a pervasive pattern of instability in affect regulation, impulse control, interpersonal relationships, and self-image and is often comorbid with a number of Axis I disorders as well as other Axis II disorders. The current chapter briefly summarized the theoretical foundations and empirical evidence that professionals would find useful in treating this resistant disorder. Assessment and diagnosis of the disorder, as well as conceptualization from learning theory, attachment theory, risk factor research, genetic, biological, and cultural perspectives were reviewed. Medical treatments were briefly outlined as well as popular therapeutic approaches such as dialectical behavior therapy and transference-focused psychotherapy. A new perspective, an attachment theory approach to the treatment of BPD, was also outlined with a case example of its implementation.

REFERENCES

Akiskal, H. S. (1985). Borderline: An adjective in search of a noun. *Journal of Clinical Psychiatry, 46*(2), 41–48.

Alexander, M. J., & Muenzenmaier, K. (1998). Trauma, addiction, and recovery: Addressing public health epidemics among women with severe mental illness. In B. L. Levin, A. K. Blanch, & A. Jennings (Eds.), *Women's mental health services: A public health perspective* (pp. 215–239). Thousand Oaks, CA: Sage.

American Psychiatric Association. (2000). *Diagnostic and statistical manual of mental disorders* (4th ed., text rev.). Washington, DC: Author.

American Psychiatric Association. (2001, October). Practice guideline for the treatment of patients with borderline personality disorder. *American Journal of Psychiatry, 158*(Suppl.), 1–52.

Andrulonis, P. A., Glueck, B. C., & Stroebel, C. F. (1982). Borderline personality subcategories. *Journal of Nervous and Mental Diseases, 170*, 670–679.

Azouvi, P., Jokic, C., Attal, N., Denys, P., Markabi, S., & Bussel, B. (1999). Carbamazepine in agitation and aggressive behavior following severe closed-head injury: Results of an open trial. *Brain Injury, 13*, 797–804.

Becker, D. (1997). *Through the looking glass: Women and borderline personality disorder.* Boulder, CO: Westview.

Bellino, S., Paradiso, E., & Bogetto, F. (2005). Oxcarbazepine in the treatment of borderline personality disorder: A pilot study. *Journal of Clinical Psychiatry, 66*, 1111–1115.

Bell-Pringle, V. J., Pate, J. L., & Brown, R. C. (1997). Assessment of borderline personality disorder using the MMPI-2 and the Personality Assessment Inventory. *Assessment, 4*, 131–139.

Bemporad, J. R., Smith, H. F., Hanson, G., & Cicchetti, D. (1982). Borderline syndromes in childhood: Criteria for diagnosis. *American Journal of Psychiatry, 139*, 596–602.

Benazzi, F. (2000). Borderline personality disorder and bipolar II disorder in private practice depressed outpatients. *Comprehensive Psychiatry, 41*, 106–110.

Bender, D. S., Farber, B. A., & Geller, J. D. (2001). Cluster B personality traits and attachment. *Journal of the American Academy of Psychoanalysis, 29*, 551–563.

Benedetti, F., Sforzini, L., Colombo, C., Maffei, C., & Smeraldi, E. (1998). Low-dose clozapine in acute and continuation treatment of severe borderline personality disorder. *Journal of Clinical Psychiatry, 59*, 103–107.

Bowlby, J. (1969). *Attachment and loss: Vol. 1. Attachment.* New York: Basic Books.

Bowlby, J. (1973). *Attachment and loss: Vol. 2. Separation: Anxiety and anger.* New York: Basic Books.

Bradley, S. J. (1979). The relationship of early maternal separation to borderline personality in children and adolescents: A pilot study. *American Journal of Psychiatry, 136*, 424–426.

Brennan, K. A., & Shaver, P. R. (1998). Attachment styles and personality disorders: Their connections to each other and to parental divorce, parental death, and perceptions of parental caregiving. *Journal of Personality, 66*, 835–878.

Brown, G. R., & Anderson, B. (1991). Psychiatric morbidity in adult inpatients with childhood histories of sexual and physical abuse. *American Journal of Psychiatry, 148*, 55–61.

Brown, L. S. (1994). *Subversive dialogues: Theory in feminist therapy.* New York: Basic Books.

Butcher, J. N., Dahlstrom, W. G., Graham, J. R., Tellegen, A., & Kaemmer, B. (1989). *MMPI-2: Manual of administration and scoring.* Minneapolis: University of Minnesota Press.

Casimir, G. J., & Morrison, B. J. (1993). Rethinking work with "multicultural populations." *Community Mental Health Journal, 29*, 547–559.

Chavira, D. A., Grilo, C. M., Shea, M. T., Yen, S., Gunderson, J. G., Morey, L. C., et al. (2003). Ethnicity and four personality disorders. *Comprehensive Psychiatry, 44*(6), 483–491.

Clarkin, J. F., Foelsch, P. A., Levy, K. N., Hull, J. W., Delaney, J. C., & Kernberg, O. F. (2001). The development of a psychodynamic treatment for patients with borderline personality disorders: A preliminary study of behavioral change. *Journal of Personality Disorders, 15,* 487–495.

Clarkin, J. F., Levy, K. N., Lenzenweger, M. F., & Kernberg, O. F. (2004). The Personality Disorders Institute/Borderline Personality Disorder Research Foundation randomized control trial for borderline personality disorder: Rationale, methods, and patient characteristics. *Journal of Personality Disorders, 18,* 52–72.

Clarkin, J. F., Yeomans, F. E., & Kernberg, O. F. (1999). *Psychotherapy of borderline personality.* Washington, DC: American Psychiatric Press.

Clarkin, J. F., Yeomans, F. E., & Kernberg, O. F. (2006). *Psychotherapy of borderline personality: Focusing on object relations.* Washington, DC: American Psychiatric Press.

Cloninger, C. R. (1997). Special feature: Etiology of personality disorders. A commentary on Dr. Parker's tripartite model. *Journal of Personality Disorders, 11,* 370–374.

Coccaro, E. F. (1998). Neurotransmitter function in personality disorders. In K. R. Silk (Ed.), *Biology of personality disorders: Review of psychiatry* (pp. 1–25). Washington, DC: American Psychiatric Press.

Coccaro, E. F., & Kavoussi, R. J. (1997). Fluoxetine and impulsive aggressive behavior in personality-disordered subjects. *Archives of General Psychiatry, 54,* 1081–1088.

Coonerty, S. (1986). An exploration of separation-individuation themes in the borderline personality disorder. *Journal of Personality Assessment, 50,* 501–511.

Cornelius, J. R., Soloff, P. H., Perel, J. M., & Ulrich, R. F. (1990). Fluoxetine trial in borderline personality disorder. *Psychopharmacology Bulletin, 26,* 151–154.

Cornelius, J. R., Soloff, P. H., Perel, J. M., & Ulrich, R. F. (1993). Continuation pharmacotherapy of borderline personality disorder with haloperidol and phenelzine. *American Journal of Psychiatry, 150,* 1843–1848.

Cornett, C. (1993). *Affirmative dynamic psychotherapy with gay men.* Lanham, MD: Aronson.

Cowdry, R. W., & Gardner, D. L. (1988). Pharmacotherapy of borderline personality disorder: Alprazolam, carbamazepine, trifluoperazine, and tranylcypromine. *Archives of General Psychiatry, 45,* 111–119.

Crick, N. R., Murray-Close, D., & Woods, K. (2005). Borderline personality features in childhood: A short-term longitudinal study. *Development and Psychopathology, 17,* 1051–1070.

Curtois, C. A. (1999). *Recollections of sexual abuse: Treatment principles and guidelines.* New York: Norton.

Daley, S. E., Burge, D., & Hammen, C. (2000). Borderline personality disorder symptoms as predictors of 4-year romantic relationship dysfunction in young women: Addressing issues of specificity. *Journal of Abnormal Psychology, 3,* 451–460.

DeSoto, M. C., Geary, D. C., Hoard, M. K., Sheldon, M. S., & Cooper, L. (2003). Estrogen fluctuations, oral contraceptives, and borderline personality. *Psychoneuroendocrinology, 28,* 751–766.

Dimeff, L., Rizvi, S. L., Brown, M., & Linehan, M. M. (2000). Dialectical behavior therapy for substance abuse: A pilot application to methamphetamine-dependent women with borderline personality disorder. *Cognitive and Behavioral Practice, 7,* 457–468.

Divac-Jovanovic, M., Svrakic, D., & Lecic-Tosevski, D. (1993). Personality disorders: Model for conceptual approach and classification. *American Journal of Psychotherapy, 47,* 558–571.

Driessen, M., Veltrup, C., Wetterling, T., John, U., & Dilling, H. (1998). Axis I and Axis II comorbidity in alcohol dependence and the two types of alcoholism. *Alcohol Clinical and Experimental Research, 22,* 77–86.

Exner, J. E. (2003). *The Rorschach—A comprehensive system:* Vol. I.*Basic foundations and principles of interpretation* (4th ed.). Hoboken, NJ: Wiley.

Fava, M. (1997). Psychopharmacological treatment of pathologic aggression. *Psychiatric Clinic of North America, 20,* 427–431.

Fonagy, P. (1998). An attachment theory approach to treatment of the difficult patient. *Bulletin of the Menninger Clinic, 62,* 147–169.

Fonagy, P., Target, M., & Gergely, G. (2000). Attachment and borderline personality disorder: A theory and some evidence. *Psychiatric Clinics of North America, 23,* 103–122.

Fonagy, P., Target, M., Gergely, G., Allen, J. G., & Bateman, A. W. (2003). The developmental roots of borderline personality in early attachment relationships: A theory and some evidence. *Psychoanalytic Inquiry, 23*(3), 412–459.

Fossati, A., Donati, D., Donini, M., Novella, L., Bagnato, M., & Maffei, C. (2001). Temperament, character, and attachment patterns in borderline personality disorder. *Journal of Personality Disorders, 15,* 390–402.

Fossati, A., Feeney, J. A., Carretta, I., Grazioli, F., Milesi, R., Leonardi, B., et al. (2005). Modeling the relationships between adult attachment patterns and borderline personality disorder: The role of impulsivity and aggressiveness. *Journal of Social and Clinical Psychology, 24,* 520–537.

Francis, A., & Widiger, T. A. (1987). A critical review of four DSM-III personality disorders: Borderline, avoidant, dependent and passive-aggressive. In G. L. Tischler (Ed.), *Diagnosis and classification in psychiatry: A critical appraisal of DSM-III* (pp. 269–289). New York: Cambridge University Press.

Frank, H., & Paris, J. (1981). Recollections of family experience in borderline patients. *Archives of General Psychiatry, 38,* 1031–1034.

Frankenburg, F. R., & Zanarini, M. C. (2002). Divalproex sodium treatment of women with borderline personality disorder and bipolar II disorder: A double-blind placebo-controlled pilot study. *Journal of Clinical Psychiatry, 63,* 442–446.

Frankenburg, F. R., & Zanarini, M. C. (2004). The association between borderline personality disorder and chronic mental illnesses, poor health-related lifestyle choices, and costly forms of health care utilization. *Journal of Clinical Psychiatry, 65,* 1660–1665.

Frankenburg, F. R., & Zanarini, M. C. (2006). Personality disorders and medical comorbidity. *Current Opinion in Psychiatry, 19,* 428–431.

Gardner, D. L., & Cowdry, R. W. (1985). Alprazolam induced dyscontrol in borderline personality disorder. *American Journal of Psychiatry, 142,* 98–100.

Gardner, D. L., & Cowdry, R. W. (1986). Development of melancholia during carbamazepine treatment in borderline personality disorder. *Journal of Clinical Psychopharmacology, 6,* 236–239.

Gartner, A. F., Marcus, R. N., Halmi, K., & Loranger, A. W. (1989). DSM-III-R personality disorders in patients with eating disorders. *American Journal of Psychiatry, 146,* 1585–1591.

Giesen-Bloo, J., van Dyck, R., Spinhoven, P., van Tilburg, W., Dirksen, C., van Asselt, T., et al. (2006). Outpatient psychotherapy for borderline personality disorder: Randomized trial of schema-focused therapy versus transference-focused psychotherapy. *Archives of General Psychiatry, 63,* 649–658.

Goldman, S. J., D'Angelo, E. J., DeMaso, D. R., & Mezzacappa, E. (1992). Physical and sexual abuse histories among children with borderline personality disorder. *American Journal of Psychiatry, 149,* 1723–1726.

Goodwin, J. M., Cheeves, K., & Connell, V. (1989). Borderline and other severe symptoms in adult survivors of incestuous abuse. *Psychiatric Annals, 20,* 22–31.

Graybar, S. R., & Boutilier, L. R. (2002). Nontraumatic pathways to borderline personality disorder. *Psychotherapy: Theory, Research, Practice, and Training, 39,* 152–162.

Greenberg, R., Craig, S., Seidman, L., Cooper, S., & Teele, A. (1987). Transitional phenomena and the Rorschach: A test of a clinical theory of borderline personality organization. In J. S. Grotstein, M. F. Solomon, & J. A. Lang (Eds.). *The borderline patient: Emerging concepts in diagnosis, psychodynamics, and treatment* (pp. 83–94). Hillsdale, NJ: Analytic Press.

Grilo, C. M., Sanislow, C. A., & McGlashan, T. H. (2002). Co-occurrence of DSM-IV personality disorders with borderline personality disorder. *Journal of Nervous and Mental Diseases, 190,* 552–553.

Grinker, R. R., Werble, B., & Drye, R. C. (1968). *The borderline syndrome: A behavioral study of ego-functions.* New York: Basic Books.

Grootens, K. P., & Verkes, R. J. (2003). Emerging evidence for the use of atypical antipsychotics in borderline personality disorder. *Pharmacopsychiatry, 38,* 20–23.

Gunderson, J. G., Frank, A. F., & Ronningstam, E. F. (1989). Early discontinuance of borderline patients from psychotherapy. *Journal of Nervous Mental Disorders, 177,* 38–42.

Gunderson, J. G., & Sabo, A. N. (1993). The phenomenological and conceptual interface between borderline personality disorder and PTSD. *American Journal of Psychiatry, 150,* 19–27.

Gunderson, J. G., & Zanarini, M. (1987). Current overview of the borderline diagnosis. *Journal of Clinical Psychiatry, 48,* 5–11.

Gurvits, I. G., Koenigsberg, H. W., & Siever, L. J. (2000). Neurotransmitter dysfunction in patients with borderline personality disorder. *Psychiatric Clinics of North America, 23,* 27–40.

Hatzitaskos, P., Soldatos, C. R., Kokkevi, A., & Stefanis, C. N. (1999). Substance abuse patterns and their association with psychopathology and type of hostility in male patients with borderline and antisocial personality disorder. *Comprehensive Psychiatry, 40,* 278–282.

Henry, K., & Cohen, C. (1983). The role of labeling processes in diagnosing borderline personality disorder. *American Journal of Psychiatry, 140,* 1527–1529.

Herman, J. L. (1992). *Trauma and recovery.* New York: Basic Books.

Herman, J. L., & van der Kolk, B. A. (1987). Traumatic antecedents of borderline personality disorder. In B. A. van der Kolk (Ed.), *Psychological trauma* (pp. 111–126). Washington, DC: American Psychiatric Press.

Hicklin, J., & Widiger, T. A. (2000). Convergent validity of alternative MMPI-2 personality disorder scales. *Journal of Personality Assessment, 75,* 502–518.

Hirshberg, L. M. (1989). Rorschach images of symbiosis and separation in eating-disordered and in borderline and nonborderline subjects. *Psychoanalytic Psychology, 6,* 475–493.

Hodges, S. (2003). Borderline personality disorder and posttraumatic stress disorder: Time for integration? *Journal of Counseling and Development, 81*(4), 409–417.

Hollander, E., Swann, A. C., Coccaro, E. F., Jiang, P., & Smith, T. B. (2005). Impact of trait impulsivity and state aggression on divalproex versus placebo response in borderline personality disorder. *American Journal of Psychiatry, 162,* 621–624.

Horwitz, L., Gabbard, G. O., Allen, J. G., Frieswyk, S. H., Colson, D. B., Newson, G. E., et al. (1996). *Borderline personality disorder: Tailoring the psychotherapy to the patient.* Washington, DC: American Psychiatric Press.

Hovey, J. D., & Magana, C. G. (2002). Psychosocial predictors of anxiety among immigrant Mexican migrant farmworkers: Implications for prevention and treatment. *Cultural Diversity and Ethnic Minority Psychology, 8*(3), 274–289.

Irle, E., Lange, C., & Sachsse, U. (2005). Reduced size and abnormal asymmetry of parietal cortex in women with borderline personality disorder. *Biological Psychiatry, 57,* 173–182.

Jackson, K. M., & Trull, T. J. (2001). The factor structure of the Personality Assessment Inventory—Borderline Features (PAI-BOR) Scale in a nonclinical sample. *Journal of Personality Disorders, 15,* 536–545.

Jang, K. L., Dick, D. M., Wolf, H., Livesley, W. J., & Paris, J. (2005). Psychosocial adversity and emotional instability: An application of gene-environment interaction models. *European Journal of Personality, 19,* 359–372.

Janowsky, D. S., Kraus, J. E., Barnhill, J., Elamir, B., & Davis, J. M. (2003). Effects of topiramate on aggressive, self-injurious, and disruptive/destructive behaviors in the intellectually disabled: An open-label retrospective study. *Journal of Clinical Psychopharmacology, 23,* 500–503.

Jensen, H. V., & Andersen, J. (1989). An open, noncomparative study of amoxapine in borderline disorders. *Acta Psychiatrica Scandinavia, 79,* 89–93.

Kahl, K. G., Rudolf, S., Stoeckelhuber, B. M., Dibbelt, L., Gehl, H., Markof, K., et al. (2005). Bone mineral density, markers of bone turnover, and cytokines in young women with borderline personality disorder with and without comorbid major depressive disorder. *American Journal of Psychiatry, 162,* 168–174.

Kavoussi, R. J., Liu, J., & Coccaro, E. F. (1994). An open trial of sertraline in personality disordered patients with impulsive aggression. *Journal of Clinical Psychiatry, 55,* 137–141.

Kavoussi, R. J., Liu, J., & Coccaro, E. F. (1998). Divalproex sodium for impulsive aggressive behavior in patients with personality disorder. *Journal of Clinical Psychiatry, 59,* 676–680.

Kay, J. H., Altshuler, L. L., Ventura, J., & Mintz, J. (1999). Prevalence of Axis II comorbidity in bipolar patients with and without alcohol use disorders. *Annals of Clinical Psychiatry, 11,* 187–195.

Kernberg, O. F. (1967). Borderline personality organization. *Journal of the American Psychoanalytic Association, 15,* 641–685.

Kernberg, O. F. (1975). *Borderline conditions and pathological narcissism.* New York: Aronson.

Kernberg, O. F. (1996). A psychoanalytic theory of personality disorders. In J. F. Clarkin & M. F. Lenzenweger (Eds.), *Major theories of personality disorder* (pp. 106–140). New York: Guilford Press.

Knight, R. (1954). Some remarks on psychotherapy. *Digest of Neurology & Psychiatry, 22,* 150.

Kröger, C., Schweiger, U., Sipos, V., Arnold, R., Kahl, K. G., Schunert, T., et al. (2006). Effectiveness of dialectical behavior therapy for borderline personality disorder in an inpatient setting. *Behavior Research and Therapy, 44,* 1211–1217.

Kroll, J. (1993). *PTSD/borderlines in therapy: Finding the balance.* New York: Norton.

Landecker, H. (1992). The role of childhood sexual trauma in the etiology of borderline personality disorder: Considerations for diagnosis and treatment. *Psychotherapy, 29,* 234–242.

Laporte, L., & Guttman, H. (1996). Traumatic childhood experiences as risk factors for borderline and other personality disorders. *Journal of Personality Disorders, 10,* 247–259.

LaWall, J. S., & Wesselius, C. L. (1982). The use of lithium carbonate in borderline patients. *Journal of Psychiatric Treatment and Evaluation, 4,* 265–267.

Levitt, E. E., & Gotts, E. E. (1995). *The clinical application of MMPI special scales* (2nd ed.). Hillsdale, NJ: Erlbaum.

Levy, K. N., Clarkin, J. F., Yeomans, F. E., Scott, L. N., Wasserman, R. H., & Kernberg, O. F. (2006). The mechanisms of change in the treatment of borderline personality disorder with transference focused psychotherapy. *Journal of Clinical Psychology, 62,* 481–501.

Lieb, K., Zanarini, M. C., Schmahl, C., Linehan, M. M., & Bohus, M. (2004). Borderline personality disorder. *Lancet, 364,* 453–461.

Linehan, M. M. (1993). *Skills training manual for treating borderline personality disorder.* New York: Guilford Press.

Linehan, M. M., Armstrong, H. E., Suarez, A., Allmon, D., & Heard, H. L. (1991). Cognitive-behavioral treatment of chronically parasuicidal borderline patients. *Archives of General Psychiatry, 48,* 1060–1064.

Linehan, M. M., Comtois, K. A., Murray, A. M., Brown, M. Z., Gallop, R. J., Heard, H. L., et al. (2006). Two-year randomized controlled trial of follow-up of dialectical behavior therapy versus therapy by experts for suicidal behaviors and borderline personality disorder. *Archives of General Psychiatry, 63,* 757–766.

Linehan, M. M., & Heard, H. L. (1993). Impact of treatment accessibility on clinical course of parasuicidal patients. In reply to R. E. Hoffmann [Letter to the editor]. *Archives of General Psychiatry, 50,* 157–158.

Linehan, M. M., Schmidt, H., Dimeff, L. A., Craft, J. C., Kanter, J., & Comtois, K. A. (1999). Dialectical behavior therapy for patients with borderline personality disorder and drug-dependence. *American Journal on Addictions, 8,* 279–292.

Links, P., Steiner, M., Boiago, I., & Irwin, D. (1990). Lithium therapy for borderline patients: Preliminary findings. *Journal of Personality Disorders, 4,* 173–181.

Liotti, G., & Pasquini, P. (2000). Predictive factors for borderline personality disorder: Patients' early traumatic experiences and losses suffered by the attachment figure. *Acta Psychiatrica Scandinavica, 102,* 282–289.

Livesley, W. J., Jang, K. L., & Vernon, P. A. (1998). Phenotypic and genetic structure of traits delineating personality disorder. *Archives of General Psychiatry, 55,* 941–948.

Lopez, F. G. (1995). Contemporary attachment theory: An introduction with implications for counseling psychology. *Counseling Psychologist, 23,* 395–415.

Lyddon, W. J. (1990). First- and second-order change: Implications for rationalist and constructivist cognitive therapies. *Journal of Counseling and Development, 69,* 122–127.

Lyddon, W. J. (1993). Contrast, contradiction, and change in psychotherapy. *Psychotherapy, 30,* 383–390.

Lyddon, W. J., & Sherry, A. (2001). Developmental personality styles: An attachment theory conceptualization of personality disorders. *Journal of Counseling and Development, 79,* 405–414.

Mack, J. E. (1975). *Borderline states in psychiatry.* New York: Grune & Stratton.

Markovitz, P. (1995). Pharmacotherapy of impulsivity, aggression, and related disorders. In E. Hollander & D. J. Stein (Eds.), *Impulsivity and aggression* (pp. 263–267). New York: Wiley.

Markovitz, P. J., Calabrese, J. R., Charles, S. C., & Meltzer, H. Y. (1991). Fluoxetine in the treatment of borderline and schizotypal personality disorders. *American Journal of Psychiatry, 148,* 1064–1067.

Masling, J. M., Rabie, L., & Blondheim, S. H. (1967). Obesity, level of aspiration, and Rorschach and TAT measures of oral dependence. *Journal of Consulting Psychology, 31,* 233–239.

Matsunaga, H., Kaye, W. H., McConaha, C., Plotnicov, K., Pollice, C., & Rao, R. (2000). Personality disorders among subjects recovered from eating disorders. *International Journal of Eating Disorders, 27,* 353–357.

McCann, J. T., Flynn, P. M., & Gersh, D. M. (1992). MCMI-II diagnosis of borderline personality disorder: Base rates versus prototypic items. *Journal of Personality Assessment, 58,* 105–114.

McQuillan, A., Nicastro, R., Guenot, F., Girard, M., Lissner, C., & Ferrero, F. (2005). Intensive dialectical behavior therapy for outpatients with borderline personality disorder who are in crisis. *Psychiatric Services, 56,* 193–197.

Meehl, P. E. (1972). Specific genetic etiology, psychodynamics, and therapeutic nihilism. *International Journal on Mental Health, 1,* 10–27.

Meehl, P. E. (1977). Specific etiology and other forms of strong influence: Some quantitative meanings. *Journal of Medicine and Philosophy, 2,* 33–53.

Meyer, B., Pilkonis, P. A., Proietti, J. M., Heape, C. L., & Egan, M. (2001). Attachment styles and personality disorders as predictors of symptom course. *Journal of Personality Disorders, 15*, 371–389.

Mihura, J. L. (2006). Rorschach assessment of borderline personality disorder. In S. K. Huprich (Ed.), *Rorschach assessment of the personality disorders* (pp. 171–203). Mahwah, NJ: Erlbaum.

Miller, S. G. (1994). Borderline personality disorder from the patient's perspective. *Hospital and Community Psychiatry, 45*(12), 1215–1219.

Miller, S. G. (1999). Borderline personality disorder in cultural context: Commentary on Paris. *Psychiatry, 59*(2), 193–195.Millon, T. (1987). On the genesis and prevalence of the borderline personality disorder: A social learning thesis. *Journal of Personality Disorders, 1*, 354–372.

Millon, T. (1996). *Disorders of personality, DSM-IV and beyond.* New York: Wiley.

Millon, T. (2000). Sociocultural conceptions of the borderline personality. *Psychiatric Clinics of North America, 23*(1), 123–136.

Millon, T., Davis, R., & Millon, C. (1997). *MCMI-III manual* (2nd ed.). Minneapolis, MN: National Computer Systems.

Morey, L. C. (1991). *Personality Assessment Inventory: Professional manual.* Odessa, FL: Psychological Assessment Resources.

Morey, L. C. (2003). *Essentials of PAI assessment.* Hoboken, NJ: Wiley.

Morey, L. C., Waugh, M. H., & Blashfield, R. K. (1985). MMPI scales for DSM-III personality disorders: Their derivation and correlates. *Journal of Personality Assessment, 49*, 245–251.

Morgenstern, J., Langenbucher, J., Labouvie, E., & Miller, K. J. (1997). The comorbidity of alcoholism and personality disorders in a clinical population: Prevalence and relation to alcohol typology variables. *Journal of Abnormal Psychology, 106*, 74–84.

Murray, J. F. (1993). The Rorschach search for the borderline Holy Grail: An examination of personality structure, personality style, and situation. *Journal of Personality Assessment, 61*, 342–357.

Nace, E. P., Davis, C. W., & Gaspari, J. P. (1991). Axis II comorbidity in substance abusers. *American Journal of Psychiatry, 148*, 118–120.

Nace, E. P., Saxon, J. J., & Shore, N. (1983). A comparison of borderline and nonborderline alcoholic patients. *Archives of General Psychiatry, 40*, 54–56.

Negy, C., & Snyder, D. K. (2000). Relationship satisfaction of Mexican American and non-Hispanic White American interethnic couples: Issues of acculturation and clinical intervention. *Journal of Marital and Family Therapy, 26*, 293–304.

Ni, X., Chan, K., Bulgin, N., Sicard, T., Bismil, R., McMain, S., et al. (2006). Association between serotonin transporter gene and borderline personality disorder. *Journal of Psychiatric Research, 40*, 448–453.

Nickell, A. D., Waudby, C. J., & Trull, T. J. (2002). Attachment, parental bonding, and borderline personality disorder features in young adults. *Journal of Personality Disorders, 16*, 148–159.

Nickel, M. K., Nickel, C., Mitterlehner, F. O., Tritt, K., Lahmann, C., Leiberick, P. K., et al. (2004). Topiramate treatment of aggression in female borderline personality disorder patients: A double-blind, placebo-controlled study. *Journal of Clinical Psychiatry, 65*, 1515–1519.

Nielsen, A. D., Hewitt, P. L., & Habke, A. M. (1997). Borderline and schizophrenic patients: A comparison using the MCMI-II. *Journal of Psychopathology and Behavioral Assessment, 19*, 303–313.

Norden, M. J. (1989). Fluoxetine in borderline personality disorder. *Progress in Neuro-Psychopharmacology and Biological Psychiatry, 13*, 885–893.

Oquendo, M. A., & Mann, J. J. (2000). The biology of impulsivity and suicidality. *Psychiatric Clinics of North America, 23*, 11–25.

Pally, R. (2002). The neurobiology of borderline personality disorder: The synergy of "nature and nurture." *Journal of Psychiatric Practice, 8*, 133–142.

Paris, J. (1993). The treatment of borderline personality disorder in light of the research on its long-term outcome. *Canadian Journal of Psychiatry, 38,* 189–197.

Paris, J. (1994). *Borderline personality disorder: A multidimensional approach.* Washington, DC: American Psychiatric Press.

Paris, J. (1996). *Social factors in the personality disorders.* New York: Cambridge University Press.

Paris, J. (1997). Childhood trauma as an etiological factor in the personality disorders. *Journal of Personality Disorders, 11,* 34–49.

Paris, J. (1998). Does childhood trauma cause personality disorders in adults? *Canadian Journal of Psychiatry, 43,* 148–153.

Paris, J. (2002). Implications of long-term outcome research for the management of patients with borderline personality disorder. *Harvard Review of Psychiatry, 10,* 315–323.

Parker, G. (1997). Special feature: The etiology of personality disorders: A review and consideration of research models. *Journal of Personality Disorders, 11,* 345–369.

Parsons, B., Quitkin, F. M., McGrath, P. J., Stewart, J. W., Tricamo, E., Ocepek-Welikson, K., et al. (1989). Phenelzine, imipramine, and placebo in borderline patients meeting criteria for atypical depression. *Psychopharmacology Bulletin, 25,* 524–534.

Philipsen, A., Richter, H., Schmahl, C., Peters, J., Rüsch, N., Bohus, M., et al. (2004). Clonidine in acute aversive inner tension and self-injurious behavior in female patients with borderline personality disorder. *Journal of Clinical Psychiatry, 65,* 1414–1419.

Pilkonis, P. A., & Frank, E. (1988). Personality pathology in recurrent depression: Nature, prevalence, and relationship to treatment response. *American Journal of Psychiatry, 145,* 435–441.

Reich, D. B., & Zanarini, M. C. (2001). Developmental aspects of borderline personality disorder. *Harvard Review of Psychiatry, 9,* 294–301.

Reich, J. H., & Noyes, R. (1987). A comparison of DSM-III personality disorders in acutely ill panic and depressed patients. *Journal of Anxiety Disorders, 1,* 123–131.

Rifkin, A., Levitan, S. J., Galewski, J., & Klein, D. F. (1972a). Emotionally unstable character disorder: A follow-up study: Pt. I. Description of patients and outcome. *Biological Psychiatry, 4,* 65–79.

Rifkin, A., Levitan, S. J., Galewski, J., & Klein, D. F. (1972b). Emotionally unstable character disorder: A follow-up study: Pt. II. Prediction of outcome. *Biological Psychiatry, 4,* 81–88.

Rinne, T., de Kloet, E. R., Wouters, L., Goekoop, J. G., de Rijk, R. H., & van den Brink, W. (2003). Fluvoxamine reduces responsiveness of HPA axis in adult female BPD patients with a history of sustained childhood abuse. *Neuropsychopharmacology, 28,* 126–138.

Rinne, T., van den Brink, W., Wouters, L., & van Dyck, R. (2002). SSRI treatment of borderline personality disorders: A randomized, placebo-controlled clinical trial for female patients with borderline personality disorder. *American Journal of Psychiatry, 159,* 2048–2054.

Sable, P. (1997a). Attachment, detachment, and borderline personality disorder. *Psychotherapy, 34,* 171–181.

Sable, P. (1997b). Disorders of adult attachment. *Psychotherapy, 34,* 286–296.

Sabo, A. N. (1997). Etiological significance of associations between childhood trauma and borderline personality disorder: Conceptual and clinical implications. *Journal of Personality Disorders, 11,* 50–70.

Salzman, C., Wolfson, A. N., Schatzberg, A., Looper, J., Henke, R., Albanese, M., et al. (1995). Effect of fluoxetine on anger in symptomatic volunteers with borderline personality disorder. *Journal of Clinical Psychopharmacology, 15,* 23–29.

Shader, R. I., Jackson, A. H., & Dodes, L. M. (1974). The anti-aggressive effects of lithium in man. *Psychopharmacologia, 40,* 17–24.

Shaw, C., & Proctor, G. (2005). Women at the margins: A critique of the diagnosis of borderline personality disorder. *Feminism and Psychology, 15*(4), 483–490.

Sherry, A. (in press). An attachment theory approach to the short-term treatment of a woman with borderline personality disorder and comorbid diagnoses. *Clinical Case Studies.*

Sherry, A., Lyddon, W. J., & Henson, R. (in press). Adult attachment and developmental personality styles: An empirical study. *Journal of Counseling and Development.*

Sinha, B. K., & Watson, D. C. (1997). Psychosocial predictors of personality disorder traits in a non-clinical sample. *Personality and Individual Differences, 22,* 527–537.

Skodol, A. E., Buckley, P., & Charles, E. (1983). Is there a characteristic pattern to the treatment history of clinic outpatients with borderline personality? *Journal of Nervous and Mental Diseases, 171,* 405–410.

Soler, J., Pascual, J. C., Campins, J., Barrachina, J., Puigdemont, D., Alvarez, E., et al. (2005). Double-blind, placebo-controlled study of dialectical behavior therapy plus olanzapine for borderline personality disorder. *American Journal of Psychiatry, 162,* 1221–1224.

Soloff, P. H., Cornelius, J., George, A., Nathan, R. S., Perel, J. M., & Ulrich, R. F. (1993). Efficacy of phenelzine and haloperidol in borderline personality disorder. *Archives of General Psychiatry, 50,* 377–385.

Soloff, P. H., George, A., Nathan, R. S., Schulz, P. M., Ulrich, R. F., & Perel, J. M. (1986). Progress in pharmacotherapy of borderline disorders: A double blind study of amitriptyline, haloperidol, and placebo. *Archives of General Psychiatry, 43,* 691–697.

Soloff, P. H., & Millward, J. W. (1983). Developmental histories of borderline patients. *Comprehensive Psychiatry, 24,* 574–588.

Somwaru, D. P., & Ben-Porath, Y. S. (1995, March). *Development and reliability of MMPI-2 based personality disorder scales.* Paper presented at the 30th annual Workshop and Symposium on Recent Developments in Use of the MMPI-2 and MMPI-A, St. Petersburg Beach, FL.

Stern, A. (1938). Psychoanalytic investigation of and therapy in the borderline group of neuroses. *Psychoanalytic Quarterly, 7,* 467–489.

Stevenson, J., & Meares, R. (1992). An outcome study of psychotherapy for patients with borderline personality disorder. *American Journal of Psychiatry, 149,* 358–362.

Stone, M. H. (1990). *The fate of borderline patients.* New York: Guilford Press.

Strack, S. (2002). *Essentials of Millon inventories assessment.* Hoboken, NJ: Wiley.

Sullivan, P. F., Joyce, P. R., & Mulder, R. T. (1994). Borderline personality disorder in major depression. *Journal of Nervous and Mental Diseases, 182,* 508–516.

Tariot, P. N., Erb, R., Podgorski, C. A., Cox, C., Patel, S., & Jakimovich, L. (1998). Efficacy and tolerability of carbamazepine for agitation and aggression in dementia. *American Journal of Psychiatry, 155,* 54–61.

Teter, C. J., Early, J. J., & Gibbs, C. M. (2000). Treatment of affective disorder and obesity with topiramate. *Annals of Pharmacotherapy, 34,* 1262–1265.

Tidemalm, D., Elofsson, S., Stefansson, C., Waern, M., & Runeson, B. (2005). Predictors of suicide in a community-based cohort of individuals with severe mental illness. *Social Psychiatry and Psychiatric Epidemiology, 40,* 595–600.

Torgersen, S., Kringlen, E., & Cramer, V. (2001). The prevalence of personality disorders in a community sample. *Archives of General Psychiatry, 58,* 590–596.

Torgersen, S., Lygren, S., Øien, P. A., Skre, I., Onstad, S., Edvarsen, J., et al. (2000). A twin study of personality disorders. *Comprehensive Psychiatry, 41,* 416–425.

Tramantano, G., Javier, R. A., & Colon, M. (2003). Discriminating among subgroups of borderline personality disorder: An assessment of object representations. *American Journal of Psychoanalysis, 63*(2), 149–175.

Tritt, K., Nickel, C., Lahmann, C., Leiberich, P. K., Rother, W. K., Loew, T. H., et al. (2005). Lamotrigine treatment of aggression in female borderline-patients: A randomized, double-blind, placebo-controlled study. *Journal of Psychopharmacology, 19,* 287–291.

Trull, T. J. (1995). Borderline personality disorder features in nonclinical young adults: Pt. 1. Identification and validation. *Psychological Assessment, 7,* 33–41.

van den Bosch, L. M. C., Koeter, M. W. J., Stijnen, T., Verheul, R., & van den Brink, W. (2005). Sustained efficacy of dialectical behavior therapy for borderline personality disorder. *Behavior Research and Therapy, 43,* 1231–1241.

van den Bosch, L. M. C., Verheul, R., & van den Brink, W. (2001). Substance abuse in borderline personality disorder: Clinical and etiological correlates. *Journal of Personality Disorders, 15,* 416–424.

Verheul, R. van den Brink, W., & Hartgers, C. (1998). Personality disorders predict relapse in alcoholic patients. *Addictive Behaviors, 23,* 869–882.

Villeneuve, E., & Lemelin, S. (2005). Open-label study of atypical neuroleptic quetiapine for treatment of borderline personality disorder: Impulsivity as main target. *Clinical Journal of Psychiatry, 66,* 1298–1303.

Wagner, A. W., & Linehan, M. M. (1994). Relationship between childhood sexual abuse and topography of parasuicide among women with borderline personality disorder. *Journal of Personality Disorders, 8,* 1–9.

Walsh, F. (1977). The family of the borderline patient. In R. R. Grinker & B. Werble (Eds.), *The borderline patient* (pp. 158–177). New York: Aronson.

Widiger, T. A. (1992). Categorical versus dimensional classification: Implications from and for research. *Journal of Personality Disorders, 6,* 287–300.

Widiger, T. A., & Frances, A. J. (1989). Epidemiology, diagnosis, and comorbidity of borderline personality disorder. In A. Tasman, R. E. Hales, & A. J. Frances (Eds.), *American Psychiatric Press review of psychiatry* (Vol. 8, pp. 8–24). Washington, DC: American Psychiatric Press.

Widiger, T. A., & Trull, T. J. (1993). Borderline and narcissistic personality disorders. *Annuals of Clinical Psychiatry, 6,* 17–20.

Wilcox, J. (1994). Divalproex sodium in the treatment of aggressive behavior. *Annals of Clinical Psychiatry, 6,* 17–20.

Williams, C. L., & Berry, J. W. (1991). Primary prevention of acculturative stress among refugees: Application of psychological theory and practice. *American Psychologist, 46,* 632–641.

Wirth-Cauchon, J. (2001). *Women and borderline personality disorder: Symptoms and stories.* New Brunswick, NJ: Rutgers University Press.

Zanarini, M. C., & Frankenburg, F. R. (1997). Pathways to the development of borderline personality disorder. *Journal of Personality Disorders, 11,* 93–104.

Zanarini, M. C., & Frankenburg, F. R. (2001). Olanzapine treatment of female borderline personality disorder patients: A double-blind, placebo-controlled pilot study. *Journal of Clinical Psychiatry, 62,* 849–854.

Zanarini, M. C., Frankenburg, F. R., Hennen, J., & Silk, K. R. (2004). Mental health service utilization by borderline personality disorder patients and Axis II comparison subjects followed prospectively for 6 years. *Journal of Clinical Psychiatry, 65,* 28–36.

Zanarini, M. C., Frankenburg, F. R., & Parachini, E. A. (2004). A preliminary, randomized trial of fluoxetine, olanzapine, and the olanzapine-fluoxetine combination with women with borderline personality disorder. *Journal of Clinical Psychiatry, 65,* 903–907.

Zimmerman, M., & Mattia, J. I. (1999). Axis I diagnostic comorbidity and borderline personality disorder. *Comprehensive Psychiatry, 40,* 245–252.

Zlotnick, C., Rothschild, L., & Zimmerman, M. (2002). The role of gender in the clinical presentation of patients with borderline personality disorder. *Journal of Personality Disorders, 16,* 277–282.

CHAPTER 16

Other Personality Disorders

BRIAN P. O'CONNOR

DESCRIPTION OF THE DISORDERS

We are all, at least sometimes, our own worst enemies. Our natural ways of thinking, feeling, and acting occasionally get us into trouble with others or cause distress. But most of the time we eventually recover, we make reparations, we learn from our mistakes, or we may simply be tolerated or forgiven by others. For individuals with personality disorders (PDs), the episodes are not merely occasional or circumscribed, and they are not easily tolerated or changed. Instead, PDs are central, defining, maladaptive tendencies that begin early and remain chronic. They are displayed in a variety of situations, they affect many spheres of the individual's life, and they involve deviations from the standards of living and interpersonal behavior in the individual's social-cultural group. They are considered extreme and inflexible manifestations of otherwise common and normal-range personality characteristics.

The 10 official PDs are on their own axis in the *Diagnostic and Statistical Manual of Mental Disorders* (*DSM-IV-TR*; American Psychiatric Association, 2000). Unlike most Axis I disorders, the PDs on Axis II are more chronic, ingrained, resistant to change, and bearable by those who have them. People do not suddenly become ill with a PD and seek help. Rather, individuals with PDs feel normal and at home with their conditions because their disordered personalities and self-concepts are all they know and remember. They often value the very habits and features in themselves that are troublesome for others. Personality disorders are thus ego-syntonic, in contrast with the phenomenologically foreign, aversive, ego-dystonic natures of most Axis I disorders. Diagnosing PDs involves making judgments of aberrant lifestyles of persons who often value their maladaptive beliefs and habits. Individuals with PDs are usually not distressed by their lack of adjustment or by their culturally deviant personalities, but they are often unhappy people and distress can be found in their lives. Personality disorders often co-occur with and contribute to other difficulties, such as academic problems, work problems, family and relationship problems, substance abuse, violence and criminality, suicide, mortality, accidents, emergency room visits, child custody battles, and therapy failures, dropouts, and referrals. Personality disorders can exist with and without Axis I disorders, and Axis I disorders can exist with and without PDs. The axis system in the *DSM-IV-TR* requires attention to possible disorders on both axes when diagnosing clients. Typically, PDs complicate the course of Axis I disorders and influence the nature and response to psychological and pharmacological treatments. They occasionally foreshadow development of psychoses. They also tend to have a self-fulfilling, vicious cycle aspect, wherein the rigid ways of responding to life events result in experiences that ultimately maintain and deepen the problematic patterns. Individuals with PDs are often reluctant to accept professional help, and they tend to blame others for their difficulties (O'Connor & Dyce, 2001a).

The 10 *DSM-IV-TR* PDs are grouped into three clusters on the basis of descriptive similarities. The odd-eccentric Cluster A includes the Paranoid, Schizoid, and Schizotypal Personality Disorders. The dramatic-erratic Cluster B includes the Antisocial, Borderline, Histrionic, and Narcissistic Personality Disorders, which often involve labile moods and intense interpersonal conflicts. The anxious-fearful Cluster C includes the Avoidant, Dependent, and Obsessive-Compulsive Personality Disorders. Although PDs are officially categorical, you-have-it-or-you-don't disorders, many researchers now believe that PDs are instead dimensions on which different people have different scores.

In the following, the individual PDs are described in more detail. The Borderline PD is omitted in this chapter because it is described in detail in Chapter 15 of this handbook. The descriptions end with examples of popular media characters who displayed important PD features (see Hesse, Schilewe, & Thomsen, 2005, for further information). The examples are intended to serve as memorable illustrations and were not formally diagnosed using the *DSM-IV-TR*. Interested readers are referred to Gunderson and Phillips (1995), Links (1996), Livesley (2001, 2003), Magnavita (2004), Maj, Akiskal, Mezzich, and Okasha (2005), Widiger and Sanderson (1997), and Yudofsky (2005) for more detailed descriptions of the individual PDs. Good sources for further information on the prevalence of PDs include Ekselius, Tillfors, Furmark, and Fredrickson (2001), Mattia and Zimmerman (2001), Torgersen, Kringlen, and Cramer (2001), and Weissman (1993).

THE PARANOID PERSONALITY DISORDER

The Paranoid PD involves unjustified suspiciousness and distrust of others. Persons with this PD anticipate exploitation; scan their environments for signs of threat; interpret ambiguous events as having hidden, threatening meanings; perceive attacks and criticisms from others when none have been made; feel persecuted; bear grudges; and may take extraordinary measures to avoid exploitation. These forms of cognitive impairment are nevertheless accompanied by coherent speech, which is often based on faulty premises. Paranoid PD individuals are guarded, are often concerned with rank and power, and have a need to be self-sufficient. They are preoccupied with doubts about the loyalty and trustworthiness of friends, coworkers, and relationship partners, resulting in occupational difficulties, confrontations, and real or threatened lawsuits. They tend to be secretive and avoid intimacy, self-disclosure, and dependency because of the anticipated vulnerability. They have few friends and may search for subordinate allies or fringe group members, who are eventually distrusted. Suspicions about emotional and sexual infidelities result in ongoing arguments, complaints, sarcasm, vigilance, discomfort, and conflict in close relationships. There is a lack of insight into how their own behavior prompts antagonistic reactions from others, thereby confirming their preexisting, untrusting worldviews. These individuals rarely seek professional help because they blame other people for their difficulties rather than themselves. Media examples are Humphrey Bogart's character in *The Caine Mutiny* and Dale Gribble from the *King of the Hill* television show.

The estimated prevalence of the Paranoid PD in the general populations is 1%, and estimates range between 2% and 30% for the clinical population. It is more common among men than women. The Paranoid PD is less disabling than Schizophrenia, and there are no hallucinations. The paranoid delusions are less obviously false and outrageous than those in Delusional Disorder. There are fewer intense relationships and self-harming behaviors than in the Borderline PD; there is little or no history of social deviance and motivation to exploit others, as in the Antisocial PD; and there are fewer perceptual distortions and eccentric behaviors than in Schizotypal PD.

The Schizoid Personality Disorder

Prototypical features of the Schizoid PD include disinterest and detachment from social relationships and inappropriate, flat, or restricted emotional responses to others. These are loners who prefer solitary activities but who also have minimal interest in sensory experiences and who generally have low levels of pleasure in life. Schizoid individuals may appear slightly uncomfortable; they give short answers to queries; and they display little humor or eye contact and only bland facial expressions. They are eccentric, aloof, and indifferent to praise and criticism. They are apparently oblivious to the everyday interests and concerns of others and to the rewards, punishments, and subtleties of everyday social interactions. They appear unable to experience and express emotions, especially anger and aggression.

Schizoid individuals may develop attachments to animals or objects rather than people. Apart from the contacts they may have with first-degree relatives, their plans for developing relationships are rarely enacted, and opportunities are not pursued. They may claim to have friends, but these are typically only scattered acquaintances and not confidants. They are passive and indecisive in the face of life events and lack ambition. They may succeed at solitary occupations and develop stable, distant relationships in these contexts. They may have interests in fads and intellectual movements, but without social involvement. They are observers and not participants in life. They prefer solitary intellectual activities and gadgets. Some experts believe their fantasy lives may be slightly richer than their real lives, but these typically remain well hidden. Their thoughts and speech may be odd but not incoherent, and contact with reality is maintained. Media examples are Batman and Sandra Bullock's character in *The Net*, although these examples contain only some Schizoid PD elements and are not prototypical.

Prevalence of the Schizoid PD in the general population is less than 1%. It is slightly more common in men than women. The Schizoid PD involves less impairment than Schizophrenia and no hallucinations. There are fewer social contacts than in the Paranoid PD and no paranoia or verbal aggression. Unlike the Schizotypal PD, there is little social anxiety and no cognitive or perceptual distortions or eccentricities.

The Schizotypal Personality Disorder

The Schizotypal PD is an attenuated Schizophrenia-like disorder that was first recognized in studies of the adopted-away children of schizophrenics. Many such individuals had chronic but nonpsychotic symptom patterns. The Schizotypal PD involves distinct cognitive features and interpersonal deficits. Schizotypal persons often have peculiar superstitions, beliefs in magical powers, bizarre fantasies, mystical experiences, paranoid thoughts, or perceptual distortions. They may claim to be clairvoyant or telepathic or to have a sixth sense. They are prone to believing that events have particular meaning for them (ideas of reference). Their vocabulary is sometimes odd and their speech vague, abstract, and disjointed. They may ramble, but they are not as incoherent as schizophrenics. They sometimes talk to themselves and appear unkempt. Emotional expressions are restricted and flat or silly and inappropriate. They tend to be passive, unengaged, and hypersensitive to criticism. They experience persistent social anxiety associated with paranoid thoughts about unfamiliar others and perhaps from an early history of being teased. They are often socially inept and sensitive to anger and lack close contacts apart from relatives. They may be drifters and become involved in cults and fringe groups. They tend to feel isolated from others who do not share their odd beliefs and experiences. They rarely date or marry and seem to prefer their own eccentric cognitive worlds and empty lives. Film examples are Robert DeNiro's character in, *Taxi Driver* and Willy Wonka from the film *Charlie and the Chocolate Factory*.

Estimated prevalence of the Schizotypal PD in the general population is 3%, and it is more common among men than women. Schizotypal persons may display psychotic like symptoms when stressed, but there is typically less impairment and the cognitive distortions are not sufficiently severe to warrant a diagnosis of Schizophrenia. These persons are bizarre and have peculiar fantasies and perceptual illusions, but not full-blown delusions or hallucinations.

THE ANTISOCIAL PERSONALITY DISORDER

The *DSM-IV* criteria for diagnosing the Antisocial PD focus on irresponsible and harmful behaviors. There is consistent disregard for and violation of the rights of others, as manifested in a wide range of criminal-type behaviors such as assault, theft, vandalism, child and spouse abuse, substance abuse, and sadism. These social predators sometimes steal from friends and family members, and they are typically irresponsible in social and occupational roles, often failing to honor commitments. There is repeated lying for personal gain, often accompanied by an apparent inability to distinguish between the truth and the lies they tell to further their own goals. Antisocial persons are impulsive, irritable, and aggressive. They feel and show little remorse for their harmful actions, unless for manipulative reasons. Antisocial personalities can be superficially charming and ingratiating. They may have relationships, but they rarely maintain stable, mutually satisfying, intimate relationships. In their eyes, the social world is hostile and self-serving, and other people are objects to be used and abused. Antisocial personalities are egocentric manipulators and swindlers who rarely feel shame or empathy.

Although usually of average or above-average intelligence, antisocial personalities nevertheless exhibit a failure to plan, little experience of anxiety in threatening situations, a disregard for the truth, a lack of insight, and a failure to learn from past problems. Antisocial persons are impulsive, reckless, and concerned with immediate gratification. They act as if codes of conduct do not apply to them. It was previously thought that their violent behaviors were impulsive or performed for thrills, but recent evidence suggests more planning and instrumental motivation (Woodworth &

Porter, 2002). Substance abuse is common and chronic. Although the Antisocial PD occurs in high concentrations in prison populations, it can be found in many segments of society and is a major drain on social resources. The *DSM-IV-TR* diagnostic criteria focus largely on observable behaviors and are thus more narrow than the broader concept of psychopathy (Hare, 1999), which incorporates less observable personality traits such as manipulativeness, lack of remorse, and callousness. Media examples are Malcolm McDowell's character in *A Clockwork Orange*, Anthony Hopkins's character (Hannibal Lecter) in *Silence of the Lambs*, Robert DeNiro's character in *Cape Fear*, Michael Douglas's character in *Wall Street*, and the main characters in Truman Capote's *In Cold Blood*. Other famous examples are Saddam Hussein, Josef Stalin, Idi Amin, Bonnie and Clyde, and the killers Ted Bundy and Gary Gilmore.

The estimated prevalence of the Antisocial PD in the general population is 3% to 6% for men and 1% for women. Estimates for prison populations are in the 30% range. Compared to individuals with Borderline PD, antisocial persons have more distant relationships and less desire for nurturance and less concern with being abandoned. They are more calculating, aggressive, and exploitive than people with Histrionic PD, their emotions are less exaggerated, and there is more evidence of Conduct Disorder and criminality. They are more reckless and impulsive than narcissistic individuals and more concerned with material gains than with admiration.

THE HISTRIONIC PERSONALITY DISORDER

The Histrionic (definition: theatrical in manner) PD was previously termed hysterical personality and involves excessive emotionality and attention-seeking behavior. These persons are unsure of their value and are uncomfortable when they are not the center of attention. They are flamboyant in their dress and speech, and they are often inappropriately flirtatious, seductive, provocative, vain, and demanding, all apparently stemming from a need for the spotlight and for social approval. Emotional responses are shallow, shifting, and exaggerated. They talk about themselves and are concerned with their appearance. They are excitable; crave novelty and sensational experiences; are trusting, easily frustrated, and overly reactive; and they may throw temper tantrums. They appear sensitive and display interest in others and an apparent eagerness to please. They may be quick to form new relationships, but they have problems forming lasting attachments. After initially positive impressions, others may eventually perceive them as shallow and insincere. Histrionic persons become dependent, demanding, manipulative, and needy with others, and their relationships are not as intimate as they may claim. Opinions are often strongly stated, but histrionic persons are not deep or critical thinkers. They may do well in positions requiring creativity and imagination or in positions that have them in the spotlight (e.g., acting and modeling). Their speech is vague, impressionistic, and replete with exaggerated stories. Media examples are Blanche Dubois and Stanley Kowalski in *A Streetcar Named Desire*, Gloria Swanson's character in *Sunset Boulevard*, and the Samantha Jones character on *Sex in the City*. The pianist and celebrity Liberace also exhibits elements of this PD.

The estimated prevalence of the Histrionic PD in the general population is 2% to 3%, and it is twice as common among women as men (Hartung & Widiger, 1998). Histrionic individuals are more flamboyant, emotional, and uninhibited and less docile than individuals with Dependent PD. They are more juvenile, flirtatious, melodramatic, and warm and more willing to be perceived as weak or dependent than are narcissistic individuals. The Histrionic PD is not related to Conversion Disorder, as was once believed.

The Narcissistic Personality Disorder

The Narcissistic PD involves grandiose self-importance, a strong need for admiration, and a lack of empathy. These individuals believe they are unique and a cut above the masses. They require, and feel entitled to, high levels of admiration and special treatment. They have fantasies of unbounded success, beauty, brilliance, or fame and may be drawn to occupations that can provide adulation. They brag, exaggerate their accomplishments, and extract compliments from others. They both envy the accomplishments of others and believe that others are envious of them. They may appear distant and self-sufficient, but their self-esteem is fragile and they are sensitive to criticism. They often feel inadequate, undeserving, and empty, even when they are successful. Impression management victories are strongly sought but eventually feel hollow, which fuels further efforts to impress. Narcissistic persons may become outraged in response to minor slights and rejections, and then become preoccupied with revenge. Episodes of depression may soon follow. They are sensitive to their own feelings but are oblivious to the needs and feelings of others, whom they often treat as objects to be exploited. Their relationships tend to be erratic and strained as they alternate between idealization and contempt for close others. Other people are potentially admiring audiences rather than full human beings. Narcissistic individuals expect high levels of dedication from subordinates, but they have little regard for their well-being and give little in return. A media example is Jack Nicholson's character in *A Few Good Men*.

Prevalence estimates for the Narcissistic PD are in the 1% range for the general population, but run as high as 15% to 20% in clinical populations. The diagnosis is more commonly made by psychoanalysts than by other experts, and it is more common in men than in women. Narcissists have more strongly inflated self-views than histrionics. They seek admiration more than simple attention.

The Avoidant Personality Disorder

The Avoidant PD involves early, general, chronic, and engulfing shyness. It is characterized by anxious social inhibition, feelings of social and personal inferiority, and sensitivity to criticism and rejection. In first encounters, avoidant persons appear uncertain, self-effacing, and eager to please. Internally, they are preoccupied with negative thoughts about assertiveness and appearing foolish. They tend to interpret reactions from others as criticisms. They are creatures of habit whose everyday lives are limited by feelings of incompetence and fears of embarrassment over novel social activities. Avoidant persons desire closeness and normal social lives, but they have great difficulty initiating relationships. They become involved with others only when they are certain of being liked, and they require regular reassurance. Avoidant persons are often isolated, lonely, and bored, with few close relationships apart from family members. They tend to hold marginal jobs that also serve as distractions from their loneliness, and they may perform reasonably well when the positions do not require social involvement. A film example is Woody Allen's character in *Zelig*.

The estimated prevalence of the Avoidant PD is in the 0.5% to 1% range for the general population and in the 5% to 10% range for clinical populations. It is equally common in men and women. There is typically comorbidity with depression and general social anxiety. The social inhibition is more pervasive and chronic in the Avoidant PD and involves more serious social skills deficits, greater difficulties in establishing new relationships, and more problems with intimacy. The social withdrawal stems from a fear of rejection rather than from lack of social interest or an incapacity to experience closeness, as in the Schizoid PD. It is distinguished from the Dependent PD by greater wariness in forming new relationships and by fears of closeness.

The Dependent Personality Disorder

Persons with Dependent PD have a strong, pervasive need to be cared for. There is excessive fear of being alone, clinging behavior, submissiveness, and timidity. Pervasive fears of abandonment and disapproval render them unwilling to make demands on others, reluctant to disagree with others, and overly accommodating. They lack confidence in their abilities, seek advice and reassurance from others before making even minor decisions, and prefer to have others assume responsibility for most aspects of their lives. They feel anxious and helpless when alone, and they are self-sacrificing in their care for others. Dependent persons seek out relationships despite fears of being rejected. They tolerate mistreatment and perform undesirable tasks to maintain affection. They give priority to the needs of others, even while others may lose respect for, exploit, and reject them. These reactions make them feel more helpless, which increases their anxieties and discourages assertive behavior. Development of intimacy may be hampered by the obsession with maintaining relationships. They also quickly seek replacements when important relationships end. They tend to avoid positions of responsibility and become anxious and seek reassurance when placed in such positions. They consider other people to be stronger and more competent than themselves, and they tend to have jobs that involve doing tasks for others. Media examples are Bill Murray's character in *What about Bob* and Jean Stapleton's character in the television show *All in the Family*.

Estimated prevalence of the Dependent PD in the general population is 1.5%, and it is (controversially) diagnosed more frequently in women. It is associated with depression, Bipolar Disorder, social phobia, and physical symptoms. Dependent persons tend to attribute their personal problems to physical causes. The fear of abandonment is less disabling than in the Borderline PD, and dependent persons respond to threatened interpersonal losses with submission and appeasement rather than rage. They have difficulty being alone but have no particular difficulties initiating relationships, as in the Avoidant PD.

The Obsessive-Compulsive Personality Disorder

Persons with Obsessive-Compulsive PD are perfectionists who are preoccupied with rules, order, control, lists, and schedules at the expense of pleasure and efficiency. Work and productivity are more important than friendships and good times, which are likely to be planned. They are preoccupied with "shoulds" and are overly conscientious and moral. The apparent morality is based on a preoccupation with proper procedures rather than deep convictions. They are serious, inflexible, stubborn, neat, formal, punctual, and lacking in spontaneity. Carefully planned activities are ultimately not thoroughly enjoyed. They are unwilling to compromise or let themselves be convinced by others, and they can be annoying with their insistence that things be done their way. They may procrastinate over even small decisions and have difficulty completing tasks and seeing the big picture. They become anxious in the face of uncertainty, yet they can also be hard-driving, do-it-now types. They are meticulous workers and can have good careers, but at the expense of enriching social and personal lives. They are stingy in their spending on both themselves and others and tend to hoard money and possessions. They are emotionally restricted, have trouble expressing affection, and are intolerant of emotionality in others. Anger may be their most common and visible emotion, although it is rarely expressed strongly. They may become depressed as they realize the emptiness of their lifelong preoccupations with order and rules. They may seek treatment only after years of stale, broken, or unfulfilling relationships. Media examples are Jack Nicholson's character in *As Good As It Gets* and Dan Aykroyd's character in *Dragnet*.

The estimated prevalence of the Obsessive-Compulsive PD in the general population is 1%, and it is slightly more common among men than women. It is comorbid with the Avoidant PD. People with Obsessive-Compulsive PD generally do not have intrusive obsessions or compulsions. They are excessively conscientious, but not necessarily anxious and nervous. Their obsessive-compulsive tendencies are ego-syntonic rather than -dystonic.

DIAGNOSIS AND ASSESSMENT

UNIQUE CHALLENGES

There are many diagnostic challenges for PDs and extensive research literatures on the many issues (for reviews, see Clark & Harrison, 2001; Clark, Livesley, & Morey, 1997; MacKenzie, 2001; Strupp, Horowitz, & Lambert, 1997). Both conceptual and methodological refinements have been emerging in this relatively young field, but many more steps forward are still required. Building the scientific knowledge base on PDs requires good measurement, and the available methods and tools unfortunately provide us with sometimes blurry pictures.

Personality disorders are broad patterns that involve a much wider spectrum of behavior than is the case for other disorders. Specific traits or behaviors may not seem problematic when viewed in isolation, but their overall constellations may be maladaptive. Clinicians must focus on the broad constellations and must then determine whether the characteristics are stable across time and situations. Obtaining this information requires more than single interviews and single sources of information, yet there is often little time for the necessary in-depth assessments (O'Connor & Dyce, 2001a).

The data-gathering challenge is accompanied by the cognitive challenge created by within-PD variation across clients. There can be surprising differences between people who meet the criteria for the same PDs because a variety of traits appear in the criteria for each PD and not all the criteria are necessary for diagnoses. Also challenging is the fact that very few people with PDs seek help for their PDs. Instead, they typically seek treatment for more specific stresses and problems. These may have been generated, in part, by a PD, but the PD is almost never part of the presenting symptoms. For example, borderline persons may seek help for depression, substance abuse, or eating disorders; avoidant persons may seek help for anxiety; and dependent persons may seek help for mood and marital problems.

Once a working diagnosis has been formulated, clinicians must then deal with clients who are often unwilling to see their personalities as disordered. Clinicians must remain vigilant to how their own psychological makeup, cultural backgrounds, and values may act as distorting lenses that influence the degree to which they perceive particular characteristics in others as deviant and maladaptive.

Problems in differential diagnosis are also likely to be encountered because of the common comorbidities between PDs and Axis I disorders. Personality disorders were placed on a separate axis in the *DSM-III* (American Psychiatric Association, 1980) after it was realized that they often coexist with currently active psychiatric conditions. Empirical research has repeatedly confirmed that people with PDs are significantly more likely to have Axis I disorders than people without PDs (e.g., Dolan-Sewell, Krueger, & Shea, 2001; Tyrer, Gunderson, Lyons, & Tohen, 1997; Zimmerman & Coryell, 1989). A review of the literature by Van Velzen and Emmelkamp (1996) revealed that approximately 50% of patients with anxiety disorders, depressive disorders, or eating disorders also receive a PD diagnosis. The *DSM* criteria nevertheless require that PDs be differentiated from such common disorders, which can be a time-consuming challenge (Farmer, 2000; Livesley, Schroeder, Jackson, & Jang, 1994). The differences between social phobia and the Avoidant PD, between depression and the Borderline PD, and between Schizophrenia and the Schizotypal PD are sometimes difficult to perceive when dealing with real people. Furthermore, people in anxious, depressed, or psychotic like states sometimes obtain high scores on particular PD scales, highlighting the necessity of distinguishing states from traits.

Clinicians must also differentiate PDs from the symptoms caused by situational crises, medical conditions, brain trauma, medication, and substance abuse. Immigration adjustment difficulties and the expression of cultural values can also make some people seem deviant and maladjusted. Personality disorders are diagnosed when the PD symptoms are chronic, stable, and early developing. They cannot be diagnosed if the symptoms flare up exclusively during times of stress and active mental illness. The lack of insight into personality problems and the ego-syntonic nature of the symptoms are often deciding factors when diagnosing a PD rather than some other condition.

Livesley (1998) suggested simple, useful guidelines for deciding whether a PD diagnosis is warranted. A failure at any one of the following three life tasks is a major warning sign: (1) forming stable, coherent, and integrated representations of oneself and others; (2) developing the capacity for intimacy and positive relationships with other people; and (3) the ability to function adaptively in society via cooperative and prosocial behaviors. Chronic problems with any of these life tasks indicate that a client is likely to meet the general criteria for PDs.

INTERVIEWS AND TESTS

Several structured interviews, semi-structured interviews, and self-report measures are now available for PD assessments. Detailed reviews of the many tests and interviews were provided by Clark and Harrison (2001), Widiger and Sanderson (1995), and Van Velzen and Emmelkamp (1996). Some of the assessment tools consist of questions that precisely match *DSM* criteria; some involve a greater variety of questions that together focus on PD diagnoses; some focus on thematic content areas (e.g., work, social relations); and some focus on normal and/or pathological personality traits. Some tools focus on single PDs, whereas others provide scores for all PDs. The structured interviews can be time-consuming, sometimes requiring up to 4 hours. However, the self-report measures are typically considered screening devices that merely provide suggestive evidence that should be carefully investigated using interviews. Selected reliability and validity issues are discussed in the following sections.

Agreement and Stability

One frustrating problem with PD interviews, self-report tests, and clinical judgments is their sometimes low levels of diagnostic agreement. Interrater reliabilities for individual interview measures are typically slightly above the standard cutoff of .70 (Clark & Harrison, 2001). The internal consistency estimates for self-report PD scales are also typically above .70. However, the levels of agreement across different tests and interviews are often lower. Reviews by Clark et al. (1997), Clark and Harrison (2001), Klonsky, Oltmanns, and Turkheimer (2002), Oltmanns and Turkheimer (2006), Walters, Moran, Choudhury, Lee, and Mann (2004), and Zimmerman (1994) revealed that agreement indices (kappas) for structured interviews are in the .35 to .51 range. The agreement between clinical interviews and structured interviews is slightly lower (range = .21 to .38), and the agreement between structured interviews and self-report measures is lower still (kappas ranged between .08 and .42). The median degrees of agreement for studies that reported correlation coefficients varied between .39 and .51. These modest values are not scientifically or clinically acceptable (Coolidge & Segal, 1998; Perry, 1992, p. 1645). Furthermore, researchers have not been able to identify systematic sources of variation (e.g., due to type of assessment, sample, or informant) in the agreement indices (Klonsky et al., 2002). Self-reports for some PDs, such as narcissism, may have less validity than informant reports due to the lack of self-insight associated with the PD. But self-reports are nevertheless necessary in gaining information about internal states and motivations that are not observable by informants.

Also problematic is the fact that although PDs are defined as enduring patterns, PD diagnoses are not highly stable over time. For example, Zimmerman (1994) found an average stability (kappa) of .56 for less than 1-week periods, and an average stability of .51 for longer periods (for reviews, see Clark et al., 1997; McDavid & Pilkonis, 1996). Wider ranges of stability coefficients for individual PDs, and higher stability estimates, are obtained for dimensional scores than for PD diagnoses (Loranger, Lenzenweger, Garner, & Susman, 1991). Recent longitudinal studies have revealed modest stabilities for PD diagnoses and PD criteria ratings, but high rank-order stability in PD criterion counts (Clark, 2005). The generally modest stability coefficients are somewhat ambiguous because they could be caused by genuine instability in behavior, which would constitute a major problem for the PD concept, or they could be caused by measurement error. A gold standard for PD assessment is obviously not yet available.

Personality Disorder Comorbidity

Comorbidity means that two or more independent disorders exist simultaneously in the same persons. High comorbidity between PDs is a common, puzzling diagnostic phenomenon (Grant, Stinson, Dawson, Chou, & Ruan, 2005; Stuart et al., 1998; Westen & Shedler, 1999). Is it possible for someone to have more than one PD? Between 67% and 85% of patients who meet the criteria for one PD also meet the criteria for at least one other PD. Over 90% of people receiving the borderline diagnosis qualify for other PD diagnoses (Clark et al., 1997, p. 211). The mean number of potential PD diagnoses in people with at least one PD has been estimated to fall between 1.5 and 5.6 PDs by Dolan, Evans, and Norton (1995), and between three and four PDs by Widiger and Sanderson (1995, p. 381). These comorbidities are peculiar and disturbing, but fortunately not random (e.g., the Obsessive-Compulsive and Antisocial PDs rarely co-occur, as do the Schizoid and Histrionic PDs; Clark et al., 1997). Comorbidities are also higher for more severe cases and when there are earlier ages of onset (Ozkan & Altindag, 2005). Personality disorder comorbidities are recognized in the *DSM-IV-TR* manual, but the levels are clearly excessive and there are no clinical guidelines for dealing with these occurrences. In practice, clinicians often provide only one PD diagnosis in their clients' charts.

Clark et al. (1997) claimed that the various problems in PD assessment stem from both faulty measures and deficiencies in the *DSM* descriptions of PDs. If the *DSM* accounts of PDs are not accurate, then the psychometric properties of measures designed to assess PD constructs will also be poor. Personality disorder criteria are often ambiguous trait adjectives that require inferences of pathological deviation by clinicians. For example, behavioral indicators for "clinically significant impairment," "excessive social anxiety," "shallow expression of emotions," and "requires excessive admiration" are not provided. The inferential leaps required for Axis II diagnoses are generally greater than the inferential leaps required for Axis I diagnoses. The consequences are lower levels of diagnostic agreement, lower levels of stability over time, and higher comorbidities (O'Connor & Dyce, 2001b). The descriptions and conceptualizations of PDs in the *DSM* have been evolving and improving, but many challenges remain. The *DSM* was designed as a descriptive, heuristic filing system for psychiatric diagnoses (Clark et al., 1997, p. 125), and it will likely become more scientifically based with time. Descriptions of PDs can also be found in the *International Statistical Classification of Diseases-10* (World Health Organization, 1992). There are many similarities and some differences between the *DSM-IV* and the *ICD-10* with regards to PDs, and many of the same diagnostic problems.

CATEGORIES VERSUS DIMENSIONS OF PERSONALITY DISORDERS

Normal personality trait language is used to describe PDs in the *DSM-IV-TR*. Personality pathology is apparently a matter of extremeness on common trait dimensions. Yet a categorical model is used for diagnoses. This model of qualitatively distinct clinical syndromes is now widely discredited by extensive comorbidity evidence and by the heterogeneity of PD phenomena (Clark et al., 1997). More direct evidence against the categorical model comes from numerous, large-sample searches for taxons, or distinct, qualitative categories of abnormality. Most of the investigations indicate that PDs are dimension-only and not taxonic phenomena (Edens, Marcus, Lilienfeld, & Poythress, 2006; Fossati et al., 2005; Haslam, 2003; Marcus, John, & Edens, 2004; Rothschild, Cleland, Haslam, & Zimmerman, 2003; Vasey, Kotov, Frick, & Loney, 2005). Some studies suggest that psychopathy and schizotypy might be taxonic (Haslam, 2003; Skilling, Harris, Rice, & Quinsey, 2002), but subsequent studies using a variety of samples and methods have indicated that psychopathy is dimensional. Furthermore, the same basic dimensions exist in the data from clinical and nonclinical populations, and this is true for responses on both clinical and nonclinical measures (O'Connor, 2002). Normal and abnormal personalities exist in the same universe of basic psychological dimensions. The differences between clinical and nonclinical populations are matters of degree, at least in the case of PDs.

A separate and more general issue in this debate concerns the nature of the dimensions that are important to PDs. Taxometric studies focus only on scores on PD indicators, tests, or criteria that are in accordance with the *DSM* descriptions. But if PDs are rigid and extreme manifestations of normal personality characteristics, then attention should also focus on the scores on the dimensions of normal personality traits. In this view, the *DSM* PDs are located in restricted regions of the multivariate space that is defined by normal personality dimensions (O'Connor & Dyce, 2001b). Comorbidity is due to different PDs being located in neighboring regions. The assignment of clients to categories is thus rather arbitrary.

The dimensional approach also provides a much-needed conceptual framework for individuals who meet the general criteria for PDs, but not the criteria for specific PDs. In the *DSM-IV-TR,* a diagnosis of "PD Not Otherwise Specified" (PDNOS) is given to such persons. Although this PD category has no specific features, it is the most frequent diagnosis in clinical settings. The same phenomenon also exists when community samples are studied. Lenzenweger, Loranger, Korfine, and Neff (1997) assessed 2,000 university students and found that 11% met the criteria for at least one PD. Of these, half received a diagnosis of PDNOS. The fact that so many people fall into this supposedly small, leftover category indicates that the current categorical system needs refinement and elaboration. In contrast, PDNOS diagnoses are expected to be common and are consistent with the dimensional view. If PDs are located in restricted regions of the multivariate space that is defined by normal personality dimensions, then there should be very many such regions that are problematic, and not just those defined by the 10 PDs in the *DSM-IV-TR.* In this view, the official PDs are descriptions of only 10 common PD prototypes. Many other forms of PD may exist and may be defined by dimensional models, but they are likely to be, individually, more rare and thus difficult to formally define. They are nevertheless sufficiently common, as a collective (regarding the frequency of PDNOS diagnoses), to warrant attention.

A dimensional model of PDs is likely to appear in the *DSM* someday, but only if and when there is agreement on the basic dimensions of personality (Frances, 1993). A wide variety of dimensional models have been proposed (Widiger & Simonsen, 2005), but extensive tests using a variety of clinical and nonclinical data sets have revealed that very few models are empirically supported (Dyce & O'Connor, 1998). The available evidence most strongly supports the five-factor model (FFM), which consists of the dimensions of neuroticism, extraversion, openness to experience, agreeableness, and conscientiousness (Costa & Widiger, 2002). Popular interest in the FFM approach to PDs is growing, but the consensus is presently far from unanimous. A problem with all dimensional approaches is that they are models that sacrifice fine-grained detail in attempts to simplify complex worlds. The FFM captures the primary dimensions that underlie PDs, but it does not capture all of the variation in PD scores (O'Connor, 2005). The broad FFM dimensions each have specific facets, but facet-level analyses do not dramatically increase the prediction of PDs. There are also currently no cut scores for determining where on a normal personality dimension elevations are extreme and maladaptive.

CONCEPTUALIZATION

DEVELOPMENTAL ISSUES

By definition, PDs begin early, last long, and presumably are more stable than Axis I disorders. Unfortunately, little is known about their natural histories because high-quality longitudinal investigations have not been conducted (for reviews, see Perry, 1993; Stone, 2001). Although the *DSM-IV-TR* specifies that PDs must have appeared in adolescence or early adulthood for a diagnosis to be made, PDs do not suddenly emerge at this time. The relevant traits often emerge earlier in life and probably crystallize and stabilize in young adulthood. Personality disorders have genetic influences, involve consistent ways of dealing with life challenges and other people, are ego-syntonic, and are pervasive in their influence on many life domains. Their courses are thus generally steady and the prognoses grim. They are often most intense when individuals are in their 20s. There is evidence that some PDs, notably the Antisocial, Borderline, and Narcissistic PDs, fade with time. However, there is also a suspicion that, with age, some individuals merely learn to alter their behaviors around others without genuinely changing inside. Comorbid conditions, such as depression or substance abuse, and the absence of treatment can make prognoses very poor. If there is a comorbid Axis I condition, then the prognosis is poor for both the Axis I condition and the PD (Tyrer et al., 1997). A meta-analysis of studies on PDs in people over 50 years of age revealed an overall prevalence rate of 10% (Abrams & Horowitz, 1996), which is in the same range as the PD prevalence estimates for the general population. This indicates that there is probably no major reduction with age. In fact, PDs may be under diagnosed in older adults (Segal, Hersen, Van Hasselt, Silberman, & Roth, 1996).

LEARNING AND MODELING

Behavioral theories are much more common for Axis I disorders than they are for PDs. This may be due to the stronger influence of psychodynamic theories on the conceptualization of PDs and to the presumed rigid and pervasive consistency in PD behavior that is foreign to learning theories. The result has been a relatively weak empirical interest in specific learning and modeling influences. Personality disorders are not circumscribed bad habits acquired from models or from reinforcement contingencies in specific situations. Instead, individuals presumably acquire general, basic cultural worldviews, values, internal working models, and thinking styles from their home environments. Learning and modeling are thus probably quite general and abstract rather than situation-specific, and they are probably focused on basic guiding assumptions rather than changeable cognitions. Speculations along these lines for specific PDs can be found in the literature on cognitive therapies for PDs (Beck, Freeman, & Davis, 2004).

PARENTAL ISSUES

There is a lively, varied, and speculative literature on parental influences on PDs. Psychoanalytic and object relations explanations are common and remain relatively untested, apart from clinical observations. There is nevertheless a consensus that early experiences with significant others leave enduring marks on the individuals who eventually develop PDs. Harsh and neglectful parenting figure prominently in these discussions, as is true for many *DSM* disorders. But there are sometimes additional suspected parental influences that are unique to PDs. Reviews were provided by Bornstein (1993), Gunderson and Phillips (1995), Perry and Valliant (1989), Sutker, Bugg, and West (1993), Widiger and Sanderson (1997), and Widiger and Trull (1993).

Parental rage, suspicion, distrust, prejudice, and humiliation are presumably experienced by persons who develop the Paranoid PD. Parental coldness, rage, neglect, withdrawal, and social isolation occur in the Schizoid and Schizotypal PDs. Parental seductiveness, authoritarianism, and puritanical parental attitudes are said to generate deep conflicts, a need to be the center of attention, and inner feelings of low or fragile self-esteem in persons who develop the Histrionic PD. The literature on the Narcissistic PD is more extensive and focuses on parental rejection, control, low empathy, conditional regard, high expectations, disdain and neglect of childhood fears, failures, dependencies, and excessive idealization combined with inconsistent interest and devaluation. Children are objects used to boost parental (rather than child) esteem. Common themes for the Avoidant and Dependent PDs involve parental rejection, control, over protectiveness, caution, minimal parental community involvement, experiences of embarrassment, humiliation, and rejection, and premature demands for independence (Bartholomew, Kwong, & Hart, 2001; Stone, 1993). In the Obsessive-Compulsive PD, there is presumably parental pressure, disapproval, high expectations, and overemphasis on social and cultural standards. The empirical evidence is most extensive for the Antisocial PD. Common themes in the research findings include parental absence, abuse, hostility, neglect, rejection, inconsistency, poverty, crime, unsettled family circumstances, and failures to teach responsible behavior. Some of these parental behaviors may be reactions to antisocial behaviors in the children.

Many people who are exposed to the parental influences just described do not develop PDs. Twin and adoption studies have indicated that environmental influences are specific and not shared. For example, identical twins who are reared together are as similar to each another as identical twins who are reared apart (Bouchard, 1997). Shared experiences in the same family environments do not increase similarities in personality characteristics. The implication of this finding is that the family experiences just described, if accurate, are not shared and are unique to specific individuals within family environments. Numerous, complex, as-yet-unknown gene-environment interactions are probably most important (Paris, 1998). Biological and neurological predispositions presumably combine with problematic early attachment histories to create disordered personality structures.

LIFE EVENTS

Once a person has developed a PD, responses to life events tend to be inflexible and consistent with the nature of the specific PD. Life changes and stresses may be disruptive, but individuals with PDs soon return to their familiar selves. Relatively more research has focused on the early life events and psychosocial adversities that precede the onset of PDs. The lists of such events tend to consist of the same experiences that are common to many psychological disorders. Few experiences seem PD-specific. Furthermore, although the risk factors may be found in the developmental backgrounds of many individuals with PDs, not all persons who are exposed to the risks develop PDs or other disorders (Rutter & Rutter, 1993). Resilience is common, and the nature of the person-environment interactions that are involved has not yet been discovered.

Paris (2001) provided a review of the psychosocial adversities that are associated with PDs. Persons with PDs tend to have relatives with significant pathology, and the suspicion in the literature is that the effects on children are more than just genetic. Divorce, separation from parents, and family breakdowns occur at higher rates than in community samples. Retrospective studies of parenting practices have revealed problems with affection and attachment and with parental control and neglect, as described in the section on Parental Issues. Childhood sexual abuse is apparently most common and important to the Borderline PD (Chapter 15). Less research has been conducted on sexual abuse and other PDs. Physical and verbal abuse are found in the backgrounds of persons with the Antisocial PD.

Genetic Influences

There have been few twin and adoption studies focusing specifically on PDs, and confounds with Axis I conditions are common in the available data sets (Bouchard, 1997; Dahl, 1993; Jang & Vernon, 2001; Nigg & Goldsmith, 1994). Large, high-quality samples are difficult to obtain, and research is hampered by misdiagnoses and problems with the definition and assessment of PDs, as described earlier. The most clear-cut evidence currently available for genetic influences is for the Paranoid, Schizoid, Schizotypal, Borderline, and Antisocial PDs. The odd-eccentric PDs are more common in the biological relatives of diagnosed schizophrenics than in the general population (Nigg & Goldsmith, 1994), suggesting a common diathesis. There are also similarities between these PDs and Schizophrenia in responses to antipsychotic medication, especially for the Schizotypal PD. The risk for the development of Schizophrenia is higher for the Schizotypal PD than for the Schizoid PD (Siever, Bernstein, & Silverman, 1995), and genetic research indicates that the Paranoid PD is more closely related to Delusional Disorder (Axis I) than to Schizophrenia (Bernstein, Useda, & Siever, 1995). Twin research on the Antisocial PD, as well as research on the adopted children of criminals and antisocial parents, has been relatively consistent in providing evidence for the importance of genetic influences (Sutker et al., 1993). There is more criminal and antisocial behavior in the adopted-away children of biological parents with Antisocial PD than in control samples. Few data are available for the histrionic, narcissistic, and anxious-fearful.

The meager data on the heritability of PDs have focused attention on the more extensive data that exist for the heritability of normal personality traits (Bouchard, 1997; Jang & Vernon, 2001; Nigg & Goldsmith, 1994). Clear similarities exist between PDs and normal personality dimensions such as aggressiveness, social anxiety, and impulsivity. Research on identical twins reared together and apart, on fraternal and identical twins, and on adopted and nonadopted siblings, commonly reveals heritability coefficients in the 40% to 50% range for most personality traits. Very similar coefficients are obtained in genetic research on the heritability of PD-relevant traits (e.g., anxiousness, callousness, intimacy avoidance; Livesley, Schroeder, Lang, Jackson, & Vernon, 1993). Environmental factors and error account for the remaining 50% to 60% of the variation. The heritability estimates for PDs and for normal personality characteristics are also very similar (Livesley, Schroeder, Jackson, & Lang, 1994). Both genetic and environmental influences are thus substantial. Unfortunately, efforts to localize the genes involved with specific PDs have not been successful.

Peer Influences

Very few studies have been conducted on possible peer influences on PDs. This is likely due to the widespread belief that PDs are largely built in by genes and early family experiences. Impoverished or problematic peer relations are common in PDs, but these are presumably consequences and not causes of the disorders. Most of the studies involving peers have focused on conduct disordered children and persons with Antisocial PD. Exposure to deviant peers in these cases probably makes already bad situations even worse and may be due to self-selection into particular kinds of groups.

PHYSICAL FACTORS AFFECTING BEHAVIOR

There has been much less research on the physical factors affecting PDs than there has been on other *DSM* disorders. Most of the available studies have focused on PD-relevant traits rather than on PDs per se. Genetic influences are substantial, but it is not known exactly what is inherited. Speculations have focused on neurotransmitters and brain systems (Silk, 1998). Serotonin is involved in impulsiveness and aggression, and norepinephrine and dopamine are associated with the Schizotypal PD (Coccaro, 2001). Some believe that PDs are trait versions of Axis I disorders (Siever & Davis, 1991), possessing a similar biological basis. DePue and Lenzenweger (2005) proposed a neurobehavioral dimensional model of general personality disturbance. Their models focus on the familiar, broad dimensions of neuroticism and extraversion, on behavioral inhibition and activation systems, and on associated neurotransmitters. Normal and abnormal personality are probably based on the same brain systems. The challenge is to figure out the differences and details when it comes to PDs.

Persons with Schizotypal PD have neuropsychological profiles similar to those of schizophrenics, as well as enlarged ventricles and less temporal lobe gray matter (Dickey et al., 1999). The most extensive research literature on physical influences is for the Antisocial PD and psychopathy. Such individuals apparently have neurocognitive deficits that prevent them from learning from punishment, make them low in anxiety and unresponsive to emotions, generate strong cravings for stimulation, make them inattentive to sensory input, and that focus their attention on their own interests. Brain-imaging research has revealed abnormalities in the prefrontal cortex, which is involved in the inhibition of impulsive behavior (Damasio, 2000).

DRUGS AFFECTING BEHAVIOR

There are no specific research literatures on drugs and PDs, apart from what is described in the section on Medical Treatment. Alcohol and substance abuse are more common in the Antisocial PD than in other PDs, but are not considered primary causes of the disorder.

CULTURAL AND DIVERSITY ISSUES

By definition, PDs involve behavior that deviates markedly from the expectations of the individual's culture. This poses challenges for clinicians working in modern heterogeneous societies. What is deviant behavior? High levels of female submissiveness and dependence are normative in some cultures, but not in others. Paranoia sometimes occurs among prisoners, refugees, and hearing-impaired people and may not be an indication of the Paranoid PD. Personality disorders are more closely tied to cultural expectations than are other disorders (Alarcon, Foulks, & Vakkur, 1998), although there is evidence that the same constellation of PDs exists in cultures outside of North America and Europe (e.g., Yang et al., 2000).

The most challenging diversity issue regarding PDs concerns sex differences, which are relatively consistent (Hartung & Widiger, 1998; Widiger, 1998). Overall prevalence of PDs is similar in men and women. However, men receive more diagnoses of the Antisocial, Paranoid, Schizoid, Schizotypal, Narcissistic, and Obsessive-Compulsive PDs, whereas women receive more diagnoses of the Borderline, Histrionic, and Dependent PDs. Sex differences in PD prevalence rates correspond with traditional masculine and feminine sex-role orientations. However, there is controversy over the relative frequencies with which females are diagnosed with the Borderline, Histrionic, and Dependent PDs (the sex ratio in these diagnoses is approximately 3:1). It is uncertain whether men and women vary in how susceptible they are to these PDs, or whether clinicians merely perceive their male and female patients differently. There is also concern that the *DSM* criteria for PDs involve stereotypically feminine traits but not stereotypically masculine traits (e.g., the inability to identify and express emotions, excessive independence; Tavris, 1992).

BEHAVIORAL TREATMENT

Persons with PDs are unlikely to seek help. They generally believe that they do not need help and that there is no problem with their personality. When they do present for help, it is usually for a life crisis (e.g., job loss) or an Axis I condition (depression, anxiety), and they are reluctant to view themselves as contributors to their troubles. In their view, other people are the problem and are the ones who need to change. They may seek treatment when compelled by others, but often drop out prematurely or do not cooperate. A strong working therapeutic alliance is difficult to develop. Therapists often believe persons with PDs are untreatable and are unlikely to follow treatment recommendations. There is also a common belief among therapists that PD clients will not be responsive to insight-based therapies because they do not see themselves as the problem. However, there is also a belief that insight is what is most needed for these people. Therapists are often more directive in dealing with PD clients, and there is more focus on present maladaptive behaviors and thinking patterns than on past causes and problems.

The full range of familiar psychotherapy interventions are available for PDs, including psychoanalysis, brief psychodynamic therapy, cognitive therapy, dialectical behavioral therapy, interpersonal therapy, social skills and assertiveness training, and psychoeducation (Beck et al., 2004; Clarkin, Yeomans, & Kernberg, 1999; Dowson & Grounds, 1995; Livesley, 2001; Magnavita, 2004; Sperry, 1995; Stone, 1993). Psychodynamic techniques were previously the norm and remain in use today, although there is increasing emphasis on the benefits of cognitive and interpersonal approaches tailored for PDs. Enthusiastic descriptions of treatment methods for particular disorders are readily found in the literature, along with good descriptions of the therapeutic obstacles that arise when dealing with clients with particular PDs (Bockian & Jongsma, 2001; Livesley, 2003). However, few randomized, controlled studies have been conducted that focus on single disorders (Crits-Christoph, 1998). Researchers have difficulty finding pure PD cases without other PD and Axis I comorbidities. Case studies are common. Two recent meta-analyses have revealed effect sizes for psychotherapies that provide grounds for more optimism than is typically evident in the literature (Leichsenring & Leibing, 2003; Perry, Banon, & Ianni, 1999). However, there remains a widespread belief that persons with PDs are not as responsive to psychotherapy as people with only Axis I disorders.

Brief drug or psychotherapy treatments do not have immediate, substantial, and enduring effects on long-standing, ingrained personality traits. The habits of a lifetime are not easily changed. Treatment goals should be modest, perhaps involving reductions in symptoms in times of crisis, and slow, slight improvements in relationships, living habits, thinking styles, and emotional reactions (O'Connor & Dyce, 2001a). Most personality disordered individuals will never reach normal levels of adjustment. Social skills training may seem warranted in many cases, but the changes may be only superficial.

MEDICAL TREATMENT

There is a growing literature on pharmacological treatments for PDs (Kapfhammer & Hippius, 1998; Links, Heslegrave, & Villella, 1998; Markovitz, 2001). However, there are no medications designed specifically for PDs and none are that remarkably effective. Drugs are most beneficial for PDs that resemble Axis I disorders and for reducing distress in times of crises. For example, low doses of phenothiazines can be effective for schizotypal persons; persons with Avoidant PD may respond to antidepressants and tranquilizers; and Prozac is used for reducing aggressiveness. But the drugs do not change long-standing habits. Medication is most effective when there are comorbid conditions, although little is known about the long-term effects.

Case Description

Case Introduction, Presenting Complaints, and History

Mr. A. was a 29-year-old master's-level student in history who sought help at a hospital psychology clinic for symptoms of anxiety and depression. A crisis of discomfort and unhappiness had long been building up as a result of his inability of take the final steps needed to complete his degree and his inability to make friends or find a girlfriend. He tearfully described these problems and said he found it difficult to keep on living as he had been, but that he also believed that he would never change and that life was passing him by. He had previously disclosed some of his struggles to his thesis supervisor, who encouraged him to meet with a counselor at the college psychology clinic. His mother had also encouraged him to seek help. However, he said he did not feel comfortable during his one meeting with the clinic counselor and he never returned. He felt the counselor did not understand him, and he felt too embarrassed to follow his suggestion that he join a support group of other students with adjustment problems. He said he thought he would be older than the other students and he did not want to be identified as someone who needed help. He sought help at the hospital because he thought it would be more confidential and because he needed relief. He was prescribed an antidepressant and was assigned to a psychologist at the hospital clinic. The referral form stated that the problems were apparently long-standing and likely involved more than crisis reactions and depression.

Assessment

The psychologist obtained extensive descriptions of Mr. A.'s current problems and of his early experiences with family and peers. Mr. A. also completed the Minnesota Multiphasic Personality Inventory-2 and measures of depression and anxiety. His profile of scores, including those on the MMPI Personality Disorder

(continued)

scales (Morey, Waugh, & Blashfield, 1985), revealed indications of depression, social anxiety, social phobia, Avoidant PD, and weaker indications of Schizotypal PD.

Case Conceptualization

The current discomfort and unhappiness were considered flare-ups resulting from long-standing tendencies to feel socially anxious, to withdraw, and to pursue solitary diversions. Soothing the present distress with medication and talks with the psychologist were not expected to change the generating causes. Social phobia initially seemed the most likely underlying problem, but the scores on the Avoidant and Schizotypal PDs eventually made more sense. Mr. A. had deep, resistant, and rationalized convictions about himself and others that prevented him from changing. He wanted symptom relief, but apparently without fundamental personal changes. He also had a hidden sense of superiority regarding his intellectual skills and esoteric interests. The constellation of his presenting symptoms and his earlier life experiences led to the conclusion that the problems were caused by the Avoidant PD and current psychosocial stresses. His scores on schizotypy were considered by-products of his solitary, esoteric preoccupations and of the overlap between schizotypy and Avoidant PD.

Course of Treatment and Assessment of Progress

Mr. A. stayed on the antidepressant, met weekly with the psychologist, and experienced symptom relief over a 2-month period. The psychologist used behavioral and cognitive intervention methods for addressing his social anxiety. Mr. A. was initially cooperative, but his efforts became increasingly feeble and half-hearted. He said that although he could sometimes make himself behave more assertively with others, he did not enjoy doing so, he felt he was misleading himself and others, and he lost interest and returned to his solitary pursuits.

Complicating Factors

Mr. A. lived with his mother, with whom he felt close. The psychologist wished that his parents had provided firmer encouragement for normative developmental challenges. His mother's ongoing support made it easy for Mr. A. to slip back into his unassertive and solitary ways.

Follow-UP

Mr. A. stopped meeting with the psychologist altogether after 6 months; there had been a 6-week interval when there were no meetings. He said he was getting along "all right" and would call if he needed help again. Therapy ended without real change taking place.

Treatment Implications of the Case

The case was a prototypical example of both a PD and life stresses generating anxiety, depression, and the request for help. Medication and psychotherapy relieved the current distress, but the PD made the client a reluctant participant in his own treatment.

The client's self- and worldview were apparently deeply entrenched by early learning, lifelong habits, and brain chemistry. Ongoing cognitive therapy would likely be effective if there was more serious commitment from the client, who never gave himself sufficient opportunity to experience reinforcements for alternative ways of dealing with others.

SUMMARY

The 10 heterogeneous PDs in the *DSM-IV-TR* are rigid, extreme, pervasive, chronic, and maladaptive manifestations otherwise normal and common personality characteristics. Individuals with PDs often value their peculiar qualities and lack insight into how their difficulties are self-generated. Personality disorders occur in 10% to 13% of the general population and in 50% to 67% of clinical samples. Diagnosing PDs is challenging because extensive information about broad patterns is required, because PDs must be differentiated from situational crises and other disorders, and because PDs are typically not part of presenting complaints. Conceptualization of and assessment methods for PDs must be refined to reduce excessive levels of comorbidity and to increase diagnostic agreement. Personality disorders begin early, last long, and presumably are more stable than Axis I disorders. Genetic factors, neurotransmitters, and early family experiences are apparently the primary causes. However, precise details on these likely causes are not presently available, and it will be a long time before precise, accurate, and predictive models of the origins of PDs can be designed. Correlates and risk factors for PDs tend to be the same as those involved in Axis I disorders. The full range of familiar interventions is available for PDs, although therapy is considered less effective for PDs than for other conditions. Clients with PDs are reluctant to change, and therapists are often pessimistic. Modern cognitive and interpersonal treatment approaches may prove more effective than the traditionally common psychodynamic therapies for PDs. Further progress in understanding and treating PDs is essential because they complicate the courses of Axis I disorders and because they are associated with a wide variety of serious personal and social costs.

REFERENCES

Abrams, R. C., & Horowitz, S. V. (1996). Personality disorders after age 50: A meta-analysis. *Journal of Personality Disorders, 10,* 271–281.

Alarcon, R. D., Foulks, E. F., & Vakkur, M. (1998). *Personality disorders and culture: Clinical and conceptual interactions.* New York: Wiley.

American Psychiatric Association. (1980). *Diagnostic and statistical manual of mental disorders* (3rd ed.). Washington, DC: Author.

American Psychiatric Association. (2000). *Diagnostic and statistical manual of mental disorders* (4th ed., text rev.). Washington, DC: Author.

Bartholomew, K., Kwong, M. J., & Hart, S. D. (2001). Attachment. In W. J. Livesley (Ed.), *Handbook of personality disorders* (pp. 196–230). New York: Guilford Press.

Beck, A. T., Freeman, A. M., & Davis, D. D. (2004). *Cognitive therapy of personality disorders.* New York: Guilford Press.

Bernstein, D. P., Useda, D., & Siever, L. J. (1995). Paranoid personality disorder. In W. J. Livesley (Ed.), *The DSM-IV personality disorders* (pp. 45–57). New York: Guilford Press.

Bockian, N. R., & Jongsma, A. E. (2001). *The personality disorders: Treatment planner.* New York: Wiley.

Bornstein, R. F. (1993). *The dependent personality.* New York: Guilford Press.

Bouchard, T. J. (1997). The genetics of personality. In K. Blum, E. P. Noble, R. S. Sparkes, T. H. J. Chen, & J. G. Cull (Eds.), *Handbook of psychiatric genetics* (pp. 273–296). Boca Raton, FL: CRC Press.

Clark, L. A. (2005). Stability and change in personality pathology: Revelations of three longitudinal studies. *Journal of Personality Disorders, 19,* 525–532.

Clark, L. A., & Harrison, J. A. (2001). Assessment instruments. In W. J. Livesley (Ed.), *Handbook of personality disorders* (pp. 277–306). New York: Guilford Press.

Clark, L. A., Livesley, W. J., & Morey, L. (1997). Personality disorder assessment: The challenge of construct validity. *Journal of Personality Disorders, 11,* 205–231.

Clarkin, J. F., Yeomans, F. E., & Kernberg, O. F. (1999). *Psychotherapy for borderline personality.* New York: Wiley.

Coccaro, E. F. (2001). Biological and treatment correlates. In W. J. Livesley (Ed.), *Handbook of personality disorders* (pp. 124–135). New York: Guilford Press.

Coolidge, F. L., & Segal, D. L. (1998). Evolution of personality disorder diagnosis in the *Diagnostic and Statistical Manual of Mental Disorders. Clinical Psychology Review, 18,* 585–599.

Costa, P. T., & Widiger, T. A. (2002). *Personality disorders and the five-factor model of personality* (2nd ed.). Washington, DC: American Psychological Association.

Crits-Christoph, P. (1998). Psychosocial treatments for personality disorders. In P. E. Nathan & J. M. Gorman (Eds.), *A guide to treatments that work* (pp. 544–553). New York: Oxford University Press.

Dahl, A. A. (1993). The personality disorders: A critical review of family, twin, and adoption studies. *Journal of Personality Disorders, 7,* 86–99.

Damasio, R. (2000). A neural basis for sociopathy. *Archives of General Psychiatry, 57,* 128–129.

DePue, R. A., & Lenzenweger, M. F. (2005). A neurobehavioral dimensional model of personality disturbance. In M. F. Lenzenweger & J. F. Clarkin (Eds.), *Major theories of personality disorder* (pp. 391–454). New York: Guilford Press.

Dickey, C. C., McCarley, R. W., Volgmaier, M. M., Niznikiewicz, M. A., Seidman, L. J., & Hirayasu, Y. (1999). Schizotypal personality disorder and MRI abnormalities of temporal gray matter. *Biological Psychiatry, 45,* 1392–1402.

Dolan, B., Evans, C., & Norton, K. (1995). Multiple Axis-II diagnoses of personality disorder. *British Journal of Psychiatry, 166,* 107–112.

Dolan-Sewell, R. T., Krueger, R. F., & Shea, M. T. (2001). Co-occurrence with syndrome disorders. In W. J. Livesley (Ed.), *Handbook of personality disorders* (pp. 84–104). New York: Guilford Press.

Dowson, J. H., & Grounds, A. T. (1995). *Personality disorders: Recognition and clinical management.* New York: Cambridge University Press.

Dyce, J. A., & O'Connor, B. P. (1998). Personality disorders and the five-factor model: A test of facet-level predictions *Journal of Personality Disorders, 12,* 31–45.

Edens, J. F., Marcus, D. K., Lilienfeld, S. O., & Poythress, N. G., Jr. (2006). Psychopathic, not psychopath: Taxometric evidence for the dimensional structure of psychopathy. *Journal of Abnormal Psychology, 115,* 131–144.

Ekselius, L., Tillfors, M., Furmark, T., & Fredrickson, M. (2001). Personality disorders in the general population: DSM-IV and ICD-10 defined prevalence as related to sociodemographic profile. *Personality and Individual Differences, 30,* 311–320.

Farmer, R. F. (2000). Issues in the assessment and conceptualization of personality disorders. *Clinical Psychology Review, 20,* 823–851.

Fossati, A., Beauchaine, T. P., Grazioli, F., Carretta, I., Cortinovis, F., & Maffei, C. (2005). A latent structure analysis of DSM-IV narcissistic personality disorder criteria. *Comprehensive Psychiatry, 46,* 361–367.

Frances, A. (1993). Dimensional diagnosis of personality: Not whether, but when and which. *Psychological Inquiry, 4,* 110–111.

Grant, B. F., Stinson, F. S., Dawson, D. A., Chou, S. P., & Ruan, W. J. (2005). Co-occurrence of DSM-IV personality disorders in the United States: Results from the National Epidemiologic Survey on Alcohol and Related Conditions. *Comprehensive Psychiatry, 46,* 1–5.

Gunderson, J. G., & Phillips, K. A. (1995). Personality disorders. In H. I. Kaplan & B. J. Sadock (Eds.), *Comprehensive textbook of psychiatry* (6th ed., pp. 1425–1461). Baltimore: Williams & Wilkins.

Hare, R. D. (1999). *Without conscience: The disturbing world of the psychopaths among us.* New York: Guilford Press.

Hartung, C. M., & Widiger, T. A. (1998). Gender differences in the diagnosis of mental disorders: Conclusions and controversies of the DSM-IV. *Psychological Bulletin, 123,* 260–278.

Haslam, N. (2003). The dimensional view of personality disorders: A review of taxometric evidence. *Clinical Psychology Review, 23,* 75–93.

Hesse, M., Schilewe, S., & Thomsen, R. R. (2005). Rating of personality disorder features in popular movie characters. *BMC Psychiatry, 5,* 45.

Jang, K. L., & Vernon, P. A. (2001). Genetics. In W. J. Livesley (Ed.), *Handbook of personality disorders* (pp. 177–195). New York: Guilford Press.

Kapfhammer, H. P., & Hippius, H. (1998). Pharmacotherapy in personality disorders. *Journal of Personality Disorders, 12,* 277–288.

Klonsky, E. D., Oltmanns, T. F., & Turkheimer, E. (2002). Informant-reports of personality disorder: Relation to self-reports and future research directions. *Clinical Psychology: Science and Practice, 9,* 300–311.

Leichsenring, F., & Leibing, E. (2003). The effectiveness of psychodynamic therapy and cognitive behavior therapy in the treatment of personality disorders: A meta-analysis. *American Journal of Psychiatry, 160,* 1223–1232.

Lenzenweger, M. F., Loranger, A. W., Korfine, L., & Neff, C. (1997). Detecting personality disorders in a nonclinical population. *Archives of General Psychiatry, 54,* 345–351.

Links, P. S. (1996). *Clinical assessment and management of severe personality disorders.* Washington, DC: American Psychiatric Association.

Links, P. S., Heslegrave, R., & Villella, J. (1998). Psychopharmacological management of personality disorders: An outcome-focused model. In K. R. Silk (Ed.), *Biology of personality disorders* (pp. 93–127). Washington, DC: American Psychiatric Press.

Livesley, W. J. (1998). Suggestions for a framework for an empirically based classification of personality disorders. *Canadian Journal of Psychiatry, 43,* 137–147.

Livesley, W. J. (Ed.). (2001). *Handbook of personality disorders.* New York: Guilford Press.

Livesley, W. J. (2003). *Practical management of personality disorder.* New York: Guilford Press.

Livesley, W. J., Schroeder, M. L., Jackson, D. N., & Jang, K. L. (1994). Categorical distinctions in the study of personality disorder: Implications for classification. *Journal of Abnormal Psychology, 103,* 6–17.

Livesley, W. J., Schroeder, M. L., Lang, K. L., Jackson, N. D., & Vernon, P. A. (1993). Genetic and environmental contributions to dimensions of personality disorder. *American Journal of Psychiatry, 150,* 1826–1831.

Loranger, A. W., Lenzenweger, M. F., Garner, A. F., & Susman, V. L. (1991). Trait-state artifacts and the diagnosis of personality disorders. *Archives of General Psychiatry, 48,* 720–728.

MacKenzie, K. R. (2001). Personality assessment in clinical practice. In W. J. Livesley (Ed.), *Handbook of personality disorders* (pp. 307–321). New York: Guilford Press.

Magnavita, J. J. (Ed.). (2004). *Handbook of personality disorders: Theory and practice.* Hoboken, NJ: Wiley.

Maj, M., Akiskal, H. S., Mezzich, J. E., & Okasha, A. (Eds.). (2005). *Personality disorders*. Chichester, West Sussex, England: Wiley.

Marcus, D. K., John, S. L., & Edens, J. F. (2004). A taxometric analysis of psychopathic personality. *Journal of Abnormal Psychology, 113,* 626–635.

Markovitz, P. (2001). Pharmacotherapy. In W. J. Livesley (Ed.), *Handbook of personality disorders* (pp. 475–498). New York: Guilford Press.

Mattia, J. I., & Zimmerman, M. (2001). Epidemiology. In W. J. Livesley (Ed.), *Handbook of personality disorders* (pp. 107–123). New York: Guilford Press.

McDavid, J. D., & Pilkonis, P. A. (1996). The stability of personality disorder diagnoses. *Journal of Personality Disorders, 10,* 1–15.

Morey, L. C., Waugh, M. H., & Blashfield, R. K. (1985). MMPI scales for DSM-III personality disorders: Their derivation and correlates. *Journal of Personality Assessment, 49,* 245–251.

Nigg, J. T., & Goldsmith, H. H. (1994). Genetics of personality disorders: Perspectives from personality and psychopathology research. *Psychological Bulletin, 115,* 346–380.

O'Connor, B. P. (2002). The search for dimensional structure differences between normality and abnormality: A statistical review of published data on personality and psychopathology. *Journal of Personality and Social Psychology, 83,* 962–982.

O'Connor, B. P. (2005). A search for consensus on the dimensional structure of personality disorders. *Journal of Clinical Psychology, 61,* 323–345.

O'Connor, B. P., & Dyce, J. A. (2001a). Personality disorders. In M. Hersen & V. B. Van Hasselt (Eds.), *Advanced abnormal psychology* (pp. 399–417). New York: Kluwer Academic/Plenum Press.

O'Connor, B. P., & Dyce, J. A. (2001b). Rigid and extreme: A geometric representation of personality disorders in five-factor model space. *Journal of Personality and Social Psychology, 81,* 1119–1130.

Oltmanns, T. F., & Turkheimer, E. (2006). Perceptions of self and others regarding pathological personality traits. In R. F. Krueger & J. Tackett (Eds.), *Personality and psychopathology: Building bridges* (pp. 71–111). New York: Guilford Press.

Ozkan, M., & Altindag, A. (2005). Comorbid personality disorders in subjects with panic disorder: Do personality disorders increase clinical severity? *Comprehensive Psychiatry, 46,* 20–26.

Paris, J. (1998). Anxious traits, anxious attachment, and anxious-cluster personality disorders. *Harvard Review of Psychiatry, 6,* 142–148.

Paris, J. (2001). Psychosocial adversity. In W. J. Livesley (Ed.), *Handbook of personality disorders* (pp. 231–241). New York: Guilford Press.

Perry, J. C. (1992). Problems and considerations in the valid assessment of personality disorders. *American Journal of Psychiatry, 149,* 1645–1653.

Perry, J. C. (1993). Longitudinal studies of personality disorders. *Journal of Personality Disorders, 7,* 63–85.

Perry, J. C., Banon, E., & Ianni, F. (1999). Effectiveness of psychotherapy for personality disorders. *American Journal of Psychiatry, 156,* 1312–1321.

Perry, J. C., & Valliant, G. E. (1989). Personality disorders. In H. I. Kaplan & B. J. Sadock (Eds.), *Comprehensive textbook of psychiatry* (5th ed., pp. 1352–1395). Baltimore: Williams & Wilkins.

Rothschild, L., Cleland, C., Haslam, N., & Zimmerman, M. (2003). A taxometric study of borderline personality disorder. *Journal of Abnormal Psychology, 112,* 657–666.

Rutter, M., & Rutter, M. (1993). *Developing minds: Challenge and continuity across the life span*. New York: Basic Books.

Segal, D. L., Hersen, M. E., Van Hasselt, V. B., Silberman, C., & Roth, L. (1996). Diagnosis and assessment of personality disorders in older adults: A critical review. *Journal of Personality Disorders, 10,* 384–399.

Siever, L. J., Bernstein, D. P., & Silverman, J. M. (1995). Schizotypal personality disorder. In W. J. Livesley (Ed.), *The DSM-IV personality disorders* (pp. 71–90). New York: Guilford Press.

Siever, L. J., & Davis, K. L. (1991). A psycho-biological perspective on the personality disorders. *American Journal of Psychiatry, 148,* 1647–1658.

Silk, K. R. (1998). *Biology of personality disorders.* Washington, DC: American Psychiatric Press.

Skilling, T. A., Harris, G. T., Rice, M. E., & Quinsey, V. L. (2002). Identifying persistently antisocial offenders using the Hare Psychopathy Checklist and DSM antisocial personality disorder criteria. *Psychological Assessment, 14,* 27–38

Sperry, L. (1995). *Handbook of diagnosis and treatment of the DSM-IV personality disorders.* New York: Brunner/Mazel.

Stone, M. H. (1993). *Abnormalities of personality: Within and beyond the realm of treatment.* New York: Norton.

Stone, M. H. (2001). Natural history and long-term outcome. In W. J. Livesley (Ed.), *Handbook of personality disorders* (pp. 259–276). New York: Guilford Press.

Strupp, H. H., Horowitz, L. M., & Lambert, M. J. (1997). *Measuring patient changes in mood, anxiety, and personality disorders: Toward a core battery.* Washington, DC: American Psychological Association.

Stuart, S., Pfohl, B., Battaglia, M., Bellodi, L., Grove, W., & Cadoret, R. (1998). The co-occurrence of DSM-III-R personality disorders. *Journal of Personality Disorders, 12,* 302–315.

Sutker, P. B., Bugg, F., & West, J. A. (1993). Antisocial personality disorder. In P. B. Sutker & H. E. Adams (Eds.), *Comprehensive handbook of psychiatry* (pp. 337–369). New York: Plenum Press.

Tavris, C. (1992). *The mismeasure of woman.* New York: Simon & Schuster.

Torgersen, S., Kringlen, E., & Cramer, V. (2001). The prevalence of personality disorders in a community sample. *American Journal of Psychiatry, 58,* 590–596.

Tyrer, P., Gunderson, J., Lyons, M., & Tohen, M. (1997). Extent of comorbidity between mental state and personality disorders. *Journal of Personality Disorders, 11,* 242–259.

Van Velzen, C. J. M., & Emmelkamp, P. M. G. (1996). The assessment of personality disorders: Implications for cognitive and behavior therapy. *Behavior Research and Therapy, 34,* 655–668.

Vasey, M. W., Kotov, R., Frick, P. J., & Loney, B. R. (2005). The latent structure of psychopathy in youth: A taxometric investigation. *Journal of Abnormal Child Psychology, 33,* 411–429.

Walters, P., Moran, P., Choudhury, P., Lee, T., & Mann, A. (2004). Screening for personality disorder: A comparison of personality disorder assessment by patients and informants. *International Journal of Methods in Psychiatric Research, 13,* 34–39.

Weissman, M. M. (1993). The epidemiology of personality disorders: A 1990 update. *Journal of Personality Disorders, 7,* 44–62.

Westen, D., & Shedler, J. (1999). Revising and assessing Axis II: Pt. II. Toward an empirically based and clinically useful classification of personality disorders. *American Journal of Psychiatry, 156,* 273–285.

Widiger, T. A. (1998). Sex biases in the diagnosis of personality disorders. *Journal of Personality Disorders, 12,* 95–118.

Widiger, T. A., & Sanderson, C. J. (1995). Assessing personality disorders. In J. N. Butcher (Ed.), *Clinical personality assessment* (pp. 380–394). New York: Oxford University Press.

Widiger, T. A., & Sanderson, C. J. (1997). Personality disorders. In A. Tasman, J. Kay, & J. A. Lieberman (Eds.), *Psychiatry* (Vol. 2, pp. 1291–1317). Philadelphia: Saunders.

Widiger, T. A., & Simonsen, E. (2005). Alternative dimensional models of personality disorder: Finding a common ground. *Journal of Personality Disorders, 19,* 110–130.

Widiger, T. A., & Trull, T. J. (1993). Borderline and narcissistic personality disorders. In P. B. Sutker & H. E. Adams (Eds.), *Comprehensive handbook of psychiatry* (pp. 371–394). New York: Plenum Press.

Woodworth, M., & Porter, S. (2002). In cold blood: Characteristics of criminal homicides as a function of psychopathology. *Journal of Abnormal Psychology, 111,* 436–445.

World Health Organization. (1992). *The ICD-10 classification of mental and behavioral disorders: Clinical descriptions and diagnostic guidelines.* Geneva, Switzerland: Author.

Yang, J., McCrae, R. R., Costa, P. T., Jr., Yao, S., Dai, X., Cai, T., et al. (2000). The cross-cultural generalizability of Axis-II constructs: Evaluation of two personality disorder assessment instruments in the People's Republic of China. *Journal of Personality Disorders, 14,* 249–263.

Yudofsky, S. C. (2005). *Fatal flaws: Navigating destructive relationships with people with disorders of personality and character.* Washington, DC: American Psychiatric Publishing.

Zimmerman, M. (1994). Diagnosing personality disorders: A review of issues and research methods. *Archives of General Psychiatry, 51,* 225–245.

Zimmerman, M., & Coryell, W. (1989). DSM-III personality disorder diagnoses in a nonpatient sample. *Archives of General Psychiatry, 46,* 682–689.

CHAPTER 17

Bulimia Nervosa

TIFFANY M. STEWART AND DONALD A. WILLIAMSON

DESCRIPTION OF THE DISORDER

Bulimia is derived from the Greek word *boulimos*, whose literal meaning is "ox hunger" or "ravenous hunger" in English. Prior to 1979, there were reports of binge eating and binge eating and purging, but Gerald Russell (1979) was the first to depict Bulimia Nervosa (BN) as a syndrome that was distinct from Anorexia Nervosa (AN). The syndrome of BN includes excessive concern with body size and binge eating followed by some type of compensatory behavior to prevent weight gain (e.g., self-induced vomiting). The diagnostic criteria have changed considerably over the years. In 1980, *bulimia*, conceptualized as a syndrome marked by binge eating, was included in the *Diagnostic and Statistical Manual of Mental Disorders*, third edition (*DSM-III*; American Psychiatric Association, 1980). However, purging was not required for the diagnosis. Bulimia Nervosa was later established as an official diagnostic category in the *DSM-III-R* (American Psychiatric Association, 1987), which required a lack of control over eating in binge eating episodes and purgative behavior for clinical diagnosis. With publication of the *DSM-IV* (American Psychiatric Association, 1994), the diagnostic criteria for BN, summarized in Table 17.1, were revised. The current clinical description of the syndrome of BN is depicted by several core features. First, BN is depicted by recurrent episodes of binge eating, which are characterized by (a) eating a large amount of food in a discrete period of time, and (b) a sense of lack of control over eating during the episode. Binge eating episodes involve consuming an amount of food that is larger than others would eat in a similar time period under similar circumstances. Such an episode may be defined as an "objective binge." In contrast, other binges may be classified as "subjective." Such a subjective binge may include measurably small amounts of a "forbidden food" (i.e., a food that is in violation of one's idea of restrictive dieting and creates significant anxiety and weight concern). The second core feature required for the diagnosis of BN is the recurrent use of inappropriate compensatory behaviors, such as self-induced vomiting, excessive exercise, fasting, or the misuse of laxatives, diuretics, enemas, or other medications, or some combination of these methods, with the most common type of compensatory behavior being self-induced vomiting (Williamson, Martin, & Stewart, 2004). In addition,

Table 17.1

Summary of the *DSM-IV* Diagnostic Criteria for Bulimia Nervosa

1. Episodes of binge eating are recurrent. An episode of binge eating is characterized by both of the following:
   a. Eating an amount of food that is larger than most people would eat during a similar period of time (discrete period of time, e.g. 2-hour period), under similar circumstances.
   b. A feeling of lack of control over eating during the episodes of binge eating.
2. Compensatory behavior(s) for the purpose of preventing weight gain are utilized, e.g., self-induced vomiting; misuse of laxatives, diuretics, enemas, and/or other medications or supplements; restrictive eating, or excessive exercise is recurrent.
3. The binge eating and compensatory behaviors, e.g. self-induced vomiting, etc., both occur, on the average, at least twice per week for 3 months duration.
4. Self-evaluation is significantly influenced by body weight and shape.
5. The disturbance of bulimia nervosa does not occur exclusively during episodes of anorexia nervosa.

Subtypes:

Purging type: during the current episode of bulimia nervosa, the person has engaged, on a regular basis, in self-induced vomiting or the misuse of laxatives, diuretics, or enemas.

Nonpurging type: during the current episode of bulimia nervosa, the person has used other inappropriate compensatory behaviors, such as fasting or excessive exercise, but has not engaged, on a regular basis, in self-induced vomiting or misuse of laxatives, diuretics, or enemas.

the *DSM-IV* designates that recurrent binge eating and compensatory behavior both must occur at least twice a week for a period of 3 months. A third core feature necessary for a diagnosis of BN requires that overall self-evaluation is overly influenced by body shape and weight. Finally, the syndrome of BN may not occur exclusively during episodes of AN (American Psychiatric Association, 1994).

There are two subtypes of BN: purging and nonpurging types. The purging subtype, the most common, is defined by recurrent episodes of utilizing compensatory strategies, such as self-induced vomiting or the misuse of laxatives or diuretics. In contrast, the nonpurging subtype engages in binge behavior but utilizes behavior such as excessive exercise and/or fasting as compensatory strategies, and does not regularly engage in self-induced vomiting and/or the misuse of laxatives and/or diuretics to control body weight.

The Eating Disorder Not Otherwise Specified (EDNOS) category includes various forms of eating disorders that do not meet criteria for AN or BN but are still of clinical significance. In many cases, patients exhibit a mixture of features, including (a) intense fear of weight gain, (b) overconcern with body size, and (c) use of extreme methods for weight control. For example, an individual may use inappropriate compensatory behavior after consuming objectively small amounts of food (e.g., self-induced vomiting after eating one slice of cake). The diagnosis of EDNOS is given to nearly 50% of patients with eating disorders who present for eating disorder treatment (American Psychiatric Association Work Group on Eating Disorders, 2000; Thaw, Williamson, & Martin, 2001). One recent study indicated that approximately 70% of EDNOS participants moved to either AN or BN over the course of a 30-month follow-up period (Milos, Spindler, Schnyder, & Fairburn, 2005). Another recent study found that BN cases and EDNOS cases with BN symptoms, called EDNOS-BN, did not statistically differ on variables such as dietary restraint, body weight and shape concerns, and comorbid psychiatric and personality symptoms (leGrange et al., 2006). This study also found that EDNOS-BN cases engaged in clinically meaningful levels of binging and purging. These findings highlight the clinical importance of the EDNOS category. Further, these findings have significant implications for the classification of eating disorders, including BN, as body weight changes and symptom severity can move an individual from one diagnosis to another, not necessarily indicating actual "illness transition" (Wonderlich, Joiner, Keel, Williamson, & Crosby, in press).

CLASSIFICATION

Results of numerous empirical studies have raised significant concern regarding the current *DSM* classification system of eating disorders. The main concerns include (a) the validity and/or significance of the individual diagnostic criteria for AN, BN, EDNOS, and Binge Eating Disorder (BED)(e.g., the weight criteria for AN, the operational definition of the binge criterion for BN); (b) validity of the subtypes related to AN (e.g., restricting, binge-purge) and BN (e.g., purging, nonpurging); and (c) the validity of the distinctiveness of the eating disorder diagnoses (e.g., AN, BN, and EDNOS); for example, patients with AN have been found to "cross over" to develop BN, and EDNOS patients to full syndrome AN or BN (Wonderlich et al., in press).

Three-Dimensional Model Williamson, Gleaves, and Stewart (2005) conceptualized eating disorders in terms of a three-dimensional model with the utilization of taxometric analysis. In this model, binge eating is viewed as qualitatively different from normalcy, and two true dimensions, fear of fatness/compensatory behaviors, and extreme drive for thinness, are viewed as continuous with normalcy. This model is based on a series of taxometric studies conducted by Williamson, Womble, et al. (2002), Gleaves, Lowe, Green, Cororve, and Williams (2000), and Gleaves, Lowe, Snow, Green, and Murphy-Eberenz (2000). Figure 17.1 illustrates this model and positions eating disorder diagnostic categories among the three dimensions to illustrate how the current *DSM-IV* categorical approach relates to the three-dimensional approach for classification. The floor of this three-dimensional model is provided by the two continua, and the third dimension is binge eating that is discontinuous, or categorical. A fourth variable, body weight relative to height, was viewed as pertinent to this conceptual model but was not regarded as an eating disorder symptom. It should be noted that in the study reported by Williamson, Womble et al. (2002), the two continua, drive for thinness and fear of fatness/concern for body size and shape, were positively correlated. Therefore, it is possible that there is one latent dimension that accounts for these two continua. As can be seen in Figure 17.1, Anorexia Nervosa, restricting type (AN-R), obese, and normal groups are conceptualized as positioned along the two continua, whereas disorders involving binge eating including Bulimia Nervosa, purging type (BN-P), Bulimia Nervosa, nonpurging type (BN-NP), Anorexia Nervosa, binge/purge type (AN-BP), and Binge Eating Disorder (BED) are viewed as discontinuous with AN-R, obese, and normal groups.

Implications of the Three-Dimensional Model for the Study of Eating Disorders
Classification of eating disorders based on taxometric findings may provide indirect

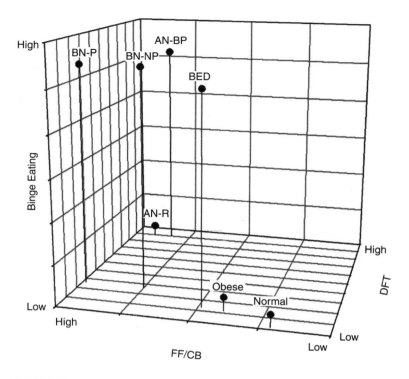

Figure 17.1   Three-Dimensional Model of eating disorders (Williamson, Gleaves, & Stewart, 2005). BN-P = Bulimia Nervosa, purging type; BN-NP = Bulimia Nervosa, nonpurging type; AN-R = Anorexia Nervosa, restricting type; AN-BP, Anorexia Nervosa, binge/purge type; BED = Binge Eating Disorder; FF/CB = Fear of fatness/concern with body size and shape. *Source:* "Categorical versus Dimensional Models of Eating Disorders: An Examination of the Evidence," by D. A. Williamson, D. H. Gleaves, and T. M. Stewart, 2005, *International Journal of Eating Disorders, 37,* pp. 1–10. Reprinted with permission.

evidence for a genetic basis for certain features of eating disorders (e.g., binge eating or anxiety sensitivity). Identification of a taxonic structure for the symptoms of eating disorders does not necessarily imply a genetic basis. However, identification of a taxonic structure may at least give a genetic etiology a higher probability than if the disorder was determined to be an extreme point on one or more continua (Meehl, 1992). There may also be ways in which a taxonic structure is related to etiology other than through genetics. It is quite possible that a taxon may represent effects of different types of specific environmental events or behavioral threshold effects (Blundell & Hill, 1993).

Strategies for assessing eating disorders will be influenced by the conceptualization of symptoms. If a symptom is viewed as being a dimension, the psychometric goal will be to assess all aspects of the construct and discriminate all regions of the dimension (Meehl, 1992; Ruscio & Ruscio, 2002). When attempting to measure a categorical construct, the goal is to sort criteria at a best cut so as to minimize misclassifications (Meehl, 1992). The three-dimensional model suggests that it may be useful to measure concerns about body size and shape, drive for thinness, and fear of fatness using continuous variables that could operationally define these characteristics. Variables such as weight status are routinely measured using continuous variables, and this approach is recommended given current evidence. Binge eating, a variable that is conceptualized as categorical, should be measured as a dichotomy (e.g., within normal limits versus outside normal limits).

Researchers (e.g., Hay & Bacaltchuk, 2002; Treasure & Schmidt, 2002) have observed that treatments for BN and BED are generally less intense and more efficacious than treatments for AN. Furthermore, efficacious pharmacologic therapy for BN and BED has been consistently reported. In contrast, effective pharmacotherapy for AN has not been reported (Treasure & Schmidt, 2002). Why are eating disorders with binge eating as a primary behavioral feature more difficult to treat? In their discussion of the three-dimensional model, Williamson et al. (2005) noted that behavioral and cognitive change may be difficult to initiate with a categorical variable, but once initiated should be more complete and dramatic because such "syndromes" are represented as a dichotomy (i.e., either within normal limits or not; Strube, 1989). It is possible that there is a genetic or biological basis for binge eating (Blundell & Stubbs, 1998; Koopmans, 1998) that is treatable by pharmacotherapy or various types of psychotherapy if binge eating is caused by a disruption of normal appetitive control mechanisms (Blundell & Hill, 1993). These speculations address why binge eating may be more easily treated, but the question of why AN-R is so resistant to treatment still requires explanation. The three-dimensional model views AN-R to be continuous with normalcy. Why is a syndrome that is an extreme level of normalcy especially difficult to treat? Williamson et al. suggested that disorders that are acquired from a culture that overvalues thinness in certain subgroups (Strong, Williamson, Netemeyer, & Geer, 2000) may be more difficult to treat than disorders that stem from disturbances of biological or psychological regulatory mechanisms. Thus, relative to other characteristics of eating disorders (e.g., restrictive eating and body image concerns), binge eating may be relatively easy to modify.

PREVALENCE

Estimates of the prevalence of eating disorders vary depending on the sampling and assessment methods. Current estimates of lifetime prevalence for BN range from 1.1% to 4.2% for females (American Psychiatric Association, 2004; American Psychiatric Association Work Group on Eating Disorders, 2000). Bulimia Nervosa is not common in males, accounting for approximately 10% of all of the cases (Williamson, Zucker, Martin, & Smeets, 2001). A recent study indicated a 0.3% to 7.3% prevalence rate in women and 0% to 2.1% prevalence in men in Western countries (Makino, Tsuboi, & Dennerstein, 2004). Another recent study reported evidence for a decrease in BN point prevalence in women from the 1980s to the present time (Keel, Heatherton, Dorer, Joiner, & Zalta, 2005), which is consistent with other recent studies (Currin, Schmidt, Treasure, & Jick, 2005; Hoek, van Hoeken, & Bartelds, 2000; Hoek, Van Son, van Hoeken, Bartelds, & Van Furth, 2005; Westenhoefer, 2001).

In addition, overall estimates in the United States across different ethnic groups suggest that Native American women have the highest prevalence rate of eating disorders overall, Caucasian and Hispanic women having the second highest, with African American and Asian women following (Crago, Shisslak, & Estes, 1996; Dorian & Garfinkel, 1999).

COMORBIDITY

Comorbid psychiatric diagnoses, such as depression, anxiety, substance abuse, and personality disorders, are often associated with BN (Hudson, Hudson, & Pope, 2005). Braun, Sunday, and Halmi (1994) reported an 82% prevalence of Axis I comorbidity among eating disorder patients. The prevalence rate of comorbid affective disorders in women with BN range from 50% to 75% (American Psychiatric Association, 2004; Braun et al., 1994; Brewerton et al., 1995; Rowe, Pickles, Simonoff, Bulik, & Silberg, 2002). Comorbid anxiety disorders have also been found to be common among patients with eating disorders (Braun et al., 1994; Brewerton et al., 1995; Bulik, Sullivan, Carter, & Joyce, 1996; Herzog, Keller, Sacks, Yeh, & Lavori, 1992; Kaye, Bulik, Thornton, Barbarich, & Masters, 2004; Milos, Spindler, Ruggiero, Klaghofer, & Schnyder, 2002; Rowe et al., 2002). In particular, Obsessive-Compulsive Disorder has been found to be associated with BN (Braun et al., 1994; Kaye et al., 2004; Milos et al., 2002; Thiel, Zuger, Jacoby, & Schussler, 1998; Thornton & Russell, 1997). In addition, substance abuse and dependence have been found in as many as 13% to 52% of individuals with BN (Brewerton et al., 1995; Bulik, Sullivan, Carter, & Joyce, 1997; Bulik et al., 2004; Dansky, Brewerton, & Kilpatrick, 2000; Dohm et al., 2002; Holderness, Brooks-Gunn, & Warren, 1994).

Axis II comorbidity is often associated with BN, typically in the form of Cluster B personality disorders (histrionic, narcissistic, borderline, and antisocial; Grilo, Levy, Becker, Edell, & McGlashan, 1996; Braun et al., 1994; Grilo, 2002). Research has shown that Borderline Personality Disorder is the predominant Axis II pathology associated with BN (Ames-Frankel et al., 1992). In addition, community-based studies have found no significant differences between prevalence rates of comorbid diagnoses between persons diagnosed with BN or subthreshold BN (Garfinkel et al., 1995; Kendler et al., 1991). A recent study indicated that there were few sex differences in personality and psychological traits associated with eating disorders (Fernandez-Aranda et al., 2004).

DIAGNOSIS AND ASSESSMENT

Comprehensive assessment for the diagnosis and treatment of BN requires a multitrait-multimethod approach. This approach includes collection of information through medical evaluation, structured interviews, self-report inventories, and self-monitoring. Thus, it is desirable for individuals with eating disorders to be evaluated by a multidisciplinary team, including a physician and/or a psychiatrist, a dietitian, and a psychologist. It is also of great value for individuals with eating disorders to be evaluated by health care professionals who have experience with eating disorders, given the complicated nature of the assessment (e.g. medical and psychological factors).

MEDICAL EXAMINATION

Medical complications are often associated with BN. These are typically related to the type of purging (i.e., vomiting, laxatives, and diuretics) and frequency of purging (Mehler, Crews, & Weiner, 2004). These medical complications include skeletal complications, reproductive system complications, endocrine abnormalities, metabolic abnormalities, and electrolyte and/or fluid disturbances (Crow, 2005; Pomeroy, 2004). A thorough medical evaluation by a physician should be conducted to evaluate any medical problems and formulate a treatment plan accordingly. More specific physical examination and medical history signs of BN may include but are not limited to salivary gland enlargement, erosion of dental enamel, peripheral edema, constipation, irregular menses, abrasions on fingers or on back of hands from self-induced vomiting, abdominal bloating or discomfort, headaches, and lethargy or fatigue (Pomeroy, 2004). It is important to note that after regular vomiting over time, it may become easier for individuals, and they may not require a finger or object to stimulate the gag reflex. This makes it easier to purge via self-induced vomiting and may reduce the likelihood of the presence of abrasions on the fingers. For a more thorough review of the medical complications of BN, refer to Mehler et al. (2004) or Pomeroy (2004).

The examination should also include height and weight to determine Body Mass Index (BMI). This index may be used to establish whether the individual is of normal weight, underweight, or overweight status. It is important to note that many BN cases will have normal weight status and thus will appear healthy upon physical presentation. In addition, percentages of body composition are valuable to assess (i.e., lean mass and fat mass) and to corroborate BMI, as BMI does not take into account such indices. Indices such as weight and, if possible, body composition should be monitored throughout the treatment process to determine progress.

DIETARY ASSESSMENT AND SELF-MONITORING

Measurement of macronutrient and caloric intake is significant in establishing a treatment plan for BN. However, due to low compliance and modest accuracy, it is recommended that self-monitoring of food intake serve as an adjunct to any assessment, versus a component that is heavily relied on for critical information. This procedure requires that the individual record the amounts and types of foods eaten, as well as behavioral, cognitive, and emotional antecedents and consequences of eating (Williamson, Prather, McKenzie, & Blouin, 1990). Self-monitoring for 2 weeks prior to entering treatment is recommended to aid in diagnosis and case formulation.

BEHAVIORAL ASSESSMENT: TEST MEALS

Test meals may serve as the key component of behavioral assessment, also serving as a key component in the treatment process for BN (Stewart & Williamson, in press). Individuals with BN often have difficulty coming forth with information about their eating habits because of shame and often minimize or omit key details about their eating habits on their self-monitoring. The test meal method of assessment may be used for directly observing eating behavior, including elements such as rate of eating, anxiety while eating, urges to binge, urges to purge, hiding of food, and food mixing. Caloric intake may be calculated during these meals. From a treatment perspective, exposure with response prevention may be employed, with the utilization of a hierarchy of feared foods (Stewart & Williamson, 2004b).

PSYCHOLOGICAL EVALUATION

Psychological assessment of BN is vital when establishing a case formulation and treatment plan. Of significant importance in the psychological assessment process is the successful establishment of rapport to obtain accurate information and to initiate an effective treatment process.

Psychological assessment may be best conceptualized as an ongoing process of information gathering. Throughout this process, factors in the etiology and symptom maintenance are formulated and revised with new information collected during the entire course of treatment. Important domains of such an assessment include a detailed weight history, the presence of body image disturbance, dysfunctional eating behaviors, and comorbid psychopathology. A thorough assessment includes multiple methods of data collection, such as structured interviews, self-report measures, and behavioral observations. Some of the most common measures that have relevance to BN are reviewed in the following section. For a more thorough review of eating disorder assessment, see Stewart and Williamson (2006). For a specific review of interviewing techniques, please see Stewart and Williamson (in press).

Semi-Structured Clinical Interviews   Two semi-structured interview formats for the purpose of diagnosing eating disorders have been developed. First, the Eating Disorder Examination, 12th edition (EDE; Fairburn & Cooper, 1993), is a widely researched interview with acceptable psychometric properties reported (Fairburn & Cooper, 1993; Rizvi, Peterson, Crow, & Agras, 2000). The EDE includes four subscales that evaluate several aspects of disordered eating, including restraint, concern with eating, concern with weight, and concern with shape, as well as a measure of overall severity. The EDE provides adequate eating disorder diagnoses and has been shown to be sensitive to the effects of treatment (Fairburn, Jones, Peveler, Hope, & O'Conner, 1993). Second, the Interview for the Diagnosis of Eating Disorders, fourth edition (IDED-IV; Kutlesic, Williamson, Gleaves, Barbin, & Murphy-Eberenz, 1998), is a semi-structured interview designed specifically for the differential diagnosis of AN, BN, and EDNOS, based on *DSM-IV* diagnostic criteria. The presence and severity of each criterion are rated by the interviewer. Historical and developmental information are also collected. Adequate validity and reliability have been reported (Kutlesic et al., 1998).

Self-Report Inventories   Psychometrically sound self-report measures that are utilized for the assessment of eating disorder symptoms, including BN include, the Eating Disorder Examination-Questionnaire (EDE-Q; Fairburn & Beglin, 1994), the Eating Attitudes Test (EAT; Garner & Garfinkel, 1979), the Eating Disorder Inventory-Revised (EDI-2; Garner, 1991), the Bulimia Test-Revised (BULIT-R; Thelen, Farmer, Wonderlich, & Smith, 1991), the Multiaxial Assessment of Eating Disorder Symptoms (MAEDS; Anderson, Williamson, Duchmann, Gleaves, & Barbin, 1999), and the Eating Inventory (EI; Stunkard & Messick, 1988).

The EDE-Q follows the questions used in the EDE to assess the central features of AN and BN. The EDE-Q can be used to screen for the presence of binging and purging and extreme concerns related to body size and shape and eating. The reliability and validity of the EDE-Q has been established. The EAT is a 40-item self-report measure developed to assess anorexic attitudes, beliefs, and behaviors. The EAT has been found to differentiate between eating disorder patients and nonclinical controls as well as to distinguish between binge eaters from individuals diagnosed with BN (Williamson et al., 1990). Psychometric properties have been found to be adequate (Gross, Rosen, Leitenberg, & Wilmuth, 1986).

The EDI-2 evaluates the cognitive and behavioral characteristics of BN and AN. The EDI-2 has eleven subscales: (1) Drive for Thinness, (2) Bulimia, (3) Body Dissatisfaction, (4) Ineffectiveness, (5) Perfectionism, (6) Interpersonal Distrust, (7) Interoceptive

Awareness, (8) Maturity Fears, (9) Asceticism, (10) Impulse Regulation, and (11) Social Insecurity. Satisfactory reliability and validity have been shown, with extensive norms established (Garner, 1991). The BULIT-R is a 28-item self-report tool developed to measure the symptoms of BN according to the *DSM-III-R* (American Psychiatric Association, 1987). The BULIT-R was found to discriminate individuals with BN, BED, obesity, and nonclinical subjects (Williamson, 1990). Satisfactory psychometric properties were reported (Thelen et al., 1991). The MAEDS is a 56-item self-report measure that is designed to assess a total of six symptom clusters: avoidance of fear foods, purgative behaviors, binge eating, fear of fatness, restrictive eating, and depression. Satisfactory validity and reliability have been reported (Anderson et al., 1999; Martin, Williamson, & Thaw, 2000). The MAEDS and the EAT are recommended as satisfactory measures of treatment outcome. Finally, the EI assesses three domains of eating behavior: dietary restraint, behavioral disinhibition, and perceived hunger. The EI has also been found to have adequate validity and reliability (Stunkard & Messick, 1988).

BODY IMAGE ASSESSMENT

From the perspective of cognitive-behavioral theory, disturbances of body image involve negative cognitive emotions and behavioral reactions to body-relevant information. In this regard, body image assessment procedures have been developed to measure subjective attitudes about bodily attributes, perceptions of actual or current body size, ideal body size, and behaviors related to body image (e.g., body checking, avoidance of feared situations, restrictive eating). This theory has direct relevance to BN (Williamson, Stewart, White, & York-Crowe, 2002). Body image assessment measures have typically been divided into four groups: (1) size estimation procedures (i.e., figural stimuli and perceptual measures for the purpose of measuring over- and underestimation of body size); (2) body dissatisfaction procedures (i.e. dissatisfaction with body size and/or shape); (3) sociocultural procedures (e.g., risk factors and internalization of the thin ideal); and (4) behavioral measures (i.e., body checking and avoidance of uncomfortable or feared situations surrounding body image). For a comprehensive review of body image assessment in the context of eating disorders, refer to Stewart and Williamson (2004a).

Dissatisfaction with size and/or shape is one of this most common and useful indices to measure when assessing body image in BN. A number of questionnaires exist to assess satisfaction with and attitudes toward body size and shape. Two of these measures are the EDI-2 subscale assessing body dissatisfaction (Garner, 1991) and the Body Shape Questionnaire (BSQ; Cooper, Taylor, Cooper, & Fairburn, 1987). Overall, these measures have been found to be reliable, valid, and easily administered procedures (Cooper et al., 1987; Garner, 1991).

Another important index for measurement is body size over- or underestimation. Assessments of body image have been created that utilize visual stimuli to assess this characteristic, as well as assess body dissatisfaction. Such measures include the Body Image Assessment (BIA; Williamson, Davis, Bennett, Goreczny, & Gleaves, 1989), the Body Morph Assessment (BMA; Stewart, Williamson, Smeets, & Greenway, 2001), and the Body Morph Assessment 2.0 (BMA 2.0; Stewart, Williamson, Allen, & Han, 2005). The BIA utilizes figural stimuli to derive a measure of body dissatisfaction. The BMA, a recently developed computer measure, assesses body image dissatisfaction utilizing a morph of a human body via an interactive computer assessment format.

Both of these measures have shown adequate validity and reliability (Stewart et al., 2005; Williamson et al., 1989).

Other aspects of body image that may be less obvious include body checking and/or behavioral avoidance related to body image. Checking of various body areas (e.g., stomach or hips) or the entire body (e.g., observation using a mirror or compulsive weighing) to detect minute changes in fatness can aid in the perpetuation of body image disturbance and eating disorder symptoms in BN. The Body Checking Questionnaire (BCQ; Reas, Whisenhunt, Netemeyer, & Williamson, 2002) was developed to measure severity of body checking; the reliability and validity of this brief self-report inventory has been established. Avoidance of situations that promote anxiety about body image is common in individuals with body image disturbance and eating disorders. The Body Image Avoidance Questionnaire (BIAQ; Rosen, Srebnik, Saltzberg, & Wendt, 1991) is a 19-item self-report measure that assesses these behavioral tendencies. This measure has been shown to be reliable and valid.

Recent literature has begun to focus on other specialized facets of body image, particularly in men (Adams, Turner, & Bucks, 2005). Men who are obsessed with body size often perceive their body as too thin and insufficiently muscular. Such "muscle dysmorphia" often lends itself to compulsive weight lifting and use of steroids. The Muscle Appearance Satisfaction Scale (MASS; Mayville, Williamson, White, Netemeyer, & Drab, 2002) was developed to meet this assessment need and has been found to be reliable and valuable in the assessment of men with this type of body image presentation. However, women have also begun to demonstrate body image symptoms that relate to the desire for increased muscularity; therefore, further research and assessment tools are needed to adequately ascertain this relationship.

Numerous assessments have been developed for the assessment of body image. These range from more holistic experiences of body image (e.g., the assessment of body image quality of life via the Body Image Quality of Life Scale); (BIQL; Cash & Fleming, 2002) to more highly specialized assessments (e.g., schemas related to body image via the Appearance Schemas Inventory; (ASI; Cash & Labarge, 1996).

Secondary Psychopathology Assessment

As previously mentioned, BN and subthreshold BN are often related to comorbid psychopathology (e.g., depression, anxiety, substance use, personality disorders). Thus, it is important to assess for the presence of comorbid disorders to construct a viable case formulation and treatment plan. The Structural Clinical Interview for *DSM-IV* Axis I Disorders (SCID-I; First, Spitzer, Gibbon, & Williams, 1996) and the Structural Clinical Interview for *DSM-IV* Axis II Disorders (SCID II; First et al., 1995) may be utilized for this purpose.

CONCEPTUALIZATION

Learning and Modeling

Learning   Figure 17.2 demonstrates the core conceptual learning model of BN. This figure was adapted from Williamson (1990). The core psychopathology of BN is typically initiated after a period of dieting. Ideally, individuals view restrictive eating as the goal. Once dietary restraint is broken by either eating a forbidden food and/or binge eating, a fear of weight gain is activated and body image concerns and anxiety

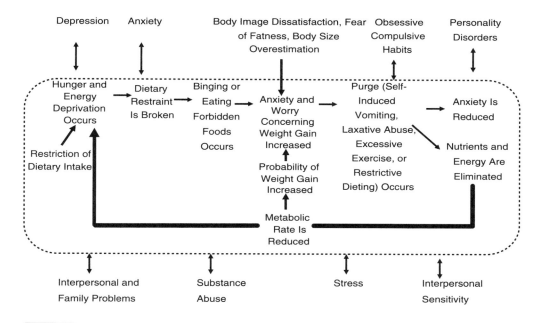

Figure 17.2 Conceptual Learning Model for Bulimia Nervosa proposed by Williamson (1990). *Source: Assessment of Eating Disorders: Obesity, Anorexia, and Bulimia Nervosa,* by D. A. Williamson, 1990, Elmsford, NY: Pergamon Press. Reprinted with permission.

are heightened. Purgative behavior then ensues as a way to release the anxiety and is negatively reinforced by the relief. Purging leads to the elimination of nutrients in the body and often a reduction and/or elimination of energy, thus resulting in energy deprivation and hunger. Such energy deprivation typically perpetuates the cycle to continue. Over time, an individual with BN learns that anxiety from binge eating can be substantially relieved by self-induced vomiting. Further, it is often realized that drive for thinness and fears of fatness can be decreased if the person engages in excessive exercise and/or other weight gain prevention activities. Thus, BN behavior is reinforced over time and becomes increasingly difficult for individuals to stop the behaviors on their own.

Modeling The sociocultural model of eating disorders assumes that the cultural context of the promotion of a thin body size as the ideal puts young women at risk for the internalization of this ideal and, in turn, the development of eating disorders. The same may be interpreted for males in the bodybuilding arena. This type of model has sustained its popularity in eating disorder literature over time; however, it has lacked a complete explanation of the mechanisms by which these contexts contribute to the risks of the development of eating disorders, or BN specifically. One study reviewed the relationship of such media on the intentional utilization of weight loss products by women (Whisenhunt, Williamson, Netemeyer, & Andrews, 2003). This study found that normal weight women with body dysphoria, when exposed to weight loss ads in print media (e.g., magazines), expressed the intention to utilize weight reduction products. This is an example of how the social context may influence behavior directly in this regard.

Another example of modeling in BN is vicarious modeling in the way of family members (e.g. mothers to daughters, sisters to sisters) and friends, roommates, and fellow dancers modeling eating disordered behaviors to each other. There is a long-standing discussion of the example of sorority houses that have designated spots for purging and sports teams who value weight so much that they support behaviors that maintain low body weight (e.g., vomiting and sauna use by jockeys).

LIFE EVENTS

The role of developmental factors and life events in the development of eating disorders has been emphasized. Developmental factors that impact BN include, but are not limited to, pubertal timing, early childhood eating and health problems, weight concerns, dieting, negative body image, general psychiatric disturbance, negative emotionality, sexual abuse, and BMI. Other factors are family interaction, functioning and/or attachment styles, family history and/or family psychopathology, low self-esteem, perfectionism, low interoceptive awareness, and participation in a weight-related exercise (e.g., dance) (Jacobi, 2005). Weight gain associated with the onset of puberty may lead to increased body image disturbance and restrictive eating. Further, Welch, Doll, and Fairburn (1997) found that bulimic women had experienced more negative life events in the year before the onset of the eating disorder than a community control group. Such events included physical illness, pregnancy, change in family structure, or sexual and/or physical abuse. Research studies and literature reviews on childhood sexual abuse and eating disorders (H. G. Pope & Hudson, 1992; Wonderlich, Brewerton, Jocic, Dansky, & Abbott, 1997) have concluded that childhood sexual abuse may be a risk factor for BN. A recent investigation found a relationship between childhood physical abuse and body image distortion (Treuer, Koperdak, Rozsa, & Furedi, 2005). However, further replication studies are needed, as many of the studies reviewed include different variables and designs.

GENETIC INFLUENCES

Biological, genetic, and environmental factors influence risk and predisposition for eating disorders. The influence of genetics on the etiology of eating disorders has been shown in family and twin studies. A well-established series of family studies has found a greater lifetime prevalence of eating disorders among relatives of individuals with BN (Bulik, 2004). Family studies indicate that BN aggregates in families (Stein et al., 1999; Strober, Freeman, Lampert, Diamond, & Lay, 2000). The heritability estimates for BN from twin studies have ranged from 28% to 83% (Bulik, Sullivan, & Kendler, 1998; Bulik, Sullivan, Wade, & Kendler, 2000; Wade, Martin, & Tiggeman, 1998). Linkage analyses of families with eating disorders, identified through a proband with BN, have yielded results suggesting a significant linkage on Chromosome 10p (Bulik et al., 2003).

Association studies utilizing affected cases and unaffected controls have focused on candidate genes involved in serotonergic and dopaminergic function, as well as on genes related to feeding behavior, such as potassium channels, and genes involved in energy balance, food intake, and body weight regulation (e.g., MC4, POMC, leptin, agouti-related protein, and neuropeptide Y; Tozzi & Bulik, 2003). More recently, contradictory findings regarding the relationship between bulimia and the estrogen receptor beta have been described (Nilsson et al., 2004). Many genetic association studies on eating disorders have been conducted to date, but few results have been replicated.

Failure to replicate findings could be due to trait heterogeneity as a result of inaccurate subtyping of eating disorders as related to behavioral phenotypes. Most studies have classified the phenotype of interest based on the full *DSM-IV* syndrome criteria (American Psychiatric Association, 1994) rather than single component behaviors. It is our belief that greater genetic homogeneity may best be determined by the investigation of the association of a more "simple" phenotype (component behavior), such as binge eating alone, rather than on full syndromes or categories (groupings of behaviors), such as the full syndrome of BN. Further, given the issues with classification and diagnosis of psychological disorders, particularly eating disorders such as BN, it is unlikely that the *DSM-IV* categories/diagnostic schema represent more potential for a genetic basis than the core behaviors that underlie these categories (Slof-Op't Landt et al., 2005). For example, the diagnostic criteria of the *DSM-IV* (American Psychiatric Association, 1994) are clinically determined. These criteria may simply represent combinations of environmentally and/or genetically influenced symptoms. These combinations of clinically determined criteria may inhibit investigations for relevant genes, as there is likely no existing gene that underlies the entire combination. However, it is likely that there are candidate genes that underlie single, or component, behaviors. Thus, it is critical that future research attempt to investigate the genetic basis of more simple behavioral phenotypes of eating disorders (e.g., binge eating) to increase the likelihood of finding more meaningful genotype-phenotype relationships.

The search for genes and mutations contributing to the development of BN is in its early stages and is continuing to evolve (Slof-Op't Landt et al., 2005). Larger scale genetic studies are needed to determine specific candidate genes and biological pathways involved in BN. For a review of the progress of genetics and eating disorders, see Slof-Op't Landt et al.

PHYSICAL FACTORS AFFECTING BEHAVIOR

Physical conditions affecting behavior may include but are not limited to complications of gastric bypass and various gastrointestinal and/or stomach-related problems that would promote and/or maintain BN symptoms. There are an increasing number of eating disorder cases in the postoperative bariatric surgery literature (Segal, Kinoshita Kussunoki, & Larino, 2004). These cases often do not meet full criteria for BN, but do meet criteria for EDNOS varieties. It has been reported that some of these patients experience a change in their previous relationship with food, marked by a fear of regaining weight (Segal et al., 2004). Thus, this leads to eating avoidance behaviors. Further, we have observed clinically that if patients experience eating too much for their new stomach size and begin vomiting, they may avoid eating to avoid this occurrence. In addition, some patients realize that if they eat too much, they will vomit automatically, and so they continue to eat too much, leading themselves into a binge-purge cycle of behavior.

Conditions that may preexist or may develop after the onset of BN that may lead to the maintenance of BN behaviors include irritable bowel syndrome (IBS), with or without constipation, peptic ulcers, and medication-induced stomach pain and gastric ulcers. Recent research has shown that women who experienced GI complaints as a child had an earlier onset of BN than those without such complaints (Gendall, Joyce, Carter, McIntosh, & Bulik, 2005). Such GI complaints were hypothesized to be related to abdominal pain associated with autonomic arousal (e.g., stress reactions) and abdominal pain associated having the sensation of a full stomach (e.g., gastric reflux, gastric and intestinal distention, and/or intestinal contractions). In treatment, such gastric difficulties maintain bulimic behaviors as the behaviors are negatively reinforced by relief from pain (e.g., vomiting relieves the sensation of the full stomach), and the full stomach may be causing the intestines to contract.

DRUGS AFFECTING BEHAVIOR

A significant source of medical and psychological complications in individuals diagnosed with BN is the use and abuse of over-the-counter supplements to increase the likelihood of weight loss or weight gain suppression, including appetite suppressants, energy pills, diuretics, and laxatives (Crow, 2005; Roerig et al., 2003). For a review of products and adverse effects, see Roerig et al. (2003). Supplements containing central nervous system stimulants such as ephedrine, caffeine, and herbal stimulants (e.g., Ma Huang) often cause an increase in heart rate, promoting anxiety, headaches, decreased concentration, nausea, and even seizures. Often, tolerance occurs with regular use and withdrawal symptoms occur with abrupt discontinuation of use.

Diuretic use and abuse are also popular among BN patients, often contributing to reflex edema. In addition, there are diuretic cocktails, including not only the diuretic itself, but caffeine and additional preparations such as analgesics and potassium salts.

In addition to the over-the-counter supplements, individuals may misuse prescription medication to avoid weight gain or promote weight loss. The individual may be prescribed medications that lead to aversive side effects (e.g., weight gain). Such medications may include antidepressants (e.g. tricyclics, selective serotonin reuptake inhibitors), mood stabilizers (lithium), antipsychotic medications (e.g., clozapine, alanzapine, risperidone), antiepileptics (e.g., valproate, abapentin), and hormones (e.g., contraceptives, corticosteroids, progestational steroids) (Ryan & Stewart, 2004). If individuals have medical problems that require medications that promote weight gain, particularly if they already have body image concerns, it is possible that they would be led to engage in eating disordered behaviors as an escape route to their perceived lack of control over their situation or discontinue use of the medication. Medications such as these often have poor compliance because of the weight gain side effect. Also, stimulant medications (e.g., Aderall) are often acquired from friends and utilized by BN patients for weight loss purposes.

CULTURAL AND DIVERSITY ISSUES

Through the years, the idea that eating disorders and body image disturbances are limited to Caucasian women has been challenged with increased evidence that eating disorders and body image disturbance are present in men and women and in persons of diverse ethnicities (e.g., African American, Latin American, and Asian populations) (Yanovski, 2000). However, it is important to note that presentations of these symptom profiles are complex, particularly with regard to BN, and not fully understood, especially with regard to minority populations. In particular, the diagnosis of BN in non-Western cultures has proven to be challenging, given cultural differences. For example, self-induced vomiting is more prevalent in Western culture, and laxative and diuretic use appears to be the more prevalent forms of purging in non-Western cultures (Keel & Klump, 2003).

When assessing and treating individuals for eating disorders, researchers and clinicians must take into account the intricate interactions among psychological, social, and ethnic aspects that play a significant part in eating disorders. Over time, several important variables have emerged in the literature, including sex, ethnicity, and culture (Stewart & Williamson, in press). This section, however, targets BN.

Men   Symptoms of body dissatisfaction are now being viewed as relatively common among men (Adams et al., 2005). In addition, a recent study demonstrated that body dissatisfaction plays a key role in the relationship between homosexuality and eating disorder symptoms (Hospers & Jansen, 2005). However, body image concerns and eating disorders are not limited to the homosexual male population. These issues affect heterosexual men as well, particularly with regard to steroid abuse (Blouin & Goldfield, 1995) and "muscle dysmorphia" (H. G. Pope, Gruber, Choi, Olivardia, & Phillips, 1997; C. G. Pope et al., 2005). Body image concerns may lead men, homosexual and heterosexual alike, to engage in eating disorder behaviors to achieve their desired body size and shape, such as excessive exercise and unhealthy eating habits and substance use. A recent study showed that male bodybuilders, a population prone to body image concerns, exhibit more severe body dissatisfaction, bulimic behavior, and negative psychological characteristics, compared with controls (athletic and nonathletic males; Goldfield, Blouin, & Woodside, 2006). Specifically, high rates of binge eating, BN, weight and shape preoccupation, and extreme behaviors to modify body size and appearance was present in male bodybuilders, especially those engaged in competition (Goldfield et al., 2006).

African American and Hispanic Women   Status of overweight and/or obesity is often a risk factor for eating disorders. African American and Hispanic girls may be at risk for eating disorders due to their greater risk for overweight and obese status. African American women have been shown to be less likely to diet than Caucasian, non-Hispanic women (Akan & Grilo, 1995). African American women and adolescents have been shown to have lower levels of body size dissatisfaction in studies of body image (Stewart et al., 2005; Williamson et al., 2005). Further, African American women appear to be protected from eating disorders by identification with an African American cultural identity that is associated with greater acceptance of larger body sizes (Pumariega, Gustavson, Gustavson, Motes, & Ayers, 1994). However, although studies have reported that African American women are less likely to develop symptoms of BN than their Caucasian counterparts, some studies have reported similar rates of BN in both populations (Field, Colditz, & Peterson, 1997; Thompson, 1992). Further, laxative and diuretic use has been reported to be higher in African American women than in Caucasians (Field et al., 1997; Pumariega et al., 1994); the data on self-induced vomiting is mixed (Emmons, 1992; Field et al., 1997).

Recent studies show that Hispanic adolescents (ages 11 to 20) had prevalence rates of eating disorders consistent with U.S. trends (Granillo, Jones-Rodriguez, & Carvajal, 2005) and comparable to that of Caucasians (Pemberton, Vernon, & Lee, 1996). Body dissatisfaction, negative affect, substance use, and low self-esteem were some of the main risk factors for the development of eating disorders in this population. Despite comparable rates of eating disorders, Hispanic girls and women (Winkleby, Gardner, & Taylor, 1996) and African American women (Stewart et al., 2005) typically choose preferences for a larger body size. In a recent study examining predictors of body image dissatisfaction and disturbed eating attitudes and behaviors in African American and Hispanic girls, approximately 13% of the Hispanic girls and 10% of the African American girls met criteria for a diagnosis of a probable eating disorder. In this study, fear of negative evaluation was a key differentiating factor between the groups with eating disorder symptoms and groups without eating disorder symptoms (Vander Wal & Thomas, 2004). Further, recent research has reported that increased identification with Western values (i.e., acculturation) is associated with higher levels of eating disorders among Hispanic individuals (Chamorrow & Flores-Ortiz, 2000; Gowen, Hayward, Killen, Robinson, & Taylor, 1999).

Asian Women   Eating disorders are an important epidemic under study in young women in developing countries. The focus on eating disorders in Asian populations has increased significantly over the past 2 decades. Research has generated conflicting results and many methodological issues associated with studying this population (Stewart & Williamson, in press). Eating disorders have been identified in China, Korea, Japan, Malaysia, Taiwan, and Singapore (Tsai, 2000). However, different areas and levels of Westernization has, in some cases, influenced the types of symptoms. In Asian women, the construct of body image in eating disorders remains unclear. For example, in some instances, there is a fear of weight gain and/or drive for thinness, as in typical Western eating disorder presentation. However, in some instances, this feature is not present, but other eating disorder behaviors, such as purging and restrictive eating, are observed (Cummins, Simmons, & Zane, 2005). This symptom pattern is believed to be determined by Asian cultures that also idealize thinness (Rieger, Touyz, Swain, & Beumont, 2001). However, this idealization of thinness is a culture-bound phenomenon, not meant to achieve an "ideal" as in Western culture, but to possibly gain approval by family, friends, or others in the community.

Acculturation   It is unclear if acculturation (members of the minority group, e.g., Asian, adapting to and adopting the dominant, e.g., Western, culture) leads to higher or lower rates of eating disorders. A recent study concluded that prevalence of eating disorders in non-Western countries is lower than that in Western countries, but appears to be increasing over time (Makino et al., 2004). There have been reports of increased eating disorders in association with Westernization in Japan, India, Hong Kong, Pakistan, Fiji, Zimbabwe, and Egypt (Anderson-Fye & Becker, 2004). In this sense, Westernization refers to the native culture's adopting the values of Western Europe and the United States, including aesthetic ideals. Recent research suggests that there is a weak relationship between acculturation and eating disorders among Asian women (Gowen et al., 1999; Haudeck, Rorty, & Henker, 1999). However, a significant relationship has been detected in Hispanic populations (Chamorrow & Flores-Ortiz, 2000; Gowen et al., 1999).

BEHAVIORAL TREATMENT

Description of Treatment

Cognitive-Behavioral Information-Processing Model   The core psychopathology in BN may be conceptualized by the cognitive-behavioral and information-processing model. See Figure 17.3 for an illustration of this model, adapted from

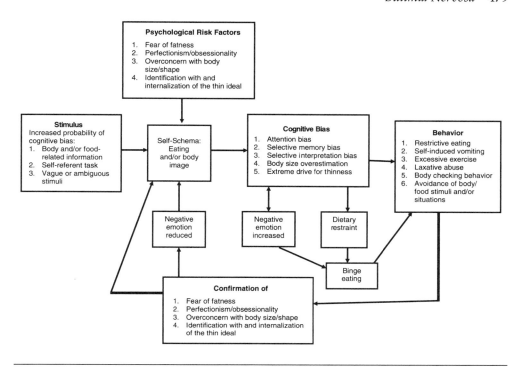

Figure 17.3 Cognitive-Behavioral and Information-Processing Model proposed by Williamson, White, et al. (2004). *Source:* "Cognitive-Behavioral Theories of Eating Disorders," by D. A. Williamson, M. A. White, E. York-Crowe, and T. M. Stewart, 2004, *Behavior Modification, 28*(6), 711–738. Reprinted with permission.

Williamson, White, York-Crowe, and Stewart (2004). It is a blend of many different theories of eating disorders and should not be viewed as a distinct or a novel theory. Figure 17.3 illustrates a model that integrates the perspectives of cognitive and behavioral theorists over the past 3 decades. Central features of this model are (a) cognitive biases, (b) body self-schema, (c) binge eating, (d) compensatory behavior, (e) negative reinforcement of compensatory behavior via reduction of negative emotion, and (f) psychological risk factors that are hypothesized to identify individuals who are vulnerable for the development of eating disorders.

As shown in Figure 17.3, the model hypothesizes that certain types of stimuli are more likely to activate cognitive biases in people with a highly developed self-schema. The key stimulus characteristics that have been found to activate cognitive biases are (a) body- or food-related information, (b) vague or ambiguous stimuli, and (c) situations that require the person to focus on his or her body and eating. The psychological risk factors (of the model) are (a) fear of fatness, (b) perfectionism and obsessionality, (c) internalization of a thin ideal size and shape, and (d) overconcern with body size and shape. The model hypothesizes that negative emotion interacts with the self-schema to activate cognitive biases. Such activation of cognitive bias likely elicits negative emotion. Thus, it is possible for cognitive biases to activate negative emotion and the self-schema for body size and shape or eating to then activate cognitive biases (Williamson, White, et al., 2004).

The experience of this feedback loop may be characterized by anxiety (e.g., feelings of fatness) and self-loathing or even obsession (e.g., body disparagement). The individual experiences this negative emotion as an aversive experience that he or she feels the need to escape or avoid. Avoidance typically consists of restrictive eating, purgative behaviors, and excessive exercise. The effect of this behavior is reduction of negative emotion, which negatively reinforces (and strengthens) the behavior (Williamson, 1990) and also confirms the usefulness to the person of engaging in this escape and avoidant behavior.

The Goals of Treatment   The goals of treatment for BN may include the following: reduction in or elimination of binge eating and purging behaviors; increasing the variety of foods eaten; improvement in attitudes related to the eating disorder; minimization of food restriction; encouragement of healthy but not excessive exercise patterns; treatment of clinical features and comorbid conditions associated with eating disorders (i.e., depression, anxiety, personality disorders); the treatment of body image disturbance; and relapse prevention. See Table 17.2 for specific goals included in a treatment program for BN (as summarized from Stewart & Williamson, 2004b, 2004c). Broader treatment targets may include affective and personality problems, perfectionism, self-esteem, identity themes, fear and anxiety, negative emotional reactions, and generalization and maintenance of behavioral change (Stewart & Williamson, 2004b).

Table 17.2
The Primary Goals of Treatment for Bulimia Nervosa

1. Enhancement of the patient's and family's knowledge of Bulimia Nervosa (BN), body image, and patient's individual case conceptualization. To define patient and family role in treatment and recovery process.
2. Correction of medical complications that have developed as a result of restrictive eating, binging, purging, laxative abuse, or any other physical complications of BN. The reduction of medical risk is the first priority in treatment and this includes the establishment of a healthy weight.
3. Establishment and stabilization of healthy eating patterns, including the establishment of a healthy schedule of eating, establishment of nutritionally sound eating, and promotion of successful accomplishment in following the recommended meal plan.
4. Establishment and stabilization of healthy exercise patterns, including establishment of a healthy schedule of exercise, establishment of a sound exercise plan, and promotion of successful accomplishment in following the recommended exercise plan.
5. Modification of comorbid psychological problems that may have aided in the onset and may aid in the maintenance of BN (e.g., depression, anxiety, personality disorders).
6. Modification of body image disturbance.
7. Maintenance of healthy weight, eating habits, and balanced and mindful perspectives and thought patterns over time.
8. Enhancement of functioning in the family and social relationships marked by improved communication with family members and greater comfort in interpersonal relationships and social situations.
9. Development of relapse prevention marked by the establishment of and adherence to specific plans for the management of high-risk situations.

Cognitive-Behavioral Therapy To date, manual-based cognitive-behavioral therapy (CBT) (Fairburn, Marcus, & Wilson, 1993) is the best known effective treatment for BN (Wilson, 2005). Cognitive-behavioral therapy was officially recommended as the treatment of choice for adults with BN by the National Institute for Clinical Excellence (NICE; 2004).

This treatment is based on the CBT model for BN and consists of cognitive and behavioral procedures to achieve goals that include (a) modification of the binge-purge cycle; (b) modification of faulty attitudes and beliefs about dieting, body image, weight regulation, and social pressures related to thinness as an ideal body shape; (c) maintenance of behavioral and attitudinal changes; and (d) relapse prevention.

Treatment should be based on the conceptualization of the specific factors that contribute to the etiology and maintenance of an individual's BN or EDNOS with BN features. The principal components of CBT include modification of irrational thinking about eating and body size, gradual introduction of three nutritionally balanced meals per day, and exposure to the consumption of forbidden foods without purging (i.e., exposure with response prevention; Rosen & Leitenberg, 1982; Williamson et al., 1998; Williamson, Martin, et al., 2004). Manualized CBT for BN, devised by Fairburn, Marcus, & Wilson (1993), includes (a) self-monitoring of food intake, precipitating factors, and binge-purge episodes; (b) regular weighing; (c) normalization and stabilization of eating patterns; (d) cognitive restructuring; and (e) relapse prevention. It is recommended that treatment begin with a focus on nutrition stabilization and refeeding because if they are malnourished, individuals with BN often have associated cognitive impairments that interfere with the effectiveness of cognitive therapy (Williamson, Martin, et al., 2004).

Wilson (2005) recently summarized evidence surrounding CBT as the treatment of choice for BN as follows: (a) CBT alone has been established as an efficacious treatment for BN and typically eliminates binge eating and purging in 30% to 50% of all cases; (b) CBT has been shown to decrease dysfunctional dieting and reduce the level of overall psychiatric symptoms; (c) CBT has been shown to reduce body image disturbance and improve self-esteem and social functioning; (d) improvement in symptoms is maintained at a reasonable level at a 1-year follow-up time period and beyond; (e) manual-based treatment has been shown to be effective in the modification of dietary restraint; (f) CBT has been shown to be more effective than antidepressant medication, primarily because CBT works primarily to completely reduce binging and purging behaviors. Further, a combination of CBT and antidepressant medication has been found to be significantly more effective than medication alone; and (g) CBT has been shown to be superior to interpersonal therapy in the short term. In addition, it was "cautiously" concluded that guided self-help programs (Fairburn, 1995) may be utilized as a first-step intervention for a subset of BN patients.

Manual-based therapies are not without their drawbacks. It is important to take into account individual needs of the patients and unique case conceptualizations even when utilizing manual-based treatment paradigms. For example, although CBT for BN is well established, it focuses heavily on the behaviors associated with BN, including binging and purging. For increased effectiveness in individuals, increased focus on some of the factors that maintain BN may be warranted, such as body image disturbance, negative affect, anxiety, and personality disorders.

Body Image Treatment   Individuals with BN have routinely demonstrated body size overestimation and reported body size dissatisfaction, compared to individuals without BN (Williamson, Cubic, & Gleaves, 1993). Individuals with BN also tend to select a smaller ideal body size (IBS) than individuals without BN (Williamson et al., 1993). Although many studies have investigated body image in BN, the majority of these studies have investigated the outcome of body image in the context of overall CBT interventions. Thus, the specific role of body image in the treatment outcome of BN is not clear. In a recent study, Peterson et al. (2004) found that BN participants did not show significant changes in IBS over the course of the treatment or follow-up time periods. This suggests that IBS may remain stable over time, even with improvement of BN symptoms and improvement of other body image–related symptoms. More research is needed to clarify the impact of these findings of the role of body image in the treatment outcome of BN, given that body image appears to play such a critical role in the etiology, maintenance, and treatment outcome of BN. It is our belief that in treating severe cases of BN, medical complications and binge eating and purging must be stabilized prior to tackling the difficult issues of body image in treatment as body image aspects of treatment are often emotional and difficult for individuals and may lead to relapse in a non-inpatient setting (Stewart, 2004; Stewart & Williamson, 2004b).

Treatment Planning and Consideration

Presence of comorbid diagnoses often complicates treatment of BN. Thus, the potential interference of secondary psychopathology on treatment adherence must be a focus in treatment planning. Effective treatment planning must account for how such additional variables may affect aspects of treatment such as the client's motivation for treatment, the therapeutic alliance, and overall treatment outcome. Studies that have investigated the impact of comorbid psychological problems on the successful treatment of BN have generally not found that comorbid problems significantly reduce the effectiveness of CBT. However, several studies have found that Borderline Personality Disorder (BPD) is associated with poorer outcome in trials of antidepressant medications and CBT (Wonderlich & Mitchell, 1997). Thus, the problems possibly instigated by Axis II disorders should be treated first or concurrently with the problems associated with the eating disorder.

MEDICAL TREATMENT

Special Medical Protocols

For more information on special protocols for the treatment of eating disorders, refer to Stewart and Williamson (2004b).

Acute Inpatient Treatment   Twenty-four-hour supervision and care may be necessary for individuals with BN who have severe medical complications and become medically unstable. In such cases, the constant supervision of nursing care is necessary to restore physical health. Without the restoration and stabilization of physical health, there is no chance for the stabilization of mental health. For individuals with BN, the 24-hour environment provides a critical support system and structure that prevent continued purgative behaviors such as self-induced vomiting, use of diet pills, compulsive exercise, and laxative use or abuse. Acute inpatient care is not needed for all BN cases. This level of care is recommended for those who are medically unstable, less than 85% of their ideal body weight, are severely depressed, or are suicidal or homicidal. These guidelines are based on the treatment philosophy that most individuals with BN can be effectively treated with partial hospitalization, and intensive outpatient and/or traditional outpatient therapy. The inpatient treatment level should be used for stabilization of patients who are in an acute medical or psychiatric crisis (e.g., out of control binging and purging) or who have not responded positively to a lower level of care. For most cases, as progress is achieved, the person moves to the next lowest level of care (e.g., partial hospitalization) until discharged to traditional outpatient therapy for long-term follow-up. For more information about this process, see to Stewart and Williamson (2004b).

Establishment of Weight Goal The goal weight range is determined by the patient's current body weight, body composition, and ideal body weight (based on BMI and standard weight-height tables). The goal of 92% of ideal body weight is recommended as the minimally acceptable weight for underweight patients. Patients should be prescribed a meal plan to gain, maintain, or lose weight based on their individual needs. It is recommended that most patients not be provided with specific goals in pounds or caloric intake levels, as such information generally leads to obsessional thinking about weight and weight gain and can make their treatment progression more difficult.

Wheelchair Protocol This protocol requires the patient to stay in a wheelchair at all times to reduce energy expenditure and to increase body weight. This protocol would apply to individuals who are extremely low in body weight due to high levels of purging or excessive exercise, or to individuals who are not complying with their prescription to not engage in physical activity per their treatment plan.

Bed Rest Protocol This protocol requires the patient to stay in bed all day, with regular checks (e.g., 15- to 30-minute intervals by nursing staff) to increase body weight and reduce energy expenditure. In this protocol, the patient may not participate in most unit activities, unless ordered by the attending physician.

Exercise and Physical Activity Individuals with BN often utilize compulsive exercise as a compensatory behavior to lose weight and/or prevent weight gain. To manage this problem, physical activity prescriptions, including regular physical activity (e.g., physical chores, such as mowing grass) as well as exercise for fitness purposes (e.g., cardiovascular and strength exercise) should be very specific, detailing the frequency, duration, and types of activity for each day. The level and type of physical activity should be prescribed by a physician or exercise physiologist. The prescription should be based on such factors as current weight and body composition, history of exercise abuse, and medical risk factors. This plan should also take into consideration how long the individual has been in treatment and likelihood for relapse.

Weight Gain Protocol If initial medical evaluation of body weight, medical health, and body composition indicates that weight gain is necessary for improved medical health, a weight gain protocol should be implemented. This protocol is designed to yield a minimum 2-pound weight gain each week after the initial week of the protocol. If the patient does not gain 2 pounds per week after 2 weeks of inpatient treatment, the following options should be considered: (a) bed rest protocol in the inpatient setting, (b) transfer to medical inpatient setting for refeeding using nasogastric tube feeding, or (c) transfer to another facility that specializes in the treatment of intractable cases.

Nutritional Supplementation   Because reestablishment of appropriate nutrition is critical to restoring health, it is necessary to use a liquid nutritional supplement for patients unable to eat 100% of their prescribed meal plan. Patients in treatment are typically supplemented routinely after noncompliance with the prescribed meal plan. Patients are given (at least) the caloric equivalent of any food item not eaten at a meal or snack. Noncompliance is defined as eating less than 100% of the prescribed meal plan.

Gastrointestinal Considerations   Disturbances in the functioning of the upper gastrointestinal (GI) tract have been reported in BN (Hadley & Walsh, 2003). These difficulties have been shown to perpetuate medical complications in the disorder itself as well as promote difficulties in refeeding and weight restoration while in treatment. Gastrointestinal disturbances that have been associated with BN include diminished gastric relaxation, delayed gastric emptying, greater gastric capacity, abnormalities of autonomic function in the GI tract, and diminished release of cholecystokinin. In treatment, all of these issues must be addressed to facilitate patient progress. Problems most common in treatment include gastric reflux, laxative withdrawal symptoms (e.g., edema), and constipation from eating at regular intervals and fully digesting food without vomiting. These issues may be best managed in treatment with proper therapy and open-ended lines of communication from the patient about what is happening so that staff can respond more aggressively if symptoms become too serious. Medications may include proton pump inhibitor agents for reflux disease, stool softeners, fiber supplements, and medically monitored enemas for constipation and medically monitored diuretics for edema.

PHARMACOTHERAPY

Pharmacotherapy is used primarily to reduce the frequency of disturbed eating behaviors (e.g., binge eating and vomiting). Antidepressant medications have been shown to be efficacious in the treatment of BN (Steffen, Roerig, Mitchell, & Uppala, 2006). In a review of the treatment of BN with antidepressants, Agras (1997) reported that the overall effectiveness of these medications in reducing the frequency of binging and purging was 70%. When compared to CBT, it has been reported that both pharmacotherapy and CBT effectively reduce symptoms of depression, frequency of binge eating and purging, and self-reported negative eating attitudes on a short-term basis (Whittal, Agras, & Gould, 1999). Thus, it has been suggested that pharmacotherapy should not be utilized as a sole treatment for BN or subthreshold bulimia (Garfinkel & Walsh, 1997). Experts have recommended that if pharmacotherapy is to be utilized, it should be in conjunction with CBT for best results, as relapse rates have been shown to be high with medication alone (Walsh, Hadigan, Devlin, Gladis, & Roose, 1991).

Different types of antidepressant medications have been tested and found to be effective, including, tricyclics, monoamine oxidase inhibitors (MAOIs), and selective serotonin reuptake inhibitors (SSRIs). It has been shown that any one of these antidepressants leads to recovery in about 25% of the BN patients treated (Agras, 1997). However, among the antidepressants, the more recently developed SSRIs, particularly fluoxetine, are the most preferred. This preference is warranted for two reasons: This class of antidepressants yields fewer side effects than tricyclic antidepressants and MAOIs, and SSRIs have been shown to have an effect of improved body satisfaction (Goldbloom & Olmsted, 1993). Sertraline has been demonstrated to be efficacious and well-tolerated in the treatment of BN (Milano, Petrella, Sabatino, & Capasso, 2004; Sloan, Mizes, Helbok, & Muck, 2004).

In summary, the eating disorder guidelines from NICE (2004) concluded that for the treatment of BN, (a) individuals should be educated and informed regarding the use of antidepressant medications. They should be informed that they can reduce binging and purging, that any benefits of the medication will be apparent early in treatment, and that the long-term effects of the medication are unknown; (b) the effective dose of fluoxetine is higher for BN than for depression; and (c) SSRIs particularly fluoxetine, are the favored medications due to the reduction of symptoms and tolerability of the medication.

Case Description

Case Introduction

Charlotte, a 28-year-old female, presented at a hospital-based eating disorders clinic at the request of her husband and family members. Her husband and parents reported that she was engaging in self-induced vomiting several times per day, and they were significantly concerned about her health. Charlotte reported that she felt out of control with her binge-purge behavior; however, she felt it was necessary to maintain her body weight (low normal weight) and had low motivation to stop purging. She was extremely resistant to entering a treatment program due to her concerns of weight gain and being away from her young son, age 2, at home.

Presenting Complaints

At entry into treatment, Charlotte was 5 feet 7 inches and 130 pounds. Her BMI was 20. She presented with resistance to treatment and expressed extreme fears of gaining weight and being fat. She admitted to restrictive eating, excessive exercise (in the past), and purging via self-induced vomiting for weight control. She also admitted to extreme fatigue, feeling cold, and being motivated to be able to better control her eating behavior. Her family expressed extreme concern regarding her ability to maintain a normal life, that is, keep her job, raise her son, and maintain her health.

History

Charlotte grew up in a large southern family in which meals typically consisted of large portions and high-fat foods. Overweight and obesity were typical in her family, beginning in family members as young as adolescence. Charlotte

(continued)

reported that around age 12, she began to become more aware of her body in relation to members of her family and her friends. She said that at that time, she feared weight gain and looking like some of her overweight family members. She reported that at approximately age 15, she began to restrict her eating gradually over time until she began to lose weight. She received many compliments on her weight loss at the time and felt she was accomplishing something good and healthy. Charlotte reports that she was eating approximately 1,200 calories a day during that time and maintained this for 2 or 3 years. She also reports beginning an exercise regimen for the first time and exercising approximately 1 hour per day during that time. However, after graduating from high school and getting a job at a local health club as an aerobics instructor, she felt the pressure to lose more weight to fit into tight-fitting aerobics clothing. Charlotte reported that at that time it became difficult to restrict her eating anymore. She increased her exercise to approximately 3 hours per day and began using compensatory behaviors, such as self-induced vomiting, on a regular basis to rid her body of excess calories. At the time of admission to the hospital, Charlotte reported that she had been utilizing self-induced vomiting as a compensatory strategy for approximately 9 years, beginning with once or twice a week in the first few years. In addition, she reported that she had begun binging on foods she feared would make her gain weight around the same time she began to use vomiting as a compensatory strategy. Over time, the binging and purging became more frequent, resulting in a frequency of at least 2 times per day over the past year. In addition, her family reports that even if she doesn't binge, she vomits everything she eats; thus, her vomiting was occurring upwards of 10 times per day.

Assessment

During the intake assessment, a clinical interview was conducted in addition to the IDED-IV to obtain a comprehensive assessment of Charlotte's current status. The IDED-IV indicated a diagnosis of Bulimia Nervosa, purging type. The MAEDS indicated a baseline level of fear of fatness ($t = 80$), restrictive eating ($t = 70$), binge eating ($t = 75$), purgative behavior ($t = 85$), depression ($t = 70$), and avoidance of fear foods ($t = 70$). The BMA 2.0 was administered to assess body size over- or underestimation and body dissatisfaction. Charlotte's scores indicated that she significantly overestimated her current body size (CBS); she was not satisfied with her CBS, as indicated by the discrepancy between her CBS and her chosen IBS (BMA t scores: CBS = 70, IBS = 40, CBS-IBS discrepancy = 30). As noted earlier, Axis I and Axis II comorbidity is common in BN cases. Charlotte did not exhibit symptoms of a comorbid Axis II disorder. She did, however, exhibit mild symptoms of depression that did not yield a full clinical diagnosis of an Axis I mood disorder.

Case Conceptualization

Course of Treatment

Charlotte's treatment consisted of entering treatment on an inpatient level for the purpose of stabilization of medical complications associated with her BN, including GI complications, electrolyte imbalances, dehydration, and fatigue. Entering treatment on the inpatient level was also intended to enable Charlotte to get her intense and frequent cycles of binge eating and purging under control. In the treatment program, she attended individual therapy, group therapy, family therapy, nutrition and dietary counseling, and therapeutic meals as outlined by Stewart and Williamson (2004c). Pharmacotherapy was utilized to help decrease her depression and anxiety so as to reduce her binge eating and purging behavior.

The primary goals of the treatment plan included the following: (a) stabilization of binge-purge behavior, (b) nutrition stabilization with a plan for weight maintenance, (c) elimination of exercise until stabilization of binging-purging had occurred, (d) reduction in depression symptoms, (e) reduction of fears of fatness and drive for thinness, (f) systematic desensitization through fear and avoided food hierarchy, and (g) relapse prevention.

The Recovery Skills Building and Relapse Prevention groups were particularly relevant to Charlotte because she had difficulty understanding how to change her behavior and go back to living everyday life without her BN behaviors. In individual therapy, identity, self-esteem, body image, and anxiety were all relevant topics. Charlotte had difficulty finding her identity without her BN behaviors and her self-loathing related to body image. In addition to discussions about relevant themes perpetuating Charlotte's BN, behavioral strategies such as behavioral contracting were utilized to aid her in engaging in healthy behaviors (e.g., a behavioral contract to engage in meal plan compliance at home). Charlotte benefited from family and couples therapy as her family support system was very important for her recovery. Once discharged to lower levels of care, even though she was an adult, her family members and husband helped her to stay motivated and compliant with her treatment plan.

Assessment of Progress

Over the course of treatment, Charlotte's body weight and composition were checked regularly utilizing bioelectrical impedance. In addition, the MAEDS was administered weekly to assess for improvement over time. The MAEDS scores were then compared over time to determine if her symptoms were improving, remaining stable, or worsening. Finally, the BMA was compared over time to assess any progress or worsening in estimation of body size and satisfaction with body size.

Complicating Factors and Medical Management

Charlotte was placed on 24-hour supervision in the inpatient facility for the first week to prevent purging. Because she purged so frequently prior to coming into the hospital program, she had difficulty controlling the purging and also had difficulty not purging small amounts of food automatically upon swallowing. Because of this, for the first week, she was put on a strict supplement feeding protocol and was prescribed a small amount of supplement every hour to aid her body and mental orientation in becoming appropriately responsive to refeeding.

Charlotte also had difficulties with dehydration, constipation, GI reflux, and esophageal inflammation and pain. An endoscope procedure was done to confirm that there were no tears in her esophagus or other, more serious

(continued)

conditions than inflammation and abrasion from vomiting. She was given a proton pump inhibitor medication for the reflux (e.g., Nexium) and a fiber supplement and stool softener for constipation. Due to her difficulty with keeping fluids down in her initial treatment period, she was put on saline IV fluids for rehydration.

Managed Care Considerations

Managed care approaches that have been developed and implemented throughout the past decade have impacted mental health services significantly, particularly impacting those individuals with severe and potentially chronic disorders (Williamson, Thaw, & Varnado, 2001). Individuals with eating disorders who require inpatient treatment fall into this category. The "continuum of care approach," including partial hospitalization, integrated with inpatient and outpatient care, was developed in response to the need for less costly alternatives to inpatient treatment for eating disorders (Williamson, Womble, & Zucker, 1998). The present case was treated with the "continuum of care" approach. We found this approach to be effective in treating the patient, as well as cost-effective. The approach was accepted by the managed care company via a process of regular reviews and updates on the patient's progress and further treatment goals from the medical and psychological staff.

Follow-up

Charlotte was at the inpatient level of care for 4 weeks to stabilize her binge-purge behavior. She was at the partial hospitalization level of care for 4 weeks and intensive outpatient level for approximately 1 week before following up in outpatient care. From that point, she was followed in traditional outpatient care by the dietitian (meal plan), psychiatrist (medications), and psychologist (behavioral treatment, including body image and family and couples counseling).

Treatment Implications of the Case

Charlotte's case was an extremely severe case of BN, binge-purge type. She had severe vomiting patterns that were hard to break even when she made a commitment to try to stop and tried to make efforts toward healthy eating patterns. Even though she was normal weight, she had medical complications that had to be taken into account in treatment on a continual basis. She was extremely resistant to treatment for a long period of time even, though her habits had very much influenced her quality of life (e.g., lost her job, her husband did not want her around her young son).

She had very low insight into her behaviors, which made therapeutic progress slow. This factor, coupled with her medical complications, low motivation for change, and slow progress in the achievement of treatment goals (e.g., following a meal plan) made the effective treatment of this case challenging. Without the positive attributes of her family support, there would have been no hope for this case. This case is an example of the importance of the strengths and weaknesses of the case conceptualization; individual scenarios have to be taken into account to develop the most effective treatment plan for the individual.

SUMMARY

Over the years, research on epidemiology, etiology, assessment, diagnosis, and treatment of BN has progressed considerably. Progress has led to a greater overall understanding of this disorder. In addition, existing treatment outcome literature suggests overall improved success in the treatment of BN and subthreshold BN. However, further progress toward the effective treatment *and* prevention of BN needs to be made.

Improvements in the existing classification scheme for the diagnosis of eating disorders, including BN, have important implications for assessment and treatment. An improvement in classification of symptoms could aid in improved understanding of the diagnosis of BN, as well as possibly its genetic underpinnings. In addition, further research is needed to investigate the genetic basis of the eating pathology associated with eating disorders such as BN. The search for genes and mutations contributing to the development and maintenance of BN is still in the early stages. Larger scale genetic studies are needed to determine the specific candidate genes and biological pathways that influence the eating pathology (e.g., binge eating) associated with BN. Further, as prevalence rates in non-Western countries continue to mount, investigations are needed to determine the factors underlying the development and maintenance of eating disorders, including BN, in these minority populations. Finally, further investigation of pharmacotherapy and behavioral treatment methods is warranted.

Research related to BN has exploded since its initial description in 1979 (Russell, 1979). Considerable progress has been made in treatment, with continued advances in the areas of genetics and classification. Additional research should focus on effective prevention strategies.

REFERENCES

Adams, G., Turner, H., & Bucks, R. (2005). The experience of body dissatisfaction in men. *Body Image, 2*(3), 271–283.

Agras, W. S. (1997). Pharmacotherapy of bulimia nervosa and binge eating disorder: Longer-term outcomes. *Psychopharmacology Bulletin, 33,* 433–436.

Akan, G. E., & Grilo, C. M. (1995). Sociocultural influences on eating attitudes and behaviors, body image, and psychological functioning: A comparison of African-American, Asian-American, and Caucasian college women. *International Journal of Eating Disorders, 18*(2), 181–187.

American Psychiatric Association. (1980). *Diagnostic and statistical manual of mental disorders* (3rd ed.). Washington, DC: Author.

American Psychiatric Association. (1987). *Diagnostic and statistical manual of mental disorders* (3rd ed., rev.). Washington, DC: Author.

American Psychiatric Association. (1994). *Diagnostic and statistical manual of mental disorders* (4th ed.). Washington, DC: Author.

American Psychiatric Association. (2004). Practice guideline for eating disorders. In *Practice guidelines for the treatment of psychiatric disorders compendium* (2nd ed., pp. 675–744). Washington, DC: Author.

American Psychiatric Association Work Group on Eating Disorders. (2000). Practice guideline for the treatment of patients with eating disorders (revision). *American Journal of Psychiatry, 157*(1), 1–39.

Ames-Frankel, J., Devlin, M. J., Walsh, B. T., Strasser, T. J., Sadik, C., Oldham, J. M., et al. (1992). Personality disorder diagnoses in patients with bulimia nervosa: Clinical correlates and changes with treatment. *Journal of Clinical Psychiatry, 53*(3), 90–96.

Anderson, D. A., Williamson, D. A., Duchmann, E. G., Gleaves, D. H., & Barbin, J. M. (1999). Development and validation of a multifactorial treatment outcome measure for eating disorders. *Assessment, 6,* 7–20.

Anderson-Fye, E. P., & Becker, A. E. (2004). Sociocultural aspects of eating disorders. In J. K. Thompson (Ed.), *Handbook of eating disorders and obesity* (pp. 565–589). Hoboken, NJ: Wiley.

Blouin, A. G., & Goldfield, G. S. (1995). Body image and steroid use in male bodybuilders. *International Journal of Eating Disorders, 18*(2), 159–165.

Blundell, J. E., & Hill, A. J. (1993). Binge eating: Psychobiological mechanisms. In C. Fairburn & G. T. Wilson (Eds.), *Binge eating: Nature, assessment, and treatment* (pp. 206–224). New York: Guilford Press.

Blundell, J. E., & Stubbs, R. J. (1998). Diet composition and the control of food intake in humans. In G. A. Bray, C. Bouchard, & W. P. T. James (Eds.), *Handbook of obesity* (pp. 243–272). New York: Marcel Dekker.

Braun, D. L., Sunday, S. R., & Halmi, K. A. (1994). Psychiatric comorbidity in patients with eating disorders. *Psychological Medicine, 24,* 859–867.

Brewerton, T. D., Lydiard, R. B., Herzog, D. B., Brotman, A. W., O'Neil, P. M., & Ballenger, J. C. (1995). Comorbidity of Axis I psychiatric disorders in bulimia nervosa. *Journal of Clinical Psychiatry, 56,* 77–80.

Bulik, C. (2004). Genetic and biological risk factors. In J. K. Thompson (Ed.), *Handbook of eating disorders* (pp. 3–16). Hoboken, NJ: Wiley.

Bulik, C. M., Devlin, B., Bacanu, S. A., Thornton, L., Klump, K.L., Fichter, M. M., et al. (2003). Significant linkage on chromosome 10p in families with bulimia nervosa. *American Journal of Human Genetics, 72,* 200–207.

Bulik, C. M., Klump, K. L., Thornton, L., Kaplan, A. S., Devlin, B., Fichter, M. M., et al. (2004). Alcohol use disorder comorbidity in eating disorders: A multicenter study. *Journal of Clinical Psychiatry, 65*(7), 1000–1006.

Bulik, C. M., Sullivan, P. F., Carter, F. A., & Joyce, P. R. (1996). Lifetime anxiety disorders in women with bulimia nervosa. *Comprehensive Psychiatry, 37,* 368–374.

Bulik, C. M., Sullivan, P. F., Carter, F. A., & Joyce, P. R. (1997). Lifetime comorbidity of alcohol dependence in women with bulimia nervosa. *Addictive Behaviors, 22,* 437–446.

Bulik, C. M., Sullivan, P. F., & Kendler, K. S. (1998). Heritability of binge-eating and broadly defined bulimia nervosa. *Biological Psychiatry, 44,* 1210–1218.

Bulik, C. M., Sullivan, P. F., Wade, T. D., & Kendler, K. S. (2000). Twin studies of eating disorders: A review. *International Journal of Eating Disorders, 27,* 1–20.

Cash, T. F., & Fleming, E. C. (2002). The impact of body image experiences: Development of the Body Image Quality of Life Inventory. *International Journal of Eating Disorders, 31,* 455–460.

Cash, T. F., & Labarge, A. S. (1996). Development of the Appearance Schemas Inventory: A new cognitive body-image assessment. *Cognitive Therapy and Research, 20,* 37–50.

Chamorrow, R., & Flores-Ortiz, Y. (2000). Acculturation and disordered eating patterns among Mexican American women. *International Journal of Eating Disorders, 28,* 125–129.

Cooper, P. J., Taylor, M. J., Cooper, Z., & Fairburn, C. G. (1987). The development and validation of the Body Shape Questionnaire. *International Journal of Eating Disorders, 6,* 485–494.

Crago, M., Shisslak, C. M., & Estes, L. S. (1996). Eating disturbances among American minority groups: A review. *International Journal of Eating Disorders, 19*(3), 239–248.

Crow, S. (2005). Medical complications of eating disorders. In S. Wonderlich, J. Mitchell, M. de Zwaan, & H. Steiger (Eds.), *Eating disorders review: Pt. 1. Academy of Eating Disorders* (pp.127–136). Seattle, WA: Radcliffe Publishing.

Cummins, L. H., Simmons, A. M., & Zane, N. W. (2005). Eating disorders in Asian populations: A critique of current approaches to the study of culture, ethnicity, and eating disorders. *American Journal of Orthopsychiatry 75*(4), 553–574.

Currin, L., Schmidt, U., Treasure, J., & Jick, H. (2005). Time trends in eating disorder incidence. *British Journal of Psychiatry, 186,* 132–135.

Dansky, B. S., Brewerton, T. D., & Kilpatrick, D. G. (2000). Comorbidity of bulimia nervosa and alcohol use disorders: Results from the National Women's Study. *International Journal of Eating Disorders, 27,* 180–190.

Dohm, F. A., Strigel-Moore, R. H., Wilfley, D. E., Pike, K. M., Hook, J., Fairburn, C. G. (2002). Self-harm and substance use in a community sample of Black and White women with binge-eating disorder and bulimia nervosa. *International Journal of Eating Disorders, 32*(3), 89–400.

Dorian, B. J., & Garfinkel, P. E. (1999). The contribution of epidemiologic studies to the etiology and treatment of the eating disorders. *Psychiatric Annals, 29*(4), 187–192.

Emmons, L. (1992). Dieting and purging behavior in Black and White high school students. *Journal of the American Dietetic Association, 92*(3), 306–312.

Fairburn, C. G. (1995). *Overcoming binge eating.* New York: Guilford Press.

Fairburn, C. G., & Beglin, S. J. (1994). Assessment of eating disorders: Interview or self-report questionnaire? *International Journal of Eating Disorders, 16*(4), 363–370.

Fairburn, C. G., & Cooper, Z. (1993). The Eating Disorder Examination (12th edition). In C. G. Fairburn & G. T. Wilson (Eds.), *Binge eating: Nature, assessment, and treatment* (pp. 317–360). New York: Guilford Press.

Fairburn, C. G., Jones, R., Peveler, R. C., Hope, R. A., & O'Connor, M. E. (1993). Psychotherapy and bulimia nervosa: The longer-term effects of interpersonal therapy, behavior therapy, and cognitive behavior therapy. *Archives of General Psychiatry, 50,* 419–428.

Fairburn, C. G., Marcus, M. D., & Wilson, G. T. (1993). Cognitive behavior therapy for binge eating and bulimia nervosa: A comprehensive treatment manual. In C. G. Fairburn & G. T. Wilson (Eds.), *Binge eating: Nature, assessment, and treatment* (pp. 361–404). New York: Guilford Press.

Fernandez-Aranda, F., Aitken, A., Badia, A., Gimenez, L., Solano, R., Collier, D., et al. (2004). Personality and psychopathological traits of males with an eating disorder. *European Eating Disorders Review, 12,* 367–274.

Field, A. E., Colditz, G. A., & Peterson, K. E. (1997). Racial/ethnic and gender differences in concern with weight and in bulimic behaviors among adolescents. *Obesity Research, 5*(5), 447–454.

First, M. B., Spitzer, R. L., Gibbon, M., & Williams, J. B. W. (1996). *Structured Clinical Interview for DSM-IV Axis I Disorders—Patient version (SCID-I, version 2.0).* New York: New York State Psychiatric Institute.

First, M. B., Spitzer, R. L., Gibbon, M., Williams, J. B. W., Davies, M., Borus, J., et al. (1995). The Structured Clinical Interview for DSM-III-R Personality Disorders (SCID-II): Pt. II. Multisite test-retest reliability study. *Journal of Personality Disorders, 9,* 92–104.

Garfinkel, P. E., Lin, E., Goering, P., Spegg, C., Goldbloom, D. S., Kennedy, S., et al. (1995). Bulimia nervosa in a Canadian sample: Prevalence and comparison of subgroups. *American Journal of Psychiatry, 152,* 1052–1058.

Garfinkel, P. E., & Walsh, B. T. (1997). Drug therapies. In D. M. Garner & P. E. Garfinkel (Eds.), *Handbook of treatment for eating disorders* (2nd ed., pp. 372–380). New York: Guilford Press.

Garner, D. M. (1991). *Eating Disorder Inventory-2 manual.* Odessa, FL: Psychological Assessment Resources.

Garner, D. M., & Garfinkel, P. E. (1979). The Eating Attitudes Test: An index of the symptoms of anorexia nervosa. *Psychological Medicine, 9,* 273–279.

Gendall, K. A., Joyce, P. R., Carter, F. A., McIntosh, V. V., Bulik, C. M. (2005). Childhood gastrointestinal complaints in women with bulimia nervosa. *International Journal of Eating Disorders, 37*(3), 256–260.

Gleaves, D. H., Lowe, M. R., Green, B. A., Cororve, M. B., & Williams, T. L. (2000). Do anorexia and bulimia nervosa occur on a continuum? A taxometric analysis. *Behavior Therapy, 31,* 195–219.

Gleaves, D. H., Lowe, M. R., Snow, A. C., Green, B. A., & Murphy-Eberenz, K. P. (2000). The continuity and discontinuity models of bulimia nervosa: A taxometric investigation. *Journal of Abnormal Psychology, 109,* 56–68.

Goldbloom, D. S., & Olmstead, M. P. (1993). Pharmacotherapy of bulimia nervosa with fluoxetine: Assessment of clinically significant attitudinal change. *American Journal of Psychiatry, 150*(5), 770–774.

Goldfield, G. S., Blouin, A. G., & Woodside, D. B. (2006). Body image, binge eating, and bulimia nervosa in male bodybuilders. *Canadian Journal of Psychiatry, 51*(3), 160–168.

Gowen, L. K., Hayward, C., Killen, J. D., Robinson, T. N., & Taylor, C. B. (1999). Acculturation and eating disorder symptoms in adolescent girls. *Journal of Research on Adolescence, 9,* 67–83.

Granillo, T., Jones-Rodriguez, G., & Carvajal, S. C. (2005). Prevalence of eating disorders in Latina adolescents: Associations with substance use and other correlates. *Journal of Adolescent Health, 36*(3), 214–20.

Grilo, C. M. (2002). Recent research of relationships among eating disorders and personality disorders. *Current Psychiatry Reports, 4,* 18–24.

Grilo, C. M., Levy, K. N., Becker, D. F., Edell, W. S., & McGlashan, T. H. (1996). Comorbidity of DSM-III-R axis I and II disorders among female inpatients with eating disorders. *Psychiatric Services, 47,* 426–429.

Gross, J., Rosen, J. C., Leitenberg, H., & Wilmuth, M. E. (1986). Validity of the Eating Attitudes Test and the Eating Disorders Inventory of bulimia nervosa. *Journal of Clinical and Consulting Psychology, 54*(6), 875–876.

Hadley, S. J., & Walsh, B. T. (2003). Gastrointestinal disturbances in anorexia nervosa and bulimia nervosa. *CNS and Neurological Disorders, 2,* 1–9.

Haudeck, C., Rorty, M., & Henker, B. (1999). The role of ethnicity and parental bonding in the eating and weight concerns of Asian-American and Caucasian college women. *International Journal of Eating Disorders, 25,* 425–433.

Hay, P., & Bacaltchuk, J. (2002). Bulimia nervosa. In United Health Foundation (Ed.), *Clinical evidence* (pp. 21–31). London: BMJ Publishing Group.

Herzog, D. B., Keller, M. B., Sacks, N. R., Yeh, C. J., & Lavori, P. W. (1992). Psychiatric comorbidity in treatment-seeking anorexics and bulimics. *Journal of the American Academy of Child and Adolescent Psychiatry, 31*(5), 810–818.

Hoek, H. W., van Hoeken, K., & Bartelds, A. I. M. (2000, November). *No increase in the incidence of anorexia and bulimia in the nineties.* Paper presented at the annual meeting of the Eating Disorders Research Society, Prien am Chimsee, Germany.

Hoek, H. W., Van Son, G. E., van Hoeken, D., Bartelds, A. I. M., & Van Furth, E. F. (2005, April). *Changes in the incidence of eating disorders.* Paper presented at the International Conference on Eating Disorders, Montreal.

Holderness, C., Brooks-Gunn, J., & Warren, M. (1994). Comorbidity of eating disorders and substance abuse: Review of the literature. *International Journal of Eating Disorders, 16,* 1–35.

Hospers, H. J., & Jansen, A. (2005). Why homosexuality is a risk factor for eating disorders in males. *Journal of Social and Clinical Psychology, 24*(8), 1188–1201.

Hudson, J. I., Hudson, R. A., & Pope, H. G. (2005). Psychiatric comorbidity and eating disorders. In S. Wonderlich, J. Mitchell, M. Zwann, & H. Steiger (Eds.), *Eating disorders review: Pt. 1. Academy for Eating Disorders* (pp. 43–58). Seattle, WA: Radcliffe Publishing.

Jacobi, C. (2005). Psychosocial risk factors for eating disorders. In S. Wonderlich, J. Mitchell, M. de Zwaan, & H. Steiger (Eds.), *Eating disorders review: Pt. 1. Academy of Eating Disorders* (pp. 59–85). Seattle, WA: Radcliffe Publishing.

Kaye, W. H., Bulik, C. M., Thornton, L., Barbarich, N., & Masters, K. (2004). Comorbidity of anxiety disorders with anorexia and bulimia nervosa. *American Journal of Psychiatry, 161,* 2215–2221.

Keel, P. K., Heatherton, T. F., Dorer, D. J., Joiner, T. E., & Zalta, A. K. (2005). Point prevalence of bulimia nervosa in 1982, 1992, and 2002. *Psychological Medicine, 36,* 119–127.

Keel, P. K., & Klump, K. (2003). Are eating disorders culture-bound syndromes? Implications for conceptualizing their etiology. *Psychological Bulletin, 129*(5), 747–769.

Kendler, K. S., MacLean, C., Neale, M., Kessler, R., Heath, A., & Eaves, L. (1991). The genetic epidemiology of bulimia nervosa. *American Journal of Psychiatry, 148,* 1627–1637.

Koopmans, H. S. (1998). Experimental studies on the control of food intake. In G. A. Bray, C. Bouchard, & W. P. T. James (Eds.), *Handbook of obesity* (pp. 273–312). New York: Marcel Dekker.

Kutlesic, V., Williamson, D. A., Gleaves, D. H., Barbin, J. M., & Murphy-Eberenz, K. P. (1998). The Interview for the Diagnosis of Eating Disorders IV: Application to DSM-IV diagnostic criteria. *Psychological Assessment, 10,* 41–48.

leGrange, D., Binford, R. B., Peterson, C. B., Crow, S. J., Crosby, R. D., Klein, M. H., et al. (2006). DSM-IV threshold versus subthreshold bulimia nervosa. *International Journal of Eating Disorders, 39*(6), 462–467.

Makino, M., Tsuboi, K., & Dennerstein, L. (2004). Prevalence of eating disorders: A comparison of Western and non-Western countries. *Medscape General Medicine, 6*(3), 49.

Martin, K. C., Williamson, D. A., & Thaw, J. M. (2000). Criterion validity of the Multiaxial Assessment of Eating Disorders Symptoms. *International Journal of Eating Disorders, 28,* 303–310.

Mayville, S. B., Williamson, D. A., White, M. A., Netemeyer, R., & Drab, D. L. (2002). Development of the Muscle Appearance Satisfaction Scale: A self-report measure for the assessment of muscle dysmorphia symptoms. *Assessment, 9,* 351–360.

Meehl, P. E. (1992). Factors and taxa, traits and types, differences of degree and differences of kind. *Journal of Personality, 60,* 117–174.

Mehler, P. S., Crews, C., & Weiner, K. (2004). Bulimia: Medical complications. *Journal of Women's Health, 13*(6), 668–675.

Milano, W., Petrella, C., Sabatino, C., & Capasso, A. (2004). Treatment of bulimia nervosa with sertraline: A randomized controlled trial. *Advances in Therapy, 21*(4), 232–237.

Milos, G., Spindler, A., Ruggiero, G., Klaghofer, R., & Schnyder, U. (2002). Comorbidity of obsessive-compulsive disorders and duration of eating disorders. *International Journal of Eating Disorders, 31,* 284–289.

Milos, G., Spindler, A., Schnyder, U., & Fairburn, C. G. (2005). Instability of eating disorder diagnoses: A prospective study. *British Journal of Psychiatry, 187,* 573–578.

National Institute for Clinical Excellence. (2004). *Eating disorders—Core interventions in the treatment and management of anorexia nervosa, bulimia nervosa and related eating disorders (NICE clinical guideline No. 9).* London: Author. Available from www.nice.org.uk.

Nilsson, M., Naessen, S., Dahlman, I., Linden Hirschberg, A., Gustafsson, J.-A., & Dahlman-Wright, K. (2004). Association of estrogen receptor β gene polymorphisms with bulimic disease in women. *Molecular Psychiatry, 9,* 28–34.

Pemberton, A. R., Vernon, S. W., & Lee, E. S. (1996). Prevalence and correlates of bulimia nervosa and bulimic behaviors in a racially diverse sample of undergraduate students in two universities in southeast Texas. *American Journal of Epidemiology, 144*(5), 450–455.

Peterson, C. B., Wimmer, S., Ackard, D. M., Crosby, R., Cavanagh, L. C., Engbloom, S., et al. (2004). Changes in body image during cognitive-behavioral treatment in women with bulimia nervosa. *Body Image 1* (2), 139–154.

Pomeroy, C. (2004). Assessment of medical status and physical factors. In J. Kevin Thompson (Ed.), *Handbook of eating disorders and obesity* (pp. 81–111). Hoboken, NJ: Wiley.

Pope, C. G., Pope, H. G., Menard, W., Fay, C., Olivardia, R., & Phillips, K. A. (2005). Clinical features of muscle dysmorphia among males with body dysmorphic disorder. *Body Image, 2*(4), 395–400.

Pope, H. G., & Hudson, J. I. (1992). Is childhood sexual abuse a risk factor for bulimia nervosa? *American Journal of Psychiatry, 149*, 455–463.

Pope, H. G., Gruber, A. J., Choi, P. Y., Olivardia, R., & Phillips, K. A. (1997). Muscle dysmorphia disorder. *Psychosomatics, 38*, 548–557.

Pumariega, A. J., Gustavson, C. R., Gustavson, J. C., Motes, P. S., & Ayers, S. (1994). Eating attitudes in African-American women: The Essence eating disorders survey. *Eating Disorders: Journal of Treatment and Prevention, 2*(1), 5–16.

Reas, D. L., Whisenhunt, B. L., Netemeyer, R., & Williamson, D. A. (2002). Development of the Body Checking Questionnaire: A self-report measure of body checking behavior. *International Journal of Eating Disorders, 31*, 324–333.

Rieger, E., Touyz, S. W., Swain, T., & Beumont, P. J. (2001). Cross-cultural research on anorexia nervosa: Assumptions regarding the role of body weight. *International Journal of Eating Disorders, 29*, 205–215.

Rizvi, S. L., Peterson, C. B., Crow, S. J., & Agras, W. S. (2000). Test-retest reliability of the Eating Disorder Examination. *International Journal of Eating Disorders, 28*, 311–316.

Roerig, J. L., Mitchell, J. E., deZwaan, M., Wonderlich, S. A., Kamran, S., Engbloom, S., et al. (2003). The eating disorders medicine cabinet revisited: A clinician's guide to appetite suppressants and diuretics. *International Journal of Eating Disorders, 33*, 443–457.

Rosen, J. C., & Leitenberg, H. (1982). Bulimia nervosa: Treatment with exposure and response prevention. *Behavior Therapy, 13*(1), 117–124.

Rosen, J. C., Srebnik, D., Saltzberg, E., & Wendt, S. (1991). Development of a body image avoidance questionnaire. *Psychological Assessment, 3*(1), 32–37.

Rowe, R., Pickles, A., Simonoff, E., Bulik, C. M., & Silberg, J. L. (2002). Bulimic symptoms in the Virginia Twin Study of adolescent behavioral development: Correlates, comorbidity, and genetics. *Biological Psychiatry, 51*, 172–182.

Ruscio, J., & Ruscio, A. M. (2002). Structure-based approach to psychological assessment: Matching measurement models to latent structure. *Assessment, 9*, 4–16.

Russell, G. F. M. (1979). Bulimia nervosa: An ominous variant of anorexia nervosa. *Psychological Medicine, 9*, 429–448.

Ryan, D., & Stewart, T. M. (2004). Medical management of obesity in women: Office-based approaches to weight management. *Journal of Obstetrics and Gynecology, 47*(4), 914–927.

Segal A., Kinoshita Kussunoki, D., & Larino, M. A. (2004). Post-surgical refusal to eat: Anorexia nervosa, bulimia nervosa or a new eating disorder? A case series. *Obesity Surgery, 14*(3), 353–360.

Sloan, D. M., Mizes, J., Helbok, C., & Muck, R. (2004). Efficacy of sertraline for bulimia nervosa. *International Journal of Eating Disorders, 36*, 48–54.

Slof-Op't Landt, M. C., van Furth, E. F., Meulenbelt, I., Slagboom, P. E., Bartels, M., Boomsma, D. I., et al. (2005). Eating disorders: From twin studies to candidate genes and beyond. *Twin Research and Human Genetics, 8*(5), 467–482.

Steffen, K. J., Roerig, J. L., Mitchell, J. E., & Uppala, S. (2006). Emerging drugs for eating disorder treatment. *Expert Opinion on Emerging Drugs, 11*(2), 315–336.

Stein, D., Lilenfeld, L. R., Plotnicov, K., Pollice, C., Rao, R., Strober, M., et al. (1999). Familial aggregation of eating disorders: Results from a controlled family study of bulimia nervosa. *International Journal of Eating Disorders, 26*, 211–215.

Stewart, T. M. (2004). Light on body image treatment: Acceptance through mindfulness. *Behavior Modification, 28*(6), 783–811.

Stewart, T. M., & Williamson, D. A. (2004a). Assessment of body image disturbances. In J. Kevin Thompson (Ed.), *Handbook of eating disorders and obesity* (pp. 495–514). Hoboken, NJ: Wiley.

Stewart, T. M., & Williamson, D. A. (2004b). Multidisciplinary treatment of eating disorders: Pt. I. Structure and costs of treatment. *Behavior Modification, 28*(6), 812–830.

Stewart, T. M., & Williamson, D. A. (2004c). Multidisciplinary treatment of eating disorders: Pt. II. Primary goals and content of treatment: A mindful approach. *Behavior Modification, 28*(6), 831–853.

Stewart, T. M., & Williamson, D. A. (2006). Eating disorders. In M. Hersen (Ed.), *Clinician's handbook of adult behavioral assessment* (pp. 253–278). Philadelphia: Brunner-Routledge.

Stewart, T. M., & Williamson, D. A. (in press). Eating disorders. In M. Hersen (Ed.), *The comprehensive handbook of interviewing*. Thousand Oaks, CA: Sage.

Stewart, T. M., Williamson, D. A., Allen, H. R., & Han, H. (2005, October). *The Body Morph Assessment Version 2.0 (BMA 2.0): Psychometrics and interesting findings.* Poster presented at the North American Society for the Study of Obesity, Vancouver, British Columbia, Canada.

Stewart, T. M., Williamson, D. A., Smeets, M. A. M., & Greenway, F. L. (2001). The Body Morph Assessment: Development of a computerized measure of body image. *Obesity Research, 9,* 43–50.

Strober, M., Freeman, R., Lampert, C., Diamond, J., & Lay, W. (2000). Controlled family study of anorexia nervosa and bulimia nervosa: Evidence of shared liability and transmission of partial syndromes. *American Journal of Psychiatry, 157,* 393–401.

Strong, S. M., Williamson, D. A., Netemeyer, R. G., & Geer, J. H. (2000). Eating disorder symptoms and concerns about body differ as a function of gender and sexual orientation. *Journal of Social and Clinical Psychology, 19,* 240–255.

Strube, M. J. (1989). Evidence for the type in Type A behavior: A taxometric analysis. *Journal of Personality and Social Psychology, 56,* 972–987.

Stunkard, A. J., & Messick, S. (1988). *The Eating Inventory.* San Antonio, TX: Psychological Corporation.

Thaw, J. M., Williamson, D. A., & Martin, C. K. (2001). Impact of altering DSM-IV criteria for anorexia and bulimia on the base rates of eating disorder diagnoses. *Eating and Weight Disorders, 6*(3), 121–129.

Thelen, M. H., Farmer, J., Wonderlich, S., & Smith, M. (1991). A revision of the bulimia test: The BULIT-R. *Psychological Assessment, 3,* 119–124.

Thiel, A., Zuger, M., Jacoby, G. E., & Schussler, G. (1998). Thirty-month outcome in patients with anorexia or bulimia nervosa and concomitant obsessive-compulsive disorder. *American Journal of Psychiatry, 155,* 244–249.

Thompson, B. W. (1992). "A way outa no way": Eating problems among African-American, Latina, and White women. *Gender and Society, 6*(4), 546–561.

Thornton, C., & Russell, J. (1997). Obsessive compulsive comorbidity in the dieting disorders. *International Journal of Eating Disorders, 21,* 83–87.

Tozzi, F., & Bulik, C. M. (2003). Candidate genes in eating disorders: Current drug targets. *CNS and Neurological Disorders, 2,* 31–39.

Treasure, J., & Schmidt, U. (2002). Anorexia nervosa. In United Health Foundation (Ed.), *Clinical evidence* (pp. 1–10). London: BMJ Publishing Group.

Treuer, T., Koperdak, M., Rozsa, S., & Furedi, J. (2005). The impact of physical and sexual abuse on body image in eating disorders. *European Eating Disorders Review, 13*, 106–111.

Tsai, G. (2000). Eating disorders in the Far East. *Eating and Weight Disorders, 5*(4), 183–197.

Vander Wal, J. S., & Thomas, N. (2004). Predictors of body image dissatisfaction and disturbed eating attitudes and behaviors in African American and Hispanic girls. *Eating Behaviors, 5*(4), 291–301.

Wade, T., Martin, N. G., & Tiggemann, M. (1998). Genetic and environmental risk factors for the weight and shape concerns characteristic of bulimia nervosa. *Psychological Medicine, 28*, 761–771.

Walsh, B. T., Hadigan, C. M., Devlin, M. J., Gladis, M., & Roose, S. P. (1991). Long-term outcome of antidepressant treatment for bulimia nervosa. *American Journal of Psychiatry, 9*, 1206–1212.

Welch, S. L., Doll, H. D., & Fairburn, C. G. (1997). Life events and the onset of bulimia: A controlled study. *Psychological Medicine, 27*, 515–522.

Westenhoefer, J. (2001). Prevalence of eating disorders and weight control practices in Germany in 1990 and 1997. *International Journal of Eating Disorders, 29*(4), 477–481.

Whisenhunt, B. L., Williamson, D. A., Netemeyer, R. G., & Andrews, C. (2003). Health risks, past usage, and intention to use weight loss products in normal weight women with high and low body dysphoria. *Eating and Weight Disorders, 8*, 114–123.

Whittal, M. L., Agras, W. S., & Gould, R. A. (1999). Bulimia nervosa: A meta-analysis of psychosocial and pharmacological treatments. *Behavior Therapy, 30*(1), 117–135.

Williamson, D. A. (1990). *Assessment of eating disorders: Obesity, anorexia, and bulimia nervosa.* Elmsford, NY: Pergamon Press.

Williamson, D. A., Cubic, B. A., & Gleaves, D. H. (1993). Equivalence of body image disturbances in anorexia and bulimia nervosa. *Journal of Abnormal Psychology, 102*, 177–180.

Williamson, D. A., Davis, C. J., Bennett, S. M., Goreczny, A. J., & Gleaves, D. H. (1989). Development of a simple procedure for assessing body image disturbances. *Behavioral Assessment, 11*, 433–446.

Williamson, D. A., Duchmann, E. G., Barker, S. E., & Bruno, R. M. (1998). Anorexia nervosa. In V. B. Van Hasselt & M. Hersen (Eds.), *Handbook of psychological treatment protocols for children and adolescents* (pp. 413–434). Hillsdale, NJ: Erlbaum.

Williamson, D. A., Gleaves, D. H., & Stewart, T. M. (2005). Categorical versus dimensional models of eating disorders: An examination of the evidence. *International Journal of Eating Disorders, 37*, 1–10.

Williamson, D. A., Martin, C. K., & Stewart, T. M. (2004). Psychological aspects of eating disorders. *Best Practice and Research Clinical Gastroenterology, 18*(6), 1073–1088.

Williamson, D. A., Prather, R. C., McKenzie, S. J., & Blouin, D. C. (1990). Behavioral assessment procedures can differentiate bulimia nervosa, compulsive overeater, obese, and normal subjects. *Behavioral Assessment, 12*, 239–252.

Williamson, D. A., Stewart, T. M., White, M. A., & York-Crowe, E. (2002). Information processing perspective on body image. In T. F. Cash & T. Prudzinsky (Eds.), *Body images* (pp. 47–54). New York: Guilford Press.

Williamson, D. A., Thaw, J. M., & Varnado, P. J. (2001). Cost-effectiveness analysis of a hospital-based cognitive-behavioral treatment program for eating disorders. *Behavior Therapy, 32*, 459–477.

Williamson, D. A., White, M. A., York-Crowe, E., & Stewart, T. M. (2004). Cognitive-behavioral theories of eating disorders. *Behavior Modification, 28*(6), 711–738.

Williamson, D. A., Womble, L. G., Smeets, M. A. M., Netemeyer, R. G., Thaw, M., Kutlesic, V., et al. (2002). The latent structure of eating disorder symptoms: A factor analytic and taxometric investigation. *American Journal of Psychiatry, 159*, 412–418.

Williamson, D. A., Womble, L. G., & Zucker, N. L. (1998). Cognitive behavior therapy for eating disorders. In T. S. Watson & F. M. Gresham (Eds.), *Child behavior therapy: Ecological considerations in assessment, treatment, and education* (pp. 335–355). New York: Plenum Press.

Williamson, D. A., Zucker, N. L., Martin, C. K., & Smeets, M. A. M. (2001). Etiology and management of eating disorders. In H. E. Adams & P. B. Sutker (Eds.), *Comprehensive handbook of psychopathology* (3rd ed., pp. 641–670). New York: Plenum Press.

Wilson, G. T. (2005). Psychological treatment of eating disorders. *Annual Review of Clinical Psychology1*, 439–465.

Winkelby, M. A., Gardner, C. D., & Taylor, C. B. (1996). The influence of gender and socioeconomic factors on Hispanic/White differences in body mass index. *Preventative Medicine, 25*(2), 203–211.

Wonderlich, S. A., Brewerton, T. D., Jocic, Z., Dansky, B., & Abbott, D. W. (1997). Relationship of childhood sexual abuse and eating disorders. *Journal of the American Academy of Child Adolescent Psychiatry, 36,* 1107–1115.

Wonderlich, S. A., Joiner, T. E., Keel, P. K., Williamson, D. A., & Crosby, R. D. (in press). Eating disorder diagnoses: Empirical approaches to classification. *American Psychologist.*

Wonderlich, S. A., & Mitchell, J. E. (1997). Eating disorders and comorbidity: Empirical, conceptual, and clinical implications. *Psychopharmacology Bulletin, 33,* 381–390.

Yanovski, S. Z. (2000). Eating disorder, race, and mythology. *Archives of Family Medicine, 9*(1), 88.

CHAPTER 18

Organic Disorder

GERALD GOLDSTEIN

DESCRIPTION OF THE DISORDER

In 1992, a distinguished group of psychiatrists and neurologists wrote a comment in the *American Journal of Psychiatry* entitled "Now Is the Time to Retire the Term 'Organic Mental Disorders'" (Spitzer et al., 1992). The paper was a critique of what was viewed as the outdated distinction between "organic" and "nonorganic" mental disorders philosophically based on the outmoded concept of mind-body dualism. They proposed that the then forthcoming fourth edition of the *Diagnostic and Statistical Manual of Mental Disorders* (*DSM-IV*; American Psychiatric Association, 1994) should abandon the category of Organic Mental Disorders and replace it with two new categories: "secondary disorders" for those disorders related to some physical illness or "substance induced disorders." The traditional organic mental disorders, described in the past as organic brain syndrome or acute or chronic brain syndrome, would be replaced by the term "delirium, dementia, and amnestic disorders" under the rubric of "cognitive impairment disorders." The authors of this paper were eminently successful: *DSM-IV* did abandon the term Organic Mental Disorders and replaced it with new terminology very close to what was suggested in the paper. Beyond that change, the term "organic brain syndrome" has essentially been abandoned in clinical practice, replaced with the Delirium, Dementia, and Amnestic Disorder categories. When a cognitive impairment disorder is diagnosed, an effort is also made to indicate the associated physical disorder, such as dementia due to head trauma (294.1) or substance use disorder such as alcohol-induced persisting dementia (291.2), often referred to as alcohol dementia.

This distinction is not merely a matter of classification, but has two scientific bases. As a result of the biological revolution in psychiatry generating a massive amount of research, it has become clear that many of the mental disorders previously thought to be environmentally acquired actually have a biological basis. Typically, genetic factors are involved, and we appear to be on the edge of discovery of actual genetic mechanisms for some of the disorders. Very few authorities now view Schizophrenia or autism as environmentally acquired disorders, and in some other conditions, such as depression and Obsessive-Compulsive Disorder, some biological basis is suspected, at least in some cases. In the case of some conditions, notably autism, there is impressive evidence that they are neurodevelopmental disorders (Minshew, Goldstein, & Siegel, 1997; Rutter, 1983). Thus, the distinction between organic and nonorganic mental disorders has become essentially meaningless, as many of the disorders we used to characterize in that way, such as Schizophrenia versus organic brain syndrome, both turn out to be neurobiological disorders. That is not to say that there are no environmentally acquired mental disorders; rather, for probably most of the disorders there is a vulnerability component in which environmental forces interact with neurobiological factors to produce an illness. Perhaps the most obvious example is alcoholism. If there were no alcohol in the environment we would have no alcoholism, but there is impressive evidence showing that individuals who acquire alcohol dependence often have strong family histories of the disorder, suggestive of a genetic vulnerability (Hill et al., 2004).

The second scientific consideration involves our increased knowledge of the traditional organic mental disorders: delirium, dementia, and amnesia. This increased knowledge has supported the capability of making more refined diagnoses. These three conditions are complex disorders, and diagnoses without further qualification are rarely, if ever, useful for treatment and management. In the case of delirium, which is a usually transient disturbance of consciousness, appropriate medical treatment that can often reverse the process without residual consequences is dependent on identification of the cause. It may be associated with a number of medical conditions or with substance abuse. Dementia research has essentially become a separate branch of neuroscience. *DSM-IV* contains a lengthy list of conditions dementia may be due to, for example, dementia due to Parkinson's disease, with each item on the list representing a field of independent research. There has been a major thrust in the area of Alzheimer's disease, and although we do not yet know the specific cause, a great deal is known about its genetics, pathology, and course. When *DSM-IV* was published, the term "dementia of the Alzheimer's type" was used because a definitive diagnosis could not be made in a living individual and it was necessary to do a brain autopsy to identify the specific pathology. Now, using PET scanning, it is possible to identify the amyloid pathology that produces the disease in living patients (Klunk et al., 2004). Substantial progress has been made in other areas. For example, the gene has been identified for Huntington's disease; there is an increasing understanding of the dementia associated with cerebral vascular disease; and the prions or "slow viruses" associated with Creutzfeldt-Jakob or mad cow disease, a form of dementia, have been discovered (Couzin, 2006; Soto, Estrada, & Castilla, 2006).

These considerations are meant to provide a context for describing what used to be called organic mental disorders. First, what we now mean by the term in general is the presence of delirium, dementia, or amnesia. These disorders are produced by some medical condition or substance use. Delirium is a usually transient impairment of consciousness; dementia is a usually gradual deterioration of cognitive abilities; and amnesia is a specific impairment of memory with relatively good preservation of other cognitive abilities. In this chapter, we do not go into any detail about delirium because it is typically a temporary condition treated in acute medical facilities, particularly when it is associated with a life-threatening illness. Pure amnesia is a relatively rare condition that is sometimes transient, as in the case of recovery from a severe head injury; when associated with structural damage to the hippocampus or related systems, it can be permanent. The major condition seen in most clinical psychiatry and psychology practice is dementia, which is quite common, particularly among elderly individuals. We therefore focus mainly on dementia.

Dementia is typically thought of as a progressive disorder characterized by gradual deterioration of cognitive function. However, there are also nonprogressive dementias. Severe head trauma may result in an impairment of cognitive abilities that is substantial and permanent but that does not progress. This distinction is of crucial importance for rehabilitation planning; one may be fighting off the inexorable progression of a degenerative process, or one may be dealing with an individual who is significantly impaired but who will not get progressively worse during the foreseeable future.

The most common form of progressive dementia is Alzheimer's disease. It is a disease of the elderly most typically appearing in significant form after age 60. Usually most notable is deterioration of memory, which often appears as the first sign of the disorder, but other abilities, including general intelligence, language, and problem solving, eventually become involved. Unlike some of the other dementias, there is no apparent movement disorder; gait, dexterity, and speech articulation may remain well preserved, although the content of language may be impaired.

Less common than Alzheimer's disease is a group of disorders associated with neurobiological abnormalities that are developmental and genetic. In the case of one of these disorders, Huntington's disease, the genetic basis has been clearly established and the responsible gene abnormality has been identified (Gusella, MacDonald, Ambrose, & Duyao, 1993). The disease appears in early adulthood and is characterized by a unique movement disorder, known as chorea, and gradual deterioration of cognitive function. A form of Parkinson's disease, known as Lewy body dementia, is characterized by the movement abnormalities of Parkinson's disease, but also by significant cognitive impairment (McKeith et al., 2004). Multiple sclerosis and amyotrophic lateral sclerosis are progressive deteriorative, or more precisely demyelinating diseases of the central nervous system often associated with impairment of memory and other cognitive abilities. Neuropsychological studies have been devoted to seeking cognitive differences among several of the different forms of dementia (e.g., Butters, Goldstein, Allen, & Shemansky, 1998).

The condition *DSM-IV* calls vascular dementia was at one time called cerebral vascular disease or cerebral arteriosclerosis. It was once thought to be more common than Alzheimer's disease, but that no longer seems to be the case. It is currently viewed as a relatively vaguely defined disorder and may be reconceptualized in *DSM-V*. To make the diagnosis there must be evidence of neurological abnormalities of the type associated with cerebral vascular disease, such as abnormal reflexes, ophthalmological findings indicative of atherosclerosis, and abnormal laboratory results. It was called "multi-infarct dementia" in *DSM-III* (American Psychiatric Association, 1980), consistent with the belief that it was produced by a series of usually minor strokes and the presence of significant hypertension. However, the failure to document this history in substantial numbers of patients led to the switch to the vascular dementia term.

Among young adults the most common form of dementia is associated with traumatic injury to the brain. The traumatic dementias are dementias because they involve often significant impairment of cognitive function, but they are generally not progressive. They are often associated with seizures or physical damage to parts of the body other than the brain. The individual with traumatic brain injury confined to a wheelchair because of damage to an extremity or the spinal cord is not uncommon.

Typically traumatic brain injury is at its worst at the time of the trauma; there may be a period of loss of responsiveness or coma, but there is commonly substantial recovery, often aided by rehabilitation efforts, and a return to normal or near normal premorbid function.

Considering the area broadly, there are two forms of traumatic brain injury: closed-head injury, in which the skull is not penetrated and the brain damage is produced largely by its impact against the skull, and focal or open-head injury, in which the skull is penetrated and brain damage consists of a missile destroying a circumscribed area of tissue in a specific portion of the brain. Usually, closed-head injury produces generalized impairment of memory, attention, and intellectual function, whereas open-head injury produces consequences that are dependent on the localized site of the lesion. Thus, an individual with an open-head injury to the middle, left side of the brain may acquire significant speech and language difficulties, called aphasia, and damage to the posterior portions of the brain could produce difficulties with visual perception.

Dementia may be produced by essentially any form of medical disorder, including infection, cancer, cardiovascular disease, malnutrition, and toxic and metabolic disorders. It has also been associated with substance dependence, notably alcoholism, and other, but apparently not all, addictive substances. The concept of "alcohol dementia" has been controversial for many years; some authorities assert that it is the direct consequence of alcohol itself, whereas others believe that it develops as a result of the consequences of alcoholism, notably malnutrition and liver disease. People with alcoholism often have numerous head injuries, and there is a theory that some of the cognitive deficits that are observed in individuals with alcoholism preceded becoming alcoholic and are developmental phenomena (Tarter, Hegedus, Goldstein, Shelly, & Alterman, 1984). In general, however, dementia results from numerous different illnesses and may be produced by many causes. Prevalence of specific causes may vary over time and across cultures. For example, general paresis, a brain disease associated with syphilis that was fairly common at one time, is barely existent now. The diseases encephalitis and meningitis resulting from infection are still found in some parts of the world, but in other places are quite uncommon. Brain disorders associated with HIV/AIDS infection apparently did not exist until the relatively recent appearance of the disease. Some of the dementias have notable epidemiologies. Multiple sclerosis is found most commonly in cold northern climates in individuals of Scandinavian descent. Infectious disorders such as encephalitis and AIDS dementia are relatively more common in areas in which there is a high density of the particular infectious agent involved. On the other hand, there appear to be no epidemiological considerations in Huntington's disease; it matters only whether one inherits the gene.

DIAGNOSIS AND ASSESSMENT

Unlike many of the other mental disorders, dementia and delirium may be diagnosed in primary care settings by medical procedures, including the physical examination and various laboratory methods. Thus, for example, Huntington's and Parkinson's disease may be diagnosed by direct observation of abnormal movements; severe, focal vascular disease can be detected by observation of a stroke or paralysis of one side of the body. These diagnoses can be confirmed by tests of sensory function and reflexes that constitute a portion of the physical neurological examination. The physical examination is typically accompanied by a variety of laboratory procedures, some of which are parts of a routine medical evaluation and others of which are specialized neurological procedures. The electroencephalogram (EEG) is widely used; in some settings it has become almost routine to do computerized tomography (CT scan) or magnetic resonance imaging (MRI) of the head and sometimes of the spinal cord. Beyond these procedures is a variety of relatively new neuroimaging techniques that we mention but do not describe in detail here. Positron emission tomography (PET) evaluates brain metabolism through tracing an injected radioactive substance. It has recently become important for evaluation of dementia because a dye (Pittsburgh B) has been developed that, when used during the PET procedure, can identify the amyloid bodies that constitute the major pathology of Alzheimer's disease (Klunk et al., 2004). Single photon emission tomography and related procedures evaluate cerebral blood flow. Diffusion tensor imaging is an MRI-related method for evaluating the intactness of fiber tracts (Sotak, 2002). Magnetic resonance spectroscopy is also an MRI-related procedure used to evaluate brain metabolism at a molecular biological level. Functional MRI is a technology for monitoring ongoing brain activity while the subject is taking an MRI. With this procedure it is possible to do behavioral testing and directly observe associated brain activity. These advanced procedures are not used routinely in clinical evaluation, and some are used essentially exclusively for research.

While these procedures are available for identification of brain dysfunction, the diagnoses of delirium, dementia, amnesia, and the class of disorders identified in *DSM-IV* as Cognitive Disorder Not Otherwise Specified (294.9) are defined behaviorally. Thus, for example, the diagnosis of Alzheimer's disease is based on the presence of memory impairment and other cognitive disturbances. It is unlikely that any patient has been diagnosed with Alzheimer's disease solely on the basis of amyloid bodies seen on PET scan without a history of cognitive impairment. The procedures used to make these diagnoses are conducted at two levels: screening and detailed assessment. Screening is typically accomplished with delirium or dementia rating scales. There are several delirium rating scales: the Delirium Rating Scale (deRooij, Schurmans, van der Mast, & Levi, 2005), the NEECHAM Confusion Scale (Champagne, 1987), and the Memorial Delirium Assessment Scale (Lemiengre et al., 2006). These scales are generally designed to be used by bedside nurses and include a combination of behavioral and physical status items. For example, the NEECHAM Confusion Scale consists of 9 items and evaluates ratings of attention, processing commands, appearance, motor and verbal behavior, vital function, oxygen saturation, and urinary continence. The most popular of the dementia scales are the Mini-Mental State Examination (Folstein, Folstein, & McHugh, 1975 and the Mattis (1998) Dementia Rating Scale. A dementia rating scale developed by Blessed, Tomlinson, and Roth (1968) was widely used in the past, but the Mini-Mental scale and the Mattis scale are more commonly used at present. These scales are short cognitive tests that briefly evaluate orientation, attention, memory, language comprehension, spatial abilities, and judgment. Some clinicians use less formal mental status examinations that typically contain the basic elements of these scales.

More refined assessment is accomplished within the framework of two disciplines: behavioral neurology and clinical neuropsychology. Behavioral neurology is the branch of clinical neurology that specializes in brain disorders that have behavioral components. General neurology is concerned with the entire nervous system, including disorders of peripheral nerves, the spinal cord, and all aspects of brain disease. Areas of interest may include spinal cord injuries, diseases of the sensory and motor systems, epilepsy, and such specific disorders as stroke, head injury, multiple sclerosis, and Parkinson's disease. Behavioral neurologists are competent in all of these areas as neurologists, but focus their practice primarily on patients with cognitive disorders involving general cognitive ability, memory, language, skilled movement, and perceptual abilities. It is probably fair to say that behavioral neurologists use as their major assessment paradigm an extension of the neurological examination that focuses on purposive or complex behavior. One could characterize this practice as a significant extension of the mental status examination, but the extensive detail sometimes needed to make precise diagnoses of specific syndromes goes well beyond the mental status examination if it is construed only as a screening procedure. However, the examination method is clinical and does not involve extensive use of instrumentation or quantitative procedures. The writings of Luria (1973) and Geschwind (1984) provide excellent examples of how behavioral neurologists approach assessment.

Clinical neuropsychology is concerned with essentially the same kinds of patients as those for behavioral neurology. However, clinical neuropsychologists are psychologists and use the methods of psychology in their approach to assessment. Most prominently, there is heavy emphasis on quantitative methods in the form of psychological testing. Clinical neuropsychology grew out of two traditions, with roots in clinical psychology and behavioral neurology. However, over the years it has become a separate discipline, combining the two with elements of psychiatry and neuroscience. From early in its history clinical psychology has been involved with the assessment of cognitively disabled and brain-damaged patients. There is a long history of the use of psychological tests to evaluate mental retardation, and indeed the first intelligence tests were utilized for that purpose. Clinical psychologists were asked to determine whether their tests could be helpful in the diagnosis of organic brain syndrome and in differentiating between organic brain syndrome and other disorders associated with cognitive dysfunction, notably Schizophrenia. The common practice then was to use the available tests, including the Rorschach test, Human Figure drawings, the Bender-Gestalt Test, and the Wechsler intelligence scales. In different settings, other psychologists were beginning what was essentially a basic science of the neurobiological bases of behavior largely involving animal studies but also some human research. The names of Karl Lashley, Donald Hebb, Elliot Stellar, Wolfgang Khler, and Harry Harlow are probably the most familiar ones representing this area. A group of European cognitively oriented psychologists and psychiatrists who came to the United States at the beginning of World War II, including Kurt Goldstein, Heinz Werner, and Martin Scheerer, made an important contribution to what was to become neuropsychology. Another group of psychological scientists collaborated with neuroscientists and neurologists in another branch of this development. Probably most notable in this group was Ward Halstead, who collaborated with a neuroscientist, Heinrich Klüver, and three neurosurgeons, Percival Bailey, Earl Walker, and Paul Bucy, all of whom were interested in the frontal lobes, in doing the basic research that ultimately gave rise to the Halstead-Reitan neuropsychological test battery, currently the most widely used comprehensive test battery in clinical neuropsychology. Later collaborations of this type took place between Hans-Lukas Teuber and Mortimer Mishkin, both of whom were psychologists involved in neuroscience research, and Morris Bender, a neurologist. In later years, this kind of relationship was formed between Karl Pribram, a neurosurgeon, and numerous psychologists (e.g., Mirsky, Rosvold, & Pribram, 1957; Prigatano & Pribram, 1982).

Over the years a confluence emerged among these groups that established the discipline of clinical neuropsychology generally defined as an area of clinical practice with a specific focus on brain function and central nervous system disorders and based on the science that attempts to relate brain function to behavior, now known as experimental neuropsychology or behavioral neuroscience. Thus, the psychologists that became members of this discipline, many of whom started out as clinical psychologists, developed expertise in various aspects of neuroscience and clinical aspects of neurological disorders and established their own procedures, now known as neuropsychological assessment. As the field developed in the United States patterns of practice emerged, with leadership coming from two distinctly different schools, one led by Arthur Benton and the other by Ralph Reitan. Later, there was further fragmentation associated with the introduction of the so-called process approach to clinical neuropsychology and the introduction of Luria's theory and methods to the United States following translation of his books from Russian and increased availability of his test materials. Despite these different schools, the discipline remains identifiable as an entity with a universal interest in brain-damaged patients and their assessment and treatment.

These preliminary remarks are necessary for an understanding of the nature of assessment in clinical neuropsychology. Not all neuropsychologists use the same tests, and when they do, they are not always scored or interpreted in the same way. There are, however, numerous general areas of agreement among the various groups. First, a competent diagnostic evaluation of patients can be accomplished only with an adequate assessment. Most neuropsychologists agree that it is necessary to administer some form of test battery consisting of diverse tests, although there is sharp disagreement between the view that a standard battery should be administered containing the same tests given in the same way to all patients and the view that the test battery used should be individualized in accordance with the nature of the case and the referral question (Goldstein, 1997; Milberg, Hebben, & Kaplan, 1996). In any event, a neuropsychological assessment generally consists largely of tests of cognitive function that evaluate the areas of general intellectual ability, abstract reasoning and problem solving, attention, memory, language, spatial cognition, and perceptual and motor skills. Most neuropsychologists now use quantitative tests of these areas that have satisfactory psychometric status with regard to various forms of validity, reliability, and adequate norms. The general requirement for the tests used to be characterized as neuropsychological tests is that they are sensitive to the condition of the brain. Operationally, that means that there has been adequate peer-reviewed published research involving patients with some form of brain disorder and demographically comparable controls that shows that there are differences between patients and controls that at least reach the level of statistical significance and ideally that have high levels of sensitivity and specificity. One may use other tests as part of the battery, but those tests should not be used to diagnose brain damage. For example, one might want to use tests that estimate premorbid function or educational achievement.

It should be noted that clinical neuropsychologists function in various settings and do not work only with adult psychiatric patients. Some work almost exclusively with children; others work with children and adults in general medical settings, particularly those that serve neurological and neurosurgical patients. Many neuropsychologists work in rehabilitation settings, most of which provide services to individuals who have sustained stoke or head injuries. They may work with many patients with dementia of the Alzheimer's type, but much of their work is with patients whose disorders lie primarily within the purview of neurology and neurosurgery and who are rarely seen in psychiatric settings. These patients have a broad variety of clinically distinct conditions or syndromes that account for much of the corpus of the practice of behavioral neurology and clinical neuropsychology. A thorough review of these disorders is contained in a book edited by Heilman and Valenstein (2003). Probably the most well known of these syndromes is aphasia, a disturbance of speech and language usually associated with left hemisphere stroke, but these syndromes exist across essentially the entire range of cognitive function, including disorders of attention, learning and memory, reasoning abilities or executive function, spatial cognition, skilled movement, and perceptual abilities. Sometimes these syndromes are quite specific and precise. A classic example is a condition known as alexia without agraphia, in which the patient can write but not read to the extent that there is an inability to read what had just been written. It is not clinically useful, and often not accurate, to describe individuals with these syndromes as having dementia. There may be a variable degree of loss of general intellectual function in many of these patients, but often intellectual function is quite intact with the exception of the areas involved in the syndrome. Patients with severe amnesia who may have essentially no recall of recent events may maintain an average level of general intelligence (IQ). Many neuropsychologists, particularly those who practice in neurological and neurosurgical settings, devote a great deal of effort to identifying these specific syndromes utilizing neuropsychological assessment procedures. Such assessments often contribute significantly to neurological diagnosis and provide the basis for rehabilitation planning, which, in the case of patients of this type, requires specific knowledge of the pattern of preserved and impaired abilities. This relationship among assessment, planning, and implementation is probably best established in the areas of aphasia and specific learning disability rehabilitation.

The assessment tasks of clinical neuropsychologists working in psychiatric settings have areas of difference and overlap with those performed by workers in neurological and neurosurgical settings. Initially, clinical neuropsychologists started working in psychiatric facilities because clinicians wanted their expertise with regard to distinguishing between brain-damaged and psychiatric patients. The representative case was the individual with subtle or more blatant cognitive dysfunction, but available diagnostic methods did not establish whether it was produced by a neurological disorder or an environmentally acquired mental illness. In most instances, the puzzling cases involved patients for whom the diagnosis of Schizophrenia was being considered. The question was whether the patient did indeed have Schizophrenia or, using the terminology of the time, an organic brain syndrome. A substantial research literature emerged in response to this question (Goldstein, 1978), and numerous tests were proposed that effectively distinguished between brain-damaged and schizophrenic patients.

Changes since that time involved numerous considerations. First, the question as raised turned out to be something of a pseudo-issue since research with the CT scan when it developed showed that patients with definitive diagnoses of Schizophrenia had prominent evidence of structural brain damage clearly visualized by the CT scan. The interests of neuropsychologists then gravitated toward finding associations between CT scan results, and associated procedures such as cerebral blood flow studies, and performance on neuropsychological tests. A great deal of evidence was produced at that time relating performance on tests of problem solving, notably the Wisconsin Card Sorting Test, to abnormalities in the frontal lobes of patients with Schizophrenia (Goldberg & Weinberger, 1988). These studies extended into a broad field of investigation of the neuropsychology of Schizophrenia, often involving a number of neuroimaging technologies and numerous neuropsychological tests and experimental procedures. In clinical practice neuropsychologists have a great interest in examining cognitive profiles of patients with Schizophrenia. These profiles tend to be quite diverse, and there have been investigations of cognitive heterogeneity in Schizophrenia, looking for possible subtypes (Goldstein, 1994; Seaton, Goldstein, & Allen, 2001).

Aside from diagnostic considerations, neuropsychological assessment has found an important place in treatment and rehabilitation planning for individuals with Schizophrenia. There is substantial evidence that neuropsychological tests are robust predictors of outcome and are superior predictors to symptom profiles (Green, Kern, Braff, & Mintz, 2000). Cognitive function appears to be at the basis of the disorder and tends to remain stable over time, whereas symptoms tend to be transient and changeable. There are two roles for neuropsychological assessment in this area. One relates to forming treatment plans based on anticipated outcomes predictable from the tests. The other is in the process of cognitive rehabilitation, in which the tests are used to identify impaired and preserved abilities and training programs are designed and implemented to remediate the deficits. There have been numerous studies evaluating teaching patients with Schizophrenia to improve their performance on the Wisconsin Card Sorting Test, a procedure that mainly assesses cognitive flexibility (Green, Satz, Ganzell, & Vaclav, 1992).

In addition to the area of Schizophrenia, neuropsychological assessment is now commonly used with patients with other psychiatric disorders. Neuropsychological studies of patients with such disorders as Major Depression, Bipolar Disorder, and Obsessive-Compulsive Disorder have found patterns of cognitive ability that have potential relevance to the clinical phenomenology and course of these disorders. There has been extensive neuropsychological work done with the neurodevelopmental disorders, notably Autistic Disorder, Asperger's Disorder, and Attention-Deficit/Hyperactivity Disorder. It is therefore not unusual to refer a patient with depression for a neuropsychological assessment, not primarily to rule out brain damage, but to obtain a cognitive profile that might be helpful in treatment planning and management.

With regard to dementia, there is a group of neuropsychologists particularly interested in the elderly who have focused those interests on assessment of late-middle-aged and elderly individuals for reduction in cognitive function, with frank dementia as an end-state. Most recently, a related interest has developed in mild cognitive impairment or signs of cognitive dysfunction in elderly individuals that might reflect normal aging or the early signs of progressive dementia (Lopez et al., 2006). Neuropsychological assessment in this area to some extent concerns the diagnosis of dementia itself, but is more often concerned with the pattern of cognitive dysfunction that characterizes different forms of dementia and patterns that distinguish between these different forms, such as Alzheimer's disease and Lewy body dementia. Competence is also often an issue, and the neuropsychologist is asked to offer an opinion as to the patient's self-management capacity. Neuropsychological assessment of individuals with moderate to severe dementia has to be designed in consideration of the sometimes limited capacity of these individuals to take formal tests. Indeed, special tests and test batteries have been developed for assessment of significantly impaired elderly individuals (Panisset, Roudier, Saxton, & Boller, 1994). Sometimes it is not possible to go beyond the screening instruments mentioned earlier, such as the Mini-Mental State Examination or the Mattis Dementia Rating Scale. An extensive technical literature has emerged documenting specific aspects of memory failure, changes in language and related communicative abilities, and conceptual reasoning. Thus, an assessment report should be able to make statements such as "This patient demonstrates the rapid forgetting, relatively preserved procedural memory, and word-finding difficulty characteristic of Alzheimer's disease."

Neuropsychological assessment of children is a specialized area requiring backgrounds in child psychology and psychopathology, development of the nervous system, and neurobehavioral illnesses of childhood. The *DSM* categorization into disorders usually first diagnosed in infancy, childhood, or adolescence and disorders that are categorized in the delirium, dementia, and amnestic disorder section should not be taken to mean that some of the child diagnoses are not neurobehavioral disorders. This point is particularly the case for mental retardation, but most authorities would view autism, Attention-Deficit/Hyperactivity Disorder, and the rarer forms of developmental conditions such as Asperger's and Rett's Disorder as neurobehavioral disorders. Child clinical neuropsychologists are highly involved in assessment and treatment of children with specific learning disabilities, and there is an extensive neuropsychological literature on dyslexia, dyscalculia, and other learning disabilities. Child neuropsychologists use tests that are frequently similar to those used for adults, but a great deal more refinement is present regarding age norms, and the test materials are made suitable for children. Other tests are quite different, particularly those used for infants and young children. Assessment material is also available, often in the form of structured interviews and questionnaires to obtain information from parents. There is also great interest in head injury because trauma is the most common cause of acquired neurological damage in children, and the consequences of trauma for children are quite different from what happens to adults.

Regardless of setting, the vast majority of neuropsychologists use neuropsychological tests as their major assessment instrument and may actually use many of the same tests. However, some use a standard procedure, often the Halstead-Reitan neuropsychological test battery or the Luria-Nebraska Neuropsychological Battery, and others use individual tests selected on the basis of the disorder being evaluated, the referral question, the patient's demographics, and practical concerns such as testing time available. Some practitioners take a compromise approach, having different relatively fixed batteries for several assessment areas. Thus, one might have a battery for elderly patients, for head-injury patients, and for children being evaluated for Attention-Deficit/Hyperactivity Disorder.

We will not go into extensive detail about specific tests. Two extensive volumes, Lezak, Howieson, and Loring (2004) and Spreen and Strauss (1998), provide descriptions of most of these tests. However, we note that a comprehensive assessment typically contains tests of general intelligence, abstract reasoning, attention, memory, language, spatial cognition, and perceptual and motor skills. Some clinicians add tests of educational achievement, personality, and effort, particularly if there is a malingering issue. These test batteries are interpreted according to a scheme devised by Reitan (Reitan & Wolfson, 1993) using four methods of inference. The first is general level of performance on the entire battery, usually summarized as a single or small number of index scores, sometimes called impairment indexes. The second method involves pathognomonic signs, which provide definitive evidence of neurological dysfunction. Such signs never occur in normal individuals. The third method is right-left comparisons, in which functioning of the right and left side of the body, or right and left hemispace in the case of vision, are compared to each other, looking for abnormal asymmetries. This method is essentially taken from the neurological examination in which the neurologist may compare reflexes on the right and left sides of the body or vision in the right and left visual fields in order to lateralize brain damage. This examination is based on the principle that for many functions the right hemisphere of the brain controls the left side of the body and vice versa. The fourth method involves performance profiles or patterns of cognitive performance that specifically characterize a disorder. Much work in this area has been done with the Wechsler intelligence scales, where subtest profiles were sought that characterized particular disorders such as Schizophrenia or autism or specific damage to one or the other cerebral hemisphere. Generally, neuropsychologists use these four methods, each of which has its limitations but work reasonably well when used in combination, in making their interpretations.

CONCEPTUALIZATION

In this section we comment on the conceptual aspects of the *DSM* category of delirium, dementia, and amnesia in the areas of learning and modeling, life events, genetic influences, physical factors affecting behavior, drugs affecting behavior, and cultural and diversity issues. However, because the disorders we are discussing are so broad, no one thing can be said for any of these topics that is pertinent to all of those disorders. We therefore proceed by taking a topic and concentrating on a disorder in which it is particularly pertinent. Thus, as an obvious example, life events have nothing to do with whether one acquires Huntington's disease because the only consideration is whether one has the gene. However, life events have a great deal to do with whether one sustains a severe brain injury in a car accident.

LEARNING AND MODELING

The relevance of learning and modeling to brain disorders occurs mainly in the case of the neurodevelopmental disorders. Although they are classified in *DSM-IV* as disorders usually first diagnosed in infancy, childhood, or adolescence, many of them fit equally appropriately into the delirium, dementia, and amnestic and other cognitive disorders category. We here focus on the disorder of autism. It is generally agreed that autism is a neurodevelopmental disorder characterized by inability to form social relationships, abnormal language development, and restrictive repetitive or stereotypic behavior. It is often associated with mental retardation. It is a chronic disorder that appears before age 3 and persists into adulthood. It is thought to be irreversible, and there is no definitive medical cure.

Learning and modeling are important considerations in autism because there is recent, increasingly encouraging evidence that with early detection appropriate education and training can significantly improve outcome in later years (Siegel, Goldstein, & Minshew, 1996). This early education emphasizes communication skills (Yoder & Stone, 2006) and symbolic play (Kasari, Freeman, & Paparella, 2006). There is a great emphasis on teaching joint attention, impairment of which is felt to be a core deficit area in autism during the early years (Whalen, Schreibman, & Ingersoll, 2006). There are widely accepted general programs, such as Treatment and Education of Autistic and related Communications Handicapped Children, created by Eric Schopler and colleagues (e.g., Cox & Schopler, 1993). Outcome studies have supported the common belief that early intervention during the preschool years can result in better cognitive function, communication, and social skills than would be the case without such intervention. Thus, although it is well established that autism is a neurodevelopmental disorder, there appears to be sufficient plasticity in children to positively alter through education and modeling what otherwise could be very unfortunate outcomes.

Within the area of learning there is a broader issue of whether individuals with significant structural brain damage are capable of new learning. The earlier view was that brain damage significantly compromises the ability to learn new information. In some forms of brain damage there is a spontaneous recovery of function to a greater or lesser degree, but systematic educational efforts to teach new information may be largely ineffective. Probably beginning with development of speech and language therapy and later of cognitive rehabilitation methods, efforts have been made to develop educational systems to teach new information to brain-damaged individuals for the purpose of promoting recovery and restoring premorbid function. From a scientific standpoint, a major methodological problem involved demonstrating that any improvements with education or training were the result of teaching rather than spontaneous recovery of function. Numerous research strategies involving such methods as multiple baseline designs or working with chronic patients who were stable for lengthy periods of time have to a large extent been successful in demonstrating improvement beyond spontaneous recovery. The major class of exceptions is patients with rapidly progressive disorders, where the course of the disease counteracts rehabilitative efforts. However, even in slowly progressive disease such as multiple sclerosis, it is possible to demonstrate improvement with systematic training in such areas as memory (Allen, Goldstein, Heyman, & Rondinelli, 1998).

These considerations would suggest that a conceptualization of dementia as a necessarily progressive disorder is incorrect. The question of reversibility is more complex. There are clearly remissions associated with some forms of dementia, but whether actual improvements associated with educational and rehabilitative methods signify reversibility of the disorder is questionable. For example, in autism, although education can clearly improve social functioning, the assumption is that the autism is still present in individuals who show such improvement. *DSM-IV* recognizes that dementia may be progressive, static, or remitting depending on the disease process and the availability of adequate treatment. There is now substantial evidence coming from the autism and general cognitive rehabilitation literature that the application of educational methods can positively alter outcome.

LIFE EVENTS

In the case of neurobehavioral disorders, it may be more appropriate to combine life events and lifestyle. The life events literature in the area of Schizophrenia in particular stresses the matter of how adverse life events can negatively influence course of illness and produce particularly unfortunate outcomes such as suicide. This pattern does not appear to have much applicability to the neurobehavioral disorders. Rather, a number of other factors appears to be relevant. Most obviously, a chance life event can produce the disorder, notably brain injury resulting from an accident or a violent act. Moving to an area in which an epidemic of some neurological disorder occurs is another possibility. Unintentional exposure to infection sometimes occurs. Quite frequently, however, characteristics of lifestyle may make an individual vulnerable to neurobehavioral disease. There are numerous clear examples. Persistent alcohol dependence can lead to alcohol dementia. Risky sexual behavior can result in AIDS dementia or dementia associated with other forms of sexually transmitted diseases. Unhealthy dietary habits leading to obesity may put one at risk for stroke or vascular dementia. Head trauma resulting from an accident may be associated with impulsive behavior such as driving while intoxicated. The health promotion and behavioral health literature focuses on this area, stressing prevention.

Whether life events can alter the severity and course of neurobehavioral disorders as they do some psychiatric disorders has not really been studied. There are a few well-established considerations. In autism, any change in the environment, even if minor, can be very upsetting and could provoke symptoms that were not present before the change (*DSM-IV*). In multiple sclerosis there is some support for the view that adverse life events can trigger a relapse episode (Brown, Tennant, Dunn, & Pollard, 2005). In Huntington's disease there is an increased risk of suicide particularly during the early course of the illness, when independent function begins to diminish (Paulsen, Hoth, Nehl, & Stierman, 2005; Schoenfeld et al., 1984).

GENETIC INFLUENCES

There is a clear and less clear influence of genetic factors on the neurobehavioral disorders. The clearest case is Huntington's disease, which is a classic genetic disease. The genetics are well understood, with a 50% probability that the offspring will acquire the disease if one parent has it. There are several other disorders in which a genetic influence is strongly suspected but they are not strongly hereditary in that there is not a particularly remarkable association in families, and the genetic mechanism has not been discovered. The major disorders in this category are multiple sclerosis and autism. In both cases, strenuous efforts have been made to determine whether these are acquired diseases, primarily looking at toxic and infectious possibilities, but the results were largely negative. On the other hand, the gene has not been discovered for either of these disorders, and there is not an established group of candidate genes (Muhle, Trentacoste, & Rapin, 2004). The status of autism and multiple sclerosis with regard to genetics is quite similar, with substantial evidence from population and laboratory studies of a genetic influence, but thus far the specific loci have not been found. The possibility that Alzheimer's disease has a genetic component has been raised since the discovery of a specific lipoprotein APOE4 in the brains of people with Alzheimer's disease, but this work is very early in its development.

PHYSICAL FACTORS AFFECTING BEHAVIOR

By definition, the neurobehavioral disorders are those conditions that alter behavior as the result of a general medical condition. However, it is not uncommon for a brain disorder to be accompanied by a physical illness that, though sometimes resulting from brain disease, does not directly involve cognitive function. Probably the most common of these disorders involve physical damage. In the case of trauma, an accident can lead to injury of the brain but can also produce paralysis of the arms or legs or partial or total destruction of the eyes or ears. Thus, the person brain-injured in an accident may often be paralyzed and confined to a wheelchair or totally or partially blind or deaf. In the case of stroke, there may be loss of function of one side of the body, usually involving arms and legs to some extent, and there may be partial loss of vision.

Multiple sclerosis involves progressive paralysis and sometimes less deterioration of vision.

An important area of concern is the general health status of individuals with neurobehavioral disorders. Patients who have had strokes typically have histories of cardiovascular disease that requires continued treatment. Patients who have had severe head injury may have seizures. Individuals with Huntington's disease have particular nutritional requirements involving an increased caloric intake. The reverse is true for patients confined to wheelchairs who often become obese because of their sedentary status. In particular, elderly people with significantly severe dementia are at risk for developing infections or malnutrition because of impaired capacity for self-care.

Some of the neurobehavioral disorders are intrinsically biologically determined and will appear and sometimes progress regardless of health maintenance or lifestyle. Diseases like multiple sclerosis, Huntington's disease, and autism are constitutional and cannot be prevented by any form of health maintenance practices. Other disorders are directly related to health maintenance and self-care, notably the substance use disorders and cardiovascular disorders associated with obesity and other poor health habits. This distinction is significant because on the one hand it discourages the false hope that arises from efforts to prevent or treat incurable illnesses, sometimes attaining the level of being victimized by charlatanism, while it encourages the view that good health maintenance may prevent or ameliorate the progression of numerous disorders.

We have indicated that essentially any disease process that affects any part or organ of the body can also affect the brain. Thus the brain may acquire cancer, infection, vascular disease, respiratory disorders, metabolic disorders, autoimmune disorders, and the effects of trauma. There are implications for brain function from numerous systemic illnesses, such as diabetes, lung disease, and hypertension. Additionally, there are some diseases that affect only the brain or central nervous system. The major ones are Alzheimer's disease, Huntington's disease, and multiple sclerosis. The particular disease involved has strong implications for severity, morbidity, and mortality. There are also treatment implications. Infection is often reversible through use of antibiotics, and although brain trauma may recover spontaneously or with the support of rehabilitation, other disorders, such as brain cancer, are often fatal if not treatable by neurosurgery; still others, such as multiple sclerosis, are slowly progressive but not medically treatable in a curative sense. Other disorders are directly related to health maintenance and self-care, notably the substance use disorders and cardiovascular disorders associated with obesity and other poor health habits.

DRUGS AFFECTING BEHAVIOR

Drugs relevant to the neurobehavioral disorders may be classified into three categories. There are the drugs that are used to treat other medical disorders aside from brain disorders. Drugs for diabetes, hypertension, and heart disease may be used with brain-damaged patients having these disorders. Hopefully, by effectively treating the systemic illness, brain function may be improved as well. Similarly, psychiatric drugs for depression, mania, or anxiety may be used with brain-damaged patients with these disorders. The second class is those drugs that directly treat neurological symptoms. Included here are the anticonvulsant medications used to treat epilepsy and anti-Parkinsonian medication to reduce the motor symptoms of Parkinson's disease. Sometimes anticonvulsant medication, notably sodium valproate, is used to relieve agitation in combination with depression in patients with dementia.

The third class of drugs is the cognitive enhancers. These are medications specifically designed to improve cognitive function in individuals with dementia. At present, the most popular of these drugs is Aricept, but many drugs preceded it and many are forthcoming. Whether these drugs are effective in slowing down the course of Alzheimer's disease has become a major question in pharmacological research. Some of this investigation involves behavioral effects such as mood, agitation, and symptoms of psychosis and some with formal cognitive changes. There are numerous reports of positive results in the literature (e.g., Gauthier et al., 2002), and much work is in process.

Culture and Diversity Issues

A major issue that has arisen in neuropsychological assessment has to do with whether neuropsychological tests are culture-fair. But the matter goes beyond fairness because there is the question of whether a competent and adequate neuropsychological evaluation can be given by someone who does not speak the language of the patient. Some authorities indicate that there are difficulties in that regard, and ideally the examiner should give the examination in the language of the patient (Nell, 2004). A related matter has to do with whether translations of tests written in one language are adequate in other languages. A controversy has arisen concerning whether it is best to use "culture-fair" or "culture-specific" tests. That is, should tests emphasize culturally and ethnically neutral material or cognitive competence of individuals in their own cultures? In the past, declarations were made that tests were culture-fair because they were nonverbal, but this assertion has been proven not to be the case (Rosselli & Ardila, 2003). Rather, it seems necessary to prospectively develop tests proven by empirical research to be culture-fair. The practice of adjusting test scores for socioeconomic status has also been controversial (Reitan & Wolfson, 1995). These matters are of sufficient importance to lead to the development of a specialized area of research in neuropsychology that deals with cultural and diversity matters and that has already produced an extensive literature representing various views. Neuropsychological tests are different from neurodiagnostic procedures in general because scores are frequently significantly correlated with educational level and other surrogates of sociocultural status. Beyond that, different cultures view testing differently, and some do not even use tests. Thus, the impact of placing an individual in a testing situation that might be completely alien may be a significant consideration in interpreting test results. Nell points out, for example, that test wiseness, as in reconciling speed and accuracy to get an optimal score, may not be present in individuals from cultures that do not utilize tests. Though he does not reject entirely the use of tests in these cultures, he supports such methods as more extensive use of more lengthy interviews than those usually conducted and employment of individuals drawn from the target culture to translate and administer the tests.

Another matter of cultural relevance concerns epidemiology. Different neurobehavioral disorders have different incidence and prevalence rates in different cultures. In an extreme form, some disorders are pandemic in some cultures while they barely exist in others. Factors such as climate, prevalence of poverty, and to some extent genetics all play roles. In some parts of the world neuropsychologists may provide services to large numbers of patients with a disease that neuropsychologists located elsewhere may never or rarely see in their practices. The most dramatic example of this discrepancy is in the case of HIV/AIDS. Because it can result in dementia, HIV/AIDS is of importance to neuropsychology. *DSM-IV* lists Dementia Due to HIV Disease (294.9) as a form of dementia, and there is now abundant research evidence for that inclusion (Heaton et al., 1995). In some African countries HIV/AIDS is epidemic, some having a prevalence of over 20% (e.g., Gouws, White, Stover, & Brown, 2006), while in other countries it is typically less than 1% (e.g., in Tijuana, Mexico; Brouwer et al., 2006).

The genetics data are of great interest because of the specificity found. There have been numerous population studies of multiple sclerosis. In one of them, conducted in Ireland, the interest was in HLA alleles, thought to be important for development of multiple sclerosis. A significant difference was found in the prevalence rate of multiple sclerosis in two Irish counties. While the implicated alleles were found to be more common in subjects in both counties than in normal controls, the sample in one county had a significantly higher rate of one of the haplotypes studied, suggesting a differential predisposition to multiple sclerosis (McGuigan et al., 2005). Several other neurobehavioral disorders have a greater or lesser connection with genetics, with population movements creating interactions of this type between the gene pool and geographic location. Alcoholism has been shown to be influenced by genetic factors, and the question has been raised of why alcoholism is so infrequent in oriental countries. At one time it was thought that the genes that encode enzymes of alcohol metabolism have an allele found in East Asian individuals that protects against alcoholism (Chen et al., 1999). This view is held less strongly currently, but the possibility of a genetic factor influencing this protection has not been ruled out.

In summary, cultural and diversity issues impact the problem of neurobehavioral disorders in numerous ways. The assessment process may be substantially affected by sociocultural differences, particularly when the cultural background of the tester and the culture in which the test was produced differ from that of the patient. Culture and geography influence the relative prevalences and incidences of the neurobehavioral disorders sometimes in a Draconian way, as in the case of the HIV/AIDS epidemics. Population migration of groups with differing genetic constitutions may substantially influence the frequency of appearance of some diseases, with the distance between locations sometimes being very small.

BEHAVIORAL TREATMENT

The treatment of patients with neurobehavioral disorders is substantially different from the treatment of most psychiatric disorders. Psychotherapy, a major method used in varying forms by clinical psychologists and psychiatrists, is rarely used except during the course of head-injury rehabilitation. Psychopharmacological agents are used primarily for treatment of ancillary disorders such as depression following a head injury, but not as direct treatment for the head injury itself. Educational and vocational counseling may be used for younger individuals, mostly people who have had head injuries or veterans with battle wounds, if there is potential for return to school or work.

The choice of treatment used is largely dependent on the severity of the dementia. With more severely impaired patients, treatment is largely case management, in which a professionally trained individual, usually a nurse or social worker, follows the patient and works with the family or other caretakers to provide an optimal adjustment and to solve problems as they occur. If the individual is in a nursing home, the caseworker, when available, works with nursing home staff. In institutional settings in particular clients may receive reality orientation therapy or some systematic program to maintain orientation to time, space, and person and contact with the environment. During the end-stage of the illness, individuals may require assistance in self-care, often including personal hygiene, toileting, dressing, and eating.

For patients with moderate or mild dementia the treatment of choice is speech-language therapy or cognitive rehabilitation. Speech-language therapy is typically used for patients with aphasia and constitutes a variety of methods depending on the severity of impairment and the type of language disorder. Special programs are available for difficulties in pronunciation, word finding difficulties, disability in forming sentences, difficulties in comprehension of spoken or written language, and handwriting and calculation deficits. Speech-language pathology is an independent discipline for professional individuals who assess and treat patients with speech and language disturbances.

A form of treatment generally known as cognitive rehabilitation aims to remediate or restore cognitive abilities impaired as a result of brain damage. The methods used are specific to the domain of function being addressed, so that cognitive rehabilitation can involve treatment of disorders of abstract reasoning and problem solving, attention, memory, perceptual and motor abilities, and spatial cognition. As indicated, language disorders are typically treated by speech-language pathologists. Cognitive rehabilitation is available at most rehabilitation hospitals and is generally implemented or supervised by clinical neuropsychologists. Numerous programs are available, many of which are manualized and supported with specifically programmed software in cases in which a computer is used in the procedure. Sometimes cognitive rehabilitation includes treatment of specific maladaptive behaviors such as assaultiveness or incontinence, generally using behavior therapy designs. The training is sometimes supported by appropriate prosthetics that may be as simple as a notepad that the patient learns to use to record things to be remembered or more elegant, small computerlike devices that contain information the patient may need to access. Sometimes the training consists largely of teaching the patient to use the device.

The training generally consists of a fixed number of sessions during which the patient is taught or coached to use some method that will support improvement of some target ability. The clearest examples come from memory retraining. The design of this training is based on a combination of educational technology and the theoretical psychology of memory. Memory improves with the number of repeated trials, and efforts have been made to apply knowledge from the experimental psychology of memory to rehabilitation. Such basic concepts as the distinction between massed and spaced learning, the organization of lists into semantic categories, and, perhaps most important, the application of self-initiated cues to support remembering have all been applied. In the case of cuing, a great deal of emphasis has been placed on imagery and organization. For example, patients are taught to form pictorial images based on words in a list or to make up stories connecting the words. Other techniques, such as errorless learning, are also used to prevent making errors during learning, thereby benefiting retention. More practical methods, such as teaching a patient to keep a notebook to record appointments and other things to be remembered or to use a personal reminder, are often used. Extensive reviews concerning memory training are found in Wilson and Moffat (1984) and Beers and Goldstein (1998).

A comprehensive system of training attention was developed by Sohlberg and Mateer (1987). This is a manualized computer-supported method that has specific training programs for levels of attention. The levels trained are focused, sustained, selective, alternating, and divided attention. A training program for spatial cognition was devised some time ago involving teaching right hemisphere stroke patients to do the Wechsler Block Design test, seeking generalization to improved activities of daily living (Ben-Yishay, Diller, Gerstman, & Gordon, 1970). Programs have been developed for unilateral neglect, the half visual field inattention syndrome found in some stroke patients, particularly those with right cerebral hemisphere strokes. The most well-known programs for abstraction and problem-solving ability are those that successfully improve performance on the Wisconsin Card Sorting Test by patients with Schizophrenia (Green et al., 1992). Although patients with structural brain lesions were not included in this research, the technique itself represents a model for doing cognitive rehabilitation through the use of task simplification and cuing. Goldman (1990) and collaborators developed a series of programs involving complex attentional and problem-solving abilities for individuals with chronic alcoholism based on the Trail Making Test and other neuropsychological tests of learning and speed of information processing.

We have provided only some examples of a multitude of training programs designed for rehabilitation of patients with brain damage. These programs are often available in the form of kits containing a manual and the necessary equipment and software. Many of them are computer-assisted. In addition to the training programs, there has been some movement toward the development of "cognitive prostheses," which are devices patients may use to support memory, direction finding, and other cognitive abilities. Commercially available personal reminders and hand-held computers are sometimes helpful, but for some neurologically impaired individuals these require special engineering.

MEDICAL TREATMENT

As indicated, this group of patients have medical illnesses or problems that typically require treatment specific to those individual problems. Thus, patients who sustained head trauma may be taking anticonvulsant drugs, patients with stroke may be taking antihypertensive agents, and patients with infection may be taking antibiotics. The list goes on through essentially the entire gamut of diseases. Other than pharmacological treatment, the most used medical treatment for neurological disorders is surgery where it is indicated. Patients with brain cancer may receive radiation therapies. Patients with mobility disabilities often receive physical and occupational therapy. These patients may also receive treatment by physiatrists, who may coordinate programs of medication and physical interventions such as fitting of prosthetics and nerve regeneration procedures. There is an extensive technology of wheelchair design developed by rehabilitation engineers with expertise in that area. Manual and motorized chairs are now often designed around the pattern of sensory and manual impaired and preserved abilities demonstrated by the patient.

With regard to psychiatric medications, as indicated, the traditional anti-anxiety, antidepression, and antipsychotic drugs are sometimes used to treat the secondary consequences of neurobehavioral disorders. Patients with psychoses who sustain brain damage are typically continued on their antipsychotic medications. The anti-anxiety and antidepression drugs may be used as indicated. There are several specific problems that sometimes arise in the case of some of the neurobehavioral disorders. Suicide may emerge as a high risk during the earlier stages of multiple sclerosis and

Huntington's disease and may be appropriately managed with antidepressant medication. There is frequently an association between alcoholism and depression, and antidepression medication may be a consideration in such cases. However, as dementia progresses into the severe range, the likelihood of depression diminishes. In some cases, patients who sustained head injury may develop problems with impulsivity, and antimanic or other medication that controls impulsivity may be required.

The cognitive enhancers have been taking on an increasingly important role in the treatment of dementia. As indicated, they are a class of medications designed to alternatively improve cognitive function in dementia or delay the progression of the illness. Most of these drugs are cholinesterase inhibitors, the most widely used being donepezil (Aricept). Numerous studies have documented that use of this drug is associated with improvement on objective measures of cognitive function in patients with severe Alzheimer's disease (Gauthier et al., 2002; Winblad et al., 2006). Other, similar drugs are rivastigmine, galantamine, metrifonate, and memantine, all of which have been reported to have cognitive enhancement effects. These drugs are being used in extensive research efforts, and the present findings are apparently quite promising with regard to improvement and preservation of function.

SOME TYPICAL SCENARIOS

Because of the enormous diversity of the neurobehavioral disorders associated with structural brain damage it is not possible to provide a single case description that is representative of anything but the specifics of the disorder chosen. Therefore, we here outline some of the presentations and courses of some of these disorders, focusing on those most commonly seen by clinicians in neuropsychiatric settings. We review history, presentation at onset, course, and outcome.

ALZHEIMER'S DISEASE

Individuals who go on to develop Alzheimer's disease typically have a normal infancy and childhood and continue functioning normally until, at the earliest, late middle age. There is now some suggestion that these individuals may exhibit subtle signs of cognitive dysfunction relative to peers (Snowdon et al., 1996), but that is not well established and is not sufficient to significantly impede normal development. During late middle age the individual may experience what is now termed mild cognitive impairment (MCI), usually marked by incidents of forgetfulness or language difficulties, notably verbal fluency. Not all individuals with MCI eventually develop Alzheimer's disease. That becomes apparent when memory failures become more prominent. After they do develop MCI, there is a somewhat varied course of cognitive deterioration that persists throughout the remainder of life. Several large epidemiological studies of survival showed that Alzheimer's disease increases the risk of mortality. For some time it has been estimated that survival is about 5 years from time of onset of the illness. A recent study puts the figure at 5.9 years (Ganguli, Dodge, Shen, Pandav, & deKosky, 2005). During that time there is an inexorable course of deterioration, eventually involving all cognitive abilities and self-care capacity, including language, which may become unintelligible during the last stages of the illness. Pneumonia and dehydration are often listed as causes of death.

HEAD INJURY

Head trauma is probably the most common neurological disorder in young adults. Assuming a car accident as the cause, the patient is often found unresponsive or unconscious. A scale called the Glasgow Coma Scale examines for eye opening, motor response, and verbal response. At the extreme there is no response to questions, no movement to command, and no eye opening even to a painful stimulus, with varying degrees in between. The coma may persist; if it lasts more than 4 weeks it is rated as extremely serious. When the patient wakes up from coma, a period of amnesia follows, called posttraumatic amnesia. It has what is called an anterograde-retrograde characteristic, in which memory is worst from the period just before the accident and during the accident itself and improves as time gets closer to the present. When the individual is fully alert and conscious it is appropriate to do a neuropsychological assessment or at least an extended mental status examination. Assessments at that time often reflect varying patterns of cognitive deficits, generally involving memory or the ability to learn new information. Depending on the site of the injury, there may be impairments of abstract reasoning and problem solving, language, spatial cognition, attention, or various perceptual and motor skills. If the injury is not extremely severe with substantial destruction of brain tissue, some degree of recovery may be anticipated over the following year. Sometimes recovery is not substantial, and sometimes the patient returns to apparently normal premorbid function. Recovery may be complicated by seizures or a personality change. The change has been described by Max et al. (2006) as in some cases involving the voluntary regulation of affect. Change resulting in Posttraumatic Stress Disorder has also been reported (Glaesser, Neuner, Lutgehetmann, Schmidt, & Elbert, 2004). Particularly in the case of younger individuals, management issues often involve ability to return to school or work. Often the recovery process begins in an inpatient unit, transferring to an outpatient rehabilitation facility in which counseling, speech-language therapy, cognitive rehabilitation, and physical therapy for any sensory or motor injuries sustained are available. An important extension of rehabilitation is supported employment, in which the trainee is provided with a real job, but a job coach is present at the work site who provides instruction, counseling, and support. It is generally reasonable to anticipate a good outcome in these cases if complicating factors can be minimized.

MULTIPLE SCLEROSIS

Individuals who go on to develop multiple sclerosis are typically normal until their mid-20s, at which time the first symptoms appear. These early signs may be an apparent difficulty with dexterity or difficulty walking because of dragging a foot. There may be changes in vision. The course that follows may take one of two directions. There is a progressive type of the disease in which deterioration of movement is linear, with no pauses in the progression. There is also a relapsing-remitting type in which there are periods of stability or improvement, followed by a reoccurrence of symptoms and further progression. In both cases, there is ultimate progression of disability. Cognitive changes are most notable during the final stages but are detectable through careful observation or formal testing through much of the course of the illness. The major impairments are in memory and attention, with good preservation of language. Currently treatment is available with immunosuppressant drugs that may slow the progression of the disorder. The disease is marked particularly by progressive loss of the ability to walk, but sometimes there are visual changes if the optic nerve is involved. Because of the increasing disability associated with the disease fatigue is often a major problem, as is susceptibility to other health problems. Pressure ulcers, urinary tract infections, and influenza are not uncommon, and the cause of death is not always the multiple sclerosis itself.

SUMMARY

Hopefully, these scenarios provide some impression of the diversity of the neurobehavioral disorders and of the differences in symptoms, course, implications for health status in general, and outcome. Although these are often incurable, progressive, and sometime rapidly terminal illnesses, there are recent signs of hope in the form of the cognitive enhancers for Alzheimer's disease, the effectiveness of speech-language therapy, cognitive rehabilitation, supported employment for head injury, and the use of immunosuppressants for multiple sclerosis.

REFERENCES

Allen, D. N., Goldstein, G., Heyman, R. A., & Rondinelli, T. (1998). Teaching memory strategies to persons with multiple sclerosis. *Journal of Rehabilitation Research and Development, 35,* 405–410.

American Psychiatric Association. (1980). *Diagnostic and statistical manual of mental disorders* (3rd ed.). Washington, DC: Author.

American Psychiatric Association. (1994). *Diagnostic and statistical manual of mental disorders* (4th ed.). Washington, DC: Author.

Beers, S. R., & Goldstein, G. (1998). Assessment and planning for memory retraining. In G. Goldstein & S. R. Beers (Eds.), *Human brain function—Assessment and rehabilitation: Vol. 4. Rehabilitation* (pp. 229–246). New York: Plenum Press.

Ben-Yishay, Y., Diller, L., Gerstman, L., & Gordon, W. (1970). Relationship between initial competence and ability to profit from cues in brain-damaged individuals. *Journal of Abnormal Psychology, 78,* 248–259.

Blessed, G., Tomlinson, B. E., & Roth, M. (1968). The association between quantitative measures of dementia and of senile changes in the cerebral grey matter of elderly subjects. *British Journal of Psychiatry, 114,* 797–811.

Brouwer, K. C., Strathdee, S. A., Magis-Rodriguez, C., Bravo-Garcia, E., Gayet, C., Patterson, T. L., et al. (2006). Estimated numbers of men and women infected with HIV/AIDS in Tijuana, Mexico. *Journal of Urban Health, 83,* 299–307.

Brown, R. F., Tennant, C. C., Dunn, S. M., & Pollard, J. D. (2005). A review of stress-relapse interactions in multiple sclerosis: Important features and stress-mediating and-moderating variables. *Multiple Sclerosis, 11,* 477–484.

Butters, M. A., Goldstein, G., Allen, D. N., & Shemansky, W. J. (1998). Neuropsychological similarities and differences among Huntington's disease, multiple sclerosis, and cortical dementia. *Archives of Clinical Neuropsychology, 13,* 721–735.

Champagne, M. T. (1987). The NEECHAM Confusion Scale: Assessing acute confusion in the hospitalized elderly. *Gerontologist, 27,* 4a.

Chen, C. C., Lu, R. B., Chen, Y. C., Wang, M. F., Chang, Y. C., Li, T. K., et al. (1999). Interaction between the functional polymorphisms of the alcohol-metabolism genes in protection against alcoholism. *American Journal of Human Genetics, 65,* 795–807.

Couzin, J. (2006). Cell biology: The prion protein has a good side? You bet. *Science, 311,* 1091.

Cox, R. D., & Schopler, E. (1993). Aggression and self-injurious behaviors in persons with autism: The TEACCH (Treatment and Education of Autistic and related Communications Handicapped Children) approach. *Acta Paedopsychiatrica, 56,* 85–90.

deRooij, S. E., Schurmans, M. J., van der Mast, R. C., & Levi, M. (2005). Clinical subtypes of delirium and their relevance for daily clinical practice: A systematic review. *International Journal of Geriatric Psychiatry, 20,* 609–615.

Folstein, M. F., Folstein, S. E., & McHugh, P. R. (1975). Mini-Mental State: A practical method for grading the cognitive state of patients for the clinician. *Journal of Psychiatric Research, 12,* 189–198.

Ganguli, M., Dodge, H. H., Shen, C., Pandav, R. S., & deKosky, S. T. (2005). Alzheimer disease and mortality: A 15-year epidemiological study. *Archives of Neurology, 62,* 779–784.

Gauthier, S., Feldman, H., Hecker, J., Vellas, B., Emir, B., Subbiah, P., et al. (2002). Functional, cognitive, and behavioral effects of donepezil in patients with moderate Alzheimer's disease. *Current Medical Research Opinion, 18,* 347–354.

Geschwind, N. (1984). Cerebral dominance in biological perspective. *Neuropsychologia, 22,* 675–83.

Glaesser, J., Neuner, F., Lutgehetmann, R., Schmidt, R., & Elbert, T. (2004). Posttraumatic stress disorder in patients with traumatic brain injury. *BMC Psychiatry, 4,* 5.

Goldberg, T. E., & Weinberger, D. R. (1988). Probing prefrontal function in schizophrenia with neuropsychological paradigms. *Schizophrenia Bulletin, 14,* 179–183.

Goldman, M. S. (1990). Experience-dependent neuropsychological recovery and the treatment of chronic alcoholism. *Neuropsychology Review, 1,* 75–101.

Goldstein, G. (1978). Cognitive and perceptual differences between schizophrenics and organics. *Schizophrenia Bulletin, 4,* 160–185.

Goldstein, G. (1994). Neurobehavioral heterogeneity in schizophrenia. *Archives of Clinical Neuropsychology, 9,* 265–276.

Goldstein, G. (1997). The clinical utility of standardized or flexible battery approaches to neuropsychological assessment. In G. Goldstein & T. Incagnoli (Eds.), *Contemporary approaches to neuropsychological assessment* (pp. 67–91) New York: Plenum Press.

Gouws, E., White, P. J., Stover, J., & Brown, T. (2006). Short term estimates of adult HIV incidence by mode of transmission: Kenya and Thailand as examples. *Sexually Transmitted Infections, 82,* 51–55.

Green, M. F., Kern, R. S., Braff, D. L., & Mintz, J. (2000). Neurocognitive deficits and functional outcome in schizophrenia: Are we measuring the "right stuff"? *Schizophrenia Bulletin, 26,* 119–136.

Green, M. F., Satz, P., Ganzell, S., & Vaclav, J. F. (1992). Wisconsin Card Sorting Test performance in schizophrenia: Remediation of a stubborn deficit. *American Journal of Psychiatry, 149,* 62–67.

Gusella, J. F., MacDonald, M. F., Ambrose, C. M., & Duyao, M. P. (1993). Molecular genetics of Huntington's disease. *Archives of Neurology, 50,* 1157–1163.

Heaton, R. K., Grant, I., Butters, N., White, D. A., Kirson, D., Atkinson, J. H., et al. (1995). The HNRC 500: Neuropsychology of HIV infection at different disease stages—HIV Neurobehavioral Research Center. *Journal of the International Neuropsychological Society, 1,* 231–251.

Heilman, K. M., & Valenstein, E. (Eds.). (2003). *Clinical neuropsychology* (4th ed.). New York: Oxford University Press.

Hill, S. Y., Shen, S., Zezza, N., Hoffman, E. K., Perlin, M., & Allan, W. (2004). A genome wide search for alcoholism susceptibility genes. *American Journal of Medical Genetics. B: Neuropsychiatry Genetics, 128,* 102–113.

Kasari, C., Freeman, S., & Paparella, T. (2006). Joint attention and symbolic play in young children with autism: A randomized controlled intervention study. *Journal of Child Psychology and Psychiatry, 47,* 611–620.

Klunk, W. E., Engler, H., Nordberg, A., Wang, Y., Blomqvist, G., Holt, D. P., et al. (2004). Imaging brain amyloid in Alzheimer's disease with Pittsburgh Compound-B. *Annals of Neurology, 55,* 306–319.

Lemiengre, J., Nelis, T., Joosten, E., Braes, T., Foreman, M., Gastmans, C., et al. (2006). Detection of delirium by bedside nurses using the confusion assessment method. *Journal of the American Geriatric Society, 54,* 685–689.

Lezak, M. D., Howieson, D. B., & Loring, D. W. (Eds.). (2004). *Neuropsychological assessment* (4th ed.). New York: Oxford University Press.

Lopez, O. L., Becker, J. T., Jagust, W. J., Fitzpatrick, A., Carlson, M. C., DeKosky, S. T., et al. (2006). Neuropsychological characteristics of mild cognitive impairment subgroups. *Journal of Neurology, Neurosurgery, and Psychiatry, 77,* 159–165.

Luria, A. R. (1973). *The working brain.* New York: Basic Books.

Mattis, S. (1998). *Dementia Rating Scale (DRS).* Odessa FL: Psychological Assessment Resources.

Max, J. E., Levin, H. S., Schachar, R. J., Landis, J., Saunders, A. E., Ewing-Cobbs, L., et al. (2006). Predictors of personality change due to traumatic brain injury in children and adolescents 6 to 24 months after injury. *Journal of Neuropsychiatry and Clinical Neuroscience, 18,* 21–32.

McGuigan, C., Dunne, C., Crowley, J., Hagan, R., Rooney, G., Lawlor, E., et al. (2005). Population frequency of HLA haplotypes contributes to the prevalence difference of multiple sclerosis in Ireland. *Journal of Neurology, 252,* 1245–1248.

McKeith, I., Mintzer, J., Aarsland, D., Burn, D., Chiu, H., Cohen-Mansfield, J., et al. (2004). Dementia with Lewy bodies. *Lancet Neurology, 3,* 19–28.

Milberg, W. P., Hebben, N., & Kaplan, E. (1996). The Boston process approach to neuropsychological assessment. In I. Grant & K. M. Adams (Eds.), *Neuropsychological assessment of neuropsychiatric disorders* (2nd ed., pp. 58–80). New York: Oxford University Press.

Minshew, N. J., Goldstein, G., & Siegel, D. J. (1997). Neuropsychologic functioning in autism: Profile of a complex information processing disorder. *Journal of the International Neuropsychological Society, 3,* 303–316.

Mirsky, A. F., Rosvold, H. E., & Pribram, K. H. (1957). Effects of cingulectomy on social behavior in monkeys. *Journal of Neurophysiology, 20,* 588–601.

Muhle, R., Trentacoste, S. V., & Rapin, I. (2004). The genetics of autism. *Pediatrics, 113,* 472–486.

Nell, V. (2004). Translation and test administration techniques to meet the assessment needs of ethnic minorities, migrants, and refugees. In G. Goldstein & S. R. Beers (Eds.), *Comprehensive handbook of psychological assessment: Vol. 1. Intellectual and neuropsychological assessment* (pp. 333–338). Hoboken NJ: Wiley.

Panisset, M., Roudier, M., Saxton J., & Boller, F. (1994). Severe impairment battery: A neuropsychological test for severely demented patients. *Archives of Neurology, 51,* 41–45.

Paulsen, J. S., Hoth, K. F., Nehl, C., & Stierman, L. (2005). Critical periods of suicide risk in Huntington's disease. *American Journal of Psychiatry, 162,* 725–731.

Prigatano, G. P., & Pribram, K. H. (1982). Perception and memory of facial affect following brain injury. *Perceptual and Motor Skills, 54,* 859–69.

Reitan, R. M., & Wolfson, D. (1993). *The Halstead-Reitan Neuropsychological Test Battery: Theory and clinical applications* (2nd ed.). Tucson, AZ: Neuropsychology Press.

Reitan, R. M., & Wolfson, D. (1995). The influence of age and education on neuropsychological test results. *Clinical Neuropsychologist, 9,* 151–158.

Rosselli, M., & Ardila, A. (2003). The impact of culture and education on non-verbal neuropsychological measurement: A critical review. *Brain and Cognition, 52,* 326–333.

Rutter, M. (1983). Cognitive deficits in the pathogenesis of autism. *Journal of Child Psychology and Psychiatry and Allied Disciplines, 24,* 513–531.

Schoenfeld, M., Myers, R. H., Cupples, L. A., Berkman, B., Sax, D. S., & Clark, E. (1984). Increased rate of suicide among patients with Huntington's disease. *Journal of Neurology, Neurosurgery, and Psychiatry, 47,* 1283–1287.

Seaton, B. E., Goldstein, G., & Allen, D. N. (2001). Sources of heterogeneity in schizophrenia: The role or neuropsychological functioning. *Neuropsychology Review, 11,* 45–67.

Siegel, D. J., Goldstein, G., & Minshew, N. J. (1996). Designing instruction for the high-functioning autistic individual. *Journal of Developmental and Physical Disabilities, 8,* 1–19.

Snowdon, D. A., Kemper, S. J., Mortimer, J. A., Greiner, L. H., Wekstein, D. R., & Markesbery, W. R. (1996). Linguistic ability in early life and cognitive function and Alzheimer's disease in late life: Findings from the Nun Study. *Journal of the American Medical Association, 275,* 528–532.

Sohlberg, M. M., & Mateer, C. A. (1987). Effectiveness of an attention-training program. *Journal of Clinical and Experimental Neuropsychology, 9,* 117–130.

Sohlberg, M. M., & Mateer, C. A. (2001). Improving attention and managing attentional problems: Adapting rehabilitation techniques to adults with ADD. *Annals of the New York Academy of Science, 931,* 359–375.

Sotak, C. H. (2002). The role of diffusion tensor imaging in the evaluation of ischemic brain injury: A review. *NMR Biomedicine, 15,* 561–569.

Soto, C., Estrada, L., & Castilla, J. (2006). Amyloids, prions and the inherent infectious nature of misfolded protein aggregates. *Trends in Biochemical Science.*

Spitzer, R. L., First, M. B., Williams, J. B., Kendler, K., Pincus, H. A., & Tucker, G. (1992). Now is the time to retire the term "organic mental disorders." *American Journal of Psychiatry, 149,* 240–244.

Spreen, O., & Strauss, E. (Eds.). (1998). *A compendium of neuropsychological tests* (2nd ed.). New York: Oxford University Press.

Tarter, R. E., Hegedus, A., Goldstein, G., Shelly, C., & Alterman, A. I. (1984). Adolescent sons of alcoholics: Neuropsychological and personality characteristics. *Alcoholism, Clinical and Experimental Research, 8,* 216–222.

Whalen, C., Schreibman, L., & Ingersoll, B. (2006). The collateral effects of joint attention training on social initiations, positive affect, imitation, and spontaneous speech in young children with autism. *Journal of Autism and Developmental Disorders, 36,* 655–664.

Wilson, B. A., & Moffat, N. (Eds.). (1984). *Clinical management of memory problems.* Rockville MD: Aspen.

Winblad, B., Kilander, L., Eriksson, S., Minthon, L., Batsman, S., Wetterholm, A. L., et al. (2006). Donepezil in patients with severe Alzheimer's disease: Double-blind, parallel-group, placebo-controlled study. *Lancet, 367,* 1057–1065.

Yoder, P., & Stone, W. L. (2006). Randomized comparison of two communication interventions for preschoolers with autism spectrum disorders. *Journal of Consulting and Clinical Psychology, 74,* 426–435.

Indebtedness is expressed to the Medical Research Service, Department of Veterans Affairs, for support of this work.

CHAPTER 19

Alcohol Abuse

F. MICHLER BISHOP

DESCRIPTION OF THE DISORDER

Despite similarities, many therapists find the treatment of most typical psychotherapeutic problems more rewarding and less difficult than that of alcohol abuse. Their beliefs and feelings about relapse are distinctly different as well. This chapter has two goals: (1) to encourage and motivate therapists to include clients who are having problems with alcohol in their practice, as there are many such clients who are not getting treatment and would benefit from it; and (2) to encourage and motivate therapists to develop an individualized, evidence-based approach for such clients, especially as we now have numerous ways to help them.

Why are therapists so hesitant to treat people with addictive problems? Certainly, therapists are concerned about helping people with serious health problems. According to Thomas Babor (2003, p. 1341), the lead author of *Alcohol: No Ordinary Commodity—Research and Public Policy*, sponsored jointly by the World Health Organization and the Society for the Study of Alcohol, "No other product so widely available to consumer use, not even tobacco, accounts for as much premature death and disability as alcohol." At least three factors may contribute to therapist hesitancy.

1. Clients suffering from many typical psychotherapeutic problems, including depression, anxiety, bipolar disorders, Obsessive-Compulsive Disorder, and Attention-Deficit/Hyperactivity Disorder, are in almost all cases motivated to get better. They want help. They do not want to be so depressed that they cannot get out of bed, and they do not want to be so anxious that they cannot make a speech, go to a meeting, or, in the case of agoraphobia, leave the house. When they come into a therapist's office, they want to feel better, and the therapist wants to help them feel better. They may have multiple problems, but they often appear motivated to get rid of them. Whether or not an individual client makes much progress is another matter, but to many therapists, the client has a problem, and the therapist believes that he or she knows how to help.

   In contrast, clients who are abusing alcohol are usually ambivalent and have "conflicting wants." They want to enjoy a fuller, less tumultuous life, *and* they want to continue to engage in their addictive behavior(s) as much as they can without getting into trouble. In one client's words, "I want to have a better life, but, at the same time, I seem to want to continue to drink and fool around, at least on occasion." Such clients can easily confuse and frustrate a therapist. They are motivated to change only sporadically and unpredictably. They may abstain or cut down for months or even years and then begin to abuse alcohol all over again, even to the point of becoming dependent. (Note: Clients who come for anger management problems are often equally ambivalent and undermotivated and often equally frustrating for many therapists. On a less serious level, procrastinators want to have a cleaner house or a less hectic life, but, at the same time, want to relax and put it off to tomorrow.)

2. When depressed or anxious clients relapse, therapists are sympathetic and know how to help them feel better and, ultimately, do better. However, when clients with alcohol problems relapse, many therapists believe that more choice is involved and they may not be as sympathetic. In truth, anxious and depressed clients may have contributed to their relapse by "choosing" to fall back into some old behavioral patterns, for example, staying home rather than going to the gym or to a self-help meeting; they may have stopped their medication as well. However, many therapists do not conceptualize or feel about an addictive relapse in the same way. No doubt, clients with addictive problems may cause an automobile accident or gamble away all of a family's savings, but a relapse into Major Depression or agoraphobia may also have serious consequences for everyone involved.

3. Therapists find working with the more traditional psychotherapeutic clients more rewarding. If they get better, such clients are often quite appreciative. That may not be the case with addictive clients, who may wonder which is worse, the "disease" or the cure. In addition, clients suffering from the more traditional psychotherapeutic problems may keep coming for appointments even though they do not really need them, and these are not difficult sessions for therapists.

Technically, according to the *Diagnostic and Statistical Manual of Mental Disorders* (*DSM-IV*), alcohol abuse is distinct from alcohol dependence; however, despite dissenters, abuse and dependence are increasingly being seen as existing on the same continuum, and the next version of the *DSM* may reflect this new thinking (Kahler, 2006). Currently, the criteria in the *DSM-IV* for a diagnosis of abuse focuses on the harmful consequences of repeated misuse, for example, in terms of relationships, job performance, and legal problems. A diagnosis of dependence involves additional factors, such as tolerance, withdrawal, and compulsive use. It is important to note that clinicians commonly meet people at serious risk because of alcohol misuse who do not meet the criteria for abuse or dependence but who can clearly benefit from treatment. As you will see in the case studies discussed at the end of the chapter, problems with alcohol consumption vary considerably between people and vary considerably across a lifetime. Vaillant (1996, p. 248), who has conducted one of the few long-term studies of alcohol addiction, starting over 50 years ago in Boston, concluded, "Rather than progressing, chronic alcohol abuse often appears merely to fluctuate in severity." Like dieting, people typically abuse alcohol on an on-again, off-again basis.

In the general population, alcohol use and misuse occur along a continuum and vary considerably with regard to age, gender, and ethnicity. The 2001–2002 National

Epidemiologic Survey of Alcohol and Related Conditions (Grant, Dawson, Stinson, Chou, Dufour, and Pickering, 2006; http://niaa.census.gov), for example, found that in the 18 to 29 age group, approximately 10% of White males abuse alcohol in contrast to approximate 6% of White females; abuse in the African American population in the same age group was approximately 7% for males and 2% for females. For Hispanic/Latino population, the numbers were 9% and 3%; for the Asian population, 5% and 4%; and for the Native American population 15% and 7%. Looking at the nation as a whole, although 9% of males 18 to 29 years old abuse alcohol, only 2% of the above-65 group does. Similar statistics are found for alcohol dependence, suggesting that on average approximately 8% of the population suffers from abuse or dependence with wide differences depending on age, gender, and ethnicity. Beyond abuse and dependence, "risky" and "problem" drinkers make up a large percentage of the total drinking population, and even moderate drinkers may engage in risky behavior. That is, they may have one or two more drinks than usual at a party, but insist on driving home anyway; tests would clearly show that, although not swerving on the road, their reaction times are significantly slower.

Over the past 70 years, most treatment has focused on the severely dependent people. Some of the myths about alcoholism stem from this group; they do comprise a difficult population to treat effectively, especially if "effective" means nothing but abstinence. However, there are many, many people who are abusing alcohol regularly or occasionally who could benefit from treatment. And the research is very clear that some of these people may be able to moderate their drinking.

It is also important to remember (and, sometimes, to tell clients) that several studies indicate that approximately 75% of the people who have problems with alcohol resolve those difficulties on their own without treatment (as do the majority of people who are addicted to heroin and cocaine; Finney, Moos, & Timko, 1999; L. C. Sobell, Cunningham, & Sobell, 1996; L. C. Sobell, Ellingstad, & Sobell, 2000; Toneatto, Sobell, Sobell, & Rubel, 1999; Tucker & King, 1999; Walters, 2000). This "natural recovery" has been well documented, and our role as therapists may be simply to accelerate this process. On the other hand, most of the people who find their way to a therapist's office have usually tried to moderate and then tried to abstain many, many times. They are not among the people who will recover naturally and, in fact, are often in serious difficulty and have finally reached out for professional help; consequently, they are often complex cases, but interesting and enjoyable as well.

DIAGNOSIS AND ASSESSMENT

To some degree, therapists in the alcohol treatment field face a marketing problem: How can we get more clients to come and talk to us and to come sooner rather than later? We know that many people who could benefit from treatment do not seek it.

What Is a Client Seeking?

In the tradition of Carl Rogers (2003), who created client-centered therapy, let us first consider what clients want from diagnosis and assessment. Many clients are looking for answers to three questions:

- Do I have a problem?
- How serious is it?
- What can I do about it?

In the initial session, fear, ambivalence, anger, and confusion are typical, especially ambivalence. The first appointment may be like going for an annual medical checkup. The client may have put off making the appointment for months or even years. Fearful questions abound: What will I find out? What will the therapist say? What will he or she say I have to do?

A client—even an adolescent or mandated client—has probably already spent quite a bit of time and effort trying to figure out whether he or she has a problem. Research suggests that many people have not sought out treatment because they have the preconceived notion that a therapist or counselor is going to say "You have to stop" and "You have to go to AA." That may *not* be what many therapists are going to say, but that is what many people *think* they are going to say, and clients may have already readied themselves to defend against such suggestions.

Consequently, it is especially important to make new clients feel comfortable and that they have found someone who is empathetic, nonjudgmental, and expert enough to help them resolve their difficulties. No one starts drinking saying to himself or herself, "Let's see how I can mess up my life." Traditionally, alcohol counseling has been aggressively confrontational, but many years of research by Miller and his associates (Miller, Benefield, & Tonigan, 1993) demonstrate that this is not an effective approach; in fact, such an approach usually increases the likelihood of relapse. In addition, recent research by Meyers, Miller, and their colleagues (Meyers, Miller, Hill, & Tonigan, 1999; Miller, Meyers, & Tonigan, 1999; see also Smith & Meyers, 2004) also suggests that there are more empathetic, supportive ways than the traditional Johnson (Johnson, 1989) interventionist approach to motivate people to enter treatment.

Note: There are many myths in the alcohol treatment field. One is that all "addicts" and "alcoholics" lie. This is part of the moral, characterological approach that has been so prevalent in the field for so many years. Fortunately, research indicates that this is *not* so (L. C. Sobell, Toneatto, & Sobell, 1994). Clients lie when telling the truth will get them thrown out of a program, cause them to lose their jobs, lead to a breakup in a relationship, or cause their therapist, at least in their minds, to react in a judgmental fashion. If telling the truth will not cause painful consequences, if they can feel assured that the consultation room's door is sealed tight, and if they feel that the therapist will not judge them critically, then more often than not, they will share their concerns about their use and their lapses and relapses and their feelings about other issues that may haunt their lives. As is true in regular psychotherapy, clients may lie by omission for many sessions before telling their therapist about some especially upsetting event or behavior. Clients may be willing to talk about many issues but be afraid that they will be judged if they disclose that they regularly overdrink; they are afraid that they will be judged as they know society judges them, and as they may be judging themselves.

What Should the Therapist Seek?

The problem of getting people with alcohol problems into treatment and engaged in therapy is not trivial. A depressed person may eagerly seek treatment. A person with an alcohol problem often avoids it. That makes answers to two questions critically important: What can a therapist do to enhance the likelihood that someone will come for the first session? and What can the therapist do during the first session to increase the likelihood that the client will return?

The research into brief interventions and motivational interviewing make very clear that clients may make significant changes after very brief interactions with a therapist, counselor, nurse, or doctor (see later discussion). Although there is insufficient evidence to tell a therapist what to do in all cases, there is research evidence that strongly suggest what *not* to do:

- There are no data that support being strongly confrontational with a client. Instead, there are data that suggest that such behavior will increase drinking and shorten the time to relapse.
- There are no research data to support the idea that a client must acknowledge that he or she is an alcoholic or an addict before he or she can begin to recover.
- Sending someone to AA may help, but there is no evidence that every client *must* go in order to "recover."
- There are no research data that suggest that inpatient treatment works better than outpatient treatment for all people.

The most important objective of the first session is to get a second session. It makes sense to do whatever is reasonable to motivate a client to make and to keep a second appointment (see the menu of options later in the chapter). And if clients do not show up for the next appointment, a simple telephone call has been shown to significantly increase follow-up visits (Koumans, Muller, & Miller, 1967). The style and tone—what some people in the motivational interviewing field call the "spirit" of the approach—contribute significantly to whether a client returns, but providing practical suggestions will probably also increase the return rate. Ideally, clients will leave the first session (1) feeling heard; (2) with more information regarding their problem, the severity of the problem, and what they can do; and (3) with one or more practical things to do between sessions.

During the first session, therapists seek answers to many questions, including the following:

1. Is there a problem, or are there problems?
2. If there are multiple problems, how many problems are there, and how do they seem to interact?
3. How serious are the various problems?
4. How ready is the client to work on the various problems?
5. What stage of change (see later discussion) do clients seem to be in for each problem?
6. What other forms of therapy have they tried? What have they learned that has been helpful?
7. What is the evidence from their past that they *can* change? (What addictive behavior, if any, have they changed? What nonaddictive behaviors have they changed?)
8. What do they know about cognitive-behavioral therapy, rational-emotive behavioral therapy, or some other form of therapy?
9. What are their external resources (family, children, employment, religion, hobbies)?
10. What does an addictive episode look like from beginning to end?
11. What do they get from or like about their addictive behavior?
12. What might they like to change about their addictive behavior?

13. What should be focused on first?
14. What might they be willing to do during the coming week?
15. What might derail them, and how likely is it that they will be derailed?

For a general clinical practitioner, the Alcohol Use Disorders Identification Test (AUDIT; Babor & Grant, 1989; Saunders, Aasland, Babor, De la Fuente, & Grant, 1993) is the best brief screening instrument available, especially as it is also good for detecting problem drinking, and it is free. It also is better than the well-known CAGE test for assessing problem drinking; a score of 8 or more on the AUDIT indicates that a person is at risk for alcohol-related problems. It is also reportedly more effective than the CAGE with women and African American and Mexican American clients (Steinbauer, Cantor, Holzer, & Volk, 1998). The Brief Drinker's Profile provides therapists with an interview format to use to assess drinking patterns, quantity, frequency, family history, and recent history of alcohol problems. It is available online as part of the Drinkers Check-up (www.drinkerscheckup.com; Hester, Squires, & Delaney, 2005). There are many other, related instruments available, most in the public domain (cf. http://casaa.unm.edu); Miller, Westerberg, and Waldron (2003) provide an excellent review for both adults and adolescents.

SUBSEQUENT SESSIONS: ONGOING ASSESSMENT

Being active in a session may be common to some therapists, but many therapists, both those trained in psychodynamic therapies and those trained in Rogerian-like approaches, have a tendency to listen during a session and do little else. Considering that many therapists are empathetic people and want to help others feel better, it is easy for a therapist to slide into talking about the client's depression or anxiety, and the session may be practically over before getting to the addictive problem. Prior to any session, reviewing the notes and then the menu of options helps a therapist decide on which three or four exercises or approaches might work best. Doing a cost-benefit analysis, a standard functional analysis, or a time effects analysis (see Bishop, 2001) often reveals new aspects of the addictive behavioral patterns, as well as other issues that the client may not have mentioned in prior sessions.

CONCEPTUALIZATION

Like religion and politics, most people have impassioned beliefs on one side or the other about how addictions ought to be treated. In the United States, the vast majority of treatment providers strongly believe in the 12-step approach, and the vast majority of treatment facilities are 12-step-focused. Over time, many factors have been thought to cause addictions, including moral decrepitude, characterological weakness, spiritual disconnectedness, family system dynamics, cognitive deficits, genetic predispositions, and, most recently, brain chemistry imbalances, and treatments reflects the underlying assumptions of each.

Originally, alcoholism was conceptualized as a primary, progressive disease. Now there is more evidence that this is not the case. As Vaillant (2003, p. 1048) notes, "One of the most surprising findings was that alcohol abusers—if after one or two decades they did not remit or become alcohol-dependent—could continue to abuse alcohol for decades more without clear progression to dependence." What may occur varies tremendously from person to person and over time. People move back and

Table 19.1
Relapse Rates

Alcoholism	30%–60%
Asthma	60%–80%
Cocaine dependence	40%–50%
Diabetes	30%–50%
Nicotine dependence	60%–80%
Opioid dependence	20%–50%

Source: From "Myths about the Treatment of Addiction" (pp. 309–314), by C. P. O'Brien and A. T. McClellan, in *Principles of Addiction Medicine,* third edition, A. W. Graham and T. K. Schultz (Eds.), 1998, Chevy Chase, MD: American Society of Addiction Medicine.

forth between periods of abstinence, controlled drinking, and full alcohol abuse. Some people may spend relatively long periods—2, 3, and even more than 5 years—being abstinent, and then resume drinking (Schuckit, Tipp, Smith, & Bucholz, 1997). O'Brien and McClellan (1998) have argued that addictions are not dissimilar from many other human health problems. Like diabetes, asthma, and hypertension, all share the following characteristics: (a) Relapse rates are high (see Table 19.1); (b) no one gene or factor (e.g., personality, familial, environmental) *causes* the problem; (c) even when a genetic predisposition may exist, a variety of lifestyle factors and behavioral factors—diets high in sugar and/or cholesterol, lack of exercise, smoking, stress—all seem to affect whether any of these afflictions manifest themselves; (d) behavioral and lifestyle decisions affect the severity and rates of relapse; and (e) patients have difficulty continuing to follow what has been shown to help: medications and various behavioral and diet changes.

The public health model suggests that any public health problem results from a combination of three factors: the agent (in this case, alcohol), the host (in this case, the drinker), and the environment. As a result, laws are common limiting the age at which alcohol may be purchased and the hours and places it may be sold; evidence-based treatment approaches have been created and tested; and medications have been developed and are being developed to interrupt or stop the effects of ethanol on the body.

When a new client sits down in a therapist's office, it is important to keep the following in mind:

1. The client may be suffering from a problem very similar to a serious, chronic, life-threatening illness. If this is the case, the therapist needs to figure out how to help him or her accept this reality and learn to manage the problem (and the accompanying other psychological and practical problems) as effectively as possible. The best model may be an internist model; many internists help people manage chronic illnesses without becoming judgmental or exasperated, despite the fact that many patients ignore their advice and relapse frequently.
2. On the other hand, a client's addiction may be like an addiction to nicotine, in which case, he or she can overcome the problem completely. At a certain point

in his or her life, the client may choose to abstain and stick to that decision for the remainder of his or her life.

3. Finally, a client may be able to resolve his or her alcohol problems by moderating his or her behavior, a common path for millions of people.

Because clients with addictive behaviors are not always clear about what they want, Prochaska and DiClemente's (DiClemente, 2006; Prochaska & DiClemente, 1982; Prochaska, DiClemente, & Norcross, 1992) well-known transtheoretical model of change has been helpful in conceptualizing treatment (see, however, criticism of the model, e.g., Sutton, 2005, West, 2005). Although there are six stages in that model—precontemplation, contemplation, preparation, action, maintenance, and termination—it may help to think of clients as coming in three general types. The vast majority, approximately 80% to 85%, are ambivalent, not sure about what they want to do or what they can do. About 10% know they want to change; they know that they want to stop or moderate their drinking and are motivated to do so. The remaining 10% do not think they have a problem; they are in precontemplation; they are in therapy because someone threatened to leave them or to fire them or because a judge mandated them to come. The goal of therapy is to help them move from one stage of change to the next.

Our job would be simpler if we had only to sense where our client was in terms of the stages of change model and could proceed to use techniques that have been shown to be effective at that stage. But most of our clients have multiple problems, addictive as well as nonaddictive, and are in different stages on each. They may want to cut down or stop cocaine use but not drinking; at the same time, they may claim they do not have an anger management problem, but their spouse says they do; they also seem to be suffering from two or three other diagnosable psychiatric disorders. Where to begin and how to help is always a challenge. The stages of change model helps in at least three ways. It can help therapists decide, given the stage of the client on a particular problem, which techniques to use. It helps clients understand that change does not usually come in a straight line; slips and full-blown relapses are common. And the model helps prevent therapist burnout. It helps us be more accepting of the real nature of change without becoming demoralized.

LEARNING AND MODELING

As will become more evident in the section on Behavioral Treatments, most of the prevalent, evidence-based, non-medication treatments are based on the idea that people have learned how to drink and can learn how to drink less or not at all. The underlying assumption is that humans can direct their own behavior change. Brief interventions and, more specifically, motivational interviewing are based on the idea that if people are given responsibility for behavior change, feedback about their behavior, and treatment in an empathetic manner, they will change their behavior. Social skills training, behavioral marital therapy, behavior contracting, behavioral self-control training, and the community reinforcement approach (CRA) all explicitly teach clients a variety of skills to help them cope better with urges and high-risk situations. Some include components or modules to improve interpersonal communications and marital and family relationships. Other approaches focus on changing the drinker's environment and the manner in which that environment reinforces both drinking and nondrinking behavior. For example, both the CRA and its related community reinforcement and family therapy (CRAFT) explicitly work to enhance behavior change by altering the way reinforcement occurs. The latter approach teaches concerned significant others how to respond differently to both the drinking and the nondrinking behavior of the identified person, that is, how to not reinforce drinking behavior and how to reinforce nondrinking behavior.

Many other aspects of human functioning are being examined for clues into addictive behavioral patterns, including individual differences in time perspective (Keough, Zimbardo, & Boyd, 1999), self-control strength (based on the idea that human energy resources are finite; Muraven, Collins, & Nienhaus, 2002), and the impact of behavioral economics (Tucker, Vuchinich, Black, & Rippens, 2006).

Marlatt and Gordon's (1985) seminal cognitive-behavioral model of relapse has been updated (Witkiewitz & Marlatt, 2004) to reflect the dynamic, multidimensional nature of relapse. The new model incorporates research findings into the impact on relapse of numerous factors, such as differences in self-efficacy, affect states, social support, motivation, coping skills, and outcome expectancies. The result is a much more complex, nonlinear model reflecting the interactive nature of many intrapersonal and interpersonal factors.

LIFE EVENTS

DiClemente (2003) asserts that the paths to developing alcohol problems and the paths to recovering from or resolving those problems are very similar. For example, initially, young people are not contemplating drinking or using drugs. But then they begin to consider doing so, often weighing the pros and cons. Without realizing it, they may begin to hang out with the young people in their school or neighborhood who are drinking or using, and one day, when offered, they may take a puff or a swig to experiment or to bond with their friends. Eventually, they move into the action and then into the maintenance phase, drinking more frequently and reorganizing their life and friendships to accommodate their new lifestyle.

Recovering, as we discussed earlier, often follows a similar pathway—if not so smoothly—but in reverse. The basic therapeutic approach of standard psychodynamic therapy focuses on life events, those that occurred many, many years ago as well as those that happened between sessions. Most current, empirically supported approaches do not spend much, if any, time on the past. However, there is ample evidence suggesting that life events may trigger genetic predispositions to drink. In addition, it is probably wise to remember that clients come into a therapist's office expecting to talk about their troubles, including the troubles they have had in earlier years. People like to talk about themselves, and one part of building a good therapeutic relationship involves listening carefully to what clients say. Moreover, therapists may be able to use past life events as motivational handles; they may be able to help their clients realize that alcohol use was an understandable way to cope with situations when they were young, but now the old way of coping has become addictive and destructive. How do they feel about repeating the old pattern again and again?

GENETIC INFLUENCES

To many readers, it may be obvious that people may inherit a predisposition to alcohol problems, but that may not be the case at all for a particular client. She may accept that "alcoholism runs in the family," but from that point on things are very confusing. Is she like her aunt who goes to AA regularly, her uncle who died "from drinking too much," or her mother who does not drink much at all or her father who "drinks every day" and occasionally is verbally abusive of all the family members? As a teenager, she always had to "walk on eggshells" around him, and she never dared to bring home friends because she never knew what condition he would be in.

Clients may be in a therapist's office in the hopes that he or she can give them a clear, unequivocal answer. In most instances, the therapist cannot. As with many physical ailments—diabetes, hypertension, and asthma—there is a genetic component. For example, twin studies indicate that 50% to 60% of alcohol dependence may be attributable to genetic factors (Tsuang, Bar, Harley, & Lyons, 2001). But it is difficult to know to what extent any one person has inherited a particular predisposition. And will the genetic predisposition manifest itself? Will other factors—environmental factors or lifestyle behaviors, to name only two—activate it? Inheriting a genetic predisposition to have problems with alcohol is not the same thing as a genetic predisposition to have blue eyes. A genetic predisposition in this case does not mean someone cannot do anything about it. Discussing with a client that she may have a genetic predisposition to problems with alcohol may help her to be more accepting of herself and her problems, and it may motivate her to do something more serious about it.

PHYSICAL FACTORS AFFECTING BEHAVIOR

No doubt, some clients who are abusing alcohol are doing so because they find it an effective, easily accessible, fast-acting analgesic. Alcohol is the only legal, fast-acting antidepressant on the market (albeit, also a depressant in approximately 2 hours). It is also a fast-acting anti-anxiety medication; others exist, for example, Xanex and Valium, but they require a prescription and people get in trouble with them as well. The combined impact may, for some, reduce the physical pain that they are experiencing and cause them to develop alcohol problems.

Similarly, people who are obese or physically disabled may find solace in alcohol. And for many people, alcohol facilitates social connections. Of course, as members of AA note, some people eventually substitute "rum for relationships," but for many others, it is a way to join in with other people. If a client frequently experiences feelings of isolation, rejection, and alienation, drinking with someone or alone may alleviate or eliminate those feelings.

DRUGS AFFECTING BEHAVIOR

Polysubstance abuse is common, if not the norm. Many, if not most, of our clients use and abuse a variety of drugs, and they may be dependent on one or more of them. Alcohol is more commonly the trigger to other drug use than the reverse. For example, men who occasionally abuse cocaine often begin with alcohol (and often end the evening with unprotected sex). However, if other drugs are not available, alcohol may be substituted. In the well-known case of Vietnam soldiers (Robins, Helzer, & Davis, 1975), when beer and liquor were not available, many used and abused, and some became addicted to readily available heroin. However, when they returned to the States, the vast majority quit heroin on their own and returned to alcohol; some of those men also then went on to become dependent on alcohol. In a study of natural recovery from cocaine use (Toneatto et al., 1999), 56% reported switching to other drugs (e.g., cannabis and alcohol) as a way to maintain their decision to stop using cocaine.

CULTURAL AND DIVERSITY ISSUES

All cultures in all parts of the worlds have discovered a way to produce alcoholic beverages. Babylonians are supposed to have believed that the best decisions could be arrived at by discussing the issue first sober and then intoxicated. Wine is an integral part of many rituals in many religions, perhaps the most famous being Holy Communion among Christians, but wine is also an important part of the seder and of the Jewish wedding ceremony. Although three of the world's major religions—Buddhism, Islam, and Mormonism—specifically prohibit the consumption of alcohol, not all members follow that prohibition. And toasting of important events is common throughout the world. Consequently, it is not surprising that in almost all cultures alcohol is used and abused. However, whereas in the United States drinking more than 14 drinks per week is considered heavy drinking, such consumption in many European cultures is quite common. For example, many French, Spanish, and Italians routinely drink wine with both lunch and dinner and are not considered to be problem drinkers.

Ethnic groups in the United States are groups in only the most superficial sense. I doubt many "non-Hispanic White" readers would put much credence in any statement about "Europeans" suggesting that Greeks, Swedes, Germans, and English (to name only a few) think and behave in a manner similar enough to be grouped in a meaningful way. Even within a country with a relatively homogeneous population (becoming rarer and rarer these days), there are significant differences in the way people from different economic and social strata think and behave.

As noted earlier, the NIAAA study (Grant et al., 2006) found considerable ethnic differences in alcohol abuse and dependence. Castro, Proescholdbell, Abeita, and Rodriquez (1999), in their review of ethnic and cultural issues in the treatment of substance abuse, argue that ethnicity per se does not predispose someone to develop a substance abuse problem. However, "adverse life conditions such as poverty, racial discrimination, and alienation from mainstream social institutions" (p. 500), may contribute to the development of an addiction. They quote a 1993 Substance Abuse and Mental Health Services Administration study that showed the following: Non-Hispanic Whites made up approximately 74.4% of the U.S. population in 1993 and 81% of the heavy drinkers entering treatment; African Americans made up 11.9% of the population, but only 9% of the heavy drinkers entering treatment; the numbers for the Hispanic/Latino population were 9.7% and 9.0% The same report found considerable variations in the "primary substance upon treatment entry" for alcohol: non-Hispanic Whites, 67.8%; African Americans, 39.0%; Hispanics/Latinos, 46.2%; Asian Americans and Pacific Islanders, 48.8%; and American Indians/Native Americans, 81.6%. In contrast, 41.9% of African Americans entered treatment for cocaine, and 34.2% of Hispanics/Latinos entered for heroin.

In my office in New York City, I see people from a wide variety of cultures. It becomes increasingly important to listen to them carefully and to their concerned significant others. What is problematic about my client's behavior? What are the cultural norms of the ethnic group that he or she comes from? It is not uncommon for two people in a couple to each come from separate ethnic groups, each with distinct cultural habits and norms. I need to try to understand how these norms have relevance and significance for the psychotherapeutic problems at hand.

BEHAVIORAL TREATMENT

In the opening to their chapter entitled "What Works? A Summary of Alcohol Treatment Outcome Research," Miller, Wilbourne, and Hettema (2003) ask what readers would do if they learned that they had a life-threatening illness. Naturally, they would seek out medical advice. But, the authors ask, "If your doctor told you, 'I really don't pay much attention to that scientific stuff—it's hard to understand, and it's not really relevant to what I do,' chances are you would find another doctor" (p. 13). Over the past 30 years, there has been a dramatic increase in research looking at what works in the treatment of addictions. However, despite good research evidence that a variety of approaches are effective, few are widely used; in addition, those that are most popular have either no research support or very, very little.

Is there a best approach? The research data do not indicate that there is one best approach. This is also true for most other human afflictions and problems (e.g., asthma, divorce, trauma). But there are now several approaches that have strong empirical support. Over the past 30 years, Miller and his associates have periodically reviewed the literature to find an answer to the question "What works?" According to their latest review (Miller, Wilbourne, & Hettema, 2003), 18 approaches have good empirical support (see Table 19.2). The ranking is based on a "cumulative evidence score" (CES) based on the "inferential strength of the design" and the methodological quality of each study for each treatment modality. (Ten others approaches also have positive

Table 19.2
What Works?

	CES (Cumulative Evidence Score)	Studies with Positive Findings (%)
Brief intervention	390	74
Motivational enhancement	189	72
Acamprosate	116	100
Community reinforcement	110	86
Self-change manual (bibliotherapy)	110	59
Opiate antagonist (e.g., naltrexone)	100	83
Behavioral self-control training	85	52
Behavior contracting	64	80
Social skills training	57	55
Marital therapy—behavioral	44	56
Aversion therapy, nausea	36	50
Case management	33	80
Cognitive therapy	21	40
Aversion therapy, covert sensitization	18	38
Aversion therapy, Apneic	18	67
Family therapy	15	50
Acupuncture	14	67
Client-centered therapy	5	50

Table 19.3
What Works?

	Number of Studies	Studies with Positive Findings (%)
Acamprosate	5	100
Community reinforcement	7	86
Opiate antagonist (e.g., naltrexone)	6	83
Behavior contracting	5	80
Case management	4	80
Brief intervention	34	74
Motivational enhancement	18	72
Aversion therapy, Apneic	3	67
Acupuncture	3	67
Self-change manual (bibliotherapy)	17	59
Marital therapy—behavioral	9	56
Social skills training	20	55
Antidepressant—SSRIs	15	53
Behavioral self-control training	31	52
Aversion therapy, nausea	6	50
Family therapy	4	50
Client-centered therapy	8	50

CES scores, but they were not included because they have been tested in only one or two studies.)

Miller and his associates (Miller, Wilbourne, & Hettema, 2003) do not suggest that CES scores suggest how much better one approach is over the other. That is, brief interventions, with a score of 380, are not more than 3 times as effective as CRAFT, with a score of 110, or over 8 times more effective than cognitive therapy (50).

If one ignores methodological quality and focuses only on modalities with 50% or more studies with positive results (see Table 19.3), the rank orders shift, but the list remains essentially the same: Cognitive therapy (40), aversion therapy, and covert sensitization (38) are not included; antidepressant therapy (selective serotonin reuptake inhibitors [SSRIs]), with 53% studies with positive outcomes, is.

What May Not Work

From the list of 48 different treatment modalities, it is equally important to note what does *not* have much empirical support, especially because the list includes the most popular techniques in the alcohol treatment field over the past 50 years (see Table 19.4). For example, there is no empirical evidence that confrontational counseling is effective; not one study out of 12 found it to be effective. (Note: That should not be interpreted to suggest that a therapist cannot be confrontational at times with clients; it is the style and manner that count.) The list also includes AA. That does not mean that AA has not helped millions of people over the past 90 or so years. As Moos (2006) has suggested, AA is very effective with those that take to it. But professionals are on weak ethical and professional grounds when they insist that all clients must go to AA—or, in fact, must

Table 19.4
What May Not Work?

	CES (Cumulative Evidence Score)	Number of Studies	Studies with Positive
Findings			
Problem solving	−26	4	25
Relapse prevention	−38	22	36
Alcoholics Anonymous (AA)	−94	7	14
Confrontational counseling	−183	12	0
Psychotherapy	−207	19	16
General alcoholism counseling	−284	23	9
Educational tapes, lectures, etc.	−443	39	13

do any particular thing. Some people have argued that the very large-scale MATCH study demonstrated that AA worked just as well as motivational interviewing, but, in fact, the study included 12-step facilitation therapy, a manual-driven, professionally delivered approach.

On the positive side, after more than 30 years of extensive and intensive research by thousands of scientists, practitioners now have a menu of treatment options to offer their clients. We do not have to, nor should we, practice one particular approach. There is plenty of room and there are plenty of reasons for us to use our professional judgment and intuition to suggest and use a wide variety of effective techniques.

What Can a Client and Therapist Do? A Menu of Options

Most clients who come into a therapist's office have already tried everything they know. Many of them have other mental health issues as well and, as a result, are not especially easy to help. They have moments of motivation, but for the most part, they are ambivalent. In most cases, they would very much like to be able to get away with a double life: They would like to be able to drink when and where and how much they feel like and not have the consequences that sometimes or always follow.

Imagine a client walking into a therapist's office. What can he consider doing to help himself resolve his alcohol problems? We now know that there are a number of different approaches that he can choose from (see Table 19.5).

At the same time, the therapist also has a list of different treatment approaches to choose from (see Table 19.6).

The key question, especially in the first session but often in later sessions as well, is which approach may work best with a particular client. What is this client willing and able to do? Ultimately, the client may be the best guide. Therapy is a cybernetic activity. Good therapists always use feedback as to what a client is receptive to and what he or she is not receptive to. But it is critical that therapists know the options available and are flexible enough to try them. In the following sections, I have briefly discussed nine approaches that have moderate to strong research support. Therapists who become familiar with the various components of these approaches will mix and

Table 19.5
A Menu of Client Treatment Options

Medications: Antabuse, naltrexone, Campral, Suboxone, SSRIs, etc.
Therapy (But what kind?)
Self-change manuals/bibliotherapy
Self-help meetings
Drinker's checkup, online meetings, exercise, chat rooms
Cost benefit analysis/decisional balance
Social skills training
Value hierarchy exercise
Drinking log
ABC for urge coping
ABC for emotional and behavioral problems
Outpatient group
Inpatient stay

---

match components from each as the situation seems to warrant, especially because some of the approaches include similar techniques.

Motivational Interviewing

Tables 19.5 and 19.6 clearly show that motivational interviewing (MI; Miller & Rollnick, 2002) has considerable empirical support. Therapist style is central to the approach. Readers who were trained in a Rogerian, client-centered approach will find much that is familiar; those with a different training background, especially those who were trained in a strong, confrontational alcoholism treatment approach, may find the motivational interviewing approach quite foreign. However, there are many training opportunities available (see www.motivationalinterview.org.).

Table 19.6
A Menu of Therapist Treatment Options

Motivational interviewing
Brief interventions
Case management
Social skills training
In-session exercises
Value hierarchy exercise
   Cost-benefit analysis/decisional balance
   ABC for urge coping
   ABC for emotional and behavioral problems
Suggest/assign homework
   Recommend websites, books and tapes
   Drinking log
   Loss list
Facilitate attending SMART recovery meetings
Facilitate attending AA meetings
Facilitate medication
Facilitate outpatient group treatment
Facilitate inpatient treatment

Several aspects of MI involve a distinctly empathetic style. Therapists are taught to "roll with the resistance" and to "avoid argumentation." The acronym FRAMES captures the essence of MI:

- Clients are given Feedback about their alcohol use, often including probable alcohol levels given their levels of drinking.
- The Responsibility for change is assumed to be the client's.
- Clients are also given Advice and a Menu of options in terms of what they might do to help themselves.
- At the same time, as mentioned earlier, the therapist Expresses Empathy and Supports Self-efficacy.

As with any other skill, learning the central MI techniques, for example, how to "develop discrepancy" and how to "support self-efficacy," takes time and practice. Several studies have demonstrated that more effective therapists—regardless of the technique—are more empathetic (Miller, 2003; Miller et al., 1993). Research (Hester, 1994) also clearly indicates that more people do better when they are given a choice, that is, a menu of options. Reviewing the many treatment options sends a strong message of hope: There is more than one way out of this mess. Discussing treatment options may be especially motivating for people who have already tried and failed at one or two treatment modalities.

Many investigations of motivational interviewing have demonstrated that it may not take multiple sessions to cause people to make significant changes in their lives. Outcomes may not be significantly better with more therapy.

BRIEF INTERVENTIONS

What constitutes a brief intervention varies considerably. Most people (clients as well as practitioners) continue to believe that going to therapy means making a commitment to a once-per-week (or more) meeting for an extended time period, perhaps years. In contrast to that therapeutic model, brief interventions are indeed brief. They may be as brief as 5 minutes and as long as six sessions. Numerous studies show that such interventions are effective (this was a review of the research literature, not a "study," Bishop, 2002). McCrady's (2000) review found only two treatment modalities, brief interventions and relapse prevention, that met the criteria for empirically validated treatments established by the American Psychological Association's Division 12 Task Force. In the very large-scale MATCH study (Project MATCH Research Group, 1997), four sessions of motivational enhancement therapy (MET) produced the same results as 12 sessions of cognitive-behavioral therapy or 12-step facilitation therapy. Many brief interventions involve what are called "opportunistic" settings, such as an emergency room or an internist's office (e.g., Blow et al., 2006; Israel, Hollander, Sanchez-Craig, Booker, Miller, Gingrich, & Rankin, 1996). In the Israel et al. study, 3 hours of cognitive-behavioral counseling delivered by a nurse in an internist's office (as compared to simple advice to cut back on drinking) 1 year later resulted in a 70% reduction in drinking, an 85% reduction in psychosocial problems, and 345 fewer visits to doctors; the advice group also decreased their drinking by 46%, but there was no reduction in psychosocial problems or visits to doctors. On the other hand, Heather (1995) cautions against embracing brief interventions too enthusiastically and has noted that we still do not know why they work (Heather, 2003).

What can we learn from the brief intervention research? Even a few meetings with someone may have a significant impact on his or her drinking. Drinkers with more severe problems will probably benefit from more intensive therapy (Hester, 1994), but we should not always assume that we have failed because someone does not return for more sessions; more therapy may not have been more successful at that moment in time. In line with the internist model discussed earlier, we will serve more clients more effectively when we are open to working with someone who appears after a period of time (perhaps a long period of time) because of a relapse or only because he or she thinks a booster session would be a good, preventive idea. It is also not totally unreasonable to suggest to someone who calls that he or she could come in for a session or two and that that might be sufficient.

Behavior Contracting and Behavioral Self-Control Training

Behavior contracting and some form of behavior self-control training (BSCT) may be especially helpful for clients who want to moderate their drinking. As discussed in the Diagnosis and Assessment section, moderation or controlled drinking may work for a minority of clients. Of course, if the therapist thinks that a particular client will probably not be able to drink alcohol in a moderate fashion, she certainly should discuss her concerns with her client. As noted earlier, in King and Tucker's (2000) study, people who are successful at moderating usually succeed within about five attempts. If clients have tried many more times than that before, the prognosis may not be good. However, clients may be adamant and will discontinue therapy if the therapist is adamant in return. Therapists could consider a contract, as Hester (2003) suggests: They will work together with the client, using a BSCT approach, for a specified period of time, perhaps 6 weeks; if the client still has problems, she or he will agree to using BSCT for abstinence for 2 to 4 weeks, a "sobriety sampling" approach.

Before embarking on some form of BSCT, the therapist should also consider whether a brief intervention or some form of self-help book, manual, or computer program might not work equally as well with her client. But if her client seems to want to work with her, in some sense as a coach as well as therapist, then BSCT may be very effective. The essence of BSCT involves the following (as listed in Hester, 2003, p. 154):

1. Setting limits on the number of drinks per day and on peak blood-alcohol levels.
2. Self-monitoring of drinking behaviors.
3. Changing the rate of drinking.
4. Practicing assertiveness in refusing drinks.
5. Setting up a reward system for achievement of goals.
6. Learning which antecedents result in overdrinking and which in moderation.
7. Learning other coping skills instead of drinking.
8. Learning how to avoid relapsing back into heavy drinking.

Many readers may already be doing some of these steps with their clients. That is, they may already be helping their clients practice refusing drinks, using role-playing or some other methods. They may already be routinely exploring the circumstances that tend to lead to moderate drinking and which to overdrinking. For self-monitoring, they may want to give their clients the kind of cards used in BSCT for that purpose.

Clients are taught to record each drink, what they were drinking, where, when, and with whom. If therapists have already asked clients to keep a drinking log, they know that simply being more aware of drinking behavior usually leads to significant changes in drinking. Behavior self-control training also teaches clients how to calculate the standard ethanol content or standard drinks; in brief, one 12-ounce beer, one 5-ounce glass of wine, and one jigger (1.5 ounces) of 80-proof liquor all have the same alcohol (and ethanol) content. Of course, it is a rare client who measures his or her drinks. But I have never had a client refuse to buy a jigger and measure drinks for a week. The last time I asked a client to do that, the client's wife had been complaining that he often drank too much; she was pleased that he was no longer using cocaine after 10 years, but this new problem was equally troublesome for her. Although he said he had only two drinks per night, when he returned to the next session after measuring his drinks, it turned out that he made each drink with two to three jiggers of scotch. He was smiling, but he was also more aware of what he had done—switch one problem for another—and we could begin to work on that.

Behavior self-control training routinely gives clients information about the health risks of various levels of drinking and then contracts with them about their "regular" and "absolute" limits and maximum drinks per week, and it encourages clients not to drink every day. An MI approach mixes readily with BSCT; that is, it is relatively easy to work empathetically with a client to figure out what is reasonable for the coming week. In addition, setting reasonable goals at the beginning helps build a client's sense of self-efficacy. Exploring what a client thinks he or she may be able to do inevitably helps a therapist gain more insight into how significant a problem a client has with alcohol. Finally, there is some evidence that a therapist can increase the likelihood that clients will succeed if the therapist, uses a number of specific questions (Bishop, 2001, pp. 212–217; Gollwitzer, 1999). To learn more about the BSCT approach, consult Hester (2003), Hester and Delaney (1997), and the website www.behaviortherapy.com.

CASE MONITORING AND CASE MANAGEMENT

Case monitoring and management (Stout et al., 1999; Zweben, Rose, Stout, & Zywiak, 2003) are approaches that most therapists can immediately begin to incorporate into their practices. The empirical support is moderate (only four studies), but 80% of the studies resulted in a positive finding. In traditional therapy, most clients come once per week. But there is little evidence that there is any good reason for this practice, and Freud saw people irregularly as well as on a regular basis. Again, the internist model may be the best to follow. Internists accept that patients are not particularly good at taking care of their health and that many come for an appointment only when there is a crisis; for example, only 50% of people with serious diabetes take their insulin, and fewer than 30% alter their lifestyle (O'Brien & McLellan, 1998). Despite the fact that diabetes can have serious consequences for patients and their family, few internists take a moralist, confrontational approach. They continue to work to see what they can do to be of help. O'Brien and McClellan note that "maintenance treatments will be needed to ensure that symptom remission continues" (p. 312).

Zweben et al. (2003) make a distinction between case management and case monitoring. Case management involves much more work on the part of the therapist, who takes much more responsibility for the client's care. In the case monitoring approach, clients are expected to find the resources they need (Stout et al., 1999). However, in both cases, the therapist is attempting to help clients stay on track by using flexible and occasional contacts, often by telephone only. More contacts are initiated by the therapist shortly after treatment and when there is cause for concern about lapsing and relapsing (e.g., a family wedding is approaching). The therapist, as in MI, provides empathetic, nonjudgmental support, while at the same time being ready and open to renewing or facilitating more intensive treatment when the need arises. The contact with the client may start with an assessment of addictive problems, but normally includes inquiries into other problems that many clients grapple with (e.g., depression, HIV, housing, employment, and family problems).

Several cautionary notes: Finding the line between being concerned and being intrusive requires sensitivity. Dentists routinely send us checkup reminders, but most internists don't, and most clients are not used to therapists calling them. Therapists may want to ask their clients whether they would appreciate such calls. Moreover, engaging in what I call "Zen caring" may help; if a client has relapsed, of course I care, but not to the extent of being disappointed or irritated. Disappointment and irritation are signs that I have become invested in my client's progress. That may lead to lying on my client's part, who, because of my behavior or tone, has begun to feel bad if I feel bad.

Many therapists also see quite disturbed clients; in these cases, maintaining boundaries may be difficult. Limiting telephone calls to 10 minutes may be a wise idea, unless a client has agreed to be charged for a full telephone session. Moreover, when a therapist falls into the trap of doing for his client what the client can do for himself, that does not encourage the development of self-efficacy.

SELF-HELP MANUALS (BIBLIOTHERAPY)

Like BSCT, self-help manuals may be most appropriate for clients who are interested in moderating their drinking; however, research indicates that some of those clients will eventually turn to abstinence (Miller, Leckman, Delaney, & Tinkcom, 1992). Numerous studies have shown that self-help manuals and books provide effective treatment for many people with alcohol problems (e.g., Miller & Taylor, 1980; Miller, Wilbourne, et al., 2003). Having a variety of self-help books available increases the options a therapist is able to extend to clients. Many excellent ones exist, including Granfield and Cloud's (1999) *Coming Clean*; Miller and Munoz's (2004) *Controlling Your Drinking: Tools to Make Moderation Work for You*; Rotgers, Kern, and Hoeltzel's (2002) *Responsible Drinking: A Moderation Management Approach to Problem Drinking*; Sanchez-Craig's (1993) *Saying When: How to Quit Drinking or Cut Down*; M. B. Sobell and Sobell's (1993) *Problem Drinker: Guided Self-Change Treatment*; and Tate's (1993) *Alcohol: How to Give It Up and Be Glad You Did*. Self-directed help is also available online at www.drinkerscheckup.com, www.nova.edu/gsc and www.smartrecovery.org.

SOCIAL SKILLS TRAINING

Social skills training is a component of many cognitive-behavioral therapies, including Beck's cognitive therapy (Beck, 1976; Beck, Wright, Newman, & Liese, 1993), Ellis's rational-emotive behavior therapy (Ellis, 1993, 1996; Ellis & Velten, 1992), and Monti's coping skills training (Monti, Kadden, Rohsenow, Cooney, & Abrams, 2002). It is also a part of O'Farrell and Fals-Stewart's (2000, 2003) behavioral marital therapy and CRAFT. Monti's coping skills training includes drink refusal skills, giving and receiving positive feedback, listening skills, and developing social support, among others. Behavioral marital therapy provides sessions specifically structured to increase positive exchanges between spouses, plan shared recreational activities that both may enjoy, create "behavior change agreements" for particularly troubling behaviors, and develop better listening and speaking skills; those trained in Rogerian active listening will recognize the techniques employed.

BEHAVIORAL MARITAL AND FAMILY THERAPY

Therapists should definitely consider involving concerned significant others in treatment, as there is plenty of research evidence showing that doing so improves outcomes.

Behavioral couples therapy has been shown to be effective in most studies. Although there are many aspects of this therapeutic approach (outlined in brief in O'Farrell & Fals-Stewart, 2003), therapists can integrate aspects of the approach and may already have been doing so.

Daily Sobriety Contract   Fals-Stewart and O'Farrell and their associates (O'Farrell & Fals-Stewart, 2003; Fals-Stewart, O'Farrell, Birchler, Córdova, Kelley, 2005) have developed a relatively simple way for husbands and wives to help each other. Let us assume for this example that it is the husband that is recovering. Each morning they meet for a few minutes. The husband states "his intent not to drink or use drugs that day, and the spouse expresses support for the patient's efforts to stay abstinent" (O'Farrell & Fals-Stewart, 2003, pp. 193–195). The husband may also ask that the wife not bring up or bother him about past behavior, and the wife records what happened the previous day on a calendar provider by the therapist. If attendance at AA meetings is part of the contract, that is also recorded if it has occurred.

Taking Antabuse has been a part of many of O'Farrell and Fals-Stewart's (2003) studies; if that is included in the treatment plan, the wife gives the husband the pill, he takes it, and she expresses her appreciation for his doing so. As I discuss later in the section on medication, many people stop taking Antabuse even though it may be very helpful in providing periods of sobriety and stability. Other forms of medications could be included on the contract, but no research looking at the impact of a sobriety contract and such medications has been done to date.

Most of the studies have also involved carefully structured behavioral marital and/or family therapy. Hallmarks of this approach include the following:

- The therapist is careful to control the focus of and work in the session, while at the same time providing an empathetic, supportive environment for the client and the client's spouse.
- The addictive behavior is addressed first; then the focus may shift to learning new and better techniques for resolving marital conflicts.
- The couple agrees to discuss anger over past drinking and fears about future drinking only in session with the therapist.
- Specific communication skills techniques are taught and practiced in session, first on relatively minor issues and then, in a careful stepped-up approach, on more emotionally charged issues.

O'Farrell and Fals-Stewart (2003) report that this approach seems to work best when the client is older, has at least a high school education, and has a more serious alcohol problem, and the relationship is threatened. It also helps when the couple is living together (or willing to get back together) and is desirous of resolving their difficulties.

Behavioral marital therapy has been shown to positively affect not only drinking behavior but also domestic violence. For example, whereas 9.1% of wives reported incidents of violence in a national survey, 53.4% of the wives in one study (O'Farrell & Murphy, 1999) reported violence before treatment; after treatment, the rate dropped to 18.2%, a significant improvement but still more than twice the national norm. However, 1 year after treatment, for wives of remitted husbands, the rate had dropped to 10.3%. Children also appear to benefit more from the impact of behavioral couples counseling than when the client is involved only in individual-based treatment (Kelley & Fals-Stewart, 2002).

COMMUNITY REINFORCEMENT APPROACH AND COMMUNITY REINFORCEMENT AND FAMILY THERAPY

The community reinforcement approach offer therapists another empirically supported approach to work with individuals and, when possible, with family members and other concerned significant others (CSO). Both CRA and CRAFT are based on the idea that the drinking behavior of the identified person is being inadvertently reinforced by members of the person's community. "Community" in this program most often means the spouse, but may also include parents and even people in other parts of the person's environment, that is, the workplace, school, or place of worship. The aim of treatment is to change the manner in which the environment responds to the drinker's drinking behavior. The CRAFT approach was developed to help CSOs respond differently to the drinker's drinking, with three aims in mind: (1) to help the drinker reduce his or her drinking, (2) to motivate the drinker to enter treatment, and (3), at the same time, to improve the psychosocial quality of the CSO's life, including his or her life with the drinker.

One of the most appealing aspects of CRA and CRAFT is their focus on clients' learning how to relate in a more positive manner and to enjoy life more. Careful functional analyses of (a) drinking behaviors and of (b) pleasurable, nondrinking behaviors are central to both approaches. Smith and Meyer (2004) provide clear charts to help the therapist and the drinker better understand the external triggers (who, where, and when) and the internal triggers (thoughts, physical feelings, and emotional feelings) that may contribute to drinking. Similarly, the short- and long-term consequences of drinking are carefully examined. Later, a Happiness Scale is used to help assess how happy or unhappy the person (or the CSO, if the therapist is working with a CSO) is in 12 different areas of life.

Both approaches include problem-solving training, drink refusal training based on Monti's (Monti et al., 2002) work, social and recreational counseling, and relationship therapy. In the relationship training portion, a similar Happiness Scale is used, and the couple working together identify specific areas they would like to improve. Finally, the couple is specifically trained on what to do in the case of lapses and relapses; this includes helping the CSO develop an early warning system, based on the notion that it is the CSO who often realizes a relapse is imminent before the drinker himself or herself.

Meyers and his associates (Meyers & Wolfe, 2004; Smith & Meyers, 2004) emphasize the importance of teaching CSOs to behave differently both when the drinker does *not* drink and when he or she does. This way, the CSO learns the difference between being a positive reinforcer and being an enabler. Offering CSOs a vision and a way toward a more enjoyable life helps overcome some of the initial anger and hostility toward any suggestions of treating the drinker in a more positive manner.

Self-Help Groups

Alcoholics Anonymous Although AA does not appear to have strong empirical support (see earlier remarks), it appears very effective for those who like it (Moos, 2006). There is ample empirical support that those who participate in AA do better over time (Hoffman & Miller, 1992; Moos & Moos, 2005; Schuckit et al., 1997). Moos and Moos, for example, followed more than 300 people with alcohol problems for 16 years; over 70% eventually participated in AA at one time or another. Participation varied considerably. For example, participants of two groups (AA only and treatment plus AA) who continued with AA went, on average, to 35 to 40 meetings per year. Members of another group, who initially had not been going to AA but subsequently entered treatment, later attended AA for about 6 weeks and 20 meetings per year. Overall, there was a positive correlation between participation in AA and higher remission rates, especially when AA participation averaged 40 meetings or more per year. Vaillant (2003) also found that AA attendance was strongly related to the prevention of relapse in both of his two groups; in the Harvard group, five of the nine alcohol-dependent men who achieved stable abstinence attended between 30 and 2,000 meetings. Schuckit et al. also found AA attendance was one of the predictors of abstention for more than 5 years (as were more years of problems with alcohol and older age). On the other hand, there is not adequate research evidence to warrant pushing every client to attend AA meetings. In the Moos and Moos study, in the treatment only group, remission rates did not differ over the 16 years between those who attended and did not attend AA. (For more information, see the "Big Book," officially titled *Alcoholics Anonymous* [AA World Services, 2001] and *Twelve Steps and Twelve Traditions* [AA World Services, 2002], as well AA's website, alcoholicsanonymous.org.)

Self-Management and Recovery Training The SMART Recovery® program is worth considering because those who have been involved in its development have attempted to create a self-help program based on what the research shows works. The program is abstinence-focused and recognized by the National Institute on Alcohol Abuse and Alcoholism [NIAAA] (note: referred to later in the section on ethnicity) and the National Institute on Drug Abuse as providing effective self-help; its Four Point Program™ includes (1) Enhancing and Maintaining Motivation to Abstain; (2) Coping with Urges; (2) Managing Thoughts, Feelings and Behavior (Problem Solving); and (4) Balancing Momentary and Enduring Satisfactions of Life (Lifestyle Balance). Many of the exercises in the group's facilitator's guide, tool box, and member's manual have been drawn from research and manuals on motivational interviewing, cognitive-behavioral therapy, and relapse prevention, and the facilitators are taught many of the skills intrinsic to motivational interviewing (e.g., open-ended questions, avoiding argumentation, rolling with resistance, and decisional balance exercises, called cost-benefit analyses in SMART). Ellis's (1962, 1994) well-known ABC technique is also widely used, particularly because it is so popular with participants. The SMART Recovery program focuses on what has happened in the past 2 weeks and what might happen in the next 2 weeks that could contribute to a relapse (e.g., an upcoming office party). Participants who want to discuss issues arising from more intense experiences, such as sexual abuse, are encouraged to seek professional help. (See www.smartrecovery.org for more information.)

Moderation Management Unlike SMART Recovery and AA, which both focus on abstinence, Moderation Management (MM) teaches people how to moderate their consumption of alcohol. It provides another resource for clients. Moderation Management meetings, like SMART Recovery meetings, encourage crosstalk, and the group focuses on "Nine Steps toward Moderation and Positive Lifestyle Change." Members are encouraged to begin by abstaining for 30 days. The organization also has a list of 10 "ground rules," including "MM members accept responsibility for their own actions and have a sincere desire to reduce their drinking to a nonharmful level," "MM has a zero tolerance policy toward drinking and driving," and "Problems related to the abuse of illegal drugs are outside the scope of MM meetings" (www.moderation.org; see also Humphrey & Klaw, 2001; Rotgers et al., 2002).

Note: Other self-help groups are Secular Organizations for Sobriety (www.secular-humanism.org/sos) and Women for Sobriety (www.womenforsobriety.org; see also McGrady, Horvath, & Delaney, 2003).

MEDICAL TREATMENT

More than 200 medications were reportedly under development in 2006 as pharmaceutical companies race to find a chemical solution to addictions (Denizet-Lewis, 2006). Buprenorphine, which became available in 2005, already makes it much easier to help clients overcome and/or manage their opioid addiction. Clients no longer have to go to a methadone clinic at 8 AM each morning. Like anyone else with a life-threatening health problem, they can go to a doctor's office, get a prescription, fill it, and take the medicine as prescribed. They can go on business trips and on vacation, something that is practically impossible with methadone treatment.

While medications are often the first approach for many other health problems in this country, most clients seeking help for alcoholism are completely unaware of the medical option, despite the fact that we now have three medications that can be helpful. This is probably partly due to the fact that medications for alcohol abuse have not been marketed to the public or to internists and psychiatrists the way other medications for depression, erectile dysfunction, and allergies have been.

ANTABUSE

Antabuse is an excellent choice if a client wants to abstain completely for a number of weeks or months. Usually the goal is to end months of daily battles against the urge to drink, battles that almost inevitably end in failure. Antabuse completely alters the equation. If a client feels an urge or has a thought about having a drink, both are quickly and easily rejected. Drinking is simply not an option, as violent nausea will follow. The exhausting inner arguments are silenced.

But most clients reject Antabuse, and those who start, being human, often stop. They may convince themselves that they should be able to abstain without medication; this is common among clients suffering from other ailments, such as Major Depression and diabetes.

Or they may want to have a drink *if* they want to. Antabuse is usually taken one time per day, in the morning. Marital behavior therapy and CRA often include Antabuse. (For more on disulfram, see Ehrenreich & Krampe, 2004; Fuller & Gordis, 2004.)

NALTREXONE

Naltrexone is another potentially very helpful adjunct to therapy for some clients. The advantage of naltrexone is that people can drink while taking it, but they do not feel the normal effects of alcohol. In general, people do not overdrink while on the drug. A client learns that more drinks will not have the desired effect, and this effectively alters the inner dialogue and subsequent behavior. Sinclair (2001, p. 7) reasons that "the benefits [of naltrexone] are caused by the drug acting not directly but rather by extinction." When a client has taken naltrexone, drinking behavior is no longer reinforced. Once naltrexone is stopped, a return to drinking may be caused by relearning of the drinking behavior. Consequently, he suggests that clients be encouraged to carry a naltrexone pill with them at all times and to take it if they anticipate drinking, thereby preventing the reinforcing effects of alcohol and the relearning of drinking behavior.

When naltrexone appeared on the market in 1994, it was hailed as the "cure" for alcoholism. Such enthusiasm disappeared rapidly when it became evident that most people would not use it; they did not want to give up the opportunity and the ability to feel the way they wanted to feel when they wanted to feel it. We can only assume that when it became apparent that the new drug was not going to be as popular as originally thought, no meaningful expenditure for marketing followed. Vivitrol, an injectable, month-long version, recently approved, may help, but, at this point in time, unlike insulin, it requires a monthly doctor visit.

CAMPRAL

Campral is another medication that may be helpful for some clients. It has been very popular in Europe for over 10 years, but the research results in this country have not been as positive. Nevertheless, the FDA has approved Campral and it appears to work on completely different neurotransmitters (compared to Antabuse and naltrexone). It is important to remember that a drug may be helpful to an individual but not appear to be effective when the results of a group are considered. According to some clients, Campral has made it remarkably easier for them to abstain; it may help some clients have fewer urges and cope better with those they have.

The recently published COMBINE study (Anton et al., 2006) compared a variety of combined medical and nonmedical therapeutic approaches for the treatment of alcohol dependence and included nine groups. Four groups received medical management, similar to what someone might receive when initiating treatment for diabetes or for AIDS. Four groups received both medical management and a special alcohol treatment counseling called combined behavioral intervention (CBI). All eight groups received naltrexone, acamprosate, naltrexone and acamprosate, or a placebo. A ninth group did not receive any pill or medical management, but only CBI. The results and interactions are too complex to discuss here, but, as expected, all groups dramatically reduced their drinking. The rate of days abstinent increased from 25.2% to 73.1% and drinks per day decreased by 44%; drinks per week decreased from 66 to 13, an 89% overall reduction in alcohol consumption.

Medical management plus naltrexone and medical management plus CBI both worked better during the treatment period. Combining naltrexone and CBI with medical management did not improve the results. Acamprosate had no significant impact in any of the treatment conditions. Interestingly, during treatment, medical management plus a placebo was better than CBI alone. Does this mean that clients should not bother with behavioral therapy but only see a medical doctor? Probably not, but it does suggest the power (autosuggestion) of taking medication even if that medication is fake and, as a result, the importance for therapists to include such an intervention in their menu of options. Finally, during the last 16 weeks of the 1-year follow-up, no significant group effects were found.

Besides the three drugs just discussed, SSRIs, although not leading to higher abstinence rates, appear to help clients reduce their consumption of alcohol.

Caution: Therapists must be careful not to function outside the boundaries of their licenses. Most readers cannot prescribe and probably do not keep abreast of all of the side effects of many medications; that is the job of psychiatrists and psychopharmacologists. But they may explain this option to clients and may help their clients get medical help and follow through with their doctor's advice. Moreover, in the next 10 years, pharmaceutical research will offer many more ways to help people resolve their addiction problems. It is likely that no one medication will do the trick for everyone, but each new option may bring new hope for individual clients.

Case Description

Given that alcohol misuse, abuse, and dependence come in many forms and levels of severity, no one case would sufficiently illustrate the manner in which a variety of techniques can be integrated to help individual clients. I have selected three: Ed, Carlos, and Shari.

Ed

When Ed first walked into my office, I could immediately see that he was uncomfortable. Dressed all in black—black T-shirt, black, rumpled jacket, black loafers, no socks—he told me that he had never been to a therapist before. I asked him what had brought him in, and he said that his wife and family "had had it." Their main complaint was that he was too difficult to enjoy being around. He was argumentative, demanding, and often disrespectful and obnoxious. He was clearly troubled about his daughter's comment, but was less so about his wife's remarks. In his view, she had always been dissatisfied. Despite his success in his career as an architect—it turned out that Ed always has ample work because he is willing to do any type of job, from designing the renovation of a small New York City kitchen to designing an entire high-end fashion clothing store interior in SoHo—and his belief that he had been a good husband and a father, he thought of her as unappreciative and critical. He then went on to tell me about a recent gallery opening followed by dinner with his wife and daughter. The opening had been mostly business; he had gotten tired of waiting for his wife and daughter— who were late—and had had a few extra drinks to cope. Then, when they were at the restaurant, the service was extremely slow, Ed was tired and impatient to get home, and when the food finally arrived, he claimed that it was cold. It had been very unpleasant, and his daughter had told him that she no longer wanted to have dinner with him if he was going to drink.

As is often the case when someone first walks into my office, Ed was trying to figure out what he could do, what he should do, and, to some extent, what he could get away with *not* doing. I'm a father as well, and I know I want my children to enjoy the time we spend together, so I told him about William Glasser's (1989) three questions: What do you want? What are you doing? and How do you like it? The first question is the tricky one, I said. "Which do you want most, your daughter to enjoy dinner with you or to drink as much as you want?" I admitted it was a hard question. "No," he said. "When you put it that way, I suppose my real goal is to have a good relationship with Allie." We sat for a few moments. What could he do? We discussed some options: Antabuse, naltrexone, Campral? He was interested that such medications existed, but uninterested in trying any of them.

Over the next 10 minutes, I developed a pretty good picture of his drinking behavior. I already knew that his everyday routine was typical of many men who live in suburbia: In the evening, he caught the 5:37 train to Hicksville, drove home from the station, changed his clothes, and poured himself a glass of bourbon. I did not ask him at the time whether he measured his drinks; I doubted it, as it is uncommon to do so. I would ask him later. Listening to him, it sounded as if he poured himself 2 to 3 ounces of alcohol for each drink. He then sat down, went through the mail, checked e-mail messages and his Blackberry, and then poured himself another drink. It turned out that he did not eat much lunch, perhaps a sandwich, and had only a small bowl of cereal and a cup of coffee for breakfast. He played tennis at least three times a week; at 145 pounds, he was slim and trim for his age.

I asked him to give me two other examples of arguments that he had had with his wife and/or children, and the pattern was clear. No doubt, he was an exacting man. He probably would not have succeeded as an architect without being somewhat compulsive and perfectionistic, but he brought that trait home with him, and after a few drinks, he was difficult, if not impossible, to be with.

Ed wanted very much to try to moderate his drinking. We discussed various strategies and developed a plan. He would switch to wine and never drink at social functions. He finds them boring and the people often irritating; they last too long, and he eventually has one drink after another. He also decided not to drink more than two glasses of wine per night and not to drink at least two nights per week. He was a very determined man, and I was reasonably confident that he might be able to adhere to his plan. However, he strongly liked to do what he wanted when he wanted and the way he wanted, so I was not surprised when, in a session that included his wife, it came out that he had resumed drinking every day of the week and that he often had a third and sometimes fourth drink. His wife, Cecile, was not happy with his change.

In a private session with Ed, we discussed his plan, and I shifted to some standard rational-emotive behavioral therapy (REBT): What was he telling himself when he took a third and fourth drink? That helped us better understand how

(*continued*)

he tended to derail his efforts and to understand the difficulties he was experiencing, and review what he wanted to do and why. He wanted to try harder to follow his plan. Another 6 months passed. His wife and his daughter, while acknowledging some improvement, still maintained that he had not taken the problem seriously enough. There had been several other incidents, including one at a business dinner; he had not followed his plan regarding not drinking at social functions. But Ed remained adamant. We again discussed medication, going a week or two without drinking at all, and Moderation Management. He remained determined to solve the problem on his own.

Another year passed. He and his wife came in every other month. Their relationship was stable but not improving. Finally, at a wedding, he got drunk—he had violated his rule again—and behaved in a very obnoxious manner to guests and to his wife. She made it very clear to him: The marriage would end if he did not stop drinking. In a subsequent session, he was unhappy, but he had decided to quit.

Three years later, he has remained abstinent, and that may not change considering the high value he puts on his family relationships. His daughter and his son—I have seen them all on occasion—are extremely happy. They say he is a changed man and much more pleasant to be around. He, too, is pleased.

Looking back, I used a combination of motivational interviewing and the three questions from William Glasser's (1989) reality therapy to help Ed clarify his goals and motivate him to make a plan. Then we created a plan, a behavioral self-control training contract, but without explicit rewards and penalties. I also taught Ed and Cecile a variety of relationship enhancing techniques common to cognitive-behavioral therapy and REBT, as well as to behavioral marital therapy and coping skills training. The aim was to not only improve their relationship but also to decrease Ed's days of overdrinking.

I saw Ed irregularly over 4 years, and continue to do so for checkups and booster sessions when needed, but now they are all focused on non-alcohol-related issues.

Carlos

In contrast to Ed, Carlos has had a long history of abuse and dependence, including inpatient stays, loss of employment, temporary loss of a professional license, and on-again-off-again periods of abstinence, moderate drinking and abuse and dependence. As a child he had been physically and verbally abused by his mother.

Carlos is a strikingly handsome, physically fit man who has made fortunes managing other people's money and his own. At the same time, he has partied hard, using a variety of drugs, primarily alcohol and cocaine. He has had many short-term relationships with a variety of attractive women, and married and divorced two. He has been living with Claire for over 6 years. Claire has two teenage sons from a previous marriage; one lives with Carlos and her in her Park Avenue apartment; the other is a junior at Brown.

When Carlos walked into my office, he looked ill. His face was puffy and slightly ashen in color, and he said he was miserable. He had been drinking heavily for the past 3 months; he had just spent the past 3 days partying with a girlfriend and her model friends, all of whom drank heavily and used a variety of club drugs. At 45, keeping up with 25- and 28-year-olds had been, he said, "too much." He was also very unhappy with his life. He had two homes, enjoyed collecting art, and said he loved Claire, but he continually had side affairs. He insisted that she thought he had been in Los Angeles the past 3 days meeting with clients. He was quite convinced that he had to stop drinking, stop using cocaine, and change many aspects of his life. I asked him about past attempts to quit and learned that he had done three 28-day stays in three different treatment centers, leaving the last one against medical advice. He was not interested in doing another one. He could not leave New York or take any time off because he had several important business meetings in the next week.

He had not had a physical for years and did not have an internist, so I gave him a referral to both an internist and a psychopharmacologist who specializes in additive medicine. He seemed relieved that I was taking his condition seriously and agreed to go to both. I did not insist that he see them before he saw me again, something I do occasionally, but urged him to see them as quickly as possible.

We discussed the benefits of Antabuse, naltrexone, and Campral, and I encouraged him to discuss the pros and cons of all three with the psychopharmacologist. We used the last 15 minutes to explore what he wanted to do before the next session, scheduled for a week later. He wanted to stop drinking; he had done so with Librium before and still had some at home from a previous psychiatrist. Concerned because he did not have a current, ongoing relationship with a medical doctor, I suggested other options available to him. He noted that if he did have serious withdrawal symptoms, he could always simply drink a little bit to ease himself down more gradually; he had done it before. I urged him to go to his local emergency room if he got in trouble, and I also gave him the telephone numbers of colleagues at two different outpatient treatment centers in New York City. We also discussed his going to self-help meetings; he had gone to AA meetings occasionally before but did not like them. I knew he spent hours in front of a computer screen, so I suggested that he visit the SMART Recovery website and consider attending an online meeting; I also gave him a handout with the dates and times of SMART Recovery meetings in New York City.

I asked how likely he thought it was that he would stop drinking. He thought it was very likely, 100%. Double checking, I asked him how committed he was to abstaining, at least for a few weeks. Again, he said he was very committed, 100%. In an attempt to explore further the potential vulnerability to his plan, I asked him what he thought might possibly derail his plan. Initially, he said he could not think of anything. Then he shared with me that he thought Claire's criticism and negativity might "make me drink." We explored that a little, but time was running out, so I asked him if he would like to make an earlier appointment than the one we already had scheduled. He did not think that was necessary. Could he make a commitment not to drink no matter what Claire said or did for 1 week? He seemed to like that idea and was very clear that that would

(*continued*)

not be difficult to do, so we parted on that note. He also went away with the telephone numbers of four professionals, and I thought it likely that he would follow up our session with a visit to both the internist and the psychiatrist I had recommended.

When he came through the door a week later, I was surprised to see how much better he looked. His color was good, he walked with an air of confidence, and he smiled easily when he came through the door. He had just come from the gym; he had been to the internist and the internist had told him that he was in fine health, with no liver damage. He had also met with the psychiatrist I had recommended and had started naltrexone; however, he doubted he was going to continue, as he was feeling so much better. I urged him to continue for a while, especially as there seemed to be no negative consequences.

I saw Carlos three more times; he left on a business trip and called to break the following appointment because he was, he said, "doing fine and too busy." I did not hear from him for 6 months, so one morning, close to noon, I called his cell number. He sounded like death, and he was amazed and appreciative that I had called. We made an appointment 3 days later, when he would be back from Los Angeles. When he walked into my office, he again looked terrible and again reported that he was miserable.

Of course, this time I knew more about him, so we could work more quickly. However, he was not inclined to return to the psychopharmacologist. He was again sure that he could stop on his own and that he could stay stopped. We discussed possible benefits of longer, more consistent therapy. At 45, he appeared to be going through a midlife crisis, not only in his relationship with Claire but also in his professional life. He had enough money so that he could do practically anything, but I knew that in his hungover, depressed condition, discussions about serious existential issues would be a waste of time. We agreed to meet again in 4 days. By that meeting, he had again stopped drinking, and he was looking, again, surprisingly better.

I have seen Carlos now for over 6 years; after that appointment, he called me once for a referral to an inpatient facility. I gave him two suggestions, and he spent 2 weeks at one of them. Then he found a therapist who thought his insistence on abstinence was the problem and who agreed to work on moderate drinking with him. There seemed little point in my saying much, and he was not asking me; I am sure he knew what I thought because we had had discussions about moderate drinking versus abstinence in the past. Two months later, he called and came in. It has been over a year, and he has remained abstinent.

Carlos still seems to be grappling with midlife issues, but that may be more in my mind than his. He oversees his considerable investments and loves decorating his two homes with new art. He continues to wonder about staying with Claire. We have explored in some depth his relationship with his mother, who is still alive and as critical as ever. We have talked about his feelings and thoughts when Claire appears to be unhappy or critical of him. Carlos grew up in a poor family; his father drank heavily, womanized a lot, and left when Carlos was 10. Carlos never saw him again. Carlos thinks he would like to be in a monogamous relationship, but he knows he will never be happy enough with Claire to "abstain" from other relationships.

I have tried to work with Carlos on an ongoing basis. Initially, he was clearly not interested in therapy; he just wanted help at that point in time. I told him I would be very open to helping him and that if the television didn't work, I first checked the plug. If that fixed it, fine, but if not, then we might have to go inside and see what was really wrong. He liked that idea, and several years later asked me if I remembered saying that and suggested that perhaps we had better spend some time "looking into the guts." We have done so to a limited degree, but not on a traditional, weekly basis at all. But when he comes in for one of his occasional visits, he is clearly more open to talking about the possible roots of his problems.

Shari

When Shari walked into my office over 2 years ago, she was a striking, intense, petite 28-year-old doing reasonably well as a film editor in New York, but not as well as she would like. She likes to socialize with a group of young people who are clearly more successful than she is. Some have already made their own independent films, and one makes over $50,000 per episode in a TV sitcom. Most of her crowd drinks a lot and some also like to do a variety of other drugs.

When I met her, her boyfriend at that time, Craig, was not happy with "that scene" and wanted her to cut down on her drinking. Originally, she thought that might be a good idea. She had recently gotten very drunk at a party and had insulted one of her friends, Elissa, someone who might have been able to help her take the next step in terms of her career. She had felt that Craig was not paying enough attention to her and that Elissa was paying too much attention to Craig, and the combination, coupled with more drinks than she could remember, created an explosive scene that she very much regretted.

Shari was not sure what she wanted to do. Perhaps, she said with a smile, she should stop, but she was not quite ready. A friend suggested that they go to AA together, and she was considering it. She was not exercising, although she had done a lot of bicycling, including touring, in the past. She smoked about a pack of cigarettes a day. She used other drugs when friends offered them in the past, but she had stopped that routine about a year before.

We started to explore her options. Would she consider stopping for a week or two? No, that did not seem right. She liked to drink Cosmopolitans. She agreed that Cosmopolitans are problematic for several reasons; they are very sweet and easy to drink, and they come straight up, without ice. They are served in a large martini glass, and it is also very difficult to know how much alcohol they have in them. Would she consider switching to wine? No, she didn't like wine very much. How about something that combined soda with alcohol? She could then order every other drink without alcohol, causing her to slow down but allowing her to always have something in her hand.

We also discussed naltrexone and Campral. She was surprised. Did I think her problem was that serious? I did. She had had two fights with two previous

(continued)

boyfriends in the past several years, both of which turned not only ugly but physical. She was very slim and was interested in doing better professionally. She was trying to write her own screenplay, but the alcohol seemed to be stopping her from fulfilling that dream. It seemed likely that her depression, being treated with Celexa, was exacerbated by alcohol, and the result was that she did not write.

I realized that we could do a number of different kinds of exercises during the session. She seemed fairly highly motivated to control her drinking. And she also wanted to do more writing. Consequently, I chose to do Ellis's ABC(DE). It is an exercise that some clients like very much. They take it home, use it on their own, and develop a much stronger sense of self-efficacy; they often feel better able to control both addictive behaviors (e.g., drinking too much) and nonaddictive behaviors (in this case, writing).

I asked her what she was telling herself when she was drinking. She did not understand my question. She had already shared with me that she often became very anxious and, in fact, had had panic attacks on two occasions.

"I think you are saying something like, 'I want to relax. I have to calm down.' You gulp the drink down so as to get the effect quickly."

"Yeah, I love those Cosmopolitans. I usually drink two in the first half-hour just to feel better."

We spent the next 20 minutes exploring what else she could say to herself to better manage her anxiety. Then we shifted to behavioral ways that she could slow her drinking down or not drink at all on 1 or 2 days a week. I reviewed my previous suggestions about switching drinks. Then I asked her how Craig might help. Would she like him to come in for a session? No, she was not serious enough about him to do that. But she did agree that she could spend more evenings with him rather than always hanging out with her crowd of friends.

At the end of the session, we decided on the following options. She would discuss going to AA with her friend. I also told her about SMART Recovery and gave her their website address. She agreed to think about changing drinks. During the session, she had agreed to try drinking only every other day and, when out with friends, to find another drink, perhaps vodka and tonic. I also gave her the name of a psychopharmacologist in case she wanted to explore medications. I made another appointment with her in a week.

She called and said she had to cancel the next session, but she had started to attend AA. I saw her the following week. For the next 6 months she went to AA, I saw her every other week, and she abstained during that time. Then she started to drink again, and not always moderately. I noticed that she often came to the session with nothing to work on; she seemed to be waiting for something to "cure" the problems. I knew from previous sessions that in her family she had always taken care of other people, but she gave me several examples of when she did not take care of herself. I suggested that she was waiting for me, the doctor, to cure her problem. What would help *her* take charge of her life more? How did she feel about setting up some achievable writing goals for the next week? She appeared interested. Someone she knew had asked her to write for a website. He wanted a 750-word article. She seemed inspired by the idea of trying to write a draft. We set an appointment for the next week, but she cancelled it. She had too much work, she said. She cancelled the next appointment as well. I called her and left a voice message. It became apparent that she was not coming back to therapy. One year passed.

Shari called in November, apologetic. Did I have time to see her? She appeared as usual, early, fashionably dressed, and smiling cutely, in a kind of coquettish manner out of the corner of her eye. At first, things did not seem to have changed that much. She had changed jobs and had a new boyfriend, but she was not very serious about him. She was drinking again, but not as often and heavily on only rare occasions. She had had no fights or unpleasant scenes since the last time we had met. She had not gone back to AA and did not want to. After listening for a while, I asked about her writing. She was still not doing much. I again suggested a consultation with a psychopharmacologist. She could get a second opinion and explore her options. She could take the prescription and not fill it.

Dr. Werstein, the psychopharmacologist, called me 3 weeks later. I had had Shari sign a release so I could talk to her. Shari had made two evening appointments and had called to cancel both, because she told Dr. Werstein, she was "too busy at the office." Shari and I met again 6 months later. She had seen Dr. Werstein and liked her, and Dr. Werstein suggested a slight increase in the Celexa, which Shari had taken. Shari and she had discussed naltrexone and Campral, but she was hesitant to start, saying that she was worried about the side effects. She had not looked either of the medications up online and did not know of any specific side effects, but she was still hesitant to start. She thought she could manage her drinking problem on her own, and she did not want to take another medication.

Following the principles of motivational interviewing, I shifted to trying to get her to talk about what she *had* managed to do already in her life. She had found a better job and one more to her liking. She was paying her own bills. However, she quickly shifted to what she had *not* managed to do: She was not writing, she was spending much too much on clothing, and she needed to find a better boyfriend; she wanted to get married and have children, and she was now 30. I shifted the focus back: I learned that she was drinking much less frequently and much less when she went out, and she had switched to wine. She had also gotten much better at managing her anxiety without using alcohol. She said that the REBT worksheets had helped and exercising helped. Here was real evidence that she could change. She had also stopped smoking, another specific example of change, and she had found a friend to bicycle with her.

Therapy is now focused on two goals and a question. The goals are (1) writing more frequently and (2) finding a better boyfriend, one who ultimately could become a true partner. The question is: Can she drink moderately over the long term?

I have tried to be of help as Shari has made several changes in her life over the past few years, including managing her drinking behavior more effectively. Like some clients, she has taken a liking to REBT and has read several books, including one on managing anxiety that she found very helpful. She is increasingly taking responsibility for her life, but she continues to have difficulty with alcohol and with writing on a consistent basis, so her career dreams remain unfulfilled.

SUMMARY

What Do We Know?

- Addictions can be treated as effectively as many other human afflictions, such as diabetes and asthma.
- A menu of evidence-based, clinically effective treatment options is available to both clients and therapists.
- Therapists can integrate aspects of each of these empirically supported approaches given the characteristics of particular clients.

What Helps?

- 1. Empathy is key. Try to ensure that clients leave feeling as if they have been heard.
- 2. Focus on the addictive problem first, then the other problems (except when that would be unempathetic and counterproductive). Watch out for the therapist tendency to want to make the client *feel* better even when the client is clearly saying he or she wants to *behave better*.
- 3. Remember, many clients would like to be able to have, in a sense, a double life; for example, they would like to be a loving husband and father *and*, on occasion, get drunk and stay out all night. Work to help them resolve that conflict.
- 4. Develop discrepancy between the conflicting wants of a client.
- 5. Roll with the resistance.
- 6. Keep the menu of options in front of you as you work. Tailor your approach to fit your client, using a variety of techniques culled from those approaches.
- 7. Look for a motivational handle or handles. Relationships matter to most clients; you may be able to motivate clients to work on changing for someone else if they will not do it for themselves.
- 8. Teach useful tools, such as social skills training, decisional balance exercises, the ABC technique, and sobriety sampling.
- 9. When appropriate, act as a supportive coach.
- 10. Negotiate a balance between the why and the how. Humans want to understand *why*. Help clients learn *how* to do better over time, but spending time understanding the roots of the problem may have motivational value.
- 11. Before each session, have a plan. Review your notes, look at your menu of options, and jot down three things you want to try to do in the session.
- 12. Throw your plan out or radically revise it if the client has changed dramatically, for the better or for the worse, since the previous session.
- 13. Practice a technique each week. Write it down on a 3 x 5 card and work on getting better at it.
- 14. Watch for your own irrational beliefs, which may impede therapeutic progress.
- 15. Often, people change slowly; work to reduce the harm your client might do to himself or herself in the coming week or weeks.

Researchers study what is able to be studied and federal research grants affect what is looked at. Over the past 10 years, because we have had new machines that have allowed us to look where no humans have looked before, we have focused almost exclusively on the brain and on brain chemistry. But the enteric nervous system in the gut (where 95% of serotonin is created) and other parts of the nervous system may play key roles as well.

Society's acceptance of depression as an illness has increased dramatically over the past 20 years. Will addictions be looked at in a less judgmental light in the near future? All religions teach people not to judge their fellow humans, and modern brain research clearly suggests that what cannot be seen with the naked eye may have a tremendous impact on an individual's ability to make choices and to lead or not lead a productive, meaningful life.

Many of the approaches discussed in this chapter, with some exceptions, ignore what historically have always been matters of the heart: beauty, love, meaningfulness, to name only a few. (Perhaps AA has been so successful with the people it has helped because it provides some of these other critical elements of a human life.) In addition, many current approaches, but not all, put almost all of the focus on the individual. They seem to ignore the impact of the environment, of poverty and class, of meaningless employment and empty lives, yet we know from research that genetic expression, neurochemistry, and behavior are all affected by the environment.

To some extent we are like climatologists, looking for answers about complex, interacting systems. What can best be done to help clients respond better to the inevitable minor squalls and major storms? Fortunately, 50 years of research has improved our understanding of both weather patterns and addictive behavior patterns; – and for addictive behaviors, we have evidence-based ways to be of help. Will therapists and treatment facilities also change in light of this research? That is another interesting question.

REFERENCES

AA World Services. (2001). *Alcoholics anonymous.* New York: Author.

AA World Services. (2002). *Twelve steps and twelve traditions.* New York: Author.

Anton, R. F., O'Malley, S. S., Ciraulo, D. A., Cister, R. A., Couper, D., Donovan, D. M., et al. (2006). Combined pharmacotherapies and behavioral interventions for alcohol dependence: The COMBINE study: A randomized controlled trial. *Journal of the American Medical Association, 295,* 2003–2017.

Babor, T. F., Caetano, R, Casswell, S., Edwards, G., Giesbrecht, N., Graham, K., et al. (2003). Alcohol: No ordinary commodity—Research and public policy. Oxford: Oxford University Press.

Babor, T. F., & Grant, M. (1989). From clinical research to secondary prevention: International collaboration in the development of the Alcohol Use Disorders Identification Test (AUDIT). *Alcohol Health and Research World, 13,* 371–374.

Beck, A. T. (1976). *Cognitive therapy and the emotional disorders.* New York: International Universities Press.

Beck, A. T., Wright, F. D., Newman, C. F., & Liese, B. S. (1993). *Cognitive therapy of substance abuse.* New York: Guilford Press.

Bishop, F. M. (2001). *Managing addictions: Cognitive, emotive and behavioral techniques.* Northvale, NJ: Aronson.

Bishop, F. M. (2002). Brief interventions for the treatment of substance abuse. In F. W. Bond & W. Dryden (Eds.), *Handbook of brief cognitive behavioral therapy* (pp. 162–185) London: Wiley.

Blow, F. D., Barry, K. L., Walton, M. A., Maio, R. F., Chermack, S. T., Bingham, C. R., et al. (2006). The efficacy of two brief intervention strategies among injured, at-risk drinkers in the emergency department: Impact of tailored messaging and brief advice. *Journal of Studies of Alcohol, 67,* 568–578.

Castro, F. G., Proescholdbell, R. J., Abeita, L., & Rodriquez, D. (1999). Ethnic and cultural minority groups. In B. S. McCrady & E. E. Epstein (Eds.), *Addictions: A guidebook for professionals* (pp. 499–526). New York: Oxford University Press.

Denizet-Lewis, B. (2006, June 25). An anti-addiction pill? *New York Times,* pp. 48–53.

DiClemente, C. C. (2006). *Addictions and change: How addictions develop and addicted people recover.* New York: Guilford Press.

Ehrenreich, H. & Krampe, H. (2004). Does disulfiram have a role in alcoholism treatment today: Not to forget about disulfiram's psychological effects. *Addiction, 99,* 26–27.

Ellis, A. (1962, 1994). *Reason and emotion in psychotherapy.* Secaucus, NJ: Citadel. Rev. ed., Secaucus, NJ: Carol Publishing Group; Revised 1994, New York: Birch Lane Press.

Ellis, A. (1993). Changing rational-emotive therapy (RET) to rational emotive behavior therapy (REBT). *Behavior Therapist, 16,* 257–258.

Ellis, A. (1996). *Better, deeper, and more enduring brief therapy: The rational behavior therapy approach.* New York: Brunner/Mazel.

Ellis, A., & Velten, E. (1992). *When AA doesn't work for you: Rational steps to quitting alcohol.* Fort Lee, NJ: Barricade Books.

Fals-Stewart, W., O'Farrell, T. J., Birchler, G. R., Córdova, J., & Kelley, M. L. (2005). Behavioral couples therapy for alcoholism and drug abuse: Where we've been, where we are, and where we're going. *Journal of Cognitive Psychotherapy, 19,* 229–246.

Finney, J. W., Moos, R. H., & Timko, C. (1999). The course of treated and untreated substance use disorders: Remission and resolution, relapse and mortality. In B. S. McCrady & E. E. Epstein (Eds.), *Addictions: A comprehensive guidebook* (pp. 30–49). New York: Oxford University Press.

Fuller, R. K., & Gordis, E. (2004). Does disulfiram have a role in addiction treatment today? *Addiction, 99,* 21–24.

Glasser, W. (1989). Control theory. In W. Glasser (Ed.), *Control theory in the practice of reality therapy* (pp. 1–15). New York: Harper & Row.

Grant, B. F., Dawson, D. A., Stinson, F. S., Chou, S. P., Dufour, M. C., & Pickering, R. C. (2006). The 12-month prevalence and trends in DSM-IV alcohol abuse and dependence, United States, 1991–1992 and 2001–2002. *Drug and Alcohol Dependence, 74,* 223–234.

Gollwitzer, P. M. (1999). Implementation intentions: Strong effects of simple plans. *American Psychologist, 54*(7), 493–503.

Granfield, R., & Cloud, W. (1999). *Coming clean: Overcoming addiction without treatment.* New York: New York University Press.

Heather, N. (1995). Interpreting the evidence on brief interventions: The need for caution. *Alcohol and Alcoholism, 30,* 287–296.

Heather, N. (2003). Brief alcohol interventions have expanded in range but how they work is still mysterious. *Addiction, 98,* 1025–1026.

Hester, R. K. (1994). Outcome research: Alcoholism. In M. Galanter & H. Kleber (Eds.), *Textbook of substance abuse treatment* (Chap. 4, pp. 35–44). Washington, DC: American Psychiatric Association Press.

Hester, R. K. (2003). Behavioral self-control training. In R. K. Hester & W. R. Miller (Eds.), *Handbook of alcoholism treatment approaches: Effective alternatives* (3rd ed., pp. 152–164). Boston: Allyn & Bacon.

Hester, R. K., & Delaney, H. D. (1997). Behavioral self-control program for Windows: Results of a controlled clinical trial. *Journal of Consulting and Clinical Psychology, 65,* 686–693.

Hester, R. K., Squires, D. D., & Delaney, H. D. (2005). The drinker's check-up: 12-month outcomes of a controlled clinical trial of a stand-alone software program for problem drinkers. *Journal of Substance Abuse Treatment, 28,* 159–169.

Hoffman, N. G., & Miller, N. S. (1992). Treatment outcomes for abstinence-based programs. *Psychiatric Annals, 22,* 402–408.

Humphrey, K., & Klaw, E. (2001). Can targeting nondependent problem drinkers and providing Internet-based services expand access to assistance for alcohol problem? A study of the Moderation Management self-help/mutual aid organization. *Journal of Studies of Alcohol, 62,* 528–532.

Israel, Y., Hollander, O., Sanchez-Craig, M., Booker, S., Miller, V., Gingrich, R., et al. (1996). Screening for problem drinking and counseling by the primary care physician-nurse team. *Alcoholism: Clinical and Experimental Research, 20,* 8, 1443–1450.

Johnson, V. E. (1989). Intervention: How to help someone who doesn't want help—A step-by-step guide for families of chemically dependent persons. Minneapolis, MN: The Johnson Institute.

Kahler, C. W. (2006). Towards an empirically supported alcohol use disorders nosology for DSM-V. *Brown University Digest of Addiction Theory and Applications, 25*(9), 8.

Kelley, M. L., & Fals-Stewart, W. (2002). Couples-versus individual-based therapy for alcohol and drug abuse: Effects on children's psychosocial functioning. *Journal of Clinical and Consulting Psychology, 70,* 417–427.

Keough, K. A., Zimbardo, P. G., & Boyd, J. N. (1999). Who's smoking, drinking, and using drugs? Time perspective as a predictor of substance use. *Basic and Applied Social Psychology, 21,* 149–164.

King, M. P., & Tucker, J. A. (2000). Behavior change patterns and strategies distinguishing moderation drinking and abstinence during the natural resolution of alcohol problems without treatment. *Psychology of Addictive Behaviors, 14,* 48–55.

Koumans, A. J. R., Muller, J. J., & Miller, C. F. (1967). Use of telephone calls to increase motivation for treatment in alcoholics. *Psychological Reports, 21,* 327–328.

Marlatt, G. A., & Gordon, J. R. (Eds.). (1985). *Relapse prevention.* New York: Guilford Press.

McCrady, B. S. (2000). Alcohol use disorders and the Division 12 Task Force of the American Psychological Association. *Psychology of Addictive Behaviors, 14,* 267–276.

McGrady, B. S., Horvath, A. T., & Delaney, S. I. (2003). Self-help groups. In R. K. Hester & W. R. Miller (Eds.), *Handbook of alcoholism treatment approaches: Effective alternatives* (3rd ed., pp. 165–187). Boston: Allyn & Bacon.

Meyers, R. J., Miller, W. R., Hill, D. E., & Tonigan, J. S. (1999). Community reinforcement and family training (CRAFT): Engaging unmotivated drug users in treatment. *Journal of Substance Abuse, 10,* 1–18.

Meyers, R. J., & Wolfe, B. L. (2004). *Get your loved one sober.* Center City, MN: Hazelden.

Miller, W. R. (2003). Enhancing motivation for change. In R. K. Hester & W. R. Miller (Eds.), *Handbook of alcoholism treatment approaches: Effective alternatives* (3rd ed., pp. 131–151). Boston: Allyn & Bacon.

Miller, W. R, Benefield, R. G., & Tonigan, J. S. (1993). Enhancing motivation for change in problem drinking: A controlled comparison of therapist styles. *Journal of Consulting and Clinical Psychology, 61,* 455–461.

Miller, W. R., Leckman, A. L., Delaney, H. D., & Tinkcom, M. (1992). Long-term follow-up of behavioral self-control training. *Journal of Studies on Alcohol, 53,* 249–261.

Miller, W. R., Meyers, R. J., & Tonigan, J. S. (1999). Engaging the unmotivated in treatment for alcohol problems: A comparison of three strategies for intervention through family members. *Journal of Consulting and Clinical Psychology, 67,* 688–697.

Miller, W. R., & Munoz, R. F. (2004). *Controlling your drinking: Tools to make moderation work for you.* New York: Guilford Press.

Miller, W. R., & Rollnick, S. (2002). *Motivational interviewing: Preparing people to change addictive behavior* (2nd ed.). New York: Guilford Press.

Miller, W. R., & Taylor, C. A. (1980). Relative effectiveness of bibliotherapy, individual and group self-control training in the treatment of problem drinkers. *Addictive Behaviors, 5,* 13–24.

Miller, W. R., Westerberg, V. S., & Waldron, H. B. (2003). Evaluating alcohol problems in adults and adolescents. In R. K. Hester & W. R. Miller (Eds.), *Handbook of alcoholism treatment approaches: Effective alternatives* (3rd ed., pp. 78–112). Boston: Allyn & Bacon.

Miller, W. R., Wilbourne, P. L., & Hettema, J. E. (2003). What works? A summary of alcohol treatment outcome research. In R. K. Hester & W. R. Miller (Eds.), *Handbook of alcoholism treatment approaches: Effective alternatives* (3rd ed., pp. 13–64). Boston: Allyn & Bacon.

Monti, P. M., Kadden, R. M., Rohsenow, D. J., Cooney, N. L., & Abrams, D. B. (2002). *Treating alcohol dependence: A coping skills training guide* (2nd ed.). New York: Guilford Press.

Moos, R. H. (2006, January). *Influencing social environments to enhance client outcomes in addiction.* Symposium presented at the Eleventh International Conference on Treatment of Addictive Behaviors, Santa Fe, NM.

Moos, R. H., & Moos, B. S. (2005). Paths of entry into Alcoholics Anonymous: Consequences for participation and remission. *Alcoholism: Clinical and Experimental Research, 29,* 1858–1868.

Muraven, M., Collins, R. L., & Nienhaus, K. (2002). Self-control and alcohol restraint: An initial application of the self-control strength model. *Psychology of Addictive Behavior, 16,* 113–120.

O'Brien, C. P., & McClellan, A. T. (1998). Myths about the treatment of addiction. In A. W. Graham & T. K. Schultz (Eds.), *Principles of addiction medicine* (2nd ed., pp. 309–314). Chevy Chase, MD: American Society of Addiction Medicine.

O'Farrell, T. J., & Fals-Stewart, W. (2000). Behavioral couples therapy for alcoholism and drug abuse. *Journal of Substance Abuse Treatment, 18,* 51–54.

O'Farrell, T. J., & Fals-Stewart, W. (2003). Marital and family therapy. In R. K. Hester & W. R. Miller (Eds.), *Handbook of alcoholism treatment approaches: Effective alternatives* (3rd ed., pp. 188–212). Boston: Allyn & Bacon.

O'Farrell, T. J., & Murphy, C. M. (1999). Marital violence before and after alcoholism treatment. *Journal of Clinical and Consulting Psychology, 63,* 256–262.

Prochaska, J. O., & DiClemente, C. C. (1982). Transtheoretical therapy: Toward a more integrative model of change. *Psychotherapy, 20,* 161–173.

Prochaska, J. O., DiClemente, C. C., & Norcross, J. C. (1992). In search of how people change: Applications to addictive behaviors. *American Psychologist, 47,* 1102–1114.

Project MATCH Research Group. (1997). Matching alcoholism treatments to client heterogeneity: Project MATCH post-treatment drinking outcomes. *Journal of Studies on Alcohol, 58,* 7–29.

Robins, L. N., Helzer, J. E., & Davis, D. H. (1975). Narcotic use in Southeast Asia and afterwards: An interview study of 898 Vietnam returnees. *Archives of General Psychiatry, 32*(8), 955–961.

Rogers, C. (2003). *Client-centered therapy.* London: Constable and Robinson.

Rotgers, F., Kern, M. F., & Hoeltzel, R. (2002). *Responsible drinking: A moderation management approach to problem drinking.* Oakland, CA: New Harbinger.

Sanchez-Craig, M. (1993). *Saying when: How to quit drinking or cut down.* Toronto: Addictions Research Foundation.

Saunders, J. B., Aasland, O. G., Babor, T. F., De la Fuente, J. R., & Grant, M. (1993). Development of the Alcohol Use Disorders Identification Test (AUDIT): Pt. II. WHO collaborative project on early detection of persons with harmful alcohol consumption. *Addiction, 88,* 791–804.

Schuckit, M. A., Tipp, J. E., Smith, T. L., & Bucholz, K. K. (1997). Periods of abstinence following the onset of alcohol dependence in 1,853 men and women. *Journal of Studies of Alcohol, 58,* 581–589.

Sinclair, J. D. (2001). Evidence about the use of naltrexone and for different ways of using it in the treatment of alcoholism. *Alcohol and Alcoholism, 36,* 2–10.

Smith, J. E., & Meyers, R. J. (2004). *Motivating substance abusers to enter treatment.* New York: Guilford Press.

Sobell, L. C., Cunningham, J. A., & Sobell, M. B. (1996). Recovery from alcohol problems with and without treatment: Prevalence in two population surveys. *American Journal of Public Health, 86*, 966–972.

Sobell, L. C., Ellingstad, T. P., & Sobell, M. B. (2000). Natural recovery from alcohol and drug problems: Methodological review of the research with suggestions for future directions. *Addiction, 95*(5), 749–764.

Sobell, L. C., Toneatto, T. & Sobell, M. B. (1994). Behavioral assessment and treatment planning for alcohol, tobacco, and other drug problems: Current status with an emphasis on clinical applications. *Behavior Therapist, 25*, 533–580.

Sobell, M. B., & Sobell, L. C. (1993). *Problem drinkers: Guided self-change treatment.*. New York: Guilford Press.

Steinbauer, J. R., Cantor, S. B., Holzer, C. E., & Volk, R. J. (1998). Ethnic and sex bias in primary care screening tests for alcohol use disorders. *Annals of International Medicine, 129*, 353–362.

Stout, R. L., Rubin, A., Zwick, W., Feldman, J., Shepard, D., & Larson, M. J. (1999). Optimizing the cost-effectiveness of alcohol treatment: A rationale for extended case monitoring. *Addictive Behaviors, 24*, 17–35.

Sutton, S. (2005). Another nail in the coffin of the Transtheoretical Model? A comment on West (2005). *Addictions, 100*, 104–105.

Tate, P. (1993). *Alcohol: How to give it up and be glad you did.* Altamonte Springs, FL: Rational Self-Help Press.

Toneatto, T., Sobell, L. C., Sobell, M. B., & Rubel, E. (1999). Natural recovery from cocaine dependence. *Psychology of Addictive Behaviors, 13*, 259–268.

Tsuang, M. T., Bar, J. L., Harley, R. M., & Lyons, M. J. (2001). The Harvard Twin Study of Substance Abuse: What we have learned. *Harvard Review of Psychiatry, 9*, 267–279.

Tucker, J. A., & King, M. P. (1999). Resolving alcohol and drug problems: Influences on addictive behavior change and help-seeking processes. In J. A. Tucker, D. M. Donovan, & G. A. Marlatt (Eds.), *Changing addictive behaviors* (pp. 97–126). New York: Guilford Press

Tucker, J. A., Vuchinich, R. E., Black, B. C., & Rippens, P. D. (2006). Significance of a behavioral economic index of reward value in predicting drinking problem resolution. *Journal of Consulting and Clinical Psychology, 74*, 317–326.

Vaillant, G. E. (1996). A long-term follow-up of male alcohol abuse. *Archives of General Psychiatry, 53*, 243–249.

Vaillant, G. E. (2003). A 60-year follow-up of alcoholic men. *Addiction, 98*, 1043–1051.

Walters, G. D. (2000). Spontaneous remission from alcohol, tobacco, and other drug abuse: Seeking quantitative answers to qualitative questions. *American Journal of Drug and Alcohol Abuse, 26*, 443–460.

West, R. (2005). Time for a change: Putting the Transtheoretical (Stages of Change) Model to rest. *Addiction, 100*, 1036–1039.

Witkiewitz, K., & Marlatt, G. A. (2004). Relapse prevention for alcohol and drug problems: That was Zen, this is Tao. *American Psychologist, 59*, 224–235.

Zweben, A., Rose, S. J., Stout, R. L., & Zywiak, W. H. (2003). Case monitoring and motivational style brief interventions. In R. K. Hester & W. R. Miller (Eds.), *Handbook of alcoholism treatment approaches: Effective alternatives* (3rd ed., pp. 113–130). Boston: Allyn & Bacon.

PART III

SPECIAL ISSUES

CHAPTER 20

Marital Distress

BRIAN D. DOSS, ALEXANDRA E. MITCHELL,
AND FELICIA DE LA GARZA-MERCER

DESCRIPTION OF THE PROBLEM

Marital distress has an enormous impact on individuals, children, and society as a whole. More than 40% of first marriages are predicted to end in divorce (Kreider, 2005), with second marriages even more likely to fail (e.g., Bramlett & Mosher, 2001). Additionally, many other marriages are either stably distressed or cycle through periods of marital distress. Even when it does not result in divorce, marital distress has been linked to elevated levels of individual mental health and substance abuse disorders (e.g., Whisman & Uebelacker, 2003) and increased negative cardiovascular, immune, and other physical health problems (e.g., Kiecolt-Glaser & Newton, 2001). Marital distress and divorce also have a profound impact on child functioning and have been linked to increased externalizing and internalizing behavior problems and poor academic achievement (e.g., Cummings & Davies, 1994). These problems, coupled with the extensive financial strains of divorce, often reduce individuals' ability to care for themselves and increase the demands on services provided by health agencies, employers, and state and federal governments.

Marital distress has a variety of emotional, behavioral, and cognitive manifestations. These components are interrelated, with difficulties in one area of relationship functioning influencing and being influenced by difficulties in another area. Relative to satisfied couples, spouses in distressed marriages may experience high levels of negative affect, report a general lack of emotional affection, and have difficulty regulating their emotions (Epstein & Baucom, 2002; Gottman, 1999). Behavioral signs of couple distress include problematic communication patterns, physical aggression between partners, and sexual difficulties (Christensen & Shenk, 1991; Snyder, 1997). The manner in which individuals think about their partner and the relationship are also related to relationship distress (Epstein & Baucom, 2002). Specifically, partners in distressed relationships often have negative attributions about their partner's behavior, unrealistic standards and dysfunctional assumptions about the relationship, and negative expectancies about their partner and the relationship. These three elements of marital distress are discussed in more detail in this chapter.

EMOTION

Couples seeking marital therapy often present with feelings of general dissatisfaction and disaffection that may be related to one or more specific emotional difficulties (Snyder & Aikman, 1999). Compared to nondistressed couples, distressed couples exhibit higher rates, longer duration, and greater reciprocity of negative relationship affect (Gottman, 1999). However, it is important to note that not all negative emotions negatively affect the marital relationship. For example, whereas time-limited anger is not related to divorce, ongoing criticism and contempt are (Gottman, Driver, & Tabares, 2002).

In addition, distressed couples often experience a general lack of emotional intimacy, which is related to marital distress for both husbands and wives (Greef & Malherbe, 2001). Based on reports from marital therapists, Geiss and O'Leary (1981) found that over half of couples seeking treatment identified a "lack of loving feelings" as a problem area in the relationship. Furthermore, 57% of couples seeking marital therapy reported emotional distance as a reason for seeking treatment (Doss, Simpson, & Christensen, 2004). Therapists identify intimacy deficits as one of the most damaging problems in relationships (Whisman, Dixon, & Johnson, 1997). The recent development of integrative behavioral couple therapy (Jacobson & Christensen, 1998), described in more detail later in the chapter, was largely in response to limitations of existing treatments to deal with a lack of loving feelings (Jacobson, 1992).

BEHAVIOR

Communication problems are one of the most common behaviors in distressed couples; however, the particular communication difficulties a couple may be experiencing can take a variety of forms. Compared to nondistressed couples, distressed couples exhibit more negative communication (i.e., criticism, disagreement) and less positive communication (i.e., problem solving, agreement, and humor; Hooley & Hahlweg, 1989; Margolin & Wampold, 1981). In addition, distressed and nondistressed couples also differ in their patterns of communication; indeed, distressed couples are more likely to reciprocate and escalate hostility exhibited by their partner, continue hostile behavior throughout a conflict, and engage in sequences of behavior in which one partner pursues an issue while the other withdraws from the conflict (Heyman, 2001).

Aggression is another common behavioral manifestation of couple distress. Approximately 60% of couples seeking treatment for marital distress have experienced physical violence in their relationship (Ehrensaft & Vivian, 1996). Based on their report of their own behavior, approximately 29% of partners were mildly aggressive (throwing objects, pushing, slapping, shoving, grabbing), and 25% of partners were severely aggressive (hitting with object, kicking, biting, beating up, forcing sex, attempting to use a weapon). Women commit aggressive acts more frequently than do men, but aggressive acts committed by men are more likely to result in injury (Archer, 2000). Male aggression toward females can take one of two forms: intimate terrorism or common couple violence (M. P. Johnson, 1995; M. P. Johnson & Ferraro, 2000). In intimate terrorism, an individual uses aggression to control his partner. In contrast, common couple violence is not related to a pattern of control, but rather occurs when arguments escalate.

Sexual difficulties are also strongly associated with marital distress (e.g., Snyder, 1997). Indeed, over 50% of couples seeking therapy report sexual difficulties in their relationship (Geiss & O'Leary, 1981). Among these couples, male partners commonly identify problems with infrequency of intercourse, orgasm, and feelings of sexual inadequacy (Snyder & Berg, 1983). Female partners commonly have difficulty with sexual arousal and orgasm. Couples with sexual difficulties often, but not always, have difficulties in other areas of their relationship (Metz & Epstein, 2002).

COGNITION

In addition to emotional and behavioral difficulties, distressed couples may also process information differently from nondistressed couples. When a distressed individual's partner exhibits negative behavior, that individual tends to attribute the cause of his or her partner's negative behavior to the partner or to himself or herself, rather than to outside events (Baucom, Sayers, & Duhe, 1989). In addition, individuals in distressed relationships often view the cause of negative behaviors as stable (likely to continue in the future) and global (likely to affect many aspects of the relationship). In contrast, individuals in satisfied relationships are likely to make external, time-limited, and specific attributions.

Partners in distressed relationships also have unrealistic standards and dysfunctional assumptions about themselves, their partners, and the relationship. For example, marital distress is associated with believing that one's partner should be able to determine what one is thinking without its being explicitly stated (Eidelson & Epstein, 1982). Having such a standard may inhibit an individual from expressing thoughts, feelings, and needs and may also result in an individual's feeling angry or hurt when his or her partner is not able to infer these thoughts, feelings, and needs. Assuming that expressing disagreement may threaten the couple relationship or that relationship difficulties arise from inherent gender differences may also lead to dysfunctional interactions between partners.

Finally, many distressed couples have negative expectancies about their partner and their marriage (Epstein & Baucom, 2002). Individuals in distressed relationships often predict that their partner will behave negatively and that their partner and their relationship are unlikely to change. Such negative expectancies may both contribute to and exacerbate cycles of negative expectations, emotions, and behavior.

DIAGNOSIS AND ASSESSMENT

MARITAL DISTRESS IN *DSM-IV* AND *DSM-V*

Currently, marital distress is not included as a psychological disorder in the fourth edition of the *Diagnostic and Statistical Manual of Mental Disorders* (*DSM-IV*; American Psychiatric Association, 2000). Indeed, the only current category for marital distress in *DSM-IV* is a V-code labeled "partner relationship problem" (p. 737). It is described as "a pattern of interaction between spouses or partners characterized by negative communication (e.g., criticisms), distorted communication (e.g., unrealistic expectations), or noncommunication (e.g., withdrawal)." This pattern must be associated with "clinically significant impairment in individual or family functioning or the development of symptoms in one or both partners." This definition focuses solely on the communication domain of marital distress, excluding emotional and cognitive aspects.

Failure to include marital distress as a formal diagnosis, and the accompanying lack of integration of marital distress into the etiology and presentation of other individual disorders, has been identified as one of the primary limitations of *DSM-IV* (e.g., First et al., 2002). Unfortunately, marital distress has also been omitted from the ongoing working groups for the creation of *DSM-V*. In an effort to improve the coverage of marital distress in *DSM-V*, Division 43 (Family Psychology) of the American Psychological Association has established a working group, cochaired by Dr. Erika Lawrence and the first author, to develop a proposal for suggested inclusions; this effort is currently ongoing. Additionally, Drs. Beach and Wamboldt are coordinating a parallel effort for inclusion of relational processes in the *DSM-V*. This group recently published a book titled *Relational Processes and DSM-V: Neuroscience, Assessment, Prevention, and Treatment* (2006).

ASSESSMENT

Clinical Interview   Assessment of couples often begins with a clinical interview to assess individual and relationship histories as well as origins and development of current difficulties. Interviews should typically be supplemented by the use of self-report questionnaires, particularly on sensitive topics such as sex and domestic violence. Some therapists conduct the full interview with both partners present. Other therapists include separate meetings with individual partners as part of the interview process. An advantage to meeting with partners separately is that each partner may feel safer talking about potentially sensitive issues such as relationship aggression. Some therapists choose not to proceed with separate interviews unless information gathered during a conjoint session indicates that it may be necessary, because not knowing what was disclosed during the separate interviews may lead the partners to feel less comfortable with the therapist. If the therapist decides to conduct separate interviews, he or she must provide clear guidelines about how he or she will handle disclosure of information by one partner in the individual session that is unknown to the other partner.

Measures of Emotion

SELF-REPORT MEASURES   Several self-report measures provide information about an individual's overall relationship satisfaction and, to varying degrees, levels of affectional communication and closeness. Perhaps the first widely used measure of martial distress, the Marital Adjustment Test (MAT; Locke & Wallace, 1959), is a 15-item instrument containing questions measuring relationship satisfaction, conflict resolution, communication, cohesion, and level of agreement about several important relationship domains. An updated and revised version of the MAT, the 32-item Dyadic Adjustment Scale (DAS; Spanier, 1976), contains four subscales assessing satisfaction, cohesion, consensus, and affectional expression in the couple relationship.

Although measures of marital adjustment and marital satisfaction assess similar constructs, there are some potential difficulties with marital adjustment measures (e.g., Heyman, Sayers, & Bellack, 1994). For example, the adjustment score of the DAS (Spanier, 1976) is based on items about both behavioral processes related to marital satisfaction and feelings of satisfaction with aspects of the marriage (Heyman et al., 1994). The first 15 items of the DAS ask the respondent to indicate the level of disagreement between partners about, rather than satisfaction with, various relational issues. Comparison of individuals' level of disagreement with their level of satisfaction in these areas indicated that individuals' ratings of disagreement and satisfaction often differ. Although the DAS remains the most widely recognized measure of relational adjustment, researchers are increasingly turning toward more pure measures of relationship satisfaction, such as the Quality of Marriage Index (Norton, 1983).

In this vein, one of the most comprehensive and well-validated measures of relationship satisfaction is the Marital Satisfaction Inventory—Revised (MSI-R; Snyder, 1997; Snyder & Aikman, 1999), a 150-item measure that assesses level of distress in several different relationship domains. In addition to validity scales, the MSI-R contains one scale that measures the individual's overall dissatisfaction with the relationship and 10 scales that assess satisfaction in specific relationship domains. These domains are affective communication, problem-solving communication, aggression, time spent together, finances, sexual dissatisfaction, marital and parental role orientation, family history of distress, parenting, and parent-child relationships. The MSI-R can be used to identify distressed couples as well as to evaluate change in specific aspects of couples' relationships during therapy (Snyder, 1997).

Rather then assessing satisfaction, other measures focus on the emotional connection between partners. One commonly used measure, the Personal Assessment of Intimacy in Relationships (PAIR; Schaefer & Olson, 1981), assesses several types of intimacy and may be particularly helpful when individuals have difficulty articulating the specific areas in which they experience intimacy deficits. The PAIR assesses different types of intimacy, including emotional (feelings of closeness), social (shared friends), sexual (general affection and sexual activity), intellectual (ability to discuss ideas and thoughts), and recreational (common interests). This measure can be used to determine both the amount of intimacy currently perceived in those areas and the amount of intimacy desired.

OBSERVATIONAL MEASURES   Observational measures are commonly used in research on marital distress but, because of time limitations and the effort needed to code observations, typically are not used in clinical settings. Observational assessments typically entail extensive coding of structured sets of videotaped interactions between spouses. Although observational systems often assess constructs in more than one domain (i.e., emotional, behavioral, and cognitive), the instruments are reviewed according to their primary domain of assessment. Information about additional systems can be found in Kerig and Baucom's (2004) book on the subject, and a review of the psychometric properties of numerous coding systems is provided in an article by Heyman (2001).

The Specific Affect Coding System (Shapiro & Gottman, 2004) can be used to identify specific emotions displayed by each partner during an interaction. A coder observes the couple's interaction and codes each change in emotion. Positive emotional communication codes include interest, validation, affection, humor, and surprise or joy. Negative emotion codes include disgust, contempt, belligerence, domineering, criticism, anger, defensiveness, sadness, and stonewalling. When no positive or negative emotion is evident, a neutral code is given.

Two observational systems have been developed specifically to assess intimate behaviors in couple relationships. The Intimacy Coding System (Dorian & Cordova, 2004) and the Couples' Intimate Behavior Rating System (Mitchell et al., in press) were both developed to examine couple behavior during discussions about relationship injuries. Such discussions provide an opportunity for couples to develop feelings of closeness when personal disclosures are responded to in an empathic manner. After viewing the entire interaction, coders or raters assess both the speaker's disclosures and the listener's response. These measures allow the therapist to identify particular behaviors, such as lack of disclosure or low levels of empathy, which may be leading to intimacy deficits.

Measures of Behavior

SELF-REPORT MEASURES   Couples may come to therapy with vague descriptions of the behaviors that they find problematic in their relationship, especially when presenting with "communication" difficulties (Doss et al., 2004). Two self-report measures may be helpful in clarifying the specific distressing behaviors in the relationship. On the Areas of Change Questionnaire (ACQ; Weiss & Birchler, 1975; Weiss, Hops, & Patterson, 1973), respondents indicate whether they would prefer that their partner increase or decrease 34 behaviors, such as companionship, housework, recreational time, sex, and work habits, and the amount of change desired in each area. The Frequency and Acceptability of Partner Behavior Inventory (FAPBI; Christensen & Jacobson, 1997; Doss & Christensen, 2006), partially adapted from the ACQ, assesses the partner's frequency of 20 positive and negative relationship behaviors as well as the acceptability of those behaviors at that frequency. In a sample of over 12,000 individuals and 500 community and therapy couples, the FAPBI was found to have four factors: Affection, Closeness, Demand, and Violation. These factors were consistent across sexes, sexual orientations, and types of romantic relationship (Doss & Christensen, in press).

For more detailed assessment of dysfunctional communication patterns, the Communication Patterns Questionnaire (CPQ; Christensen & Sullaway, 1984) is useful. The CPQ assesses communication behaviors across three phases of disagreement: when a problem arises, during the discussion of the problem, and following the discussion. Questionnaire subscales provide the therapist with information about whether the couple engages in mutually constructive communication, mutual avoidance, or demand-withdraw patterns of communication.

To assess both psychological and physical aggression in relationships, the Conflict Tactics Scales (CTS2; Straus, Hamby, Boney-McCoy, & Sugarman, 1996) is often used. On the CTS2, the Negotiation scale assesses the couple's ability to respond to disagreement by successfully discussing the topic. The remaining scales assess negative responses to conflict, including psychological aggression, physical assault, sexual coercion, and injury. Each of the scales assessing negative responses to conflict includes both Minor and Severe subscales, enabling the severity of the particular type of aggression to be assessed.

Couples may not feel comfortable discussing their sexual relationship in detail during the clinical interview; therefore, self-report instruments may be particularly useful in gathering information about this relationship domain. The Sexual Interaction Inventory (LoPiccolo, & Steger, 1974) asks each partner to rate the frequency, desired frequency, satisfaction with, desired satisfaction with, and perceptions of partner's satisfaction and desired satisfaction with 17 heterosexual behaviors. In contrast to measuring specific sexual behaviors, the Golombok Rust Inventory of Sexual Satisfaction (Rust & Golombok, 1986) screens for sexual dysfunction. The 28-item questionnaire contains 12 subscales providing information about specific areas of sexual dysfunction, including impotence, premature ejaculation, anorgasmia, vaginismus, noncommunication, infrequency, avoidance, nonsensuality, and dissatisfaction.

Observational Measures

Observational Measures   There are several observational coding systems that can be used to assess the communication behavior exhibited by a particular couple. The

Rapid Marital Interaction Coding System (Heyman, 2004) was developed as a variant of the Marital Interaction Coding System (e.g., Weiss, 1992). Coders observe a couple's interaction and, after each speaker turn, categorize an individual's behavior into a variety of positive, negative, or neutral codes. The Communications Skills Test (Floyd, 2004) is another observational assessment instrument that can be helpful in understanding how partners interact when discussing a conflictual issue. Coders provide a rating for each speaker turn, ranging from very positive to very negative depending of the behavior's influence on resolving the problem. In addition to providing information about each individual's overall ability to problem-solve, this instrument enables the therapist to examine the sequence of behaviors that the couple engages in as they attempt to discuss an issue.

As previously noted, patterns of interaction in which one partner pursues discussion of a topic while the other person withdraws from the discussion are common in distressed couples (Heyman, 2001). The Couple Interaction Rating System (Sevier, Simpson, & Christensen, 2004) was created to assess this particular pattern of communication. After watching the entire interaction, raters assess the degree to which each individual engaged in five specific behaviors. Two behaviors, blaming the partner and pressuring the partner to change, are considered components of demanding behavior. Withdrawing behavior is measured with three codes: withdrawal, avoidance, and discussion.

The previous coding systems are particularly useful for examining couple behavior during problem-solving discussions. However, couples also have discussions in which one partner has a problem outside the relationship and is seeking support from his or her partner. The Social Support Interaction Coding System (Pasch, Harris, Sullivan, & Bradbury, 2004) was created to assess couple communication during such discussions. Coders assess couple behavior after each speaker turn. There are separate codes for the helper (positive instrumental, positive emotional, positive other, negative, neutral, and off-task) and the helpee (positive, negative, neutral, and off-task). Behaviors such as giving advice and offering to help the partner in taking action are categorized as positive instrumental. The positive emotional code includes offering encouragement and reassurance. Any positive behaviors that are not instrumentally or emotionally supportive are classified as positive other. Behaviors such as blaming and criticizing are categorized as negative.

Measures of Cognition
SELF-REPORT MEASURES There are several self-report measures to assess attributions, standards, assumptions, and expectancies in relationships. The Dyadic Attribution Inventory (Baucom, Sayers, et al., 1989) is a 24-item questionnaire that provides descriptions of hypothetical relationship events concerning affection, complimenting, consideration, sharing feelings, sex, household chores, personal habits, finances, companionship, and communication. In 12 of these situations the result of the partner's behavior is positive, and in 12 it is negative. To assess the attribution given to these events, the respondent is asked to indicate whether the behavior in each event is due to the respondent, the partner, or an outside circumstance. The respondent also indicates the degree to which this causal influence is likely to continue in the future and the degree to which the cause will affect many relationship domains. The Relationship Attribution Measure (Fincham & Bradbury, 1992) is a similar measure but presents only negative hypothetical events. In addition to assessing the respondent's perception of the cause, this measure assesses whether the respondent perceives the

negative behavior as intentional, justified, or selfishly motivated and views the partner as deserving blame for the behavior.

In contrast to asking about specific behaviors, the Marital Attitude Survey (Pretzer, Epstein, & Fleming, 1991) is a 39-item measure that assesses the respondent's general thoughts about the relationship (i.e., "If my partner did things differently we'd get along better"). The instrument contains eight subscales, six assessing attributions, and two assessing expectancies. The six attribution subscales examine the respondent's attributions about his or her own behavior and personality and about his or her partner's behavior, personality, malicious intent, and lack of love. The Expectancies subscales indicate the degree to which the respondent believes the couple is able to change and expects the relationship to improve.

Two measures may enable the therapist to quickly determine the specific relationship beliefs and standards that may be leading to dysfunctional interactions in the couple relationship. The Relationship Belief Inventory (Eidelson & Epstein, 1982) contains five scales measuring beliefs that are associated with marital distress: "disagreement is destructive," "mind reading is expected," "partners cannot change," "sexual perfectionism," and "the sexes are different." A similar measure is the Inventory of Specific Relationship Standards (Baucom, Epstein, Rankin, & Burnett, 1996). This instrument assesses an individual's standards pertaining to boundaries, power, and investment in the relationship. The individual's standards for each of these dimensions are examined as they relate to finances, affection, household tasks, relation with friends and family, religion, sexual interaction, career issues, parenting, communicating negative and positive thoughts and feelings, and leisure.

OBSERVATIONAL MEASURES   Observational measures have not typically focused on couples' thought processes. One notable exception to this is the Relationship Schema Coding System (Sullivan & Baucom, 2004), which examines the extent to which individuals interpret events according to their meaning for the relationship. After watching the entire interaction, an observer rates partners on the quantity and quality of relationship processing as well as whether these thoughts are constructive or destructive. Assessing couple behavior with this measure may be helpful in identifying strengths and weaknesses in the way partners process events both inside and outside of their relationship (Sullivan & Baucom, 2004).

CONCEPTUALIZATION

Unlike any other difficulty focused on in Volume 1, marital distress is defined as occurring both within and between individuals. As such, the conceptualization of marital distress must incorporate both inter- and intra-individual etiologies and manifestations. Indeed, the origins of marital distress may lie in one or both of the spouses, in a combination of individual traits across spouses, in the couple's dynamics independent of individual difficulties, or in conflicts between the couple and their broader work, social, or cultural environments. As described in the Treatment section, different theoretical orientations place varying emphases on these domains. However, there are a number of empirical findings that shed light on marital distress.

LEARNING AND MODELING

A consistent finding in the marital distress literature is that, compared to children of nondivorced parents, children of divorced parents have a greater likelihood of divorce themselves. Therefore, there appears to be some individual mechanisms through which marital distress and divorce is transmitted though generations. Although this finding is generally accepted, there is considerable debate about the specific mechanisms of such transmission.

Perhaps the most compelling evidence for an intergenerational mechanism of divorce and marital distress is for the effects of parenting (e.g., Hetherington, Bridges, & Insabella, 1988; Hetherington & Kelly, 2002). Indeed, parenting quality has been found to largely mediate the relation between parents' divorce and their children's marital instability (Hetherington & Elmore, 2004). Compared to intact families, children in divorced families experience more parent-child and parent-parent conflict. Additionally, both mothers and fathers tend to be less firm and consistent, less emotionally warm, and more punitive (e.g., Amato, 2001; Hetherington & Stanley-Hagan, 2002). The effect of parenting on children's likelihood of subsequent divorce seems to be especially strong for mothers' parenting (Hetherington & Elmore, 2004). Parenting difficulties in the family of origin are likely related to a number of attachment difficulties frequently seen in the adult children's distressed relationships (e.g., Hazan & Shaver, 1987). However, additional evidence exists for intergenerational transmission of divorce being independently mediated through demographic risks. In particular, parents' divorce increases the likelihood of their children's young age at marriage (Hetherington & Elmore, 2004). Furthermore, as discussed later in the chapter, genetics also partially mediate the intergenerational transmission of divorce.

Life Events

Stressful life events can be an opportunity for both conflict and growth in marital relationships. Although marital distress often originates in times of high stress (Karney & Bradbury, 1995), couples often report that successfully navigating these stressors enhances marital satisfaction and commitment (e.g., Belsky & Rovine, 1990; Shapiro, Gottman, & Carrere, 2000). Couples who tend to grow from stressful life events have good communication and flexible relationship expectations and view the event as a shared challenge. Next, we explore two common potentially stressful life events that often impact marriages.

Relationship Formation   There are several early relationship factors and/or experiences that have been found to predict the likelihood of subsequent marital distress and divorce. One of the most consistent predictors of divorce risk is getting married at an early age. Indeed, Hetherington and Elmore (2004) identified early marriage as the most powerful demographic predictor of divorce. In particular, a couple who marries when the wife is a teenager is much more likely to divorce than couples where the wife was at least 20 years old (Bramlett & Mosher, 2001).

Another critical factor in a couple's subsequent success is whether they lived together (i.e., cohabited) before marriage. Numerous studies have shown cohabitation to predict higher rates of divorce (e.g., Kamp Dush, Cohan, & Amato, 2003) and marital distress (e.g., Stanley, Whitton, & Markman, 2004). Subsequent research has pointed to cohabitation before engagement as being especially problematic (Kline et al., 2004), with theory suggesting that some couples who cohabit before marriage may not have married had they not lived together originally (Stanley, Rhoades, & Markman, 2006).

Transition to Parenthood A recent meta-analysis revealed that couples with an infant have substantially lower marital satisfaction than matched couples with no children ($d = -0.38$; Twenge, Campbell, & Foster, 2003). Numerous longitudinal studies have shown relationship satisfaction declines of a full standard deviation or more in 20% to 59% of couples (e.g., Belsky & Rovine, 1990; Cowan & Cowan, 2000) and "precipitous" drops in 70% of couples (e.g., Gottman et al., 2002). Indeed, almost 33% of partners fall into the clinical range of marital distress during the first 18 months after the birth of their child (Cowan & Cowan, 1995).

Increases in marital distress during the transition to parenthood can be traced to a number of individual, couple, and child factors. For example, individual factors, such as psychological distress, life stress, lack of social support (Cowan & Cowan, 1995), and insecure attachment (Rholes, Simpson, Campbell, & Grich, 2001) all contribute to declines in satisfaction. Additionally, couple factors such as poor communication, low relationship awareness, conflict about division of labor, and the coparenting relationship all predicted increased relationship distress (Shapiro et al., 2000). Finally, child factors, including a couple's desire to have a child at that time (Cowan & Cowan, 2000) and the sex of the child (with male children leading to fewer declines in satisfaction; Cox, Paley, Burchinal, & Payne, 1999), have predicted marital satisfaction.

Genetic Influences Although the full scope of genetic influence on marital distress is unknown, there is emerging evidence that genetics play an important role in marital distress and divorce. In particular, personality, which has strong genetic heritability (e.g., Viken, Rose, Kaprio, & Koskenvuo, 1994), has been linked to marital distress (e.g., Lavee & Ben-Ari, 2004) and divorce (e.g., Jockin, McGue, & Lykken, 1996). However, the specific effects of personality on marriage seem to depend on the specific type of personality studied (with effects for neuroticism generally being strongest), sex of the individual (e.g., Lavee & Ben-Ari, 2004), and whether one considers level of or changes in marital distress (e.g., Karney & Bradbury, 1997).

Additionally, to understand the effect of genetics, it is useful to simultaneously examine the influence of genetic and social/psychological factors on marriage. For example, the problematic parenting in divorced families discussed earlier has been linked to subsequent development of personality problems in children. Personality problems in the children are then related to poor problem-solving and relationship skills that are subsequently linked to their own marital instability (Hetherington & Elmore, 2004). Are such effects better conceptualized as genetic or social/psychological influences? Studies examining both types of influences simultaneously suggest that approximately 30% to 42% of the heritability of divorce risk operates through genetic influences on personality (e.g., Jockin et al., 1996).

INDIVIDUAL MENTAL DISORDERS

The intersection of marital distress and individual psychopathology is critical to an understanding of the generally high comorbidity between these two areas. The interplay between marital and individual distress is complex, with increasing evidence that the effects of the two areas are reciprocal (Whisman & Uebelacker, 2003). Marital distress increases the probability of individual mental health problems; indeed, compared to those in nondistressed marriages, individuals in distressed marriages are 1.8 to 5.7 times more likely to have diagnosable mental health problems (Whisman & Uebelacker, 2003). Furthermore, these associations seem to be limited to marital distress rather than more general difficulties in relationships with family and friends (Whisman, Sheldon, & Goering, 2000) or even cohabiting romantic relationships (Uebelaker & Whisman, 2006). On the other hand, individual mental health problems have been shown to create disruptions in family interactions and emotional connections (e.g., Chakrabarti, Kulhara, & Verma, 1993). The relationship between marital distress and three common individual disorders is explored in greater detail next.

Depression　Meta-analyses based on representative samples of thousands of individuals reveal that marital distress and depression are correlated 0.37 and 0.42 for men and women, respectively; this correlation rises to 0.66 in individuals seeking treatment for Major Depression (Whisman, 2001). Additionally, marital distress increases threefold the likelihood of developing a major depressive episode in the following year; stated differently, approximately 33% of the cases of Major Depression among married individuals could be prevented if marital distress was eliminated (Whisman & Bruce, 1999).

Anxiety　Maritally distressed individuals are 2.5 times more likely to have an anxiety disorder than maritally satisfied individuals. Particularly comorbid types of anxiety include Generalized Anxiety Disorder (3.2 times), Panic Disorder (3.5 times), and Posttraumatic Stress Disorder (PTSD; 3.8 times), whereas simple phobia is less associated with marital distress (1.9 times; Whisman & Uebelacker, 2003). When rates of marital distress among individuals with anxiety disorders are considered, the numbers are equally striking. Approximately 50% of individuals with Obsessive-Compulsive Disorder and 70% of veterans with PTSD have clinically significantly levels of marital distress (Riggs, Hiss, & Foa, 1992).

Substance Abuse　Associations between marital distress and substance abuse are also strong. Maritally dissatisfied individuals are 3.7 times more likely to develop an alcohol use disorder in the following year (Whisman, Uebelacker, & Bruce, 2006). Furthermore, after treatment for alcohol disorders, marital distress predicts an increased likelihood and decreased time to relapse (Maisto, O'Farrell, Connors, McKay, & Pelcovits, 1988). The reverse relationship also holds; Disordered drinking leads to increase in marital distress and divorce in the following year (Leonard & Roberts, 1998). Additionally, individuals abusing illegal drugs report high levels of marital distress (Fals-Stewart, Birchler, & O'Farrell, 1999).

Physical Problems and Marriage

Discovery or development of a spouse's physical problems can have an important influence on a marriage; however, the specifics of that impact depend on both the nature of the physical problem and the strength of the marital relationship. For sudden and severe physical problems, such as a diagnosis of cancer, severe reactions such as depression, anxiety, and sexual difficulties are often found in the individual as well as his or her partner (e.g., Ptacek, Pierce, Dodge, & Ptacek, 1997). These individual difficulties often have negative impacts on the marriage, as described earlier. However, as mentioned previously, successfully navigating stressful life events such as severe illness can help couples increase intimacy and marital satisfaction (Halford, Scott, & Smythe, 2000).

In addition, there is substantial evidence that being married, especially happily married, can have a dramatic impact on the development and course of physical problems (cf. Kiecolt-Glaser & Newton, 2001). Moreover, marital distress and a lack of social support are some of the strongest predictors of physical health outcomes (Burman & Margolin, 1992). Recent efforts have begun to map the specific pathways of marriage's influence on physical health (Kiecolt-Glaser & Newton, 2001) and to determine which marital interventions may improve health outcomes (e.g., Scott, Halford, & Ward, 2004).

CULTURAL AND DIVERSITY ISSUES

There have been several studies on rates of marital distress and divorce for different ethnic groups; results tend to indicate that compared to Caucasian and Hispanic couples, African American couples are more likely and Asian American couples much less likely to get divorced (e.g., Bramlett & Mosher, 2001). These differences likely reflect a complex combination of economic, religious, and cultural factors. Cultural and diversity issues are also essential to consider when assessing and treating couples (e.g., Hardy & Laszloffy, 2002). For example, although high levels of verbal negativity are generally considered a sign of marital distress, the definition of "high" is culturally dependent. Indeed, German couples in satisfied relationships and Australian couples in distressed relationships engage in similar levels of verbal negativity (Halford, Hahlweg, & Dunne, 1990), suggesting that what may be acceptable in German society may not be acceptable in Australian society. Additionally, cultural and diversity issues play important roles in marriages in which spouses have different ethnic or cultural backgrounds. Previous research (e.g., Kurdek, 1991) suggests that these couples have somewhat higher rates of divorces and separation than couples from similar backgrounds, likely because of differences in core beliefs and values. These topics are explored in more detail in the Case Description in this chapter and in other resources (e.g., Hardy & Laszloffy, 2002). Additionally, although a full treatment is beyond the current scope of this chapter, gay and lesbian committed relationships also experience special challenges, including societal stigma, ambiguity of social roles, and often a lack of social support (cf. Green & Mitchell, 2002).

BEHAVIORAL TREATMENTS

OVERALL EFFICACY

There can be little doubt that research-based behavioral treatment (i.e., marital therapy) is, on average, an efficacious treatment for marital distress. In the most recent meta-analysis of general marital therapy, Shadish and Baldwin (2003) found a mean posttreatment effect size of .84, a large effect. This result indicates that, on average, couples in marital therapy are better off after treatment than 80% of couples in a no-treatment control group. Thus, the pre-post efficacy of marital therapy for improving marital distress has been well established. Additionally, the same meta-analysis indicated that virtually all well-developed marital therapies are approximately equally effective at the end of active treatment.

However, there are at least two reasons to be cautious about these reassuring findings. First, virtually all of the studies described in the meta-analysis were conducted in research settings, most using research staff as therapists rather than clinicians who would typically see couples. Therefore, although the results suggest that marital therapy delivered as part of a research study is a powerful treatment for marital distress, the effectiveness of marital therapy in real-world clinical settings is unclear. In the only published effectiveness study of marital therapy for marital distress to date, Hahlweg and Klann (1997) found that marital therapy in German community clinics produced an average effect size of .28, notably smaller than the effect size of .84 reported earlier. Second, the impact of marital therapy tends to decrease as time elapses from the end of treatment, leaving many, and sometimes most, couples no better off than when they originally sought treatment. As described in more detail in the following section, the long-term efficacy of marital therapy depends in part on the specific type of treatment received.

DESCRIPTION AND OUTCOME OF SPECIFIC MARITAL THERAPIES FOR MARITAL DISTRESS

Although existing evidence has not suggested important differences in the efficacy of different treatments at the end of treatment, it is important to consider the various therapeutic approaches because the amount of empirical support for the treatments varies substantially and because there appears to be variability across treatments (and studies) regarding their efficacy at long-term follow-up.

Behavioral Marital Therapy   In behavioral marital therapy (BMT), the therapist encourages change through direct instruction and skills training. Specifically, BMT utilizes three primary techniques: behavioral exchange, communication training, and problem-solving training. Behavioral exchange techniques aim to increase the frequency of positive behaviors by encouraging couples to generate and enact lists of positive relationship behaviors. Communication training teaches couples speaker and listener skills that can be used in daily conversation; problem-solving training teaches couples strategies to effectively brainstorm and solve difficult issues.

Behavioral marital therapy was the first empirically supported marital therapy and is the most researched type of marital therapy. Couples who receive BMT repeatedly demonstrate decreases in marital distress from beginning to end of treatment, with effect sizes in the medium (e.g., Shadish & Baldwin, 2005) to large (e.g., Dunn & Schwebel, 1995) range. However, in the first published long-term follow-up of BMT, Jacobson, Schmaling, and Holtzworth-Munroe (1987) found that, 2 years after treatment, over half of the couples had either the same or worse levels of marital distress as they did before beginning treatment. Snyder, Wills, and Grady-Fletcher (1991) found similar results in a 4-year follow-up of BMT. However, the largest study of BMT to date found 60% of couples had maintained clinically significant improvements 2 years following the end of treatment, significantly more than the Jacobson et al. or the Snyder et al. studies (Christensen, Atkins, Yi, Baucom, & George, 2006).

Cognitive-Behavioral Couple Therapy   Cognitive-behavioral couple therapy (CBCT) attempts to build on BMT by adding cognitive interventions to the traditional BMT interventions described earlier. In particular, CBCT uses cognitive-restructuring techniques to modify selective attention, misdirected causal attributions, and maladaptive expectancies, assumptions, and standards (Baucom, Epstein, Sayers, & Sher, 1989). However, the addition of cognitive interventions does not appear to improve the efficacy of BMT, even when paired with additional emotional expressiveness (e.g., Baucom, Sayers, & Sher, 1990; Halford, Sanders, & Behrens, 1993).

Insight-Oriented Marital Therapy   The central therapeutic task of insight-oriented marital therapy (IOMT) is resolving conflictual, emotional processes within or between spouses. These emotional processes develop over time through individual developmental issues and maladaptive relationship patterns and rules within the present marriage. As such, IOMT uses a number of therapist questions and interpretations to uncover and then restructure unconscious or subconscious expectations or dynamics. With increased insight into these maladaptive aspects of themselves and their relationship, couples are expected to more appropriately respond to their current marital difficulties (Snyder & Wills, 1989). In an outcome study of 60 couples, IOMT was shown to have similar reductions in marital distress to BMT at the end of treatment (Cohen's *d* of approximately 1.00; Snyder & Wills, 1989). However, at a 4-year follow-up, only 3% of IOMT couples were divorced, whereas 38% of BMT couples were divorced (Snyder et al., 1991). This follow-up, the longest to date in the published marital therapy literature, indicates that IOMT may address many of the concerns with decreases in efficacy in BMT over time.

Emotionally Focused Couples Therapy   Based in attachment theory, emotionally focused couples therapy (EFCT) targets cycles of negative emotions and communication in an effort to produce new interactions that permit the development of increased intimacy. In the first part of treatment, the EFCT therapist assesses the couple and attempts to de-escalate maladaptive interaction patterns. Once the couple can restructure their interactions in session, the therapist encourages deepening of emotional experiences; from this emotional sharing, opportunities for intimacy and new emotional bonds are created. In the final sessions, the therapist works to solidify couple gains and develop new solutions to previous relationship difficulties. Across several studies, EFCT resulted in a pre-post effect size of 1.28 for decreases in marital distress (S. M. Johnson, Hunsley, Greenberg, & Schindler, 1999), somewhat larger than the mean effect size of .84 reported for marital treatments in general (Shadish & Baldwin, 2003). In a recent study, 50% of couples at posttreatment and 70% of couples at 3 months were in the nondistressed range (S. Johnson & Talitman, 1997).

Integrative Behavioral Couple Therapy   Integrative behavioral couple therapy (IBCT) builds on BMT by integrating a focus on individuals' emotional reactions to their partner's behaviors in addition to attempts to modify actual behavior—the typical focus of BMT. Integrative behavioral couple therapy provides couples with an individualized relationship theme which helps them to comprehend the natural differences between them and how their interactions have turned these natural differences into the problematic patterns that are now creating their marital distress. The therapy uses three primary techniques: empathic joining (eliciting and sharing of vulnerable feelings to increase intimacy), unified detachment (developing a cognitive, detached understanding of their problematic relationship patterns), and tolerance (encouraging couples to examine both positive and negative aspects of their problem behavior, including enacting the problem behavior itself).

In an ongoing study, the largest randomized trial of marital therapy to date, 71% of couples in IBCT showed clinically significant improvement by the end of treatment, with 52% of couples ending treatment in the nondistressed range (Christensen et al.,

2004). At 2-year follow-up, 68.8% of IBCT couples were reliably improved since pre-treatment, with 47% of couples in the nondistressed range (Christensen et al., 2006). This approach and the specific techniques are illustrated in the Case Description.

Case Description

When they sought marital therapy, Dara and Gabriel, ages 40 and 47, respectively, had been married for 15 years and had two school-age children. They reported that they had been experiencing marital difficulties for approximately 1 year, but that their problems had increased in severity over the past 6 months. Neither spouse had previously sought individual or marital therapy in the past. They participated in a randomized clinical trial of marital therapy (Christensen et al., 2004, 2006) and received integrative behavioral couple therapy (IBCT). Thus, the conceptualization and treatment of their marital distress follows an IBCT framework.

Presenting Complaints

Dara and Gabriel sought couple therapy primarily for help with overwhelming financial problems and with issues of mistrust that had arisen as a result of their financial worries. Both were successful professionals who had enjoyed moderate financial success: Dara was an English teacher at a private high school, and Gabriel was a tax attorney. However, in the year preceding therapy, Gabriel's private practice began suffering. Profoundly ashamed of his failures, Gabriel was paralyzed with the fear of "losing face" with his wife. He had always been proud of his ability to take care of his family, and he relished Dara's admiration and appreciation of his support. Hence, when he experienced this first real failure, his basic sense of self was shattered. As a result of monetary deficiencies and his dread of revealing these deficiencies to Dara, Gabriel began taking large amounts of money from his and Dara's shared savings account without asking or informing her that he was doing so. When Dara accidentally discovered what Gabriel had done, she became enraged and immediately lost all trust in him—both as a husband and as a professional equal. Gabriel, on the other hand, felt that Dara was too harsh and criticizing of his behavior, and he had extreme difficulty expressing his financial anxieties to her for fear of being attacked and rejected.

Dara and Gabriel were both aware that their "financial relationship" was negatively affecting their marital, as well as their family, relationship. Their problems came to a head when Dara discovered that Gabriel had continued to withdraw additional large sums of money from their account after he had promised to mend his ways. Dara felt betrayed and devastated by what she perceived as Gabriel's abuse of her trust, their finances, and their children's college future. Gabriel, on the other hand, experienced his business and financial failures as a deep embarrassment, feeling that they reflected "what a husband shouldn't be like." As a result, Gabriel felt that Dara must be extremely disappointed in him—both as a business professional and as a man. Gabriel experienced Dara's financial suggestions as harsh criticism and would consequently retreat from arguments.

Concurrently, Gabriel's mother passed away unexpectedly, and he experienced tremendous grief over her death; although he recognized that Dara was

(continued)

supportive throughout his mourning, he nevertheless felt that she did not truly understand his pain and that she was impatient with his resultant family obligations. Whereas Dara, who had been distant from her parents and siblings, perceived their own immediate family as their true family, Gabriel felt it was natural and essential to give equal weight to his extended family; he further felt that his temporary sacrifice of time with his wife and children was necessary to both cope with his mother's death and build family cohesion.

History

Gabriel was born in Venezuela to a large Catholic family that he described as "very loving and close." He left Venezuela when he was 19 years old to pursue his BA and JD degrees in the United States, with the eventual goal of helping to support and move his family to the United States. After obtaining his degrees, Gabriel worked hard to successfully bring his entire family to the United States. He described himself as being financially independent and a successful lawyer; he was proud of and received great joy from knowing that he was able to support his family on his own. Before meeting Dara, Gabriel had been in two long-term relationships, but reported that he didn't take them seriously, referring to himself as somewhat of a "playboy," preferring to date numerous women at once.

Dara, on the other hand, grew up in what she described as an "extremely rigid" family that avoided conflict. She reported that her parents considered her the "bad girl" in the family; she felt so suffocated by their disappointment in her that she left home immediately after finishing high school. Although it was her decision to move, her parents never questioned her departure, and she experienced their lack of ambivalence as a hurtful abandonment, subsequently refusing to have any contact with them. Despite their lack of support, she was able to work full time in various jobs and concurrently acquire her BA. She immediately began teaching in a local high school and was well-liked and popular as a teacher, ultimately able to acquire a teaching position at a well-known private school. During this time Dara was in an "on again–off again" relationship with her high school boyfriend, but she came to the realization that she needed to move on. She perceived herself as an independent woman who could rely only on herself for support and decision making.

When Gabriel and Dara met, he was immediately taken with her and found her independence and financial know-how attractive and exciting. For him it was love at first sight; he knew right away that she was "the one" and that he needed her in his life. Although Dara was initially hesitant about Gabriel and confused by his intense interest in and pursuit of her, she eventually found these very qualities attractive, perceiving him as the first man who seemed to genuinely care about her and what she had to say. Further, Dara admired Gabriel's strong relationship with his family, and he encouraged her to re-embrace her own family, to much success and happiness. After 6 months of dating, Dara became pregnant; the idea of a burgeoning family thrilled Gabriel, and he insisted that they get married and share their life together. Impressed by his "huge, generous heart," Dara agreed.

Assessment

Prior to beginning treatment, Gabriel and Dara each completed the Dyadic Adjustment Scale (DAS; Spanier, 1976), the Frequency and Acceptability of Partner Behavior Inventory (FAPBI; Christensen & Jacobson, 1997; Doss & Christensen, 2006), and the Beck Depression Inventory-II (BDI-II; Beck, Steer, & Brown, 1996). Their scores on the DAS revealed distinct marital distress. Consistent with his verbal presentation, Gabriel's predominant concerns on the FAPBI revolved around Dara's being too critical of him and his recent inability to fully confide in her. He also listed Dara's criticism and lack of support as particularly troublesome. Dara's primary concerns were Gabriel's lying about and going back on his word on their financial problems. She also reported that Gabriel was too controlling, that he did not initiate sex with her as often as she would like, and that he did not participate in recreational activities with her and their sons. On the BDI-II, Gabriel reported moderate to severe depression, and Dara reported mild depression; neither reported any suicidal ideation or physical aggression.

Case Conceptualization

After initial intake and individual interviews, the therapist presented the couple with feedback and impressions of their relationship in the fourth session. The goal of this feedback session was to provide the couple with a comprehensive formulation of their relationship difficulties, the *vulnerabilities* that they brought to the relationship, the *differences* between them that activated their vulnerabilities, the *theme* that characterized their differences, the way they interacted around these differences that lead to a *polarization process* in which their financial difficulties shook the foundation of their marriage, and the subsequent *mutual trap* that kept their marriage from healing. Throughout this session, the therapist encouraged the couple to respond to, become involved with, and amend, if needed, the formulation.

The therapist began by revealing that their individual comments and completed questionnaires demonstrated that Dara and Gabriel were equally distressed about their current financial situation and the effects these difficulties were having on their relationship. However, they both reported that they were highly committed to each other, and the therapist affirmed that this commitment was a good indicator of potential progress and the success that could be achieved with therapy. It seemed that no matter what, they were determined to work and pull through to save their marriage and family.

The therapist then summarized each partner's individual history and background, how the couple met, and what initially attracted them to each other. He relayed to them that, in many ways, their disparate family and cultural backgrounds contributed greatly to the problems they were currently facing. Growing up feeling unloved and virtually abandoned by her family, Dara had learned to rely solely on herself for everything she needed. Her past negative experiences with her family left her in a vulnerable position, where she felt she could trust only herself. Gabriel, in contrast, was very close and attached to his family. However, as a result of his success, cultural background, and intense family ties, Gabriel

(continued)

had learned to tie his sense of self-worth to his ability to succeed and provide for his family. This connection between his self-worth and his success also made Gabriel highly vulnerable to any reversal of financial prosperity.

When the couple met, Gabriel gave Dara the new experience of being able to trust and rely on someone other than herself, and Dara gave Gabriel the experience of both a loving romance and the realization that he wanted to start and support his own family. Both were attracted to each other's independence and financial success, and Dara was impressed with Gabriel's active pursuit of her and his sincere interest in what she had to say. Although the pregnancy came as a surprise, they were able to turn a potentially divisive situation into a healing event that brought them even closer together through marriage and starting a family. Similarly, although they came from different religions, their families welcomed the marriage and were accepting of their differences.

Recently, however, Dara and Gabriel had encountered two major stressors. One was the death of Gabriel's mother. This unexpected trauma led to Gabriel's absence in their home during much of her illness and activated Dara's vulnerabilities about once again being abandoned by her family. Gabriel felt caught in the middle—torn between his two families and having to sacrifice time with Dara to give his mother her proper respects. The second major stressor was Gabriel's declining private practice and his concealment of spending his and Dara's shared savings account. As a result, he feared that Dara's esteemed perception and respect for him would shatter. Terrified that Dara would be overwhelmingly critical of his financial losses and ultimately leave him, his strategy was to conceal and lie about his account withdrawals.

The therapist then introduced the predominant *theme* that seemed to characterize Dara and Gabriel's relationship. This theme involved their issues of mutual trust; whereas they had previously shared a strong trust in each other, Dara now felt that she could not trust Gabriel to be honest and forthcoming about their finances, and Gabriel felt that he could no longer trust Dara with his shame and anxiety about his financial and career difficulties.

After summarizing the content of their difficulties and how their individual histories and vulnerabilities made these difficulties especially painful, the therapist turned to their *polarization process:* how they interacted in ways that exacerbated rather than ameliorated their difficulties. Their particular destructive communication pattern was a variant of the "demand-withdraw" pattern (e.g., Christensen & Heavey, 1990), in which one partner, in this case Dara, takes on a critical, demanding role and the other, Gabriel, takes on an avoidant, uncommunicative, withdrawing role. The therapist detailed how Gabriel's concealments came with large costs: Dara experienced his lying as a devastating breach of trust that forced her to once again trust and rely on only herself. Gabriel and Dara then became trapped in a cycle of Gabriel's withdrawing and hiding his feelings, fears, and losses and of Dara's eventually learning of his cover-ups and becoming more upset, critical, and demanding. As a result of her anger and feelings of betrayal, Dara would demand and criticize Gabriel even more, which would subsequently make Gabriel retreat and withdraw even more. This polarization process, resulting in emotional distance and resentment, exacerbated the original difficulties of financial dishonesty. Finally, the couple found themselves in their cyclical *mutual trap* from which they were unable to escape—Dara "pushing" Gabriel in an overwhelming and harsh way and Gabriel "pulling away," fearful of ever being able to confide in Dara with his financial problems.

As described by the therapist, "The primary goal for you two in couple therapy will be to build and regain trust in each other. Dara, you need to learn to trust Gabriel that he won't conceal his financial problems and use your saved earnings, and Gabriel, you need to trust that you can express your problems and emotions and that Dara will be able to listen to and support you." Both partners responded positively to the feedback, saying that they felt the therapist perfectly captured the cycle of problems in which they had become enmeshed.

Course of Treatment and Assessment of Progress

Therapy sessions in IBCT focus on positive or negative incidents that are relevant to the case formulation for the couple. Throughout therapy, techniques specific to IBCT, such as empathic joining, unified detachment, and tolerance building, were utilized to enhance intimacy and acceptance in Dara and Gabriel's relationship. Use of unified detachment, especially in a humorous manner, was especially helpful for the couple. Early on in therapy, Dara and Gabriel learned to jokingly, but aptly, describe their conflict cycle as a "mom-son" pattern; this allowed them to not only get emotional distance from their problem and take a more objective look at their maladaptive behaviors of demanding and withdrawing, but to acknowledge their individual and dyadic roles within this pattern as well.

For example, at the sixth session Dara detailed an incident in which she gave Gabriel several checks to deposit in their savings account. Upon receiving the checks, Gabriel noticed that one check should have been deposited in a different account; he called Dara and explained the problem and then corrected for this before depositing the money. Although this amendment was seemingly minor, it had a major impact on Dara's trust in Gabriel. She told the therapist, "This was the first time I had given him my deposits since this whole situation began, mostly because I was ill and wasn't able to go to the bank. I felt the anxiety building up in me, but I knew that I had to rely on him to deposit the checks. It was so nice when he called me and let me know, because I know that if he hadn't, later on I would have accused him of taking the money, and he would have denied it." The therapist reflected these issues, responding, "It seems like this incident was different for both of you: For you, Gabriel, knowing that Dara was able to stand by you no matter what increased your trust that Dara could support you and look up to you. And for you, Dara, Gabriel's openness increased your trust that he could be truthful with you, that he could acknowledge your feelings and your intelligence." With the therapist's help, they had been able to extract themselves from their mutual trap.

Role-playing reversed roles was also effective in helping each partner more fully understand the other's perspective and emotions. For example, toward the end of treatment, Dara discussed how she was upset that Gabriel didn't seem to make her and their children enough of a priority, and that although she knew he had a busy schedule, she wished that he would plan more time for family matters. Gabriel responded, "The way she acts makes me feel like I have to do exactly what

(continued)

she wants me to do, and that anything slightly less is never going to be okay. I can feel myself resisting when she gets so demanding like that." The therapist noted the resurgence of their "push-pull" struggle and suggested that each partner "change seats" and replay the conversation that had just taken place, but from the other person's perspective. After having the couple repeat the argument in the reverse role-play, he asked Dara, "So, now, how do you understand what 'Dara' is saying?" Dara laughed aloud and replied, "She's being so unreasonable—she doesn't understand that it's not just about her, that it's mostly about work and closing down the store. She doesn't understand that I do want to be there, but that I just may be a little late."

The therapist then turned to Gabriel, and asked him how he, from Dara's perspective, now understood what "Gabriel" was saying. "Well, he's basically telling me that the kids and I are not important enough for him to make plans in his schedule and that work is his biggest priority. When he comes late to a planned family event it makes me upset because I feel like I can't trust him to be there." After each partner was able to recognize each other's vulnerabilities about the issue, the therapist reflected to the couple, "So now you can both understand how this conflict is upsetting for the other. It's difficult for each of you to be completely satisfied because both of you are so busy and have your own schedules. Each of you then becomes increasingly more distressed, and these feelings get in the way of being able to have more flexibility. But I think the role-playing we just did really emphasized the idea that when you are able to listen and when you are able to give each other the feeling of being listened to, the push-pull struggle starts becoming more manageable and less offensive." This improved acceptance and insight ultimately bolstered their trust in each other.

Complicating Factors

Gabriel's grief over his mother's unexpected death and his resultant deep depression were the primary complicating factors in therapy. His initial BDI score indicated moderate to severe depression, and he reported that he consistently experienced disturbing nightmares and visions about his mother's death. It was clear that Gabriel's anguish and his continual reliving of the trauma were affecting not only his relationship with Dara, but his energy and motivation to succeed financially as well. However, over the course of therapy, Gabriel's BDI scores gradually decreased to a nonclinical level. This improvement seemed to be related to his increased ability to confide in Dara, his perception that Dara was better able to support and listen to him, and an overall upturn and enhancement of their relationship.

Objective Outcome Assessment

As part of the research study, follow-up assessments completed at the last therapy session and at the 2-year and 5-year marks are reported here.

Dara's and Gabriel's DAS scores at the last therapy session were 109 and 114, respectively, increasing 16 and 26 points since the initial therapy session and placing them in the range of happily married couples. In response to open-ended questions about their thoughts on therapy, Dara reported that she enjoyed therapy and their therapist greatly. Gabriel described his enthusiasm for the experience, stating that he became "closer to [his] spouse" and that "therapy came in at the right time when [he] needed it the most," ultimately "[saving their] relationship."

At the 2-year mark, the couple reported that they were "very happy" with the relationship and that "real progress" on important and problematic issues had occurred. Gabriel cited the great helpfulness of therapy and how he and his wife were able to "follow through" with what they had learned and culled from therapy even years after its termination. Their DAS scores substantiated their reports, with Dara scoring 107 and Gabriel scoring 132.

The 5-year follow-up showed the level of happiness with the relationship had increased even more; they couple reported that they were "extremely happy" with their marriage. Their DAS scores were maintained within the range of happily married couples, and each reported only two areas of concern within the relationship. It appeared that, although they still experienced mild financial difficulties, they were able to more effectively manage this distress. Each also conveyed how the relationship had become progressively stronger and richer over the years. Gabriel wrote, "Prior to therapy we were very stressed out and didn't pay much attention to each other, but now we have great communication and are best friends. We have learned how to listen to and be there for each other." Dara reported similar feelings, saying, "Life is more fulfilling now, and everything has gotten better. We are best friends—we have more similar goals, beliefs, values, and viewpoints. Being so committed to each other and providing a strong foundation for family has kept us together. Although I initially had a lot of issues with trust, therapy allowed our communication to be more complete and satisfying."

SUMMARY

Although marital distress has not traditionally received as much attention in the psychological literature as many individual mental health disorders, a growing body of research points to the profound negative impact marital distress has on adult and child functioning and society as a whole. Fortunately, the same literature has refined our understanding of the etiology and nature of marital distress. Most notably, a number of longitudinal studies have demonstrated important predictors of marital distress and the reciprocal effects between individual and marital functioning over time. Furthermore, several self-report, spouse report, and observational assessments of marital distress have been developed and validated; such assessments serve to further our understanding and treatment of marital distress. Finally, in the past 4 decades treatment of marital distress has seen important advances both in terms of the number of marital problems that can be targeted as well as the efficacy of those treatments.

Despite these successes, important challenges remain. First, it is extremely complex to consider emotional, cognitive, behavioral, and physiological aspects of marital distress simultaneously; however, a more complete conceptualization of marital distress requires an examination of the interface between these domains. Second, with the current limitations in how marital distress is included in *DSM-IV* (American Psychiatric Association, 2000), proper assessment and treatment of marital distress—both on its own and in conjunction with other individual mental disorders—is impaired.

Finally, investigations of treatment for marital distress need to focus more on dissemination of empirically supported treatments into real-world settings, assess outcomes over longer periods of time, and determine ways to intervene with couples who would not typically seek traditional forms of marital therapy.

REFERENCES

American Psychiatric Association. (2000). *Diagnostic and statistical manual of mental disorders* (4th ed., text rev.). Washington, DC: Author.

Amato, P. R. (2001). The consequences of divorce for adults and children. In R. M. Milardo (Ed.), *Understanding families into the new millennium: A decade in review* (pp. 488–506). Lawrence, KS: National Council on Family Relations.

Archer, J. (2000). Sex differences in aggression between heterosexual partners: A meta-analytic review. *Psychological Bulletin, 126,* 651–680.

Baucom, D. H., Epstein, N., Rankin, L. A., & Burnett, C. K. (1996). Assessing relationship standards: The Inventory of Specific Relationship Standards. *Journal of Family Psychology, 10,* 72–88.

Baucom, D. H., Epstein, N., Sayers, S. L., & Sher, T. G. (1989). The role of cognitions in marital relationships: Definitional, methodological, and conceptual issues. *Journal of Consulting and Clinical Psychology, 57,* 31–38.

Baucom, D. H., Sayers, S. L., & Duhe, A. (1989). Attributional style and attributional patterns among married couples. *Journal of Personality and Social Psychology, 56,* 596–607.

Baucom, D. H., Sayers, S. L., & Sher, T. G. (1990). Supplementing behavioral marital therapy with cognitive restructuring and emotional expressiveness training: An outcome investigation. *Journal of Consulting and Clinical Psychology, 58,* 636–645.

Beach, S. R. H., Wamboldt, M. Z., Kaslow, N. J., Heyman, R. E., First, M. B., Underwood, L. G., et al. (2006). *Relational processes and DSM-V: Neuroscience, assessment, prevention, and treatment.* Washington, DC: American Psychiatric Press.

Beck, A. T., Steer, R. A., & Brown, G. K. (1996). *Beck Depression Inventory* (2nd ed.). San Antonio, TX: Psychological Corporation.

Belsky, J., & Rovine, M. (1990). Patterns of marital change across the transition to parenthood: Pregnancy to three years postpartum. *Journal of Marriage and the Family, 52,* 5–19.

Bramlett, M. D., & Mosher, W. D. (2001). First marriage dissolution, divorce, and remarriage: United States. *Advance data from vital and health statistics, No. 323.* Hyattsville, MD: National Center for Health Statistics.

Burman, B., & Margolin, G. (1992). Analysis of the association between marital relationships and health problems: An interactional perspective. *Psychological Bulletin, 112,* 39–63.

Chakrabarti, S., Kulhara, P., & Verma, S. K. (1993). The pattern of burden in families of neurotic patients. *Social Psychiatry and Psychiatric Epidemiology, 28,* 172–177.

Christensen, A., Atkins, D. C., Berns, S., Wheeler, J., Baucom, D. H., & Simpson, L. E. (2004). Traditional versus integrative behavioral couple therapy for significantly and chronically distressed married couples. *Journal of Consulting and Clinical Psychology, 72,* 176–191.

Christensen, A., Atkins, D. C., Yi, J. C., Baucom, D. H., & George, W. H. (2006). *Couple and individual adjustment for two years following a randomized clinical trial comparing traditional versus integrative behavioral couple therapy.* Manuscript submitted for publication.

Christensen, A., & Heavey, C. L. (1990). Gender and social structure in the demand/withdraw pattern of marital conflict. *Journal of Personality and Social Psychology, 59,* 73–81.

Christensen, A., & Jacobson, N. S. (1997). *The frequency and acceptability of partner behavior.* Los Angeles: University of California. Unpublished measure.

Christensen, A., & Shenk, J. L. (1991). Communication, conflict, and psychological distance in non-distressed, clinic, and divorcing couples. *Journal of Consulting and Clinical Psychology, 59,* 458–463.

Christensen, A., & Sullaway, M. (1984). *Communication Patterns Questionnaire.* Unpublished Measure.

Cowan, C. P., & Cowan, P. A. (1995). Interventions to ease the transition to parenthood: Why they are needed and what they can do. *Family Relations: Journal of Applied Family and Child Studies, 44,* 412–423.

Cowan, C. P., & Cowan, P. A. (2000). *When partners become parents: The big life change for couples.* Mahwah, NJ: Erlbaum.

Cox, M. J., Paley, B., Burchinal, M., & Payne, C. C. (1999). Marital perceptions and interactions across the transition to parenthood. *Journal of Marriage and the Family, 61,* 611–625.

Cummings, E. M., & Davies, P. T. (1994). *Children and marital conflict: The impact of family dispute and resolution.* New York: Guilford Press.

Dorian, M., & Cordova, J. V. (2004). Coding intimacy in couples' interactions. In P. K. Kerig & D. H. Baucom (Eds.), *Couple observational coding systems* (pp. 243–256). Mahwah, NJ: Erlbaum.

Doss, B. D., & Christensen, A. (2006). Acceptance in romantic relationships: The frequency and acceptability of partner behavior inventory. *Psychological Assessment, 18,* 289–302.

Doss, B. D., Simpson, L. E., & Christensen, A. (2004). Why do couples seek marital therapy? *Professional Psychology: Research and Practice, 35,* 608–614.

Dunn, R. L., & Schwebel, A. I. (1995). Meta-analytic review of marital therapy outcome research. *Journal of Family Psychology, 9,* 58–68.

Ehrensaft, M. K., & Vivian, D. (1996). Spouses' reasons for not reporting existing marital aggression as a marital problem. *Journal of Family Psychology, 10,* 443–453.

Eidelson, R. J., & Epstein, N. (1982). Cognition and relationship maladjustment: Development of a measure of dysfunctional relationship beliefs. *Journal of Consulting and Clinical Psychology, 50,* 715–720.

Epstein, N. B., & Baucom, D. H. (2002). *Enhanced cognitive-behavioral therapy for couples: A contextual approach.* Washington, DC: American Psychological Association.

Fals-Stewart, W., Birchler, G. R., & O'Farrell, T. J. (1999). Drug-abusing patients and their intimate partners: Dyadic adjustment, relationship stability, and substance use. *Journal of Abnormal Psychology, 108,* 11–23.

Fincham, F. D., & Bradbury, T. N. (1992). Assessing attributions in marriage: The Relationship Attribution Measure. *Journal of Personality and Social Psychology, 62,* 457–468.

First, M. B., Bell, C. C., Cuthbert, B., Krystal, J. H., Malison, R., Offord, D. R., et al. (2002). Personality disorders and relational disorders: A research agenda for addressing critical gaps in DSM. In D. K. Kupfer, M. B. First, & D. A. Regier (Eds.), *A research agenda for DSM-V* (pp. 123–186). Washington, DC: American Psychiatric Association.

Floyd, F. J. (2004). Communication Skills Test (CST): Observational system for couples' problem-solving skills. In P. K. Kerig & D. H. Baucom (Eds.), *Couple observational coding systems* (pp. 143–158). Mahwah, NJ: Erlbaum.

Geiss, S. K., & O'Leary, K. D. (1981). Therapist ratings of frequency and severity of marital problems: Implications for research. *Journal of Marital and Family Therapy, 7,* 515–520.

Gottman, J. M. (1999). *The marriage clinic: A scientifically-based marital therapy.* New York: Norton.

Gottman, J. M., Driver, J., & Tabares, A. (2002). Building the sound marital house: An empirically-derived couple therapy. In A. S. Gurman & N. S. Jacobson (Eds.), *Clinical handbook of couple therapy* (3rd ed., pp. 373–399) New York: Guilford Press.

Greef, A. P., & Malherbe, H. L. (2001). Intimacy and marital satisfaction in spouses. *Journal of Sex and Marital Therapy, 27*, 247–257.

Green, R. J., & Mitchell, V. (2002). Gay and lesbian couples in therapy: Homophobia, relational ambiguity, and social support. In A. S. Gurman & N. S. Jacobson (Eds.), *Clinical handbook of couple therapy* (3rd ed., pp. 546–568). New York: Guilford Press.

Hahlweg, K., & Klann, N. (1997). The effectiveness of marital counseling in Germany: A contribution to health services research. *Journal of Family Psychology, 11*, 410–421.

Halford, W. K., Hahlweg, K., & Dunne, M. (1990). The cross-cultural consistency of marital communication associated with marital distress. *Journal of Marriage and the Family, 52*, 109–122.

Halford, W. K., Sanders, M. R., & Behrens, B. C. (1993). A comparison of the generalization of behavioral marital therapy and enhanced behavioral marital therapy. *Journal of Consulting and Clinical Psychology, 61*, 51–60.

Halford, W. K., Scott, J. L., & Smythe, J. (2000). Couples and coping with cancer: Helping each other through the night. In K. B. Schmaling & T. G. Sher (Eds.), *The psychology of couples and illness: Theory, research, and practice* (pp. 135–170). Washington, DC: American Psychological Association.

Hardy, K. V., & Laszloffy, T. A. (2002). Couple therapy using a multicultural perspective. In A. S. Gurman & N. S. Jacobson (Eds.), *Clinical handbook of couple therapy* (pp. 569–593). New York: Guilford Press.

Hazan, C., & Shaver, P. (1987). Conceptualizing romantic love as an attachment process. *Journal of Personality and Social Psychology, 52*, 511–524.

Hetherington, E. M., Bridges, M., & Insabella, G. M. (1998). What matters? What does not? Five perspectives on the association between marital transitions and children's adjustment. *American Psychologist, 53*, 167–184.

Hetherington, E. M., & Elmore, A. M. (2004). The intergenerational transmission of couple instability. In P. L. Chase-Lansdale, K. Kiernan, & R. J. Friedman (Eds.), *Human development across lives and generations: The potential for change* (pp. 171–203). New York: Cambridge University Press.

Hetherington, E. M., & Kelly, J. (2002). *For better or worse: Divorce reconsidered.* New York: Norton.

Hetherington, E. M., & Stanley-Hagan, M. M. (2002). Parenting in divorced and remarried families. In M. H. Bornstein (Ed.), *Handbook of parenting: Vol. 3. Being and becoming a parent* (2nd ed., pp. 233–254). Mahwah, NJ: Erlbaum.

Heyman, R. E. (2001). Observation of couple conflicts: Clinical assessment, applications, stubborn truths, and shaky foundations. *Psychological Assessment, 13*, 5–35.

Heyman, R. E. (2004). Rapid Marital Interaction Coding System (RMICS). In P. K. Kerig & D. H. Baucom (Eds.), *Couple observational coding systems* (pp. 67–94). Mahwah, NJ: Erlbaum.

Heyman, R. E., Sayers, S. L., & Bellack, A. S. (1994). Global marital satisfaction versus marital adjustment: An empirical comparison of three measures. *Journal of Family Psychology, 8*, 432–446.

Hooley, J. M., & Hahlweg, K. (1989). Marital satisfaction and marital communication in German and English couples. *Behavioral Assessment, 11*, 119–133.

Jacobson, N. S. (1992). Behavioral couple therapy: A new beginning. *Behavior Therapy, 23*, 493–506.

Jacobson, N. S., & Christensen, A. (1998). *Acceptance and change in couple therapy: A therapist's guide to transforming relationships.* New York: Norton.

Jacobson, N. S., Schmaling, K. B., & Holtzworth-Munroe, A. (1987). Component analysis of behavioral marital therapy: 2-year follow-up and prediction of relapse. *Journal of Marital and Family Therapy, 13*, 187–195.

Jockin, V., McGue, M., & Lykken, D. T. (1996). Personality and divorce: A genetic analysis. *Journal of Personality and Social Psychology, 71*, 288–299.

Johnson, M. P. (1995). Patriarchal terrorism and common couple violence: Two forms of violence against women. *Journal of Marriage and the Family, 57*, 283–294.

Johnson, M. P., & Ferraro, K. J. (2000). Research on domestic violence in the 1990s: Making distinctions. *Journal of Marriage and the Family, 62*, 948–963.

Johnson, S. M., Hunsley, J., Greenberg, L., & Schindler, D. (1999). Emotionally focused couples therapy: Status and challenges. *Clinical Psychology: Science and Practice, 6*, 67–79.

Johnson, S., & Talitman, E. (1997). Predictors of outcome in emotionally focused marital therapy. *Journal of Marital and Family Therapy, 23*, 135–152.

Kamp Dush, C. M., Cohan, C. L., & Amato, P. R. (2003). The relationship between cohabitation and marital quality and stability: Change across cohorts? *Journal of Marriage and the Family, 65*, 539–549.

Karney, B. R., & Bradbury, T. N. (1995). The longitudinal course of marital quality and stability: A review of theory, method, and research. *Psychological Bulletin, 118*, 3–34.

Karney, B. R., & Bradbury, T. N. (1997). Neuroticism, marital interaction, and the trajectory of marital satisfaction. *Journal of Personality and Social Psychology, 72*, 1075–1092.

Kerig, P. K., & Baucom, D. H. (Eds.). (2004). *Couple observational coding systems*. Mahwah, NJ: Erlbaum.

Kiecolt-Glaser, J. K., & Newton, T. L. (2001). Marriage and health: His and hers. *Psychological Bulletin, 127*, 472–503.

Kline, G. H., Stanley, S. M., Markman, H. J., Antonio Olmos-Gallo, P., St. Peters, M., Whitton, S. W., et al. (2004). Timing is everything: Pre-engagement cohabitation and increased risk for poor marital outcomes. *Journal of Family Psychology, 18*, 311–318.

Kreider, R. M. (2005). Number, timing, and duration of marriages and divorces: 2001. *Current Population Reports*. Washington, DC: U.S. Census Bureau.

Kurdek, L. A. (1991). Marital stability and changes in marital quality in newlywed couples: A test of the contextual model. *Journal of Social and Personal Relationships, 8*, 27–48.

Lavee, Y., & Ben-Ari, A. (2004). Emotional expressiveness and neuroticism: Do they predict marital quality? *Journal of Family Psychology, 18*, 620–627.

Leonard, K. E., & Roberts, L. J. (1998). Marital aggression, quality and stability in the first year of marriage: Findings from the Buffalo Newlywed Study. In T. N. Bradbury (Ed.), *The developmental course of marital dysfunction* (pp. 44–73). New York: Cambridge University Press.

Locke, H. J., & Wallace, K. M. (1959). Short marital adjustment and prediction tests: Their reliability and validity. *Marriage and Family Living, 21*, 251–255.

LoPiccolo, J., & Steger, J. C. (1974). The Sexual Interaction Inventory: A new instrument for assessment of sexual dysfunction. *Archives of Sexual Behavior, 3*, 585–595.

Maisto, S. A., O'Farrell, T. J., Connors, G. J., McKay, J. R., & Pelcovits, M. (1988). Alcoholics' attributions of factors affecting their relapse to drinking and reasons for terminating relapse episodes. *Addictive Behaviors, 13*, 79–82.

Margolin, G., & Wampold, B. E. (1981). Sequential analysis of conflict and accord in distressed and non-distressed marital partners. *Journal of Consulting and Clinical Psychology, 49*, 554–567.

Metz, M. E., & Epstein, N. (2002). Assessing the role of relationship conflict in sexual dysfunction. *Journal of Sex and Marital Therapy, 28*, 139–164.

Mitchell, A. E., Castellani, A. M., Sheffield, R. L., Joseph, J. I., Doss, B. D., & Snyder, D. K. (in press). Predictors of intimacy in couples' discussions of relationship injuries: An observational study. *Journal of Family Psychology*.

Norton, R. (1983). Measuring marital quality: A critical look at the dependent variable. *Journal of Marriage and the Family, 45*, 141–151.

Pasch, L. A., Harris, K. W., Sullivan, K. T., & Bradbury, T. N. (2004). The Social Support Interaction Coding System (SSICS). In P. K. Kerig & D. H. Baucom (Eds.), *Couple observational coding systems* (pp. 319–334). Mahwah, NJ: Erlbaum.

Pretzer, J., Epstein, N., & Fleming, B. (1991). Marital Attitude Survey: A measure of dysfunctional attributions and expectancies. *Journal of Cognitive Psychotherapy, 5,* 131–148.

Ptacek, J. T., Pierce, G. R., Dodge, K. L., & Ptacek, J. J. (1997). Social support in spouses of cancer patients: What do they get and to what end? *Personal Relationships, 4,* 431–449.

Rholes, W. S., Simpson, J. A., Campbell, L., & Grich, J. (2001). Adult attachment and the transition to parenthood. *Journal of Personality and Social Psychology, 81,* 421–435.

Riggs, D. S., Hiss, H., & Foa, E. B. (1992). Marital distress and the treatment of obsessive compulsive disorder. *Behavior Therapy, 23,* 585–597.

Rust, J., & Golombok, S. (1986). The GRISS: A psychometric instrument for the assessment of sexual dysfunction. *Archives of Sexual Behavior, 15,* 157–165.

Schaefer, M. T., & Olson, D. H. (1981). Assessing intimacy: The PAIR inventory. *Journal of Marital and Family Therapy, 7,* 47–60.

Scott, J. L., Halford, W. K., & Ward, B. G. (2004). United we stand? The effects of a couple-coping intervention on adjustment to early stage breast or gynecological cancer. *Journal of Consulting and Clinical Psychology, 72,* 1122–1135.

Sevier, M., Simpson, L. E., & Christensen, A. (2004). Observational coding of demand-withdraw interaction in couples. In P. K. Kerig & D. H. Baucom (Eds.), *Couple observational coding systems* (pp. 159–172). Mahwah, NJ: Erlbaum.

Shadish, W. R., & Baldwin, S. A. (2003). Meta-analysis of MFT interventions. *Journal of Marital and Family Therapy, 29,* 547–570.

Shadish, W. R., & Baldwin, S. A. (2005). Effects of behavioral marital therapy: A meta-analysis of randomized controlled trials. *Journal of Consulting and Clinical Psychology, 73,* 6–14.

Shapiro, A. F., & Gottman, J. M. (2004). The Specific Affect Coding System (SPAFF). In P. K. Kerig & D. H. Baucom (Eds.), *Couple observational coding systems* (pp. 191–208). Mahwah, NJ: Erlbaum.

Shapiro, A. F., & Gottman, J. M., & Carrere, S. (2000). The baby and the marriage: Identifying factors ant buffer against decline in marital satisfaction after the first baby arrives. *Journal of Family Psychology, 14,* 59–70.

Snyder, D. K. (1997). *Manual for the Marital Satisfaction Inventory—Revised.* Los Angeles: Western Psychological Services.

Snyder, D. K., & Aikman, G. A. (1999). The Marital Satisfaction Inventory—Revised. In M. E. Maruish (Ed.), *Use of psychological testing for treatment planning and outcomes assessment* (2nd ed., pp. 1173–1210). Mahwah, NJ: Erlbaum.

Snyder, D. K., & Berg, P. (1983). Determinants of sexual dissatisfaction in sexually distressed couples. *Archives of Sexual Behavior, 12,* 237–246.

Snyder, D. K., & Wills, R. M. (1989). Behavioral versus insight-oriented marital therapy: Effects on individual and interspousal functioning. *Journal of Consulting and Clinical Psychology, 57,* 39–46.

Snyder, D. K., Wills, R. M., & Grady-Fletcher, A. (1991). Long-term effectiveness of behavioral versus insight-oriented marital therapy: A 4-year follow-up study. *Journal of Consulting and Clinical Psychology, 59,* 138–141.

Spanier, G. B. (1976). Measuring dyadic adjustment: New scales for assessing the quality of marriage and similar dyads. *Journal of Marriage and the Family, 28,* 15–38.

Stanley, S. M., Rhoades, G. K., & Markman, H. J. (2006). Sliding vs. deciding: Inertia and the premarital cohabitation effect. *Family Relations, 55,* 499–509.

Stanley, S. M., Whitton, S. W., & Markman, H. J. (2004). Maybe I do: Interpersonal commitment and premarital or nonmarital cohabitation. *Journal of Family Issues, 25,* 496–519.

Straus, M. A., Hamby, S. L., Boney-McCoy, S., & Sugarman, D. B. (1996). The revised Conflict Tactics Scales (CTS2): Development and preliminary psychometric data. *Journal of Family Issues, 17*, 283–316.

Sullivan, L. J., & Baucom, D. H. (2004). The relationship schema coding system: Coding the behavioral manifestations of relationship thinking. In P. K. Kerig & D. H. Baucom (Eds.), *Couple observational coding systems* (pp. 289–304). Mahwah, NJ: Erlbaum.

Twenge, J. M., Campbell, W. K., & Foster, C. A. (2003). Parenthood and marital satisfaction: A meta-analytic review. *Journal of Marriage and Family, 65*, 574–583.

Uebelacker, L. A., & Whisman, M. A. (2006). Moderators of the association between relationship discord and major depression in a national population-based sample. *Journal of Family Psychology, 20*, 40–46.

Viken, R. J., Rose, R. J., Kaprio, J., & Koskenvuo, M. (1994). A developmental genetic analysis of adult personality: Extraversion and neuroticism from 18 to 59 years of age. *Journal of Personality and Social Psychology, 66*, 722–730.

Weiss, R. L. (1992). *The Marital Interaction Coding System—Version IV.* Eugene: Oregon Marital Studies Program.

Weiss, R. L., & Birchler, G. R. (1975). *Areas of change questionnaire.* Unpublished manuscript, University of Oregon.

Weiss, R. L., Hops, H., & Patterson, G. R. (1973). A framework for conceptualizing marital conflict, a technology for altering it, some data for evaluating it. In M. Hersen & A. S. Bellack (Eds.), *Behavior change: Methodology, concepts, and practice* (pp. 309–342). Champaign, IL: Research Press.

Whisman, M. A. (2001). The association between marital dissatisfaction and depression. In S. R. H. Beach (Ed.), *Marital and family processes in depression: A scientific foundation for clinical practice* (pp. 3–24). Washington, DC: American Psychological Association.

Whisman, M. A., & Bruce, M. L. (1999). Marital distress and incidence of major depressive episode in a community sample. *Journal of Abnormal Psychology, 108*, 674–678.

Whisman, M. A., Dixon, A. E., & Johnson, B. (1997). Therapists' perspectives of couple problems and treatment issues in couple therapy. *Journal of Family Psychology, 11*, 361–366.

Whisman, M. A., Sheldon, C. T., & Goering, P. (2000). Psychiatric disorders and dissatisfaction with social relationships: Does type of relationship matter? *Journal of Abnormal Psychology, 109*, 803–808.

Whisman, M. A., & Uebelacker, L. A. (2003). Comorbidity of relationship distress and mental and physical health problems. In D. K. Snyder & M. A. Whisman (Eds.), *Treating difficult couples: Helping clients with coexisting mental and relationship disorders* (pp. 3–26). New York: Guilford Press.

Whisman, M. A., Uebelacker, L. A., & Bruce, M. L. (2006). Longitudinal association between marital dissatisfaction and alcohol use disorders in a community sample. *Journal of Family Psychology, 20*, 164–167.

CHAPTER 21

Sexual Deviation

W. L. MARSHALL, G. A. SERRAN, L. E. MARSHALL, AND M. D. O'BRIEN

DESCRIPTION OF THE PROBLEM

The term "sexual deviation" has been used to encompass a variety of sexual behaviors; some of these represent unusual activities, and others are legally classified as offenses. For example, Laws and O'Donohue (1997) include in their edited book on sexual deviations both legal (e.g., fetishisms) and illegal (e.g., rape) sexual acts. It is difficult to understand why these two quite different types of behaviors would be described by the same pejorative label. In fact, Laws and O'Donohue mix diagnostic labels (e.g., pedophilia) with legal descriptors (e.g., rape). Presumably some people correctly diagnosed as pedophilic might never have committed an illegal sexual act with a child, thereby further confusing the use of such terminology.

We prefer to use the label "sexual deviance" for those behaviors that require a nonconsenting victim, defined by either clear unwillingness, or a failure to fully inform (e.g., a man positive for HIV who fails to tell his sexual partner), or by an inability to provide consent (e.g., a child). The use of unacceptable force during sexual relations would similarly define the act as nonconsenting, even if the partner subjected to force had earlier given, but then withdrawn, consent. We refer to these people collectively as sexual offenders. Most such offenders are male, although there is evidence that some females also commit sexual offenses (Hunter & Mathews, 1997). For all other sexual behaviors that are often included under the term sexual deviation, we use the term "sexual variations," which implies their relative statistical rarity but indicates that they do not necessarily involve a nonconsenting partner. We distinguish these two sets of sexual behaviors in the next section, but we do not provide any further discussion thereafter of the sexual variants because much less is known about them and there seems to be less research interest in them over the past 10 to 20 years (see Marshall, Marshall, & Serran, in press). The primary focus of this chapter, then, is on men who have committed sexual offenses.

590

SEXUAL VARIANTS

Fetishism refers to a sexual interest in objects (often articles of clothing, such as underwear or shoes) where the object becomes a primary source of sexual arousal. Some definitions include what is called "partialism," where a part of the body (e.g., breasts, buttocks) have become a strong focus of sexual interests (Bancroft, 1989; De Silva, 1993; Langevin, 1983). Fetishisms appear to be far more common in men than in women (Mason, 1997). The fetish may want his sexual partner to wear the desired object during intercourse, or he may enjoy the object in isolation from a partner. In the latter instances, he may fondle, suck, or smell the object as part of his masturbatory ritual. Nowadays the Internet provides numerous sites that specifically cater to a remarkable variety of fetishistic interests.

Transvestic fetishism describes the wish to wear clothes of the opposite sex for the purpose of generating sexual arousal. This behavior occurs typically in males (Blanchard, Racansky, & Steiner, 1986; Ovesey & Person, 1973), but it has been observed in females (Gamman & Makinen, 1994). It is necessary to distinguish transvestic fetishism from transsexualism and from those homosexual cross-dressing males who are, in the argot of the street, known as "drag queens" (Person & Ovesey, 1984; Zucker & Blanchard, 1997). Transsexuals are people who experience themselves as a member of the opposite sex and often seek sexual reassignment. Drag queens are male homosexuals who dress in women's clothing to sexually attract other males. Neither drag queens nor transsexuals are considered sexual deviants. Almost half of all transvestites have had one or more homosexual experiences (Brown et al., 1996).

Sexual masochism includes people who derive sexual pleasure from being humiliated or physically hurt (Baumeister & Butler, 1997). Despite popular opinion to the contrary (see Greene & Greene, 1974, for a review), sexual masochism appears to be practiced by many people who live otherwise healthy, normal, and successful lives (Scott, 1983), and most take care to avoid lasting harm (Weinberg & Kamel, 1983). However, sexual masochism is considered to be pathological if, and only if, the person is unable to enjoy sex without suffering psychological or physical pain (Coen, 1988).

Similarly, *sexual sadism,* which involves sexual excitement provoked by causing another person to suffer humiliation or physical distress (Hucker, 1997), may be practiced with a consenting partner where limits are mutually imposed on the degree of suffering and care is taken to ensure safety (Gosselin, 1987; Weinberg, 1987). There are, however, some sexual sadists for whom sexual excitement is dependent on subjecting a nonconsenting victim to humiliation and physical abuse. These latter sadists are discussed more thoroughly in the section on sexual offenders.

Given the remarkable range of human (mostly male) imagination in the sexual realm, it is not surprising that there are many other forms of sexual variations, including urophilia (where the erotic focus is on urine), coprophilia (feces), klismaphilia (enemas), zoophilia or bestiality (animals), asphyxiophilia (induced loss of consciousness due to reduced oxygen intake), infantilism (being treated as an infant), gerontophilia (sexual attraction to an older person), and triolism (observing partners having sex). This is not, it should be noted, an exhaustive list (see, e.g., Milner & Dopke, 1997, and Money, 1986, for discussions of far more extensive lists).

SEXUAL DEVIANTS

As noted, the majority of sexual offenders are male, so we restrict our focus to men who commit such acts. There are juvenile males who commit sexual offenses (see

Barbaree & Marshall, 2005); we may refer to the literature on these adolescents where it is pertinent, but for the most part we restrict ourselves to research on adult male sexual offenders.

There are numerous types of sexual offenders (we use this term as synonymous with sexual deviants), but all have in common a nonconsenting victim. Some represent what has been called "nuisance" offenders, although this does not capture either the distress they may cause victims or their potential to escalate to more intrusive and aggressive acts. We use the term "less problematic sexual offenders" to describe these perpetrators. Other types of sexual offenses involve the potential for far greater harm; we call them "seriously problematic sexual offenders."

Less Problematic Sexual Offenders *Exhibitionism* is by far the most common sexual offense (Rooth, 1973), although it is rarely reported to authorities, and, even when it is, successful prosecution is rare. Exhibitionism involves the deliberate exposure of the genitals to an unwilling observer. The exhibitionist is typically male and the victim is almost exclusively female (Murphy, 1997). This problem behavior has been self-reported by 4.3% of males in a large-scale ($N = 2,800$) anonymous survey (Långström & Seto, in press). On the other hand, surveys of adult females indicate that between 32% and 48% report having been exposed to exhibitionists (Cox, Tsang, & Lee, 1982; Gitlelson, Eacott, & Mehta, 1978; Riordan, 1999). Despite claims by exhibitionists that they do not hurt their victims, between 50% and 80% of victims report being distressed and frightened by the experience (Cox & Maletzky, 1980). Exhibitionists have very high rates of repeat offending even after effective treatment (Marshall, Eccles, & Barbaree, 1991). Also, some exhibitionists go on to commit more serious "hands-on" offenses. Freund (1990) found that 15% of exhibitionists also raped an adult female, and Firestone, Kingston, Wexler, and Bradford (2005) note that 31.3% of exhibitionists had committed other, more violent offenses.

Early researchers pointed out that some of these males expose to children (MacDonald, 1973; Mohr, Turner, & Jerry, 1964). However, current views would likely identify these men as pedophilic, with the exposure being a preliminary step to molesting a child (Murphy & Page, 2006). There is evidence that over 30% of exhibitionists also engaged in voyeurism and frottage (Abel & Osborn, 1992; Freund, 1990). Exhibitionists tend to have poor social skills and may have dysfunctional attachments to their adult partners (Lee, Jackson, Pattison, & Ward, 2002).

Frotteurism describes the behavior of men who frequent crowded areas (e.g., rush-hour public transit, shopping malls) and rub their genitals against women (and, rarely, men). Very little is known about frotteurs, presumably because they are rarely reported, or if reported, the victim rarely is willing to testify in court. Krueger and Kaplan (1997) report that *Psychlit* and *Medline* searches covering the period 1966 to 1997 revealed only 17 reports concerning frotteurs, few of which provided a sound basis from which to draw conclusions. However, Abel (personal communication, September 1978) described reports from New York transit police indicating not only very high rates of frottage among persistent offenders, but also that some of the frotteurs attempted rape in full view of, and in close proximity to, rush-hour subway train passengers. In this form frottage becomes rape, and, indeed, in all its various expressions frottage essentially meets our criteria for the sexually offensive behaviors we subsume under the term "rape" (see later description).

Voyeurs are those men who seek sexual excitement by viewing other people undressing or engaging in sex. This behavior appears to be a reasonably common source of sexual excitement among males, at least in fantasy (Crepault & Couture, 1980); it becomes problematic when it is either the exclusive form of sexual activity or when the voyeur attempts to watch others who are unaware of his presence (Hanson & Harris, 1997). These latter cases constitute criminal offenses, and those who commit these offenses are often called "peepers" (Gebhard, Gagnon, Pomeroy, & Christenson, 1965). Peeping frequently co-occurs with exhibitionism (Abel & Rouleau, 1990; Freund, 1990), and these two groups of offenders appear to share many features in common (Freund, Seto, & Kuban, 1997).

Scatologia describes people (almost always males) who are sexually excited by engaging in sexually explicit speech with another person. There are numerous telephone sites that cater to such individuals. However, when the scatophile requires for his sexual excitement that the person on the receiving telephone be unwilling, then the behavior becomes illegal and the offense is called "telephone scatologia" (Milner & Dopke, 1997). Very little is known about the characteristics of these offenders as so few are caught, despite the apparent magnitude of the problem. For example, Matek (1988, p. 113) describes the rate of obscene phone calls to be "of a different magnitude" from other sexual offenses.

Seriously Problematic Sexual Offenders   *Child molestation* involves an adult coercing an immature person into sexual activity; the level of coercion ranges from persuasion and deception to physical forcefulness. The definition of a child for these purposes varies across jurisdictions, from an upper limit of 12 years to 16 years, although for an offender to meet criteria for pedophilia, the child must be under 12 years. Some, but far from all, child molesters meet diagnostic criteria for pedophilia (see discussion in the next section). These offenders are represented in every adult age group, with some committing their first offenses after age 60 (Marshall, 2006).

Available evidence indicates that some of these offenders commit only one act or offend against only one child, whereas others far more persistently seek out child victims (Marshall, 1997). Child molesters may abuse children from their own family (incest offenders) or from the families of others (nonfamilial child molesters). Most molest female children, but a significant proportion abuse male children, and a small number molest both boys and girls. As many as 300,000 children are sexually abused every year in the United States (American Humane Association, 1988), and the rates appear to be approximately the same in other countries (Marshall, 1997). While the effects on the child victims range from almost benign to very serious long-term consequences, it appears that the majority significantly suffer as a result of the abuse. Short-term consequences for child victims of sexual abuse include loss of self-worth, emotional distress, sleep disturbances, aggression, and problems concentrating (Browne & Finkelhor, 1986; Conte & Schuerman, 1987); 27% of the 369 child victims examined in one study showed at least four problematic sequelae (Conte & Schuerman, 1987). Longer term effects have also been reported, including eating disorders, sexual problems, thwarted emotional development, and personality disorders (see Marshall, Marshall, Serran, & Fernandez, 2006, for a review of these effects).

The term *rape* is used in this chapter to include all forms of forceful imposition of sexual behaviors on a nonconsenting adult. Thus sexual assaults short of penile-vaginal penetration are subsumed under the descriptor "rape." This definition conforms to Canadian criminal law, which in 1983 did away with the legal term rape because of the difficulties in demonstrating, to the satisfaction of the courts, that penile-vaginal penetration had occurred during a sexual assault. This change in Canadian law also reduced the stressfulness of the court proceedings on the victim. Unfortunately, other countries have not followed Canada's example. Rape is almost always committed by a male on a female, although there have been examples of women who committed rape (Hunter & Mathews, 1997), and male victims of male rapists have also been reported (M. R. Koss, 1992).

Unlike child molesters, rapists are characteristically under age 40, although some persist beyond that age. Incidence studies reveal that between 25% and 35% of females will be sexually assaulted at some time during their adult life (M. P. Koss, Gidycz, & Wisniewski, 1987; Russell, 1984). However, it has been estimated that the true rate may be much higher (M. R. Koss, 1992). There are no characteristics that distinguish victims, and although most are in the age range 16 to 35 years, some victims are quite elderly. The psychological and emotional damage to victims is consistently found to be severe and in many cases long-lasting (Calhoun, McCauley, & Crawford, 2006). Many of the observed negative effects on victims of rape are the same sequelae as are faced by victims of child sexual abuse (Burgess & Holmstrom, 1979; West, 1991).

A special category of sexual offenders is that described as *sexual sadists.* We noted earlier that some men who meet criteria for sexual sadism may be content to practice their unusual desires with consenting partners. However, men we are concerned with here are those who enact sexually sadistic acts on unwilling victims, who are usually, but not always, adult women (Marshall & Hucker, 2006). These offenders are, fortunately, few in number, but they constitute a real danger to innocent victims because in addition to forcing sex on a woman they also deliberately inflict severe physical harm and extreme psychological damage (Marshall & Kennedy, 2003). Sadistic sexual offenders appear to have a high incidence of serious personality disorders, and they typically have conflicts with women (Proulx, Blais, & Beauregard, 2006).

For the purposes of the rest of this chapter we restrict our focus to exhibitionists, child molesters, and rapists as they are the only sexual deviants for whom there is a sufficient and broad body of evidence on which to develop a reasonably soundly based conceptualization of the problems. In addition, the diagnostic issues are relatively straightforward with most of the other disorders, except for the common problem of inferring recurrent sexual fantasies or urges concerning the specific behavior in the absence of an admission by the client.

DIAGNOSIS AND ASSESSMENT

Diagnosis

The latest edition of the *Diagnostic and Statistical Manual of Mental Disorders* (*DSM-IV-TR*, American Psychiatric Association, 2000, p. 566) declares that the paraphilias involve "recurrent, intense sexually arousing fantasies, sexual urges, or behaviors" involving sexual activity. These urges, fantasies, or behaviors must be both persistent (at least 6 months' duration) and "cause clinically significant distress or impairment" (p. 566). This latter requirement presents something of a puzzle because many paraphilics, and certainly many sexual offenders, are not themselves troubled by their behaviors except for transitory fears of being found out. In the case of sexual offenders, it is their victims who are distressed, but it is not clear that this is what the authors of *DSM* mean. Various other aspects of *DSM* criteria also cause concern (Marshall, 1997, 2006; O'Donohue, Regev, & Hagstrom, 2000) due to either their seemingly arbitrary nature (e.g., 6 months' duration) or to the vagueness of the criteria (e.g., Does the behavior in question have to be overt?).

However, the most problematic aspect of *DSM* criteria is that the determination of a persistent sexual interest typically requires an inference by the clinician because, at least among sexual offenders, there is a reluctance on the part of clients to admit to such a problem. The degree to which diagnosticians must rely on inference reduces the possibility of the resultant diagnoses being reliable. This, in fact, appears to be a serious problem with *DSM* paraphilia diagnoses (Marshall, in press).

Marshall and his colleagues (Marshall & Kennedy, 2003; Marshall, Kennedy, & Yates, 2002; Marshall, Kennedy, Yates, & Serran, 2002), in a series of papers examining the diagnosis of sexual sadism, found (a) little agreement across studies in the criteria used to arrive at this diagnosis; (b) the inappropriate application of the diagnosis by practicing clinicians; and (c) a failure to agree on the diagnoses of 12 clients by 15 carefully selected internationally renowned experts on sexual sadism. In a broader study of interdiagnostician agreement, Levenson (2004) compared the diagnoses applied to 295 sexual offenders who were being evaluated for civil commitment as sexually violent predators (SVP). Levenson found that none of the following diagnoses met even moderate levels of interrater reliability: pedophilia, sexual sadism, exhibitionism, and paraphilia Not Otherwise Specified (NOS). In addition, she noted that not even the general category of "any paraphilia" reached satisfactory levels of interdiagnostician reliability. In Levenson's study, as is apparently common practice at SVP hearings (Doren, 2002) in the United States, the diagnosticians used the NOS category for men convicted of rape or lesser degrees of sexual assault of adults. The *DSM* has never had a category to cover rapists, despite the fact that such behaviors appear to be no less problematic, persistent, or deviant than are those behaviors that meet *DSM* paraphilia criteria. Indeed, a rapist would seem to be in far more need of clinical attention than a fetishist.

Deficiencies of *DSM* criteria in meeting needs of researchers and clinicians has led many practitioners to either use the diagnostic labels rather loosely or to use non-*DSM* terms, such as "child molesters" or "rapists," to describe their subjects or clients. In the case of SVP hearings in the United States, the operating rules require that an offender meet criteria for a *DSM* diagnosis in order to be civilly committed (Schlank, 2006). In general practice in the United States, a client must meet *DSM* criteria in order for the treating clinician to be paid. These requirements essentially force U.S. clinicians to broaden their application of paraphilic diagnoses, particularly in the case of sexual offenders, in order to be paid by HMOs or insurance companies. This practice inevitably leads to diagnostic unreliability and makes a mockery of the diagnostic system. It also presents difficulties in comparing the results of studies across various centers.

In clinical practice and in research reports, various terms are used interchangeably to refer to men who molest children. Some studies describe all such offenders as pedophiles, others call them child molesters, and some (e.g., Freund, Heasman, & Roper, 1982) distinguish men who molest prepubescents (pedophiles) from those who abuse postpubescent children (hebephiles). Hebephilia is not a *DSM* diagnosis. The *DSM* diagnosis of pedophilia requires that the child be prepubescent, although information on the actual age of the child may not be accessible to the diagnostician. Even if this information were available, what are we to make of a man who begins molesting a child when the victim is 8 years old and continues until the child is 15? Does the man meet *DSM* criteria for pedophilia until the child pubesces, after which he is no longer a pedophile and in fact no longer meets any *DSM* criteria? This seems absurd.

The diagnostic manual, then, does not serve at all well those who treat sexual offenders. At the moment, the most sensible practice seems to be to simply describe sexual offenders in terms of their unacceptable behavior, that is, as child molesters, rapists, exhibitionists. We follow this practice in the rest of this chapter, and we restrict our focus to these three types of offenders.

ASSESSMENT

Approaches to assessment of sexual offenders reveal common targets that are evaluated across all types of offenders (Dougher, 1995; Marshall, 1996). Table 21.1 describes these common features. Assessments are typically completed to evaluate risk to reoffend, treatment needs, and changes as a result of treatment.

Risk to reoffend is sometimes assessed for court purposes (usually at sentencing or for SVP hearings), but it is also done to allocate incarcerated sexual offenders to appropriate levels of security and to assist parole decision makers. There are now empirically derived measures that serve to estimate likelihood of a re-offense. These measures are called "actuarial" instruments, based as they are on examining the relationship between various features and actual re-offense records. There are two types of actuarial instruments: those that depend on past history or static factors and those that identify changeable features of the clients (i.e., so-called dynamic factors). Various static measures have been developed, each of which seems equally accurate: STATIC-99 (Hanson & Thornton, 2000), RRASOR (Hanson, 1997), the Sex Offender Risk Appraisal Guide (SORAG; Quinsey, Harris, Rice, & Cormier, 1998) and the Minnesota Sex Offender Screening Tool—Revised (MnSOST-R; Epperson et al., 1999). It is only recently that dynamic factors have been examined and researchers have generated two scales: the STABLE-2000 and the ACUTE-2000 (Hanson, 2006). The STABLE-2000 identifies factors that are relatively stable over time but are amenable to change (e.g., intimacy deficits, poor self-regulation, deviant attitudes, sexual preoccupation). The ACUTE-2000 lists transitory factors that increase the immediate risk of a re-offense (e.g., sudden negative moods, recent interpersonal conflicts, immediate access to a victim).

Static risk scales simply establish the likelihood that the man will re-offend but do not provide information on what could be changed to reduce this risk. The items in STABLE-2000, however, identify features that treatment can address; this is therefore a useful instrument in determining areas of treatment need. The ACUTE-2000 describes

Table 21.1
Common Targets of Assessment

1. Risk for future re-offending
2. Identification of factors, people, and situations that enhance risk
3. Self-esteem/self-efficacy
4. Schema and associated perceptions, cognitions, and attitudes
5. Understanding of victim harm and empathy for victims
6. Social skills, including relationship skills and assertiveness
7. Coping style/skills
8. Emotion management
9. Self-regulation, including impulse control and sexual regulation
10. Deviant sexual interests
11. Sense of responsibility for all behaviors, including sexual behaviors

features that fluctuate, some aspects of which may be modified by treatment, but they serve better as guides for probation and parole officers supervising the offenders in the community.

The remaining features outlined in Table 21.1 are the targets of treatment, and their assessment should guide the focus of treatment providers. Therapy should address those areas in which each individual client is deficient. How assessment is done to provide a guide to therapists varies according to available resources and depends on the view the clinical team takes on how case formulation should proceed. Drake and Ward (2003), for example, argue that treatment should be preceded by a comprehensive assessment process resulting in a fully developed case formulation that can then guide the individualizing of treatment delivery. This approach leads to the use of a series of detailed interviews, an array of tests completed by the clients, and some form of sexual preference testing. Such an exhaustive evaluation is considerably costly in terms of the time and resources of the staff and markedly delays the client's entry into treatment. It is perhaps suitable only to large, institutionally based operations, and even for those it would have to have significant advantages (which have yet to be demonstrated) over alternative approaches. Nevertheless, many treatment programs do use an extensive battery of tests and interviews to generate, not so much a case formulation, but rather a baseline against which the effects of treatment can later be established.

These pre- and posttreatment assessments typically occur in programs that employ closed groups; that is, a group of offenders all start and finish the program at the same time. Such a "one size fits all" approach has been criticized (see Laws & Ward, 2006; Marshall et al., 2006) as failing to meet the needs of each individual client. Marshall et al. advocate use of a more flexible approach. They prefer to operate open-ended groups that allow each client to proceed at his own rate and within which a progressively adjusted case formulation emerges. In this view, a case formulation (whatever it relies on) should be constantly changing as the client changes with treatment and more strengths or problems emerge. Because sexual offenders are typically reluctant to reveal much about themselves until they develop trust in a therapist, this gradual approach to case formulation and problem identification would seem to be necessary. Such an approach relies on the therapist's skills in revealing and identifying issues to be focused on, but it does not provide a base against which to determine treatment gains.

The more traditional approach, like Drake and Ward's case formulation, requires a series of interviews that examines the client's history (developmental and offense history), his relationships, his capacity and style of learning, his acceptance of responsibility for his life and crimes, his ability to deal effectively with problems, and his sense of self-worth. Various tests are typically completed by clients, who evaluate the features listed in Table 21.1. These tests should have sound psychometric properties; unfortunately, they are not always chosen on this basis. Even when tests do have satisfactory psychometric qualities, we believe they still present problems. In the first place, it is not hard for any testee to recognize which answers will present him in a favorable light, and sexual offenders have an obvious interest in doing so. Second, there may be no changes revealed on some measures from pre- to posttreatment assessment simply because the client was functioning well on the issue prior to intervention. Even if change occurs on the measures over treatment, this in itself does not reveal how well a client is functioning. For example, in evaluating our intimacy training component, we found statistically significant improvements in intimacy skills with treatment, but the posttreatment scores were still over 1 standard deviation below the normative mean (Marshall, Bryce, Hudson, Ward, & Moth, 1996).

One of the targets of assessment with sexual offenders that is considered by some to be essential to their proper evaluation concerns the presumed sexual preferences that are said to drive the aberrant behaviors. The early behavioral formulations of the etiology of sexual offending suggested that conditioning processes established preferences for deviant acts, which then either initiated or maintained the behaviors (McGuire, Carlisle, & Young, 1965). As a result, it was assumed that assessing, and then treating, these deviant preferences would constitute a sufficient program to address the problematic behavior (Bond & Evans, 1967).

Phallometric testing, originally devised by Freund (1957) to determine sexual interests, quickly became established as the sine qua non of sexual offender assessment. Initially, it was thought that all sexual offenders would display deviant sexual preferences at phallometric assessments, but it soon became evident that this was not the case. Current evidence indicates that somewhat less than 50% of nonfamilial child molesters show sexual arousal to children that is approximately equal to or greater than their arousal to adults, while far fewer incest offenders appear deviant (Marshall & Fernandez, 2003). Among rapists, only 30% display deviance at phallometric testing (Marshall & Fernandez, 2003). Normal responding during such testing does not mean the man has no problem. Obviously if a man sexually abuses a child, something is clearly not normal, but it might not be that he is sexually attracted to children; there are many nonsexual reasons why a man might molest children (Freund, Watson, & Dickey, 1991). Finally, phallometric testing has not yet been shown to be reliable (Marshall & Fernandez, 2003). Nevertheless, phallometric testing remains popular and may have some value in an assessment package.

Thus, although assessments may appear to be comprehensive and based on sound knowledge of the problems that typify sexual offenders, it does not follow that they are serving useful purposes such as generating case formulations or evaluating treatment gains. Marshall et al. (2006) have outlined an approach that utilizes a therapist rating scale targeting the issues addressed in treatment. Completed early in treatment and repeated throughout, this rating scale helps the therapist to (a) identify problems in need of treatment, (b) determine when sufficient progress has been made to terminate focus on each issue, and (c) estimate how well the client is functioning on each issue at the end of treatment. Although more extensive evaluations are under way with this rating scale, we have demonstrated its interrater reliability (reported in Marshall et al., 2006) and its value in facilitating end-of-treatment report writing.

CONCEPTUALIZATION

Learning and conditioning processes have been viewed as playing a part in the development of deviant sexual behavior (Abel & Blanchard, 1974; Laws & Marshall, 1990). According to this theory, repeated association of inappropriate fantasies and sexual arousal generated by masturbation entrench a strong desire to engage in the activities and with the partners depicted in the fantasies. The "sexual preference hypothesis" (McGuire et al., 1965) that guided these ideas suggested that men who molest children do so because they had acquired a preference for children (via conditioning processes); rapists were thought to have developed a preference for forceful, nonconsenting sex as a result of similar conditioning processes. The evidence for the sexual preference hypothesis, however, is not convincing (Marshall, Anderson, & Fernandez, 1999; Marshall & Eccles, 1993), likely because there are many other factors that contribute to the development of sexual offending.

Our understanding of the development of sexual offending behavior has evolved over time based on research and theory. Marshall and Barbaree (1990) outlined a comprehensive model of etiology, including sociocultural factors (Marshall, 1985), biological influences (Marshall, 1984), and developmental experiences (Marshall, Hudson, & Hodkinson, 1993). Marshall and Marshall (2000) proposed that the origins of sexual offending lie in the offender's experience of poor quality parent-child attachments. Considerable research indicates a variety of disruptive experiences in the childhood of these offenders (Awad, Saunders, & Levene, 1984; Bass & Levant, 1992; Finkelhor, 1984; Lang & Langevin, 1991; Langevin et al., 1984; Protter & Travin, 1987; Saunders, Awad, & White, 1986). Substance abuse, physical and sexual abuse, neglect, criminal activities, and rejection are common in the family background of sexual offenders (Staryzk & Marshall, 2003). Specific to parental attachment, Smallbone and Dadds (2000) demonstrated that insecure childhood attachments were significantly associated with coercive sexual behavior.

In our view, insecure parental attachment creates vulnerability and results in low self-esteem, poor relationship skills, and an increased risk of being sexually abused, all of which can lead to heightened sexualization and adult sexual offending. Among vulnerable youngsters, sexual activity may be used as a means of comfort, pleasure, escape from distress, and control. In line with this we have found that both rapists and child molesters are more likely to use sex as a way of dealing with life's problems than are non-sex offenders (Cortoni & Marshall, 2001) and that sexual offenders respond to stress with poor coping styles (Marshall, Serran, & Cortoni, 2000). Consistent with these observations, both Proulx, McKibben, and Lusignan (1996) and Looman (1999) have shown that sexual offenders are more likely to fantasize about deviant activities when they are in negative mood states. Continued use of sex as a coping strategy might lower a man's constraints against engaging in deviant acts, particularly when an opportunity presents itself in the context of the experience of distress.

Once an attraction to deviant sex becomes entrenched, fantasizing the deviant images during masturbation may allow the elaboration of details of offending (e.g., the child is cooperative, or the woman enjoys being forced) that serve to solidify distorted views of the abuse, which may, in turn, justify an actual offense (Wright & Schneider, 1997). Enactment of deviant sex may also serve to compensate for deficiencies in the offender's life. When he is offending, the man may experience power and control, he may obtain some degree of affection or intimacy, and these experiences may produce some degree of self-affirmation. Rapists frequently report negative attitudes toward women (Marshall & Hambley, 1996), and this is expressed in their attempts to degrade or humiliate their victims (Darke, 1990). Child molesters appear to experience strong sexual satisfaction from molesting children. Howells (1979) and Finkelhor (1984) propose that emotional congruence with children is an essential aspect of child sexual abuse, and this experience enhances molesters' feelings of control and intimacy with the child victims.

More recently, Smallbone (2006) extended Marshall and Barbaree's (1990) integrated theory employing an attachment perspective. Smallbone pointed to evidence indicating that the nurturing system, attachment system, and sexual system are evolutionarily entrenched and lie in close proximity in the brain, such that the activation of one system can be expected to increase activity in each of the other two systems.

When this occurs in the context of a father-daughter relationship, for example, the adult may have trouble distinguishing his sexual feelings from his feelings of caring toward and attachment to his daughter. Under conditions where the father is stressed and otherwise sexually unsatisfied, these indirectly evoked sexual feelings, occurring while he is in close proximity to his daughter, may lead to inappropriate sexual contact. This initial experience may then subsequently be used in fantasy associated with masturbation, leading to an enhanced desire in the man for sex with his daughter. Of course, although Smallbone's theory explains the possible origin of incestuous behavior, it does not lend itself as well to describing the onset of other sexually offensive behaviors, including other forms of child molestation.

Barbaree (1990) suggests that for men to sexually offend, they must overcome whatever constraints prevent them from doing so. Intoxication is one such disinhibitor that encourages the expression of aggression (Bushman & Cooper, 1990), facilitates sexual arousal (Seto & Barbaree, 1995), and generates sexual responses to rape (Barbaree, Marshall, Yates, & Lightfoot, 1983). It is noteworthy that more than 50% of sexual offenders are intoxicated when they offend (Abracen, Looman, & Anderson, 2000; Christie, Marshall, & Lanthier, 1979; Johnson, Gibson, & Linden, 1978). Similarly, it has been shown that anger provoked by a woman facilitates sexual arousal to rape in otherwise normal males (Yates, Barbaree, & Marshall, 1984). The distorted perceptions of child molesters (Abel, Becker, & Cunningham-Rathner, 1984; Bumby, 1996) serve to disinhibit any constraints they may have against abusing children, and rapists hold views of women that also appear to reduce their constraint against sexual assault (Bumby, 1996; Marshall & Hambley, 1996).

Finally, whatever factors produce a disposition to offend, an offense cannot take place unless an opportunity arises. The confluence of factors presented earlier (i.e., a history of negative childhood experiences, feelings of low self-worth, poor peer relations, the tendency to use sex to cope with distress, conditioning of arousal to deviant sex, and the presence of disinhibitors) may lead a man to seek or take advantage of an opportunity to sexually offend. Some offenders plan their offenses in advance, some groom their victims over time until they can manipulate situations to gain access to them, and others may seize unplanned opportunities to offend. However, our view is that unless a man is primed by his history (both past and recent) to be in the vulnerable state we have described, he will not seek or take advantage of possible opportunities to offend. In fact, it is clear that sexual offenders have many opportunities to offend that they do not take advantage of (Marshall, Marshall, et al., in press), so some personal factors (those that create vulnerability) must be present to trigger or inhibit offending when an opportunity arises.

As research continues to grow, so too will our ability to formulate more sophisticated and more accurate accounts of the etiology of these problematic sexual behaviors.

BEHAVIORAL TREATMENT

Initial behavioral programs for sexual offenders developed in the 1960s and 1970s consisted primarily of strategies focused on reducing sexual arousal to deviant cues and enhancing arousal to appropriate sexual acts (see Laws & Marshall, 2003, for a history of these early approaches). Marshall (1971) pointed out that such an approach failed to provide the offender with the skills necessary to act on his changed sexual interests. He advocated adding training in social and relationship skills to the treatment of sexual offenders. Since that time, treatment programs have become more comprehensive, including a wide range of relevant components.

During the early 1980s, Marques (1982) and Pithers (Pithers, Marques, Gibat, & Marlatt, 1983) described the potential application of relapse prevention components in sexual offender treatment. Clinicians enthusiastically embraced this approach, and it remained uncritically accepted for many years as the optimal way to treat sexual offenders. Recently, Ward and his colleagues (Ward & Hudson, 1996; Ward, Hudson, & Marshall, 1994; Ward, Hudson, & Siegert, 1995) critically examined the theoretical basis of the relapse prevention approach; they argued for new ways of conceptualizing the treatment of sexual offenders. In fact, the evidence has not revealed support for the efficacy of relapse prevention approaches with sexual offenders (Marshall & Anderson, 2000). In addition, others offered criticisms of the clinical value of focusing solely on avoidance strategies (Mann, Webster, Schofield, & Marshall, 2004). It was suggested that programs adopt an overall more positive treatment model that emphasized approach goals (Marshall et al., 2005), included development of a "good lives" plan (Ward & Marshall, 2004), and markedly reduced attention to the identification of relapse prevention strategies (Marshall et al., 2006).

Within this approach to treatment, behaviors of sexual offenders are conceptualized as driven by the same needs that all people seek. It is their inability to meet their needs prosocially that we believe drives them to commit offenses. From this perspective, we need to equip sexual offenders with the skills, cognitions, and emotional capacities to meet their needs appropriately to reduce their offending behavior. The treatment targets that derive from this view include enhancement of self-efficacy/self-esteem; the development of empathy for others, and particularly for possible future victims; restructuring the offense-related schemas that produce distorted perceptions, maladaptive cognitions, and inappropriate attitudes; increasing coping skills and developing appropriate coping styles; enhancing the offender's sense of personal responsibility; facilitating a range of effective social skills (anxiety and anger management, assertiveness, relationship skills, attachment styles); modifying deviant sexual thoughts/fantasies; and developing adequate self-regulatory processes (emotional, sexual, and behavioral regulation). These targets are tied together by the overriding concept of the good lives model (Deci & Ryan, 2000), which outlines 10 areas of functioning within which humans strive to realize their potential. Ward and his colleagues (Ward, 2002; Ward & Fisher, 2006; Ward & Marshall, 2004; Ward & Stewart, 2003) have adapted this good lives model to suit the treatment needs, learning capacities, and interests of sexual offenders. Sexual offenders are assisted in determining their own unique good lives goals that fit with their interests and capacities and an associated set of detailed plans for the steps necessary to achieve these goals. A minimum set of circumstances and persons to avoid is also generated, but the emphasis throughout treatment is on developing a more positive and rewarding life.

Treatment is conducted in groups of 10 offenders and one or two therapists. High-risk/high-needs clients typically require approximately 400 hours of specialized sexual offender treatment, plus additional treatment for substance abuse, anger management, and whatever other idiosyncratic problems the client has (Marshall & Yates, 2005). The specialized sexual offender program for these high-risk/high-needs clients is best run for three 3-hour sessions per week over a 6-month period. Spacing sessions in this way allows clients to both consolidate within-sessions gains and practice between sessions their newly acquired skills. Moderate-risk/moderate-needs clients require approximately 150 hours of specialized treatment, plus whatever other programming is required. Low-risk/low-need clients have minimal specialized treatment needs, usually limited to less than 100 hours.

To achieve our goal of maintaining a positive approach to treatment that guides sexual offenders toward the development of a better life, we emphasize the importance of therapeutic processes. Marshall, Fernandez, et al. (2003) reviewed the general clinical literature on these processes and identified a range of therapist characteristics that were said to maximize benefits from psychological treatment. In two studies (Marshall, Serran, et al., 2003; Marshall, Serran, et al., 2002) it was demonstrated that four therapist characteristics (empathy, warmth, directiveness, and rewardingness) accounted for between 30% and 60% of the variance in multiple measures of treatment-induced change in sexual offender programs. These researchers also found that a strongly confrontational style on the part of the therapist was negatively related to changes in the treatment targets. These observations of the important therapist qualities were matched by reports of sexual offenders during and after treatment (Drapeau, 2005). In addition, Beech and his colleagues (Beech & Fordham, 1997; Beech & Hamilton-Giachritsis, 2005) found that a cohesive and expressive group climate also facilitated the achievement of sexual offender treatment goals, and Pfäfflin, Böhmer, Cornehl, and Mergenthaler (2005) have shown that emotional expression by sexual offenders in treatment is essential to the achievement of treatment goals. We integrate these features into the operation of our program. In addition to creating the appropriate group climate in which clients work cohesively, are active participants, and are emotionally expressive, the therapist displays the appropriate qualities, emphasizes the clients' positive attributes, points to their strengths, and maintains sufficient flexibility to respond to each client's style and learning ability and to the client's day-to-day fluctuations.

MEDICAL TREATMENT

We consider use of medications essential for some cases, but the use of medications is viewed as one element in the overall treatment of sexual offenders (Glaser, 2003). Generally, we use medications for either sexually obsessed (or addictive, compulsive, or hypersexual) clients, those whose deviant fantasies are strong and persistent, or those who seem so dangerous (i.e., high risk to re-offend associated with high risk to harm) that more drastic interventions are required.

For those offenders who seem to be sexually obsessed, we employ one of the selective serotonin reuptake inhibitors (SSRIs) that have been shown to reduce the client's sense of urgency or compulsion regarding his sexual expression (Greenberg & Bradford, 1997). Dangerous clients, or those who have strong and persistent deviant fantasies, are placed on one of the antiandrogens or hormonal medications (Bradford, 2000). We typically use luprolide acetate (i.e., Lupron) for such clients. Except for the very dangerous offenders, who may be required to remain on the antiandrogen indefinitely, all sexual offenders who are on medications will be gradually withdrawn from the drugs as they begin to make satisfactory progress in psychological treatment.

OUTCOME EVALUATIONS

Recently, two meta-analyses of outcome studies of the treatment of sexual offenders have been reported. Hanson et al. (2002) selected 43 studies that had a comparison group of untreated sexual offenders and that relied on official recidivism data for their appraisal of treatment effects. Among the 9,453 sexual offenders examined in this study, it was only the offenders treated by cognitive-behavioral methods that showed positive results. Of those treated in cognitive-behavioral programs, 9.9% sexually re-offended within the long-term follow-up period, while 17.3% of the matched untreated group were repeat offenders. These differences were statistically significant and revealed an odds ratio of 0.64. Lösel and Schmucker (2005) more recently were able to access a greater number of studies ($k = 69$, containing 80 independent comparisons involving 22,181 subjects), which were not accessible to Hanson et al. because they were either unpublished European papers or appeared in non-English-language journals. Lösel and Schmucker's meta-analysis revealed treatment effects that were significantly higher than those observed by Hanson et al. (OR = 1.70). Again, it was only the cognitive-behavioral programs that were effective. Both Hanson et al. and Lösel and Schmucker not only found significant reductions in sexual recidivism, but they also demonstrated that cognitive-behavioral treatment significantly reduced the incidence of nonsexual re-offenses. For example, in Hanson et al.'s report, 28.7% of the treated sexual offenders committed posttreatment nonsexual offenses, whereas 41.7% of the untreated group committed a nonsexual offense, resulting in an OR of 0.56. Lösel and Schmucker again report greater effects than Hanson et al. on general recidivism (OR = 1.67). Although sexual offender treatment has not been designed to reduce anything other than sexual recidivism, it has consistently been shown to reduce the overall tendency of sexual offenders to commit any crime—an unexpected but pleasing result.

We recently completed an evaluation of our Canadian prison-based program by following 534 treated clients for a mean of 5.4 years. Based on actuarial measures of risk, we estimated that 16.8% would sexually re-offend over this period, but just 3.2% actually did. These results produce an OR of 6.14, which translates into an effect size of $d = 1.00$. As observed in the meta-analyses reported earlier, we also found significant effects on nonsexual recidivism (40% estimated versus 13.6% actual). Appraisals of three other Canadian prison programs have similarly produced positive results (Barbaree, Langton, & Peacock, 2004; Looman, Abracen, & Nicholaichuk, 2000; Nicholaichuk, Gordon, Gu, & Wong, 2000).

Although not all treatment programs for sexual offenders are effective, it is evident that some are. Reports by Hanson et al. (2002), Lösel and Schmucker (2005), and Dowden, Antonowicz, and Andrews (2003) reveal that cognitive-behavioral approaches are more likely to be effective than programs that adopt a different model of treatment. Given the evidence we have reviewed on the influence of the therapist and the group climate, we suspect that cognitive-behavioral approaches that de-emphasize psychoeducational methods and avoid highly prescriptive manuals, thereby allowing the treatment provider to be genuinely psychotherapeutic, are the programs that are most likely to be effective. Indeed, it appears that the attainment of treatment goals with sexual offenders is highly dependent on the proper implementation of process issues (Burton & Cerar, 2005; Simons, Tyler, & Lins, 2005). The fact that the only four Canadian prison programs that have been evaluated and found to be effective were less prescriptively detailed and encouraged a psychotherapeutic approach supports this view, as does the fact that the most notable failure among sexual offender programs (Marques, Weideranders, Day, Nelson, & van Ommeren, 2005) followed highly detailed manuals and allowed little or no room for therapist flexibility.

Case Description

Alex was 42 years of age when he was convicted of sexual assault on a 22-year-old female. He was sentenced to 3 years in prison. Alex had prior convictions of indecent exposure (x3), sexual assault (x2), driving while intoxicated (x2), possession of an illegal substance (cocaine), and theft under $200. Given this record, the sentence of just 3 years was surprisingly short, and because he had spent 6 months in a holding cell awaiting trial, he was required to spend only a further 2 years in prison. As a result, he was quickly processed at the induction center and transferred to our prison program to ensure that he received treatment before release. Alex entered our program within 3 weeks of his arrival at our institution.

In addition to the previous sexual convictions, Alex indicated that he had exposed himself many times that were not reported. He said he had also engaged in sexual acts with two women who did not report the incidents, although he said he was forceful and they were clearly not consenting. At the induction center assessment, Alex told the interviewer that he had a drinking problem and that he was an occasional marijuana and cocaine user. He said that his use of alcohol and drugs was extreme only when he was under stress or when things went wrong in his life. It was at these times that Alex committed his offenses, although he did not try to excuse these behaviors by blaming intoxication. At an interview prior to entering our program, Alex told the interviewer that he masturbated two or three times a week but that his fantasies were almost always appropriate. Again, it was only when he was experiencing problems or when he was out of work that his sexual fantasies would involve raping a woman. This was, not surprisingly, when Alex was most likely to offend.

When Alex was arrested for the current offense, he was working as an assistant to an electronics repairman. He had held this job for 2 years, the longest time he had been continually employed. When he left school at age 17, he took a series of unskilled jobs (e.g., truck driver, delivery man for a grocery store, construction worker, small engine repairman) but did not hold any job for more than 6 to 9 months at a time. He typically quit his job and spent a lot of time out of work, during which time he made little effort to get a job. However, Alex said he really liked his last job and was interested in training so he could become a qualified electronics repairman. He noted that it paid well, something he had previously not been used to. Interestingly, Alex did not commit an offense during his steady employment as an assistant electronics repairman, which he said was the time he felt the best he has ever felt in his life. The current offense was not reported to the police by the victim until 3 years after the crime occurred, although she did report it the day after to a rape crisis center. Counseling apparently provided her with the courage to report the matter to officials.

Alex had a poor history regarding relationships. He did not date during his school years as he felt no female would like him. He reported that his parents had never encouraged personal hygiene, and as a consequence his teeth had rotted and he said he suspects he had bad body odor during his school years because he rarely bathed. Also, his clothes were rarely washed. As a result, Alex said he felt unattractive and believed that girls laughed at him. His first date occurred at age 23, shortly after he had his teeth fixed and after he began to attend more diligently to his personal hygiene. Unfortunately, this relationship did not last as his girlfriend dropped him for another man, a fact she made quite clear to Alex. This entrenched in Alex an already negative view of women, which derived from both his perceptions of his high school experiences with girls and his quite negative attitude toward his mother. Subsequently, Alex had not had any long-term relationship and had never lived with a woman.

According to his description, Alex's parents were a rather dysfunctional pair. His father was a construction worker who was alcoholic and abusive toward Alex's mother as well as toward Alex and his younger sister. Alex was aware that his father had sexually molested his sister at times when the father was intoxicated. The frequent fights between Alex's father and mother often led to the neighbors calling the police; his father was charged on two occasions with physical assault. His mother worked as a checkout clerk at a local supermarket and was also a heavy drinker. Alex viewed both his parents as neglectful and emotionally abusive toward his sister and him. He learned to steal and drink his father's alcohol at quite a young age in order to escape the unpleasant world of his family life. Such a poor home environment and its effects on Alex were exacerbated when his drunken maternal uncle began sexually touching 9-year-old Alex. This continued for 18 months until his uncle moved to another city. After this experience Alex began to masturbate quite frequently, particularly after drinking alcohol, with both serving to cope with the stress of his family life and with the personal disappointments he faced at school.

Alex was reasonably successful academically but was not a devoted student. He felt rejected by most of the other children at school, although he admitted that this might have been due to his own belief that they would reject him. He formed somewhat superficial friendships with two boys who, like Alex, felt rejected by the other students. With these two friends Alex began using drugs as well as alcohol, and together the three shoplifted and stole sports equipment from the school.

Alex admitted to all the offenses for which he had been convicted but added that he had exposed himself on numerous occasions from age 15 until his early 30s. He also said he had twice physically coerced sex from females who were clearly reluctant, although neither reported him. All the females he sexually assaulted (3 convictions plus 2 unreported) were in the age range from late teens to late 20s. He knew none of them beforehand but met each at a party or a bar. Alex either offered them a ride home from a bar, during which time he assaulted them, or he attacked them in a room at a party. On each occasion Alex was intoxicated on alcohol but had not been using any other drugs. He said that he frequented strip clubs and had a collection of pornographic DVDs which he used to stimulate masturbation. He also reported occasionally using prostitutes but said he found it less satisfying than masturbation. The content of his sexual fantasies, so Alex claimed, were usually appropriate, except when he became drunk in response to stress, at which time the sexual content of his fantasies became abusive and he imagined the woman to be resisting. Alex reported that this worried him, and he believed this had to change if he was to live offense-free. He said he was determined to enter treatment to address his problems because he finally felt he could develop a better, more satisfying life.

TREATMENT OF THE CONDITION

The main areas that needed to be addressed in Alex's treatment program were enhancement of his self-esteem, improvement in his coping style and skills, the development of better mood management, increased relationship skills, modification of his deviant sexual fantasies, substance abuse treatment, and assistance in developing elaborate future plans based on the good lives model. Initially in treatment, Alex was somewhat guarded and saw himself as much more deviant than the other group members. His defensiveness, however, did not include his offenses, about which he was quite open; it was more that he did not seem confident enough in the therapist and the group to reveal other deficient aspects to his functioning. Accordingly, the therapist adopted a relatively nonprobing style, allowing Alex to speak about issues when, and if, he felt comfortable. Whenever Alex volunteered information, he was rewarded by supportive attention from the therapist. This less challenging approach appeared to put Alex at ease, and gradually he became more forthcoming; as Alex became more open, the therapist became more probing and challenging. Now and then Alex would revert to a defensive style, particularly when the topic was threatening (e.g., early in the relationship component) or when he was having trouble in the institution with a staff member or another inmate. However, for the most part, once Alex had confidence in the group and in the therapist, he was able to point to dysfunctional ways he had responded in the past and take the necessary steps to address these dysfunctional responses.

Alex identified areas of functioning in which he felt competent (viz., work, sports, hobbies), and as a consequence his self-esteem in these areas was satisfactory. The areas in which he lacked confidence included his appearance, personal relationships, and capacity to cope with difficulties. Since having his teeth fixed, he now felt that he could develop confidence in his appearance and he had started to dress better. With assistance, Alex was able to list several features of his appearance that he considered positive, and he was encouraged to remind himself periodically of these features; the other group members also repeatedly and appropriately commented positively on Alex's appearance. Alex participated enthusiastically in the relationship component of treatment and in the component that focused on coping effectively with life's problems. Therapeutic focus on both these areas not only assisted him in gaining the skills and attitudes necessary to function well, but it also increased his confidence that he could form effective relationships and deal properly with stress.

Alex identified his past attachment style as "fearful avoidant." He said this was due to not believing he was a person someone else could feel affection for and as a result of his inability to trust others. Both these attitudes appeared to have arisen during his childhood due to his parents' neglectful and rejecting behaviors and were exacerbated by his perception that fellow students during his school years also rejected him. He said that he brought these negative attitudes to each of the relationships he had in the past and that he believed these attitudes prevented anyone from getting close to him. Alex resolved to overcome his relationship problems, and he worked hard during this component.

In the discussion of coping with stress and other difficulties that arise in life, Alex said that he had always run away from problems by getting drunk and by entering his deviant fantasy world while masturbating. It was at these times, Alex said, that his negative attitudes toward women were strongly in evidence. This avoidant style had not allowed him to develop any of the skills (e.g., problem solving and assertiveness) necessary to deal with difficult situations. Once Alex was helped to see how dysfunctional his avoidant coping style was and what a price he had to pay for adopting such a style, he enthusiastically participated in role-plays in which he practiced more appropriate coping responses. He was given instructions to deal with problems that arose in the prison by using his newly acquired skills; he not only made consistent efforts to do so, but he was mostly quite successful.

The therapist outlined procedures that Alex could employ to change the content of his masturbatory fantasies whenever they were deviant. Keeping a diary of his sexual fantasies revealed that it was only under times of stress that Alex used inappropriate fantasies and that the number of these occasions had decreased as he engaged effectively in treatment. By the time treatment focused on deviant fantasies, Alex's tendency to use such fantasies was limited even when he experienced stress. Nevertheless, masturbatory reconditioning procedures (Laws & Marshall, 1991) were described to Alex and he was told to diligently practice these procedures whenever he masturbated. He was advised to focus only on appropriate fantasies until he ejaculated, immediately after which he was to cease masturbating and rehearse repeatedly for 10 minutes every variation on his deviant fantasy. This procedure is called "verbal satiation" and is intended to associate deviant thoughts with unreinforced conditions (i.e., the absence of sexual arousal) and thereby produce extinction of the provocative property of the deviant fantasies (see Marshall, O'Brien, & Marshall, in press, for detailed descriptions of these procedures). Diary records revealed an effective decline in the frequency of deviant thoughts over the period that Alex remained in treatment and a total cessation over the 6 months posttreatment.

As a final stage in treatment, Alex was assisted in defining future goals (his good life program) that were consistent with his interests and abilities. He developed plans for becoming trained as an electronics repairman and he attended school in prison to reestablish his competence up to grade 12. Alex intended to return to active participation in sports; he said he was a good baseball player and had been invited several times in recent years to join an old-timers' league team. He also enjoyed fixing car motors and small engines as a hobby, which he had neglected in the recent past. Alex said he would check the newspapers when he was released in order to buy used motors in need of repair, which he would then fix and sell. Most of all, Alex wanted to develop a romantic relationship with a woman of his own age who did not have children at home. He was confident that if he took things slowly he could develop a good relationship that would result in a long-term commitment.

Alex formulated a set of plans that involved small, easily attainable steps that would result in the achievement of his various goals. He planned to live with his sister and brother-in-law, who were a happy and trouble-free couple; they had offered Alex a place to stay after he reestablished contact with them over a 2-year period. They understood Alex's problems, were fully aware of his offenses, and knew the kinds of things they needed to watch for to ensure that he did not slip back into problematic ways. Finally, Alex indicated an intention to attend AA meetings once released and attend a community-based alcohol abuse program. He had participated in a prison substance abuse program and was judged by the trainers to have done very well.

Alex has been released for over 5 years and has not reoffended. Although contacts have been entirely by mail, since Alex resides too far away for more personal contacts, both he and his sister report trouble-free functioning. Alex had not, at last contact, formed a permanent romantic relationship; he had dated three different women, the last of whom appears to be developing into a long-term commitment.

REFERENCES

Abel, G. G., Becker, J. V., & Cunningham-Rathner, J. (1984). Complications, consent and cognitions in sex between children and adults. *International Journal of Law and Psychiatry, 7,* 89–103.

Abel, G. G., & Blanchard, E. B. (1974). The role of fantasy in the treatment of sexual deviation. *Archives of General Psychiatry, 30,* 467–475.

Abel, G. G., & Osborn, C. (1992). The paraphilias: The extent and nature of sexually deviant and criminal behavior. *Psychiatric Clinics of North America, 15,* 675–687.

Abel, G. G., & Rouleau, J. L. (1990). The nature and extent of sexual assault. In W. L. Marshall, D. R. Laws, & H. E. Barbaree (Eds.), *Handbook of sexual assault: Issues, theories, and treatment of the offender* (pp. 9–21). New York: Plenum Press.

Abracen, J., Looman, J., & Anderson, D. (2000). Alcohol and drug abuse in sexual and nonsexual violent offenders. *Sexual Abuse: A Journal of Research and Treatment, 12,* 263–274.

American Humane Association. (1988). *Highlights of official child neglect and abuse reporting, 1986.* Denver, CO: Author.

American Psychiatric Association. (2000). *Diagnostic and statistical manual of mental disorders* (4th ed., text rev.). Washington, DC: Author.

Awad, G., Saunders, E., & Levene, J. (1984). A clinical study of male adolescent sex offenders. *International Journal of Offender Therapy and Comparative Criminology, 28,* 105–115.

Bancroft, J. (1989). *Human sexuality and its problems* (2nd ed.). Edinburgh: Churchill Livingstone.

Barbaree, H. E. (1990). Stimulus control of sexual arousal: Its role in sexual assault. In W. L. Marshall, D. R. Laws, & H. E. Barbaree (Eds.), *Handbook of sexual assault: Issues, theories, and treatment of the offender* (pp. 115–142). New York: Plenum Press.

Barbaree, H. E., Langton, C., & Peacock, E. (2004, October). *The evaluation of sex offender treatment efficacy using samples stratified by levels of actuarial risk.* Paper presented at the 23rd annual Research and Treatment Conference of the Association for the Treatment of Sexual Abusers, Albuquerque, NM.

Barbaree, H. E., & Marshall, W. L. (Eds.). (2005). *The juvenile sex offender* (2nd ed.). New York: Guilford Press.

Barbaree, H. E., Marshall, W. L., Yates, E., & Lightfoot, L. O. (1983). Alcohol intoxication and deviant sexual arousal in male social drinkers. *Behaviour Research and Therapy, 21,* 365–373.

Bass, B. A., & Levant, M. D. (1992). Family perception of rapists and pedophiles. *Psychological Reports, 71,* 211–214.

Baumeister, R. F., & Butler, J. L. (1997). Sexual masochism: Deviance without pathology. In D. R. Laws & W. O'Donohue (Eds.), *Sexual deviance: Theory, assessment, and treatment* (pp. 225–239). New York: Guilford Press.

Beech, A. R., & Fordham, A. S. (1997). Therapeutic climate of sexual offender treatment programs. *Sexual Abuse: A Journal of Research and Treatment, 9,* 219–237.

Beech, A. R., & Hamilton-Giachritsis, C. E. (2005). Relationship between therapeutic climate and treatment outcome in group-based sexual offender treatment programs. *Sexual Abuse: A Journal of Research and Treatment, 17,* 127–140.

Blanchard, R., Racansky, I. G., & Steiner, B. W. (1986). Phallometric detection of fetishistic arousal in heterosexual male cross-dressers. *Journal of Sex Research, 22,* 452–462.

Bond, I. K., & Evans, D. R. (1967). Avoidance therapy: Its use in two cases of underwear fetishism. *Canadian Medical Association Journal, 96,* 1160–1162.

Bradford, J. M. W. (2000). The treatment of sexual deviation using a pharmacological approach. *Journal of Sex Research, 3,* 248–257.

Brown, G. R., Wise, T. M., Costa, P. E., Herbst, J. H., Fagan, P. J., & Schmidt, C. (1996). Personality characteristics and sexual functioning of 188 cross-dressing men. *Journal of Nervous and Mental Diseases, 184,* 265–273.

Browne, A., & Finkelhor, D. (1986). Impact of child sexual abuse: A review of the research. *Psychological Bulletin, 99,* 16–77.

Bumby, K. M. (1996). Assessing the cognitive distortions of child molesters and rapists: Development and validation of the MOLEST and RAPE Scales. *Sexual Abuse: A Journal of Research and Treatment, 8,* 37–54.

Burgess, A. W., & Holmstrom, L. L. (1979). Rape: Sexual disruption and recovery. *American Journal of Orthopsychiatry, 49,* 648–657.

Burton, D., & Cerar, K. (2005, November). *Therapeutic alliance.* Paper presented at the 24th annual Research and Treatment Conference of the Association for the Treatment of Sexual Abusers, Salt Lake City.

Bushman, B., & Cooper, H. (1990). Effects of alcohol on human aggression: An integrative research review. *Psychological Bulletin, 7,* 341–354.

Calhoun, K. S., McCauley, J., & Crawford, M. E. (2006). Sexual assault. In R. D. McAnulty & M. M. Burnette (Eds.), *Sex and sexuality:* Vol. 3. *Sexual deviation and sexual offenses* (pp. 97–130). Westport, CT: Praeger.

Christie, M. M., Marshall, W. L., & Lanthier, R. D. (1979). *A descriptive study of incarcerated rapists and pedophiles.* Report to the Solicitor General of Canada, Ottawa.

Coen, S. J. (1988). Sadomasochistic excitement: Character disorder and perversion. In R. A. Glick & D. I. Myers (Eds.), *Masochism: Current psychoanalytic perspectives* (pp. 43–60). Hillsdale, NJ: Analytic Press.

Conte, J. R., & Schuerman, J. R. (1987). The effects of sexual abuse on children: A multidimensional view. *Journal of Interpersonal Violence, 2,* 380–390.

Cortoni, F. A., & Marshall, W. L. (2001). Sex as a coping strategy and its relationship to juvenile sexual history and intimacy in sexual offenders. *Sexual Abuse: A Journal of Research and Treatment, 13,* 27–43.

Cox, D. J., & Maletzky, B. M. (1980). Victims of exhibitionism. In D. J. Cox & R. J. Daitzman (Eds.), *Exhibitionism: Description, assessment and treatment* (pp. 289–293). New York: Garland.

Cox, D. J., Tsang, K., & Lee, A. (1982). A cross cultural comparison of the incidence and nature of male exhibitionism in college students. *Victimology, 7,* 231–234.

Crepault, C., & Couture, M. (1980). Men's erotic fantasies. *Archives of Sexual Behavior, 9,* 565–581.

Darke, J. L. (1990). Sexual aggression: Achieving power through humiliation. In W. L. Marshall, D. R. Laws, & H. E. Barbaree (Eds.), *Handbook of sexual assault: Issues, theories, and treatment of the offender* (pp. 55–72). New York: Plenum Press.

Deci, E. L., & Ryan, R. M. (2000). The "what" and "why" of goal pursuits: Human needs and the self-determination of behavior. *Psychological Inquiry, 11,* 227–268.

De Silva, P. (1993). Fetishism and sexual dysfunction: Clinical presentation and management. *Sexual and Marital Therapy, 8,* 147–155.

Doren, D. M. (2002). *Evaluating sex offenders: A manual for civil commitments and beyond.* Thousand Oaks, CA: Sage.

Dougher, M. (1995). Behavioral techniques to alter sexual arousal. In B. K. Schwartz & H. R. Cellini (Eds.), *The sex offender: Corrections, treatment and legal practice* (Vol. 1, pp. 15.1–15.8). Kingston, NJ: Civic Research Institute.

Dowden, C., Antonowicz, D., & Andrews, D. A. (2003). The effectiveness of relapse prevention with offenders: A meta-analysis. *International Journal of Offender Therapy and Comparative Criminology, 47,* 516–528.

Drake, C. R., & Ward, T. (2003). Treatment models for sex offenders: A move toward a formulation-based approach. In T. Ward, D. R. Laws, & S. M. Hudson (Eds.), *Sexual deviance: Issues and controversies* (pp. 226–243). Thousand Oaks, CA: Sage.

Drapeau, M. (2005). Research on the processes involved in treating sexual offenders. *Sexual Abuse: A Journal of Research and Treatment, 17,* 117–125.

Epperson, D. L., Kaul, J. D., Huot, S. J., Hesselton, D., Alexander, W., & Goldman, R. (1999). *Minnesota Sex Offender Screening Tool—Revised (MnSOST-R): Development, performance, and recommended risk level cut scores.* Available from www.psychology.iastate.edu/faculty/epperson/mnsost_download.htm.

Finkelhor, D. (1984). *Child sexual abuse: New theory and research.* New York: Free Press.

Firestone, P., Kingston, D. A., Wexler, A., & Bradford, J. M. W. (2005). *Long term follow-up of exhibitionists: Psychological, phallometric, and offence.* Unpublished manuscript.

Freund, K. (1957). Diagnostika homosexuality u mu? *Czecholsovakia Psychiatrie, 53,* 382–393.

Freund, K. (1990). Courtship disorder. In W. L. Marshall, D. R. Laws, & H. E. Barbaree (Eds.), *Handbook of sexual assault: Issues, theories, and treatment of the offender* (pp. 195–207). New York: Plenum Press.

Freund, K., Heasman, G. A., & Roper, V. (1982). Results of the main studies on sexual offenses against children and pubescents (a review). *Canadian Journal of Criminology, 24,* 387–397.

Freund, K., Seto, M. C., & Kuban, M. (1997). Frotteurism: The theory of courtship disorder. In D. R. Laws & W. O'Donohue (Eds.), *Sexual deviance: Theory, assessment, and treatment* (pp. 111–130). New York: Guilford Press.

Freund, K., Watson, R., & Dickey, R. (1991). Sex offenders against female children perpetrated by men who are not pedophiles. *Journal of Sex Research, 28,* 409–423.

Gamman, L., & Makinen, M. (1994). *Female fetishism.* New York: New York University Press.

Gebhard, P. J., Gagnon, J. H., Pomeroy, W. B., & Christenson, C. V. (1965). *Sex offenders.* New York: Harper & Row.

Gittleson, N. L., Eacott, S. R., & Mehta, B. M. (1978). Victims of indecent exposure. *British Journal of Psychiatry, 132,* 61–66.

Glaser, W. (2003). Integrating pharmacological treatments. In T. Ward, D. R. Laws, & S. M. Hudson (Eds.), *Sexual deviance: Issues and controversies* (pp. 262–279). Thousand Oaks, CA: Sage.

Gosselin, C. C. (1987). The sadomasochistic contract. In G. D. Wilson (Ed.), *Variant sexuality: Research and theory* (pp. 229–257). Baltimore: Johns Hopkins University Press.

Greenberg, D. M., & Bradford, J. M. W. (1997). Treatment of the paraphilic disorders: A review of the role of the selective serotonin reuptake inhibitors. *Sexual Abuse: A Journal of Research and Treatment, 9,* 349–360.

Greene, G., & Greene, C. (1974). *S-M: The last taboo.* New York: Grove Press.

Hanson, R. K. (1997). *The development of a brief actuarial risk scale for sexual offense recidivism.* (User Report 97–04). Ottawa: Department of the Solicitor General of Canada.

Hanson, R. K. (2006). Stability and change: Dynamic risk factors for sexual offenders. In W. L. Marshall, Y. M. Fernandez, L. E. Marshall, & G. A. Serran (Eds.), *Sexual offender treatment: Controversial issues* (pp. 17–31). Chichester, England: Wiley.

Hanson, R. K., Gordon, A., Harris, A. J. R., Marques, J. K., Murphy, W. D., Quinsey, V. L., et al. (2002). First report of the Collaborative Outcome Data Project on the Effectiveness of Psychological Treatment of Sex Offenders. *Sexual Abuse: A Journal of Research and Treatment, 14,* 169–195.

Hanson, R. K., & Harris, J. R. (1997). Voyeurism: Assessment and treatment. In D. R. Laws & W. O'Donohue (Eds.), *Sexual deviance: Theory, assessment, and treatment* (pp. 311–331). New York: Guilford Press.

Hanson, R. K., & Thornton, D. (2000). Improving risk assessments for sex offenders: A comparison of three actuarial scales. *Law and Human Behavior, 24,* 119–136.

Howells, K. (1979). Some meanings of children for pedophiles. In M. Cook & G. Wilson (Eds.), *Love and attraction: An international conference* (pp. 519–526). Oxford: Pergamon Press.

Hucker, S. J. (1997). Sexual sadism: Psychopathology and theory. In D. R. Laws & W. O'Donohue (Eds.), *Sexual deviance: Theory, assessment, and theory* (pp. 194–209). New York: Guilford Press.

Hunter, J. A., & Mathews, R. (1997). Sexual deviance in females. In D. R. Laws & W. O'Donohue (Eds.), *Sexual deviance: Theory, assessment, and treatment* (pp. 465–480). New York: Guilford Press.

Johnson, S. D., Gibson, L., & Linden, R. (1978). Alcohol and rape in Winnipeg, 1966–1975. *Journal of Studies on Alcohol, 39,* 1887–1894.

Koss, M. P., Gidycz, C. A., & Wisniewski, N. (1987). The scope of rape: Incidence and prevalence of sexual aggression and victimization in a national sample of higher education students. *Journal of Consulting and Clinical Psychology, 55,* 162–170.

Koss, M. R. (1992). The underdetection of rape: Methodological choices influence incidence estimates. *Journal of Social Issues, 48,* 61–75.

Krueger, R. B., & Kaplan, M. S. (1997). Frotteurism: Assessment and treatment. In D. R. Laws & W. O'Donohue (Eds.), *Sexual deviance: Theory, assessment, and treatment* (pp. 131–151). New York: Guilford Press.

Lang, R. A., & Langevin, R. (1991). Parent-child relations in offenders who commit violent sexual crimes against children. *Behavioral Sciences and the Law, 9,* 61–71.

Langevin, R. (1983). *Sexual strands.* Hillsdale, NJ: Erlbaum.

Langevin, R., Bain, J., Ben-Aron, M., Coulthard, R., Day, D., Handy, L., et al. (1984). Sexual aggression: Constructing a predictive equation. A controlled pilot study. In R. Langevin (Ed.), *Erotic preference, gender identity, and aggression in men: New research studies* (pp. 39–76). Hillsdale, NJ: Erlbaum.

Långström, N., & Seto, M. C. (in press). Exhibitionistic and voyeuristic behavior in a Swedish national population survey. *Archives of Sexual Behavior.*

Laws, D. R., & Marshall, W. L. (1990). A conditioning theory of the etiology and maintenance of deviant sexual preferences and behavior. In W. L. Marshall, D. R. Laws, & H. E. Barbaree (Eds.), *Handbook of sexual assault: Issues, theories, and treatment of the offender* (pp. 209–229). New York: Plenum Press.

Laws, D. R., & Marshall, W. L. (1991). Masturbatory reconditioning with sexual deviates: An evaluative review. *Advances in Behaviour Research and Therapy, 13,* 13–25.

Laws, D. R., & Marshall, W. L. (2003). A brief history of behavioral and cognitive-behavioral approaches to sexual offender treatment: Part 1. Early developments. *Sexual Abuse: A Journal of Research and Treatment, 15,* 75–92.

Laws, D. R., & O'Donohue, W. (Eds.). (1997). *Sexual deviance: Theory, assessment, and treatment.* New York: Guilford Press.

Laws, D. R., & Ward, T. (2006). When one size doesn't fit all: The reformulation of relapse prevention. In W. L. Marshall, Y. M. Fernandez, L. E. Marshall, & G. A. Serran (Eds.), *Sexual offender treatment: Controversial issues* (pp. 241–254). Chichester, England: Wiley.

Lee, J. K. P., Jackson, J. H., Pattison, P., & Ward, T. (2002). Developmental risk factors for sexual offending. *Child Abuse and Neglect, 26,* 73–92.

Levenson, J. S. (2004). Reliability of sexually violent predator civil commitment criteria. *Law and Human Behavior, 28,* 357–368.

Looman, J. (1999). Mood, conflict, and deviant sexual fantasies. In B. K. Schwartz (Ed.), *The sex offender: Theoretical advances, treating special populations and legal developments* (Vol. 3, pp. 3.1–3.11). Kingston, NJ: Civic Research Institute.

Looman, J., Abracen, J., & Nicholaichuk, T. P. (2000). Recidivism among treated sexual offenders and matched controls: Data from the Regional Treatment Centre (Ontario). *Journal of Interpersonal Violence, 15,* 279–290.

Lösel, F., & Schmucker, M. (2005). The effectiveness of treatment for sexual offenders: A comprehensive meta-analysis. *Journal of Experimental Criminology, 1,* 1–29.

MacDonald, J. M. (1973). *Indecent exposure.* Springfield, IL: Charles C Thomas.

Mann, R. E., Webster, S. D., Schofield, C., & Marshall, W. L. (2004). Approach versus avoidance goals in relapse prevention with sexual offenders. *Sexual Abuse: A Journal of Research and Treatment, 16,* 65–75.

Marques, J. K. (1982, March). *Relapse prevention: A self-control model for the treatment of sex offenders.* Paper presented at the 7th annual Forensic Mental Health Conference, Asilomar, CA.

Marques, J. K., Weideranders, M., Day, D. M., Nelson, C., & van Ommeren, A. (2005). Effects of a relapse prevention program on sexual recidivism: Final results from California's Sex Offender Treatment and Evaluation Project (SOTEP). *Sexual Abuse: A Journal of Research and Treatment, 17,* 79–107.

Marshall, W. L. (1971). A combined treatment method for certain sexual deviations. *Behaviour Research and Therapy, 9,* 292–294.

Marshall, W. L. (1984, March). *Rape as a socio-cultural phenomenon.* The J. P. S. Robertson Annual Lecture, Trent University, Peterborough, Ontario, Canada.

Marshall, W. L. (1985, May). *Social causes of rape.* Visiting Fellows' Public Lecture, University of Western Australia, Perth.

Marshall, W. L. (1996). Assessment, treatment, and theorizing about sex offenders: Developments over the past 20 years and future directions. *Criminal Justice and Behavior, 23,* 162–199.

Marshall, W. L. (1997). Pedophilia: Psychopathology and theory. In D. R. Laws & W. O'Donohue (Eds.), *Sexual deviance: Theory, assessment, and treatment* (pp. 152–174). New York: Guilford Press.

Marshall, W. L. (2006). Diagnostic problems with sexual offenders. In W. L. Marshall, Y. M. Fernandez, L. E. Marshall, & G. A. Serran (Eds.), *Sexual offender treatment: Controversial issues* (pp. 33–43). Chichester, England: Wiley.

Marshall, W. L. (in press). Diagnostic issues, multiple paraphilias, and comorbid disorders in sexual offenders: Their incidence and treatment. *Aggression and Violent Behavior: A Review Journal.*

Marshall, W. L., & Anderson, D. (2000). Do relapse prevention components enhance treatment effectiveness? In D. R. Laws, S. M. Hudson, & T. Ward (Eds.), *Remaking relapse prevention with sex offenders: A sourcebook* (pp. 39–55). Newbury Park, CA: Sage.

Marshall, W. L., Anderson, D., & Fernandez, Y. M. (1999). *Cognitive behavioural treatment of sexual offenders.* Chichester, England: Wiley.

Marshall, W. L., & Barbaree, H. E. (1990). An integrated theory of sexual offending. In W. L. Marshall, D. R. Laws, & H. E. Barbaree (Eds.), *Handbook of sexual assault: Issues, theories, and treatment of the offender* (pp. 257–275). New York: Plenum Press.

Marshall, W. L., Bryce, P., Hudson, S. M., Ward, T., & Moth, B. (1996). The enhancement of intimacy and reduction of loneliness among child molesters. *Legal and Criminological Psychology, 1,* 95–102.

Marshall, W. L., & Eccles, A. (1993). Pavlovian conditioning processes in adolescent sex offenders. In H. E. Barbaree, W. L. Marshall, & S. M. Hudson (Eds.), *The juvenile sex offender* (pp. 118–142). New York: Guilford Press.

Marshall, W. L., Eccles, A., & Barbaree, H. E. (1991). The treatment of exhibitionists: A focus on sexual deviance versus cognitive and relationship features. *Behaviour Research and Therapy, 29,* 129–135.

Marshall, W. L., & Fernandez, Y. M. (2003). *Phallometric testing with sexual offenders: Theory, research, and practice.* Brandon, VT: Safer Society Press.

Marshall, W. L., Fernandez, Y. M., Serran, G. A., Mulloy, R., Thornton, D., Mann, R. E., et al. (2003). Process variables in the treatment of sexual offenders: A review of the relevant literature. *Aggression and Violent Behavior: A Review Journal, 8,* 205–234.

Marshall, W. L., & Hambley, L. S. (1996). Intimacy and loneliness, and their relationship to rape myth acceptance and hostility toward women among rapists. *Journal of Interpersonal Violence, 11,* 586–592.

Marshall, W. L., & Hucker, S. J. (2006). Severe sexual sadism: Its features and treatment. In R. D. McAnulty & M. M. Burnette (Eds.), *Sex and sexuality:* Vol. 3.*Sexual deviation and sexual offenses* (pp. 228–250). Westport, CT: Praeger.

Marshall, W. L., Hudson, S. M., & Hodkinson, S. (1993). The importance of attachment bonds in the development of juvenile sex offending. In H. E. Barbaree, W. L. Marshall, & S. M. Hudson (Eds.), *The juvenile sex offender* (pp. 164–181). New York: Guilford Press.

Marshall, W. L., & Kennedy, P. (2003). Sexual sadism in sexual offenders: An elusive diagnosis. *Aggression and Violent Behavior: A Review Journal, 8,* 1–22.

Marshall, W. L., Kennedy, P., & Yates, P. (2002). Issues concerning the reliability and validity of the diagnosis of sexual sadism applied in prison settings. *Sexual Abuse: A Journal of Research and Treatment, 14,* 310–311.

Marshall, W. L., Kennedy, P., Yates, P., & Serran, G. A. (2002). Diagnosing sexual sadism in sexual offenders: Reliability across diagnosticians. *International Journal of Offender Therapy and Comparative Criminology, 46,* 668–676.

Marshall, W. L., & Marshall, L. E. (2000). The origins of sexual offending. *Trauma, Violence, and Abuse: A Review Journal, 1,* 250–263.

Marshall, W. L., Marshall, L. E., & Serran, G. A. (in press). Strategies in the treatment of paraphilias: A critical review. *Annual Review of Sex Research.*

Marshall, W. L., Marshall, L. E., Serran, G. A., & Fernandez, Y. M. (2006). *Treating sexual offenders: An integrated approach.* New York: Routledge.

Marshall, W. L., O'Brien, M. D., & Marshall, L. E. (in press). Modifying sexual preferences. In A. Beech, L. Craig, & K. Browne (Eds.), *Assessment and treatment of sexual offenders: A handbook.* Chichester, England: Wiley.

Marshall, W. L., Serran, G. A., & Cortoni, F. A. (2000). Childhood attachments, sexual abuse, and their relationship to adult coping in child molesters. *Sexual Abuse: A Journal of Research and Treatment, 12,* 17–26.

Marshall, W. L., Serran, G. A., Fernandez, Y. M., Mulloy, R., Mann, R. E., & Thornton, D. (2003). Therapist characteristics in the treatment of sexual offenders: Tentative data on their relationship with indices of behaviour change. *Journal of Sexual Aggression, 9,* 25–30.

Marshall, W. L., Serran, G. A., Moulden, J., Mulloy, R., Fernandez, Y. M., Mann, R. E., et al. (2002). Therapist features in sexual offender treatment: Their reliable identification and influence on behaviour change. *Clinical Psychology and Psychotherapy, 9,* 395–405.

Marshall, W. L., Ward, T., Mann, R. E., Moulden, H., Fernandez, Y. M., Serran, G. A., et al. (2005). Working positively with sexual offenders: Maximizing the effectiveness of treatment. *Journal of Interpersonal Violence, 20,* 1–19.

Marshall, W. L., & Yates, P. M. (2005). Comment on Mailloux et al.'s (2003) study "Dosage of treatment of sexual offenders: Are we overprescribing?" *International Journal of Offender Therapy and Comparative Criminology, 49,* 221–224.

Mason, F. L. (1997). Fetishism: Psychopathology and theory. In D. R. Laws & W. O'Donohue (Eds.), *Sexual deviance: Theory, assessment and treatment* (pp. 75–91). New York: Guilford Press.

Matek, O. (1988). Obscene phone callers.*Journal of Social Work and Human Sexuality, 7,* 113–130.

McGuire, R. J., Carlisle, J. M., & Young, B. G. (1965). Sexual deviations as conditioned behavior: A hypothesis. *Behaviour Research and Therapy, 2,* 185–190.

Milner, J. S., & Dopke, C. A. (1997). Paraphilia not otherwise specified: Psychopathology and theory. In D. R. Laws & W. O'Donohue (Eds.), *Sexual deviance: Theory, assessment, and treatment* (pp. 394–423). New York: Guilford Press.

Mohr, J. W., Turner, R. E., & Jerry, M. B. (1964). *Pedophilia and exhibitionism.* Toronto: University of Toronto Press.

Money, J. (1986). *Lovemaps: Clinical concepts of sexual/erotic health and pathology, paraphilia, and gender transposition in childhood, adolescence, and maturity.* New York: Irvington.

Murphy, W. D. (1997). Exhibitionism: Psychopathology and theory. In D. R. Laws & W. O'Donohue (Eds.), *Sexual deviance: Theory, assessment, and treatment* (pp. 22–39). New York: Guilford Press.

Murphy, W. D., & Page, J. (2006). Exhibitionism. In R. D. McAnulty & M. M. Burnette (Eds.), *Sex and sexuality:* Vol. 3. *Sexual deviation and sexual offenses* (pp. 1–20). Westport, CT: Praeger.

Nicholaichuk, T., Gordon, A., Gu, D., & Wong, S. (2000). Outcome of an institutional sexual offender treatment program: A comparison between treated and matched untreated offenders. *Sexual Abuse: A Journal of Research and Treatment, 12,* 139–153.

O'Donohue, W. T., Regev, L. C., & Hagstrom, A. (2000). Problems with the DSM-IV diagnosis of pedophilia. *Sexual Abuse: A Journal of Research and Treatment, 12,* 95–105.

Ovesey, L., & Person, E. (1973). Gender identity and sexual psychopathology in men: A psychodynamic analysis of homosexuality, transsexualism, and transvestism. *Journal of the American Academy of Psychoanalysis, 1,* 53–72.

Person, E. S., & Ovesey, L. (1984). Homosexual cross-dressers. *Journal of the American Academy of Psychoanalysis, 12,* 167–186.

Pfäfflin, F., Böhmer, M., Cornehl, S., & Mergenthaler, E. (2005). What happens in therapy with sexual offenders? A model of process research. *Sexual Abuse: A Journal of Research and Treatment, 17,* 141–151.

Pithers, W. D., Marques, J. K., Gibat, C. C., & Marlatt, G. A. (1983). Relapse prevention with sexual aggressors: A self-control model of treatment and maintenance of change. In J. G. Greer & I. R. Stuart (Eds.), *The sexual aggressor: Current perspectives on treatment* (pp. 214–239). New York: Van Nostrand Reinhold.

Protter, B., & Travin, S. (1987). Sexual fantasies in the treatment of paraphilic disorders: A bimodal approach. *Psychiatric Quarterly, 58,* 279–297.

Proulx J., Blais, E., & Beauregard, E. (2006). Sadistic sexual aggressors. In W. L. Marshall, Y. M. Fernandez, L. E. Marshall, & G. A. Serran (Eds.), *Sexual offender treatment: Controversial issues* (pp. 61–77). Chichester, England: Wiley.

Proulx, J., McKibben, A., & Lusignan, R. (1996). Relationship between affective components and sexual behaviors in sexual aggressors. *Sexual Abuse: A Journal of Research and Treatment, 8,* 279–289.

Quinsey, V. L., Harris, G. T., Rice, M. E., & Cormier, C. A. (1998). *Violent offenders: Appraising and managing risk.* Washington, DC: American Psychological Association.

Riordan, S. (1999). Indecent exposure: The impact upon the victim's fear of sexual crime. *Journal of Forensic Psychiatry, 10,* 309–316.

Rooth, G. (1973). Exhibitionism, sexual violence and paedophilia. *British Journal of Psychiatry, 122,* 705–710.

Russell, D. E. J. (1984). *Sexual exploitation: Rape, child sexual abuse, and workplace harassment.* Thousand Oaks, CA: Sage.

Saunders, E., Awad, G. A., & White, G. (1986). Male adolescent sex offenders: The offenders and the offense. *Canadian Journal of Psychiatry, 127,* 375–380.

Schlank, A. (2006). The civil commitment of sexual offenders: Lessons learned. In W. L. Marshall, Y. M. Fernandez, L. E. Marshall, & G. A. Serran (Eds.), *Sexual offender treatment: Controversial issues* (pp. 45–60). Chichester, England: Wiley.

Scott, G. G. (1983). *Erotic power: An exploration of dominance and submission.* Secaucus, NJ: Citadel Press.

Seto, M. C., & Barbaree, H. E. (1995). The role of alcohol in sexual aggression. *Clinical Psychological Review, 15*, 545–566.

Simons, D., Tyler, C., & Lins, R. (2005, November). *Influence of therapist characteristics on treatment progress.* Paper presented at the 24th annual Research and Treatment Conference of the Association for the Treatment of Sexual Abusers, Salt Lake City.

Smallbone, S. W. (2006). An attachment-theoretical revision of Marshall and Barbaree's integrated theory of the etiology of sexual offending. In W. L. Marshall, Y. M. Fernandez, L. E. Marshall, & G. A. Serran (Eds.), *Sexual offender treatment: Controversial issues* (pp. 93–107). Chichester, England: Wiley.

Smallbone, S. W., & Dadds, M. R. (2000). Attachment and coercive sexual behaviour. *Sexual Abuse: A Journal of Research and Treatment, 12*, 3–15.

Starzyk, K. B., & Marshall, W. L. (2003). Childhood, family, and personological risk factors for sexual offending. *Aggression and Violent Behavior: A Review Journal, 8*, 93–105.

Ward, T. (2002). Good lives and the rehabilitation of offenders: Promises and problems. *Aggression and Violent behavior: A Review Journal, 7*, 513–528.

Ward, T., & Fisher, D. (2006). New ideas in the treatment of sexual offenders. In W. L. Marshall, Y. M. Fernandez, L. E. Marshall, & G. A. Serran (Eds.), *Sexual offender treatment: Controversial issues* (pp. 143–158). Chichester, England: Wiley.

Ward, T., & Hudson, S. M. (1996). Relapse prevention: A critical analysis. *Sexual Abuse: A Journal of Research and Treatment, 8*, 177–200.

Ward, T., Hudson, S. M., & Marshall, W. L. (1994). The abstinence violation effect in child molesters. *Behaviour Research and Therapy, 32*, 431–437.

Ward, T., Hudson, S. M., & Siegert, R. J. (1995). A critical comment on Pithers' relapse prevention model. *Sexual Abuse: A Journal of Research and Treatment, 7*, 167–175.

Ward, T., & Marshall, W. L. (2004). Good lives, aetiology and the rehabilitation of sex offenders: A bridging theory. *Journal of Sexual Aggression, 10*, 153–169.

Ward, T., & Stewart, C. A. (2003). The treatment of sex offenders: Risk management and good lives. *Professional Psychology: Research and Practice, 34*, 353–360.

Weinberg, T. S. (1987). Sadomasochism in the United States: A review of recent sociological literature. *Journal of Sex Research, 23*, 50–59.

Weinberg, T., & Kamel, W. L. (Eds.). (1983). *S and M: Studies in sadomasochism.* Buffalo, NY: Prometheus.

West, D. J. (1991). The effects of sex offences. In C. R. Hollin & K. Howells (Eds.), *Clinical approaches to sex offenders and their victims* (pp. 55–73). Chichester, England: Wiley.

Wright, R. D., & Schneider, S. L. (1997). Deviant sexual fantasies as motivated self-deception. In B. K. Schwartz & H. R. Cellini (Eds.), *The sex offender: New insights, treatment innovations and legal developments* (Vol. 2, pp. 8.1–8.14). Kingston, NJ: Civic Research Institute.

Yates, E., Barbaree, H. E., & Marshall, W. L. (1984). Anger and deviant sexual arousal. *Behavior Therapy, 15*, 287–294.

Zucker, K. J., & Blanchard, R. (1997). Transvestic fetishism: Psychopathology and theory. In D. R. Laws & W. O'Donohue (Eds.), *Sexual deviance: Theory, assessment, and treatment* (pp. 253–279). New York: Guilford Press.

CHAPTER 22

Adults with Intellectual Disabilities

PETER STURMEY

DESCRIPTION OF THE DISORDER

The term "intellectual disabilities" (ID) refers to a very wide range of conditions that are (a) identified early during development, often before 11 years and often much earlier; (b) characterized by significantly slower intellectual development, as manifested in lower final mental ages, global deficits in most or all aspects cognition; and (c) deficits in daily functioning below that expected by the local culture. Until recently, most Americans used the term "mental retardation," but this term has now been replaced with "intellectual disabilities." Traditional classification schemes subdivide ID into four degrees of severity: mild, moderate, severe, and profound. "Unspecified ID" is used where ID is suspected, but degree of impairment cannot be directly assessed, such as in some people with cerebral palsy. Formerly, the term "borderline ID" was used for people with an IQ beyond the formal cutoff for ID, but who had significant intellectual problems and related problems in daily functioning. The *Diagnostic and Statistical Manual of Mental Disorders,* fourth edition (*DSM-IV*; American Psychiatric Association, 2000) defined these degrees of ID only by IQ scores. In Europe it is conventional to combine severe and profound ID into one classification, referred to as "severe" ID.

The range of daily functioning in adults with ID is indeed very wide. Those who meet the psychometric criteria for mild ID and who may have been in special education as children and adolescents may no longer use services. They may be married, work, have children, and have no gross problems in adapting to daily living most of the time. In contrast, some adults with profound ID and multiple disabilities may be medically fragile, have associated biomedical problems, such as cerebral palsy, seizure disorders and sensory impairments, and a shortened life span, and require complete assistance in all aspects of daily functioning for their entire lives. The functioning of most people with ID lies somewhere in between these two extremes.

A few forms of genetic and other biomedical forms of ID, such as Down syndrome, can be detected in utero. Services may identify some of the infants and young children with the most severe forms of ID, such as those associated with some known genetic syndromes, prenatal trauma, infections, and acquired brain damage, at birth or early infancy because these conditions are often associated with concomitant biomedical problems and grossly delayed developmental milestones that are readily apparent. In contrast, services identify many children with less severe forms of ID only during the first few years of school, when academic failure becomes apparent, especially after education depends on adequate reading, writing, and arithmetic skills. Upon graduation from high school, many young adults who were formally diagnosed with mild ID and were in special education no longer use services for people with ID. We know little about these people as adults.

Rates of intellectual development of children with ID vary considerably and gradually decelerate compared to their typical peers. Intellectual growth associated with each degree of ID differs in rate, mental age as adults, and the age at which relative deceleration stops (Fisher & Zeaman, 1970). Thus, adults with profound ID may have a few or no words and may have some basic self-help skills, such as spoon feeding and locomotion. In contrast, some adults with mild ID may work, live independently or with occasional professional or informal assistance, have some functional social, problem-solving, and academic skills that enable them to function independently or semi-independently, and have satisfying social and personal lives.

Intellectual disability is characterized by global deficits in all or almost all aspects of cognition, including reaction time, attention, motivation, use of abstract language, intellectual skills and adaptive behavior necessary for daily living (Baroff & Olley, 1999). The nature of ID is clarified when contrasted with related developmental conditions. For example, *DSM-IV* characterizes specific learning disabilities (SLD) by deficits that are specific to one domain of functioning. Functioning in the affected domains is *at least 2 standard deviations below IQ* (American Psychiatric Association, 2000, p. 46.) Intellectual disability may also be contrasted with Pervasive Developmental Disorder (PDD), which is characterized by *qualitative* differences in language, reciprocal social interaction skills, and stereotyped behavior, interests, and activities that are pervasive and deviant relative to the person's mental age (American Psychiatric Association, 2000, p. 45.) Many, but not all, people with PDDs also have ID.

Zigler, Balla, and Hodapp (1984) proposed that ID can be better thought of as two groups of conditions reflecting etiology. Nonorganic forms of ID account for the majority of people with ID and are characterized by mild and moderate IQ. They are associated with poverty, lack of education, large family size, no specific etiology, and low income. People with nonorganic forms of ID often have at least one first-degree relative who also has mild or moderate ID. The term "organic forms of ID" refers to ID where there is a known biomedical cause. These biomedical causes include (a) hormonal causes; (b) nutritional deficiencies during uterine development, infancy, and childhood; (c) perinatal infections; (d) exposure to toxins; (e) various kinds of brain trauma, including road traffic accidents, problems during birth, falls, near-drowning and violence, including child abuse; and (f) genetic causes, which may be chromosomal or single gene causes (Durkin & Stein, 1996.) The pattern of organic etiologies changes dramatically over time. For example, in the past, ID due to maternal tertiary syphilis during pregnancy was relatively common, whereas it is now very rare, as it can be readily detected and treated. By contrast, Fetal Alcohol Syndrome, due to maternal consumption of alcohol, and AIDS-related ID have increased (Baumeister & Woodley-Zanthos, 1996.) Organic forms of ID are often less strongly related to income and social class. They are not associated with a family pattern of ID, unless there is some heritable form of ID.

Intellectual disability is associated with negative evaluation, discrimination, and stigmatization. In the past many people with ID were ostracized as a threat to society. The disability was a justification for institutionalization, other forms of segregation, sterilization, and, indeed, murder. Currently, adults with ID often face social rejection, lack of access to independent housing, work, and medical, dental, and psychological treatment and other services. Society continues to debate the issue of termination of fetuses and live infants with severe biomedical problems who have or are at high risk for ID.

DIAGNOSIS AND ASSESSMENT

Traditional Approaches

Traditionally, three criteria have been used to diagnose ID: (1) significantly below average intelligence, (2) deficits in adaptive behavior, and (3) detection during the developmental period. Each criterion deserves individual examination. *DSM-IV* operationalizes significantly subaverage intelligence as "an IQ of approximately 70 or below on an individually administered IQ test (for infants, a clinical judgment or significantly subaverage intelligence)" (American Psychiatric Association, 2000, p. 46.) However, the IQ used to define ID has varied considerably and continues to vary among states, countries, and different laws within one country. Thus, past definitions used an IQ of 85 or lower to define ID. Currently, various U.S. laws use IQ criteria of below 75, 70, or 69. The IQ must be derived from an accurately normed test that is developed using accurate sampling from the relevant population and whose norms remain stable during the time in which it is used. Adequacy of test norms is not trivial. It determines client eligibility for services. Scullin (2006) demonstrated that after the publication of the third revision of the Wechsler Intelligence Scale for Children (WISC-III) in 1991, nationwide declines in the number of students with ID reversed. Decreasing rates of placement may have reflected the upward drift in the norms of the old WISC after publication and the increase in placement may have reflected the greater difficulty of the new, accurately normed test. Thus, people who formerly were ineligible for services became eligible after new tests were introduced (Kanaya, Scullin, & Ceci, 2003). Such drifts in IQ test norms may also result in apparently large changes in individual IQs. These changes, such as a 10-point drop in IQ when a person is retested with a recently normed test, might be mistaken for some morbid change.

DSM-IV defines deficits in adaptive behavior as

the person's effectiveness in meeting the standards expected for his or her age by his or her cultural group . . . in at least two of the following areas: communication, self-care, home living, social/interpersonal skills, use of community resources, self-direction, functional academic skills, work, leisure, health and safety. (American Psychiatric Association, 2000, p. 46)

Adaptive behavior is conventionally assessed by instruments such as the Vineland Scales of Adaptive Behavior or similar measures. Although these measures may more or less accurately measure a client's current functioning, they fail to capture an essential component of the definition, namely, whether such a deficit is expected in the person's culture. Thus, a 4-year-old with only 20 words might be regarded as a serious cause for concern in one setting and a cute child in another. Martin, King, Jaccoby, and Jacklin (1984) observed that children acquired toileting skills much earlier in a 1947 cohort than in a 1975 cohort, which acquired toileting skills at approximately 24 months. This might reflect the introduction of disposable diapers and washing machines and changes in expectation for adaptive behavior. In contrast, infants in other cultures may routinely acquire toileting skills at 6 months (de Vries & deVries, 1977).

The final criterion is that ID must be detected during the developmental period. *DSM-IV* operationalizes this as "onset . . . before age 18 years" (American Psychiatric Association, 2000, p. 46). Many laws differ from one another on this criterion and may use 21 or 22 years. A clinically important question involves a small number of people who experience acquired brain damage or a psychotic disorder in late teenage years, score below 70 on IQ tests, and have deficits in adaptive behavior. Services often dispute such people's diagnosis and eligibility for services.

AMERICAN ASSOCIATION ON INTELLECTUAL DISABILITIES SUPPORTS DEFINITION

The American Association on Intellectual Disabilities (AAID) has offered an alternate approach to defining ID. They noted that ID is not necessarily an inherent or permanent quality of the person. Rather, it may reflect the formal and informal supports available to the person. They defined ID as follows:

> Mental retardation is not something you have, like blue eyes, or a bad heart. Nor is it something you are, like short, or thin. It is not a medical disorder, nor a mental disorder. Mental retardation is a particular state of functioning that begins in childhood and is characterized by limitation in both intelligence and adaptive skills. Mental retardation reflects the "fit" between the capabilities of individuals and the structure and expectations of their environment. (American Association on Mental Retardation, 2002, p. 48)

The AAID also developed a multidimensional conception of ID that includes cognitive abilities, adaptive behavior, participation and social roles, health, and the person's environmental and cultural context. They suggested that ID and the differing degrees of ID should be defined in terms of the intensity and duration of supports a person needs, rather than IQ. The AAID developed its own manual to assess ID based on this definition (American Association on Mental Retardation, 2002). MacMillan, Gresham, and Siperstein (1993) criticized the AAID's definition of ID because it eliminated the traditional degrees of ID defined by IQ scores, depended too much on the assessment of adaptive behavior, which might be unreliable, and raised the IQ cutoff to 75 from 70. Perhaps the most stinging criticism has been the conspicuous failure of most practitioners and researchers to adopt this definition over the past decade.

DISABILITY, IMPAIRMENT, AND HANDICAP

The World Health Organization (2001) further parses aspects of ID by distinguishing three constructs. *Impairment* is damage or weakening of functioning at the level of the cell or organ or psychological process. *Disability* refers to limitations in daily functioning that result from impairment. *Handicap* is the negative personal evaluation by others related to disability. For example, a person with ID might have multiple biological impairments related to rubella damage as a fetus. These impairments may result in failure to exhibit typical motor, sensory, educational, and other adaptive behavior functioning. Other people might negatively evaluate a person who is blind and cannot walk by turning away from the person or assuming he or she is sick. Each of these three terms implies a different kind of intervention. Impairment might be prevented or remediated by medical or other interventions. Disability might be removed by prostheses, training, or therapy. Handicap might be reduced by exposing the public to disability, by education, or by training efforts to reduce discrimination.

SHIFTING FASHIONS IN DIAGNOSIS

Between 1976 and 2004 the number of children diagnosed with ID in the American education system fell from nearly 1 million to fewer than 600,000 (U.S. Department of Education, 2004). MacMillan and colleagues (MacMillan, Gresham, Siperstein, & Bocian, 1996) showed that school services did not diagnose many children who met psychometric criteria for ID, including deficits in adaptive behavior. Instead, they often diagnosed these children with SLDs or emotional disorders, even though they did not meet the diagnostic criteria for these disorders. School districts labeled children as having ID only if they met the criterion for ID, persistently failed on reading and writing, evidenced behavioral disorders, and could not be educated with currently available resources. Further, MacMillan, Gresham, and Bocian (1998) noted that the IQs of children labeled with SLDs have also dropped. These observations suggest that the American education system has become reluctant to use the term intellectual disability unless doing so accesses additional resources for children who cannot be served with the resources associated with other diagnostic labels.

CONCEPTUALIZATION

LEARNING AND MODELING

Learning and modeling are essential and important processes in the development of nonorganic forms of mental retardation, where biological causes are absent and environmental restrictions are obvious. Even within a single organic form of ID, the developmental outcomes are so varied that environmental variables must be very important. Consider the different outcomes for people with Down syndrome: One person with Down syndrome may be nonverbal and nonambulatory and function with profound ID; another person with Down syndrome may be a movie actor.

Functional Analysis of Retarded Behavior Bijou (1961/1995) applied behavior analysis to child development. He emphasized the importance of the child's context and the continuous interactions between the child and his or her environment. He also emphasized the behavioral processes that lead to the acquisition of elaborated behavior, such as reinforcement, extinction, shaping, acquisition of novel reinforcers, maintenance of operant behavior, and discrimination and generalization, which may result in acquisition of complex behavior, such as decision making, problem solving, and self-regulatory behavior. Subsequent observational studies of young children and interactions with their caregivers have confirmed that there are strong relationships between the child's language and social environment and subsequent intellectual outcomes (Hart & Risley, 1995).

Bijou (1966) extended these notions to address the development of ID by emphasizing the observable behavior of people with ID rather than retarded development as an intrapsychic trait. Thus, the behavior of a person with ID can be characterized as less behavior, slower behavior, and some behavioral excesses compared to a typically developing person. Various behavioral and physical characteristics of the person with ID may make learning less likely. Consider the interactions of people with ID, which may be fewer and shorter, perhaps because the person with ID does not reinforce other people's interactions if interacting with them is more effortful or punishing than other activities. Observational studies of family homes have found environmental characteristics, such as fewer language models, less reinforcement for language, and more punishment, in homes where children have slower development (Hart & Risley, 1995). Studies have also implicated learning in the development of severe challenging behaviors in people with ID. For example, Oliver, Hall, and Murphy (2005) observed the development of self-injury in young children with ID. They observed that over a 2-year period mutual reinforcement developed between caregiver and child, such that as the child grew older, self-injury was more likely to evoke a social response from caregivers.

The notion that learning lies at the base of retarded and nonretarded behavior stimulated habilitation based on applied behavior analysis (ABA), prompted services to promote client growth through learning, and encouraged training parents and staff to teach adults with ID effectively. Observations that some clients moved from institutions to community group homes *failed* to learn new adaptive behaviors or even *lost* skills in the absence of structured approaches to promote learning (Fleming & Stenfert Kroese, 1990) highlighted the need for services to take positive action to ensure that adults with ID learn important and meaningful skills.

LIFE EVENTS

Much less attention has been given to life events in people with ID than to other clinical groups, perhaps because the etiology of ID is unrelated to life events. However, several studies have reported correlations between life events and a variety of mental health and behavioral problems in adults with ID (Owen et al., 2004) and Pervasive Development Disorder (Ghazzhuiddin, Alessi, & Greden, 1995). Life events for people with ID may be somewhat different than for other people in that they report problems with relationships with staff, changes in residence, bereavement, illness, and injury.

GENETIC INFLUENCES

Nonorganic Forms of Intellectual Disability   Genetic influences on mild ID is controversial. This is because of the association with repugnant aspects of eugenics and related social policies, racial politics, faking of research data (Kamin, 1974), controversial viewpoints on the heritability of IQ (Herrnstein & Murray, 1994), and debate over the efficacy and funding of early intervention for children at risk for ID. Most people agree that first-degree relatives of people with mild ID are at greater risk of mild ID. However, the cause is unclear. Some attribute the pattern to the high heritability of intelligence, others to the effects of shared common environmental deprivation. Recently, Spinath, Harlaar, Ronald, and Plomin (2004) reported a large-scale empirical twin study of the heritability of mild ID. They observed the concordance of mild ID, defined as scoring in the lowest 5% on a composite measure of verbal and nonverbal tests in children ages 2, 3, and 4 years, in 73 monozygotic, 53 same-sex dizygotic, and 55 opposite-sex dizygotic twins. Spinath et al. selected these twins from a large sample of 4,758 twins in a British cohort born between 1994 and 1995. They used the prob and wise concordance as a measure of the risk that a cotwin would be affected if the other twin was affected. Concordance rates were 74%, 45%, and 36% for monozygotic, same-sex dizygotic, and opposite-sex dizygotic twins, respectively. That is, if one monozygotic twin had mild ID, there was a 74% chance that the cotwin also had mild ID. When compared to heritability of intelligence in the entire sample of twins, Spinath et al. found that the heritability of mild ID was *higher* that in the rest of the sample. They concluded that there was a greater genetic influence on heritability of mild cognitive impairment than intelligence generally and that there might be specific genetic influences on the heritability of mild ID that were not present in the general population. They estimated that the group heritability was approximately .49 (confidence interval = .29 to .69). Although this estimated heritability is quite high, approximately 50% of the variability in mild ID was due to environmental variation and error variance. Heritability is a characteristic of a specific population located at a particular place and time, not a characteristic of an individual. Heritability may also vary as the environment varies from time to time and place to place. Hence, we cannot confidently generalize these observed values of heritability to other populations.

Organic Forms of Intellectual Disability   Organic forms of ID may arise from a wide range of biological causes, including genetic causes. There are many genetic forms of ID, including chromosomal abnormalities and single recessive and dominant genes. A few chromosomal causes, such as Down and Fragile-X syndromes, are relatively common; each has a prevalence of approximately 0.1%. By contrast, there are hundreds of very rare single gene causes. For example, tuberose sclerosis is caused by a single dominant gene associated with severe or profound ID, significant medical problems, and shortened life span. Its prevalence is approximately 1 in 25,000 (Devlin, Shepherd, Crawford, & Morrison, 2006.) Phenylketonuria (PKU) is another genetic form of ID, but it is caused by a recessive single gene. If untreated, it results in profound ID. The prevalence of PKU is approximately 1 in 14,000 live births (March of Dimes, 2006).

Some genetic causes are important, as genetic counseling and treatment specific to each disorder may be possible. For example, there is no syndrome-specific treatment for tuberose sclerosis. Genetic counseling is not possible, as it appears to arise as a spontaneous mutation. In contrast, PKU is completely preventable. If the condition is detected early and the child put on a restricted protein diet immediately for many years, ID will be prevented. There are often associations related to many specific syndromes that offer education and support to parents and may support research.

PHYSICAL FACTORS AFFECTING BEHAVIOR

Medical problems may be more difficult to detect in people with ID than in the general population. For example, some people with ID may not communicate discomfort or more subtle aspects of poor health; in other cases, people may disregard their complaints. Ensuring that people with ID receive high-quality, responsive medical, dental, and nursing services is often challenging.

Some physical problems interact with behavioral issues (O'Neill et al., 1997). Painful physical conditions might set the occasion to escape from situations associated with them. For example, a person with ID might experience discomfort after prolonged periods of sitting or because a chair is too low, resulting in discomfort associated with working at a surface that is too high. If the person does not effectively communicate or is ignored, then other people might inadvertently shape maladaptive behavior.

Medication for General Medical Conditions   The health of people with mild ID is broadly comparable to people of average intelligence, although there is some reduction in life span compared to the general population. People with organic forms of ID associated with severe and profound ID may have significantly reduced life expectancy. Many people with mild ID, perhaps because of low income, lack of health insurance, lack of knowledge, and services being difficult to access, may have many preventable medical problems and lack preventive medical services. Thus, they are at risk for illnesses related to obesity, lack of exercise, poor diet, and seizure disorders (Surgeon General, 2002), which may also impact behavior management. Some medications for physical conditions, such as refractory seizure disorders and untreated hypothyroidism, may further impair cognitive functioning and also impact behavior problems. Treatment teams must balance the risks and benefits of managing health problems that come with risks of additional cognitive and behavioral impairment.

Psychotropic Medications   Psychotropic medications are used very commonly with adults with ID. Medication to manage seizure disorders also has psychotropic effects. Perhaps a third to a half of all adults with ID receive psychotropic medications (Singh, Ellis, & Wechsler, 1997). Lott et al. (2004) analyzed the pattern of prescriptions in a sample of 2,344 individuals with ID living in community settings between 1998 and 2000, of whom 82% lived in their own home or in a group home; 57% of males and 43% of females received prescriptions for psychotropic medications and/or seizure medications. The most commonly prescribed classes of medications were anticonvulsants, mood stabilizers, and lithium (34% of prescriptions), antipsychotics (32%), antidepressants (17%), and anxiolytic medications (12%.) Sixty percent of persons received polypharmacy; 14% received five or more psychotropic medications. During the study period, large changes in prescription practices were observed: There were fewer prescriptions for old antipsychotic medications, such as haloperidol and thioridazine; and there were more prescriptions for atypical antipsychotic medications, such as olanzapine and risperidone, and for other medications, such as valproic acid and clonazepam.

Much of the use of psychotropic medication is problematic. Common practices include off-label prescriptions (Haw & Stubbs, 2005), polypharmacy (Hurley, Folstein, & Lam, 2003), and use for treatment of behavior disorders, such as self-injury, aggression, tantrums, and property destruction (Aman, Sarphare, & Burrow, 1995) without psychiatric diagnoses (Clarke, Kelley, Thinn, & Corbett, 1990) and poor or absent monitoring of side effects. Recent comprehensive reviews have revealed that the majority of published studies on psychotropic medications had many basic flaws (Matson et al., 2000; Matson, Bielecki, Mayville, & Matson, 2003.) It may be that much psychotropic medication is prescribed in the absence of good program design, simple preventive behavioral practices, and treatment plans. What was once seen as an institutional blight is now common practice in community services, where monitoring and oversight of dispersed, multiagency services is difficult. Integrating the use of psychotropic medication with accurate psychiatric diagnoses and behavioral interventions remains a significant challenge.

Cultural and Diversity Issues

Cultural issues impinge on the definition and conceptualization of disability as well as the availability and nature of supports for people with ID and their families. The adaptive behavior component of the definition of ID includes references to "the person's effectiveness in meeting the standard expected *for his or her age by his or her cultural group*" (American Psychiatric Association, 2000, p. 46, italics added). As noted earlier, expectations of adaptive behavior vary widely within and between cultures and within a culture over time. Thus, whether a person with a given behavioral repertoire will be identified as a person with ID will vary according to these local expectations. For example, a 2-year-old who is incontinent may be developmentally delayed in one culture and developmentally typical in another. A 2-year-old who is incontinent might have been seen as developmentally delayed in the 1950s and today might be seen as typically developing.

Tests are often normed within a narrow range of cultures. We cannot assume that a test that is reliable and valid in one culture will also be reliable and valid in another culture. Several studies have shown that the adoption of test norms from one culture to another is inappropriate (Gannotti & Handwerker, 2002; Naglieri & Rojahn, 2001), including assessments of adaptive behavior (Reschley & Ward, 1991.) This may lead to over- or under diagnosis of minority persons with ID.

Family Adjustment   Most adults with ID live with their family, and most families adjust well to having a member with ID. Adaptation in the early years is probably most challenging. When their family members are adults, the majority of families have established and effective ways of coping. Indeed, many report benefits of having a person with ID in their family, such as learning tolerance, patience, and pride in their family member's achievements. Family adaptation may be enhanced by problem-focused coping, having multiple roles, social support, and religious beliefs. These patterns of adaptation may differ among cultures and may vary with acculturation (Magana, Schwartz, Rubert, & Szapocznik, 2006). Some families of people with ID do continue to experience periods of distress and may experience health and other problems related to the burden of long-term care and declining physical capacity as they age.

There is extensive research on the cultural beliefs about the nature of disability in general and developmental disability in particular, including work on the nature and extent of family and social support networks and religious and other cultural beliefs. For example, in some cultures members may believe that ID is a biomedical problem that should be aggressively treated and that family members in particular should engage in sustained efforts to address their child's disability. Other cultures may view ID as God's punishment for the sins of the parents and that the appropriate action of family members is to bear their punishment, because to fight it would be to sin further. Practitioners should become familiar with these cultural differences in order to understand the family's frame of reference and understanding of ID.

Cultural and ethnic identity may also be related to adaptation in adults with ID. Frison, Wallander, and Browne (1998) studied social adaptation in African American students with ID. They found that ethnic identification and intergenerational church support buffered against maladjustment. Cultural issues may also impinge on health. For example, although the survival of infants with Down syndrome has increased from less than 50% in 1942–1952 to 91% in 1980–1996, large disparities in mortality existed between ethnic groups in the United States. The Centers for Disease Control reported that in 1997 the median life span of White Americans with Down syndrome was 50 years, whereas for African Americans and others with Down syndrome it was only 25 and 11 years, respectively (Friedman, 2001). In an editorial, the CDC noted that the data may be inaccurate, as death certificates may be incomplete. These data do raise the possibility that differences in care, perhaps especially cardiac care, might be responsible for these large disparities in mortality between ethnic groups in the United States. Researchers have yet to conduct studies confirming these explanations.

BEHAVIORAL TREATMENT

TEACHING SKILLS

Teaching skills to enhance the competence of adults with ID is a basic strategy to foster adaptation to community living, well-paid, enjoyable work, and independent living. Many social and problem-solving skills also buffer against mental health and behavioral disorders. Early models of community services placed considerable emphasis on staff training and organizational support as essential components of community services, especially for adults with more severe behavioral challenges (Felce, de Kock, Mansell, & Jenkins, 1984). These early models of community services were highly structured. They involved clear definitions of staff roles and behavior and staff training and support. Unfortunately, community services largely did not adopt these empirically supported models. Instead, they adopted ideologically palatable but unevaluated models. In the United States a free market of private providers developed with varying degrees of oversight. Thus, currently, there are wide variations in whether community services teach their clients skills or structure their services to foster independence and personal growth (Perry & Felce, 2005). Staff training, support, and consultation may address this need to varying degrees (Jones et al., 2001).

Bijou's (1996) functional analytic model of the behavior of people with ID has been very influential in developing behavioral interventions to enhance the skills and lifestyle of adults with ID. Behavioral interventions should conform to Baer, Wolf, and Risley's (1968) six dimensions of ABA. They should be (a) applied, that is, address behavior that society deems to be significant; (b) behavioral, that is, pragmatic and measuring the behavior directly through reliable, quantifiable observation, rather than simply accepting self-report of behavior; (c) analytical; that is, there should be a believable demonstration that the intervention caused the change, typically by the use of small n experimental designs that show a reliable relationship between the independent and dependent variables; (d) technological; that is, intervention should be operationalized so that another person can replicate the intervention; (e) conceptually systematic by relating the intervention to the behavioral concepts, such as reinforcement and stimulus control; and (f) effective, by producing changes so large that the client and society recognize them as being important. Applied behavior analysis interventions must program for generality of behavior change across time and settings (Stokes & Baer, 1977). Finally, ABA interventions must have goals, use procedures, and produce effects that society recognizes as important and valued (Wolf, 1978).

Reinforcer Assessment Applied behavior analysis uses reinforcement to increase operant behavior. A reinforcer is a stimulus that, when presented contingent upon a behavior, results in the increase in the future probability of that behavior. If the stimulus is presented, it is referred to as a positive reinforcer. If the stimulus is removed, it is referred to as a negative reinforcer. Reinforcers may be unconditioned, such as food or warmth. Others are acquired through stimulus pairings, such as tokens and money. It is best that therapists assess reinforcers directly through presenting stimulus arrays and observing approach and avoidance responses, rather than using third-party reports alone, which are often inaccurate (Green et al., 1988).

Reid, Parsons, and Green (1998) conducted stimulus preference assessments of work task with three adults with ID ages 30, 49, and 73 who also had severe physical disabilities. The study took place at a company that published books and advertising materials. Work tasks included stamping addresses and applying labels. To enhance the validity of the assessment the company's actual materials were used, staff who would be in the workplace participated, and the participants sampled the work task for several minutes prior to assessment. Two sets of materials were placed in front of each client. If the client pointed or touched the materials, that was a choice. The authors presented all possible combinations of pairs of tasks. During assessments all three participants made reliable choices between work tasks, and the preferred tasks identified in the prework assessment were also chosen on the job. The authors suggested that assessment of client preferences for work tasks would enhance the clients' experience of work and give the clients a realistic experience of the jobs they were to do.

Differential Reinforcement   Therapists use reinforcers in procedures such as differential reinforcement of behavior, where members of one response class are reinforced and other responses are not. Initially, little behavior change may occur during differential reinforcement, as there may be few opportunities to reinforce. However, after time, the response rate will slowly increase and there will be a new higher rate of responding. When a response class is reinforced, there is a broad change in behavior. Not only does the operant increase, but behavior becomes more orderly and predictable and other, nonreinforced behavior decreases. Thus, reinforcement has many potentially desirable effects on behavior.

Thompson, Iwata, Hanley, Dozier, and Samaha (2003) evaluated the effects of fixed ratio-1 (FR-1), extinction (EXT), and differential reinforcement of other behavior (DRO) on appropriate and maladaptive behavior in nine adults with mild through profound ID who worked in a workshop program. Target responses included adaptive behaviors, such as communicative or vocational behaviors. The authors also recorded negative vocalization and problem behaviors, such as head hitting. Reinforcers were identified using stimulus preference assessments. All nine participants emitted more appropriate responses during the FR-1 condition than the EXT and DRO conditions. Generally, participants emitted more responses during the DRO than EXT condition.

Reinforcer Deprivation and Satiation   The time since last reinforcement also influences operant behavior. For example, reinforcer deprivation results in a subsequent increase in operant behavior, whereas reinforcer satiation results in a subsequent decrease in the behavior. Deprivation and satiation can both be used as intervention methods. For example, it may be advisable to ensure that clients have little or no access to the reinforcer prior to a teaching session. Primary reinforcers are very susceptible to satiation. Thus, use of the primary reinforcers is undesirable if alternative reinforcers are available. Although using multiple primary reinforcers may be helpful, establishing secondary reinforcers as soon as possible is preferred because secondary reinforcers are less susceptible to satiation. They can be exchanged for primary re-inforcers later, when the client can select reinforcers that are most powerful at that particular point in time.

Klatt, Sherman, and Sheldon (2000) investigated the effects of reinforcer deprivation on engagement in leisure activities in three men with severe or profound ID. The study took place in the men's apartments during free time. Klatt et al. first conducted stimulus preference assessments of leisure items and then observed the proportion of time clients engaged with leisure materials following 1 to 4 days, 2 hours, or 15 minutes of deprivation of the leisure materials. For highly preferred leisure materials, client engagement in leisure activity was higher during the 1 to 4 day and 2 hour deprivation conditions and lowest during the 15 minute deprivation. For less preferred materials, deprivation had no effect on engagement, as less preferred materials were always associated with little engagement. Klatt et al. replicated these results when regular staff implemented these procedures. This study supports the use of reinforcer deprivation to enhance reinforcer effectiveness. It also shows the effects of reinforcer satiation on reducing adaptive behavior.

Some studies have used reinforcer satiation as an effective treatment for maladap-tive behavior, which is useful when extinction would be undesirable, impractical, or dangerous. For example, Hagopian, LeBlanc, and Maglieri (2000) treated excessive medical complaining in a young man with ID who was medically fragile. Prior to intervention they identified that attention was the likely reinforcer maintaining com-plaining. Thus, to reduce attention as a powerful reinforcer, the intervention involved delivering high rates on noncontingent attention. This led to large reductions in ex-cessive complaints, without the undesirable side effects of extinction. Thus, attention satiation was both effective and acceptable in reducing the maladaptive behavior.

Stimulus Control and Transfer of Stimulus Control of Operant Behavior　If a stimulus is reliably present during the availability of reinforcement and is reliably absent during the nonavailability of reinforcement, then that antecedent stimulus can also affect behavior. When such an antecedent stimulus does affect behavior, that behavior is said to be under stimulus control. The stimulus that is associated with the availability of reinforcement is called the S-D and the stimulus associated with the nonavailability of reinforcement is called the S-delta. Interventions using stimu-lus control procedures are very desirable because they may affect behavior quickly, whereas reinforcement procedures typically affect behavior gradually.

Transfer of stimulus control occurs when stimulus control is shifted from one set of stimuli to another. This occurs commonly in prompting procedures. Here an effective but inappropriate antecedent is inserted into the teaching situation to elicit the be-havior of interest. For example, hand-over-hand prompting might be used to prompt a person to spoon-feed. However, because abrupt withdrawal of this prompt will re-sult in the behavior of interest not occurring, the prompt is faded gradually until the naturally occurring antecedents come to control the response of interest. For example, the trainer might gradually move the prompt up the client's arm to the shoulder and then fade out the distance between trainer and client until the presence of the spoon and food alone elicit spoon-feeding. When the spoon and associated stimuli result in feeding, then transfer of stimulus control from the artificial prompt to more desirable discriminative stimuli has occurred.

An example of stimulus control intervention procedures comes from Wacker and Berg (1983), who taught five students, ages 18 and 19 years, with moderate or severe

ID to assemble complex 30- to 40-step vocational tasks using pictures as antecedents. In baseline the authors presented a model of the completed task and instructed the participants to complete the task. During training the authors used transfer of stimulus control to the pictures by teaching correct use of picture prompts in three steps. In step 1 the participants learned to turn the pages of a book containing the pictures. In step 2 participants selected the piece depicted in the picture and placed it on the table but did not assemble the piece. In step 3 the students selected and assembled the piece depicted in the picture. The trainers taught each step using modeling, verbal correction following errors, and intermittent contingent praise. This was effective in teaching these tasks to the clients. Further, the clients also used other picture prompts to learn novel vocational tasks that were not trained.

Parsons, Reid, Green, and Browning (2001) used transfer of stimulus control procedures by training job coaches to fade assistance systematically, thereby increasing independent job performance of workers with ID in community settings. They trained both off-site and in the workplace. Training staff to fade prompts accurately in the nonwork setting resulted in correct implementation of fading in the work settings and increased client independence at work.

Generalization　Generalization occurs when the effects of reinforcement spread to nonreinforced stimuli or responses. For example, generalization occurs when teaching a client to greet one staff person by saying "Hello" is subsequently followed by saying "Hello" to other staff members and peers, and when the client also says "Hi," even though reinforcement has not occurred in these situations or for these responses. Generalization must be carefully planned. For example, one might identify all the people and situations a client might greet and all the different ways a client might greet someone. The therapist then designs the intervention using a sample of these stimulus combinations and should probe for generalization when no training has occurred. A therapist can enhance generalization by reinforcing all examples of generalized responding, training with many examples, people, and settings, and varying the training stimuli and situations in minor irrelevant ways (Stokes & Baer, 1977).

Neef, Lensbower, Hockersmith, DePalma, and Gray (1990) evaluated different methods of promoting generalized use of washing and dryer machines in four adults ages 31 to 64 with mild through severe ID. Training occurred in a day habilitation center adjacent to the clients' laundry. Generalization probes took place in the clients' residences. Neef et al. compared single case training and general case training. In single case training, intervention took place with only one washing machine and one drying machine. General case training took place with two additional machines, carefully chosen to sample all stimulus and response variations in the task. For example, in general case training participants had to pull, press, and lift a lever to open the lid and to set the temperature; they received training on panels in several different locations on the machines. Although single case training improved participant performance compared to baseline, client performance remained poor. Only during general case training did generalization occur to all the untrained machines. Careful analysis of the kind of generalization expected to occur prior to training and careful selection of training stimuli resulted in generalization to untrained stimuli.

Discrimination　Discrimination is when a response occurs in the presence of some but not other stimuli. This occurs after responses are reinforced in the presence of one set of stimuli and are not reinforced in the absence of those stimuli. For example, in language interventions a therapist may reinforce saying "green" in the presence of green objects, but not in the presence of blue objects. Subsequently, the person says "green" only in the presence of green, but not blue, objects. Thus, as time proceeds and further discrimination training takes place, a person may learn other discriminations, such as bright-dark, saturated-unsaturated, and hunter green–apple green. Discrimination lies at the basis of language and concept formation.

Sievert, Cuvo, and Davis (1988) presented an interesting application of discrimination training as part of a package to teach eight adults with mild ID and related disabilities self-advocacy skills. One component of the training was to teach the participants to discriminate between descriptions of rights violations and nonviolations. In a group training procedure, the instructor first stated the right and conditions necessary for that right. For example, one has the right to marry and must obtain a license to do so. During discrimination training, the presenter described scenarios some of which involved a rights violations and others that did not. If the participants correctly identified the scenario, the instructor praised their correct responses. If the participants did not make a correct response, the instructor prompted correct responses using a prompt hierarchy. During baseline, participants correctly discriminated only 51% of rights scenarios (range 43% to 78%), and after training participants discriminated correctly on 98% of rights scenarios (range 93% to 100%).

Extinction   If the reinforcer maintaining the behavior is known and the contingency between that response and the reinforcer is disrupted, either by withholding the reinforcer or by presenting it noncontingently, then the behavior will reduce in frequency. Extinction has other effects on behavior, including a general breakdown in the predictability of behavior, increases in other responses, and increases in novel behavior. Extinction may also be accompanied by a temporary increase in the behavior of interest and negative emotional side effects, such as crying. Therapists sometimes reduce undesirable operant behavior using extinction. In practice, extinction is usually combined with differential reinforcement, as this combination of procedures results in faster reduction of the target behavior than extinction alone. A therapist can also teach other useful responses using the differential reinforcement component of the treatment package.

An example of the use of extinction and DRO comes from Rehfeldt and Chambers (2003). The participant was a 23-year-old man with mild ID and autism taking several psychotropic medications. Inappropriate verbal behavior consisted of perseverative topic, such as sirens, alarms, and the dentist, and excessive coughing. Prior to intervention, the researchers conducted a functional analysis in which they exposed the client to conditions that mimicked possible environmental contingencies. Thus, in the attention condition, each time the client emitted an inappropriate verbal behavior another person made a comment. In the demand condition he was taught a vocational task that he typically performed. Each time he emitted an inappropriate verbal behavior he was given a 30-second break contingent upon that behavior. In the alone condition, which is used as an assessment of automatic reinforcement ("self-stimulation"), he remained in his room with no interaction. During the tangible condition he was provided with access to items he liked, such as writing about sirens, contingent on appropriate verbal behavior. During this initial functional assessment the client emitted most inappropriate verbal responses during the attention condition, leading the authors to conclude that his inappropriate verbal behavior was maintained by attention. Therefore, treatment consisted of attention extinction and differential reinforcement of alternative (DRA) behavior. That is, each time he made an inappropriate verbal response the experimenter did not make eye contact or any comment. When he made appropriate verbal remarks, the experimenter gave him 5 seconds of attention and eye contact. This intervention resulted in significant reduction in inappropriate verbal behavior, but also led to a dramatic increase in appropriate verbal behavior.

Shaping Shaping is a procedure that combines extinction and differential reinforcement to gradually change some feature of behavior, such as topography, latency, or duration. In shaping, the therapist identifies the final target behavior and some current approximation to the final target behavior. After the therapist takes baseline data, he or she identifies variations in the currently reinforced responses that approximate more closely to the target response. Those responses alone are differentially reinforced. Other, previously reinforced responses are extinguished. Shaping produces a slow and gradual change in the person's behavior and requires considerable skill and patience on the part of the behavior change agent.

As part of a smoking cessation intervention, Rea and Williams (2002) taught four men ages 22 to 43 with mild ID to blow into a CO detector. Because breathing could not be observed, a piece of Christmas tinsel was attached to the end of the monitor so that the researchers could reliably observe air movement. The experimenters recorded the number of seconds each breath lasted. During baseline the experimenters instructed the participant to hold his breath and cover his nose for as long as possible and then exhale as long as possible. They held daily shaping sessions which consisted of one or two 3-trial sessions. The initial target value was set within the baseline durations. Once the participant met or exceeded that criterion on all three trials, the experimenters increased the criterion by 1 second. After the participant exhaled for 15 seconds, the experimenter also shaped a "hold breath" procedure for 15 seconds. The shaping procedure was effective and subsequently CO levels could be taken as part of a smoking reduction intervention.

Chaining Chaining occurs when an organism emits complex series of different responses in a certain sequence. Many adaptive behaviors, such as cleaning an apartment or preparing a snack, are response chains. In a response chain each previous response and/or its products function as the conditioned reinforcer for the preceding response and as the discriminative stimuli for the next response. Hence, teaching a response chain involves bring responses under the stimulus control of previous responses and involves discrimination training. This can be done by any of three methods. In all three methods the therapist first task-analyzes the response chain, for example, by observing a person performing the task correctly. In backward chaining the therapist teaches the last response first, and then the last two steps, and so on. In forward chaining the therapist teaches the first step, then the first and second steps, and so on. In the whole-task method the entire chain is taught with full prompting, and prompting is gradually faded out over time.

A study by Luyben, Funk, Morgan, Clark, and Delulio (1986) illustrates use of response chains to teach age-appropriate leisure skills. They taught three men ages 24 to 52 with IQs of 22 to 52 to pass a soccer ball using a 9-step task analysis. There were 20-minute training sessions. During these sessions the experimenter modeled the step, gave instructions and used imitative and physical prompts and reinforcement using forward training. Participants progressed from one step to the next only after they met criterion for the current step. During baseline the three participants performed no correct passes, and after intervention they performed 91% to 99% of steps correctly. Thus, chaining was an effective procedure to teach passing a soccer ball.

Punishment   When a stimulus reliably follows a response and the future probability of that response decreases, then that stimulus is said to be a punisher. Positive punishers involve the presentation of a stimulus, such as saying "Excuse me," and negative punishers involve the removal of a stimulus after a behavior, such as a loss of tokens. Stimuli to be used as punishers should be empirically determined by observation of client behavior rather than assumed on the basis of third-party reports.

Punishment remains a controversial topic. Explicit acknowledgment of the use of punishment is unacceptable to many practitioners. However, punishment is an integral part of all of our lives; many of our behaviors reduce in frequency after we stub our toe or another person scowls at us. People do not consider these forms of punishment to be problematic. Rather, many people consider the explicit programmatic use of aversive consequences in the absence of other procedures to be controversial.

One example of punishment in a skills training intervention comes from Azrin, Sneed, and Foxx's (1973) dry bed training procedure. Dry bed training is a multi-component package that includes requiring the person to clean up the mess, wash sheets, and repeatedly practice going to the bathroom at night contingent upon a toileting accident. This package is highly effective, but many people have debated the importance and acceptability of this component of the package.

Stimulus Equivalence   Earlier, we saw that discrimination training was a primitive kind of conceptual behavior. The concept of stimulus equivalence builds on this to describe more elaborate forms of conceptual behavior. In stimulus equivalence training, the instructor presents a sample stimulus, such as a word, and then presents an array of comparison stimuli, such as pictures, line drawings, and other words. The person then responds, for example, by pointing to one of the comparison stimuli to indicate which of the comparison stimuli match the sample. Often this training procedure is done on computers to facilitate teaching and data collection. Once participants learns one set of stimulus-stimulus relationships, they can then learn other, new relationships. When this is done many untrained relationships emerge. For example, suppose a client is taught that "one dollar" and "$1" and "100 ¢" are equivalent. If the client then learns that "a buck" is the same as "one dollar," then the client will also learn many other untaught relationships (Miller, Cuvo, & Borakove, 1977).

Self-Control   Applied behavior analysis addresses self-control as an example of response-response relationships. Self-control consists of a controlling response that influences the probability of a controlled response. For example, removing a distracting stimulus (the controlling response) might make engaging in work (the controlled response) more likely. Analysis and intervention focuses on (a) identifying the controlling responses, such as self-recording, setting targets, accurate self-reinforcement; and (b) the variables that influence the controlling response, such as the antecedents and contingencies maintaining the controlling responses.

Watanabe and Sturmey (2003) taught three men with autism ages 22 to 40 years in a community day program to select the order of their activities. In one condition the staff selected the order of the activities for the clients, and in the other condition, the clients wrote down the order of the activities. When the clients selected their own order of activities they engaged in appropriate behavior longer than when the staff chose the order of the activities. In this example, the controlling behavior (writing a schedule) increased the controlled behavior (client engagement).

Rule-Governed Behavior A final important distinction is that between contingency and rule-governed behavior. Rule-governed behavior is behavior in verbally competent people who can state rules about contingencies. This can occur either by instructions from other people or can be generated by oneself. Contingency shapes behavior changes gradually and is responsive to consequences, whereas rule-governed behavior is relatively insensitive to contingencies.

Taylor and O'Reilly (1997) taught four adults with mild and moderate ID to use self-stated rules to shop in community settings. The authors first developed a 21-step task analysis of shopping in a grocery store. They then taught the participants to self-instruct and self-reinforce aloud by stating the steps of the task analysis, following those steps, and praising their own correct responses. Training took place in a classroom setting and a grocery store. The authors then taught the participants to fade these overt self-instructions by stating them progressively more softly. They then instructed the participants to state the instructions to themselves. Taylor and O'Reilly showed that the participants learned to self-instruct and grocery shop independently. They then blocked self-instruction by requiring the participant to count random numbers aloud. When participants did this, they no longer shopped independently. This study showed that participants learned to self-instruct and also supported the notion that it was the privately stated self-instructions that controlled shopping behavior.

Training Others All ABA interventions depend on people to implement them. Hence, interest in staff, family, and indeed peer training and motivation is a central issue (Reid & Parsons, 1995). Typical training procedures, such as verbal or written instruction, are often ineffective. Unfortunately, services commonly use written instruction to train staff as it is quick and easy to document. Hence, much staff training does not result in changes in staff behavior or delivery of services or desired changes in client behavior. Behavioral skills training consists of brief instructions and a rationale for treatment, modeling, rehearsal, and feedback and is highly effective and efficient in teaching staff skills (Brienes & Sturmey, in press; Sarokoff & Sturmey, 2004). Effective training also should include procedures to ensure appropriate generalization of staff behavior, such as multiple exemplars and general case training as a component of staff training (Ducharme & Feldman, 1992).

An interesting application of behavioral skills training comes from Likins, Salzberg, Stowitscheck, Lignugaris/Kraft, and Curl (1989), who taught a person with ID to coach a coworker with ID. They evaluated two procedures to teach three women with mild ID to prepare chef salads in a supported work site at a university canteen. The authors developed a 19-step task analysis. They used the number of steps performed independently as the dependent variable. During baseline the work coach told the participants to make a chef salad like the one they had just made. In the first intervention the job coach modeled one step. Once the participant mastered a step, they added an additional step. In the Quality Control condition the authors trained a coworker with ID to (a) accurately model making a salad; (b) discriminate peer errors, such as food touching the table; (c) model the checking procedure; and (d) provide accurate feedback to their peer. During baseline participants completed fewer than 20% of steps correctly. Modeling alone increased correct performance to only 60% of steps for one participant and only approximately 33% of steps for the other two participants. Following the

Quality Control procedure, participants completed approximately 90% of steps correctly. During baseline the supervisor judged that most of the salads made could not be sold to customers. After the Quality Control training, the supervisors considered that all of the salads that two of the participants made could be sold to customers, and that three of four that the third participant made could also be sold. Hence, teaching Quality Control procedures to peers using behavioral skills training resulted in highly functional work performance in adults with ID in community settings.

Typical Applications   Most applied skills teaching interventions do not use single procedures. Rather, they usually include multiple procedures to maximize the likelihood of behavior change. Thus, typical interventions with people with ID often include antecedents, consequences, staff or family training, and monitoring to ensure implementation and maximal change in client behavior.

CHALLENGING BEHAVIORS

Challenging behaviors, such as aggression, self-injury, and tantrums, are more common in adults with ID than in the general population. For example, Rojahn and Tasse (1996) reported data from statewide databases in New York and California: Aggression occurred in approximately 12% of both populations, and self-injury occurred in approximately 8% of both populations. Other challenging behaviors, such as running away, pica, and regurgitation, occur much less frequently. These challenging behaviors result in negative consequences for the clients, their families, their peers, and those who work with them. These negative consequences may include (a) potentially life-threatening medical interventions; (b) restraint; (c) limitations on personal freedoms and lifestyle; (d) client, peer, family member, and staff distress; (d) restrictive or aversive treatments; (e) multiple psychotropic medications; (f) family breakdown; and (g) institutionalization. In contemporary community services restrictive behavioral procedures are used quite commonly, even though they are also often ineffective (Feldman, Atkinson, Foti-Gervais, & Condillac, 2004; Robertson et al., 2005). Investigations into abuse in community services also periodically reveal problems related to poor behavioral interventions, as in Cornwall, United Kingdom (Healthcare Commission, 2006) and Washington, DC, United States (Boo, 1999).

Early behavioral studies indicated that challenging behaviors were amenable to contingency management procedures, such as extinction, time-out from positive reinforcement, and various differential reinforcement procedures. By the 1980s, researchers had developed and evaluated a wide array of behavioral treatment procedures. However, such approaches, although often successful, had significant limitations: (a) They were excessively technological and divorced from the conceptual basis of ABA (Baer et al., 1968); (b) they were perhaps not maximally effective; (c) they were not always individualized; (d) they sometimes relied on contingency management procedures excessively; and (e) they sometimes used more restrictive behavioral procedures than was necessary.

Carr (1977) published an influential review identifying the different contingencies, such as attention, escape from aversive stimuli, and automatic reinforcement, that might maintain self-injurious behavior. Subsequent naturalistic (Oliver et al., 2005) and experimental (Kahng, Iwata, & Lewis, 2002) studies confirmed that environmental variables that maintain challenging behaviors vary significantly from person to person. These variables accurately predict effective and ineffective treatments.

Researchers and practitioners have applied this model to a wide range of challenging behaviors, such as aggression and tantrums. Use of functional assessment and functional analysis has repeatedly been shown to result in more effective treatment (Didden, Duker, & Korzilius, 1997), including adults with mild ID (Didden, Korzilius, van Oorsouw, & Sturmey, 2006). Hence, current standards of practice require careful preassessment analysis of the functions of challenging behaviors (O'Neill et al., 1997) and individualized treatment plans that are based on that analysis.

Applied behavior analysis emphasizes experimental control through small *n* research designs (Baer et al., 1968). However, most practitioners use descriptive methods, such as brief psychometric instruments (Sturmey, 1994); staff interviews; observation in the natural environment, such as observations of approach and avoidance responses (Smith, Bihm, Tavkar, & Sturmey, 2005); and mini-experiments (DesRochers, Hile, & Williams-Mosely, 1997). These methods result in a hypothesis about the function of the target behavior, possible functionally equivalent behaviors to increase, and current environmental variables that can be modified and that may have a large impact to increase desirable replacement behavior and reduce the challenging behavior. (The case study in this chapter illustrates this approach.) The clinician uses the functional assessment and analysis to derive a hypothesis concerning the challenging behavior and to identify functionally equivalent replacement behavior, contingencies that maintain the target behavior that may be modified, establishing operations, such as periods of reinforcer deprivation that can be changed, and the form of extinction to be used.

Eliminating Restrictive Treatment   Restrictive procedures were formerly associated with institutions. However, there is now evidence that community services also commonly used these procedures with adults with ID, often in the absence of regulation and professional input. For example, Feldman et al. (2004) conducted interviews with service providers for 607 clients with ID and behavior problems; 92% lived in community settings, such as foster homes, group homes, and semi-independent living arrangements. Of clients who had dangerous behavior problems, 39% had formal intervention procedures with restrictive procedures, but an additional 20% had *informal* intervention programs with restrictive procedures. Of clients who had nondangerous behavior problems, 21% had formal and 20% had informal programs involving restrictive procedures. For the entire sample of people with intrusive interventions, the most commonly used procedures were psychotropic medication (65%), physical restraint (12%), confinement time-out (11%), mechanical restraint (6%), and seclusion (5%). Surprisingly, restrictive procedures were commonly used informally for both dangerous and nondangerous behavior. For example, 21 of 112 (19%) clients were physically restrained for dangerous behavior, and 10 of 116 clients (9%) were retrained for nondangerous behaviors. Informal programming also had a number of undesirable practices, such as lack of supervisory feedback to staff. Staff rated informal programs as less effective than formal programs. Use of restrictive procedures such as restraint is only weakly related to client challenging behavior (Sturmey, 1999; Sturmey, Lott, Laud, & Matson, 2005). This observation suggests that factors other than client behavior, such as staff training, supervision, policies, and regulation, may be more important determinants of the use of restrictive procedures. Restrictive behavioral practices can often be eliminated or greatly reduced by better regulation, staff training, and oversight. Usually, effective practices involve identifying at risk clients, monitoring the use of restrictive procedures and combinations of goal setting, and feedback to reduce restraint (Sturmey & McGlynn, 2003).

Cognitive-Behavior Therapy   There has been recent interest in the development of cognitive-behavior therapy for people with mild ID (Stenfert Kroese, Dagnan, & Loumidis, 1997). For example, Lindsay (Lindsay, Allan, MacLeod, Smart, & Smith, 2003) has published several case studies of sexual offenders with mild ID with very promising results, and J. L. Taylor and colleagues (J. L. Taylor, Novaco, Gillmer, Robertson, & Thorne, 2005) have published several randomized controlled trials of anger management that have included some people with mild ID. This approach seems promising. However, it is not clear what proportion of people with mild ID can successfully participate in cognitive-behavior therapy and whether cognitive strategies add anything beyond behavioral methods of intervention (Sturmey, 2004, 2006).

MEDICAL TREATMENT

There is no single medical treatment for ID, especially for adults. Where there is a specific biomedical etiology of ID there may be specific biomedical interventions to treat or prevent ID. For example, PKU is an inherited metabolic disorder. It results in an inability to digest protein effectively, and the subsequent undigested protein and its by-products cause brain damage. Placing the infant on a very low protein diet early in life can prevent ID and minimize more subtle cognitive disability (Baumeister & Woodley-Zanthos, 1996). There are many such interventions for specific forms of ID. However, they are applicable only to rare conditions and not the common nonorganic forms of ID. Although various dietary and mineral supplements have been proposed and marketed to boost intelligence, there is little evidence of efficacy from controlled studies (Singh, Ellis, Mattila, Mulick, & Poling, 1998).

Adults with ID do have significant preventable health problems, related to poor diet, inactivity, and lack of preventive health care. This results in preventable disability and medical problems There are now many interventions to address the physical health of adults with ID, including exercise programs, modifying diet, teaching self-regulation of lifestyle, and staff and parent training (Surgeon General, 2002). Implementation of these practices by services is variable.

Case Description

Case Introduction

This case description is typical of much behavioral work carried out in community settings with adults with ID and illustrates the use of functional behavioral assessment. The author's comments are presented in italics to illustrate the development of clinical hypotheses as assessment proceeded. This behavioral, hypothesis-driven approach to case formulation (Sturmey, 1996, 2007a, 2007b) reflects the earlier work of contributors such as Wolpe and Turkat (1985).

The author worked for a community, for-profit company that operated approximately six group homes for adults with ID. Initially, the two owners contacted the author because of a client with severe self-injury that had resulted in the client's receiving sutures to his head approximately once per month for the preceding year. They wished to add a helmet to prevent self-injury and needed a consult

(continued)

from someone to document that this was appropriate. The author conducted a functional assessment that identified his self-injury was probably reinforced by access to food and leisure items and that he had weak communication skills that staff were insensitive to. This self-injury was treated by teaching him to communicate for food and leisure items and by teaching staff to prompt and respond early to his requests. His self-injury and emergency room visits decreased without need for a restraint. Subsequently the owners asked the author to work with a variety of clients, including the two women in this case study.

In the author's experience, this pattern of referral is quite common. The service in question was unable to manage a severe problem. They did not have the basic technical expertise to know to conduct a functional assessment. Absent such skills, they initially pursued restrictive procedures, such as restraint without other positive strategies. Often the referral of one major problem opens the door to many other, less significant, but still serious problems that are not being dealt with effectively.

Presenting Complaints

The company owners referred two women with mild ID who shared a room in the group home. When the women returned from work they would go into their room, and about once a week major fights would begin.

The presence of poor social behavior between the two women immediately suggested that a replacement behavior should be some form of cooperative and mutually reinforcing social behavior. The temptation in such situations is to remove the provocative stimuli to prevent the problem from occurring, that is, separate the two women into different bedrooms. This solution merely prevents the problem from happening. However, it does not treat the problem, and it disrupts everyone else's lives unnecessarily.

It is also noteworthy that the problem is highly situation-specific. Namely, the aggression takes place only (a) between these two women and not with other residents, (b) only in their bedroom and not elsewhere, and (c) only after work and not at other times. This is a classic example of the situation-specific nature of behavior generally, as well as behavior problems specifically. Part of the assessment should include analysis of what forms of adaptive social behavior these women have with other people and in other situations, so that these other behaviors can be encouraged in these problem situations. The situation-specific nature of the problem suggests that this is not a skills deficit problem, but rather a problem relating to environmental design. One might ask what it is about these situations that fails to support relevant adaptive behavior, and what it is about the other situations that does support relevant adaptive behavior.

History

The referral agents mentioned that this problem had gradually gotten worse over time, but no specific cause could be identified.

History is often incomplete and garbled. In any case, history often has few implications for treatment. In this case, one cannot be sure if the residents' behavior got worse or if staff became less tolerant. If it was the former, a gradual increase is suggestive of shaping of progressively more severe forms of aggression and/or extinction of socially appropriate behavior. Part of the assessment should include an evaluation of whether staff prompt and reinforce socially appropriate behavior to compete with aggression.

Assessment

A brief phone interview with the case manager and shift supervisor broadly confirmed these details. They also noted that Miss Madison, the resident who bit Miss Hammond, often arrived at the group home in a state of agitation and was a whirlwind of frenetic activity that annoyed everyone.

Staff cannot observe aggressive behavior as it occurs behind closed doors. However, the client-to-client injuries can serve as a reliable measure of the most intense and most clinically significant forms of aggressive behavior. The clinician will have to live without a comprehensive data collection system that measures other, less intense forms of aggressive behavior.

The reports that Miss Madison arrives at home in a state of agitation is suggestive of a response chain. Perhaps increases in motor activity reliably precede mild forms of aggressive behavior and finally result in biting Miss Hammond. Presumably this is followed by some consequence. It might be the removal of Miss Hammond for treatment, permitting Miss Madison to return to her frenetic activity, or staff attention in the form of reprimands to Miss Madison. The fact that staff described Miss Madison's behavior as annoying might also suggest that she is aversive to other people. Perhaps intervention should address this in some way.

Note that, even though the clinician has not yet observed the clients, the case formulation is already developed and has strong implications to guide assessment and treatment. Perhaps Miss Madison's aggression is the terminal behavior in a response chain that is reinforced by removal of others, including her roommate, and access to preferred motor activity. Thus, assessment should focus on observation in the home when they return from work. A treatment plan might include differential reinforcement of behavior incompatible with agitation upon arrival at home, teaching socially appropriate behavior to the two women, making Miss Madison more reinforcing to others in some way, and contingency management of aggression.

The author conducted informal observations of the clients on several occasions in the group home that confirmed much of what had been reported. The two women avoided each other much of the time. Periodically, they told each other to go away and gave each other mean looks. It appeared that each functioned as an aversive stimulus for the other. To test this hypothesis the author conducted a series of mini-experiments. I asked the women to interact with each other, shake hands, wave to each other, or say "Hi" to each other. They vigorously refused, often turned away from one another, and finally confirmed this hypothesis by referring to one another as "a stinky bitch."

These observations suggest that Miss Madison's biting Miss Hammond might result from Miss Hammond's close physical proximity and that biting was negatively reinforced by subsequent removal of Miss Hammond.

These observations confirmed a wide range of aggressive social behavior only between the two roommates and not other residents or staff. The strongly aversive nature of the women for each other may have resulted from the repeated pairings of one another with aversive stimuli such as biting and arguing. An important implication of this is that the intervention must also change the women from aversive to appetitive stimuli.

(continued)

Case Conceptualization

A functional assessment is a concise statement that distills the essential elements of the case formulation and their implications for treatment (Sturmey, 1996, 2007a, 2007b). Functional approaches to case formulation identify only the variables from the current environment that have a large effect on the behavior of interest and can be modified (Haynes & O'Brien, 1990). Therefore, the case conceptualization can be stated as follows:

Miss Madison's behavior consists of a response chain in which she gets off the bus, engages in excessive motor activity, and engages in progressively more intense forms of verbal aggression, which are negatively reinforced by the temporary removal of Miss Hammond. Finally, they come into close proximity with each other, Miss Madison bites Miss Hammond and Miss Hammond is removed for prolonged periods of time. Therefore, treatment should involve the following elements:

(a) Intervention must occur early in the response chain to promote incompatible behavior. In this case, the moment Miss Madison comes off the bus she will be asked to engage in 5 minutes of muscle relaxation and slow breathing on her bed. If she becomes excited again, she should repeat the exercises until calm. Staff should teach relaxation to Miss Madison using instruction, modeling, and verbal praise for relaxation.

(b) Miss Madison and Miss Hammond will engage in prosocial behavior every evening. The two women both identified preferred leisure activities as jigsaw puzzles, and Miss Hammond also identified making a drink for other people as a preferred activity. Therefore, the two women should engage in leisure activities across the table from one another. Initially they did so at opposite ends of the table. At the end of the activity Miss Hammond made drinks for herself and Miss Madison. Over time, staff decreased the distance between the two women. Staff also introduced shared activities requiring them to hand items to each other. Staff progressively increased the duration of the activities and used verbal praise when the two residents carried out the activities. The author modeled this procedure for the staff and gave them feedback on their performance when they used it.

Course of Treatment and Assessment of Progress

Within a couple of weeks Miss Madison engaged in her own version of relaxation. She could remain on her bed in a fairly still fashion and could breathe slowly with staff prompts, but usually used thoracic rather than diaphragmatic breathing. When she began to get agitated around the house she would engage in her breathing exercises, but she required staff prompts to lie down periodically. This procedure alone seemed quite effective in reducing negative interactions between the two women.

Over a 3-month period, the women learned to tolerate each other's presence during leisure activities quite well. A number of unanticipated positive changes also occurred. These included Miss Madison's requesting certain drinks from Miss Hammond and both women cooperating on cleaning up after snacks. At the end of 3 months they could sit next to each other for an extended period of time with no problems. Additionally, they would look at and smile at each other and refrain from making abusive comments. At the end of 3 months there were no more incidents of biting.

Complicating Factors

There were no major complicating factors, other than monitoring implementation, training new staff, and retraining current staff. One limitation was that there was little contact with the residents' psychiatrist and integration of this treatment with psychotropic medication, due to the limited number of hours available for consultation.

Managed Care Considerations

Community-based services for adults with ID have expanded enormously, and their costs continue to increase considerably. States are involved in aggressive monitoring of rates for services. In this case, after a year or so the state reduced reimbursement rates. The group home company, which was relatively small, was no longer financially viable. A Borg-like conglomerate, which was busy assimilating small services across several states, purchased it. As part of the corporate assimilation, full-time professional staff were transformed into part-time consultants with flexible hours but no benefits. Professional staff who had worked there many years were outsourced.

Follow-Up

These residents were monitored at least monthly. There was no regression at 1-year follow-up, as shown by an absence of injuries to Miss Hammond. Both women seemed friendly and much happier in each other's company. Group home staff and the owners of the company reported being very happy with the progress.

TREATMENT IMPLICATIONS OF THE CASE

Functional assessment is a very pragmatic approach to case formulation and treatment design. It has a strong conceptual basis in learning theory. It allows a clinician to design effective individualized interventions, to increase appropriate behavior, and to effectively reduce undesirable behavior.

SUMMARY

Intellectual disabilities are characterized by global deficits in all aspects of cognition and deficits in meeting the local cultural expectations for adaptive behavior and occur during the developmental period. Accurate diagnosis of ID depends on adequate case findings, changes in conceptualization of ID, and measurement of intelligence and adaptive behaviors. There have been large changes in patterns of diagnosis and service use depending on the willingness of services to diagnose ID and changes in relevant test norms.

Behavior analysis has made significant contributions to the conceptualization of ID and habilitation and treatment of challenging behavior. Life events are relatively unimportant compared to other conditions. However, a wide range of biomedical causes exists, mostly associated with severe and profound ID. The majority of people with ID have mild and moderate ID, most of which has no specific known etiology. It is important that services address biomedical conditions associated with ID. Biomedical conditions may also be associated with challenging behaviors. Many people with ID take psychotropic medication for aggression and self-injury. Their use is controversial due to common off-label prescription, polypharmacy, and ambiguous empirical research support.

Cultural issues may be important when defining ID, especially with regard to conceptualization of ID, defining and measuring ID, and working with families. Most families adjust well to having a family member with ID. Adjustment problems are common during the first 2 years after diagnosis. Families also may face challenges periodically, such as those related to caregiver aging and disability.

Behavioral analysis has made important contributions to teaching a wide range of skills to people with ID, including self-help and community, leisure, social, and problem-solving skills. Behavior analytic approaches should have strong conceptual and empirical bases. Behavior analysis has also been effective in developing technologies to disseminate these approaches by training other people to teach people with ID.

Challenging behaviors are relatively common in people with ID and represent a significant challenge to family adaptation and services. Behavioral interventions should be based on an understanding of the functions of the behaviors of interest. Behavioral interventions have strong empirical support in a wide range of applications.

REFERENCES

Aman, M. G., Sarphare, G., & Burrow, W. H. (1995). Psychotropic drugs in group homes: Prevalence and relation to demographic/psychiatric variables. *American Journal on Mental Retardation, 99,* 500–509.

American Association on Mental Retardation. (2002). *Mental retardation: Definitions, classification and system of supports.* Washington, DC: Author.

American Psychiatric Association. (2000). *Diagnostic and statistical manual of mental disorders* (4th ed., text rev.). Washington, DC: Author.

Azrin, N. H., Sneed, T. J., & Foxx, R. M. (1973). Dry-bed training: Rapid elimination of childhood enuresis. *Behavior, Research and Therapy, 12,* 147–156.

Baer, D. M., Wolf, M., & Risley, T. R. (1968). Some current dimensions of applied behavior analysis. *Journal of Applied Behavior Analysis, 1,* 91–97.

Baroff, G. S., & Olley, J. G. (1999). *Mental retardation: Nature, cause, and management.* Philadelphia: Taylor/Francis.

Baumeister, A. A., & Woodley-Zanthos, P. (1996). Prevention: Biological factors. In J. W. Jacobson & J. A. Mulick (Eds.), *Manual of diagnosis and professional practice in mental retardation* (pp. 229–242). Washington, DC: American Psychological Association.

Bijou, S. W. (1966). A functional analysis of retarded behavior. In R. Ellis (Ed.), *International review of research in mental retardation* (Vol. 1, pp. 1–19). New York: Academic Press.

Bijou, S. W. (1995). *Behavior analysis of child development.* Reno, NV: Context Press. (Original work published 1961)

Boo, K. (1999, December 5). System loses lives and trust. *Washington Post,* p. A1. Retrieved August 13, 2006, from http://www.babcockcenter.org/Reading/Boo120599.htm.

Brienes, N. E., & Sturmey, P. (in press). Reducing student stereotypy by improving teachers' implementation of discrete-trial teaching. *Journal of Applied Behavior Analysis.*

Carr, E. G. (1977). The motivation of self-injurious behavior: A review of some hypotheses. *Psychological Bulletin, 84,* 800–816.

Clarke, D. J., Kelley, S., Thinn, K., & Corbett, J. A. (1990). Psychotropic medication and mental retardation: Pt. 1. Disabilities and the prescription of drugs for behavior and for epilepsy in three residential settings. *Journal of Mental Deficiency Research, 34,* 385–395.

DesRochers, M. N., Hile, M. G., & Williams-Mosely, T. L. (1997). Survey of functional assessment procedures used with individuals who display mental retardation and severe problem behaviors. *American Journal on Mental Retardation, 101,* 535–546.

Devlin, L. A., Shepherd, C. H., Crawford, H., & Morrison, P. J. (2006). Tuberous sclerosis complex: Clinical features, diagnosis, and prevalence within Northern Ireland. *Developmental Medicine and Childhood Neurology, 48,* 495–499.

de Vries, M. W., & deVries, M. R. (1977). Cultural relativity of toilet training readiness: A perspective from East Africa. *Pediatrics, 60,* 170–177.

Didden, R., Duker, P., & Korzilius, H. (1997). Meta-analysis study of treatment effectiveness for problem behaviors with individuals who have mental retardation. *American Journal on Mental Retardation, 101,* 387–399.

Didden, R., Korzilius, H., van Oorsouw, W., & Sturmey, P. (2006). Behavioral treatment of challenging behaviors in individuals with mild mental retardation: Meta-analysis of single subject research. *American Journal on Mental Retardation, 111,* 290–297.

Ducharme, J. M., & Feldman, M. A. (1992). Comparison of staff training strategies to promote generalized teaching skills. *Journal of Applied Behavior Analysis, 25,* 165–179.

Durkin, M. S., & Stein, M. (1996). Classification in mental retardation. In J. W. Jacobson & J. A. Mulick (Eds.), *Manual of diagnosis and professional practice in mental retardation* (pp. 67–74). Washington, DC: American Psychological Association.

Felce, D., de Kock, U., Mansell J., & Jenkins J. (1984). Providing systematic individual teaching for severely disturbed and profoundly mentally-handicapped adults in residential care. *Behaviour Research and Therapy, 22,* 299–309.

Feldman, M. A., Atkinson, L. L., Foti-Gervais, L., & Condillac, R. (2004). Formal versus informal interventions for challenging behavior in persons with intellectual disability. *Journal of Intellectual Disability Research, 48,* 60–68.

Fisher, M. A., & Zeaman, D. (1970). Growth and decline of retarded intelligence. In N. R. Ellis (Ed.), *International review of research in mental retardation* (Vol. 4, pp. 151–190). New York: Academic Press.

Fleming, I., & Stenfert Kroese, B. (1990). Evaluation of a community care project for people with learning difficulties. *Journal of Mental Deficiency Research, 34,* 351–364.

Friedman, J. M. (2001, June 8). Racial disparities in median age at death of persons with Down syndrome: United States, 1968–1997. *Morbidity and Mortality Weekly Report, 50*(22), 463–465.

Frison, S. L., Wallander, J. L., & Browne, D. (1998). Cultural factors enhancing resilience and protecting against maladjustment in African American adolescents with mild mental retardation. *American Journal on Mental Retardation, 102,* 613–626.

Gannotti, M. E., & Handwerker, W. P. (2002). Puerto Rican understandings of child disability: Methods for the cultural validation of standardized measures of child health. *Social Sciences and Medicine, 55,* 2094–2105.

Ghazzhuiddin, M., Alessi, N., & Greden, J. F. (1995). Life events and depression in children with pervasive developmental disorders. *Journal of Autism and Developmental Disorders, 25,* 495–502.

Green, C. W., Reid, D. H., White, L. K., Halford, R. C., Brittain, D. P., & Gardner, S. M. (1988). Identifying reinforcers for persons with profound handicaps: Staff opinion versus systematic assessment of preferences. *Journal of Applied Behavior Analysis, 21,* 31–43.

Hagopian, L. P., LeBlanc, L. A., & Maglieri, K. A. (2000). Non-contingent attention for the treatment of excessive medical complaints in a medically fragile man with mental retardation. *Research in Developmental Disabilities, 21,* 215–221.

Hart, B., & Risley, T. R. (1995). *Meaningful differences in the everyday experience of young American children.* Baltimore, PA: Brooks.

Haw, C., & Stubbs, J. (2005). A survey of off-label prescribing for inpatients with mild intellectual disability and mental illness. *Journal of Intellectual Disability Research, 49,* 858–865.

Haynes, S. W., & O'Brien, W. H. (1990). Functional analysis in behavior therapy. *Clinical Psychology Review, 10,* 649–668.

Healthcare Commission. (2006). *Joint investigation into the provision of services for people with learning disabilities at Cornwall partnership NHS trust.* London: Commission for Healthcare Audit and Inspection.

Herrnstein, R. J., & Murray, C. (1994). *Bell curve: Intelligence and class structure in American life.* New York: Free Press.

Hurley, A. D., Folstein, M., & Lam, N. (2003). Patients with and without intellectual disability seeking outpatient psychiatric services: Diagnoses and prescribing pattern. *Journal of Intellectual Disability Research, 47,* 39–50.

Jones, E., Felce, D., Lowe, K., Bowley, C., Pagler, J., Gallagher, B., et al. (2001). Evaluation of the dissemination of active support training in staffed community residences. *American Journal on Mental Retardation, 106,* 344–358.

Kahng, S., Iwata, B. A., & Lewis, A. B. (2002). Behavioral treatment of self-injury, 1964 to 2000. *American Journal on Mental Retardation, 107,* 212–221.

Kamin, L. J. (1974). *The science and politics of IQ.* Potomac, MD: Erlbaum.

Kanaya, T., Scullin, M. H., & Ceci, S. J. (2003). The impact of rising IQ scores on American society via mental retardation. *American Psychologist, 58,* 776–790.

Klatt, K. P., Sherman, J. A., & Sheldon, J. B. (2000). Effects of deprivation on engagement in preferred activities by persons with developmental disabilities. *Journal of Applied Behavior Analysis, 33,* 495–506.

Likins, M., Salzberg, C. L., Stowitschek, J. J., Lignugaris/Kraft, B., & Curl, R. (1989). Co-worker implemented job training: The use of coincidental training and quality-control checking on the food preparation skills of trainees with mental retardation. *Journal of Applied Behavior Analysis, 22,* 381–393.

Lindsay, W. R., Allan, R., MacLeod, F., Smart, N., & Smith, A. H. (2003). Long-term treatment and management of violent tendencies of men with intellectual disabilities convicted of assault. *Mental Retardation, 41,* 47–56.

Lott, I. T., McGregor, L., Engelman, L., Touchette, P., Tournay, A., Sandman, C., et al., (2004). Longitudinal prescribing patters for psychoactive medications in community-based individuals with developmental disabilities: Utilization of pharmacy records. *Journal of Intellectual Disability Research, 48,* 563–571.

Luyben, P. D., Funk, D. M., Morgan, J. K., Clark, K. A., & Delulio, D. W. (1986). Team sports for the severely retarded: Training a side-of-the-foot soccer pass using a maximum-to-minimum prompt reduction strategy. *Journal of Applied Behavior Analysis, 19,* 431–436.

MacMillan, D. L., Gresham, F. M., & Bocian, K. M. (1998). Discrepancy between definitions of learning disabilities and school practices: An empirical investigation. *Journal of Learning Disabilities, 31,* 314–326.

MacMillan, D. L., Gresham, F. M., & Siperstein, G. N. (1993). Conceptual and psychometric concerns about the 1992 AAMR definition of mental retardation. *American Journal on Mental Retardation, 98*, 325–335.

MacMillan, D. L., Gresham, F. M., Siperstein, G. N., & Bocian, K. M. (1996). The labyrinth of IDEA: School decisions on referred students with subaverage general intelligence. *American Journal on Mental Retardation, 101*, 161–174.

Magana, S., Schwartz, S. J., Rubert, M. P., & Szapocznik, J. (2006). Hispanic caregivers of adults with mental retardation: Importance of family functioning. *American Journal on Mental Retardation, 111*, 250–262.

March of Dimes. (2006). *Phenylketonuria*. Retrieved August 10, 2006, from http://www.marchofdimes.com/professionals/681_1219.asp.

Martin, J. A., King, D. R., Jaccoby, E. E., & Jacklin, C. (1984). Secular trends and individual differences in toilet-training progress. *Journal of Pediatric Psychology, 9*, 457–467.

Matson, J. L., Bamburg, J. W., Mayville, E. A., Pinkston, J., Bielecki, J., Kuhn, D., et al. (2000). Psychopharmacology and mental retardation: A 10 year review (1990–1999). *Research in Developmental Disabilities, 21*, 263–296.

Matson, J. L., Bielecki, J., Mayville, S. B., & Matson, M. L. (2003). Psychopharmacology research for individuals with mental retardation: Methodological issues and suggestions. *Research in Developmental Disabilities, 24*, 149–157.

Miller, M. A., Cuvo, A. J., & Borakove, L. S. (1977). Teaching naming of coin values comprehension before production versus production alone. *Journal of Applied Behavior Analysis, 10*, 735–736.

Naglieri, J. A., & Rojahn, J. (2001). Intellectual classification of Black and White children in special education programs using the WISC-III and the Cognitive Assessment System. *American Journal on Mental Retardation, 106*, 359–367.

Neef, N. A., Lensbower, J. J., Hockersmith, I., DePalma, V., & Gray, K. (1990). In vivo versus simulation training: An interactional analysis of range and type of training exemplars. *Journal of Applied Behavior Analysis, 23*, 447–458.

Oliver, C., Hall, S., & Murphy, G. (2005). The early development of self-injurious behavior: Evaluating the role of social reinforcement. *Journal of Intellectual Disability Research, 49*, 591–599.

O'Neill, R. E., Horner, R. H., Albin, R. W., Sprague, J. R., Storey, K., & Newton, J. S. (1997). *Functional assessment and program development for problem behavior: A practical handbook* (2nd ed.). New York: Brooks.

Owen, D. M., Hastings, R. P., Noone, S. J., Chinn, J., Harman, K., Roberts, J., et al. (2004). Life events as correlates of problem behavior and mental health in a residential population of adults with developmental disabilities. *Research in Developmental Disabilities, 25*, 309–320.

Parsons, M. B., Reid, D. H., Green, C. W., & Browning, L. B. (2001). Reducing job coach assistance for supported workers with severe multiple disabilities: An alternative off-site/on-site model. *Research in Developmental Disabilities, 22*, 151–164.

Perry, J., & Felce, D. (2005). Factors associated with outcome in community group homes. *American Journal on Mental Retardation, 110*, 121–135.

Rea, J., & Williams, D. (2002). Shaping exhale durations for breath CO detection for men with mild mental retardation. *Journal of Applied Behavior Analysis, 35*, 415–418.

Rehfeldt, R. A., & Chambers, M. R. (2003). Functional analysis and treatment of verbal perseverations displayed by an adult with autism. *Journal of Applied Behavior Analysis, 36*, 259–261.

Reid, D. H., & Parsons, M. B. (1995). *Motivating human service staff: Supervisory strategies for maximizing work effort and work enjoyment*. Morganton, NC: Habilitative Management Consultants.

Reid, D. H., Parsons, M. B., & Green, C. W. (1998). Identifying work preferences among individuals with severe multiple disabilities prior to beginning supported work. *Journal of Applied Behavior Analysis, 31,* 281–285.

Reschley, D. J., & Ward, S. M. (1991). Use of adaptive behavior measures and overrepresentation of Black students with mild mental retardation. *American Journal on Mental Retardation, 95,* 257–268.

Robertson, J., Emerson, E., Pinkney, L., Caesar, E., Felce, D., Meek, A., et al. (2005). Treatment and management of challenging behaviors in congregate and noncongregate community-based supported accommodation. *Journal of Intellectual Disabilities Research, 49,* 63–72.

Rojahn, J., & Tasse, M. (1996). Psychopathology in mental retardation. In J. W. Jacobson & J. A. Mulick (Eds.), *Manual of diagnosis and professional practice in mental retardation* (pp. 147–156). Washington, DC: American Psychological Association.

Sarokoff, R. A., & Sturmey, P. (2004). The effects of instruction, feedback, rehearsal, and modeling on staff implementation of discrete trial teaching. *Journal of Applied Behavior Analysis, 37,* 535–538.

Scullin, M. H. (2006). Large state-level fluctuations in mental retardation classifications related to introduction of renormed intelligence test. *American Journal on Mental Retardation, 111,* 322–335.

Sievert, A. L., Cuvo, A. J., & Davis, P. K. (1988). Training self-advocacy skills to adults with mild handicaps. *Journal of Applied Behavior Analysis, 21,* 299–309.

Singh, N. N., Ellis, C. R., Mattila, M. J., Mulick, J. A., & Poling, A. (1998). Vitamin, mineral, and dietary treatments. In A. Reis & M. G. Aman (Eds.), *Psychotropic medication and developmental disabilities: The international consensus handbook* (pp. 311–320). Columbus, Ohio: Nisonger Center.

Singh, N. N., Ellis, C. R., & Wechsler, H. (1997). Psychopharmacoepidemiology of mental retardation: 1966 to 1995. *Journal of Child and Adolescent Psychopharmacology, 7,* 255–266.

Smith, A. J., Bihm, E. B., Tavkar, P., & Sturmey, P. (2005). Approach-avoidance and happiness indicators in unstructured settings: A preliminary analysis of persons with developmental disorders. *Research in Developmental Disabilities, 26,* 297–313.

Spinath, F. M., Harlaar, N., Ronald, A., & Plomin, R. (2004). Substantial genetic influence on mild mental impairment in early childhood. *American Journal on Mental Retardation, 109,* 34–43.

Stenfert Kroese, B., Dagnan, D., & Loumidis, K. (1997). *Cognitive behavior therapy for people with learning disabilities.* New York: Brunner-Routledge.

Stokes, T. F., & Baer, D. M. (1977). An implicit technology of generalization. *Journal of Applied Behavior Analysis, 10,* 349–367.

Sturmey, P. (1994). Assessing the functions of aberrant behaviors: A review of psychometric instruments. *Journal of Autism and Developmental Disorders, 24,* 293–304.

Sturmey, P. (1996). *Functional analysis in clinical psychology.* Chichester, England: Wiley.

Sturmey, P. (1999). Correlates of restraint use in an institutional population. *Research in Developmental Disabilities, 20,* 339–346.

Sturmey, P. (2004). Cognitive therapy with people with intellectual disabilities: A selective review and critique. *Clinical Psychology and Psychotherapy, 11,* 223–232.

Sturmey, P. (2006). On some recent claims for the efficacy of cognitive therapy for people with intellectual disabilities. *Journal of Applied Research in Intellectual Disabilities, 19,* 109–118.

Sturmey, P. (2007a). *Clinical case formulation: A behavioral approach.* Chichester, England: Wiley.

Sturmey, P. (Ed.). (2007b). *Functional analysis in clinical treatment.* New York: Elsevier.

Sturmey, P., Lott, J. D., Laud, R., & Matson, J. L. (2005). Correlates of restraint use in an institutional population: A replication. *Journal of Intellectual Disabilities Research, 49,* 501–506.

Sturmey, P., & McGlynn, A. P. (2003). Restraint reduction. In D. Allen (Ed.), *Responding to challenging behavior in persons with intellectual disabilities: Ethical approaches to physical intervention* (pp. 203–218). Kidderminster, United Kingdom: British Institute of Learning Disabilities.

Surgeon General. (2002). *Closing the gap: A national blueprint to improve the health of persons with mental retardation* (Report of the Surgeon General's conference on Health Disparities and Mental Retardation). Retrieved August 11, 2006, from http://www.nichd.nih.gov/publications/pubs/closingthegap/index.htm.

Taylor, I., & O'Reilly, M. F. (1997). Toward a functional analysis of private verbal self-regulation. *Journal of Applied Behavior Analysis, 30,* 43–58.

Taylor, J. L., Novaco, R. W., Gillmer, B. T., Robertson, A., & Thorne, I. (2005). Individual cognitive-behavioral anger treatment for people with mild-borderline intellectual disabilities and histories of aggression: A controlled trial. *British Journal of Clinical Psychology, 44,* 367–382.

Thompson, R. H., Iwata, B. A., Hanley, G. P., Dozier, C. L., & Samaha, A. L. (2003). The effects of extinction, noncontingent reinforcement, and differential reinforcement of other behavior as control procedures. *Journal of Applied Behavior Analysis, 36,* 221–238.

Turkat, I. D. (Ed.). (1985). *Behavioral case formulation.* New York: Plenum Press.

U.S. Department of Education. (2004). *U.S. Department of Education Statistics.* Retrieved August, 10, 2006, from http://nces.ed.gov/programs/digest/d04/tables/dt04_052.asp.

Wacker, D. P., & Berg, W. K. (1983). Effects of picture prompts on the acquisition of complex vocational tasks by mentally retarded adolescents. *Journal of Applied Behavior Analysis, 16,* 417–433.

Watanabe, M., & Sturmey, P. (2003). The effect of choice-making opportunities during activity schedules on task engagement of adults with autism. *Journal of Autism and Developmental Disabilities, 33,* 535–538.

Wolf, M. M. (1978). Social validity: The case for subjective measurement or how applied behavior analysis is finding its heart. *Journal of Applied Behavior Analysis, 11,* 203–214.

Wolpe, J., & Turkat, I. D. (1985). Behavioral formulation of clinical cases. In I. D. Turkat (Ed.), *Behavioral case formulation* (pp. 5–26). New York: Plenum Press.

World Health Organization. (2001). *International classification of functioning, disease, and health (ICF).* Geneva, Switzerland: Author.

Zigler, E., Balla, D., & Hodapp, R. (1984). On the definition and classification of mental retardation. *American Journal of Mental Retardation, 89,* 215–230.

CHAPTER 23

Older Adults

BARRY A. EDELSTEIN, SARAH A. STONER, AND ERIN WOODHEAD

In 2003, 12% (35.9 million) of the U.S. population was 65 years or older (He, Sengupta, Velkoff, & DeBarros, 2005). During the same period, one out of every 14 people on earth (440 million) was 65 years or older, which was approximately 7% of the total population. The ratio of men to women decreases with age. For example, in 2002 there were 92 men per 100 women in the age range of 55 to 64, and 46 men per 100 women among adults 85 and older (Smith, 2003) in the United States. Approximately 80% of the 50,000 centenarians in the United States are women. The U.S. older population is rapidly increasing, boosted by aging baby boomers and greater longevity. In 2011, the first of the baby boomers will turn 65. The size of the U.S. older adult population is expected to double by 2020 (U.S. Census Bureau, 2004).

The majority of older adults in the United States are White, accounting for approximately 82% of adults age 65 and older. African Americans account for 8.2%, Asian or Pacific Islanders for 2.8%, Hispanic individuals (of any race) for 5.7%, and American Indian and Native Alaskan Native Americans for less than 1% (Administration on Aging, 2004). The older adult population of the United States is less diverse than the younger population. For example, non-Hispanic Whites had the oldest age distribution in 2002. Among individuals 65 to 74, 80% were non-Hispanic Whites, whereas among individuals 85 and older, 87% were non-Hispanic Whites (U.S. Census Bureau, 2004).

A smaller percentage of older adults in the United States live in poverty today than in the past. For example, in 1959, 35% of adults 65 and older lived below the poverty line (He et al., 2005). In 2003, the proportion was 10%. Women are currently more likely than men to be living in poverty (13% versus 7%), and older Blacks (34%) and Hispanics (20%) are more likely than non-Hispanic Whites (8%; He et al., 2005).

Work habits and social characteristics of older adults have changed over the years and vary considerably by age. Though older adults are less likely to be a member of the labor force than in past years, in 2003 approximately 50% of men and over 66% of women 70 and older worked part time (He et al., 2005). Approximately 75% of older adults living alone in 2003 were women, with the greatest proportion (57%) being 85 and older. Many individuals are surprised to learn that only approximately

4.5% of older adults age 75 to 84 live in nursing homes. This proportion increases with age, with approximately 18% of those 85 and older living in nursing homes. Approximately 75% of nursing home residents are women (He et al., 2005).

The principal goal of this chapter is to acquaint readers with age-related issues and information that can inform their assessment, case conceptualization, treatment formulation, and treatment implementation. The take-home message is that older adults are different from younger adults across multiple, clinically relevant domains. We begin with a discussion of age-related myths and biases that can negatively influence the assessment and intervention process. Strategies for addressing these are offered. The aging of the body is then discussed so that readers can appreciate the extent of normal biological changes and their implications for assessment and treatment. Suggestions for accommodating the associated deficits of these changes are offered. Discussion of the aging body is followed by consideration of several common chronic medical conditions that can complicate the assessment and treatment process and pharmacological consequences that can also contribute to the complexity of one's case conceptualization and treatment. Psychiatric manifestations of these and other medical conditions are presented to broaden the reader's scope of potential factors contributing to client clinical presentations.

Social relationships, both positive and negative, are then considered in light of their potential contributions to the psychological functioning of the older adult. Finally, age-related assessment considerations are addressed, with emphasis on the paucity of psychometrically sound assessment instruments for older adults and the need for caution when considering the psychometric properties of assessment instruments that were created for younger adults before employing them with older adults.

AGE-RELATED MYTHS AND BIASES

Many myths and biases regarding the aging process are apparent in today's society. Such myths often create a negative impression on the aging process and lead to stereotypes against older adults. Although many research studies have successfully challenged the myths and biases related to aging, the false beliefs can still have damaging effects.

Six main myths regarding older adults are perpetuated in today's society (Rowe & Kahn, 1998). These myths imply that older adults are sick, incapable of learning new information or skills, unable to benefit from healthy changes or risk-reduction strategies, dependent solely on their genetics in regard to how well they age, incapable of sexual desires or interests, and unable to be a productive part of society. Rowe and Kahn provide discrediting information and statistics for each myth, thereby indicating that many age-related stereotypes and myths are no more than false beliefs.

Despite the fact that myths relating to later life can be discredited with empirical evidence, the myths nevertheless are damaging and permeate society with an unfavorable image of aging. For example, Bonnesen and Burgess (2004) found that the term "senior moment" was printed 181 times in newspapers across the country during a 10-year period. The phrase was used for several purposes; for example, "senior moment" was used to describe minor and major memory problems and situations in which someone made a mistake. The phrase had a positive meaning in only 9.9% of its usage. Additional instances of ageism and ageist stereotypes can be found throughout the media and health care services (Ory, Kinney Hoffman, Hawkins, Sanner, & Mockenhaupt, 2003).

Age-related stereotypes, biases, and myths can be very damaging. Self-stereotypes against aging may develop when individuals who accept the negative myths and biases linked to aging become increasingly older and are faced with membership in the demographic group of which they hold negative beliefs (Levy, 2003). Furthermore, myths and biases associated with aging can be detected in individuals' attitudes toward others. A meta-analysis of attitudes toward younger and older adults revealed that individuals tend to rate younger adults as more attractive, competent, and favorable than older adults (Kite, Stockdale, Whitley, & Johnson, 2005).

Several strategies may be employed for combating myths and biases against older adults. Education about the facts and myths of aging, particularly for professionals who interact with older adults, may help decrease the influence of these false beliefs (Ory et al., 2003; Thornton, 2002). Increased interaction between members of different generations may also help to discredit myths (Ory et al., 2003). When witnessing an age-related myth or bias, these false beliefs should be discredited so that they are not perpetuated (Thornton, 2002). An increase in research findings pertaining to older adults can also help to expand knowledge pertaining to aging (Ory et al., 2003; Thornton, 2002).

OLDER ADULT SEXUALITY

Among the many myths related to aging, myths about sexuality, or lack of sexuality, in older adults lead to beliefs that older adults do not, should not, and cannot engage in sexual activities. However, sexual activity among older adults is not uncommon or unnatural.

Sexual behavior among older adults is a topic that is historically under researched, yet this lack of data does not reflect a lack of sexual activity (Burgess, 2004). Studies that have examined sexual behavior in older adults (i.e., Beutel, Schumacher, Weidner, & Brähler, 2002; Bortz, Wallace, & Wiley, 1999; Bretschneider & McCoy, 1988; Marsiglio & Donnelly, 1991; Matthias, Lubben, Atchison, & Schweitzer, 1997) provide evidence that older adults desire and engage in sexual behaviors. For example, sexual intercourse was reported to occur at least occasionally by 83% of men and 64% of women over age 80 residing in retirement facilities (Bretschneider & McCoy, 1988), and 55% of adults age 66–70, 45% of adults age 71–75, and 24% of adults over 76 sampled in another study experienced intercourse during the prior month (Marsiglio & Donnelly, 1991). Among a sample of individuals over 70, 30% reported having intercourse during the prior month (Matthias et al., 1997); 50% of German males over age 61 reported engaging in intercourse at least once during the previous year (Beutel et al., 2002). In an examination of men over 80, 12% of the individuals reported having intercourse an average of once a week, and 5% reported having intercourse at least twice per week (Bortz et al., 1999). Aside from intercourse, Bortz et al. found that a desire for sexual activity at least twice per week was experienced by approximately 20% of their sample of men over 80 years old. Rates of sexual behaviors vary across studies, depending on the sample and measurement of sexual activity.

Older adults often face some challenges with sexuality in later life, however. One significant challenge for women regards the lack of a sexual partner (Burgess, 2004). Women's life spans exceed men's by an average of 7 years. Older women are more likely to outlive their spouse, and there are more older women than older men. However, men may also face the problem of not having a sexual partner (Beutel et al., 2002). Age-related physical changes also present challenges that can influence sexual functioning, though sexual problems that may occur during later life are not necessarily due to the process of aging (O'Donohue & Graber, 1996). For example, sexual functioning may be impacted by medications used to treat other disorders (Agronin, 2004). Changes in physical appearance may alter one's body image, self-esteem, and identity; these changes may impact one's feelings of sexual desirability (Badeau, 1995). Likewise, older adults may be susceptible to believing society's myths that older adults should not engage in sexual activities and are sexually undesirable, thereby creating challenges for older adults who wish to continue engaging in sexual activity (O'Donohue & Graber, 1996).

Privacy, or lack of privacy, may also contribute to the challenges facing those who desire sexual activities during later life. Older adults residing in nursing facilities, for example, may have difficulty finding the privacy needed to engage in sexual activities (Agronin, 2004; Burgess, 2004; O'Donohue & Graber, 1996). Additionally, problems may arise when one partner in a couple has dementia; the other partner may question whether sexual activities are ethical and whether the affected partner maintains the capability to consent to such sexual activities (Agronin, 2004).

Older adults may have concerns about engaging in sexual behaviors that relate to their current health conditions. Individuals may be apprehensive over the safety of sexual behaviors following a heart attack, stroke, or other physical illnesses (Badeau, 1995). Many older adults are capable of returning to sexual activities following such illnesses and should be encouraged to discuss their concerns with their physicians.

Myths pertaining to lack of sexual activity in later life are false and can be potentially damaging. Many older adults engage in sexual activities, and problems relating to sexual behavior should not be assumed to be caused by the aging process.

SEXUAL ORIENTATION

Sexual orientation is an important topic for consideration when working with older adults. Older gay men and lesbians have experienced years of stigmatization and discrimination for their sexual orientation and may therefore be hesitant to reveal their orientation for fear of further discrimination (Brotman, Ryan, & Cormier, 2003). Indeed, in one study's sample, 73% of gay men and lesbians of varying ages reported a belief that policies and employees of retirement and nursing facilities discriminate against individuals with a homosexual orientation; 33% of the participants reported that they would not reveal their sexual orientation if they were residents of a retirement facility (Johnson, Jackson, Arnette, & Koffman, 2005). Furthermore, some gay men and lesbians have expressed concern over the possibility of losing their independence and living in retirement facilities after experiencing much discrimination regarding their sexual orientation during their lifetime (Brotman et al., 2003).

Of the many societal challenges facing gay men and lesbians, the concept of "family" is an important concern. Many gay men and lesbians incorporate same-sex partners and friends into their concept of family, so that these members become "fictive kin" (Brotman et al., 2003). However, health care systems may discount or minimize these relationships and not recognize support for older adults provided by individuals other than biological family members. A common misconception is that older adults who are gay or lesbian lack social support due to a lack of biological children or legal spouse. However, one study found that older gay men and lesbians averaged 6.3 people in their social support network (Grossman, D'Augelli, & Hershberger, 2000).

Indeed, an individual's homosexual orientation does not indicate a lack of adequate social support (Brotman et al., 2003; Grossman et al., 2000).

Diversity in Older Adults

Older adults are diverse with regard to culture, ethnicity, educational level, background, and sexual orientation. The considerable heterogeneity among older adults with regard to these demographics should not be disregarded. The misconception that older adults are all the same (uniformity myth) is incorrect. For example, according to the 2000 U.S. census data, 18% of adults over 65 belong to a racial minority group (Federal Interagency Forum on Aging-Related Statistics, 2004), and this percentage is expected to increase to 39% by 2050 (Federal Interagency Forum on Aging-Related Statistics, 2004). Recommendations for increasing awareness of the vast amount of diversity existing among older adults include learning about, teaching, and discussing diversity among older adults (Hinrichsen, 2006).

THE AGING BODY

There are many physiological, sensory, and cognitive changes related to normal aging. Age-related declines in these domains tend to be linear through the 8th and 9th decades (Rowe & Devons, 1996), yet there is great variability in the rate of decline between individuals. Furthermore, declines in one domain are not necessarily indicative of decline in another. Many changes that commonly occur during the aging process are labeled "normal," yet caution is warranted when using this term. "Normal" changes may imply that declines or changes in functioning do not indicate disease or interference in one's life. Age-related changes that are particularly relevant for assessment and treatment are discussed next, as are their implications.

Physiological Changes

Age-related changes may be observed in many parts of the body, including the brain, nervous, cardiovascular, pulmonary, and gastrointestinal systems (see Rowe & Devons, 1996, for an overview). Physiological changes that commonly occur with aging may have a psychological impact on individuals. For example, age-related changes in the cardiovascular system may include a decrease in heart muscle tone (Leaf, 1973, as cited in Markson, 1993). Changes affecting cardiovascular functioning include thickening of the left ventricular wall, increase in systolic blood pressure, slower maximum heart rate following exercise, and increased stroke volume (Rowe & Devons, 1996). Numerous age-related changes that occur within the cardiovascular system do not typically affect the heart's functioning during resting periods, but may impact the heart's functioning during periods of exercise (Wei, 2004). The heart is a vital organ, and problems associated with the cardiovascular system may remind individuals of their own mortality and lead to associated anxiety (Whitbourne, 1998).

Age-related declines are also noticeable in the pulmonary system, although these changes may be greatly influenced by environmental factors, such as smoking. Although lung capacity remains roughly equivalent in older as compared to younger individuals, the lungs and the chest wall surrounding the lungs become stiffer with age. Such stiffness causes a decrease in the amount of air that is expelled from the lungs and an increase in the residual volume of air in the lungs (Rowe & Devons,

1996). Older adults may experience fatigue during physical activity due to less efficient gas exchange in the lungs (Whitbourne, 1998). Additionally, shortness of breath and difficulty breathing may approximate symptoms experienced during panic attacks, which can be a frightening sensation for many individuals (Whitbourne, 1998).

Changes in the cardiovascular and pulmonary systems are not readily observable by others, but age-related changes of skin and body composition are more noticeable. As individuals age, the cell structure of skin changes so that wrinkles form and skin appears different than it did during younger years (Whitbourne, 1998). Individuals also tend to experience a decrease in muscle mass and an increase in fat deposits around the waist and hips (Whitbourne, 1998). These changes alter one's appearance and may influence one's identity and self-esteem. Additionally, loss of muscle mass and other common changes in the body, such as decreased bone density and increased pain in joints, can decrease mobility. Muscle loss commonly occurs in older age and may result in movements that are less stable. Decreases in bone density cause bones to be less capable of bearing stress and more susceptible to bone fractures. Pain in joints may increase as cartilage thins and provides less protection between bones. Movements may become painful, and the potential for injury from falls increases. These changes can contribute to a decrease in a sense of well-being, as well as an increase in the potential for depression or anxiety (Whitbourne, 1998). Decreases in mobility may also hinder participation in social activities.

Older adults experience numerous age-related changes in their body, and concerns regarding these changes should not be dismissed as unimportant. Some older adults report physical symptoms that are caused by psychological disorders, such as depression. Likewise, some older adults may report feelings of depression or fatigue that are caused by a physical disorder, such as cardiovascular disease (Ouslander, 1983).

Sensory and Perceptual Changes   Age-related changes in vision, hearing, taste, touch, and smell are common among older adults. Physical changes in sensory receptors may be subtle, occurring slowly over an extended period of time (Nusbaum, 1999), so that these changes may not be readily detectable to the individual experiencing these changes or to those with whom the individual interacts. Declines in sensation may eventually impact several aspects of an individual's life, however.

Approximately 92% of adults over 70 use eyeglasses to correct their vision, and 14% of individuals 70–74 and 32% of individuals over age 80 experience difficulties with vision despite using eyeglasses (Desai, Pratt, Lentzner, & Robinson, 2001). Visual impairments are caused by numerous changes in the visual system, including gradual hardening of the crystalline lens, which decreases one's ability to change focus between near and far objects (accommodation; Kasthurirangan & Glasser, 2006; Weale, 2003). Cataracts are another common reason for visual difficulties in later life. Cataracts occur when areas of the crystalline lens of the eye become opaque and hardened (Kline & Li, 2005). There are several types of cataracts, with nuclear cataracts being most strongly correlated with age. Nuclear cataracts are opaque areas on the center of the lens that obstruct vision, causing an increased sensitivity to glare, clouded vision, and a change in color appearances due to the cataract blocking some short-wavelength light (Kline & Li, 2005). Cortical and subcapsular cataracts are more closely related to diabetes. Overall, cataracts occur in more than half of adults over 70 (Desai et al., 2001). Age-related macular degeneration is another leading cause of vision loss among older adults (National Eye Institute, 2005). Macular degeneration occurs when either cells in the area of the retina known as the macula begin to dysfunction or new blood vessels form behind the macula and shift its position in the eye. Central vision is affected by age-related macular degeneration, so that objects in the center of the field of vision are blurred and straight lines may appear wavy.

Visual impairments can have an emotional impact (Owsley et al., 2006; Savikko, Routasalo, Tilvis, Strandberg, & Pitkälä, 2005). For example, in a focus group discussion regarding emotions experienced by individuals with age-related macular degeneration, 65% of emotional comments were negative, relating to frustration, fear, sadness, and inadequacy (Owsley et al., 2006). Individuals with more advanced macular degeneration also reported increased role difficulties, increased dependence on others, decreased social functioning, and decreased overall mental health as compared to those with less advanced macular degeneration (Owsley et al., 2006). Individuals with poorer vision in another study experienced more loneliness than those with better vision (Savikko et al., 2005).

Visual impairments among older adults may create problems in psychological testing. For example, inaccurate information may be recorded on paper-and-pencil measures due to difficulty reading the material. Individuals with cataracts are more susceptible to environmental glare, so that reading tests on glossy paper or undergoing testing in a room with bright lighting may be difficult. There are some steps practitioners can take, however, to minimize or accommodate visual difficulties. DeAngelis (2002) recommends several strategies for minimizing the adverse effects of structural changes in the visual system, such as increasing illumination by using a variety of light sources in a room. Poor lighting may increase difficulty in seeing clearly, and bright light from one source may increase the amount of glare in the room. Interference from glare may be reduced by arranging for the client to sit away from windows and other sources of bright light. Use of corrective eyeglasses will help ensure that older adults are able to see as well as possible during the testing session. It is important to always ask the person being evaluated whether he or she wears corrective lenses and encourage their use. Printing information in contrasting colors (e.g., blue letters on a yellow background) will increase the contrast between written letters and the background, so that they may be viewed more easily. Use of a 16-point font for printed material can also be helpful. Print that is too small or too large can impair reading performance.

Hearing Hearing impairment in one or both ears affects approximately 30% of adults over 70 and almost 50% of adults over 85 (Desai et al., 2001). Exposure to loud noise, reactions to radiation or chemotherapy used during cancer treatment, ear infections, injury to the head, cognitive declines, and slowed temporal processing are factors that may contribute to hearing impairment (Connelly, 2005; Gordon-Salant, 2005). Sound waves may be blocked from reaching the middle ear due to disease, excess ear wax, or other conditions that interfere with efficient sound wave conduction, resulting in conductive hearing loss. Hearing loss may also be due to dysfunction of the inner ear or auditory nerve, resulting in sensorineural hearing loss. Some individuals may experience both sensorineural and conductive hearing loss, which is termed mixed hearing loss (Connelly, 2005). Behaviors exhibited by individuals that may be indicative of hearing impairment include asking for others to repeat statements, complaints that others mumble, and showing difficulty understanding others in noisy or reverberant environments where sounds may be distorted (Cook & Hawkins, 2006; Helfer & Wilber, 1990).

Individuals with hearing loss may experience depressive symptoms, low self-efficacy, loneliness, smaller social networks, and paranoia (Kramer, Kapteyn, Kuik, & Deeg, 2002; National Council on the Aging, 1999; Strawbridge, Wallhagen, Shema, & Kaplan, 2000). For example, Strawbridge et al. found that individuals with moderate or worse hearing impairments were twice as likely to endorse depressive symptoms as individuals without hearing impairment.

Depending on the cause of hearing impairment, hearing loss may be alleviated with hearing aids or other strategies (Gordon-Salant, 2005). In some instances of conductive hearing loss, hearing may be improved by treating the cause of the problem (i.e., removal of ear wax). Hearing aids may be beneficial for individuals experiencing sensorineural or mixed hearing loss (Connelly, 2005). Many older adults not currently using hearing aids may benefit from their use (Davis, 2003). However, many individuals may find hearing aids problematic due to having unrealistic expectations of their efficacy, stigmas attached to use of hearing aids, or the high financial cost of obtaining a hearing aid. Additionally, hearing aids are incapable of completely eliminating background noise, although some models may be able to adjust for background noise (Cook & Hawkins, 2006). Although hearing aids amplify sound intensity, they do not reduce any cognitive demands of listening, such as memory demands or ability to alternate attention between speakers (Gordon-Salant, 2005).

Aside from use of hearing aids, hearing difficulties may be partially alleviated through some simple steps (Portis, 2006). Sitting directly in front of a person with hearing impairment will allow the listener to see the speaker's face and mouth while talking, which may make lip reading easier. Adequate room lighting will also allow individuals to see a speaker's face clearly. Mumbling, talking rapidly, and blocking one's face with one's hands or other objects may distort the sound and make listening more difficult, so these behaviors should be avoided. Background noise, such as music or traffic noise, should be kept to a minimum to reduce distractions. Level of reverberation can be reduced through avoiding rooms with high ceilings or hard floors, as reverberation will distort sounds. Finally, individuals who report difficulty hearing should be encouraged to have their hearing tested and use a hearing aid if one is recommended.

Taste and Smell   The sensations of taste and smell are often combined into one sense, called "chemosensation" (Rawson, 2003). Declines in chemosensation may occur with age, but these declines are inconsistent (Rawson, 2003). However, changes in perception of taste and smell are important to consider when assessing and treating older adults, as some of these changes may occur with the development of certain disorders (i.e., Alzheimer's disease, Parkinson's disease). Likewise, changes in chemosensation may become a source of frustration or annoyance for many individuals, especially if complaints and concerns regarding these changes are not taken seriously (Rawson, 2003).

Several researchers have found that declines in taste qualities are inconsistent throughout later life (e.g., Fukunaga, Uematsu, & Sugimoto, 2005; Nordin, Razani, Markison, & Murphy, 2003). For example, a decrease in sensitivity to salt and sucrose occurs with aging, yet perception of sour tastes does not appear to be affected by age (Fukunaga et al., 2005; Rawson, 2003; see Mojet, Christ-Hazelhof, & Heidema, 2001, for review). Changes in chemosensation may reduce one's enjoyment of and interest in food, increasing risk for malnutrition. On the other hand, risk for obesity may increase, as these changes could cause an individual to need to add more salt or sugar to their food to detect those tastes, or individuals may overeat due to the limited sensory feedback from taste and smell (Nusbaum, 1999). Environmental risks may also occur with declines in chemosensations. Individuals experiencing declines in chemosensation may not be able to detect when food has spoiled; however, they can develop strategies to prevent consumption of spoiled food (Rawson, 2003). Likewise, individuals with decreased chemosensation may not smell smoke as readily as others (Nusbaum, 1999), posing another environmental danger; this can be compensated for through the use of smoke detectors. Although psychological testing results may not be directly influenced by an individual's decreased chemosensation, chemosensation declines may occur with Alzheimer's disease, Parkinson's disease, and other neurological disorders (Nusbaum, 1999; Rawson, 2003).

TOUCH

Older adults may experience a decline in tactile sensitivity (Stevens, Alvarez-Reeves, Dipietro, Mack, & Green, 2003). Tactile and thermal sensitivity in the extremities, such as the toes or fingers, appears to decline at a greater rate than sensitivity to touch in other parts of the body, such as the lip (Stevens et al., 2003; Stevens & Choo, 1996, 1998). However, changes in sensations relating to touch have not been studied as extensively as other age-related changes. Declines in tactile sensitivity may limit sensory feedback, which could be influential on tasks utilizing fine motor skills, such as writing or using utensils (Nusbaum, 1999).

COGNITION AND MEMORY

Changes in cognition and memory may occur with age. Declines in cognitive performance and executive functioning of individuals throughout later life has been well documented and include declines in explicit memory, executive functioning, and information processing speed (e.g., Keller, 2006; Rowe & Kahn, 1998; Salthouse, 1996; Span, Ridderinkhof, & van der Molen, 2004; Zelazo, Craik, & Booth, 2004).

Concerns about memory and cognitive declines are common among older adults and are expressed equally among individuals with mild cognitive impairment and those with no significant cognitive impairment (Cargin, Maruff, Collie, & Masters, 2006). Although a large percentage of older adults experience declines in memory and cognition, significant cognitive declines are not detectable in a majority of older adults (Keller, 2006). A lack of motivation to perform as well as possible or one's acceptance of the stereotype that older adults can't perform as well as younger adults on some tasks may partially account for some of the memory and cognitive performance differences between younger and older adults (Bienenfeld, 1990; Chasteen, Bhattacharyya, Horhota, Tam, & Hasher, 2005). Additionally, declines in cognition and memory across the life span are highly variable among individuals.

Changes in memory or cognitive functioning may sometimes be compensated for by using accommodative strategies (Salthouse, 1998). For example, older adults experiencing difficulty dividing attention between tasks can focus on completing one task at a time. Declines in memory and cognition may become problematic, however, if three criteria are met: dramatic changes in memory and cognitive functioning in a short period of time, measured performance on tasks that are at least 2 standard deviations below a comparative group's mean, and an inability to perform normal activities due to the cognitive and memory declines (Salthouse, 1998).

Sleep

Adults are at greater risk for sleep disorders as they age. In a study of over 9,000 community-dwelling older adults in the United States, over half were found to experience chronic sleep disruptions (Foley et al., 1995). Women are more likely to report sleep problems but less likely to nap during the day than men (Foley et al., 1995). These authors found that 19.2% of the participants had difficulty falling asleep, 29.7% awakened during the night, 18.8% awakened too early, 24.6% took naps during the day, 12.7% did not feel rested after awakening from sleep, 42.7% had difficulty initiating or maintaining sleep, and 28.7% reported insomnia. Insomnia appears to be more prevalent among older adults who are in poor health and take medications (Ancoli-Israel & Cooke, 2005). Symptoms of depression, physical disabilities, respiratory symptoms, and poorer health were associated with a higher frequency of overall sleep complaints.

The architecture of older adult sleep differs from that of younger adults. An examination of the sleep cycles of older adults reveals more fragmented patterns of sleep. Older adults also experience a shorter duration of stage 3 and stage 4 slow-wave sleep (Ancoli-Israel & Cooke, 2005; Neubauer, 1999), the deeper stages of sleep. The duration of REM sleep does not appear to change with aging. In general, older adults tend to experience less total nighttime sleep than do younger adults. However, there is no reason to believe that they require less sleep. They are also more likely to nap during the daytime.

A variety of factors can disrupt sleep (e.g., pain, medical illnesses, psychiatric disorders, alcohol, medications, nicotine, and poor sleep habits; Neubauer, 1999). Individuals with dementia, for example, experience an increased number of awakenings and an increased proportion of stage 1 sleep (Mathews, Adetunji, Budur, Mathews, & Ramachandran, 2004). Depression and anxiety are associated with an increased risk of insomnia (Ford & Kamerow, 1989).

Insufficient sleep can significantly impact the daily functioning of an older adult. For example, it is associated with a greater need to nap, impaired cognitive abilities, slowed reaction time, impaired interpersonal relationships, and increased mortality (Ancoli-Israel & Cooke, 2005). One should not assume that poor sleep is simply due to aging. A discussion of the sleep difficulties and a thorough sleep history that focuses on possible contributing factors are warranted.

Interested readers are referred to www.sleepfoundation.org and www.asda.org for more information on sleep and its disorders.

Age-Related Health and Medical Issues

Approximately 88% of older adults report having at least one chronic medical condition (King, Rejeski, & Buchner, 1998). Generally, women have a higher prevalence of chronic disease than men. For instance, of 1,000 males over 65, approximately 380 report arthritic symptoms, whereas approximately 517 women report similar symptoms (National Center for Health Statistics [NCHS], 1995). This gender difference could be due in part to older women frequently living longer than older men, or it could be due to psychosocial factors, such as older women having lived with less paid employment, less strenuous physical activity, and a greater feeling of vulnerability to illness (Verbrugge, 1990).

The five most common chronic illnesses for women over 65, in order of prevalence, are arthritis, hypertension, all types of heart disease (coronary heart disease, angina, myocardial infarction), any type of cancer, and sinusitis. For men over 65, the five most common, in order of prevalence, are hypertension, arthritis, all types of heart disease, any type of cancer, and diabetes (NCHS, 2004). It is important for mental health professionals to have some knowledge of the common chronic diseases among older adults to understand how these could impact assessment and treatment. Additionally, it is important to be aware of commonly used medications, their adverse effects, and how their interaction may produce adverse effects. Finally, it is important to understand the relations between physical diseases and their psychiatric manifestations.

COMMON CHRONIC DISEASES AMONG OLDER ADULTS

Arthritis   Arthritis is delineated as either osteoarthritis or rheumatoid arthritis. Osteoarthritis is the more common condition. Approximately half of older adults over 65 have osteoarthritis in at least one joint (University of Pittsburgh Medical Center [UPMC], 2006). Women are more likely than men to develop osteoarthritis. There also are cultural differences regarding who is more likely to develop the disease. For example, Whites are at the highest risk for developing osteoarthritis, and African American women are more likely than White women to develop osteoarthritis in the knee, and less likely to develop this disease in the hand (UPMC, 2006).

Rheumatoid arthritis is an autoimmune disease that usually affects the same joint on both sides of the body. Risk factors for rheumatoid arthritis include long-term smoking, family history of the disease, and a history of persistent depression. With either type of arthritis, one usually has to limit activities, deal with chronic pain, and depend on others for tasks such as writing. In older adults, arthritis can combine with other age-related declines, such as sensory impairments, to produce a high level of disability (Taylor, 1999). These consequences of arthritis have implications for both assessment and treatment. It is important to recognize that arthritis may affect an older adult's ability to write and perform well on manual dexterity or motor speed tasks. Arthritis may also negatively affect sleep quality (sleep latency and efficiency), which has recently been linked to all-cause mortality in adults over 60 (Dew et al., 2003). Additionally, older adults with arthritis may be limited in the number and frequency of pleasant activities they can perform, which may make treatment planning more difficult. These functional limitations could lead to depression and social isolation.

Diseases of the Cardiovascular System   Cardiovascular disease (CVD) refers to diseases of the heart and can include coronary artery disease, hypertension, heart failure, peripheral vascular disease, and cardiac arrhythmia (National Institutes of Health [NIH], 2006; UPMC, 2006). Heart disease is one of the leading causes of death in the United States and is often caused by atherosclerosis, a common CVD. Blood clots often form with atherosclerosis, which decrease blood flow. These blood clots, which often break up and travel through the artery, can lead to myocardial infarction (heart attack) or angina (chest pain).

Congestive heart failure occurs when the heart is unable to pump the required amount of blood throughout the body. This causes blood to back up in the veins and leads to edema (swelling), usually first apparent in the feet, ankles, and legs. In this condition, the heart does not work as efficiently as it used to, thereby causing the individual to easily become short of breath or tired when engaging in activities (American Heart Association, 2006). Individuals diagnosed with congestive heart failure may need to make considerable lifestyle changes, which may affect quality of life. Finding ways to accommodate these lifestyle changes are appropriate goals for a treatment plan. A client with congestive heart failure may experience certain cognitive declines, which may need to be taken into account during the assessment process. In one study, individuals with congestive heart failure had cognitive deficits in the areas of working memory, attention, learning, executive functioning, and psychomotor speed (Bennett, Sauve, & Shaw, 2005).

Hypertension is often referred to simply as high blood pressure and often occurs as a result of arteriosclerosis, though there can be other causes. Arteriosclerosis is commonly referred to as "hardening of the arteries." Hypertension exerts stress on the heart, lungs, brain, kidneys, and blood vessels, which eventually may lead to damage in these organs. Hypertension can also have significant cognitive consequences. In one longitudinal study, older adults with hypertension showed a faster decline in logical reasoning tasks (ability to solve problems) compared to those within a normal blood-pressure range. Older adults with hypertension may have diminished cognitive function in other domains (e.g., nonverbal memory, motor speed, and manual dexterity; Waldstein, Brown, Maier, & Katzel, 2005). Additionally, Kuo et al. (2005) found that hypertension was associated with quicker decline on a measure of physical function (SF-36).

Cerebrovascular Disease   Cerebrovascular disease causes damage to the blood vessels in the brain, often resulting in a stroke. A stroke is defined as an interruption of blood supply to any part of the brain and is also referred to as a cerebrovascular accident (NIH, 2006). The most common type of stroke is an ischemic stroke. An ischemic stroke is caused by arteries clogged by fatty deposits (atherosclerosis). A second type of stroke is a hemorrhagic stroke, which results from bleeding in the brain. In a hemorrhagic stroke, small blood vessels in the brain become weak and burst. Individuals with hypertension are at the highest risk of stroke, and risk increases with age, family history of stroke, smoking, diabetes, high cholesterol, and heart disease. If blood flow to the brain is stopped for more than a few seconds, brain cells die, which could lead to permanent damage.

Strokes can lead to memory impairment and vascular dementia. It is appropriate to refer a client to a neuropsychologist for a more thorough evaluation of the client's memory complaints and to determine whether the stroke is contributing to the client's memory problems. Often, a current medical examination is also required to rule out other possible causes of the memory impairment.

Chronic Obstructive Pulmonary Disease   Chronic obstructive pulmonary disease (COPD) includes a group of lung diseases that often limit airflow and lead to varying degrees of air sac enlargement, inflammation, and lung tissue destruction. The most common forms of COPD are emphysema and bronchitis (UPMC, 2006). Common symptoms include shortness of breath, lasting from a few months to a number of years, wheezing, coughing, and decreased exercise tolerance. Chronic obstructive pulmonary disease can lead to cardiac arrhythmia, pneumonia, or dependence on mechanical ventilation. As with diseases of the cardiovascular system, COPD can limit one's ability to engage in physical activity. Individuals with these disorders may present for treatment for anxiety or depression due to the lifestyle changes often required by these disorders.

Diabetes Mellitus   Diabetes mellitus is a disease characterized by hyperglycemia (high blood sugar levels). Individuals with diabetes usually do not make enough insulin, or their body does not use insulin properly, which leads to the hyperglycemia. Diabetes mellitus is divided into Type 1 diabetes (insulin-dependent) and Type 2 diabetes (non-insulin-dependent). Type 2 diabetes is more prevalent in older adults than Type I Diabetes. Older adults with diabetes may show declines in processing speed and verbal memory. Prior to age 70, the potential decline in cognitive functioning can be controlled in diabetics with antidiabetic treatments that control blood glucose levels. After age 70, diabetes may contribute to pathological changes that may lead to vascular dementia or Alzheimer's disease (Messier, 2005). A recent review of the literature on Type 2 diabetes and cognitive decline provides further support for this relationship, but many of the studies in this area lacked a control group, and this research is particularly lacking in women with Type 2 diabetes (Coker & Shumaker, 2003).

MEDICATION USE AMONG OLDER ADULTS

Adults over 65 buy 30% of all prescription drugs and 40% of all over-the-counter (OTC) drugs, yet represent only 13% of the U.S. population (U.S. Food and Drug Administration [FDA], 1997). Because many older adults have more chronic illnesses than do younger adults, adults over 65 consume more prescription and OTC medications than any other age group. Older adults often have multiple medications to manage, which can lead to potentially serious side effects and interactions.

Side Effects   Older adults can be particularly sensitive to the effects of certain medications due to age-related changes in organ function and loss of muscle tissue that may affect the concentration level of the drug in the blood (FDA, 1997). For example, older adults absorb medications at a slower rate than younger adults, which may result in an increase in the time it takes for the drug to go into effect (American Geriatrics Society, 2002). Older adults also have an increase in receptor sensitivity for many medications (Lawson, 1991). Older adults are at high risk for medication complications due to their changing physiology, comorbid medical illnesses, and psychosocial losses (Pinals, 2001).

Many drugs have a potential side effect of cognitive impairment, which can complicate the assessment of dementia or self-reported memory complaints. Certain classes of drugs have an increased risk of side effects of cognitive impairment in older adults, including benzodiazepines, opioids, anticholinergics, and tricyclic antidepressants (Gray, Lai, & Larson, 1997). It is recommended that older adults not be prescribed tricyclic depressants, such as Elavil, because of the anticholinergic actions of these drugs. Certain cardiovascular drugs (e.g., quinidine, tocainide, and lidocaine) produce side effects of delirium, confusion, delusions, and hallucinations. Additionally, antiparkinsonian agents (e.g., levodopa) may produce serious side effects, including hallucinations, illusions, insomnia, and psychotic symptoms, which are often more prevalent in individuals at an advanced Parkinson's stage (Gray et al., 1997). The fact that many older adults are on multiple medications increases the likelihood of side effects. In addition, these side effects may be more severe in older adults. It is important for the clinician to determine whether presenting symptoms are indicative of a psychological problem or due to medication adverse effects, or both.

Interactions   The FDA (1997) has warned that, of all the other problems older adults face when taking medications, medication interaction is the most serious.

This is especially troublesome given that the average older adult is taking four prescription medications plus two OTC medications (FDA, 1997). Taking multiple medications is often unavoidable, and potential interactions always should be considered. For example, taking antacids can interfere with the absorption of certain drugs for Parkinson's disease, heart disease, and high blood pressure. Risk factors, such as moderate alcohol consumption, can increase adverse drug reactions by as much as 24% (Onder, Landi, Della Vedova, Atkinson, & Pedone, 2002). Many older adults consider complementary and alternative medicine to treat some of their medical illnesses. Herbal supplements can interact with prescription and OTC medications (Bressler, 2005). Thus, clinicians need to be aware of all the medications that are being taken by an older adult, including alternative medicines (e.g., herbal remedies).

Medication Adherence   As mentioned, older adults are prescribed more medications than any other age group and often do not respond appropriately to the medication because of poor adherence. In a study of more than 3,000 adults over 65 in 11 countries, approximately 12.5% of participants reported not fully adhering to their medication regimen (Cooper et al., 2005). Nonadherence rates as high as 45% have been reported (Morrow, Leirer, & Sheikh, 1988). Other researchers have proposed that self-reported medication adherence is a belief-laden construct, which is best predicted by personal health locus of control beliefs and not by medical factors (McDonald-Miszczak, Maki, & Gould, 2000).

Several researchers (e.g., Park, Morrell, Frieske, & Kincaid, 1992) have examined the effect of external cognitive supports on medication adherence. These researchers found that young-old adults demonstrated a high rate of adherence, which was not enhanced by various external supports, such as an organizational chart and/or a medication organizer. However, old-old participants had a lower rate of adherence (by about 10%) and frequently did not adhere to their regimen because of forgetting to take medications. As mentioned, beliefs about medication adherence, rather than medical factors such as number of medications, can be an important factor in determining adherence. McDonald-Miszczak, Maris, Fitzgibbon, and Ritchie (2004) found that older adults with a higher perceived ability to relate to their health care professionals placed a higher level of importance on medication adherence and took their medical conditions more seriously. Clinicians working with older adults may consider asking about medication adherence and providing suggestions (e.g., medication organizer, talking pill box) to older adults to increase their adherence.

PSYCHIATRIC MANIFESTATIONS OF PHYSICAL DISEASE

As previously noted, it is important for the clinician to appreciate the nature and presentation of the more common, and the chronic, diseases of older adulthood. Some of these diseases (e.g., COPD, diabetes mellitus, cancer, hypothyroidism, and coronary artery disease) can be preceded by a psychiatric disorder, occur as a comorbid disorder, occur as a manifestation of the physical disease, or result in psychiatric disorders. We discuss a few of these disorders to illustrate the importance of acquiring this information and using it in the context of one's assessment and formulation of interventions.

PARKINSON'S DISEASE

Depression can be the initial presenting complaint of individuals with Parkinson's disease. Starkstein, Preziosi, Bolduc, and Robinson (1990) reported that 29% of their participants with Parkinson's disease had a history of depression *prior to* the appearance of any motor symptoms. Todes and Lee (1985) reported similar premorbid findings. Parkinson's disease is also often accompanied by depression (Frazer, Leicht, & Baker, 1996; Leentjens, 2004), with an estimated 41% of individuals with Parkinson's disease displaying either major depression (50%) or dysthymia (50%; Starkstein et al., 1990). The presentation of depression in Parkinson's disease is more likely to be characterized by greater anxiety and "less self-punitive ideation" than the depression seen among individuals without Parkinson's disease (Cummings, 1992). Anxiety, particularly generalized anxiety, panic, and social phobia disorders, are often associated with Parkinson's disease (Walsh & Bennett, 2001). Approximately 40% of Parkinson's disease patients experience anxiety disorders (Richard, Schiffer, & Kurlan, 1996).

CANCER

The prevalence rates for depression among cancer patients ranges from 6% to 41% (McDaniel, Musselman, Porter, Reed, & Nemeroff, 1995); these rates vary depending on whether somatic criteria are included (Rodin, Craven, & Littlefield, 1993). The teasing apart of symptoms can be aided by knowledge of the presentations of cancer and depressive symptoms (Koven, Shreve-Neiger, & Edelstein, in press). For example, if fatigue is worse in the morning, depression may be the causal factor; if insomnia does not appear to be caused by pain, depression might be a likely cause (Edelstein, Martin, & Koven, 2003). A diagnosis of pancreatic cancer can be preceded by symptoms of anxiety (Passik & Roth, 1999) and depression (Gillam, 1990; Holland et al., 1986). Depression also can precede lung (Hughes, 1985), head, and neck cancer (Davies, Davies, & Delpo, 1986). The side effects of cancer treatment (e.g., anorexia, fatigue, insomnia; Frazer et al., 1996; Greenberg, 1989) and the pain associated with cancer can often complicate the assessment of depression.

CHRONIC OBSTRUCTIVE PULMONARY DISEASE

Depression and anxiety are common symptoms associated with COPD. Approximately 25% to 50% of individuals with COPD experience depressive symptoms (Murrell, Himmelfarb, & Wright, 1983). Van Manen et al. (2002) found that patients with severe COPD are 2.5 times more likely to experience depression than are control patients. The inability to get sufficient oxygen is one of the symptoms of COPD. Thus, anxiety associated with COPD is often related to the hypoxia and dyspnea that result from oxygen deprivation (Frazer et al., 1996). The anxiety-related attempts by patients to increase their oxygen intake can further burden the respiratory system, which can, in turn, exacerbate respiratory distress and anxiety (Frazer et al., 1996).

DIABETES MELLITUS

A meta-analysis by Anderson, Freedland, Clouse, and Lustman (2001) revealed that having diabetes doubles the odds of developing comorbid depression when compared with individuals without diabetes. The lifetime risk of developing depression among individuals with diabetes is approximately 32% (Frazer et al., 1996; Lustman, Griffith, Clouse, & Cryer, 1986). The depression has its own unfortunate sequelae, often resulting in impaired cognitive and physical functioning and poorer compliance with dietary and medical regimens (Ciechanowski, Katon, & Russo, 2000). Finally, individuals with diabetes and depression have a greater likelihood of developing diabetic complications than individuals without depression (de Groot, Anderson, Freedland, Clouse, & Lustman, 2001).

CARDIOVASCULAR DISEASE

Depression often precedes coronary heart disease in men. Ford and colleagues (1998) found that men who reported clinical depression were 2.12 times more likely to develop coronary disease than men who did not report depression, and 2.12 times more likely to experience a subsequent myocardial infarction (heart attack). The latter relation held even when the depression preceded the myocardial infarction by 10 years. In a study of 100 stable outpatients with coronary heart disease, Bankier, Januzzi, and Littman (2004) found frequent comorbid psychiatric diagnoses among the patients, with a mean of 1.7 psychiatric disorders per patient. The following percentages of disorders were found: "single past major depressive episode (29%), current dysthymic disorder (15%), recurrent major depressive disorder with current major depressive episode (31%), current alcohol abuse (19%), posttraumatic stress disorder (29%), current generalized anxiety disorder (24%), current binge-eating disorder (10%), and current primary insomnia (13%)" (p. 645).

SOCIAL RELATIONSHIPS

The social relationships of older adults are different in nature and structure than those of younger adults (e.g., Antonucci, 2001). The number of social contacts decreases with age, but the quality of these relationships and the amount of emotional support that stems from these relationships generally remain stable with age (e.g., Antonucci, 1990; Bossé, Aldwin, Levenson, Spiro, & Mroczek, 1993). Older adults actively select which relationships will provide them with the most rewards. This selection process often starts in young adulthood (Carstensen, 1992). Changes in social relationships in older adulthood have implications for therapy with older adults. It is important to determine who is potentially available in a client's network as a source of social support (Antonucci, 2001), and it is helpful to know the structure of an older adult's social network to better understand his or her social relationships and some of the reasons he or she may have sought therapy.

SOCIAL RELATIONSHIPS AND HEALTH

Relation to Physical Health   Social relationships among older adults serve as a protective buffer against physical health problems (Berkman & Syme, 1979). Older adults who reported having at least one confidant are less likely to have deficits in basic activities of daily living and stamina and mobility. In addition, subjective reports of higher social interaction adequacy are protective against strength and range-of-motion declines (Hays, Saunders, Flint, Kaplan, & Blazer, 1997). Members of older adults' social networks can exert a positive influence on their health behaviors (Hays et al., 1997). Older adults identify, on average, three to five individuals in their social networks who exert a positive influence on their health behaviors, by either encouraging them to engage in healthy behaviors or discouraging them from engaging in unhealthy behaviors (Tucker, 2002).

The absence of meaningful social interactions can also affect the health of older adults. For example, Sorkin, Rook, and Lu (2002) found that greater loneliness and low levels of emotional support and companionship contributed to an increased probability of having a diagnosed heart condition. Consistent with these results, Seeman (2000), in a comprehensive review of the literature, concluded that social relationships among older adults have the potential for both health-promoting and health-damaging effects. Therefore, it is important to identify individuals in older adults' social network who are encouraging them to maintain healthy behaviors, particularly if those individuals can be incorporated into treatment goals involving pleasant events scheduling or other forms of behavioral activation.

Relation to Mental Health   Among older adults, having fewer social support resources is related to higher levels of depression and higher levels of suicidal ideation (Vanderhorst & McLaren, 2005). Vanderhorst and McLaren examined the contribution of marital status, social support resources, and "sense of belonging" in the community in the prediction of depressive symptoms and suicidal ideation. Many researchers have argued in support of the beneficial effects of marriage on mental health (e.g., Peters & Liefbroer, 1997). Interestingly, Vanderhorst and McLaren found that social support was predictive of depressive symptoms and suicidal ideation above and beyond what is predicted by marital status. Thus, social support appears to offer an additional protective contribution beyond what is contributed by marital status.

It is important for older adults to maintain friendships outside of their current living situation for their mental health. For example, social support from friends living outside of a retirement community has been associated with lower levels of depression, when compared to individuals who had friends only within the retirement community (Potts, 1997). Higher levels of social support appear to be related to lower levels of depressive symptoms. Thus, an older adult with high levels of social support may not be the typical client seen for treatment of depression. Indeed, low levels of social support have been related to a higher probability of seeking appropriate mental health services (Phillips & Murrell, 1994). Therefore, those who are not satisfied with their current level of social support are more likely to seek mental health services, making an understanding of social support networks in older adults that much more important.

GENDER DIFFERENCES IN OLDER ADULT SOCIAL RELATIONSHIPS

Many authors (e.g., Moen, 2001; Turk-Charles, Rose, & Gatz, 1996) have highlighted important gender differences in older adult social relationships. Many of these gender differences are also present in younger adults, such as women reporting more confidants than men. However, some gender differences are particular to older adult social relationships, such as the increased emotional support older adult women receive from their children and grandchildren (Turk-Charles et al., 1996).

When conceptualizing an older adult's presenting problems, it is important to be aware of both the general social changes that occur with age and how these changes may manifest differently across genders. For instance, older women report a greater intimacy with their social contacts than do older men and generally report more confidants than men (Candy, Troll, & Levy, 1981). However, older men are more likely to have a larger number of acquaintances (Vaux, 1985). Women are also more likely to report stronger bonds and more contact with their children and grandchildren (Turk-Charles et al., 1996). For older women, the larger amount of social support they experienced when younger may lead to a stronger feeling of isolation in older adulthood, as social support generally decreases for both men and women in very old age (Turk-Charles et al., 1996). This occurs in both White and African American populations, with older women becoming more depressed than older men when dealing with the loss of close members of their social support networks (Husaini et al., 1991).

Negative Social Interactions

Recently, more attention has been paid to the impact of negative social interactions. For many years researchers assumed that all social relationships were beneficial, but recent research indicates that negative social interactions can have an impact on older adult emotional health (e.g., Newsom, Nishishiba, Morgan, & Rook, 2003; Rook, 1990). Although negative exchanges occur with less frequency than positive social exchanges among older adults (Rook, 2001), negative exchanges more consistently affect both daily positive and daily negative mood ratings, whereas positive exchanges affect only daily positive exchanges. Moreover, Newsom et al. found that positive exchanges are more likely to have an immediate impact on positive affect, whereas negative exchanges have a longer lasting impact, sometimes lasting a few months after the negative interaction occurred.

More recent research provides support for the disproportional impact of negative interactions on emotional well-being (Newsom, Rook, Nishishiba, Sorkin, & Mahan, 2005), with negative interactions related to both reduced well-being and higher ratings of psychological distress. From an intervention standpoint, it is important to keep in mind that negative interactions encountered by certain individuals are relatively stable across a number of years, indicating that for some individuals, social interactions are a source of chronic stress. For older adults, these relationships may be particularly difficult to terminate (Krause & Rook, 2003). Additionally, older adults who report negative interactions in one relationship are likely to report them across many relationships. Overall, the nature and number of social relationships among older adults are important considerations, whether one is broadly examining their influences on physical and mental health or seeking sources of conflict that have contributed to the presenting problem.

ASSESSMENT CONSIDERATIONS

Most of our current psychological assessment instruments were created with, and for use with, individuals under 65 (young adults). The field has been slow to respond to the paucity of instruments created for older adults, or at least developed with appropriate older adult normative data. Few of the instruments developed for young adults have adequate psychometric support for their use with older adults. Though all psychometric characteristics are important, norms, content validity, and construct validity should receive considerable attention when selecting assessment instruments. One more factor to consider is that many of the available self-report assessment instruments are inadequate when used with cognitively impaired older adults. In light of that, we discuss assessment and measurement issues that one should consider when selecting an assessment instrument for use with older adults.

Assessment Methods

Psychologists have long been encouraged to use multiple methods of assessment (e.g., Campbell & Fiske, 1959; Haynes & O'Brien, 2000) to ensure accurate, reliable, and valid information. One of the principal reasons for this recommendation is that each method (e.g., interviews, direct observations, self-reports, reports by others, psychophysiological recordings) has strengths and weaknesses. Moreover, it is difficult to determine what the particular method is contributing to the outcome of the assessment (i.e., method variance). The weaknesses or idiosyncrasies of any single method can be minimized by using two or more assessment methods. In addition, each method can capture both unique and overlapping information.

This multimethod approach to assessment becomes constrained as the cognitive skills of the client diminish. The reliability and validity of self-report become questionable, ruling out interviews and the use of self-report instruments. There is a necessary shift from more traditional, nomothetic to more behavioral, idiographic assessment approaches as one moves from cognitively intact to cognitively impaired individuals (Edelstein et al., 2003). One must rely to a greater extent on reports by others (e.g., family, staff members) and on direct observation. In the latter case, one must turn to analyses of controlling environmental variables to explain or account for the client's behavior.

Normative Data   Attention to appropriate normative data is important because of age-related changes in abilities, knowledge, and experiences. For the same reason one would eschew adolescent norms when using an assessment instrument with a 30-year-old, one should do the same when using an assessment instrument with an 80-year-old when normative data are available only for adults up to age 65. Edelstein et al. (2003) have illustrated negative and positive bias of norms with the following examples. There are often age-related declines in fluid abilities, with older adults performing more poorly than younger adults on tasks that require these abilities. A clinician might administer a task that requires fluid abilities (e.g., matrix reasoning) to an older adult and conclude that he or she is experiencing cognitive deficits. In contrast, a clinician might administer a vocabulary test to an older adult and conclude that this is a particular strength of the individual. However, the clinician must consider the fact that crystallized intelligence (as indexed by vocabulary) is maintained in old age and often improves with age.

Reliability   The type of reliability that is probably most sensitive to age differences is internal consistency. One approach to increasing internal consistency estimates is to increase the number of items on an assessment instrument. Though time considerations may be a limiting factor for all age groups, fatigue and pain are more likely limiting factors for older adults. Older adults are more likely than younger adults to experience chronic diseases (e.g., arthritis) that can limit their participation. Reliability estimates may be low across age groups if items are interpreted differently due to differences in life experiences (i.e., cohort differences).

Content Validity   Content validity is one of the two most important types of validity to examine when considering using an assessment instrument with older adults that was developed for younger adults. Content validity represents the extent to which an assessment instrument samples the domain of interest. The item content must be relevant to the age period of the individuals being assessed. For example, a measure of depression should include items that represent the experience and behavior of older adults who are depressed. This is particularly important as there is evidence that psychological symptoms of disorders among older adults may differ from those of younger adults (Himmelfarb & Murrell, 1983). For example, some of the fears of older adults are not experienced by younger adults or may be experienced with less intensity or with less disruption of everyday activities (Kogan & Edelstein, 2004). Content validity problems also arise when an assessment instrument contains health-related items that are not the direct focus of the instrument. For example, scores on the Center for Epidemiologic Studies Depression scale can be affected by such health conditions as chronic lung disease, bone and joint disease, visual impairments, and peripheral vascular disease (Grayson, MacKinnon, Jorm, Creasey, & Broe, 2000), independent of depression.

Construct Validity   Measures of constructs can evidence age-related differences (Kaszniak, 1990). For example, the factor structure of instruments can change across age groups. Tulsky, Zhu, and Ledbetter (1997) reported age-related differences in factor loadings on the perceptual organization and processing speed factors of the Wechsler Adult Intelligence Scale—Third Edition. Construct validity must be established for the age group being assessed. It is important to remember that validity resides with the measures obtained, not with the instrument with which they are obtained.

SUMMARY

Older adults offer many challenges to the clinician, who is often inadequately prepared to incorporate the unique and often complex age-related factors into the assessment, case conceptualization, and intervention processes. The presence of physical diseases, their pharmacological treatment, and the potential psychological consequences of both contribute to the complexities of arriving at an accurate and valid conceptualization of an older adult's presenting problems. We have offered foundational knowledge and discussed relevant issues that should enable the reader to begin to meet the challenges of working with older adults. Interested readers are directed to the following web sites relevant to clinical practice with older adults: http://www.apa.org/pi/aging/publications.html#FactSheets and http://www.apa.org/pi/aging/practitioners.pdf.

REFERENCES

Administration on Aging. (2004, September). *Census 2000 data on the aging.* Retrieved June 10, 2006, from http://www.aoa.gov/prof/Statistics/Census2000/minority-sumstats.asp.

Agronin, M. E. (2004). Sexuality and aging. In J. Sadavoy, L. F. Jarvik, G. T. Grossberg, & B. S. Meyers (Eds.), *Comprehensive textbook of geriatric psychiatry* (pp. 789–814). New York: Norton.

American Geriatrics Society. (2002). *Age-related pharmacokinetic changes.* Retrieved June 1, 2006, from http://www.geriatricsyllabus.com/syllabus.

American Heart Association. (2006). *Congestive heart failure.* Retrieved May 30, 2006, from http://www.americanheart.org.

Ancoli-Israel, S., & Cooke, J. R. (2005). Prevalence and comorbidity of insomnia and effect on functioning in elderly populations. *Journal of the American Geriatrics Society, 53,* S264–S271.

Anderson, R. J., Freedland, K. E., Clouse, R. E., & Lustman, P. H. (2001). The prevalence of comorbid depression in adults with diabetes: A meta-analysis. *Diabetes Care, 24,* 1069–1078.

Antonucci, T. C. (1990). Social supports and social relationships. In R. H. Binstock & L. K. George (Eds.), *Handbook of aging and the social sciences* (pp. 205–226). San Diego: Academic Press.

Antonucci, T. C. (2001). Social relations: An examination of social networks, social support, and sense of control. In J. E. Birren & K. W. Schaie (Eds.), *Handbook of the psychology of aging* (pp. 427–453). San Diego: Academic Press.

Badeau, D. (1995). Illness, disability and sex in aging. *Sexuality and Disability, 13*(3), 219–237.

Bankier, B., Januzzi, J. L., & Littman, A. B. (2004). The high prevalence of multiple psychiatric disorders in stable outpatients with coronary heart disease. *Psychosomatic Medicine, 66,* 645–650.

Bennett, S. J., Sauve, M. J., & Shaw, R. M. (2005). A conceptual model of cognitive deficits in chronic heart failure. *Journal of Nursing Scholarship, 37,* 222–228.

Berkman, L. F., & Syme, S. L. (1979). Social networks, host resistance, and mortality: A nine-year follow-up study of Alameda County residents. *American Journal of Epidemiology, 109,* 186–204.

Beutel, M., Schumacher, J., Weidner, W., & Brähler, E. (2002). Sexual activity, sexual and part-nership satisfaction in ageing men: Results from a German representative community study. *Andrologia, 34*(1), 22–28.

Bienenfeld, D. (1990). Psychology of aging. In D. Bienenfeld (Ed.), *Verwoerdt's clinical geropsy-chology* geropsychiatry (3rd ed., pp. 26–34). Baltimore: Williams & Wilkins.

Bonnesen, J., & Burgess, E. (2004). Senior moments: The acceptability of an ageist phrase. *Journal of Aging Studies, 18*(2), 123.

Bortz, W. M., Wallace, D. H., & Wiley, D. (1999). Sexual function in 1,202 aging males: Differen-tiating aspects. *Journal of Gerontology: Series A, Biological Sciences and Medical Sciences, 54*(5), M237–M241.

Bossé, R., Aldwin, C. M., Levenson, M. R., Spiro, A., & Mroczek, D. K. (1993). Change in social support after retirement: Longitudinal findings from the normative aging study. *Journal of Gerontology, 46,* 9–14.

Bressler, R. (2005). Herb-drug interactions: Interactions between saw palmetto and prescription medications. *Geriatrics, 60,* 32–34.

Bretschneider, J. G., & McCoy, N. L. (1988). Sexual interest and behavior in healthy 80–102-year-olds. *Archives of Sexual Behavior, 17*(2), 109–129.

Brotman, S., Ryan, B., & Cormier, R. (2003). The health and social service needs of gay and lesbian elders and their families in Canada. *Gerontologist, 43*(2), 192–202.

Burgess, E. (2004). Sexuality in midlife and later life couples. In J. H. Harvey, A. Wenzel, & S. Sprecher (Eds.), *The handbook of sexuality in close relationships* (pp. 437–454). Mahwah, NJ: Erlbaum.

Campbell, D. T., & Fiske, D. W. (1959). Convergent and discriminant validation by the multitrait-multidimensional matrix. *Psychological Bulletin, 56,* 81–105.

Candy, S. G., Troll, L. E., & Levy, S. G. (1981). A developmental exploration of friendship functions in women. *Psychology of Women Quarterly, 5,* 456–472.

Cargin, J. W., Maruff, P., Collie, A., & Masters, C. (2006). Mild memory impairment in healthy older adults is distinct from normal aging. *Brain and Cognition, 60,* 146–155.

Carstensen, L. L. (1992). Social and emotional patterns in adulthood: Support for socioemotional selectivity theory. *Psychology and Aging, 7,* 331–338.

Chasteen, A. L., Bhattacharyya, S., Horhota, M., Tam, R., & Hasher, L. (2005). How feelings of stereotype threat influence older adults' memory performance. *Experimental Aging Research, 31,* 235–260.

Ciechanowski, P. S., Katon, W. J., & Russo, J. E. (2000). Depression and diabetes: Impact of depressive symptoms on adherence, function, and costs. *Archives of Internal Medicine, 160*(21), 3278–3285.

Coker, L. H., & Shumaker, S. A. (2003). Type 2 diabetes mellitus and cognition: An understudied issue in women's health. *Journal of Psychosomatic Research, 54,* 129–139.

Connelly, P. E. (2005). Hearing loss: Types of hearing loss. *Better Hearing Institute.* Retrieved June 1, 2006, from http://www.betterhearing.org/hearing_loss.

Cook, J., & Hawkins, D. (2006). Hearing loss and hearing aid treatment options. *Mayo Clinic Proceedings, 81*(2), 234–237.

Cooper, C., Carpenter, I., Katona, C., Schroll, M., Wagner, C., Fialova, D., et al. (2005). The AdHOC study of older adults' adherence to medication in 11 countries. *American Journal of Geriatric Psychiatry, 11,* 1067–1076.

Cummings, J. L. (1992). Depression and Parkinson's disease: A review. *American Journal of Psychiatry, 149,* 443–454.

Davies, A. D. M., Davies, C., & Delpo, M. C. (1986). Depression and anxiety in patients undergoing diagnostic investigations for head and neck cancers. *British Journal of Psychiatry, 149,* 491–493.

Davis, A. (2003). Population study of the ability to benefit from amplification and the provision of a hearing aid in 55–74 year-old first-time hearing aid users. *International Journal of Audiology, 42,* 39–52.

DeAngelis, S. (2002). Visual impairment in the older adult: Breaking down the barriers to communication. *Access, 16*(10), 36–39.

de Groot, M., Anderson, R., Freedland, K. E., Clouse, R. E., & Lustman, P. J. (2001). Association of depression and diabetes complications: A meta-analysis. *Psychosomatic Medicine, 63*(4), 619–630.

Desai, M., Pratt, L. A., Lentzner, H., & Robinson, K. N. (2001). Trends in vision and hearing among older Americans. *Aging Trends, No. 2.* Hyattsville, MD: National Center for Health Statistics. Retrieved June 1, 2006, from http://www.cdc.gov/nchs/data/agingtrends/02vision.pdf.

Dew, M. A., Hoch, C. C., Buysse, D. J., Monk, T. H., Begley, A. E., Houck, P. R., et al. (2003). Healthy older adults' sleep predicts all-cause mortality at 4 to 19 years of follow-up. *Psychosomatic Medicine, 65,* 63–73.

Edelstein, B., Martin, R. R., & Koven, L. P. (2003). Assessment in geriatric settings. In J. R. Graham & J. A. Naglieri (Eds.), *Comprehensive handbook of psychology:* Vol. 10. *Assessment psychology* (pp. 389–414). New York: Wiley.

Federal Interagency Forum on Aging-Related Statistics. (2004). *Older Americans 2004: Key indicators of well-being.* Washington, DC: U.S. Government Printing Office.

Foley, D. J., Monjan, A. A., Brown, S. L., Simonsick, E. M., Wallace, R. B., & Blazer, D. G. (1995). Sleep complaints among elderly persons: An epidemiologic study of three communities. *Sleep, 18,* 425–432.

Ford, D. E., & Kamerow, D. B. (1989). Epidemiologic study of sleep disturbances and psychiatric disorders: An opportunity for prevention? *Journal of the American Medical Association, 262,* 1479–1483.

Ford, D. E., Mead, L. A., Chang, P. P., Cooper-Patrick, L., Wang, N. Y., & Klag, M. J. (1998). Depression is a risk factor for coronary artery disease in men: The precursors study. *Archives of Internal Medicine, 158,* 1422–1426.

Frazer, D. W., Leicht, M. L., & Baker, M. D. (1996). Psychological manifestations of physical disease in the elderly. In L. L. Carstensen, B. A. Edelstein, & L. Dornbrand (Eds.), *The practical handbook of clinical gerontology* (pp. 217–235). Thousand Oaks, CA: Sage.

Fukunaga, A., Uematsu, H., & Sugimoto, K. (2005). Influences of aging on taste perception and oral somatic sensation. *Journal of Gerontology: Series A, Biological Sciences and Medical Sciences, 60A*(1), 109–113.

Gillam, J. H., III. (1990). Pancreatic disorders. In W. R. Hazzard, R. Andres, E. L. Bierman, & J. P. Blass (Eds.), *Principles of geriatric medicine and gerontology* (2nd ed., pp. 640–644). New York: McGraw-Hill.

Gordon-Salant, S. (2005). Hearing loss and aging: New research findings and clinical implications. *Journal of Rehabilitation Research and Development, 42*(4), 9–24.

Gray, S. L., Lai, K. V., & Larson, E. B. (1997). Drug-induced cognition disorders in the elderly: Incidence, prevention, and management. *Drug Safety, 21,* 101–122.

Grayson, D. A., MacKinnon, A., Jorm, A. F., Creasey, H., & Broe, G. A. (2000). Item bias in the Center for Epidemiologic Studies Depression Scale: Effects of physical disorders and disability in an elderly community sample. *Journal of Gerontology: Psychological Science and Social Science, 55*(5), P273–P282.

Greenberg, D. B. (1989). Depression and cancer. In R. G. Robinson & P. V. Rabins (Eds.), *Depression and coexisting disease* (pp. 103–115). New York: Igaku-Shoin.

Grossman, A. H., D'Augelli, A. R., & Hershberger, S. L. (2000). Social support networks of lesbian, gay, and bisexual adults 60 years of age and older. *Journal of Gerontology: Psychological Sciences, 55B*(3), P171–P179.

Haynes, S. N., & O'Brien, W. H. (2000). *Principles and practice of behavioral assessment.* New York: Springer.

Hays, J. C., Saunders, W. B., Flint, E. P., Kaplan, B. H., & Blazer, D. G. (1997). Social support and depression as risk factors for loss of physical function in later life. *Aging and Mental Health, 1,* 209–220.

He, W., Sengupta, M., Velkoff, V. A., & DeBarros, K. A. (2005). *Current population reports, 65+ in the United States: 2005.* Washington, DC: U.S. Government Printing Office.

Helfer, K., & Wilber, L. (1990). Hearing loss, aging, and speech perception in reverberation and noise. *Journal of Speech and Hearing Research, 33*(1), 149–155.

Himmelfarb, S. & Murrell, S. A. (1983) Reliability and validity of five mental health scales in older persons. *Journal of Gerontology, 38* 333-339.

Hinrichsen, G. A. (2006). Why multicultural issues matter for practitioners working with older adults. *Professional Psychology: Research and Practice, 37*(1), 29–35.

Holland, J. C., Korzun, A. H., Tross, S., Silberfarb, P., Perry, M., Comis, R., et al. (1986). Comparative psychological disturbance in patients with pancreatic and gastric cancer. *American Journal of Psychiatry, 143,* 982–986.

Hughes, J. E. (1985). Depressive illness and lung cancer. *European Journal of Surgical Oncology, 11,* 15–20.

Husaini, B. A., Moore, S. T., Castor, R. S., Neser, W., Whitten-Stovall, R., Linn, J. G., et al. (1991). Social density, stressors, and depression: Gender differences among the Black elderly. *Journals of Gerontology, 46,* P236–P242.

Johnson, M. J., Jackson, N. C., Arnette, J. K., & Koffman, S. D. (2005). Gay and lesbian perceptions of discrimination in retirement care facilities. *Journal of Homosexuality, 49*(2), 83–102.

Kasthurirangan, S., & Glasser, A. (2006). Age related changes in accommodative dynamics in humans. *Vision Research, 46*(8/9), 1507–1519.

Kaszniak, A.W. (1990). Psychological assessment of the aging individual. In J.E. Birren & K.W. Schaie (Eds.), *Handbook of the psychology of aging* (3rd. ed., pp. 427-445). New York: Academic Press

Keller, J. (2006). Age-related neuropathology, cognitive decline, and Alzheimer's disease. *Ageing Research Reviews, 5*(1), 1–13.

King, A. C., Rejeski, W. J., & Buchner, D. M. (1998). Physical activity interventions targeting older adults: A critical review and recommendations. *American Journal of Preventive Medicine, 15,* 315–333.

Kite, M., Stockdale, G., Whitley, B., & Johnson, B. (2005). Attitudes toward younger and older adults: An updated meta-analytic review. *Journal of Social Issues, 61*(2), 241–266.

Kline, D. W., & Li, W. (2005). Cataracts and the aging driver. *Ageing International, 30*(2), 105–121.

Kogan, J., & Edelstein, B. (2004). Modification and psychometric examination of a self-report measure of fear in older adults. *Journal of Anxiety Disorders, 18,* 397–409.

Koven, L. P., Shreve-Neiger, A., & Edelstein, B. (in press). Interview of older adults. In M. Hersen (Ed.), *Handbook of interviewing: Adults.* Thousand Oaks, CA: Sage.

Kramer, S. E., Kapteyn, T. S., Kuik, D. J., & Deeg, D. J. H. (2002). The association of hearing impairment and chronic diseases with psychosocial health status in older age. *Journal of Aging and Health, 14*(1), 122–137.

Krause, N., & Rook, K. S. (2003). Negative interaction in late life: Issues in the stability and generalization of conflict across relationships. *Journals of Gerontology: Series B, Psychological Sciences and Social Sciences, 58,* 88–99.

Kuo, H. K., Jones, R. N., Milberg, W. P., Tennstedt, S., Talbot, L., Morris, J. N., et al. (2005). Effect of blood pressure and diabetes mellitus on cognitive and physical functions in older adults: A longitudinal analysis of the advanced cognitive training for independent and vital elderly cohort. *Journal of the American Geriatrics Society, 53,* 1154–1161.

Lawson, D. H. (1991). Epidemiology. In D. M. Davies (Ed.), *Textbook of adverse drug reactions* (4th ed., p. 11). New York: Oxford University Press.

Leentjens, A. F. G. (2004). Depression in Parkinson's disease: Conceptual issues and clinical challenges. *Journal of Geriatric Psychiatry and Neurology, 17,* 120–126.

Levy, B. R. (2003). Mind matters: Cognitive and physical effects of aging self-stereotypes. *Journal of Gerontology: Psychological Sciences, 58B*(4), P203–P211.

Lustman, P. J., Griffith, L. S., Clouse, R. E., & Cryer, P. E. (1986). Psychiatric illness in diabetes mellitus: Relationship to symptoms and glucose control. *Journal of Nervous and Mental Diseases, 174,* 736–742.

Markson, E. W. (1993). Physiological changes, illness, and health care use in later life. In B. B. Hess & E. W. Markson (Eds.), *Growing old in America* (pp. 173–186). New Brunswick, NJ: Transaction.

Marsiglio, W., & Donnelly, D. (1991). Sexual relations in later life: A national study of married persons. *Journal of Gerontology, 46*(6), S338–S344.

Mathews, M., Adetunji, B., Budur, K., Maghews, M., & Ramachandran, S. (2004). An overview of sleep disorders in the older patient. *Clinical Geriatrics, 12*(9), 37–42.

Matthias, R. E., Lubben, J. E., Atchison, K. A., & Schweitzer, S. O. (1997). Sexual activity and satisfaction among very old adults: Results from a community-dwelling Medicare population survey. *Gerontologist, 37*(1), 6–14.

McDaniel, J. S., Musselman, D. L., Porter, M. R., Reed, D. A., & Nemeroff, C. B. (1995). Depression in patients with cancer: Diagnosis, biology, and treatment. *Archives of General Psychiatry, 52,* 88–99.

McDonald-Miszczak, L., Maki, A. S., & Gould, N. O. (2000). Self-reported medication adherence and health status in late adulthood: The role of beliefs. *Experimental Aging Research, 26,* 189–207.

McDonald-Miszczak, L., Maris, P., Fitzgibbon, T., & Ritchie, G. (2004). A pilot study examining older adults' beliefs related to medication adherence: The BERMA survey. *Journal of Aging and Health, 16,* 591–614.

Messier, C. (2005). Impact of impaired glucose tolerance and Type 2 diabetes on cognitive aging. *Neurobiology of Aging, 26,* 26–30.

Moen, P. (2001). The gendered life course. In R. H. Binstock & L. K. George (Eds.), *Handbook of aging and the social sciences* (pp. 179–196). San Diego: Academic Press.

Mojet, J., Christ-Hazelhof, E., & Heidema, J. (2001). Taste perception with age: Generic or specific losses in threshold sensitivity to the five basic tastes? *Chemical Senses, 26*(7), 845–860.

Morrow, D. G., Leirer, V. O., & Sheikh, J. (1988). Adherence and medication instructions: Review and recommendations. *Journal of the American Geriatrics Society, 36,* 1147–1160.

Murrell, S. A., Himmelfarb, S., & Wright, K. (1983). Prevalence of depression and its correlates in older adults. *American Journal of Epidemiology, 117,* 173–185.

National Center for Health Statistics. (1995). *Prevalence of selected chronic conditions by age and sex.* Retrieved May 30, 2006, from http://www.cdc.gov/nchs/agingact.htm.

National Center for Health Statistics. (2004). *Prevalence of selected chronic conditions by age, sex, and race/ethnicity.* Retrieved May 30, 2006, from http://www.cdc.gov/nchs/agingact.htm.

National Council on the Aging. (1999, May). *The consequences of untreated hearing loss in older persons.* Washington, DC: National Council on the Aging. Retrieved May 5, 2006, from http://www.ncoa.org/attachments/UntreatedHearingLossReport %2Edoc.

National Eye Institute. (2005). *Age-related macular degeneration: What you should know.* U.S. Department of Health and Human Services. Retrieved June 27, 2006, from http://www.nei.nih.gov/health/maculardegen/webAMD.pdf.

National Institutes of Health. (2006). *MedlinePlus medical encyclopedia.* Retrieved May 30, 2006, from http://www.nlm.nih.gov/medlineplus/encyclopedia.html.

Neubauer, D. N. (1999). Sleep problems in the elderly. *American Family Physician, 59*(9), 2551–2560.

Newsom, J. T., Nishishiba, M., Morgan, D. L., & Rook, K. S. (2003). The relative importance of three domains of positive and negative social exchanges: A longitudinal model with comparable measures. *Psychology and Aging, 18,* 746–754.

Newsom, J. T., Rook, K. S., Nishishiba, M., Sorkin, D. H., & Mahan, T. L. (2005). Understanding the relative importance of positive and negative social exchanges: Examining specific domains and appraisals. *Journals of Gerontology: Series B, Psychological Sciences and Social Sciences, 60,* 304–312.

Nordin, S., Razani, L. J., Markison, S., & Murphy, C. (2003). Age-associated increases in intensity discrimination for taste. *Experimental Aging Research, 29,* 371–381.

Nusbaum, N. J. (1999). Aging and sensory senescence. *Southern Medical Journal, 92*(3), 267–275.

O'Donohue, W., & Graber, B. (1996). Sexual dysfunction. In M. Hersen & V. B. Van Hasselt (Eds.), *Psychological treatment of older adults: An introductory text* (pp. 299–313). New York: Plenum Press.

Onder, G., Landi, F., Della Vedova, C., Atkinson, H., & Pedone, C. (2002). Moderate alcohol consumption and adverse drug reactions among older adults. *Pharmacoepidemiology and Drug Safety, 11,* 385–392.

Ory, M., Kinney Hoffman, M., Hawkins, M., Sanner, B., & Mockenhaupt, R. (2003). Challenging aging stereotypes: Strategies for creating a more active society. *American Journal of Preventive Medicine, 25*(3, Suppl. 2), 164–171.

Ouslander, J. G. (1983). Psychiatric manifestations of physical illness in the elderly. *Psychiatric Medicine, 1*(4), 363–388.

Owsley, C., McGwin, G., Scilley, K., Dreer, L. E., Bray, C. R., & Mason, J. O. (2006). Focus groups with persons who have age-related macular degeneration: Emotional issues. *Rehabilitation Psychology, 51*(1), 23–29.

Park, D. C., Morrell, R. W., Frieske, D., & Kincaid, D. (1992). Medication adherence behaviors in older adults: Effects of external cognitive supports. *Psychology and Aging, 7,* 252–256.

Passik, S. D., & Roth, A. J. (1999). Anxiety symptoms and panic attacks preceding pancreatic cancer diagnosis. *Psycho-Oncology, 8,* 268–272.

Peters, A., & Liefbroer, A. C. (1997). Beyond marital status: Partner history and well-being in old age. *Journal of Marriage and the Family, 59,* 687–699.

Phillips, M. A., & Murrell, S. A. (1994). Impact of psychological and physical health, stressful events, and social support on subsequent mental health help seeking among older adults. *Journal of Consulting and Clinical Psychology, 62,* 270–275.

Pinals, S. L. (2001). Geriatric psychopharmacology: Antidepressant and antipsychotic medications in the elderly. *Journal of Geriatric Psychiatry, 34,* 43–59.

Portis, T. (2006). *Sensible strategies for better communication with people who are hard of hearing: American Academy of Audiology.* Retrieved June 1, 2006, from http://www.audiology.org/consumer/guides/communicating.php.

Potts, M. K. (1997). Social support and depression among older adults living alone: The importance of friends within and outside of a retirement community. *Social Work, 42,* 348–362.

Rawson, N. E. (2003). Age-related changes in perception of flavor and aroma. *Generations, 27*(1), 20–26.

Richard, I. H., Schiffer, R. B., & Kurlan, R. (1996). Anxiety and Parkinson's disease. *Journal of Neuropsychiatry & Clinical Neurosciences, 8,* 383–392.

Rodin, G., Craven, J., & Littlefield, C. (1993). *Depression in the medically ill.* New York: Brunner/Mazel.

Rook, K. S. (1990). Stressful aspects of older adults' social relationships: Current theory and research. In M. A. P. Stephens, J. H. Crowther, S. E. Hobfoll, & D. L. Tennenbaum (Eds.), *Stress and coping in later-life families* (pp. 173–192). Washington, DC: Hemisphere.

Rook, K. S. (2001). Emotional health and positive versus negative social exchanges: A daily diary analysis. *Applied Developmental Science, 5,* 86–97.

Rowe, J. W., & Devons, C. A. (1996). Physiological and clinical considerations of the geriatric patient. In E. W. Busse & D. G. Blazer (Eds.), *The American Psychiatric Press textbook of geriatric psychiatry* (2nd ed.) Washington, DC: American Psychiatric Press.

Rowe, J., & Kahn, R. (1998). *Successful aging.* New York: Pantheon Books.

Salthouse, T. A. (1996). The processing-speed theory of adult age differences in cognition. *Psychological Review, 103*(3), 403–428.

Salthouse, T. A. (1998). Cognitive and information-processing perspectives on aging. In I. H. Norduhus, G. R. VandenBos, S. Berg, & P. Fromholt (Eds.), *Clinical geropsychology.* Washington, DC: American Psychological Association.

Savikko, N., Routasalo, P., Tilvis, R., Strandberg, T., & Pitkälä, K. (2005). Predictors and subjective causes of loneliness in an aged population. *Archives of Gerontology and Geriatrics, 41*(3), 223–233.

Seeman, T. E. (2000). Health promoting effects of friends and family on health outcomes in older adults. *American Journal of Health Promotion, 14,* 362–370.

Smith, D. (2003). The older population in the United States: March 2002. *Current Population Reports,* 2–5. Washington, DC: Retrieved January 4, 2006, from http://www.census.gov/prod/2003pubs/p20–546.pdf.

Sorkin, D., Rook, K. S., & Lu, J. L. (2002). Loneliness, lack of emotional support, lack of companionship, and the likelihood of having a heart condition in an elderly sample. *Annals of Behavioral Medicine, 24,* 290–298.

Span, M., Ridderinkhof, K., & van der Molen, M. (2004). Age-related changes in the efficiency of cognitive processing across the life span. *Acta Psychologica, 117*(2), 155–183.

Starkstein, S. E., Preziosi, T. J., Bolduc, P. L., & Robinson, R. G. (1990). Depression in Parkinson's disease. *Journal of Nervous and Mental Disorders, 178,* 27–31.

Stevens, J., Alvarez-Reeves, M., Dipietro, L., Mack, G., & Green, B. (2003). Decline of tactile acuity in aging: A study of body site, blood flow, and lifetime habits of smoking and physical activity. *Somatosensory and Motor Research, 20*(3/4), 271–279.

Stevens, J., & Choo, K. (1996). Spatial acuity of the body surface over the life span. *Somatosensory and Motor Research, 13*(2), 153–166.

Stevens, J., & Choo, K. (1998). Temperature sensitivity of the body surface over the life span. *Somatosensory and Motor Research, 15*(1), 13–28.

Strawbridge, W. J., Wallhagen, M. I., Shema, S. J., & Kaplan, G. A. (2000). Negative consequences of hearing impairment in old age: A longitudinal analysis. *Gerontologist, 40*(3), 320–326.

Taylor, S. E. (1999). *Health psychology.* New York: McGraw-Hill.

Thornton, J. (2002). Myths of aging or ageist stereotypes. *Educational Gerontology, 28*(4), 301–312.

Todes, C. J., & Lee, A. J. (1985). The pre-morbid personality of patients with Parkinson's disease. *Journal of Neurological and Neurosurgical Psychiatry, 48,* 97–100.

Tucker, J. S. (2002). Health-related social control within older adults' relationships. *Journals of Gerontology: Series B, Psychological Sciences and Social Sciences, 57,* 387–395.

Tulsky, D., Zhu, J., & Ledbetter, M. F. (1997). *WAIS-III/WMS-III: Technical manual.* San Antonio, TX: Psychological Corporation.

Turk-Charles, S., Rose, T., & Gatz, M. (1996). The significance of gender in the treatment of older adults. In L. L. Cartsensen, B. A. Edelstein, & L. Dornbrand (Eds.), *The practical handbook of clinical gerontology* (pp. 107–128). Thousand Oaks, CA: Sage.

U.S. Census Bureau. (2004). *Global population profile: 2002—International population reports.* Washington, DC: U.S. Government Printing Office, U.S. Agency for International Development.

U.S. Food and Drug Administration. (1997). *Medications and older people.* Retrieved May 30, 2006, from http://www.fda.gov/fdac/features/1997/697_old.html.

University of Pittsburgh Medical Center. (2006). *Diseases and conditions.* Retrieved May 30, 2006, from http://www.upmc.com/DiseasesConditions.htm.

Vanderhorst, R. K., & McLaren, S. (2005). Social relationships as predictors of depression and suicidal ideation in older adults. *Aging and Mental Health, 9,* 517–525.

van Manen, J. G., Bindels, P. J. E., Dekker, F. W., Jzermans, C. J. I. van der Zee, J. S., & Schadé, E. (2002). Risk of depression in patients with chronic obstructive pulmonary disease and its determinants. *Thorax, 57,* 412–416.

Vaux, A. (1985). Variations in social support associated with gender, ethnicity, and age. *Journal of Social Issues, 41,* 89–110.

Verbrugge, L. M. (1990). The twain meet: Empirical explanations of sex differences in health and mortality. In M. G. Ory & H. R. Warner (Eds.), *Gender, health, and longevity: Multidisciplinary perspectives* (pp. 159–199). New York: Springer.

Waldstein, S. R., Brown, J. R. P., Maier, J. K., & Katzel, L. I. (2005). Diagnosis of hypertension and high blood pressure levels negatively affect cognitive function in older adults. *Annals of Behavioral Medicine, 29,* 174–180.

Walsh, K., & Bennett, G. (2001). Parkinson's disease and anxiety. *Postgraduate Medicine, 77,* 89–93.

Weale, R. A. (2003). Epidemiology of refractive errors and presbyopia. *Survey of Ophthalmology, 48*(5), 515–543.

Wei, J. (2004). Understanding the aging cardiovascular system. *Geriatrics and Gerontology International, 4*(Suppl. 1), S298–S303.

Whitbourne, S. K. (1998). Physical changes in the aging individual: Clinical implications. In I. H. Norduhus, G. R. VandenBos, S. Berg, & P. Fromholt (Eds.), *Clinical geropsychology*. Washington, DC: American Psychological Association.

Zelazo, P. D., Craik, F. I. M., & Booth, L. (2004). Executive function across the life span. *Acta Psychologica, 115,* 167–183.

CHAPTER 24

Insomnia

DANIEL J. TAYLOR, CHRISTINA M. McCRAE, PHILIP GEHRMAN,
NATALIE DAUTOVICH, AND KENNETH L. LICHSTEIN

DESCRIPTION OF THE DISORDER

Insomnia is typically characterized as a complaint of difficulty initiating or maintaining sleep, or nonrefreshing sleep. Chronic insomnia affects approximately 15.9% of adults, making it more prevalent than heart disease, cancer, AIDS, neurological disease, breathing problems, urinary problems, diabetes, and gastrointestinal problems (Lichstein, Durrence, Riedel, Taylor, & Bush, 2004). Insomnia is particularly pervasive in primary care clinics, where it is reported by as many 50% of patients (Katz & McHorney, 1998; Simon & VonKorff, 1997). Prevalence of insomnia in psychology clinics is currently unknown, but is likely at least as high as in medical clinics because it is a symptom of many mental disorders (Taylor, Lichstein, & Durrence, 2003).

Researchers estimate the total annual direct cost (e.g., medication, physician visits) of insomnia to be $13.9 billion, with total costs (i.e., including indirect costs) of $30 billion to $35 billion per year (Walsh & Engelhardt, 1999). Indirect costs include absenteeism, increased accidents, and poor job performance (Leger, Massuel, & Metlaine, 2006). In addition, insomnia is also a risk factor for increased psychopathology, including depression, anxiety disorders, substance use and abuse, and suicidal ideation (Taylor et al., 2003). Thus, insomnia poses a significant public health burden and strains the resources of physicians, psychologists, and employers. Fortunately, several empirically validated treatments are available. However, these treatments are often underutilized either because of misinformation or insufficient training. This chapter reviews current conceptualizations of insomnia, recommends insomnia assessment techniques, and discusses empirically validated treatments of insomnia.

DIAGNOSIS AND ASSESSMENT

Insomnia is a very heterogeneous disorder, requiring careful assessment and conceptualization to ensure that patients receive the most appropriate treatment. There are several diagnostic classification systems to choose from when deciding if a person indeed has insomnia. The *Diagnostic and Statistical Manual of Mental Disorders* (*DSM-IV-TR*; American Psychiatric Association, 1994) classification system is the one most often used by mental health practitioners. In this system, there are four main diagnostic options for insomnia: Primary Insomnia, Insomnia Related to Another Mental Disorder, Sleep Disorder Due to a General Medical Condition, and Substance-Induced Sleep Disorder. A diagnosis of Primary Insomnia (Table 24.1) is made when there is a subjective complaint of poor sleep that is not exclusively the result of another condition. The other three diagnoses are essentially subcategories of secondary or comorbid insomnia.

Table 24.1

DSM-IV and *ICSD-2* Diagnostic Systems for Insomnia

DSM-IV CRITERIA FOR PRIMARY INSOMNIA

A. Difficulty initiating or maintaining sleep, or of nonrestorative sleep, at least 1 month.
B. The sleep disturbance causes clinically significant distress or impairment.
C. The sleep disturbance does not occur exclusively in relation to another sleep disorder.
D. The sleep disturbance does not occur exclusively in relation to another mental disorder.
E. The disturbance is not the direct result of a substance or medical condition.

ICSD-2 CRITERIA FOR INSOMNIA

A. A complaint of difficulty initiating sleep, difficulty maintaining sleep, waking up too early, or sleep that is chronically nonrestorative or poor in quality.
B. The above sleep difficulty occurs despite adequate opportunity and circumstances for sleep.
C. At least one of the following forms of daytime impairment related to the nighttime sleep difficulty is reported by the patient:
   1. Fatigue/malaise
   2. Attention, concentration, or memory impairment
   3. Social/vocational dysfunction or poor school performance
   4. Mood disturbance/irritability
   5. Daytime sleepiness
   6. Motivation/energy/initiative reduction
   7. Proneness for errors/accidents at work or while driving
   8. Tension, headaches, and/or GI symptoms in response to sleep loss
   9. Concerns or worries about sleep

ICSD-2 INSOMNIA SUBTYPE CLASSIFICATIONS

Adjustment insomnia	Occurs in response to an identifiable stressor (lasts from a few days to weeks).
Psychophysiological insomnia	When excessive arousal interferes with sleep (often a conditioned response).
Paradoxical insomnia	Subjective complaint of insomnia in the absence of objective evidence.
Idiopathic insomnia	Onset early in life without evidence of precipitating factors and with chronic course.
Inadequate sleep hygiene	Lifestyle and behavioral factors (e.g. excessive caffeine use) produce the sleep disturbance.
Insomnia due to a mental disorder	
Insomnia due to a drug or substance	
Insomnia due to a medical condition	

Within the sleep medicine community, a more specialized classification system has been created called the *International Classification of Sleep Disorders*, now in its second edition (*ICSD-2*; American Academy of Sleep Medicine, 2005). The *ICSD-2* specifies (Table 24.1) generic criteria for insomnia followed by additional criteria for each of eight adult subtypes and one subtype specific to children, which is not addressed here. The generic criteria are similar to those for *DSM-IV-TR* Primary Insomnia, but the *ICSD-2* goes beyond the *DSM-IV-TR* in the necessity of daytime complaint. This classification system is more often used by sleep medicine physicians. However, in truth, the diagnostic categories of the *DSM-IV-TR* are sufficient to determine which treatment is to be used.

Differential Diagnosis

As mentioned, once a patient is determined to have insomnia, it is necessary to determine etiology. Primary Insomnia is the term used when no coexisting disorder that could be influencing sleep has been identified, and thus it is assumed that no other disorder is causing the insomnia (National Institutes of Health, 2005). However, when another significant mental or physical disorder is present, determining if insomnia was caused by the other disorder is next to impossible. Therefore, the panel from National Institutes of Health state-of-the-science conference on insomnia gave the following recommendations:

> Most cases of insomnia are comorbid with other conditions. Historically, this has been termed "secondary insomnia." However, the limited understanding of mechanistic pathways in chronic insomnia precludes drawing firm conclusions about the nature of these associations or the direction of causality. Furthermore, there is concern that the term "secondary insomnia" may promote undertreatment. Therefore, we propose that the term "comorbid insomnia" may be more appropriate. Common comorbidities include psychiatric disorders, particularly depression and substance use disorders; cardiopulmonary disorders; and conditions associated with chronic somatic complaints (i.e., musculoskeletal syndromes such as rheumatoid arthritis or lower back pain) that may disrupt sleep. Other associated sleep disorders can also contribute to insomnia, particularly obstructive sleep apnea, restless legs syndrome, or periodic limb movement disorder. (National Institutes of Health, 2005, pp. 1049–1050.)

ASSESSMENT TECHNIQUES

Clinical Interview

A thorough clinical interview is at the heart of the insomnia assessment process. The sleep history gathered during the interview will be the basis for determining whether the insomnia is primary or comorbid. Unfortunately, no validated interview schedule currently exists, but Morin (1993) provided an excellent Insomnia Interview Schedule in his earlier treatment manual.

Presenting Problem   As with any problem, details about the conditions under which it began are a good place to start. Chronic insomnia often begins during periods of life stress (precipitating factors), but then continues to be a problem after the stress has passed. Insomnia typically follows a varying course, with periods of good sleep interrupted by periods of poor sleep. Situational factors associated with good and poor periods should be explored.

TYPICAL DAY AND NIGHT Next, it is useful to have patients walk through a typical day by describing the time they wake up in the morning and their daily routine. Detailed information about their bedtime routine, if any, is then collected, followed by the course of a typical night of sleep. This information can be very useful for identifying inadequate sleep hygiene behaviors that can interfere with sleep and need to be addressed during treatment.

PHYSIOLOGIC HYPERAROUSAL The role of hyperarousal can then be explored, with questions about feeling tense and alert in bed. Consistent with the conditioning model of insomnia, patients will often report that they feel very sleepy but then suddenly wake up when they get into bed. Excessive worrying and rumination in bed can be indications of high cognitive arousal that may interfere with sleep. Patients will often report that they are not able to "turn off" their mind in order to fall asleep. Excessive physiologic arousal is a cue to consider the use of relaxation therapies during treatment.

CIRCADIAN RHYTHMS A factor often overlooked in the differential diagnosis of insomnia, circadian rhythms should always be assessed. As described in the Conceptualization section, a mismatch between an individual's endogenous circadian rhythms and his or her desired sleep-wake schedule can lead to insomnia. Treatment of the problem is not likely to be successful if it does not include interventions to align these different schedules. One way to explore circadian rhythm misalignment is to ask, "If you could go to bed and wake up at any time, what would be the ideal schedule for your body?" The emphasis is on physiological tendencies, not personal preferences. Individuals with a delayed sleep phase will describe very late bedtimes and wake times in response to this question, with the opposite pattern for those with an advanced phase. If a patient takes 2 hours to fall asleep on nights with a bedtime of 11 PM, but falls asleep quickly with a 2 AM bedtime, then delayed sleep phase is the likely cause of the problem rather than insomnia. A brief self-report measure such as the Morningness-Eveningness Scale (Horne & Ostberg, 1976) is generally helpful in determining circadian phase.

Mental Health A thorough mental health history should be a part of the standard assessment process for any client, paying particular attention to mood and anxiety disorders, as these are most likely to be associated with insomnia (Taylor, Lichstein, Durrence, Riedel, & Bush, 2005). However, patients with any mental disorder are more likely to experience poor sleep, so all mental disorders should be assessed. Structured clinical interviews such as the Structured Clinical Interview for the *DSM-IV* (First, Spitzer, Miriam, & Williams, 1996) are very useful in ensuring the most valid and reliable diagnoses for the majority of Axis I disorders.

Physical Health Although it is not necessary to have each patient undergo a thorough medical examination, it is recommended when possible. It may be helpful to work in conjunction with the patient's primary care provider to assist in this process. A number of medical conditions can impair sleep, which may not be readily seen during a medical history alone, such as hyperthyroidism. However, if a medical examination is not possible, a thorough medical history should suffice. If an adequate trial of treatment is unsuccessful, a full medical examination should be performed.

Insomnia can also be the result of other sleep disorders such as sleep apnea (i.e., repeated cessation of breathing during sleep), so particular attention should be paid to assessing for other symptoms of disturbed sleep. In general, an overnight sleep study is not in order unless the patient has obvious symptoms of another sleep disorder or has failed a trial of an empirically validated insomnia treatment. However, there is disagreement in the field as to the exact prevalence of undiagnosed sleep disorders such as apnea in patients with insomnia, especially in older adults.

A suspicion of sleep apnea should be raised if the patient reports heavy snoring, daytime sleepiness, and waking up gasping or choking during the night. Common risk factors of apnea include being >30 years old, male or postmenopausal female, obesity, a large neck (i.e., >17 inches for men and >16 inches for women), and craniofacial abnormalities (Guilleminault & Abad, 2004; Malhotra & White, 2002). Complaints of itchy, tingling legs at night suggest the possible presence of restless legs syndrome.

Finally, a number of pharmacologic products, both legal and illegal, can impair sleep and should be considered. Often, patients are told to take prescription medications at night to avoid daytime side effects, but the sleep-interfering impact is overlooked. It is useful to ask patients for a list of their current medications, including vitamins and herbal products. A *Physicians' Desk Reference* or similar drug reference can be used to look for insomnia as a potential side effect. Again, working with a patient's health care provider is essential when pharmacologic factors are suspected.

SELF-REPORT INSTRUMENTS

The information collected through the clinical interview can be complemented with myriad self-report measures. Moul and colleagues (Moul, Hall, Pilkonis, & Buysse, 2004) reviewed the available instruments and made recommendations. We list a few of the options consistent with current recommendations for sleep research and/or clinical practice (Buysse, Ancoli-Israel, Edinger, Lichstein, & Morin, in press).

Overall Sleep   To assess overall sleep and sleep quality, the most common strategy is to have patients fill out a sleep diary each day by completing questions about their bedtime, the time it took to fall asleep, and other aspects of their sleep and waking time. A 2-week sleep diary is an invaluable way to examine sleep patterns not apparent in the patient's history, particularly as patients often give inaccurate retrospective estimates of sleep. Sleep diaries are also an essential tool when using *sleep restriction,* described later in the chapter. The Pittsburgh Sleep Quality Index is another self-report questionnaire that can provide information about overall sleep and sleep quality; it assesses global severity of sleep disturbance regardless of the source of the disturbance (Buysse, Reynolds, Monk, Berman, & Kupfer, 1989).

Insomnia   There are several insomnia-specific questionnaires that can provide useful information for the initial assessment as well as for tracking progress over the course of treatment. The Insomnia Severity Index is a brief instrument designed for use as a screening and outcome measure (Bastien, Vallieres, & Morin, 2001). The Dysfunctional Beliefs and Attitudes about Sleep Scale is a very useful instrument designed to assess inaccurate or maladaptive sleep-related cognitions that can increase worry about sleep and can later be targets of cognitive therapy, as described later (Morin, Stone, Trinkle, Mercer, & Remsberg, 1993). Although other instruments exist, these are the two most commonly used.

Daytime Functioning Self-report instruments can also be used to evaluate the daytime consequences of insomnia. The Epworth Sleepiness Scale and Sleep Wake Activity Inventory both measure excessive daytime sleepiness (Johns, 1991; Rosenthal, Roehrs, & Roth, 1993). The Functional Outcomes of Sleepiness Questionnaire can be used to assess various domains of daytime functioning (Weaver et al., 1997). The Quality of Life of Insomniacs Questionnaire can be used to measure quality of life (Rombaut, Maillard, Kelly, & Hindmarch, 1990), but is commonly overlooked in favor of more widely known generic quality of life instruments, such as the SF-36 (J. E. Ware & Sherbourne, 1992). The Multidimensional Fatigue Inventory (Smets, Garssen, Bonke, & De Haes, 1995) and the Fatigue Severity Scale (Krupp, LaRocca, Muir-Nash, & Steinberg, 1989) are often used to measure the problem of fatigue in insomnia patients. Numerous questionnaires are available to assess psychiatric symptoms, but because none has been specifically evaluated in patients with insomnia, the choice of a measure is open to the clinician.

Objective Sleep Measures

The biggest limitation in self-report measures of sleep is their inherent tendency to reflect estimation biases. This problem is compounded by the fact that sleep is by definition a state of reduced alertness, so one would not expect patients to be able to accurately describe their sleep patterns. Thus, some practitioners prefer more objective measures of sleep in assessing insomnia.

Polysomnography Polysomnography (PSG), more colloquially referred to as a sleep study, is considered the gold standard measure of sleep. Polysomnography involves the measurement of EEG and other physiological parameters to delineate sleep into its five stages, yielding quantitative measures of sleep quantity and continuity. However, current guidelines state that the diagnosis of insomnia should be based on self-report, and the PSG is only routinely recommended if there is a suspicion of other sleep disorders for which PSG is a valid measure (Sateia, Doghramji, Hauri, & Morin, 2000).

Actigraphy Actigraphy is an alternative method for objectively measuring sleep. Actigraphs are wrist-worn devices, similar to a watch, that record movement. The movement data can then be scored based on an algorithm to estimate sleep and wake periods (Lichstein et al., 2006). Periods of relative high activity are scored as wake and periods of inactivity are scored as sleep. An advantage of actigraphy is that several days or even weeks of data can be collected without substantial cost or subject burden, making it useful for observing objective patterns in sleep over time that would not be captured by a single night of PSG. Another major advantage of actigraphy is that it is conducted in the individual's home environment. This method can also be useful for tracking sleep changes over the course of treatment (Vallieres & Morin, 2003).

CONCEPTUALIZATION

Learning, Behavior, and Life Events

Several theoretical models conceptualizing insomnia currently exist. One of the first empirically supported learning models of chronic insomnia, Bootzin's (1972) stimulus control model, is based primarily on operant conditioning principles. According to this model, falling asleep produces positive reinforcement, and the stimuli associated with sleep become discriminative stimuli for sleep. Poor sleep occurs when strong cues (i.e., discriminative stimuli) for sleep have not been established, or when cues for sleep-incompatible activities have been established. For good sleepers, the bed, bedroom, and bedtime are strong cues (i.e., discriminative stimuli) for sleep. Poor sleepers develop habits (worrying, watching TV, snacking in the bed or bedroom) that may make the bed, bedroom, and bedtime strong cues for wake. Classical conditioning principles may also play a role as the bed, bedroom, and bedtime are repeatedly paired with the anxiety and frustration associated with trying to fall asleep. Over time, the internal cues associated with this anxiety and frustration (i.e., mind racing, anticipatory anxiety, physiological arousal) begin to serve as cues for further arousal and sleep disruption.

Bootzin's (1972) model was followed by the developmental model of Spielman, Saskin, and Thorpy (1987). This model (Figure 24.1) outlines three types of factors that contribute to insomnia: *predisposing* factors (conditions or traits that make an individual vulnerable to developing insomnia), *precipitating* factors (conditions that contribute to the onset of the insomnia), and *perpetuating* factors (conditions that serve to maintain the insomnia). Whereas predisposing factors generally remain constant over time, the contributions of precipitating and perpetuating factors vary.

In this model, life events frequently operate as precipitating factors that trigger the onset of insomnia. Such events can be transient (i.e., a major exam, a public speaking engagement) or more enduring (i.e., death of a loved one, job-related stress, unemployment, hospitalization, diagnosis with a major illness). An event does not need to have strong negative emotional salience or negative consequences to contribute to insomnia. For example, a wedding or the birth of a child is generally considered a positive event that, nonetheless, can trigger insomnia in susceptible individuals. Insomnia that develops in response to a life event may resolve on its own, particularly for transient events. However, in cases of chronic insomnia, precipitating factors have their major impact at the initiation of insomnia, followed by a gradual lessening as the role of perpetuating factors grows and strengthens over time. This model

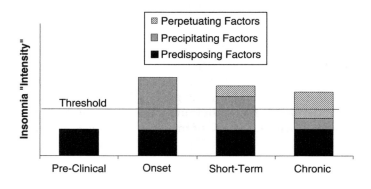

Figure 24.1   Developmental Model of Insomnia. *Source:* "Treatment of Chronic Insomnia by Restriction of Time in Bed," by A. J. Spielman, P. Saskin, and M. J. Thorpy, 1987, *Sleep, 10,* pp. 45–55. Copyright 1987 by Elsevier Sciences. Reprinted with permission.

is complementary to Bootzin's (1972) model in that the behaviors Bootzin describes are thought of as both *predisposing* and *perpetuating* factors in Spielman et al.'s (1987) model.

Morin (1993) developed a cognitive-behavioral model of insomnia to supplement the behavioral models supplied by Bootzin and Spielman (Figure 24.2). This model reiterated the previous behavioral theories, but also focused on the maladaptive thoughts patients with insomnia often have, which serve as *predisposing* and *perpetuating* factors. Morin's research (Morin et al., 1993) found that patients with insomnia had a wide variety of maladaptive thoughts about sleep, such as "I won't be able to function if I don't get a full 8 hours of sleep." Similar to Beck, Rush, Shaw, and Emery (1979), Morin believed that if you identified and challenged or restructured maladaptive thoughts, the patient's insomnia would improve.

Finally, Harvey (2002) presented a purely cognitive model (Figure 24.3) of insomnia building on Morin's (1993) work. This model focused on "selective attention and monitoring, distorted perception of sleep and daytime deficits, erroneous beliefs, and counterproductive safety behaviors." Harvey proposed that these nighttime and daytime thought processes resulted in an upward spiral of increasing of maladaptive worry and subsequent physiological arousal and emotional distress, which results in chronic insomnia.

In addition to these models, certain behaviors affect the body's circadian rhythm, thus impacting sleep and sometimes presenting as insomnia. The circadian clock regulates the sleep-wake cycle. Insomnia complaints can occur as the result of dysfunctions related to the timing of the sleep period within the 24-hour day. Examples of circadian rhythm disorders include jet lag (due to rapid time zone changes), night or shift work, and phase advance syndrome or phase delay syndrome. Jet lag, which occurs when there is rapid east or west travel across time zones, results from a mismatch between

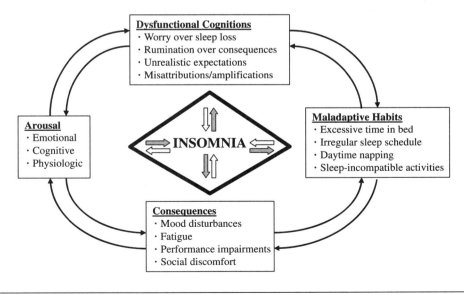

Figure 24.2 Cognitive Behavioral Model of Insomnia. *Source: Insomnia: Psychological Assessment and Management*, by C. M. Morin, 1993, New York: Guilford Press. Copyright 1993 by Guilford Press. Reprinted with Permission.

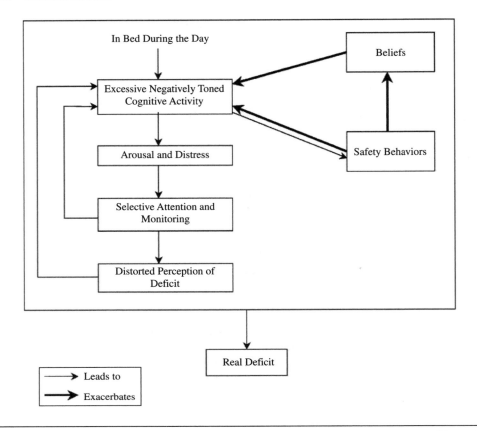

Figure 24.3   Cognitive Model of Insomnia. *Source:* "A Cognitive Model of Insomnia," by A. G. Harvey, 2002, *Behavior Research and Therapy*, 40 (8), pp. 869–893. Copyright 2002 by Elsevier Sciences. Reprinted with permission.

the internal circadian rhythm and the local time. Shift work (night shift or rotating day and night shifts) disrupts the circadian rhythm, resulting in not enough sleep and poor quality sleep. For phase delay syndrome, sleep is significantly delayed (3:00 AM) in relation to the desired sleep time, making it difficult to get up in the morning to meet work and other obligations. Interestingly, other than delayed timing, sleep is otherwise normal. Shift workers and college students are likely to develop this disorder. For phase advance syndrome, normal sleep is advanced in relation to desired time (8:00 PM bedtime, 3:00 AM awakening). This disorder is often seen in older adults.

GENETIC INFLUENCES

Although virtually no research has been conducted specifically on the genetics of insomnia, other evidence suggests that genetic influences may be involved. For instance, epidemiologic surveys of twin pairs have found a higher concordance rate for insomnia among monozygotic twins compared to dizygotic twins, with heritability estimates in the range of .2 to .4 (Heath, Kendler, Eaves, & Martin, 1990; McCarren, Goldberg, Ramakrishnan, & Fabsitz, 1994). One difficulty in interpreting these results is that they did not use standard diagnostic criteria for insomnia, and so the results are more reflective of sleep complaints in general. More recently two family studies have been conducted using *DSM-IV* criteria for insomnia (Bastien & Morin, 2000; Dauvilliers et al., 2005). In both studies there was evidence of familial aggregation of insomnia. Based on these results it can be concluded that there are genetic influences, but the nature of the genes involved remains unknown.

PHYSICAL AFFECTING BEHAVIOR

Various studies have shown that compared to good sleepers, people with insomnia exhibit physiological hyperarousal (e.g., in terms of body temperature, metabolic rate, heart rate) prior to sleep onset and during sleep (Bonnet & Arand, 1996, 1998, 2000; Freedman & Sattler, 1982; Monroe, 1967). In addition, people with insomnia either cannot or take longer to fall asleep during the day (for a review, see Riedel & Lichstein, 2000). Based on these and other findings, Bonnet and Arand (1997) proposed that Primary Insomnia is a disorder of central nervous system hyperarousal. However, there are some problems with these data; the studies used small sample sizes and the measures used are not a direct analog of arousal.

In addition, insomnia is frequently comorbid with medical and psychiatric illnesses. Medical conditions known to disrupt sleep include asthma, head injury, fibromyalgia, pulmonary disease, arthritis, headaches, Alzheimer's disease, Parkinson's disease, and seizures. Factors related to medical conditions are also frequently cited for causing sleeping difficulties (i.e., nocturia, coughing, difficulty breathing, pain; Hoch, Buysse, Monk, & Reynolds, 1992). Psychiatric disorders that can disturb sleep include depression, anxiety, Bipolar Disorder, Posttraumatic Stress Disorder (PTSD), and Schizophrenia.

DRUGS AFFECTING BEHAVIOR

Insomnia can sometimes be caused by certain prescription medications (e.g., imipramine, steroids, L-dopa, clonidine), over-the-counter medications (OTC; e.g., Anacin, Excedrin, some diet pills, some nasal decongestants), substances of abuse (i.e., alcohol, cocaine, narcotics, amphetamines), and common substances (i.e., caffeine, nicotine). Prescription medications that are particularly disruptive of sleep include certain antidepressants (i.e., selective serotonin reuptake inhibitors) and beta adrenoreceptor agonists, or beta-blockers (used to treat hypertension, cardiac arrhythmias, and angina).

Hypnotic medications are commonly used to treat insomnia. However, chronic use of hypnotic medication can produce hypnotic-dependent insomnia, a disorder characterized by a pattern of tolerance or dependence and rebound insomnia on discontinuation. Attempts to significantly reduce the dosage or stop taking the medication altogether produce withdrawal symptoms (nausea, muscle tension, aches, irritability, restlessness, and nervousness) and a return of insomnia (rebound insomnia). As a result, usage of the hypnotic medication is maintained despite diminished therapeutic effectiveness. Women and the elderly are disproportionately high users of hypnotic medications and, as a result, are particularly susceptible to hypnotic-dependent insomnia. Fortunately, some studies have shown that behavioral treatment of insomnia can both improve sleep and help hypnotic-dependent patients withdraw from their medications (Lichstein & Johnson, 1993).

CULTURAL AND DIVERSITY ISSUES

Various cultural factors have been found to have a differential impact on the health and illnesses of cultural groups (Consedine, Magai, & Horton, 2005). In general, insomnia increases with age. Specifically, a review of 20 studies reporting a wide age range found that the majority of studies (60%) showed an increase of prevalence and severity of insomnia with age (Lichstein et al., 2004). Further, research clearly shows that difficulty maintaining sleep increases with age, and modest evidence shows difficulty initiating sleep and early morning awakening may also increase with age (Lichstein et al., 2004). The majority of studies reviewed (73%) also point to a greater prevalence of insomnia among women than men, with higher remission rates in males perhaps contributing to the higher prevalence in females (Foley et al., 1995).

Insomnia and Race   The majority of multicultural research on insomnia has focused primarily on African American and Caucasian American populations. The bulk of these studies have found a higher prevalence of and more severe insomnia among Caucasian American s (Blazer, Hays, & Foley, 1995; Jean-Louis et al., 2001; Whitney et al., 1998). However, the data were somewhat mixed, with two studies finding a higher prevalence of insomnia in adult African Americans and adult non–Caucasian Americans (Bixler, Vgontzas, Lin, Vela-Bueno, & Kales, 2002; Karacan et al., 1976). These prevalence rates also seem to vary between age groups within different ethnicities. African Americans show a bimodal pattern of insomnia, with the peaks of insomnia occurring in the middle years (30s to 50s) and in the later years (70s to 80s) of life (Lichstein et al., 2004). Despite this pattern, insomnia is still less prevalent in older African Americans than in older Caucasian Americans (Durrence & Lichstein, 2006). Finally, the majority of studies found the highest incidence of insomnia and most severe sleep complaints to be among African American females (Foley et al., 1995; Karacan, Thornby, & Williams, 1983).

There are several limitations associated with the study of cultural factors in relation to insomnia. First, associated variables such as socioeconomic status and health-related concerns may account for differences in nocturnal sleep quality that are misperceived as resulting from membership in a specific cultural group. Additionally, differences in the *prevalence* of insomnia across cultural groups may result from differences in the *incidence* and remission rates of insomnia across these groups as opposed to actual prevalence rates (Foley et al., 1995). Similarly, although prevalence rates are typically reported, these rates may not reflect the severity of the insomnia (e.g., amount of wake time after sleep onset). Finally, there are few studies that report within-group differences in addition to between-group differences.

BEHAVIORAL TREATMENTS

Unfortunately, there is no algorithm research suggesting the "best" treatment in each situation. Most insomnia treatment studies to date have focused mainly on healthy individuals with a complaint of only primary chronic insomnia. Treatment options available include (a) treating primary chronic insomnia with cognitive-behavioral therapies, (b) treating secondary or comorbid insomnia with cognitive-behavioral therapies or medication while letting someone else treat the other disorder, (c) treating the more pressing of two disorders (i.e., suicidal depression) while taking a wait-and-see approach with insomnia, and (d) using medication when the patient is uninterested in or unable to complete cognitive-behavioral therapies.

It may be more appropriate to treat acute insomnia with medication, but it is important to monitor patients so that they do not develop a psychological dependence on the medications, which are approved only for 2 weeks to 6 months depending on the compound. Steps can also be taken to reduce the impact of acute insomnia during a stressful life event by normalizing sleeplessness in these situations as being appropriate and time-limited. This could help to circumvent the patient's developing perpetuating behaviors that may turn the insomnia into a chronic disorder. It is important to note that this acute behavioral treatment has not been empirically tested to determine the long-term effects on the development of chronic insomnia.

COGNITIVE-BEHAVIORAL TREATMENTS

Cognitive-behavioral treatments work by targeting the behavioral habits and cognitive patterns that perpetuate poor sleep. Although pharmacological treatments are useful for acute insomnia, cognitive and behavioral approaches are preferred for chronic insomnia and can be used to effectively treat both Primary Insomnia (Morin, Culbert, & Schwartz, 1994; Morin, Hauri, et al., 1999) and insomnia comorbid with other disorders (Currie, Wilson, Pontefract, & deLaplante, 2000; Lichstein, Wilson, & Johnson, 2000; Stepanski & Rybarczyk, 2006). Meta-analyses indicate that behavioral interventions significantly improve sleep in 70% to 80% of patients, resulting in patients falling asleep approximately 30 minutes sooner, sleeping approximately 30 minutes longer, and having approximately 1 less awakening per night (Morin et al., 1994; Murtagh & Greenwood, 1995). Cognitive-behavioral treatments present no physical tolerance or dependency risks and are more effective in sustaining sleep improvements over time than either medication alone or medication and behavioral treatments combined (Morin, Colecchi, Stone, Sood, & Brink, 1999). Additionally, patients rate cognitive-behavioral treatment as more appropriate and acceptable than medication.

There are a wide variety of cognitive-behavioral treatment options for insomnia, including stimulus control, sleep restriction, relaxation, biofeedback, cognitive therapy, and sleep hygiene. Common features of these treatments include (a) collaboration between patient and therapist, (b) daily monitoring, (c) homework assignments, and (d) a clear rationale for techniques.

We offer next some brief examples of the most common methods used, in order of declining empirical support determined by a critical review by the Standards of Practice Committee of the American Academy of Sleep Medicine (Chesson et al., 1999; Morin, Hauri, et al., 1999). These reviews found that stimulus control therapy, progressive muscle relaxation therapy, and paradoxical intention therapy were "well established" treatments. In addition, sleep restriction and electromyogram biofeedback were deemed "probably efficacious," but did not reach the "well established" level because there were not enough well-designed efficacy studies available. Multicomponent treatments such as cognitive behavioral therapy of insomnia (CBTi) were originally listed as only "probably efficacious," however CBTi has since met criteria for being "well established." It is important to note that the multicomponent therapies comprised multiple "well established" therapies, but there are no data to show that the multicomponent therapy is more efficacious than the single therapies. Several excellent treatment manuals give more detailed instructions on the use of the various cognitive and behavioral techniques (Lichstein & Morin, 2000; Morin, 1993; Morin & Espie, 2003; Perlis, Jungquist, Smith, & Posner, 2005; Perlis & Lichstein, 2003).

Stimulus Control   Stimulus control is the most effective single cognitive-behavioral intervention (Morin et al., 1994). It is based on the idea that the bedroom is a weak discriminative stimulus for sleeping because it is often used for activities other than sleep (i.e., eating, watching TV, worrying; Bootzin, 1972). Stimulus control therapy and sleep restriction therapy are slightly more effective (50% to 60% improvement) than other single modality therapies (progressive muscle relaxation, 40%; paradoxical intention, 30%). The goal of stimulus control is to strengthen sleep-compatible associations with the bed and bedroom and to break sleep-incompatible ones. Typically the patient is told to avoid using the bed or bedroom for anything but sleep or sex. Additionally, when awake in bed for more than 15 to 20 minutes, the patient is to get out of bed and engage in a nonstimulating activity in another room, returning to bed again only when sleepy. This instruction is to be repeated as often as necessary throughout the night.

Sleep Restriction   Although sleep restriction was listed as "probably efficacious" by the Standards of Practice Committee, it is listed next because it is as effective as stimulus control as a single treatment, even though fewer studies have been performed with it as single treatment (Morin et al., 1994; Murtagh & Greenwood, 1995). Indeed, one reason few data exist examining sleep restriction as a single treatment is because most newer multimodal treatments of insomnia actually combine stimulus control with sleep restriction.

Traditional sleep restriction limits or restricts the time allowed for sleep each night by eliminating napping and restricting the amount of time spent in bed (TIB) at night (Spielman, Saskin, & Thorpy, 1987). Typically, the patient keeps a sleep diary for 2 to 3 weeks to establish how much time each night is actually spent sleeping. Based on the average amount of time the person sleeps each night, the therapist determines a prescribed sleep amount for the patient (not less than 5.5 hours). This amount is typically equal to either the person's average total sleep time (TST) or to the TST plus 30 minutes (Spielman et al., 1987). Because the initial TIB is based on pretreatment data, it frequently underestimates the individual's actual sleep need. Sleep restriction takes this into account by increasing the TIB in 15- to 30-minute increments each week that sleep efficiency (TST/TIB × 100%) reaches 90% or higher (some clinicians prefer to use $\geq$ 87%). When sleep efficiency falls below 85% in a given week, the TIB is decreased by 15 to 30 minutes.

The goal of sleep restriction is to regulate the sleep-wake cycle by tailoring the time spent in bed to the patient's true sleep need, thus strengthening the homeostatic and circadian sleep regulation systems (Borbely, 1982). By restricting the TIB each night, sleep restriction initially results in progressive sleep deprivation; as a result, the homeostatic system places increasing pressure on the individual to sleep. By instituting a set bedtime and wake time, patients send a stronger signal for sleepiness at bedtime because they are regularizing their circadian cycle, which can become dysregulated when they sleep in or vary their bedtime considerably, especially on weekends.

An alternative form of sleep restriction, sleep compression, has also shown effectiveness in treating insomnia (e.g., Lichstein, Riedel, Wilson, Lester, & Aguillard, 2001). The goal of sleep compression is to gradually reduce time in bed until the patient's optimal time in bed has been established. This intervention may be more acceptable to patients who find the sleep restriction technique too drastic.

Progressive Muscle Relaxation   Although several relaxation interventions exist (e.g., imagery, meditation, biofeedback), progressive muscle relaxation (PMR) has the most evidence as a treatment for insomnia and has been shown to be more effective than placebo, wait-list, and no-treatment controls. Progressive muscle relaxation involves alternately tensing (~4 to 7 seconds) and relaxing (~20 to 45 seconds) different muscle groups throughout the body: hands, wrists, arms, shoulders, feet, ankles, thighs, buttocks, abdomen, shoulders, neck, forehead, face, jaw, and shoulders (Jacobson, 1929). Focused attention on feelings of relaxation and the comparison and contrast between the feelings of relaxation and tension is intended to teach the patient greater appreciation for the relaxation experience. This technique typically takes 10 to 30 minutes. Homework involves instructing the patient to practice the relaxation at home just prior to bedtime and during nighttime awakenings. Practice is extremely important to develop a deeper level of relaxation, so sometimes a daily practice session is added.

OTHER RELAXATION METHODS   As mentioned, many other relaxation techniques exist, but to date only meditation, imagery, and autogenic training have been assessed for the treatment of insomnia. Although these treatments have shown effectiveness in at least one clinical trial, other studies found no benefit, and the reviewers felt overall evidence did not support a recommendation of these techniques as single treatments. Other relaxation methods are sometimes recommended, such as diaphragmatic breathing, hypnosis, and thought stopping, but these techniques have no empirical backing as treatments of insomnia.

Paradoxical Intention   Paradoxical intention aims to reduce the patient's performance anxiety about falling asleep through instructions to get in bed and try to stay awake rather than try to fall asleep. All research on this technique has focused on patients with sleep-onset insomnia and has produced mixed results, with four studies showing it to be more effective than control and two studies failing to find a difference. Because this intervention is less effective than the single treatments of stimulus control, sleep restriction, and PMR, it is rarely recommended over those interventions, but may be useful to those who do not benefit from the other methods.

Biofeedback   Biofeedback procedures teach patients to control physiological responses (e.g., muscle tension) through visual or auditory feedback. Every study ever performed with biofeedback as a treatment for insomnia shows it to be an effective treatment; however, two found that it was no more effective than placebo. Because improvements appear to be comparable to PMR, which take less time for the patient to learn and requires no expensive equipment, this method is not recommended over stimulus control, sleep restriction, or PMR, again unless the patient fails to benefit from those other methods.

Cognitive Behavioral Therapy of Insomnia   Cognitive behavioral therapy of insomnia generally refers to the combination of sleep hygiene, one or more behavioral techniques (usually stimulus control, sleep restriction, and PMR), and traditional cognitive therapy (Beck et al., 1979). The combination of several techniques produces a wide swath of interventions, which can address the various factors that may be maintaining an individual's insomnia (cognitive or physiological arousal, conditioning, worry). Cognitive behavioral therapy of insomnia is consistent with a multifactorial model of insomnia and is rapidly becoming the treatment standard. It has been shown to be more effective than control in several randomized clinical trials, and two studies have shown CBTi to be as effective as medication at posttreatment and more effective than medication at follow-up (Jacobs, Pace-Schott, Stickgold, & Otto, 2004; Morin, Colecchi, et al., 1999). What follows are the two components of CBTi that have not yet been discussed.

SLEEP HYGIENE   Sleep hygiene typically consists of psychoeducational training on reducing or eliminating behaviors that *may* be interfering with sleep (i.e., nicotine, alcohol and caffeine use, smoking, exercising too close to bedtime). Sometimes sleep hygiene is defined more broadly to include the bedroom environment as well (too much light, heat, cold, or noise). Although research shows that sleep hygiene education is ineffective as a single treatment, most behavioral sleep medicine specialists utilize it as an adjunct treatment to guard against behaviors that might sabotage effectiveness of the more active treatments. Of note, this is the technique most nonspecialists are familiar with and is often the only nonpharmacological treatment they offer their patients with insomnia, which may result in these nonspecialists and their patients unfairly deducing that behavioral treatments are ineffective.

COGNITIVE THERAPY   Cognitive therapy targets maladaptive thoughts that interfere with sleep. Over time, patients often develop dysfunctional thoughts and beliefs about their sleep and the negative effects of sleep loss. Some worry that they may never sleep well again; others have unrealistic beliefs about how much sleep they need and become focused on sleeping 8 hours every night. Treatment focuses on identifying these maladaptive thoughts, challenging their validity, and replacing them with more adaptive thoughts (Morin, Savard, & Blais, 2000). A more adaptive thought for an unrealistic belief about sleep need would be, "I will still be able to function if I don't get a full 8 hours of sleep. I may feel a little tired, but that's okay. Everyone feels tired during the day sometimes." Daily thought logs are used to identify maladaptive thoughts, the situations in which they occur, and the patient's reaction to them (angry, frustrated). More adaptive thoughts and beliefs reduce the patient's arousal, and sleep improves. Cognitive therapy alone has not been empirically tested and thus should be used only in combination with other empirically validated treatments.

MEDICAL TREATMENTS

Medication is the most common form of treatment offered to people with chronic and transient insomnia. The reasons for this are likely multifactorial: (a) Few physicians or therapists are trained in cognitive and behavioral therapies of insomnia, (b) physicians are often uninformed about the utility and efficacy of these therapies, (c) cognitive and behavioral therapies take more time and effort on the part of the patient and physician, and (d) many nonspecialists accept the misconception that insomnia is always a secondary disorder, which will dissipate once the "primary" disorder has been addressed. There are three main classes of hypnotic medications currently used to treat insomnia: benzodiazepines, nonbenzodiazepine hypnotics, and antidepressants. Although none of these drugs are approved for more than transient or short-term (<6 months) use, they are in actuality often used indefinitely. Barbiturates were once popular hypnotics but are rarely used today because of their many detrimental side effects.

Table 24.2
Medications Commonly Used to Treat Insomnia

Drug	Trade Name	Dosage (mg)	Half-Life (hrs)
BENZODIAZEPINES			
Chlordiazepoxide	Librium	10–25	24–28
Clonazepam	Klonopin	0.5–3	30–40
Diazepam	Valium	2–10	30–100
Estazolam	ProSom	1–2	8–24
Flurazepam	Dalmane	15–30	48–120
Lorazepam	Ativan	.5–2	10–20
Temazepam	Restoril	15–30	8–20
Triazolam	Halcion	0.125–0.25	2–6
Quazepam	Doral	7.5–15	48–120
NONBENZODIAZEPINE HYPNOTICS			
Eszopiclone	Lunesta	2–3 adult, 1 elderly	5–7
Rozerem	Ramelteon	8–64	1.2
Zaleplon	Sonata	5–10	1
Zolpidem	Ambien	5–10	1.5–2.4
ANTIDEPRESSANTS			
Amitriptyline	Elavil	25–150	5–45
Nefazodone	Serzone	50–150	6–18
Sinequan	Doxepin	25–150	10–30
Trazodone	Desyrel	25–150	3–14

Source: Principles and Practices of Sleep Medicine, 4th Edition, by M. H. Kryger, T. Roth, and W. C. Dement, 2005, Philadelphia, PA : Elsevier/Saunders. Copyright 2005 by Elsevier/Saunders. Reprinted with Permission.

BENZODIAZEPINES

Benzodiazepine receptor agonists (Table 24.2) became the hypnotics of choice in the 1960s as a "safe" alternative to barbiturates. They were said to be nonaddictive and less lethal in overdose. Later evidence showed that benzodiazepines often produce tolerance, rebound insomnia upon withdrawal, and daytime residual effects, including cognitive (particularly amnesia) and psychomotor impairment, including greater risk for falls and hip fractures in older adults (Ray, Griffin, & Downey, 1989; Roth, Hajak, & Ustun, 2001). Withdrawal after long-term use can result in sleep disturbance, irritability, increased tension and anxiety, panic attacks, hand tremor, sweating, difficulty in concentration, dry retching and nausea, some weight loss, palpitations, headache, muscular pain and stiffness, and a host of perceptual changes (Petursson, 1994). However, using a slow taper paired with relaxation training is effective for reducing benzodiazepines use without substantial worsening of sleep (Lichstein & Johnson, 1993).

NONBENZODIAZEPINE HYPNOTICS

Newer nonbenzodiazepine alternatives (Table 24.2) are now starting to replace benzodiazepine receptor agonists as the hypnotics of choice. These new compounds are said to be nonaddictive and have fewer side effects than benzodiazepines, which are no longer recommended for treatment of insomnia (Langer, Mendelson, & Richardson, 1999). These newer medications do have a better side effect profile than benzodiazepines, but there is some disagreement about their freedom from dependence. Many of these medications had enough addictive potential for the Drug Enforcement Agency to label them Class IV narcotics. In addition, reports of negative side effects have begun to surface recently, including rebound insomnia, subjective ratings suggestive of abuse potential, anxiety, sleep-related eating disorder, and short-term memory decrements (Besset, Tafti, Villemin, Borderies, & Billiard, 1995; Elie, Ruther, Farr, Emilien, & Salinas, 1999; Mintzer & Griffiths, 1999; Morgenthaler & Silber, 2002; Rush, Baker, & Wright, 1999; Troy et al., 2000). Because none of these medications has been assessed for periods of longer than 6 months, which is the duration they are most likely to be taken by patients with chronic (i.e., >6 months) insomnia, we do not yet know the long-term consequences of these medications.

Zolpidem (Ambien) is the oldest nonbenzodiazepine hypnotic. This drug has been approved for 2-week use and is effective in improving sleep-onset latency and total sleep time, but not middle of the night awakenings. Others have found that this medication can be effective in treating sleep efficiency and total sleep time for as many as 12 weeks of nonnightly use. Patients who take zolpidem should not be active for at least 7 to 8 hours after taking the medication.

Zaleplon (Sonata) is a somewhat newer compound that has a very short half-life. It too has been shown to be effective in improving sleep-onset latency, but because of the rapid metabolism, taking this medication at bedtime does not help with middle of the night awakenings or total sleep time. However, because patients can be active within 4 hours of taking this medication, it may be appropriate to take in the middle of the night to treat maintenance insomnia or early morning awakenings, as long as the patient does not plan to get out of bed for another 4 hours.

Eszopiclone (Lunesta) is one of the newest members of this class. Eszopiclone has been shown to improve sleep-onset latency, wake time after sleep onset, and total sleep time. In addition, the medication has shown effectiveness for as long as 6 months (Krystal et al., 2003).

Rozerem (Ramelteon) is the newest member of these nonbenzodiazepine hypnotics. It does not act on the GABA receptors, but instead appears to act on the melatonin receptors. This is the only drug in this class that is not listed as a controlled substance, as it shows little to no potential for abuse. This medication appears to improve only sleep-onset problems, although it may also be useful for patients with irregular schedules or delayed sleep phase syndrome.

ANTIDEPRESSANTS

Antidepressants remain the most frequently prescribed medication for insomnia, despite never being approved for such use by the FDA (Walsh & Schweitzer, 1999). Some hypothesize that physicians prescribe these medications more often because they feel that hypnotics (a) are more likely to produce tolerance and withdrawal symptoms with long-term use, (b) are more dangerous and closely regulated because they are Schedule IV narcotics, (c) cost more, and (d) have more side effects. Studies have found that unlike benzodiazepines, antidepressant medications have almost no abuse potential (Rush et al., 1999).

The antidepressants most likely to be used as insomnia medications are the tricyclic antidepressants (TCAs), although in much smaller dosages than would normally be used for depression (Table 24.2). The TCAs are used because one of their chief side effects is sedation. To date, five randomized, double-blind, placebo-controlled trials have examined the efficacy of TCAs in treating insomnia (Hajak et al., 2001; Riemann et al., 2002; Rodenbeck et al., 2003; Walsh et al., 1998; J. C. Ware & Pittard, 1990). Data from these studies indicate that TCAs have mixed effects on sleep latency, total sleep time, and number of awakenings. Trazodone appears to be the most effective, but the effectiveness does not seem to last longer than 1 week (Walsh et al., 1998).

Although studies have found that, unlike benzodiazepines, antidepressant medications have almost no abuse potential (Rush et al., 1999), TCAs do have serious side effects. These include daytime sedation with subsequent risk of falls in elderly, priapism (painful sustained erection), orthostatic hypotension, cardiac dysrhythmias, anticholinergic effects (i.e., dry mouth, constipation, confusion, blurred vision, lightheadedness, difficulty urinating, and loss of bladder control), and death associated with overdose (McCall, 2002). When one weighs the risks associated with these drugs, they do not appear to be attractive treatment options.

OVER-THE-COUNTER MEDICATIONS

The most commonly *used* treatments for insomnia by patients are OTC sleep aids. However, because these compounds are not regulated by the FDA, it is difficult to ensure consistency of dosage between manufacturers.

The most prevalent of these are the antihistamines doxylamin and diphenhydramine, sometimes combined with nonsteroidal anti-inflammatory drugs (e.g., Tylenol PM). The sleep-promoting ability of these products has not been well studied, so the efficacy, side effects, and potential for tolerance and dependence are unknown (McCall, 2002; Pillitteri, Kozlowski, Person, & Spear, 1994). However, data suggest that tolerance to antihistamines develops rapidly, in as few as 4 days, so they are not recommended as a treatment for insomnia (Richardson, Roehrs, Rosenthal, Koshorek, & Roth, 2002).

Herbal OTC remedies commonly used by insomnia patients include melatonin and valerian. Two controlled trials have been performed examining the efficacy of these compounds in patients with insomnia (Coxeter, Schluter, Eastwood, Nikles, & Glasziou, 2003; Montes, Uribe, Sotres, & Martin, 2003). In these studies, neither melatonin nor valerian was significantly better at improving sleep than placebo. However, another study of medically ill patients with sleep-onset insomnia did show significant improvement in patients taking melatonin as opposed to placebo (Andrade, Srihari, Reddy, & Chandramma, 2001). One recent study found melatonin to be effective in older adults with low melatonin levels (Zhdanova et al., 2001). A subsequent study found that melatonin was not an effective hypnotic in patients with Alzheimer's disease (Singer et al., 2003).

ALCOHOL

Patients often try alcohol at bedtime as a "homeopathic" remedy. One study found that 28% of insomnia patients used alcohol as a hypnotic, with 67% reporting good effectiveness (Roehrs & Roth, 1997). Using alcohol as a sleep aid is strongly discouraged because although it may help patients fall asleep, the metabolism of alcohol causes reduced REM and deep sleep and increased awakenings during the night. Further, alcohol can act as a central nervous system stimulant, may increase nocturnal awakenings, and has a high abuse potential.

COMBINATION TREATMENTS

Pharmacological and psychological interventions for chronic insomnia have comparable efficacy (Jacobs et al., 2004; Morin, Colecchi, et al., 1999). Pharmacological treatments have the advantage of being easy to use and easy to administer. For this reason, they are often preferable in cases of acute, short-term, or transient insomnia. However, psychological treatments are more effective in long-term treatment of chronic insomnia, which is one reason no medications have been approved for use longer than 6 months. This, combined with the fact that psychological treatments pose no risk for tolerance or dependence and do not have the side effects of medications, makes psychological treatments preferable for the management of chronic insomnia. The few studies that combined these two treatment approaches indicate that patients using sleep medications and psychological treatment do no better than those with psychological treatment only (Hauri, 1997; Jacobs et al., 2004; Morin, Colecchi, et al., 1999).

OTHER TREATMENT-RELATED ISSUES

Other treatment-related issues that need to be taken into consideration are length and cost of treatment and use of behavioral interventions with specific populations, such as older adults and pediatric patients. The length of psychotherapy treatment is typically 6 to 10 sessions, each lasting 30 to 60 minutes (Lichstein & Morin, 2000). Obviously, such long treatments represent a major barrier to the routine provision of behavioral interventions in some settings. Fortunately, behavioral interventions can be effectively administered in 4 sessions or fewer (Chambers & Alexander, 1992; Edinger & Sampson, 2003; McCurry, Logsdon, Vitiello, & Teri, 1998). The alternative treatment, medication, can be as short as 1 night (transient insomnia) to indefinite (chronic insomnia). Treating patients with medication indefinitely has several drawbacks. For one, no medication for the treatment of insomnia has been tested past 6 months, so we know frighteningly little about the long-term effects of these medications.

Cost of treatment also depends on modality. Behavioral treatments range from $50 to $100 per session for 2 to 10 sessions, whereas the nonbenzodiazepine medications can cost from $1 to $10 per pill (Perlis & Youngstedt, 2000). Thus, behavioral intervention may cost more initially ($100 to $1,000), but medications end up being much more expensive in the long run. For instance, if a patient takes a nonbenzodiazepine hypnotic that costs $3 every night for 1 year, the cost would be slightly over $1,000 per year. The average duration of chronic insomnia is 9.4 years (Lichstein et al., 2004), so if these patients were to treat their insomnia with medication for the duration of the illness, the cost on average would be over $10,000. That is considerably more than the behavioral treatments and does not account for the side effects of such long treatment.

PATIENT AGE

Hypnotic medication may be contraindicated in older adults because these individuals are at greater risk of polypharmacy and medication-related side effects (McCrae et al., 2003, 2005). Conversely, older adults are as likely to benefit from cognitive and behavioral treatments as younger adults (Morin et al., 1994). Practitioners are sometimes hesitant to treat insomnia directly in older adults because it is frequently comorbid with other disorders. However, several studies have now shown that it is possible to effectively treat insomnia comorbid with other disorders using cognitive and behavioral techniques (Lichstein, McCrae, & Wilson, 2003; Lichstein et al., 2000; for a review, see Stepanski & Rybarczyk, 2006).

Pediatric patients experience some sleep problems that are similar to those experienced by adults (i.e., difficulties falling asleep, frequent night awakenings) and some that are unique (i.e., enuresis, head banging). Childhood sleep problems can be successfully treated using behavioral techniques, including education, establishing appropriate bedtime rituals, extinction techniques, and scheduled awakenings (Mindell, 1999; Ramchandani, Webb, & Stores, 2000). As this list demonstrates, pediatric behavioral treatments differ from those of adults. The nature of the intervention is altered as the parents and more specifically the parent-child interaction is frequently involved. For an excellent treatment resource, see *A Clinical Guide to Pediatric Sleep: Diagnosis and Management of Sleep Problems* (Mindell & Owens, 2003).

Case Description

A 24-year-old single White female college graduate from an upper-class family who was working as a massage therapist and had been suffering from insomnia since she was a junior in college (approximately 5 years) presented to a university psychology clinic for treatment of her insomnia. At intake, the therapist interviewed the patient with the Structured Clinical Interview for *DSM* Axis I Disorders (SCID) and the Insomnia Interview Schedule (Morin, 1993), and asked the patient to complete a 1-week sleep diary before the next session. The patient self-reported nightly insomnia, with sleep-onset latency and wake time after sleep onset of 2.5 hours, an estimated total sleep time of 5.5 hours (compared to the 8 she used to get in college before her insomnia started), and a time in bed of 11 hours, for an estimated sleep efficiency of 50%. The SCID revealed the patient had diagnoses of Attention-Deficit/Hyperactivity Disorder (ADHD; per self-report), PTSD, and Major Depression, the latter two in partial remission. She was taking 300 mg of trazodone for insomnia, 150 mg of Wellbutrin and 300 mg of Effexor for depression, and 60 mg of Ritalin (30 mg at 8 AM & 12 PM) for ADHD. The patient denied any medical problems and was very athletic, training for multiple triathlons. The patient had taken Ambien in the past, but stopped when she started eating in her sleep.

During the second session the therapist explained the sleep restriction and stimulus control rationales and worked with the patient to develop a prescribed sleep period of 12:30 AM–7:30 AM. During the subsequent week the patient altered this sleep schedule somewhat to 10:45 PM–7:45 AM but still improved her total sleep time to 7.3 hours, sleep-onset latency to 20 minutes, wake time after sleep onset to 90 minutes, and her sleep efficiency to 81%, as assessed by sleep diaries. Over the course of the next 4 sessions, the therapist continued to monitor the patient's sleep pattern with her weekly sleep diary and slowly increased her time in bed by 15 minutes each week. Sleep hygiene education was introduced

(continued)

in the third session, with no major changes being necessary. The therapist attempted to train the patient in progressive muscle relaxation, but the patient was uninterested, favoring the use of books on tape to relax. The patient only marginally adhered to her prescribed sleep schedule due to her hectic exercise schedule and her flexible work schedule, which allowed her to sleep in when she wanted. Although the patient continued to have some difficulty waking up at night, she was able to stop taking trazodone and improved her average total sleep time to 8 hours and her sleep efficiency to 90% by going to bed at 11:45 PM and waking up at 7:30 AM.

The insomnia was mostly resolved within approximately 8 to 10 weeks. The focus of therapy then shifted to her depression and PTSD. Through the use of cognitive and behavioral techniques, her depression decreased and her feelings of safety around the therapist increased, all while she withdrew from all medications except 75 mg of Effexor and 40 mg of Ritalin. Therapy eventually terminated when the patient moved away after 9 months of weekly and then 3 months of bimonthly therapy.

SUMMARY

Insomnia is a very heterogeneous disorder with myriad possible etiologies and maintaining factors. However, research has shown that cognitive and behavioral interventions such as stimulus control, sleep restriction, PRM, or the combination of these interventions with sleep hygiene and cognitive therapy (i.e., CBTi) are the most effective treatments of chronic Primary Insomnia. In addition, CBTi has been shown to be as effective as medication in the short term and more effective in the long term for the treatment of chronic Primary Insomnia. Many of these cognitive-behavioral treatment methods have also been shown to be effective in treating insomnia comorbid with other disorders; however, more research in this area is needed. To date, little is known about the effectiveness of treatments for acute insomnia, but a defensible approach would be to treat it with medication while monitoring the patient to ensure he or she does not develop chronic or hypnotic-dependent insomnia.

REFERENCES

American Academy of Sleep Medicine. (2005). *International classification of sleep disorders: Diagnostic and coding manual* (2nd ed.). Westchester, IL: Author.

American Psychiatric Association. (1994). *Diagnostic and statistical manual of mental disorders* (4th ed.). Washington, DC: Author.

Andrade, C., Srihari, B. S., Reddy, K. P., & Chandramma, L. (2001). Melatonin in medically ill patients with insomnia: A double-blind, placebo-controlled study. *Journal of Clinical Psychiatry, 62*(1), 41–45.

Bastien, C., & Morin, C. (2000). Familial incidence of insomnia. *Journal of Sleep Research, 9,* 49–54.

Bastien, C., Vallieres, A., & Morin, C. (2001). Validation of the Insomnia Severity Index as an outcome measure for insomnia research. *Sleep Medicine, 2,* 297–307.

Beck, A. T., Rush, A. J., Shaw, B. F., & Emery, G. (1979). *Cognitive therapy of depression.* New York: Guilford Press.

Besset, A., Tafti, M., Villemin, E., Borderies, P., & Billiard, M. (1995). Effects of zolpidem on the architecture and cyclical structure of sleep in poor sleepers. *Drugs under Experimental and Clinical Research, 21*(4), 161–169.

Bixler, E. O., Vgontzas, A. N., Lin, H. M., Vela-Bueno, A., & Kales, A. (2002). Insomnia in central Pennsylvania. *Journal of Psychosomatic Research, 53*(1), 589–592.

Blazer, D. G., Hays, J. C., & Foley, D. J. (1995). Sleep complaints in older adults: A racial comparison. *Journals of Gerontology: Series A, Biological Sciences and Medical Sciences, 50*(5), M280–284.

Bonnet, M. H., & Arand, D. L. (1996). The consequences of a week of insomnia. *Sleep: Journal of Sleep Research and Sleep Medicine, 19*(6), 453–461.

Bonnet, M. H., & Arand, D. L. (1997). Hyperarousal and insomnia. *Sleep Medicine Reviews, 1*(2), 97–108.

Bonnet, M. H., & Arand, D. L. (1998). Heart rate variability in insomniacs and matched normal sleepers. *Psychosomatic Medicine, 60*(5), 610–615.

Bonnet, M. H., & Arand, D. L. (2000). Activity, arousal, and the MSLT in patients with insomnia. *Sleep: Journal of Sleep and Sleep Disorders Research, 23*(2), 205–212.

Bootzin, R. R. (1972). A stimulus control treatment for insomnia. *American Psychological Association 80th Annual Convention Proceedings, 7*, 395–396.

Borbely, A. A. (1982). A two process model of sleep regulation. *Human Neurobiology, 1*, 195–204.

Buysse, D. J., Ancoli-Israel, S., Edinger, J. D., Lichstein, K. L., & Morin, C. M. (in press). Recommendations for a standard research assessment of insomnia. *Sleep.*

Buysse, D. J., Reynolds, C. F., III, Monk, T. H., Berman, S. R., & Kupfer, D. J. (1989). The Pittsburgh Sleep Quality Index: A new instrument for psychiatric practice and research. *Psychiatry Research, 28*(2), 193–213.

Chambers, M. J., & Alexander, S. D. (1992). Assessment and prediction of outcome for a brief behavioral insomnia treatment program. *Journal of Behavior Therapy and Experimental Psychiatry, 23*(4), 289–297.

Chesson, A. L., Jr., Anderson, W. M., Littner, M., Davila, D., Hartse, K., Johnson, S., et al. (1999). Practice parameters for the nonpharmacologic treatment of chronic insomnia: An American Academy of Sleep Medicine report (Standards of Practice Committee of the American Academy of Sleep Medicine). *Sleep, 22*(8), 1128–1133.

Consedine, N. S., Magai, C., & Horton, D. (2005). Ethnic variation in the impact of emotion and emotion regulation on health: A replication and extension. *Journals of Gerontology: Series B, Psychological Sciences and Social Sciences, 60*(4), P165–P173.

Coxeter, P. D., Schluter, P. J., Eastwood, H. L., Nikles, C. J., & Glasziou, P. P. (2003). Valerian does not appear to reduce symptoms for patients with chronic insomnia in general practice using a series of randomised n-of-1 trials. *Complementary Therapies in Medicine, 11*(4), 215–222.

Currie, S. R., Wilson, K. G., Pontefract, A. J., & deLaplante, L. (2000). Cognitive-behavioral treatment of insomnia secondary to chronic pain. *Journal of Consulting and Clinical Psychology, 68*(3), 407–416.

Dauvilliers, Y., Morin, C., Cervena, K., Carlander, B., Touchon, J., Besset, A., et al. (2005). Family studies in insomnia. *Journal of Psychosomatic Research, 58*, 271–278.

Durrence, H. H., & Lichstein, K. L. (2006). The sleep of African Americans: A comparative review. *Behavioral Sleep Medicine, 4*(1), 29–44.

Edinger, J. D., & Sampson, W. S. (2003). A primary care "friendly" cognitive behavioral insomnia therapy. *Sleep, 26*(2), 177–182.

Elie, R., Ruther, E., Farr, I., Emilien, G., & Salinas, E. (1999). Sleep latency is shortened during 4 weeks of treatment with zaleplon, a novel nonbenzodiazepine hypnotic: Zaleplon Clinical Study Group. *Journal of Clinical Psychiatry, 60*(8), 536–544.

First, M. B., Spitzer, R. L., Miriam, G., & Williams, J. B. W. (1996). *Structured Clinical Interview for DSM-IV Axis I Disorders—Clinician version (SCID-CV)*. Washington, DC: American Psychiatric Press.

Foley, D. J., Monjan, A. A., Brown, S. L., Simonsick, E. M., Wallace, R. B., & Blazer, D. G. (1995). Sleep complaints among elderly persons: An epidemiologic study of three communities. *Sleep, 18*(6), 425–432.

Freedman, R. R., & Sattler, H. L. (1982). Physiological and psychological factors in sleep-onset insomnia. *Journal of Abnormal Psychology, 91*(5), 380–389.

Guilleminault, C., & Abad, V. C. (2004). Obstructive sleep apnea syndromes. *Medical Clinics of North America, 88*(3), 611–630, viii.

Hajak, G., Rodenbeck, A., Voderholzer, U., Riemann, D., Cohrs, S., Hohagen, F., et al. (2001). Doxepin in the treatment of primary insomnia: A placebo-controlled, double-blind, polysomnographic study. *Journal of Clinical Psychiatry, 62*(6), 453–463.

Harvey, A. G. (2002). A cognitive model of insomnia. *Behavior Research and Therapy, 40*(8), 869–893.

Hauri, P. J. (1997). Can we mix behavioral therapy with hypnotics when treating insomniacs? *Sleep, 20*(12), 1111–1118.

Heath, A., Kendler, K., Eaves, L., & Martin, N. (1990). Evidence for genetic influences on sleep disturbance and sleep pattern in twins. *Sleep, 13*(4), 318–335.

Hoch, C. C., Buysse, D. J., Monk, T. H., & Reynolds, C. F., III. (1992). Sleep disorders and aging. In J. E. Birren, R. B. Sloane, & G. D. Cohen (Eds.), *Handbook of mental health and aging* (pp. 557–581). San Diego: Academic Press.

Horne, J. A., & Ostberg, O. (1976). A self-assessment questionnaire to determine morningness-eveningness in human circadian rhythms. *International Journal of Chronobiology, 4*(2), 97–110.

Jacobs, G. D., Pace-Schott, E. F., Stickgold, R., & Otto, M. W. (2004). Cognitive behavior therapy and pharmacotherapy for insomnia: A randomized controlled trial and direct comparison. *Archives of Internal Medicine, 164*(17), 1888–1896.

Jacobson, E. (1929). *Progressive relaxation: A physiological and clinical investigation of muscular states and their significance in psychology and medical practice*. Chicago: University of Chicago Press.

Jean-Louis, G., Magai, C. M., Cohen, C. I., Zizi, F., von Gizycki, H., DiPalma, J., et al. (2001). Ethnic differences in self-reported sleep problems in older adults. *Sleep, 24*(8), 926–933.

Johns, M. W. (1991). A new method for measuring daytime sleepiness: Epworth Sleepiness Scale. *Sleep, 14*(6), 540–545.

Karacan, I., Thornby, J. I., Anch, M., Holzer, C. E., Warheit, G. J., Schwab, J. J., et al. (1976). Prevalence of sleep disturbance in a primarily urban Florida county. *Social Science and Medicine, 10*(5), 239–244.

Karacan, I., Thornby, J. I., & Williams, R. L. (1983). Sleep disturbance: A community survey. In C. G. E. Lugaresi (Ed.), *Sleep/wake disorders: Natural history, epidemiology, and long-term evolution* (pp. 37–60). New York: Raven Press.

Katz, D. A., & McHorney, C. A. (1998). Clinical correlates of insomnia in patients with chronic illness. *Archives of Internal Medicine, 158*(10), 1099–1107.

Krupp, L. B., LaRocca, N. G., Muir-Nash, J., & Steinberg, A. D. (1989). The Fatigue Severity Scale: Application to patients with multiple sclerosis and systemic lupus erythematosus. *Archives of Neurology, 46*(10), 1121–1123.

Kryger, M. H., Roth, T., & Dement, W. C. (2005). *Principles and practice of sleep medicine* (4th ed.). Philadelphia, PA: Elsevier/Saunders.

Krystal, A. D., Walsh, J. K., Laska, E., Caron, J., Amato, D. A., Wessel, T. C., & Roth, T. (2003). Sustained efficacy of eszopiclone over 6 months of nightly treatment: Results of a randomized, double-blind, placebo-controlled study in adults with chronic insomnia. *Sleep, 26*(7), 793–799.

Langer, S. Z., Mendelson, W., & Richardson, G. (1999). Symptomatic treatment of insomnia. *Sleep, 22*(Suppl. 3), S437–S445.

Leger, D., Massuel, M. A., & Metlaine, A. (2006). Professional correlates of insomnia. *Sleep, 29*(2), 171–178.

Lichstein, K. L., Durrence, H. H., Riedel, B. W., Taylor, D. J., & Bush, A. J. (2004). *Epidemiology of sleep: Age, gender, and ethnicity.* Mahwah, NJ: Erlbaum.

Lichstein, K. L., & Johnson, R. S. (1993). Relaxation for insomnia and hypnotic medication use in older women. *Psychology and Aging, 8*(1), 103–111.

Lichstein, K., McCrae, C., & Wilson, N. (2003). Secondary insomnia: Diagnostic issues, cognitive-behavioral treatment, and future directions. In M. Perlis & K. Lichstein (Eds.), *Treating sleep disorders: Principles and practice of behavioral sleep medicine* (pp. 286–304). Hoboken, NJ: Wiley.

Lichstein, K. L., & Morin, C. M. (Eds.). (2000). *Treatment of late-life insomnia.* Thousand Oaks, CA: Sage.

Lichstein, K. L., Riedel, B. W., Wilson, N. M., Lester, K. W., & Aguillard, R. N. (2001). Relaxation and sleep compression for late-life insomnia: A placebo-controlled trial. *Journal of Consulting and Clinical Psychology, 69*(2), 227–239.

Lichstein, K. L., Stone, K. C., Donaldson, J., Nau, S. D., Soeffing, J. P., Murray, D., et al. (2006). Actigraphy validation with insomnia. *Sleep, 29*(2), 232–239.

Lichstein, K. L., Wilson, N. M., & Johnson, C. T. (2000). Psychological treatment of secondary insomnia. *Psychology and Aging, 15*(2), 232–240.

Malhotra, A., & White, D. P. (2002). Obstructive sleep apnoea. *Lancet, 360*(9328), 237–245.

McCall, W. (2002). Pharmacologic treatment of insomnia. In T. Lee-Chiong, M. Sateia & M. Carskadon (Eds.), *Sleep Medicine* (pp. 169–176). Philadelphia: Hanley and Belfus.

McCarren, M., Goldberg, J., Ramakrishnan, V., & Fabsitz, R. (1994). Insomnia in Vietnam era veteran twins: Influence of genes and combat experience. *Sleep, 17*(5), 456–461.

McCrae, C. S., Rowe, M. A., Tierney, C. G., Dautovich, N. D., DeFinis, A. L., & McNamara, J. P. H. (2005). Sleep complaints, subjective and objective sleep patterns, health, psychological adjustment, and daytime functioning in community-dwelling older adults. *Journal of Gerontology: Psychological Sciences, 60B*(4), 182–189.

McCrae, C. S., Wilson, N. M., Lichstein, K. L., Durrence, H. H., Taylor, D. J., Bush, A. J., et al. (2003). "Young old" and "old old" poor sleepers with and without insomnia complaints. *Journal of Psychosomatic Research, 54*(1), 11–19.

McCurry, S. M., Logsdon, R. G., Vitiello, M. V., & Teri, L. (1998). Successful behavioral treatment for reported sleep problems in elderly caregivers of dementia patients: A controlled study. *Journals of Gerontology: Series B, Psychological Sciences and Social Sciences, 53*(2), P122–P129.

Mindell, J. A. (1999). Empirically supported treatments in pediatric psychology: Bedtime refusal and night wakings in young children. *Journal of Pediatric Psychology, 24*(6), 465–481.

Mindell, J. A., & Owens, J. A. (2003). *A clinical guide to pediatric sleep: Diagnosis and management of sleep problems.* Philadelphia: Lippincott, Williams, & Wilkins.

Mintzer, M. Z., & Griffiths, R. R. (1999). Triazolam and zolpidem: Effects on human memory and attentional processes. *Psychopharmacology, 144*(1), 8–19.

Monroe, L. J. (1967). Psychological and physiological differences between good and poor sleepers. *Journal of Abnormal Psychology, 72*(3), 255–264.

Montes, L. G. A., Uribe, M. P. O., Sotres, J. C., & Martin, G. H. (2003). Treatment of primary insomnia with melatonin: A double-blind, placebo-controlled, crossover study. *Journal of Psychiatry and Neuroscience, 28*(3), 191–196.

Morgenthaler, T. I., & Silber, M. H. (2002). Amnestic sleep-related eating disorder associated with zolpidem. *Sleep Medicine, 3*(4), 323–327.

Morin, C. M. (1993). *Insomnia: Psychological assessment and management.* New York: Guilford Press.

Morin, C. M., Colecchi, C., Stone, J., Sood, R., & Brink, D. (1999). Behavioral and pharmacological therapies for late-life insomnia: A randomized controlled trial. *Journal of the American Medical Association, 281*(11), 991–999.

Morin, C. M., Culbert, J. P., & Schwartz, S. M. (1994). Nonpharmacological interventions for insomnia: A meta-analysis of treatment efficacy. *American Journal of Psychiatry, 151*(8), 1172–1180.

Morin, C. M., & Espie, C. A. (2003). *Insomnia: A clinical guide to assessment and treatment.* New York: Kluwer Academic/Plenum Press.

Morin, C. M., Hauri, P. J., Espie, C. A., Spielman, A. J., Buysse, D. J., & Bootzin, R. R. (1999). Non-pharmacologic treatment of chronic insomnia (An American Academy of Sleep Medicine review). *Sleep, 22*(8), 1134–1156.

Morin, C. M., Savard, J., & Blais, F. C. (2000). Cognitive therapy. In K. L. Lichstein & C. M. Morin (Eds.), *Treatment of late-life insomnia* (pp. 207–230). Thousand Oaks, CA: Sage.

Morin, C., Stone, J., Trinkle, D., Mercer, J., & Remsberg, S. (1993). Dysfunctional beliefs and attitudes about sleep among older adults with and without insomnia complaints. *Psychology and Aging, 8*, 463–467.

Moul, D. E., Hall, M., Pilkonis, P. A., & Buysse, D. J. (2004). Self-report measures of insomnia in adults: Rationales, choices, and needs. *Sleep Medicine Reviews, 8*(3), 177–198.

Murtagh, D. R., & Greenwood, K. M. (1995). Identifying effective psychological treatments for insomnia: A meta-analysis. *Journal of Consulting and Clinical Psychology, 63*(1), 79–89.

National Institutes of Health. (2005). National Institutes of Health State of the Science Conference statement on manifestations and management of chronic insomnia in adults. *Sleep, 28*(9), 1049–1057.

Perlis, M. L., Jungquist, C., Smith, M. T., & Posner, D. (2005). *Cognitive behavioral treatment of insomnia: A session-by-session guide.* New York: Springer.

Perlis, M. L., & Lichstein, K. L. (2003). *Treating sleep disorders: Principles and practice of behavioral sleep medicine.* Hoboken, NJ: Wiley.

Perlis, M. L., & Youngstedt, S. D. (2000). The diagnosis of primary insomnia and treatment alternatives. *Comprehensive Therapy, 26*(4), 298–306.

Petursson, H. (1994). The benzodiazepine withdrawal syndrome. *Addiction, 89*(11), 1455–1459.

Pillitteri, J. L., Kozlowski, L. T., Person, D. C., & Spear, M. E. (1994). Over-the-counter sleep aids: Widely used but rarely studied. *Journal of Substance Abuse, 6*(3), 315–323.

Ramchandani, P., Webb, V. V., & Stores, G. (2000). A systematic review of treatment of settling problems and night waking in young children. *Western Journal of Medicine, 173*(1), 33–38.

Ray, W. A., Griffin, M. R., & Downey, W. (1989). Benzodiazepines of long and short elimination half-life and the risk of hip fracture. *Journal of the American Medical Association, 262*(23), 3303–3307.

Richardson, G. S., Roehrs, T. A., Rosenthal, L., Koshorek, G., & Roth, T. (2002). Tolerance to daytime sedative effects of H1 antihistamines. *Journal of Clinical Psychopharmacology, 22*(5), 511–515.

Riedel, B. W., & Lichstein, K. L. (2000). Insomnia and daytime functioning. *Sleep Medicine Reviews, 4*(3), 277–298.

Riemann, D., Voderholzer, U., Cohrs, S., Rodenbeck, A., Hajak, G., Ruther, E., et al. (2002). Trimipramine in primary insomnia: Results of a polysomnographic double-blind controlled study. *Pharmacopsychiatry, 35*(5), 165–174.

Rodenbeck, A., Cohrs, S., Jordan, W., Huether, G., Ruther, E., & Hajak, G. (2003). The sleep-improving effects of doxepin are paralleled by a normalized plasma cortisol secretion in primary insomnia: A placebo-controlled, double-blind, randomized, cross-over study followed by an open treatment over 3 weeks. *Psychopharmacology, 170*(4), 423–428.

Roehrs, T., & Roth, T. (1997). Hypnotics, alcohol, caffeine: Relation to insomnia. In M. R. Pressman & W. C. Orr (Eds.), *Understanding sleep: Evaluation and treatment of sleep disorders* (pp. 339–355). Washington, DC: American Psychological Association.

Rombaut, N., Maillard, F., Kelly, F., & Hindmarch, I. (1990). The Quality of Life of Insomniacs Questionnaire (QOLI). *Medical Science Research, 18,* 845–847.

Rosenthal, L., Roehrs, T. A., & Roth, T. (1993). The Sleep-Wake Activity Inventory: A self-report measure of daytime sleepiness. *Biological Psychiatry, 34*(11), 810–820.

Roth, T., Hajak, G., & Ustun, T. B. (2001). Consensus for the pharmacological management of insomnia in the new millennium. *International Journal of Clinical Practice, 55*(1), 42–52.

Rush, C. R., Baker, R. W., & Wright, K. (1999). Acute behavioral effects and abuse potential of trazodone, zolpidem and triazolam in humans. *Psychopharmacology, 144*(3), 220–233.

Sateia, M., Doghramji, K., Hauri, P., & Morin, C. (2000). Evaluation of chronic insomnia. *Sleep, 23*(2), 1–24.

Simon, G. E., & VonKorff, M. (1997). Prevalence, burden, and treatment of insomnia in primary care. *American Journal of Psychiatry, 154*(10), 1417–1423.

Singer, C., Tractenberg, R. E., Kaye, J., Schafer, K., Gamst, A., Grundman, M., et al. (2003). A multicenter, placebo-controlled trial of melatonin for sleep disturbance in Alzheimer's disease. *Sleep, 26*(7), 893–901.

Smets, E. M., Garssen, B., Bonke, B., & De Haes, J. C. (1995). The Multidimensional Fatigue Inventory (MFI) psychometric qualities of an instrument to assess fatigue. *Journal of Psychosomatic Research, 39*(3), 315–325.

Spielman, A. J., Saskin, P., & Thorpy, M. J. (1987). Treatment of chronic insomnia by restriction of time in bed. *Sleep, 10,* 45–55.

Stepanski, E. J., & Rybarczyk, B. (2006). Emerging research on the treatment and etiology of secondary or comorbid insomnia. *Sleep Medicine Reviews, 10*(1), 7–18.

Taylor, D. J., Lichstein, K. L., & Durrence, H. H. (2003). Insomnia as a health risk factor. *Behavioral Sleep Medicine, 1*(4), 227–247.

Taylor, D. J., Lichstein, K. L., Durrence, H. H., Riedel, B. W., & Bush, A. J. (2005). Epidemiology of insomnia, depression, and anxiety. *Sleep, 28*(11), 1457–1464.

Troy, S. M., Lucki, I., Unruh, M. A., Cevallos, W. H., Leister, C. A., Martin, P. T., et al. (2000). Comparison of the effects of zaleplon, zolpidem, and triazolam on memory, learning, and psychomotor performance. *Journal of Clinical Psychopharmacology, 20*(3), 328–337.

Vallieres, A., & Morin, C. (2003). Actigraphy in the assessment of insomnia. *Sleep, 26,* 902–906.

Walsh, J. K., & Engelhardt, C. L. (1999). The direct economic costs of insomnia in the United States for 1995. *Sleep, 22*(Suppl. 2), S386–S393.

Walsh, J. K., Erman, M., Erwin, C. W., Jamieson, A., Mahowald, M., Regestein, Q., et al. (1998). Subjective hypnotic efficacy of trazodone and zolpidem in DSM-III-R primary insomnia. *Human Psychopharmacology: Clinical and Experimental, 13,* 191–198.

Walsh, J. K., & Schweitzer, P. K. (1999). Ten-year trends in the pharmacological treatment of insomnia. *Sleep, 22*(3), 371–375.

Ware, J. C., & Pittard, J. T. (1990). Increased deep sleep after trazodone use: A double-blind placebo-controlled study in healthy young adults. *Journal of Clinical Psychiatry, 51*(Suppl.), 18–22.

Ware, J. E., Jr., & Sherbourne, C. D. (1992). The MOS 36-item short-form health survey (SF-36): Pt. I. Conceptual framework and item selection. *Medical Care, 30*(6), 473–483.

Weaver, T., Laizner, A., Evans, L., Maislin, G., Chugh, D., Lyon, K., et al. (1997). An instrument to measure functional status outcomes for disorders of excessive sleepiness. *Sleep, 20,* 835–843.

Whitney, C. W., Enright, P. L., Newman, A. B., Bonekat, W., Foley, D., & Quan, S. F. (1998). Correlates of daytime sleepiness in 4,578 elderly persons: The Cardiovascular Health Study. *Sleep, 21*(1), 27–36.

Zhdanova, I. V., Wurtman, R. J., Regan, M. M., Taylor, J. A., Shi, J. P., & Leclair, O. U. (2001). Melatonin treatment for age-related insomnia. *Journal of Clinical Endocrinology and Metabolism, 86*(10), 4727–4730.

CHAPTER 25

Health Anxiety and Its Disorders

GORDON J. G. ASMUNDSON AND STEVEN TAYLOR

DESCRIPTION OF THE DISORDER

All of us have experienced health anxiety—anxiety stemming from the belief that bodily sensations or changes are indicative of disease—at some time in our lives. Like other forms of anxiety, anxiety about our health can serve an adaptive function in that it sometimes motivates us to seek medical care when such care is needed. To illustrate, concern and worry about acute head pain and imbalance in a person with a family history of stroke may prompt that person to seek immediate medical attention and thereby reduce the risk of mortality. The extent to which one experiences health anxiety varies considerably from person to person; as such, contemporary models (e.g., Salkovskis & Warwick, 1986; Taylor & Asmundson, 2004) conceptualize it along a continuum ranging from mild to severe. Potentially maladaptive expressions of health anxiety, characterized by undue suffering and impairment in social and occupational functioning, typically occur when the anxiety is out of proportion with the objective degree of medical risk. Low health anxiety in the face of high health risk (i.e., underestimates of the probability of having or contacting a disease) is discussed elsewhere (e.g., Taylor, 1999). The focus of this chapter is high health anxiety in the face of low health risk.

CORE FEATURES OF SEVERE HEALTH ANXIETY

Severe health anxiety is characterized by several core cognitive, somatic, and behavioral features. The core cognitive feature is disease conviction—the belief that one has a serious disease. People with severe health anxiety usually resist the notion that that their "symptoms" are due to anything other than disease. That is, they are convinced that the bodily sensations and changes that they are experiencing are due to some sort of serious physical malady rather than somatic sensations arising from benign bodily perturbations (e.g., trembling associated with muscle tension), symptoms of minor disease (e.g., chest pain associated with dyspepsia), and autonomic nervous system arousal.

As a consequence of their disease conviction, people with severe health anxiety become preoccupied with, and fearful of, the possibility of having to suffer the agony of having a serious disease. While disease conviction is most closely associated with the fear of currently having a disease, fear of contracting a disease can also be prominent. Recurring images of disease and death, often intrusive in nature, are not uncommon in people with severe health anxiety (Warwick & Salkovskis, 1989). Other dysfunctional beliefs (see Table 25.1) may accompany disease conviction and, together with disease conviction and preoccupation, motivate maladaptive coping behaviors. These beliefs appear to influence attention and memory, both of which become biased toward disease-related stimuli (e.g., Owens, Asmundson, Hadjistavropoulos, & Owens, 2004; Pauli & Alpers, 2002).

Fear of currently having a disease is typically accompanied by reassurance seeking behavior, whereby the person looks for repeated affirmation from others (e.g., family physician, family members) that there is nothing wrong with his or her health. Receiving reassurance provides some relief from health anxiety; unfortunately, the effects are transient, typically lasting no more than 24 hours (Haenen, de Jong, Schmidt, Stevens, & Visser, 2000). In fact, reassurance seeking appears to perpetuate severe

Table 25.1
Common Dysfunctional Beliefs of People with Severe Health Anxiety

Focus	Examples of Beliefs
Meaning of bodily sensations and changes	I'm healthy only when I don't have any bodily sensations. Bodily complaints are always a sign of disease. Red blotches are signs of skin cancer. Joint pain means that my bones are degenerating. Real symptoms aren't caused by anxiety.
Meaning and consequences of disease	If I get sick I'll be in great pain and suffering. People will avoid or reject me if I get really ill. Serious diseases are everywhere. People don't recover from serious diseases.
Viewing self as weak and vulnerable	My circulatory system is very sensitive. I need to avoid exertion because I'm physically frail. Illness is a sign of failure and inadequacy. If I'm ill people will abandon me.
Doctors and medical tests	Doctors should be able to explain all bodily complaints. Doctors can't be trusted because they often make mistakes. If a doctor refers me for further medical tests, then he or she must believe that there's something seriously wrong with me. Medical evaluations are unreliable if you don't have symptoms at the time of the test. Medical evaluations are unreliable if you don't give your doctor a complete and detailed description of your symptoms.
Adaptiveness of worry and bodily vigilance	Worrying about my health will keep me safe. I need to frequently check my body to catch the first signs of illness. I need to carefully watch my health, otherwise something terrible will happen.

Adapted from *Treating Health Anxiety: A Cognitive-Behavioral Approach*, by S. Taylor and G. J. G. Asmundson, 2004, New York: Guilford.

health anxiety in the long term (Taylor & Asmundson, 2004; Warwick & Salkovskis, 1990). Other common behavioral reactions—recurrent bodily checking (e.g., frequent breast self-examinations, repeated palpation of internal lumps or external abrasions), checking medical textbooks or the Internet for information about dreaded diseases, and trying various remedies (e.g., herbal preparations, gold bracelets)—also serve to perpetuate fear of currently having a disease. For example, repeatedly palpating a lymph node to check for swelling presumed to be indicative of cancer will actually lead to swelling and tenderness, which, in turn, are interpreted as evidence of cancer. Fear of catching a disease, on the other hand, is typically associated with phobic avoidance, such as staying away from hospitals, limiting contact with people who are sick or who deal with sick people, and not touching public door handles or other things that might have been handled by sickly people (e.g., public telephones, shopping carts, library books).

HEALTH ANXIETY DISORDERS

There are several expressions of health anxiety that can be generally classified as health anxiety disorders. These include Hypochondriasis, as defined in the *Diagnostic and Statistical Manual of Mental Disorders*, fourth edition, text revision (*DSM-IV-TR*; American Psychiatric Association, 2000), and several other clinically significant conditions that center on anxiety regarding health, including symptom presentations that fall short of full diagnostic criteria for Hypochondriasis as well as disease phobia. These are described in more detail later in the chapter. Delusional Disorder, somatic type, another condition characterized by unshakable and unfounded beliefs of having health conditions such as emitting foul odors from the skin or being infested with subcutaneous parasites, is discussed in more detail elsewhere (Taylor & Asmundson, 2004).

Hypochondriasis, as defined in the *DSM-IV-TR*, is a somatoform disorder characterized primarily by preoccupation with fears and beliefs about having a serious disease based on misinterpretation of benign (i.e., harmless) bodily sensations (Criterion A). The focus of concerns can range from highly specific bodily concerns, such as chest tightness and pain (Barsky & Klerman, 1983), to symptoms that are vague, variable, and generalized (e.g., diffuse bodily aching). Preoccupation must persist despite appropriate medical evaluation and reassurance (Criterion B); disease-related beliefs cannot be of delusion intensity or restricted to concerns about defects in appearance (Criterion C); there must be significant distress or impairment in important areas of functioning (Criterion D); and the preoccupation has to last at least 6 months (Criterion E). When these criteria are met and disease preoccupation is not better accounted for by another disorder (e.g., Obsessive-Compulsive Disorder, Major Depressive Disorder), a diagnosis of Hypochondrias is made. The *DSM-IV-TR* subtypes of Hypochondriasis are defined according to insight. Hypochondriasis with poor insight is diagnosed when, for most of the time during the course of the disorder, the person does not recognize that his or her concern about having a serious disease is excessive or unreasonable. It is noteworthy that people with Hypochondriasis usually resist the idea that they are suffering from a mental disorder.

Gureje, Üstün, and Simon (1997) used the term *abridged hypochondriasis* to refer to presentations of severe health anxiety that are missing one or more of the requisite *DSM-IV-TR* diagnostic criteria for Hypochondriasis. Abridged hypochondriasis might be diagnosed when a person is preoccupied with fears of having a serious disease but eventually responds to medical reassurance (i.e., Criterion B), if he or she is still able to function reasonably well (i.e., Criterion D), or if he or she has significant but transient anxiety lasting less than 6 months (i.e., Criterion E). We (Taylor & Asmundson, 2004) and others (Marks, 1987; Pilowsky, 1967) also conceptualize disease phobia—a *DSM-IV*-defined specific phobia characterized by the fear of being exposed to contagions or contracting a disease—as an abridged form of Hypochondriasis. Although disease phobia is commonly a feature of full-blown Hypochondriasis, it can exist on its own, without the other features of Hypochondriasis. Like other specific phobias, it is accompanied by distress, apprehension, avoidance of situations that are associated with disease (e.g., hospitals, sick people, public washrooms), and somatic symptoms of anxiety (Côté et al., 1996).

Severe health anxiety also frequently occurs as a feature of other anxiety disorders, particularly Panic Disorder (e.g., worry about dying during panic attacks), Obsessive-Compulsive Disorder (e.g., intrusive thoughts about contamination from germs), and unipolar mood disorders (e.g., worry that sleeplessness and weight loss are symptoms of an undiagnosed physical condition). It should be noted that there is controversy as to whether the health anxiety disorders are best conceptualized as anxiety disorders, masked forms of depression, somatoform disorders, or personality disorders (e.g., see Goodstein, 1985; Lesse, 1967; Mayou, Kirmayer, Simon, Kroenke, & Sharpe, 2005).

Prevalence

The majority of studies have found that severe health anxiety is equally common among women and men (Asmundson, Taylor, & Cox, 2001). Estimates suggest that full Hypochondriasis has a lifetime prevalence in the general population of 1% to 5% and occurs in 2% to 7% of primary care outpatients (American Psychiatric Association, 2000). Abridged hypochondriasis is more common than the full-blown disorder (Kirmayer & Robbins, 1991; Looper & Kirmayer, 2001); however, the lifetime prevalence of each form of abridged hypochondriasis is unknown. The point prevalence of disease phobia is 3% to 4% (Agras, Sylvester, & Oliveau, 1969; Malis, Hartz, Doebbeling, & Noyes, 2002). Collectively, these prevalence estimates suggest that health anxiety disorders, as a group, are problems that are as common as or more common than many of the major psychiatric disorders, such as Schizophrenia.

Course

Severe health anxiety typically arises when a person is under stress, seriously ill or recovering from a serious ailment, or has suffered the loss of a family member (Barsky & Klerman, 1983). It also can occur or be exacerbated when a person is exposed to disease-related media information via the popular media or medical information resources (Taylor & Asmundson, 2004). Severe health anxiety most commonly develops in early adulthood, although it can arise at any age (American Psychiatric Association, 2000). The course of full-blown Hypochondriasis is often chronic (American Psychiatric Association, 2000), persisting for years in over 50% of cases (Barsky, Fama, Bailey, & Ahern, 1998; Robbins & Kirmayer, 1996). It is most likely to become chronic in people who experience many unpleasant bodily sensations, who believe they have a serious medical condition, and who have a comorbid psychiatric disorder such as Major Depression (Barsky, Cleary, Sarnie, & Klerman, 1993; Noyes et al., 1994a, 1994b). Little is known about the course of other health anxiety disorders. Although the course of transient Hypochondriasis is, by definition, less than 6 months, people with this disorder are likely to experience future episodes of excessive health anxiety (Barsky et al., 1993).

It is unclear whether health anxiety changes with age. Research conducted to date has been based largely on cross-sectional (cohort) studies, the results of which have been mixed. Some studies suggest that health anxiety is greater in older than younger people (Altamura, Carta, Tacchini, Musazzi, & Pioli, 1998; Gureje et al., 1997), whereas other research has found no difference between age groups (Barsky, Frank, Cleary, Wyshak, & Klerman, 1991). Few studies of health anxiety have been conducted in children; however, available data indicate a significant proportion of children between 8 and 15 years of age report significant worry about their health (Wright & Asmundson, 2003). Longitudinal studies are needed to further examine if and how health anxiety changes with age.

Cost

Severity of health anxiety is often unrelated to objective measures of physical health (Barsky, Wyshak, & Klerman, 1986). Even so, as noted, severe health anxiety can seriously impair social and occupational functioning. People with severe health anxiety, compared to those without, are less likely to be employed outside the home. On the other hand, they are more likely to visit primary care physicians and specialists, to have medical laboratory tests and surgical procedures, to have greater physical limitations, to take more days of bed rest, and to be living on disability benefits (Barsky et al., 1986, 1998; Barsky, Ettner, Horsky, & Bates, 2001; Escobar et al., 1998; Hollifield, Paine, Tuttle, & Kellner, 1999). Consequently, the health anxiety disorders exert a considerable economic burden on the health care system.

DIAGNOSIS AND ASSESSMENT

Hypochondriasis and disease phobia are, as described earlier, diagnosed according to the criteria set forth in the *DSM-IV-R*. The various presentations of abridged hypochondriasis, with the exception of disease phobia, are indicated when health anxiety is clinically significant despite not meeting full diagnostic criteria for Hypochondriasis. Diagnosis and treatment planning should always begin with a careful assessment. Assessment is, in part, a theory-driven exercise that serves to inform case formulation and treatment planning; thus, assessment, case formulation, and treatment planning are influenced by the theoretical orientation from which a practitioner views psychopathology. Our approach is based on a contemporary cognitive-behavioral model of health anxiety that emphasizes the importance of cognitive, somatic, and behavioral features of the condition (Taylor & Asmundson, 2004). All of these features are important considerations in assessment. Next we discuss assessment targets and provide a brief overview of assessment methods.

Assessment Targets

The first two steps in assessment involve (1) ruling *out* general medical conditions that might account for the presenting problems, and (2) ruling *in* a *DSM-IV-TR* diagnosis of Hypochondriasis, one of the abridged presentations of hypochondriasis, or disease phobia. Both steps are important to determine whether an empirically supported treatment for excessive health anxiety, such as cognitive-behavioral treatment, is indicated. Health anxiety disorders are not a diagnosis of exclusion; that is, the absence of a medically identified basis for the patient's physical concerns does not necessarily indicate that he or she is suffering from excessive health anxiety. The patient's problems may be due to a general medical condition that was not identified by medical tests. This is one reason why ruling out general medical conditions is insufficient for a diagnosis; the clinician needs to obtain sufficient evidence that the patient's physical concerns are associated with excessive health anxiety.

By the time people with severe health anxiety are referred to a mental health professional they have often had numerous medical evaluations, particularly in the case of Hypochondriasis. These evaluations are usually conducted at the insistence of the patient, not the family physician, and result in failure to identify a general medical condition that could account for the concerning bodily sensations or changes. Some doctors try to placate the patient by providing medically unnecessary tests; however, such forms of "assessment" are not helpful and may perpetuate health anxiety. Repeated testing can serve to reinforce the patient's mistaken belief that she or he has a serious disease and, in some cases, can have iatrogenic effects (e.g., scarring and pain due to repeated exploratory surgeries, postsurgical infection).

It is possible for a patient to have a diagnosed general medical condition *and* severe health anxiety. In these cases, a diagnosis of Hypochondriasis would be made if the general medical condition did not fully account for the patient's concerns about disease (American Psychiatric Association, 2000). Because disease-related fears and beliefs are common in other psychiatric conditions, these also need to be ruled out before arriving at a diagnosis of one of the health anxiety disorders.

A thorough psychological assessment should include consideration of current *DSM-IV-TR* Axes I and II diagnoses to assess for comorbid disorders. It should also include an evaluation of core features of health anxiety, personal history, current living arrangements, and reasons for seeking treatment. As detailed earlier and elsewhere (Taylor & Asmundson, 2004), core features of health anxiety include dysfunctional beliefs and strength of conviction (e.g., beliefs such as "Healthy people never experience bodily sensations"), troubling bodily sensations or changes, disease fears, and avoidance or other safety behaviors. Consideration of personal history and current life circumstances helps to identify the learning experiences that may have contributed to the development of severe health anxiety and determine current stressors and relationships that may contribute to its maintenance, respectively. It is also important to explore reasons why a person is seeking treatment, so impediments to treatment adherence (e.g., unwillingness to accept an alternative to disease-based explanations for concerning bodily sensations or changes, presenting because he or she has been pressured to do so by a physician or family member) can be addressed.

Assessment Tools

Assessment tools used for treatment planning come in several forms, including hospital medical records, clinician-administered structured clinical interviews, self-report questionnaires, and prospective monitoring forms. Hospital medical records are important for charting the course of the patient's problems. Although others are available (see, e.g., the Structured Diagnostic Interview for Hypochondriasis; Barsky et al., 1992), we recommend using one of two structured interviews. The Structured Clinical Interview for *DSM-IV* (SCID-IV; First, Spitzer, Gibbon, & Williams, 1996) provides a comprehensive assessment of a range of Axis I disorders, including Hypochondriasis and specific phobias. The SCID-IV has the advantage of covering a wide range of current and lifetime disorders, but can take up to 2 hours to administer. The Health Anxiety Interview (Taylor & Asmundson, 2004), on the other hand, provides a faster (i.e., 30 minutes) yet comprehensive evaluation of the nature and history of health concerns associated with hypochondriasis and the other health anxiety disorders; however, its content is limited to the health anxiety disorders and does not cover other common disorders.

There are numerous self-report measures of hypochondriasis and related constructs. The most widely used of these are described in detail by Stewart and Watt (2001) and Speckens (2001) and are reproduced in the appendixes of Taylor and Asmundson (2004). The questionnaires differ in several ways, including breadth of assessment, time required for administration and scoring, availability of norms, and the amount of research on their reliability and validity. The choice of scale depends partly on the purpose of the assessment. We recommend the Whiteley Index (Pilowsky, 1967) in situations requiring quick assessment of health anxiety. Unlike other brief measures, norms and screening cutoff scores are available, and it is short enough for periodic readministration throughout treatment to monitor progress. If time permits a more detailed assessment of health anxiety, then the Illness Attitude Scales (Kellner, 1986) is a good choice. This measure is easy to score, there are a good deal of data on its reliability and validity, and norms are available. Factor analytic findings (e.g., Hadjistavropoulos, Frombach, & Asmundson, 1999) indicate that it comprises four subscales that denote several core features of health anxiety, including (a) fear of illness, disease, pain, and death; (b) symptom interference with lifestyle; (c) treatment experience (including reassurance seeking and the effects of receiving reassurance); and (d) disease conviction.

Prospective monitoring methods are useful in assessment and can be used throughout therapy to monitor the course of treatment. Prospective monitoring involves use of a daily diary or checklist. Patients can be asked to complete the diary each day for 1 or 2 weeks prior to treatment and at regular intervals (e.g., every 4 weeks) throughout treatment. This provides a wealth of information regarding the patient's specific health concerns and health behaviors on an episode-by-episode basis.

CONCEPTUALIZATION

We have previously suggested that a comprehensive conceptualization of health anxiety disorders should explain associated predisposing, precipitating, perpetuating, and protective factors (Taylor & Asmundson, 2004). *Predisposing factors* are those that make one more vulnerable to severe health anxiety and include, for example, learning experiences and physical factors that produce intense but benign bodily sensations. *Precipitating factors* are those that trigger health anxiety, such as stressful life events. *Perpetuating factors,* such as avoidance or persistent checking behavior, help maintain the condition or make it worse. *Protective factors* are those that prevent health anxiety from spiraling out of control and becoming excessive. Next we discuss a variety of factors that predispose, precipitate, and perpetuate excessive health anxiety. Less is known about factors that protect against excessive health anxiety and, as such, we do not discuss these in detail.

DEVELOPMENTAL ISSUES

There are several developmental issues that might predispose a person to develop severe health anxiety later in life. Childhood history of severe disease, whether in oneself or in a family member, is associated with Hypochondriasis in adulthood (American Psychiatric Association, 2000; Fritz & Williams, 1988; Robbins & Kirmayer, 1996). Likewise, childhood diseases, particularly those involving severe pain or discomfort, can induce fear of future disease. Hospitalization and separation from nurturing caregivers can add to distress, particularly when the child is strongly attached to her or his caregiver.

LEARNING AND MODELING

Learning experiences most likely influence health anxiety by shaping health-related beliefs and coping behaviors. Aside from learning that accompanies the developmental issues described earlier, there are other avenues through which learning can predispose and precipitate health anxiety, including learning that occurs in the context of parental issues and stressful life events (Taylor & Asmundson, 2004). These issues are summarized next.

Parental Issues Early learning experiences arising from particular patterns of parent-child interaction might predispose a person to develop severe health anxiety as a child or later in life. Three types of parent-child patterns have been studied: parental modeling (i.e., where the child observes that parents are excused from home and work responsibilities or receive special attention when sick); parental overprotection (i.e., where parents treat the child as frail and vulnerable, teaching the child to believe that he or she is sickly or at risk for getting sick); and parental reinforcement of illness behavior. Illness behavior—appearing sickly—is reinforced when parents give the child toys, food treats, attention, sympathy, special care, or excused absences from school or home chores whenever complaints of not feeling well are voiced.

Most (Baker & Merskey, 1982; Bianchi, 1971; Parker & Lipscombe, 1980; Schwartz, Gramling, & Mancini, 1994; Watt & Stewart, 2000; Whitehead et al., 1994), but not all (Barsky, Wool, Barnett, & Cleary, 1994), retrospective studies suggest that severe health anxiety in adulthood is associated with childhood exposure to these parental patterns. Supporting the importance of parental modeling, longitudinal studies suggest that parental ill health is correlated with medically unexplained symptoms in offspring during childhood and adulthood (Craig, Boardman, Mills, Daly-Jones, & Drake, 1993; Hotopf, Mayou, Wadsworth, & Wessely, 1999).

It is important to note that we do not advocate a "blame your parents" model of health anxiety (see Taylor & Asmundson, 2004). Although the available research suggests that parent-child interactions may be important in the onset and maintenance of severe health anxiety, they are only one of several factors. Similarly, parental overprotection, reinforcement, and modeling are not involved in all cases of severe health anxiety.

Life Events As noted, severe health anxiety usually begins during early adulthood and is often precipitated by stressful life events, including stress associated with activities of daily living (e.g., work demands, financial issues), serious and painful disease or recovery from such, or loss of a family member (American Psychiatric Association,

2000; Barsky & Klerman, 1983; Robbins & Kirmayer, 1996). Stress is associated with increases in somatic complaints, health anxiety, and physician visits that are disproportionate to actual medical morbidity (Kellner, Pathak, Romanik, & Winslow, 1983); however, stressful events are likely insufficient precipitators of severe health anxiety. Most people experience stressful life events and do not develop a health anxiety disorder. But stress does produce arousal-related bodily sensations or changes that may be misinterpreted by some people as being indicative of disease. Likewise, being sick or experiencing an accident- or disease-related death of someone close may lead vulnerable people to ruminate about the fragility of life and dangerousness of the world. This in turn may promote worry about personal well-being.

Barsky et al. (1994) compared general medical clinic outpatients with or without Hypochondriasis with regard to history of childhood trauma. Hypochondriasis was associated with a higher frequency of sexual abuse (29% vs. 7%), childhood physical violence (32% vs. 7%), and major parental upheaval (29% vs. 9%) before age 17. Stressors such as physical or sexual abuse may lead a child to believe that he or she is weak, helpless, and generally vulnerable, thereby contributing to health-related anxiety; however, when compared to normal control participants, many psychiatric populations (e.g., those with Panic Disorder, Bulimia Nervosa, Borderline Personality Disorder) have increased prevalence of sexual abuse, physical abuse, and other sorts of stressful life events (Paris, 1998; Taylor, 2000). This suggests that life stressors play, at most, a nonspecific role in predisposing one toward severe health anxiety; that is, life stressors likely influence health anxiety disorders and many other disorders.

GENETIC INFLUENCES

Early studies failed to find evidence of genetic factors in severe health anxiety. Noyes, Holt, Happel, Kathol, and Yagla, (1997), for example, found no increase in the rate of Hypochondriasis among the relatives of 19 patients with Hypochondriasis attending a general medical clinic compared with the relatives of 24 patients without Hypochondriasis from the same clinic. Similarly, using a twin study method, Torgersen (1986) found that the concordance rate for lifetime history of somatoform disorders did not significantly differ between monozygotic (MZ) and dizygotic (DZ) twin pairs, despite the twofold greater genetic similarity of the former to the latter twins. These finding are difficult to interpret given the small samples employed and, in case of the Torgersen study, the low population base rates of Hypochondriasis.

Studies with larger samples of twin pairs (DiLalla, Carey, Gottesman, & Bouchard, 1996; Gottesman, 1962) suggest that genetic factors account for up to 35% of the variance in scores on the Hypochondriasis scale (Hs) of the Minnesota Multiphasic Personality Inventory; however, these findings are also limited in that the Hs scale measures awareness of bodily sensations and not severe health anxiety. To address the limitations of previous studies, we recently assessed the relative effects of genetic and environmental influences on the variance of severe health anxiety (i.e., after controlling for medical morbidity) in 88 MZ and 65 DZ twin pairs (Taylor, Thordarson, Jang, & Asmundson, 2006). Results indicated that genetic factors play a modest role in severe health anxiety, accounting for 10% to 37% of variance in scores on measures of health anxiety after controlling for general medical morbidity. The relevant genes have yet to be identified but may include the genes implicated in the modulation of emotion, such as the serotonin transporter gene. The most important determinants appear to be environmental in nature, accounting for 63% to 90% of variance.

Severe health anxiety is often precipitated by benign bodily sensations or changes that are misinterpreted as being indicative of disease. Consequently, factors that contribute to a "noisy" body may also influence health anxiety. For example, brief periods of activity following prolonged inactivity (and physical deconditioning) can lead to shortness of breath, lightheadedness, rapid heart rate, and aches and pain, which, in turn, might be misinterpreted as signs of disease. Similarly, autonomic arousal, a concomitant of both positive and negative emotions, stimulates palpitations, muscle tension, shortness of breath, gastrointestinal distress, and increased urinary frequency. People with severe health anxiety often fail to recognize that their upsetting bodily sensations and changes may be simply the concomitants of physical overexertion or emotional arousal.

CULTURAL AND DIVERSITY ISSUES

Cultural factors, such as societal values and expectations, can also influence how a person interprets bodily sensations and changes and whether treatment seeking is initiated. There appear to be cross-cultural differences in which bodily sensations and changes tend to be feared the most (Escobar, Allen, Hoyos Nervi, & Gara, 2001). People in the United States and Canada appear to have particularly high concerns about immunologically based symptoms, such as those related to viruses, "sick building syndrome," and "multiple chemical sensitivity." On the other hand, people in the United Kingdom and Germany are more concerned with gastrointestinal and cardiopulmonary symptoms, respectively (Escobar et al., 2001). Clinicians need to be cautious when diagnosing health anxiety disorders in people whose beliefs about disease have been reinforced by healers who hold opinions divergent from reassurances provided by physicians (American Psychiatric Association, 2000).

BEHAVIORAL TREATMENT

There are several treatments based, at least in part, on behavioral principles that are similar to one another: psychoeducation, cognitive therapy, exposure and response prevention, behavioral stress management, and cognitive-behavior therapy. All explicitly avoid giving reassurance because of the concern that reassurance perpetuates severe health anxiety.

PSYCHOEDUCATION

Psychoeducation involves providing a person with information about the nature of her or his presenting concerns and about treatment strategies. The advantage of psychoeducation is that it is simple to administer and can be delivered in groups. Specific content depends on the type of treatment that the person receives. If treatment is based on a cognitive-behavioral model, then psychoeducation will involve an explanation of the model (supplemented using a version of Figure 25.1, adapted to the specific characteristics of the patient) and examples of treatment strategies. Here we like to use the "noisy body" analogy as a means of introducing people to a cognitive-behavioral approach wherein troubling sensations are relabeled harmless "bodily noise" rather than indications of physical dysfunction or disease. Psychoeducation differs from the

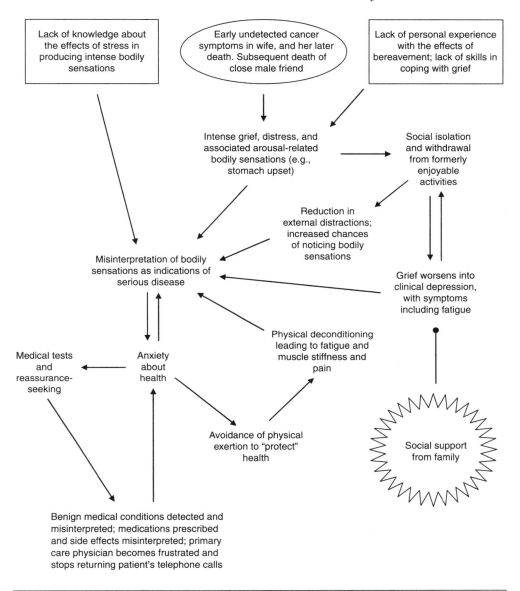

Figure 25.1 Relationships among elements in Mr. C.'s case formulation. Boxes indicate predisposing factors, ellipse represents precipitating factor, and star represents protective factor. The remaining elements are involved in the perpetuation (maintenance) of Mr. C.'s problems.

provision of reassurance in that the patient is presented with new information. By comparison, the provision of reassurance involves the repeated presentation of old information (e.g., reminding patients each week that they are healthy, or repeatedly performing medical tests to placate patients). Coping strategies (e.g., relaxation training) are also often used in psychoeducation, but systematic exposure exercises are usually not included.

Three studies have examined the merits of group psychoeducation as the main component of treatment (Avia et al., 1996; Bouman, 2002; Lidbeck, 1997). Findings suggest that psychoeducation is associated with significant reductions in Hypochondriasis, superior to wait-list control, with gains maintained at follow-ups of up to a year. Bouman found that psychoeducation was associated with a mean reduction of 40% in the frequency of medical service utilization (as indicated by comparing the frequency of doctor visits 6 months before versus 6 months after treatment). Participants reported that they valued the opportunity to share their concerns during the psychoeducational program, and most were relieved to learn that they were not the only ones suffering from excessive health anxiety.

EXPOSURE AND RESPONSE PREVENTION

Common features of the health anxiety disorders include fear and avoidance of stimuli that the person associates with disease. Accordingly, clinicians have combined various forms of exposure therapy to reduce severe health anxiety: in vivo exposure (e.g., exposure to hospitals, doctors), interoceptive exposure (e.g., physical exercise to induce rapid heartbeat), and imaginal exposure (e.g., imagining that one has developed cancer). Exposure is conducted in treatment sessions and as homework assignments. Response prevention is often combined with exposure to encourage the patient to delay or refrain from bodily checking and from seeking medical reassurance. Uncontrolled trials indicated that exposure and response prevention tends to be successful in reducing health anxiety (e.g., Logsdail, Lovell, Warwick, & Marks, 1991; Visser & Bouman, 1992). In a controlled study, Visser and Bouman (2001) found this treatment to be effective and superior to a wait-list control, with gains maintained at 7-month follow-up.

BEHAVIORAL STRESS MANAGEMENT

Behavioral stress management emphasizes the role of stress in producing harmless but unpleasant bodily sensations (i.e., bodily noise). The person is encouraged to practice various stress management exercises (e.g., relaxation training, time management, problem solving) as a means of managing stress. We also encourage reintroduction of regularly scheduled pleasurable activities to promote a healthy lifestyle (i.e., behavioral activation; Taylor & Asmundson, 2004). These strategies collectively reduce the bodily sensations that fuel health anxiety and increase a sense of well-being. Behavioral stress management was originally developed as a control condition (controlling, for example, nonspecific treatment factors) in a randomized, controlled study comparing cognitive-behavior therapy, behavioral stress management, and wait-list control (Clark et al., 1998). Although planned as a control condition, behavioral stress management also proved to be effective at reducing health anxiety. This serendipitous result has led to the use of behavioral stress management in the treatment of Hypochondriasis. By providing strategies for effective coping, behavioral stress management may have a nonspecific, beneficial effect on a person's overall symptom profile. If behavioral stress management is used, it is important that patients understand that the rationale for using stress management is to reduce unpleasant but *harmless* bodily sensations; it is not meant as a means of avoiding sensations believed to be dangerous (Taylor & Asmundson, 2004).

Cognitive-Behavior Therapy

Cognitive-behavior therapy incorporates psychoeducation and, if warranted, exposure and response prevention along with cognitive restructuring and behavioral exercises. Cognitive restructuring might be used, for example, to examine beliefs about the meaning of bodily sensations. Behavioral exercises are used to further test beliefs and to examine the effects of hypochondriacal behavior patterns. For example, to test the effects of reassurance seeking, the patient could be encouraged to refrain from this behavior for a period of time. Often, patients discover that reassurance seeking drives their fears and feelings of vulnerability. Once patients refrain from reassurance seeking they often find that they are less preoccupied with their health and feel less vulnerable because they are not exposed to daily reminders of morbidity and mortality.

Many uncontrolled trials have suggested that cognitive-behavior therapy can effectively reduce severe health anxiety (e.g., Martinez & Botella, 2005; Stern & Fernandez, 1991). Trials comparing cognitive-behavior therapy to wait-list controls, other treatment conditions, and medical treatment as usual have also produced results suggesting the superiority of cognitive-behavior therapy (e.g., Barsky & Ahern, 2004; Clark et al., 1998; Warwick, Clark, Cobb, & Salkovskis, 1996). Therapists in most cognitive-behavior therapy studies have implemented treatment on an individual basis, although Stern and Fernandez found that group treatment was also effective. In addition to being economical, group treatment for Hypochondriasis can foster a sense of acceptance and social support (Bouman, 2002).

Meta-analytic Findings

Our recent meta-analysis examined 25 treatment trials of full-blown or abridged hypochondriasis (Taylor, Asmundson, & Coons, 2005). Although there was not a large number of studies for inclusion, the meta-analytic findings provided some suggestive results, which were consistent with the results of individual studies that compared two or more treatments and with the results of narrative reviews (e.g., Asmundson et al., 2001). The most commonly examined psychosocial interventions were cognitive-behavioral interventions (e.g., psychoeducation, exposure and response prevention, cognitive therapy, cognitive-behavior therapy, behavioral stress management). The meta-analyses suggested that effect sizes were larger for all psychosocial interventions than for wait-lists. There was some evidence that a combination of cognitive and behavioral interventions (i.e., cognitive-behavior therapy) was more effective than either intervention alone or pharmacotherapy, with treatment gains maintained at 12-month follow-up.

MEDICAL TREATMENT

General Considerations

Primary care physicians play an important role in encouraging patients to try a course of cognitive-behavior therapy or pharmacotherapy. Patients referred for such treatment are typically those who have not responded to simpler interventions, such as physician assurance that their health is fine. To avoid unnecessary medical evaluations, the patient, mental health practitioner, and primary care physician can generate a tailored list of guidelines for when a physician should be consulted (see Taylor &

Asmundson, 2004). Specific guidelines for seeking medical care will depend on the nature of the patient's physical health. For elderly or infirm patients, frequent (e.g., monthly) medical check-ups may be medically necessary.

MEDICATION

Case studies and a small number of trials suggest that the following medications can be helpful in reducing Hypochondriasis: clomipramine (25–225 mg/day; Kamlana & Gray, 1988; Stone, 1993), imipramine (125–150 mg/day; Lippert, 1986; Wesner & Noyes, 1991), fluoxetine (20–80 mg/day; Fallon et al., 1996; Viswanathan & Paradis, 1991), fluvoxamine (300 mg/day; Fallon et al., 2003), paroxetine (up to 60 mg/day; Oosterbaan, van Balkom, van Boeijen, de Meij, & van Dyck, 2001), and nefazodone (200–500 mg/day; Kjernisted, Enns, & Lander, 2002). These medications can reduce all aspects of severe health anxiety, including disease fears and beliefs, pervasive anxiety, somatic symptoms, avoidance, and reassurance seeking (Fallon, 2001; Wesner & Noyes, 1991). In clinical studies these medications are typically administered over a period of 12 weeks, although they may be taken over a much longer period (e.g., years) in routine clinical practice in order to prevent relapse. Little is currently known about the long-term efficacy of various medications for treating severe health anxiety, or about the relapse rates once the medications are discontinued.

There has been only one placebo-controlled pharmacotherapy study (Fallon et al., 1996). Results indicated that there was no significant difference in the proportion of responders in either condition, although there were trends favoring fluoxetine (for patients completing 12 weeks of treatment, 80% of fluoxetine patients were classified as responders, compared to 60% of placebo patients). More recent results, based on an increased sample size, apparently indicate that fluoxetine is superior to placebo, both in terms of outcome after 12 weeks and at 9-month follow-up (B. A. Fallon, personal communication, September 10, 2002).

Medications examined in our recent meta-analysis (Taylor et al., 2005) were various selective serotonin reuptake inhibitors (SSRIs)—paroxetine, fluvoxamine, fluoxetine—as well as the compound nefazodone. The meta-analyses suggested that effect sizes were larger for all SSRI interventions and nefazodone than for wait-lists. Fluoxetine was especially promising; however, effect sizes for it and all other medications were smaller than for cognitive-behavior therapy.

SELECTING BETWEEN MEDICATION AND PSYCHOTHERAPY

Walker, Vincent, Furer, Cox, and Kjernisted (1999) reported that the majority (74%) of a sample of 23 people with severe health anxiety interested in seeking treatment for their concerns identified cognitive-behavior therapy as their preferred treatment (and 48% indicated they would accept only cognitive-behavior therapy), whereas only 4% preferred medication. Given that cognitive-behavior therapy and some medications (e.g., fluoxetine, nefazodone) may be roughly equivalent in efficacy, at least in the short term, and that there is no evidence that one treatment works any faster than another, some clinicians let the patients choose between the two (Enns, Kjernisted, & Lander, 2001). The availability of choices might enhance treatment acceptability and adherence. Patients failing to benefit from one intervention could be placed on another.

Notwithstanding, there are several noteworthy problems in using pharmacotherapy to treat severe health anxiety. There are case reports of patients failing to benefit from one or more of these drugs (e.g., Stone, 1993; Viswanathan & Paradis, 1991). Even for short (8–12 weeks) trials using drugs with few side effects, 13% to 21% of patients drop out of treatment (Taylor et al., 2005), some become preoccupied with side effects (e.g., Stone, 1993; Wesner & Noyes, 1991), and, in some cases, symptoms worsen during drug treatment as patients become alarmed by side effects like gastrointestinal discomfort (Fallon, 2001; Oosterbaan et al., 2001).

Case Description

Case Introduction

Mr. C., a 69-year-old widower and retired civil engineer, presented with a 2-year history of bodily complaints, persistent anxiety, and depressive symptoms. This case highlights several of the issues important for understanding and treating severe health anxiety. These include diagnostic issues and questions of how to conceptualize and treat severe health anxiety in the context of other psychiatric conditions. Other important issues raised by the case include the role of interpersonal factors in health anxiety, such as patterns of interaction with family, doctors, and mental health professionals. Finally, the case illustrates one of the circumstances in which "less is more." Although we have sophisticated, empirically supported cognitive-behavioral techniques, sometimes the most effective treatment consists of some simple behavioral interventions. The case has been disguised to protect patient privacy and confidentiality. This was done according to the guidelines set out by Clifft (1986) in a way that does not compromise its didactic value.

Presenting Complaints

Mr. C. described several bodily concerns, including muscle stiffness and pain, nausea (without vomiting), stomach pain, and bloating. His main concerns were abdominal sensations, which he feared were indications of cancer. He also worried that he might succumb to kidney or liver failure as a result of the medications he had taken. Mr. C. described daily anxiety and preoccupation with his unpleasant bodily sensations. His health anxiety persisted despite medical reassurance that there was no evidence of serious disease.

Mr. C. reported suffering from intermittent bouts of depressed mood, in which he felt sad and despondent for several days at a time. These episodes occurred once every few weeks. He also described a persistent lack of interest in formerly enjoyable activities, along with lack of appetite (without notable weight loss), chronic weakness and fatigue, and concentration difficulties. There was no evidence of suicidal ideation.

History

Course of Presenting Problems

Mr. C.'s physical and emotional problems developed 2 years ago, shortly after his wife died of pancreatic cancer. Her early symptoms, which were not

(continued)

immediately recognized by her primary care physician as indicators of cancer, consisted of abdominal pain, nausea, loss of appetite, unexplained weight loss, and jaundice. Shortly after her death, while Mr. C. isolated himself from others and was intensely grieving, he began to have recurrent bouts of abdominal discomfort and worried that he too might have cancer. He also noticed muscle stiffness and pain, which he feared were signs of serious disease. Mr. C.'s physical and emotional problems worsened 5 months later, when a close male friend died of complications associated with kidney failure.

Mr. C.'s grief worsened during the 7 months after his friend's death, to the point that his primary care physician thought he was clinically depressed. Mr. C.'s children and grandchildren rallied to his aid, offering him emotional and social support, and his depressive symptoms gradually abated over the course of the next 12 months. His health anxiety, however, persisted unabated.

Treatment History

Mr. C. underwent numerous medical investigations, including evaluations from specialists in gastroenterology, rheumatology, and internal medicine. He was found to have borderline hypertension and gastritis. A small, benign kidney cyst was identified and removed. His kidneys were otherwise unremarkable, and there was no evidence that the cyst caused any of his symptoms. There was no evidence of cancer, liver disease, or rheumatologic disease. The consensus of medical option was that Mr. C. was in good health for his age.

Mr. C. was treated by his primary care physician with ranitidine for gastritis (150 mg, twice daily) and alprazolam for anxiety (0.25 mg, three times daily). He was prescribed paroxetine (10 mg/day) for depression but discontinued because of side effects, primarily consisting of jitteriness and gastrointestinal upset. He was also prescribed chlorthalidone (12.5 mg/day) for hypertension but quickly discontinued this medication because of side effects consisting of nausea and dizziness. After discontinuing paroxetine and chlorthalidone, Mr. C. became increasingly preoccupied about whether those medications had harmed his body, and also worried about the side effects of ranitidine and alprazolam.

Mr. C.'s primary care physician advised him to manage his hypertension by reducing his sodium intake and by increasing his physical activity. The primary care physician also offered to prescribe a muscle relaxant for Mr. C.'s muscle stiffness and pain. Mr. C. declined because of concerns about adverse side effects. He also declined a referral to a psychiatrist for pharmacologic treatment because of concerns about side effects. Mr. C.'s primary care physician eventually persuaded Mr. C. to see a psychologist for "stress management."

Personal and Family History

Mr. C. was the eldest of four children, raised in a medium-size city. He recalled having a happy childhood and reported being a capable, conscientious student who obtained good grades at school and eventually completed an engineering degree at a local university. Regarding his general medical history, Mr. C. said he rarely became ill; "I never gave my health a second thought—I thought I'd always be healthy." He could not recall ever having a serious medical illness and could not recall any family members suffering from serious illness. Both of his elderly parents were still alive, as were his two sisters and brother. Mr. C. was not aware of any family history of psychopathology.

Mr. C. married at age 24, and the couple had three children. He stated that he had never experienced any difficulties in occupational or social functioning. He reported that his relationship with his wife and children had always been good. At the time of the intake evaluation, Mr. C. was living alone but had regular contact with his children, a daughter and two sons, who lived nearby.

Assessment

Chart Review

Prior to conducting the initial assessment interview, the therapist reviewed Mr. C.'s hospital records, along with other records supplied by the referring physician. The records provided ample documentation of extensive medical investigations that revealed no evidence of serious medical pathology. The records also contained information that Mr. C. had been reassured about his health many times by several medical specialists, and yet he continued to request further medical tests. The records indicated that Mr. C.'s health anxiety and demands for medical tests and reassurance began shortly after the death of his wife 2 years earlier. The records revealed no evidence of prior psychopathology.

Clinical Interview

When Mr. C. presented to his first session with the cognitive-behavioral therapist, he was assessed with the SCID-IV (First et al., 1996), supplemented to include questions assessing dysfunctional beliefs, maladaptive behaviors, and patterns of interpersonal interaction related to health anxiety. The interview also provided an opportunity for the therapist to make behavioral observations and to collect information relevant to a mental status examination.

Throughout the interview Mr. C. was agitated and repeatedly interrupted the therapist with questions about symptoms and treatments. These questions were clearly intended to elicit reassurance; for example, "I get this dull, aching pain in my stomach. Do you think that could be serious?"; "I saw in a magazine that psychiatric drugs and blood pressure pills cause kidney and liver damage. What do you think?"; "Do I look yellow? Do you think I have jaundice?" Rather than getting sidetracked by these questions, the therapist replied with variants of the following: "I can see that you're really worried about your health. I'll be in a better position to answer all your questions once I've done a thorough assessment."

Mr. C. was able to provide a detailed history of the various medical tests and their results, including the dates of testing and the names of doctors. His history was quite accurate when compared to his medical records, which suggested that his recent and remote memory were intact. However, on several occasions during the interview he lost track of the therapist's questions, which was consistent with his reported concentration difficulties. Although Mr. C. expressed concerns about his health, he was able to acknowledge that his worries might be excessive. For example, he wondered whether his stomach problems were caused by

(continued)

something other than cancer, such as stomach irritation due to medication or the effects of stress.

Results from the SCID-IV suggested that Mr. C. had previously met *DSM-IV* diagnostic criteria for Major Depressive Disorder (single episode, moderate severity), arising shortly after his wife's death, worsening after the death of his close friend, and then gradually abating. (Note that the duration of depressive symptoms was in excess of what would be expected simply from bereavement; American Psychiatric Association, 2000.) At the time of the intake evaluation, Mr. C. had depressive symptoms, but these were not sufficient for a diagnosis of Major Depressive Disorder.

Diagnosis of his bodily complaints and anxiety symptoms was more of a conundrum. According to *DSM-IV-TR*, a separate diagnosis of Hypochondriasis is not made if health concerns occur only during major depressive episodes. Mr. C.'s health anxiety and depression arose simultaneously, shortly after the death of his wife. But as his depression abated, his health anxiety persisted, suggesting that the latter was not simply a feature of depression. This suggested a diagnosis of Hypochondriasis.

Additional interview questions included as part of the SCID-IV indicated that Mr. C. held the following beliefs: (a) "If I experience symptoms [i.e., unpleasant bodily sensations] then I must be ill"; (b) "Real symptoms aren't caused by anxiety or stress"; (c) "Medications can seriously damage your body"; (d) "If I have symptoms then the best thing to do is to rest"; and (e) "Repeated medical tests are required because doctors often fail to detect serious diseases."

The interview also revealed evidence of maladaptive behaviors, such as avoidance of physical exertion whenever he felt weak or in pain, focusing on his stomach whenever he felt queasy, checking and rechecking medical pamphlets for information on side effects, and seeking reassurance from doctors or family members about symptoms and side effects. His reassurance seeking from his primary care physician persisted to the point that the physician no longer returned Mr. C.'s telephone calls. Mr. C. was considering changing doctors because he worried that he was not receiving proper medical care.

Self-Report Measures

Mr. C. completed two self-report measures: the Whiteley Index (Pilowsky, 1967) and the short version of the Pleasant Events Schedule (MacPhillamy & Lewinsohn, 1982). The pretreatment score on the Whiteley Index, at 12 of a possible 14, was substantially elevated and consistent with significantly elevated health anxiety. The Pleasant Events Schedule revealed that although there were several activities that he considered to be potentially enjoyable, he participated in very few of them. If increasing his participation in formerly enjoyable activities was to be used as a component of treatment (i.e., "behavioral activation" as used in the treatment of depression and health anxiety; Jacobson et al., 1996; Taylor & Asmundson, 2004), then Mr. C.'s responses suggested that the following activities were worth considering: going for walks, going out with friends, gardening or caring for houseplants, visiting interesting outdoor places (e.g., zoo, reserve, park, riverside, harbor), listening to music, or watching television.

For a 2-week period, Mr. C. was also asked to complete a prospective monitoring form in which, for each particularly intense episode of abdominal distress, he noted the situation in which it occurred, along with emotions and thoughts at the time. Monitoring provided several important pieces of information about the roles of environmental stimuli and cognitions. To illustrate, one episode of abdominal distress began with Mr. C. sitting at home alone. Having skipped breakfast, he was sitting with his morning coffee reading a newspaper. Suddenly he felt queasy. He focused his attention on his stomach and noticed that his stomach was now becoming quite painful and that the pain had "spread all around the abdomen to my back." This led him to worry about his kidneys. He then telephoned for reassurance from his primary care physician. During other episodes he reported that the pain abated when a friend or relative came over to visit, or when he was engaged in diverting activities such as household chores.

Case Conceptualization

The case formulation sought to delineate the predisposing, precipitating, perpetuating, and protective factors involved in Mr. C.'s problems. The formulation for Mr. C. is illustrated in Figure 25.1. The hypothesized predisposing factors involved a lack of knowledge about the bodily effects of stress, a lack of experience with bereavement, and a lack of experience in coping with grief. These factors, in aggregate, made it very difficult for Mr. C. to deal with his losses. The fact that Mr. C. had always enjoyed good physical health also probably contributed to his problems adjusting to the fact that he was developing health problems (e.g., hypertension) and was likely to experience more of these problems in the not too distant future.

Figure 25.1 suggests that many factors interacted in various ways to perpetuate or maintain Mr. C.'s problems. His profound grief and distress over the loss of his wife and close friend were associated with strong arousal-related sensations such as pain and nausea. Given (a) his lack of knowledge about the effects of stressors such as interpersonal loss in producing arousal-related bodily sensations, (b) his lack of experience with bereavement, and (c) that his arousal-related abdominal sensations resembled his wife's prodromal symptoms of pancreatic cancer, Mr. C. drew the understandable but erroneous conclusion that his abdominal distress was a sign of cancer. Because Mr. C. isolated himself in his house after the loss of his wife and friend, the reduction in external distractions increased the chances that he would notice and focus on bodily sensations such as unpleasant stomach sensations. His misinterpretation of his abdominal sensations made him anxious, which, in turn, exacerbated the sensations. His anxiety about his health prompted him to seek medical testing and reassurance, which further exacerbated his health anxiety (Figure 25.1). His health anxiety also led him to avoid physical exertion in an effort to avoid further exacerbating his abdominal and other unpleasant bodily sensations. This led to physical deconditioning, which, in turn, led to increased fatigue and muscle stiffness and pain.

Figure 25.1 also suggests that Mr. C.'s lack of experience and skills in coping with bereavement made his grief particularly intense, which led to social isolation and withdrawal from formerly enjoyable activities. Isolation and

(continued)

withdrawal in turn cut him off from sources of reinforcement in his life, thereby worsening his grief to the point that he developed Major Depressive Disorder (cf. Jacobson et al., 1996). The latter was associated with fatigue and weakness, which he misinterpreted as further evidence that he, like his wife, had developed cancer.

Figure 25.1 shows that the main protective factor for Mr. C. appeared to be the social support of his children, grandchildren, and friends. At the behest of Mr. C.'s primary care physician, his family encouraged Mr. C. to socialize more often with them. This social support apparently prevented his depression from persisting. But given the number of factors contributing to his misinterpretation of bodily sensations (Figure 25.1), social support (which unfortunately entailed reassurance) was insufficient for reducing his health anxiety.

Course of Treatment and Assessment of Progress

The case formulation suggested that various cognitive-behavioral interventions might be useful, such as cognitive restructuring exercises to directly challenge dysfunctional beliefs, and behavioral exercises to teach him about the effects of stress or anxiety on bodily sensations and how the odds of detecting an unpleasant bodily sensation are influenced by the tendency to focus on one's body or on one's external environment. The case formulation, however, was insufficient for developing a treatment plan for Mr. C.; it was necessary to consider how he interacted with the therapist. Mr. C. had difficulty concentrating, was easily sidetracked, and repeatedly asked for reassurance on a range of different medical topics. These factors made it difficult to conduct cognitive restructuring, as the therapist soon discovered. Therefore, the therapist simplified the treatment program to target Mr. C.'s main problems. Treatment essentially consisted of (a) eliciting Mr. C.'s primary concerns (i.e., distressing abdominal sensations) and providing education about the effects of stress and selective attention on the experience of bodily sensations (using handouts in Taylor & Asmundson, 2004); and (b) behavioral activation exercises (i.e., exercises that afforded a sense of enjoyment or mastery, scheduled at least daily, such as those described earlier). He was encouraged to persist in these activities even if he experienced abdominal discomfort or initial fatigue.

These activities served several important functions. They helped prove to Mr. C. that he was capable of physical activity and that this was good for his health (e.g., it reduced fatigue and muscle pain and challenged the view that he was weak and would be damaged by physical activity). These activities also reduced abdominal distress, which would be expected if his stomach problems were stress-related rather than cancer-related. The exercises provided Mr. C. with exposure to positively reinforcing activities, which further reduced his depressive symptoms. The physical aspects of the exercises were also useful in reducing his hypertension.

Mr. C. was seen for 10 weekly one-to-one 50-minute sessions. In addition to the interventions described earlier, the following were used. He was educated about the self-defeating effects of persistently seeking reassurance from physicians (e.g., the iatrogenic effects of repeated medical tests, along with the risk of exhausting and alienating one's doctor through repeated requests for reassurance). The therapist asked Mr. C. to test for himself the effects of not seeking reassurance for a period of time (e.g., for a few days, to begin with) from health professionals and family members. He was also encouraged to avoid reading medical texts or articles, either in print or on the Internet, because they fueled his health concerns.

In consultation with the therapist, Mr. C., and the primary care physician, it was agreed that Mr. C. would refrain from talking about his bodily concerns with family members and from seeking reassurance from family. His daughter, who often drove him to appointments, was also interviewed by the therapist with Mr. C.'s permission. The treatment plan was explained to her, and she readily agreed that it was important for her and the other family members to stop reinforcing Mr. C.'s health preoccupation by offering needless reassurance. Family members agreed to refrain from offering reassurance. When Mr. C. tried to elicit reassurance, he would receive replies such as "Dad, you know it's against hospital rules for me to reassure you. Let's talk about something else. Tell me about your garden." According to guidelines worked out by Mr. C., his physician, and the therapist, if Mr. C. felt especially ill he would seek medical attention.

Over the course of treatment, Mr. C. admitted that his bodily complaints and health anxiety had abated, and his mood had continued to improve. His daughter, in a separate interview, noted that the family had seen an improvement in the physical and emotional well-being of their pater familias. Weekly administration of the Whiteley Index revealed consistent gradual decrements in total scores and a nadir at 3 of a possible 14 points being reached at 7 weeks. The primary care physician also reported that Mr. C.'s blood pressure had declined to the point that he was no longer borderline hypertensive. Mr. C. felt that because he was coping better he did not need to continue using alprazolam at 0.25 mg, 3 times daily. He gradually reduced the dose, under the supervision of the prescribing physician, to 0.125 mg, once a day.

By the end of treatment Mr. C.'s view of himself and his problems had changed. Instead of seeing himself as a victim of disease in need of constant medical testing and reassurance, he averred, "I need to forget about aches and pains and live it up a little. I have to overcome this myself."

Complicating Factors

The case of Mr. C. illustrates how depressive symptoms such as concentration difficulties can make it difficult for the patient to benefit from treatment. There were several other potential complications, which were avoided in Mr. C.'s treatment. One was "doctor shopping," in which the patient consults multiple physicians in the search for reassurance. Mr. C. was informed of this problem and advised to remain with his current primary care physician. Doctor shopping can lead to unnecessary (e.g., repeated) medical tests and undue reassurance.

A further potential complicating factor concerns medical morbidity. As Mr. C. ages he will quite likely eventually develop some serious disease, possibly cancer. This complication did not arise in his cognitive-behavioral treatment but is an issue that he will probably need to deal with in the future. It was difficult to predict how he would respond. Some people with severe health anxiety become

(continued)

highly distressed when they develop a serious disease. Other health-anxious patients react with relief because they (and their doctors) finally have objective proof of real disease.

Managed Care

In managed care settings, people with severe health anxiety might be treated in only 10 sessions, as in the case of Mr. C. However, other patients may require longer courses of treatment. For a given patient, it can be difficult to accurately predict the number of sessions required. This is because there are few empirically supported predictors of treatment outcome, aside from observations that patients with mild health anxiety tend to require fewer sessions than those with severe anxiety (Taylor & Asmundson, 2004). Insurance providers may need to be informed of the uncertainty about the number of sessions needed. Even patients who initially fail to benefit from a short course of treatment, such as 10 sessions, may benefit from a longer course of treatment. Given the substantial economic costs that severe health anxiety places on the health care system—in terms of visits to primary care physicians and specialists, medical laboratory tests, and exploratory surgical procedures—even a long course of cognitive-behavior therapy (e.g., 30–40 sessions) may lead to an overall reduction in health care costs.

Follow-Up

Mr. C. was advised to recontact the cognitive-behavioral clinic if he required further assistance in coping with health anxiety. It was explained to him that therapy can be helpful even for people who have serious, medically verified diseases, because it can help them cope with the stress associated with physical illness. Mr. C. did not recontact the clinic, nor was their any indication from his primary care physician that Mr. C. was in need of further therapy.

TREATMENT IMPLICATIONS OF THE CASE

The way people with severe health anxiety interact with their health care providers can interfere with effective treatment. Mr. C., like many patients with excessive health anxiety, was so preoccupied with his concerns that he frequently interrupted the therapist with requests for reassurance and was difficult to engage in a dialogue because he insisted on discussing his symptoms in great detail. Compounding this situation, Mr. C. had concentration difficulties, which interfered with his ability to attend to and remember what the therapist was saying. Given these problems, it was not surprising that cognitive restructuring interventions were ineffective. To circumvent some of these difficulties, the therapist gave Mr. C. printed psychoeducational handouts and also kept treatment as simple as possible.

SUMMARY

Given the wide range of interventions available for treating health anxiety (Taylor & Asmundson, 2004), it may be tempting for the therapist to attempt to implement multiple techniques, such as sophisticated cognitive restructuring methods, in the hope that more interventions will lead to better treatment outcomes. The present case illustrates the opposite principle of "less is more"; a small number of consistently practiced interventions can be helpful, even when more complex interventions seem unlikely to succeed.

Finally, the case shows that severe health anxiety need not have its origins in childhood experiences with disease. Many adults with a health anxiety disorder have had serious childhood illnesses, or as children witnessed family members become seriously ill; however, as the case of Mr. C. amply illustrates, the treating clinician should not assume that the origins of excessive health anxiety are invariably rooted in the patient's childhood.

REFERENCES

Agras, S., Sylvester, D., & Oliveau, D. (1969). The epidemiology of common fears and phobias. *Comprehensive Psychiatry, 10,* 151–156.

Altamura, A. C., Carta, M. G., Tacchini, G., Musazzi, A., & Pioli, M. R. (1998). Prevalence of somatoform disorders in a psychiatric population: An Italian nationwide survey. *European Archives of Psychiatry and Clinical Neuroscience, 248,* 267–271.

American Psychiatric Association. (2000). *Diagnostic and statistical manual of mental disorders* (4th ed., text rev.). Washington, DC: Author.

Asmundson, G. J. G., Taylor, S., & Cox, B. J. (2001). *Health anxiety: Clinical and research perspectives on hypochondriasis and related disorders.* New York: Wiley.

Avia, M. D., Ruiz, M. A., Olivares, M. E., Crespo, M., Guisado, A. B., Sanchez, A., et al. (1996). The meaning of psychological symptoms: Effectiveness of a group intervention with hypochondriacal patients. *Behavior Research and Therapy, 34,* 23–31.

Baker, B., & Merskey, H. (1982). Parental representations of hypochondriacal patients from a psychiatric hospital. *British Journal of Psychiatry, 141,* 233–238.

Barsky, A. J., & Ahern, D. K. (2004). Cognitive behavior therapy for hypochondriasis: A randomized controlled trial. *Journal of the American Medical Association, 291,* 1464–1470.

Barsky, A. J., Cleary, P. D., Sarnie, M. K., & Klerman, G. L. (1993). The course of transient hypochondriasis. *American Journal of Psychiatry, 150,* 484–488.

Barsky, A. J., Cleary, P. D., Wyshak, G., Spitzer, R. L., Williams, J. B. W., & Klerman, G. L. (1992). A structured diagnostic interview for hypochondriasis: A proposed criterion standard. *Journal of Nervous and Mental Diseases, 180,* 20–27.

Barsky, A. J., Ettner, S. L., Horsky, J., & Bates, D. W. (2001). Resource utilization of patients with hypochondriacal health anxiety and somatization. *Medical Care, 39,* 705–715.

Barsky, A. J., Fama, J. M., Bailey, E. D., & Ahern, D. K. (1998). A prospective 4- to 5-year study of DSM-III-R hypochondriasis. *Archives of General Psychiatry, 55,* 737–744.

Barsky, A. J., Frank, C. B., Cleary, P. D., Wyshak, G., & Klerman, G. L. (1991). The relation between hypochondriasis and age. *American Journal of Psychiatry, 148,* 923–928.

Barsky, A. J., & Klerman, G. L. (1983). Overview: Hypochondriasis, bodily complaints, and somatic styles. *American Journal of Psychiatry, 140,* 273–283.

Barsky, A. J., Wool, C., Barnett, M. C., & Cleary, P. D. (1994). Histories of childhood trauma in adult hypochondriacal patients. *American Journal of Psychiatry, 151,* 397–401.

Barsky, A. J., Wyshak, G., & Klerman, G. L. (1986). Hypochondriasis: An evaluation of the DSM-III criteria in medical outpatients. *Archives of General Psychiatry, 43,* 493–500.

Bianchi, G. N. (1971). Origins of disease phobia. *Australian and New Zealand Journal of Psychiatry, 5,* 241–257.

Bouman, T. K. (2002). A community-based psychoeducational group approach to hypochondriasis. *Psychotherapy and Psychosomatics, 71,* 326–332.

Clark, D. M., Salkovskis, P. M., Hackmann, A., Wells, A., Fennell, M., Ludgate, J., et al. (1998). Two psychological treatments for hypochondriasis: A randomised controlled trial. *British Journal of Psychiatry, 173,* 218–225.

Clifft, M. A. (1986). Writing about psychiatric patients: Guidelines for disguising case material. *Bulletin of the Menninger Clinic, 50,* 511–524.

Côté, G., O'Leary, T., Barlow, D. H., Strain, J. J., Salkovskis, P. M., Warwick, H. M. C., et al. (1996). Hypochondriasis. In T. A. Widiger, A. J. Frances, H. A. Pincus, R. Ross, M. B. First, & W. W. Davis (Eds.), *DSM-IV sourcebook* (Vol. 2, pp. 933–947). Washington, DC: American Psychiatric Association.

Craig, T. K. J., Boardman, A. P., Mills, K., Daly-Jones, O., & Drake, H. (1993). The South London Somatisation Study I: Longitudinal course and the influence of early life experiences. *British Journal of Psychiatry, 163,* 579–588.

DiLalla, D. L., Carey, G. G., Gottesman, I. I., & Bouchard, T. J., Jr. (1996). Heritability of MMPI personality indicators of psychopathology in twins reared apart. *Journal of Abnormal Psychology, 105,* 491–499.

Enns, M. W., Kjernisted, K., & Lander, M. (2001). Pharmacological management of hypochondriasis and related disorders. In G. J. G. Asmundson, S. Taylor, & B. J. Cox (Eds.), *Health anxiety: Clinical and research perspectives on hypochondriasis and related conditions* (pp. 193–219). New York: Wiley.

Escobar, J. I., Allen, L. A., Hoyos Nervi, C., & Gara, M. A. (2001). General and cross-cultural considerations in a medical setting for patients presenting with medically unexplained symptoms. In G. J. G. Asmundson, S. Taylor, & B. J. Cox (Eds.), *Health anxiety: Clinical and research perspectives on hypochondriasis and related conditions* (pp. 220–245). New York: Wiley.

Escobar, J. I., Gara, M., Waitzkin, H., Silver, R. C., Holman, A., & Compton, W. (1998). DSM-IV hypochondriasis in primary care. *General Hospital Psychiatry, 20,* 155–159.

Fallon, B. A. (2001). Pharmacologic strategies for hypochondriasis. In V. Starcevic & D. R. Lipsett (Eds.), *Hypochondriasis: Modern perspectives on an ancient malady* (pp. 329–351). New York: Oxford University Press.

Fallon, B. A., Qureshi, A. I., Schneier, F. R., Sanchez-Lacay, A., Vermes, D., Feinstein, R., et al. (2003). An open trial of fluvoxamine for hypochondriasis. *Psychosomatics, 44,* 298–303.

Fallon, B. A., Schneier, F. R., Marshall, R., Campeas, R., Vermes, D., Goetz, D., et al. (1996). The pharmacotherapy of hypochondriasis. *Psychopharmacology Bulletin, 32,* 607–611.

First, M. B., Spitzer, R. L., Gibbon, M., & Williams, J. B. W. (1996). *Structured Clinical Interview for DSM-IV.* New York: New York State Psychiatric Institute, Biometrics Research Department.

Fritz, G. K., & Williams, J. R. (1988). Issues of adolescent development for survivors of childhood cancer. *Journal of the American Academy of Child and Adolescent Psychiatry, 27,* 712–715.

Goodstein, R. K. (1985). Common clinical problems in the elderly: Camouflaged by ageism and atypical presentation. *Psychiatric Annals, 15,* 299–312.

Gottesman, I. I. (1962). Differential inheritance of psychoneuroses. *Eugenics Quarterly, 9,* 223–227.

Gureje, O., Üstün, T. B., & Simon, G. E. (1997). The syndrome of hypochondriasis: A cross-national study in primary care. *Psychological Medicine, 27,* 1001–1010.

Hadjistavropoulos, H. D., Frombach, I. K., & Asmundson, G. J. G. (1999). Exploratory and confirmatory factor analytic investigations of the Illness Attitudes Scale in a non-clinical sample. *Behavior Research and Therapy, 37,* 671–684.

Haenen, M. A., de Jong, P. J., Schmidt, A. J. M., Stevens, S., & Visser, L. (2000). Hypochondriacs' estimation of negative outcomes: Domain-specificity and responsiveness to reassuring and alarming information. *Behavior Research and Therapy, 38,* 819–833.

Hollifield, M., Paine, S., Tuttle, L., & Kellner, R. (1999). Hypochondriasis, somatization, and perceived health and utilization of health care services. *Psychosomatics, 40,* 380–386.

Hotopf, M., Mayou, R., Wadsworth, M., & Wessely, S. (1999). Childhood risk factors for adults with medically unexplained symptoms: Results from a national birth cohort study. *American Journal of Psychiatry, 156,* 1796–1800.

Jacobson, N. S., Dobson, K. S., Truax, P. A., Addis, M. E., Koerner, K., Gollan, J. K., et al. (1996). A component analysis of cognitive-behavioral treatment for depression. *Journal of Consulting and Clinical Psychology, 64,* 295–304.

Kamlana, S. H., & Gray, P. (1988). Fear of AIDS. *British Journal of Psychiatry, 15,* 1291.

Kellner, R. (1986). *Somatization and hypochondriasis.* New York: Praeger.

Kellner, R., Pathak, D., Romanik, R., & Winslow, W. W. (1983). Life events and hypochondriacal concerns. *Psychiatric Medicine, 1,* 133–141.

Kirmayer, L. J., & Robbins, J. M. (1991). Three forms of somatization in primary care: Prevalence, co-occurrence, and sociodemographic characteristics. *Journal of Nervous and Mental Diseases, 179,* 647–655.

Kjernisted, K. D., Enns, M. W., & Lander, M. (2002). An open-label clinical trial of nefazodone in hypochondriasis. *Psychosomatics, 43,* 290–294.

Lesse, S. (1967). Hypochondriasis and psychosomatic disorders masking depression. *American Journal of Psychotherapy, 21,* 607–620.

Lidbeck, J. (1997). Group therapy for somatization disorders in general practice: Effectiveness of a short cognitive-behavioral treatment model. *Acta Psychiatrica Scandinavica, 96,* 14–24.

Lippert, G. P. (1986). Excessive concern about AIDS in two bisexual men. *Canadian Journal of Psychiatry, 31,* 63–65.

Logsdail, S., Lovell, K., Warwick, H. M., & Marks, I. (1991). Behavioral treatment of AIDS-focused illness phobia. *British Journal of Psychiatry, 159,* 422–425.

Looper, K. J., & Kirmayer, L. J. (2001). Hypochondriacal concerns in a community population. *Psychological Medicine, 31,* 577–584.

MacPhillamy, D., & Lewinsohn, P. M. (1982). The Pleasant Events Schedule: Studies on reliability, validity, and scale intercorrelation. *Journal of Consulting and Clinical Psychology, 50,* 363–380.

Malis, R. W., Hartz, A. J., Doebbeling, C. C., & Noyes, R. (2002). Specific phobia of illness in the community. *Hospital and Community Psychiatry, 24,* 135–139.

Marks, I. (1987). *Fears, phobias, and rituals.* New York: Oxford University Press.

Martinez, M. P., & Botella, C. (2005). An exploratory study of the efficacy of a cognitive-behavioral treatment for hypochondriasis using different measures of change. *Psychotherapy Research, 15,* 392–408.

Mayou, R., Kirmayer, L. J., Simon, G., Kroenke, K., & Sharpe, M. (2005). Somatoform disorders: Time for a new approach in DSM-V. *American Journal of Psychiatry, 162,* 847–855.

Noyes, R., Holt, C. M., Happel, R. L., Kathol, R. G., & Yagla, S. J. (1997). A family study of hypochondriasis. *Journal of Nervous and Mental Diseases, 185,* 223–232.

Noyes, R., Kathol, R. G., Fisher, M. M., Phillips, B. M., Suelzer, M., & Woodman, C. L. (1994a). One-year follow-up of medical outpatients with hypochondriasis. *Psychosomatics, 35,* 533–545.

Noyes, R., Kathol, R. G., Fisher, M. M., Phillips, B. M., Suelzer, M., & Woodman, C. L. (1994b). Psychiatric comorbidity among patients with hypochondriasis. *General Hospital Psychiatry, 16,* 78–87.

Oosterbaan, D. B., van Balkom, A. J. L. M., van Boeijen, C. A., de Meij, T. G. J., & van Dyck, R. (2001). An open study of paroxetine in hypochondriasis. *Progress in Neuro-Psychopharmacology and Biological Psychiatry, 25,* 1023–1033.

Owens, K. M. B., Asmundson, G. J. G., Hadjistavropoulos, T., & Owens, T. J. (2004). Attentional bias toward illness threat in individuals with elevated health anxiety. *Cognitive Therapy and Research, 28*, 57–66.

Paris, J. (1998). Does childhood trauma cause personality disorder in adults? *Canadian Journal of Psychiatry, 43*, 148–153.

Parker, G., & Lipscombe, P. (1980). The relevance of early parental experiences to adult dependency, hypochondriasis and utilization of primary physicians. *British Journal of Medical Psychology, 53*, 355–363.

Pauli, P., & Alpers, G. W. (2002). Memory bias in patients with hypochondriasis and somatoform pain disorder. *Journal of Psychosomatic Research, 52*, 45–53.

Pilowsky, I. (1967). Dimensions of hypochondriasis. *British Journal of Psychiatry, 113*, 89–93.

Robbins, J. M., & Kirmayer, L. J. (1996). Transient and persistent hypochondriacal worry in primary care. *Psychological Medicine, 26*, 575–589.

Salkovskis, P. M., & Warwick, H. M. (1986). Morbid preoccupations, health anxiety and reassurance: A cognitive-behavioral approach to hypochondriasis. *Behavior Research and Therapy, 24*, 597–602.

Schwartz, S. M., Gramling, S. E., & Mancini, T. (1994). The influence of life stress, personality, and learning history on illness behavior. *Journal of Behavior Therapy and Experimental Psychiatry, 25*, 135–142.

Speckens, A. E. M. (2001). Assessment of hypochondriasis. In V. Starcevic & D. R. Lipsitt (Eds.), *Hypochondriasis: Modern perspectives on an ancient malady* (pp. 61–88). New York: Oxford University Press.

Stern, R., & Fernandez, M. (1991). Group cognitive and behavioral treatment for hypochondriasis. *British Medical Journal, 303*, 1229–1231.

Stewart, S. H., & Watt, M. C. (2001). Assessment of health anxiety. In G. J. G. Asmundson, S. Taylor, & B. J. Cox (Eds.), *Health anxiety: Clinical and research perspectives on hypochondriasis and related conditions* (pp. 95–131). New York: Wiley.

Stone, A. B. (1993). Treatment of hypochondriasis with clomipramine. *Journal of Clinical Psychiatry, 54*, 200–201.

Taylor, S. (2000). *Understanding and treating panic disorder.* New York: Wiley.

Taylor, S., & Asmundson, G. J. G. (2004). *Treating health anxiety: A cognitive-behavioral approach.* New York: Guilford Press.

Taylor, S., Asmundson, G. J. G., & Coons, M. J. (2005). Current directions in the treatment of hypochondriasis. *Journal of Cognitive Psychotherapy, 19*, 291–310.

Taylor, S., Thordarson, D. S., Jang, K. L., & Asmundson, G. J. G. (2006). Genetic and environmental origins of health anxiety: A twin study. *World Psychiatry, 5*, 47–50.

Taylor, S. E. (1999). *Health psychology* (4th ed.). Boston: McGraw-Hill.

Torgersen, S. (1986). Genetics of somatoform disorders. *Archives of General Psychiatry, 43*, 502–505.

Visser, S., & Bouman, T. K. (1992). Cognitive-behavioral approaches in the treatment of hypochondriasis: Six single case cross-over studies. *Behavior Research and Therapy, 30*, 301–306.

Visser, S., & Bouman, T. K. (2001). The treatment of hypochondriasis: Exposure plus response prevention versus cognitive therapy. *Behavior Research and Therapy, 39*, 423–442.

Viswanathan, R., & Paradis, C. (1991). Treatment of cancer phobia with fluoxetine. *American Journal of Psychiatry, 148*, 1090.

Walker, J., Vincent, N., Furer, P., Cox, B., & Kjernisted, K. (1999). Treatment preference in hypochondriasis. *Journal of Behavior Therapy and Experimental Psychiatry, 30*, 251–258.

Warwick, H. M., Clark, D. M., Cobb, A. M., & Salkovskis, P. M. (1996). A controlled-trial of cognitive-behavioral treatment of hypochondriasis. *British Journal of Psychiatry, 169,* 189–195.

Warwick, H. M., & Salkovskis, P. M. (1989). Cognitive and behavioral characteristics of primary hypochondriasis. *Scandinavian Journal of Behavior Therapy, 18,* 85–92.

Warwick, H. M., & Salkovskis, P. M. (1990). Hypochondriasis. *Behavior Research and Therapy, 28,* 105–117.

Watt, M. C., & Stewart, S. H. (2000). Anxiety sensitivity mediates the relationships between childhood learning experiences and elevated hypochondriacal concerns in young adulthood. *Journal of Psychosomatic Research, 49,* 107–118.

Wesner, R. B., & Noyes, R. (1991). Imipramine: An effective treatment for illness phobia. *Journal of Affective Disorders, 22,* 43–48.

Whitehead, W. E., Crowell, M. D., Heller, B. R., Robinson, J. C., Schuster, M. M., & Horn, S. (1994). Modeling and reinforcement of the sick role during childhood predicts adult illness behavior. *Psychosomatic Medicine, 56,* 541–550.

Wright, K. D., & Asmundson, G. J. G. (2003). Health anxiety in children: Development and psychometric properties of the Childhood Illness Attitudes Scale. *Cognitive Behavior Therapy, 34,* 194–201.

CHAPTER 26

Compulsive Hoarding

SUZANNE A. MEUNIER, NICHOLAS A. MALTBY, AND DAVID F. TOLIN

DESCRIPTION OF THE DISORDER

Compulsive hoarding has been conceptualized as a subtype of Obsessive-Compulsive Disorder (OCD). In recent years, some researchers have suggested that the defining features of compulsive hoarding include (a) acquisition of and failure to discard a large number of possessions that appear to be useless or of limited value, (b) living spaces sufficiently cluttered so as to preclude activities for which those spaces were designed; and (c) significant distress or impairment in functioning caused by the hoarding (Frost & Hartl, 1996). Because compulsive hoarding has not received a great deal of empirical study, there are many unanswered questions about the syndrome. For example, it is unclear where compulsive hoarding fits within the current nosology and whether there are different subtypes of hoarding. Compulsive hoarding has been associated with a poor response to treatments commonly used for OCD (Abramowitz, Franklin, Schwartz, & Furr, 2003; Black, Monahan, et al., 1998; Mataix-Cols, Marks, Greist, Kobak, & Baer, 2002; Saxena et al., 2002; Steketee & Frost, 2003).

A cognitive-behavioral model that details the defining features and potential contributing factors has been offered (Frost & Hartl, 1996; Frost & Steketee, 1998; Frost & Tolin, 2007; Steketee & Frost, 2003), which may provide a basis for developing assessment strategies to clarify these issues and to serve as the basis for a new approach to treatment of compulsive hoarding. In this chapter, we review the basic components of the cognitive-behavioral model of compulsive hoarding and empirical findings relevant to these questions.

According to the developing cognitive-behavioral model of compulsive hoarding (Frost & Hartl, 1996; Frost & Steketee, 1998; Frost & Tolin, 2007; Steketee & Frost, 2003), the defining features of hoarding (acquisition, difficulty discarding, clutter) result from deficits in information processing and rigid beliefs about and attachments to possessions that produce emotional distress and avoidance behaviors.

INFORMATION-PROCESSING DEFICITS

Information-processing deficits include attentional, memory, categorization, and decision-making difficulties. Each of these is hypothesized to be directly linked to the disorganization and difficulty discarding experienced by compulsive hoarders.

Attention   Compulsive hoarding may be associated with impairments in sustained attention and response inhibition. Problems with distractibility and short attention span are frequently observed during treatment (Steketee, Frost, Wincze, Greene, & Douglass, 2000). Symptoms of inattention have been reported at a greater frequency in hoarding versus nonhoarding populations (Hartl, Duffany, Allen, Steketee, & Frost, 2005; Meunier, Tolin, Frost, Steketee, Brady, et al., 2006). Problems sustaining attention could promote clutter when compulsive hoarders have difficulty focusing on organizing or discarding their possessions and lose track of their higher level goals.

Theorists have suggested that individuals with compulsive hoarding may also possess a "creative attentional bias" that is driven by visual cues and causes them to be drawn to and absorbed in nonessential details of a possession (Frost & Tolin, in press). A hoarder may demonstrate selective thinking by attending only to specific features of the possession (e.g., aesthetics, utility) thereby ignoring other important features (e.g., cost, available space). Hoarders may fail to process information regarding negative consequences of saving, thereby making them more likely to decide to save a possession.

Memory   People suffering from hoarding problems show some deficits in verbal and visual memory performance and use less effective organizational strategies for remembering (Hartl et al., 2004); however, these differences are fairly small. Perhaps more important, compulsive hoarders report significantly less confidence in their memory and more catastrophic assessments of the consequences of forgetting that are not accounted for by actual differences in memory performance. As a result, they report a stronger desire to keep possessions in sight so they will not be forgotten (Hartl et al., 2004). Thus, decreased memory confidence may lead individuals with hoarding problems to adopt inefficient organizational strategies.

Categorization   Individuals with compulsive hoarding appear to have an under inclusive cognitive style that causes them to view each possession as unique (Wincze, Steketee, & Frost, 2005). Each unique item may be viewed as its own category, producing a number of categories to maintain and remember. The need to remember the location of each object, rather than a category of objects, places an increased load on memory processes. As organizing tasks become more inefficient and complicated, an individual may be more likely to avoid such activities, resulting in the accumulation of clutter. Categorization problems have been observed in compulsive hoarding populations such that hoarders take more time, create more categories, and report more anxiety than do OCD and nonclinical control groups, especially when working with their own possessions (Wincze et al., 2005).

Decision Making   Decision-making problems have been repeatedly demonstrated in compulsive hoarding populations (Frost & Gross, 1993; Frost & Shows, 1993). Individuals with compulsive hoarding take more time than do healthy controls to make decisions about discarding their possessions (Maltby, Tolin, & Kiehl, 2006). The aforementioned deficits in attention, memory confidence, and categorization are likely contributors to decision-making difficulties, making the amount of effort required to make decisions overwhelming. Perfectionistic beliefs (discussed later) may also contribute to decision-making impairments. Consequently, people with holding problems may avoid tasks that involve making difficult decisions.

BELIEFS ABOUT POSSESSIONS

Individuals with compulsive hoarding appear to hold very rigid beliefs about their possessions that can further exacerbate problems in decision making. Four basic types of beliefs about possessions have been identified: emotional attachment to possessions, memory-related concerns, responsibility for possessions, and desire for control over possessions (Steketee, Frost, & Kyrios, 2003). These beliefs may cause compulsive hoarders to save possessions to avoid emotional distress or negative outcomes.

Emotional Attachment to Possessions   Research findings have indicated that compulsive hoarding is associated with excessive emotional attachment to possessions (Cermele, Melendez-Pallitto, & Pandina, 2001; Frost & Gross, 1993; Frost, Hartl, Christian, & Williams, 1995). Several different types of emotional attachments have been observed. Emotional attachments may result in the acquisition or saving of possessions based on the experience of positive or negative emotions. Emotional attachments may be related to the aesthetic qualities of the object or to the object's perceived association with emotionally significant people, places, or events. Aesthetic qualities that may produce an emotional attachment include the object's shape, color, and texture. Some individuals with compulsive hoarding express a desire to buy something simply because they like it and may collect multiples of a common household item because "they are pretty." The attachments to objects may be associated with feelings of pleasure or satisfaction, as demonstrated with compulsive buyers (Christenson et al., 1994).

Other types of emotional attachments seen among people with compulsive hoarding may be related to elevated levels of depression and anxiety (Coles, Frost, Heimberg, & Steketee, 2003; Frost, Steketee, Williams, & Warren, 2000). Objects may be imbued with human qualities, causing a person to save items due to concerns that they would "hurt its feelings." Compulsive hoarders may view their possessions as friends or family and feel that losing their things would be similar to the death of a loved one.

Just as possessions can come to represent a significant other, they can also represent a part of an individual's own identity. An unimportant flyer may develop significance as a symbol of the experience of attending a fair where it was acquired. The person may feel as though discarding the flyer would be like losing that experience and therefore part of his or her identity. Some individuals with compulsive hoarding report that they save objects because the possessions are central to their perceptions of themselves or the person that they would like to become. For example, a person may collect broken appliances from roadsides because they are a "handyman" or save art supplies in hopes of becoming an artist. Despite collecting these items, these individuals may rarely engage in behaviors that are associated with these roles, such that the handyman never repairs the appliance and the artist does not create artwork.

That is, these persons' sense of personal identity is derived from what they have, rather than from what they do (Frost & Tolin, 2007; Tolin, Frost, & Steketee, 2007).

Memory-Related Concerns   In addition to low memory confidence, individuals with compulsive hoarding report more catastrophic consequences of forgetting information (Hartl et al., 2004). As a result, they may opt to use compensatory strategies to prevent these consequences. In fact, strong desires to keep possessions in sight and to remember the location of those possessions have been reported by hoarding populations (Hartl et al., 2004). Anecdotally, we have observed patients who report that their memories are qualitatively different (e.g., "My memory is in bright colors rather than black and white") when holding an item associated with the memory. These individuals also report a concern that discarding the possession would result in the loss of an associated memory or its vividness.

Responsibility for Possessions   Individuals with compulsive hoarding appear to have an exaggerated sense of responsibility about what they save (Frost & Gross, 1993; Frost et al., 1995). Although the beliefs expressed by hoarders may appear sensible in a wasteful culture (e.g., a belief that people should recycle), their application of the belief may be too broad or applied in a rigid fashion. Thus, an item might be saved if it has any possibility of being used in the future, even though the probability of use is extremely low. In addition, people with hoarding problems may experience particularly severe distress at the idea of being wasteful. Anecdotally, some individuals with compulsive hoarding have described a perfectionistic application of their belief such that throwing away just one item with a potential use would make them "wasteful" and therefore a "bad person."

Desire for Control over Possessions   Beliefs about controlling possessions through acquisition and saving have been linked to attempts to control one's environment (Furby, 1978). People with compulsive hoarding problems appear to have stronger desires to maintain control over their possessions than do people with nonhoarding OCD and nonclinical controls (Steketee et al., 2003). Hoarding patients appear to experience significant distress about others touching or using their possessions, which can interfere with attempts to help them organize or discard things. The distrust of family and friends that we have observed in individuals with hoarding problems often seems to contribute to their rejection of help and consequently to their feeling overwhelmed by the task of addressing their clutter. Their distrust may also become a self-fulfilling prophecy in which family members who are frustrated by the clutter discard things without the hoarding patient's knowledge.

DISTRESS AND AVOIDANCE

Information-processing deficits appear to make organization and decision-making tasks much more difficult and time-consuming for individuals with compulsive hoarding problems. In addition, their beliefs about possessions seem to result in intense emotional reactions that lead to acquiring and saving behaviors. People who hoard frequently report feeling overwhelming levels of distress when attempting to address their clutter, leading them to avoid clutter-related tasks. The avoidance of organization or discarding can help to maintain their beliefs about the possessions by limiting their opportunities to test their veracity. Avoidance also limits opportunities to develop more efficient organization and decision-making skills.

UNIQUE PRESENTATIONS

To date, subtypes of compulsive hoarders have not been identified. Two possible subtypes may be characterized by self-neglect. Squalor syndrome (also referred to as Diogenes syndrome) involves domestic squalor with a tendency to hoard rubbish (Jackson, 1997). Animal hoarding involves the collection of a large number of animals with the failure to provide proper care for them. In both cases, the hoarder's home is often unsanitary and poses potentially serious threats to his or her health and safety.

Squalor   Descriptions of squalor in the literature have been offered mostly in the context of squalor syndrome. Initial reports of the syndrome described individuals who engaged in extreme neglect of self and environment (Clark, Mankikar, & Gray, 1975; MacMillan & Shaw, 1966). It has been suggested that squalor syndrome typically affects geriatric populations; however, there have been cases of squalor described in individuals who are in their 30s and 40s (Grignon, Bassiri, Bartoli, & Calvet, 1996; Vostanis & Dean, 1992). The psychiatric histories of those who present with squalor syndrome vary widely, with only half receiving a psychiatric diagnosis (Clark et al., 1975; Shah, 1995). One hypothesis about the origins of squalor syndrome focuses on frontal lobe dysfunction, which is associated with some features observed in squalor syndrome, including disinhibition, lack of initiative, and apathy (Shah, 1995). In fact, several of the psychiatric conditions that have been associated with squalor (e.g., dementia, Schizophrenia, cerebrovascular accident) share frontal lobe symptoms.

Several characteristic features of squalor have been described. Individuals whose hoarding is characterized by squalor frequently neglect personal and domestic hygiene. Individuals may hoard rubbish (e.g., bags of litter, old newspapers) in addition to neglecting the cleanliness of their home. Social withdrawal and a rejection of any help offered to them are often observed. Most patients who live in conditions of squalor are single or widowed and live alone (Clark et al., 1975; MacMillan & Shaw, 1966). It is unclear whether rejection of help is based on a lack of recognition of the problem or refusal to allow others in their home. We have observed cases in which hoarding patients continue to maintain social relationships and personal hygiene despite their poor domestic hygiene. Despite their ability to maintain outward appearances, they are likely to experience social impairment due to the rejection of help and refusal to allow others to come into their homes. In these cases, the refusal of help appears to be associated with a fear of social rejection if the state of their home was discovered.

Animal Hoarding   Animal hoarding has been defined by accumulation of a large number of animals while failing to provide basic care of the animals or their environment (Patronek, 1999). In addition, an animal hoarder does not recognize the negative impact of their collecting of animals on their own health and well-being (Patronek, 1999). In contrast, those who hoard animals justify their behavior based on perceptions of their special relationships with animals. They often perceive themselves as animal lovers who are saving the animals from death (Patronek, 2001). Animal hoarders may also describe their animals as their children or their only friends (Hoarding of Animals Research Consortium [HARC], 2002). Furthermore, one study revealed that animal hoarders often believe that they possess unique abilities to communicate and empathize with animals (HARC, 2000).

The living conditions of individuals who hoard animals are typically substandard. Animal urine and feces are often present in living areas (Patronek, 1999). In some cases, accumulation of animal waste becomes so severe that the structure of the home is damaged and the environment is toxic (HARC, 2002). Despite these poor living conditions, people who hoard animals report that their animals are healthy and well cared for (HARC, 2000).

Squalor and animal hoarding appear similar in regard to the living conditions and threats to health and safety that result. The two syndromes may be more distinct in regard to the level of insight into the risks posed by their homes. Individuals living in squalor may be aware of some of the consequences of their behavior, but reject assistance due to concerns about social judgment and rejection. Animal hoarders appear to be more homogeneous in their failure to recognize the risks. Their self-perceptions and beliefs about the well-being of their animals may at times be so fixed as to appear delusional.

DIAGNOSIS AND ASSESSMENT

SUGGESTED DIAGNOSTIC CRITERIA

The first systematic definition of compulsive hoarding identified three defining features: acquisition of and failure to discard possessions, clutter that interferes with appropriate use of living space, and associated significant distress and impairment (Frost & Hartl, 1996). This definition has distinguished hoarding from collecting of objects generally considered interesting and valuable.

Acquisition Excessive acquisition may take the form of compulsive buying, acquiring free things (e.g., extra newspapers, promotional give-aways, discarded items from the street), or stealing (Frost & Gross, 1993; Frost et al., 1998). With an estimated point prevalence of nearly 6% (Koran, Faber, Aboujaoude, Large, & Serpe, 2006), compulsive buying has been considered an impulse control disorder (Black, Repertinger, Gaffney, & Gabel, 1998). Acquisition does appear to be an impulsive behavior in the respect that it is positively reinforced by the experience of pleasure (e.g., buying items due to their appealing aesthetic qualities). However, excessive acquisition also resembles compulsive behavior in the respect that a person may feel urges to acquire and feel that the behavior is uncontrollable. Some items that are acquired have limited objective value; others are collected in amounts beyond what an individual can reasonably use, thereby rendering them useless to that person despite their objective value.

Difficulty Discarding Individuals with compulsive hoarding are characterized by difficulty discarding objects that most people consider to be useless or that have limited value. As described earlier, information-processing deficits and beliefs about the instrumental and emotional value of the possessions contribute to their difficulties (Frost et al., 1995). Individuals with hoarding problems often avoid tasks that require decision making because it is experienced as aversive. Beliefs about possessions can contribute to the distress experienced during discarding by activating fears of making mistakes or being unable to tolerate the loss of the item.

Clutter   Excessive acquisition and difficulty discarding possessions constitute hoarding pathology only when accompanied by extreme clutter. Clutter is extreme when it prevents normal use of space, including the inability to eat at the kitchen table, sit on the couch, or shower in the bathtub. In fact, a room may no longer serve any function beyond the storage of clutter. In extreme cases, clutter may extend from the floor to the ceiling, blocking an entire room or leaving only narrow pathways for walking. Family members may be able to limit the spread of clutter into some living areas.

Distress and Interference   Compulsive hoarding has been associated with significant emotional distress. Individuals with compulsive hoarding experience anxiety and grief like feelings of loss when attempting to discard possessions (Frost & Hartl, 1996; Frost et al., 1998). High rates of depression have been found in samples of hoarding patients, (Frost, Steketee, Tolin, & Brown, 2006; Frost, Steketee, Williams, et al., 2000), which might be related to feelings of loss or grief.

Clinically significant hoarding prevents the normal use of space for basic activities of daily living, including cooking, moving throughout the house, and in some cases even sleeping. The inability to complete these tasks can make hoarding a dangerous problem by introducing health risks from fire and falling hazards and poor sanitation (Kim, Steketee, & Frost, 2001). Health department officials who investigated hoarding-related complaints were surveyed to assess the impact of hoarding problems; they indicated that clutter was a substantial risk to the person's health in the majority of cases (Frost, Steketee, & Williams, 2000). Furthermore, hoarding was judged to contribute directly to the individual's death in 6% of the cases investigated. Studies have demonstrated greater family, work, and social impairment among individuals with hoarding problems compared to those with anxiety problems (Farchione et al., 2003; Frost, Steketee, Williams, et al., 2000).

Limited Insight   Individuals with compulsive hoarding often demonstrate limited insight into the severity of the problem and its resulting impairment. In fact, many hoarding patients report that they do not consider their behavior unreasonable (Frost & Gross, 1993). In cases of individuals with poor insight, the problem may come to the attention of professionals only as a result of complaints from family members or neighbors. A study of hoarders receiving social services revealed that providers rated the majority of them as possessing poor insight that could not be attributed to observable cognitive impairment (Steketee, Frost, & Kim, 2001). Low insight can provide challenges in attempts to assess the problem through self-report measures; patients and observers tend to disagree more on verbal reports of hoarding severity than on pictorial ratings of severity (Frost, Steketee, Tolin, & Renaud, in press).

ASSESSMENT

Measures that assess the defining features and proposed vulnerabilities that underlie compulsive hoarding are necessary to gain an improved understanding of the problem. Several attempts have been made to develop such measures.

The Hoarding Scale (Frost & Gross, 1993; Frost et al., 1998) is a self-report measure that measures difficulty discarding and associated beliefs, emotional reactions, and decision-making deficits. The scale demonstrated internal reliability and construct, convergent, and discriminant validity. It also reliably distinguished OCD patients with hoarding from other anxious and nonclinical populations and was able to identify subclinical levels of hoarding behavior (Frost & Gross, 1993). Unfortunately, the measure does not include items assessing other defining features.

The Saving Inventory—Revised (SI-R; Frost, Steketee, & Grisham, 2004) includes items that assess symptoms of hoarding in accordance with the defining features. A factor analysis of the items revealed three factors: compulsive acquisition, difficulty discarding, and cluttered living spaces. These three subscales demonstrate good internal and test-retest reliability and convergent validity. The measure can also be used to distinguish between hoarding and nonhoarding OCD patients.

The Saving Cognitions Inventory (Steketee et al., 2003) was designed to assess hoarding-related beliefs and emotional reactions. The scale consists of four subscales: Emotional Attachment to Possessions, Memory Concerns, Desire to Control Possessions, and Responsibility for Possessions. These demonstrate good internal consistency and convergent and discriminant validity. The Memory Concerns, Desire to Control Possessions, and Responsibility for Possessions subscales each independently predicted hoarding severity when controlling for other variables (Steketee et al., 2003).

Although these measures represent a significant improvement over previous attempts to assess hoarding with OCD symptoms, several important constructs remain in need of assessment. Severity of distress and impairment associated with hoarding symptoms must be measured. Scales that do not rely on self-reports of symptoms are also needed, as many hoarding patients have poor insight into their problem. The Clutter Image Rating (CIR; Frost, Steketee, Tolin, & Renaud, in press) was designed to overcome these limitations. This pictorial scale contains nine equidistant photographs of severity in a living room, kitchen, and bedroom. The CIR shows strong internal consistency and test-retest reliability; unlike verbal measures of clutter severity, the CIR also demonstrates good correspondence between patient and therapist ratings.

Is Hoarding a Subtype of Obsessive-Compulsive Disorder?

Hoarding   The appropriate location for hoarding in our nosology is unclear. Currently, it is included as a symptom of Obsessive-Compulsive Personality Disorder (OCPD; American Psychiatric Association, 2000); however, researchers and clinicians have commonly considered hoarding to be a variant of OCD. Evidence for this conceptualization has been mixed. Classification of hoarding as an impulse control disorder has also been proposed, due to the symptoms of excessive acquisition. Although compulsive hoarding may have associations with these and other psychiatric problems, there is evidence that supports the classification of compulsive hoarding as an independent syndrome.

Similarities between Compulsive Hoarding and Obsessive-Compulsive Disorder   Multiple studies have examined the relationship between compulsive hoarding and other subtypes of OCD symptoms. A relationship between hoarding and OCD symptoms has been found in student, community, and clinical samples (Frost & Gross, 1993; Frost et al., 1998; Frost, Krause, & Steketee, 1996). Approximately 18% to 33% of individuals with OCD report hoarding symptoms (Frost et al., 1996; Rasmussen & Eisen, 1989; Samuels et al., 2002; Sobin et al., 2000). Hoarding has been reported as the primary symptom type for 11% of individuals in one sample (Saxena et al., 2002). Doubting and checking symptom subscales have shown the strongest correlations with hoarding symptoms (Frost & Gross, 1993).

Severity of OCD and hoarding symptoms may be related. Self-identified hoarders have reported greater nonhoarding OCD symptoms than do community controls (Frost & Gross, 1993). Patients with OCD with and without hoarding symptoms report similar symptom severity on the Yale-Brown Obsessive-Compulsive Scale (Y-BOCS; Frost, Steketee, Williams, et al., 2000). In addition, severity ratings of hoarding symptoms are modestly correlated with severity ratings of nonhoarding OCD symptoms (Frost et al., 2004). Also, the severity of acquisition and difficulty discarding symptoms is greater among hoarders who scored high on OCD symptom severity (Frost et al., 2004).

Similar behaviors and cognitions have been found in hoarding and nonhoarding OCD populations. Hoarders exhibit excessive doubting, checking, and reassurance seeking prior to discarding possessions (Rasmussen & Eisen, 1989, 1992). An inflated sense of responsibility related to the use of possessions has been identified in hoarding populations (Frost & Gross, 1993; Frost et al., 1995). Similarly, individuals with OCD often report an inflated sense of responsibility to prevent harm (Obsessive Compulsive Cognitions Working Group [OCCWG], 2005). In addition, people with hoarding problems report poor memory confidence and consequently may attempt to keep their possessions in sight (Frost & Hartl, 1996). Patients with OCD also perceive their memory as unreliable and therefore tend to employ maladaptive compensatory strategies (Tolin et al., 2001). Individuals who hoard also report beliefs related to perfectionism and intolerance of uncertainty (Tolin, Brady, & Hannan, 2006), which have also been associated with checking and ordering symptoms of OCD (OCCWG, 2005).

Differences between Compulsive Hoarding and Obsessive-Compulsive Disorder Despite these similarities, evidence suggests that compulsive hoarding may be distinct from OCD. Hoarding symptoms have been associated with greater impairment and poorer response to treatment when compared to other OCD symptom types. As a result, theorists have suggested that compulsive hoarding may involve distinct biological, cognitive, and behavioral mechanisms (Frost & Tolin, 2007). Observations of hoarding behavior in the absence of other OCD symptoms also support the independence of the two disorders.

Several studies have attempted to identify independent domains of OCD symptoms using factor analysis of the Y-BOCS symptom checklist (Baer, 1994; Hantouche & Lancrenon, 1996; Leckman et al., 1997; Mataix-Cols et al., 2002; Mataix-Cols, Rauch, Manzo, Jenike, & Baer, 1999; Van Oppen, Hoekstra, & Emmelkamp, 1995). Studies using the Y-BOCS to measure OCD symptoms produced a hoarding symptoms factor; however, two studies produced a factor with combined hoarding and symmetry/ordering symptoms (Baer, 1994; Hantouche & Lancrenon, 1996). Studies utilizing confirmatory factor analysis (Summerfeldt, Richter, Antony, & Swinson, 1999) and cluster analysis (Calamari, Wiegartz, & Janeck, 1999) have also suggested that hoarding symptoms are distinct from other OCD symptoms.

Several studies have linked OCD and other anxiety disorders to impulse control disorders (Black & Moyer, 1998; McElroy, Keck, Pope, Smith, & Strakowski, 1994; Schlosser, Black, Repertinger, & Freet, 1994). Some theorists have proposed that these disorders may exist along a compulsive-impulsive spectrum (McElroy, Keck, & Phillips, 1995). Individuals with hoarding problems often engage in compulsive buying and acquisition of free things. Compulsive buying has been categorized as an impulse control disorder (McElroy et al., 1995). Several studies have demonstrated relationships between impulse control disorders and compulsive hoarding. Individuals with compulsive buying (Frost, Steketee, & Williams, 2002) and compulsive gambling (Frost, Meagher, & Riskind, 2001) problems have endorsed high levels of hoarding symptoms. In addition, OCD patients with hoarding problems have reported a greater frequency of trichotillomania and skin picking than those without hoarding problems (Samuels et al., 2002).

Individuals with compulsive hoarding report more depression and greater family, work, and social impairment when compared to nonhoarding OCD and anxiety populations (Frost, Steketee, Williams, et al., 2000). Studies indicate that hoarding symptoms are a predictor of poorer response to standard pharmacological and behavioral treatments for OCD, as demonstrated by greater dropout rates and less improvement (Abramowitz et al., 2003; Black, Monahan, et al., 1998; Mataix-Cols et al., 1999, 2002; Saxena et al., 2002; Winsberg, Cassic, & Koran, 1999). One potential explanation for this poorer treatment response is the tendency for people with hoarding problems to view their behavior as reasonable (Frost & Gross, 1993; Frost, Steketee, & Williams, 2000). Findings indicate that hoarding patients often report little distress or recognition of a problem (Grisham, Frost, Steketee, Kim, & Hood, 2006). In contrast, OCD patients typically demonstrate recognition of the irrational and maladaptive nature of their obsessions and compulsions (Frost et al., 1996).

In a sample of 75 hoarding patients, 68% denied any symptoms of nonhoarding-related OCD, suggesting that hoarding often occurs in the absence of other OCD symptoms. Conversely, hoarding behavior has been reported in association with a number of other psychiatric disorders, including Schizophrenia (Luchins, Goldman, Lieb, & Hanrahan, 1992), organic mental disorders (Greenberg, Witztum, & Levy, 1990), dementia (Finkel et al., 1997; Hwang, Tsai, Yang, Liu, & Lirng, 1998), brain injury (Anderson, Damasio, & Damasio, 2005; Eslinger & Damasio, 1985), Social Phobia (Frost, Steketee, Tolin, & Brown, 2006; Samuels et al., 2002), Generalized Anxiety Disorder (GAD; Frost, Steketee, Tolin, & Brown, 2006), eating disorders (Frankenburg, 1984), and depression (Frost, Steketee, Tolin, & Brown, 2006; Frost, Steketee, Williams, et al., 2000). One study revealed that hoarding correlated only moderately with other OCD symptoms and symptoms of depression (Wu & Watson, 2005), which may suggest that hoarding is a syndrome that is separate from but often comorbid with these other psychological disorders.

A recent study investigated presence of hoarding symptoms reported by individuals presenting for treatment of nonhoarding-related anxiety problems (such that OCD patients reporting hoarding concerns were excluded). Results revealed that 14% of Social Phobia patients, 11% of OCD patients, and 27% of GAD patients endorsed significant hoarding symptoms (Meunier, Tolin, Frost, Steketee, & Brady, 2006). Prevalence of hoarding symptoms reported by individuals with GAD in that study is consistent with prevalence rates (18% to 33%) reported in studies of individuals with OCD. These findings provide support to the notion that hoarding may be an independent condition that can be comorbid with a variety of other forms of psychopathology.

CONCEPTUALIZATION

Currently, there are no well-developed models of the etiology of compulsive hoarding. However, research findings suggest that several factors may be involved in its development. First, hoarding behaviors may be learned through observations of family members who serve as models. Second, life events involving the development of emotional attachments in relationships and/or trauma and loss may cause individuals to hold on to their possessions. Third, genetics and other biological factors may contribute to hoarding behavior. Fourth, cultural and gender differences may also affect the development of hoarding.

Learning and Modeling

A high frequency of hoarding behaviors has been observed among first-degree relatives of individuals with compulsive hoarding (Frost & Gross, 1993; Samuels et al., 2002; Winsberg et al., 1999). Although genetic factors may account for these findings, an alternative explanation is that people with hoarding problems learn acquisition and saving behaviors from family members.

Life Events

Attachments in Relationships Theorists have suggested that hoarding behaviors may develop from experiences of emotional deprivation (Seedat & Stein, 2002) such that hoarders' emotional attachments to possessions replace dysfunctional attachments to people. In fact, hoarding has been related to feelings of rejection and ambivalent or insecure attachments (Frost et al., 1999; Krause, White, Frost, Steketee, & Kyrios, 2000). Furthermore, research evidence has demonstrated that individuals with compulsive hoarding exhibit social impairment. Compulsive hoarding has been associated with low marriage rates, social anxiety and withdrawal, and dependent personality features (Frost, Steketee, Williams, et al., 2000; Kim et al., 2001).

Although a relationship between hoarding symptoms and social impairment exists, its directional nature is unclear. A chaotic family environment in early childhood appears to be related to hoarding (Krause et al., 2000). Despite this evidence, it is difficult to determine the degree to which social impairment influences the development of hoarding pathology or results from hoarding-related behaviors.

Traumatic and Loss Experiences Individuals with compulsive hoarding may possess beliefs that the world is dangerous, and consequently they feel vulnerable (Frost & Hartl, 1996). As a result, possessions may begin to function as "safety signals" that reduce feelings of vulnerability or loss (Greenberg et al., 1990; Shafran & Tallis, 1996; Steketee & Frost, 2003). In fact, people with hoarding problems describe themes related to loss experiences (Frost & Steketee, 1998). Loss experiences (e.g., death of a loved one) have been reported coincidentally with the onset of hoarding problems (Grisham et al., 2006).

Several studies have demonstrated a relationship between traumatic experiences and the development of hoarding symptoms. When compared to community controls, people with hoarding problems reported experiencing more different types of trauma experiences as well as a greater number of traumas (Hartl et al., 2005). As a result of their trauma experiences, hoarders were more likely than community controls to receive a diagnosis of Posttraumatic Stress Disorder (Hartl et al., 2005). The types of traumas that occurred more frequently in hoarding populations include witnessing a crime, having something taken by threat or force, being handled roughly, physical abuse, sexual abuse, rape, and forced sexual activity before the age of 18 years (Cromer,

Schmidt, & Murphy, 2006; Hartl et al., 2005). The occurrence of stressful life events has been shown to influence the age of onset of hoarding behavior (Grisham et al., 2006). Although traumatic experiences appear to influence the development of hoarding symptoms, the traumas may have differential effects on the various components of compulsive hoarding (e.g., clutter, difficulty discarding, acquisition; Cromer et al., 2006).

GENETIC INFLUENCES

As previously described, individuals who hoard often report histories of hoarding behaviors in family members (Frost & Gross, 1993; Samuels et al., 2002; Winsberg et al., 1999). Evidence from two studies indicates that genetic correlates of hoarding may exist (Lochner et al., 2005; Zhang et al., 2002). Specifically, one study examined three groups of sibling pairs: those concordant for hoarding, those discordant for hoarding, and those concordant for the absence of hoarding (Zhang et al., 2002). Results suggested that specific locations on three chromosomes may be associated with hoarding (Zhang et al., 2002). A separate study indicated that genotypes associated with hoarding may be limited to specific populations (Lochner et al., 2005).

PHYSICAL FACTORS AFFECTING BEHAVIOR

Physical Conditions   Just as people with hoarding problems tend to avoid clutter-related tasks due to emotional distress, we have observed hoarding patients who appear to avoid their clutter as a result of physical distress. Fatigue and physical pain have been described as limitations to sorting and organizing possessions. Specifically, these individuals often report that their physical distress limits the amount of time and energy that they are able to devote to these tasks. In addition, these individuals are often reluctant to allow others to handle their possessions, which further limits opportunities to reduce their clutter.

Neurobiological Mechanisms   Neural mechanisms of compulsive hoarding have received little empirical study. To date, there have been two published neuroimaging studies of compulsive hoarding that have produced inconsistent findings. Saxena and colleagues (2004) conducted a resting positron emissions tomography study of compulsive hoarders, nonhoarding OCD patients, and healthy controls. Results revealed that compulsive hoarders exhibited significantly lower glucose metabolism in posterior cingulate and cuneus when compared to healthy controls, and lower glucose metabolism in dorsal anterior cingulate when compared to nonhoarding OCD patients. Mataix-Cols and colleagues (2004) conducted a symptom provocation functional magnetic resonance imaging study in which OCD patients and healthy controls were scanned while imagining scenarios related to the content of symptom-related pictures. Results revealed that viewing hoarding-related pictures was associated with increased activation in left precentral gyrus and right orbit frontal cortex for OCD patients when compared to healthy controls. Furthermore, higher self-reported anxiety during hoarding imagery was associated with greater activation in left precentral gyrus.

The discrepancy in findings is likely due to several factors. First, examination of neural mechanisms during resting states may not be sufficient to detect differences between hoarding and nonhoarding populations. Assessment of neural activity during a task that requires compulsive hoarders to make decisions about their possessions might be a more accurate reflection of neural substrates of compulsive hoarding. Second, Mataix-Cols and colleagues (2004) utilized a sample that consisted mainly of nonhoarding OCD patients. Thus, results reflect brain activity in nonhoarding OCD patients asked to imagine hoarding scenarios, which may be very different from brain activity in hoarding patients. Third, symptom provocation tasks that require participants to imagine that a possession is theirs and that they were going to discard it may not be particularly provoking to compulsive hoarding patients. Fears about making the "wrong decision" cannot be addressed using this method because the task did not require participants to engage in decision making. Symptom provocation tasks that require participants to decide whether to discard their own possessions and then implement their decision may produce more meaningful results. In a preliminary symptom provocation study in which participants made actual decisions about whether to keep or discard possessions (Maltby et al., 2006), hoarders (compared to healthy controls) displayed excessive hemodynamic responding in lateral orbitofrontal cortex and parahippocampal gyrus, suggesting that hoarding may be characterized by effortful memory search and focal deficits in the processing of reward and changes in reward contingencies, particularly when these are perceived to be punishing.

CULTURAL AND DIVERSITY ISSUES

Individuals from different cultural backgrounds may have different values about the acquisition and use of possessions. It has been suggested that individuals who are deprived of material goods may learn to hold on to whatever they acquire, leading to compulsive hoarding later in life (Adams, 1973). In addition, gender differences in those who present for treatment of compulsive hoarding have been found.

Material Deprivation Upon hearing descriptions of hoarding behavior, many people assume that it occurs among certain cohorts of people who have experienced conditions of material deprivation in childhood, such as those endured by survivors of the Holocaust or the Great Depression. In fact, case studies of individuals who experience deprivation in childhood have been described in the literature (Greenberg et al., 1990; Shafran & Tallis, 1996). Empirical study has revealed that self-identified "packrats" did not differ from controls in regard to material deprivation in childhood (Frost & Gross, 1993). Thus, the theory that hoarding results from personal experience with material deprivation, though appealing, is not supported by the evidence.

Gender Differences Patients who present for treatment of compulsive hoarding at our clinic have been primarily female. There is no clear explanation for this observation. Females commonly demonstrate more negative affectivity (McCrae et al., 2002) and use of avoidant coping styles than do males (Ptacek, Smith, & Zanas, 1992; Speltz & Bernstein, 1976). Distress experienced when confronting clutter and subsequent avoidance have been considered defining features of compulsive hoarding. However, the same argument can be applied to gender differences in treatment seeking populations for a variety of psychological disorders.

BEHAVIORAL TREATMENT

Hoarding symptoms have been identified as a poor predictor of response to treatments effective for OCD (Steketee & Frost, 2003). Case reports have highlighted several problems that emerge in the treatment process, including treatment refusal, lack of treatment adherence, poor insight, and a lack of attempts to resist hoarding behaviors (Damecour & Charron, 1998; Greenberg, 1987; Greenberg et al., 1990; Shafran & Tallis, 1996). In fact, individuals with compulsive hoarding may present for treatment only as a result of pressure from family or health officials (Frost, Steketee, & Williams, 2000). During treatment, hoarding patients exhibit variable motivation and poor adherence to treatment (Christensen & Greist, 2001; Hartl & Frost, 1999; Steketee et al., 2000; Tolin, Frost, & Steketee, 2007a). People with hoarding problems have been found to have poorer insight when compared to people with OCD (Frost et al., 1996). These observed differences in insight and motivation may explain why hoarding patients appear to be more likely than OCD patients to drop out of treatment prematurely (Ball, Baer, & Otto, 1996; Mataix-Cols et al., 2002).

Because people with hoarding problems appear to receive suboptimal benefit from treatments based on conceptualizations of OCD, alternative approaches must be developed. Compulsive hoarding has been clearly defined only in recent years, and its defining features are undergoing continued empirical investigation. The cognitive-behavioral model described earlier provides a framework for an alternative treatment conceptualization. Based on this model, Steketee and Frost (2007) have developed a novel cognitive-behavioral treatment guide that highlights the importance of addressing the low motivation, information-processing deficits, and beliefs about possessions that may interfere with treatment. A summary of specific strategies to address these difficulties is provided next.

ENHANCEMENT OF MOTIVATION

Limited insight and low motivation is often described in individuals with compulsive hoarding (e.g., Christensen & Greist, 2001). Even when compulsive hoarders recognize that they have a problem with clutter, they persist in their beliefs that their behaviors are reasonable. When presenting for treatment, they may report that they just need assistance organizing their possessions. As with many other ego-syntonic problems, it may be difficult for the therapist to motivate behavior change. Direct challenges of these patients' beliefs may result in activation of their distress and may negatively impact the working relationship between therapist and patient. Therefore, Frost and Steketee (1999) argue for utilization of the principles of motivational interviewing (Miller & Rollnick, 2002). Rather than attempting to motivate patients through the use of rational arguments, motivational interviewing was designed to help patients to explore and resolve their ambivalence about behavior change. This approach may help foster views of treatment as a collaborative process.

BUILDING CONCEPTUAL MODELS

In accordance with a collaborative approach to treatment, Frost and Steketee (1999) argue for patients' involvement in developing the case conceptualization and functional analysis of their hoarding-related behaviors. Because individuals with hoarding problems tend to view their beliefs and behaviors as ego-syntonic, the degree to which they identify with the conceptualization for treatment may be an important factor in their motivation and adherence. Each patient develops his or her model through discussions with the therapist. The model includes all of the features from the cognitive-behavioral model that are pertinent to each individual's case (e.g., information-processing deficits, beliefs about and attachments to possessions, distress and avoidance). Because patients may view only certain aspects of their problem as warranting concern, explanations of the relationships between various features of the problem are provided in the discussion. This strategy may help patients to understand how their behaviors may contribute to undesired circumstances and increase the likelihood that they will consider changing their beliefs and behaviors. The model is developed during the initial sessions of treatment and is continually revised as its components change. It also serves as a guide for the treatment plan, which is also collaboratively devised.

SORTING

To gather information about symptoms to develop the conceptual model, sorting of possessions is done during most sessions. During sorting exercises, beliefs about possessions and manifestations of information-processing problems are likely to emerge. In keeping with the collaborative approach to the treatment process, the tone during sorting is focused on exploration of the difficulties in the service of a better understanding. Any urges to exert pressure to discard possessions should be resisted. Sorting can also be presented as an opportunity to develop and practice skills for organizing and making decisions about possessions.

Although sorting can be conducted in many locations, the practice of sorting in the patient's home may be particularly important. Many items that need sorting and organizing cannot be transported to an office. Practice of new skills with a variety of items and in naturalistic environments may be important to patients' mastery and continued use of the skills after the termination of treatment. Therefore, effort should be exerted to arrange to have at least some sessions in the patient's home.

NONACQUISITION

Reduction of clutter in living spaces is a common goal in treatment. This goal can be achieved in two ways: reducing existing clutter and preventing the acquisition of new possessions that contribute to clutter. Therefore, some treatment sessions should address compulsive acquisition behaviors. Beliefs and emotional attachments that drive acquisition behaviors must be identified and included in the conceptual model. Based on this conceptualization, nonacquiring sessions can be integrated into the treatment plan. A nonacquisition session should be conducted in a location where the patient has experienced difficulty resisting urges to acquire (e.g., stores, yard sales, roadsides). Sessions are focused on testing and challenging the patient's beliefs through the use of behavioral experiments and increasing tolerance of urges to acquire.

COGNITIVE STRATEGIES

Several cognitive strategies may be useful in addressing hoarding-based beliefs about possessions. Frost and Steketee (1999) outline how these techniques can be employed in the treatment of compulsive hoarding. Their suggestions are reviewed next.

Downward Arrow   The downward arrow technique (Beck, 1995) involves use of Socratic questioning to explore beliefs related to the likelihood of potential outcomes and the significance of their consequences. The purpose of this technique is to help individuals to recognize that they may be overestimating the likelihood of negative outcomes and underestimating their abilities to cope with any negative consequences when they do occur. Beliefs that may be explored with hoarding patients include those related to organizing or discarding possessions and resisting urges to acquire. Examples include the likelihood that that they will have no sense of identity by throwing out their craft supplies or the possibility that they are "stupid" if they do not have some bit of information at their fingertips.

Behavioral Experiment   Behavioral experiments may be utilized when discussion alone does not provide enough information to resolve questions about potential outcomes of a situation. In these instances, a specific hypothesis about expected outcomes is developed. Based on the hypothesis, the therapist and patient develop a behavioral experiment that will test the belief as if they were conducting a scientific experiment. The collaborative spirit of treatment is applied when creating the experiment. As with most empirical questions, there may be many ways to test the belief, and it is important to select a method that the patient is willing to attempt. At times, the experiment that the therapist and patient develop may test only a portion of the belief, so subsequent experiments may be needed to gather enough information about the original hypothesis. For example, a patient may express the belief that he or she will feel an intense sense of loss that will last forever if he or she throws away a broken knick-knack. Possible experiments are placing the object in a garbage bag and putting it in the garage, giving the object to someone else for a week, or throwing the object in the garbage on trash day. In some cases, the patient may not be willing to throw the object out immediately, but may be willing to test his or her emotional reactions to similar conditions. The outcome of each experiment must be assessed and related back to the original hypothesis. The information gained from the experiment may help a patient become more willing to attempt more difficult experiments.

Challenging Questions   Challenging questions are used during sorting and nonacquisition tasks to help patients in their decision-making process through the use of critical thinking skills. As previously reviewed, individuals with hoarding problems often focus on nonessential details about a possession. These questions are aimed at assisting them in evaluating their possessions based on all of the positive and negative consequences associated with owning them. Patients are encouraged to identify the questions that aid them in their decision making. As treatment progresses, patients are asked to generate these questions from memory to ensure that they will be able to use them with assistance from the therapist. Examples include "Do I really need it?"; "How many will be enough?"; "Do I have a specific plan to use this item within a reasonable time frame?"; and "Could I get by without it?"

Addressing Treatment Adherence

As described earlier, individuals with compulsive hoarding demonstrate poor adherence to treatment. Assessment of patients' readiness for change should be conducted prior to treatment and monitored throughout. In addition, hoarding patients may exhibit varying levels of readiness for change for different hoarding behaviors.

Clarification of their goals for treatment may help the therapist to develop the treatment plan that capitalizes on their existing motivation to make changes. When ambivalence about change arises, motivational interviewing strategies can be implemented.

Low motivation for change can also be observed in treatment-interfering behaviors. Hoarding patients will often cancel sessions, particularly when the session is planned to occur in their home. They may attempt to use sessions to discuss current stressors, thereby avoiding tasks aimed at reducing clutter. They sometimes fail to complete homework assignments, including bringing items from home to sort during office visits. Even those who complete their assignments may exert the minimum amount of effort such that the amount of time that they invest is insufficient for them to benefit significantly from treatment. Explanations of these behaviors often involve physical (low energy, pain) or psychosocial (feeling overwhelmed by current stressors, having insufficient time) themes.

Several strategies can be utilized to address these problems. Telephone sessions may be used so that the patient is cued to begin the homework task and continue working throughout the contact with the therapist. The goal is to fade the initiation of tasks from mostly therapist-initiated to patient-initiated. As treatment progresses, the therapist may simply call the patient when he or she is to begin working and check in with him or her after an agreed-upon duration. Later in treatment, the patient may simply leave a message for the therapist with a report about his or her homework practice.

Identifying helpers to assist the patient in completion of clutter-related tasks may also be of benefit. Individuals with hoarding problems often report feeling overwhelmed by the prospect of the task at hand due to their fatigue, pain, or stress. Helpers may serve to reduce the physical labor involved with reducing clutter. Although helpers may be used to speed the initial reduction of clutter, it is important to assess the patients' ability to maintain their home once they have reached their goal. If it appears that they will not be able to maintain the condition of their home on their own, problem-solving about ways that they can get the help that they will need to keep living spaces usable may be needed. As with all treatment planning, patients are actively involved in these decisions. Their behaviors that are interfering with the treatment process should be incorporated into the conceptual model and discussed in relation to their clutter problem.

EMPIRICAL FINDINGS

Intervention strategies based on the cognitive-behavioral model of compulsive hoarding have been used in a few small studies and have indicated positive results (Cermele et al., 2001; Hartl & Frost, 1999; Saxena et al., 2002; Steketee et al., 2000). In an open trial of 10 compulsive hoarding patients (Tolin et al., 2007a), significant decreases from pre- to posttreatment were noted on the SI-R and CIR. At midtreatment, 40% ($n = 4$) of treatment completers were rated "much improved" or "very much improved"; at posttreatment, 50% ($n = 5$) received this rating. Adherence to homework assignments was strongly related to symptom improvement.

MEDICAL TREATMENT

Several studies have investigated the treatment of compulsive hoarding using medications and combination treatments. Serotonin reuptake inhibitor (SRI) medications have been effective treatments for OCD. Results indicate that only small numbers of individuals with hoarding problems are classified as treatment responders using these treatments (Abramowitz et al., 2003; Black, Monahan, et al., 1998; Christensen & Greist, 2001; Mataix-Cols et al., 1999, 2002; Saxena et al., 2002; Winsberg et al., 1999). As with behavioral treatments, OCD patients with hoarding symptoms generally appear to fare less well than their nonhoarding counterparts (Mataix-Cols et al., 1999, 2002), although in a recent open trial of paroxetine (Saxena, Brody, Maidment, & Baxter, 2007), OCD patients with and without compulsive hoarding appeared to respond equally well to treatment.

Poor treatment response may be partly due to problems with the conceptualization of the disorder. Because it is unclear whether hoarding is a subtype of OCD, the application of OCD conceptualizations may not be ideal. The development of the cognitive-behavioral model may help to guide the selection of appropriate treatments for hoarding problems. In addition, neurobiological differences between hoarding and OCD are currently being examined using functional magnetic resonance imaging studies. Knowledge gained from these studies may provide insight into the parts of the brain that affect hoarding behaviors and the types of medications that may be able to address these brain functions.

Case Description

Robyn is a 32-year-old, single woman who presented for treatment of her hoarding behaviors. She had cluttered rooms in two houses. In her room at her aunt's house, the floor was covered with clothes, papers, and other belongings; however, her bed was uncluttered. Because her aunt imposed restrictions in her house, Robyn's room was much less cluttered than her room in her parents' house, which was filled several feet high with possessions such that her bed and her closets were unusable. In addition, the room smelled and was unsanitary. Because she was unable to sleep in her bedroom, Robyn decided to live with her aunt. When moving, she made no attempt to bring her possessions with her. Robyn's mother also had hoarding problems. Therefore, she put no pressure on Robyn to reduce or organize her clutter. In fact, Robyn's mother actively supported hoarding behaviors, extolling how Robyn was not wasteful and was acting responsibly toward her possessions.

During treatment, Robyn exhibited many of the beliefs about possessions reviewed earlier. She expressed strong emotional attachments to her possessions and attributed human qualities to them, which appeared to be the main reason behind her saving behavior. She expressed fears that she would lose her memories of her life if she discarded her possessions because she believed that she needed the items to be visual cues of important experiences that she has had. Robyn also believed that she was responsible for saving the world from ecological disaster, causing her to recycle all items she could. She was proud of being responsible and not wasteful, and she believed that if others acted as she did, the world would be better off. She also expressed get pride in being able to use her possessions to "always have the answers." For example, if

(continued)

she wanted to know the name of the hairdresser that she used 10 years ago, she knew that she had her business card somewhere. She believed that her behaviors had many positive effects on her life even though they contributed to the clutter.

Robyn also exhibited signs of information-processing deficits that contributed to her difficulty discarding possessions. She had difficulty maintaining attention during categorizing and decision-making tasks. She sorted items easily if there was no threat of discarding; however, her decision-making process slowed down substantially when she was sorting with the intention of discarding items. Frequently, she would spend 15 to 20 minutes trying to decide what to do with a single item. Even when she successfully sorted her possessions, she would rarely place the sorted items into an organizational system. As a result, progress was slow because these sorted items would quickly become mixed up with new objects and need to be sorted again. She also demonstrated difficulty sorting due to the tendency to develop a large number of specialized categories for her possessions. She discriminated various types of papers from each other and would remove the thicker covers from magazines and place them in a separate bin for recycling. She did this for many other types of recyclables as well. Recycling became a chore that demanded many recycling containers and specialized trips to the recycling center that provided the most categories of recycling. This was also complicated by her desire not to be wasteful, as she would not discard the containers holding her recyclables unless they were full. When the recycling center announced that they would be recycling only two broad categories, paper and plastic, Robyn did not know what to do. She brought all her recyclables back to her home and began storing them in her basement.

Robyn expressed distress while engaging in tasks aimed at reducing clutter. She described frustration and anxiety during organizing because she had difficulty making decisions and worried that she would mistakenly discard something of value. In practice, this led her to avoid recycling because it was such a chore, and her house began to fill up with things waiting to be recycled. Robyn also stated that she was unable to sort her possessions because it made her tired. Fatigue limited the amount of time she could put into organization. She appeared to find the feeling of fatigue so objectionable that she used it as a reason to avoid organizing. Due to her difficulty tolerating these distressed states, she avoided making decisions about her possessions, which caused an increasingly worse clutter problem.

Like many hoarders, Robyn was only partially engaged in the idea of treatment. She did not want help "throwing things out"; rather, she wanted to be able to find her possessions more easily. She stated that she was not looking to have a "neat" room, just a better organized one. She reported that she decided to seek treatment due to pressure to clean up from her aunt, with whom she lived. During treatment, she often asked to be "fixed," but then rejected most suggestions related to change. She demonstrated poor homework compliance and often canceled sessions due to her fatigue. After a year of weekly treatment sessions, she had made only minimal gains that seemed unlikely to remain if treatment ceased.

SUMMARY

The empirical findings described earlier represent advancements in our understanding of compulsive hoarding. The cognitive-behavioral model of hoarding provides a framework for these investigations and may guide future studies that will clarify unanswered questions about the syndrome. First, it appears that compulsive hoarding may be a unique syndrome that simply shares some similar features with other disorders. The relationships between compulsive hoarding and other syndromes are now being examined due to development of specific diagnostic criteria. Second, presence of different subtypes of compulsive hoarding can be studied. Unique presentations of the syndrome involving squalor or animals have been identified. In addition to these unique presentations, we have observed individual differences in the rigidity of beliefs about possessions and the amount of avoidance behavior exhibited. It is unclear whether these differences will translate into clusters of compulsive hoarders that constitute separate subtypes. Third, potential indicators of poor treatment response have been identified using the model. Specifically, poor motivation and lack of insight into the problems associated with hoarding behaviors may render traditional exposure-based treatments ineffective. Effectiveness of alternative treatment strategies developed from the model is currently being tested.

Despite these advancements, several research areas require further development. The study of compulsive hoarding has been restricted by a lack of appropriate assessment strategies. In addition, there has been limited examination of potential etiological factors (e.g., learning and biological mechanisms) that contribute to the development of hoarding behaviors. Current cognitive-behavioral and neurobiological models of compulsive hoarding can be improved through the clarification of etiological mechanisms, which may result in improved behavioral and medical treatments.

REFERENCES

Abramowitz, J. S., Franklin, M. E., Schwartz, S. A., & Furr, J. M. (2003). Symptom presentation and outcome of cognitive-behavioral therapy for obsessive-compulsive disorder. *Journal of Consulting and Clinical Psychology, 71*, 1049–1057.

Adams, P. L. (1973). *Obsessive children.* New York: Brunner/Mazel.

American Psychiatric Association. (2000). *Diagnostic and statistical manual of mental disorders* (4th ed., text rev.). Washington, DC: Author.

Anderson, S. W., Damasio, H., & Damasio, A. R. (2005). A neural basis for collecting behavior in humans. *Brain, 128,* 201–212.

Baer, L. (1994). Factor analysis of symptom subtypes of obsessive compulsive disorder and their relation to personality and tic disorders. *Journal of Clinical Psychiatry, 55*(Suppl.), 18–23.

Ball, S. G., Baer, L., & Otto, M. W. (1996). Symptom subtypes of obsessive-compulsive disorder in behavioral treatment studies: A quantitative review. *Behavior Research and Therapy, 34,* 47–51.

Beck, J. S. (1995). *Cognitive therapy: Basics and beyond.* New York: Guilford Press.

Black, D. W., Monahan, P., Gable, J., Blum, N., Clancy, G., & Baker, P. (1998). Hoarding and treatment response in 38 nondepressed subjects with obsessive-compulsive disorder. *Journal of Clinical Psychiatry, 59,* 420–425.

Black, D. W., & Moyer, T. (1998). Clinical features and psychiatric comorbidity of subjects with pathological gambling behavior. *Psychiatric Services, 49,* 1434–1439.

Black, D. W., Repertinger, S., Gaffney, G. R., & Gabel, J. (1998). Family history and psychiatric comorbidity in persons with compulsive buying: Preliminary findings. *American Journal of Psychiatry, 155,* 960–963.

Calamari, J. E., Wiegartz, P. S., & Janeck, A. S. (1999). Obsessive-compulsive disorder subgroups: A symptom-based clustering approach. *Behavior Research and Therapy, 37,* 113–125.

Cermele, J. A., Melendez-Pallitto, L., & Pandina, G. J. (2001). Intervention in compulsive hoarding: A case study. *Behavior Modification, 25,* 214–232.

Christensen, D. D., & Greist, J. H. (2001). The challenge of obsessive-compulsive disorder hoarding. *Primary Psychiatry, 8,* 79–86.

Christenson, G. A., Faber, R. J., de Zwaan, M., Raymond, N. C., Specker, S. M., Ekern, M. D., et al. (1994). Compulsive buying: Descriptive characteristics and psychiatric comorbidity. *Journal of Clinical Psychiatry, 55,* 5–11.

Clark, A. N. G., Mankikar, G. D., & Gray, I. (1975). Diogenes syndrome. *Lancet, 1,* 366–368.

Coles, M. E., Frost, R. O., Heimberg, R. G., & Steketee, G. (2003). Hoarding behaviors in a large college sample. *Behavior Research and Therapy, 41,* 179–194.

Cromer, K., Schmidt, N. B., & Murphy, D. L. (2006, March). *Elucidating the relationship between hoarding and traumatic life events.* Paper presented at the Anxiety Disorders Association of America, Miami, FL.

Damecour, C. L., & Charron, M. (1998). Hoarding: A symptom, not a syndrome. *Journal of Clinical Psychiatry, 59,* 267–272.

Eslinger, P. J., & Damasio, A. R. (1985). Severe disturbance of higher cognition after bilateral frontal lobe ablation: Patient EVR. *Neurology, 35,* 1731–1741.

Farchione, T., Tolin, D. F., Saxena, S., Maidment, K. M., Steketee, G., & Frost, R. O. (2003, November). Patterns of comorbidity in compulsive hoarding. In R. O. Frost & F. Neziroglu (Chairs), *Diagnostic and treatment issues in compulsive hoarding.* Symposium, Boston.

Finkel, S., Costa, E., Silva, J., Cohen, G., Miller, S., & Sartorius, N. (1997). Behavioral and psychological signs and symptoms of dementia: A consensus statement on current knowledge and implications for research and treatment. *International Journal of Geriatric Psychiatry, 12,* 1060–1061.

Frankenburg, F. R. (1984). Hoarding in anorexia nervosa. *British Journal of Medical Psychology, 57*(Pt. 1), 57–60.

Frost, R. O., & Gross, R. (1993). The hoarding of possessions. *Behavior Research and Therapy, 31,* 367–382.

Frost, R. O., & Hartl, T. L. (1996). A cognitive-behavioral model of compulsive hoarding. *Behavior Research and Therapy, 34,* 341–350.

Frost, R. O., Hartl, T., Christian, R., & Williams, N. (1995). The value of possessions in compulsive hoarding: Patterns of use and attachment. *Behavior Research and Therapy, 33,* 897–902.

Frost, R. O., Kim, H. J., Morris, C., Bloss, C., Murray-Close, M., & Steketee, G. (1998). Hoarding, compulsive buying and reasons for saving. *Behavior Research and Therapy, 36,* 657–664.

Frost, R. O., Krause, E., White, L., Ax, E., Chowdry, F., Williams, L., et al. (1999, November). *Compulsive hoarding: Patterns of attachment to people and possessions.* Paper presented at the annual meeting of the Association for the Advancement of Behavior Therapy, Toronto, Ontario, Canada.

Frost, R. O., Krause, M. S., & Steketee, G. (1996). Hoarding and obsessive-compulsive symptoms. *Behavior Modification, 20,* 116–132.

Frost, R. O., Meagher, B. M., & Riskind, J. H. (2001). Obsessive-compulsive features in pathological lottery and scratch ticket gamblers. *Journal of Gambling Studies, 17,* 5–19.

Frost, R. O., & Shows, D. L. (1993). The nature and measurement of compulsive indecisiveness. *Behavior Research and Therapy, 31,* 683–692.

Frost, R. O., & Steketee, G. (1998). Hoarding: Clinical aspects and treatment strategies. In M. A. Jenike, L. Baer, & W. E. Minichiello (Eds.), *Obsessive-compulsive disorder: Practical management* (3rd ed., pp. 533–554). St. Louis, MO: Mosby Yearbook Medical.

Frost, R. O., & Steketee, G. (1999). Issues in the treatment of compulsive hoarding. *Cognitive and Behavioral Practice, 6,* 397–407.

Frost, R. O., Steketee, G., & Grisham, J. (2004). Measurement of compulsive hoarding: Saving Inventory—Revised. *Behavior Research and Therapy, 42,* 1163–1182.

Frost, R. O., Steketee, G., Tolin, D. F., & Brown, T. A. (2006, March). *Comorbidity and diagnostic issues in compulsive hoarding.* Paper presented at the annual meeting of the Anxiety Disorders Association of America, Atlanta, GA.

Frost, R. O., Steketee, G., Tolin, D. F., & Renaud, S. (in press). *Development and validation of the Clutter Image Rating.* Manuscript submitted for publication.

Frost, R. O., Steketee, G., & Williams, L. (2000). Hoarding: A community health problem. *Health and Social Care in the Community, 8,* 229–234.

Frost, R. O., Steketee, G., & Williams, L. (2002). Compulsive buying, compulsive hoarding, and obsessive-compulsive disorder. *Behavior Therapy, 33,* 201–214.

Frost, R. O., Steketee, G., Williams, L. F., & Warren, R. (2000). Mood, personality disorder symptoms, and disability in obsessive compulsive hoarders: A comparison with clinical and nonclinical controls. *Behavior Research and Therapy, 38,* 1071–1081.

Frost, R. O., & Tolin, D. F. (2007). Compulsive hoarding. In S. Taylor, J. S. Abramowitz, & D. McKay (Eds.), *Obsessive-compulsive disorder: Subtypes and spectrum conditions.* New York: Elsevier.

Furby, L. (1978). Possessions: Toward a theory of their meaning and function throughout the life cycle. In P. B. Bates (Ed.), *Life span development and behavior* (Vol. 1, pp. 297–336). New York: Academic Press.

Greenberg, D. (1987). Compulsive hoarding. *American Journal of Psychotherapy, 41,* 409–416.

Greenberg, D., Witztum, E., & Levy, A. (1990). Hoarding as a psychiatric symptom. *Journal of Clinical Psychiatry, 51,* 417–421.

Grignon, S., Bassiri, D., Bartoli, J. L., & Calvet, P. (1996). Association of Diogenes syndrome with a compulsive disorder. *Canadian Journal of Psychiatry, 41,* 315–316.

Grisham, J. R., Frost, R. O., Steketee, G., Kim, H. J., & Hood, S. (2006). Age of onset of compulsive hoarding. *Journal of Anxiety Disorders, 20,* 675–686.

Hantouche, E. G., & Lancrenon, S. (1996). Typologie moderne des symptomes et des syndromes obsessionnels-compulsifs: resultats d'une large etude francaise chez 615 patients [Modern typology of symptoms and obsessive-compulsive syndromes: Results of a large French study of 615 patients]. *Encephale, 22*(Spec. No. 1), 9–21.

Hartl, T. L., Duffany, S. R., Allen, G. J., Steketee, G., & Frost, R. O. (2005). Relationships among compulsive hoarding, trauma, and attention-deficit/hyperactivity disorder. *Behavior Research and Therapy, 43,* 269–276.

Hartl, T. L., & Frost, R. O. (1999). Cognitive-behavioral treatment of compulsive hoarding: A multiple baseline experimental case study. *Behavior Research and Therapy, 37,* 451–461.

Hartl, T. L., Frost, R. O., Allen, G. J., Deckersbach, T., Steketee, G., Duffany, S. R., et al. (2004). Actual and perceived memory deficits in individuals with compulsive hoarding. *Depression and Anxiety, 20,* 59–69.

Hoarding of Animals Research Consortium. (2000). People who hoard animals. *Psychiatric Times, 17,* 25–29.

Hoarding of Animals Research Consortium. (2002). Health implications of animal hoarding. *Health and Social Work, 27,* 125–136.

Hwang, J. P., Tsai, S. J., Yang, C. H., Liu, K. M., & Lirng, J. F. (1998). Hoarding behavior in dementia: A preliminary report. *American Journal of Geriatric Psychiatry, 6*, 285–289.

Jackson, G. A. (1997). Diogenes syndrome: How should we manage it? *Journal of Mental Health, 6*, 113–116.

Kim, H. J., Steketee, G., & Frost, R. O. (2001). Hoarding by elderly people. *Health and Social Work, 26*, 176–184.

Koran, L. M., Faber, R. J., Aboujaoude, E., Large, M. D., & Serpe, R. T. (2006). Estimated prevalence of compulsive buying behavior in the United States. *American Journal of Psychiatry, 163*, 1806–1812.

Krause, E., White, L., Frost, R. O., Steketee, G., & Kyrios, M. (2000, November). *Attachment deficits among compulsive hoarders: Implications for theory and treatment.* Paper presented at the annual meeting of the Association for the Advancement of Behavior Therapy, New Orleans, LA.

Leckman, J. F., Grice, D. E., Boardman, J., Zhang, H., Vitale, A., Bondi, C., et al. (1997). Symptoms of obsessive-compulsive disorder. *American Journal of Psychiatry, 154*, 911–917.

Lochner, C., Kinnear, C. J., Hemmings, S. M., Seller, C., Niehaus, D. J., Knowles, J. A., et al. (2005). Hoarding in obsessive-compulsive disorder: Clinical and genetic correlates. *Journal of Clinical Psychiatry, 66*, 1155–1160.

Luchins, D. J., Goldman, M. B., Lieb, M., & Hanrahan, P. (1992). Repetitive behaviors in chronically institutionalized schizophrenic patients. *Schizophrenia Research, 8*, 119–123.

MacMillan, D., & Shaw, P. (1966). Senile breakdown in standards of personal and environmental cleanliness. *British Medical Journal, 2*, 1023–1037.

Maltby, N., Tolin, D. F., & Kiehl, K. A. (2006, May). *Compulsive hoarding: Is there evidence for dysfunctional error processing?* Paper presented at the annual meeting of the Society of Biological Psychiatry, Toronto, Ontario, Canada.

Mataix-Cols, D., Marks, I. M., Greist, J. H., Kobak, K. A., & Baer, L. (2002). Obsessive-compulsive symptom dimensions as predictors of compliance with and response to behavior therapy: Results from a controlled trial. *Psychotherapy and Psychosomatics, 71*, 255–262.

Mataix-Cols, D., Rauch, S. L., Manzo, P. A., Jenike, M. A., & Baer, L. (1999). Use of factor-analyzed symptom dimensions to predict outcome with serotonin reuptake inhibitors and placebo in the treatment of obsessive-compulsive disorder. *American Journal of Psychiatry, 156*, 1409–1416.

Mataix-Cols, D., Wooderson, S., Lawrence, N., Brammer, M. J., Speckens, A., & Phillips, M. L. (2004). Distinct neural correlates of washing, checking, and hoarding symptom dimensions in obsessive-compulsive disorder. *Archives of General Psychiatry, 61*, 564–576.

McCrae, R. R., Costa, P. T., Jr., Terracciano, A., Parker, W. D., Mills, C. J., De Fruyt, F., et al. (2002). Personality trait development from age 12 to age 18: Longitudinal, cross-sectional, and cross-cultural analyses. *Journal of Personality and Social Psychology, 83*, 1456–1468.

McElroy, S. L., Keck, P. E., & Phillips, K. A. (1995). Kleptomania, compulsive buying, and binge-eating disorder. *Journal of Clinical Psychiatry, 56*(Suppl. 4), 14–26.

McElroy, S. L., Keck, P. E., Pope, H. G., Smith, A. M., & Strakowski, S. M. (1994). Compulsive buying: A report of 20 cases. *Journal of Clinical Psychiatry, 55*, 242–248.

Meunier, S. A., Tolin, D. F., Frost, R. O., Steketee, G., & Brady, R. E. (2006, March). *Prevalence of hoarding symptoms across the anxiety disorders.* Paper presented at the annual meeting of the Anxiety Disorders Association of America, Atlanta, GA.

Meunier, S. A., Tolin, D. F., Frost, R. O., Steketee, G., Brady, R. E., & Brown, T. A. (2006, November). *ADHD symptoms in compulsive hoarders.* Paper presented at the annual meeting of the Association of Behavioral and Cognitive Therapies, Chicago.

Miller, W., & Rollnick, S. (2002). *Motivational interviewing: Preparing people for change* (2nd ed.). New York: Guilford Press.

Obsessive Compulsive Cognitions Working Group. (2005). Psychometric validation of the Obsessive Beliefs Questionnaire and the Interpretation of Intrusions Inventory: Pt. 2. Factor analyses and testing of a brief version. *Behavior Research and Therapy, 43,* 1527–1542.

Patronek, G. J. (1999). Hoarding of animals: An under-recognized public health problem in a difficult-to-study population. *Public Health Reports, 114,* 81–87.

Patronek, G. J. (2001). The problem of animal hoarding. *Municipal Lawyer, 42,* 6–19.

Ptacek, J. T., Smith, R. E., & Zanas, J. (1992). Gender, appraisal, and coping: A longitudinal analysis. *Journal of Personality, 60,* 747–770.

Rasmussen, S. A., & Eisen, J. L. (1989). Clinical features and phenomenology of obsessive compulsive disorder. *Psychiatric Annals, 19,* 67–73.

Rasmussen, S. A., & Eisen, J. L. (1992). The epidemiology and differential diagnosis of obsessive compulsive disorder. *Journal of Clinical Psychiatry, 53*(Suppl.), 4–10.

Samuels, J., Bienvenu, O. J., III, Riddle, M. A., Cullen, B. A., Grados, M. A., Liang, K. Y., et al. (2002). Hoarding in obsessive compulsive disorder: Results from a case-control study. *Behavior Research and Therapy, 40,* 517–528.

Saxena, S., Brody, A. L., Maidment, K. M., & Baxter, L. R., Jr. (2007). Paroxetine treatment of compulsive hoarding. *Journal of Psychiatric Research, 41,* 481–487.

Saxena, S., Brody, A. L., Maidment, K. M., Smith, E. C., Zohrabi, N., Katz, E., et al. (2004). Cerebral glucose metabolism in obsessive-compulsive hoarding. *American Journal of Psychiatry, 161,* 1038–1048.

Saxena, S., Maidment, K. M., Vapnik, T., Golden, G., Rishwain, T., Rosen, R. M., et al. (2002). Obsessive-compulsive hoarding: Symptom severity and response to multimodal treatment. *Journal of Clinical Psychiatry, 63,* 21–27.

Schlosser, S., Black, D. W., Repertinger, S., & Freet, D. (1994). Compulsive buying: Demography, phenomenology, and comorbidity in 46 subjects. *General Hospital Psychiatry, 16,* 205–212.

Seedat, S., & Stein, D. J. (2002). Hoarding in obsessive-compulsive disorder and related disorders: A preliminary report of 15 cases. *Psychiatry and Clinical Neuroscience, 56,* 17–23.

Shafran, R., & Tallis, F. (1996). Obsessive-compulsive hoarding: A cognitive-behavioral approach. *Behavioral and Cognitive Psychotherapy, 24,* 209–221.

Shah, A. (1995). Squalor syndrome: A viewpoint. *Australian Journal on Aging, 14,* 160–162.

Sobin, C., Blundell, M. L., Weiller, F., Gavigan, C., Haiman, C., & Karayiorgou, M. (2000). Evidence of a schizotypy subtype in OCD. *Journal of Psychiatric Research, 34,* 15–24.

Speltz, M. L., & Bernstein, D. A. (1976). Sex differences in fearfulness: Verbal report, overt avoidance, and demand characteristics. *Journal of Behavior Therapy and Experimental Psychiatry, 7,* 117–122.

Steketee, G., & Frost, R. O. (2003). Compulsive hoarding: Current status of the research. *Clinical Psychology Review, 23,* 905–927.

Steketee, G., & Frost, R. O. (2007). *Compulsive hoarding and acquiring: Therapist guide.* New York: Oxford University Press.

Steketee, G., Frost, R. O., & Kim, H.-J. (2001). Hoarding by elderly people. *Health and Social Work, 26,* 176–184.

Steketee, G., Frost, R. O., & Kyrios, M. (2003). Beliefs about possessions among compulsive hoarders. *Cognitive Therapy and Research, 27,* 467–479.

Steketee, G., Frost, R. O., Wincze, J., Greene, K., & Douglass, H. (2000). Group and individual treatment of compulsive hoarding: A pilot study. *Behavioral and Cognitive Psychotherapy, 28,* 259–268.

Summerfeldt, L. J., Richter, M. A., Antony, M. M., & Swinson, R. P. (1999). Symptom structure in obsessive-compulsive disorder: A confirmatory factor-analytic study. *Behavior Research and Therapy, 37*, 297–311.

Tolin, D. F., Abramowitz, J. S., Brigidi, B. D., Amir, N., Street, G. P., & Foa, E. B. (2001). Memory and memory confidence in obsessive-compulsive disorder. *Behavior Research and Therapy, 39*, 913–927.

Tolin, D. F., Brady, R. E., & Hannan, S. E. (2006). *Obsessive beliefs and symptoms of obsessive-compulsive disorder in a clinical sample.* Manuscript submitted for publication.

Tolin, D. F., Frost, R. O., & Steketee, G. (2007). *Buried in treasures: Help for compulsive acquiring, saving, and hoarding.* New York: Oxford University Press.

Tolin, D. F., Frost, R. O., & Steketee, G. (2007a). An open trial of cognitive-behavioral therapy for compulsive hoarding. *Behaviour Research and Therapy, 45*, 1461–1470.

Van Oppen, P., Hoekstra, R. J., & Emmelkamp, P. M. (1995). The structure of obsessive-compulsive symptoms. *Behavior Research and Therapy, 33*, 15–23.

Vostanis, P., & Dean, C. (1992). Self-neglect in adult life. *British Journal of Psychiatry, 161*, 265–267.

Wincze, J., Steketee, G., & Frost, R. O. (2005). *Categorization in compulsive hoarding.* Unpublished manuscript.

Winsberg, M. E., Cassic, K. S., & Koran, L. M. (1999). Hoarding in obsessive-compulsive disorder: A report of 20 cases. *Journal of Clinical Psychiatry, 60*, 591–597.

Wu, K. D., & Watson, D. (2005). Hoarding and its relation to obsessive-compulsive disorder. *Behavior Research and Therapy, 43*, 897–921.

Zhang, H., Leckman, J. F., Pauls, D. L., Tsai, C. P., Kidd, K. K., & Campos, M. R. (2002). Genomewide scan of hoarding in sib pairs in which both sibs have Gilles de la Tourette syndrome. *American Journal of Human Genetics, 70*, 896–904.

Author Index

North, M., 153
Norton, K., 447
Norton, P. J., 301
Norton, R., 567
Note, B., 112
Note, I., 112
Nothen, M. M., 180
Novaco, R. W., 276, 635
Novella, L., 411
Noyes, R., 173, 180, 403, 704, 709, 714, 715
Nuechterlein, K. H., 355, 363
Nugter, M. A., 353
Nunes, E., 101
Nusbaum, N. J., 651, 654
Nutt, D., 206, 253
Nuzzarello, A., 188

O'Brien, C. P., 528, 539
O'Brien, G. T., 181, 182
O'Brien, M. D., 607
O'Brien, T. P., 152
O'Brien, W. H., 4, 14, 16, 78, 79, 80, 81, 143, 144, 638, 664
Ocepek-Welikson, K., 417
Ochsner, K., 104
O'Cleirigh, C. M., 183
O'Connor, B. P., 439, 445, 448, 449, 454
O'Connor, M. E., 470
O'Donohue, W., 20, 590, 594, 649
O'Donovan, M. C., 369
Oei, T. P. S., 182
O'Farrell, T. J., 540, 541, 542, 573
Offord, D. R., 43, 566
O'Hara, M. W., 329
Ohara, Y., 115
Øien, P. A., 411
Oinals, D. A., 372
Okasha, A., 439
Okazaki, S., 215
Okiishi, J. C., 51
Oldham, J. M., 468
Oldridge, M. L., 366
O'Leary, D., 356
O'Leary, K. D., 564, 565
O'Leary, T., 87, 704
Olfson, M., 42, 332, 377
Olga, J. R., 206, 214
Olivardia, R., 477
Olivares, M. E., 712
Oliveau, D., 704
Oliver, C., 621, 633
Olivier, B., 356, 358
Ollendick, T., 145, 151, 374
Olley, J. G., 617
Olmstead, M. P., 485
Olsen, S., 363
Olson, D. H., 567
Oltmanns, T. F., 447
O'Malley, S. S., 545
Onder, G., 659
O'Neil, P. M., 468
O'Neill, M. L., 264, 266, 267, 273
O'Neill, R., 6, 7, 143, 622, 634
Onstad, S., 147, 148, 272, 411
Oosterbaan, D. B., 714, 715

Opdyke, D., 153
Opler, L. A., 363
Oquendo, M. A., 412
Orbach, G., 373
O'Reilly, D., 352
O'Reilly, M. F., 632
Origoni, A. E., 364
Orlandi, V., 372
Orme, J., 15
Orr, S., 269
Orsillo, S. M., 142, 155
Ortiz, T., 117
Ortmann, J., 326
Ory, M., 647, 648
Osborn, C., 592
Oseasohn, R., 101
Osher, F. C., 360, 367
Oskarsson, H., 180
Ossorio, P. G., 30
Ost, L. G., 140, 144, 145, 152, 153, 154, 155, 217
Ost, L.-G., 85
Ostberg, O., 677
Osterlind, S., 19
Ott, S. L., 356
Otto, K., 147
Otto, M., 65, 69, 176, 177, 183, 188, 217, 218, 220, 221, 688, 692, 741
Ouslander, J. G., 651
Overall, J. E., 363
Ovesey, L., 591
Owen, D. M., 621
Owen, M. J., 368, 369
Owens, J. A., 265, 276, 693
Owens, K. M. B., 702
Owens, T. J., 702
Owsley, C., 652
Oxman, T. E., 360
Ozkan, M., 448

Pace-Schott, E. F., 688, 692
Padesky, C. A., 333
Padgett, D. K., 373
Page, A., 142, 143
Page, J., 592
Pagler, J., 625
Paine, S., 705
Pakkenberg, B., 370
Paley, B., 572
Pallanti, S., 113, 114, 250
Pally, R., 412
Palmer, B. A., 358
Palmer, B. W., 355
Panasetis, P., 265, 267
Pancheri, P., 372
Pandav, R. S., 516
Pandina, G. J., 730, 744
Panisset, M., 506
Pankey, J., 89
Pankratz, V. S., 358
Pankratz, W. J., 332
Pantelis, C., 247, 248
Papageorgiou, C., 211, 295
Paparella, T., 508
Pape, S., 356
Paquette, V., 117
Parachini, E. A., 420

Paradis, C., 156, 714, 715
Paradiso, E., 419
Paris, J., 404, 405, 410, 411, 412, 417, 451, 709
Park, D. C., 659
Parker, C., 88
Parker, G., 63, 298, 411, 708
Parker, W. D., 740
Parron, D. L., 41
Parsons, B., 417
Parsons, M. B., 626, 628, 632
Parsons, T., 335
Pasch, L. A., 569
Pascual, J. C., 419
Pasquini, P., 405, 410
Passik, S. D., 660
Pate, J. L., 408
Patel, S., 419
Pater, A., 364
Pathak, D., 179, 709
Patrick, C., 36, 37, 373
Patronek, G. J., 732, 733
Patterson, G. R., 568
Patterson, M. D., 141
Patterson, T. L., 364, 513
Pattison, P., 355, 592
Pauli, P., 702
Pauls, D. L., 111, 180, 739
Paulsen, J. S., 355, 362, 510
Paulson, J., 5
Paulus, M. J., 320
Paulus, M. P., 319
Pavlov, I. P., 84
Paykel, E. S., 319
Payne, C. C., 572
Payne, D., 355
Payne, J., 357
Payne, M. E., 328
Peabody, C. G., 367
Peacock, E., 603
Pearlson, G. D., 369
Pecknold, J. C., 190
Pedone, C., 659
Pelcovits, M., 573
Pelletier, O., 301
Pemberton, A. R., 477
Penn, D., 354, 355, 356, 357, 358, 367, 373, 375
Pennebaker, J. W., 305
Perel, J. M., 189, 337, 417, 418, 420
Perez, M., 320, 323, 324, 374
Perez-Stable, E. J., 337
Peri, T., 265
Perkins, D., 103, 354, 356, 357, 377
Perlin, M., 499
Perlis, M. L., 686, 692
Perron, G., 295
Perry, J., 447, 449, 450, 454, 625
Perry, K. J., 209, 211, 212, 274
Perry, M., 660
Perry, P. J., 331
Pershad, D., 249
Person, D. C., 691
Person, E., 591
Persons, J. B., 123, 130, 333
Perto, G., 371

Subject Index